# MACHINE DESIGN

## *Other Related Books*

1. Advanced Mechanics of Materials *by* Kumar & Ghai
2. Applied Mechanics (in S.I. Units) *by* I.B. Prasad
3. Applied Stress Analysis *by* Sadhu Singh.
4. Automobile Engineering *by* Banga and Nathu Singh
5. Automobile Engineering *by* G.B.S. Narang
6. Automobile Mechanics *by* Dr. N.K. Giri
7. Engineering Metrology *by* R.K. Jain
8. Experimental Stress Anslysis *by* Dr. Sadhu Singh
9. Fluid Machines (in S.I. Units) *by* S.S. Ratan
10. Fluid Mechanics (in S.I. Units) *by* Dr. A.K. Jain
11. Fundamental of Gas Dynamics *by* Dr. K.L. Yadao
12. Gas Dynamics with Applications *by* S.K. Kulshrestha
13. Gas Turbine Theory and Jet Propulsion *by* J.K. Jain
14. Heat and Mass Transfer by C.P. Arora
15. I.C. Engines (in S.I. Units) by P.L. Ballaney
16. Internal Combustion Engine Theory and Practice *by* S.P. Sen
17. Introduction to Power Plant Technology *by* G.D. Rai
18. Machine Design *by* G.R. Nagpal
19. Machine Design *by* R.K. Jain
20. Machine Design *by* Dr. Sadhu Singh
21. Machine Design Data Handbook *by* Dr. Sadhu Singh
22. Machine Tool Engineering *by* G.R. Nagpal
23. Machine Tool Technology *by* Kundaswamy
24. Manual of Practicals in Mechanical Engineering *by* Tewari
25. Materials and Metallurgy *by* V.K. Manchanda
26. Mechanical and Industrial Measurements *by* R.K. Jain
27. Mechanical Engineering Handbook *by* Banga and Sharma
28. Mechanical Estimating and Costing *by* Banga and Sharma
29. Metal Cutting Science and Production Technology *by* Jain & Agarwal
30. Non Conventional Sources of Energy *by* G.D. Rai
31. Numerical Control of Machine Tools *by* Dr. Koren and Benuri
32. Production Technology *by* R.K. Jain
33. Power Plant Engineering *by* G.R. Nagpal
34. Refrigeration and Air Conditioning (in S.I. Units) *by* P.L. Ballaney
35. Renewable and Conventional Energy Technology *by* S.Rao, Parulekar and Narayan Khedhar
36. Robotics : Principles and Practice *by* Jain and Agarwal
37. Solar Energy Utilization *by* G.D. Rai
38. Strength of Materials (in S.I. Units) *by* Sadhu Singh
39. Thermal Engineering (in S.I. Units) *by* P.L. Ballaney
40. Thermal Engg. *by* Dr. K.L. Yadav
41. Theory of Hydraulic Machines (in S.I. Units) *by* V.P. Vasandani
42. Theory of Elasticity *by* Dr. Sadhu Singh
43. Theory of Plasticity *by* Dr. Sadhu Singh
44. Welding Processes and Technology *by* Dr. R.S. Parmar

# MACHINE DESIGN

**G.R. NAGPAL**
*B.Sc., B.Sc. Engineering (Mechanical)*
*M.Tech. (Mech. Engineering)*
*Head of Department in Mech. Engg.*
*Y.M.C.A. Institute of Engineering*
*Faridabad (Haryana)*

**KHANNA PUBLISHERS**
*Operational Office :*
B-35/9, G.T. Karnal Road Industrial Area,
(Near Telephone Exchange), Delhi-110033
*Phones* : 011-27224179, 011-45033819 • *Mob.* 09811541460
*email* : contactus@khannapublishers.in

*Published by :*

Romesh Chander Khanna & Vineet Khanna
*for* **KHANNA PUBLISHERS**
2-B, Nath Market, Nai Sarak
Delhi- 110 006 (India)

**Website : www.khannapublishers.in**



*Hologram & Description*

To all readers of our books, to prevent yourself from being defrauded by piraters, please make sure that there is an Hologram on the cover of our books with the below specifications. If you find any book without Hologram and Description, please mail us at **contactus@khannapublishers.in**

Thanking you

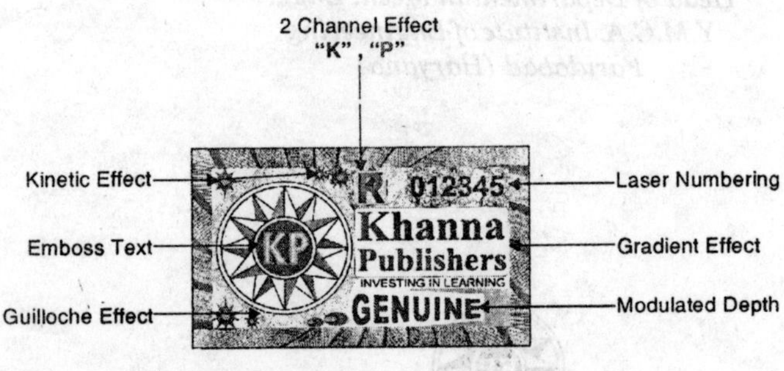


**ISBN No. 978-81-7409-148-3**

***First Edition : 1997***
***Third Edition :***
***Fourth Reprint : 2021***

***Price :* ₹ 369.00**

# Preface

This book on Machine Design has been written to meet the requirements of Engineering Degree, Diploma and A.M.I.E. (Sec. B) students. Efforts have been made to present in simple language the fundamental principles required for the correct design of separate elements which compose the machine. The text contains many illustrative examples and solutions as well as a large number of problems to be worked by student. Objective type problems have been added to make the subject matter more clear.

Although every care has been taken to eliminate errors and omissions but still if there be any omissions or errors the author will be thankful to the readers for bringing them to his notice.

The author will welcome constructive suggestions and criticisms from the readers to make this book more useful.

The author is thankful to Sh. R.C. Khanna for his most co-operative attitude and for bringing out this book in a very short time.

— G.R. Nagpal

# Contents

# Contents

# 1

# Introduction

## 1.1. Machine Design

Engineering design is a decision making process to create plans for making a component which would satisfy the requirements of the customer. Economic considerations are usually of prime importance when the design of new components is undertaken. In general, the lowest overall cost of parts designed is desired.

It is thus a creative process which starts from a requirement and defines a system and the methods of its realisation or implementation so as to satisfy the requirement. The common aim of design is to encourage originality.

The success of a new product is often critically dependent on the excellence of its design.

Design by inference is a creative activity. There is a need for flair and originality in design, this being the hall mark of a good designer.

A machine is a combination of stationary and moving parts constructed for the useful purpose of generating, transforming, or utilising mechanical energy. Machine design acquaints the reader with the fundamentals of designing the most commonly used parts, elements and units of various machines. The design may lead to an entirely new machine or an improvement of existing machine. The objective is to produce a machine which is not only sufficiently rugged to function properly for a reasonable life but is also cheap enough.

The design engineer should possess the knowledge of the following subjects :

(*i*) Mechanics of materials

(*ii*) Mechanisms

(*iii*) Strength of materials

(*iv*) Metallurgy

(*v*) Workshop processes

(*vi*) Workshop organisation.

Design process is very complex and iterative. It requires not only a detailed knowledge of the specific field but also principles of

(*i*) CAD

(*ii*) CAM

(*iii*) CIM

(*iv*) Concurrent engineering

(*v*) DFM (Design for manufacture)

(*vi*) DFA (Design for assembly)

(*vii*) Group Technology

(*viii*) Value engineering etc.

The overall design should not only be functionally sound but also cost effective and economically viable.

The design engineer should be a man of sound judgement and wide experience, and qualities which are usually acquired only after considerable time has been spent in actual professional work.

Design lay outs require both empirical and scientific design. Empirical design involves the use of tables, charts, and formulas which have been established from the experimental studies and scientific computations. Scientific design which requires a broad knowledge of the subjects like mechanics, mathematic, strength of materials, metallurgy etc. is used when a new component is to be designed to operate under special specified conditions for which data are not available.

For the economy of performance correct mechanical, hydraulic, thermodynamic and other principles must be applied.

### 1.1.1 Classification of Machine Design

Machine design can be classified as follows :

(*a*) Rational design

(*b*) Empirical design

(*c*) Combined rational and empirical design

(*d*) Design by experience.

In rational design mathematics is used to determine the size of the element whereas in empirical design data derived from machines and designs in actual use are used. Such data is tabulated in various hand books for ready reference. In combined rational and empirical design both mathematics and standard data are used in design whereas some parts are designed based on number of informations derived from careful observation and experience.

Design of a machine may proceed along the following lines :

(*i*) Machine is visualised which will satisfy functional requirements. It is profitable to analyse the various possible designs and to select the best possible design.

(*ii*) Preliminary analyses of forces which will act on various parts of the machine.

(*iii*) Determination of general proportions of the parts of machine.

(*iv*) Selection of materials for making different parts.

(*v*) To decide the manufacturing processes.

(*vi*) Preparation of production drawings.

(*vii*) Modifications based on :

(*a*) practical experience

(*b*) cost

(*c*) requirements for quantity production.

It is desirable that the machine designed should be cheaper. Some of the factors for making a cheaper product are as follows :

(*i*) Use of castings in place of forgings and machined parts.

(*ii*) Adoption of fabrication by welding.

(*iii*) In corporation of standard parts.

(*iv*) A reduction to the minimum of the amount of costly materials used.

(*v*) Allowing proper tolerances on the various dimensions.

## 1.2 Design Process

While designing a component or machine the following procedure (Fig. 1.1) may be adopted :

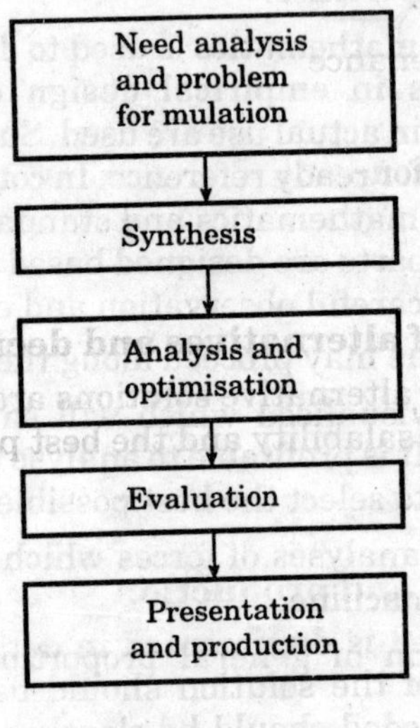


Fig. 1.1. Design process.

(*i*) Problem formulation

(*ii*) Problem analysis

(*iii*) Problem synthesis

(*iv*) Evaluation of alternatives and decision making

(*v*) Presentation and production.

**1.2.1 Need analysis and problem formulation.** While designing a new component it should be ensured that need exists for such a component. This can be done by gathering as much information as possible by surveying the market and by studying the similar components already available in the market. Once it is established that need exists for the component being designed then the problem should be stated as clearly as possible. The problem should be studied in greater details. The broader the definition the greater will be possibility of creative solutions.

**1.2.2 Synthesis.** In this stage of design making process a number of possible solutions are suggested including the previous solutions available (if any). The design engineer should have up to date knowledge keeping in view the various developments that have taken place regarding the part to be designed.

### 1.2.3 Analysis and optimisation

In this stage the criteria to be used in selecting the best design are identified taking into consideration the following factors :

(*a*) Manufacturing cost
(*b*) Reliability
(*c*) Safety
(*d*) Ease of maintenance
(*e*) Repairs
(*f*) Ease of operation
(*g*) Sales appeal.

### 1.2.4 Evaluation of alternatives and decision taking

In this phase all the alternative solutions are evaluated on the basis of overall cost and salability and the best possible solution is finally chosen.

### 1.2.5 Presentation and production

The solution finalised is documented in details. Detailed and dimensional drawings of the solution should be made available. Tolerances wherever needed should be clearly stated. Tolerances should be as large as possible to reduce the manufacturing cost. The materials out of which the designed parts are to be made, should be specified.

## 1.3 To Prepare Final Drawing

Working drawings are prepared after assembly drawing has been made and all possible revisions have been taken into account. The working drawing should possess the following information.

(*i*) It should be clear, concise and complete. All dimensions that are needed for manufacturing and assembly should be mentioned clearly.
(*ii*) Type of finish to be used should be given.
(*iii*) Standard symbols should be used.
(*iv*) Bill of materials should be prepared in tabular form.
(*v*) If the manufacturing process involves any special method such as lapping, heat treatment etc., then such process should be indicated in a foot note.

## 1.4 Design Procedure

When a new machine or an element of the machine is to be designed the various considerations involved are as follows.

(*i*) To state the problem completed and clearly.

(*ii*) To decide the kinematic arrangement of parts of the machine and to carry out detailed analysis of their motion.

(*iii*) To determine the nature of the forces and their magnitude acting on different elements of the machine.

(*iv*) To select proper materials for each elements of the machine and to determine the allowable stresses in the different materials.

(*v*) To determine the size of each element.

(*vi*) To prepare detailed drawings of the various elements of the machine designed.

(*vii*) To select the economical manufacturing processes by which various elements are to be manufactured.

(*viii*) To fabricate prototypes and to test the prototypes for acceptable performance. Any flaws revealed during testing should be removed by making alterations in the preliminary design of the component.

The design should be such that

(*a*) It is easier to manufacture the various parts

(*b*) It is easier to assemble the various parts

(*c*) As far as possible standard parts should be used

(*d*) There should be safety of operation and adjustment for wear.

## 1.5 Design Requirements

The machine designed should comply with the requirements of the standards set up by the state standards institute. The basic requirements of an engineering component designed are as follows.

(*i*) Its overall cost should be minimum.

(*ii*) It should be of good quality. Although it is difficult to define quality in absolute terms however the essential characteristics of quality may be grouped as under :

(*a*) Specificational quality

(*b*) Functional quality

(*c*) Aesthetical quality

(*d*) Usage quality.

Specificational quality includes conformance to basic design specifications based on standards. The component designed should function properly. Aesthetic quality of the product refers to the quality characteristics to provide for the aesthetic value demanded by users whereas usage quality may consist of simplity, economy and higher trouble-free working life of the component.

(*iii*) It should function properly. The element designed should be reliable in working and should have higher working efficiency.

(*iv*) It should be lighter in weight.

(*v*) It should be sufficiently strong, rigid and wear resistant.

(*vi*) The design should conform to the safety codes.

The various items that the designer should consider in designing equipment for operator safety are as follows.

(*a*) Covers or enclosures should be provided for moving components that are in close proximity to the operator.

(*b*) Parts which may cause injury to the operator should not project from the equipment.

(*c*) Sharp corners and edges should be avoided.

(*vii*) It should be easier to make the adjustments and to lubricate the parts designed.

## 1.6 Design Factors Relating to Customer's Requirements for Economic Design

While designing a component the following factors from customer's requirement point of view should be considered.

(*i*) The size and weight should be kept as small as possible.

(*ii*) The component should be free from noise.

(*iii*) It should be easier to transport the component.

(*iv*) It should be reliable, durable, and strong.

(*v*) Its energy consumption should be low.

(*vi*) It should have operational safety.

(*vii*) Manufacturing cost and maintenance cost should be low.

(*viii*) The component should be reliable and should have more service life.

(*ix*) The component should have good appearance.

(*x*) The overall cost of the component should be low.

(*xi*) The component should have good appearance.

## 1.7 Design Factors Relating to Manufacturing Requirements for Economic Design

While designing a component/machine the designer should decide about the following factors from manufacturing point of view:

(*i*) Materials to be used.

(*ii*) Manufacturing processes to be used.

(*iii*) Equipment required to manufacture the component.

(*iv*) Tooling required for manufacturing the components.

(*v*) Inspection and testing stages.

(*vi*) Manufacturing cost.

As far as possible standard materials available should be used. The manufacturing of components designed should be easier and minimum inspection should be needed to check the accuracy of the components. The overall manufacturing cost should be low.

### 1.7.1 Standardisation

Standardisation is defined as the adoption of prescribed regulations and specifications as they pertain to materials, methods and equipment. Standardisation of design helps in reducing cost, simplifying replacement and elimination of unnecessary variation in sizes.

A standard is a set of specifications for parts, materials or processes intended to achieve uniformity, efficiency and a specified quality. One of the important purpose of a standard is to place a limit on the number of items in the specifications so as to provide a reasonable inventory of tooling sizes, shapes and varieties.

The advantages of standardisation are in reducing cost, simplifying replacement and reducing the quantities of material in stock. The designer should be always on the alert to use parts for which patterns and dies are available instead of making new designs which serve the purpose no better.

Standardisation has got the following uses :

1. It makes the mass production possible, thereby, reducing the manufacturing costs and labour requirements.
2. The standardisation of specifications and methods of testing the machine elements helps in improving their quality and hence the service life.
3. The repair and maintenance of the machines is simplified since the worn out or damaged parts can easily be replaced by the standard ones.
4. It reduces the time and efforts needed to create and manufacture new machines since the standard elements and units can be used to assemble a new machine.

## 1.8 Computer Aided Design (C.A.D.)

Computer aided design (C.A.D.) can be defined as the use of computer systems to assist in the creation, modification, analysis and optimisation of a design. The computer systems consist of hardware and software to perform the specialised design functions. The C.A.D. hardware consists of the following :

(*i*) Computer.

(*ii*) Graphics display terminals.

(*iii*) Key boards.

C.A.D. software consists of the computer programme to implement computer graphics on the system.

A C.A.D. system permits a more thorough engineering analysis and a large number of design alternatives can be investigated. Design errors are also reduced through the greater accuracy provided by the system. Computer aided design systems provide the designer with the first promising relief from the repetitive drudgery. Computers work at high speeds and are very accurate. In C.A.D. system the parameters of a design can be changed and the calculations quickly repeated until the combination for optimum result is obtained.

Use of a C.A.D. system provides better engineering drawings, more standardisation in drawings, better documentation of design, fewer drawing errors and greater legibility. The greater is the quantity of modification of drawings or repetition of parts of the drawing. The greater will be the improvement of productivity of the C.A.D. system. Unless this occurs the time of preparing drawing on the C.A.D. system is comparable to that for ordinary drafting.

### 1.8.1 Functions of C.A.D.

The various mechanical engineering design related tasks which are performed by a computer as follows :

(*i*) Geometric modelling.

(*ii*) Engineering analysis.

(*iii*) Design review and valuation.

(*iv*) Automated drafting.

(*v*) Parts classification and coding.

(*vi*) Manufacturing data base.

1. **Geometric modelling.** It deals with computer compatible mathematical description of the geometry of an object. Mathematical description allows the image of the object to be displayed and manipulated on a graphics terminal through signals from a CAD computer system.

2. **Engineering analysis.** This is concerned with stress-strain calculations, heat transfer computations and use of differential equations to describe the dynamic behaviour of the system being designed.

3. **Design Review and Evaluation.** Design accuracy can be checked conveniently on graphics terminal, semi-automatic dimensioning and tolerancing routines. A procedure called layering is often useful in design review. Generally layering involves over laying the geometric image of the final shape of the machined part on the top of the image of the rough costing. Another procedure is interference checking. This is particularly useful in the design of the assembled structures.

Kinematics is one of the most important evaluation features available on C.A.D. systems. The available kinematic packages provide the capability to estimate the motion of simple designed mechanisms. This helps in visualisation of the operation of the mechanisms and helps to ensure against interference with other components.

4. **Automated Drafting.** It is used for the creation of a hard copy engineering drawing directly from C.A.D. data base.

5. **Part classification and coding.** C.A.D. can be used to develop a part classification and coding.

6. **Manufacturing database.** C.A.D. helps in preparing manufacturing data base for the component to be designed and manufactured.

The four phases of CAD are shown in Fig. 1.1 (*a*).

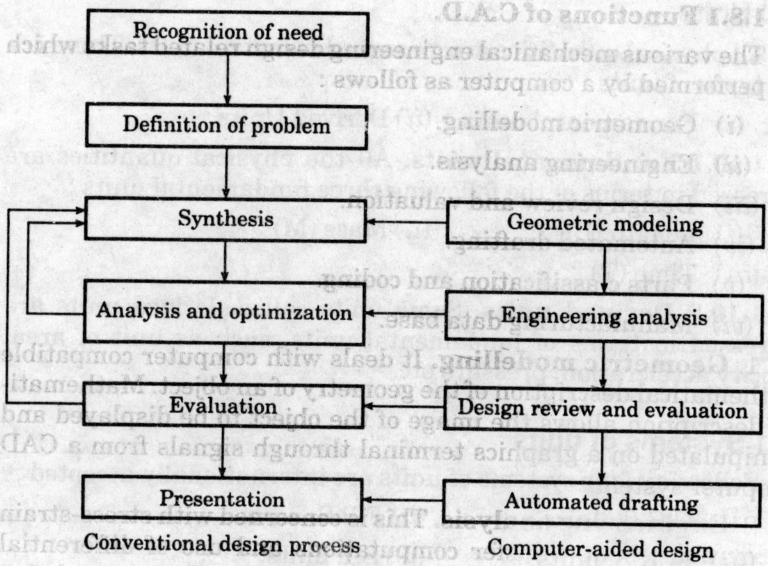


Fig. 1.1 (a)

## 1.9. Product Cycle

Fig. 1.2 shows the various steps in the product cycle (design and manufacturing). The product cycle begins with a concept, an idea for a product. The concept is cultivated, refined analysed improved and translated into a plan for the product through the design engineering process. Then a set of engineering drawings is prepared showing how the product will be manufactured. Manufacturing is followed by quality control, testing and delivery to the customer.

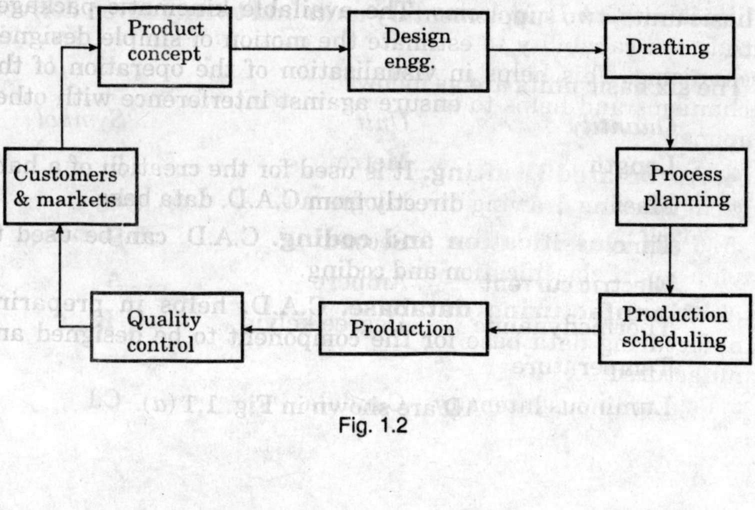


Fig. 1.2

## 1.10 Units

All physical quantities are measured in certain units. There are two types of units :

(*i*) Fundamental units. (*ii*) Derived Units.

**1.10.1 Fundamental units.** All the physical quantities are expressed in terms of the following three fundamental units :

(*i*) Length (L) (*ii*) Mass (M)

(*iii*) Time (T).

**1.10.2 Derived units.** Some units called derived units are expressed in terms of fundamental units, such as unit of area, velocity acceleration, pressure etc.

## 1.11 Systems of units

Following four systems of units are internationally accepted :

(*i*) C.G.S. units. (*ii*) F.P.S. units.

(*iii*) M.K.S. units. (*iv*) S.I. units.

**C.G.S. units.** In this system the fundamental units of length, mass and time are taken as centimetre, gram and second respectively.

**F.P.S. units.** In this system the fundamental units of length, mass and time are foot, pound and second respectively.

**M.K.S. units.** In this system the fundamental units of length, mass and time are metre, kilogram and second.

The M.K.S. units are called as gravitational units or engineer's units.

**S.I. units (International systems of units).** This system has six basic units, two supplementary units and twenty seven derived units.

The six basic units are as follows :

| *Quantity* | *Unit* | *Symbol* |
|---|---|---|
| Length | Metre | m |
| Mass | kilogram | kg |
| Time | Second | S |
| Electric current | Ampere | A |
| Thermodynamic Temperature | Degree kelvin | °K |
| Luminous intensity | Candala | Cd |

There are two supplementary units. One for measure of plane angle called the radian (rad) and other for solid angle called Stearadian (Sr). Some of the derived units are shown in Table 1.1.

**Table 1.1**

| *Units* | *Symbol* |
|---|---|
| Volume | $m^3$ |
| Area | $m^2$ |
| Density (mass) | $kg/m^3$ |
| Velocity | m/s |
| Acceleration | $m/s^2$ |
| Angular velocity | rad/s |
| Angular acceleration | $rad/s^2$ |
| Force | Newton (N) |
| Torque | Nm |
| Pressure | $N/m^2$ |
| Dynamic Viscosity | $NS/m^2$ |
| Kinematic Viscosity | $m^2/s$ |
| Power | W |
| Work, Energy | J |
| Thermal conductivity | W/mK |
| Specific heat | J/kg, °k |
| Entropy | J/°k |
| Frequency | Hertz (Hz) |

where N = Newton

*m* = metre

J = Joule

W = Watt

Pa = Pascal

$$1 \text{ N/m}^2 = 1 \text{ Pa}$$

$$1 \text{ MPa} = 10^6 \text{ Pa} = 10^6 \text{ N/m}^2 = 10^6 \text{ N/m}^2$$

$$1 \text{ kW} = 10^3 \text{ W}$$

$$1\text{kN} = 1000\text{N}$$

$$1 \text{ MN} = 10^6 \text{ N}$$

$$1 \text{ J} = 1 \text{ N–m}$$

$$1 \text{ W} = 1 \text{ J/s}$$

$$1 \text{ Hz} = 1 \text{ cycle/s}$$

### 1.11.1 Comparison of S.I. and M.K.S. system

Table 1.2 indicates the units of some of the quantities in S.I. and M.K.S. system

**Table 1.2**

| *Quantity* | *S.I. system* | *M.K.S. system* |
|---|---|---|
| Length | m | m |
| Volume | $m^3$ | $m^3$ |
| Area | $m^2$ | $m^2$ |
| Force | N | kg |
| Velocity | m/s | m/s |
| Angular Velocity | rad/s | rad/s |
| Torque | Nm | kg-cm |
| Moment of a force | Nm | kg-cm |
| Pressure | $N/m^2$ | $kg/cm^2$ |
| Work, Energy | J | kg-cm |
| Heat | J | K-cal |
| Temperature | °K | °C |
| Power | W | kg/s |

## PROBLEMS

**1.** What is machine design ?

**2.** Explain the steps involved while designing a new component.

**3.** State the design requirements.

**4.** Write short notes on the following :

(*a*) Design procedure

(*b*) Functional quality

(*c*) Usage quality.

**5.** Discuss the factors relating to customer's requirement while designing a component.

**6.** Discuss the factors relating to manufacturing requirements while designing a new component.

**7.** Discuss the qualities of design engineer.

**8.** Discuss product cycle.

**9.** Write short notes on the following :

(*a*) Standardisation of design

(*b*) S.I. Units.

**10.** Describe the design procedure.

**11.** What are the requirements of a design engineer ?

**12.** State the S.I. units of the following in S.I. system :

(*a*) Force (*b*) Power

(*c*) Work (*d*) Temperature

(*e*) Pressure (*f*) Area

(*g*) Volume.

# 2

# Engineering Materials

## 2.0. Introduction

Selection of proper material for making different components is based on several factors such as availability of materials economy, case of handling and fabrication, strength and durability. The proper material is one that meets the engineering requirements.

A particular material is selected for a given application keeping in view the properties of materials. Metal parts for steam engines, I.C. engines, valves and other similar services are stressed at temperatures ranging from 100°C to 1000°C. The Metals used for such parts should be able to retain a large percentage of their strength at high temperatures and should not creep. The materials of the friction surfaces of friction clutches should have the properties of high coefficient of friction, removal of heat effectively and should protect the surface against scoring. The blades of hydraulic turbines should possess adequate strength and resistance to corrosion. Until recently the material used for these blades was stainless steel which is quite expensive and difficult to machine. These blades can be made from carbon or less expensive alloy steel and then faced with thin coating of stain less steel. It is important that materials be used in such a way as to take full advantage of their natural characteristics. For example a moulded plastic part may take advantage of the natural colour of material and insulating properties which could not be employed if sheet metal were used. The other considerations are economy and availability. The cost of material is an important factor. The cost should be as low as possible. Sometimes a material is selected even though it has inferior properties because the right material is too expensive or not available. A high material cost may be accompanied by easier fabrication with a significant saving in labour. Although copper is expensive yet it is preferred as it is the best conducting material available today. Material selected should retain its properties. For example an insulating material should be capable of retaining its properties even after getting wet or greasy. The ease of manufacturing operations possible with a particular material claim due consideration.

The various properties of materials depend on nature and behaviour of materials. The nature of material involves their atomic and molecular structure which in turn depends upon the bonding forces and energies associated with the solid state. The response of the material to imposed conditions can often be traced directly to its basic structure and its internal forces and energies. Mechanical behaviour depends on the nature of the interatomic forces which exist in the solid. The behaviour of solid materials involves their response to all sorts of conditions such as mechanical, thermal, electrical, radiological and chemical. For many purposes the mechanical properties of solids may be satisfactorily explained by reference to the micro structure only. It is observed that many of the properties of engineering interest depend more upon the presence of defects than upon the perfection of the structure at the atomic level. This is particularly true of crystalline solids in which metals form by for the largest and important subdivision.

## 2.1 Selection of Materials

Selection of a materials is one of the decisions the designer is called upon to make. The decision is usually made before the dimensions of the part are determined.

In order to use and work the various materials correctly it is important to know the various properties of materials. For the proper selection of materials it is essential to have a thorough understanding to nature and behaviour of materials. The material structure is an important factor in determining the properties of materials. The finer structure has a more compact coherence than the rougher one. It is because of this reason that steel is stronger than cast iron. Choice of materials depends upon several factors such as :

(*i*) Availability of materials.

(*ii*) Economy

(*iii*) Ease of handling and fabrication.

(*iv*) Ability of the material to be machined shaped, joined, hardened etc.

(*v*) Strength.

(*vi*) Durability.

(*vii*) Corrosion resistance.

The material selected for making a component should be easily available and the cost of the material should be low. It should be easier to give the required shape to the material and the material should be sufficient strong to resist the external forces. The material selected should be durable and should have sufficient resistance to corrosion.

A piece of material contains millions of crystalline grains and each gain consists of million of atoms. As a large number of units are involved therefore it is satisfactory to study the average behaviour of the units. The various properties of materials are compared by numerical values of the strengths and deformations developed in them under the different systems of forces. Now-a-days the problem is of selecting the most suitable material from hundreds of materials available.

## 2.2 Properties of Materials

The various properties of materials are classified as follows :

(*i*) *Physical Properties.* They include density, porosity, structure, feasibility, shape and size.

(*ii*) *Mechanical Properties.* They include, strength, stiffness, elasticity, plasticity, toughness, hardness, brittleness, and creep.

(*iii*) *Magnetic Properties.* They include permeability and hysteresis.

(*iv*) *Thermal Properties.* They include thermal conductivity specific heat, latent heat and thermal stresses.

(*v*) *Electrical Properties.* They include dielectric strength conductivity and resistivity.

(*vi*) *Chemical Properties.* They include chemical composition, corrosion resistance, acidity, and alkalinity.

### 2.2.1 Mechanical Properties

(*i*) **Strength.** It is defined as resistance by which the material opposes the deformation. If the resistance offered by the material to the external loads is more the material is said to be stronger. The maximum load withstood by a specimen of the metal before destruction is called ultimate strength. The load acting per unit area of specimen is called stress and the deformation produced is called strain.

(*ii*) **Elasticity.** It is defined as the ability of a material to return to its original dimensions after suffering a deformation or strain due to stress resulting from some applied force. The greatest stress that can be applied without the material suffering permanent deformation represents the elastic limit. A perfectly elastic body, after the application and removal of load, returns to its original size and shape. The modulus of elasticity of a material is an index of its elastic stiffness and is ratio of stress to corresponding strain within proportional limit.

(*iii*) **Plasticity.** Plasticity of a material is defined as its ability to retain any deformation produced in it without fracture under the action of external load. A plastic material does not recover its shape after removal of load, reaching equilibrium after a certain amount of distortion.

(*iv*) **Stiffness.** Stiffness of a metal is defined as its resistance to elastic deformation. A material which undergoes a slight deformation under the action of load is said to possess high degree of stiffness.

(*v*) **Toughness.** It is the ability of a material to resist fracture under impact loads, *i.e.* suddenly applied loads. Tough materials can withstand large deformation together with high stress without fracture. Materials used for structural parts and machine parts should be tough as they are to resist occasional high loads or heavy shocks.

(*vi*) **Brittleness.** Brittle materials are those which shatter before much strain has taken place. Glass and cast iron are brittle materials.

(*vii*) **Ductility.** It is defined as the ability of a material to be drawn out without rupture. Ductility may be measured in terms of the percentage elongation obtained during a tensile test to destruction. A material having more percentage elongation will have more ductility.

(*viii*) **Malleability.** A material which can be hammered into thin sheets is called malleable. Gold, copper, aluminium are malleable.

(*ix*) **Tenacity.** It is defined as the ability of a material to resist fracture under the action of a tensile force. It is measured in terms of the ultimate tensile stress.

(*x*) **Machinability.** Machinability of a material is the ease with which it can be cut, drilled and shaped. It depends upon hardness, ductility and strength of materials. Machining involves a series of pulses in which the cutting tool moves into the material, first compressing and then shearing the metal ahead of itself. The lower the shear strength relative to tensile and compressive strengths, the more easily the metal can be removed and finer surface finish can be obtained. Grey cast iron and low carbon steels have good machinability.

(*xi*) **Weldability.** It is the capacity of metal to be welded under the fabrication conditions imposed into a specific, suitably designed structure and to perform satisfactorily in the intended service. The following metals have good weldability in the descending order. Iron carbon steel, cast steel, cast iron, low alloy steels, stainless steels.

(*xii*) **Hardness.** Hardness is the resistance to abrasion, scratching and indentation or to wear. When a material is to be selected to resist wear, erosion or plastic deformation hardness is generally the most important property. The hardness of a material can be checked by the following three tests :

(*i*) Brinell hardness test.

(*ii*) Rockwell hardness test.

(*iii*) Vickers pyramid test.

The hardness measured by Brinell hardness test is expressed in Brinell hardness number (B.H.N.) whereas hardness measured by Rockwell hardness test is expressed as HRC or HRB depending on whether C scale or B scale has been used during hardness test. The hardness measured by Vickers pyramid test is expressed as Diamond pyramid number (D.P.N.).

Following are the hardness values for important metals and alloys (as B.H.N.).

(*i*) Aluminium = 21 — 24.

(*ii*) Brass (70% Cu, 30% Zn) = 70, (when annealed),

(*iii*) Bronze (94% Cu, 5% Sn) = 74, (when annealed),

(*iv*) Copper (annealed) = 47,

(*v*) Duralumin (heat treated) = 95,

(*vi*) Grey Cast Iron = 150 — 225,

(*vii*) Iron, commercial, pure = 69,
(*viii*) Magnesium = 41,
(*ix*) Malleable cast iron = 110 — 145,
(*x*) Nickel = 85,
(*xi*) Steel, structural = 120,
(*xii*) Steel, high carbon, heat treated = 550,
(*xiii*) Wrought iron = 100,
(*xiv*) Monel metal = 166.

**Example 2.1.** *Compare ductility, malleability, tenacity and hardness of C.I., mild steel, hard steel, and wrought iron.*

**Solution.** The various properties are indicated in Table 2.1.

**Table 2.1**

| *Material* | *Ductile* | *Malleable* | *Tenacious* | *Hardness* |
|---|---|---|---|---|
| Cast iron | No | No | Not much | Very hard |
| Mild steel | Yes | Yes | Yes | Moderately soft |
| Hard steel | Not much | Not much | Yes | Hard |
| Wrought iron | Yes | Yes | Yes | Soft |

### 2.2.2 Thermal Properties

(*i*) *Specific heat.* Specific heat of a substance is defined as the amount of heat required to raise the temperature of unit mass of the substance through 1°C. Its units are kcal per kg per °C.

(*ii*) *Thermal capacity.* Thermal capacity of a mass of material is defined as the amount of heat required to raise the temperature of the whole mass through 1°C. It depends upon the amount of material and specific heat of the material.

(*iii*) *Linear Expansion.* When a solid material is heated it expands. Consider a metal rod having a length $L_0$ at temperature 0°C. When it is heated to a temperature $T$°C, its length is increased to $L_t$

$\therefore$ Increase in length $(\Delta L) = L_t - L_0$

Rise in temperature = $T$°C

Increase in length depends upon the nature of the material of the rod and is

(*i*) Directly proportional to rise in temperature

(*ii*) Directly proportional to the original length.

$$\Delta L \propto L_0 T$$

or $$\Delta L = \alpha \, . \, L_0 \, . \, T.$$

where α is a constant and is called coefficient of linear expansion and depends upon the type of material of the rod. It is defined as the fractional increase in length per degree rise in temperature.

$$\therefore \qquad \alpha = \frac{\Delta L}{L_0 \times T}$$

Table 2.2 indicates the value of coefficient of linear expansion for some of the materials.

**Table 2.2**

| *Materials* | *Coefficient of linear expansion* ($\times 10^{-6}$ °C) |
|---|---|
| Aluminium | 23 |
| Bakelite | 28 |
| Brass | 19 |
| Copper | 17 |
| Cast iron | 11.1 |
| Glass | 3 |
| Lead | 29 |
| Mercury | 60 |
| Mild steel | 12.1 |
| Nickel | 13 |
| Platinum | 9 |
| Silver | 19 |
| Tungsten | 4.5 |
| Zinc | 30 |

(*iv*) **Thermal Stresses.** When the temperature of a metal rod changes, expansion or contraction of the rod takes place. If the ends of the rod are fixed so as to prevent expansion or contraction then tensile or compressive stress called thermal stresses are set up in the rod. Sometimes the value of these stresses exceed the breaking stress of rod. Therefore, a provision is always made for expansion or contraction in metallic structures. For example a long steam pipe is provided with expansion joints. Small gaps are often left between successive lengths of railway line to allow for expansion. Similarly iron girders used in construction of bridges are not rigidly fixed to their piers but are capable of sliding over them to a small extent. Consider a rod having length $L$ and fixed at ends $P$, $Q$. If the temperature of rod is increased by $T$°C, then increase in length $\Delta L$ is given by the relation.

$$\Delta L = \alpha . L . T.$$

$$\therefore \quad \frac{\Delta L}{L} = \alpha T.$$

If the rod is prevented from expansion it will exert a force $F$ on the wall. If $A$ is the cross-section area of the rod them

$p$ = Thermal stress = $F/A$

and
$$\frac{p}{\frac{\Delta L}{L}} = E$$

where $E$ is Young's modulus.

$$\therefore \quad p = \frac{\Delta L}{L} . E$$

$$\therefore \quad p = \alpha . T . E.$$

(*v*) *Thermal conductivity.* The heat conducting property of a material is measured by its thermal conductivity. The thermal conductivity is high in case of good conductors of heat. Metals in general are good conductors of heat. Materials like wood, glass, wool or paper are poor conductors of heat.

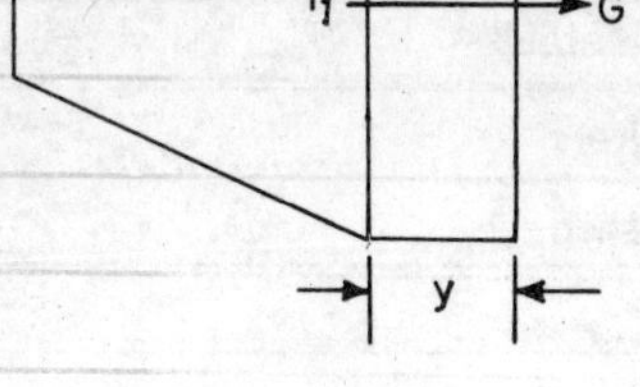

Fig. 2.1

Consider a slab of solid material as shown in Fig. 2.1.

$A$ = Area of cross-section through which heat flows by conduction to be measured perpendicularly to the direction heat of flow.

$y$ = Thickness.

Let the temperature at left hand face be $T_1$ and at right hand face $T_2$. $T_1$ being more than $T_2$.

The amount of heat $Q$ flowing from left hand face to right hand face in time $t$ is given by

$$Q \propto \frac{A\,(T_1 - T_2)\,t}{y} \;;\; Q = \frac{K.A.\,(T_1 - T_2)\,t}{y}$$

where $K$ is a constant and is called coefficient of thermal conductivity and is defined is the amount of heat in calories which flows through a cm. cube of material in one second when its opposite faces are kept at a temperature difference of 1°C. Table 2.3 indicates the values of thermal conductivity for some materials.

**Table 2.3**

| *Material* | *Thermal Conductivity (cal. / cm sec °C)* |
|---|---|
| Aluminium | 0.5 |
| Bronze | 0.16 |
| Bismuth | 0.019 |
| Brass | 0.310 |
| Copper | 0.92 |
| Cork | 0.0001 |
| Gold | 0.70 |
| Glass | 0.0025 |
| Iron | 0.16 |
| Monel Metal | 0.06 |
| Lead | 0.08 |
| Silver | 0.97 |
| Tungsten | 0.48 |
| Zinc | 0.26 |
| Ebonite | 0.0004 |
| Cast Iron | 0.13 |

## 2.3 Melting Point

Melting point of a solid is defined as the temperature at which it starts melting. When heat is added to a solid, its thermal energy increases until the atoms (or molecules) on the surface begin to break away from their equilibrium positions. The temperature at which melting begins depends on the amount of thermal energy required, which is turn depends upon the characteristics of the inter atomic and molecular bonds. Melting point is high for solids with stronger bonds. Table 2.4 indicates the melting point of some metals.

**Table 2.4**

| *Metal* | *Melting Point (°C)* |
|---|---|
| Aluminium | 600 |
| Chromium | 1890 |
| Cast Iron | 1150—1300 |
| Copper | 1083 |
| Cobalt | 1492 |
| Iron | 1537 |
| Lead | 327 |
| Magnesium | 650 |
| Nickel | 1453 |
| Platinum | 1769 |
| Silver | 961 |
| Tin | 232 |
| Tungsten | 3410 |
| Zinc | 419 |

## 2.4 Type of Engineering Materials

Materials used for making components are of two types.

(*i*) Metallic materials

(*ii*) Non-metallic materials.

**2.4.1 Metallic materials.** Metallic materials used in engineering are classified into two categories.

(*a*) Ferrous metals

(*b*) Non-ferrous metals.

Ferrous metals are those in which chief constituent is iron. In addition to iron they may contain C, S, P, Mn etc. The various ferrous metals used in engineering are as follows :

(*i*) Pig iron

(*ii*) Cast iron

(*iii*) Wrought iron

(*iv*) Plain carbon steels

(*v*) Alloy steels.

Non ferrous materials are those materials which do not contain iron. The principal non-ferrous metals commonly used are copper, zinc, aluminium, tin, lead etc. The commonly used non-ferrous metals alloys are gun metal, brass, bronze, etc.

**2.4.2 Non-metallic materials.** They include plastics, rubber, leather, wood, glass, carbon etc.

## 2.5 Pig Iron

The molten metal obtained from blast furnace is poured into moulds where it solidifies to form what is known as Pig Iron. Pig iron is available in the market in the form of billets and is used for making wrought iron, cast iron and steels. Pig iron contains about 93% pure iron. Its chemical composition is as follows :

C = 3 to 4%

Si = 0.5 to 3%

S = up to 0.1%

P = 0.25 to 1%

Mn = 0.1 to 1%.

Pressure of large amount of carbon makes the pig iron very bard and brittle and therefore it is not suitable for making castings and other useful articles without refining.

## 2.6 Cast Iron

Cast iron is produced by melting and refining pig iron in cupola furnace. It consist of iron, carbon, silicon, phosphorus, and manganese in varying amounts. The amount of carbon in cost iron is 2 to 4%. Cast iron has the following properties :

(*i*) It can be economically cast into complicated shapes.

(*ii*) It has the capacity of damping out vibrations is supports and frames of moving machinery.

(*iii*) It has resistance to wear, abrasion and corrosion.

(*iv*) It can be machined easily.

(*v*) It has high compressive strength.

(*vi*) Cast iron is brittle, has no plasticity and has low resistance to tension.

(*vii*) It can not be forged, magnetised or tempered.

(*viii*) It is difficult to be welded.

(*ix*) The impact strength of most cast iron is low.

### 2.6.1 Types of Cast Iron

Cast iron in general contains 2 to 4% carbon. Other constituents present in cast iron are about S = 0.02 to 0.1%, phosphorus upto 1% and manganese 0.5 to 1%. The carbon present in cast iron exists in two forms namely.

(*i*) Combined form.

(*ii*) Free form or graphite.

In combined form carbon exists in a state of chemical combination as iron carbide called cementite. Cementite is very hard and hence cast iron containing carbon in combined form is very hard and can not be easily machined. Graphite is soft and cast iron containing carbon in graphite form is soft and machinable. The type and properties of cast iron (C.I.) depend on whether the carbon is present in combined form or graphite form. The various types of cast iron are as follows :

(*i*) White cast iron.

(*ii*) Grey cast iron.

(*iii*) Malleable cast iron.

(*iv*) Nodular or spheroidal cast iron.

(*v*) Chilled cast iron.

(*vi*) Alloy cast iron.

**White Cast Iron.** It contains carbon in combined form. The iron on breaking shows a silvery white crystalline fracture. It is very hard and brittle and unmachinable. It has high compressive strength but a low resistance to impact. It has very limited applications.

Its percentage composition is as follows.

C = 1.75 to 2.3%

Si = 0.85 to 1.2%

Mn = 0.1 to 0.5%

S = 0.1 to 0.35%

P = 0.05 to 0.20%

**Grey Cast Iron.** It contains carbon in free form. It is soft and dark grey in colour. It is easily machinable and is the usual product of the iron foundry. It is widely used for cylinders, cars wheels, columns, automobiles, locomotives and pipes. Its percentage composition is as follows :

C = 2.5 to 3.5%

Si = 1 to 2.50%

Mn = 0.4 to 1%

S = 0.02 to 0.15%

P = 0.15 to 1%

For pressure vessels grey cast iron is useful up to 340°C and for other application it can be usefully employed up to 425°C, when grey cast iron is repeatedly heated at about 425°C grain growth, distortion and brittleness is produced.

**Malleable Cast Iron.** It is obtained by annealing white cast iron at 950 to 1000°C with the object of separating carbon in finely divided form. It is tough, machinable and malleable. It is of two types :

(*a*) White heart malleable cast iron.

(*b*) Black heart malleable cast iron.

White heart malleable cast iron on breaking shows a brightly crystalline fracture whereas the fracture of black heart malleable is dark grey or black. White heart malleable cast iron castings exhibit non-uniform mechanical properties, thicker sections are harder and less ductile. The maximum thickness of castings is limited to about 18 mm.

Typical composition of white heart malleable cast iron is as follows :

C = 32—3.6%

P = 0.1%

Si = 04—1.1%

S = 01—0.3%

Mn = 01-0.40%

A typical composition of black heart malleable cast iron is as follows :

C = 2.2 to 2.8%

P = 0.1%

Si = 0.7 to 1.1%

S = 0.03 to 0.1%

Mn = 0.3 to 0.38%

Malleable cast iron is less brittle and more ductile. Malleable cast iron is used where small intricate jobs are needed which should possess shock resistance. It is used for motor parts like differential and steering gear housings, axles, brake pedals, structural components for railway carriages, agricultural and textile machinery, spanners, cranks etc. Black heart malleable cast iron is quite commonly used.

**Nodular Cast Iron.** It is obtained by the addition of magnesium into molten cast iron. This causes the graphite to take a spheroidal or nodular form.

It behaves like steel and gives better machined surfaces. It has high strength, ductility and impact strength. It is used for hydraulic cylinders, cylinder heads, gears, cams, gear boxes, liners of I.C. engines, and heat resisting furnaces. The composition of nodular cast iron (as cast) is as follows :

C = 3.3%

Mn = 0.4%

P = 0.03%

Ni = 0.75%

Mg = 0.06%

Si = 0.6%

This iron is also called spheroidal graphite cast iron, ductile cast iron or high strength cast iron. It has high yield point as compared to malleable cast iron and can resist quite high loads without permanent deformation. It can be welded and galvanised easily.

## 2.7. Wrought Iron

Wrought iron is pure form of iron and contains iron about 99.8%. It is obtained by remelting pir iron in puddling process.

**Properties.** Properties of wrought iron are as follows :

(*i*) It can be rolled, drawn, forged and welded.

(*ii*) It is ductile and malleable and can be used for wire drawing the sheets.

**Table 2.5 indicates the properties of C.I. and cast steels.**

**Mechanical Properties and Applications of Cast Irons and Cast Steels**

| *IS Designation* | *Tensile strength kg/mm²* | *Stress kg/mm²* | *Elongation per cent (gauge length $5.65\sqrt{A}$)* | *BHN* | *Typical Applications* |
|---|---|---|---|---|---|
| **Grey C.I. Castings** | | Transverse rupture stress | | | **Flywheels, pulleys, low speed gears, machine tool parts like beds and frames.** |
| Grade—15 | 13 to 19 | 28.5 to 41.7 | — | 146 to 197 | |
| 20 | 17 to 24 | 33.5 to 46.4 | — | 179 to 223 | |
| 25 | 22 to 28 | 38.6 to 51.0 | — | 197 to 241 | |
| 30 | 27 to 31 | 43.6 to 52.5 | — | 207 to 241 | |
| 35 | 32 to 35 | 55.3 to 57.3 | — | 207 to 241 | |
| 40 | 37 to 40 | 62.7 to 63.7 | — | 241 to 320 | |
| **Spheroidal or Nodular** | | Minimum proof stress | | | Intricate castings frames for machines, dies for press formings. |
| **Graphite Cast Iron** | | 0.2 percent | | | |
| IS Grade—SG 80/2 | 80 | 48 | 2 | 260 to 330 | |
| SG 60/2 | 60 | 40 | 2 | 210 to 280 | |
| SG 42/12 | 42 | 28 | 82 | 187 max. | |

| | | | | | |
|---|---|---|---|---|---|
| **Cast Steels** | | Yield strength (10.5 per cent proof stress) | | | Complicated castings. |
| IS - CS 65 | 65 | 40 | 17 | 190 | |
| CS 85 | 85 | 71 | 12 | 248 | |
| CS 125 | 125 | 102 | 5 | 363 | |
| **Alloy Cast Iron** | | Yield strength | | | Castings where toughness, stremgth, wear-resistance is required as in crank shafts of automobile engines. |
| Nickel C.I. | 25 | 12 | — | 180 min. | |
| Ni-Mo C.I. | 30 | 18 | — | 220 min. | |

(*iii*) It possesses the property of recovering rapidly from overstrain which enables it to accommodate sudden shock without injury.

**Uses.** It is used for railway couplings, chains, crane hooks and anchors, steam, oil and water pipes.

## 2.8. Steel

Steel is an alloy mainly of iron and carbon. It also contains little amount of sulphur and phosphorus manganese and silicon. Steel basically differs from cast iron in the amount of carbon contents contained in it. In steel the carbon in present in the combined form. The amount of carbon present in steel is up to 1.5%. Higher percentage of carbon makes the steel tough and hard.

## 2.9. Classification of Steels

Steels are classified as follows :

(*i*) Plain carbon steels (*ii*) Alloy steels.

## 2.10. Plain Carbon Steels

Plain carbon steels owe their properties to the presence of amount of carbon. These steels, according to their carbon contents are classified as follows :

(1) Dead mild steel. (2) Mild steel.

(3) Medium carbon steel. (4) High carbon steel.

Plain carbon steels are designated by the letter C followed by a number representing average carbon percentage content in hundredth of a percent. For example a plain carbon steel designated as C-30 contains carbon 0.30%.

Table 2.6 shows typical applications of plain carbon steels.

**Table 2.6**

| *Type of steel* | *Carbon%* | *Typical applications* |
|---|---|---|
| Dead mild steel | 0.06 to 0.15 | Thin sheets and wires, boiler, plate, ship plates, welded and solid drawn tubes, nails screws. |
| Mild steel | 0.15 to 0.45 | |
| | 0.15 to 0.3% | Bars, plates |
| | 0.15 to 0.45 | Axles, shafts, connecting rods. |
| Medium carbon steel | 0.45% to 0.8% | |
| | 0.45 to 0.6 | Crankshafts, scraper blades |
| | 0.6 to 0.8% | Drop hammerdies, automobile springs, anvils. |
| High carbon steel | 0.8 to 1.5 | |
| | 0.8 to 0.9 | Punches,chisels, hand tools, railway rails. |
| | 0.9 to 1.1 | Springs, shear blades, dies taps, milling cutters, broaches. |
| | 1.1 to 1.2 | Lathe tools, wood working tools |
| | 1.2 to 1.3 | Files |
| | 1.3 to 1.5 | Metal cutting saws, dies for wire drawing. |

Table 2.7 shows strength of some varieties of steel.

**Table 2.7**

| *Types of steel* | *Ultimate strength kg/cm²* | *Yield point kg/cm²* | *Elastic limit kg/cm²* |
|---|---|---|---|
| Carbon steel (C-0.05% to 0.15%) | 4100 | 2730 | 2170 |
| Carbon steel (C-0.15% to 0.25%) | 4700 | 3010 | 2450 |
| Carbon steel (C-0.25% to 0.35%) | 4500 | 3220 | 2940 |
| Carbon steel (C-0.35% to 0.45%) | 5950 | 3850 | 3500 |
| Nickel steel (Ni-0.25% t0 3.75%) | 5400 | 3600 | 3200 |

**Table 2.8**
**Typical uses of Carbon Steels**

| *Steel Designation* | *Typical uses* |
|---|---|
| C10 | Used for making camshafts, cams, light duty gears, worms, gudgeon pins, selector forks, spindles, pawls, ratchets, chain wheels, etc. |
| C15 | Used for lightly stressed parts. |
| C30 | Used for cold formed levers-Hardened and tempered tie rods, cables, sprockets, hubs and bushes-steel tubes. |
| C35 | Steel for low stressed parts, automobile tubes and fasteners. |
| C35 Mn75 | Steel for making low stressed parts in machine structures, cycle and motorcycle framer tubes, fish paltes for rails and fasteners. |
| C40 | Used for crankshafts, shafts, spindles, automobile axle beams, push rods, connecting rods, studs, bolts, lightly stressed gears, etc. |
| C45 | Used for spindles of machine tools, bigger gears, bolts and shafts. |
| C50 | Used for making keys, shafts cylinders, machine components requiring moderate wear resistance. In surface hardened condition it is also suitable for large-pitch worms and gears. |

*(Contd...)*

| *Steel Designation* | Typical uses |
|---|---|
| C50Mn1 | Rail steel. Also used for making spike bolts, gear shafts, rocking levers and cylinder liners. |
| C55Mn75 | Used for making gears, cylinders, cams, keys, crank shafts, sprockets and machine parts requiring moderate wear resistance for which toughness is not of primary importance. |
| C60 | Steel for making spindles for machine tools, hardened screws and nuts, couplings, crank shafts, axles and pinions. |

**Example 2.2.** *State the carbon percentage in plain carbon steels used for the following components :*

*(i) Hammers* *(ii) Stamping and pressing tools*
*(iii) Blacksmith's tools* *(iv) Chisels*
*(v) Slotting and turning tools*
*(vi) Drills* *(vii) Taps*
*(viii) Dies* *(ix) Broaches*
*(x) Razors* *(xi) Reamers*
*(xii) Files* *(xiii) Axles*
*(xiv) Knives.*

**Solution.** The various plane carbon steels used for different components mentioned are as follows :

| *Name of component* | *Carbon per cent in carbon steel* |
|---|---|
| (*i*) Hammers | 0.6-0.7 |
| (*ii*) Stamping and pressing tools | 0.6-0.7 |
| (*iii*) Blacksmith's tools | 0.7-0.9 |
| (*iv*) Chisels | 0.8-0.9 |
| (*v*) Slotting and turning tools | 1.3 |
| (*vi*) Drills | 1.2-1.3 |
| (*vii*) Taps | 1.1-1.2 |
| (*viii*) Dies | 0.9-1.1 |
| (*ix*) Broaches | 1% |
| (*x*) Razors | 1.2% |
| (*xi*) Reamers | 1% |

*Contd...*

| Name of component | Carbon per cent in carbon steel |
|---|---|
| (xii) Files | 1.3% |
| (xiii) Axles | 0.4% |
| (xiv) Knives | 1.4% |

## 2.11 Alloys Steels

Alloy steels are those which in addition to iron and carbon contain alloying elements like nickel, chromium, vanadium, tungsten, molybdenum cobalt, manganese, silicon etc. Each of these alloying elements give a typical property to steel.

The effect of alloying elements is as follows :

*(i)* **Nickel.** Nickel increases toughness and strength of steel. It makes the steel corrosion resistant. It improves the ductility. It is generally added to low and medium carbon steels. The amount added may be up to 36%.

*(ii)* **Chromium.** Chromium is added to steel to increase the depth to which the steel may be hardened. The amount added may be up to 18%. Steel containing upto 1.5 chromium possesses more tensile strength and hardness.

*(iii)* **Vanadium.** It acts as a deoxidiser and helps in degasification of steel in molten state. The addition of vanadium up to 0.2% in low and medium carbon steels increases tensile strength and elastic limit without loss in ductility.

*(iv)* **Tungsten.** Addition of tungsten makes the steel hard though and wear-resistant. The amount added varies from 0.5 to 15%. High percentage of tungsten makes the steel to retain its hardness even when highly heated. 6 to 18% tungsten is added in high speed steels which are used for making cutting tools, dies, punches, drills, reamers, and milling cutters.

*(v)* **Molybdenum.** It forms carbides and also dissolves in ferrite to some extent and gives hardness and toughness to steel. While molybdenum is used alone in a few steels is finds its greatest use when combined with other alloying elements such as nickel chromium or both.

*(vi)* **Manganese.** It acts as a deoxidizer and counteracts the undesirable effect of sulphur. Addition of manganese from 1 to 1.5% makes the steel strong and tough. When added from 11 to 14% in steel containing carbon 0.8 to 1.5 makes the steel very hard and tough.

(*vii*) **Cobalt.** It refines grains and improves hardness toughness and tensile strength. It is added from 1 to 12% in high speed steel. It improves magnetic properties of steel.

(*viii*) **Silicon.** It improves hardness, elastic limit and magnetic permeability of steel. The amount added is up to 2%.

## 2.12 Some Common Alloy Steels

(*i*) **Nickel steels.** In these steels nickel is the principal alloying element. The amount added may be upto 36%.

Steel having carbon 0.2 to 0.35% and nickel up to 5% are tough, resistant to fatigue and have more tensile strength. Nickel steel containing 36% nickel is called Invar. It has least co-efficient of expansion and is mainly used for measuring instruments.

(*ii*) **Chromium steels.** In these steels chromium is the principal alloying element. Addition upto 2% makes the steel more strong and hard but the ductility is reduced. Addition of both nickel and chromium improves the ductility of steel. Chromium steels are used for surgical instrument drills, files, wrenches etc.

(*iii*) **Stainless steel.** These steels contain mainly chromium and nickel and are classified as follows :

(*a*) **Martensitic Stainless Steels.** They contain approximately 11 to 14% chromium and 0.1% to 0.3% carbon. These steel can be cold worked and work hardened. They are used for making springs, steam turbine blades, cutlery, and ball bearings.

(*b*) **Ferritic Stainless Steel.** They contain chromium from 15 to 30% and cannot be heat treated. They are resistant to corrosion and have great strength. They are used for household utensils, surgical instruments, and are used for making components used in brewery, chemical industries and automobile. They are also known as straight stainless steels.

(*c*) **Austenitic Stainless Steels.** These steels contain chromium and nickel. They contain 15 - 20% chromium and 8 to 10% nickel 18/8 (chromium = 18% and nickel = 8%) steel is most commonly used. These steels cannot be hardened by heat treatment. They are used for household equipment, heat exchangers and dairy equipment.

(*iv*) **High Speed Steel.** High speed steels can withstand high temperature without losing hardness. Therefore, they are used for making tools. The tools made up of high speed steels can be run at high speeds as compared to tools made up of carbon steels. Drills, milling cutters, tools for lathe, and shaper are made up of high speed steel. The various high speed steels are as follows :

(*i*) *Tungsten high speed steel.* It is also known as 18 - 4 - 1 high speed steel as it contains tungsten 14% chromium 4% and vanadium 1%. Such steels contain carbon 0.7%.

(*ii*) *Molybdenum high speed steels.* It contains molybdenum 6%, tungsten 6%, chromium 4%, vanadium 2%.

(*iii*) *Cobalt high speed steels.* In these steels the amount of cobalt is upto 15%. A typical cobalt high speed steel has the following composition :

| | |
|---|---|
| C | = 0.8% |
| Tungsten, (W) | = 14% |
| Chromium, (Cr) | = 4% |
| Vanadium, (V) | = 2% |
| Cobalt, (Co) | = 8% |
| Molybdenum, (Mo) | = 0.5%. |

(*v*) **Cemented Carbide.** It is a very hard material and is made by mixing tungsten metal powder with finely divided powder of lamp black (carbon). The mixture is heated to about 1600°C in an atmosphere of hydrogen. Carbide obtained is used for making tool tips. Carbide tools can be used at high cutting speed and they can resist high temperature.

(*vi*) **Manganese Steel.** It contains 10 to 15% manganese with carbon 1 to 1.5%. This steel is non magnetic, has high percentage of elongation and can be forged. It is used for stone crushing rollers, cranks and connecting rods of locomotives.

Alloy steels are designed by the number representing carbon percentage followed by chemical symbol of the alloying elements and then number indicating the average content of element being mentioned. For example an alloy steel designated as 30 $Ni_4\,Cr_1$ means alloy steel containing.

C = 0.3% Ni = 4%

Cr = 1%.

Table 2.9 shows applications and composition of some of alloy steels.

**Table 2.9**

| Type of steel | I.S. specification 1570/1961 | Average Chemical Composition (%) | | | | | | | | | | | Applications |
|---|---|---|---|---|---|---|---|---|---|---|---|---|---|
| | | C | Mn | Si | S | P | Cr | Ni | Mo | W | V | Co | |
| High speed steels | T70 W 18 Cr4 VI | 0.70 | 0.40 | 0.35 | 0.025 | 0.025 | 4.15 | — | — | — | 1.20 | — | Milling Cutters, Broaches |
| | T75 W18 Co6 Cr4 VI Mo 75 | 0.75 | 0.40 | 0.36 | 0.025 | 0.025 | 4.20 | — | 0.75 | 18.25 | 5.25 | 5.50 | Machining Blades, Lathe Tools |
| | T75 W18 Co10 Cr4 V2 Mo75 | 0.75 | 0.40 | 0.35 | 0.025 | do | do | — | do | do | 1.80 | 0.25 | High Tensile material |
| | T123 W14 Co5 Cr4 VI | 1.25 | do | do | do | do | do | — | 0.60 | do | 4.00 | 5.00 | Heavy duty cutting tools valve seats |
| Die steel | | 0.85 | 1.90 | 0.25 | — | — | 0.30 | — | — | 13.25 | 0.15 | — | Blanking and stamping dies |
| Stainless steels | 3O Cr 13 | 0.32 | 0.50 | 0.50 | 0.025 | 0.030 | 53.00 | 1.55 | — | — | — | — | Pump valves, parts, Air craft parts |
| | O4 Cr 19 Ni9 | 0.06 | 1.05 | do | do | do | 99.00 | 9.50 | — | — | — | — | Domestic and table wares surgical brewing equipment |
| | O5 Cr 18 Nill Mo3 | do | do | do | do | do | 17.50 | 12.55 | 2.55 | — | — | — | Domestic and table wares surgicale equipment |
| Spring steel | 55Si2 Mn90 | 0.55 | 0.90 | 1.70 | 0.03 | 0.03 | — | — | — | — | — | — | Springs |
| Ball Bearing Steel | 105 Cr1 | 1.00 | 0.40 | 0.25 | 0.025 | 0.025 | 1.00 | — | — | — | — | — | Ball bearings-suitable for parts of maximum hardness |
| | T33 W9 Cr3 V38 | 0.32 | 0.30 | 0.22 | 0.025 | 0.025 | 3.50 | — | — | 9.00 | 0.40 | — | Large forge tools, hot working dies |
| Hot Work Steels | T35 Cr 5 Mo5 V30 | 0.035 | 0.37 | 1.00 | — | — | 1.00 | — | 1.40 | — | — | — | For casting dies |
| | T90 Mn2 W50 Cr-45 | 0.90 | 1.50 | 0.22 | 0.025 | 0.025 | 0.45 | — | — | 0.50 | 0.50 | — | Cold punches, engraving tools press tools, precision instruments. |
| Cold work Steels | T160 Cr12 | 1.60 | 0.37 | do | do | do | 12.00 | — | 0.80 | — | | — | Punching dies, sheets, blades |

Table 2.10 shows properties of the alloy steel other than heat resisting steels.

**Table 2.10**

| *Designation (ISI Grade)* | *Tensile strength (kg/cm$^2$)* | *Yield Strength (kg/cm$^2$)* | *Minimum Elongation (%)* | *Brinell Hardness Number (BHN)* |
|---|---|---|---|---|
| (1) | (2) | (3) | (4) | (5) |
| 20 Mn 2 | 6000-7500 | 4400 | 18 | 170-217 |
| | 7000-8500 | 5000 | 16 | 201-248 |
| 27 Mn 2 | 6000-7500 | 4400 | 18 | 170-217 |
| | 7000-8500 | 5000 | 16 | 201-248 |
| 37 Mn 2 | 6000-7500 | 4400 | 18 | 170-217 |
| | 7000-8500 | 5400 | 18 | 201-248 |
| | 8000-9500 | 6000 | 16 | 229-277 |
| | 9000-10500 | 7000 | 15 | 255-311 |
| 35 Mn 2 Mo 28 | 7000-8500 | 5400 | 18 | 201-148 |
| | 8000-9500 | 6000 | 16 | 229-277 |
| | 9000-10500 | 7000 | 15 | 255-311 |
| | 10000-11500 | 8000 | 13 | 285-341 |
| 40 Cr 1 | 7000-8500 | 5400 | 18 | 201-248 |
| | 8000-9500 | 6000 | 16 | 229-277 |
| | 9000-10500 | 7000 | 16 | 255-311 |
| 40 Cr 1 Mo 28 | 7000-8500 | 5000 | 18 | 201-248 |
| | 8000-9500 | 6000 | 16 | 229-277 |
| | 9000-10500 | 7000 | 15 | 255-311 |
| | 10000-11500 | 8000 | 13 | 955-341 |
| 30 Ni 1 Cr 1 | 15500 | 13000 | 8 | 444 |

### 2.12.1 Indian Standard Code for Designation of Steel

1. According to this standard, a steel may be designated by a group of symbols indicating the important characteristics in the following order.

(*a*) Tensile strength, (*b*) Carbon content,

(*c*) Alloy content, (*d*) Sulphur and phosphorus limits,
(*e*) Weldability, (*f*) Surface finish,
(*g*) Surface condition, (*h*) Steel quality, and
(*i*) Treatment.

2. If considered necessary, one of the following prefixes precede the designation of steel to avoid confusion with designation of other materials to indicate, if required, its form.

(*i*) S - for wrought steel

(*ii*) CS - for cast steel.

3. For steels, specially those which are standardised on the basis of their ultimate tensile strength ; without detailed composition the symbol 'St' is to be followed by the minimum ultimate tensile strength expressed in $kg/mm^2$.

*e.g.* St, 40 steel means a steel having ultimate tensile strength of 40 $kg/mm^2$.

Table 2.10 (A) shows the various standardised steels specified by tensile strength and their typical uses. IS : 1570 - 1961 also specifies the ultimate tensile strength and corresponding minimum percentage elongation for round and flat test pieces for these steels.

**Table 2.10 (A)**

| *General Classification* | *Steel Designation* | *Typical Uses* |
|---|---|---|
| General structural steels, available in the form of bar sections, tubes plates and strips | St 30 | Structural steel sheets for plain drawn parts, tubes for oil well casing, strain, water and air passages, cycle, motorcycle and automobile tubes, river bars and wire. |
| | St 32<br>St 34 | Steels for locomotive carriage and car structures, screw stock. |
| | St 37 | Structural steel for chemical pressure vessels. |
| | St 39 | Structural steel for ship, chemical vessels, air receivers and fasterners. |

(*Contd*...)

| General Classification | Steel Designation | Typical Uses |
|---|---|---|
| | St 42 | Structural steel for bridges and building construction, railway rolling stock, screw spikes and oil well casing. |
| | St 44 | Structural steel for railway rolling stock pressure vessels, fasteners, and valve fittings for compressed gas cylinders. |
| | St 47 | Structural steel for railway rolling stock, pressure parts of marine and land boilers, and rivets for air receives. |
| | St 50 | Structural steel for mines, forgings for marine engines and machine parts. |
| Medium tensile structural steels | St 52 | Steel for railway wheels, disc wheel centres for railway and electric tramway cars and seamless tubes. |
| | St 55 | High tensile steel for locomotive carriage wagon and tramway axles, bolts, and seamless and welded tubes. |
| | St 58 | High tensile steel for bridges and general construction, and bars and wire for concrete reinforcement. |
| | St 63 | High tensile steel for tramway axles and seamless tubes. |
| High tensile steels | St 66<br>St 78<br>St 88 | High tensile steel for locomotive, carriage and wagon wheels and tyres, and machine parts for heavy loading. |

4. For plain carbon steels, the letter 'C' is to be followed by the average carbon content in hundredth of a per cent.

*e.g.* C 30 plain carbon steel contains carbon 0.30%.

5. For alloys steels, the average carbon content in hundredths of a per cent is to be used without the prefix 'C'.

The member representing the carbon content is followed by the symbols for one or more of predominating alloying elements followed by the members indicating their average contents.

20 Cr 18 Ni 2 means alloy steel contains.

C = 0.2%

Cr = 18%

Ni = 2%

15 Cr 65 means C = 0.15% and Cr = 0.65%.

6. For carbon and alloy tools steels the letter 'T' is to be followed by the average carbon content in hundredths of a per cent.

In case, where only a maximum limit for carbon is specified the carbon range may be assumed as 10 points (0.10 per cent) which is the standard range in the current manufacturing practice. The average carbon content may, therefore, be taken as 5 points (0.05 per cent) less than the maximum limit. Where maximum carbon content specified is less than ten points (0.10 per cent) the carbon index shall be the maximum divided by two.

7. The alloy index is to consist of chemical symbols of the significant elements arranged in descending order of percentage contents. The nominal or average percentage of each alloying element is to indicated by an index number following its chemical symbol.

Where the minimum contents of Nimbium, Titanium, etc., are specified as stabilizers, they are to be considered as significant alloying elements and indicated as the end of the designation.

| *Average Alloy Content* | *Index Number* |
|---|---|
| Upto 1 per cent | Average alloying content upto 2 decimal places underhand by a bar except in cases, such as Boron, Nitrogen, etc., where it is to be indicated by the alloy symbol only. |
| 1 to 10 per cent | Rounded to the nearest, whole number, where necessary, to distinguish two steels of the same type having overlapping ranges of alloying contents, the alloying contents may be rounded off to one place of decimal, the decimal digit being underlined by a bar. |
| 10 per cent and over | Rounded to the nearest whole number. |

Where only the minimum limit is indicated for an alloying element, the range may be taken as 10 points (0.10 per cent) over the minimum limit and the average taken as 5 points (0.05 per cent) more than the minimum.

8. Where two or more significant alloying elements have the same alloy index in the same steel, the chemical symbols are to be grouped together followed by the alloy index.

9. Sulphur and lead content in free cutting steel are to be treated and indicated as alloying elements.

10. The letter 'K' is to be used to indicate steel with special limits for the maximum sulphur and phosphorus.

11. Guaranteed weldability of steel is to be indicated by the following symbols :

(*i*) *w* — fusion weldable

(*ii*) *wp* — pressure weldable

(*iii*) *wr* — weldable by resistance

(*iv*) *ws* — weldable by spot welding

12. Finish is indicated by the following symbols.

(*i*) *F* — Black sheet,

(*ii*) *F2* — Black sheet suitable for enamelling and galvanising,

(*iii*) *F3* — Pickled surface, free from scale, moderately rough surface permissible

(*iv*) *F4* — Double pickled surface : having a smooth surface ; slight grooves and pores perm issible suitable for ordinary drawing

(*v*) *F5* — Suitable for deep drawing and spray painting,

(*vi*) *F6* — Suitable for extra deep drawing, spray painting and plaining,

(*vii*) *F7* — Cold finished.

13. To indicate surface condition following symbols are used.

(*i*) *J* — Bright drawn or bright rolled,

(*ii*) *J2* — Precision ground, skinned ;

(*iii*) *J3* — pickled or descaled ;

(*iv*) *J4* — Shot blasted or sand blasted,

(*v*) *J5* — Deseamed or scarfed and *J6* - Reeled.

14. To indicate steel quality,

(*ii*) *E* — Stabilized against stress corrosion or intergrannular attack,

(*iii*) *L* — control cooled to ensure freedom from flakes,

(*iv*) *D* — Fully killed (deoxidized),

(v) *D2* — Semi skilled,

(vi) *R* — Rimming quality,

(vii) *G* — Grain size controlled,

(viii) *H* — Hardenability controlled,

(ix) *I* — Inclusion controlled, and

(x) *M* — Structural homogeneity guaranteed by macro-etch test.

15. The following symbols are to be used to indicate treatment give to the steel :

(i) *a* — Annealed or softened,

(ii) *c* — Case carburised,

(iii) *d* — Hard drawn, cold reduce

(iv) *h*—Hot rolled,

(v) *n*—Normalised,

(vi) *o*—Spherodised,

(vii) *p*—Patented,

(viii) *q*—Hardened and tempered,

(ix) *s*—Stress relieved,

(x) *t*—Tempered.

Properties of some of carbon steels are as indicated in table 2.11.

**Table 2.11 Properties of Carbon Steels**

| *Designation (ISI Grade)* | *%C* | *%Mn* | *Tensile Strength kg/cm²* | *Minimum elongation percentage* | *Brinell, hardness (BHN)* |
|---|---|---|---|---|---|
| *C* 07 | 0.12 max | 0.50 max | 3200-4000 | 27 | — |
| *C* 10 | 0.15 max | 0.30-0.60 | 3400-4200 | 26 | — |
| *C* 14 | 0.10-0.18 | 0.40-0.70 | 3700-4500 | 26 | 137 |
| *C* 15 | 0.20 max | 0.30-0.60 | 3700-4900 | 25 | 137 |
| *C* 15 **Mn 75** | 0.10-0.20 | 0.60-0.90 | 4200-5000 | 25 | 163 |
| *C* 20 | 0.15-0.20 | 0.60-0.10 | 4400-5200 | 24 | 156 |
| *C* 25 | 0.20-0.30 | 0.30-0.60 | 4400-5400 | 27 | 170 |
| *C* 25 **Mn 75** | 0.20-0.30 | 0.00-0.90 | 4700-5700 | 22 | 207 |
| *C* 30 | 0.25-0.35 | 0.60-0.90 | 5000-6000 | 21 | 179 |

*Contd...*

| *Designation (ISI Grade)* | *%C* | *%Mn* | *Tensile Strength kg/cm²* | *Minimum elongation percentage* | *Brinell, hardness (BHN)* |
|---|---|---|---|---|---|
| *C* 35 | 0.30-0.40 | 0.35-0.60 | 5200-6200 | 20 | 187 |
| *C* 35 **Mn 75** | 0.30-0.40 | 0.60-0.90 | 5500-6500 | 20 | 223 |
| *C* 40 | 0.35-0.45 | 0.60-0.90 | 5800-6800 | 18 | 217 |
| *C* 45 | 0.40-0.50 | 0.60-0.90 | 6300-7100 | 15 | 229 |
| *C* 50 | 0.45-0.55 | 0.60-0.90 | 6600-7800 | 13 | 241 |
| *C* 50 **Mn 1** | 0.45-0.55 | 1.0-1.10 | 7200 (min) | 11 | 255 |
| *C* 55 **Mn 75** | 0.50-0.60 | 0.60-0.90 | 7200 (min) | 13 | 265 |
| *C* 60 | 0.55-0.65 | 0.50-0.80 | 7500 (min) | 11 | 255 |
| *C* 65 | 0.60-0.70 | 0.50-0.80 | 7500 (min) | 10 | 255 |

Table 2.11 *A* indicates the percentage composition of some of alloy steels.

**Table 2.11 A**

**Alloy Steels - other than Stainless and Heat-Resisting Types**

(*Ref. IS : 1570 - 1961*)

| *Steel Designation* | | *Percentage Composition* | *Uses* |
|---|---|---|---|
| **(A) Creeping Resisting Steels** | | | |
| (*i*) | 10Mo 55 | C = 0.15 max. ; Si = 0.10-0.35 ; Mn = 0.40-0.70 ; Ni = 0.30 max. ; Cr = 0.25 max. ; Mo = 0.45-0.65. | (*i*) and (*ii*)-Steam Pipes, Boiler tubing, Carburised Gears, Pipe Fittings and Plates for use in the steam service (upto 300°C). |
| (*ii*) | 20Mo55 | C = 0.15-0.25 ; Si = 0.10-0.35 ; Mn = 0.40-0.70 ; Ni = 0.30 max. ; Cr = 0.25 max. ; Mo = 0.45-0.65. | |
| (*iii*) | 15Cr90Mo55 | C= 0.10-0.20 ; Si = 0.10-0.35 ; Mn = 0.40-0.70 ; Ni = 0.30 max. ; Cr = 0.70-1.10 ; Mo = 0.45-0.65. | (*iii*) and (*iv*) same uses as above ; in addition, for Bolts and Forgings in steam service in the H. and T. state (moderate temperature). |

| Steel Designation | | Percentage Composition | Uses |
|---|---|---|---|
| (*iv*) | 40Cr1Mo60 | C = 0.35-0.45 ;<br>Si = 0.10-0.35 ;<br>Mn = 0.40-0.70 ;<br>Cr = 1.00-1.50 ;<br>Mo = 0.50-0.20. | |
| (*v*) | 35Cr1V25Mo 65 | C = 0.25-0.45 ;<br>Si = 0.20-0.50 ;<br>Mn = 0.40-0.70 ;<br>Ni = 0.30 max. ;<br>Cr = 1.00-1.50 ;<br>Mo = 0.50-0.80 ;<br>V = 0.20-0.30. | Forgings, Bolts and Nuts for high temperature service in the H. and T. state. |

## (B) Steels for Heavy Duty and Highly Stressed Parts :

| | | | |
|---|---|---|---|
| (*i*) | 15NiCr1 Mo12 | C = 0.12-0.18 ;<br>Si = 0.10-0.35 ;<br>Mn = 0.60-1.00 ;<br>Ni = 1.00-1.50 ;<br>Cr = 0.75-1.25 ;<br>Mo = 0.08-0.15. | (*i*), (*ii*) and (*iii*)—Heavy Duty Gears, Heavy Vehicles and Automobile Transmission Components. These are C.H. steels. |
| (*ii*) | 15Ni2Cr1 Mo15 | C, Si Mn and Cr contents are same as in (*i*) and<br>Ni = 1.50-2.00 ;<br>Mo = 0.10-0.20. | |
| (*iii*) | 16NiCr2 Mo20 | C = 0.12-0.20 ;<br>Si = 0.10-0.35 ;<br>Mn = 0.40-0.70 ;<br>Ni = 1.80-2.20 ;<br>Cr = 1.40-1.70 ;<br>Mo = 0.15-0.25. | |
| (*iv*) | 13Ni3Cr80 | C = 0.10-0.15 ;<br>Si = 0.10-0.35 ;<br>Mn = 0.40-0.70 ;<br>Ni = 3.00-3.50 ;<br>Cr = 0.60-1.00. | |
| (*v*) | 35Ni1Cr60 | C = 0.30-0.40 ;<br>Si = 0.10-0.35 ;<br>Mn = 0.60-0.90 ;<br>Ni = 1.00-1.50 ;<br>Cr = 0.45-0.75. | Aircraft and Heavy Vehicle Crankshaft and Connecting Rods, Gear shaft, Chain parts, Clutches Gears, Camshafts, etc. |

*Contd...*

| | | | |
|---|---|---|---|
| (*vi*) | 30Ni4Cr1 | C = 0.2-0.34 ;<br>Si = 0.10-0.35 ;<br>Mn = 0.40-0.70 ;<br>Ni = 3.00-4.30 ;<br>Cr = 1.10-1.40.<br>C = 0.35-0.45 ; | Highly stressed Gears and other components requiring tensile strength of the order of 160 kg/mm$^2$ and where minimum distortion due to heat treatment is essential. |
| (*vii*) | 40Ni2Cr1 Mo28 | C = 0.35-0.45 ;<br>Si = 0.10-0.35 ;<br>Mn = 0.40-0.70 ;<br>Ni = 1.25-1.75 ;<br>Cr = 0.90-1.30 ;<br>Mo = 0.20-0.35. | High strength machine parts, collets ; spindles, screws, High tensile Bolts Gears and Pinions, Axle Shafts, Tappets, Crankshafts, Connecting, Rods, Boring Bars. |
| (*viii*) | 31Ni2Cr65 Mo55 | C = 0.27-0.35 ;<br>Si = 0.10-0.35 ;<br>Mn = 0.40-0.70 ;<br>Ni = 2.25-2.75 ;<br>Cr = 0.50-0.80 ;<br>Mo = 0.40-0.70. | Bolts, Studs, Shafts, Crankshafts, Connecting Rods, Gears, Axles, Mandrel. |

**Table 2.11 B**

## Carbon and Carbon-Manganese Free-cutting Steels

(*Ref : IS : 1570 — 1961*)

| *Steel Designation and percentage Composition* | *Uses* |
|---|---|
| 10S11<br>(C = 0.15 max ;<br>Si =0.05-0.30 ;<br>Mn = 0.60-0.90 ;<br>S = 0.08-0.13 ;<br>P = 0.06 max.) | Low-duty bolts, nuts and studs. |
| 14Mn1S14<br>(C = 0.14-0.18 ;<br>Si = 0.05-0.30 ;<br>Mn = 1.20-1.50 ;<br>S = 0.10-0.18 ;<br>P = 0.06 max.) | C.H. steel for camshafts, Tappet Rollers, Lightly stressed gears, Gudgeon pins and all relatively lightly stressed gun and general details requiring high wear hardness. |
| 25Mn1S14<br>(C = 0.20-0.30 ;<br>Si = 0.25 max. ;<br>Mn = 1.00-1.50 ;<br>S = 0.10-0.18 ;<br>P = 0.06 max.) | Welded parts ; may be substituted for C30 and C35 where improved machining, deeper hardening and higher physical properties are required. |

*Contd...*

| *Steel Designation and percentage Composition* | *Uses* |
|---|---|
| 40S18 (C = 0.35-0.45 ; Si = 0.25 max. ; Mn = 0.80-1.20 ; S = 0.14-0.22 ; P = 0.06 max.) | Bolts and Machine details in general. |
| 40Mn2S12 (C = 0.35-0.45 ; Si = 0.25 max. ; Mn = 1.30-1.70 ; S = 0.08-0.15 ; P = 0.06 max.) | Bolts and Machine details in general ; these are basically oil hardening steels and may be substituted for C45 and C50 where improved machining deeper hardening and higher physical properties are desired. |

**Table 2.11 C**
**Tensile Properties for Carbon-Manganese Free Cutting Steels (Stress Values in N/mm$^2$)**

| *Designation* | *Condition Hot Rolled or Normalised* | | *Cold Drawn Bars 20 to 40 mm dia.* | | | |
|---|---|---|---|---|---|---|
| | $\sigma_{ut}$ | %$\delta$ | $\sigma_{ut}$ | %$\delta$ | $\sigma_{ut}$ | %$\delta$ |
| 10S11 | 370-490 | 24 | 460 | 10 | | |
| 14Mn1S14 | 440-540 | 22 | 520 | 11 | | |
| 25Mn1S14 | 500-600 | 20 | 560 | 10 | | |
| 40S18 | 550-650 | 17 | 600 | 10 | 600-750<br>700-850 | 18 |
| 11S25 | 370-490 | 22 | 440 | 11 | | 17 |
| | | | | | 600-750 | 18 |
| 40Mn2S12 | 600-700 | 15 | 640 | 8 | 700-850 | 18 |
| | | | | | 800-950 | 16 |

$\sigma_{ut}$ = ultimate tensile stress

$\delta$ = Elongation.

**Table 2.11 (D) indicates properties of some of the materials.**

**Table 2.11 (D)**

| *Material IS Designation* | | *U.T.S* | *Tensile Yield Strength* | *Endurance Limit Strength* | *Torsional Endurance Limit* |
|---|---|---|---|---|---|
| St 34 | | 330 | 200 | 170 | 100 |
| St 37 | | 360 | 220 | 180 | 110 |
| St 42 | | 410 | 250 | 200 | 120 |
| St 50 | | 490 | 290 | 250 | 150 |
| St 70 | | 690 | 410 | 350 | 200 |
| C 10 | | 340-500 | 250 | 180 | 100 |
| C 30 | | 500-600 | 330 | 250 | 150 |
| C 40 | | 580-680 | 380 | 300 | 180 |
| C35Mn75 | | 550-650 | 360 | 275 | 160 |
| C 50 | | 600-800 | 400 | 300 | 180 |
| C 60 | | 850-1050 | 570 | 400 | 200 |
| *IS 210 Cast Iron* | | | | | |
| Grade 20 | FG 200 | 200 | | 100 | 80 |
| Grade 25 | FG 260 | 260 | | 120 | 100 |
| *IS 1030 Cast Steel* | | | | | |
| Grade 1 | 20-40 | 400 | | 160 | 100 |
| Grade 2 | 25-45 | 450 | | 180 | 110 |

**Example 2.3.** *Compare the following properties of cast iron, wrought iron and steel.*

(*i*) *Structure*

(*ii*) *Strength*

(*iii*) *Melting point*

(*iv*) *Magnetisation*

(*v*) *Specific gravity.*

(*i*) **Structure.** Cast iron has crystalline structure, wrought iron has fibrous structure whereas structure of steel is granular.

(*ii*) **Strength.** Cast iron has ultimate 6.5 t/cm$^2$, wrought iron has ultimate tensile strength of 3.85 tonne/cm$^2$ and ultimate tensile strength of steel is 11 tonnes/cm$^2$.

(*iii*) **Melting point.** The melting point of cast iron is 1200°C and melting point of wrought iron is about 1500°C whereas melting point of steel varies from 1280 to 1400°C.

Table 2.12 indicates the values of physical constants for some common materials.

**Table 2.12**

| *Material* | *Modulus of elasticity E (kg/cm$^2$)* | *Modulus of rigidity G, (kg/cm$^2$)* | *Poisson's ratio 1/m* | *Density, ρ (gm/cm$^3$)* |
|---|---|---|---|---|
| Aluminium (alloys) | $0.724 \times 10^6$ | $0.267 \times 10^6$ | 0.334 | 2.73 |
| Brass | $0.970 \times 10^6$ | $0.350 \times 10^6$ | 0.30-0.40 | 8.45 |
| Bronze | $1.110 \times 10_6$ | — | — | 8.73 |
| Carbon steel | $2.060 \times 10_6$ | $0.800 \times 10^6$ | 0.292 | 7.82 |
| Cast iron gray | $1.020 \times 10_6$ | $0.422 \times 10^6$ | 0.211 | 7.20 |
| Copper | $1.230 \times 10_6$ | $0.390 \times 10^6$ | 0.260 | 8.96 |
| Inconel | $2.180 \times 10_6$ | $0.775 \times 10^6$ | 0.299 | 8.96 |
| Magnesium | $0.457 \times 10_6$ | $0.169 \times 10^6$ | 0.350 | 1.80 |
| Molybdenum | $3.375 \times 10_6$ | $1.195 \times 10^6$ | 0.307 | 10.80 |
| Monel metal | $1.828 \times 10_6$ | $0.668 \times 10^6$ | 0.320 | 8.83 |
| Nickel silver | $1.300 \times 10_6$ | $0.492 \times 10^6$ | 0.322 | 8.69 |
| Nickel steel | $2.000 \times 10_6$ | $0.780 \times 10^6$ | 0.291 | 7.75 |
| Phosphor-bronze | $1.132 \times 10_6$ | $0.422 \times 10^6$ | 0.349 | 8.16 |
| Stainless steel (18-8) | $1.940 \times 10_6$ | $0.745 \times 10^6$ | 0.305 | 7.75 |
| Titanium | $1.055 \times 10_6$ | — | — | 4.48 |
| Tungsten | $4.153 \times 10^2$ | $1.770 \times 10^6$ | 0.170 | 19.30 |

The mechanical properties of grey iron castings according to ISI (IS-210-1962) are given in table 2.12 (*a*).

**Table 2.12 (*a*)**

| *ISI grade* | *Minimum tensile strength, kg/cm²* | *Temperature rapture stress* | Brinell hardness number |
|---|---|---|---|
| 15 | 1300-1900 | 2850-4170 | 149-197 |
| 50 | 1700-2400 | 3350-4640 | 179-223 |
| 25 | 2200-2800 | 3860-5100 | 197-241 |
| 30 | 2700-3100 | 3360-5250 | 207-241 |
| 35 | 4200-3500 | 5530-5730 | 207-241 |
| 40 | 3000-4500 | 6270-6370 | 241-320 |

Let $$r = \frac{\text{Ultimate shear strength}}{\text{Ultimate tensile strength}}$$

Table 2.12 (*b*) shows the values of *r* for some of the materials.

**Table 2.12 (*b*)**

| *Material* | *r* |
|---|---|
| Aluminium | 0.60 |
| Cast iron | 1.28 |
| Steel | 0.75 |
| Copper | 0.90 |

## 2.13 Non-Aerrous Metals

They are those metals which do not contain iron as base. The principal non-ferrous metals used in industry are copper, zinc; tin, lead and aluminium. Due to their sate existence they are more expensive than ferrous metals and are therefore used for work pieces whose special characteristics must be superior to those of ferrous metals. Following properties make these metals perfectable as compared to iron.

(*i*) They can be easily cast.

(*ii*) They can be cold worked.

(*iii*) They possess high resistance to corrosion.

(*iv*) They are good conductors of heat and electricity.

## 2.14 Copper

It is extracted from copper ores, the main ore being copper pyrites ($CuFeS_2$). It contains about 30% copper. The ore is first powdered, concentrated and then raised. Roasting helps in removing water, $CO_2$ and Sulphur. The ore is now melted in a reverberatory furnace. Silica is added to the charge which forms slag with impurities like iron and alumina. The molten metal is then oxidised in Bessemer converter. The product so obtained is called blister copper. To get copper of highest purity (99.9%) the final refining is done by electrolytic process. It has bright red colour, its melting point is 1083°C and specific gravity 8.9.

**Properties.** 1. It has good conductivity of heat and electricity.

2. It is soft, malleable and ductile.

3. It has good corrosion resistance.

**Uses.** 1. As it is good conductor of electricity it is used for making electrical transmission wires and cables.

2. It is used in heat exchangers.

3. Copper sheets are used for damp proofing of buildings.

## 2.15 Zinc

Zinc is extracted from zinc ores. The chief ore is zinc blende (ZnS).

It contains about 67% of zinc. The ore is crushed, concentrated and then roasted in excess of air when the ore is converted into zinc oxide. The metallic zinc is obtained from zinc oxide by reducing process. It has bluish white colour, it melting point is 420°C and specific gravity 7.

**Properties.** 1. It has high corrosion resistance.

2. It is a good conductor of heat and electricity.

**Uses.** It is used for galvanising steel parts such as tube wires, sheets etc.

## 2.16 Tin

This is extracted from tin ore called tin stone ($SnO_2$). Tin stone contains about 78% of tin. The ore is first roasted to remove arsenic and sulphur. The roasted ore is then mixed with coal and line and heated in a reverberatory furnace, at about 1200°C. By this reduction process with coal, oxygen is separated from tin stone and raw tin is obtained. Tin is manufactured as blocks, ingots, bars and foils. It has white colour, its melting point is 230°C and specific gravity 7.3.

**Properties.** 1. It is soft, ductile, and corrosion proof.

2. It is a good conductor of heat and electricity.

3. It has good adherence power to steel, copper and similar metals. It can be alloyed with other metals.

**Uses.** 1. It is used as protective coating on iron and steel sheets.

2. It is used for the manufacture of tin-lead solder.

## 2.17 Lead

The important ore of lead is galena (PbS). It contains about 86% lead. The ore is first roasted to remove sulphur

$$2PbS + 3\ O_2 \rightarrow 2PbO + 2SO_2$$

Lead oxide is then mixed with some amount of lime and heated in a furnace to get the metallic lead. The Fig. 2.2 indicates the manufacturing process for lead.

It has bluish grey colour. Its melting point is 326°C and its specific gravity is 11.4.

**Properties.** 1. It is soft and can be easily bent and hammered.

2. It can be easily cast.

3. It is resistant to corrosion.

4. It is malleable and ductile.

**Uses.** 1. It is used for water pipes and roof coverings.

2. It is used for outer coverings of electric ground cables.

## 2.18 Aluminium

The main ore of aluminium is Bauxite. ($Al_2O_3.\ 2H_2O$). The ore is first dried and ground. It is then mixed with sodium hydroxide and heated. The impurities are thus removed and pure aluminium oxide is obtained. Aluminium is then obtained from aluminium oxide by electrolysis.

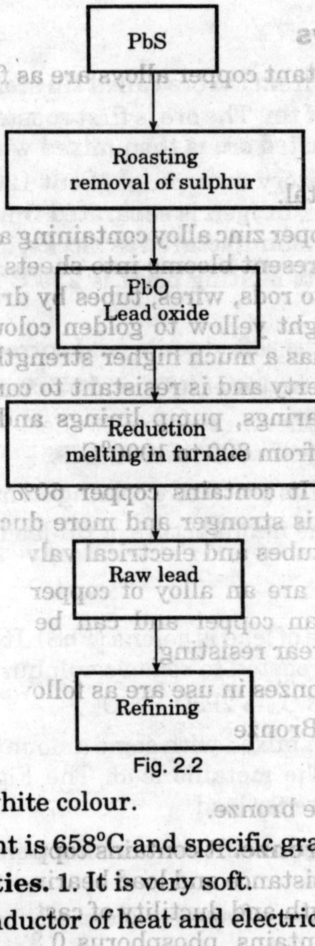


Fig. 2.2

It has silvery white colour.

Its melting point is 658°C and specific gravity 2.7.

**2.18.1 Properties.** 1. It is very soft.

2. It is good conductor of heat and electricity.

3. It is highly resistant to corrosion.

4. It is easily alloyable.

5. It can be easily worked, rolled and drawn.

**2.18.2 Uses.** 1. It is used for making electric cables.

2. It is used for making reflectors.

3. It is used for making various parts of internal combustion engine such as piston.

## 2.19 Non-Ferrous Metal Alloys

Alloy is a mixture of two or more metals made by melting together. Alloying results in an increase in strength and hardness as well as in the cutting and casting properties.

## 2.20 Copper Alloys

The most important copper alloys are as follows :

(*i*) Brass

(*ii*) Bronze

(*iii*) Muntz metal.

**Brass.** It is a copper zinc alloy containing at least 50% of copper. It is worked from present blooms into sheets and bands by hot or cold rolling, and into rods, wires, tubes by drawing and extrusion process. It is of bright yellow to golden colour. It is soft ductile, non-magnetic and has a much higher strength than copper. It has a good casting property and is resistant to corrosion. It is used for making bushes, bearings, pump linings and valves. Its melting temperature varies from 800 to 1000°C.

**Muntz Metal.** It contains copper 60% and zinc 40%. It is wear-resistant and is stronger and more ductile than brass. It is used for condenser tubes and electrical valve stems.

**Bronzes.** They are an alloy of copper and tin. They have a higher strength than copper and can be easily cast. They are non-corrosive and wear resisting.

The common bronzes in use are as follows :

(*i*) Phosphor Bronze

(*ii*) Gun metal

(*iii*) Manganese bronze.

(*i*) **Phosphor bronze.** It contains copper, tin and phosphorus. It has good wear resistance and load bearing capacity. Phosphorus increases the strength and ductility of castings. A common type of phosphor bronze contains, phosphorus 0.3%, tin 6%, and copper 93.7%. Phosphor bronze is used for making bearings, gears and springs. Phosphor bronze used for making springs contains about 0.5% phosphorus.

(*ii*) **Gun Metal.** It is an alloy of copper, tin and zinc. It contains:

Copper = 88%

Tin = 10%

Zinc = 20%

It is corrosion resistant. It is suitable for making bearings, glands, valves, and boiler fittings.

(*iii*) **Manganese Bronze.** It is an alloy of copper, zinc, iron and manganese. A common type of manganese bronze contains :

Copper = 59%

Zinc = 39%

Manganese = 1%

Iron = 1%.

It is hard and resistant to corrosion. It can be only hot worked. It is used for making ship propellers, pumps, valves, gears etc.

## 2.21 Nickel Alloys

(*i*) *German silver.* It contains about 62% copper, 18% zinc and 20% nickel. It is of silvery white colour and is ductile. It is used for making electrical resistance wires, valves and utensils.

(*ii*) *Monel metal.* It contains about 67% Nickel, 31% copper, 1% iron and small additions of manganese, silicon etc. It is resistant to corrosion and is tough, ductile and can be easily machined. It can be hot rolled, cold drawn and annealed.

It is used for making pump impellers, and in chemical industry.

## 2.22 Bearing Metals

Bearing metal should possess the following properties :

(*i*) It should have high compressive strength so that it can resist the bearing pressure.

(*ii*) It should have low coefficient of friction.

(*iii*) It should have high thermal conductivity so that heat produced due to friction is dissipated easily.

(*iv*) It should be able to resist the temperature without loosing strength.

(*v*) It should be wear resistant.

(*vi*) It should maintain a continuous oil film.

(*vii*) It should be able to embed in itself any dirt or grit present in lubricating oil.

(*viii*) It should be shock resistant.

The various bearing metals are classified as follows :

(*i*) Copper base bearing metals.

(*ii*) Tin base bearing metals.

(*iii*) Lead base bearing metals.

(*iv*) Cadmium base bearing metals.

(*i*) **Copper Base Bearing Metals.** Copper base bearing metals contain copper 85% and tin 10% and the remaining is zinc and lead. These alloys are stronger and harder and are used for heavy loads.

(*ii*) **Tin Base Bearing Metals.** The most commonly used alloy is babbit metal which contains 85% tin, antimony 10% and copper 5%. It has low coefficient of friction and is used where bearings are subjected to higher pressure and load.

(*iii*) **Lead Base Bearing Metal.** It contains lead, tin, antimony and copper. Lead may be 0 to 30% and antimony 10 to 15%. Bearings of this metal are used for light loads.

(*iv*) **Cadmium Base Bearing Metal.** It contains cadmium 95%, silver 5% and very small amount of irridium. It has more compressive strength and has more favourable properties at higher temperature.

Table 2.13 indicates some of the non-ferrous metal alloys and their specific applications.

**Table 2.13**

| *Name* | *Composition* | *Typical Uses* |
|---|---|---|
| Muntz metal | Cu = 60%<br>Zn = 40% | Condenser tubes, Electrical valve stems. |
| Gun metal | Cu = 88%<br>Tin = 10%<br>Zinc = 20% | Valves, glands, boiler fittings |
| Brass | Copper = 63%<br>Zinc = 37% | House hold utensils, and general castings |
| Constantan | Copper = 50%<br>Nickel = 50% | Standard resistances |
| Bronze | Copper = 93.7<br>Tin = 6%<br>Phosphorus = 0.3% | Springs, turbine boiler, bearings. |
| White metal | Lead = 80%<br>Bismuth = 20% | Bearing linings. |

| Manganese bronze | Copper = 59%<br>Zinc = 39%<br>Manganese = 1%<br>Iron = 1% | Ship proppelloers, pumps, valves, gears. |
|---|---|---|
| German silver | Copper = 62%<br>Zinc = 18%<br>Nickel = 20% | Electrical resistance wires, values, utensils. |
| Monel metal | Nickel = 63 to 70%<br>Iron = 3%<br>Manganese = 2%<br>Silicon = 4% | Condenser tubes, pump impellers. |
| | Carbon = 0.24%<br>Remaining is copper | |
| German silver | Copper = 50%<br>Zinc = 30%,<br>Nickel = 20% | House and shop fittings. |
| Duralumin | Aluminium = 95%<br>Copper = 3.5%<br>Manganese = 0.5%<br>Silicon = 0.4%<br>Magnesium = 0.6% | Aircraft parts, extruded sections, sheets |
| Bell metal | Copper = 66.7%<br>Tin = 33.3% | Bells. |
| Alnico | Steel = 50%<br>Nickel = 20%<br>Aluminium = 20%<br>Cobalt = 10% | Permanent magnets. |

## 2.23 Heat Treatment of Steel

Heat treatment of steel is defined as the process of heating the steel fairly slowly to some pre-determined temperature and then cooling through suitable means. The ultimate structure of steel depends upon the rate of cooling. Heat treatment of steel enables to achieve desired properties in steel so as to make it suitable for a particular use.

## 2.24 Purposes of Heat Treatment

The various purposes of heat treatment are as follows :

(*i*) To harden the metal.

(*ii*) To relieve internal stresses and eliminate the effect of cold working.

(*iii*) To soften the metal.

(*iv*) To improve machinability.

(*v*) To refine grain structure.

(*vi*) To improve mechanical properties such as ductility, hardness tensile, strength etc.

Heat treatment process consists in the following operations :

(*i*) Heating the metal to definite temperature. The temperature to which steel is heated depends upon the composition of steel, and type of structure required.

(*ii*) Keeping the metal at this temperature for a sufficient these so that the necessary charges may take place.

(*iii*) Cooling the metal. The rate at which the metal is cooled depends upon the type of structure required.

## 2.25 Terms and Definitions

(*i*) **Ferrite.** It is a solid solution of carbon in alpha iron. It consists of pure iron grains. It is soft, ductile magnetic and of low strength.

(*ii*) **Cementite.** It is the carbide of iron ($Fe_3C$). It is hard, brittle and magnetic.

(*iii*) **Austentite.** It is a solid solution of carbon in gamma iron. It is non-magnetic.

(*iv*) **Pearlite.** It is made up of ferrite and cementite and contains about 0.83% carbon. It is very strong.

(*v*) **Martensite.** It is obtained by cooling quickly the steel from austenitic condition. It is a super-saturated solution of carbon in ferrite. It is very hard and brittle. It consists of needle like crystals.

(*vi*) **Troostite and Sorbite.** Troostite is obtained by tempering martensite in the region of 400°C. It is soft and ductile. Sorbite is obtained by heating the troostite in the region of 400 to 675°C. It is more softer and ductile.

(*vii*) **Eutectoid Steel.** Plain carbon steel containing exactly 0.83% carbon is called a eutectoid steel.

(*viii*) **Hype-eutectoid Steels.** Steels containing less than 0.83% carbon are called hypo-eutectoid steels.

(*ix*) **Hypereutectoid Steels.** Steels containing more than 0.83% carbon are called hypereutectoid steels.

## 2.26 Heat Treatment Processes for Steel

The various heat treatment proceses are as follows :

(*i*) Hardening (*ii*) Tempering

(*iii*) Annealing (*iv*) Normalising

(*v*) Case hardening.

## 2.27 Hardening

It is used to harden the steel. It consists in heating the steel to a temperature with in the hardening range. The hardening temperature for steels having 0.83% carbon or more is about 30 to 50°C above the lower critical temperature whereas for steel having less than 0.83% carbon it is 30 to 50°C above the higher critical temperature. The steel is kept at this temperature for sufficient time so that through penetration of temperature inside the steel takes place. After this the steel is cooled quickly. Quick cooling is called quenching. Quick cooling forces the steel to be transformed from austenite to martensite which is very hard substance and therefore makes the steel hard.

The hardening temperature for high speed steels and alloys steels varies from 1100°C to 1300°C. High carbon steels can be hardened by quenching in oil whereas low carbon steels require a faster cooling rate which is achieved by quenching in water. When quenched in water carbon has not time to combine again with iron to become iron carbide. The structure retains its state produced during heating. Martensitic structure is obtained which is quite hard and thus makes the steel hard.

## 2.28 Annealing

During cold working or hot working residual stresses are built in and in addition the material usually has a higher hardness due to these working operations. These operations change the structure of material so that it is no longer represented by equilibrium diagram. This process of heat treatment is used to soften the steel so that it can be easily machined. It relieves the metal from internal streses that have been set up in it during cold working. It increases the ductility of metal and refines grain size. Annealing consists of heating steel to a particular temperature holding it at that temperature for sometime and then cooling slowly. The steel may be cooled either in furnace or by dumping it in ash or sand. According to the material being heat treated and the object of operation annealing is classified into two types :

(*i*) Process annealing (*ii*) Full annealing.

**Process Annealing.** It consists in heating the metal to a temperature below the lower critical temperature usually in the range of 550 - 650°C, keeping the metal at this temperature for a sufficient period to allow the necessary changes to take place and then cooling slowly. This brings about recrystallisation and new grains are formed and softening of metal takes place. It is generally used for removing internal strains caused during cold working operations in mild steel products such as sheets, strips and wires.

**Full Annealing.** It is used to soften the steel in order that it can be easily machined and the various operations such as bending, rolling, pressing etc. can be easily performed on it. Further it produces fine grained steels having superior mechanical properties. This process consists in heating the hypoeutectoid steels to about 20 to 30°C above the higher critical point and heating to about 20 to 30°C above the lower critical point the hyperentectoid steels. After keeping the steel at these temperatures steel is cooled slowly in sand, lime or ash. The annealing temperature for mild steel is 840—870°C and for high speed steel it is about 760 to 780°C. When the steel is heated to annealing temperature its structure is converted into austenitic form and then by slow cooling pearlite plus ferrite to pearlite plus cementite are obtained which are softer and those make the steel soft.

## 2.29 Tempering

The steel obtained after hardening process is hard, brittle and highly stressed. This makes the steel unsuitable for practical purposes. It becomes therefore necessary to submit the steel to further heat treatment before use so that the mechanical properties of steel may be improved. It is obtained by carrying out tempering process on steel. Tempering consists in heating the hardened steel to a suitable temperature below the lower critical point followed by cooling through suitable means. In tempering process the transformation of martensite (of hardened steel) into pearlite takes place which makes the steel tough, soft and ductile. The tempering process has the following main purposes :

(*i*) It causes stress relief.

(*ii*) It reduces hardness and brittleness and increases ductility and toughness.

The most common methods used to temper steel are as follows:

(*i*) Brine or salt bath, (*ii*) Oil bath,

(*iii*) Lead bath, (*iv*) Water bath,

(*v*) Muffle furnace.

Table 2.14 indicates the approximate tempering temperatures.

**Table 2.14**

| *Tempering temperature* (°C) | *Temper colour* | *Applications* |
|---|---|---|
| 220 | Pale yellow | Light turning tools, hacksaw, blades and scrapers. |
| 230 | Pale straw | Planning and shaping tools, hammer faces and screwing dies for brass. |
| 240 | Dark straw | Reamers, shear blades millin cutters. |
| 250 | Brown | Taps, dies, punches, boring tools. |
| 260 | Brownish purple | Punches, reamers, stone cutting tools, gauges. |
| 270 | Purple | Press tools, surgical tools axes. |
| 280 | Dark purple | Cold chisels, chisels for wood. |
| 290 | Bright blue | Cold chisels for wrought iron, screw drivers. |
| 300 | Deep blue | Springs. |

## 2.30 Normalising

This process is mainly useful for low and medium carbon steels. When the steel is cold worked its structure gets distorted and it becomes brittle.

Therefore, the steel becomes unsuitable for working. To restore the steel to its normal conditions the steel is normalised. Normalising serves the following purposes :

(*i*) It refines the structure of steel.

(*ii*) It removes internal stresses.

(*iii*) It increases toughness.

Normalising consists in heating the steel to about 30 to 50°C above the higher critical point and than cooling in air. Normalising results in a finer and more dispersed pearlite. Normalised steels have the following properties :

(*i*) They are less ductile than annealed steels but they have higher tensile and yield strength.

(*ii*) They have finer grain structure and possess better shock resistance.

Table 2.15 shows the comparison of normalised and annealed steels.

**Table 2.15**

| *Carbon (%)* | *Heat treatment* | *Tensile strength (kg/mm$^2$)* | *Elongation (%)* |
|---|---|---|---|
| 0.16-0.22 | Normalised | 39 | 67 |
| | Annealed | 33 | 65 |
| 0.38-0.43 | Normalised | 47 | 35 |
| | Annealed | 39 | 35 |
| 0.55-0.62 | Normalised | 68 | 20 |
| | Annealed | 50 | 25 |
| 0.88-0.95 | Normalised | 81 | 13 |
| | Annealed | 57 | 18 |

## 2.31 Case Hardening

It is the process of producing hard outer surface of steel components while the core remains tough. This process of heat treatment is used for gears, cams etc. which should possess a hard wear resistant surfaces and tough shock resistant cores. In this process a high carbon surface is formed on low carbon steel components.

The various case hardening proceses are as follows.

(*i*) Carburising (*ii*) Cyaniding (*iii*) Nitriding.

**Carburising.** It is a method of giving a hardened case to components of low carbon steel by heating the steel components in contact with a carbonaceous material. Depending upon the type of carbonaceous material used, the various carburising processes are as follows :

(*i*) Pack carburising (*ii*) Gas carburising

(*iii*) Liquid carburising.

**Pack Carburising.** In this process the steel components are placed in a metal box containing carbonaceous material such as bones, charred leather and charcoal. The list is sealed with fire clay. The contents of the box are heated in a furnace to temperature of 900 to 950°C. The component are kept at this temperature for sufficient time according to the depth of case required. In this process the outer surface of steel components absorbs carbon from packing material. Then the steel components are cooled slowly in the box to room temperature. The components are then hardened by the hardening process.

**Cyaniding.** This method is used to produce hard surd surface on low carbon steel parts by heating them in a molten salt bath containing sodium cyanide (20 to 40%), sodium carbonate (30 to 40%) and the rest being sodium chloride, the bath being at a temperature of 850–900°C. The immersion time varies from 15 minutes to one hour. Quenching in water or oil follows cyaniding. In this process the case produced consists mainly of nitrides in the surface layers and the inner layers are richer in carbon. This is a cheaper process and gives higher output.

**Nitriding.** This process is used to produce very hard surface on a piece of steel. This consists in heating the steel in the presence of ammonia gas at about 500°C for sufficient time which may vary from 20 to 100 hours according to the depth of hard case required and the size of steel parts. In this process ammonia gas dissociates as follows.

$$NH_3 = 3H + N$$

The atomic nitrogen so produced reacts with iron and forms nitrides which render a very hard surface to steel. This process is quite suitable for steels having some alloying elements such a chromium (1.0 to 1.8%), aluminium (0.75 to 1.25%) and molybonum (0.1—0.3%). The amount of carbon in such steels varies from 0.2 to 0.4%.

In this process it takes about 30 hours to produce a case depth of 0.25 mm and about 80 hours to produce a case depth of 0.75 mm. This method is employed for hardening various components such as dies, cylinder liners, valves, rollers, crankshafts etc.

**Advantages.**

(*i*) It gives a very hard case resistant to corrosion.

(*ii*) As no quenching is needed after nitriding therefore the possibility of cracking and distortion is negligible and hence the components can be machine finished before treatment.

(*iii*) The steel components after nitriding can retain their hardness up to 500°C whereas the hardness of carburised steels start falling at about 200°C.

**Disadvantages.**

(*i*) This process proves to be economical only when large number of components are to be hardened.

(*ii*) The hardness of nitrided steel components is lost if they get overheated.

## 2.32 Casting

It is one of the most important method of the manu- facturing proceses. Casting consists of pouring a molten metal into a previously prepared cavity or mold and permitting it to solidify and thereby acquire the desired shape. The metals most frequently cast are cast iron, steel, aluminium brass, bronze, magnesium and certain zinc alloys. Grey cast iron has got excellent castable properties and therefore it is most widely used in castings. Of the various types of steels medium carbon steel is most commonly used in steel castings. All steel casting should be annealed to relieve them of internal streses. Casting is quite useful for the production of large objects such ao lathe and other machines beds and frames, large propels and rollers. The shrinkage of parts made by casting takes place when the metal is cooled.

Table 2.16 shows the linear shrinkage of castings of some of the materials.

**Table 2.16. Linear Shrinkage of Castings**

| *Castings* | *Linear Shrinkage* |
|---|---|
| Bar iron, rolled | 1: 55 |
| Brass | 1 : 65 |
| Bronze | 1 : 63 |
| Cast iron | 1 : 96 |
| Gun metal | 1 : 134 |
| Steel castings | 1 : 50 |
| Steel, puddled | 1 : 72 |
| Steel, wrought | 1 : 64 |
| Tin | 1 : 128 |
| Zinc | 1 : 624 |

### 2.32.1. Heat Treatment of Cast Iron

(*i*) **Stress Relief.** In this heat treatment process the cast iron parts are heated to 425 to 540°C. The parts are heated at this temperature for about 30 minutes to 5 hours and then they are slowly cooled in the furnace. By the process though internal stresses are reduced yet there is a slight decrease in hardness or strength at room temperature.

(*ii*) **Annealing.** It is carried out by heating cast iron to 760°C to 815°C (up to 980°C in case of alloyed cast iron) for some time and then cooling slowly. It is carried out to soften cast iron in order to facilitate machining of cast iron.

(*iii*) **Hardening.** This process of heat treatment is used to harden cast iron. It is carried out at by heating at 815°C to 870°C, quenching and then tempering to improve hardness and resistance to wear. Quenching is generally done in oil. However water and air quenching are also used.

## 2.33 Plastics

Plastics are the organic materials which can be moulded into various shapes through the application of heat and pressure. They are prepared from natural and synthetic resins. Natural resins include shellac, wax, wood resins and amber etc. Synthetic resins are prepared by the recurring chemical reaction of a simple organic compound. The molecular of simple organic compound combine and form a high molecular weight composition. Plastic polyethylene is composed of polymers which are formed by ethylene molecules called monomers (Fig. 2.2).

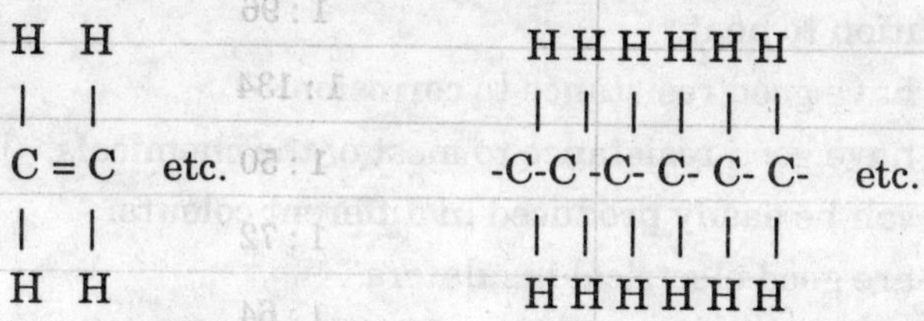

(*a*) Ethylene monomer (*b*) Polyethylene polymer

Fig. 2.2

Resin is the substitute word usually used in place of plastic synthetic resins are of two types namely : (*i*) Thermosets, (*ii*) Thermoplastics.

## 2.34 Terms and Definitions

(*i*) **Monomer, polymer, polymerisation**. Monomer is a substance consisting of short molecules. They link together to form long molecules called polymers. The process in which indefinite repetition of original molecules called monomers of synthetic resins combine together and give rise to polymers is called polymerisation.

(*ii*) **Fillers.** Fillers are added to plastics to reduce the consumption of plastic and to give certain specific properties to plastics. They are usually in the form of minute particles or long fibres. The commonly used fillers are wood, flour, paper, pulp, asbestos and mica. Asbestos when added makes the plastics resistant to heat and electricity.

(*iii*) **Plasticisers.** These materials are added to plastics to improve toughness, plasticity and flexibility so that the moulding of plastics becomes easy. These materials also counteract the brittleness of moulded parts. Plasticisers are generally added to thermoplastics. Camphor is used as plasticiser.

(*iv*) **Pigments and Dyes.** They are added to plastics to obtain desired colour shades in the plastic components.

(*v*) **Stabilisers.** They protect plastics from light and heat.

## 2.35 Properties of Plastics

Different plastics have different properties. Some of common properties of plastics are as follows :

(*i*) Light weight combined with adequate strength.

(*ii*) Easy to mould into different shapes.

(*iii*) They have low thermal conductivity and provide good insulation to heat.

(*iv*) They have good resistance to corrosion.

(*v*) They have good resistance to most of the chemicals.

(*vi*) They can be easily produced in different colours.

(*vii*) They are good electrical insulators.

(*viii*) As compared to metals they have better resistance to shock and vibration.

## 2.36 Type of Plastics

Plastics are of two types.

1. *Thermo plastics*

(*i*) Cellulose derivatives

(*ii*) Polyhydrocarbons, such as polyethylene polystrene, polypropylene.

(*iii*) Vinyl polymers

(*iv*) Linear polyesters.

2. *Thermosetting plastics*

(*i*) Formaldehyde resins (*ii*) Epoxy resins

(*iii*) Silicon resins (*iv*) Polyester resins.

## 2.37 Thermosetting Plastics

These plastics after heating and pressing acquire a permanent shape and do not soften on reheating. They are thus more suitable for high temperature application than thermoplastic materials. They undergo chemical change during moulding. They are brittle and require some filler to make them hard and tough. As compared to thermo-plastics, thermosetting plastics are stronger and cheaper. Their scrap can not be reused.

The thermo-setting plastics, because of their resistance to melting and to solvents have a very wide use. A typical application is in lacquers to be employed as protective lining in chemical reaction vessel.

## 2.37.1. Types of Thermosetting Plastics

Thermosetting resins include the following :

| | |
|---|---|
| (*i*) Phenol formaldehyde. | (*ii*) Phenol furfural. |
| (*iii*) Urea formaldehyde. | (*iv*) Melamine formaldehyde. |
| (*v*) Polyesters. | (*vi*) Silicons. |

**Phenol Formaldehyde.** It is obtained by mixing phenol and formaldehyde. It is also known as Bakelite. It has high resistance to heat, water and electricity. It has mechanical strength and hardness. It is used for electric plugs, switches radio cabinets, tooling, forming dies, gears and bearings, cameras, ash trays, aeroplane parts, and brake linings. It has good resistance to alcohol oil, greases and to weak acids and alkalis.

**Phenol Furfural.** It is obtained from husgs of rice, sugarcane refuse, oats shells etc. It is dark coloured and has good resistance to moisture and electricity. It can be easily mould. It has high strength and durability. It has used for making brake linings and electrical components. It has better moisture resistance than phenol formaldehyde plastics.

**Urea Formaldehyde.** It is obtained by mixing urea and formaldehyde. It is light coloured plastic and has high resistance to oil, water, weak acids and alkalis. It is used for making clock cases, buttons, electric switches and plugs, lighting fittings, toilet seats etc. It has good resistance to most solvents and common chemicals.

**Melamine Formaldehyde.** It is obtained by the condensation of melamine and formaldehyde. It is hard and has high resistance to moisture and heat. It has excellent electrical properties. It is mainly used for circuit breakers switch panels and lamp reflectors.

**Polysters.** They have high dielectric strength and good colourability. They are mainly used for aircraft parts and car bodies.

**Silicones.** They are water repellent and can withstand high temperatures up to about 260°C. They are used as an additive to oils, waxes, rubbers etc.

## 2.38 Thermoplastics

These plastics become hard during moulding and cooling but can be softened on reheating and can be remoulded. The thermoplastic materials are injection molded and compression moulding method is seldom used. They can be moulded from powder form at relatively low temperatures (100°C) by comparatively small pressures.

## 2.39 Types of Thermoplastics

Thermoplastic resins are as follows :

*Cellulose nitrate.* It is obtained by treating purified cotton linters with a mixture of nitric acid and sulphuric acid. It is highly inflammable and tough. It is used for toys, combs, handles and coverings, brushes, spectacle frames, toilet goods, shoes, and typewriter keys.

**Cellulose acetate.** Cellulose acetate is prepared by the action of acetic acid to cellulose. As compared to cellulose nitrate it is superior in moldability and resistance to moisture. It is tough and durable. It has good impact strength. It provides good electric insulation. It is used for extruded sheets, tubes, toilet articles, coatings, photographic films, lamp shades radio cabinets, buttons and buckles.

**Ethyl cellulose.** It exhibits toughness and good resistance to chemicals. It is mainly used for forming dies, coatings, tool handles, and telephones. It has good resistance to acids and alkalis.

**Cellulose acetate butyrate.** It is made by treating cellulose with both acetic acid and butyric acid. It can be easily machined and moulded. It is resistant to most of the household chemicals but is adversely affected by alcohol and strong alkalis.

It possesses high resistance to impact. It is tough and absorbs less moisture. It is used for helmets, coatings insulating tapes, machinery guards, special purposes hoses, instrument panels, pens, furniture.

**Polythene.** It is wax-like material and is chemically inert to most liquids. It has high electrical resistivity and is very tough. It is used as an electrical insulating material.

**P.V.C. (Polyvinyl chloride).** It is a rubber like material and is non-inflammable. It is widely used as an insulating cover on electrical cables, gloves conveyor belting, toys, dolls, special purpose hose and tubing. It has good resistance to acids, alkalis and most common chemicals.

**Teflin.** It is a wax like material. It has high electrical resistance and a very low coefficient of friction. It does not absorb water and is resistant to chemicals. It is used for electrical insulation and for gaskets.

**Cellulose propionate.** It has better heat resistance than cellulose acetate. It is easily machined and moulded. It is used for pens and pencils and telephone hand sets.

Table 2.17 shows average properties of plastics.

**Table 2.17. Average Properties of Plastics**

| *Materials* | *P (kg/cm$^3$)* | *E (10$^6$ kg/cm$^2$)* | *K (k.cal/hr m$^o$C* |
|---|---|---|---|
| **Thermoplastics** | | | |
| Cellulose acetate moulded | 0.0013 | 175 (B) | 0.12 |
| Teflon | 0.0023 | 45 (T)<br>56 (C) | 0.22 |
| Polystrene general purpose | 0.00104 | 350 (T) | — |
| Polyethylene medium density | 0.00093 | 42 (T) | 0.30 |
| **Thermosetting plastics :** | | | |
| Exposy, general purpose | 0.00112 | 455 (T) | 0.67 |
| Phenolic, moulded type | 0.0014 | 700 (T) | 0.193 |
| Silicon mineral filled, moulded | 0.0019 | 805 (B) | 0.178 |

**Note.** Modulus of elasticity measured in compression (C) tension (T) and bending (B).

Table 2.18 indicates average properties of ceramics.

**Table 2.18. Average Properties of Ceramics**

| *Material* | *P (kg/cm$^3$)* | *E (kg/cm)$^2$* | *K (k, cal/hr m$^o$C* | *Tensile strength* |
|---|---|---|---|---|
| Polyerystaline glass | 0.0025 | $0.88 \times 10^6$ | 1.68 | 1400 kg/cm$^2$ |
| Fused silica glass | 0.0022 | $0.705 \times 10^6$ | 1.19 | - |
| Moulded graphite | 0.0015 | $0.056 \times 10^6$ | 119 | 4200 kg/cm$^2$ |

*(Contd...)*

| *Material* | *P (kg/cm³)* | *E (10⁶ kg/cm²)* | *K (k, cal/hr m°C* | *Tensile strength* |
|---|---|---|---|---|
| Alumina ceramics | 0.0037 | $3.15 \times 10^6$ | — | 2800 kg/cm² |
| Tungsten carbide | 0.015 | $7 \times 10^6$ | 104 | — |

## 2.40 Rubber

Rubber is used for seals and diaphragms, for water lubricated bearings, for parts subjected to vibrations and for belts. Where high strength is required textile cords or fabrics are coated with rubber to withstand the applied loads, the rubber largely serving to insulate the cards from each other. For severe service steel wires may be coated with rubber and used as load carrying medium such as in tyres and heavy duty conveyor belts.

## 2.41 Glass

It is an inorganic material and is obtained by fusing together one or more oxides of silicon, boron, phosphorus, sodium, potassium, calcium magnesium etc. The mixture is heated to as high temperature as 1400 – 1500°C for varying periods of time. The product is then cooled quickly so that different components have no time to separate as definite crystals. It is hard, brittle and transparent. It is an amorphous substance having a homogeneous texture. Its tensile strength varies from 420–840 kg/cm² and compressive strength is nearly 7000 kg/cm². Its melting point is from 850 – 950°C.

## 2.42 Wood

Wood is a natural polymer and its molecular structure is based on the cellulose chain whose cell wall consists of cellulose fibres arranged parallel to its axis. The wood is the intermediate and in fact the main zone of tree.

Colour and odour of wood are generally due to the presence of chemical compounds in wood cells and are greatly variable not only in different species but even in different parts of the same tree.

Wood on exposure to atmosphere either absorbs or looses moisture depending upon whether it contains less or more moisture than the atmosphere. The wood tissues lose moisture when subjected to drying conditions. Water is lost first from the cell cavities and then from cell walls. Woods shrink most severely in tangential direction and less so in radial direction. There is minimum almost negligible shrinkage in longitudinal direction. The cell walls absorb large amount of water resulting in swelling of its surface when exposed to moisture. Wood has more strength in the longitudinal direction as compared to the transverse direction due to its directed cell structure. The strength of wood is defined by its compressive strength, tensile strength and flexural strength.

## 2.43 Leather

It is quite flexible and can withstand considerable wear. It is used for making washers and packings.

## 2.44 Materials Abbreviations

The abbreviations for some of the materials are indicated in Table 2.19.

**Table 2.19**

| *Material* | *Abbreviation* |
|---|---|
| Aluminium | Al |
| Cast iron | C.I. |
| Malleable cast iron | M.C.I. |
| Wrought iron | W.I. |
| Gunmetal | G.M. |
| Lead | Pb |
| Manganese | Mn |
| Platinum | Pt |
| Steel | Steel |
| Cast steel | C.S. |
| Forged steel | F.S. |
| Mild steel | M.S. |
| Nickel | Ni |
| Nickel steel | Ni S |
| Zinc | Zn |
| High speed steel | H.S.S. |

**Example 2.4.** *State the type of steel represented by the following:*

(*a*) $C_{20}$ (*b*) $C_{25}$ *Mn 73*

(*c*) *09 Cr 18 Nl 8 Mo 3* (*d*) *35 Mn 2 Mo 43*

(*e*) *St 45* (*f*) *14 Cr 68.*

**Solution.**

(*a*) $C_{20}$ is a plain carbon steel containing 0.20% carbon.

(*b*) $C_{25}$ Mn 73 is a plain carbon steel containing 0.25% carbon and 0.73% manganese.

(*c*) 0.09 Cr 18 Nl 8 Mo 3 is an alloy steel and contains

C = 0.09%

Cr = 18%

NI = 8%

Mo = 3%.

(*d*) 35 Mn 2 Mo 43 steel contains

C = 0.35%

Mn = 2%

Mo = 4.3%.

(*e*) St 45 steel is a steel having ultimate tensile strength of 45 $kg/mm^2$.

(*f*) 14 Cr 68 is an alloy steel containing

C = 0.14%

and Cr = 0.68%.

## PROBLEMS

**2.1.** State the factors which affect the selection of a material.

**2.2.** Described the following mechanical properties of materials.

(*a*) Strength (*b*) Ductility

(*c*) Malleability (*d*) Machinability

(*e*) Weldability.

**2.3.** Write short notes on the following :

(*a*) Thermal conductivity (*b*) Coefficient of linear expansion

(*c*) Thermal stresses (*d*) Melting point.

**2.4.** How do you classify engineering materials ? Describe any three ferrous metals.

**2.5.** (*a*)Define plain carbon steels.

(*b*) Name the plain carbon steels.

State their applications.

**2.6.** What is an alloy steel ? Describe high speed steels and stainless steels.

**2.7.** Write short notes on the following :

(*a*) Manganese steel (*b*) cemented carbides.

**2.8.** State the factors which make non-ferrous metals preferable as compared to ferrous metals.

**2.9.** State the properties and applications of the following :

(*a*) Copper (*b*) Zinc

(*c*) Aluminium (*d*) Tin

(*e*) Lead.

**2.10.** State the composition, properties and uses of the following :

(*a*) Gun metal (*b*) Muntz metal

(*c*) Monel metal (*d*) Phosphor bronze

(*e*) Brass (*f*) Bearing metal

(*g*) Babbit metal.

**2.11.** State the purposes of heat treatment of steel.

**2.12.** Describe the following heat treatment proceses for steel.

(*a*) Hardening (*b*) Normalising

(*c*) Annealing (*d*) Carburising

(*e*) Tempering.

**2.13.** Describe the following :

(*a*) Plastics (*b*) Rubber

(*c*) Wood (*d*) Leather

(*e*) Glass.

**2.14.** Write short notes on the following :

(*a*) Casting (*b*) Grey cast iron

(*c*) Chilled cast iron.

**2.15.** Discuss heat treatment of C.I.

**2.16.** State the type of steel represented by the following :

| | |
|---|---|
| (*a*) 31 Ni 3 Cr 65 Mo 55 | (*b*) 20 Mo 55 |
| (*c*) 40 Cr 1 Mo 60 | (*d*) St 60 |
| (*e*) 16 Cr 70 | (*f*) 40 Mn 2 Mo 50 |
| (*g*) C 24 Mn 72 | (*h*) C 38. |

**2.17.** State the materials commonly used to manufacture the following parts :

(*a*) Pulley (*b*) Shaft
(*c*) Leaf spring (*d*) Key
(*e*) Gear for gear box of a lathe
(*f*) Rivets for structures (*g*) Bush for a bearing
(*h*) Screw jack body (*i*) Flywheel
(*j*) Bell-crank lever (*k*) Punch used on a press
(*l*) Flanges of a flange coupling
(*m*) Bolt (*n*) Sprockets
(*o*) Chains (*p*) Belts
(*q*) Crankshaft.

# 3

# Stress Analysis

## 3.0 Introduction

When a machine or machine member is designed so that it can function properly for a specified length of time, it is required that the machine member should resist the stresses produced in it due to external forces called applied loads. Further it is necessary to determine the nature of action of force in a member which may cause it to fail. The action that initiates failure is called 'Mode of failures'.

While designing a machine the various links should be so built up or constructed that they can withstand the forces to which they are subjected. Relative motion must be known before these forces can be ascertained. Design methods for the various machine elements are based on the theories of mechanics, strength of materials, metallurgy, mechanisms etc. These theories or more or less simplified approximations and attention should be directed to the limitations imposed by the assumptions made. Stresses and deformations are produced in a body by the forces acting on it. It is natural to assume that the resultant effect at any chosen point is the sum of the effects of various loads.

The problem of mechanical strength is one of the most important feature of the design of machine parts. Machine parts should be so designed that stress concentrations at points of high loading are avoided as much as possible.

## 3.1 Load

Any external force to which a machine part is subjected is called a 'Load'. In the design process following information about load should be known :

(*i*) Magnitude of load (*ii*) Direction of load

(*iii*) Type of load.

The direction of load acquaints the designer with the type of stress set up with in the machine part by the load whereas intensity of stress will depend upon the magnitude of load. The various types of loads are as follows :

(*i*) Steady load or static load

(*ii*) Varying load

(*iii*) Shock load.

A static load can be axial tension or compression, a shear load, a bending load, a torsional load or any combination of these. Static load is applied gradually increasing from zero to its final value and then either does not change its magnitude, direction or point of application with time or change them very slightly,

$$n = \text{Factor of safety} = F_u/F$$

where $F_u$ = ultimate load

$F$ = safe load

The failure of components subjected to loads that vary or fluctuate between different magnitudes is called fatigue failure.

Shock load or impact load is defined as the load which is applied very rapidly to the machine part. The shock factor ($k_s$) is defined as follows.

$$k_s = \frac{\sigma_s}{\sigma}$$

where

$\sigma_s$ = stress produced by shock or suddenly applied load.

$\sigma$ = stress produced by same load applied gradually.

$K_s$ = 1.5 to 2 for heavy shocks

= 1 to 1.5 for minor shocks

= 1 for gradually applied or steady loads.

In cyclic loading (fatigue loading) the fracture of the machine part occurs at stresses very much lower than their ultimate statical strength.

When a machine element is subjected to static loading $t$ may fail in two manners namely.

(*i*) Failure due to yielding

(*ii*) Failure due to fracture, rupture or breaking.

In case of materials subjected to cyclic loads the endurance limit is the criterion for failure.

Static loads can be determined accurately out the values of fluctuating loads and impact loads are more uncertain. Considerations must also be given to the long term effects of corrosion and high temperatures.

For the same magnitude of load a machine part can resist dead load more easily than varying load. Similarly a machine part can resist varying load more easily than shock load.

## 3.2 Stress

When a material is loaded it gets deformed (strained) and internal reactive forces called stresses are set up in the material and act to resist the applied forces. The direction and tendency of applied forces dictates the type of stress and the area involved over which the stress is distributed. A stress indicates force per unit area. It is expressed in kg/cm$^2$.

$$f = \frac{P}{A}$$

where $f$ = Unit stress in kg/cm$^2$

$P$ = Total force in kg either parallel to or perpendicular to area $A$ which is in cm$^2$.

## 3.3 Type of Stresses

Stresses are classified as follows :

(*a*) Tensile stress (*b*) Compressive stress

(*c*) Shear stress (*d*) Bending stress

(*e*) Torsional stress.

## 3.4 Tensile Stress

A tensile load is one which tries to stretch or elongate the material and stress set up due to this action is called Tensile stress. Consider mild steel bar (Fig. 3.1) of length $L$ and diameter $d$. When it is subjected to a tensile load $P$ it will elongate by an amount $\Delta L$

and will get contract laterally. The application of load $P$ produces reactive stresses with in the bar through which the load is transmitted to the support. The bar is said to be under tension and tensile stress and strain are defined as follows :

$$L = \text{Original length}, P = \text{Tensile load}$$

$$A = \text{Cross-sectional area of bar} = \frac{\pi}{4} d^2$$

$$\Delta L = \text{Extension}, f_t = \text{Tensile stress} = P/A$$

$$e = \text{Longitudinal strain} = \Delta L/L$$

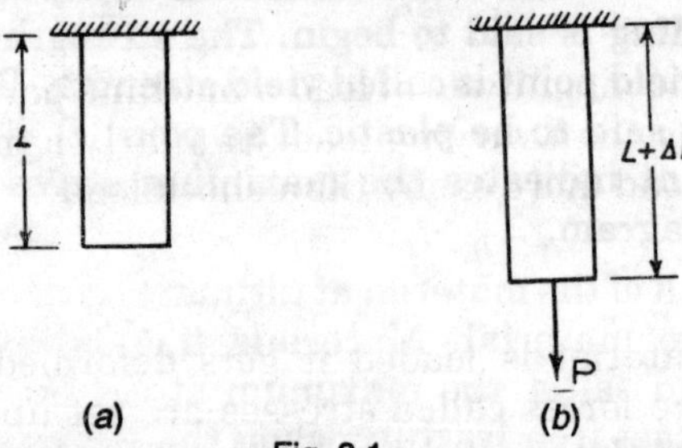


Fig. 3.1.

As the magnitude of load $P$ is further increased such that finally failure of material takes place, the corresponding values of $\Delta L$ can be measured for different values of $P$. A graph plotted between values of stress and strain is called stress strain diagram. Fig. 3.2 shows the stress-strain diagram for a standard specimen of ductile material like mild steel loaded in tension till fracture takes place. In this diagram point $A$ is called limit of proportionality. This is the point at which the curve begins to deviate from straight line up to this point, stress is proportional to strain *i.e.* Hooke's law is obeyed.

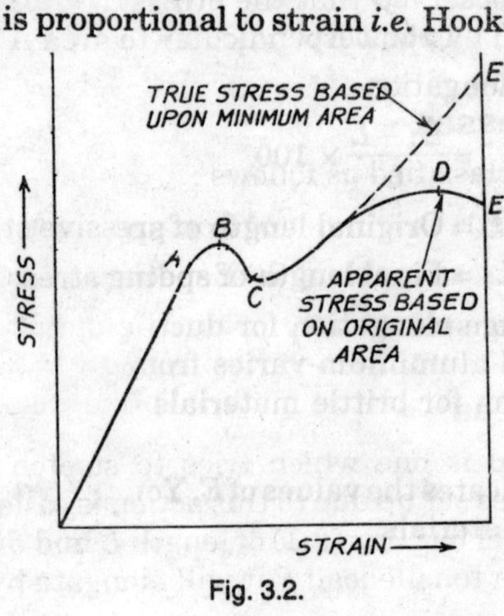


Fig. 3.2.

$$\text{Stress} \propto \text{Strain}$$

$$\frac{\text{Stress}}{\text{Strain}} = E$$

where $E$ is called Young's modulus of elasticity. Point $B$ represents elastic limit which indicates limit of elastic behaviour of material that is material returns back to its original position on the removal of load. Thus elastic limit is defined as the maximum stress which can be applied to a material without obtaining a permanent set. Hooke's law is not obeyed. Point $C$ is called Yield point. The material has now passed from an elastic condition into plastic state and at this point Yielding is said to begin. The strength of material corresponding to yield point is called yield strength. Beyond this point the material is said to be plastic. The point $D$ is called Ultimate point. This point indicates the maximum stress reached on the stress-strain diagram.

The strength of the material at ultimate point is called ultimate strength of the material. Materials like mild steel exhibit a downward trend after the maximum stress is reached whereas materials like cast iron fracture when the stress corresponding to ultimate strength is reached. After point $D$ the extension continues with an apparent decrease in stress until fracture takes place at point $E$ which is called Breaking point. It is observed that material appears to have lower stress at point of fracture. This is because of the fact that the material contracts radially with increased load and when maximum load is reached the specimen begins to neck and cross sectional area reduces quite rapidly. If the value of cross-sectional area at fracture is used instead of original cross-sectional area it is observed that the stress at fracture is somewhat more as indicated by point $E'$.

Percentage elongation

$$= \frac{L_1 - L}{L} \times 100$$

where $L$ = Original length of specimen

$L_1$ = Final length of specimen

The percentage elongation for ductile materials such as mild steel, copper and aluminium varies from 15 to 75% whereas percentage elongation for brittle materials like cast iron is less than 5%.

Table 3.1 indicates the values of $E$, Young's modulus of elasticity for some of the materials.

**Table 3.1**

| *Materials* | $E\ (kg/cm^2)$ |
|---|---|
| Aluminium | $0.7 \times 10^6$ |
| Cast iron (grey) | $0.91 \times 10^6$ |
| Copper | $1.19 \times 10^6$ |
| Molybodenum | $2.94 \times 10^6$ |
| Nickel | $2.1 \times 10^6$ |
| Steel | $2.1 \times 10^6$ |
| Tungsten | $3.5 \times 10^6$ |

Fig. 3.3 shows stress-strain diagram for a brittle material like cast iron.

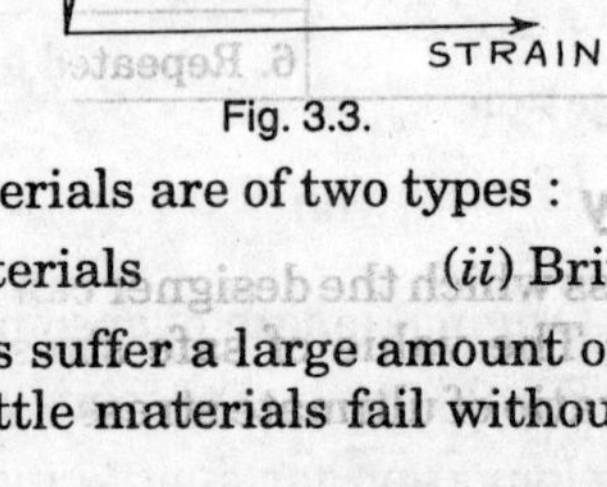


Fig. 3.3.

Engineering materials are of two types :

(*i*) Ductile materials (*ii*) Brittle materials.

Ductile materials suffer a large amount of deformation before failure. Whereas brittle materials fail without a great amount of deformation.

### 3.4.1 Static Failure And Its Prediction

Failures that are caused by the material being defective or by the fabrication not meeting specifications are problems of production and not of design. The obvious cause of a structural failure is the fact that the stresses imposed on the member by service loads are greater than its strength and the immediate concern is to find feasible means of eliminating and forecasting such failures.

The general procedure in this case is to check the balance between the stress and strength, that is, to re-evaluate the loads, the stresses and the strength in the failed part. There are five types of structural damage which machine parts may experience, viz., excessive elastic deformation, elastic buckling, plastic deformation, creep and fracture. Three basic types of fracture are commonly observed in materials. Cleavage fractures follow the cube faces of the ferrite crystals whereas in the shear fractures, translation always occurs in the direction having the minimum inter atomic distance and usually along the planes having the greatest atomic density. Consequently, either of the two modes of fracture can be identified by a microscopic examination. The shear mode of fracture is associated with a grey and silky appearance of the fracture surface whereas the cleavage mode causes the surface to be bright and granular.

The factors influencing the type of failure for metals are given below :

| *Conductive to shear failure* | *Conductive to cleavage failure* |
|---|---|
| 1. High shear stresses. | 1. High tensile stresses. |
| 2. Low tensile stresses. | 2. Low shear stresses. |
| 3. High temperature. | 3. Low temperature. |
| 4. Slow rate of loading. | 4. High rate of loading. |
| | 5. High stress concentrations. |
| | 6. Repeated loads. |

## 3.5 Factor of Safety

The greatest stress which the designer can allow in the material is called safe stress. The value of safe stress must be less than ultimate stress. The ratio of ultimate stress and safe stress is called Factor of safety.

$$\text{Factor of safety} = \frac{\text{Limit stress}}{\text{Safe stress}}$$

The limit stress of a material is that stress beyond which failure by rupture may be expected.

The safe stress is also called working stress or allowable stress.

The limit stress is the maximum stress to which a machine part can be subjected without being fractured or damaged. For brittle materials limit stress is the ultimate stress of material.

$$\text{F.S.} = \frac{f_u}{\text{Safe stress}}$$

For ductile materials the limit stress is the yield stress.

$$\text{F.S.} = \frac{\text{Yield stress}}{\text{Safe stress}}$$

For materials subjected to varying load the limit stress is the endurance limit ($f_e$).

$$\text{F.S.} = \frac{f_e}{\text{Safe stress}}$$

where F.S. = Factory of safety

$f_u$ = Ultimate stress.

The values of factor of safety for some of the materials for different types of loads are indicated in table 3.2.

**Table 3.2**

| *Material* | *Steady load* | *Varying load* | | *Shock load* |
|---|---|---|---|---|
| | | *Stress always of same kind* | *Stress alter-nating* | |
| Cast Iron | 4 | 6 | 12 | 16 |
| Wrought Iron | 4 | 6 | 8 | 13 |
| Steel | 4 | 6 | 8 | 12 |
| Soft metals and alloys | 5 | 6 | 8 | 12 |
| Leather | 8 | 10 | 14 | 16 |
| Timber | 6 | 10 | 15 | 20 |

The ulitmate strength for some of the materials is shown in table 3.3.

**Table 3.3**

| *Material* | *Ultimate strength kg/cm²* |
|---|---|
| Cast Iron (grey) | 1400 |
| Cast Steel | 5000 |
| Mild Steel | 4200 |
| Nickel-chromium Steel | 9000 |

*Contd...*

| *Material* | *Ultimate strength kg/cm²* |
|---|---|
| Aluminium | 900 to 4000 |
| Brass | 1700 |
| Copper | 3000 |
| Gun Metal | 2500 |
| Leather | 200 to 350 |

The factor of safety is used to account for the unknowns and uncertainties involved on the design. The factor of safety depends upon the following factors :

(*i*) Type of load.

(*ii*) Type of material.

(*iii*) Degree of economy required.

(*iv*) Type of Machine part and working conditions.

(*v*) Degree of safety to human life and property required.

In general it is not economical to use safety factors large enough to eliminate all possibilities of failure resulting from the worst possible combination of circumstances. The designer should try to reduce the probability of failure to a suitable level which necessarily depends on each particular application. A more through and detailed analysis of the problem may show that smaller factors of safety can be used which may justify the additional engineering expense involved.

Table 3.4 indicates strengths of some varieties of steel.

**Table 3.4**

| *Material* | *Ultimate Strength (kg/cm²)* | *Yield Point (kg/cm²)* | *Elastic Point (kg/cm²)* |
|---|---|---|---|
| Carbon Steel (C=0.05 to 0.15%) | 4220 | 2720 | 2170 |
| Carbon Steel (C=0.15 to 0.25%) | 4690 | 3010 | 2450 |
| Carbon Steel (C=0.25 to 0.35%) | 4900 | 3220 | 2940 |
| Carbon Steel (C=0.35 to 0.45%) | 5950 | 3850 | 3500 |
| Nickel Steel ($N_1$ = 3.25 to 3.75%) | 5400 | 3600 | 3200 |

**3.5.1. Statistical Considerations in deciding Factor of Safety**

The statistical considerations help in predicting the variation in strength of materials used for component as well as the variation in forces or loads acting on them.

Let $P$ = Actual load acting on the component.

This should be smaller than the capacity of the component to sustain the load.

$\overline{P}$ = Mean load.

$\Delta P$ = Tolerance on mean load.

The variation in load may be $\overline{P} + \Delta P$ to $\overline{P} - \Delta P$.

Fig. 3.3.1 shows normal distribution of load.

Let $C$ = Capacity of the component

$\overline{C}$ = Mean capacity

$\Delta C$ = Tolerance on capacity

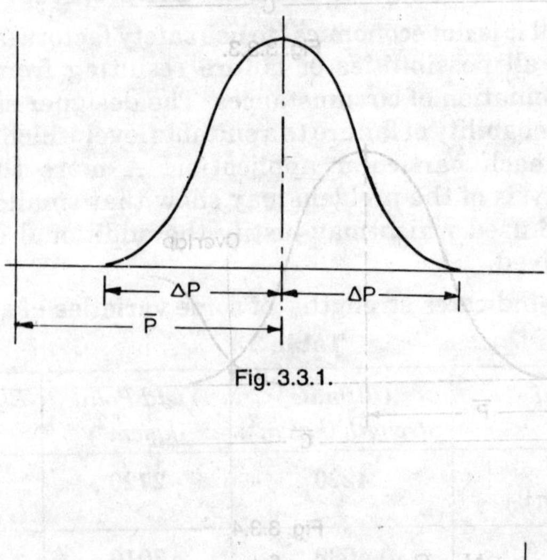


Fig. 3.3.1.

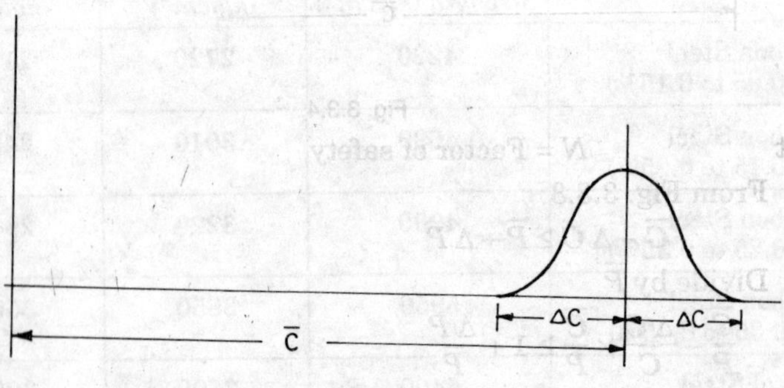


Fig. 3.3.2.

Fig. 3.3.2 shows variation in the capacity of the component. The capacity should always be more than the load acting on the component. This is represented in Fig. 3.3.3.

Tolerances on load and capacity are considered as it is difficult to fix exact values of load and capacity. In some cases the possibility of failure is tolerated up to certain limit. In such cases the load curve and the capacity curve may over - lap as shown in Fig. 3.3.4.

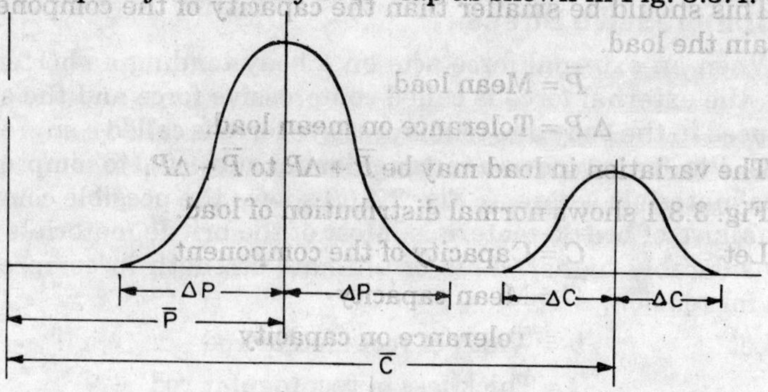


Fig. 3.3.3.

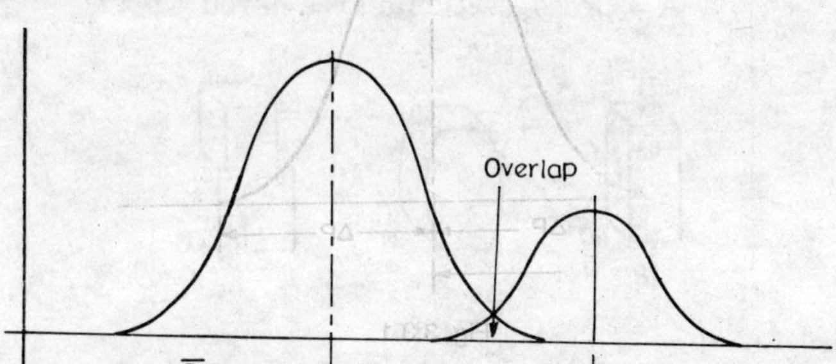


Fig. 3.3.4.

Let $N$ = Factor of safety

From Fig. 3.3.3

$$\overline{C} - \Delta C \geq \overline{P} + \Delta P$$

Divide by $\overline{P}$

$$\frac{\overline{C}}{\overline{P}} - \frac{\Delta C}{\overline{C}} \times \frac{\overline{C}}{\overline{P}} \geq 1 + \frac{\Delta P}{\overline{P}}$$

Now $\frac{\overline{C}}{\overline{P}} = N$

$$\frac{\overline{C}}{P}\left[1-\frac{\Delta C}{C}\right] \geq 1+\frac{\Delta P}{P}$$

$$N \geq \frac{1+\frac{\Delta P}{P}}{1-\frac{\Delta C}{C}}$$

## 3.6 Compressive Stress

When an external force acts on a body tending a shorten the body, the external force is called compressive force and the stress produced in the body due to compressive force is called compressive stress. Fig. 3.4 (*a*) shows a rectangular bar subjected to compressive forece materials where as Fig. 3.4 (*c*) shows the possible compressive failure of brittle materials. Most of the brittle materials have a considerably higher value of ultimate strength in compressive than for tension.

Let $b$ = Width of rectangular rod

$t$ = Thickness of rectangular rod

$P$ = Compressive force

$A$ = Cross–sectional area of rod = $b \times t$

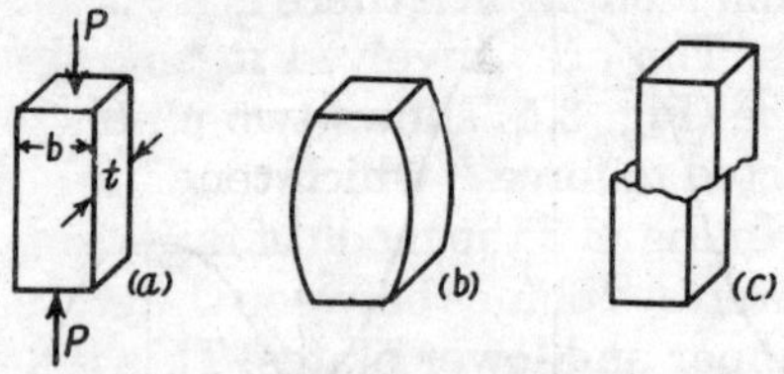

Fig. 3.4

$f_c$ = Compressive stress

$$= \frac{P}{A} = \frac{P}{b \times t}.$$

## 3.7 Poisson's Ratio

It is defined as the ratio of lateral strain to longitudinal strain.

$\mu$ = Poisson's Ratio

$$= \frac{e_1}{e_2}$$

where $e_1$ = Lateral strain

and $e_2$ = Longitudinal strain

For steel the approximate value of Poisson's ratio is 0.3. Typical values of Poisson's ratio are given in table 3.5.

**Table 3.5**

| *Material* | *Poisson's ratio* (μ) |
|---|---|
| Aluminium | 0.34 |
| Aluminium alloys | 0.32 |
| Copper | 0.35 |
| Iron | 0.28 |
| Cast Iron (grey) | 0.20 |
| Magnesium | 0.33 |
| Titanium | 0.34 |

## 3.8 Shear Stress

When a load acts on a body tending to cut or shear it across, the stress at a section along which there is a tendency to cut is called a Shearing stress. The area involved in shearing is parallel to the direction of force (Fig. 3.5) shows two plates joined together by a rivet and subjected to force $P$ which tends to slip or slide one plate over the other. In Fig. 3.5 the mode of failure shown is due to shear of rivet at the interface planes between the plates due to the relative motion of the upper and lower plates. This type of failure is called single shear of rivet.

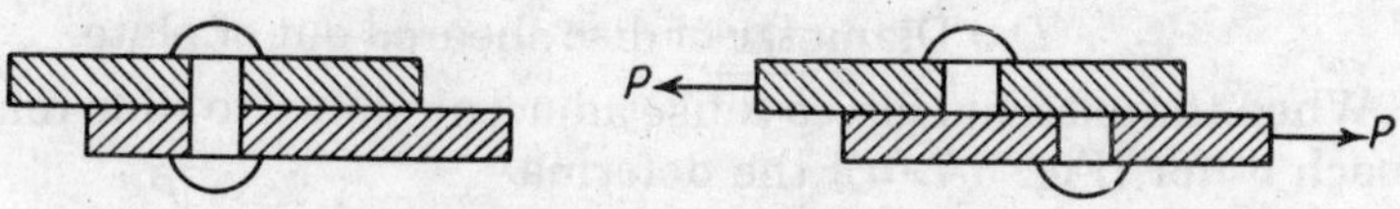


Fig. 3.5. Single shear.

Fig. 3.6 shows a failure that occurs due to the relative motion of centre plate with respect to both the upper and lower plates and this mode of failure is called double shear.

Let $d$ = Rivet diameter

$f_s$ = Shear stress in rivet material

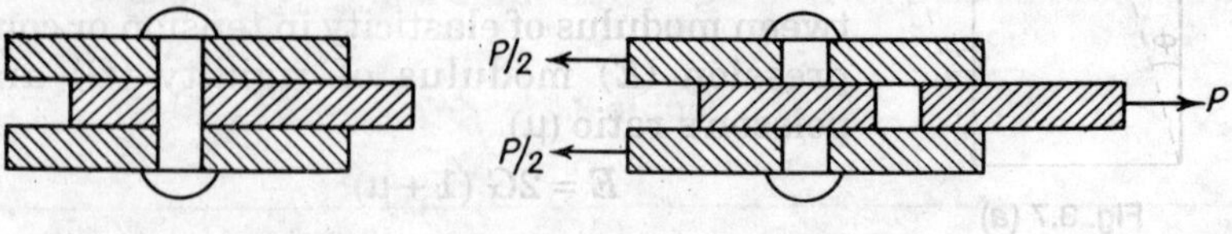


Fig. 3.6. Double shear.

when the rivet is in single shear

$$A = \text{Area under shear} = \frac{\pi}{4} d^2$$

$$\therefore \quad P = A \times f_s = \frac{\pi}{4} d^2 \times f_s$$

when the rivet is in double shear

$$A = \text{Area in shear} = 2 \times \frac{\pi}{4} d^2$$

$$P = A \times f_s = 2 \times \frac{\pi}{4} d^2 \times f_s$$

Fig. 3.7 shows a punch shearing out a cylindrical disc from of plate with the shearing area being equal to outside surface of disc Sheared Area $(A) = \pi.D\, t$

$$P = A \times f_s$$

$$= \pi D t \times f_s$$

$$\therefore \quad f_s = \frac{P}{\pi D t}$$

where $t$ = Thickness of plate

$P$ = Force applied

$f_s$ = Ultimate shear stress of plate

$D$ = Diameter of disc sheared out of plate.

When the external forces cause adjacent planes to slide relative to each other [Fig. 3.7 (*a*)] the deformations are called shearing deformations.

The shearing strain or angular deformation ($\phi$) is proportional to the shearing stress for values within the elastic range and Hooke's law for shear becomes

$$\frac{f_s}{\phi} = G$$

where $f_s$ = shear stress. The constant of proportionality $G$ is called modulus of

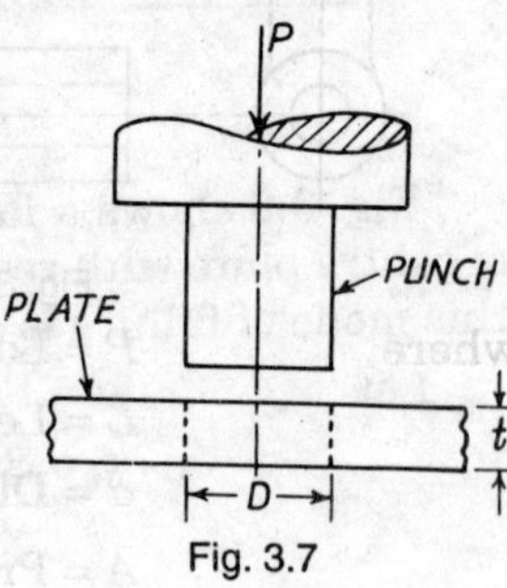


Fig. 3.7

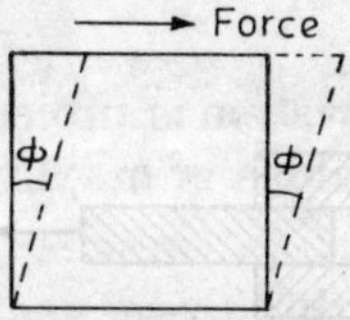

Fig. 3.7 (*a*)

rigidity. The following relationship exists between modulus of elasticity in tension or compression ($E$) modulus of rigidity ($G$) and poisson's ratio ($\mu$)

$$E = 2G\,(1 + \mu)$$

## 3.9 Bearing Stress

It is a particular type of local compression and occurs between two members held in contact when one presses against the another. Consider a member as shown in Fig. 3.8 in which if load is applied by pins. The distribution of pin pressure will not be uniform but will be in accordance with the shape of the surfaces in contact and the deformation characteristics of two materials. The distribution of stress will be similar to that shown in Fig. 3.9.

Bearing stress is calculated by dividing the load by the projected area.

$f$ = Bearing stress (kg/cm$^2$)

$$f = \frac{P}{A} = \frac{P}{L \times d}$$

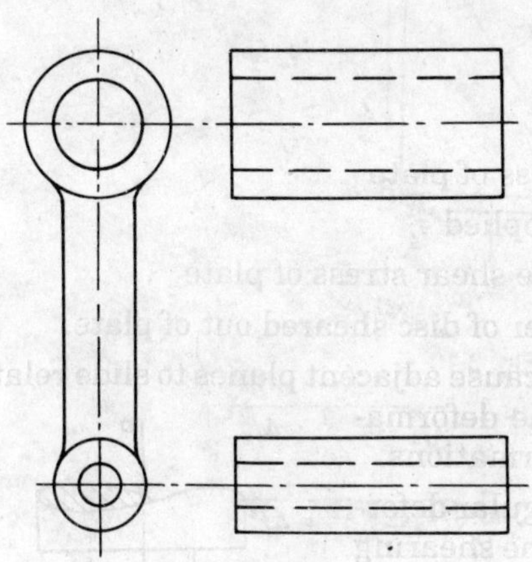
Fig. 3.8.

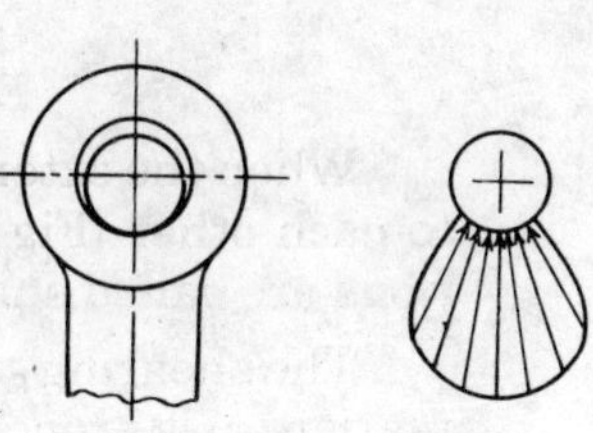
Fig. 3.9.

where $P$ = Load in kg

$L$ = Length of pin in cm

$d$ = Diameter of pin in cm

$A$ = Projected area in cm$^2$

## 3.10 Combined Stresses

(*a*) **Two dimensional stress field.** When a system is subjected to direct stresses and shear stresses then the values of maximum principal stresses are calculated as follows :

Consider a two dimensional system on which the stresses acting are as mentioned below (Fig. 3.10).

$f_x$ = Direct tensile or compressive stress acting on plane *AB*.

$f_y$ = Direct tensile or compressive stress acting on *CB*.

$f_{xy}$ or $f_s$ = Shear stress acting along plane *AB*. and plane *CB*.

$f$ = Principal stress.

$$= \frac{1}{2}\ \frac{(f_x + f_y)}{2} \pm \frac{1}{2}\sqrt{(f_x - f_y)^2} + 4\ F_s^2$$

Therefore two principal stresses will be given by the equations as follows.

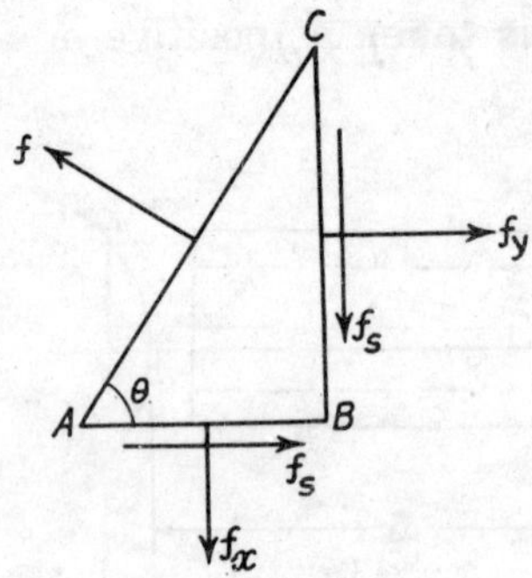


Fig. 3.10

$$f_1 = \frac{1}{2}(f_x + f_y) + \frac{1}{2}\sqrt{(f_x - f_y)^2 + 4f_s^2}$$

$$f_2 = \frac{1}{2}(f_x + f_y) - \frac{1}{2}\sqrt{(f_x - f_y)^2 + 4f_s^2}$$

These stresses will act on mutually perpendicular planes given by the equation as follows :

$$\tan 2\theta = \frac{2\,f_s}{f_x - f_y}$$

The maximum shear stress is given by

$$f_{s\,(max)} = \frac{1}{2}\sqrt{(f_x - f_y)^2 + 4f_s^2}$$

or
$$f_{s\,(max)} = \frac{1}{2}\,|f_1 - f_2|$$

The two planes having shear stress maximum and mutually perpendicular are found from the following equation :

$$\tan 2\theta = \frac{f_x - f_y}{-2 \times f_s}$$

If $f_s = 0$, $f_x$ and $f_y$ are the principal stresses.

## 3.11 Mohr Circle

It is a graphical method to find principal stresses. In this method $ON = f_x$, $OM = f_y$. From $M$ and $N$ take $MS = NR$ = shear stress ($f_s$) and join $SR$. With $SR$ as diameter and $C$ as centre, draw a circle. Then from the circle [Fig. 3.11 (*a*)]

$$f_1 = \text{Principal stress (max)} = OB$$
$$f_2 = \text{Principal stress (min)} = OA$$
$$f_{s\,max} = \text{Maximum shear stress} = CP$$

Tensile stress is taken as positive and compressive stress is taken as negative.

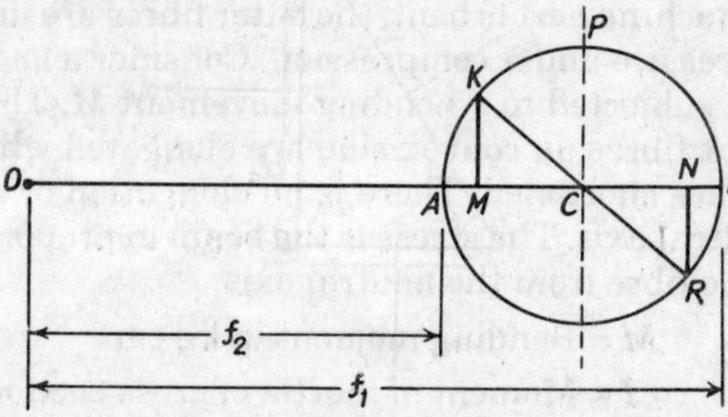


Fig. 3.11 (*a*).

(*b*) **Three dimensional stress field.** Fig. 3.11 (*b*) shows a general three dimensional stress element showing three normal stresses $f_x$, $f_y$ and $f_z$ and six shear stresses $f_{xy}$, $f_{yx}$, $f_{yz}$, $f_{zy}$, $f_{zx}$ and $f_{xz}$. The three principal stresses will be given by the three roots of the following determinant

$$\begin{vmatrix} f_x - f & f_{xy} & f_{xz} \\ f_{xy} & f_y - f & f_{yz} \\ f_{xz} & f_{yz} & f_z - f \end{vmatrix}$$

Maximum shear stress $f_{s\,(max)}$ will be given by

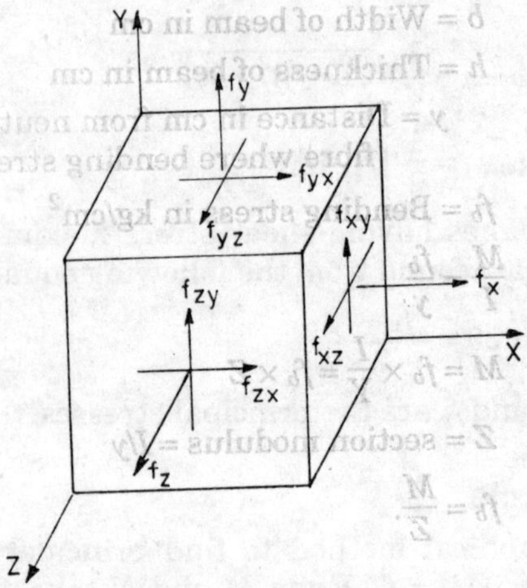


Fig. 3.11 (*b*)

$$f_{s\,max} = \text{Largest of } \frac{|f_1 - f_2|}{2}, \frac{f_2 - f_3 f}{2}$$

and $$\frac{|f_3 - f_1|}{2}$$

## 3.12 Bending Stress

When a machine part is bent, the outer fibres are under tension and inner fibres are under compression. Consider a beam shown in Fig. 3.12 and subjected to a bending movement $M$. The beam gets bent such that fibres on convex side are elongated while fibres on concave side are shortened. There is no elongation or compression along the neutral axis. The stress is the beam in proportional to the distance of the fibre from the neutral axis.

Let $M$ = Bending moment in kg cm

$I$ = Moment of inertia of cross-sectional area about the neutral axis in $cm^4$

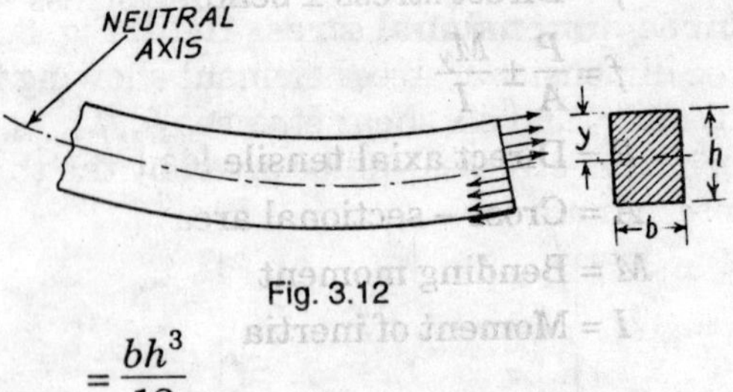


Fig. 3.12

$$= \frac{bh^3}{12}$$

$b$ = Width of beam in cm

$h$ = Thickness of beam in cm

$y$ = Distance in cm from neutral surface to the fibre where bending stress is to be found

$f_b$ = Bending stress in kg/cm$^2$

$$\frac{M}{I} = \frac{f_b}{y}$$

$$M = f_b \times \frac{I}{Y} = f_b \times Z$$

where $Z$ = section modulus = $I/y$

$$\therefore \quad f_b = \frac{M}{Z}.$$

During bending a straight beam is considered to behave so that plane sections remain plane and hence unit fibre strains and stresses are proportional to the distance of fibre from the neutral surface. The following assumptions should be satisfied.

(*i*) The beam is straight so that fibre strains are proportional to distance from neutral surface.

(*ii*) The cross-section is uniform.

(*iii*) The forces acting on the beam must be perpendicular to the axis of beam and the plane of forces acting on the beam must contain the bending axis of the beam to prevent the beam being to subjected to a torsional moment in addition to bending.

## 3.13 Combined Bending and Direct Stresses

When a machine part is subjected to bending and direct loads the combined stresses ($f$) at the outer surfaces are calculated as follows :

$$f = \text{Direct stress} \pm \text{bending stress}$$

$$f = \frac{P}{A} \pm \frac{M_y}{I}$$

where $P$ = Direct axial tensile load

$A$ = Cross – sectional area

$M$ = Bending moment

$I$ = Moment of inertia

**Table 3.8 (*d*)**

| *Section* | *Moment of inertia (I)* | *Section modulus (Z)* | *Radius of gyration (K)* |
|---|---|---|---|
| 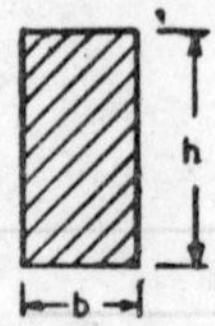 | $\frac{bh^3}{12}$ | $\frac{bh^2}{6}$ | $\frac{h}{\sqrt{12}}$ |
| 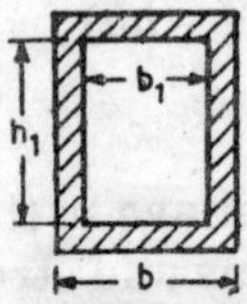 | $\frac{bh^3 - b_1 h_1^3}{12}$ | $\frac{bh^3 - b_1 h_1^3}{6h}$ | $\sqrt{\frac{bh^3 - b_1 h_1^3}{12(bh - b_1 h_1)}}$ |
| 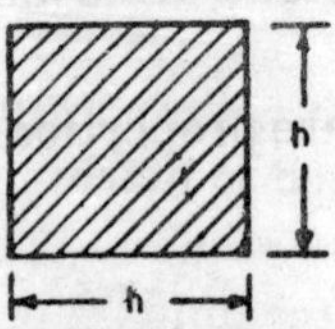 | $\frac{h^4}{12}$ | $\frac{h^3}{6}$ | $\frac{h}{\sqrt{12}}$ |
| 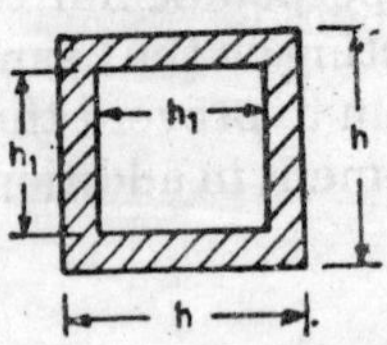 | $\frac{h^4 - h_1^4}{12}$ | $\frac{h^4 - h_1^4}{6h}$ | $\sqrt{\frac{h^2 + h_1^2}{12}}$ |
| 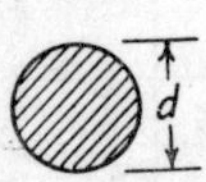 | $\frac{\pi d^4}{64}$ | $\frac{\pi d^3}{32}$ | $\frac{d}{4}$ |
| 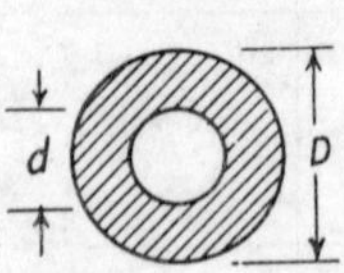 | $\frac{\pi(D^4 - d^4)}{64}$ | $\frac{(\pi D^4 - d^4)}{32D}$ | $\frac{\sqrt{D^2 + d^2}}{4}$ |

*(Contd...)*

| Section | Moment of inertia (I) | Section modulus (Z) | Radius of gyration (K) |
|---|---|---|---|
|   | $\frac{\pi a^3 b}{64}$ | $\frac{\pi a^2 b}{32}$ | $\frac{a}{4}$ |
| 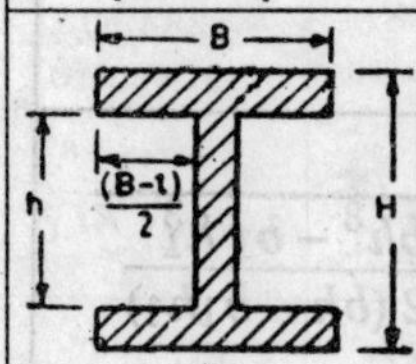  | $\frac{BH^3 - bh^3}{12}$ | $\frac{BH^3 - bh^3}{6h}$ | $\sqrt{\frac{BH^3 - bh^3}{12\,(BH - bh)}}$ |

The plus sign indicates tension and negative sign indicates compression.

Table 3.8 (*d*) indicates the moment of inertia, section modulus and radius of gyration of some important sections used in machine design.

Table 3.9 shows the values of maximum shear force, maximum bending moment and maximum deflection of a beam under various types of loads.

**Table 3.9**

| | Loading | Maximum shear force(F) | Maximum bending moment (M) | Deflection (Y) |
|---|---|---|---|---|
| **Cantilever with end load** | 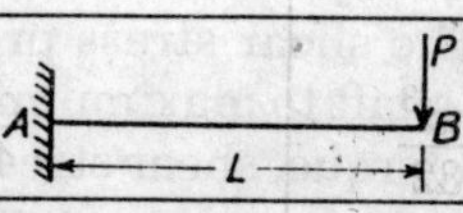  | P | $M = P \times L$ at A | $\frac{PL^3}{3EI}$ |
| **Cantilever intermediate load (W)** | 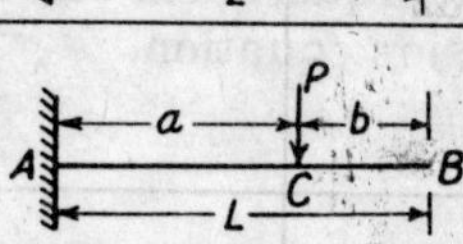  | P | $M = P \times a$ at A | $\frac{F}{EI}(3a^2L - a^3)$ |
| **Cantilever with uniform load (W)** | 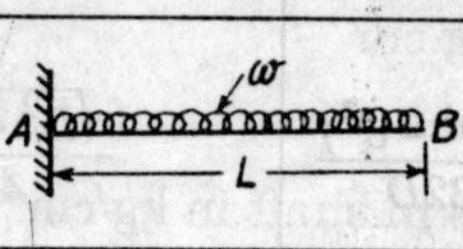  | $P = W \times L$ | $M = \frac{WL}{2}$ at A | $\frac{WL^3}{8EI}$ |
| **End supports centre load** | 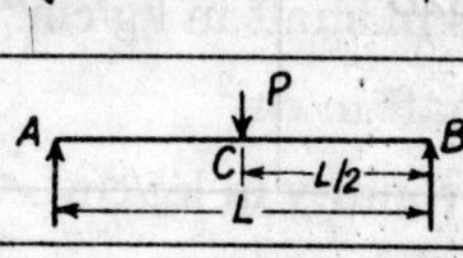  | $\frac{P}{2}$ | $\frac{PL}{4}$ at C | $\frac{PL^3}{48\,EI}$ at C |

| | Loading | Maximum shear force(F) | Maximum bending moment (M) | Deflection (Y) |
|---|---|---|---|---|
| End supports intermediate load | 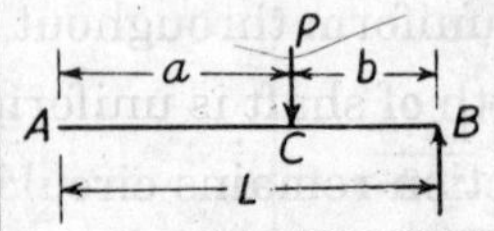 | $\frac{Pd}{L}$ | $M = \frac{P.a.b}{L}$ at C | $\frac{PB}{3\,E.I.L}\left[\frac{a(a+2b)^{3/2}}{2}\right]$ |
| End support uniform load | 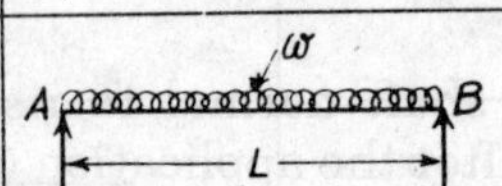 | $\frac{P}{2}$ | $M = \frac{PL}{8}$ at centre | $\frac{5PL^3}{384\,EI}$ at centre |
| One end fixed other supported | 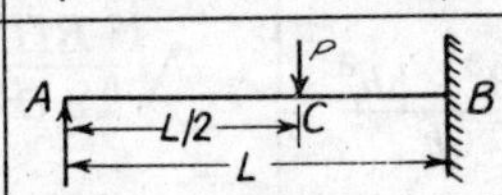 | $\frac{11}{16}P$ | $M = \frac{3}{16}PL$ at B | $\frac{7}{768}\,\frac{PL^3}{EI}$ |
| Both ends fixed with centre load | 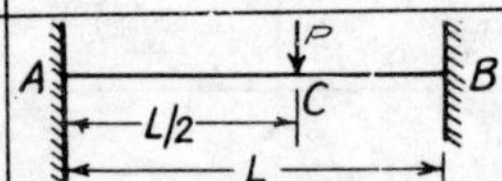 | $\frac{P}{2}$ | $M = \frac{PL}{8}$ at A and B | $\frac{PL^3}{192EI}$ at C |
| Both ends fixed with uniform load | 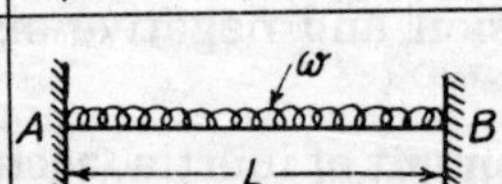 | $\frac{P}{2}$ | $M = \frac{PL}{12}$ | $\frac{PL^3}{384EI}$ at centre |

$L$ = Length of beam

$P$ = Load

$W$ = Uniform distributed load

$P = W \times L$

$E$ = Young's modulus of elasticity

$I$ = Moment of inertia of beam.

## 3.14 Torsional Stress

The stress produced in a shaft subjected to a twisting moment or torque is called shear stress. The shear stress produced varies linearly from zero at the centre of shaft to maximum at the surface of shaft. The relationship between torque, shear stress and angle of twist is given by the following torsion equation.

$$\frac{T}{I_p} = \frac{f_s}{r} = \frac{G\,\theta}{L}$$

where $T$ = Torque in kg cm

$I_p$ = Polar moment of inertia of shaft in $cm^4$

$f_s$ = Shear stress in shaft in $kg/cm^2$

$r$ = Radius of shaft in $cm^2$

$G$ = Modulus of rigidity in $kg/cm^2$

$\theta$ = Angle of twist in radians

$L$ = Length of shaft in cm.

The above torsion equation is based on the following/assumptions :

(*i*) The material of shaft is uniform throughout.

(*ii*) The twist along the length of shaft is uniform throughout.

(*iii*) The shaft circular in section remains circular after loading.

(*iv*) A plane section of the shaft normal to its axis before loading remains plane after the application of torque.

From torsion equation

$$\frac{T}{I_p} = \frac{f_s}{r}$$

$$T = \frac{I_p}{r} \times f_s = z_p \times f_s$$

where $z_p$ = polar section modulus = $\frac{I_p}{r}$.

The torque ($T$) is obtained from a consideration of horse power transmitted by the rotating shaft

$$\text{H.P.} = \frac{2\pi NT}{4500}$$

where H.P. = Horse power ; $T$ = Torque in kg–cm

$N$ = R.P.M. of shaft

In S.I. units $P$ = Power (watts) = $\frac{2\pi NT}{60}$

where $T$ = Torque in Nm; $N$ = R.P.M. of shaft.

The values of polar moment of inertia and polar section modulus for some of the sections are given in Table 3.10.

**Table 3.10**

| *Section* | $I_p$ | $z_p$ |
|---|---|---|
| 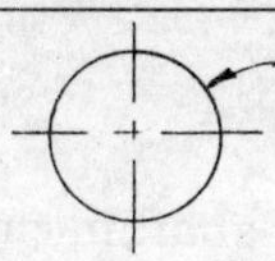 | $\frac{\pi}{32} d^4$ | $\frac{\pi}{16} d^3$ |
| 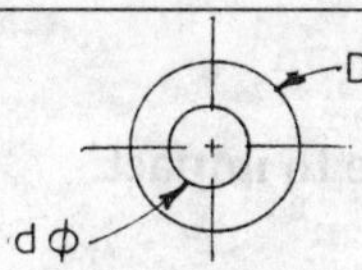 | $\frac{\pi}{32} (D^4 - d^4)$ | $\frac{\pi}{16} \frac{(D^4 - d^4)}{D}$ |

## 3.15 Design of Members Subjected to Impact Torsion

Sometimes suddenly applied energy loads may produce impact stresses in torsion members. Such as in a rotating shaft torsional impact stress is produced by the sudden transfer of kinetic energy of a flywheel when the shaft is stopped suddenly.

Let $\theta$ = Angle of twist

$L$ = Length of shaft

$T$ = Equivalent static torsional moment

$E$ = Kinetic energy

= Work done by the equivalent torque

$$E = \frac{1}{2} T.\theta. \qquad ...(i)$$

Now for a circular shaft

$$\frac{T}{I_p} = \frac{C\theta}{L}$$

where $I_p$ = Polar moment of inertia of shaft

$C$ = Modulus of rigidity

$$\therefore \quad \theta = \frac{T\,.\,L}{C\,.\,I_p} \qquad ...(ii)$$

From (*i*) and (*ii*), we get

$$\theta = \sqrt{\frac{2 \times L \times E}{C\,.I_p}} \qquad ...(iii)$$

Again
$$\theta = \frac{T\,.\,L}{C\,.\,I_p}$$

and
$$\frac{T}{I_p} = \frac{f_s}{r} = \frac{f_e}{d/2}$$

$$T = I_p \frac{f_s}{d/2}$$

$$\therefore \quad \theta = \frac{T\,.\,L}{C\,.\,I_p} = \frac{I_p\,.\,f_s \times L}{\frac{d}{2}\,.C\,.\,I_p}$$

$$\theta = \frac{2\,.\,f_s\,.\,L}{C\,.\,d} \qquad ...(iv)$$

where $f_s$ = Maximum shear stress due to impact.

From (*iii*) and (*iv*), we get

$$\frac{2f_s \cdot L}{Cd} = \sqrt{\frac{2\,LE}{C\,I_p}}$$

$$f_s^2 = \frac{2\,L.\,E}{C\,I_p} \times \frac{C^2\,d^2}{4\,.L^2}$$

$$= \frac{1}{2} \cdot \frac{CE\,.d^2}{I_p\,.\,L} = \frac{1}{2} \cdot \frac{C\,.\,E\,.\,d^2}{\frac{\pi}{32}\,d^4 \times L}$$

$$= \frac{4\,C\,.\,E}{\frac{\pi}{4}\,d^2\,.\,L} = \frac{4\,CE}{A\,.\,L}$$

where $A$ = Cross-sectional area of shaft

$$f_s = \sqrt{\frac{4\,CE}{AL}}\,.$$

**Example 3.1.** *A circular mild steel shaft 100 cm long and 8 cm in diameter has a flywheel fitted at one end and rotates at 240 R.P.M. The flywheel weighs 80 kg and its radius of gyration is 28 cm. If the shaft is suddenly stopped determine the following :*

(*a*) *Maximum angle of twist*

(*b*) *Maximum shear stress*

*Take* $C = 0.8 \times 10^6$ *kg/cm²*.

**Solution.** $d$ = Shaft diameter = 8 cm

$C$ = Modulus of rigidity = $0.8 \times 10^6$ kg/cm²

$N$ = R.P.M. of shaft = 240

$\omega$ = Angular velocity of flywheel

$$= \frac{2\pi\,N}{60} = \frac{2\pi \times 240}{60} = 25.12 \text{ rad/sec.}$$

$W$ = Weight of flywheel = 80 kg

$I_p$ = Polar moment of inertia of shaft

$$= \frac{\pi}{32}\,d^4 = \frac{\pi}{32} \times 8^4 = 40^2 \text{ cm}^4$$

$E$ = Kinetic energy of flywheel

$$= \frac{1}{2} \cdot I\omega^2$$

where $I$ = Moment of inertia of flywheel

$$= \frac{W}{g}\,k^2 = \frac{80}{981} \times 28^2 = 64 \text{ kg cm}^2$$

$$k = \text{radius of gyration of flywheel} = 28 \text{ cm}$$

$$\therefore \quad E = \frac{1}{2} I\omega^2$$

$$= \frac{1}{2} \times 64 \times (25.12)^2 = 20193 \text{ kg cm.}$$

we have proved that $\theta = \frac{\sqrt{2 . L . E}}{C . I_p}$

$$= \sqrt{\frac{2 \times 100 \times 20193}{0.8 \times 10^6 \times 40^2}} = 0.112 \text{ radians}$$

$$f_s = \text{Maximum shear stress}$$

$$= \sqrt{\frac{4.C.E}{A . L}}$$

$$= \sqrt{\frac{4 \times 0.8 \times 10^6 \times 20193}{\frac{\pi}{4} \times 8^2 \times 100}} = 3600 \text{ kg/cm}$$

## 3.16 Combined Bending and Torsion

A rotating shaft carrying gears, pulleys and sheaves etc. is subjected to both bending and twisting when used for power transmission. In such cases shaft diameter is calculated as follows :

(*i*) According to Guest's theory equivalent torque should be used to find the shaft diameter

$d$ = Shaft diameter

$T$ = Torque acting on shaft

$M$ = Bending moment acting on shaft

$f_s$ = Shear stress in shaft

$r$ = Radius of shaft

$T_e$ = Equivalent torque

$$= \sqrt{T^2 + M^2}$$

Now $$\frac{T_e}{I} = \frac{f_s}{r}$$

$$T_e = \frac{\pi}{32} . d^4 \times \frac{f_s}{d}/2 = \frac{\pi}{16} f_s . d^3$$

(*ii*) According to Rankine's theory, the diameter of shaft can be calculated taking into account the equivalent bending moment.

$$M_e = \frac{1}{2}\,(M + \sqrt{M^2 + T^2})$$

where $M_e$ = Equivalent bending moment

$T$ = Torque applied on shaft

$M$ = Bending moment acting on shaft

$$\frac{M_e}{I} = \frac{f_b}{y}$$

$$M_e = \frac{I}{y} \times f_b = \frac{\frac{\pi}{64} d^4}{d/2} \times f_b$$

$$M_e = \frac{\pi}{32}\, d^3 \times f_b$$

where $d$ = Shaft diameter

$f_b$ = Bending stress

(*iii*) According to maximum strain theory

$$M_e = \frac{1}{2}\,(1 - \sigma)\, M + \frac{1}{2}\,(1 + \sigma)\sqrt{M^2 + T^2}$$

where $\sigma$ = Poisson's ratio

When a shaft is subjected to combined torsion and bending service factors like shock factor ($K_m$) and fatigue factor ($K_t$) should be used. Table 3.11 indicates the values of these factors.

**Table 3.11**

| *Type of loading* | $K_m$ | $K_t$ |
|---|---|---|
| Rotating shafts | | |
| (*i*) Steady load | 1.5 | 1.0 |
| (*ii*) Load applied suddenly minor shocks | 1.5 to 2.0 | 1 to 1.5 |
| (*iii*) Load applied suddenly, major shocks | 2 to 3.0 | 1.5 to 3.0 |
| Stationary shafts | | |
| (*i*) Gradually applied load | 1.0 | 1.0 |
| (*ii*) Suddenly applied load | 1.5 to 2.0 | 1.5 to 2.0 |

When these factors are taken into account the above formulae become as follows.

$$T_e = \sqrt{(K_m \cdot M)^2 + (K_t \cdot T)^2} = \frac{\pi}{16} f_s \cdot d^3$$

$$M_e = \frac{1}{2}[K_m \cdot M + \sqrt{(K_m \cdot M)^2 + (K_t \cdot T)^2}] = \frac{\pi}{32} d^3 \cdot f_b$$

## 3.17 Columns

A long vertical bar subjected to an axial compressive load is called a column.

### 3.15.1 Terms and definitions.

(*i*) **Slenderness ratio** It is the ratio of length of column to the minimum radius of gyration of the cross-sectional area of the column. A column is said to short column when slenderness ratio is less that 32 and if the slenderness ratio is between 32 to 120 the column is said to be medium column and if slenderness ratio is more than 120 the column is called long column.

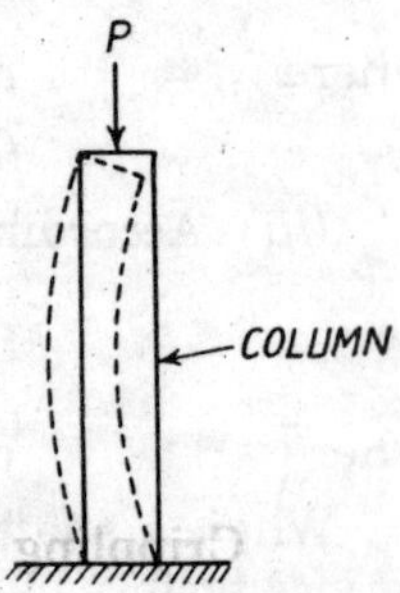

Fig. 3.14. Buckling of column.

(*ii*) **Buckling load.** It is the minimum load at which the column tends to have lateral displacement or tends to buckle (Fig. 3.14). Buckling load is also called crippling or critical load.

(*iii*) **End conditions**

A loaded column can have any one of the following end conditions.

(*i*) Both ends hinged [Fig. 3.15 (*a*)]

(*ii*) One end fixed and other hinged [Fig. 3.15 (*b*)]

(*iii*) Both ends fixed [Fig. 3.15 (*c*)]

(*iv*) One end rigidly fixed and other entirely free [Fig. 3.15 (*d*)].

Fig. 3.15 shows bending of column according to different end conditions.

Let $L$ = length of column

$l$ = Equivalent length

$= L$ when both ends are hinged

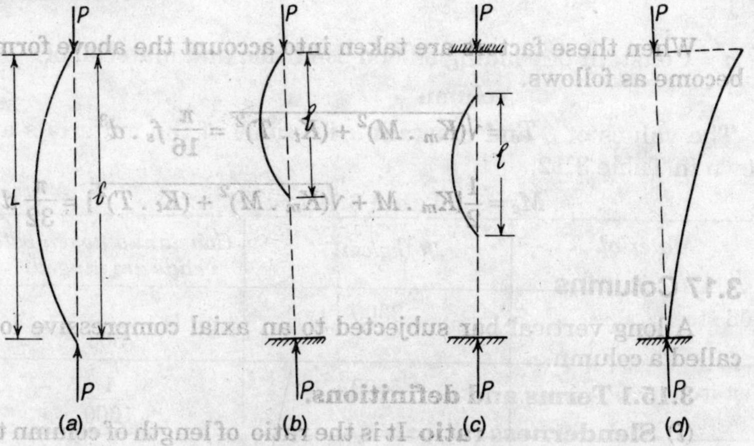


Fig. 3.15.

$= \frac{L}{\sqrt{2}}$ when one ends is fixed and other hinged

$= L/2$ when both ends are fixed

$= 2L$ when one end is fixed and other entirely free

Crippling load is calculated as follows :

(*i*) Using Euler's formula :

$$P = \frac{\pi^2 EI}{l^2}$$

where $P$ = Crippling load

$E$ = Young's modulus of elasticity

$I$ = Moment of inertia

$l$ = Equivalent length

(*ii*) Using Rankine Gordon formula

$$P = \frac{f_c \cdot A}{1 + a\left(\frac{1}{K}\right)^2}$$

where $f_c$ = Intensity of stress at yield point in compression

$A$ = Area of cross-section of column

$K$ = Least radius of gyration of cross section of column

$a$ = Constant depending on end condition and material of column

The values of $f_c$ and constant $a$ for some of the materials are shown in Table 3.12.

**Table 3.12**

| *Material* | *ft (kg/cm²)* | *Constant a (when both ends are hinged)* |
|---|---|---|
| Mild steel | 3300 | $\frac{1}{7500}$ |
| Cast iron | 5600 | $\frac{1}{1600}$ |
| Wrought iron | 2500 | $\frac{1}{9000}$ |
| Timber | 500 | $\frac{1}{750}$ |

## 3.18 Eccentric Loading

Some machine parts like frames of a punching machine, portable hydraulic riveter etc. are subjected to an eccentric load. An eccentric load is one whose line of action is parallel to but does not coincide with the centroidal axis of the supporting member. Fig. 3.16 shows an eccentric load $P$ acting on a rod. The distance $e$ is called eccentricity. The stresses produced by such load are as follows :

(*i*) Direct compressive stress as if the load passed through centre of gravity of rod.

$f_c$ = Direct compressive stress

$= P/A$

(*ii*) Bending stress due to bending moment

$f_b$ = bending stress

$$= \frac{M \times y}{I}$$

where $M$ = Bending moment $= P \times e$

$I$ = Moment of inertia

$y$ is positive on the same side of centre of gravity as $P$ and negative on the opposite side.

$f$ = Combined stress $= fc \times fb$

$$= \frac{P}{A} + \frac{P \times e \times y}{I}$$

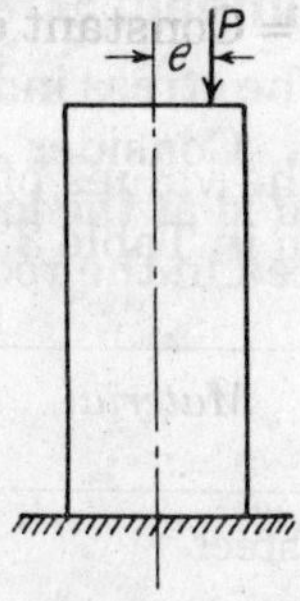


Fig. 3.16.

## 3.19 Resilience

It is the energy stored in a material due to external loading within elastic limit. The amount of resilience is equal to the work required to deform the material from zero stress to stress $f$ when the stress $f$ does not exceed elastic limit.

$$\text{Resilience } (U) = \frac{fV}{2E}$$

where $V$ = Volume of the body subjected to stress $f$

$E$ = Modulus of elasticity

Resilience per unit volume is called modulus of resilience.

$$\text{Modulus of resilience} = \frac{f^2}{2E}$$

Table 3.13 indicates the modulus of resilience for various types of loading.

**Table 3.13**

| *Type of loading* | *Modulus of resilience* |
|---|---|
| Tension or compression | $\frac{f^2}{2E}$ |
| Shear, simple transverse | $\frac{f^2}{2G}$ |
| Bending in beam End simple supported, concentrated load at centre | $\frac{f^2}{24E}$ |
| Torsion (*a*) Solid circular | $\frac{f^2}{4G}$ |
| (*b*) Hollow circular | $\frac{f^2}{4G}\left[1+\left(\frac{D^2}{D_1}\right)^2 I^2\right] D_1 > D_2$ |
| Helical spring (*a*) Axial load | $\frac{f^2}{4G}$ |
| (*b*) Axial twist | $\frac{f^2}{8E}$ |

## 3.20 Impact Stress

The stress induced in a body due to falling load is called impact stress. Consider a weight $W$ falling from a height $h$ on a collor provided at the lower end of a rod (Fig. 3.17). The maximum stress induced in the rod is given by the following equation.

$$f = \frac{W}{A}\left(1 + \sqrt{1 + \frac{2h\,AE}{W + L}}\right)$$

where $A$ = Cross sectional area of rod.

$L$ = Length of rod.

$E$ = Modulus of elasticity.

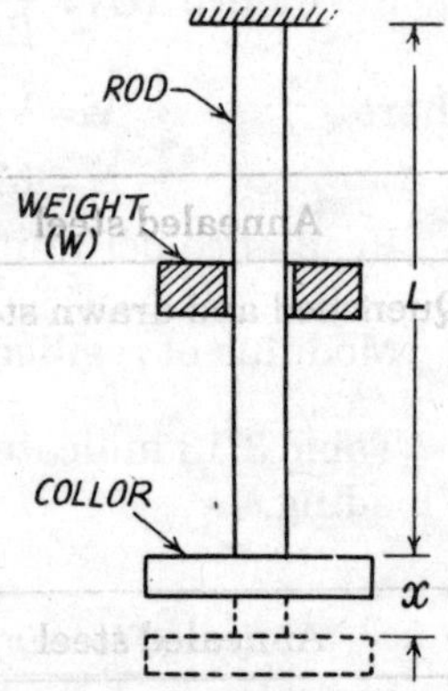


Fig. 3.17

## 3.21 Stress Concentration

In machine parts the presence of discontinuities (stress raisers) like holes, abrupt changes in cross-section fillets, keyways, and notches cause high local stresses. The effect is called stress concentration. These local stresses may give rise to cracks during service conditions which may lead to failure of machine part. Stress concentration is very serious in brittle materials during static loading as compared to ductile materials. In ductile material the phenomenon of stress concentration is quite serious during cyclic e loading. The measure of stress concentration is stress concentration factor. The stress concentration factor ($K_t$) is defined as follows :

$$K_t = \frac{\text{Maximum localised stress at discontinuity}}{\text{Nominal stress}}$$

The nominal stress is calculated by usual formulas of strength of materials for minimum cross-section. This stress concentration factor depends upon size of discontinuity or its geometric form and is also called form stress factor.

Any discontinuity in a machine part alters the stress distribution in the neighbourhood of the discontinuity so that elementary stress equations no longer describe the state of stress in the part. Fig. 3.18 shows a uniform bar intension. It is observed that force flow lines are uniformly spaced whereas in case of the bar having notches Fig. 3.19 the force flow lines will have to bend near the notches and thus stress concentration will take place. The severity of the stress concentration is proportional to the amount of bending of flow lines. The machine parts should be so shaped that stress concentration at points of high loading are avoided as much as possible.

Table 3.14 shows stress concentration factors for key ways, gear teeth and screw threads.

**Table 3.14**

| | *Profiled keyways* | | *Sled-Runner Keyways* | |
|---|---|---|---|---|
| | *Bending* | *Torsion* | *Bending* | *Torsion* |
| Annealed steel | 1.6 | 1.3 | 1.3 | 1.3 |
| Quenched and drawn steel | 2.0 | 1.6 | 1.6 | 1.6 |
| | *Gear Tooth Pressure Angle* | | | |
| | $14\frac{1}{2}^o$ | | $20^o$ | |
| Annealed steel | 1.6 | | 1.5 | |
| Quenched and drawn steel | 2.2 | | 2.0 | |
| | *Screw Threads* | | | |
| | *Cut threads* | | *Rolled threads* | |
| Annealed steel | 2.8 | | 2.2 | |
| Quenched and drawn steel | 3.8 | | 3.0 | |

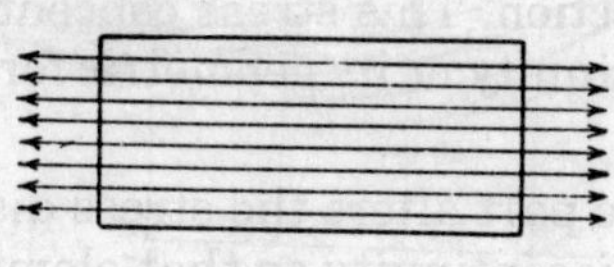

Fig. 3.18.

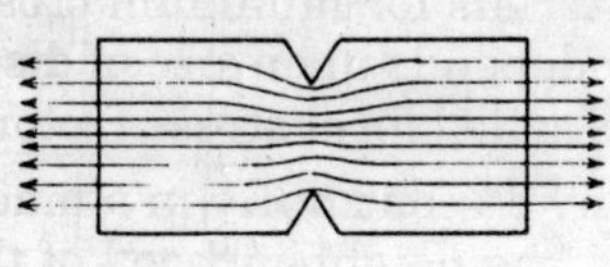

Fig. 3.19.

Fig. 3.20 shows the variation of stress concentration factor ($K_t$) for a bar with a transverse hole subjected to tension or simple compression.

where $b$ = width of rod

$d$ = diameter of hole

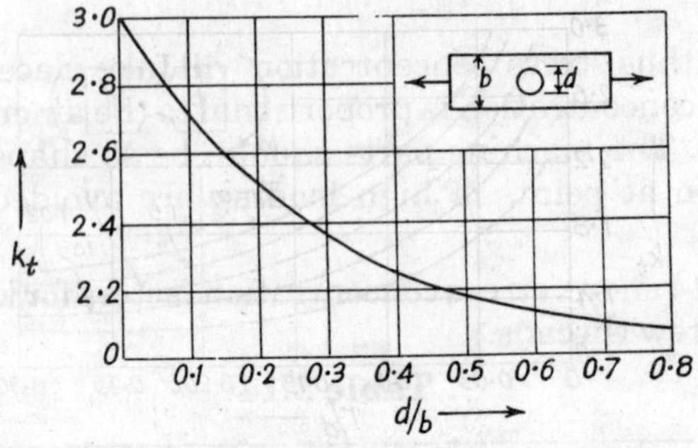


Fig. 3.20.

Fig. 3.21 shows variation of stress concentration factor for a rectangular bar with a transverse hole and subjected to bending.

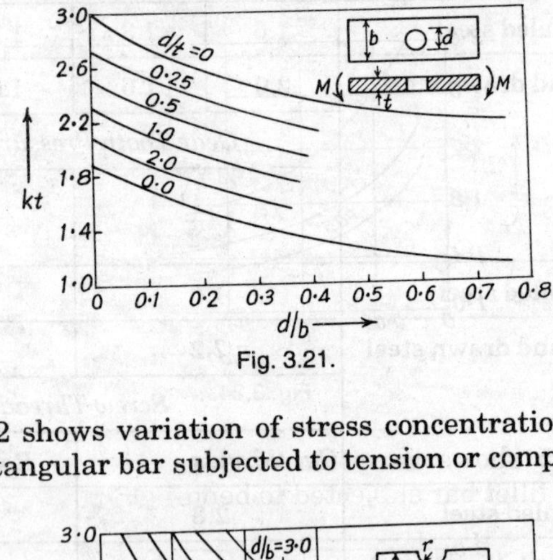


Fig. 3.21.

Fig. 3.22 shows variation of stress concentration factor for a notched rectangular bar subjected to tension or compression.

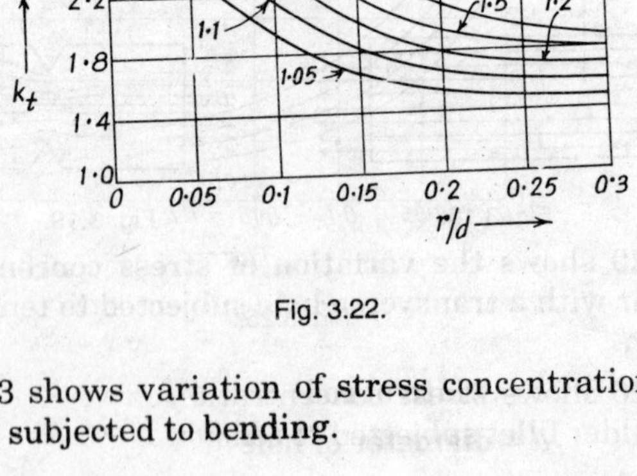


Fig. 3.22.

Fig. 3.23 shows variation of stress concentration factor for a notched bar subjected to bending.

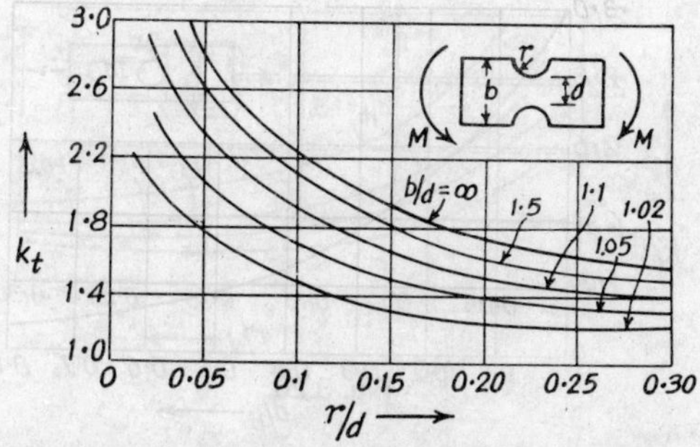


Fig. 3.23.

Fig. 3.24 shows variation of stress concentration factor for rectangular fillet bar intension or simple compression.

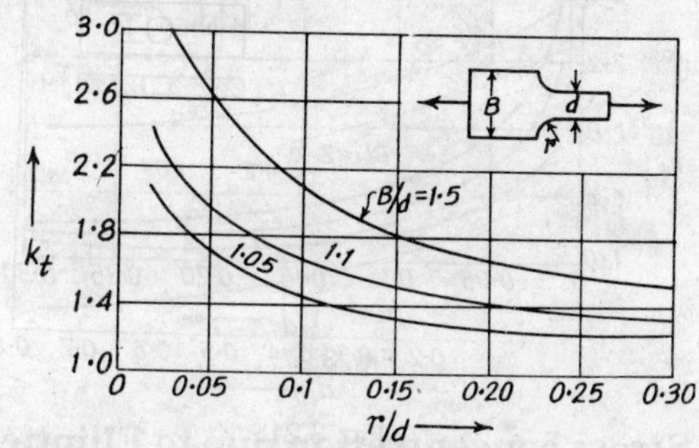


Fig. 3.24.

Fig. 3.25 shows variation of stress concentration factor for rectangular fillet bar subjected to bending.

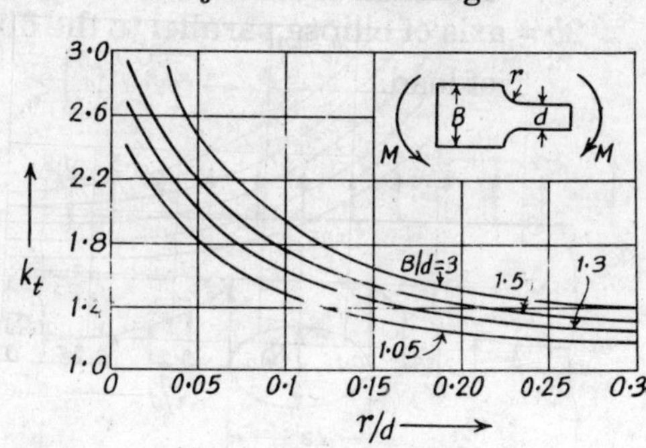


Fig. 3.25.

Fig. 3.26 shows stress concentration factor for a round shaft with a shoulder fillet subjected to tension.

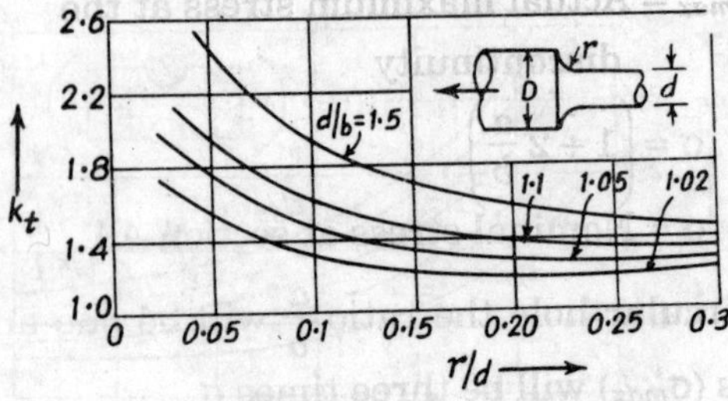


Fig. 3.26.

Fig. 3.27 shows variation of stress concentration factor for round shaft with shoulder fillet of radius $r$ in tension.

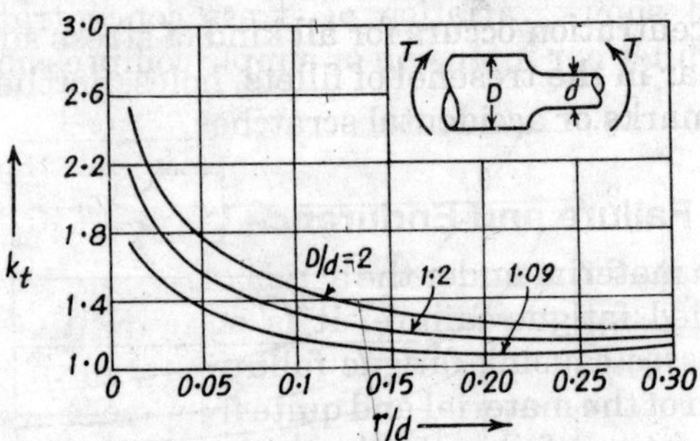


Fig. 3.27.

### 3.19.1. Stress concentration due to Elliptical Hole

Fig. 3.28 shows a bar with an elliptical hole.

Let $2a$ = axis of ellipse perpendicular to the direction of load.

$2b$ = axis of ellipse parallel to the direction of load.

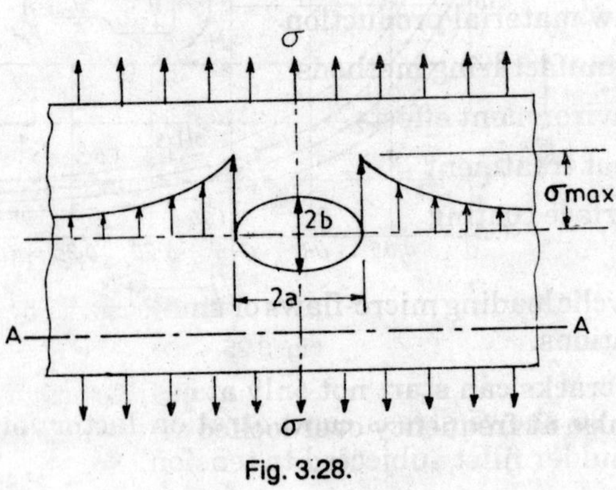


Fig. 3.28.

$\sigma_{max}$ = Actual maximum stress at the discontinuity

$$\sigma = \left(1 + 2\frac{a}{b}\right)$$

where $\sigma$ = Nominal stress at section $AA$.

In case of circular hole the ratio $\frac{a}{b}$ will be one and therefore maximum stress ($\sigma_{max}$) will be three times $\sigma$.

So that $K_t = \frac{\sigma_{max}}{\sigma} = 3$

where $K_t$ = Theoretical or geometric concentration factor.

Stress concentration occurs for all kind of stress such as axial, bending or shear in the tresenel of fillets, holes, notches, keyways, splines, tool - marks or accidental scratches.

## 3.22 Fatigue Failure and Endurance Limit

Failure of a material under the action of repeated or fluctuating stresses is called fatigue failure. It is observed that the actual maximum stresses causing fatigue failure are much blow the ultimate strength of the material and quite frequently even below the elastic limit. A fatigue failure begins with a small crack, the crack develops at the discontinuity present in the material. Once a crack has started stress concentration effect becomes greater and the crack progresses more rapidly. As the stresses area decreases in size the stress increases in magnitude until finally the remaining area fails suddenly.

Fatigue failure has its origin in some interval imperfections in the material in the form of minute inclusions. These imperfections can be due to the following reasons.

(*i*) Raw material production

(*ii*) Manufacturing methods

(*iii*) Environment effects

(*iv*) Heat treatment

(*v*) Surface coating

Under cyclic loading micro-flaws or small cracks begin to appear at these locations.

Fatigue cracks can start not only at easily recognized changes of form but also at frequency over looked stress raisers such as file and tool marks, grinding scratches quenching crack or part number and inspection stamps etc.

These cracks tend to extend across the section on repeated loading and a stage is reached when the net sound section is reduced so much that fracture takes place. Such failures called fatigue failures or progressive failures are quite damaging because such failures take place with no warning. Fatigue failure takes place at stresses very much lower than ultimate statical strength.

Smooth surface finish increases fatigue limit. The degree of smoothness of surface reduces in the following order of machining operations.

(*i*) Polishing (*ii*) Grinding

(*iii*) Turning (*iv*) Presence of scale.

The surface strength is generally increased by some kind of heat treatment surface hardening by carburising, nitriding or cyaniding are the examples of such treatments which may improve fatigue behaviour. Corrosive atmosphere is highly deteriorating for fatigue behaviour because corrosion causes cracks on the surface. Fatigue strength of most of the materials reduces with increase in temperature.

### 3.22.1. Brittle Materials with Fluctuating Loads

Although successful applications can be sites, brittle materials are usually considered unsatisfactory where the load is fluctuating. In such case higher factor of safety should be used.

Endurance limit is the maximum induced stress that the material can withstand without failure on an indefinite member of repetitions of stress. A pair of wheels and axle of a railway car is an example of repeated stresses.

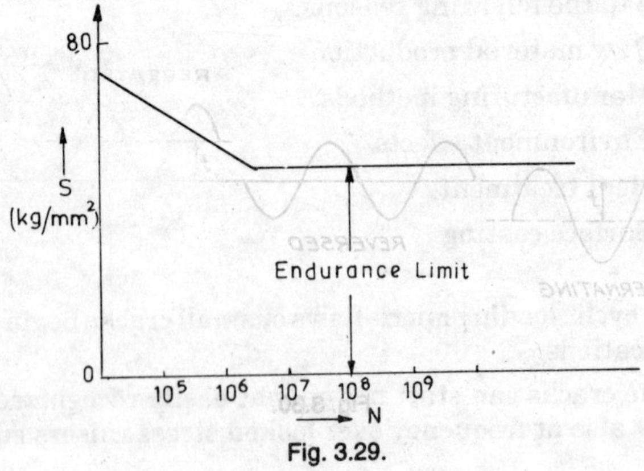


Fig. 3.29.

An $S$-$N$ curve is the plot of stress ($S$) on a specimen and number of cycles ($N$) required to produce failure during fatigue. Fig. 3.29 shows a typical $S$-$N$ curve (on log scale) for $C$ 50 steel. As shown a knee occurs in the graph and beyond this knee failure will never occur no matter how the great number of cycles. The endurance strength corresponding to the knee is called the Endurance Limit or Fatigue Limit.

Table 3.13 ($A$) indicates endurance limit ($\sigma_e$) for some of the materials.

**Table 3.13 (A)**

| *Material* | $\sigma_e$ For reversible bending (standard specimen) | Life (cycles) |
|---|---|---|
| Non ferrous materials such as Al and Mg | $\sigma_e = 0.3\ \sigma_t$ | $5 \times 10^8$ |
| Cast iron and cast steels | $\sigma_e = 0.4\ \sigma_t$ | $10^6$ |
| Steel ($BHN$ < 400 or $\sigma_t$ > 140 kg/mm$^2$) | $\sigma_e = 0.5\ \sigma_t$ | $10^6$ |

Fig. 3.30 shows the types of stresses applied on a material during fatigue failure.

Fatigue strength of a material depends upon the following factors :

(*i*) Surface conditions

(*ii*) Type of stress

(*iii*) Amplitude of stress variation

(*iv*) Size of discontinuities.

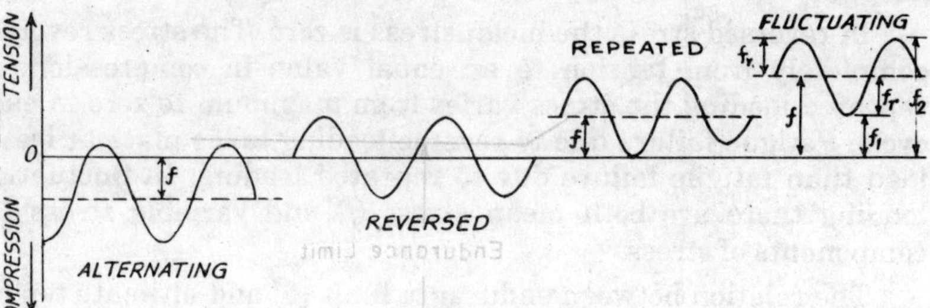


Fig. 3.30.

The various stresses used are as follows :

$$f = \text{Mean stress} = \frac{f_1 \times f_2}{2}$$

$$f_1 = \text{Minimum stress}$$

$$f_2 = \text{Maximum stress}$$

$$f_r = \text{Reversed stress}$$

**Stress ratio (R).** It is defined as the algebraic ratio of the maximum stress to the minimum stress in a stress cycle.

$$R = \text{Stress ratio}\ \frac{f_1}{f_2}$$

where $f_1$ = Minimum stress

$f_2$ = Maximum stress.

**Range of stress.** It is the algebraic difference between the maximum and minimum stress in a stress cycle.

$$f_R = \text{Range of stress} = f_2 - f_1.$$

**Variable Stress or stress amplitude** ($f_v$) . It is equal to one half of the range of stress.

$$f_v = \frac{f_R}{2} = \frac{f_2 - f_1}{2}$$

Various types of variable loading are as follows (See Fig. 3.30).

(*i*) Alternating loading

(*ii*) Reversed loading

(*iii*) Repeated loading

(*iv*) Fluctuating loading.

Under cyclic loading microflaws or small cracks begin to appear at the discontinuities in the material. These cracks tend to grow during cyclic loading and finally lead to fracture.

In reversed stress the mean stress is zero. The stress reverses completely from tension to an equal value in compression. In repeated loading the stress varies from maximum to zero in each cycle. Fatigue failure due to reverse loading takes place at lesser load than fatigue failure due to repeated loading. In fluctuating loading there are both mean stress ($f$) and variable stress ($f_v$) components of stress.

The relation between endurance limit ($f_e$) and ultimate tensile stress ($f_u$) is given by the following equation for unnotched and polished specimen.

(i) $$f_e = \left(\frac{1}{2} \text{ to } \frac{5}{8}\right) \times f_u \text{ for ferrous metals}$$
$$= \left(\frac{1}{4} \text{ to } \frac{1}{3}\right) \times f_u \text{ for non-ferrous metals}$$
$$= 0.35\, f_u \text{ for cast iron in tension}$$
$$= 0.10\, f_u \text{ for cast iron in compression.}$$

(ii) The endurance limit for wrought ferrous materials for any stress variation may be found from the following equation.

$$f_e = \frac{3\, f_{er}}{2 - R}$$

where $R$ = Stress ratio = $\frac{\text{Minimum stress}}{\text{Maximum stress in a cycle}} = \frac{f_1}{f_2}$

$f_{er}$ = Endurance limit for completely. reversed stress cycle in kg/cm$^2$

(iii) $$f_{et} = 0.55\, f_{eb}$$

where $f_{et}$ = Endurance limit for reversed torsion

$f_{eb}$ = Endurance limit for reversed bending.

(iv) For any type of torsional stress cycle

$$f_e = \frac{2\, f_{er}}{1 - R}$$

where $f_{er}$ = Endurance limit for completely reversed torsion

(v) When tension is numerically the maximum stress in any stress cycle then the endurance limit is calculated as follows :

$$f_e = \frac{6\, f_{er}}{1 - 5R}$$

## 3.23 Modifying Factors for Endurance Limit

Fatigue strength (endurance limit) of a material depends upon the following factors.

(i) Surface conditions
(ii) Type of stress
(iii) Amplitude of stress
(iv) Size of discontinuities
(v) Manufacturing methods and heat treatment.

Taking into account the above factors the working equation for endurance limit can be written as follows.

$$\sigma_E = \sigma_e \,.\, K_F \,.\, K_S \,.\, K_L$$

where $\sigma_E$ = Actual endurance limit
$K_F$ = Surface finish factor
$K_S$ = Size factor
$K_L$ = Load factor.

The values of surface finish factor ($K_F$) are indicated in Table 3.14.

**Table 3.14.**

| $f_u$ (kg/cm²) | *Machined Surface* | *Hot rolled Surface* |
|---|---|---|
| 4100 | 0.9 | 0.74 |
| 5100 | 0.89 | 0.65 |
| 7100 | 0.85 | 0.54 |
| 8200 | 0.83 | 0.49 |
| 9200 | 0.81 | 0.45 |
| 12200 | 0.74 | 0.33 |
| 14300 | 0.71 | 0.28 |

The values of size factor ($K_S$) may be taken as follows.

$$K_S = 1.0 \text{ when } d < 10 \text{ mm}$$
$$= 0.85 \text{ when } d = 10 \text{ to } 50 \text{ mm}$$
$$= 0.75 \text{ when } d > 50 \text{ mm}$$

where $d$ = test piece diameter.

The dimension $d$ corresponds to the section depth for non-round sections in bending.

The values of load factor ($K_L$ are given in table 3.15).

**Table 3.15**

| $K_L$ | *Type of loading* |
|---|---|
| 0.84 | Reversed axial loading (steels) |
| 1.0 | Reversed bending load |
| 1.0 | Reversed axial loading (cast iron) |
| 0.71 to 1.0 | Reversed axial loading (Non ferrous metals) |
| 0.58 | Reversed torsional (Steels) |
| 0.80 | Reversed torsional (cast iron) |
| 0.49 | Reversed torsional (copper) |

## 3.24 Fatigue Stress Concentration Factor ($K_f$)

Due to the presence of discontinuities (stress raisers) the fatigue resistance of the parts is lowered. The effect of such stress raisers may be expressed in the form of a factor called fatigue stress concentration factor ($K_f$) which is defined as follows :

$$K_f = \frac{\sigma_{e1}}{\sigma_{e2}}$$

where $\sigma_{e1}$ = Endurance limit of notch free specimen

$\sigma_{e2}$ = Endurance limit of notched specimen.

The fatigue stress concentration factor ($K_f$) is related to the form factor ($K_t$) as follows :

$$K_f = 1 + q(K_t - 1)$$

$$q = \frac{K_{f-1}}{k_{t-1}}$$

where $q$ = Notch sensitivity factor for fatigue loading. The typical values of notch (q) sensitivity factor are indicated in table 3.16

**Table 3.16**

| *Material* | *Annealed* | *Heat treated and drawn at 555°C* |
|---|---|---|
| Cast Iron | 0.00 to 0.05 | — |
| C 30 steel | 0.18 | 0.46 |
| C 50 steel | 0.26 | 0.50 |
| C 85 steel | — | 0.57 |
| Stainless steel | 0.16 | — |
| Cr-Ni steel | — | 0.7 |
| Copper | 0.07 | — |

A wide variation exists in the notch sensitivity of different materials.

Fine grained materials are highly sensitive to notches and notch sensitivity factor ($q$) for these materials is almost 1.

But coarse grained materials are less notch sensitive. So notches have little effect on the fatigue strength of cast iron. However brittle materials are usually considered unsatisfactory where load is fluctuating.

From the equation $q = \frac{K_{f-1}}{K_{t-1}}$

it can be seen that $q = 1$ when $K_f = K_t$ which defines a fully notch sensitive material. On the other hand when $K_{f=1}$ then $q = 0$ which defines a material insensitive to notches.

## 3.25 Designing for Fatigue Loading

The design of a machine element due to fatigue loading depends upon the type of stress cycle.

(*i*) **Completely reversed cycle**. For completely reversed cycle the design equation is as follows.

$$f_v \leq \frac{f_e}{n \,.\, K_f}$$

where $f_v$ = variable stress

$f_e$ = Endurance limit

$n$ = Factor of safety,

$k_f$ = Fatigue stress concentration factor

A similar equation can be written for completely reversed shearing stress cycle.

(*ii*) **Stress cycle other than completely reversed stress cycle**. In this case both variable stress and mean stress contribute to failure. Experiments were conducted to investigate the failure under fluctuating stresses. Fig. 3.31 shows the results of variable loading with failure points marked thereupon.

Gerber argued that the maximum value that stress amplitude assumes will be the endurance limit in fully reversed stress. Good man's relationship was more simplified. Although test data generally falls closer to the parabolic curve but due to scatter in the points the straight line relationship, is usually preferred in engineering design.

(*a*) **Soderberg criterion**. According to Soderberg criterion the failure line is taken as the straight line joining the endurance limit ($f_e$) and yield strength ($f_y$) as shown in Fig. 3.32.

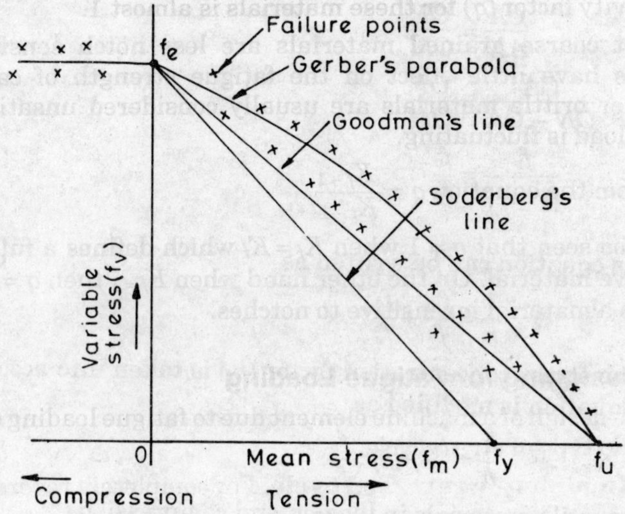


Fig. 3.31.

Fig. 3.32 shows a typical Soderberg's triangle *OMP*.

By using a suitable factor of safety ($n$) to both endurance limit and yield strength a line *RN* can be drawn parallel to the line *PM*.

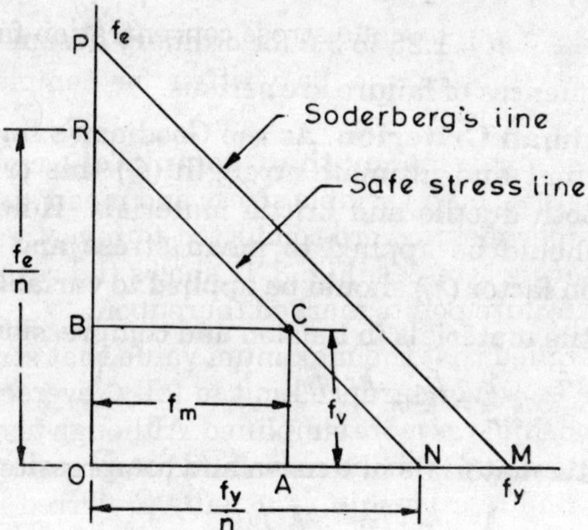


Fig. 3.32.

The line *RN* can be taken as safe stress line (design line). For any value of mean stress *OA* the permissible stress amplitude ($f_v$) is given by *OB* and *vice-versa.*

From similar triangles $OMP$ and $NCA$

$$\frac{CA}{AN} = \frac{OP}{OM}$$

$$\frac{CA}{ON - OA} = \frac{OP}{OM}$$

$$\frac{f_v}{\frac{f_y}{n} - f_m} = \frac{f_c}{f_y}$$

This equation can be written as

$$\frac{1}{n} = \frac{f_m}{f_y} + \frac{f_v}{f_e}$$

when the stress concentration factor ($k_f$) is taken into account the above equation is modified as

$$\frac{1}{n} = \frac{f_m}{f_y} + k_f \cdot \frac{f_v}{f_e}$$

for ductile materials in tension and compression

and $$\frac{1}{n} = \frac{f_{ms}}{f_{ys}} + \frac{k_f \cdot k_{vs}}{f_{es}}$$

for ductile materials in torsion.

Soderberg equation is particularly applicable to ductile material.

$n = 1.25$ to $3.0$ for ordinary design 73 and 3 to 7 when consequences of failure are serious.

(*b*) **Goodman Criterion**. As the Goodman's line connects the endurance limit and ultimate strength ($f_u$) this criterion can be applied to both ductile and brittle materials. However the form factor ($k_t$) should be applied to mean stress and fatigue stress concentration factor ($k_f$) should be applied to variable stress.

For ductile materials in tension and compression

$$\frac{1}{n} = \frac{f_m}{f_u} + \frac{k_f \cdot f_v}{f_e}$$

For brittle materials in tension and compression

$$\frac{1}{n} = \frac{k_t \cdot f_m}{f_u} + \frac{k_f \cdot f_v}{f_e}$$

For ductile materials in torsion

$$\frac{1}{n} = \frac{f_{ms}}{f_{us}} + \frac{k_f \cdot f_{vs}}{f_{es}}$$

For brittle materials in torsion

$$\frac{1}{n} = \frac{k_t \cdot f_{ms}}{f_{us}} + \frac{k_f \cdot f_{vs}}{f_{es}}$$

where $n$ = Factor of safety

$f_m$ = Mean normal stress

$f_{ms}$ = Mean shear stress

$f_{us}$ = Ultimate shear stress

$f_{vs}$ = Variable stress in shear

$f_{es}$ = Endurance limit in shear

$k_t$ = Theoretical stress concentration factor

$k_f$ = Actual stress concentration factor based on notch sensitivity of the material.

## 3.26 Theories of Failure Applied to Fatigue Loading

From Soderberg's criterion

$$\frac{1}{n} = \frac{f_m}{f_y} + \frac{k_f \cdot f_v}{f_e}$$

for ductile materials in tension and compression.

Multiplying both sides by $f_y$, we get

$$\frac{f_y}{n} = f_m + k_f \cdot f_v \cdot \frac{f_y}{f_e}$$

Now $\frac{f_y}{n}$ = Equivalent normal stress = $f_{ne}$

$$\therefore \quad f_{ne} = f_m + k_f \cdot f_v \cdot \frac{f_y}{f_e}$$

We know that

$$\frac{1}{n} = \frac{f_{ms}}{f_{ys}} + \frac{k_f \cdot f_{vs}}{f_{es}}$$

for ductile materials in torsion.

Multiplying both sides by $f_{ys}$.

$$\frac{f_{ys}}{n} = f_{ms} + k_f \cdot f_{vs} \cdot \frac{f_s}{f_{es.}}$$

But $\frac{f_{vs}}{n} = f_{se}$

equivalent shear stress.

$$f_{se} = f_{ms} + K_f \cdot f_{vs} \cdot \frac{f_{ys}}{f_{es}}.$$

(*i*) **Maximum normal stress theory.** According to this theory

$$f_{ne(max)} = \frac{1}{2} f_{ne} + \frac{1}{2}\sqrt{f_{ne}^2 + 4f_{se}^2}$$

so design equation will be

$$f_{ne\,(max)} = \frac{f_y}{n} = \frac{1}{2}[f_{ne} + \sqrt{f_{ne}^2 + 4f_{se}^2}].$$

(*ii*) **Maximum shear stress theory**

$$f_{se(italicmax)} = \frac{1}{2}\sqrt{f_{ne}^2 + 4f_{se}^2}$$

The design equation will be

$$\frac{f_y}{2n} = \frac{1}{2}\sqrt{f_{ne}^2 + 4f_{se}^2}$$

or
$$\frac{f_y}{n} = \sqrt{f_{ne}^2 + 4f_{se}^2}.$$

(*iii*) **Distortion energy theory**. The design equation for a two dimensional case will be

$$\frac{f_y}{n} = \sqrt{f_1^2 + f_2^2 - f_1 f_2} = \sqrt{f_{ne}^2 + 3f_{se}^2}.$$

## 3.27 Designing to Avoid Fatigue Failure

Following means help in reducing stress concentration due to cyclic loading.

(*i*) **Proper material selection**. Material selected for making a component should be free from stress raisers like cavities, cracks etc. Fine grained materials should be preferred because in such materials the grain boundaries largely act as barriers to cracks. Further the materials selected should be perfectly homogeneous. Brittle materials are usually considered unsatisfactory where load is fluctuating.

(*ii*) **Use of fillets**. Circular fillets help in reducing the stress concentration. Fig. 3.33 shows typical stress concentration factor for fillets of different radii.

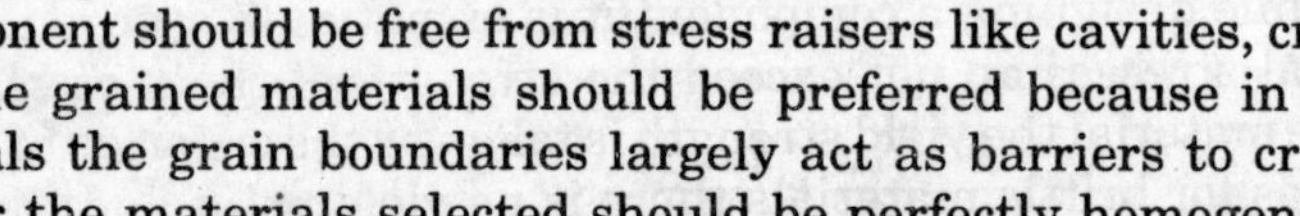


Fig. 3.33.

The sites of stress concentrations that are intentionally introduced in machine parts to fulfil some purpose must be carefully planned so as to have minimum possible stress concentration factor. Such stress concentrations include fillets, shoulders, notches, holes etc. If it is not possible to reduce the stress concentration factor due to requirements of assembly, then the stress concentration may be relieved.

(*iii*) **Proper machining and fabrication**. Poor machining resulting into bad surface finish is many times the cause of fatigue failure. Good surface finish that does not produce any grooves etc. on the surface increase the fatigue resistance of the component. Special care should be taken while producing grooves, fillets, notches etc. Their radii should bend smoothly into the adjacent surfaces.

Surfaces should be finished smoothly without leaving a nick or blemish on the surface. Special care must be taken for making grooves, notches, fillets or shoulders. Their radii must blend smoothly into adjacent surfaces.

Fabrication methods such as forging welding may result into stress raisers. If the direction of forging flow changes sharply, there is high probability of fatigue crack initiation. Welded joints need careful designing since they cause stress raisers.

(*iv*) **Special methods to improve fatigue strength**. Fatigue strength is increased by surface strengthening processes like case hardening, nitriding and cyaniding.

## 3.28 Theories of Failure

While designing a component it is essential to assure that the interval stresses do not exceed the strength of the material. For ductile material the yield strength is taken as the criterion of failure whereas for brittle materials there is no yield point and therefore ultimate strength is taken as criterian of failure. Further while designing components of brittle materials must be considered that ultimate compressive strength is much greater than ultimate tensile strength whereas the strength of ductile materials are about same in tension and compression.

Two types of mechanical failures occur in materials when they are subjected to static loading.

(*i*) Yielding failure (*ii*) Fracture failure.

Yielding or permanent deformation is a pronounced sliding along certain angular planes in the material. It takes place without rupture. In a ductile material the resistance to sliding is smaller than its resistance to separation. In ductile material failure takes place by yielding. In a brittle material the resistance to separation is less than its resistance to sliding. Failure takes place by fracture with little or no plastic deformation.

Following three theories are commonly used to explain failure of components due to various combination of stresses.

(*i*) **Maximum principal stress theory (Rankine theory).** According to the maximum principal stress theory also called Rankine's theory yielding at a point occurs only when the maximum principal stress on any plane passing through that point reaches a value equal to elastic limit as computed in simple tension test.

Let $f_{max}$ (tensile) be the largest of the positive principal stresses and $f_{max}$ (compressive) be the largest of the negative principal stresses.

then $f_{max} \leq$ Allowable stress

or $f_{max}$ (tensile) $\leq \frac{f_{yt}}{n}$

$f_{max}$ (Compressive) $\leq \frac{f_{yc}}{n}$

For materials with no distinct yield point the ultimate strength should be used in place of yield strength.

$f_{max}$ (tensile) $\leq \frac{f_{ut}}{n}$

$f_{max}$ (Compressive) $\leq \frac{f_{uc}}{n}$

where $\sigma_{yt}$ or $f_{yt}$ = yield stress in tension

$f_{ye}$ = yield stress in compression

$\sigma_{ut}$ or $f_{ut}$ = ultimate strength in tension

$\sigma_{uc}$ or $f_{uc}$ = ultimate strength in compression

$n$ = Factor of safety.

(*ii*) **Maximum shear stress theory (or Guest's theory).** According to this theory failure (yielding) takes place when maximum induced shear stress reaches value equal to shear stress at the instant of yielding in a simple tension test.

The design criterion will be $f_{s\,(max)} = \frac{f_{sy}}{n}$

where $f_{s\,(max)}$ = Maximum shear induced stress

$f_{sy}$ = yield stress in shear

$n$ = Factor of safety

But shear stress at yielding is half the yield stress in tension

$$f_{sy} = \frac{f_{yt}}{2}$$

Therefore the design criterior becomes

$$f_{s(max)} = \frac{f_{sy}}{n} = \frac{f_{yt}}{2n}$$

where $f_{yt}$ = yield stress in tension.

(*iii*) **Distortion energy theory or Von Misses Hencky theory**. According to this theory the failure criterion is based on distortion energy. The criterion is obtained by comparing the distortion energy per unit volume at a point in a machine element with the distortion energy per unit volume at the failure in simple tension test.

For analysis and design purposes it is convenient to define a Von Misses stress as follows for three dimensional stress state

$$f' = \sqrt{f_1^2 + f_2^2 + f_3^2 - f_1 f_2 - f_2 f_3 - f_3 f_1}$$

For two dimensional stress state

$$f' = \sqrt{f_1^2 + f_2^2 - f_1 f_2}$$

where $f'$ = Von Misses stress = $\frac{f_{yt}}{n}$.

$n$ being the factor of safety and $f_1$, $f_2$, $f_3$ being the principal stresses and $f_{yt}$ is the yield stress in tension.

Further $f' = \sqrt{f_x^2 + f_y^2 + 3f_{xy}^2}$

where

$f_x$ = Direct or normal stress (Tension or Compression). It may be due to either bending or axial loading or a combination of the two.

$f_y$ = Direct or normal stress (Tension or Compression) and in a direction normal to the stress, $f_x$.

$f_{xy}$ = Shear stress.

(*iv*) **Maximum strain theory or St. Venant theory** : According to this theory failure of a component occurs when the maximum strain under actual loading reaches a limiting value as determined from standard tensile test.

Let $\sigma_1$ , $\sigma_2$ and $\sigma_3$ be the principal stresses.

$E$ = Young's modulus of elasticity

$\upsilon$ = Poisson's ratio

For two dimensional stress system.

$$\frac{\sigma_1}{E} - \frac{\upsilon\,\sigma_2}{E} = \frac{\sigma_{yt}}{E}$$

**3.28.1. Theories for Ductile and Brittle materials** :-They are as follows :

1. **Ductile materials :**

(*i*) Under combined static loading the machine parts made of ductile materials will fail by yielding.

(*ii*) The working stress is based on yield point stress.

(*iii*) The maximum shear stress theory will be used for the design.

2. **Brittle materials:**

(*i*) Failure takes place by fracture.

(*ii*) Ultimate strength is used as the basis for determining the allowable stress.

(*iii*) Maximum principal stress theory should be used for design.

**3.28.2. Factors influencing type of Failure**

Various factors which play an important role during failure of a component are as follows.

1. **Type and range of stress distribution.** Failure will depend on the magnitude of load applied and whether the load applied is static or fluctuating.

2. **Type of material.** Type of failure is affected by the inherent material properties against the external load conditions.

3. **Strain rate.** Speed of deformation influences the strain rate and type of failure. For example a material that evidences ductile failure under simple tension at ordinary testing speeds may show brittle failure when loaded at high velocity.

4. **Temperature .** Usually resistance to slip decreases with increase in temperature. Thus material becomes weak at high temperature.

5. **Surface treatment.** Presence of discontinuities in metal component reduce its strength.

Various surface treatments introduce residual compressive stress in the surface of the part. This compressive stress counteracts tensile stress resulting from the externally applied load, thus reducing the probability of a cleavage failure. In this category belong, shot peening, carburizing, induction hardening, nitriding etc.

## 3.29 Comparison of Theories

Fig. 3.34 shows comparison of three theories of failure for ductile materials taking principal stresses $\sigma_1$ and $\sigma_2$ as the co-ordinates. It is observed that distortion energy theory predicts yielding with greatest accuracy in all the four quadrants whereas maximum shear stress theory always gives results which are conservative. Also the maximum normal stress theory gives conservative results only when the signs of the two principal stresses are alike. Distortion energy theory is used when margin of safety is to be held within close limits and the designer is trying for the best possible job of designing without actually testing the parts. This theory is also applied in case the job is combined to identify reasons as to why a part failed and redesign the component. This is the best theory for ductile materials. Maximum shear stress theory is applied where quick solutions are desired without too close tolerances.

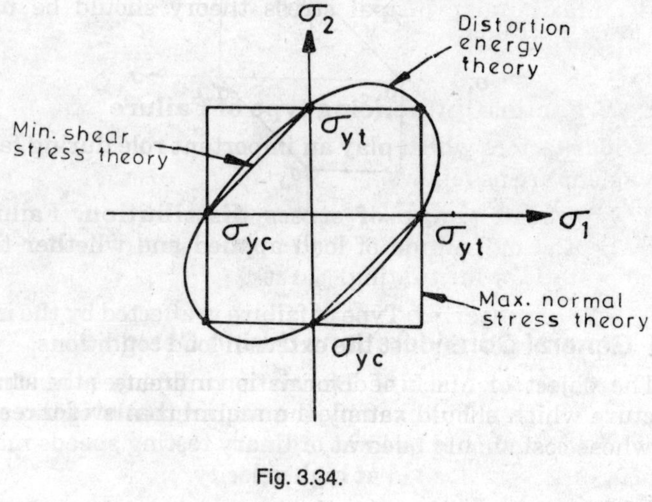


Fig. 3.34.

This theory is widely used by designers for predicting failure of ductile materials by yielding. Maximum normal stress theory is of importance for comparison purposes. This theory is generally applied to the failure of brittle materials.

Distortion energy theory is in better agreement with data for the yielding of bodies under combined stresses. Maximum shear stress theory is in good agreement with experimental results being slightly on safeside particularly for brittle materials.

In general the predictions based on maximum normal stress theory do not agree with experimental results and infact may even give results an unsafe side.

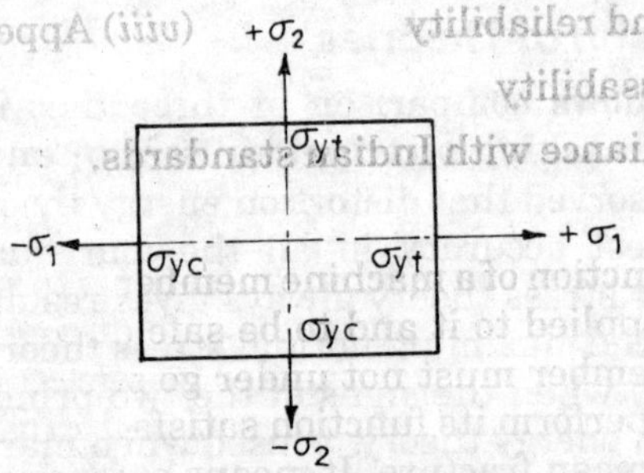


Fig. 3.35.

Fig. 3.35 shows working area of maximum normal stress theory whereas the working area for maximum shear stress theory can be represented by Fig. 3.36.

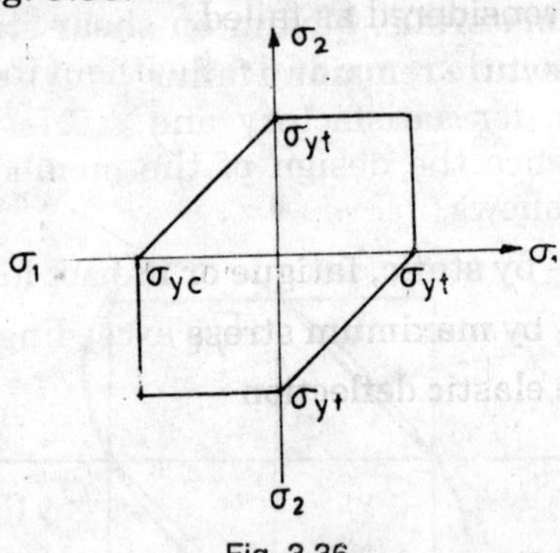


Fig. 3.36.

## 3.30 General Considerations during Design

The object of Machine Design is to create a machine or a structure which should satisfy the requirements of the customer and whose cost should be low.

Design of any member involves a proper balance between the stress induced in the member and strength of the member. The obvious cause of a structural failure is the fact that the stresses imposed on the member by the service loads are greater than its strength.

While designing a machine element the following factors should be considered adequately by the designer.

(*i*) Strength (*ii*) Stiffness
(*iii*) Wear resistance (*iv*) Materials
(*v*) Weight (*vi*) Safety
(*vii*) Life and reliability (*viii*) Appearance
(*ix*) Processability
(*x*) Compliance with Indian standards.
(*xi*) Cost

The main function of a machine member is to resist the external loads that are applied to it and to be safe during use. In resisting the loads the member must not under go structural damage *i.e.* it must not fail to perform its function satisfactorily. The failure does not necessarily mean fracture. It means any action in the member resulting from the application of loads which causes the member to cease to function satisfactorily.

When a machine part is no longer able to perform its function satisfactorily it is considered as failed.

Even though fracture remains a failure criterion for many of the machine members, for satisfactory and efficient working other failures also influence the design of the member. The modes of failure may be as follows.

(*i*) Fracture - by static, fatigue or impact load.
(*ii*) Yielding - by maximum stress exceeding the yield point.
(*iii*) Excessive elastic deflection
(*iv*) Wear
(*v*) Buckling
(*vi*) Corrosion fatigue and caustic embrittlement.

Selection of proper material helps in reducing the factor of safety. Depending on application of machine part materials having suitable properties should be chosen. For example low damping capacity material is required where resonance is desired as in tuning forks, and bells, but materials with high damping capacity is desirable in many machine members to prevent accumulation of serious resonant stresses, to decrease vibrations, chatter and noise. Resilience and toughness should be considered when member is subjected to shock loads. Weight may be desirable in case of foundation, fly wheels etc. but it is undesirable in other cases such as air craft parts, connecting rods etc. Resistance to fatigue should be the basis for the design of members subjected to cyclic loading. This property is measured by endurance limit.

Strength and rigidity are important properties of materials. Strength measured by the ultimate strength is necessary prevent failure of members by rupture. Rigidity is of importance in members whose deflections are limited by service requirements. For example, in a speed reducer, the rigidity of the shaft determines the stress concentration in the tooth face, influences the alignment and also fixes the natural frequency of vibration. Rigidity is a function of Modulus of elasticity and is practically independent of ultimate strength in the case of steels. In many designs, rigidity is the design criterion rather than the yield strength.

Ductility is the property of a material to absorb more overloads as it is capable of relatively large plastic deformation before fracture. Ductility is measured by the percentage elongation which takes place in a material at fracture. The material having less than 5% elongation is termed as brittle and one with more than 5% elongation is termed as ductile. Other properties of materials such as resistance to wear, corrosion, case of casting or forging, case of machining, friction characteristics etc. should be considered while deciding materials for making machine parts. In general, materials can be correctly chosen by comparing weight, size and cost.

Factor of safety and other service factors such as

(*i*) Stress concentration factor

(*ii*) Surface factor

(*iii*) Size factor

(*iv*) Shock factor etc.

should be properly chosen.

The selection of proper values of factor of safety and other service factor such as size factor, stress concentration factor, surface factor etc., depends on material of part/machine to be designed, type of machine, the kind of load, possibility of an accidental over load being placed on the machine part etc. The selection depends upon and reflects the judgement and experience of the design engineer.

Safety factors and service factors are taken into account while designing a component in order to achieve the following.

(*i*) Operational Safety (*ii*) Reliability

(*iii*) Durability (*iv*) Economy

Machine parts should be shaped so that stress concentrations at points of high loading are avoided as much as possible. Suitable adjustments also be made when the surface conditions of machine parts vary with the type of machining. It is observed that poor surface finish reduces the fatigue limit considerably as compared to smooth surface finish. The reason for this reduction is the sites of stress concentration that are left on the surface due to poor surface finish. In fatigue loading the surface conditions and presence of stress raiser greatly influence the fatigue life of a component.

For example,

A sharp circular groove 0.1 mm deep may reduce endurance limit by about 60%.

Corrosive atmosphere is highly deteriorating the fatigue behaviour because corrosion causes racks on the surface or eats away the material. These cracks while acting as sites of stress concentration are also further easily attacked by the corrosion and hence fatigue strength is largely reduced.

Use of factor of safety and other service factors in Machine design leads to a safe, reliable and economical design. Optimum values of factor of safety and service factors should be taken from standard tables, codes, graphs, machine design data books etc. The judgement and experience of the design engineer plays a significant role in selecting proper values of factor of safety and service factors.

## 3.31 Optimum Design

It aims at minimising undesireable effects such as

(*i*) Cost

(*ii*) Stress

(*iii*) Deflection

(*iv*) Vibrations

(*v*) Space occupancy

(*vi*) Dead weight etc.

or maximising the desireable effects such as.

(*i*) power to be transmitted

(*ii*) load carrying capacity

(*iii*) Speed capabilities etc.

This gives unique solution.

Three types of equations mentioned below are generally used for optimum design.

(*i*) Primary Design Equation (P.D.E). It expresses the quantity to be minimised or maximised.

(*ii*) Subsidiary Design Equation (S.D.E). It expresses either functional requirement or significant un desireable effect.

(*iii*) Limit Equations (L.E). They can give the satisfactory range of values of certain parameters, such as strength of materials or dimensions of the component etc.

**Example 3.2.** *A rod of medium carbon steel supports a load of 10,000 kg in tension as shown in Fig. 3.37. Find the dimensions of cross-section of the rod if*

*(a) Cross section is rectangular having width equal to three time thickness.*

*(b) When-section is circular. The allowable tensile stress in rod material is 600 kg/cm*$^2$.

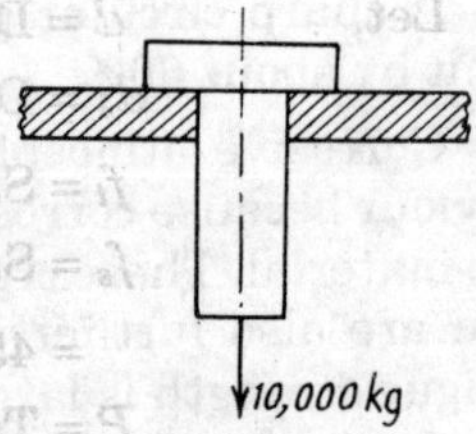


Fig. 3.37.

**Solution.**

(*a*) Let $b$ = Width of rod

$t$ = Thickness

$b = 3t$ (given)

$P$ = Tensile load = 10,000 kg

The rod will fail in tension

$A$ = Area under tensile failure = $b \times t$

$f_t$ = Tensile stress = 600 kg/cm$^2$

$$P = A \times f_t$$

$$10{,}000 = b \times t \times 600 = 3t \times t \times 600$$

$$t = 2.4 \text{ cm}$$

$$b = 7.2 \text{ cm}$$

(*b*) Let $d$ = Diameter of circular rod

$A$ = Area under tensile failure

$$= \frac{\pi}{4} d^2$$

$$P = A \times f_t$$

$$10{,}000 = \frac{\pi}{4} d^2 \times 600$$

$$d = 4.6 \text{ cm.}$$

**Example 3.3.** *A rod is fitted into a yoke and secured there to by a pin as shown in Fig. 3.30. Determine rod diameter and pin diameter if the assembly is subjected to a tensile load of 1000 kg. The allowable tensile stress is 600 kg/c m$^2$ and safe shear stress is 450 kg/cm$^2$.*

**Solution.**

Let, $d$ = Diameter of rod

$d_1$ = Diameter of pin

$f_t$ = Safe tensile stress = 600 kg/cm$^2$

$f_s$ = Safe shear stress

= 450 kg/cm$^2$

$P$ = Tensile load = 1000 kg.

(*i*) **To find rod diameter, d.** Consider tensile failure of rod.

$$A = \text{Area under tension} = \frac{\pi}{4} d^2$$

$$P = A \times f_t$$

$$1000 = \frac{\pi}{4} d^2 \times 600$$

$$d = 2.12 \text{ cm}$$

(*ii*) **To find pin diameter, $d_1$.** The tensile load will try to shear the pin at $X$ and $Y$ simultaneously. Therefore the pin is in double shear

$$A = \text{Area of the pin in double shear}$$

$$= 2 \times \frac{\pi}{4} d_1^2$$

$$P = A \times f_s = 2 \times \frac{\pi}{4} d_1^2 \times f_s$$

$$1000 = 2 \times \frac{\pi}{4} d_1^2 \times 450$$

$$d_1 = 1.2 \text{ cm.}$$

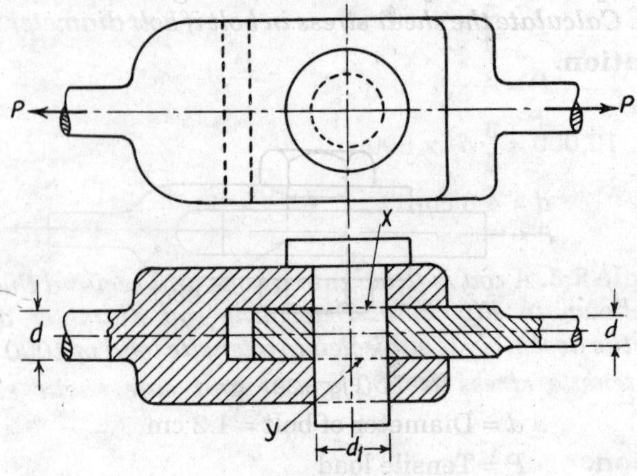


Fig. 3.38.

**Example 3.4.** *A hollow wrought iron rod is subjected to a tensile load of 1000 kg acting along its axis. If the outside diameter and inside diameter of rod are 20 mm and 15 mm respectively calculate the following :*

*(a) Safe tensile stress in the rod*

*(b) Factor of safety if the ultimate tensile stress is 3000 kg/cm².*

**Solution.**

$$P = \text{Tensile load} = 1000 \text{ kg}$$

$$A = \text{Area of rod under tension}$$

$$= \frac{\pi}{4}(D^2 - d^2)$$

where

$$D = \text{Outside diameter} = 20 \text{ mm} = 2 \text{ cm}$$

$$d = \text{inside diameter} = 15 \text{ mm} = 1.5 \text{ cm}$$

$$P = A \times f_t$$

$$f_t = \text{Safe tensile stress}$$

$$= \frac{P}{A} = \frac{1000}{\frac{\pi}{4}[(2)^2 - (1.5)^2]} = 728 \text{ kg/cm}^2$$

$$\text{Factor of safety} = \frac{\text{Ultimate stress}}{\text{Safe stress}} = \frac{3000}{728} = 4.12.$$

**Example 3.5.** *The eye bar shown in Fig. 3.39 is to carry a load of 400 kg. Calculate the shear stress in bolt if bolt diameter is 12 mm.*

**Solution.**

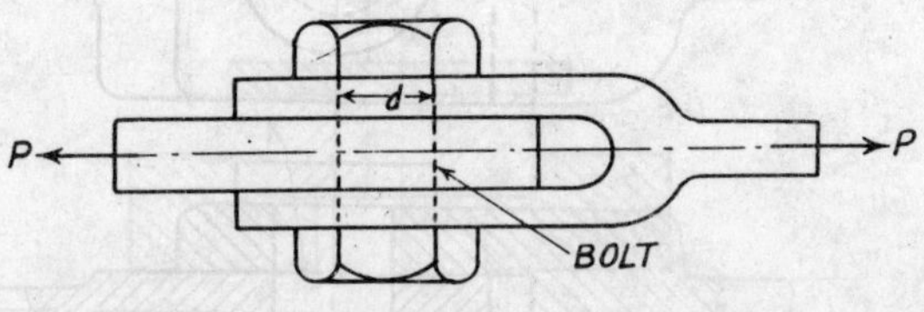


Fig. 3.39.

Let $d$ = Diameter of bolt = 1.2 cm

$P$ = Tensile load

$f_s$ = Shear stress in bolt

The bolt is in double shear

$A$ = Area under shear

$$= \frac{\pi}{4} d^2 \times 2 = \frac{\pi}{2} d^2$$

$$P = A \times f_s = \frac{\pi}{2} d^2 \times f_s$$

$$400 = \frac{\pi}{2} \times (1.2)^2 \times f_s$$

$$f_s = 176.9 \text{ kg/cm}^2.$$

**Example 3.6.** *Fig. 3.40 shows a punch and die set. Determine the load required to punch a hole of 18 mm diameter. The thickness of plate is 10 mm and ultimate shear strength of the plate is 3000 kg/cm².*

**Solution.**

This is a case of shear. The area under shear= $\pi dt$.

where $t$ = Thickness of plate

$d$ = Diameter of hole

$P$ = Area × ultimate shear stress

$= \pi\, dt \times 3000$

$= \pi \times 1.8 \times 1 \times 3000$

$= 16{,}956$ kg.

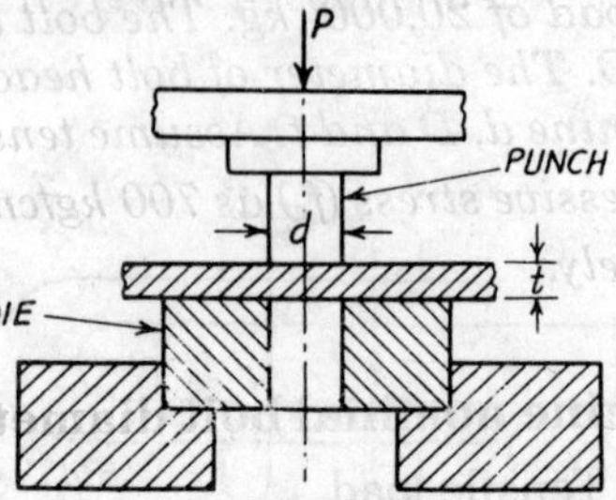


Fig. 3.40.

**Example 3.7.** *Calculate the smallest size of a hole that can be punched in a 9 mm thick steel plate. The allowable crushing stress in punch is $4 \times 10^3 kg/cm^2$ and the ultimate shear stress in plate material is $2 \times 10^3 kg/cm^2$.*

**Solution.**

Let $d$ = Minimum diameter of hole that can be punched

$t$ = Thickness of plate = 9 mm

Ultimate shear stress

$$f_s = 2 \times 10^3 \text{ kg/cm}^2$$

Ultimate crushing stress,

$$f_c = 4 \times 10^3 \text{ kg/cm}^2$$

$P_e$ = Crushing resistance of punch

$$= \frac{\pi}{4} d^2 \times f_c$$

$P_s$ = Shear force to punch the hole

= Shear area × Shear stress = $\pi d \,.\, t \,.\, f_s$

In order to punch the hole

$$P_c \geq P_s$$

$$\frac{\pi}{4} d^2 f_c \geq \pi dt \times f_s$$

$$d \geq \frac{4 \times f_s \times t}{f_c}$$

$$\geq \frac{4 \times 2 \times 10^3 \times 9}{4 \times 10^3} \geq 18 \text{ mm.}$$

$\therefore$ $d$ = 18 mm.

**Example 3.8.** *A bolt of diameter d is fixed in a plate (Fig. 3.41) and subjected to a load of 20,000 kg. The bolt is enlarged near its head to a diameter D. The diameter of bolt head is 1.5 D and head thickness is t. Determine d, D and t. Assume tensile stress ($f_t$), shear stress ($f_s$) and compressive stress ($f_c$) as 700 kg/cm$^2$, 450 kg / cm$^2$ and 300 kg/cm$^2$ respectively.*

**Solution.**

(*a*) **To determine nominal bolt diameter** *d*

$$P = \text{Tensile load}$$

Let $d_c$ = Core diameter of bolt

The bolt will fail in tension and the load is resisted by the core area of threaded end of bolt.

$$A = \text{Area under tension}$$

$$= \frac{\pi}{4} d_c^2$$

$$P = A \times f_t$$

$$20{,}000 = \frac{\pi}{4} d_c^2 \times 700$$

$$d_c = 6.03 \text{ cm}$$

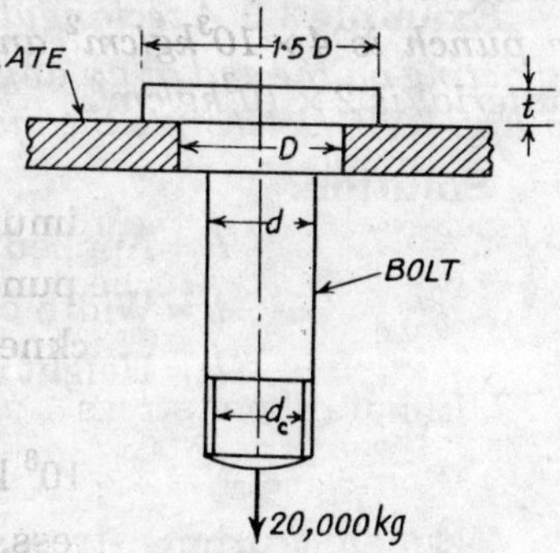

Fig. 3.41

The nominal diameter ($d$) is calculated by the following relation in case of coarse threads

$$d_c = 0.84d$$

$$d = \frac{d_c}{0.84} = \frac{6.03}{0.84} = 7.2 \text{ cm.}$$

(*b*) **To determine** ($D$)

The plate is under compression by the bolt head

$$A = \text{Area under compression}$$

$$= \frac{\pi}{4}(D_1^2 - D^2)$$

where $D_1 = 1.5D$

$$P = A \times f_c$$

$$= \frac{\pi}{4}(D_1^2 - D^2) \times f_c$$

$$20{,}000 = \frac{\pi}{4}(1.5D^2 - D^2) \times 300$$

where $D_1 = 1.5D$

$D = 8.2$ cm.

**(c) To determine plate thickness (t)**

Consider the shearing of bolt head

$$A = \text{Area under shear} = \pi . D . t$$

$$P = A \times f_s$$

$$20{,}000 = \pi \times D \times t \times 450$$

$$20{,}000 = \pi \times 8.2 \times t \times 450$$

$$t = 1.72 \text{ cm.}$$

**Example 3.9.** *A rectangular cantilever beam with a load of 2000 kg acting on the end at an angle of 30° from the horizontal is shown in Fig. 3.42. Determine the maximum stress in the beam.*

**Solution.**

$P$ = Applied load = 2000 kg

$b$ = Width of beam = 2 cm

$h$ = Height of beam = 4 cm

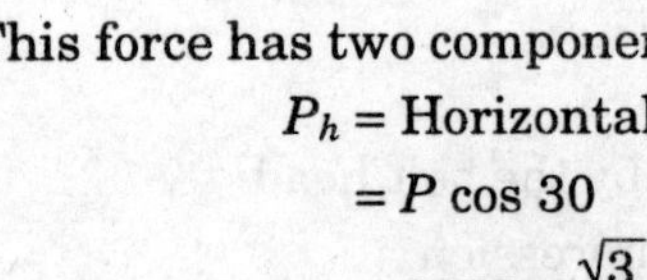


Fig. 3.42.

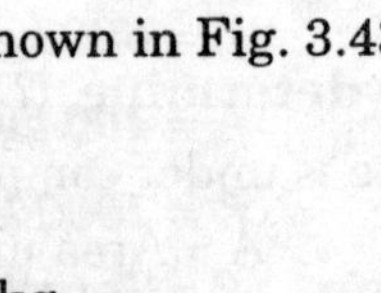


Fig. 3.43.

This force has two components as shown in Fig. 3.43.

$P_h$ = Horizontal force

$= P \cos 30$

$$= 2000 \times \frac{\sqrt{3}}{2} = 1732 \text{ kg}$$

$P_v$ = Vertical force = $P \sin 30$

$$= 2000 \times \frac{1}{2} = 1000 \text{ kg}$$

$M$ = Maximum bending moment

$= P_y \times 20 = 1000 \times 20 = 2 \times 10^4$ kg–cm

$M = f \times Z$, where $Z$ = Section modulus

$= \frac{bh^2}{6}$

$f$ = Bending stress

$$2 \times 10^4 = f \times \frac{bh^2}{6} = f \times \frac{2 \times 4^2}{6}$$

$f = 1875$ kg/cm$^2$

$A$ = Cross – sectional area of beam

$= b \times h = 2 \times 4 = 8$ cm$^2$

$f_t$ = Direct tensile stress due to $P_h$

$$= \frac{P_h}{A} = \frac{1732}{8} = 215.25 \text{ kg/cm}^2$$

$f_m$ = Maximum tensile stress on the bottom of beam

$= f + f_t = 1875 + 215.25$

$= 2090.25$ kg/cm$^2$

$f_1$ = Stress in top fiber of beam

$= -f + f_t = -1875 + 215.25$

$= -1659.75$ kg/cm$^2$ (compressive).

**Example 3.10.** *Design a cotter foundation bolt to support a tensile load of 8000 kg. A flat steel cotter is used to make the joint. The end of the bolt is made square in section (Fig. 3.44). Assume the material of the cotter and bolt to the same. Take the following permissible stresses*

$f_t = 600$ *kg/cm*$^2$

$f_s = 400$ *kg/cm*$^2$

and $f_c = 1000$ *kg/cm*$^2$.

**Solution.** $P$ = Tensile load = 8000 kg

$d$ = Diameter of bolt

$S$ = Size of square end of bolt

$b$ = Width of cotter

(*a*) **To find diameter** (*d*)

The bolt will fail in tension

$A$ = Area under tensile failure

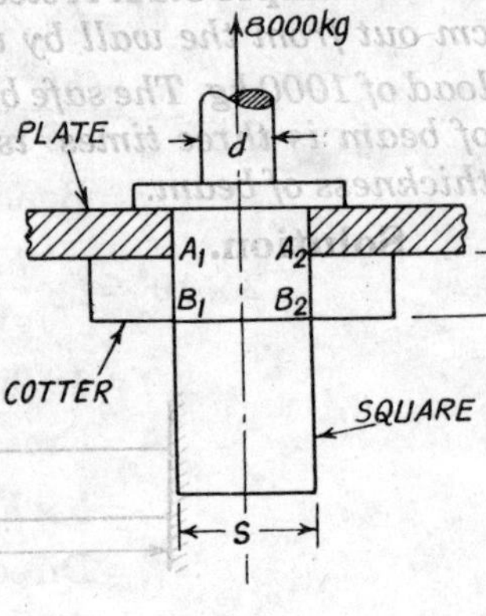


Fig. 3.44

$$= \frac{\pi}{4} d^2$$

$$P = A \times f_t$$

$$8000 = \frac{\pi}{4} d^2 \times 600$$

$$d = 4.12 \text{ cm}$$

(*b*) **To find *S***

Consider compression of cotter at $B_1B_2$

$A$ = Area under compression

$= S \times t$

$$P = S \times t \times f_c$$

$$8000 = S \times \frac{S}{4} \times 1000$$

Assuming thickness of cotter as $S/4$

$$8000 = \frac{S^2}{4} \times 1000$$

$$S = 5.7 \text{ cm}$$

$$t = \frac{5.7}{4} = 1.42 \text{ cm.}$$

Now the square end of bolt will fail in tension at the cotter

$$A = \text{Area under tension} = S^2 - S \times t$$

$$8000 = A \times \text{Induced tensile stress}$$

$$= [(S^2 - S \times t)] \times \text{Induced tensile stress}$$

Induced tensile stress

$$= \frac{8000}{(5.7)^2 - 5.7 \times 1.42} = 333.3 \text{ kg/cm}^2$$

which is safe.

(*c*) To find width (*b*) of cotter

The cotter will fail in double shear at $A_1B_1$ and $A_2B_2$

$$A = \text{Shearing area} = 2 \times b \times t$$

$$P = A \times f_s$$

$$8000 = 2 \times b \times 1.42 \times 400$$

$$b = 7.1 \text{ cm.}$$

**Example 3.11.** *A steel beam rectangular in section extends 250 cm out from the wall by which it is supported. It sustains an end load of 1000 kg. The safe bending stress in 700kg/cm*$^2$. *The thickness of beam is three times its width (Fig. 3.45) calculated width and thickness of beam.*

**Solution.**

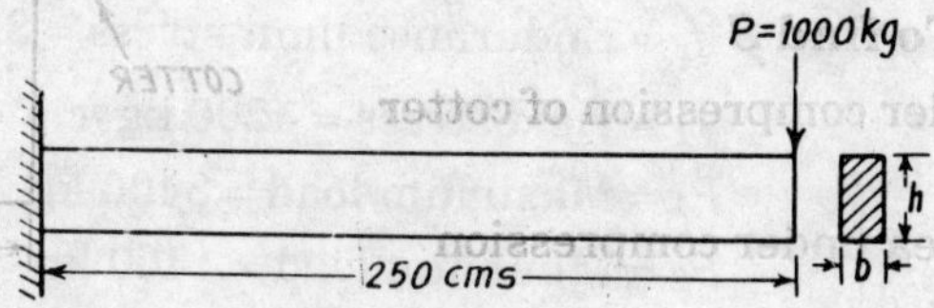


Fig. 3.45.

The dangerous section of the beam will be at the support where bending is maximum.

Let $b$ = Width

$h$ = Thickness = $3b$

$M$ = Maximum bending moment

$= 1000 \times 250 = 25 \times 10^4$ kg cm.

$I$ = Moment of inertia of rectangular section

$$= \frac{bh^3}{12}$$

$$y = \frac{h}{2}$$

$$Z = \text{Section modulus} = \frac{I}{y} = \frac{bh^3}{12} \times \frac{2}{h} = \frac{bh^2}{6}$$

$f$ = Safe bending stress = 700 kg/cm$^2$

$$M = Z \times f$$

$$25 \times 10^4 = \frac{bh^2}{6} \times 700$$

$$25 \times 10^4 = \frac{b\,(3b)^2 \times 700}{6}$$

$b = 6.2$ cm.

$h = 3 \times b$

$= 3 \times 6.2 = 18.6$ cm.

**Example 3.12.** *(a) Calculate the diameter of a uniform circular rod subjected to a maximum load of 3400 kg and a minimum load of 1400 kg in tension. The yield stress in 4200kg/cm$^2$ and endurance limit is 3200 kg/cm$^2$. Factor of safety is 1.5.*

*(b) What will be diameter of rod if stress concentration factor is 1.8.*

**Solution.** (*a*) $f_e$ = Endurance limit stress = 3200 kg/cm$^2$

$f_1$ = yield stress = 4200 kg /cm$^2$

$P_1$ = Maximum load = 3400 kg

$P_2$ = Minimum load = 1400 kg

$P$ = Average load

$$= \frac{3400 + 1400}{2} = 2400 \text{ kg}$$

Variable or range load

$$= P_r = P_1 - P = 3400 - 2400 = 1000 \text{ kg.}$$

$f$ = Working stress

$$= \frac{f_1}{\text{Factor of safety}}$$

$$= \frac{4200}{1.5} = 2800 \text{ kg/cm}^2$$

$A$ = A cross sectional area of rod.

$f_2$ = Average stress

$$= \frac{P}{A} = \frac{2400}{A}$$

$f_r$ = Range stress

$$= \frac{P_r}{A} = \frac{1000}{A}$$

Now $$f = f_2 + \frac{f_1}{f_e} \times f_r$$

$$2800 = \frac{2400}{A} + \frac{4200}{3200} \times \frac{1000}{A}$$

$$A = 1.325 \text{ cm}^2$$

Let $d$ = Diameter of rod

$$A = \frac{\pi}{4} d^2$$

$$1.325 = \frac{\pi}{4} d^2$$

$$d = 1.3 \text{ cm}$$

(b) $K$ = Stress concentration factor

$$f = f_2 + \frac{f_1}{f_e} \times f_r \times k$$

$$2800 = \frac{2400}{A} + \frac{4200}{3200} \times \frac{1000}{A} \times 1.8$$

$$A = 1.7 \text{ cm}^2$$

$$\therefore \quad 1.7 = \frac{\pi}{4} d^2$$

$$\mathbf{d = 1.47 \text{ cm.}}$$

**Example 3.13**. *A steel rod of ultimate strength 6000 kg / cm² and a yield strength of 4000 kg/cm² is subjected to a cyclic torque varying from 3200 kg cm to 1200 kg/cm². Calculate diameter of rod assuming the following data :*

*Factor of safety = 2*

*Endurance limit = 0.5 × ultimate strength*

*Surface finish factor = 0.6*

*Size factor = 0.8*

*Stress concentration factor = 1.4.*

**Solution.** $f_e$ = Endurance limit stress

$= 0.5 \times 6000 = 3000 \text{ kg/cm}^2$

$f_1$ = Yield stress = 4000 kg/cm²

$T_1$ = Maximum torque = 3200 kg/cm

$T_2$ = Minimum torque

$= -1200$ kg cm

$T$ = Average torque

$$= \frac{T_1 + T_2}{2}$$

$$T = \frac{3200 - 1200}{2} = 1000 \text{ kg cm}$$

$T_r$ = Varying torque

$$= \frac{T_1 - T_2}{2} = \frac{3200 - (-1200)}{2}$$

$= 2200$ kg cm

$f_2 =$ Safe average stress

$= \frac{T \times r}{I}$

where $r =$ Radius of rod $= D/2$

$I =$ Moment of inertia of rod

$= \frac{\pi}{32} D^4$

$D =$ Diameter of rod

$$f_2 = 1000 \times \frac{D}{2} \times \frac{32}{\pi D^4} = \frac{1000 \times 16}{D^3}$$

$f_r =$ Safe varying stress

$$= \frac{T_r \times 16}{\pi D^3} = \frac{2200 \times 16}{\pi D^3}$$

$f_{es} =$ endurance limit due to size and surface factor

$= 3000 \times 0.6 \times 0.8 = 1440$ kg/cm$^2$

$K =$ Stress concentration factor

$f =$ Working stress

$$= \frac{f_1}{\text{Factor of safety}} = \frac{4000}{2}$$

$= 2000$ kg/cm$^2$

$$f = f_2 + \frac{f_1}{f_e} . f_r \times K$$

$$2000 = \frac{1000 \times 16}{\pi D^3} + \frac{4000}{1440} \times \frac{2200 \times 16}{\pi D^3} \times 1.4$$

$D = 2.9$ cm. **Ans.**

**Example 3.14.** *A circular rod of 2 cm diameter is loaded by a steady tensile load of 2400 kg. The yield point stress for the shaft material is 2950 kg/cm$^2$. Find maximum shear stress induced and factor of safety.*

**Solution.**

$\sigma =$ Tensile stress induced in the rod (this will be the principal stress)

$= F/A$

where $F$ = Tensile load = 2400

$A$ = Area of cross-section of the rod

$$= \frac{\pi}{4} \times 2^2 = 3.14 \text{ cm}^2$$

$$\sigma = \frac{2400}{3.14} = 764 \text{ kg/cm}^2$$

$\tau$ = Maximum shear stress induced

$$= \frac{\sigma}{2} = \frac{764}{2}$$

$$= \mathbf{382 \text{ kg/cm}^2} \quad \textbf{Ans.}$$

$\sigma_y$ = yield stress = 2950 kg/cm$^2$

$n$ = Factor of safety

$$= \frac{\sigma_y}{\sigma} = \frac{2950}{764} = 3.86. \quad \textbf{Ans.}$$

**Example 3.15.** *A mild steel shaft of 4 cm diameter is subjected to a pure torque at a shear stress of 600 kg/cm$^2$. Determine factor of safety by*

(*i*) *Maximum shear stress theory*

(*ii*) *Distortion energy theory.*

*Assume yield stress in tension as 3200 kg/cm$^2$.*

**Solution.** $\tau$ = shear stress = 600 kg/cm$^2$

$\sigma_y$ = yield stress = 3200 kg/cm$^2$.

Let $\sigma_1$ and $\sigma_2$ be the principal stresses

$\sigma_1 = \tau$ = 600 kg/cm$^2$ (Tensile)

$\sigma_2$ = 600 kg/cm$^2$ (Compressive)

(*i*) By maximum shear stress theory

$n$ = Factor of safety

$\tau_{max}$ = Maximum shear stress induced

$$= \frac{1}{2}[600 - (-600)] = 600 \text{ kg/cm}^2$$

$\tau_y$ = Maximum shear stress at yield point

$$= \frac{\sigma_y}{2} = \frac{3200}{2} \text{ kg/cm}^2$$

$$n = \frac{\tau_y}{\tau_{max}} = \frac{3200}{2 \times 600} = 2.67$$

(*ii*) By distortion energy theory

$$\sigma' = \text{Von Misses stress}$$
$$= \sqrt{\sigma_1^2 + \sigma_2^2 - \sigma_1 \sigma_2}$$
$$= \sqrt{600^2 + (-600)^2 - 600(-600)}$$
$$= 1040 \text{ kg/cm}^2$$
$$\eta = \frac{\sigma_y}{\sigma'} = \frac{3200}{1040} = 3.1.$$

**Example 3.16.** *Following stresses act at a point on a body*

$$\sigma_x = 800 \text{ kg/cm}^2$$
$$\sigma_y = 450 \text{ kg/cm}^2$$
$$\tau_{xy} \text{ (shear stress)} = 630 \text{ kg/cm}^2$$

*The yield stress is 3200 kg/cm². Calculate the factor of safety using*

(*a*) *Maximum shear stress theory*

(*b*) *Distortion energy theory.*

**Solution.** Let $\sigma_1$ and $\sigma_2$ be the principal stresses

$$\sigma_y = \text{yield stress in tension}$$
$$= 3200 \text{ kg/cm}^2$$
$$\sigma_{1,2} = \frac{\sigma_x + \sigma_y}{2} \pm \frac{1}{2}\sqrt{(\sigma_x - \sigma_y)^2 + 4\,\tau_{xy}^2}$$
$$\sigma_{1,2} = \frac{800 + 450}{2} \pm \frac{1}{2}\sqrt{(800 - 450)^2 + 4 \times 630^2}$$
$$= 625 + \frac{1}{2} \times 1598$$
$$\sigma_1 = 625 + \frac{1}{2} \times 1598 = 625 + 799$$
$$= 1424 \text{ kg/cm}^2 \text{ (Tensile)}$$
$$\sigma_2 = 625 - \frac{1}{2} \times 1598$$
$$= -174 \text{ kg/cm}^2 \text{ (Compressive)}$$

(*a*) **Using maximum shear stress theory**

$$\tau_{max} = \text{maximum shear stress induced}$$
$$= \text{largest of } \frac{1}{2}\,|\sigma_1 - \sigma_2|\,,\ \frac{1}{2}\,|\sigma_1|\,,\ \frac{1}{2}\,|\sigma_2|$$
$$= \frac{1}{2}\,|1598|\,,\ \frac{1}{2}\,|1424|\,,\ \frac{1}{2}|174|$$
$$= 799,\ 712,\ 87$$

$$\therefore \quad \tau_{max} = 799 \text{ kg/cm}^2$$
$$\tau_y = \text{Shear stress at yield point}$$
$$= \frac{\sigma_y}{2} = \frac{3200}{2} = 1600 \text{ kg/cm}^3$$
$$n = \text{Factor of safety}$$
$$= \frac{\tau_y}{\tau_{max}} = \frac{1600}{799} = 2. \textbf{ Ans.}$$

(*b*) **Using distortion energy theory**

$$\sigma' = \text{Maximum stress}$$
$$= \sqrt{\sigma_1^2 + \sigma_2^2 - \sigma_1\sigma_2}$$
$$= \sqrt{1424^2 + (-174)^2 - 1424(-174)}$$
$$= 1518 \text{ kg/cm}^2$$
$$n = \text{Factor or safety}$$
$$= \frac{\sigma_y}{\sigma'} = \frac{3200}{1518} \doteq 2.1. \textbf{ Ans.}$$

**Example 3.17.** *A mild steel tube having external diameter 84 mm and internal diameter 80 mm is subjected to an internal pressure of 60 kg/cm$^2$. The tube is subjected to a twisting moment of 850 kg/cm. Considering the tube as a thin cylinder determine the factor of safety based on the following three theories.*

(*i*) *Maximum principal stress theory*

(*ii*) *Maximum shear stress theory*

(*iii*) *Distortion energy theory*

*Take elastic limit stress as 2900 kg/cm$^2$.*

**Solution.**
$$p = \text{Pressure} = 60 \text{ kg/cm}^2$$
$$D = \text{Outer diameter} = 84 \text{ mm} = 8.4 \text{ cm}$$
$$d = \text{Inside diameter} = 80 \text{ mm} = 8 \text{ cm}$$

$$t = \text{Thickness} = \frac{84-80}{2} = 2 \text{ mm}$$

$$T = \text{Twisting moment} = 850 \text{ kg/cm}$$

$$f_l = \text{Longitudinal stress}$$

$$= \frac{pd}{ut} = \frac{60 \times 8}{2 \times 0.2} = 600 \text{ kg/cm}^2$$

$$f_c = \text{Circumferential stress}$$

$$= \frac{pd}{2t} = \frac{60 \times 8}{2 \times 0.2} = 1200 \text{ kg/cm}^2$$

$$J = \text{Polar moment of inertia}$$

$$f_s = \text{Shear stress due to torsion}$$

$$\frac{T}{J} = \frac{f_s}{R}, \text{ where } R = \frac{D}{2} = \frac{84}{2}$$

$$= 42 \text{ mm} = 4.2 \text{ cm}$$

$$\frac{850}{\frac{\pi}{32}(D^4 - d^4)} = \frac{f_s}{\frac{D}{2}}$$

$$\frac{850}{\frac{\pi}{32}(8.4^4 - 8^4)} = \frac{f_s}{\frac{8.4}{2}}$$

$$f_s = 41.3 \text{ kg/cm}^2$$

$$f_1 = \text{Maximum principal stress}$$

$$= \frac{f_e + f_l}{2} + \frac{1}{2}\sqrt{(f_c - f_l)^2 + 4f_s^2}$$

$$= \frac{1200 + 600}{2} + \frac{1}{2}\sqrt{(1200 - 600)^2 + 4 \times 41.3^2}$$

$$= 900 + \frac{1}{2} \times 605.6 = 1202.8 \text{ kg/cm}^2$$

$$f_2 = \text{Minimum principal stress}$$

$$= 900 - \frac{1}{2} \times 605.6 = 697.2 \text{ kg/cm}^2$$

(*a*) According to maximum principal stress theory

$$f_{max} = \text{Maximum stress induced}$$

$$= f_1 = 1202.8 \text{ kg/cm}^2$$

$$f_y = \text{yield stress} = 2900 \text{ kg/cm}^2$$

$$n = \text{Factor of safety}$$

$$= \frac{f_y}{f_{max}} = \frac{2900}{1202.8} = 2.41$$

(*b*) **According to maximum shear stress theory**

$$f_{s(max)} = \text{Maximum shear stress induced}$$

$$= \frac{1}{2}[f_1 - (-60)]$$

$$= \frac{1}{2}[1202.8 + 60] = 631.4 \text{ kg/cm}^2$$

$$f_{sy} = \text{Shear stress at yield point}$$

$$= \frac{1}{2} \times f_y = \frac{2900}{2} = 1450 \text{ kg/cm}^2$$

$$n = \text{Factor of safety} = \frac{f_{sy}}{f_{s\,(max)}}$$

$$= \frac{1450}{631.4} = 2.3$$

(*c*) **According to distortion energy theory**

$$f' = \text{Maximum stress induced}$$

$$= \sqrt{f_1^2 + f_2^2 + f_3^2 - f_1 f_2 - f_2 f_3 - f_1 f_3}$$

where $f_3$ = Pressure in the tube = $-$ 60 kg/cm$^2$

$$f' = \sqrt{1202.8^2 + 697.2^2 + 60^2 - 1202.8 \times 697.2 + 697.2 \times 60 + 1202.8 \times 60}$$

$$= 1054.4 \text{ kg/cm}^2$$

$$n = \text{Factor of safety}$$

$$= \frac{f_y}{f'} = \frac{2900}{1054.4} = 2.75. \textbf{ Ans.}$$

**Example 3.18.** *At a point in a machine number the stress along x-axis direction is found to be 30 kg/cm$^2$ (compressive) along y-axis direction the stress is found to be 90 kg/cm$^2$ (compressive) and a shear stress of 24 kg/cm$^2$ also acts as shown in Fig. 3.46. Calculate the maximum principal stress minimum principal stress and maximum shear stress taking third principal stress as zero.*

**Solution.** $f_x$ = stress along $x$-axis

$$= -30 \text{ kg/cm}^2 \text{ (Compressive)}$$

$f_y$ = stress along $y$-axis

$= 90 - 90$ kg/cm$^2$ (Compressive)

$f_s$ = shear stress = 24 kg/cm$^2$

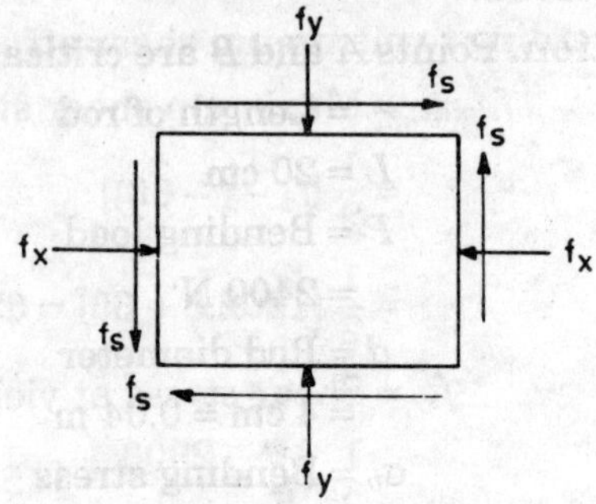


Fig. 3.46.

$f_1$ = Maximum principal stress

$$= \frac{f_x + f_y}{2} + \frac{1}{2}\sqrt{(f_x - f_y)^2 + 4f_s^2}$$

$$= \frac{-30 - 90}{2} + \frac{1}{2}\sqrt{[-30-(-90)]^2 + 4 \times 24^2}$$

$$= -60 + \frac{76.8}{2} = -60 + 38.4$$

$= -21.6$ kg/cm$^2$ (Compressive)

$f_2$ = Minimum principal stress = $-60 - 38.4$

$= -98.4$ kg/cm$^2$ (Compressive)

$f_3$ = Third principal stress = 0

$f_{s\,(max)}$ = Maximum shear stress

$$= \frac{1}{2}\ |f_1 - f_2|\ ,\ \frac{1}{2}\ |f_2 - f_3|\ ,\ \frac{1}{2}\ |f_1 - f_3|$$

$$= \frac{1}{2}[-21.6-(-98.4)],\ \frac{1}{2}[-98.4-0],\ \frac{1}{2}[-21.6]$$

$= 38.4,\ -49.2,\ -10.8$ kg/cm$^2$

Hence maximum shear stress is 49.2 kg/cm$^2$ (compressive).

**Example 3.19.** *A circular rod 4 cm diameter and 20 cm long is supported at one end as*

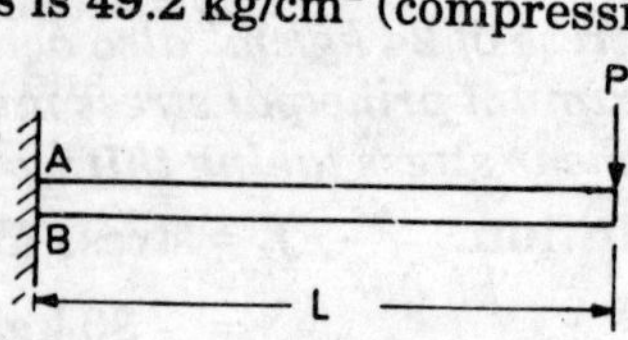


Fig. 3.47.

*a cantilever (Fig. 3.47). It is subjected to a bending load of 2400 Newtons. Determine the tensile, compressive and shear stress induced in the rod.*

**Solution.** Points $A$ and $B$ are critical

$= $ Length of rod

$L = 20$ cm

$P = $ Bending load

$= 2400$ N

$d = $ Rod diameter

$= 4 \text{ cm} = 0.04$ m

$\sigma_b = $ Bending stress

$$\frac{M}{I} = \frac{\sigma_b}{y} \qquad \ldots(i)$$

where $M = $ Bending moment

$= P \times L = 2400 \times 20$

$= 48000 \text{ N cm} = 480$ Nm

$$I = \frac{\pi}{64} d^4 = \frac{\pi}{64} (0.04)^4$$

$$y = \frac{d}{2} = \frac{0.04}{2} = 0.02 \text{ m}$$

Substituting various values in equation (*i*)

$$\frac{480}{\frac{\pi}{64}(0.04)^4} = \frac{\sigma_b}{0.02}$$

$\sigma_b = 76.4 \times 10^6 \text{ N/m}^2$

$= 76.4 \times 10^6 \text{ Pa} = 76.4$ MPa

$\sigma_1 = $ Maximum principal stress

$\sigma_1 = \sigma_b = \sigma_x$

$= 76.4$ MPa at point $A$ (Tensile)

$= -76.4$ MPa at point $B$ (Compressive)

$\tau_{max} = $ Maximum shear stress at points $A$ and $B$

$$= \frac{\sigma_1}{2} = \frac{76.4}{2} = 38.2 \text{ kg/cm}^2.$$

**Example 3.20.** *A mild steel circular rod 4.8 cm, diameter and 24 cm long is supported at one end as a cantilever and is loaded as shown in Fig. 3.48. Determine tensile stress, compressive stress and shear stress.*

**Solution.** $M$ = Bending moment = $P \times L$

where $P$ = Load = 250 kg

$L$ = Length of rod = 24 cm

$M = 250 \times 24 = 6000$ kg cm

$T$ = Torque = 2350 kg cm

$d$ = Diameter of rod = 4.8 cm

$f_b$ = Bending stress

$$\frac{M}{I} = \frac{f_b}{y}$$

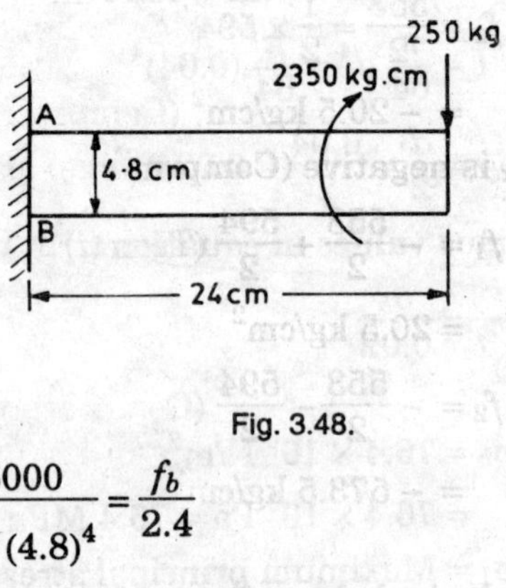


Fig. 3.48.

$$\frac{6000}{\frac{\pi}{64}(4.8)^4} = \frac{f_b}{2.4}$$

where $y = \frac{d}{2} = \frac{4.8}{2} = 2.4$ cm

$f_b = 553$ kg/cm$^2$

$f_x = f_b = 553$ kg/cm$^2$ (tensile) at $A$.

$= -553$ kg/cm$^2$ (Compressive) at $B$

The points $A$ and $B$ being the critical points.

Use torsion equation

$$\frac{T}{J} = \frac{f_s}{r}$$

where $$r = \frac{d}{2} = 2.4 \text{ cm}$$

$$\frac{2350}{\frac{\pi}{32}(4.8)^4} = \frac{f_s}{2.4}$$

$$f_s = 108 \text{ kg/cm}^2 \text{at points } A \text{ and } B$$

The maximum principal stress ($f_1$) and minimum principal stress ($f_2$) are found as follows

$$f_1 = \frac{f_x}{2} + \frac{1}{2}\sqrt{f_x^2 + 4f_s^2}$$

$$= \frac{553}{2} + \frac{1}{2}\sqrt{553^2 + 4 \times 108^2}$$

$$= \frac{553}{2} + \frac{1}{2} \times 594$$

$$= 573.5 \text{ kg/cm}^2 \text{ (tensile at } A\text{)}$$

$$f_2 = \frac{553}{2} = \frac{1}{2} \times 594$$

$$= -20.5 \text{ kg/cm}^2 \text{ (Compressive at } A\text{)}$$

Assuming that $f_x$ is negative (Compressive) at point $B$.

$$f_1 = -\frac{553}{2} + \frac{594}{2} \text{ (Tensile at point } B\text{)}$$

$$= 20.5 \text{ kg/cm}^2$$

$$f_2 = -\frac{553}{2} - \frac{594}{2} \text{ (Compressive at point } B\text{)}$$

$$= -573.5 \text{ kg/cm}^2$$

The maximum principal shear stress ($f_{s(max)}$) is given by

$$F_{s(max)} = \pm\frac{1}{2}\sqrt{f_x^2 + 4f_s^2}$$

$$= \pm\frac{1}{2}\sqrt{553^2 + 4 \times 108^2}$$

$$= 297 \text{ kg/cm}^2 \text{ at point } A$$

$$= -297 \text{ kg/cm}^2 \text{ at point } B.$$

**Example 3.21.** *A circular rod 4.8 cm diameter and 24 cm long is supported at one end as cantilever and is loaded as shown in Fig.*

*3.49. Determine the tensile, compressive and shear stresses produced in the rod due to loading.*

**Solution.**

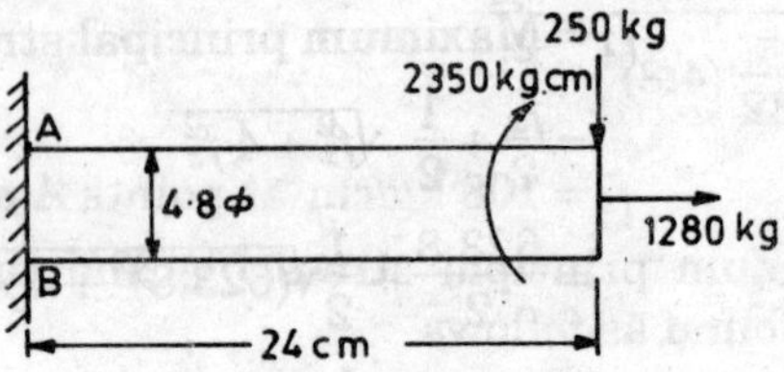


Fig. 3.49.

$d$ = Rod diameter

= 48 mm = 4.8 cm

$P$ = load = 250 kg

$L$ = Length of rod = 24 cm

$T$ = Torque = 2350 kg cm

$f$ = Direct stress

$= \frac{P}{A}$, where $A$ = cross sectional area

$$= \frac{1280}{\frac{\pi}{4} \times 4.8^2} = 70.8 \text{ kg/cm}^2$$

$M$ = Bending moment = $P \times L$

= 250 × 24 kg/cm = 6000 kg cm

$f_b$ = Bending stress

$$\frac{M}{I} = \frac{f_b}{y}$$

$$\frac{6000}{\frac{\pi}{64}(4.8)^4} = \frac{f_b}{2.4}$$

$f_b$ = 553 kg/cm

Now $\frac{T}{J} = \frac{f_s}{r}$, where $f_s$ = shear stress

$$\frac{2350}{\frac{\pi}{32} \times (4.8)^4} = \frac{f_s}{\frac{4.8}{2}}$$

$f_s = 108 \text{ kg/cm}^2$

**Point A**

$$f_x = f + f_b$$
$$= 70.8 + 553 = 623.8 \text{ kg/cm}^2$$
$$f_1 = \text{Maximum principal stress}$$
$$= \frac{f_x}{2} + \frac{1}{2}\sqrt{f_x^2 + 4 f_s^2}$$
$$= \frac{623.8}{2} + \frac{1}{2}\sqrt{(623.8)^2 + 4 \times 108^2}$$
$$= 311.9 + \frac{1}{2} \times 660$$
$$= 641.9 \text{ kg/cm}^2 \text{ (Tensile)}$$
$$f_2 = 311.9 - 330$$
$$= -18.1 \text{ kg/cm}^2 \text{ (compressive)}$$

The max. shear stress ($f_{s(max)}$) is given by

$$f_{s(max)} = \frac{1}{2}\sqrt{f_x^2 + 4 f_s^2}$$
$$= \frac{1}{2}\sqrt{(623.8)^2 + 4 \times 108^2} = 330 \text{ kg/cm}^2$$

**Point B**

$$f_x = \text{Normal stress in } x \text{ direction}$$
$$= f - f_b = 70.8 - 553 = -482.2 \text{ kg/cm}^2$$
$$f_1 = \frac{f_x}{2} + \frac{1}{2}\sqrt{f_x^2 + 4 f_s^2}$$
$$= -\frac{482.2}{2} + \frac{1}{2}\sqrt{(-482.2)^2 + 4 \times 108^2}$$
$$= -241.1 + \frac{1}{2} \times 528$$
$$= 22.9 \text{ kg/cm}^2 \text{ (Tensile)}$$
$$f_2 = -241.1 - \frac{1}{2} \times 528$$
$$= -505 \text{ kg/cm}^2 \text{ (compressive)}$$
$$f_{s\,(max)} = \frac{1}{2}\sqrt{f_x^2 + 4 f_s^2}$$
$$= \frac{1}{2}\sqrt{(-482)^2 + 4 \times 108^2} = 264 \text{ kg/cm}^2.$$

**Example 3.22.** *A material has a yield strength of 700 kg / cm$^2$. Compute the factor of safety for the following stress states :*

*(a)* $\sigma_1 = 500$ *kg/cm*$^2$, $\sigma_2 = 500$ *kg/cm*$^2$, $\sigma_3 = 0$

*(b)* $\sigma_1 = 500$ *kg/cm*$^2$, $\sigma_2 = 0$, $\sigma_3 = -200$ *kg/cm*$^2$.

*Use :* *(i) Maximum normal stress theory*

*(ii) Maximum shear stress theory.*

**Solution.** (*i*) According to maximum normal stress theory

(*a*) $n$ = factor of safety

$\sigma_y$ = yield stress = 700 kg/cm$^2$

$$n = \frac{\sigma_y}{\sigma_1} = \frac{700}{500} = 1.4$$

where $\sigma_1, \sigma_2, \sigma_3$ are principal stresses.

(*ii*) According to maximum shear stress theory

$n$ = factor of safety

$\tau_{max}$ = Maximum shear stress

$$= \frac{1}{2}\,|\sigma_1 - \sigma_2|, \frac{1}{2}\,|\sigma_2 - \sigma_3|, \frac{1}{2}\,|\sigma_3 - \sigma_1|$$

$$= \frac{1}{2}\,|500 - 500|, \frac{1}{2}\,|500 - 0|, \frac{1}{2}\,|0 - 500|$$

$$= 0, 250, -250$$

$\tau_{ys}$ = Yield stress in shear

$$= \frac{\sigma_y}{2} = \frac{700}{2} = 350 \text{ kg/cm}^2$$

$$n = \frac{350}{250} = 1.4.$$

(*b*) (*i*) According to maximum normal stress theory

$n$ = Factor of safety

$$= \frac{\sigma_y}{\sigma_1} = \frac{700}{500} = 1.4.$$

(*ii*) According to maximum shear stress theory

$\tau_{max}$ = Maximum shear stress

$$= \frac{1}{2}\,|\sigma_1 - \sigma_2|, \frac{1}{2}\,|\sigma_2 - \sigma_3|, \frac{1}{2}\,|\sigma_3 - \sigma_1|$$

$$= \frac{1}{2}\,|500 - 0|,\ \frac{1}{2}\,|0 - (200)|,\ \frac{1}{2}\,|-200 - 500|$$

$$= 250,\ 100,\ -350$$

$$n = \frac{\tau_{ys}}{\tau_{max}} = \frac{350}{350} = 1.$$

**Example 3.23.** *A connecting rod having a rectangular cross-section is loaded in tension by a force 5 kN. If the yield strength of the material is 350 MPa and factor of safety for uncertainties in strength is 1.3 and factor of safety for uncertainties for load is 2.3 find the cross-sectional dimensions of the rod. Take width of rod as five times its thickness.*

**Solution.**

$$ns = 1.3$$

$$n_L = 2.3$$

$n$ = Total factor of safety

$$= 1.3 \times 2.3 = 2.99$$

$P$ = Load = 5 kN = $5 \times 10^3$ N

$B$ = Width of rod

$T$ = Thickness of rod

$A$ = Area of cross-section

$$= B \times T = 5T \times T = 5T^2$$

$\sigma$ = Tensile stress

$$= \frac{P}{A} = \frac{5 \times 10^3}{5T^2}$$

$$= \frac{10^3}{T^2} = \frac{1000}{T^2} \text{ Pa}$$

$\sigma_y$ = Yield stress = 350 MPa = $350 \times 10^6$ Pa

$$n = \frac{\sigma_y}{\sigma}$$

$$\sigma = \frac{\sigma_y}{n}$$

$$\frac{1000}{T^2} = \frac{350 \times 10^6}{2.99}$$

$$T = \sqrt{\frac{2.99}{350 \times 10^2}} \text{ metre}$$

$$T = \frac{2.92}{10^3}\text{ m} = \frac{2.92}{10^3} \times 10^3 = 2.92\text{ mm}$$

$$B = 5T = 5 \times 2.92 = 14.6\text{ mm.}$$

**Example 3.24.** *Calculate the maximum stress induced when the rectangular rod with fillet is loaded as shown in Fig. 3.50. The thickness of rod is 12 mm.*

**Solution.** $r$ = Fillet radius = 3 mm

$B$ = Width = 100 mm = 10 cm

$d$ = Smaller width = 90 mm = 9 cm

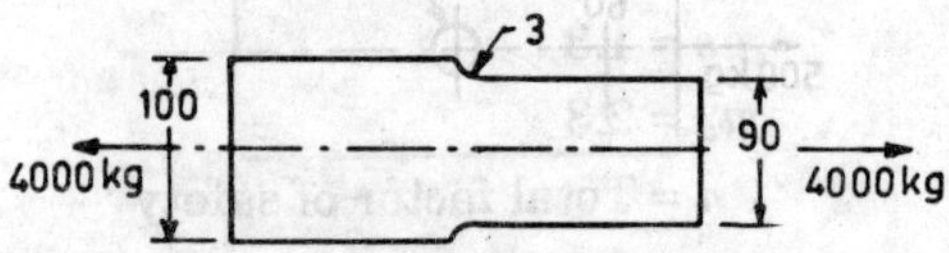


Fig. 3.50.

$t$ = Thickness of rectangular rod

= 12 mm = 1.2 mm

$$\sigma = \text{Nominal stress} = \frac{4000}{A}$$

where $A$ = Minimum cross-section area = $d \times t$

$$= \frac{4000}{9 \times 1.2} = 370\text{ kg/cm}^2$$

$K_t$ = Theoretical stress concentration factor

$$\frac{B}{d} = \frac{10}{9} = 1.11$$

$$\frac{r}{d} = \frac{3}{90} = 0.033$$

From Fig. 3.24 the value of

$K_t = 2.1.$

Corresponding to the values of

$$\frac{B}{d} = 1.11$$

and

$$\frac{r}{d} = 0.033$$

$\sigma_{max}$ = Maximum stress

$$K_t = \frac{\sigma_{max}}{\sigma}$$

$$2.1 = \frac{\sigma_{max}}{370}$$

$$\sigma_{max} = 778 \text{ kg/cm}^2.$$

**Example 3.25.** *Calculate the maximum stress when a rectangular rod is subjected to a load of 500 kg (Fig. 3.51). The rod is 6 mm thick.*

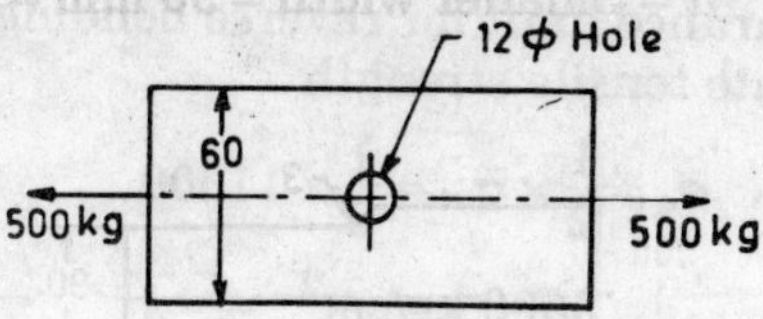


Fig. 3.51.

**Solution.** $d$ = Hole diameter

$= 12 \text{ mm} = 1.2 \text{ cm}$

$b$ = Width = 60 mm = 6 cm

$t$ = Thickness of plate = 6 mm 0.6 cm

$$\frac{d}{t} = \frac{12}{6} = 2$$

$$\frac{d}{b} = \frac{12}{60} = 0.2$$

From Fig. 3.52 the value of $K_t = 2.5$

Corresponding to $\frac{d}{b} = 0.2$

$\sigma$ = Nominal stress

$P$ = Load

$A$ = Minimum cross-sectional area

$= b \,.\, t - d \,.\, t = 6 \times 0.6 - 1.2 \times 0.6$

$= 3.6 - 0.72 = 2.88 \text{ cm}^2$

$$\sigma = \frac{P}{A} = \frac{500}{2.88} = 173.6 \text{ kg/cm}^2$$

$\sigma_{max}$ = Maximum stress = $K_t \times \sigma$

$= 2.5 \times 173.6 = 434 \text{ kg/cm}^2.$

**Example 3.26.** *A steel connecting rod is subjected to a reverse axial load of 20000 kg. Determine diameter of the rod using a factor of safety 2.3. Assume no column action and following stresses :*

$$\sigma_{ut} = 11000 \text{ kg/cm}^2$$

$$\sigma_y = 9000 \text{ kg/cm}^2.$$

**Solution.** $p$ = Load = 20000 kg

$d$ = Diameter of rod

$\sigma_e$ = Endurance limit.

Now the endurance limit for reverse bending may be taken as half of the ultimate tensile strength

$$\sigma_e = \frac{1}{2} \times \sigma_{ut} = \frac{1}{2} \times 11000$$

$$= 5500 \text{ kg/cm}^2$$

$\sigma_m$ = Mean stress = 0

$\sigma_v$ = Variable stress

$$= \frac{P}{A} = \frac{20000}{(\pi/4)\, d^2}$$

$$= \frac{80000}{\pi\, d^2}$$

$\sigma_E$ = Actual endurance limit

$= \sigma_e \,.\, K_F \,.\, K_S \,.\, K_L$

$K_F$ = Surface finish factor

= 0.74 (From table 3.14)

$K_S$ = Size factor = 0.85 (say)

$K_L$ = Load factor

= 0.84 for reversed axial load (From Table 3.15)

$$\sigma_E = 5500 \times 0.74 \times 0.85 \times 0.84 = 2906 \text{ kg/cm}^2$$

$n$ = Factor of safety = 2.3

$$\frac{1}{n} = \frac{\sigma_m}{\sigma_y} + K_t \,.\, \frac{\sigma_v}{\sigma_E} \quad \text{Let } K_f = I$$

$$\frac{1}{2.3} = 0 + \frac{1 \times \sigma_v}{2906}$$

$$\sigma_v = \frac{2906}{2.3} = 1263 \text{ kg/cm}^2$$

$$\therefore \quad 1263 = \frac{80000}{\pi d^2}$$

$$d = 4.5\text{cm.} \quad \textbf{Ans.}$$

**Example 3.27.** *A hot rolled steel shaft is subjected to a torsional load that varies from — 1000 kg-cm to 4400 kg-cm. Determine the diameter of the shaft using a factor of safety = 1.6.*

*Take $f_{ut} = 5000$ kg/cm², $fy_t = 3200$ kg–cm².*

**Solution.** $d$ = Diameter of shaft

$f_{es}$ = Endurance limit

$$= \frac{1}{2} \times f_{ut} \text{ (assume)}$$

$$= \frac{1}{2} \times 5000 = 2500 \text{ kg-cm}^2$$

$T_{max}$ = Maximum torque = 4400 kg-cm

$T_{min}$ = Maximum torque = – 1000 kg-cm

$f_{ys}$ = Yield stress in shear

$f_{yt}$ = Yield stress in tension

$f_{ys} = 0.6 \times f_{yt}$ (say)

$$= 0.6 \times 3200 = 1920 \text{ kg/cm}^2$$

Let $k_f$ = Stress concentration factor = 1

$$T_m = \text{Mean torque} = \frac{1}{2}(T_{\max} + T_{min})$$

$$= \frac{1}{2}(4400 - 1000) = 1700 \text{ kg-cm.}$$

$$T_v = \text{Variable torque} = \frac{1}{2}(T_{max} - T_{min})$$

$$= \frac{1}{2}[4400 - (-1000)] = 2700 \text{ kg-cm}$$

$f_{ms}$ = Mean shear stress

$$= \frac{T_m}{Z_p}, \quad \text{where } Z_p = \text{section modulus}$$

$$= \frac{T_m}{\frac{\pi}{16}d^3} = \frac{1700}{(\pi/16)\, d^3} = \frac{16 \times 1700}{\pi d^3} = \frac{2721}{\pi d^3}$$

$f_{vs}$ = Variable shear stress

$$= \frac{T_v}{(\pi/16)\, d^3} = \frac{2700 \times 16}{\pi d^3} = \frac{43200}{\pi d^3}$$

$f_{ES}$ = Actual endurance limit in shear

$= f_{es} \,.\, K_F \,.\, K_S \,.\, K_L$

where $K_F$ = Surface finish factor

= 0.65 for hot rolled steel with

$f_{ut}$ = 5000 kg/cm$^2$ (From Table 3.14)

$K_S$ = Size factor

= 0.85 (say)

$K_L$ = Load factor

= 0.58 for reversed torsion load on steel

$f_{ES} = 2500 \times 0.65 \times 0.85 \times 0.58$

= 801 kg/cm$^2$

$n$ = Factor of safety = 1.6

We know that for ductile materials

$$\frac{1}{n} = \frac{f_{ms}}{f_{ys}} + \frac{k_f \,.\, f_{vs}}{f_{ES}}$$

$$\frac{1}{1.6} = \frac{27200}{\pi\, d^3} \frac{1}{1920} + 1 \times \frac{43200}{\pi d^3} \times \frac{1}{801}$$

$d$ = 3.3 cm.

**Example 3.28.** *A hot rolled steel shaft is subjected to a torsional load that varies from 3200 kg-cm clockwise to 1200 kg-cm anticlockwise as an applied bending moment at a critical section varies from 4200 kg-cm to -2200 kg-cm. The shaft is of uniform cross-section and no keyway is present at the critical section. Find diameter of the shaft using factor of safety 1.8.*

*Given : $f_{ut}$ = 5000 kg/cm$^2$*

*$f_y$ = 4000 kg/cm$^2$.*

**Solution.** $M_{max}$ = Maximum bending moment = 4200 kg-cm

$M_{min}$ = Minimum bending moment = 2200 kg-cm

$f_e$ = Endurance limit

$= 0.5 \times f_{ut}$ (say)

$$= 2500 \text{ kg/cm}^2$$

(*a*) To find equivalent normal stress due to bending

$$M_m = \text{Mean bending moment}$$

$$= \frac{1}{2}[4200 - 2200] = 1000 \text{ kg–cm}$$

$$M_v = \text{Variable bending moment}$$

$$= \frac{1}{2}[M_{max} - M_{min}]$$

$$= \frac{1}{2}[4200 - (-2200)]$$

$$= 3200 \text{ kg/cm}$$

$$f_m = \text{Mean bending stress}$$

Use bending equation, $\frac{M_m}{I} = \frac{f_m}{y}$

$$f_m = \frac{32 \,.\, M_m}{\pi \times d^3} \qquad \text{where } d = \text{shaft diameter}$$

$$= \frac{32 \times 1000}{\pi d^3} = \frac{10190}{d^3} \text{ kg/cm}^2$$

$$f_v = \text{Variable stress}$$

$$= \frac{32 \,.\, M_v}{\pi d^3} = \frac{32 \times 3200}{\pi d^3}$$

$$= \frac{32600}{d^3} \text{ kg/cm}^2$$

$$f_E = \text{Actual endurance limit}$$

$$= f_e \,.\, K_F \,.\, K_S \,.\, K_L$$

$$= 2500 \times 0.66 \times 0.85 \times 1$$

$$= 1402 \text{ kg/cm}^2$$

$$(K_f = 0.66, K_S = 0.85, K_L = 1)$$

Let $f_{ne}$ = Equivalent safe normal stress we know that according to Soderberg's criteria

$$f_{ne} = f_m + k_f \,.\, f_v \,.\, \frac{f_y}{f_E}$$

$$= \frac{10190}{d^3} + \frac{1 \times 32600}{d^3} \times \frac{4000}{1402}$$

$$= \frac{103199}{d^3} \quad \text{if } k_f = 1$$

(*b*) **To find equivalent shear stress due to torsional load**

$T_m$ = Mean torque

$$= \frac{1}{2}[3200 - 1200] = 1000 \text{ kg cm.}$$

$T_v$ = Variable torque

$$= \frac{1}{2}[T_{max} - T_{min}]$$

$$= \frac{1}{2}[3200 - (-1200)] = 2200 \text{ kg cm}$$

$f_{ms}$ = Mean shear stress

Use torsion equation $\frac{T_m}{J} = \frac{f_{ms}}{r}$

$$f_{ms} = \frac{16 \,.\, T_m}{\pi d^3} = \frac{16 \times 1000}{\pi d^3}$$

$$= \frac{5096}{d^3} \text{ kg/cm}^2$$

$f_{vs}$ = Variable shear stress

$$= \frac{16 \,.\, T_v}{\pi d^3} = \frac{16 \times 2200}{\pi d^3} = \frac{11210}{d^3} \text{ kg/cm}^2$$

$f_{ES}$ = Actual endurance limit in shear

$$= f_e \,.\, K_F \,.\, K_S \,.\, K_L$$

where $K_F = 0.66$

$K_S = 0.85$

$K_L = 0.58$ (Reversed torsional load for steel)

$$f_{ES} = 2500 \times 0.66 \times 0.85 \times 0.58 = 813 \text{ kg/cm}^2$$

Let $f_{se}$ = Equivalent shear stress

$K_f = 1$

$$f_{se} = f_{ms} + K_f \,.\, f_{vs} \,.\, \frac{f_{ys}}{f_{ES}}$$

$$= \frac{5096}{d^3} + 1 \times \frac{11210}{d^3} \times \frac{2000}{813}$$

$$= \frac{38188}{d^3}$$

(**Take** $f_{ys}$ **= yield stress in shear**

$$= 0.5 \times f_y = 0.5 \times 4000 = 2000 \text{ kg/cm}^2)$$

According to maximum shear stress theory

$$f_{se(max)} = \frac{1}{2}\sqrt{f_{ne}^2 + 4 f_{se}^2}$$

$$f_{se(max)} = \frac{1}{2} \cdot \frac{1}{d_p} \sqrt{(103199)^2 + 4 \times 38188^2}$$

$$= \frac{55000}{d^3}$$

$$f_{ys} = \text{yield stress in shear}$$

$$= \frac{f_y}{2} = \frac{4000}{2}$$

$$= 2000 \text{ kg/cm}^2$$

$$n = \text{Factor of safety} = \frac{f_{ys}}{f_{se(max)}}$$

$$1.8 = \frac{2000}{55000} \times d^3$$

$$d = 3.68 \text{ cm.}$$

**Example 3.29.** *A steel shaft is subjected to a torque that varies between 2000 kg-cm clockwise to 1000 kg-cm anticlockwise at a point where bending moment varies between 4000 kg-cm to 2000 kg-cm. Find shaft diameter.*

*Given* $\sigma_{ut} = 3600 \text{ kg/cm}^2$

$\sigma_y = 2800 \text{ kg/cm}^2$

$F.O.S. = 2.5.$

**Solution.**

$M_{max}$ = Maximum bending moment

= 4000 kg-cm

$M_{min}$ = Minimum bending moment

= 2000 kg -cm

$M_m$ = Mean bending moment

$$= \frac{1}{2}[M_{max} - M_{min}]$$

$$= \frac{1}{2}[4000 - 2000] = 1000 \text{ kg-cm}$$

$$M_v = \text{Variable bending moment}$$

$$= \frac{1}{2}[M_{max} - (-M_{min})]$$

$$= \frac{1}{2}[4000 - (-2000)] = 3000 \text{ kg-cm}$$

$$T_{max} = \text{Maximum torque} = 2000 \text{ kg-cm}$$

$$T_{min} = \text{Minimum torque} = 1000 \text{ kg-cm}$$

$$T_m = \text{Mean torque} = \frac{1}{2}[2000 - 1000]$$

$$= 500 \text{ kg-cm}$$

$$T_v = \text{Variable torque} = \frac{1}{2}[2000 - (-1000)]$$

$$= 1500 \text{ kg cm}$$

Let $d$ = Shaft diameter

$\sigma_m$ = Mean bending stress

$\sigma_v$ = Variable bending stress

Using bending equation,

$$\frac{M_m}{I} \quad \frac{}{y}$$

$$\sigma_m = \frac{M_m}{I} \times y$$

$$= \frac{1000}{\frac{\pi}{64} d_4} \times \frac{d}{2} = \frac{10191}{d^3} \qquad \text{...(1)}$$

$$\sigma_v = \frac{M_v}{I} \times y$$

$$= \frac{3000}{\frac{\pi}{64} d^4} \times \frac{d}{2} = \frac{30573}{d^3} \qquad \text{...(2)}$$

$\sigma_b$ = Safe bending stress

we know that according to Soderberg relation

$$\sigma_b = \frac{\sigma_m + \sigma_v \times \sigma_y}{\sigma_E}$$

where $\sigma_E$ = Endurance limit

$= 0.5\ \sigma_{ut}$

$$= \frac{3600}{2} = 1800 \text{ kg/cm}^2$$

$$\sigma_b = \frac{10191}{d^3} + \frac{30573}{d^3} \times \frac{2800}{1800} = \frac{57749}{d^3}$$

Let $f_{sm}$ = Mean shear stress

$f_{sv}$ = Variable shear stress

Using torsion equation

$$\frac{T_m}{J} = \frac{f_{sm}}{r}$$

where $r = \dfrac{d}{2}$

$$f_{sm} = \frac{T_m}{J} \times r = \frac{500}{\frac{\pi}{36} d^4} \times \frac{d}{2} = \frac{2547}{d^3}$$

$$f_{sv} = \frac{T_v}{J} \times \frac{d}{2}$$

$$= \frac{1500}{\frac{\pi}{32} d^4} \times \frac{d}{2} = \frac{7641}{d^3}$$

$f_s$ = Mean shear stress

$$= f_{sm} + f_{sv} \times \frac{f_v}{f_E}$$

where $f_y$ = yield stress in shear

$$f_y = \frac{\sigma_v}{2} = \frac{2800}{2} = 1400 \text{ kg/cm}^2$$

$f_E$ = Endurance limit in shear

$$= \frac{\sigma_E}{2} = \frac{1800}{2} = 900 \text{ kg/cm}^2$$

$$f_s = \frac{2547}{d^3} + \frac{7641}{d^3} \times \frac{1400}{900} = \frac{14433}{d^3}$$

$\sigma_1$ = maximum principal stress

$$= \frac{\sigma_u}{F.O.S.} = \frac{2800}{2.5} = 1120 \text{ kg/cm}^2$$

$$\sigma_1 = \frac{\sigma_b}{2} + \frac{1}{2}\sqrt{\sigma_b^2 + 4f_s^2}$$

$$1120 = \frac{1}{2} \times \frac{57749}{d^3} + \frac{1}{2}\sqrt{\left(\frac{57.749}{d^3}\right)^2 + 4 \times \left(\frac{14.433}{d^3}\right)^2}$$

$$d = 4.1 \text{ cm.}$$

**Example 3.30.** *A wall bracket of uniform rectangular section is shown in Fig. 3.52. (a) It is subjected to a pull of 5000 Newtons acting at 30° to horizontal. The stress in the material of bracket is limited to $3 \times 10^7 N/m^2$. Design the section of the bracket taking depth of the section as thrice the width.*

**Solution.**

$$P = \text{Pull} = 5000 \text{ N}$$

$$\sigma = \text{Safe stress}$$

$$= 3 \times 10^7 \text{ N/m}^2$$

**Due to $P$ the bracket is subjected to**

**(*i*) bending moment and axial force due to horizontal component ($P_H$) of $P$**

**(*ii*) bending moment due to vertical component ($P_V$) of $P$.**

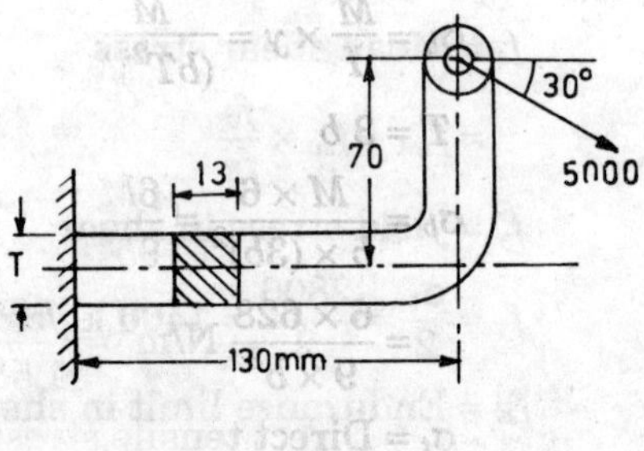


Fig. 3.52 (*a*).

**The section near the support is subjected to maximum bending moment.**

$$P_H = \text{Horizontal component of } P$$

$$= P \cos 30 = 5000 \times \cos 30 = 4335 \text{ N}$$

$$P_V = \text{Vertical component of } P$$

$$= P \sin 30 = 5000 \times \frac{1}{2} = 2500 \text{ N}$$

$M_1$ = Moment due to $P_H$

$$= \frac{4335 \times 70}{1000} = 303 \text{ Nm.}$$

$M_2$ = Maximum moment at support due to $P_V$

$$= P_V \times 130$$

$$= \frac{2500 \times 130}{1000} = 325 \text{ Nm.}$$

$M$ = Total bending moment at support

$$= M_1 + M_2 = 303 + 325 = 628 \text{ Nm.}$$

Use bending equation

$$\frac{M}{I} = \frac{\sigma_b}{y}$$

where $\sigma_b$ = Bending stress, $I$ = Moment of inertia

$$= \frac{bT^3}{12}$$

$$y = \frac{T}{2}$$

$b$ = Width of bracket

$T$ = Thickness of bracket

$$\sigma_b = \frac{M}{I} \times y = \frac{M}{(bT^2)/6}$$

Now $T = 3\,b$

$$\sigma_b = \frac{M \times 6}{b \times (3b)^2} = \frac{6M}{9b^3}$$

$$= \frac{6 \times 628}{9 \times b^3} \text{ N/m}^2 = \frac{628}{1.5b^3} \text{ N/m}^2$$

$\sigma_t$ = Direct tensile stress due to $P_H$

$$= \frac{P_H}{b \times T} = \frac{4335}{b \times 3b} = \frac{4335}{3b^2}$$

$$\sigma = \sigma_b + \sigma_t$$

$$3 \times 10^7 = \frac{628'}{1.5\,b^3} + \frac{4335}{3b^2}$$

Solving, we get $b = 0.02$ m

$T = 0.06$ m.

**Example 3.31.** *Determine the maximum stress induced in the shaft which transmits 24 kW at 450 RPM. The diameter of shaft is 30 mm as shown in Fig. 3.52 (b). Take stress concentration into account.*

**Solution.** $d$ = Shaft diameter = 30 mm

$P$ = Power

$= 24 \text{ kW} = 24 \times 10^3$ watts

$T$ = Torque transmitted

$N = RPM = 450$

$$P = \frac{2\,\pi\,NT}{60}$$

$$24 \times 10^3 = \frac{2\pi \times 450 \times T}{60}$$

$$T = 509.5 \text{ Nm}$$

$f_s$ = Shear stress

$$\frac{T}{J} = \frac{f_s}{r} \quad \text{where } r = \frac{d}{2}$$

$$f_s = \frac{T \times r}{J} \quad \text{where } J = \frac{\pi}{32}\,d^4$$

$$= \frac{16\,T}{\pi\,d^3}$$

$$f_s = \frac{16 \times 509500}{\pi\,(30)^3}$$

$$= 96 \text{ N/mm}^2$$

$K_t$ = Stress concentration factor

= 1.2 from Fig. 3.52

Maximum stress induced

$$= 1.2 \times 96 = 115.2 \text{ N/mm}^2.$$

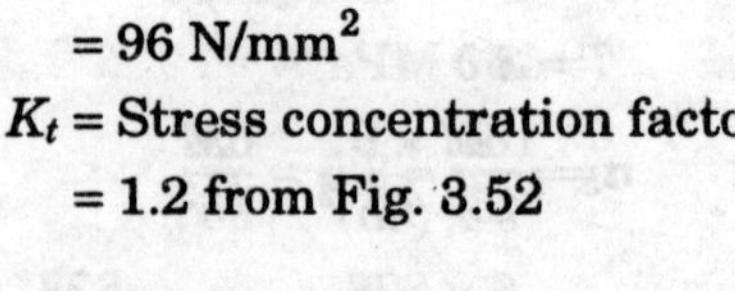


Fig. 3.52 (*b*).

**Example 3.32.** *A hub is press fitted an a shaft. An element in the hub is subjected to a radial. Compressive stress of 30 MPa and a hoop stress of 60 MPa. Determine factor of safety if (a) hub is made of mildsteel with yield stress of 320 MPa. Use maximum shear stress theory. (b) hub is made of cast iron with $\sigma_{ut}$ = 180 MPa and $\sigma_{uc}$ = 620 MPa.*

**Solution.**

(*a*) **Using maximum shear stress theory**

**Let**

$$\sigma_1 = 60 \text{ MPa}$$

$$\sigma_2 = 30 \text{ MPa (Compressive)}$$

$$f_{s(max)} = \text{Maximum shear stress}$$

$$= \frac{\sigma_1 - \sigma_2}{2}$$

$$= \frac{60 - (-30)}{2}$$

$$= 45 \text{ MPa}$$

$$n = \text{Factor of safety}$$

$$f_{yt} = \text{Yield stress in tension}$$

$$f_{s(max)} = \text{Maximum shear stress}$$

$$= \frac{f_{sy}}{n}$$

**where**

$$f_{sy} = \text{yield shear stress}$$

$$= \frac{f_{yt}}{2} = \frac{320}{2}$$

$$= 160 \text{ MPa}$$

$$n = \frac{160}{45} = 3.5$$

(*b*) *Using Mohr theory for Brittle materials $\sigma_1$ and $\sigma_2$ are the principal stresses.*

$$\sigma_{ut} = \text{Ultimate stress in tension}$$

$$= 180 \text{ MPa}$$

$$\sigma_{uc} = \text{Ultimate stress in Compression}$$

$$\sigma_{uc} = 620 \text{ MPa}$$

$$\frac{\sigma_1}{\sigma_{ut}} + \frac{\sigma_2}{\sigma_{uc}} = \frac{1}{n}$$

$$\frac{60}{180}+\left(\frac{-30}{-620}\right)=\frac{1}{n} \qquad n = 2.6.$$

**Example. 3.33.** *A mildsteel lever connected to steel shaft of 50 mm diameter is subjected to a force (F) at one end as shown in Fig. 3.53. If yield stress is 360 MPa and factor of safety is 2.8 determine the value of force using.*

(*a*) *Maximum shear stress theory.*

(*b*) *Mises Hencky theory.*

**Solution.**

**Let** $\sigma_{yt}$ = **Yield stress = 360 MPa**

$F$ = **Force**

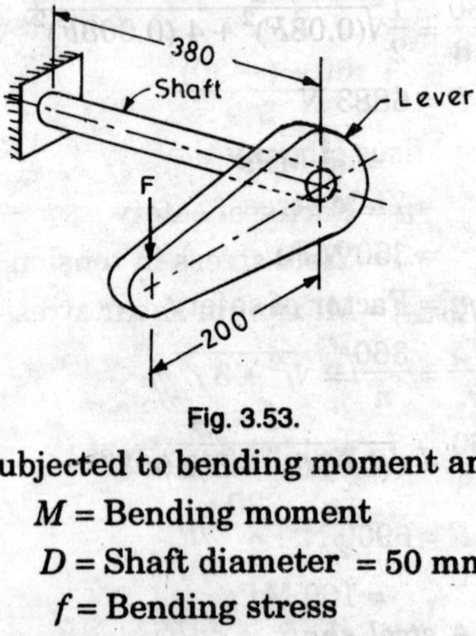


Fig. 3.53.

**The shaft is subjected to bending moment and torque.**

$M$ = **Bending moment**

$D$ = **Shaft diameter = 50 mm**

$f$ = **Bending stress**

**Using bending equation**

$$\frac{M}{I}=\frac{f}{y}$$

$$M = I\frac{f}{y}=\frac{\pi}{64}D^4\times\frac{f}{\frac{D}{2}}=\frac{\pi}{32}D^3.\times f$$

**Now** $M = F \times 380$ **N** $mm$

$$F\times 380=\frac{\pi}{32}\times 50^3\times f$$

$f = 0.03$ **FMPa**

$T$ = **Torque** $= F \times 200$

$$f_s = \text{shear stress}$$
$$= \frac{16T}{\pi D^3}$$
$$= \frac{16 \times F \times 200}{\pi \times 50^3} = 0.008 \text{ FMPa.}$$
$$f_{sy} = \text{Yield shear stress} = \frac{f_{yt}}{2} = \frac{360}{2} = 180 \text{ MPa}$$

(*a*) According to maximum shear stress theory

$$f_{s\,(max)} = \text{Maximum shear stress}$$
$$\frac{f_{sy}}{n} = \frac{1}{2}\sqrt{f^2 + 4f_s^2}$$
$$\frac{180}{2.8} = \frac{1}{2}\sqrt{(0.03F)^2 + 4\,(0.008F)^2}$$
$$F = 6883 \text{ N}$$

(*b*) According to Mises Hencky theory

$$\sigma_{yt} \text{ or } f_{yt} = \text{Yield stress.}$$
$$= 360 \text{ MPa}$$
$$n = \text{Factor of safety}$$
$$\frac{f_{yt}}{n} = \frac{360}{n} = \sqrt{f^2 + 3\,f_s^2}$$
$$\frac{360}{2.8} = \sqrt{(0.03F)^2 + 3(0.008F)^2}$$
$$F = 6900 \text{ N.}$$

**Example 3.34.** *A steel shaft is subjected to a torque varying between 80 Nm to 480 Nm. Determine the shaft diameter using the following data :*

*Stress concentration factor ($k_F$L) due to keyway = 1.5*

*Factor of safety (n) = 2*

*Yield stress = 280 MPa*

*Endurance limit = 200 MPa*

*Correction factor for torsion = 0.6*

*Surface finish factor = 0.8*

*Size factor = 0.82.*

**Solution.** $T_m$ = Mean torque

$$= \frac{1}{2} [T_{max} + T_{min}]$$

$$= \frac{1}{2} [480 + 80]$$

$= 280$ Nm.

$f_m$ = Mean shear stress

$D$ = Shaft diameter

$$f_m = \frac{16\, T_m}{\pi D^3}$$

$$= \frac{16 \times 280 \times 1000}{\pi \times D^3}$$

$$= \frac{448 \times 10^4}{\pi D^3}$$

$T_V$ = Variable torque

$$= \frac{1}{2} [T_{max} - T_{min}]$$

$$= \frac{1}{2} [480 - 80]$$

$= 200$ Nm.

$f_V$ = Variable stress

$$= \frac{16\, T_v}{\pi D^3} = \frac{16 \times 200 \times 1000}{\pi D^3}$$

$$= \frac{320 \times 10^4}{\pi D^3}$$

$K_f = 1.5$

$K_F$ = Surface finish factor

$= 0.8$

$k_s$ = Size factor

$= 0.82$

$k_L$ = Load correction factor

$= 0.6$

$f_e$ = Corrected Endurance limit

$= 200 \times K_F \times K_S \times K_L$

$= 200 \times 0.8 \times 0.82 \times 0.6$

$= 117$ MPa

$$f_{ys} = \text{Yield stress in shear}$$
$$= \frac{f_{yt}}{2}$$
$$= \frac{280}{2} = 140 \text{ MPa}$$
$$n = \text{Factor of safety} = 2$$

According to Soderberg equation,

$$\frac{1}{n} = \frac{f_m}{f_{ys}} + \frac{f_V \times k_f}{f_e}$$

$$\frac{1}{2} = \frac{448 \times 10^4}{\pi D^3} \times \frac{1}{140} + \frac{320 \times 10^4 \times 1.5}{\pi D^3 \times 117}$$

$$D = 30.5 \text{ mm.}$$

**Example 3.35.** *Using optimum design method, derive the equation for optimum design of tension rod.*

**Solution.**

Let $C$ = Cost/Unit weight

$W$ = Weight /Volume

$V$ = Volume

$= A \times L$

$C_m$ = Material cost

$A$ = Area of rod (cross-sectional)

$L$ = Length of rod

The primary design equation (P.D.E.) will be

$$C_m = C \,.\, W \,.\, V$$
$$= C.W.A.L$$

Let $P$ = Axial load

Subsidiary Design Equation (SDE) is written assuming no yielding is tolerated.

$$\tau_{max} = \text{Max shear stress}$$
$$= \frac{P}{2\,.\,A}$$

The limit equation (L.E.) will be

$$\tau_{max} < \frac{\sigma_y}{2n}$$

where $\sigma_y$ = Yield stress

$$n = \text{Factor of safety}$$

$$C_m = C.W.A.L$$

But $$A = \frac{P}{2\,\tau_{max}}.$$

$$C_m = C.W.L.\,\frac{P}{2\,(\tau_{max})}$$

For minimum cost

$$\tau_{max} = \frac{\sigma_y}{2n}$$

$$C_m = C.W.L.\left[P \times \frac{2n}{2\,.\,\sigma_y}\right]$$

$$= PLn\left[\frac{cw}{\sigma_y}\right]$$

$$= P.L.N.K$$

where $$K = \frac{C.W}{\sigma_y}$$

and is called material selection factor or material parameter. By selecting the material having minimum value of this factor, the design with minimum cost can be achieved.

## Problems

**3.1.** Define load and stress. Discuss different types of loads.

**3.2.** Write short notes on the following :

(*a*) Tensile stress (*b*) Compressive stress

(*c*) Shear stress.

**3.3.** Sketch a stress-strain diagram for a ductile material and explain the following :

(*a*) Limit of proportionality (*b*) Elastic limit

(*c*) Yield strength (*d*) Ultimate strength.

**3.4.** Define factor of safety state factor of safety commonly used for different type of loading :

**3.5.** Describe the following :

(*a*) Bearing stress (*b*) Combined stresses

(*c*) Bending stress (*d*) Torsional stress.

**3.6.** Explain how the diameter of a rotating shaft is calculated when the shaft is subjected to bending moment ($M$) and torque ($T$).

**3.7.** Define a column. Explain the following :

(*a*) Slenderness ratio (*b*) Blucking load

(*c*) Euler's formula

(*d*) Rankine Gordon formula.

**3.8.** What is resilience ? Define modulus of resilience.

**3.9.** Write short notes on the following :

(*a*) Impact stress.

(*b*) Effect of concentric loading on a machine part.

(*c*) Endurance limit.

(*d*) Mohr circle.

**3.10.** (*a*) Explain stress concentration in a machine part subjected to external load. (*b*)Define stress concentration factor.

**3.11.** (*a*) Define the following :

(*i*) Variable loading

(*ii*) Endurance diagram and endurance limit.

(*iii*) Stress concentration factor

(*iv*) Size and surface finish factor.

(*b*) A simply supported beam has a concentrated load at the centre which fluctuates from a value of $P$ and $4P$. The span of the beam is 50 cm and its cross-section is circular with a diameter of 6 cm. Taking for the beam material an ultimate stress of 70 kg/mm$^2$ a yield stress of 50 kg/mm$^2$, endurance limit of 33 kg/mm$^2$ for reversed bending, and a factor of safety of 1.3, calculate the maximum value of $P$ .Take a size factor of 0.85 and a surface finish factor of 0.9.

**3.12.** Discuss various types of loads.

**3.13.** Write short notes on the following :

(*a*) Stress concentration due to elliptical hole.

(*b*) Brittle materials with fluctuating loads.

(*c*) S-N curve for fatigue loading.

(*d*) Stress ratio, range of stress and variable stress for cyclic loading.

(*e*) Modifying factors for endurance limit.

(*f*) Fatigue stress concentration factor.

**3.14.** Describe the types of stress cycles considered while designing for fatigue loading.

**3.15.** Describe the theories of failure applied to fatigue loading design.

**3.16.** (*A*) Describe the following theories of failure.

(*a*) Maximum principal stress theory

(*b*) Maximum shear stress theory

(*c*) Distortion energy theory.

(*B*) Compare the field of above theories for due (*p*) materials.

**3.17** Write short notes on the following :

(*a*) Factors affecting factor of safety.

(*b*) Methods to avoid fatigue failure.

**3.18.** A mild steel shaft 50 mm diameter carries a torque that fluctuates 25% each way from the average value of 30000 kg-cm. The stress concentration factor is 1.9. The factor of safety based on yield point is 2.5. If the endurance limit in shear is equal to 0.6 of the yield point in shear determine the minimum value of yield point in shear which the material must have if the shaft is to be safe for continuous operation.

**3.19.** Calculate the force *P* for a plate (Fig. 3.5) if factor of safety of 3 and material of plate is *C* 40 steel.

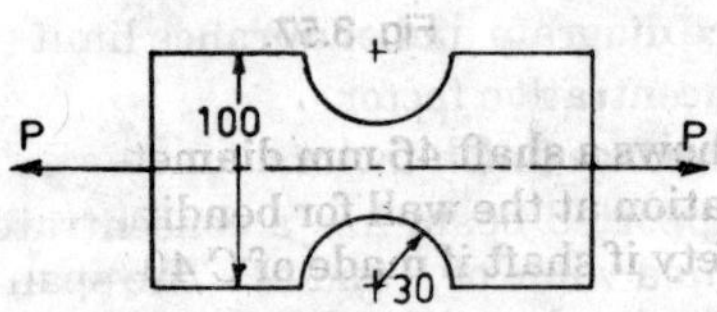


Fig. 3.54.

**3.20.** A shaft is subjected to load system as shown in Fig. 3.54. Find the values of lengths *L* and $L_1$ if the bending stress at the groove and the at the fillet are to be equal. Stress concentration should be taken into account.

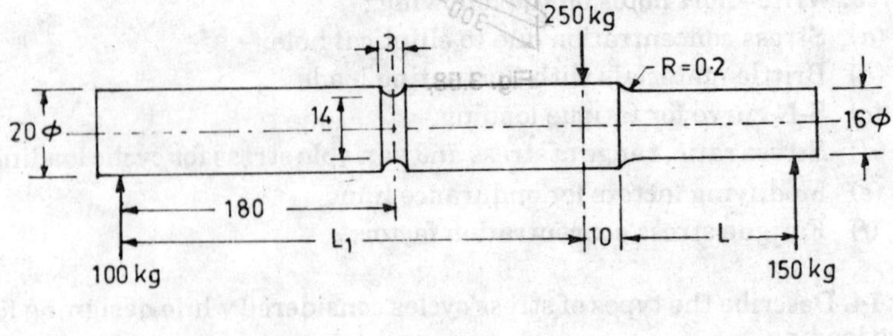


Fig. 3.55.

**3.21.** Find the length $S$ for a rotating shaft (Fig. 3.56) of the bending stress at the fillet is equal to the stress at the centre.

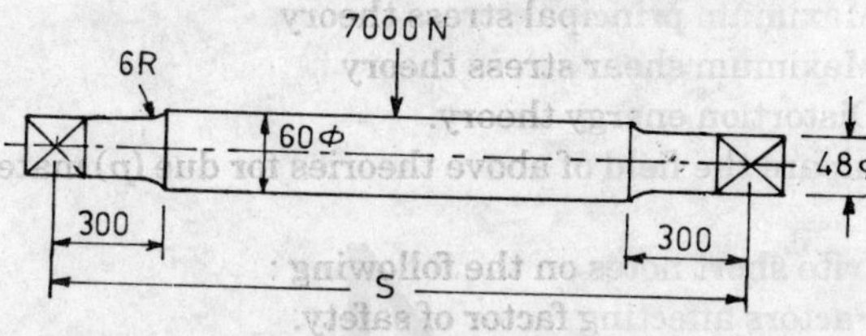


Fig. 3.56.

**3.22.** A beam 24 mm thick is subjected to a bending moment ($M$) of 20,000 kg-cm. Determine the maximum value of bending stress (Fig. 3.57).

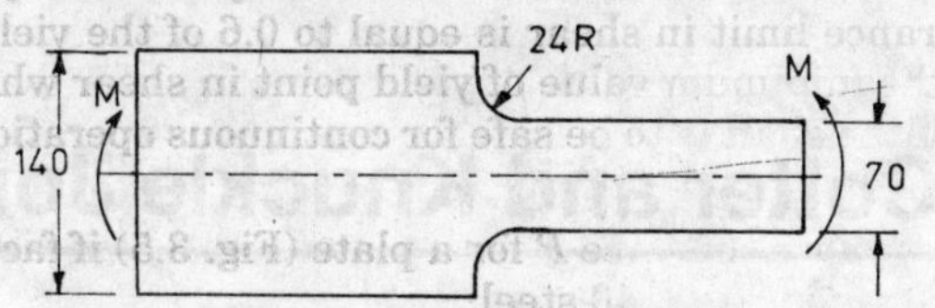


Fig. 3.57.

**3.23.** Fig. 3.58 shows a shaft 46 mm diameter is rigidly attached to the wall stress concentration at the wall for bending and torsion is 3. Find the value of factor of safety if shaft if made of $C$ 40 steel.

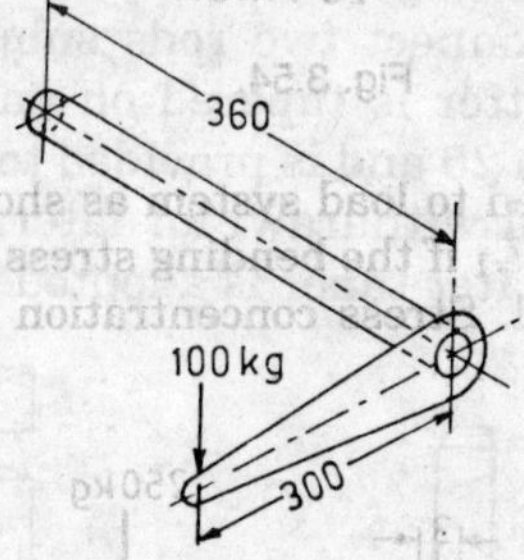


Fig. 3.58.

# 4

# Cotter and Knuckle Joints

## 4.1 Cotter

A cotter is a flat weldge shaped piece of rectangular cross section. It is used to connect two rods subjected to a tensile or compressive load. A cotter is tapered on one side or both sides. Usually the taper is 1 in 25 and is provided to facilitate the driving of cotter in position and withdrawl for lateral adjustment of connected parts. When greater taper is adopted a locking device such

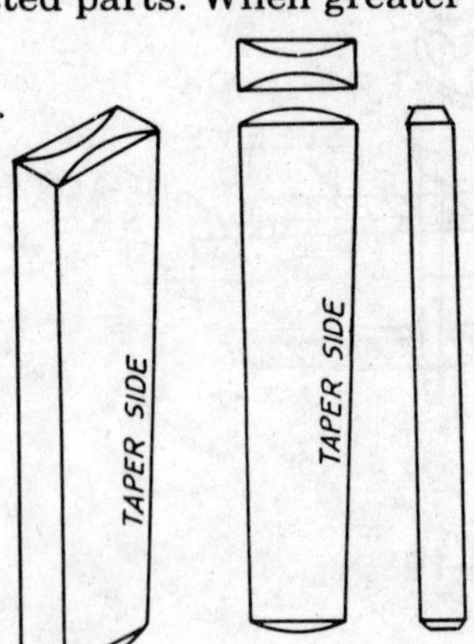


Fig. 4.1.

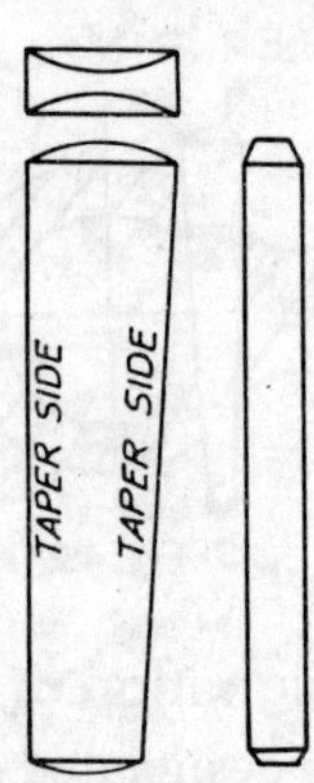


Fig. 4.2.

as a taper pin is used to prevent cotter from coming out. The ends of cotter are made narrower having round wedges on both sides to facilitate the hammering for fixing and removing. A cotter is generally made of mild steel. Fig. 4.1 shows cotter with taper on one side and Fig. 4.2 shows cotter with taper on both sides.

## 4.1 (*a*) Comparison of Cotters and Keys

Cotters are generally driven at right angles or the axes of the connected parts which are subjected to tensile or compressive stresses along their axes whereas the keys are normally driven parallel to the axis of the shafts which are subjected to torsional or twisting stresses. A cotter resists shear over two transverse sections whereas a key resists shear over longitudinal section. Both keys and cotter give a temporary joint.

**4.1.1 Taper pins.** They are used as fasteners for light work.

Pins are of two types :

(*i*) Cylindrical pins of straight pins

(*ii*) Conical pins or taper pins.

Fig. 4.3 shows the use of cylindrical pin and Fig. 4.4 shows use of a taper pin. The diameter of large end of pin is one fourth of shaft diameter and taper on pin is 1 : 48.

Taper pins are made of ordinary steel or of carbon steel containing carbon 0.10. The mean diameter of pin is 0.2*d* to 0.25*d* where *d* is shaft diameter standard taper pins may be used as fasteners for light work by placing them tangent to the shaft or on diameter. Hollow shaft are connected frequently big means of a sleeve and taper pins [As shown in Fig. 4.2, Fig. 4.2 (*a*) and Fig. 4.2 (*b*)].

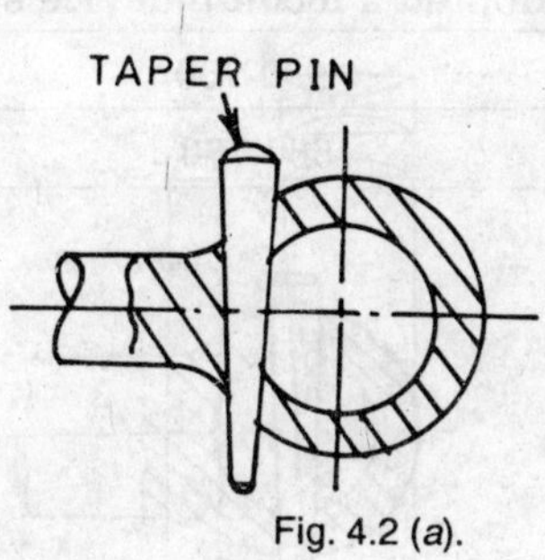


Fig. 4.2 (*a*).

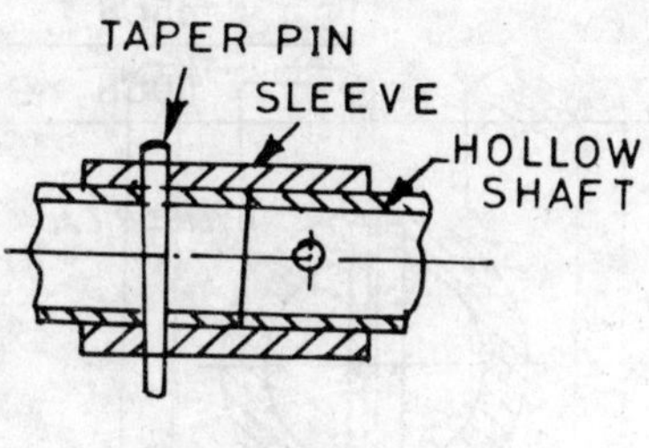


Fig. 4.2 (*b*).

## 4.1 (*b*) Designation of pins (IS 2393-1980)

Pins are designated as follows.

(*i*) **Cylindrical pins.** They are designated by the nominal diameter, the tolerance on diameter and nominal length of pin.

For example a pin of nominal diameter 12 mm, tolerance $h_7$ and nominal length 18 mm shall be represented as

Cylindrical pin 12 $h_7 \times 18$ IS : 2393

(*ii*) **Solid taper pins.** They are designated by the nominal diameter and nominal length.

For example a solid taper pin of 10 mm nominal diameter and 60 mm nominal length shall be designated as

Solid taper pin *A* 10 × 60 IS : 6688.

(*iii*) **Split taper pins.** They are designated by their nominal diameter and nominal length.

For example a split taper pin of 12 nominal diameter and 50 mm nominal length is represented as

Split taper pin *C* 12 × 50 IS : 6688.

Cylindrical pins and taper pins are made of *C* 40 steel.

### 4.1.2 Materials used for Cotter, Gib and Knuckle Joints

The properties of the materials used for cotter, gib and knuckle joints are indicated in Table 4.1.

**Table 4.1**

| *I.S. Code* | *Designation* | *Tensile Strength* ($N/mm^2$) |
|---|---|---|
| IS 1570-1979 | Steel | |
| | 30*C*8 | 500-600 |
| | 40*C*8 | 580-670 |
| | 45*C*8 | 630-700 |
| | 50*C*8 | 660-780 |

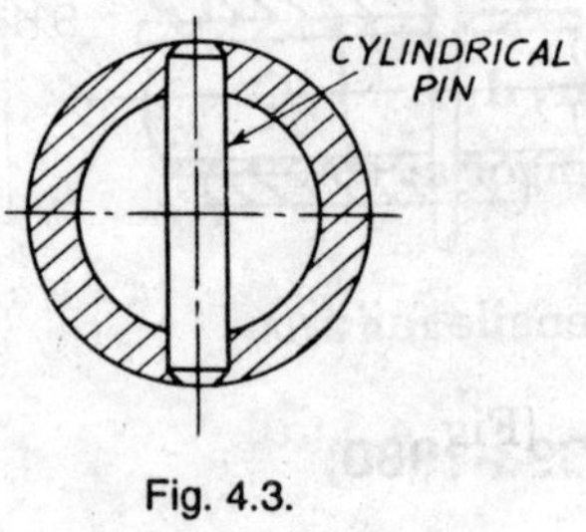


Fig. 4.3.

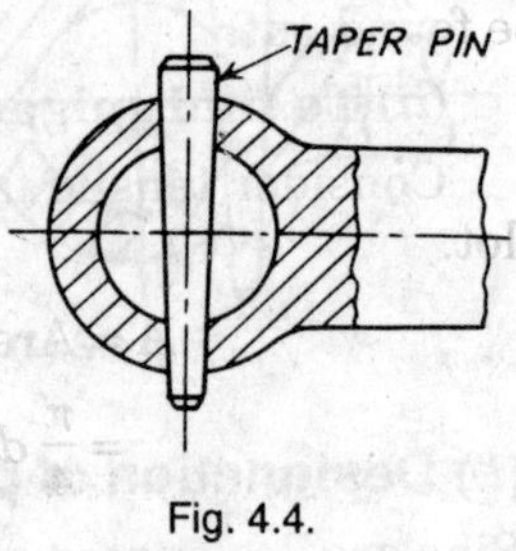


Fig. 4.4.

## 4.2 Cotter Joint

It is used to connect two rods for temporary works. One of the rods is made with a socket end and other rod is made with a spigot end. A cotter is driven tightly through socket and spigot ends. The cotter tapers in width and not in thickness (Fig. 4.5). The usual taper provided on cotter is 1 in 25. If a greater taper is required a locking device should be used.

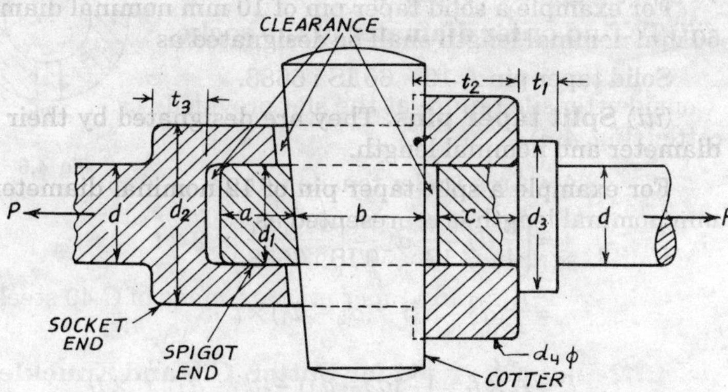


Fig. 4.5.

Let a tensile force $P$ acts on the joint and $f_t$, $f_s$ and $f_c$ be tensile stress, shear stress and crushing stress respectively. It is assumed that the socket end, spigot end and cotter are made of same material.

(*i*) **To find rod diameter** $d$. Consider tensile failure of rod.

$$A = \text{Area under tensile failure}$$

$$= \frac{\pi}{4} d^2$$

$$P = A \times f_t = \frac{\pi}{4} d^2 \times f_t \qquad ...(1)$$

From this equation the diameter of rod can be found out.

(*ii*) **To find spigot diameter, $d_1$**

Consider tensile failure of spigot at cotter slot.

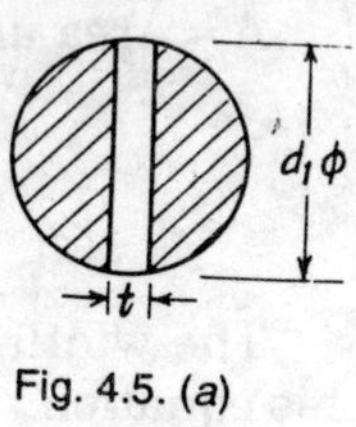


Fig. 4.5. (*a*)

$$A = \text{Area under tensile failure}$$

$$= \frac{\pi}{4} d_1^2 - d_1 \times t \quad \text{[Fig. 4.5 (a)].}$$

where $t$ = Thickness of cotter

$$P = A \times f_t$$

$$P = \left(\frac{\pi}{4} d_1^2 - d_1 \, . \, t\right) \times f_t \qquad ...(2)$$

Assuming, $t = 0.4\, d$, the diameter $d_1$ can be found from equation (2). The diameter $d_1$ is also called inner diameter of socket.

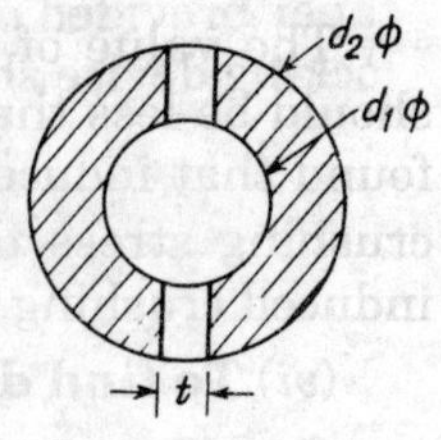

Fig. 4.6

(*iii*) **To find outer diameter of the socket $d_2$**

Consider tensile failure at the slot provided for cotter (Fig. 4.6).

$$A = \text{Area under tensile failure}$$

$$= \left(\frac{\pi}{4} d_2^2 - \frac{\pi}{4} d_1^2\right) - \left(\frac{d_2 - d_1}{2}\right) \times 2 \times t$$

$$= \frac{\pi}{4} (d_2^2 - d_1^2) - (d_2 - d_1) \times t$$

$$P = A \times f_t = [\frac{\pi}{4} (d_2^2 - d_1^2) - (d_2 - d_1) \, .t] \times f_t \qquad ...(3)$$

From equation (3) the diameter $d_2$ can be found.

(*iv*) **To find collor diameter d$_3$**

$$A = \text{Area that resists crushing of collor}$$

$$= \frac{\pi}{4} (d_3^2 - d_1^2)$$

$$P = \frac{\pi}{4} (d_3^2 - d_1^2) \times f_c \qquad ...(4)$$

The diameter $d_3$ can be found from this equation.

(*v*) **To find width of cotter b.**

The cotter will fail in double shear

$A$ = Area under shear (Fig. 4.7).

$$= 2 \times b \times t$$

$$P = A \times f_s$$

$$= 2 \, . \, b \, . \, t \, . \, f_s \qquad ...(5)$$

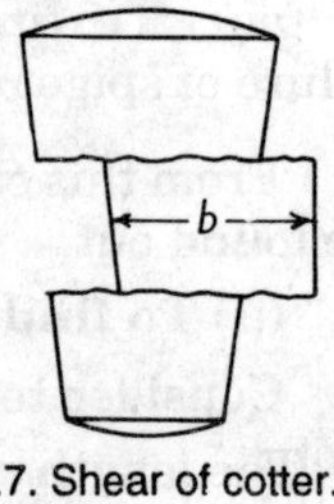

Fig. 4.7. Shear of cotter.

The width of cotter $b$ can be found from this equation.

**To check induced crushing stress.** The spigot or cotter may fail by crushing

$A$ = Area under crushing

$= d_1 \times t$

$P = A \times$ induced crushing stress, $f_{c_1}$

$= d_1 \times t \times f_{c1}$.

The value of $f_{c_1}$ is calculated from this equation. This value should be less than the allowable value of crushing stress. If it is found that induced crushing stress $f_{c_1}$ is more than the allowable crushing stress than either $d_1$ or $t$ may be increased to obtain induced crushing stress less than allowable crushing stress.

(*vi*) **To find diameter, $d_4$**

Consider crushing failure of cotter or socket

$A$ = Area under crushing

$$= \frac{d_4 - d_1}{2} \times 2 \times t$$

$= (d_4 - d_1) \times t$

$P = A \times f_c$

$$= (d_4 - d_1) \times t \times f_c \qquad ...(6)$$

The diameter $d_4$ is calculated from equation (6).

(*vii*) **To find length 'c' of socket end.** Consider shear failure of socket end

$A$ = Area under shear

$= 2c\ (d_4 - d_1)$

$P = A \times f_s$

$$= 2c\ (d_4 - d_1) \times f_s \qquad ...(7)$$

From equation (7) the length $c$ can be found.

(*viii*) **To find length 'a' of spigot end.** Consider shearing failure of spigot end. It is in double shear.

$A$ = Area under double shear

$= 2 \,.\, a \,.\, d_1$

$P = A \times f_s$

$$= 2 \,.\, a \,.\, d_1 \times f_s \qquad ...(8)$$

The length $a$ can be found from this relation.

(*ix*) **To determine thickness of collor, $t_1$.** Consider shearing of collor

$A$ = Area under shear

$= \pi\, d_1 \,.\, t_1$

$$P = A \times f_s$$
$$= \pi\, d_1\, t_1 \times f_s \qquad ...(9)$$

The thickness of collor is calculated from this relation.

(*x*) **To check the cotter for induced bending stress.** When the cotter is driven into position it may bend. The load is assumed to be uniformly distributed on the cotter in the spigot end while in socket end the load is uniformly varying (Fig. 4.8). The bending moment (*M*) will be maximum at the centre and is given by

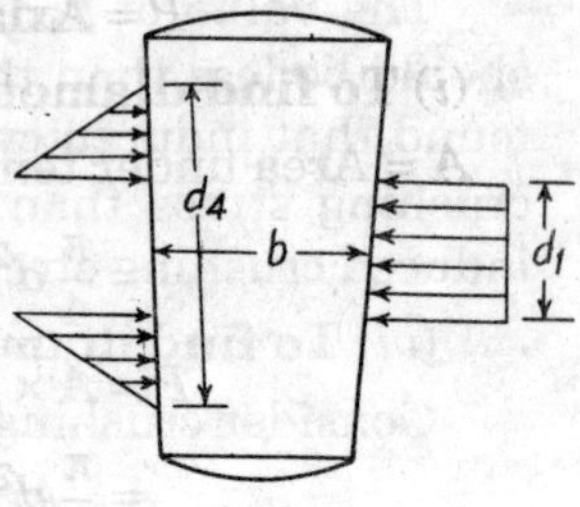


Fig. 4.8.

$$M = \frac{P}{2}\left[\frac{d_1}{4} + \left(\frac{d_4 - d_1}{6}\right)\right]$$

$$M = Z \times fb$$

where $Z$ = Section modulus

$f_b$ = Induced bending stress.

$$f_{t1} = \frac{M}{Z} = \frac{P}{2}\,\frac{\left[\frac{d_1}{4} + \left(\frac{d_4 - d_1}{6}\right)\right]}{\frac{tb^2}{6}}.$$

The induced bending stress $ft_1$ should be less than the allowable bending stress in cotter. If it is observed that the induced bending stress is more than allowable bending stress than the value of $b$ or $t$ should be increased.

The following proportions in terms of diameter $d$ may be adopted.

| | |
|---|---|
| $d_1 = 1.2\,d$ | $t_1 = 0.45\,d$ |
| $d_2 = 1.75\,d$ | $t_2 = d$ |
| $d_3 = 1.5\,d$ | $t_3 = 0.5\,d$ |
| $d_4 = 2.4\,d$ | $a = c = 0.75\,d$ |
| Clearance | = 2 to 3 mm |
| Length of cotter | = 4 $d$ |
| Taper in cotter | = 1 : 25. |

**Example 4.1.** *Design a cottered joint to connect two rods of equal diameter transmitting an axial force of 6000 kg. The safe stresses for cotter and rods are as follows :*

$f_t = 700\ kg/cm^2$,

$f_s = 450\ kg/cm^2$,

$f_c = 1100\ kg/cm^2$.

**Solution.** Cotter joint is shown in Fig. 4.5.

$P$ = Axial force = 6000 kg.

(*i*) **To find diameter 'd'.** Consider tensile failure of rod.

$A$ = Area under tensile failure

$$= \frac{\pi}{4} d^2$$

$$P = A \times f_t$$

$$= \frac{\pi}{4} d^2 \times f_t$$

$$6000 = \frac{\pi}{4} d^2 \times 700$$

$$d = 3.3 \text{ cm.}$$

(*ii*) **To find spigot diameter '$d_1$'.** Consider tensile failure of spigot at cotter slot.

$A$ = Area under tensile failure

$$= \frac{\pi}{4} d_1^2 - d_1 \times t$$

where $t$ = Thickness of cotter

$$= 0.4\, d = 0.4 \times 3.3 = 1.32 \text{ cm}$$

$$P = A \times f_t = \left(\frac{\pi}{4} d_1^2 - d_1 \times 1.32\right) \times 700$$

$$6000 = \left(\frac{\pi}{4} d_1^2 - d_1 \times 1.32\right) \times 700$$

$$0.785\, d_1^2 - 1.32\, d_1 - 8.55 = 0$$

$$d_1 = 4.24 \text{ cm.}$$

(*iii*) **To find outer diameter of socket '$d_2$'.** Consider tensile failure at the slot provided for cotter.

$A$ = Area under tensile failure

$$= \frac{\pi}{4} (d_2^2 - d_1^2) - (d_2 - d_1) \times t$$

$$P = A \times f_t$$

$$6000 = \left(\frac{\pi}{4} (d_2^2 - d_1^2) - (d_2 - d_1) \times t\right) \times f_t$$

$$= \left( \frac{\pi}{4} [d_2^2 - (4.24)^2] - (d_2 - 4.24) \times 1.32 \right) \times 700$$

$d_2 = 5.57$ cm.

(*iv*) **To find collor diameter '$d_3$'.** Consider crushing of collor.

$$A = \text{Area under crushing} = \frac{\pi}{4} (d_3^2 - d_1^2)$$

$$P = A \times f_c = \frac{\pi}{4} (d_3^2 - d_1^2) \times f_c$$

$$6000 = \frac{\pi}{4} [d_3^2 - (4.24)^2] \times 1100$$

$$d_3 = 5 \text{ cm}$$

(*v*) **To find width of cotter 'b'.** The cotter will fail in double shear.

$$A = \text{Area under shear} = 2 \times b \times t$$

$$P = A \times f_s$$

$$6000 = 2 \,.\, b \,.\, t \,.\, f_s = 2b \times 1.32 \times 450$$

$$b = 5.1 \text{ cm}$$

To check the induced crushing stress $f_{c_1}$ consider crushing of cotter.

$$A = \text{Area under crushing} = d_1 \times t$$

$$P = d_1 \times t \times f_{c_t}$$

$$6000 = 4.24 \times 1.32 \times f_{c_1}$$

$f_{c_1} = 1071.42 \text{ kg/cm}^2$ which is within safe limits.

(*vi*) **To find diameter '$d_4$'.** Consider crushing failure of cottor or socket.

$$A = \text{Area under crushing}$$

$$= (d_4 - d_1) \,.\, t$$

$$P = (d_4 - d_1) \,.\, t \,.\, f_t$$

$$6000 = (d_4 - 4.24) \times 1.32 \times 700$$

$$d_4 = 10.74 \text{ cm.}$$

(*vii*) **To find length 'c' of socket end.** Consider shear failure of socket end.

$$A = \text{Area under shear}$$

$$= 2c\ (d_4 - d_1)$$

$$P = A \times f_s = 2c\ (d_4 - d_1) = f_s$$

$$6000 = 2c\,(10.74 - 4.24) \times 450$$
$$c = 1.1 \text{ cm.}$$

(*viii*) **To find length a' of spigot end.** Consider shearing of spigot end. It is in double shear

$$A = \text{Area under shear} = 2\,a\,d_1$$
$$P = A \times f_s$$
$$P = 2a \times d_1 \times f_s$$
$$6000 = 2a \times 4.24 \times 450$$
$$a = 1.57 \text{ cm.}$$

(*ix*) **To determine thickness of collor '$t_1$'.** Consider shearing of collor

$$A = \text{Area under shear} = \pi\,d_1\,.\,t_1$$
$$P = \pi\,d_1\,.\,t_1\,.\,f_s$$
$$6000 = \pi \times 4.24 \times t_1 \times 450$$
$$t_1 = 1 \text{ cm.}$$

(*x*) **To check the cotter for induced bending stress.**

$$f_b = \text{Induced bending stress}$$
$$= \frac{M}{Z} = \frac{\frac{P}{2}\left(\frac{d_1}{4} + \frac{(d_4 - d_1)}{6}\right)}{\frac{tb^2}{6}}$$
$$= \frac{\frac{6000}{2}\left(\frac{4.24}{4} + \frac{10.74 - 4.24}{6}\right)}{\frac{1.32 \times (5.1)^2}{6}} = 1021 \text{ kg/cm}^2$$

This is less than given compressive stress, hence safe.

(*xi*) **Taper in cotter = 1 : 25**

Clearance = 2 to 3 mm

Length of cotter = $4d = 4 \times 3.3 = 13.2$ cm.

## 4.3 Sleeve and Cotter Joint

This joint is used to join two circular rods (Fig. 4.9). The two ends of rods are made to meet at the centre of the sleeve and one cotter for each rod is used to make the joint. The dimensions of the joint in terms of diameter of rod are as follows :

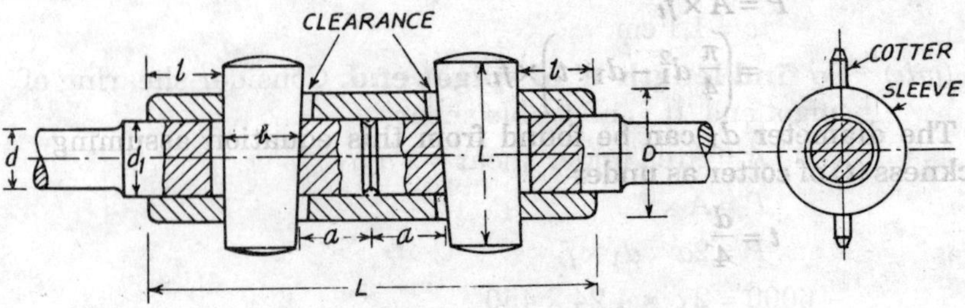


Fig. 4.9. Sleeve and cotter joint.

$d$ = Diameter of rod

$d_1$ = Diameter of enlarged end of rod

= 1.25 $d$

$s$ = Length of enlarged end of rod

= 4.5 $d$

$D$ = Outside diameter of sleeve

= 2.5 $d$

$L$ = Length of sleeve = 8 $d$

$t$ = Thickness of cotter = $\frac{d_1}{4}$

$b$ = Width of cotter = 1.25 $d$

$L_1$ = Length of cotter = 4 $d$

Taper in cotter = 1 : 25

Clearance = 3 mm.

Various dimensions of the joint are calculated as follows :

(*i*) **To find rod diameter, d.** Consider tensile failure of rod.

$$A = \text{Area under tension} = \frac{\pi}{4} d^2$$

$$P = A \times f_t$$

$$P = \frac{\pi}{4} d^2 \times f_t$$

The diameter $d$ can be found from this equation.

(*ii*) **To calculate diameter 'd'$_1$ of enlarged end of rod.** Consider tensile failure of enlarged end across slot.

$$A = \text{Area under tensile failure}$$

$$= \left( \frac{\pi}{4} d_1^2 - d_1 \, . \, t \right)$$

$$P = A \times f_t$$

$$= \left(\frac{\pi}{4} d_1^2 - d_1 . t\right) \times f_t.$$

The diameter $d_1$ can be found from this equation assuming thickness ($t$) of cotter as under

$$t = \frac{d}{4}.$$

(*iii*) **To calculate outer diameter of sleeve, D.** Consider tensile failure of sleeve across slot for cotter.

$$A = \text{Area under tensile failure}$$

$$= \frac{\pi}{4}(D^2 - d_1^2) - (D - d_1)\, t$$

$$P = A \times f_t$$

$$= \left(\frac{\pi}{4}(D^2 - d_1^2) - (D - d_1) \times t\right) \times f_t.$$

From this equation diameter $D$ can be found.

(*iv*) **To calculate width 'b' of cotter.** Consider shearing failure of cotter, the cotter being in double shear.

$$A = \text{Area under shear} = 2 . b . t$$

$$P = A \times f_s = 2 . b . t . f_s.$$

From this equation width '$b$' of cotter can be found.

(*v*) **To determine distance 'a'.** Consider failure of enlarged end of rod by shear which may fail in double shear.

$$A = \text{Area under shear} = 2 . a . d_1$$

$$P = A \times f_s = 2a \times d_1 \times f_s.$$

From this equation the distance $a$ can be found.

(*vi*) **To determine distance, 1.** Consider shear failure of sleeve end which may fail in double shear.

$$A = \text{Area under shear} = 2 . l\,(D - d_1)$$

$$P = A \times f_s = 2 . l, (D - d_1) \times f_s.$$

The length $l$ is calculated from this relation.

(*vii*) **To check the sleeve or cotter for induced crushing stress.** Consider failure of sleeve or cotter by crushing.

$$A = \text{Area under crushing} = (D - d_1) . t$$

$$P = A \times f_{c_1} = (D - d_1)\, t \times f_{c_1}$$

From this equation the induced crushing stress $f_{c_1}$ can be found. This should be less than the allowable crushing stress.

(*viii*) **To check the rod or cotter for induced crushing stress.** Consider crushing failure of rod or cotter by crushing.

$$A = \text{Area under crushing} = d_1 \,.\, t$$

$$P = A \times f_{c_2} = d_1 \,.\, t \,.\, f_{c_2}.$$

From this equation the value of induced crushing stress $f_{c_2}$ in rod or cotter can be found. This should be less than allowable crushing stress.

**Example 4.2.** *Design a sleeve and cotter joint to resist a tensile load of 5000 kg. Assume the stresses as follows :*

$$f_t = 650 \text{ kg/cm}^2$$

$$f_s = 550 \text{ kg/cm}^2$$

$$f_c = 1400 \text{ kg/cm}^2.$$

**Solution.** $P$ = Tensile load = 5000 kg.

(*i*) **To find rod diameter 'd'.** Consider tensile failure of rod.

$$A = \text{Area} = \frac{\pi}{4} d^2$$

$$P = A \times f_t = \frac{\pi}{4} d^2 \times f_t$$

$$5000 = \frac{\pi}{4} d^2 \times 650$$

$$d = 3.13 \text{ cm.}$$

(*ii*) **To calculate diameter '$d_1$' of enlarged end of rod.** Consider tensile failure of enlarged end of rod across slot.

$$A = \text{Area under tensile failure} = \frac{\pi}{4} d_1^2 - d_1 \,.\, t$$

$$P = A \times f_t$$

$$= \left(\frac{\pi}{4} d_1^2 - d_1 \,.\, t\right) \times f_t$$

$$= \left(\frac{\pi}{4} d_1^2 - d_1 \frac{d_1}{4}\right) f_t = \left(\frac{\pi}{4} d_1^2 - \frac{d_1^2}{4}\right) \times f_t$$

$$\left[\text{As } t = \frac{d_1}{4}\right]$$

$$5000 = \left(\frac{\pi}{4} d_1^2 - \frac{d_1^2}{4}\right) \times 650$$

$$d_1 = 3.79 \text{ cm.}$$

$$t_1 = \frac{d_1}{4} = \frac{3.79}{4} = 0.95 \text{ cm.}$$

(*iii*) **To calculate outer diameter of sleeve, D.** Consider tensile failure of sleeve across slot or cotter.

$$A = \text{Area under tensile failure}$$

$$= \frac{\pi}{4}(D^2 - d_1^2) - (D - d_1) \times t$$

$$P = A \times f_t = \left[\frac{\pi}{4}(D^2 - d_1^2) - (D - d_1) \times t\right] \times f_t$$

$$5000 = \frac{\pi}{4}[D^2 - (3.79)^2 - (D - 3.79) \times 0.95] \times 650$$

$$D = 5.98 \text{ cm.}$$

But from general proportions,

$$D = 2.5\, d = 2.5 \times 3.13 = 7.82 \text{ cm.}$$

(*iv*) **To calculate width of cotter.** Consider shearing failure of cotter, the cotter being in double shear.

$$A = \text{Area under double shear} = 2 \times b \times t$$

$$P = A \times f_s = 2 \times b \times t \times f_s$$

$$5000 = 2 \times b \times 0.95 \times 550$$

$$b = 4.78 \text{ cm.}$$

(*v*) **To determine distance, a.** Consider failure of enlarged end of rod by shear which may fail in double shear.

$$A = \text{Area under shear} = 2 \,.\, a \,.\, d_1$$

$$P = A \times f_s = 2 \,.\, a \,.\, d_1 \times f_s$$

$$5000 = 2 \times a \times 3.79 \times 550$$

$$a = 1.2 \text{ cm.}$$

(*vi*) **To calculate distance, 1.** Consider shear failure of sleeve end which may fail in double shear.

$A$ = Area under shear = $2 \,.\, l \,.\, (D - d_1)$

$P = A \times f_s = 2 \,.\, l \,.\, (D - d_1) \times f_s$

$5000 = 2 \,.\, l \,.\, (7.82 - 3.79) \times 550$

$l = 1.15$ cm.

(*vii*) **To check the sleeve or cotter for induced crushing stress.** Consider failure of sleeve or cotter by crushing.

$A$ = Area under crushing = $(D - d_1) \times t$

$P = (D - d_1) \times t \times f_{c_1}$

$5000 = (7.82 - 3.79) \times 0.95 \times f_{c_1}$

$f_{c_1} = 1305.6$ kg/cm$^2$.

Thus induced crushing stress $f_{c_1}$ less than allowable crushing stress 1400 kg/cm$^2$, hence safe.

(*viii*)**To check rod or cotter for induced crushing stress.** Consider crushing failure of rod or cotter by crushing.

$A$ = Area under crushing = $d_1 \times t$

$P = d_1 \times t \times f_{c_2}$

$5000 = 3.79 \times 0.95 \times f_{c_2}$

$f_{c_2} = 1388.8$ kg/cm$^2$.

which is less than 1400 kg/cm$^2$ hence safe.

(*ix*) **Other dimensions.** They are as follows :

$L_1$ = Length of cotter = $4d$

$= 4 \times 3.13 = 12.52$ cm

$L$ = Length of sleeve = $8d$

$= 8 \times 3.13 = 25.04$ cm

Taper of cotter = 1 : 25

Clearance = 3 mm.

## 4.4 Knuckle Joint

It is used to join rods in tension or compression (Fig. 4.10). The joint allows angular movement between the rods. This joint can be readily disconnected for adjustment or repairs. Knuckle joint consists of the following parts.

(*i*) Eye end rod (*ii*) Forked end rod

(*iii*) Pin (*iv*) Collor

(*v*) Taper pin

**Typical examples.** Where knuckle joint can be used are, valves and eccentric rods, tension links in bridge structure, tie rod joint for roof truss etc.

Let $P$ = Tensile force acting on the joint

$f_t$ = Tensile stress of the materials of different parts of the joint

$f_s$ = Shear stress

$f_c$ = Crushing stress

The various dimensions of the joint are calculated as follows :

(*i*) **To determine rod diameter, d.** Consider tensile failure of rod

$$A = \text{Area under tension} = \frac{\pi}{4} d^2$$

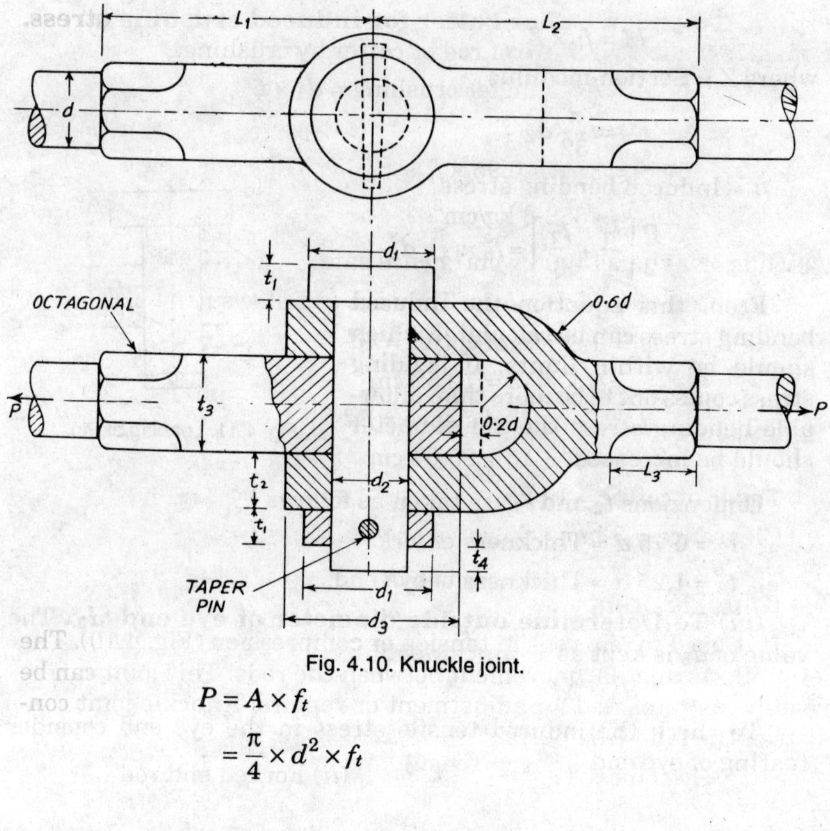


Fig. 4.10. Knuckle joint.

$$P = A \times f_t$$

$$= \frac{\pi}{4} \times d^2 \times f_t$$

The rod diameter $d$ can be calculated from this equation.

(*ii*) **To find pin diameter, $d_2$.** The pin is subjected to double shear

$$A = \text{Area under shear} = 2 \times \frac{\pi}{4} \times d_2^2$$

$$P = A \times f_s = 2 \times \frac{\pi}{4} d_2^2 \times f_s$$

The diameter $d_2$ can be found from this relation.

The pin can also fail under bending because of the clearance between pin and eye and fork ends.

Assuming the load to be uniformly distributed on the pin in the eye end and varying uniformly on the pin in the fork end, the maximum bending will take place at the mid section of the pin. Fig. 4.11 shows loading of pin.

$$M = \text{Maximum bending moment} = \frac{P}{2}\left[\frac{t_3}{4} + \frac{t_2}{3}\right]$$

$$M = f_b \times Z$$

where $Z$ = Section modulus

$$= \frac{\pi}{32} d_2^3$$

$f_b$ = Induced bending stress

$$= \frac{P}{2}\left[\frac{t_3}{4} + \frac{t_2}{3}\right] = f_b \times \frac{\pi}{32} d_2^3$$

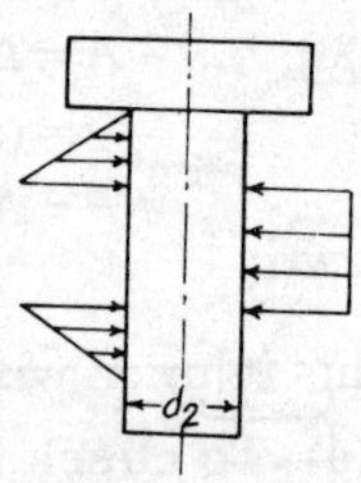

Fig. 4.11. Loading of Pin.

From this equation the induced bending stress can be calculated which should be within limits. If bending stress comes out to be more than allowable bending stress the pin diameter should be increased.

Dimensions $t_2$ and $t_3$ are taken as follows :

$t_2 = 0.75\ d$ = Thickness of fork

$t_2 = 1.25\ d$ = Thickness of eye end.

(*iii*) **To Determine outside diameter of eye end '$d_3$'.** The value of $d_3$ is kept as

$$d_3 = 2d$$

To check the induced tensile stress in the eye end consider tearing of eye end.

$$A = \text{Area under tearing} = (d_3 - d_2) \times t_3$$
$$P = A \times f_{t_1} = (d_3 - d_2) \times t_3 \times f_{t_1}$$

From this equation the induced tensile stress can be found. This stress should be less than allowable tensile stress. If the value of $f_{t_1}$ comes out to be more than allowable value of tensile stress than the diameter $d_3$ should be increased.

Similarly the induced tensile stress $f_{t_2}$ can be calculated for fork end by considering the tearing of fork end

$$A = \text{Area under tearing} = 2 \times (d_3 - d_2) \times t_2$$
$$P = 2 \times (d_3 - d_2) \times t_2 \times f_{t_2}$$

The relation will help us to check the induced tensile stress.

(*iv*) **To check the eye end and fork end against induced shearing stress.** Consider failure of eye end by shearing

$$A = \text{Area under shear} = (d_3 - d_2) \times t_3$$
$$P = A \times f_{s_1} = (d_3 - d_2) \times t_3 \times f_{s_1}$$

The induced shear stress $f_{s_1}$ can be found from this relation. This should be less than allowable shear stress.

Similarly to calculate the induced shear stress $f_{s_2}$ in fork end consider failure of fork end by shearing

$$A = \text{Area under shear}$$
$$= (d_3 - d_2) \times 2 \times t_2$$
$$P = A \times f_{s_2}$$
$$= (d_3 - d_2) \times 2 \times t_2 \times f_{s_2}$$

This relation will help us to find the induced shear stress $f_{s_2}$.

(*v*) **To check the eye end and fork end against induced crushing stress.** Consider crushing failure of eye end.

$$A = \text{Area under crushing} = d_2 \times t_3$$
$$P = d_2 \times t_3 \times f_{c_1}$$

The induced crushing stress $f_{c_1}$ in eye end can be calculated from this relation. This stress should be less than the allowable crushing stress.

Similarly the induced crushing stress $f_{c_2}$ in fork end can be found by considering crushing of fork end

$$A = \text{Area under crushing} = 2 \times t_2 \times d_2$$
$$P = A \times f_{c_2} = 2 \times t_2 \times d_2 \times f_{c_2}$$

The induced crushing stress $f_{c_2}$ in the fork end can be calculated from this equation. This stress $f_{c_2}$ should be less than given value of crushing stress.

(*vi*) **Other dimensions are calculated as follows :**

$t_1$ = Thickness of collor or thickness of pin head

$= 0.5\ d$

$L_1 = 4d$

$L_2 = 4.5\ d$

$t_4 = \dfrac{d}{8}$

$d_1$ = Diameter of pin head or diameter of collor

$= 1.5\ d$

$L_3 = 1.2\ d$

Diameter of taper pin = 0.2 *d*.

**Example 4.3.** *Design a knuckle joint to connect two mild steel rods. The joint is subjected to a tensile load of 14000 kg. Assume the working stress for both the pin and rod material as follows :*

$f_t = 800\ kg/cm^2$

$f_s = 650\ kg/cm^2$

$f_c = 1200\ kg/cm^2$

**Solution.** Knuckle joint is shown in Fig. 4.10.

$P$ = Tensile load = 14,000 kg

(*i*) **To determine rod diameter, d.** Consider tensile failure of rod.

$A$ = Area under tensile failure $= \dfrac{\pi}{4} d^2$

$$P = A \times f_t = \frac{\pi}{4} d^2 \times f_t$$

$$14{,}000 = \frac{\pi}{4} d^2 \times 800$$

$d = 4.7$ cm.

(*ii*) **To calculate pin diameter, d₂.** The bending stress in the pin is given by

$$f_b = \frac{\frac{P}{2}\left[\frac{t_3}{4} + \frac{t_2}{3}\right]}{\frac{\pi}{32} d_2^3}$$

where $f_b$ = Bending stress = 800 kg/cm$^2$

$t_2$ = Thickness of fork

= 0.75 $d$ = 0.75 × 4.7 = 3.52 cm.

$t_3$ = Thickness of eye end

= 1.25 $d$ = 1.25 × 4.7 = 5.87

$$800 = \frac{\frac{14000}{2}\left[\frac{5.87}{4} + \frac{3.52}{3}\right]}{\frac{\pi}{32} d_2^3}$$

$d_2$ = 6.1 cm.

To check the pin against shearing, consider the shearing of pin. The pin is in double shear.

$A$ = Area under shear = $2 \times \frac{\pi}{4} d_2^2$

$P = A \times f_s$

$$14{,}000 = 2 \times \frac{\pi}{4} d_2^2 \times f_{s_1}$$

$$14{,}000 = 2 \times \frac{\pi}{4} (6.1)^2 \times f_{s_1}$$

$f_{s_1}$ = 239.72 kg/cm$^2$.

Therefore the induced shear stress $f_{s_1}$ is less than allowable shear stress of 650 kg/cm$^2$. This shows that pin is safe against shearing.

(*iii*) **To determine the outside diameter of eye end, $d_3$.**

The value of $d_3$ is kept as follows :

$d_3 = 2d$ = 2 × 4.7 = 9.4 cm.

To check the induced tensile stress $f_{t_1}$ in the eye end consider tearing of eye end.

$A$ = Area under tearing = $(d_3 - d_2) \, . \, t_3$

= (9.4 – 6.1) × $t_3$

$P = A \times f_{t_1}$

$$14,000 = (9.4 - 6.1) \times 5.87 \times f_{t_1}$$

$$f_{t_1} = 622.76 \text{ kg/cm}^2$$

This is less than the allowable tensile stress 800 kg/cm$^2$, thus eye end is safe against tearing.

Similarly to find induced tensile stress $f_{t_2}$ can be found in fork end by considering tearing of fork end.

$$A = \text{Area under tearing} = 2t_2 \, (d_3 - d_2)$$

$$P = A \times f_{t_2} = 2t_2 \, (d_3 - d_2) \, ft_2$$

$$14,000 = 2 \times 3.52 \, (9.4 - 6.1) \times f_{t_2}$$

$$f_{t_2} = 602 \text{ kg/cm}^2$$

which is less than 800 kg/cm$^2$, hence safe.

(*iv*) **To check the eye end and fork and against induced shearing stress.** Consider failure of eye end by shearing

$$A = \text{Area under shear} = (d_3 - d_2) \, . \, t_3$$

$$P = A \times f_{s_1} = (d_3 - d_2) \, . \, t_3 \times f_{s1}$$

$$14,000 = (9.4 - 6.1) \times 5.87 \times f_{s_1}$$

$$f_{s_1} = 622.76 \text{ kg/cm}^2$$

Thus the induced stress $f_{s_1}$ in eye end is less than allowable shear stress 650 kg/cm$^2$, hence safe.

To find induced shear stress $f_{s_2}$ in fork end consider failure of fork end by shearing

$$A = \text{Area under shear} = 2 \, (d_3 - d_2) \, . \, t_2$$

$$P = A \times f_{s_2} = 2 \times (d_3 - d_2) \times t_2 \times f_{s_2}$$

$$14,000 = 2 \times (9.4 - 6.1) \times 3.52 \times f_{s2}$$

$$f_{s2} = 602 \text{ kg/cm}^2$$

which is less than 650 kg/cm$^2$, hence safe.

(*v*) **To check the eye end and fork end against induced crushing stress.** Consider crushing failure of eye end

$$A = \text{Area under crushing} = d_2 \times t_3$$

$$P = A \times f_{c_1} = d_2 \times t_3 \times f_{c_1}$$

$$14,000 = 6.1 \times 5.87 \times f_{c_1}$$

$$f_{c_1} = 391.1 \text{ kg/cm}^2$$

Thus the induced crushing stress $f_{c_1}$ in eye end is less than allowable crushing stress 1200 kg/cm$^2$, hence safe.

To find induced crushing stress $f_{c_2}$ in fork end consider crushing failure of fork end

$$A = \text{Area under crushing} = 2 \times t_2 \times d_2$$

$$P = A \times f_{c_2} = 2 \times t_2 \times d_2 \times f_{c_2}$$

$$14{,}000 = 2 \times 3.52 \times 6.1 \times f_{c_2}$$

$$f_{c_2} = 326.1 \text{ kg/cm}^2$$

This is less than 1200 kg/cm$^2$ hence safe.

(*vi*) **Other dimensions.** They are as follows :

$$L_1 = 4d = 4 \times 4.7 = 18.8 \text{ cm.}$$

$$L_2 = 4.5d = 4.5 \times 4.7 = 21.15 \text{ cm.}$$

$$L_3 = 1.2d = 1.2 \times 4.7 = 5.64 \text{ cm.}$$

$$t_1 = 0.5\,d = 0.5 \times 4.7 = 2.35 \text{ cm.}$$

$$d_1 = 1.5\,d = 1.5 \times 4.7 = 7.05 \text{ cm.}$$

$$t_4 = \frac{d}{8} = \frac{4.7}{8} = 0.59 \text{ cm.}$$

Diameter of taper pin

$$= 0.2\,d = 0.2 \times 4.7 = 0.94 \text{ cm.}$$

## 4.5 Gib and Cotter

A gib is used along with a cotter in gib and cotter joints to achieve the following purposes.

(*i*) Gib helps to use parallel holes.

(*ii*) It increases the bearing area of contact between the mating surfaces.

(*iii*) The friction between cotter and the outer cover (strap) causes the strap to open out as shown by dotted lines in Fig 4.12. This is prevented by the use of gib (Fig. 4.13).

When one gib is used the cotter is provided with taper only on one side and when two gibs are used cotter is tapered on both sides (Fig. 4.14). The gib and cotter are parallel along their outside edges and taper on their inside edges.

Cotter with gib Cotter with one gib Cotter with two gibs

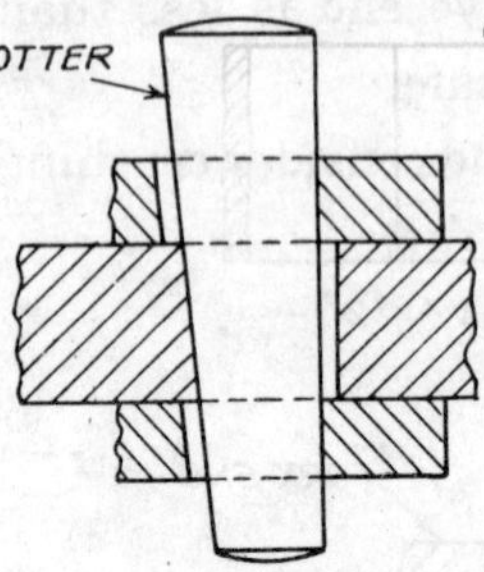

Cotter with gib
Fig. 4.12.

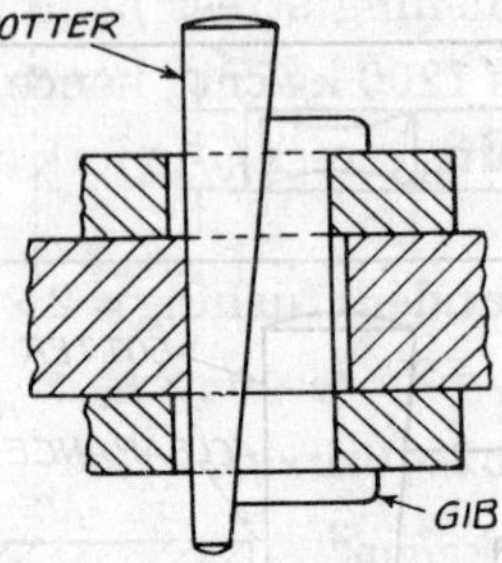

Cotter with one gib
Fig. 4.13.

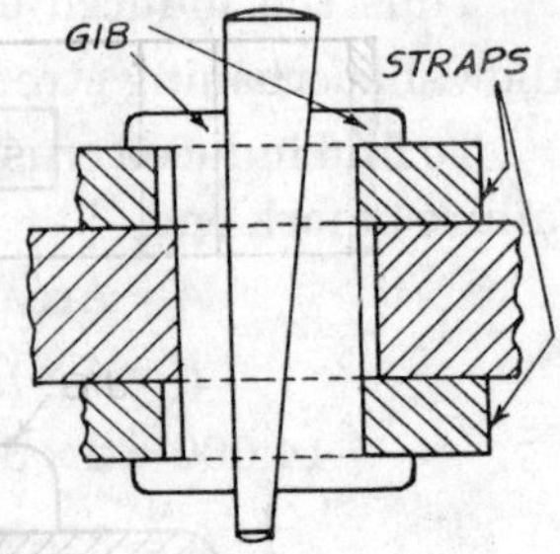

Cotter with two gibs
Fig. 4.14.

## 4.6 Gib and Cotter Joint

This joint (Fig. 4.15) is mostly used for square rod ends. One of the ends is formed into the shape of a fork. A rectangular hole is made in both the rod ends to accommodate gib and cotter. Gib is provided to increase the bearing area of contact between the mating surfaces. Secondly when the cotter without gib is driven in position it tends to bend the lower part of socket end away from the rod and this is prevented by using a gib.

**Example 4.4.** *Design a gib and cotter joint for square rods. The joint is to resist a tensile load of 6000 kg. Rods, gib and cotter are made up of same material.*

*Take* $f_t = 260\ kg/cm^2$,

$f_s = 210\ kg/cm^2$,

*and* $f_c = 620\ kg/cm^2$.

**Solution.**

Let $s$ = Each side of square section rod

$b$ = Width of strap

$B$ = Total width of gib and cotter

$t$ = Thickness of cotter = Thickness of gib

$t_1$ = Thickness of strap

$P$ = Tensile load = 6000 kg.

(*i*) **To find, s.** Consider tensile failure of rod.

$A$ = Area under tension = $s^2$

$P = A \times f_t$

$6000 = s^2 \times 260$

$s$ = 4.8 cm.

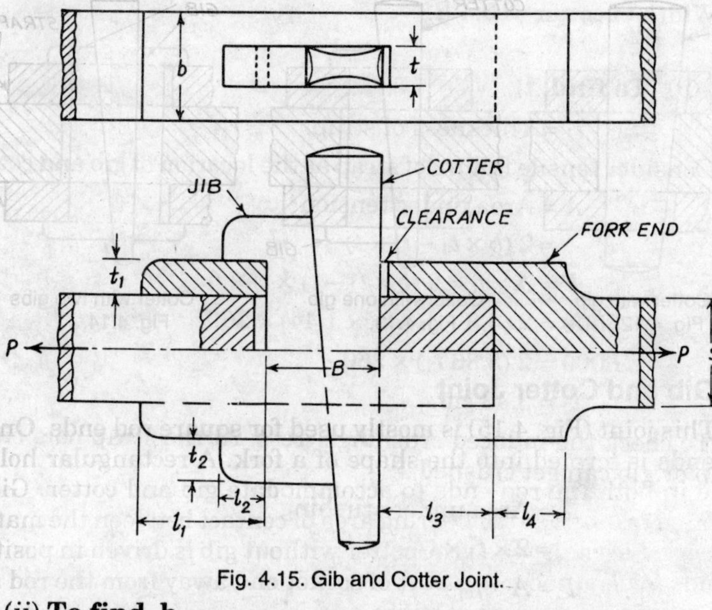


Fig. 4.15. Gib and Cotter Joint.

(*ii*) **To find, b.**

$b$ = Width of strap

The width of strap is generally taken equal to $s$.

$b = s = 4.8$ cm.

(*iii*) **To find, t.**

$t = 0.3 \times b = 0.3 \times 4.8 = 1.44$ cm.

(*iv*) **To find, B.**

Consider shearing failure of gib and cotter.

$A$ = Area under double shear $= 2 \, . \, B \, . \, t$

$P = A \times f_s$

$P = 2 \times B \times t \times f_s$

$6000 = 2 \times B \times 1.44 \times 210$

$B = 9.92$ cm.

Single gib is used to make the joint.

Width of gib $= 0.55\,B = 0.55 \times 9.92 = 5.45$ cm.

Width of cotter $= 0.45\,B\,B = 0.45 \times 9.92 = 4.47$

In case two gibs are used with the cotter.

Width of each gib $= 0.3\,B$

Width of cotter $= 0.4\,B$.

(*v*) **To find, $t_1$.**

$t_1$ = Thickness of strap.

Consider tensile failure of strap at the location of gib and cotter.

$$A = \text{Area under tension}$$
$$= 2\,(b \times t_1 - t_1 \times t)$$
$$P = A \times f_t = 2\,(b \times t_1 - t_1 \times t) \times f_t$$
$$6000 = 2\,(4.8 \times t_1 - t_1 \times 1.44) \times 260$$
$$6000 = 2\,(3.36\,t_1) \times 260$$
$$t_1 = 3.43 \text{ cm.}$$

To check the induced crushing stress. At the strap hole either strap or gib can get crushed.

$$A = \text{Area under crushing}$$
$$= 2 \times t_1 \times t$$
$$P = A \times f_{c_1}$$
$$f_{c_1} = \frac{P}{A} = \frac{6000}{2 \times 3.43 \times 1.44}$$
$$= 607.4 \text{ kg/cm}^2.$$

Therefore induced crushing stress $f_{c_1}$ is less than allowable crushing stress 620 kg/cm$^2$, hence safe.

(*vi*) **To find, $l_3$.**

$l_3$ = Length of rod end.

Consider shearing of rod end.

$$A = \text{Area under shear} = 2\,.\,l_3\,.\,s$$
$$P = A \times f_s = 2 \times l_3 \times s \times f_s$$
$$6000 = 2 \times l_3 \times 4.8 \times 210$$
$$l_3 = 2.98 \text{ cm.}$$

(*vii*) **To find, $l_1$.**

$l_1$ = Length of rod end.

Consider shearing of strap.

$$A = \text{Area under shear} = 2\,(2 \times l_1 \times t_1)$$
$$P = A \times f_s$$
$$P = 2 \times 2 \times l_1 \times t_1 \times f_s$$
$$6000 = 4l_1 \times 3.43 \times 210$$

$l_1 = 2.1$ cm.

Other dimensions are taken as follows :

$l_2 = t = 1.44$ cm

$t_2 = 1.3 \times t = 1.3 \times 1.44 = 1.87$ cm

$l_4 = \frac{2}{3} \times s = \frac{2}{3} \times 4.8 = 3.2$ cm.

Clearance = 3 mm

$L$ = Length of cotter

$= 4 \times s = 4 \times 4.8 = 19.2$ cm.

Taper on gib and cotter

= 1 : 25.

## 4.7 Gib and Cotter Joint for Strap end of a Connecting Rod

Fig. 4.16 shows a gib and cotter joint for strap end of a connecting rod.

Let $P$ = Maximum tensile load

$b$ = Width of strap

$t_1$ = Thickness of strap at thinnest part

$t$ = Thickness of cotter

$L$ = Combined width of cotter and gib

The various dimensions are calculated as follows :

(*i*) **To determine $t_1$.**

Consider tearing of strap

$A$ = Area under tearing = $2b \times t_1$

$P = A \times f_t$

where $f_t$ = Safe tensile stress

= 420 kg/cm$^2$ for wrought iron

= 490 kg/cm$^2$ for steel.

$P = 2\, b\, t_1 \times f t_1$

From this equation the value of $t_1$ can be found.

(*ii*) **To determine, L.**

Consider double shear failure of cotter and gib

$A$ = Area under shear = $2 \,.\, L \,.\, t$

where $t$ = Thickness of cotter

$$= \frac{b}{4}$$

$$P = A \times f_s$$

$$P = 2 \,.\, L \,.\, t \times f_s$$

where $\quad f_s$ = Safe shear stress.

The value of length $L$ can be found from this equation.

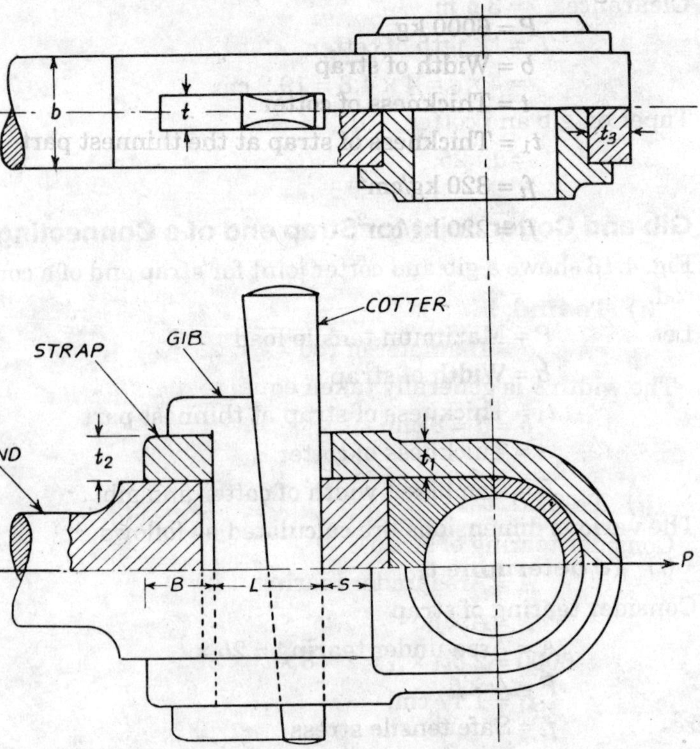


Fig. 4.16.

(*iii*) **Other dimensions are assumed as follows :**

$$t_2 = 1.2\ t_1 \text{ to } 1.5\ t_1$$

$$t_3 = 1.17\ t_1 \text{ to } 1.5\ t_1$$

$$S = 2t_1$$

$$B = 2.5\ t_1$$

Width of cotter $= 0.45\ L$

Width of gib $= 0.55\ L$.

**Example 4.5.** *Design a gib cotter joint for the strap end of a connecting rod subjected to a pull of 6000 kg. The diameter of the circular part of the rod adjacent to the strap end is 8 cm. Safe tensile stress in the material of strap is 320 kg/cm² and safe shear stress in cotter and gib is 220 kg/cm².*

**Solution.**

Fig. 4.16 shows gib and cotter joint for the strap end of a connecting rod.

$P = 6000$ kg.

$b$ = Width of strap

$t$ = Thickness of cotter

$t_1$ = Thickness of strap at the thinnest part

$f_t = 320$ kg/cm$^2$

$f_s = 220$ kg/cm$^2$.

(*i*) **To find, b.**

$d$ = Diameter of rod = 8 cm.

The width $b$ is generally taken equal to $d$.

$b = d = 8$ cm.

(*ii*) **To find, $t_1$.**

Consider tearing of strap

$A$ = Area under tearing = $2\ b\ t_1$

$P = A \times f_t$

$6000 = 2\ bt_1 \times f_t = 2 \times 8 \times t_1 \times 320$

$t_1 = 1.17$ cm.

(*iii*) **To calculate, L.**

$L$ = Combined width of cotter and gib

$t$ = Thickness of cotter

$= \frac{b}{4} = \frac{8}{4} = 2$ cm.

Consider double shear failure of cotter and gib.

$A$ = Area under double shear = $2\ .\ L\ .\ t$

$P = A \times f_s = 2\ Lt \times f_s$

$$6000 = 2 \,.\, L \,.\, 2 \times 220$$
$$L = 6.82 \text{ cm.}$$

Width of cotter $= 0.45\, L$

$$= 0.45 \times 6.82 = 3.1 \text{ cm}$$

Width of gib $= L - 3.1$ cm

$$= 6.82 - 3.1 = 3.72 \text{ cm.}$$

*(iv)* **To determine, $t_2$.**

$$t_2 = 1.5\, t_1 = 1.5 \times 1.17 = 1.75 \text{ cm.}$$

*(v)* **To determine, $t_3$.**

$t_3$ = Thickness of strap across the cotter hole

$$A_1 = A_2$$

where $A_1$ = Area of thinnest part of the strap

$A_2$ = Area of cross section of the strap at the cotter hole

$$A_1 = 2\, t_1 \times b$$
$$A_2 = 2 \,.\, t_3\, (b - t)$$
$$2t_1 \,.\, b = 2\, t_3\, (b - t)$$
$$2 \times 1.17 \times 8 = 2 \times t_3\, (8 - 2)$$
$$t_3 = 1.56 \text{ cm.}$$

Other dimensions are as follows :

$$S = 2t_1 = 2 \times 1.17 = 2.34 \text{ cm}$$
$$B = 2.5 \times t_1 = 2.5 \times 1.17 = 2.92 \text{ cm.}$$

**Example 4.6.** *Design a cotter for connecting piston rod to the cross head of the engine having cylinder diameter 20 cm and steam pressure of 8 kg/cm². Assume that all parts are made up of same material for which allowable stresses are as follows :*

$$f_t = 550 \text{ kg/cm}^2$$
$$f_s = 450 \text{ kg/cm}^2$$
$$f_c = 850 \text{ kg/cm}^2.$$

**Solution.** Fig. 4.17 shows the cotter joint for connecting piston rod with cross head.

Let $d$ = Diameter of piston rod at the cotter

$d_1$ = Diameter of piston rod at the back end

$d_2$ = Diameter of parallel part of piston rod

$d_3$ = Diameter of socket at cotter hole

$b$ = Width of cotter

$t$ = Thickness of cotter

$D$ = Diameter of cylinder = 20 cm

$p$ = Steam pressure

$= 8 \text{ kg/cm}^2$

$P$ = Maximum load on piston

$$= \frac{\pi}{4} D^2 \times p = \frac{\pi}{4} \times 20^2 \times 8 = 2512 \text{ kg.}$$

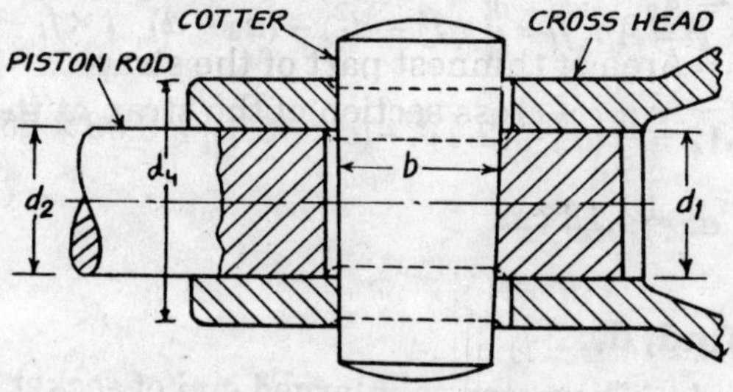


Fig. 4.17.

(*i*) **To find, d.**

Consider tensile failure of piston rod at cotter

$$A = \text{Area under tension} = \frac{\pi}{4} d^2 - d \times t$$

$$P = A \times f_t$$

$$= \left( \frac{\pi}{4} d^2 - d \times t \right) \times f_t$$

Assume $t = 0.3\, d$

$$2512 = \left( \frac{\pi}{4} d^2 - d \times 0.3\, d \right) \times 550$$

$$d = 3.1 \text{ cm.}$$

$$t = 0.3d = 0.3 \times 3.1 = 0.93 \text{ cm.}$$

(*ii*) **To find width of cotter, b.**

Consider double shear failure of cotter

$A$ = Area under shear = $2 \, . \, b \, . \, t$

$$P = A \times f_s$$

$$P = 2\,bt \times f_s$$

$$2512 = 2 \, . \, b \times 0.93 \times 450$$

$$b = 3 \text{ cm.}$$

**(*iii*) To find, d₃.**

Consider tensile failure of socket at cotter hole

$A$ = Area under tearing

$$= \frac{\pi}{4}(d_3^2 - d^2) - (d_2 - d) \, . \, t$$

$$P = A \times f_t = \frac{\pi}{4}(d_3^2 - d^2) - (d_3 - d) \, . \, t \times f_t$$

$$2512 = \frac{\pi}{4}\left\{d_3^2 - (3.1)^2 - (d_3 - 3.1)\right\} \times 0.93 \times 550$$

$$d_3 = 4.13 \text{ cm.}$$

**(*iv*) To find, $d_4$**

$d_4$ = Diameter of enlarged end of socket

Consider crushing of socket

$A$ = Area under crushing

$$= (d_4 - d) \, . \, t.$$

$$P = A \times f_c$$

$$2512 = (d_4 - d) \times t \times f_c$$

$$= (d_4 - 3 \, . \, 1) \times 0.93 \times 850$$

$$d_4 = 6.22 \text{ cm.}$$

**(*v*) To find, $d_1$**

Let the taper on piston rod, 1 : 20.

$L$ = Tapered length of piston rod

$= 2.2 \times d$ (assume) $= 2.2 \times 3.1 = 9.82$ cm.

$$d_1 = d - \frac{1}{20} \times \frac{6.82}{2}$$

$$= 3.1 - \frac{6.82}{40} = 2.93 \text{ cm.}$$

(*vi*) **To find, $d_2$**

$$d_2 = d + \frac{1}{20} \times \frac{6.82}{2}$$

$$= 3.1 + \frac{1}{20} \times \frac{6.82}{2} = 3.27 \text{ cm.}$$

## 4.8 Suspension Link

Suspension links are used in suspension bridges. Fig. 4.18 shows a suspension link. The load, $P$ acting on the link is shared by the side links.

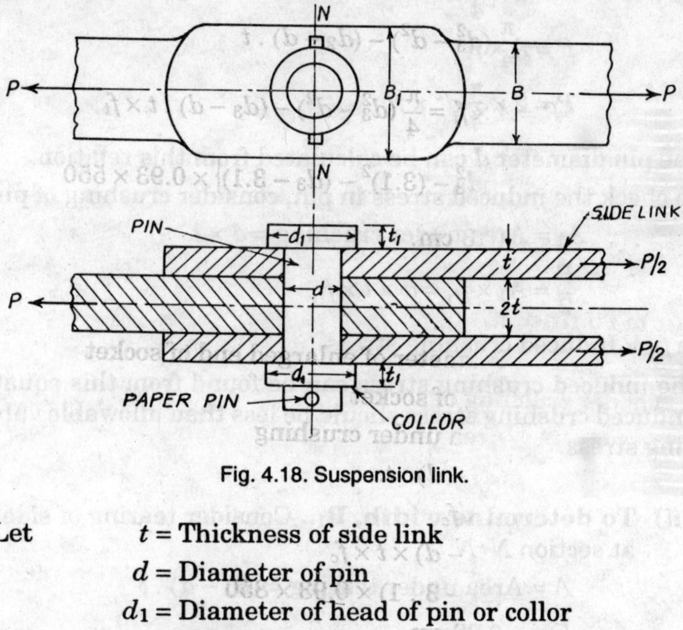


Fig. 4.18. Suspension link.

Let $t$ = Thickness of side link

$d$ = Diameter of pin

$d_1$ = Diameter of head of pin or collor

$t_1$ = Thickness of head of pin or collor

$B$ = Width of side link

$B_1$ = Width of enlarged end of link

$f_t$ = Tensile stress

$f_s$ = Shear stress

$f_c$ = Crushing stress.

(*i*) **To determine width, B.** Consider tensile failure of the side link

$$A = \text{Area under tensile failure}$$
$$= B \times t$$
$$\frac{P}{2} = A \times f_t = B \times t \times f_t.$$

The width $B$ can be calculated from this relation.

(*ii*) **To find pin diameter, d.** The pin is in double shear

$$A = \text{Area under double shear}$$
$$= 2 \times \frac{\pi}{4} d^2$$
$$P = A \times f_s$$
$$P = 2 \times \frac{\pi}{4} d^2 \times f_s.$$

The pin diameter $d$ can be calculated from this relation.

To check the induced stress in pin, consider crushing of pin

$$A_1 = \text{Area under crushing} = d \times t$$
$$\frac{P}{2} = A_1 \times f_{t_1} = d \times t \times f_{t_1}$$

where $f_{t_1}$ = Induced crushing stress.

The induced crushing stress can be found from this equation. This induced crushing stress should be less than allowable value of crushing stress.

(*iii*) **To determine width, B₁.** Consider tearing of side link at section $N$–$N$

$$A = \text{Area under tearing} = (B_1 - d) \cdot t$$
$$\frac{P}{2} = A \times f_t$$
$$\frac{P}{2} = (B_1 - d) \cdot t \cdot f_t$$

The width $B_1$ can be found from this equation. The minimum value of $B_1$ is given by

$$B_1 = B + d$$

other dimensions are as follows.

$$t_1 = 0.3d$$
$$d_1 = 1.5d$$

$\therefore$ Diameter of taper pin $= 0.2d$.

**Example 4.7.** *Design a suspension link for a steel structure subjected to a load of 10 tonnes. The thickness of each side link is 1.2 cm. The safe stresses in tension, shear and crushing are 900 kg/cm², 600 kg/cm² and 1400 kg/cm² respectively.*

**Solution.**

Suspension link is shown in Fig 4.18.

$$P = 10{,}000 \text{ kg}$$

(*i*) **To find width, B.** Consider tensile failure of side link

$$\frac{P}{2} = B \times t \times f_t$$

$$\frac{10000}{2} = B \times 1.2 \times 900$$

$$B = 4.61 \text{ cm.}$$

(*ii*) **To find pin diameter, d.** Consider shear failure of pin, the pin being in double shear

$$P = 2 \times \frac{\pi}{4} d^2 \times f_s$$

$$10{,}000 = 2 \times \frac{\pi}{4} d^2 \times 600$$

$$d = 3.2 \text{ cm.}$$

To check the pin against induced crushing stress $f_{c_1}$ consider crushing of pin.

$$A_1 = \text{Area under crushing}$$

$$= d \times t$$

$$\frac{P}{2} = d \times t \times f_{c_1}$$

$$5000 = 3.2 \times 1.2 \times f_{c_1}$$

$$f_{c_1} = 1302 \text{ kg/cm}^2$$

which is within safe limits of 1400 kg/cm².

(*iii*) **To determine width, B₁.** Consider tearing of side link at section *N-N*

$$\frac{P}{2} = (B_1 - t) \,.\, t \,.\, f_t.$$

$$5000 = (B_1 - 1.2) \times 1.2 \times 900.$$

$B_1 = 7.81$ cm.

The width $B_1$ should not be less than

$$B + d = 4.61 + 3.2 = 7.81$$

which is same as calculated.

Other dimensions are as follows :

$d_1$ = Diameter of head of pin or diameter of collor

$= 1.5 \times d = 1.5 \times 3.2 = 4.8$ cm.

$t_1$ = Thickness of head of pin or thickness of collor

$= 0.3\ d = 0.3 \times 3.2 = 0.96$ cm.

Diameter of taper pin

$= 0.2\ d = 0.3 \times 3.2 = 0.64$ cm.

## 4.9 Coupler or Turn Buckle

It is used to connect two rods which are subjected to tensile loading. The ends of roads are threaded, one rod having right hand threads and the other having left hand threads. When the coupler is given one revolution the ends of the rods either approach or recede from each other (Fig. 4.19). The various dimensions of coupler are as calculated as follows :

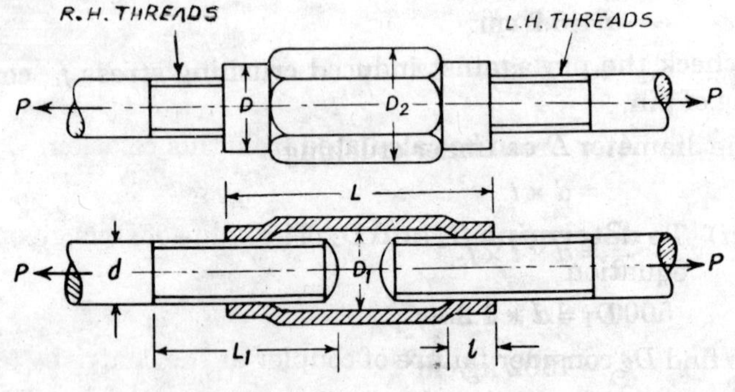


Fig. 4.19. Coupler.

Let $d$ = Diameter of rod

$d_c$ = Core diameter of rod

$D$ = Outside diameter of coupler at the ends

$D_1$ = Inside diameter of coupler at the centre

$D_2$ = Outside diameter of the coupler at the centre

$L$ = Total length of coupler

$l$ = Length of screwed portion of coupler

$L_1$ = Length of threaded portion in each rod

$f_t$ = Permissible tensile stress

$f_s$ = permissible shear stress in the nut

(*i*) **To determine, *d*.** Consider failure of rod by tearing

$$A = \text{Area under tensile failure} = \frac{\pi}{4} d_c^2$$

$$P = A \times f_t$$

$$= \frac{\pi}{4} d_c^2 \times f_t$$

From this equation $d_1$ (core diameter) can be obtained.

$$d = \frac{d_c}{0.84}$$

(*ii*) **To determine *D*.** Consider failure of coupler at the ends by tearing

$$A = \text{Area under tearing}$$

$$= \frac{\pi}{4} (D^2 - d^2)$$

$$P = A \times f_t.$$

$$= \frac{\pi}{4} (D^2 - d^2) \times f_t$$

The diameter $D$ can be calculated from this relation.

(*iii*) **To determine $D_1$ and $D_2$.** The value of $D_1$ is given by the equation

$$D_1 = d + 6 \text{ mm}$$

To find $D_2$ consider failure of coupler at the centre by tearing

$$A = \text{Area under tearing failure}$$

$$= \frac{\pi}{4} (D_2^2 - D_1^2)$$

$$P = A \times f_s.$$

$$= \frac{\pi}{4} (D_2^2 - D_1^2) \times f_t$$

From this equation the value of $D_2$ can be found.

(*iv*) **To determine the length *l*.** Consider failure of threads in the coupler by shearing.

$$A = \text{Area under shear} = \pi\, dl$$

$$P = A \times f_s$$

$$P = \pi\, dl \times f_s$$

The length $l$ can be found from this equation.

In general practice the value of length $l$ is kept as follows :

$$l = 1.25\, d \text{ for steel couplers}$$

$$= 1.5\, d \text{ to } 2d \text{ for cast iron couplers.}$$

(*v*) **Other dimensions are assumed as follows :**

$$L = 6d$$

$$L_1 = \frac{L}{2}.$$

**Example 4.8.** *Design a steel coupler to connect two round tie rods of a wall crane to resist a pull of 6000 kg. The permissible stresses in the material of coupler are 750 kg/cm$^2$ and 400 kg/cm$^2$ in tension and shear respectively.*

**Solution.**

Coupler is shown in Fig. 4.19.

$$P = \text{Tensile force} = 6000 \text{ kg.}$$

(*i*) **To determine diameter (*d*) of rod.** Consider tensile failure of rod.

$$P = \frac{\pi}{4} d_o^2 = f_t$$

$$6000 = \frac{\pi}{4} d_c^2 \times 750$$

$$d_c = 3.2 \text{ cm.}$$

$$d = \frac{d_c}{0.84} \times 3.8 \text{ cm}$$

(*ii*) **To Determine *D*.** Consider failure of coupler at the ends by tearing

$$A = \text{Area under tearing}$$

$$= \frac{\pi}{4}(D^2 - d^2)$$

$$P = A \times f_t$$

$$6000 = \frac{\pi}{4}(D^2 - 3.8^2) = 750$$

$$D = 4.96 \text{ cm.}$$

(*iii*) **To determine $D_1$ and $D_2$.** The value of $D_1$ is given by the equation

$$D_1 = d + 6 \text{ mm} = 3.8 + 0.6 = 4.4 \text{ cm.}$$

To find $D_2$ consider the failure of coupler at the centre by tearing

$$P = \frac{\pi}{4}(D_2^2 - D_1^2) \times f_t$$

$$6000 = \frac{\pi}{4}[D_2^2 - (4.4)^2] \times 750$$

$$D_2 = 5.44 \text{ cm.}$$

(*iv*) **To determine the length, *l*.** Consider the failure of threads in the coupler by shearing

$$A = \text{Area under shear} = \pi\, dl$$

$$P = A \times f_s$$

$$6000 = \pi\, dl \times 400$$

$$6000 = \pi \times 3.8 \times l \times 400$$

$$l = 1.26 \text{ cm.}$$

In general practice the length $l$ is not kept less than 1.25 $d$.

$$\therefore \quad l = 1.25 \times 3.8 = 4.75 \text{ cm.}$$

Therefore we keep the length $l$ as 4.75 cm.

(*v*) **Other dimensions are assumed as follows :**

$$L = 6\,d = 6 \times 3.8 = 22.8 \text{ cm.}$$

$$L_1 = \frac{L}{2}$$

$$= \frac{22.8}{2} = 11.4 \text{ cm.}$$

**Example 4.9.** *A tube of outside diameter 4 cm is connected to the fork end by a pin and subjected to a tensile load of 1000 kg. (Fig. 4.20). Assuming the allowable stresses for pin, tube and fork as 600 kg/cm², 800 kg/cm² and 1050 kg/cm² in shear, tension and crushing respectively determine the following :*

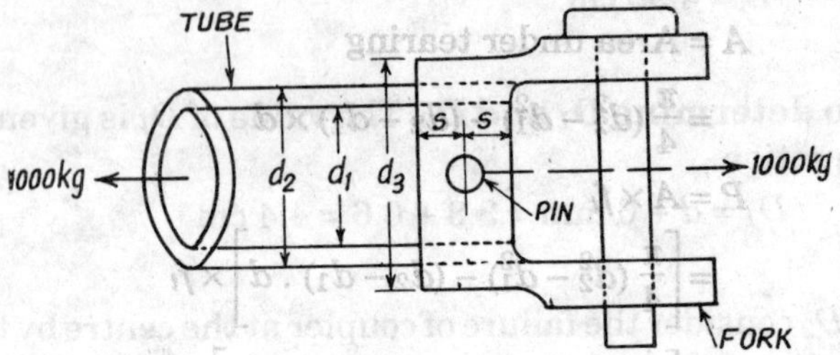


Fig. 4.20.

(*a*) *Diameter of pin* (*b*) *Thickness of tube*

(c) *Minimum thickness of fork* (*d*) *The length s.*

**Solution.**

Let,
$d_1$ = Inside diameter of tube
$P$ = Tensile load = 1000 kg.
$d$ = Pin diameter.

(*i*) **To determine pin diameter, *d*.** The pin is under double shear.

$$A = \text{Area under shear}$$
$$= 2 \times \frac{\pi}{4} d^2$$
$$P = A \times f_s$$
$$= 2 \times \frac{\pi}{4} d^2 \times f_s$$
$$1000 = 2 \times \frac{\pi}{4} d^2 \times 600$$
$$d = 1.1 \text{ cm.}$$

(*ii*) **To determine inside diameter $d_1$ of tube.** Consider crushing of pin in the tube.

$$A = \text{Area under crushing}$$
$$= (d_2 - d_1) \times d$$

$$P = A \times f_c$$
$$1000 = (d_2 - d_1) \times d \times 1050$$
$$1000 = (4 - d_1) \times 1.1 \times 1050$$
$$d_1 = 3.13 \text{ cm.}$$

The diameter $d_1$ can also be found by considering tearing of tube at the pin section.

$$A = \text{Area under tearing}$$
$$= \frac{\pi}{4}(d_2^2 - d_1^2) - (d_2 - d_1) \times d$$
$$P = A \times f_t$$
$$= \left[\frac{\pi}{4}(d_2^2 - d_1^2) - (d_2 - d_1) \, . \, d\right] \times f_t$$
$$1000 = \left[\frac{\pi}{4}(4^2 - d_1^2) - (4 - d_1) \times 1.1\right] \times 800$$
$$d_1 = 3.03 \text{ cm.}$$

Hence take $d_1 = 3.13$ cm.

So that the pin is safe in crushing.

$$\text{Thickness of tube} = \frac{d_2 - d_1}{2} = \frac{4 - 3.13}{2} = 0.43 \text{ cm.}$$

(*iii*) **To find minimum thickness of fork.**

Let $d_3$ = Outer diameter of fork.

Considering of crushing of pin in the fork.

$$A = \text{Area under crushing}$$
$$= (d_3 - d_2) \times d$$
$$P = A \times f_c$$
$$= (d_3 - d_2) \times d \times f_c$$
$$1000 = (d_3 - 4) \times 1.1 \times 1050$$
$$d_3 = 4.87 \text{ cm.}$$

$$\text{Thickness of fork} = \frac{d_3 - d_2}{2} = \frac{4.87 - 4}{2} = 0.435 \text{ cm.}$$

(*iv*) **To find length *s*.** Considering shearing of tube which is in double shear.

$$A = \text{Area under shear}$$
$$= 2 \times (d_2 - d_1) \times s$$

$$P = A \times f_s$$
$$= 2\,(d_2 - d_1) \times s \times f_s$$
$$1000 = 2\,(4 - 3.13) \times s \times 600$$
$$s = 0.96 \text{ cm.}$$

**Example 4.10.** *A cotter foundation bolt with a circular end is to be designed to take up a load of 8000 kg, calculate the following :*

(*a*) *Diameter of bolt*

(*b*) *Diameter of enlarged end of bolt*

(*c*) *Thickness of cotter*

(*d*) *Width of cotter.*

*Take* $f_t = 650$ *kg/cm*$^2$,

$f_s = 550$ *kg/cm*$^2$,

$f_c = 1050$ *kg/cm*$^2$.

**Solution.**

Fig. 4.21 shows a cotter foundation bolt with a circular end.

Let $d$ = Diameter of bolt

$d_1$ = Diameter of enlarged end of bolt

$t$ = Thickness of cotter

$b$ = Width of cotter

$P$ = Tensile load = 11000 kg.

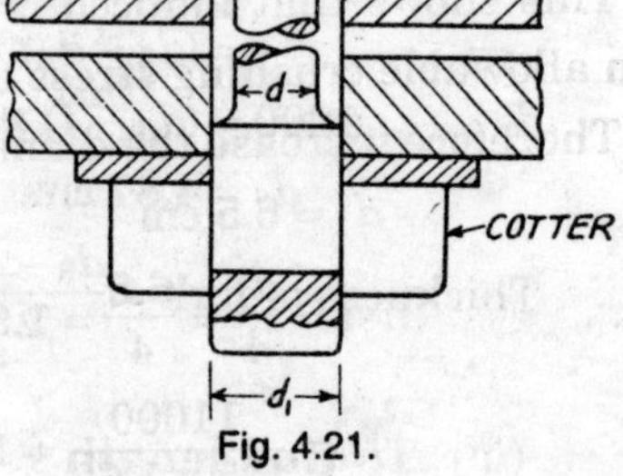

Fig. 4.21.

(*i*) **To determine diameter of bolt, *d*.** Consider tensile failure of bolt.

$A$ = Area under tension

$$= \frac{\pi}{4} d^2$$
$$P = A \times f_t$$
$$P = \frac{\pi}{4} d^2 \times f_t$$
$$11000 = \frac{\pi}{4} d^2 \times 650$$
$$d = 4.64 \text{ cm.}$$

(*ii*) **To determine diameter $d_1$ of enlarged end.** Consider tensile failure of enlarged end at the slot provided for cotter.

$$A = \text{Area under tensile failure}$$

$$= \frac{\pi}{4} d_1^2 - d_1 \times t$$

$$P = A \times f_t$$

$$= \left[\frac{\pi}{4} d_1^2 - d_1 \times t\right] \times f_t$$

$$= \left[\frac{\pi}{4} d_1^2 - d_1 \times \frac{d_1}{4}\right] \times f_t$$

Assuming thickness of cotter

$$= \frac{d_1}{4}$$

$$11000 = \left[\frac{\pi}{4} d_1^2 - \frac{d_1^2}{4}\right] \times 650$$

$$d_1 = 5.62 \text{ cm.}$$

$$t = \frac{d_1}{4} = \frac{5.62}{4} = 1.4 \text{ cm.}$$

To check the cotter for induced crushing stress, consider the crushing of cotter by enlarged end of bolt.

$$A = \text{Area under compression}$$

$$= d_1 \times t$$

$$P = A \times f_{c_1}$$

$$11000 = d_1 \times t \times f_{c_1}$$

$$= 5.64 \times 1.4 \times f_{c_1}$$

$$f_{c_1} = 1392 \text{ kg/cm}^2.$$

This shows that induced crushing stress $f_{c_1}$ in cotter is more than allowable crushing stress of 1050 kg/cm$^2$.

Therefore increase the diameter $d_1$ and let it be equal to

$$d_1 = 6.5 \text{ cm}$$

$$\therefore \quad t = \frac{d_1}{4} = \frac{6.5}{4} = 1.62 \text{ cm.}$$

$$\therefore \quad f_{c_1} = \frac{11000}{6.5 \times 1.62} = 1044.63 \text{ kg/cm}^2$$

which is less than 1050 kg/cm$^2$ hence safe.

(*iv*) **To find width *b* of cotter.** Consider shear failure of cotter, the cotter being in double shear.

$$A = \text{Area under shear} = 2 \times b \times t$$

$$P = A \times f_s = 2 \times b \times t \times f_s$$

$$11000 = 2 \times b \times 1.62 \times f_s = 3.24 \times b \times 550$$

$$b = 6.17 \text{ cm.}$$

**Example 4.11.** *Fig. 4.22 shows a cottered joint. Determine the maximum load P that should be applied for the following allowable stresses.* $\sigma_1 = 4 \times 10^7$ *N/m²*, $\sigma_c = 8 \times 10^7$ *N/m²*, $\tau = 2 \times 10^7$ *N/m². Cotter is 12 mm thick.*

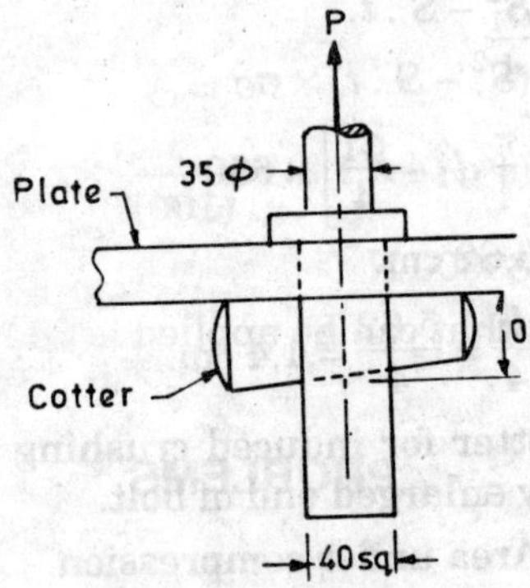


Fig. 4.22.

**Solution.** Consider cylindrical parts of bolt in tension.

$D$ = Diameter

$$= 35 \text{ mm} = 3.5 \text{ cm}$$

$$P = \frac{\pi}{4} D^2 \times \sigma_t$$

$$= \frac{\pi}{4}\left(\frac{3.5}{100}\right)^2 \times 4 \times 10^7$$

$$= 38460 \text{ N}$$

Consider cotter

The cotter is in double shear

$$A = \text{Area in double shear}$$

$$= 2 \, . \, B \, . \, t$$

where $B$ = Width of cotter = 8 cm

$t$ = Thickness of cotter = 1.2 cm

$\tau$ = Shear stress = $2 \times 10^7$ N/m$^2$

$$P = 2 \,.\, B \,.\, t \times \tau$$

$$= 2 \times \frac{8}{100} \times \frac{1.2}{100} \times 2 \times 10^7$$

$$= 38400 \text{ N}$$

Consider square part of bolt

$S$ = Size of square = 4 cm

The cotter is in compression in square part

$A$ = Area in compression

$$= S^2 - S \,.\, t.$$

$$P = (S^2 - S \,.\, t) \times \sigma_C$$

$$= (4^2 - 4 \times 1.2) \times \frac{1}{(100)^2} \times 8 \times 10^7$$

$$= 89600 \text{ N}$$

Hence safe load that can be applied is 38400 N.

## PROBLEMS

**4.1.** Define a cotter. Of what material it is usually made ?

**4.2.** (*a*) Why taper is provided in a cotter ?

(*b*) What is the taper usually given to cotters ?

(*c*) Why a single taper cotter is preferred over double taper cotter ?

**4.3.** What are the advantages of rounding off the edges of the cotter ?

**4.4.** Explain the use of a gib.

**4.5.** Two round steel rods of 5 cm diameter are connected by a sleeve and cotter joint. Design the joint assuming safe stresses as follows :

$f_t$ = 700 kg/cm$^2$,

$f_s$ = 500 kg/cm$^2$,

$f_c$ = 1250 kg/cm$^2$.

**4.6.** Design a coupler to connect two portions of a round tie rod of an iron roof truss. The maximum pull that the rod is to sustain is 5000 kg. Assume safe stresses as follows :

$f_s = 450 \text{ kg/cm}^2$

$f_t = 800 \text{ kg/cm}^2$.

**4.7.** Design a gib and cotter joint for two square rods, the size of each square rod being 7 cm × 7 cm. The rods, gib and cotter are made of same material. The allowable stresses are as follows :

$f_t = 250 \text{ kg/cm}^2$

$f_s = 200 \text{ kg/cm}^2$

$f_c = 650 \text{ kg/cm}^2$.

**4.8.** Design a cotter joint to safely resist a load of 8000 kg which acts along the axes of the rods connected by cotter. The material of cotter and rods will permit the following safe stresses.

$f_t = 600 \text{ kg/cm}^2$

$f_c = 900 \text{ kg/cm}^2$

$f_s = 400 \text{ kg/cm}^2$.

**4.9.** Design a cotter joint for 50 mm diameter rods.

Take $f_s = 0.8 f_t$

and $f_c = 2f_t$.

**4.10.** Design a knuckle joint to withstand a load of 7000 kg.

Assume $f_t$ 600 kg/cm$^2$

$f_s = 450 \text{ kg/cm}^2$

and $f_c = 850 \text{ kg/cm}^2$.

**4.11.** Design a suitable joint for fastening the piston rod to the cross head of an engine having cylinder diameter of 2.2 cm and steam pressure of 9 kg/cm$^2$ gauge.

**4.12.** Compare a cotter and a key.

**4.13.** Write short notes on the following.

(*i*) Designation of pins

(*ii*) Use of taper pins.

# 5

# Riveted Joints

## 5.0 Introduction

In engineering practice fastenings are used to join together parts in machines and structures. The fastening may be of temporary nature or permanent nature.

**Temporary fastenings.** A temporary fastenings can be unfastened without breaking parts. Bolts, nuts, studs, keys, cotters are temporary fastenings.

**Permanent fastenings.** In permanent fastening parts joined together have to broken to separate the parts. Riveting, welding, soldering, brazing are example of permanent fastenings.

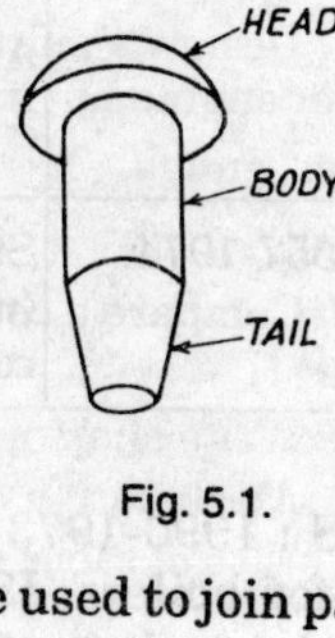


Fig. 5.1.

## 5.1 Rivet

A round bar of steel or wrought iron provided with a head on one side and a tail on the other side is called a rivet (Fig. 5.1). Rivets are used to join parts together permanently.

## 5.2 Rivet Materials

Mild steel and wrought iron are quite commonly used for making rivets. Copper and aluminium rivets are used where corrosion resistance or light weight is required. The material used should be strong and ductile.

Aluminium rivets are easier to instal because of high ductility and low strength.

For air craft aluminium alloy and nickel alloy rivets are preferred because of their low weight.

Table 5.1 indicates the essential mechanical properties of rivet materials.

**Table 5.1**

| *IS No.* | *Material* | *Tensile strength N/mm², min.* | *Shear strength N/mm², min* | *Percentage Elongation, min.* |
|---|---|---|---|---|
| IS : 1990-1973 | Steel Grade | | | |
| | Fe-360 BR | 360-440 | | 26 |
| | Grade Fe-410 BR | 410-500 | | 23 |
| IS : 9086-1979 | Aluminium alloy | | | |
| IS : 9087-1979 | Alloy No. 1 | 270 | 170 | — |
| | 2 | 270 | 180 | — |
| | 3 | 410 | 260 | — |
| IS : 9088-1979 | Nickel alloy : | | | |
| | Alloy No. 1 | 490 | 350 | — |
| | 2 | 650 | 450 | — |
| IS : 7557-1974 | Steel wire (upto 20 mm) cold forged rivets | 330-450 | | 25 |

IS : 1990-1973 specifies the properties for steel rivet and stay bars for boilers. IS : 1148-1973 and IS : 1149-1973 specifies the material for hot rolled steel (upto 40 mm dia) and high tensile steel respectively for rivets for structural purposes.

### 5.2.1 Testing of Rivets

Rivets are tested by two tests

(*i*) Bend test

(*ii*) Flattening test.

In the bend test the rivets are bent cold and hammered until the two parts of the shank are at 180° and touch each other without cracking.

In the flattening test the rivet head is flattened while hot until its diameter is 2.5 times the shank diameter without cracking at the edges.

## 5.3 Method of Riveting

While connecting plates of rivets the first steps is to drill holes in plates. The rivet is then applied by passing its body (shank) through the hole in the plates to be connected. The clearance between hole and rivet is 1 mm for rivets up to 24 mm diameter and the clearance is 1.5 mm for larger diameter rivets. After inserting the rivet the protruding part of the rivet called tail is up set to form a second closing head. This process is called riveting. Best results are obtained by hot riveting *i.e.* the head should be formed when hot.

Steel rivets up to 12 mm diameter can be driven cold whereas rivets of larger diameter are driven when hot. Seconds rivet head is made by hand hammers or pneumatic hammer. Fig. 5.2 shows a rivet before and after being driven.

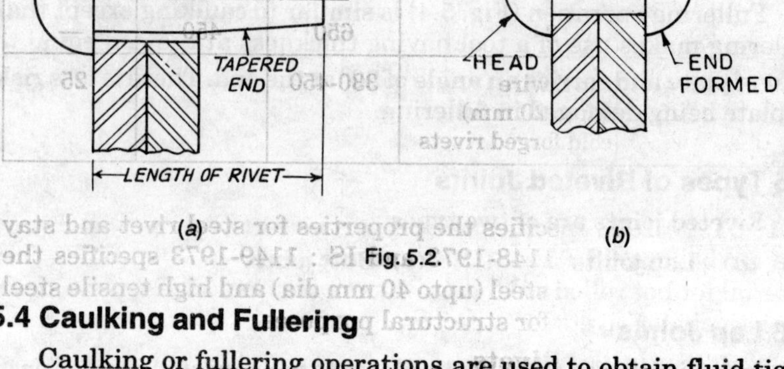


Fig. 5.2.

## 5.4 Caulking and Fullering

Caulking or fullering operations are used to obtain fluid tight joints in boilers and others pressure vessels. In caulking (Fig. 5.3) the edge of one plate is pressed tightly against the plate on which it rests by means of a blunt chisel like tool called caulking tool about 5 mm thick and 38 mm in breadth the edge ground to an angle of 80°. The edges to be caulked is beveled to an angle of 80°. The tool is placed on the edge of rivet head or plate and moved along these edges after every blow, care should be taken to prevent injury to the plate.

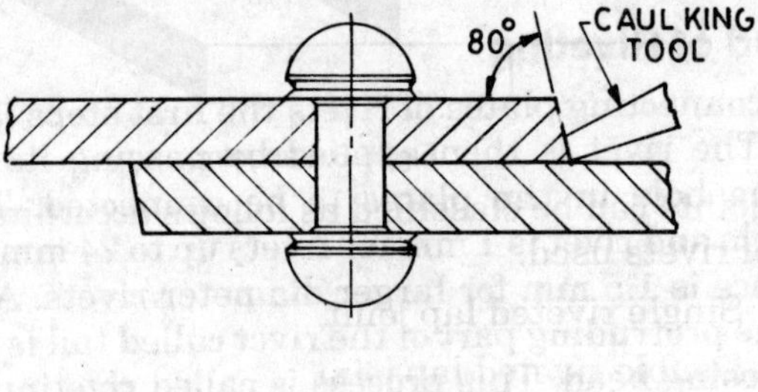


Fig. 5.3. Caulking.

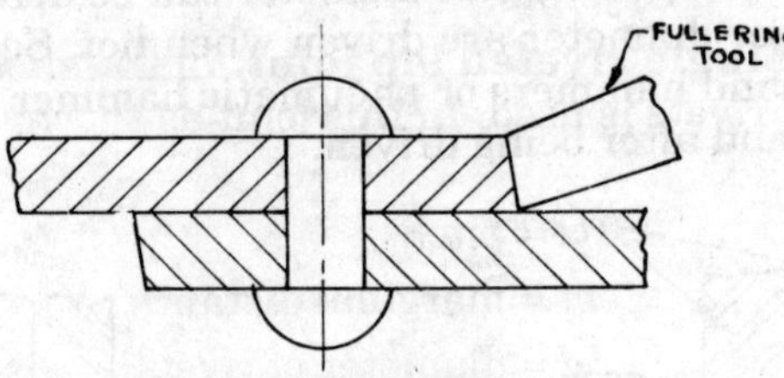


Fig. 5.4. Fullering.

Fullering operation (Fig. 5.4) is similar to caulking except that fullering makes use of a tool having thickness at the end equal to that of plate and carries an angle of 80° at the end. There is less risk of plate being damaged in fullering.

## 5.5 Types of Riveted Joints

Riveted joints are of two types :

(*a*) Lap joints (*b*) Butt joints

## 5.6 Lap Joints

In lap joints the edges of the plates to be connected overlap each other (Fig. 5.5) and then joined by rivets.

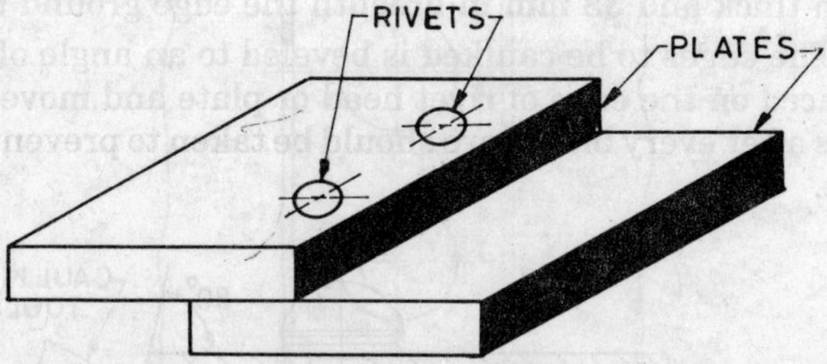


Fig. 5.5. Lap joint.

Lap joints can be classified as follows according to the number of rows of rivets used.

(*i*) Single riveted lap joint.

(*ii*) Double riveted lap joint.

(*iii*) Triple riveted lap joint.

Double riveted and triple riveted lap joints may be chain riveted or zig-zag riveted joints.

**5.6.1 Single riveted lap joint.** In the single riveted lap joint one row of rivets is used. In this joint as shown in Fig. 5.6 and Fig. 5.7.

$$p = \text{pitch}$$
$$m = \text{marginal distance}$$
$$d = \text{diameter of rivets}$$
$$t = \text{thickness of plates.}$$

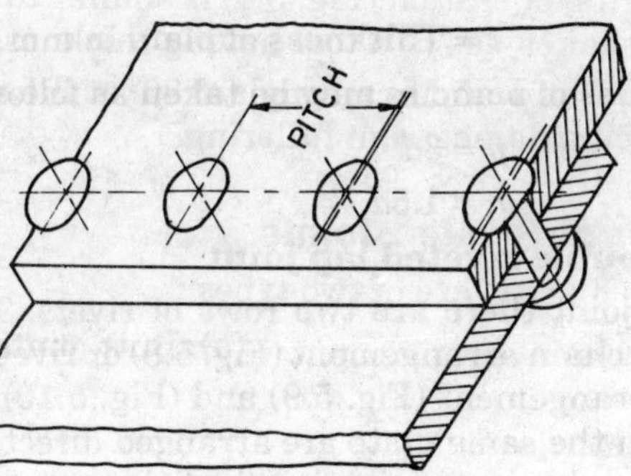


Fig. 5.6. Single riveted lap joint.

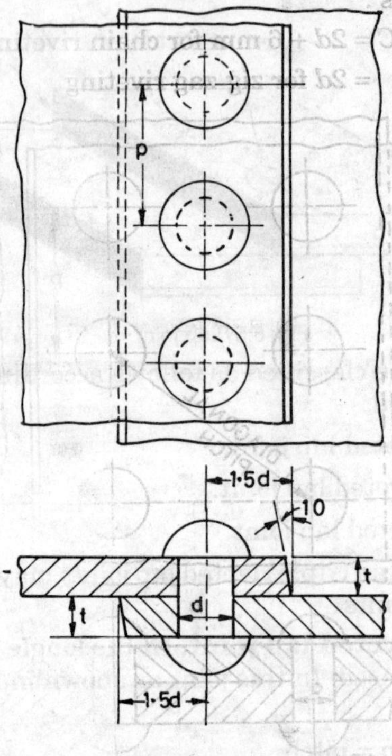


Fig. 5.7. Single riveted lap joint.

The diameter of rivet in various riveted joints can be founded by using the following relation.

$$d = 6.05\sqrt{t}$$

where $d$ = Rivet diameter in mm.

$t$ = Thickness of plate in mm.

The values of $p$ and $m$ may be taken as follows :

$$p = 3d$$

$$m = 1.5d.$$

### 5.6.2 Double riveted lap joint

In this joint there are two rows of rivets. The rivets may be arranged in chain arrangement (Fig. 5.8) or rivets may be placed in a zig-zag arrangement (Fig. 5.9) and (Fig. 5.10). In chain riveting the rivets on the same plate are arranged directly opposite to each other whereas in zig-zag riveting rivets in one row are placed facing between the two rivets of other row.

The distance between rows of rivets ($C$) known as row pitch is calculated as follows :

$$C = 2d + 6 \text{ mm for chain riveting}$$

$$= 2d \text{ for zig-zag riveting}$$

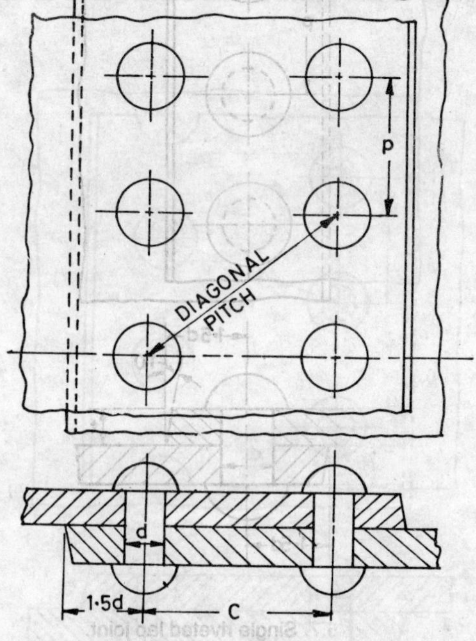


Fig. 5.8. Double-riveted lap joint (Chain Riveting)

$$p = 3\,d$$

$$m = 1.5\,d$$

$$pd = \text{Diagonal pitch}$$

$$= \frac{2p + d}{3}$$

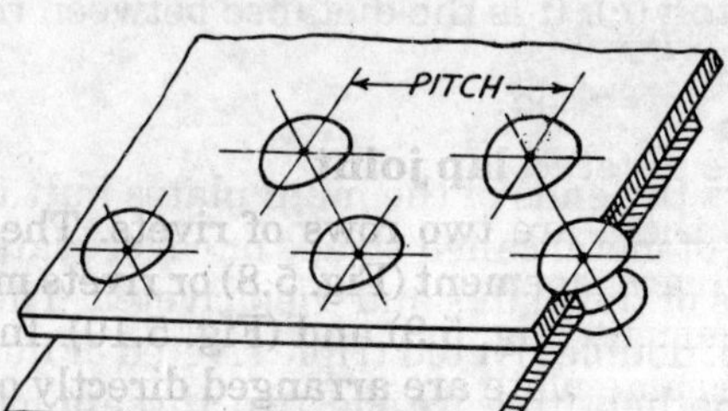


Fig. 5.9.

**Definitions**

(*i*) **Pitch,** ($p$). It is the distance between the centre of one rivet to the centre of the next adjacent rivet in the same row.

(*ii*) **Margin or marginal distance,** ($m$). It is the distance between the edge of the plate to the centre line of the adjacent row of rivets.

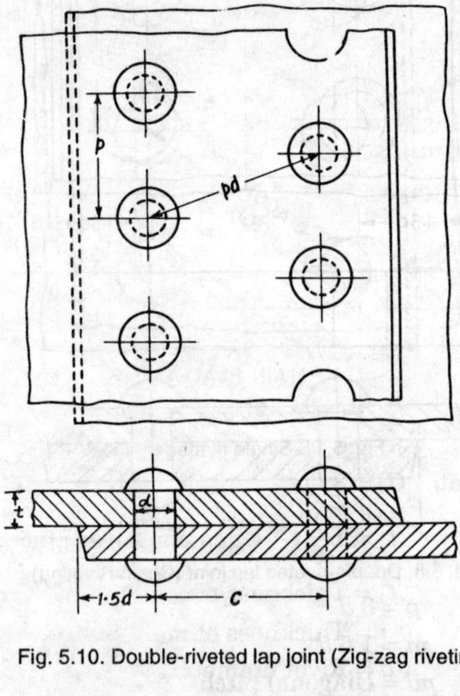


Fig. 5.10. Double-riveted lap joint (Zig-zag riveting).

(*iii*) **Diagonal pitch** ($pd$). It is the distance between the centre of one rivet to the centre of next rivet in the adjoining row.

(*iv*) **Row pitch** ($c$). It is the distance between rows of rivets.

## 5.7 Butt Joints

In butt joints the ends of the main plates butt up against each other and strips of metal called straps or cover plates are placed on one or both sides of the plates and then riveted. The joint is said to be single riveted, double riveted triple riveted or quadruple riveted depending on whether three are one, two, three or four rows of rivets respectively going through each plate. Fig. 5.11 shows a single riveted single cover butt joint.

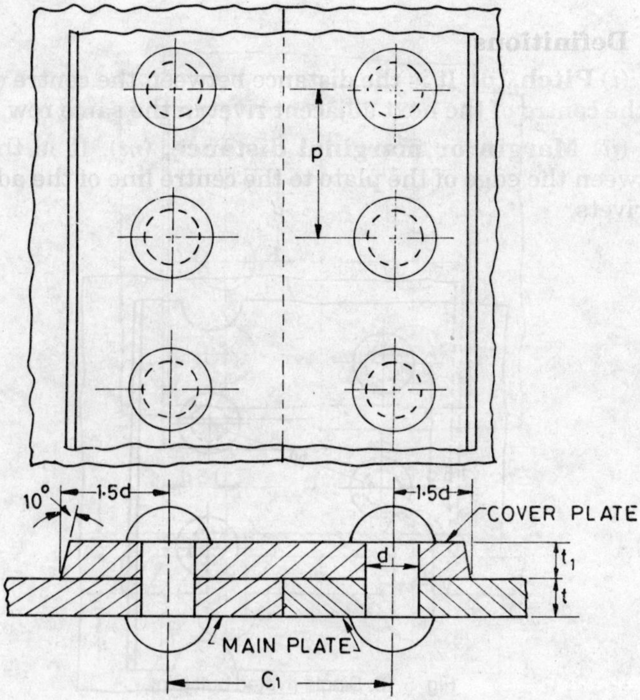


Fig. 5.11. Single riveted butt joint.

In this joint $C_1 = 3d$

$$t_1 = 1\frac{1}{8}t \quad \text{when one cover plate is used}$$

$t_1$ = Thickness of cover plate

$t$ = Thickness of main plates

$d$ = Rivet diameter.

Fig. 5.12 (*a*) and Fig. 5.13 (*b*) shows a single riveted butt joint with two cover plates. In this joint

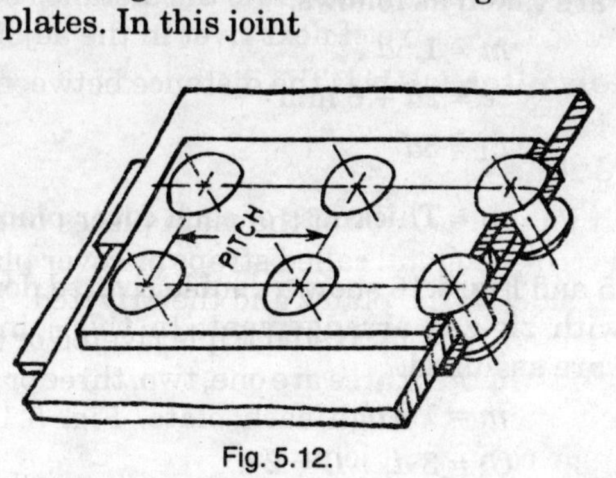


Fig. 5.12.

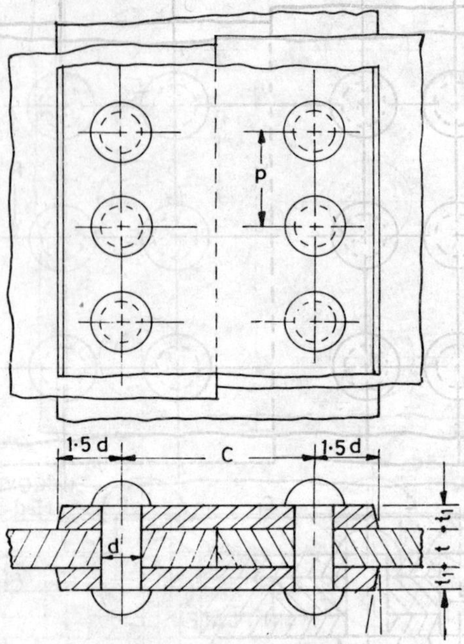


Fig. 5.13. Single riveted butt joint.

$$C_1 = 3d$$

$$t_1 = \frac{5}{8}t \quad \text{when two cover plates are used.}$$

$$p = 3d$$

**5.7.1 Double riveted double cover butt joint.** In this joint the two cover plates are used, to connect the plates together. Fig. 5.14 shows a double riveted double cover (strap) butt joint. In this joint the rivets have been arranged in chain arrangement. The dimensions are taken as follows.

$$m = 1.5d$$

$$c = 2d + 6 \text{ mm}$$

$$c_1 = 3d$$

$$t_1 = \text{Thickness of each cover plate} = \frac{5}{8}t.$$

Fig. 5.15 and Fig. 5.16 show a double riveted double cover plate butt joint with zig-zag arrangement. In this joint the following dimensions are assumed.

$$m = 1.5\,d$$

$$C_1 = 3\,d, \quad C = 2\,d$$

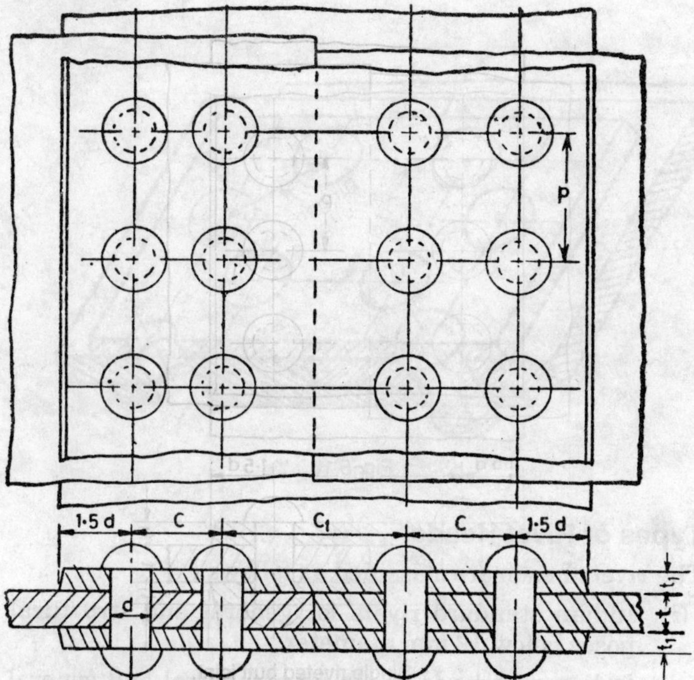


Fig. 5.14. Double riveted double cover butt joint (Chain Riveting).

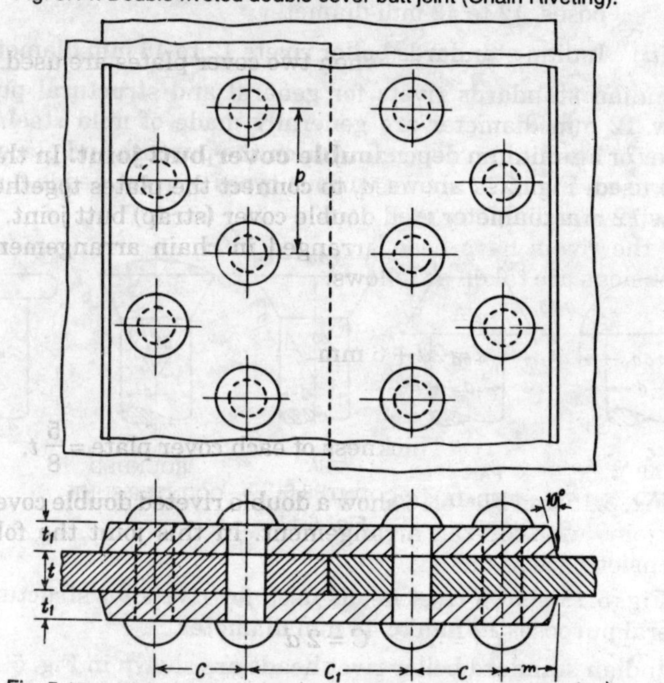


Fig. 5.15. Double riveted double cover butt joint (Zig-zag riveting).

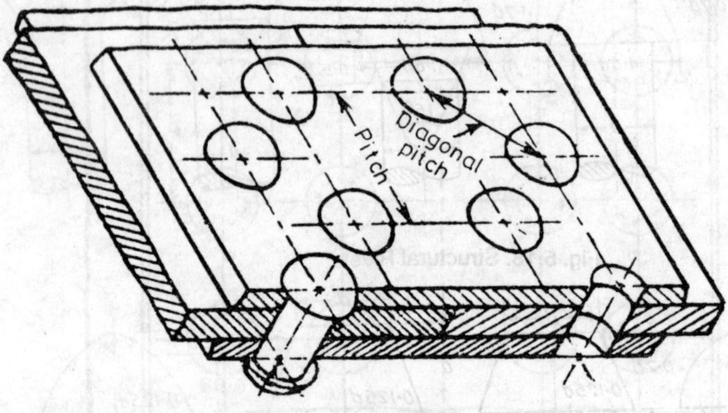


Fig. 5.16.

## 5.8 Types of Rivet Heads

The rivets heads are classified as follows :

(*i*) Indian standard rivets for general and structural purposes below 12 mm diameter.

(*ii*) Indian standards rivets for structural and general purposes, 12 to 48 mm diameter.

(*iii*) Indian standards boiler rivets 12 to 48 mm diameter.

Indian standards rivets for general and structural purposes below 12 mm diameter are generally made of mild steel, brass, copper or aluminium depending upon the purpose and place where to be used. Fig. 5.17 shows various types of rivet heads for rivets below 12 mm diameter :

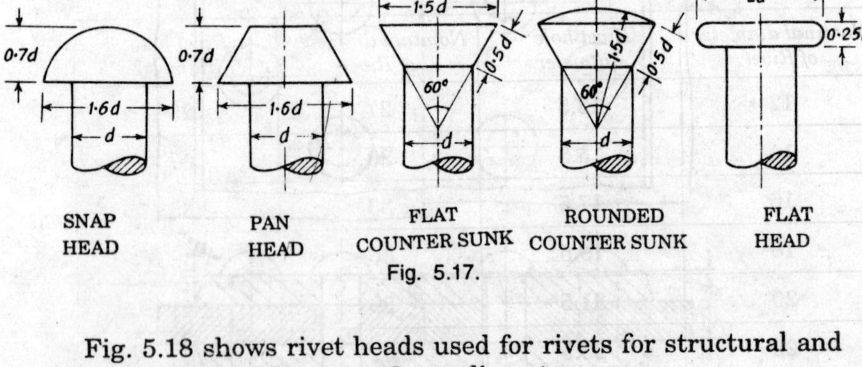


Fig. 5.17.

Fig. 5.18 shows rivet heads used for rivets for structural and general purposes 12 mm to 48 mm diameter.

Indian standard boiler rivet heads are shown in Fig. 5.19.

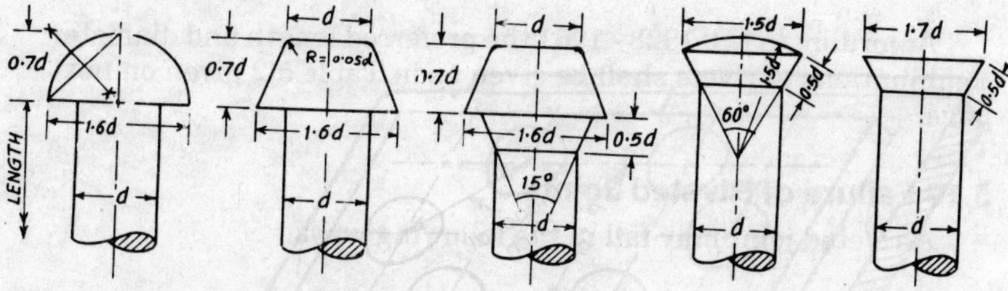


Fig. 5.18. Structural Rivets.

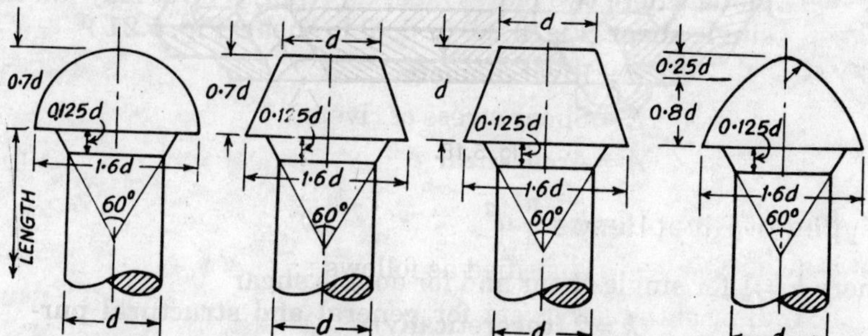


(i) Snap Head (ii) Pan Head Type (i) (iii) Pan Head Type (ii) (iv) Conical Head

Fig. 5.19. Boiler Rivets.

## 5.9 Rivet Hole Diameter

In structural and pressure vessel riveting, the diameter of rivet hole is usually 1.5 mm larger than nominal diameter of rivet.

Table 5.1 gives diameters of rivets and corresponding rivet holes in mm for boiler joints.

**Table 5.1**

| *Nominal diameter of Rivet* | *Rivet hole diameter* | *Nominal diameter of Rivet* | *Rivet hole diameter* |
|---|---|---|---|
| 12 | 13.5 | 27 | 29 |
| 14 | 15.5 | 30 | 32 |
| 16 | 17.5 | 33 | 35 |
| 18 | 19.5 | 36 | 38 |
| 20 | 21.5 | 39 | 41 |
| 22 | 23.5 | 42 | 44 |
| 24 | 25.5 | 48 | 50 |

According to I.S. 1928 - 1961 the preferred length and diameter combinations of rivets shall be given as in Table 5.2 given on next page.

## 5.10 Failure of Riveted Joints

A riveted joint may fail in the following ways.

(*i*) **Shearing of rivets.** The rivets may fail in shear at the plane where two plates meet together. A rivet may fail in single shear (Fig. 5.20) or double shear (Fig. 5.21.)

$d$ = Rivet diameter

$f_s$ = Shear stress of rivets.

$A$ = Area shear

$$= k \times \frac{\pi}{4} d^2$$

where $k = 1$ for single shear and for double shear

$k = 2$ (theoretically)

$= 1.75$ to $1.875$ (practically)

$$P_s = \text{Shear strength} = A \times f_s$$

$$= n.k \times \frac{\pi}{4} d^2 \times f_s$$

where $n$ = Number of rivets in one pitch length

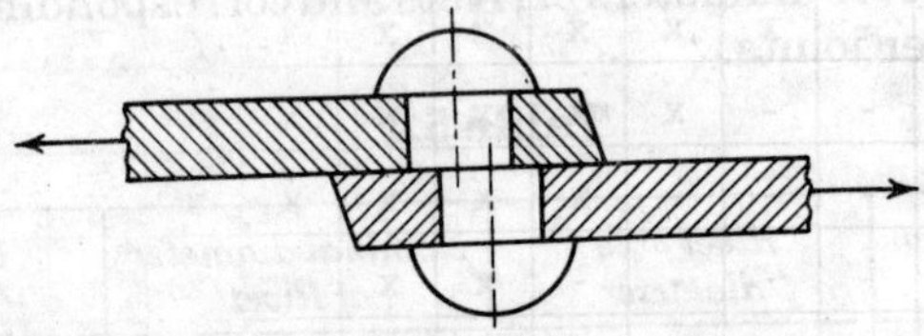

Fig. 5.20. Rivets in single shear.

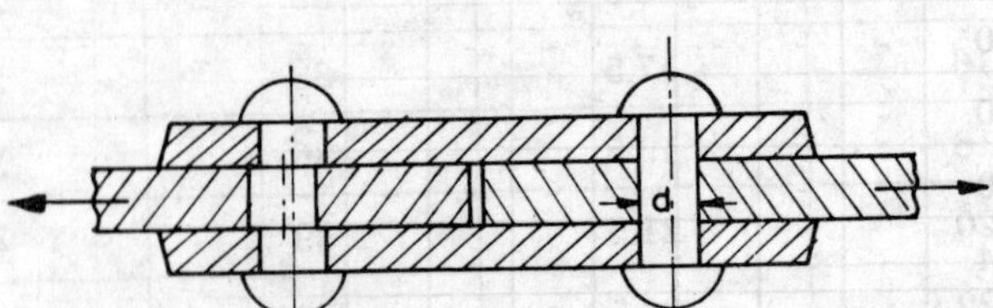


Fig. 5.21. Rivets in double shear.

## TABLE 5.2

| *Length* | *Diameter* | | | | | | | | | | | | | |
|---|---|---|---|---|---|---|---|---|---|---|---|---|---|---|
| | *12* | *14* | *16* | *18* | *20* | *22* | *24* | *27* | *30* | *33* | *36* | *39* | *42* | *48* |
| 28 | x | - | - | - | - | - | - | - | - | - | - | - | - | - |
| 31.5 | x | x | - | - | - | - | - | - | - | - | - | - | - | - |
| 35.5 | x | x | x | - | - | - | - | - | - | - | - | - | - | - |
| 40 | x | x | x | x | - | - | - | - | - | - | - | - | - | - |
| 45 | x | x | x | x | x | - | - | - | - | - | - | - | - | - |
| 50 | x | x | x | x | x | x | - | - | - | - | - | - | - | - |
| 56 | x | x | x | x | x | x | x | - | - | - | - | - | - | - |
| 63 | x | x | x | x | x | x | x | x | - | - | - | - | - | - |
| 71 | x | x | x | x | x | x | x | x | x | - | - | - | - | - |
| 80 | x | x | x | x | x | x | x | x | x | - | - | - | - | - |
| 85 | - | x | x | x | x | x | x | x | x | x | - | - | - | - |
| 90 | - | x | x | x | x | x | x | x | x | x | - | - | - | - |
| 95 | - | x | x | x | x | x | x | x | x | x | x | - | - | - |
| 100 | - | - | x | x | x | x | x | x | x | x | x | - | - | - |
| 106 | - | - | x | x | x | x | x | x | x | x | x | x | - | - |
| 112 | - | - | x | x | x | x | x | x | x | x | x | x | - | - |
| 118 | - | - | - | x | x | x | x | x | x | x | x | x | x | - |
| 125 | - | - | - | - | x | x | x | x | x | x | x | x | x | x |
| 132 | - | - | - | - | - | x | x | x | x | x | x | x | x | x |
| 140 | - | - | - | - | - | x | x | x | x | x | x | x | x | x |
| 150 | - | - | - | - | - | - | x | x | x | x | x | x | x | x |
| 160 | - | - | - | - | - | - | x | x | x | x | x | x | x | x |
| 180 | - | - | - | - | - | - | - | x | x | x | x | x | x | x |
| 200 | - | - | - | - | - | - | - | - | x | x | x | x | x | x |
| 224 | - | - | - | - | - | - | - | - | - | x | x | x | x | x |
| 250 | - | - | - | - | - | - | - | - | - | - | - | x | x | x |

Preferred numbers are indicated by ×,

(*ii*) **Tearing of plate along the centre line of a row of rivets.** The plate may tear along the line of minimum section that is along the line through the centre of holes. (Fig. 5.22)

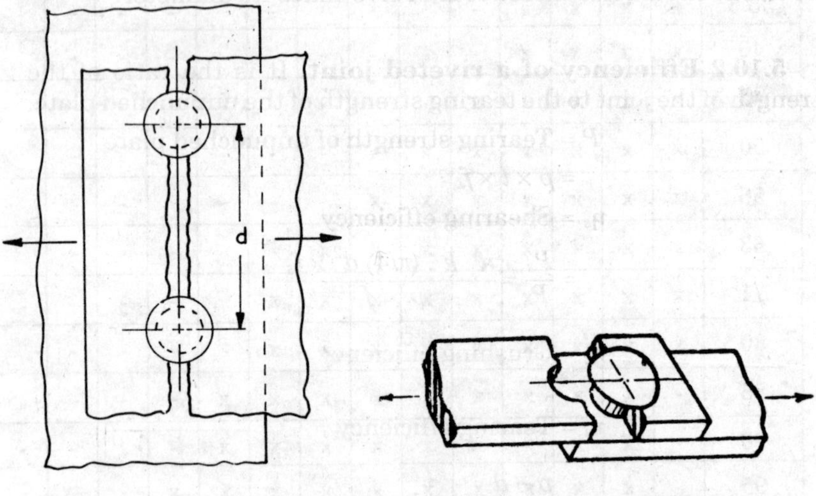


(*a*) (*b*) Tearing of plate.

Fig. 5.22.

$f_t$ = Tensile stress of plates

$A$ = Area of plate under tearing $= (p - d) \cdot t$ .

$P_t$ = Tearing strength $= (p - d) \cdot t \cdot f_t$.

where $t$ = Thickness of plate

$p$ = pitch

(*iii*) **Crushing of rivets and plates**. The rivets may fail under crushing (Fig. 5.23).

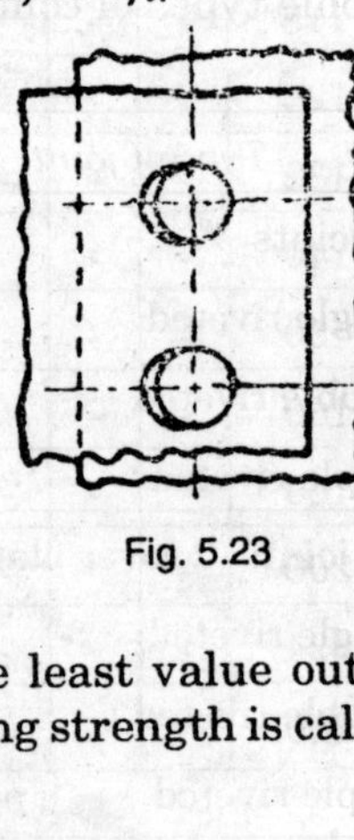

Fig. 5.23

$f_c$ = Crushing stress of rivets.

$A$ = Area under crushing

$= n \cdot d \cdot t$

$P_c$ = crushing strength

$= A \times f_c = n \cdot d \cdot f_c \cdot t$

**5.10.1. Strength of a riveted joint.** The least value out of shearing strength, tearing strength and crushing strength is called strength of the riveted joint.

Rivets should always be placed at right angles to the acting forces, and the maximum stress induced in them should be either shear or crushing. In a long rivet the initial stress set up at the junction of the shank and the point, when the rivet cools is dangerous. This initial stress increases with the relative length of the rivets, and in a very long rivet, it may cause the head to snap off without any load. For this reason, the length of the rivet between the heads should not exceed four or five times its diameter.

**5.10.2 Efficiency of a riveted joint.** It is the ratio of the strength of the joint to the tearing strength of the unpunched plate.

$P$ = Tearing strength of unpunched plate

$= p \times t \times f_t$

$\eta_s$ = Shearing efficiency

$$= \frac{P_s}{P} = \frac{n \,.\, k \,.\, (\pi/4)\, d^2 \times f_s}{p \,.\, t\, f_t}$$

$$\eta_c = \text{Crushing efficiency} = \frac{P_c}{P} = \frac{n \,.\, d \,.\, t \,.\, f_c}{p \times t \times f_t}$$

$$\eta_t = \text{Tearing efficiency} = \frac{P_t}{P} = \frac{(p-d) \,.\, t \,.\, f_t}{p \,.\, t \,.\, f_t}$$

$$= \frac{p-d}{p}$$

The lowest of the three efficiencies is called as the efficiency of the joint.

Table 5.4 indicates the average efficiency and maximum pitch for some types of commercial boiler joints.

**Table 5.4**

| *Type of joint* | *Efficiency (%)* | *Maximum pitch (cms)* |
|---|---|---|
| Lap joints | | |
| Single riveted | 45-65 | $1.31\, t + 4.128$ |
| Double riveted | 63-70 | $2.62\, t + 4.128$ |
| Triple riveted | 72-80 | $3.47\, t + 4.128$ |
| Butt joints (2 cover plates) | | |
| Single riveted | 55-60 | $1.75\, t + 4.128$ |
| Double riveted | 70-85 | $3.5\, t + 4.128$ |
| Triple riveted | 80-90 | $6\, t + 4.128$ |

The Indian Boiler Regulations (I.B.R.) allows a maximum of 85% efficiency for the best riveted joint.

## 5.11 Thickness of Cover Plate

According to I.B.R. the thickness ($t_1$) of cover plate in butt joints is as follows :

$t_1 = 1.125\, t$ for chain riveted single cover plate.

$= 1.125\, t \left(\frac{p-d}{p-2d}\right)$ for single cover plate alternate rivet in outer row being omitted.

$t_1 = 0.625\, t$ for double cover plates of equal width having chain riveting

$= 0.625\, t \frac{p-d}{p-2d}$ for double cover plates of equal width and every alternate rivet in the outer rows being omitted

$t_1 = 0.625\, t$ for narrow strap on the outside

$= 0.75\, t$ for wide strap on the inside.

According to I.B.R. the thickness of cover plate should not be less than 10 mm.

**5.11.1 Spacing of rows of rivets.** According to I.B.R. the spacing of rows of rivets is taken as follows :

(*i*) For lap and butt joints with equal number of rivets in each row

$C$ = Spacing of rows of rivets.

$= 0.33\, p + 0.67\, d$ for zig zag rivets.

$= 2\, d$ for chain rivets.

(*ii*) In joints in which number of rivets in outer row is one half of the number of rivets in each of inner rows and in which inner rows are zig zag the distance should not be less that $0.2\, p + 1.15\, d$ between outer row and inner row.

The distance between the rows in which there are full numbers of rivets (zig-zag) shall not be less than $0.165\, p + 0.67\, d$.

In all above cases $p$ is the pitch of rivets in outer rows.

## 5.12 Procedure to Design Circumferential Lap Joint for a Boiler

(*i*) **To find rivet diameter.** Diameter of rivet ($d$)

$$= 6.05 \sqrt{t}$$

where $t$ is the thickness of plate in millimetre.

(*ii*) **To find shell plate thickness.** Thickness of boiler shell plate ($t$) is calculated as follows :

$$t = \frac{pD}{2 \cdot f_t \cdot \eta} + C$$

where $p$ = Gauge pressure of steam in boiler

$D$ = Diameter of boiler shell

$f_t$ = Permissible tensile stress

$\eta$ = Longitudinal efficiency of the joint

$C$ = Corrosion allowance = 0.1 cm to 0.3 cm.

The thickness of boiler shell should not be less than 7 mm. The longitudinal joint in a boiler shell is usually a butt joint with two cover plates. The circumferential joint is a lap joint with one ring over lapping the other alternatively. The longitudinal joints are staggered because the shell is made up of a number of rings and this is done for convenience of connecting rings at places where both longitudinal and circumferential joints occur.

(*iii*) **To find number of rivets.** As the circumferential joint is a lap joint the rivets will be in single shear.

$P_s$ = Shear strength

$$= N \times \frac{\pi}{4} d^2 \times f_s$$

$F$ = Total shearing force due to steam pressure

$$= \frac{\pi}{4} D^2 \times p.$$

where $N$ is the number of rivets.

$$\therefore \quad P_S = F$$

$$N \times \frac{\pi}{4} d^2 f_s = \frac{\pi}{4} D^2 \times p$$

$$N = \frac{\frac{\pi}{4} D^2 \cdot p}{\frac{\pi}{4} d^2 \cdot f_s} = \left(\frac{D}{d}\right)^2 \frac{p}{f_s}$$

Again considering crushing of rivets.

$$P_s = \text{Crushing strength}$$
$$= N \,.\, d \,.\, t \,.\, f_c.$$
$$P_s = F$$
$$N \,.\, d \,.\, t \,.\, f_c = \frac{\pi}{4} D^2 \,.\, p$$
$$N = \frac{\frac{\pi}{4} D^2 \,.\, p}{d \,.\, t \,.\, f_c}$$

The greater of two values of $N$ will be taken as the number of rivets.

(*iv*) **To find number of rivets in one row ($n$).** The number of rivets in one row of a circumferential lap joint can be found as follows.

$$n = \frac{\pi(D + t)}{p}$$

(*v*) **To find number of rows. z**. The number of rows of rivets ($z$) is found as follows.

$$z = \frac{\text{Total number of rivets}}{\text{Number of rivet in one row}} = \frac{N}{n}$$

From the number of rows the type of joint can be decided. Then the rivets should be adjusted and pitch should be decided.

(*vi*) **To find overlap of the plate ($s$).** The overlap ($s$) of the plate is calculated as follows.

$$s = (z - 1) \times c + 2 \times m.$$

where $c$ = pitch between rows of rivets

$m$ = Marginal distance = 1.5 $d$

(*vii*) **To find specific resistance to slipping.** The allowable value of specific resistance ($f$) to slipping is given by the relation

$$f = \frac{F}{\frac{\pi}{4} d^2 \times N}$$

where $N$ = Number of rivets in the joint.

(*viii*) **To find efficiency of the joint**

$$\eta = \text{Efficiency of the joint}$$

$$= \frac{p-d}{p}$$

(*ix*) **Diameter of rivet hole ($d_1$)**

$d_1$ = Diameter of rivet hole

$= \sqrt{5t} - 0.4$ cm for lap joints

$= \sqrt{5t} - 0.5$ cm for single riveted butt joint.

$= \sqrt{5t} - 0.6$ cm for double riveted butt joint.

where $t$ = Thickness of plate in cm.

Table 5.5 indicates the suggested types of joints.

**Table 5.5**

| *Diameter of shell (cm)* | *Type of joint* |
|---|---|
| 60 - 180 | Double riveted |
| 90 - 210 | Triple riveted |
| 150 - 270 | Quadruple riveted |

Table 5.6 shows suggested values of minimum thickness boiler shell plate.

**Table 5.6**

| *Diameter of shell, cm* | Minimum thickness |
|---|---|
| 90 and under | 0.625 cm |
| 90 - 135 | 0.800 cm |
| 135 - 180 | 0.950 cm |
| 180 and over | 1.250 cm |

Table 5.7 indicates the efficiency and maximum pitch of commercial boiler joints.

**Table 5.7**

**Typical Efficiency of Commercial Boiler Joints**

| *Type of joint* | *Typical efficiency (%)* | **Maximum efficiency (%)* | $p_m$ |
|---|---|---|---|
| (1) Lap joints : | | | |
| (*i*) Single riveted | 46-60 | 63.0 | $1.31\,t + 4.128$ |
| (*ii*) Double riveted | 62-70 | 77.5 | $2.62\,t + 4.128$ |
| (*iii*) Triple riveted | 73-80 | 86.6 | $3.47\,t + 4.128$ |
| (2) Butt joints : (2 cover plates) | | | |
| (*i*) Single riveted | 54-60 | 63.3 | $1.75\,t + 4.128$ |
| (*ii*) Double riveted | 70-82 | 85.6 | $3.5\,t + 4.128$ |
| (*iii*) Triple riveted | 80-90 | 95.0 | $6\,t + 4.128$ |
| (*iv*) Quadruple riveted | 85-93 | 98.1 | — |

## 5.13. Riveted Joints for General Purposes

The usual procedure to design a riveted joint for general purpose is as follows :

(*i*) $d$ = Diameter of rivet

$= 605\sqrt{t}$ when $t \geq 8$ mm

where $t$ = Thickness of plate in millimetre

when $t$ is less than 8 mm, equate shear strength = Crushing strength to find rivet diameter.

(*ii*) The pitch is calculated by equating tearing strength of plate to shearing strength or crushing strength of rivets which even is less.

(*iii*) Maximum pitch ($p$) = $3d$

Minimum pitch = $2d$

(*iv*) $c$ = Distance between rows of rivets

$= 2d + 6$ mm for chain riveting

$= 2d$ for zig-zag riveting

* The maximum efficiencies are valid for ideal equal strength joints with tensile stress = 7.7 kg/sq. mm., crushing stress = 13.3 kg/sq. mm. and shear stress = 6.16 kg/sq. mm.

The distance $c$ should not be less than $0.6\,p$ for zig-zag riveting and should not be less than $0.8\,p$ for chain riveting.

(*v*) $m$ = Marginal distance

$= 1.5\,d$

(*vi*) $t_1$ = Thickness of cover plate

$= 0.625\,t$ for double cover plate

$= 1.125\,t$ for single cover plate.

## 5.14 Permissible Stresses

The permissible stresses for the design of riveted joints used in bridges, machine frames, building structure etc. are taken as follows. The permissible stresses in riveted joints used in bridges buildges building structures machine frames are as follows. These stresses are for mild steel structure with a factor of safety of about 2.

Shear stress on power driven rivets = 1060 kg/cm.

Plates in tension = 1400 kg/cm$^2$

Crushing stress for power driven rivets

Single shear = 2250 kg/cm$^2$

Double shear = 2750 kg/cm$^2$.

Table 5.8 indicates the values of design stress for rivets and plates of different materials.

**Table 5.8**

| *Material of Plate and Rivet* | **Design Stress for Rivets (kg/mm$^2$)* | | |
|---|---|---|---|
| | *Shear* | *Crushing* | *Tension* |
| (*i*) Carbon Steel | 7.70 | 15.40 | 9.65 |
| (*ii*) Chrome-Silico-Manganese Steel | 10.50 | 21.00 | 13.20 |
| (*iii*) Stainless Steel | 6.28 | 12.56 | 7.85 |

### 5.14.1 Assumption for design of riveted joints

While designing a riveted joint the following assumptions are made.

1. Rivets completely fill the holes.

*Crushing Stress (design) for plates may be taken as 1.6 times the value for tension given above.

2. The load distribution among the rivets is according to the shear area.
3. The distribution of tensile stress over the section of the metal between the rivets is uniform.
4. There is no bending stress in the rivets.
5. The weakening effect of the rivet holes on the plate is ignored.
6. The effect of friction between adjacent surfaces on the strength of the joint is negligible.

## 5.15 Factor of Safety

The factor of safety for some of the riveted joints is indicated in table 5.9.

**Table 5.9**

| *Type of joint* | *Factor of safety* |
|---|---|
| Butt joint | |
| (*a*) With two equal cover plates | 4 |
| (*b*) With two unequal cover plates | 4.25 |
| (*c*) With single cover plates | 4.75 |
| Lap joint | 4.75 |

**Example 5.1.** *Design a double riveted double cover plate butt joint to connect two plates together. Each plate is 9 mm thick. Assume the safe stresses as follows :*

$$f_t = 400 \text{ kg/cm}^2$$

$$f_s = 300 \text{ kg/cm}^2$$

$$f_c = 600 \text{ kg/cm}^2$$

*Sketch the joint.*

**Solution.**

Fig. 5.24 shows a double riveted double cover plates butt joint with chain riveting.

$t$ = Thickness of plate = 9 mm.

$N$ = Number of rivets per pitch = 2

(*i*) **To find rivet diameter** (*d*)

$$d = 6.05\sqrt{t} = 6.05\sqrt{9} = 18.15 \text{ mm}$$

We adopt $d = 19 \text{ mm} = 1.9 \text{ cm}$

(*ii*) **To find thickness of cover plate, $t_1$**

$$t_1 = 0.625 \times t = 0.625 \times 9 = 5.62 \text{ mm}$$

(*iii*) **To find pitch, *p*. The rivets are in double shear.**

$$P_s = \text{Shear strength} = N \times 1.875 \times \frac{\pi}{4} d^2 \times f_s$$

where $N$ = Number of rivets per pitch length = 2

$$= 2 \times 1.875 \times \frac{\pi}{4} \times (1.9)^2 \times 300 = 3188 \text{ kg.}$$

$$P_c = \text{Crushing strength}$$

$$= N \cdot d \cdot t \cdot f_c = 2 \times 1.9 \times 0.9 \times 600 = 4332 \text{ kg.}$$

**This shows that shear strength is less than crushing strength. To find pitch equate tearing strength of plate to shear strength.**

$$P_t = P_s$$

$$(p - d) \cdot t \cdot f_t = 3188$$

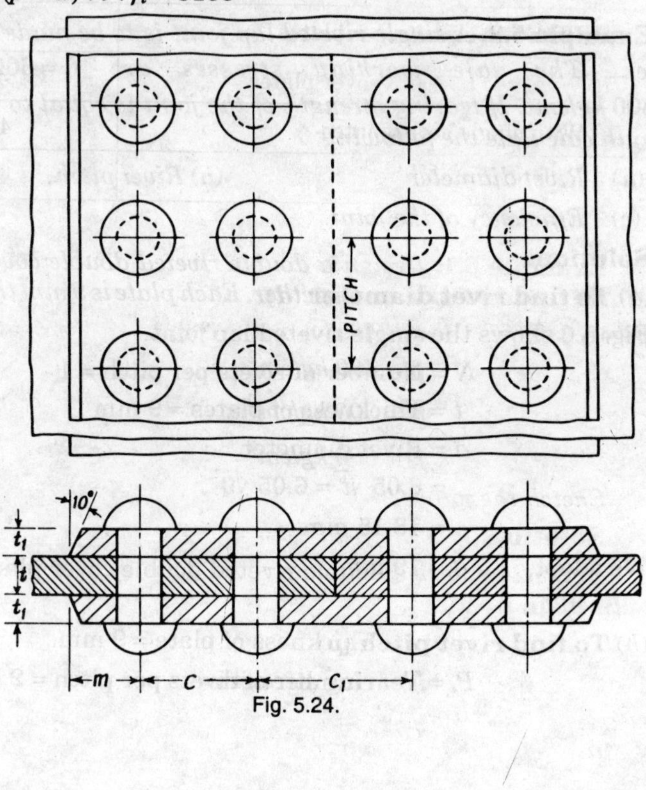


Fig. 5.24.

$(p - 1.9) \times 0.9 \times 400 = 3188$

$$p = 10.75 \text{ cm.}$$

(*iv*) **To find efficiency of the joint (η)**

$$\eta = \frac{\text{Strength of the joint}}{p \times t \times f_t} \times 100$$

where $p \times t \times f_t$ = Tearing strength of solid plate.

Strength of the joint = Least value out of shear strength, crushing strength and tearing strength

∴ Strength of the joint = 3188 kg.

$$\eta = \frac{3188}{10.75 \times 0.9 \times 400} \times 100 = 82.3\%.$$

(*v*) **To find distance between rows of rivets**

$$c_1 = 3d = 3 \times 1.9 \times 5.7 \text{ cm}$$

$$c = 0.8p = 0.8 \times 10.75 = 8.6 \text{ cm}$$

$m$ = Marginal distance

$= 1.5d = 1.5 \times 1.9 = 2.85$ cm.

**Example 5.2.** *A single riveted lap joint is to be made of 9 mm plates. The safe working stresses are $f_s = 600$ kg/cm$^2$, $f_t = 800$ kg/cm$^2$. If tearing strength of the joint is equal to shearing strength calculate the following.*

(*a*) *Rivet diameter* (*b*) *Rivet pitch.*

(*c*) *Efficiency of the joint.*

**Solution.**

(*a*) **To find rivet diameter (*d*).**

Fig. 5.6 shows the single riveted lap joint.

$N$ = Number of rivets per pitch = 1

$t$ = Thickness of plates = 9 mm

$d$ = Rivet diameter

$= 6.05 \sqrt{t} = 6.05 \sqrt{9}$

$= 18.15$ mm.

We adopt, $d = 19$ mm.

(*b*) **To find rivet pitch (*p*)**

$P_t$ = Tearing strength

$$= (p - d) \, . \, t \, . \, f_t.$$

$$P_s = \text{Shearing strength} = N \times \frac{\pi}{4} d^2 \times f_s$$

$$P_t = P_s$$

$$(p - d) \, . \, t \, . \, f_t = N \, . \, \frac{\pi}{4} d^2 \, . \, f_s$$

$$(p - 1.90) \times 0.9 \times 800 = 1 \times \frac{\pi}{4} \times (1.90)^2 \times 600$$

$$p = 4.45 \text{ cm.}$$

According to I.B.R.

Minimum pitch = $2d = 2 \times 1.95 = 3.9$ cm

Maximum pitch = $1.31 \times t + 4.128$

$= 1.31 \times 0.9 + 4.128 = 5.307$ cm.

The value of pitch 4.45 cm lies between the minimum and maximum values.

(*c*) **To determine efficiency** ($\eta$)

$$\eta = \frac{(p - d) \, . \, t \, . \, f_t}{p \times t \times f_t} \times 100$$

$$= \frac{p - d}{p} \times 100 = \frac{4.45 - 1.90}{4.45} \times 100$$

$$= 56.2\%$$

**Example 5.3.** *Two mild steel plates 7 mm thick are to be joined together by a triple riveted lap joint with zig-zag riveting. If the allowable stresses are 900 kg/cm$^2$ 700 kg/cm$^2$ and 1400 kg/cm$^2$ in tension, shear and crushing respectively determine the following*

(*a*) *Rivet diameter*

(*b*) *Rivet pitch*

(*c*) *Distance between rows of rivets.*

(*d*) *Efficiency of the joint.*

**Solution.** Fig. 5.25 shows a triple riveted lap joint with zig-zag riveting.

$t$ = Thickness of plates = 7 mm

(*i*) **To find rivet diameter (*d*).** As the thickness of plates is less than 8 mm therefore, to find rivet diameter proceed as follows

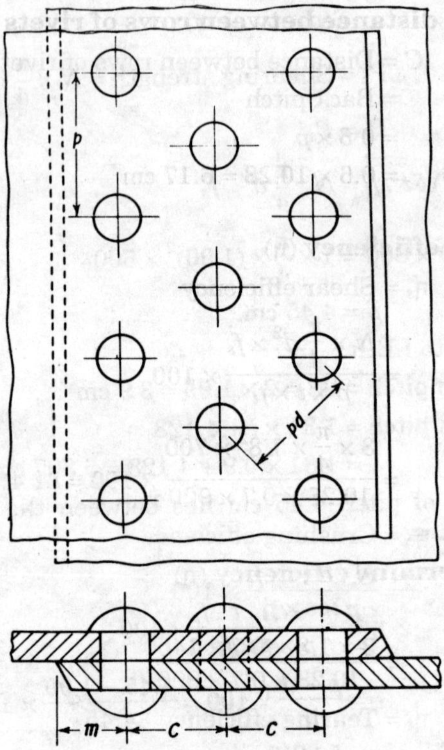


Fig. 5.25.

Shear strength = crushing strength

$$N \times \frac{\pi}{4} d^2 \, . \, f_s = N \, . \, d \, . \, t \, . \, f_c$$

where $N$ = Number of rivets per pitch = 3

$$3 \times \frac{\pi}{4} d^2 \times 700 = 3 \times d \times 0.7 \times 1400$$

$$d = 1.78 \text{ cm.} \approx 1.8 \text{ cm (say).}$$

**(*ii*) To find pitch (*p*)**

To find pitch equate tearing strength of plate to shearing strength of rivets.

$$(p - d) \, . \, t \, . \, f_t = N \times \frac{\pi}{4} d^2 \times f_s$$

$$(p - 1.8) \times 0.7 \times 900 = 3 \times \frac{\pi}{4} \times 1.8^2 \times 700$$

$$p = 10.28 \text{ cm.}$$

(*iii*) **To find distance between rows of rivets**

$$C = \text{Distance between rows of rivets}$$
$$= \text{Back pitch}$$
$$= 0.6 \times p$$
$$= 0.6 \times 10.28 = 6.17 \text{ cm}$$

(*iv*) **To find efficiency ($\eta$)**

$$\eta_s = \text{Shear efficiency}$$
$$= \frac{N \times \frac{\pi}{4} d^2 \times f_s}{p \times t \times f_t} \times 100$$
$$= \frac{3 \times \frac{\pi}{4} \times 1.8^2 \times 700}{10.28 \times 0.7 \times 900} \times 100 = 82.4\%$$
$$\eta_c = \text{Crushing efficiency}$$
$$= \frac{N \,.\, d \,.\, t \,.\, f_c}{p \times t \times f_t} \times 100$$
$$= \frac{3 \times 1.8 \times 0.7 \times 1400}{10.28 \times 0.7 \times 900} \times 100 = 81.7\%$$
$$\eta_t = \text{Tearing efficiency}$$
$$= \frac{p - d}{p} \times 100$$
$$= \frac{10.28 - 1.8}{10.28} \times 100 = 82.5\%.$$

Hence efficiency of the joint = 81.7%.

**Example 5.4.** *Two plates 12 mm thick are to be joined by a triple riveted double cover plate butt joint. The rivet pitch is to be same in all rows and chain riveting is to be used. If the allowable stresses in tension are shear and 800 kg/cm² and 600 kg/cm² respectively, determine the following :*

(*a*) *Rivet diameter*

(*b*) *Rivet pitch*

(*c*) *Distance between rows of rivets*

(*d*) *Strap (cover plate) thickness*

(*e*) *Efficiency of the joint*

(*f*) *Marginal distance.*

**Solution.**

Fig. 5.26 shows a triple riveted butt joint with chain riveting

$t$ = Thickness of plate

= 12 mm.

(*i*) **To find rivet diameter (d)**

$$d = 6.05\sqrt{t} = 6.05\sqrt{12} = 20.93 \text{ mm.}$$

We adopt, $d = 21 \text{ mm} = 2.1 \text{ cm}$

(*ii*) **To find pitch (p)**

The rivets are in double shear

$N$ = Number of rivets per pitch length

= 3

Tearing strength = shear strength

$$(p - d) \,.\, t \,.\, f_t = N \times 1.875 \times \frac{\pi}{4} d^2 \,.\, f_s.$$

assuming that the rivets in double shear are 1.875 times as strong as those in single shear

$$(p - 2.1) \times 1.2 \times 800 = 3 \times 1.875 \times \frac{\pi}{4} \times 2.1^2 \times 600$$

$$p = 14.27 \text{ cm.}$$

According to I.B.R. the maximum pitch is given by

Maximum pitch $= 6t + 4.128$

$= 6 \times 1.2 + 4.128 = 11.328$ cm.

We adopt $p = 11.5$ cm.

(*iii*) **To find distance between rows of rivets**

$C$ = Distance between rows of rivets

$= 0.8\, p = 0.8 \times 11.5 = 9.2$ cm.

(*iv*) **To find cover plate (strap) thickness**

$t_1$ = Thickness of cover plate

$= 0.625 \times t = 0.0625 \times 1.2 = 0.75$ cm.

(*v*) **To find efficiency of the joint**

$\eta_s$ = shearing efficiency

$$= \frac{N \times \frac{\pi}{4} d^2 \times f_s \times 1.875}{(p - d) \,.\, t \,.\, f_t}$$

$$= \frac{3 \times \frac{\pi}{4} \times 2.1^2 \times 600 \times 1.875}{(11.5 - 2.1) \times 1.2 \times 800}$$

$$\eta_s = 1.27 = 127\%$$

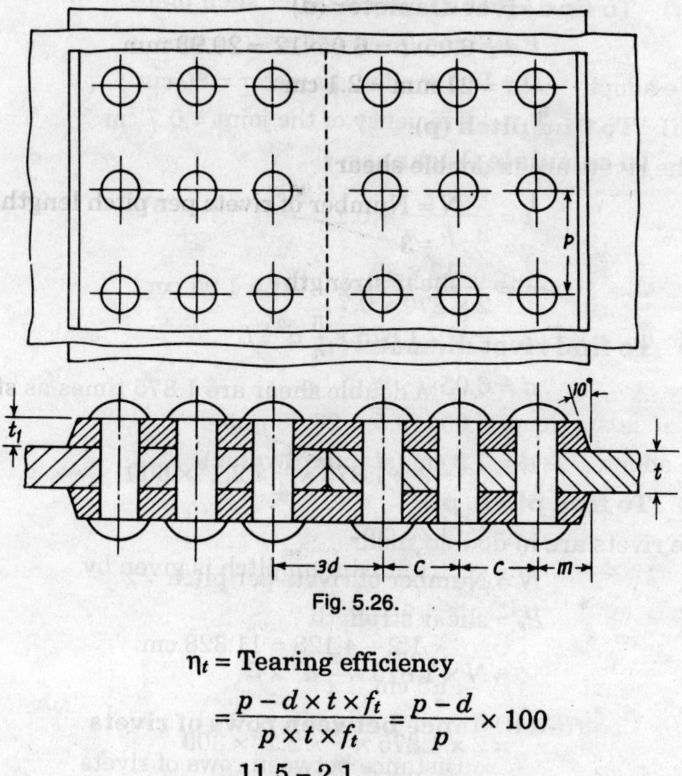


Fig. 5.26.

$$\eta_t = \text{Tearing efficiency}$$

$$= \frac{p - d \times t \times f_t}{p \times t \times f_t} = \frac{p - d}{p} \times 100$$

$$= \frac{11.5 - 2.1}{11.5} \times 100$$

$$= 0.817 = 81.7\%.$$

Hence efficiency of the joint is 8.17%.

***(vi)* To find marginal distance**

Marginal distance, $m = 1.5 \times d$

$$= 1.5 \times 2.1 = 3.15 \text{ cm.}$$

**Example 5.5.** *Design a double riveted butt joint with two cover plates for the longitudinal seam of a boiler shell of 80 cm diameter. The maximum steam pressure is 12 kg/cm². The allowable stresses* *are $f_s = 300$ kg/cm$^2$, $f_t = 370$ kg/cm$^2$ and $f_c = 550$ kg/cm$^2$. The efficiency of the joint is 70%. The corrosion allowance is 0.1 cm.*

**Solution.**

Fig. 5.14 shows a double riveted double cover butt joint.

$t$ = Thickness of boiler shell plate

$P$ = Steam pressure = 12 kg/cm$^2$

$D$ = Boiler shell diameter = 80 cm.

$\eta$ = Efficiency of the joint = 0.7 cm.

(*i*) **To calculate thickness, *t***

$$t = \frac{PD}{2 \cdot f_t \cdot n} + 0.1$$

$$= \frac{12 \times 80}{2 \times 370 \times 0.7} + 0.1 = 1.95 \text{ cm}$$

(*ii*) **To find rivet diameter, *d***

$$d = 6.05\sqrt{t}$$

$$= 6.05\sqrt{19.5} = 26.68 \text{ mm}$$

We adopt, $d = 7.2$ cm (standard value)

(*iii*) **To find pitch, *p*.**

The rivets are in double shear

$N$ = Number of rivets per pitch = 2

$P_s$ = shear strength

$$= N \times 1.875 \times \frac{\pi}{4} d^2 \times f_s$$

$$= 2 \times 1.875 \times \frac{\pi}{4} \times 2.7^2 \times 300$$

$$= 6438 \text{ kg.}$$

$P_c$ = Crushing strength

$$= N \cdot d \cdot t \cdot f_s$$

$$= 2 \times 2.7 \times 1.95 \times 550 = 5791.5 \text{ kg.}$$

As crushing strength is less than shear strength therefore to find pitch equate tearing strength of plate equal to crushing strength.

$$(p - d) \cdot t \cdot f_t = 5791.5$$

$$(p - 2.7) \times 1.95 \times 370 = 5791.5$$

$$p = 10.72 \text{ cm.}$$

According to I.B.R.

Maximum pitch $= 3.5t + 4.128$

$= 3.5 \times 1.95 + 4.128 = 11$ cm.

Minimum pitch $= 2d = 2 \times 2.7 = 5.4$

Hence we adopt,

$$p = 10.72 \text{ cm.}$$

(*iv*) **To find efficiency of the joint**

Efficiency of the joint

$$= \frac{\text{Strength of joint}}{p \times t \times f_t} \times 100$$

$$= \frac{5791.5}{10.72 \times 1.95 \times 370} \times 100 = 74.87\%.$$

(*v*) **To calculate cover plate thickness, $t_1$**

$$t_1 = 0.625\, t = 0.625 \times 1.95 = 1.22 \text{ cm.}$$

**Example 5.6.** *Design a triple riveted double cover plate with unequal cover plates butt joint for longitudinal seam of a boiler if the inside diameter of largest course of the drum is 100 cm and steam pressure is 19 kg/c m². Assume the allowable stresses as $f_s = 600$ kg/cm² $f_t = 800$ kg/cm² and $f_s = 1300$ kg/cm². Corrosion allowance is 0.1 cm.*

**Solution.**

Fig. 5.27 shows the joint

$$P = 19 \text{ kg/cm}^2$$

$$D = 100 \text{ cm.}$$

(*i*) **To find thickness *t* of boiler shell**

$$t = \frac{PD}{2 f_{t.\eta}} + 0.1$$

$$= \frac{19 \times 100}{2 \times 800 \times 0.8} + 0.1 = 1.58 \text{ cm}$$

Assuming the efficiency as 80%.

(*ii*) **To find diameter of riveted, *d***

$$d = 6.05 \sqrt{t}$$

$$= 6.05 \sqrt{15.8} = 24 \text{ mm} = 2.4 \text{ cm.}$$

We adopt, $d = 2.4$ cm.

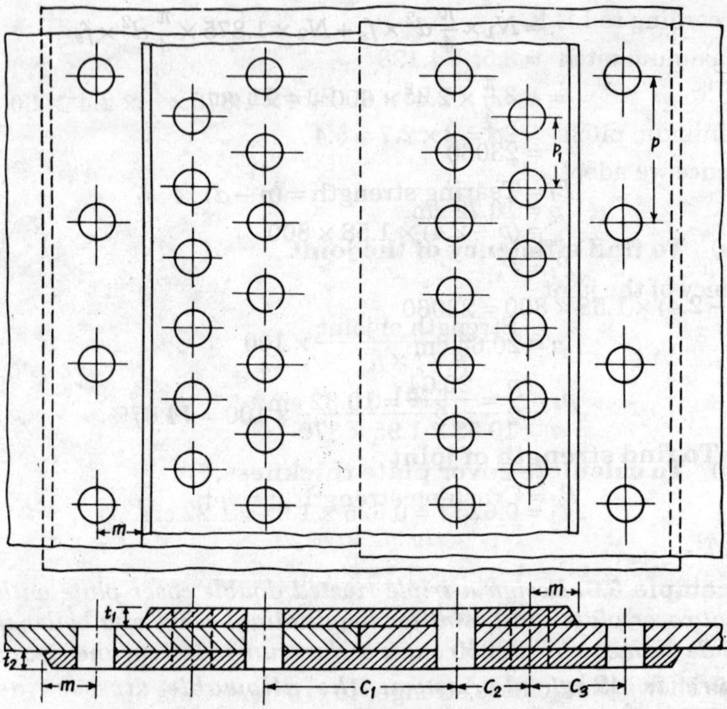


Fig. 5.27.

**(*iii*) To find thickness of cover plates**

$t_1$ = Thickness of upper cove plate *i.e.*, thick ness of narrow butt strap

$= 0.625 \times t = 0.625 \times 1.58 = 0.988$ cm

$t_2$ = Thickness of lower cover plate *i.e.* thick ness of wide butt strap.

$t_2 = 0.75 \times t = 0.75 \times 1.58 = 1.18$ cm.

**(*iv*) To find pitch, *p***

$p$ = Pitch between rivets in outer row

$N$ = Total number of rivets per pitch length

= 5

Out of these five rivets the rivets in single shear and double shear are as follows :

$N_1$ = Rivets in single shear = 1

$N_2$ = Number of rivets in double shear = 4

$P_s$ = Shear strength of all the rivets

$$= N_1 \times \frac{\pi}{4} d^2 \times f_s + N_2 \times 1.875 \times \frac{\pi}{4} d^2 \times f_s$$

$$= 1 \times \frac{\pi}{4} \times 2.4^2 \times 600 + 4 \times 1.875 \times \frac{\pi}{4} \times 2.4^2 \times 600$$

$$= 23060$$

$$P_t = \text{Tearing strength} = (p - d) \, . \, t \, . \, f_t$$

$$= (p - 2.4) \times 1.58 \times 800$$

$$P_t = P_s$$

$$(p - 2.4) \times 1.58 \times 800 = 23060$$

$$p = 20.64 \text{ cm}$$

$$p_t = \frac{p}{2} = \frac{20.64}{2} = 10.32 \text{ cm.}$$

(*v*) **To find strength of joint**

$$P_c = \text{Crushing strength of rivets}$$

$$= N_1 \, . \, d \, . \, t_2 \, . \, f_c + N_2 \, . \, d \, . \, t \, . \, f_c.$$

$$= 1 \times 2.4 \times 1.18 \times 1300 + 4 \times 2.4 \times 1.58 \times 1300$$

$$= 23400 \text{ kg}$$

$$P_s = 23060$$

This shows that joint is stronger in crushing than shear.

The joint may fail by tearing the plate between rivets in second row and shearing the rivet in outer row, in that case strength will be given by

$$P_1 = (p - 2d) \, . \, t \, . \, f_t + \frac{\pi}{4} d^2 \, . \, f_s$$

$$= (20.64 - 2 \times 2.4) \times 1.58 \times 800 + \frac{\pi}{4} \times 2.4^2 \times 600$$

$$= 22734 \text{ kg.}$$

Again the joint may fail by tearing the plate between rivets in third row and shearing of two rivets in double shear in second row and shearing of one rivet in single shear in outer row. In this case strength is calculated as follows :

$$P_2 = (P - 2d) \, . \, t \, . \, f_t + 2 \times \frac{\pi}{4} d^2 \times f_s \times 1.875 + \frac{\pi}{4} d^2 \, . \, f_s \, .$$

$$= (20.64 - 2 \times 2.4) \times 1.58 \times 800 + 2 \times \frac{\pi}{4} \times 2.4^2 \times 600 \times 1.875$$

$$+ \frac{\pi}{4} \times 2.4^2 \times 600$$

$= 32907$ kg.

Hence strength of the joint $= P_1 = 22734$ kg.

(*vi*) **To find efficiency of the joint**

$$P = \text{Strength of unpunched plate}$$
$$= p \times t \times f_t$$
$$= 20.64 \times 1.58 \times 800 = 26088 \text{ kg}$$

$$\text{Efficiency} = \frac{22734}{26088} \times 100 = 87\%.$$

The efficiency is greater than assumed efficiency of 80% hence design is satisfactory.

(*vii*) **To find distance between rows of rivets**

$$c_1 = 3d = 3 \times 2.4 = 7.2 \text{ cm}$$
$$c_3 = 0.2p + 1.15d$$
$$= 0.2 \times 20.64 + 1.15 \times 2.4 = 6.88 \text{ cm}$$
$$c_2 = \text{Distance between inner rows}$$
$$= 0.165p + 0.67d$$
$$= 0.165 \times 20.64 + 0.67 \times 2.4$$
$$= 3.4 + 1.6 = 5 \text{ cm}$$
$$m = \text{Marginal distance} = 1.5\,d$$
$$= 1.5 \times 2.4 = 3.6 \text{ cm.}$$

**Example 5.7.** *It is required to design longitudinal and circumferential riveted joints for a boiler of diameter 160 cm. The steam pressure in the boiler is 14 kg/cm². In longitudinal joint which is quadruple riveted double cover plate butt joint with unequal cover plates there are 8 rivets in double shear and 3 rivets in single shear. The pitch (p) in the outermost row is twice the pitch of rivets in next inner row and the pitch of rivets in third and fourth row from outermost row is p / 4. The efficiency of the longitudinal joint is 80%. The allowable stresses are as follows :*

$$f_s = 600 \text{ kg/cm}^2$$
$$f_t = 800 \text{ kg/cm}^2$$
$$f_c = 1200 \text{ kg/cm}^2$$

*Corrosion allowance is 0.1 cm.*

**Solution.**

The joint is shown in Fig. 5.28.

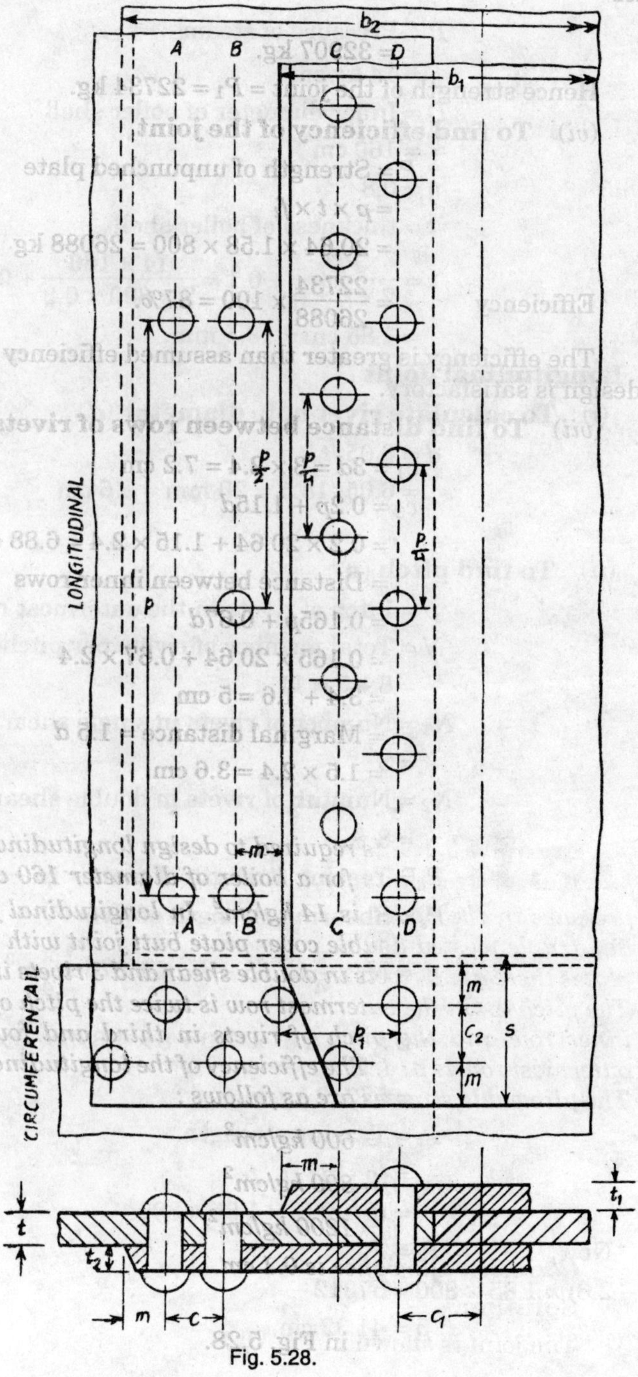
b2
A
B
C
D
b1
p/2
p/4
p/4
LONGITUDINAL
p
m
A
B
C
D
CIRCUMFERENTAIL
m
c2
s
m
p1
m
t
t1
t2
m
c
c1

Fig. 5.28.

$P$ = Pressure of steam

$= 14 \text{ kg/cm}^2$

$D$ = Inner diameter of boiler shell

$= 160$ cm

$\eta = 0.8$

$t$ = thickness of boiler shell

$$= \frac{PD}{2 \times f_t \times \eta} + 0.1 = \frac{14 \times 160}{2 \times 800 \times 0.8} + 0.1$$

$= 1.85$ cm $= 18.5$ mm.

**Longitudinal Joint**

(*i*) **To calculate rivet hole diameter (*d*)**

$d = 6.05\sqrt{t}$

$= 6.05\sqrt{18.5} = 26$ mm $= 2.6$ cm

(*ii*) **To find pitch (*p*)**

$p$ = Pitch of rivets in the outermost row

$N$ = Total member of rivets per pitch length

$= 8 + 3 = 11$

$N_1$ = Number of rivets in single shear

$= 3$

$N_2$ = Number of rivets in double shear

$= 8$

$P_t$ = Tearing strength of plate = $(p - d) \cdot t \cdot f_t$

$P_s$ = Shearing strength of rivets

$$= N_1 \times \frac{\pi}{4} d^2 \cdot f_s + N_2 \times 1.875 \times \frac{\pi}{4} d^2 \times f_s$$

$$= 3 \times \frac{\pi}{4} \times 2.6^2 \times 600 + 8 \times 1.875 \times \frac{\pi}{4} \times 2.6^2 \times 600$$

$= 57312$ kg.

$P_t$ = Tearing strength

$= (p - d) \cdot t \cdot f_t$

$= (p - 2.6) \times 1.85 \times 800$

Now, $P_t = P_s$

$(p - 2.6) \times 1.85 \times 800 = 57312$

$p = 41.32$ cm.

**(iii) To calculate thickness of cover plates**

$t_1$ = Thickness of upper cover plate *i.e.* thickness of narrow cover plate

$= 0.625 \times t$

$= 0.625 \times 1.85 = 1.15$ cm.

$t_2$ = Thickness of lower cover plate *i.e.*, thickness of wider cover plate (strap)

$= 0.75 \times t = 0.75 \times 1.85 = 1.38$ cm

$m$ = Marginal distance $= 1.5\,d = 1.5 \times 2.6 = 3.9$ cm.

$c$ = Back pitch $= 2.5\,d = 2.5 \times 2.6 = 6.5$ cm

$c_1 = 3d = 3d \times 2.6 = 7.8$ cm.

$b_1$ = Width of narrower strap

$= 2(2m + c) = 2(2 \times 3.9 + 6.5) = 28.6$ cm.

$b_1$ = Width of wider strap

$= 2[3c + 2m]$

$= 2[3 \times 6.5 + 2 \times 3.9] = 54.6$ cm.

**(iv) To find efficiency of the joint**

$P_1$ = Strength of joint along $AA$

= Tearing strength of plate

$= (p - d) \,.\, t\, f_t$

$= (41.32 - 2.6) \times 1.85 \times 800 = 57312$ kg

$P_2$ = Strength of joint along $B$–$B$

= Tearing strength of plate along $B$–$B$ + Shearing of rivet in row $A$–$A$

$$= (p - 2d) \,.\, t \,.\, f_t + 1 \times \frac{\pi}{4} d^2 f_s$$

$$= (41.32 - 2 \times 2.6) \times 1.85 \times 800 + \frac{\pi}{4} \times 2.6^2 \times 600$$

$= 56651$ kg

$P_3$ = Strength of joint along $C$–$C$

= Tearing strength at $CC$ + shear strength of two rivets in single shear at $B$-$B$ + shear strength of one rivet in single shear at $A$-$A$

$$= (p - 4d) \,.\, t \,.\, f_t + 2 \times \frac{\pi}{4} d^2 f_s + \frac{\pi}{4} d^2 f_s$$

$$= (41.32 - 4 \times 2.6) \times 1.85 \times 800 + 2 \times \frac{\pi}{4} \times 2.6^2 \times 600$$

$$+ \frac{\pi}{4} \times 2.6^2 \times 600$$

$$= 55313 \text{ kg.}$$

$P_4$ = Strength of joint at *D-D*

= Tearing strength at *D-D* + strength of 4 rivets in double shear at *C-C* + shear strength of 2 rivets in single shear at *B-B* + shear strength of one rivet in single shear at *A-A*

$$= (p - 4d) \,.\, t \,.\, f_t + 4 \times 1.875 \times \frac{\pi}{4} d^2 f_s + 2 \times \frac{\pi}{4} d^2 f_s + \frac{\pi}{4} d^2 \times f_s$$

$$= (41.32 - 4 \times 2.6) \times 1.85 \times 800 + 4 \times 1.875 \times \frac{\pi}{4}$$

$$\times 2.6^2 \times 600 + 2 \times \frac{\pi}{4} \times 2.6^2 \times 600 + \frac{\pi}{4} \times 2.6^2 \times 600$$

$$= 79192 \text{ kg}$$

$P_s$ = Shear strength of the joint

= 57312 kg

$P_c$ = Crushing strength of joint

$$= (N_1 \times d \times t_2 + N_2 \times d \,.\, t)\, f_0$$

$$= (3 \times 2.6 \times 1.38 + 8 \times 2.6 \times 1.85) \times 1200$$

$$= 59088 \text{ kg}$$

This shows that out of all strengths the least strength of the joint is when the joint fails at *C-C* by tearing

Strength of the joint = $P_3$

= 55313 kg.

$$\text{Efficiency} = \frac{\text{Strength of the joint}}{p \times t \times f_t} \times 100$$

$$= \frac{55313}{41.32 \times 1.85 \times 800} \times 100$$

$$= 90.45\%.$$

**Circumferential Joint**

$d = 2.6$ cm

$t = 1.85$ cm

(*i*) **To find number of rivets**

As the joint is a lop joint, therefore, the rivets will be in single shear

$$P_s = \text{Shear resistance of rivets}$$

$$= \frac{\pi}{4} d^2 . f_s \times N$$

$$= \frac{\pi}{4} \times 2.6^2 \times 600 \times N$$

$$= 3183 \times N \text{ kg}$$

where $N$ = Number of rivets

$F$ = Total shearing force due to steam pressure

$$= \frac{\pi}{4} D^2 \times P$$

$$= \frac{\pi}{4} \times 160^2 \times 14 = 281344 \text{ kg}$$

Now $F = P_s$

$$281344 = 3183 \times N$$

$$N = 88.38 = 90 \text{ (say)}$$

Again the number of rivets can be found by equating crushing strength to total shearing force due to steam pressure.

$$P_c = \text{Crushing strength}$$

$$= N . d . t . f_c = N \times 2.6 \times 1.85 \times 1200$$

$$= 5772 \times N \text{ kg}$$

$$P_c = F$$

$$5772 \times N = 281344$$

$$N = 48.74 = 49 \text{ (say)}$$

Hence $N = 90.$

As the diameter of boiler shell is 160 cm therefore, the joint will be double riveted as indicated by Table 5.4.

$\therefore$ $n$ = Number rivets per row $= \frac{N}{2}$

$$= \frac{90}{2} = 45.$$

(*ii*) **To find pitch**

$$p_1 = \text{pitch of rivets} = \frac{\pi(D+t)}{n}$$

$$= \frac{\pi(160+1.85)}{45} = 11.3 \text{ cm}$$

Efficiency of the joint

$$= \frac{p_1 - d}{p_1} \times 100 = \frac{11.3 - 2.6}{11.3} \times 100 = 77\%.$$

(*iii*) **To find distance between rows of rivets**

$C_2$ = spacing between row of rivets

$= 0.33\, p_1 + 0.67\, d$

$= 0.33 \times 11.3 + 0.67 \times 2.6$

$= 3.73 + 1.74 = 5.47$ cm.

Minimum value of $C = 0.6 \times p_1 = 0.6 \times 11.3 = 6.78$ cm

We adopt $C_2 = 6.8$ cm

$m$ = Marginal distance

$= 1.5 \times d = 1.5 \times 2.6 = 3.9$ cm

$S$ = Overlap of the plate

$S = 2m + C_2 = 2 \times 3.9 + 6.8 = 14.6$ cm.

## 5.16 Lozenge (Diamond) Joint

Lozenge joint is used to join two plates of a girder for roof or bridge work. In this joint the rivets are arranged as shown in Fig. 5.29.

In this joint the following values may be taken

$C_1 = 3d$

$C = 2.5\, d$

$p = 4d$

$m = 1.5\, d$

$S = m$

$d$ = Rivet diameter $= 6.05\sqrt{t}$

$t_1 = 0.75\, t$.

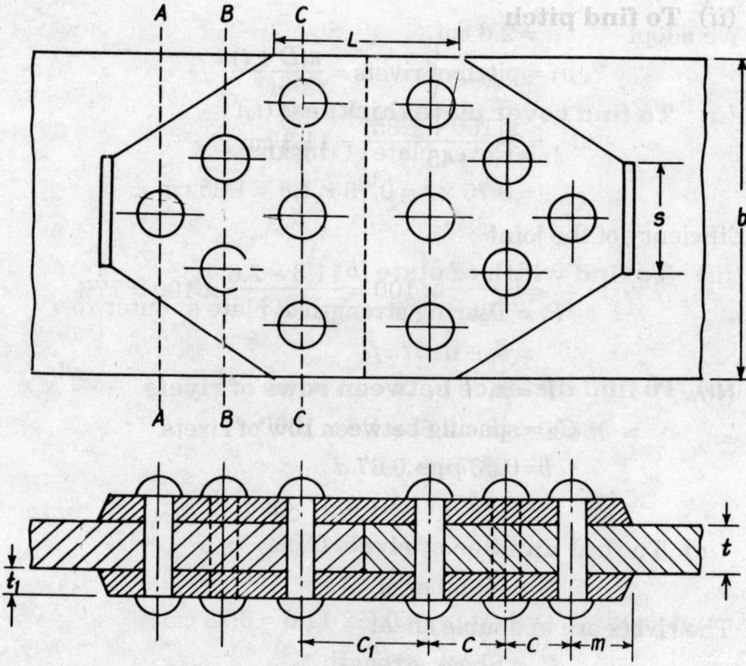


Fig. 5.29.

**Example 5.8.** *Design Lozenge joint having double cover plates for mild steel flat tie bars 18 mm thick to carry a load of 38000 kg. The safe stresses are as follows :*

$$f_s = 700\ kg/cm^2$$

$$f_t = 1000\ kg/cm^2$$

$$f_c = 1500\ kg/cm^2$$

*The plate is not weakened by more than one rivet hole.*

**Solution.**

Fig. 5.29 shows a Lozenge joint

$t$ = Thickness of plates

= 18 mm = 1.8 cm

$P$ = 38000 kg.

(*i*) **To find rivet hole diameter (d)**

$$d = 6.05\sqrt{t} = 6.05\sqrt{18}$$

$$= 6.05 \times 4.24 = 25.65 \text{ mm}$$

$$= 2.565 \text{ cm}$$

We adopt $d = 2.6$ cm.

(*ii*) **To find cover plate thickness ($t_1$)**

$$t_1 = \text{Cover plate of thickness}$$
$$= 0.75 \times t = 0.75 \times 1.8 = 1.35 \text{ cm.}$$

(*iii*) **To find width of plate ($b$)**

$$P_t = \text{Tearing strength of plate at outer row}$$
$$= (b - d) \,.\, t \,.\, f_t$$

Now, $P = p_t$

$$38000 = (b - 2.6) \times 1.8 \times 1000$$
$$b = 23.7 \text{ cm.}$$

(*iv*) **To find number of rivets ($N$)**

$$N = \text{Number of rivets}$$

The rivets are in double shear

$$P_s = \text{Shear strength}$$
$$= N \times 1.875 \times \frac{\pi}{4} d^2 \times f_s$$
$$= N \times 1.875 \times \frac{\pi}{4} \times 2.6^2 \times 700$$
$$= 6965 \times N \text{ kg}$$

Put $P = P_s$

$$38000 = 6965 \times N$$
$$N = \frac{38000}{6965} = 5.45$$
$$P_c = \text{Crushing strength}$$
$$= N \,.\, d \,.\, t \,.\, f_c = N \times 2.6 \times 1.8 \times 1500$$
$$= 7020 \times N \text{ kg}$$

Put $P = P_c$

$$38000 = 7020 \times N$$
$$N = \frac{38000}{7020} = 5.4$$

We adopt $N = 6$.

The rivets are arranged as shown in Fig. 5.29.

(*v*) **To find efficiency of the joint**

$P_s$ = Shearing strength of 6 rivets

$$= 6 \times \frac{\pi}{4} d^2 \times 1.875 \times f_s$$

$$= 6 \times \frac{\pi}{4} \times 2.6^2 \times 1.875 \times 700$$

= 41789 kg.

$P_c$ = Crushing strength of 6 rivets

$= 6 \times d \,.\, t \,.\, f_c$

$= 6 \times 2.6 \times 1.8 \times 1500 = 42120$ kg.

$Pt$ = Tearing strength along $A$–$A$.

= 38000 kg.

$P_1$ = Strength of joint at $B$–$B$.

= Tearing strength of 2 rivets at $B$-$B$ + shear strength of one rivet at $A$-$A$.

$$= (b - 2d) \,.\, t \,.\, f_t + 1.875 \times \frac{\pi}{4} d^2 \times f_s$$

$$= (23.7 - 2 \times 2.6) \times 1.8 \times 1000 + 1.875 \times \frac{\pi}{4} \times 2.6^2 \times 700$$

= 40265 kg.

$P_2$ = Strength of joint at $C$–$C$.

= Tearing strength of 3 rivets at $C$-$C$ + Shear strength of two rivets at $B$-$B$ + Shear strength of one rivet at $A$-$A$.

$$= (b - 3d) \,.\, t f_t \,. \; + 2 \times 1.875 \times \frac{\pi}{4} d^2 f_s$$

$$+ 1.875 \times \frac{\pi}{4} d^2 \times f_s$$

$$= (23.7 + 3 \times 2.6) \times 1.8 \times 1000$$

$$+ 2 \times 1.875 \times \frac{\pi}{4} \times 2.6^3 \times 700 + 1.875$$

$$\times \frac{\pi}{4} \times 2.6^2 \times 700 = 49515 \text{ kg.}$$

Hence lowest strength of the joint is at $A$-$A$ and is equal to 38000.

Strength of solid plate = $b \times t \times f_t$

$$\text{Efficiency} = \frac{38000}{b \times t \times f_t} \times 100$$

$$= \frac{38000}{23.7 \times 1.8 \times 1000} \times 100 = 89\%.$$

(*vi*) **To find pitch and distances between rows of rivets**

$$p = \text{pitch} = 4\,d$$

$$= 4 \times 2.6 = 10.4 \text{ cm}$$

$$c_1 = 3\,d = 3 \times 2.6 = 7.8 \text{ cm}$$

$$c = 2.5\,d = 2.5 \times 2.6 = 6.5 \text{ cm}$$

$$m = \text{Margin} = 1.5 \times 2.6 = 3.9 \text{ cm.}$$

## 5.17 Eccentric Load on Riveted Connections

When a load is applied eccentrically to a group of rivets forming a riveted connection the effect of both moment or torque and direct load should be taken into account. Consider a typical riveted joint show in Fig. 5.30 in which a group of four rivets support the eccentric load *P* with an eccentricity of '*e*'.

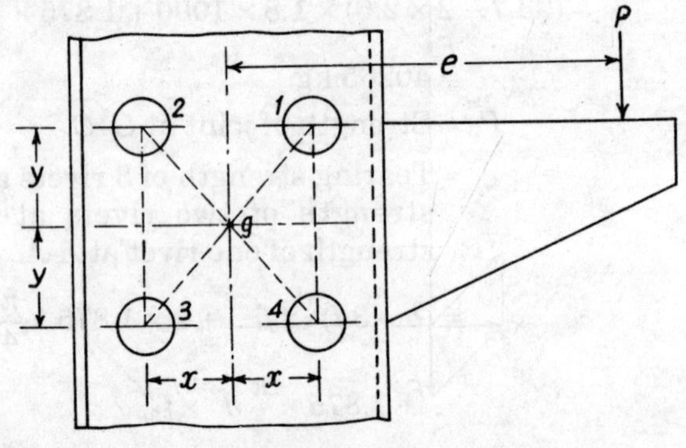


Fig. 5.30.

To find diameter of rivets proceed as follows :

(*i*) Locate the centre of gravity of the group of rivets. In this case as the rivets are of same size and they are symmetrically placed the centre of gravity of group of rivets will be at *g*.

(*ii*) Introduce at centre of gravity two forces $P_1$ and $P_2$ equal and opposite in vertical direction and each equal to *P*.

$$P_1 = P_2 = P$$

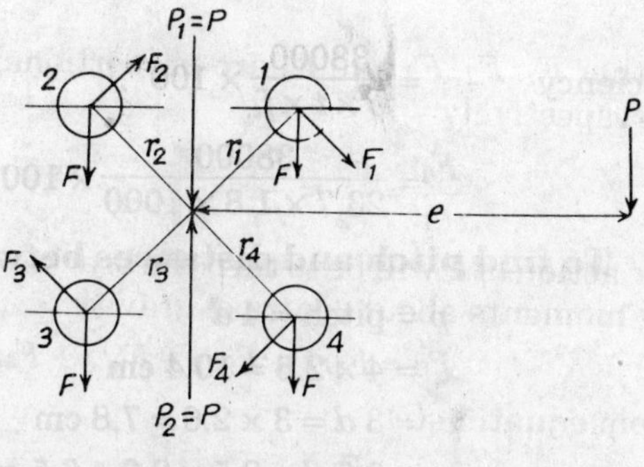


Fig. 5.31.

(*iii*) Primary shear force ($F$) on each rivet is given by

$$F = \frac{P}{n} = \frac{P}{4}$$

where $n$ = Number of rivets.

This force acts vertically downward at the centre of each rivet.

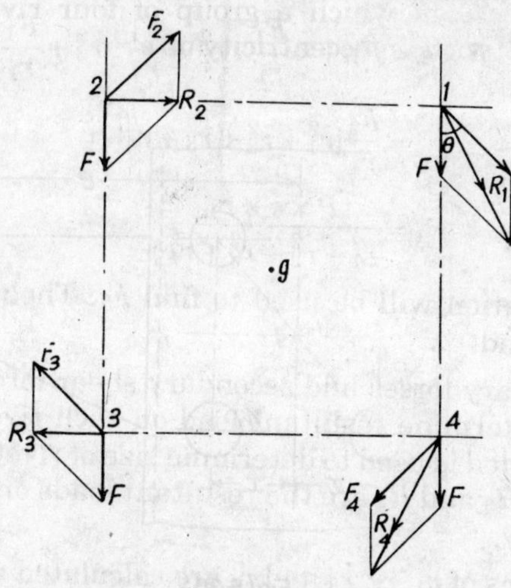


Fig. 5.32.

(*iv*) The turning moment = $P \times e$.

This turning moment produces secondary shear forces $F_1, F_2, F_3$ and $F_4$ respectively on rivet 1, 2, 3 and 4 (see Fig. 5.31). The forces $F_1, F_2, F_3$ and $F_4$ are different in magnitude and direction of these forces are at right angle to their respective moment arms that is $F_1$ will act at right angle to $r_1$, $F_2$ will act right angle to $r_2$, $F_3$ will act at right angle to $r_3$ and $F_4$ will act at right angle to

$r_4$. Further $F_1$, $F_2$, $F_3$ and $F_4$ are proportional to distances $r_1$, $r_2$, $r_3$ and $r_4$ respectively.

$$\frac{F_1}{r_1} = \frac{F_2}{r_2} = \frac{F_3}{r_3} = \frac{F_4}{r_4} \quad ...(i)$$

The action of $P$ will be to turn the bracket in clockwise direction. Taking moments about centre of gravity.

$$Pe = F_1 r_1 + F_2 r_2 + F_3 r_3 + F_4 r_4 \quad ...(ii)$$

From equation (*i*)

$$F_2 = \frac{F_1}{r_1} \times r_2$$

$$F_3 = \frac{F_1}{r_1} \times r_3$$

$$F_4 = \frac{F_1}{r_1} \times r_4$$

Substituting these values in equation (*ii*)

$$P \times e = F_1 r_1 \times \frac{F_1}{r_1} \cdot r_2^2 + \frac{F_1}{r_1} \cdot r_3^2 + \frac{F_1}{r_1} \cdot r_4^2$$

$$= \frac{F_1}{r_1}[r_1^2 + r_2^2 + r_3^2 + r_4^2]$$

$$F_1 = \frac{P \times e \times r_1}{r_1^2 + r_2^2 + r_3^2 + r_4^2}.$$

This equation will be used to find $F_1$. Then forces $F_2$, $F_3$ and $F_4$ can be found.

The primary forces and secondary shear forces are added vectorially to determine resultant load on each rivet. The maximum resultant loaded is used to determine size of rivet. As shown in Fig. 5.32, $R_1$, $R_2$, $R_3$ and $R_4$ are the resultant loads on rivets, 1, 2, 3 and 4 respectively.

The values of $r_1$, $r_2$, $r_3$ and $r_4$ are calculated as follows :

$$r_1 = \sqrt{x^2 + y^2} = r_2 = r_3 = r_4$$

Graphically resultant load $R_1$ can be found as follows :

$$R_1 = \sqrt{F_1^2 + F^2 + 2F_1 \cdot F \cdot \cos\theta}$$

where $\theta$ = Angle between $F_1$ and $F$

Let $d$ = Rivet diameter

$f_s$ = Safe shear stress in rivet material

$\varphi$ = Maximum load out of $R_1$, $R_2$, $R_3$ and $R_4$.

The rivet is in single shear

$$Q = \frac{\pi}{4} d^2 \times f_s$$

The rivet diameter is found from this equation.

**Example 5.9.** *A group of six rivets supports a load of 4200 kg. (Fig. 5.33). If all the rivets are of same size determine diameter of the rivet. The shear stress is limited to 500 kg/cm². Also calculate the bearing stress if the plate thickness is 1.2 cm.*

**Solution.**

As shown in the Fig 5.33

$P$ = Eccentric load = 4200 kg

$e$ = Eccentricity = 16 cm.

$g$ = Centre of gravity

$n$ = Number of rivets = 6

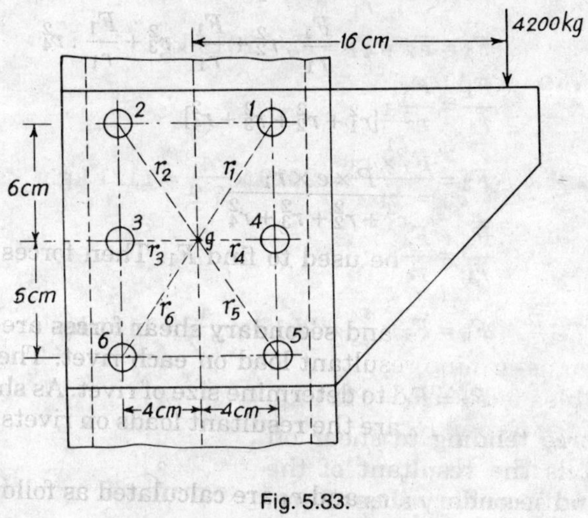


Fig. 5.33.

$F$ = Primary shear force.

$$= \frac{P}{n}$$

$$= \frac{P}{6} = \frac{4200}{6} = 700 \text{ kg.}$$

Let $F_1$, $F_2$, $F_3$, $F_4$, $F_5$, and $F_6$ be the secondary shear forces on rivet 1, 2, 3, 4, 5, and 6 respectively.

$$r_1 = \text{Arm length} = \sqrt{6^2 + 4^2} = 7.2 \text{ cm.}$$

$$r_1 = r_2 = r_5 = r_6 = 7.2 \text{ cm}$$

$$r_3 = r_4 = 4 \text{ cm.}$$

$$P \times e = \frac{F_1}{r_1}\left[r_1^2 + r_2^2 + r_3^2 + r_4^2 + r_5^2 + r_6^2\right]$$

$$4200 \times 16 = \frac{F_1}{7.2}\left[7.2^2 + 7.2^2 + 4^2 + 4^2 + 7.2^2 + 7.2^2\right]$$

$$F_1 = 2019 \text{ kg.}$$

$$\frac{F_1}{r_1} = \frac{F_2}{r_2}$$

$$\therefore \quad F_2 = F_1 \times \frac{r_2}{r_1} = 2019 \times \frac{7.2}{7.2} = 2019 \text{ kg.}$$

$$\frac{F_1}{r_1} = \frac{F_5}{r_5}$$

$$\therefore \quad F_5 = F_1 \times \frac{r_5}{r_1} = F_1$$

$$F_1 = F_2 = F_5 = F_6 = 2019 \text{ kg.}$$

$$\frac{F_1}{r_1} = \frac{F_3}{r_3}$$

$$F_3 = \frac{F_1 \times r_3}{r_1} = 2019 \times \frac{4}{7.2} = 1121 \text{ kg.}$$

$$\frac{F_1}{r_1} = \frac{F_4}{r_4}$$

$$F_4 = F_1 \times \frac{r_4}{r_1} = 2019 \times \frac{4}{7.2} = 1121 \text{ kg.}$$

$$\therefore \quad F_3 = F_4 = 1121 \text{ kg.}$$

The force tending to shear off each rivet is the resultant of the primary and secondary shear force. The resultant forces $R_1, R_2, R_3, R_4, R_5$ and $R_6$ on rivet 1, 2, 3, 4, 5, and 6 respectively can be found graphically.

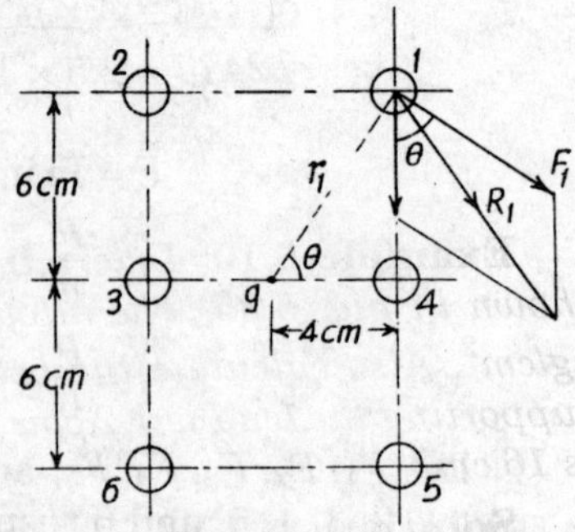

Fig. 5.34.

The maximum resultant force $R_1$ will be on rivet 1.

$R_1$ is the resultant of $F$ and $F_1$. The force $F$ acts vertically downward and the force $F_1$ acts at right angle to $r_1$. From force diagram (Fig. 5.34)

$$R_1 = 2477 \text{ kg.}$$

Analytically the resultant load $R_1$ is calculated as follows :

$$\theta = \text{Angle between forces } F_1 \text{ and } F.$$

$$\cos\theta = \frac{4}{r_1} = \frac{4}{7.2}$$

$$R_1 = \sqrt{F^2 + F_1^2 + 2F\,F_1\cos\theta}$$

$$= \sqrt{700^2 + 2019^2 + 2 \times 700 \times 2019 \times \frac{4}{7.2}}$$

$$= 2477 \text{ kg.}$$

(*ii*) **To calculate rivet diameter, (d)**

Let $d$ = Rivet diameter

$f_s$ = Shear stress = 500 kg/cm$^2$

The rivet is in single shear

$$A = \text{Area under shear} = \frac{\pi}{4} d^2$$

$$R_1 = A \times f_s = \frac{\pi}{4} d^2 \times f_s$$

$$2477 = \frac{\pi}{4} d^2 \times 500 \quad d = 2.5 \text{ cm.}$$

(*iii*) **To calculate bearing stress**

$f_b$ = Bearing stress

$t$ = Thickness of plate = 1.2 cm.

$A$ = Area of rivet in bearing = $d \,.\, t$

$$R_1 = A \times f_b = d \,.\, t \,.\, f_b$$

$$2477 = 2.5 \times 1.2 \times f_b$$

$$f_b = 825.67 \text{ kg/cm}^2.$$

**Example 5.10.** *Determine the diameter of rivet for the joint shown in Fig. 5.35. The allowable shear stress in the rivet is 500 kg/cm$^2$. Also calculate the bearing stress of the thickness of plate supporting the load is 1.2 cm. The distance between centres of rivets is 16 cm.*

**Solution.**

As shown in Fig. 5.35

$P$ = Eccentric load = 2400 kg.

$e$ = Eccentricity = 18 cm.

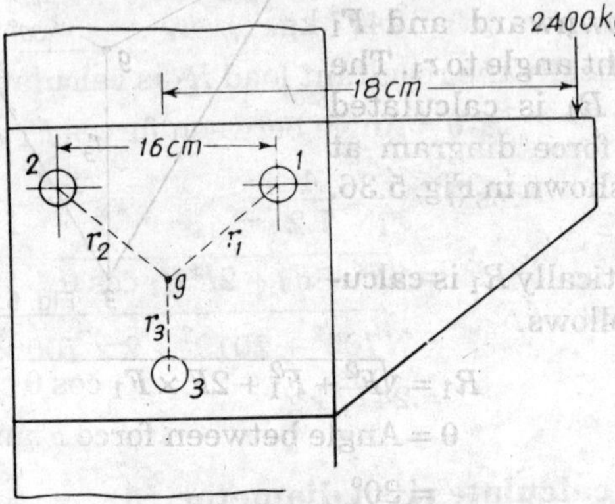


Fig. 5.35.

$n$ = Number of rivets = 3

$F$ = Primary shear force on each rivet

$$= \frac{P}{3} = \frac{2400}{3} = 800 \text{ kg.}$$

The centre of gravity is $g$.

The distance of centre of gravity from centre of rivets 1, 2, and 3 is $r_1$, $r_2$ and $r_3$ respectively

$$r_1 = r_2 = r_3 = \frac{8}{\cos 30} = 9.24 \text{ cm.}$$

Let $F_1$, $F_2$ and $F_3$ be the secondary shear forces on rivet 1, 2 and 3 respectively,

$$P \times e = \frac{F_1}{r_1}[r_1^2 + r_2^2 + r_3^2]$$

$$2400 \times 18 = \frac{F_1}{9.24}[9.24^2 + 9.24^2 + 9.24^2]$$

$$F_1 = 1558 \text{ kg.}$$

$$\frac{F_1}{r_1} = \frac{F_2}{r_2} = \frac{F_3}{r_3}$$

as $$r_1 = r_2 = r_3$$

$$\therefore \quad F_1 = F_2 = F_3 = 1558 \text{ kg.}$$

(*i*) **To calculate $R_1$**

The rivet 1 is heavily loaded.

$R_1$ = Resultant load acting on rivet – 1

$R_1$ is the resultant of $F$ and $F_1$. The force $F$ acts vertically downward and $F_1$ acts at right angle to $r_1$. The resultant $R_1$ is calculated from the force diagram at rivet 1 as shown in Fig. 5.36.

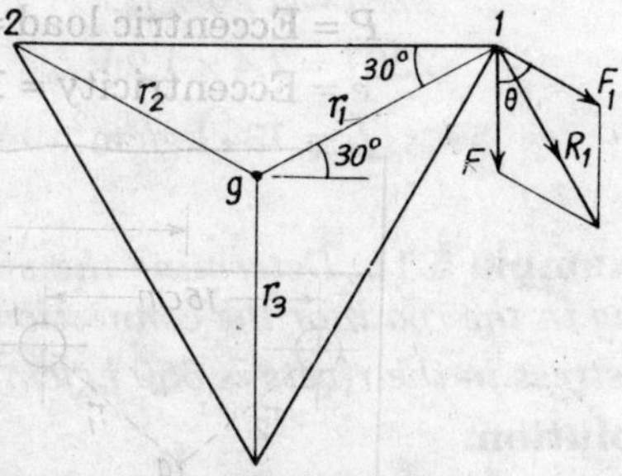


Fig. 5.36.

Analytically $R_1$ is calculated as follows.

$$R_1 = \sqrt{F^2 + F_1^2 + 2F \times F_1 \cos\theta}$$

where $\theta$ = Angle between force $F$ and $F_1$

$= 30°$

$$R_1 = \sqrt{800^2 + 1558^2 + 2 \times 800 \times 1558 \times \cos 30}$$

$= 2287$ kg.

(*ii*) **To find rivet diameter, *d***

$d$ = rivet diameter

$f_s$ = Shear stress in rivet

$= 500 \text{ kg/cm}^2$

The rivet is in single shear

$A$ = Area under shear

$$= \frac{\pi}{4} d^2$$

$$R_1 = A \times f_s$$

$$2287 = \frac{\pi}{4} d^2 \times 500$$

$d = 2.4$ cm.

(*iii*) **To find bearing stress**

$f_b$ = Bearing stress

$t$ = Thickness of plate

$= 1.2$ cm

$A$ = Area under bearing $= d \times t$

$$R_1 = A \times f_b$$

$$2287 = d \times t \times f_b$$

$$2287 = 2.4 \times 1.2 \times f_b$$

$$f_b = 794 \text{ kg/cm}^2.$$

**Example 5.11.** *Determine the size of rivets to resist a pull of 4800 kg in the road for the connection shown in Fig. 5.37. The safe shear stress in the rivets is 650 kg/cm$^2$.*

**Solution.**

$P$ = Load = 4800 kg

$n$ = Number of rivets = 4

$F$ = Primary shear force

$$= \frac{4800}{4} = 1200 \text{ kg}$$

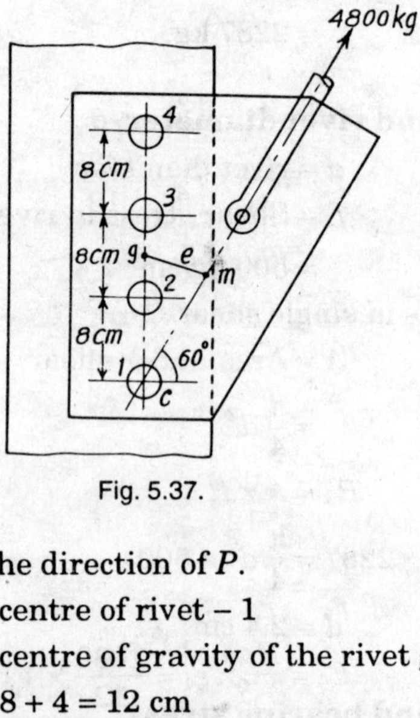


Fig. 5.37.

This force acts in the direction of $P$.

$c$ = centre of rivet – 1

$g$ = centre of gravity of the rivet group.

$cg = 8 + 4 = 12$ cm

$e$ = Eccentricity = $gm$.

In $\Delta\, gmc$ $\quad \dfrac{gm}{gc} = \sin 30.$

$$gm = gc \sin 30 = 12 \times \frac{1}{2} = 6 \text{ cm}.$$

$\therefore$ $\quad e$ = Eccentricity = $gm$ = 6 cm.

Twisting moment $= P \times e = 4800 \times 6$

$$= 28800 \text{ kg cm.}$$

$$28800 = \frac{F_1}{r_1} [r_1^2 + r_2^2 + r_3^2 + r_4^2]$$

$F_1, F_2, F_3$ and $F_4$ are the secondary forces on rivets 1, 2, 3 and 4 respectively and $r_1, r_2, r_3, r_4$ are the arms at which $F_1, F_2, F_3$ and $F_4$ act respectively.

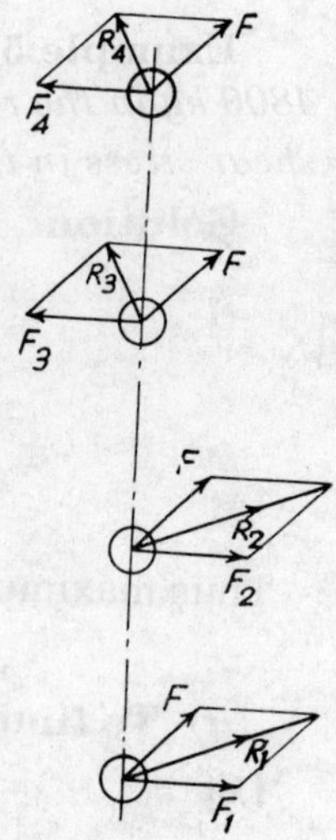

Fig. 5.38.

$$r_1 = 12 \text{ cm}$$

$$r_2 = 4 \text{ cm}$$

$$r_3 = 4 \text{ cm}$$

$$r_4 = 12 \text{ cm}$$

$$28800 = \frac{F_1}{12} [12^2 + 4^2 + 4^2 + 12^2]$$

$$F_1 = 1080 \text{ kg}$$

$$\frac{F_1}{r_1} = \frac{F_2}{r_2}$$

$$F_2 = \frac{F_1}{r_1} \times r_2 = \frac{1080}{12} \times 4$$

$$= 360 \text{ kg.}$$

$$\frac{F_3}{r_3} = \frac{F_1}{r_1}$$

$$\therefore \quad F_3 = \frac{F_1}{r_1} \times r_3$$

$$= \frac{1080}{12} \times 4 = 360 \text{ kg}$$

$$\frac{F_4}{r_4} = \frac{F_1}{r_1}$$

$$\therefore \quad F_4 = \frac{F_1}{r_1} \times r_4 = \frac{1080}{12} \times 12 = 1080 \text{ kg.}$$

(*i*) **To find maximum resultant force.** The resultant forces $R_1$, $R_2$, $R_3$ and $R_4$ can be calculated from force diagram as shown in Fig. 5.38 or these values can be found as follows :

$R_1$ is the resultant of $F$ and $F_1$

$$R_1 = \sqrt{F^2 + F_1^2 + 2F F_1 \cos \theta}$$

where $\theta$ = Angle between $F$ and $F_1 = 60^\circ$.

$$R_1 = \sqrt{1200^2 + 1080^2 + 2 \times 1200 \times 1080 \cos 60}$$
$$= 2202 \text{ kg.}$$
$$R_2 = \sqrt{F_2 + F_2^2 + 2F\,F_2 \cos 60}$$
$$= \sqrt{1200^2 + 360^2 + 2 \times 1200 \times 360 \times \cos 60}$$
$$= 1489 \text{ kg.}$$
$$R_3 = \sqrt{F^2 + F_3^2 - 2F\,F_3 \cos 60}$$
$$= \sqrt{1200^2 + 360^2 - 2 \times 1200 \times 360 \cos 60}$$
$$= 906 \text{ kg.}$$
$$R_4 = \sqrt{F^2 + F_4^2 - 2F\,F_4 \cos 60}$$
$$= \sqrt{1200^2 + 1080^2 - 2 \times 1200 \times 1080 \cos 60}$$
$$= 601 \text{ kg.}$$

Thus maximum resultant force acts rivet - 1 and is equal to

$$R_1 = 2202 \text{ kg.}$$

(*ii*) **To find rivet diameter, *d***

Let $d$ = Rivet diameter

$f_s$ = Shear stress = 650 kg/cm²

The rivet is in single shear

$A$ = Area under shear

$$= \frac{\pi}{4} d^2 \times f_s$$
$$R_1 = \frac{\pi}{4} d^2 \times f_s$$
$$2202 = \frac{\pi}{4} \times d^2 \times 650$$
$$d = 2.1 \text{ cm.}$$

**Example 5.12.** *A bracket is supported by means of four rivets as shown in Fig. 5.38 (a). Determine the diameter of rivets made of C 12 Steel. Use factor of safety equal to 1.8.*

**Solution.** $P$ = Load = 2T = 2000 kg

$F$ = Primary shear force on each rivet

$$= \frac{P}{4} = \frac{2000}{4} = 500 \text{ kg}$$

$e$ = Eccentricity = 110 mm = 11 cm

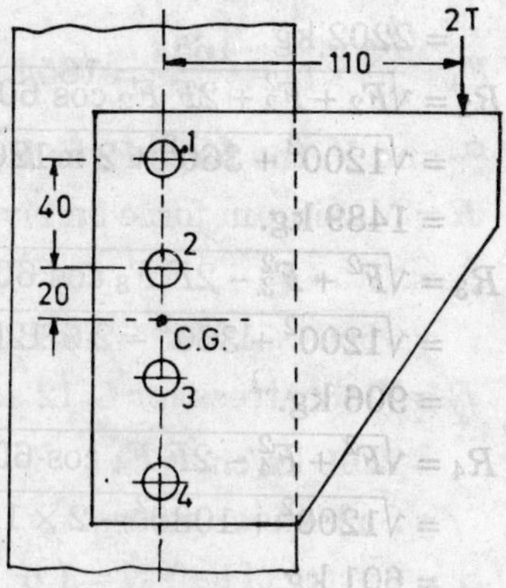


Fig. 5.38 (*a*).

$$M = \text{moment of } P \text{ about C.G.}$$
$$= P \times e = 2000 \times 11$$
$$= 22000 \text{ kg cm}$$

Let $F_1$, $F_2$, $F_3$ and $F_4$ be the secondary shear forces due to $M$. On rivet 1, 2, 3, and 4 respectively. Let $r_1$, $r_2$, $r_3$ and $r_4$ distance of these rivets from C.G.

$$r_1 = 6 \text{ cm}$$
$$r_2 = 2 \text{ cm}$$
$$r_3 = 2 \text{ cm}$$
$$r_4 = 6 \text{ cm.}$$

$$M = 22000 = \frac{F_1}{r_1}[r_1^2 + r_2^2 + r_3^2 + r_4^2]$$

$$= \frac{F_1}{6}[6^2 + 2^2 + 2^2 + 6^2]$$

$$F_1 = 1654 \text{ kg}$$

$$\frac{F_1}{r_1} = \frac{F_2}{r_2}$$

$$F_2 = \frac{F_1}{r_1} \times r_2$$

$$= \frac{1654}{6} \times 2 = 551.1 \text{ kg}$$

$$F_3 = \frac{F_1}{r_1} \times r_3 = \frac{1654}{6} \times 2 = 551.1 \text{ kg}$$

$$F_4 = \frac{F_1}{r_1} \times r_4 = \frac{1654}{6} = 1654 \text{ kg.}$$

Out of $F_1$, $F_2$, $F_3$ and $F_4$ the force $F_2$ or $F_4$ is maximum

$R$ = Maximum force on rivet

$= \sqrt{F^2 + F_1^2}$

$= \sqrt{500^2 + 1654^2} = 1686$ kg

$f_y$ = Yield stress for $C$ 12 steel

$= 2100$ kg/cm$^2$

$f$ = Safe shear stress

F.O.S. = Factor of safety = 1.8

$$f = \frac{f_y}{\text{F.O.S.}} = \frac{2100}{1.8} = 1167 \text{ kg/cm}^2$$

$d$ = Rivet diameter

$$R = \frac{\pi}{4} d^2 \times f$$

$$1686 = \frac{\pi}{4} d^2 \times 1167$$

$d = 1.36$ cm.

## PROBLEMS

**5.1.** (*a*) Sketch a rivet and name its parts.

(*b*) State the materials commonly used for making rivets.

(*c*) Testing of rivets.

**5.2.** (*a*)Name the different types of riveted joints.

(*b*) Sketch and dimension the following riveted joints to join plates 9 mm thick.

(*i*) Single riveted lap joint.

(*ii*) Single riveted single cover plate butt joint.

(*iii*) Triple riveted double cover plate butt joint with zig-zag riveting.

**5.3.** Name, sketch and dimension the rivet heads used in boiler construction.

**5.4.** Name and sketch the rivet heads used in structural work.

**5.5.** Define the following :

(*a*) Pitch

(*b*) Marginal distance

(*c*) Diagonal pitch.

**5.6.** (*a*) Discuss the modes of failure of riveted joints.

(*b*) What do you mean by strength and efficiency of a riveted joints.

**5.7.** Design a single riveted lap joint to connect two mild steel plates 11 mm thick. Assume the safe stresses as follows :

$$f_s = 300 \text{ kg/cm}^2,$$

$$f_t = 400 \text{ kg/cm}^2,$$

$$f_c = 550 \text{ kg/cm}^2.$$

**5.8.** Design a double strap, double riveted butt joint for the longitudinal seam of a boiler joint, 90 cm diameter to carry a maximum steam pressure of 11 kg/cm$^2$ gauge. The allowable stresses are as follows :

$$f_s = 300 \text{ kg/cm}^2$$

$$f_t = 400 \text{ kg/cm}^2$$

$$f_c = 550 \text{ kg/cm}^2.$$

**5.9.** Design longitudinal and circumferential joints for a boiler of 140 cm diameter to carry a working pressure of 13 kg/cm$^2$. The joint is to be triple riveted, double cover plates with unequal cover plates. The safe stresses are as follows :

$$f_s = 600 \text{ kg/cm}^2$$

$$f_t = 300 \text{ kg/cm}^2$$

$$f_c = 1300 \text{ kg/cm}^2.$$

**5.10.** Two mild steel tie rods 30 cm wide and 19 mm thick of a bridge are to be joined by a butt joint having two straps. Design the joint taking stresses as

$$f_s = 700 \text{ kg/cm}^2$$

$$f_c = 1400 \text{ kg/cm}^2$$

$$f_t = 950 \text{ kg/cm}^2$$

shear resistance in double shear may be taken as 15% more than single shear.

**5.11.** A double cover butt joint is made up of two 16 mm thick mild steel plates. The joint is subjected to a tension load of 15000 kg. Design and sketch the joint assuming that plates are not weakened by more than one rivet hole in the outer most row. The safe stresses are

600 kg/cm$^2$, 800 kg/cm$^2$ and 1400 kg/cm$^2$ in shear, tension and compression respectively.

**5.12.** Fig. 5.39 shows a plate riveted to a vertical member by rivets of 14 mm diameter. Calculate the load $P$ that can be carried by the joint if the safe stress in shear of rivets is 550 kg/cm$^2$ and the safe crushing stress of rivets is 1050 kg/cm$^2$.

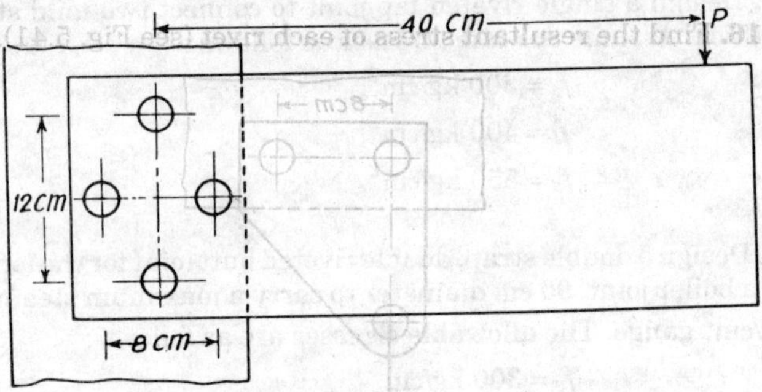


Fig. 5.39.

**5.13.** Fig. 5.40 shows a riveted joint with an eccentric load of 1800 kg. Calculate the rivets diameter if the safe shear stress in rivets is 600 kg/cm$^2$. Also find the crushing stress in rivet if the thickness of plate is 16 mm.

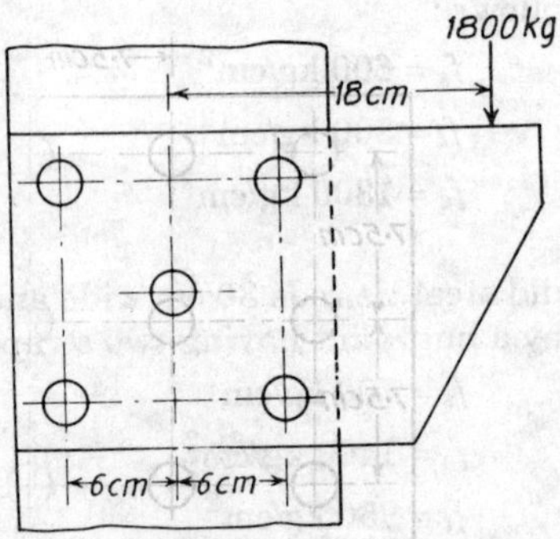


Fig. 5.40.

**5.14.** Design a double riveted lap joint to connect two plates together. The plates are 14 mm thick. The safe stresses are as follows :

$$f_s = 450 \text{ kg/cm}^2$$

$$f_t = 800 \text{ kg/cm}^2$$

$$f_c = 1500 \text{ kg/cm}^2$$

sketch the joint.

**5.15.** Design a double riveted double cover plate butt joint with zig-zag riveting for two plates 17 mm thick. The ultimate stresses are 2000 kg/cm$^2$ in shear, 3200 kg/cm$^2$ in tension and 4800 kg/cm$^2$ in bearing. Use a factor of safety of 4.

**5.16.** Find the resultant stress of each rivet (see Fig. 5.41).

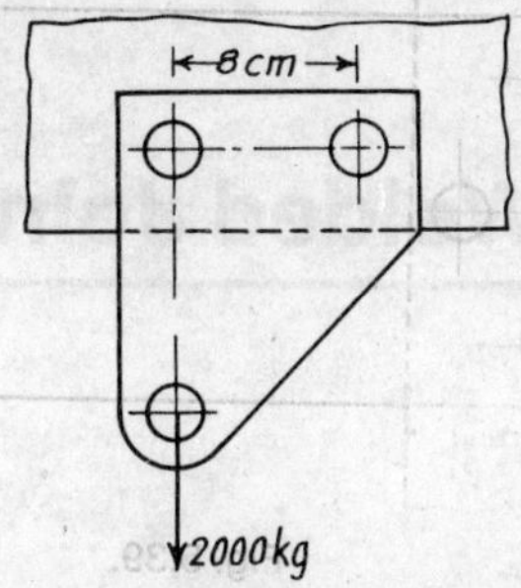


Fig. 5.41.

**5.17.** Determine the permissible load $P$ for the riveted joint shown in Fig. 5.42. If the resultant shear stress for the most highly stressed rivet is 1020 kg/cm$^2$ and rivets are 2.5 cm diameter.

(**Ans.** 18455 kg)

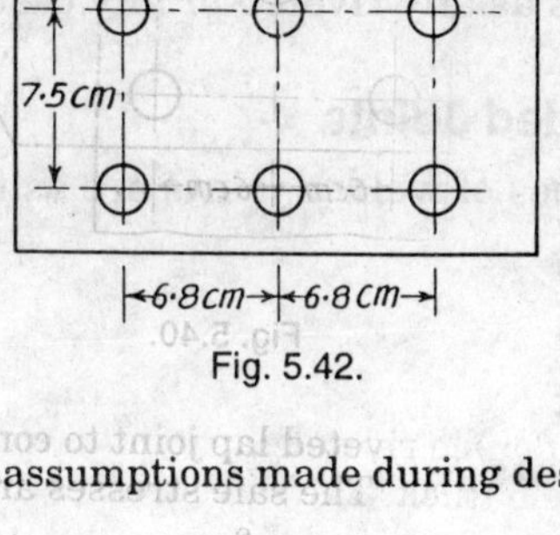


Fig. 5.42.

**5.18.** Discuss the assumptions made during design of riveted joint.

# 6

# Welded Joints

## 6.0 Introduction

Welding is used to join together two or more pieces of metals permanently. It enables a junction to be made between two or more pieces of metal, the contacting surfaces of which have been raised to a plastic or molten condition by the application of heat with or without added metal and with or without the application of pressure. Welding enables the production of leak proof joints that will withstand high temperatures and pressures. Welding has greatly replaced riveting in ship building and structural work. Welding produces stronger and permanent joint. Because of development made in welding technique welded joints have become as reliable and free from faults as any riveted or any cast construction.

## 6.1 Types of Welded Joints

The various types of welded joints are as follows :

(*i*) Butt joints

(*ii*) Lap joints

(*iii*) Edge joint

(*iv*) Corner joints

(*v*) Tee joints.

Fig. 6.1 shows butt joints whereas the lap joints are shown in Fig. 6.2. The edge joints is shown in Fig. 6.3 and Fig. 6.4 shows corner joint whereas *T* joint is shown in Fig. 6.5.

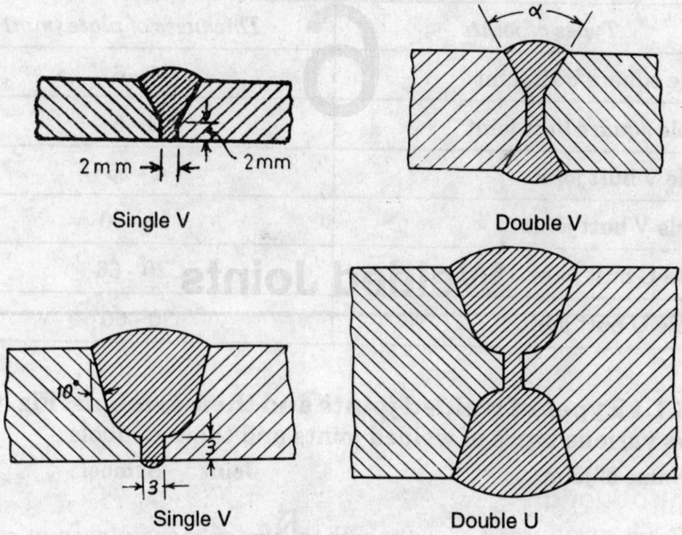


Fig. 6.1. Butt joints.

The angle α in *V*-joints varies from 55°–70°.

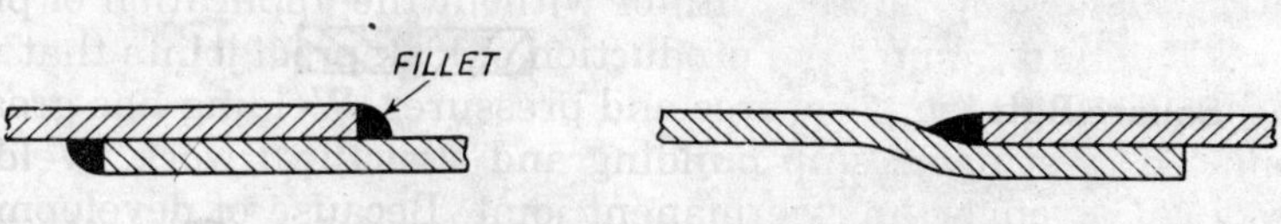


Fig. 6.2. Lap Joints.

Edge Joint
Fig. 6.3.

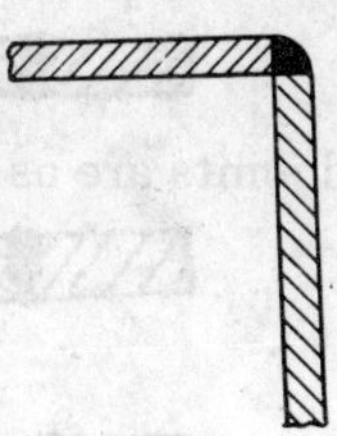

Corner Joint
Fig. 6.4.

Double fillet *T* joint
Fig. 6.5.

Table 6.1 indicates the thickness of plates for which different types of butt joints are used.

**Table 6.1**

| *Types of joints* | *Thickness of plate (mm)* |
|---|---|
| Single square butt joint | 1 - 6 |
| Double square butt joint | 3 - 8 |
| Single V butt joint | 4 - 25 |
| Double V butt joint | 12 - 60 |
| Single U butt joint | 20 - 60 |
| Double U butt joint | 30 - 60 |

**6.1.1 Types of welded joints and their symbols.** Fig. 6.5 (*a*) shows various types of welded joints and their symbols.

Name of joint — Joint — Symbol

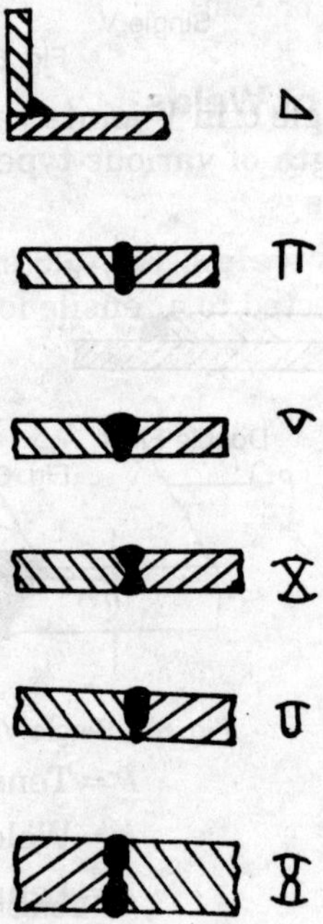

Fillet

Square Butt

Single-V Butt

Double-V Butt

Single-U Butt

Double-U Butt

Single Bevel Butt

Double Bevel Butt

Single-J Butt

Double-J Butt

Spot

Sealing Run

Stud

Bead (Edge or Seal)

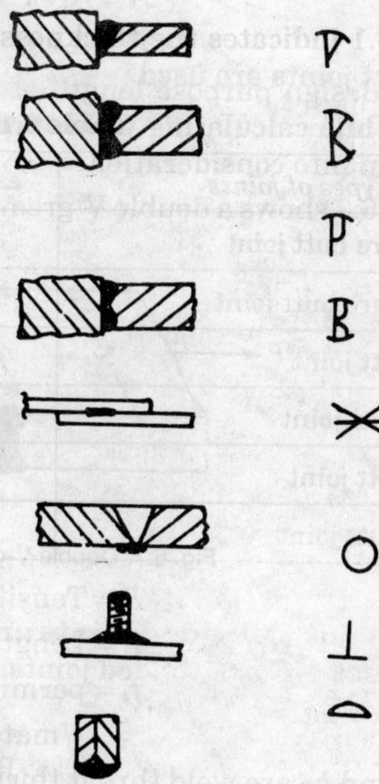

## 6.2 Strength of Welds

The strength of various type of welds (welded joints) is calculates as follows :

(*i*) **Butt welds.** Fig. 6.6 shows a single *V* groove butt weld subjected to a tensile load *P*.

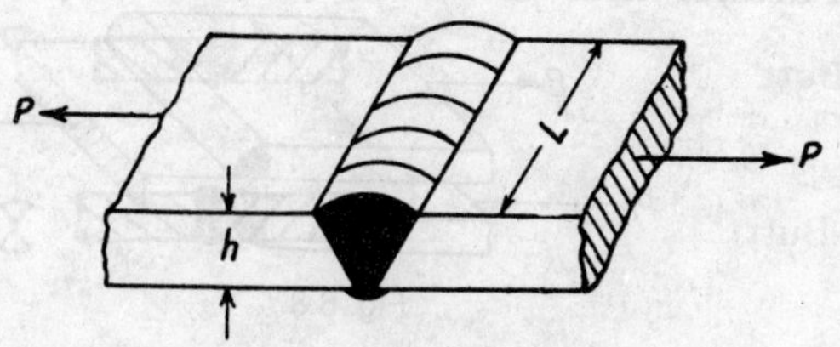


Fig. 6.6. Single V-groove butt weld.

Let $P$ = Tensile load

$h$ = Weld throat

$l$ = Length of weld

$f_t$ = Permissible stress for the weld in tension.

$$A = \text{Area of weld} = h \times l$$

$$P = A \times f_t = h \times l \times f_t.$$

For design purpose length of weld is taken equal to width of plate. While calculating weld throat and reinforcement of weld is not taken into consideration.

Fig. 6.7 shows a double V-groove butt weld subjected to a tensile load $P$.

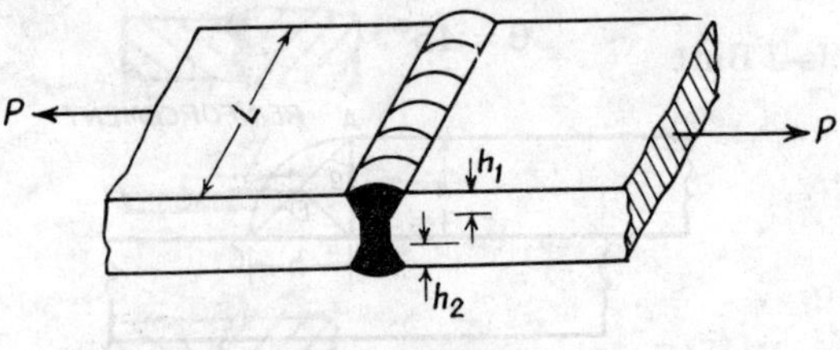


Fig. 6.7. Double V-groove butt weld.

$P$ = Tensile load

$L$ = Length of weld

$f_t$ = permissible tensile stress in weld material.

$h_1$ and $h_2$ are weld throat thickness of $V$ at the top and bottom.

$$A = \text{Area of weld} = (h_1 + h_2) \times L$$

$$P = A \times f_t$$

$$= (h_1 + h_2) \times L \times f_t$$

(*ii*) **Fillet welds.** They are of two types :

(*a*) Transverse fillet welds.

(*b*) Parallel fillet welds.

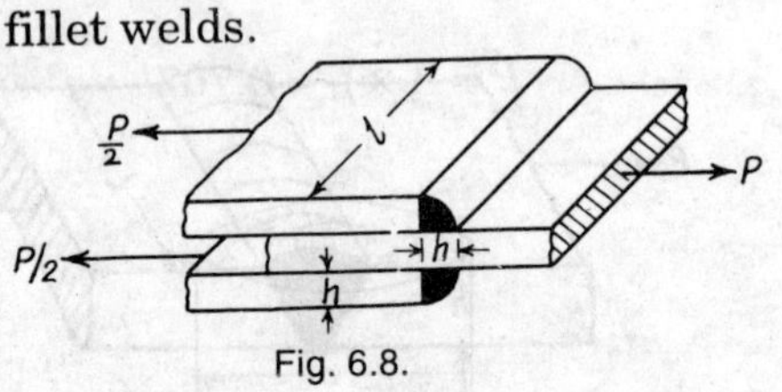


Fig. 6.8.

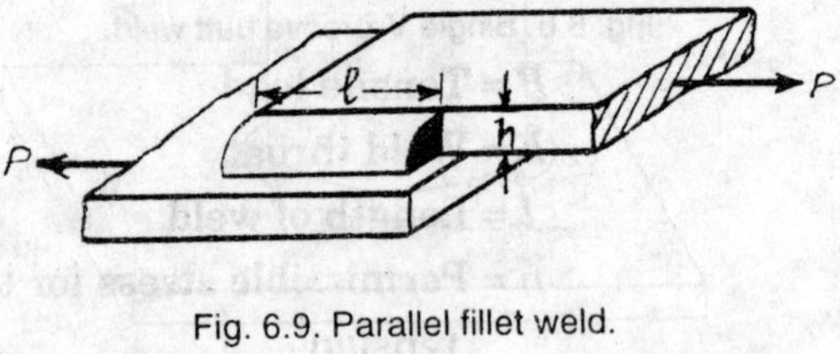


Fig. 6.9. Parallel fillet weld.

Fig. 6.8 shows a transverse fillet joint with two fillets. Transverse fillet welds are assumed to fail in tension whereas parallel fillet welds (Fig. 6.9) are assumed to fail in shear.

Fig. 6.10 shows a 45° fillet weld with equal legs $h$

$$AB = BC = h$$
$$= \text{size of weld}$$
$$\theta = 45^\circ$$

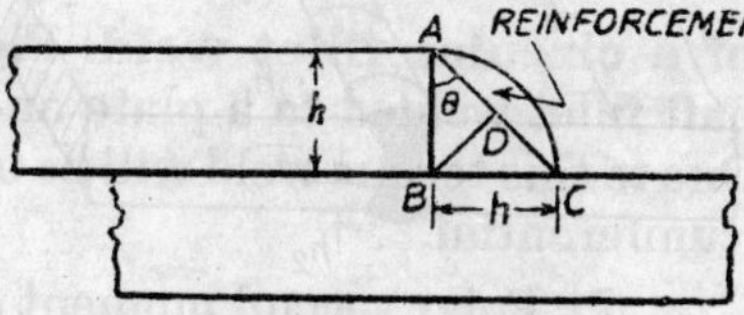


Fig. 6.10. Fillet weld.

$BD$ is perpendicular to $AC$ and is called throat length

$$BD = \text{Throat length}$$

In $\Delta\, BDA$
$$\frac{BD}{AB} = \sin\theta = \sin 45$$
$$BD = AB \sin 45 = h \sin 45 = 0.707\, h$$
$$l = \text{Length of weld}$$
$$A = \text{Area resisting the load is the throat area}$$
$$= BD \times l = 0.707 \times h \times l$$

(*i*) In transverse fillet weld which is assumed to fail in tension.
For single fillet :

$$P = A \times f_t = 0.707h \times l \times f_t$$

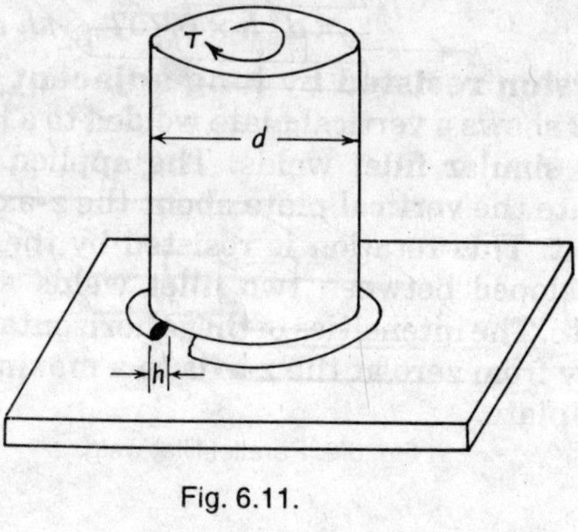


Fig. 6.11.

For double fillet : $P = 2 \times 0.707 \times h \times l \times f_t$.

(*ii*) In parallel fillet weld which is assumed to fail in shear.

For single fillet :

$$P = A \times f_s = 0.707 \times h \times l \times f_s$$

For double fillet :

$$P = A \times f_s = 2 \times 0.707\ hl \times f_s.$$

(*iii*) **Special cases of fillet welds**

(*a*) **Torsion of a circular fillet weld.** Fig. 6.11 shows a circular shaft fillet welded to a plate and subjected to a torque $T$. Due to this torque weld will be under shear. The weld is circumferential.

$J$ = Polar second moment of area of weld section

$T$ = Torque acting on shaft

$d$ = Shaft diameter

$r$ = Radius of shaft = $d/2$

$h$ = Leg of weld

$f_s$ = Shear stress in weld material

$$f_s = \frac{T \times r}{J} = \frac{T \times (d/2)}{\pi\, dh\, (d/2)^2}$$

$$f_s = \frac{2T}{\pi\, d^2\, h}$$

The maximum value of shear stress occurs on throat of weld which is inclined at 45° to the horizontal plane. The length of throat is $h \sin 45 = 0.707\, h$. In that case maximum shear stress will be

$$f_s = \frac{2T}{\pi\, d^2\, h \times 0.707} = \frac{2.83\, T}{\pi h\, d^2}.$$

(*b*) **Torsion resisted by long adjacent fillet welds.** Fig. 6.12 shows a vertical plate welded to a horizontal plate by two similar fillet welds. The applied torque $T$ tries to rotate the vertical plate about the $z$-axis through its mid point. This rotation is resisted by the shearing stresses developed between two fillet welds and the horizontal plate. The intensities of these horizontal shearing stresses vary from zero at the z-axis to a maximum at the ends of the plate.

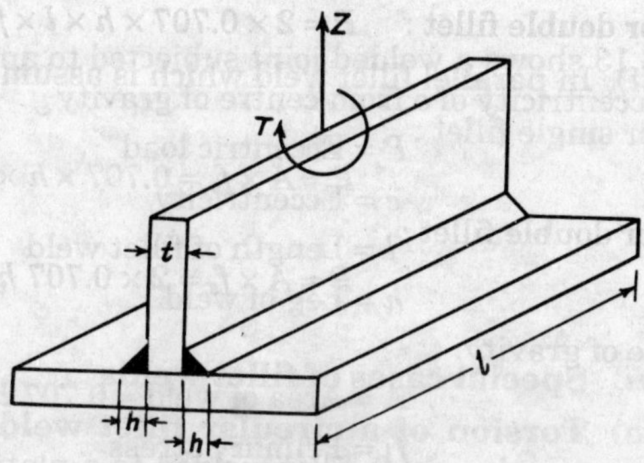


Fig. 6.12.

Let $l$ = Length of weld

$h$ = Leg of weld

$T$ = Torque applied about the vertical plane

$f_s$ = Shear stress in weld material

The maximum value of shear stress will be in the throat and is given by the following relation.

$$f_s = \frac{T \times \frac{l}{2}}{2h_1 \times \frac{l^3}{12}} = \frac{3T}{h_1 l^2}$$

The maximum value of shear stress will be in the throat and is given by the relation,

$$f_s = \frac{3\,T}{0.707\,hl^2} = \frac{4.24\,T}{hl^2}.$$

where $h_1$ = Throat length = 0.707 $h$

## 6.3 Eccentrically Loaded Welded Joints

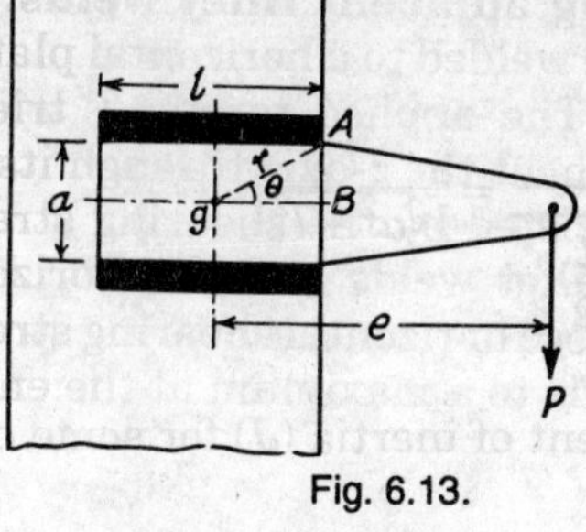


Fig. 6.13.

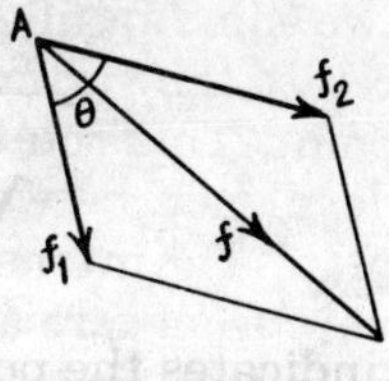


Fig. 6.14.

Fig. 6.13 shows a welded joint subjected to an eccentric load $P$ with an eccentricity of $e$ from centre of gravity $g$.

$P$ = Eccentric load

$e$ = Eccentricity

$l$ = Length of fillet weld

$h$ = Leg of weld

$g$ is centre of gravity.

$A$ = Area of weld = 0.707 $hl$

$f_1$ = Primary stress

$$= \frac{P}{A} = \frac{P}{0.707\, h.l.}$$

$$f_2 = \text{Secondary stress} = \frac{T \times r}{J}$$

$gA = r$

where $T$ = Twisting moment = $P \cdot e$

$J$ = Polar moment of inertia of weld

$$f_2 = \frac{T \times r}{J} = \frac{P \cdot e \cdot r}{J}$$

The maximum stress will occur where $r$ is maximum.

The resultant stress can be calculated from stress diagram (Fig. 6.14). The stress $f_1$ acts vertically downward and $f_2$ acts at right angle to distance $r$.

The resultant stress can be calculated as follows :

$f$ = resultant stress

$$= \sqrt{f_1^2 + f_2^2 + 2 f_1 \cdot f_2 \cos\theta}$$

where $\theta$ = Angle between $f_1$ and $f_2$.

$$\cos\theta = \frac{gB}{gA}$$

$$= \frac{\frac{1}{2}}{\sqrt{\left(\frac{a}{2}\right)^2 + \left(\frac{l}{2}\right)^2}} = \frac{l}{\sqrt{a^2 + l^2}}$$

Table 6.2 indicates the polar moment of inertia ($J$) for some of welds with the weld treated as a line.

**Table 6.2**

| *Outline of Welded Joint* | $J$ |
|---|---|
| 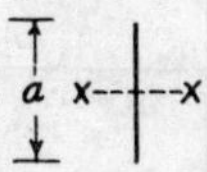 | $\frac{a^2}{12}$ |
| 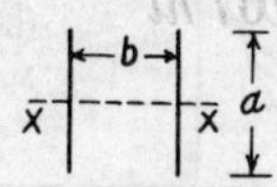 | $\frac{a(3b^2 + a^2)}{6}$ |
| 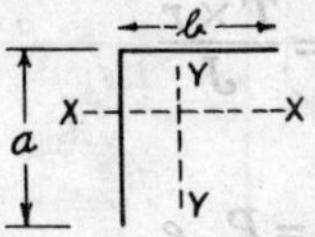 | $\frac{(b+a)^4 - 6b^2a^2}{12\,(a+b)}$ |
| 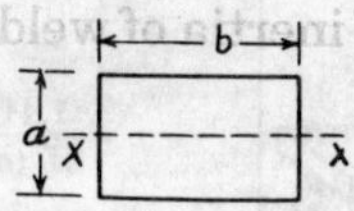 | $\frac{(a+b)^3}{6}$ |
| 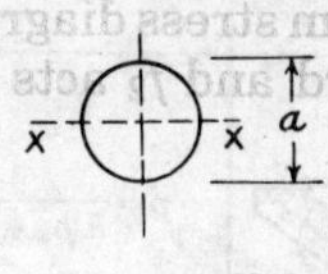 | $\frac{\pi\, d^3}{4}$ |

Fig. 6.15 indicates the induced stresses for different types of loading on welded joints. The symbols used are as follows :

$P$ = Load

$M$ = Bending moment

$T$ = Twisting moment

$L$ = Length of weld

$h$ = Size of weld

$p$ = Normal stress

$f_s$ = Average shear stress

| *Type of weld and load* | *Stresses* | *Type of weld and load* | *Stresses* |
|---|---|---|---|
| 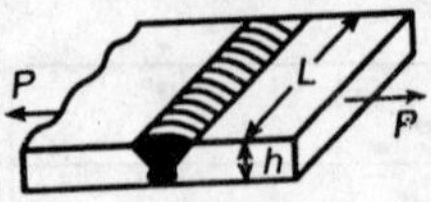 | $p = \frac{P}{hL}$ | 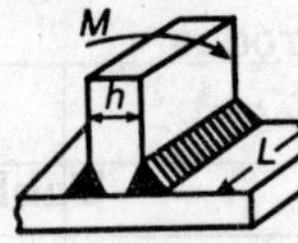 | $p = \frac{6\,M}{Lh^2}$ |
| 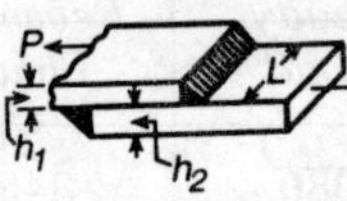 | $p = \frac{1.414\,P}{(h_1 + h_2)\,L}$ | 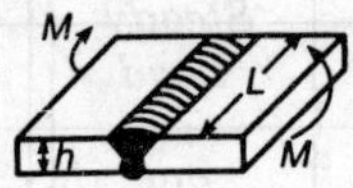 | $p = \frac{6M}{Lh^2}$ |
| 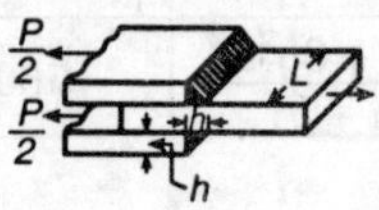 | $p = \frac{0.707\,P}{h\,.\,L}$ | 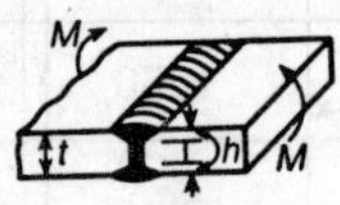 | $p = \frac{3\,t\,M}{Lh\,(3t^2 - 6th + 4h^2)}$ |
| 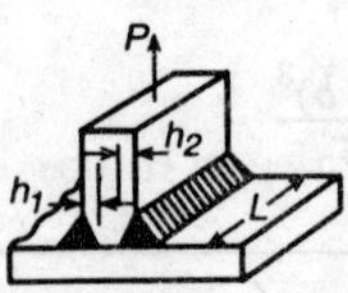 | $p = \frac{P}{(h_1 + h_2\,L)}$ | 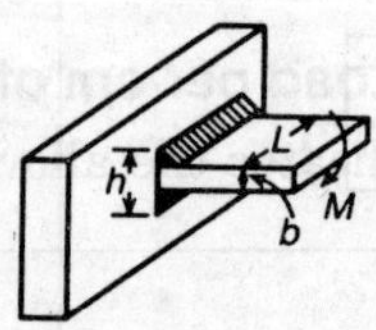 | $p = \frac{1.414\,M}{hL\,(h + b)}$ |
| 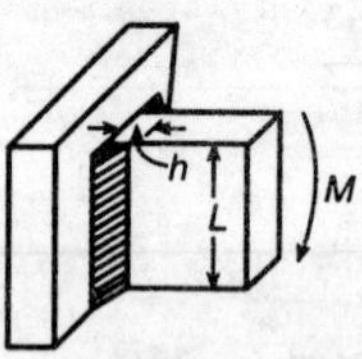 | $p = \frac{4.24\,M}{hL^3}$ | 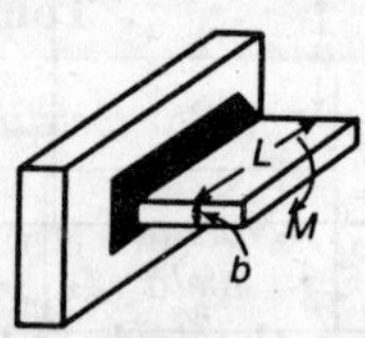 | $p = \frac{4.24\,M}{h[b_2 + 3L(b + 4)]}$ |
| 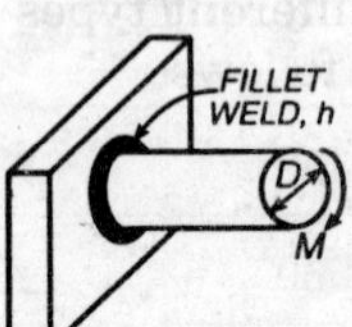 | $p = \frac{5.66\,M}{\pi\,hD^2}$ | 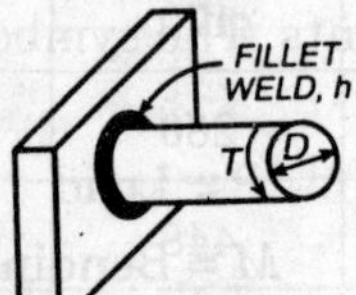 | $f_b = \frac{2.83\,T}{\pi\,hD_2}$ |
| 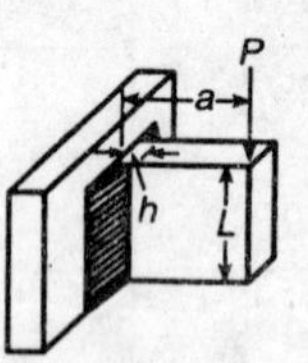 | $p_{(max)} = \frac{4.24Pa}{hL^2}$<br>$f_{s_1} = \frac{0.707\,P}{hL}$ | 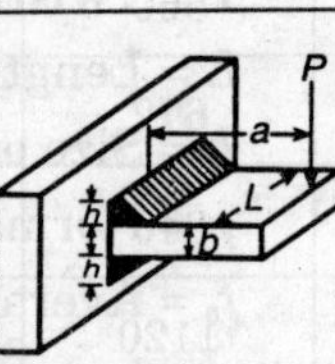 | $f_{s_1} = \frac{0.707\,P}{hL}$<br>$p_{\max} = \frac{P}{hl(b + h)}$<br>$\sqrt{\frac{2a^2 + (b + h)^2}{2}}$ |

Fig. 6.15.

## 6.4 Design Stress for Welds

Table 6.3 indicates the design stresses in kg/cm$^2$ for welds made with mild steel electrodes.

**Table 6.3**

| *Types of Load* | *Bare Electrodes* | | *Coated Electrodes* | |
|---|---|---|---|---|
| | *Steady Load* | *Reversed Load* | *Steady Load* | *Reversed Load* |
| Fillet welds (all) | 795 | 210 | 980 | 345 |
| Butt welds Tension | 910 | 350 | 1120 | 560 |
| Compression | 1050 | 350 | 1260 | 560 |
| Shear | 560 | 210 | 700 | 350 |

## 6.5 Allowable Load per cm of Weld

Table 6.4 indicates the allowable static load per linear cm. of weld in kg.

**Table 6.4**

| *Size of Weld (mm)* | *Bar welding rod* | | *Shield arc* | |
|---|---|---|---|---|
| | *Normal weld* | *Parallel weld* | *Normal weld* | *Parallel weld* |
| 3 × 3 | 170 | 135 | 210 | 170 |
| 5 × 5 | 280 | 225 | 350 | 280 |
| 8 × 8 | 448 | 360 | 560 | 448 |
| 10 × 10 | 560 | 450 | 700 | 560 |
| 12 × 12 | 672 | 540 | 840 | 672 |
| 15 × 15 | 840 | 675 | 1050 | 840 |
| 20 × 20 | 1120 | 900 | 1400 | 1120 |

## 6.6 Stress Concentration Factor

The stress concentration factor for different types of welds is indicated in table 6.5.

**Table 6.5**

| *Type of weld* | *Stress concentration factor* |
|---|---|
| **1. Static load** | 1.0 |
| (*i*) Reinforced butt weld | 1.2 |
| **2. Fatigue load** | |
| (*i*) Toe of transverse fillet weld | 1.5 |
| (*ii*) T-Butt joint with sharp corners | 2.0 |
| (*iii*) Parallel fillet weld | 2.7 |

Since abrupt changes in form occur in welds, stress concentrations are present as the force passes from one portion of the assembly to the other Fig. 6.16 show butt weld in tension. Stress concentration takes places at points *B* the sharp cornered notches and the point *A* where the force spreads into the reinforcement. Fig. 6.17 shows a fillet weld in tension. The stress concentration occurs at toe and heel points *A* and *B*.

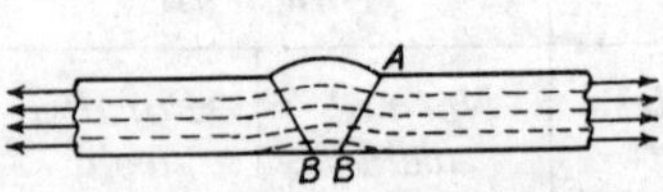

Fig. 6.16.

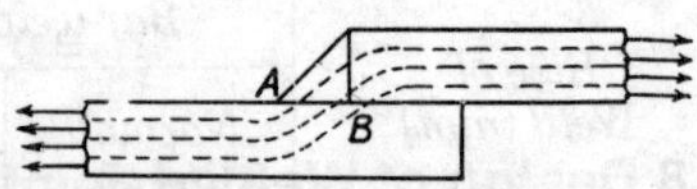

Fig. 6.17.

In case of fatigue loading the stress concentration factor should be taken into account. For design purpose Nominal stress *x*-stress concentration factor should not exceed the design stress.

## 6.7 Fillet Welds Under Varying Loads

For fillet welds under varying load the following design values should be used which are based on A.W.S. (American Welding Society) Code.

Let $$k = \frac{\text{Minimum load}}{\text{Maximum load}}$$

$$= +1, \text{ steady load}$$

$$= 0 \text{ Released load}$$

= − 1, completely reversed load.

Allowable fatigue strength ($F$) is given by

$$F = \frac{900}{1 - \frac{k}{2}} \text{ kg/cm for } 2 \times 10^6 \text{ cycles.}$$

$$= \frac{1260}{1 - \frac{k}{2}} \text{ kg/cm for } 0.6 \times 10^6 \text{ cycles.}$$

$$= \frac{1500}{1 - \frac{k}{2}} \text{ kg/cm for } 0.1 \times 10^6 \text{ cycles.}$$

The above values should be used if they are less than 1570 kg/cm. If the computed value is more than 1570 kg/cm the latter value should be used.

The relation between fatigue strength and number of cycles is as follows :

$$F_1 = F_2 \left( \frac{N_2}{N_1} \right)^C$$

where $F_1$ = Fatigue strength for $N_1$ cycles

$F_2$ = Fatigue strength for $N_2$ cycles

$C$ = Constant

= 0.18 for plates in axial loading

= 0.13 for butt welds.

## 6.8 Design of Welded Joints

While designing welded joints it is assumed that

(*i*) The load is distributed uniformly along the entire length of the weld.

(*ii*) The stress is spread over the effective section uniformly.

(*iii*) Suitable stress concentration factors and factors of safety are employed to account for the unknown factors like.

(*a*) Change of physical properties due to high rate of cooling.

(*b*) Thermal stresses in welds.

(*c*) Homogeneity of weld metal.

(*iv*) Proper type of welded joint is used.

(*v*) It is desirable to relate minimum weld size to plate thickness as indicated in Table 6.6.

**Table 6.6**

| *Plate thickness (mm)* | *Minimum size of the weld (mm)* |
|---|---|
| 3 to 5 | 3 |
| 6 to 8 | 5 |
| 10 to 16 | 6 |
| 18 to 24 | 10 |
| 26 to 55 | 14 |
| over 38 | 20 |

**Example 6.1.** *A plate 6 cm wide and 13 mm thick is welded to another plate by two parallel fillet welds as shown in Fig. 6.18 and carries a tensile load of 4000 kg. Determine the length of each weld if the allowable working stress in shear for the weld material is 780 kg/cm².*

**Solution.**

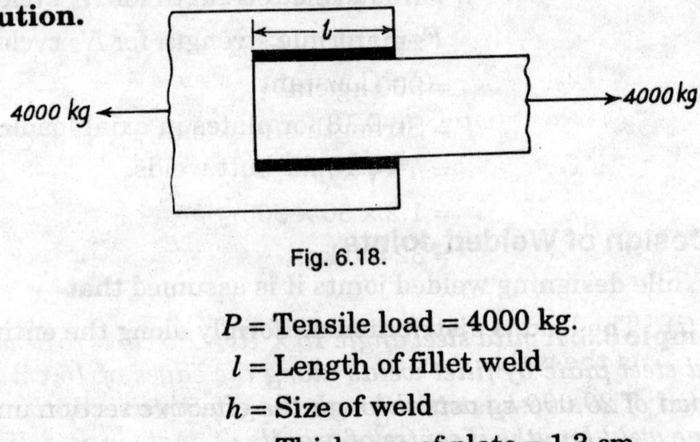


Fig. 6.18.

$P$ = Tensile load = 4000 kg.

$l$ = Length of fillet weld

$h$ = Size of weld

= Thickness of plate = 1.3 cm.

$f_s$ = Allowable shear stress in weld material

= 780 kg/cm²

$$P = 2 \times 0.707 \times h \times l \times f_s$$

$$4000 = 2 \times 0.707 \times 1.3 \times l \times 780$$

$$l = 2.79 \text{ cm.}$$

Allowing 1.25 cm for starting and stopping of the weld, the net length of each weld will be 2.79 + 1.25 = 4.04 cm.

**Example 6.2.** *Two plates are to be joined to gether by a single V groove butt weld. Each plate is 1.2 cm thick and 30 cm wide. Calculate the strength of the joint if the allowable tensile stress in weld material is 900 kg/cm².*

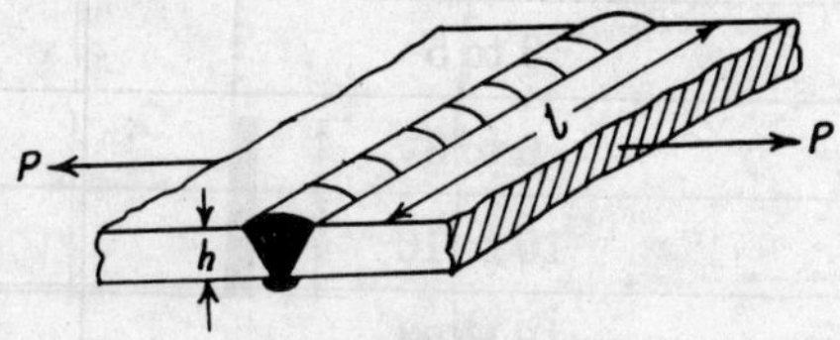


Fig. 6.19.

**Solution.**

Fig. 6.19 shows the joint

$L$ = Length of weld
= Width of plate
= 30 cm

$h$ = Size of weld
= Thickness of plate
= 1.2 cm

$f_t$ = Allowable tensile stress in weld material
= 900 kg/cm$^2$

$P$ = Strength of the joint
$= h \times l \times f_t$
$= 1.2 \times 50 \times 900$
= 32400 kg.

**Example 6.3.** *A mild steel angle 15 × 10 × 1.5 cm is to be welded to a mild steel plate by fillet welds along the edges of 15 cm leg. A tensile load of 20,000 kg acts through the gravity axis of the angle. Determine weld lengths if centre of gravity of angle is at a distance of 5 cm from end B as shown in Fig. 6.20. The allowable shear stress in weld material is 730 kg/cm².*

**Solution.**

$P$ = Tensile load
= 20,000 kg

$a$ = 10 cm

$b$ = 5 cm

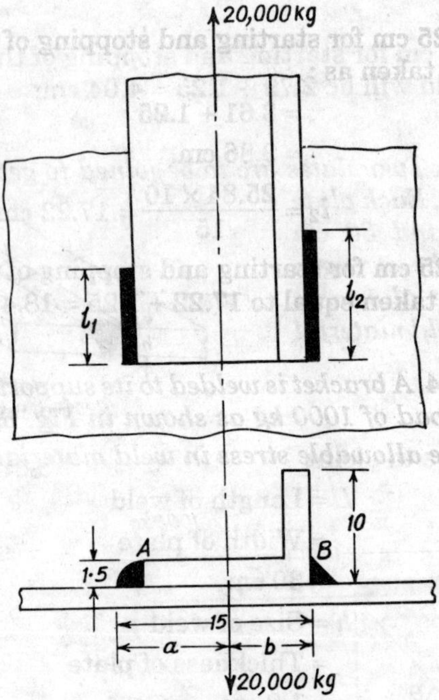


Fig. 6.20.

$f_s$ = Safe shear stress in welded materials

= 730 kg/cm$^2$

$h$ = Size of weld.

= Thickness of angle = 1.5 cm

$l_1$ = Length of weld on side $A$

$l_2$ = Length of weld on side $B$

$l$ = Total length of fillet weld

$= l_1 + l_2$

It is a case of parallel fillet weld

$$P = 0.707 \times h \times l \times f_s$$

$$20{,}000 = 0.707 \times 1.5 \times l \times 730$$

$$l = 25.84 \text{ cm}$$

$$a + b = 10 + 5 = 15 \text{ cm}$$

$$l = \frac{l \times b}{15} = \frac{25.84 \times 5}{15}$$

$$= 8.61.$$

Allowing 1.25 cm for starting and stopping of weld the welded length $l_1$ will be taken as :

$$= 8.61 + 1.25$$

$$= 9.86 \text{ cm.}$$

$$l_2 = \frac{25.84 \times 10}{15} = 17.22 \text{ cm.}$$

Allowing 1.25 cm for starting and stopping of weld the welded length $l_2$ will be taken equal to $17.22 + 1.25 = 18.47$ cm.

**Example 6.4.** *A bracket is welded to its support and is subjected to an eccentric load of 1000 kg as shown in Fig. 6.21 calculate the size of weld if the allowable stress in weld material is 950 kg/cm$^2$.*

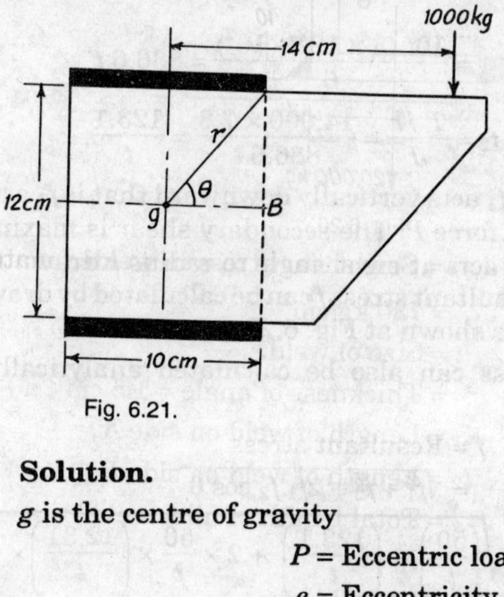

Fig. 6.21.

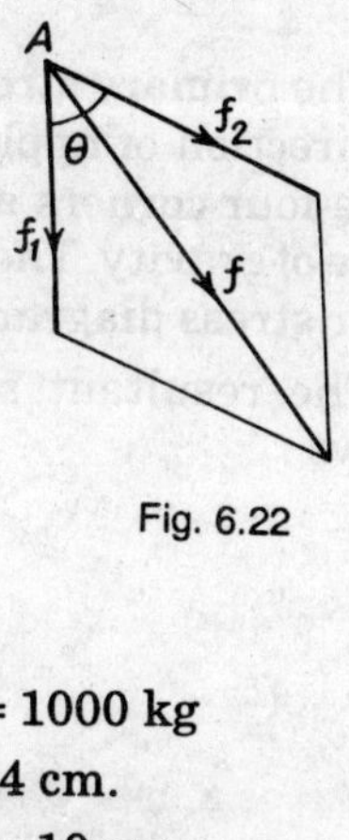

Fig. 6.22

**Solution.**

$g$ is the centre of gravity

$$P = \text{Eccentric load} = 1000 \text{ kg}$$

$$e = \text{Eccentricity} = 14 \text{ cm.}$$

$$l = \text{Length of weld} = 10 \text{ cm}$$

$$a = 12 \text{ cm}$$

$$A = \text{Area of weld}$$

$$= t \times l$$

$$f_1 = \text{Primary shear stress}$$

$$= \frac{P}{2 \cdot t \cdot l} = \frac{1000}{2 \times t \times l} = \frac{50}{t}$$

where $t$ = Size of weld

$$f_2 = \text{Secondary shear stress}$$

$$= \frac{T \times r}{J}$$

where $T$ = Twisting moment

$$= P \times e = 1000 \times 14$$

$$= 14{,}000 \text{ kg/cm}$$

$$r = \sqrt{\left(\frac{a}{2}\right)^2 + \left(\frac{l}{2}\right)^2}$$

$$= \sqrt{(6)^2 + (5)^2} = 7.8 \text{ cm}$$

$$J = \text{Polar moment of inertia of weld}$$

$$= \frac{l \,.\, t\,(3a^2 + l^2)}{6}$$

$$= \frac{10t\,(3 \times 12^2 + 10^2)}{6} = 886.6\,t$$

$$f_2 = \frac{T \,.\, r}{J} = \frac{14{,}000 \times 7.8}{886.6\,t} = \frac{123.1}{t}.$$

The primary stress $f_1$ acts vertically downward that is $f_1$ acts in the direction of applied force $P$. The secondary shear is maximum at the four corners and acts at right angle to radius $r$ drawn from centre of gravity. The resultant stress $f$ can be calculated by drawing vector stress diagram as shown at Fig. 6.22.

The resultant stress can also be calculated analytically as follows :

$$f = \text{Resultant stress}$$

$$= \sqrt{f_1^2 + f_2^2 + 2 f_1 f_2 \cos\theta}$$

$$= \sqrt{\left(\frac{50}{t}\right)^2 + \left(\frac{123.1}{t}\right)^2 + 2 \times \frac{50}{t} \times \left(\frac{12.31}{t}\right) \times \frac{5}{7.8}}$$

$$= \frac{159.8}{t}$$

where $\theta$ = Angle, between $f_1$ and $f_2$

$$\cos\theta = \frac{gB}{r} = \frac{5}{7.8}$$

Now the maximum stress is based on throat area therefore 0.707 $h$ should be considered in place of $t$.

$$\therefore \quad f = \frac{159.8}{0.707\,h}$$

But $$f = 950 \text{ kg/cm}^2$$

$$950 = \frac{159.8}{0.707\,h}$$

$$h = 0.24 \text{ cm.}$$

Hence size of weld ($h$) is 2.4 mm.

**Example 6.5.** *A bracket is welded to a stanchion by three fillets as shown in Fig. 6.23. An eccentric load of 2000 kg is to be applied. Determine the size of welds if the allowable stress in weld is 850 kg/cm².*

**Solution.**

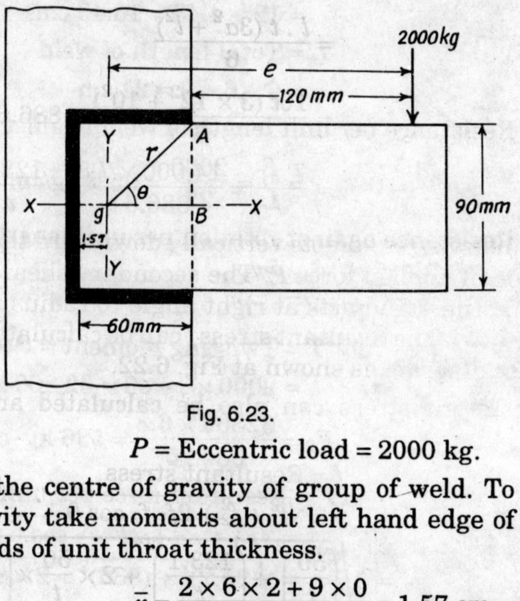


Fig. 6.23.

$$P = \text{Eccentric load} = 2000 \text{ kg.}$$

Let $g$ be the centre of gravity of group of weld. To calculate centre of gravity take moments about left hand edge of the plate assuming welds of unit throat thickness.

$$\bar{x} = \frac{2 \times 6 \times 2 + 9 \times 0}{2 \times 6 + 9} = 1.57 \text{ cm.}$$

$I_{xx}$ = Moment of inertia of the weld lengths about horizontal axis $XX$

$$= 2 \times 6 \times (4.5)^2 + \frac{9^3}{12} = 303.75 \text{ cm}^3$$

$I_{yy}$ = Moment of inertia about $y$–$y$ axis

$$I_{yy} = 2 \times \frac{6^3}{12} + 2 \times 6 \times (3 - 1.57)^2 + 9 \times (1.57)^2$$

$$= 82.5 \text{ cm}^4.$$

$$I = I_{xx} + I_{yy} = 303.75 + 82.5$$
$$= 386.25 \text{ cm}^4$$
$$r = \text{Maximum radius}$$
$$= \sqrt{gB^2 + AB^2}$$
$$= \sqrt{(6 - 1.57)^2 + (4.5)^2} = 6.3 \text{ cm}$$
$$\cos\theta = \frac{gB}{r} = \frac{6 - 1.57}{6.3}$$
$$= \frac{4.43}{6.3} = 0.7$$
$$c = \text{Eccentricity of load}$$
$$= 12 + 4.43 = 16.43 \text{ cm.}$$
$$L = \text{Total length of weld}$$
$$= 6 + 6 + 9 = 21 \text{ cm}$$

$F_1$ = Resistance per unit length of weld against translation

$$= \frac{P}{L} = \frac{2000}{21} = 95.2 \text{ kg/cm.}$$

$F_2$ = Resistance against rotation per unit length of weld

$$= \frac{T \times r}{T}$$

where $T$ = Twisting moment $= P \times e$

$$= 2000 \times 16.43 = 32{,}860 \text{ kg–cm}$$
$$F_2 = \frac{32860 \times 6.3}{386.25} = 536 \text{ kg–cm}$$
$$F = \text{Resultant force per unit length of weld}$$
$$= \sqrt{F_1^2 + F_2^2 + 2F_1F_2\cos\theta}$$
$$= \sqrt{(95.2)^2 + (536)^2 + 2 \times 95.2 \times 536 \times 0.7}$$
$$= 606.5 \text{ kg/cm.}$$

Permissible stress $= 850 \text{ kg/cm}^2$

Let $h$ is the size of weld.

$$0.707 \times h \times 1 \times 850 = 606.5$$
$$h = 1.11 \text{ cm.}$$

where $h$ = size of weld

**Example 6.6.** *A plate 100 cm long is welded at right angle to another plate by a 1.2 cm fillet weld as shown in Fig. 6.12. Calculate* *the permissible shear stress intensity in the weld material if the maximum torque that the welded joint can the sustain is 12,000 kgm.*

**Solution.**

The welded joint is shown in Fig. 6.12

$$l = \text{Length of the weld} = 100 \text{ cm.}$$

$$h = \text{Leg of weld} = 1.2 \text{ cm}$$

$$T = \text{Torque acting about the vertical plane}$$

$$= 12000 \text{ kgm} = 12 \times 10^5 \text{ kg cm}$$

$$f_s = \frac{4.24\,T}{hl^2} = \frac{4.24 \times 12 \times 10^5}{1.2 \times (100)^2} = 424 \text{ kg/cm}^2.$$

**Example 6.7.** *A shaft of 8 cm diameter is welded to a flat plate by a 1.3 cm fillet weld as shown in Fig. 6.11. Calculate the maximum torque that can be applied to the joint if permissible shear stress intensity in weld material is 650 kg/cm².*

**Solution.**

Fig. 6.11 shows the joint

$$d = \text{Shaft diameter} = 8 \text{ cm}$$

$$h = \text{Weld throat} = 1.3 \text{ cm}$$

$$f_s = \text{Permissible shear stress} = 650 \text{ kg/cm}^2$$

Now, $$f_s = \frac{2.83\,T}{\pi d^2 h}$$

$$T = \frac{\pi d^2 h \times f_s}{2.83}$$

$$= \frac{\pi \times 8^2 \times 1.3 \times 650}{2.83} = 60{,}004 \text{ kg cm.}$$

**Example 6.8.** *Determine size of weld for an eccentric loaded weld as shown in Fig. 6.23 (a). The allowable stress in weld material is 700 kg/cm².*

**Solution.** Let, $G(\bar{x}, \bar{y})$ is C.G. of weld.

$$h = \text{size of weld}$$

$$\bar{x} = \frac{A_1x_1 + A_2x_2 + A_3x_3}{A_1 + A_2 + A_3}$$

$$= \frac{2 \times 5h \times 2.5 + 7.5 \times h \times 0}{2 \times 5h + 7.5 \times h} = 1.44 \text{ cm}$$

where $A_1$, $A_2$, $A_3$ are the areas of welds 1, 2 and 3 respectively

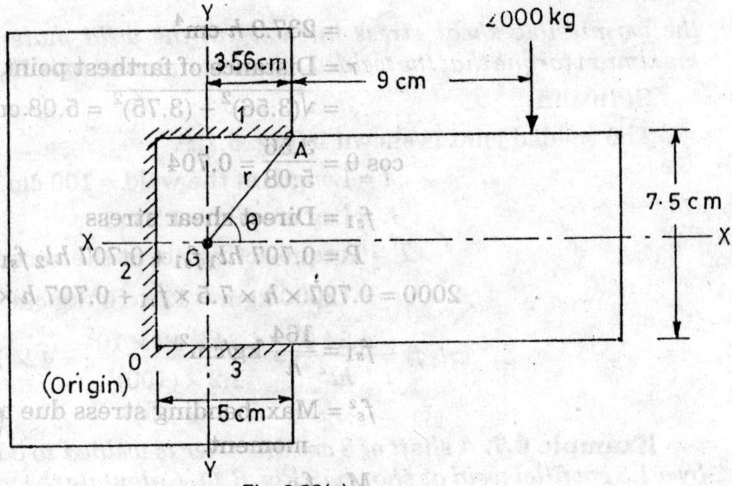


Fig. 6.23(*a*)

$\bar{y} = 3.75$ cm.

$e$ = Eccentricity of load

$= 9 + 5 - 1.44 = 12.56$ cm

$P$ = load = 2000 kg

$M$ = Turning moment of load about $G$

$= P \times e$

$= 2000 \times 12.56 = 27120$ kg cm

$I_{xx}$ = Moment of inertia about $XX$

$$= \frac{h \times 7.5^3}{12} + \frac{2 \times 5 \times h^2}{12} + (5 \times 2 \times h) \times 3.75^2$$

$$= \frac{7.5^3\, h}{12} + 2 \times 5 \times h \times 3.75^2 \left(\text{neglect } \frac{2 \times 5 \times h^2}{12}\right)$$

$= 190.4\, h$ cm$^4$

$$I_{yy} = \frac{2 \times h \times 5^3}{12} + (2 \times h \times 5)(2.5 - 1.44)^2 + \frac{7.5 \times h^3}{12} + 7.5 \times h \times 1.44^2$$

$$\left(\text{Neglect } \frac{7.5\, h^3}{12}\right)$$

$= 47.5\, h$ cm$^4$

$J$ = Polar moment of inertia

$= I_{xx} + I_{yy} = 190.4\, h + 47.5\, h$

$$= 237.9\,h\ \text{cm}^4$$

$$r = \text{Distance of farthest point } A \text{ from } G$$

$$= \sqrt{(3.56)^2 + (3.75)^2} = 5.08 \text{ cm}$$

$$\cos\theta = \frac{3.56}{5.08} = 0.704$$

$$f_{s1} = \text{Direct shear stress}$$

$$P = 0.707\,hl_1\,f_{s1} + 0.707\,hl_2\,f_{s1}$$

$$2000 = 0.707 \times h \times 7.5 \times f_{s1} + 0.707\,h \times (2 \times 5), f_{s1}$$

$$f_{s1} = \frac{164}{h} \text{ kg/cm}^2$$

$$f_s^2 = \text{Max. bending stress due to turning moment.}$$

$$\frac{M}{I_y} = \frac{f_{s2}}{y}$$

where $y = r = 5.08$ cm

$$f_{s2} = \frac{27120 \times 5.08}{237.9\,h} = \frac{576}{h} \text{ kg/cm}^2$$

$$f_s = \text{Resultant stress}$$

$$= \sqrt{f_{s1}^2 + f_{s2}^2 + 2f_{s1}\,.\,f_{s2}\,.\cos\theta}$$

$$700 = \sqrt{\left(\frac{164}{h}\right)^2 + \left(\frac{576}{h}\right)^2 + \left(2 \times \frac{164}{h} \times \frac{576}{h}\right) \times 0.704}$$

$$h = 0.94 \text{ cm.}$$

**Example 6.9.** *Fig. 6.23 (b) shows a plate 70 mm wide and 12 mm thick joined with another plate by a single transverse weld and a double parallel weld. Determine the length of parallel fillet weld of the joint is subjected to both static and fatigue loading. Given* $\sigma_t = 80$ *MN/m*$^2$, $\tau = 50$ *MN/m*$^2$, *and stress concentration factor 1.4 for transverse weld and 2.5 for parallel weld.*

**Solution.** $B$ = Width of plate = 70 mm

$t$ = thickness of plate = 15 mm

$A$ = Cross sectional area of plate in tension

$= B \times t$

$\sigma_t$ = Safe tensile stress

$F = B \times T \times \sigma_t$

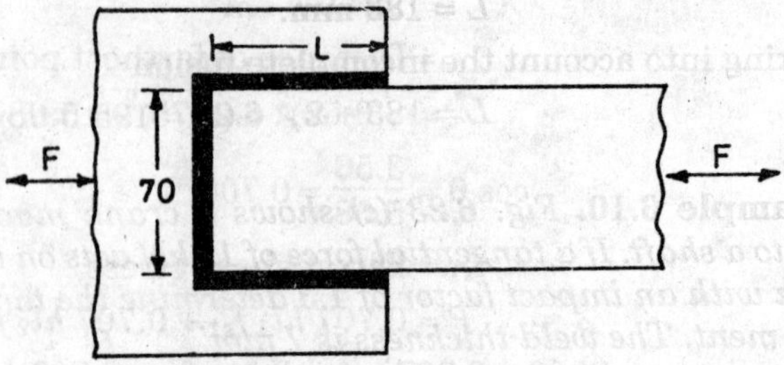


Fig. 6.23 (*b*).

$$F = 70 \times 15 \times 80 = 84 \text{ kN}$$

Let $L$ = Length of parallel fillet weld

$p$ = Total load that can be carried by the weld.

$$P = 0.707\, h \times 80 \times \tau + 0.707\, h \times 2L \times \tau$$

$$84 \times 10^3 = 0.707 \times 12 \times 80 \times 50 + 0.707 \times 12 \times 2 \times L \times 50$$

$$L = 59 \text{ mm}$$

$$L_1 = \text{Total length of weld} = L + 2S$$

where $S$ is the length of weld that takes into account the incomplete fusion at the beginning and end of weld

$$L_1 = L + 2S = 59 + 2 \times 6.25 = 71.5 \text{ mm}$$

For fatigue loading taking into account the effect of stress concentration.

$$P = 0.707 \times 12 \times 80$$

$h$ = size of weld = $t$ = 12 mm

$\tau$ = Shear stress = 50 MN/m$^2$

$$P = 0.707\, h \times 70 \times \tau + 0.707 \times h \times 2L \times \tau$$

$$84 \times 10^3 = 0.707 \times 12 \times 70 \times 50 + 0.707 \times 12 \times 2 \times L \times 50$$

$$L = 64 \text{ mm}$$

To account for incomplete fusion at the beginning and end of weld, the total length of weld will be

$$= 64 + 2 \times 6.25$$

$$L = 76.5 \text{ mm}$$

Taking into account the effect of stress concentration during fatigue loading.

$$84 \times 10^3 = P = \frac{0.707 \times 12 \times 70 \times 50}{1.4} + \frac{0.707 \times 2 \times L \times 12 \times 50}{2.5}$$

$$L = 183 \text{ mm.}$$

Taking into account the incomplete fusion

$$L = 183 + 2 \times 6.25 = 195.5 \text{ mm.}$$

**Example 6.10.** *Fig. 6.23 (c) shows a crank made of a plate welded to a shaft. If a tangential force of 12 kN acts on the other end of crank with an impact factor of 1.3 determine the torsional stress in weld ment. The weld thickness is 7 mm.*

**Solution.** $P$ = Force = 12 kN

$h$ = Distance of $P$ from central axis of shaft

= 160 mm

$M$ = Moment of force

$= P \times h = 12 \times 160 = 1920$ kN-mm

$t$ = Weld thickness = 7 mm

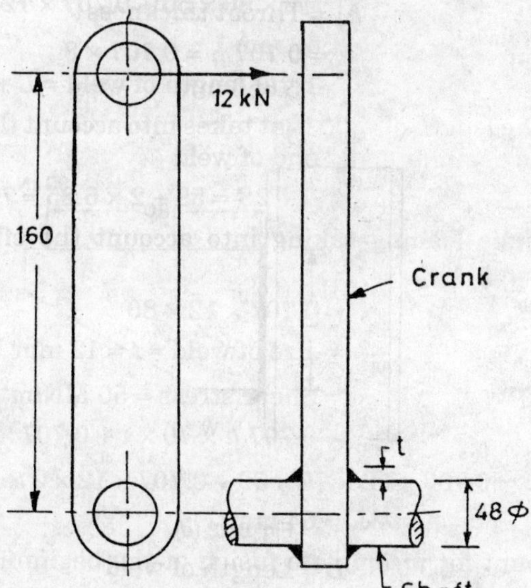


Fig. 6.23 (*c*).

$J$ = Polar moment of area of weld

$$= \frac{\pi}{32}[(D + 2\,t)^4 - D^4]$$

$$= \frac{\pi}{32}[(48 + 2 \times 7)^4 - 48^4] = 929039 \text{ mm}^4$$

$Z$ = Modulus of resistance

$$= \frac{J}{24+7} = \frac{929039}{31} = 29969 \text{ mm}^3$$

$K$ = Impact factor = 1.3

$M = Z \times f$

where $f$ = Torsional stress in weld

$$f = \frac{M}{Z} = \frac{1920 \times 10^3 \times 1.3}{2 \times 29969} = 42 \text{ N/mm}^2.$$

**Example 6.11**. *A bracket plate 18 mm thick is welded to the flange of a column by fillet welds on either side of the plate as shown in Fig 6.23 (d). If the size of weld is 8 mm, determine the length of the weld required taking allowable stress for the weld as 80 N/mm².*

**Solution.** $h$ = Size of weld = 8 mm

$h_1$ = Throat thickness

$= 0.707\, h = 0.707 \times 8$

$= 5.656$ mm

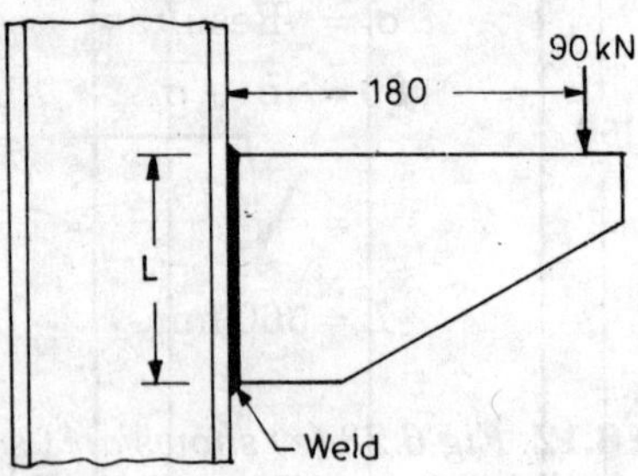


Fig. 6.23 (*d*).

$L$ = Length of weld

$A$ = Area resisting the load

$= h_1 \times L = 5.656 \times L$

Since weld is provided on both sides.

$A_1$ = Total area of weld

$= 2 \times A = 2 \times L \times h_1 = 2 \times L \times 5.656$

$P$ = Force = 90 KN

$$\sigma = \text{Direct stress} = \frac{P}{A_1}$$

$$= \frac{90 \times 1000}{2 \times L \times 5.656} = \frac{7956}{L} \text{ N/mm}^2$$

$$M = \text{Bending moment}$$

$$= P \times 180 = 90 \times 10^3 \times 180$$

$$= 162 \times 10^5 \text{ N mm}$$

$$I = \text{Moment of inertia of weld}$$

$$= \frac{h_1 \,.\, L^3 \times 2}{12} = \frac{5.656 \times L^3 \times 2}{12} = 0.94\, L^3$$

$$Z = \text{Section modulus}$$

$$Z = \frac{I}{\frac{L}{2}} = \frac{0.94\, L^3 \times 2}{L} = 1.88\, L^2$$

$$\sigma_b = \text{Bending stress} = \frac{M}{Z}$$

$$= \frac{162 \times 10^5}{1.88\, L^2} \text{ N/mm}^2 = \frac{86 \times 10^5}{L^2} \text{ N/mm}^2$$

$$\sigma_r = \sqrt{\text{Resultant stress}}$$

$$80 = \sqrt{\sigma^2 + \sigma_b^2}$$

$$= \sqrt{\left(\frac{7956}{L}\right)^2 + \left(\frac{86 \times 10^5}{L^2}\right)^2}$$

$$L = 360 \text{ mm.}$$

**Example 6.12**. *Fig 6.23 (e) shows an I section beam welded all around. Leg of weld is 5 mm. Determine the stresses in the fillets of the weld. The load (P) is 90 KN.*

**Solution.** $P$ = Load = 90 KN

Assuming that the shear stress is only taken by the vertical welds of the I-section

$L$ = Effective length of the weld on each side of web

$= 250 - 6 \times 2 = 238$ mm

$f_s$ = Mean shear stress

$h$ = Size of weld = 5 mm

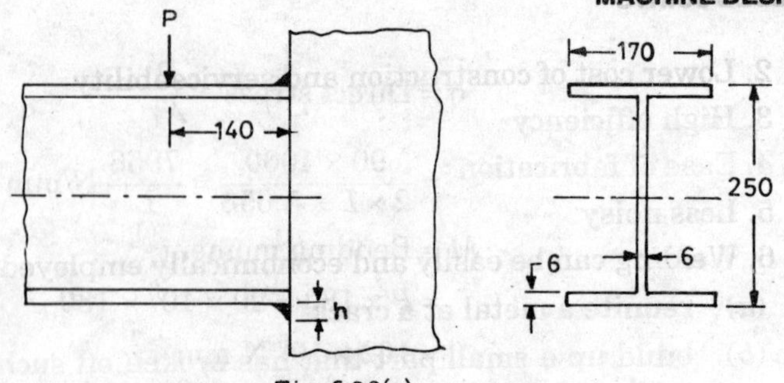


Fig. 6·23(e)

$$P = 2 \times 0.7\, h \times L \times f_s$$

$$90 \times 10^3 = 2 \times 0.7 \times 5 \times 238 \times f_s.$$

$$f_s = 54 \text{ N/mm}^2$$

$$M = \text{Bending moment} = P \times \text{Eccentricity}$$

$$= P \times 140 = 90 \times 10^3 \times 140$$

$$= 126 \times 10^5 \text{ N mm}$$

$$t = \text{Throat thickness}$$

$$= 0.7\, h = 0.7 \times 5 = 3.5 \text{ mm}$$

$$I = \text{Moment of inertia of weld}$$

$$= \frac{t\,L^3}{12} = \frac{3.5 \times 238^3}{12} = 3.93 \times 10^6 \text{ mm}^4$$

$$f_b = \text{Bending stress}$$

$$\frac{M}{I} = \frac{f_b}{y}$$

$$\text{where } y = \frac{L}{2}$$

$$\frac{126 \times 10^5}{3.93 \times 10^6} = \frac{f_b}{119}$$

$$f_b = 61 \text{ N/mm}^2$$

$$f = \text{Resultant stress} = \sqrt{f_s^2 + f_b^2}$$

$$= \sqrt{54^2 + 61^2} = 81.46 \text{ N/mm}^2.$$

**Example 6.13**. *State the advantages of welded joints over riveted joints.*

**Solution**. Because of developments made in welding the welded joints have become as reliable and free from faults as any riveted or any cast construction. Various advantages of welded joints are as follows : 1. Lighter weight

2. Lower cost of construction and serviceability
3. High efficiency
4. Ease of fabrication
5. Less noisy
6. Welding can be easily and economically employed to
   (a) reunite a metal at a crack
   (b) build up a small part that has broken off such as a gear tooth
   (c) repair a worn surface such as the blade of a hydraulic turbine and the surface of a bearing.

## PROBLEMS

**6.1.** (a) What is a welded joint ? Discuss various type of welded joints and state their symbols. (b) State the advantages of welded joint.

**6.2.** Describe how to find the strength of the following weld joints.

(a) Butt welds

(b) Fillet welds

(c) Eccentrically loaded welded joints.

**6.3.** Write short notes on the following :

(a) Fillet welds under varying loads.

(b) Stress concentration factor.

**6.4.** Compare the strength of welded joints shown in Fig. 6.24.

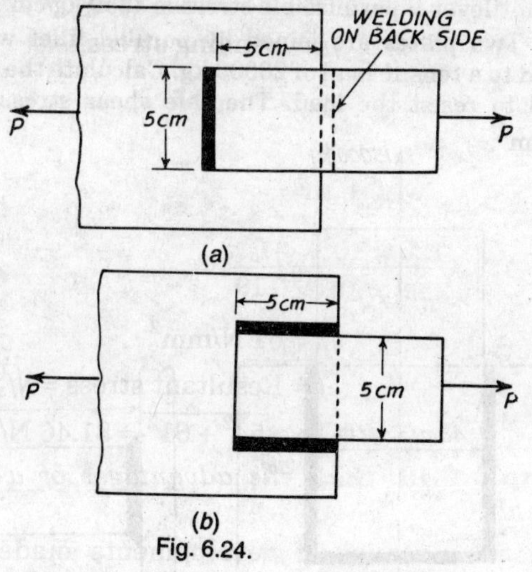


Fig. 6.24.

**6.5.** A rectangular beam as shown in Fig. 6.25 is welded to side member. A maximum load of 1100 kg is applied repetitiously. Assuming the shear load distributed over the entire weld calculate the size of weld required for $4 \times 10^6$ cycles.

**6.6.** A bracket supports a load of 2600 kg and is welded to vertical member by four fillets as shown in Fig. 6.26. Determine the size of weld if stress in throat section is not to exceed 800 kg/cm$^2$. The throat section may be taken as 0.707 times size of weld.

**6.7.** A plate 12 cm wide is joined to another plate by 1.2 cm fillet weld as shown in Fig. 6.27. Design the welded joint of the allowable shear load per linear cm is 600 kg.

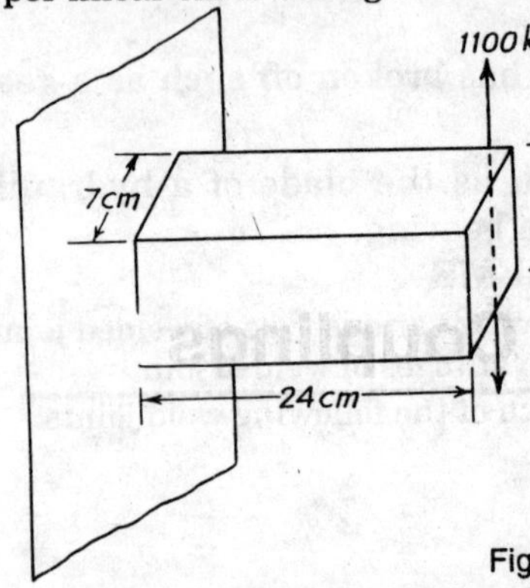


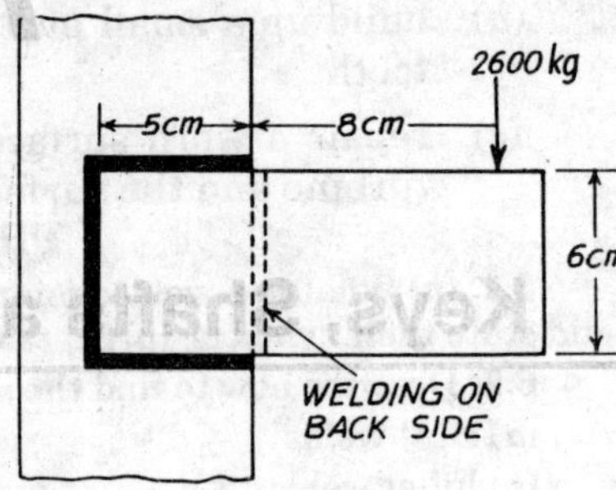


Fig. 6.25. Fig. 6.26.

**6.8.** (*a*) A hollow circular shaft of internal diameter 8 cm and external diameter 11 cm and 40 cm long is welded to the vertical plate by an all round fillet. Determine size of weld if it is to have some strength as that of pipe (Fig. 6.28). (*b*) Find the maximum load *P* that can be applied at the end of cantilever if permissible stress is 1250 kg/cm$^2$.

**6.9.** Two plates are joined by parallel fillet welds. The plates are subjected to a tensile load of 20000 kg. Calculate the length of 12 mm weld required to resist the load. The safe shear stress in weld material is 780 kg/cm$^2$.

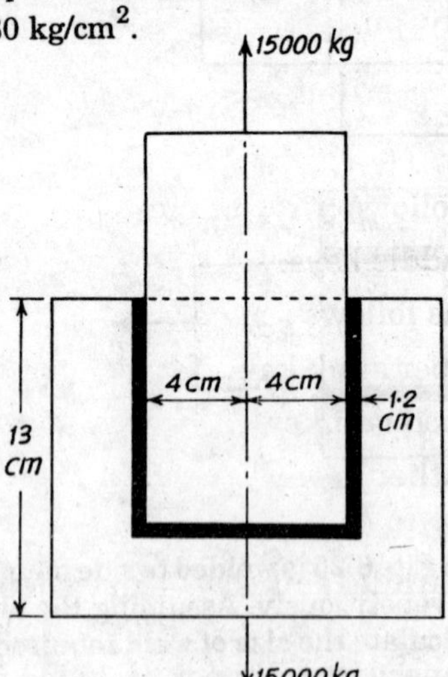


Fig. 6.27.

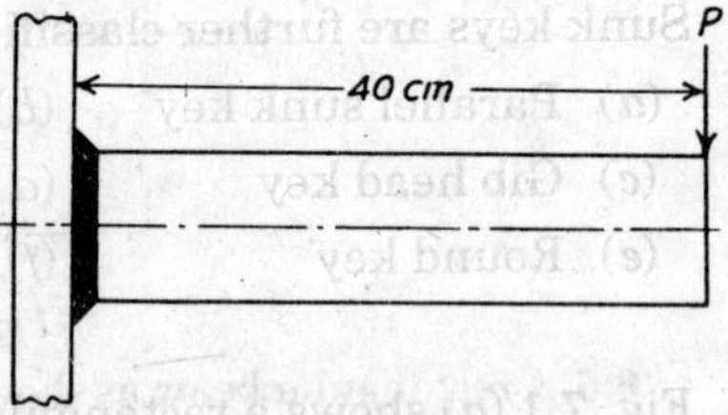


Fig. 6.28.

# 7

# Keys, Shafts and Couplings

## 7.1 Keys

A key is a wedge shaped piece made up of steel. A key is used to prevent relative motion between shafts and the member to which it is connected such as hub of gear or pulley. To accommodate the key, a groove called keyway is cut both in shaft and hub. After assembly key is partly in the shaft and partly in the hub. Keys have been standardised and are generally proportioned to the shaft diameter.

## 7.2 Types of Keys

The various types of keys are as follows :

(*a*) Sunk keys (*b*) Saddle keys.

Sunk keys are further classified as follows :

(*a*) Parallel sunk key (*b*) Taper sunk key

(*c*) Gib head key (*d*) Wood ruff key

(*e*) Round key (*f*) Feather key.

Fig. 7.1 (*a*) shows a rectangular parallel sink key. The various proportions are as follows :

The rectangular key may be tapered and taper provided is 1 : 100 (Fig. 7.1 (*c*)).

$$L = \text{Length of key} = 1.5\,d \text{ to } 3\,d$$

$$b = \text{Width of key} = \frac{d}{4}$$

$$t = \text{Thickness of key} = \frac{d}{6}$$

$$d = \text{Shaft diameter.}$$

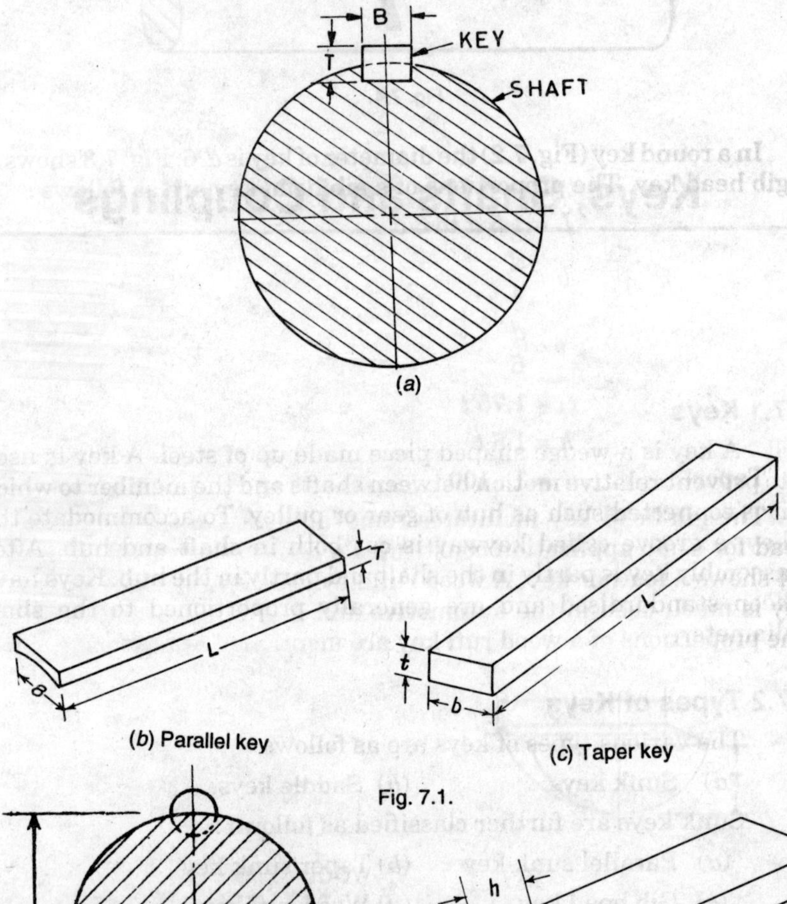


(a)

(b) Parallel key

(c) Taper key

Fig. 7.1.

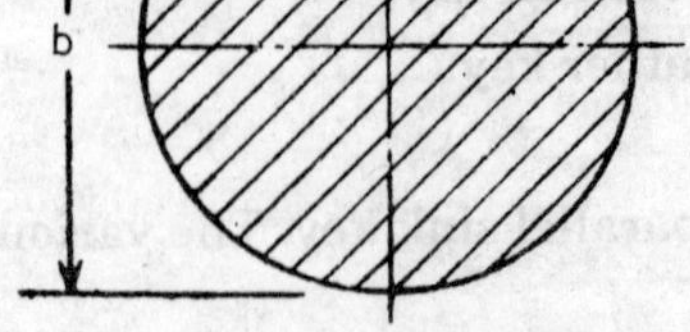


Fig. 7.2

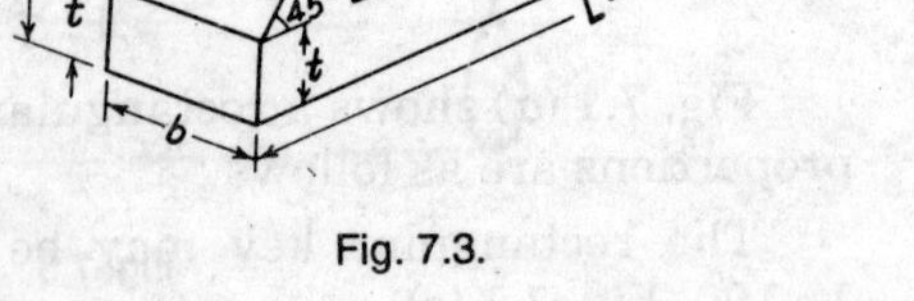


Fig. 7.3.

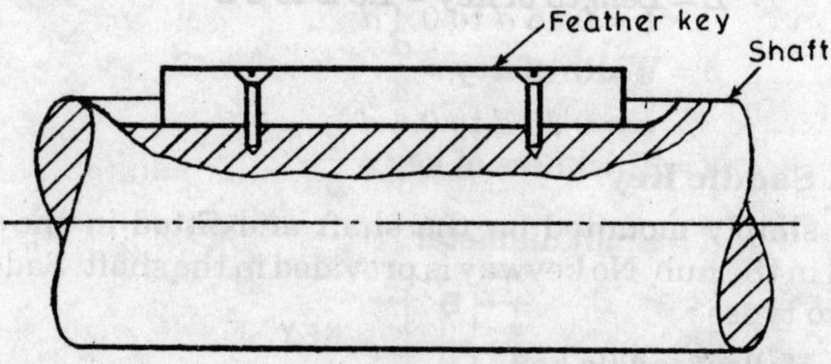


Fig. 7.4.

In a round key (Fig. 7.2) the diameter of key is $d/6$. Fig. 7.3 shows a gib head key. The proportions of a gib head key are as follows :

$$L = 1.5\,d \text{ to } 3\,d$$

$$b = \frac{d}{4}$$

$$t = \frac{d}{6}$$

$$t_1 = 1.75\,t$$

$$h = 1.5\,t$$

$$\text{Taper} = 1 : 100.$$

The gib head key facilitates removal although the projecting head for some application constitutes a hazard for workmen. Fig. 7.4 shows a feather key. A wood ruff key is shown in Fig. 7.5. This key is much used in the automotive and machine tool industries. The proportions of a wood ruff key are mentioned at next page.

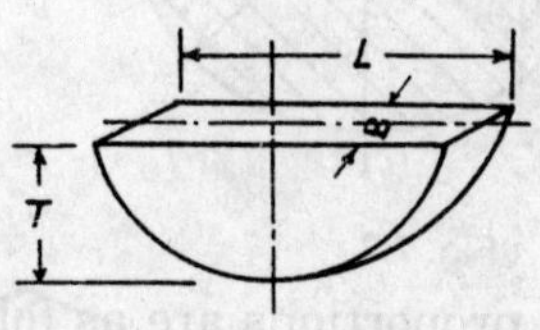


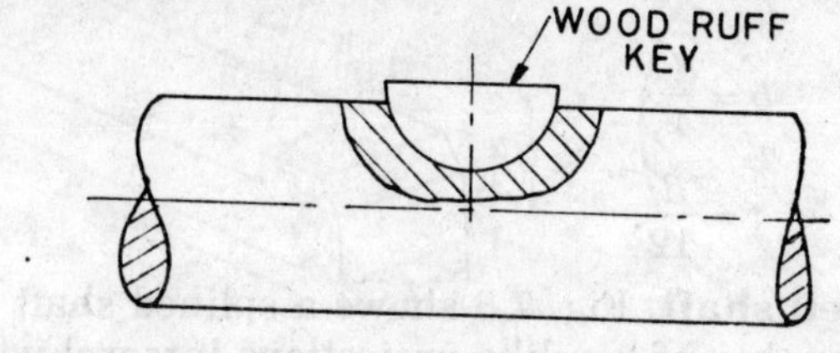


Fig. 7.5.

$$b = 0.15\,d \text{ to } 0.4\,d$$
$$t = 0.16\,d$$
$$h = 0.35\,d \text{ to } 0.4\,d$$

### 7.2.1 Saddle Key

It is simply mounted on the shaft and fitted in the keyway provided in the hub. No keyway is provided in the shaft. Saddle keys are of two types :

(*a*) Hollow saddle key

(*b*) Flat saddle key.

Hollow saddle key is suitable for light duty. In this key the bottom of key is shaped to fit the curved surface of the shaft. (Fig. 7.6). In this shaft the various dimensions are as follows :

$$b = \frac{d}{4}$$

$$t = \frac{d}{12}$$

$$L = \text{Length} = 1.5\,d \text{ to } 3\,d$$

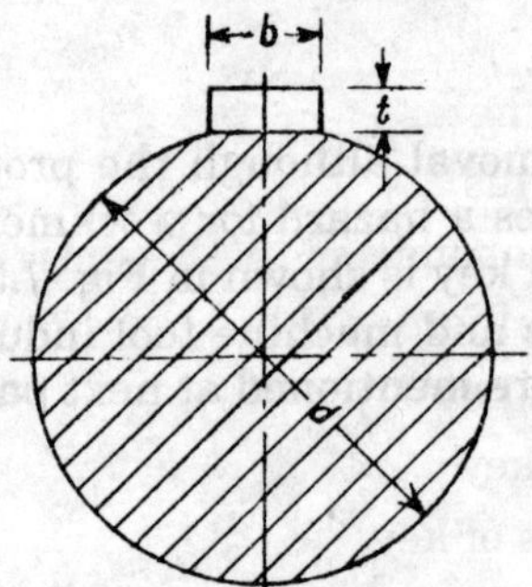


Fig. 7.6.

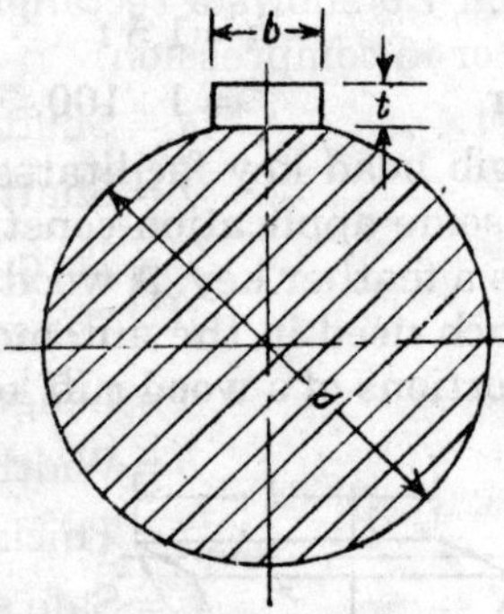


Fig. 7.7.

Flat key has both surfaces flat. Its proportions are as follows (Fig. 7.7).

$$b = \frac{d}{4}$$

$$t = \frac{d}{12}.$$

**7.2.2 Splined shaft.** Fig. 7.8 shows a splined shaft and hub. Splined shaft number of key like projections integral with it and equally speed round the circumference. These engage with corresponding recesses in a splined hub. It is quite commonly used in automobile industry. A spline is designed in same way as a rectangular key.

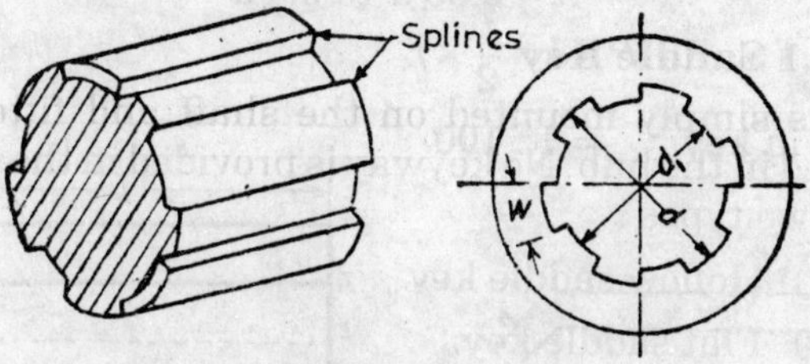


Fig. 7.8.

$d$ = Shaft diameter

$W$ = Width of spline = $d/4$

$d_1$ = Root diameter of shaft = 0.75 $d$

$t$ = Thickness of spline = 0.125 $d$

$L$ = Length of spline = 1.5 $d$.

## 7.3 Strength of Sunk Keys

Fig. 7.9 shows a rectangular sunk key. Key may fail either in shear or in compression.

Let

$d$ = Shaft diameter

$r$ = Shaft radius

$T$ = Torque transmitted by the shaft

$P$ = Tangential force at the shaft radius

$l$ = Length of key

$b$ = Width of key

$t$ = Thickness of key

$f_s$ = Safe shear stress in key

$f_c$ = Crushing stress induced in the key

(*i*) **Shearing failure of key**

$A$ = Area that resists shearing of key

= Area $ABCD = l \times b$ (see Fig.7.9(*a*))

$$P = A \times f_s$$

$$P = l \times b \times f_s$$

(*ii*) **Crushing failure of key**

$A$ = Area that resist crushing

= Area $ABEF$ [see Fig.7.9(*a*)]

$$= l \times \frac{t}{2}$$

where $AB = l$ and $BE = t/2$

$$P = l \times \frac{t}{2} \times f_c$$

Taper in key $= 1 : 100.$

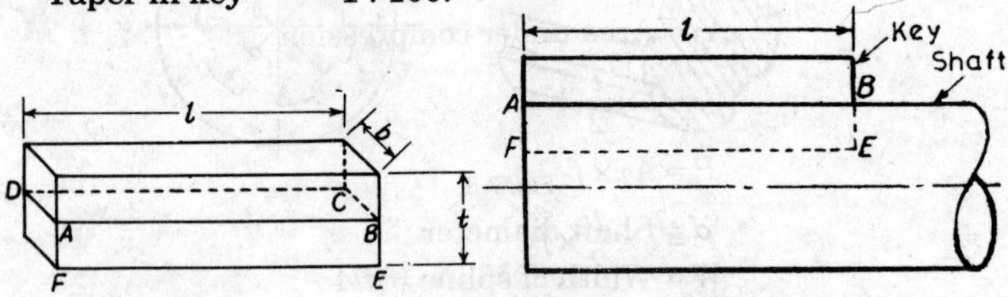


(a) Fig. 7.9 (b)

Fig. 7.9 (b) shows a rectangular sunk key fitted into a shaft such that half of thickness of key is in the shaft.

**Example 7.1.** *Determine the length, width and thickness of a mild steel rectangural sunk key required for a 80 mm diameter mild steel shaft to resist a torque of 50,000 kg cm. Take*

$$f_s = 500 \text{ kg/cm}^2 \text{ and } f_c = 1200 \text{ kg/cm}^2.$$

**Solution.**

Let $f_s$ = Safe shear stress = 500 kg/cm$^2$

$f_c$ = Crushing stress = 1200 kg/cm$^2$

$d$ = Shaft diameter = 8 cm.

$r$ = Radius of shaft = 4 cm.

$T$ = Torque = 50,000 kg cm.

$L$ = Length of key

$b$ = Width of key

$t$ = Thickness of key

$P$ = Force responsible for shearing or crushing of key = $T/r$

$$= \frac{50{,}000}{4} = 12{,}500 \text{ kg.}$$

$l$ = Length of key = 1.5 $d$ (assume)

$= 1.5 \times 8 = 12$ cm.

Considering shearing of key

$$A_1 = \text{Area under shear} = l \times b$$
$$P = A_1 \times f_s = l \times b \times f_s$$
$$12{,}500 = 12 \times b \times 500$$
$$b = 2.1 \text{ cm.}$$

Considering compression of key

$$A_3 = \text{Area under compression}$$
$$= l \times \frac{t}{2}$$
$$P = A_2 \times f_c$$
$$P = l \times \frac{t}{2} \times f_c$$
$$12{,}500 = 12 \times \frac{t}{2} \times 1200$$
$$t = 1.73 \text{ cm.}$$

**Example 7.2.** *(a) A medium carbon steel shaft transmits 40 H.P. at 450 R.P.M. The diameter of shaft is 4 cm. A square key is used whose one side is equal to ¼ the shaft diameter and whose length is equal to 1.5 times the shaft diameter. Find the dimensions of key and check the key for the induced shearing stress and crushing stress. (b) Determine the factor of safety of the key in shear and crushing if the yield stress in shearing and crushing are 3000 kg/cm² and 3800 kg/cm² respectively.*

**Solution.**

$$d = \text{Shaft diameter} = 4 \text{ cm.}$$
$$b = \text{Width of key}$$
$$= \frac{4}{4} = 1 \text{ cm.}$$
$$t = \text{Thickness of key}$$
$$= \frac{4}{4} = 1 \text{ cm.}$$
$$l = \text{Length of key} = 1.5 \times d = 1.5 \times 4 = 6 \text{ cm.}$$
$$N = \text{R.P.M. of shaft} = 450$$
$$\text{H.P.} = 40$$

Now, $$\text{H.P.} = \frac{2\pi \,.\, N \,.\, T}{4500}$$

$$40 = \frac{2\pi \times 450 \times T}{4500}$$

Torque, $T = 63.04$ kg-cm. = 6304 kg-cm.

$P$ = Tangential force at shaft radius

$$= \frac{T}{r}$$

where $r$ = Radius of shaft

$$= \frac{6304}{2} = 3152 \text{ kg}$$

Let $f_s$ = Shear stress induced in key

$f_c$ = Crushing stress induced in key

Strength of key for failure by crushing is given by

$$P = l \times \frac{t}{2} \times f_c$$

$$3152 = 6 \times \frac{1}{2} \times f_c$$

$$f_c = 1050.66 \text{ kg/cm}^2.$$

Strength of key for failure by crushing given by,

$$P = l \times b \times f_s$$

$$3152 = 6 \times l \times f_s$$

$$f_s = 525.33 \text{ kg/cm}^2.$$

Factor of safety (F.O.S.) in shear

$$= \frac{\text{Yield stress}}{\text{Induced stress}}$$

$$= \frac{3000}{525.33} = 5.71$$

$$\text{F.O.S. in crushing} = \frac{4000}{1050.66} = 3.8.$$

**Example 7.3.** *A gear with a hub 9 cm. long is fastened to a 6 cm. diameter mild steel shaft by a rectangular key made up of mild steel. The ultimate shear stress in key is 2000 kg/cm² and ultimate crushing stress is 4400 kg/cm². Using a factor of safety of 4 calculate the width and thickness of key when the shaft transmits a torque of 24,000 kg-cm.*

**Solution.**

$T$ = Torque = 24,000 kg-cm.

$d$ = Shaft diameter

= 6 cm

$r = \frac{d}{2} = 3$ cm

Safe stress in shearing of key ($f_s$)

$= \frac{2000}{4} = 500$ kg/cm$^2$

Safe stress in crushing ($f_c$)

$= \frac{4400}{4} = 1100$ kg/cm$^2$

$\left(\text{Safe stress} = \frac{\text{Ultimate stress}}{\text{F.O.S}}\right)$

$l$ = Length of key

= Length of hub = 9 cm.

$P$ = Force responsible for shearing or crushing of key

$= \frac{T}{r} = \frac{24000}{3} = 8000$ kg.

Considering shear failure of key

$$P = L \times b \times f_s$$

$$8000 = 9 \times b \times 500$$

$$b = 1.77 \text{ cm.}$$

Consider crushing failure of key

$$P = L \times \frac{t}{2} \times f_c$$

$$8000 = 9 \times \frac{t}{2} \times 1100$$

$$t = 1.62 \text{ cm.}$$

**Example 7.4.** *An automobile engine shaft has 6 splines and is required to resist a torque of 3000 kg-cm. If the maximum pressure on the splines is 80 kg/cm$^2$ determine the dimensions of spline and shaft diameter.*

**Solution.**

Let $d$ = Shaft diameter

$W$ = Width of spline = 0.25 $d$

$t$ = Thickness of spline = 0.125 $d$

$l$ = Length of spline = 1.5 $d$.

$d_1$ = Root diameter of shaft = 0.75 $d$

$p$ = Pressure on splines = 80 kg/cm.$^2$

$n$ = Number of splines

$T$ = Torque = 3000 kg–cm.

$T = p \times A \times r_m$

where $r_m$ = Mean radius from the centre of shaft to the centre of spline.

$$= \frac{d_1 + t}{2}$$

$$r_m = \frac{0.75\,d + 0.125\,d}{2} = 0.437\,d$$

$A$ = Area of splines

$= n \times l \times t$

$T = p\,.\,A\,.\,r_m$

$3000 = 80 \times nlt \times 0.437\,d$

$= 80 \times 6 \times 1.5\,d \times 0.125\,d \times 0.437\,d$

$d$ = 4.24 cm.

$l = 1.5\,d = 1.5 \times 4.24 = 6.36$ cm

$d_1$ = Root diameter of shaft

$= 0.75 \times d = 0.75 \times 4.2S = 3.18$ cm

$t$ = Thickness of spline = 0.125 $d$

$= 0.125 \times 4.24 = 0.53$ cm

$W$ = Width of spline

$= 0.25d = 0.25 \times 4.24 = 1.06$ cm.

**Example 7.4.** (*a*). *A mild steel solid machine shaft 6 cm. diameter transmits a torque of 15000 kg cm. A rectangular key is used. Key length is 1.5 times shaft diameter, width is 1/4 shaft diameter and thickness is 1/6 shaft diameter. Calculate the following:*

(*a*) *induced shear stress and crushing stress in the key ; and*

(*b*) *factor of safety in shear and crushing if yield stress in shearing and crushing are 3000 kg/cm$^2$ and 4200 kg/cm$^2$ respectively.*

**Solution.** $D$ = Shaft diameter = 6 cm.

$T$ = Torque = 15000 kg–cm.

$b$ = Width of key

$$= \frac{D}{4} = \frac{6}{4} = 1.5 \text{ cm}$$

$t$ = Thickness of key

$$= \frac{D}{6} = \frac{6}{6} = 1 \text{ cm}$$

$L$ = Length of key

$$= 1.5\,D = 1.5 \times 6 = 9 \text{ cm}$$

$R$ = Radius of shaft = 3 cm

$P$ = Force on key

$$= \frac{T}{R} = \frac{15000}{3} = 5000 \text{ kg.}$$

(*a*) To find induced shear stress ($f_s$) consider shearing of key

$$P = L \,.\, b \,.\, f_s$$

$$5000 = 9 \times 1.5 \times f_s$$

$$f_s = 370.4 \text{ kg/cm}^2.$$

To find induced crushing stress ($f_c$) consider of key

$$P = L \,.\, \frac{t}{2} \,.\, f_c$$

$$5000 = 9 \times \frac{1}{2} \times f_c$$

$$f_c = 1111 \text{ kg/cm}^2.$$

(*b*) To find factor of safety (F.O.S.)

$$\text{F.O.S. in shear} = \frac{\text{yield stress}}{f_s} = \frac{3000}{370.4} = 8.1$$

$$\text{F.O.S. in crushing} = \frac{\text{yield stress}}{f_c} = \frac{4200}{1111} = 3.78.$$

## 7.4 Shaft

A shaft is a rotating or stationary member usually of circular cross section. Shafts may be solid shafts or hollow shafts. Shafts are used for power transmission and elements like gears, pulleys, flywheels, cranks, sprockets and other power transmission elements are mounted on the shafts. A short rotating shaft is called a spindle. Shafts may be subjected to bending tension, compression or torsional loads acting singly or in combination with one another.

(*i*) **Pure torsion.** When a shaft is subjected purely to torsion then the stress induced is shear stress. The shaft diameter is calculated as follows :

$$T = \frac{\pi}{16} f_s d^3$$

where $T$ = Torque applied on shaft

$f_s$ = Shear stress induced in the shaft

$d$ = Diameter of shaft

For hallow shaft

$$T = \frac{\pi}{16} \cdot f_s \cdot \left(\frac{D^4 - d^4}{D}\right)^3$$

where $D$ is outside diameter and $d$ is the inside diameter of shaft.

(*ii*) **Combined bending and torsion.** When shaft is subjected to both bending and torsional loads then the diameter of shaft is determine using various theories of failure. For this see Chapter 3.

### 7.4.1. Design Stress.

The design stress for shaft may be taken as follows :

(*i*) For shaft without key ways

Design stress, $f_s$ = 0.3 × elastic limit in tension

= 0.18 × ultimate tensile strength

whichever is smaller.

Design stress, $f_t$ = 0.6 × elastic limit in tension

= 0.36 × ultimate tensile strength

whichever is smaller.

(*ii*) For shafts with key ways

Design stress = 0.75 × Design stress without key way.

## 7.5 Materials for Shafts

The shafts for light loads are made up of carbon steel ranging from 0.15 to 0.5% of carbon. For medium and heavy loads alloy steels such as nickel, chromium steels are commonly used. Shafts over 125 mm diameters are usually forged from nickel chromium steel and then machined to size. Table 7.1 indicates the values of ultimate tensile stress, shear stress and compression stress for different materials used for shafts.

**Table 7.1**

| *Materials* | *Carbon (%)* | *Ultimate strength (kg/cm²)* | | |
|---|---|---|---|---|
| | | *Tension* | Compres-sion | *Shear* |
| Commercial cold rolled | 0.10-0.25 | 4909 | 4900 | 2460 |
| Commercial turned | 0.10-0.25 | 4200 | 4200 | 2100 |
| | 0.15-0.25 | 4600 | 4600 | 2300 |
| Hot rolled or forged | 0.25-0.35 | 4920 | 4920 | 2460 |
| | 0.35-0.45 | 5300 | 5300 | 2650 |
| | 0.45-0.55 | 5640 | 5640 | 2820 |
| $3\frac{1}{2}$% Nickel | 0.15-0.25 | 6000 | 6000 | 3000 |
| Chrome Vanadium | 0.25-0.35 | 6320 | 6320 | 3160 |

The materials recommended by Indian Standards (I.S. 1570-1978) are indicated in Table 7.1 (*a*).

**Table 7.1** (*a*)

| *Designation* | *Tensile strength (N/mm²)* | *Yield stress (N/mm²)* |
|---|---|---|
| 40C8 | 570-670 | 322 |
| 45C8 | 618-700 | 353 |
| 50C8 | 647-765 | 373 |
| 50C12 | 706 min | 392 |

Materials used for shafts should possess the following properties :

(1) Good machinability.
(2) High strength.
(3) High wear resistance.
(4) Good heat treatment properties.
(5) Low notch sensitivity factor.

## 7.6 Standard Shaft Sizes

The length of shafting should not be more than 7 metres.

The following are the common sizes of transmission shafts (Dimensions are in millimeters)

25 to 60 mm by 5 mm increments

60 to 110 mm by 10 mm increments

110 to 140 mm by 15 mm increments

140 to 500 mm by 20 mm increments.

### 7.6.1 Shafts Subjected to Combined Torsional, Bending and Axial Loading.

In such case the maximum shear stress induced in shaft may be calculated

$P$ = Axial load

$f$ = Direct stress

$$= \frac{P}{A} \times \alpha$$

where $A$ = Area of cross–section of shaft

$$= \frac{\pi}{4} D^2$$

where $D$ = Shaft diameter

$\alpha$ = Constant, depending on the magnitude of column action to unsupported length of shaft between the bearings value of $\alpha$ depends upon $\frac{L}{K}$ ratio called slenderness ratio for column action

where $L$ = Shaft length between supporting bearings

$K$ = Radius of gyration of shaft.

The value of $\alpha$ is calculated by Euler's formula when slenderness ratio $\left(\frac{L}{K}\right)$ is more than 115

$$\alpha = \frac{f_{yc} \cdot \left(\frac{L}{K}\right)^2}{n \cdot \pi^2 \cdot E}$$

where $f_{yc}$ = Yield stress in compression

$n$ = Constant for the type of column end support

= 1.0 for hinged ends

= 2.25 for fixed ends.

If $L/K$ ratio is less than 115 then the value of $\alpha$ is calculated as follows

$$\alpha = \frac{1}{1 - 0.0044\left(\frac{L}{K}\right)}$$

If there is no column action of the shaft due to axial load,

$\alpha = 1$

$K_s$ = Shock and fatigue factor for shear

$f_s$ = Shear stress

$T$ = Torque on shaft

$$K_s \cdot \frac{T}{J} = \frac{f_s}{R}$$

where $R$ = Shaft radius

$$\frac{K_s\,T}{\frac{\pi}{32}D^4} = \frac{f_s}{\frac{D}{2}}$$

$$f_s = \frac{16K_s \cdot T}{\pi D^3}$$

$f_b$ = Bending stress

$M$ = Bending moment

$K_b$ = Shock and fatigue factor for bending

$$\frac{K_b\,M}{I} = \frac{f_b}{y}$$

$$\frac{K_b\,M}{\frac{\pi}{64}D^4} = \frac{f_b}{\frac{D}{2}}$$

$$f_b = \frac{32 \cdot K_b \cdot M}{\pi D^3}.$$

Then maximum shear stress $(f_s)_{max}$ induced in shaft is given by

$$(f_s)_{max} = \sqrt{(f_s)^2 + \frac{1}{4}(f_b + f)^2}.$$

**7.6.2. Shock and Fatigue Factor.**

These factors take care of shock and fatigue loading of shafts

$K_s$ = Shock and fatigue factor for torque

= 1.0 for gradually applied load

= 1.0 to 1.5 for suddenly applied load, minor shocks

= 1.5 to 3.0 for suddenly applied load, major shocks

Design torque $= K_s \,.\, T$

$K_s$ = Shock and fatigue factor for bending

= 1.5 for gradually applied or steady load

= 1.5 to 2.0 for suddenly applied load, minor shocks

= 2 to 3 for suddenly applied load, heavy shocks.

Design bending moment $= K_b \,.\, M$

Taking into account the shock and fatigue factor,

$T_e$ = Equivalent torque $= \sqrt{(K_s T)^2 + (K_b M)^2}$.

$M_e$ = Equivalent bending moment

$$= \frac{1}{2}[K_b\, M + \sqrt{(K_b\, M)^2 + (K_s \,.\, T)^2}].$$

### 7.6.3. Design of Axles.

Axles do not transmit any torque and are subjected to the effect of bending loads only. An axle may be rotating along with the supported parts or the axle may be stationary relative to them.

Bending equation to be used during design is

$$\frac{M}{I} = \frac{f_b}{y}$$

where $M$ = Bending moment

$I$ = Moment of inertia $= \frac{\pi}{64} D^4$

$f_b$ = Bending stress

$y = \frac{D}{2}$

$D$ = Axle diameter

$$M = f_b \,.\, \frac{I}{Y} = f_b \,.\, Z$$

where $Z$ = Section modulus

$$= \frac{\pi}{32} D^3.$$

**7.6.3.1 Shock and Fatigue Factor for Axles.** This factor takes into account the effect of shock and fatigue. The bending moment should be modified by taking into account this factor

$K_b$ = Shock and fatigue factor

(*i*) *For stationary axles*

$K_b$ = 1.0 for gradually applied and steady loads
= 1.5-2.0 for suddenly applied load with minor shock.

(*ii*) *Rotating axles*

$K_b$ = 1.5 for gradually applied and steady loads
= 1.5-2.0 for suddenly applied load with minor shocks
= 2.0-3.0 for suddenly applied load with heavy shock.

**7.6.4. Design Stress for Axles ($f_b$).**

It depends on the type of steel used for making axles.

(*i*) For axles made of steel purchased under definite specifications.

$f_b = 0.6 \times$ elastic limit in tension
$= 0.36 \times$ ultimate tensile strength in tension whichever is smaller.

(*ii*) For commercial steel axles

$f_b = 1120$ kg/cm$^2$ without allowance for key way
$= 840$ kg/cm$^2$ with allowance for key way.

**Example 7.5.** *A mild steel shaft is required to transmit 700 H.P. at 100 R.P.M. 28 the angle of twist is 1° in 1.4 m length of shaft and allowable shear stress in shaft material is 600kg/cm$^2$, determine suitable diameter of shaft. Take modulus of rigidity as $0.8 \times 10^6$ kg/cm$^2$.*

**Solution.** $T$ = Average torque

H.P. = 700

$$\text{H.P.} = \frac{2\,\pi\,NT}{4500}$$

$$700 = \frac{2\pi \times 100 \times T}{4500}$$

$$T = 5016 \text{ kg cm} = 50{,}1600 \text{ kg cm.}$$

Using torsion equation

$$\frac{T}{I} = \frac{f_s}{r}$$

where $I = \frac{\pi}{32} d^4$

= Moment of inertia of shaft

$f_s$ = Shear stress = 600 kg/cm.$^2$

$r$ = Shaft radius

$d$ = Shaft diameter

$$\frac{501{,}600}{\frac{\pi}{32} d^4} = \frac{600}{\frac{d}{2}}$$

$$d = 16.2 \text{ cm}$$

$C$ = Modulus of rigidity = $0.8 \times 10^6$ kg/cm$^2$

$\theta$ = Angle of twist = 1°

$= \frac{\pi}{180}$ radian

$L$ = Length of shaft = 140 cm

Again $\frac{T}{I} = \frac{C\,\theta}{L}$

$$\frac{501{,}600}{\frac{\pi}{32} d^4} = \frac{0.8 \times 10^6 \times \frac{\pi}{180}}{140}$$

$$d = 15.1 \text{ cm}$$

We adopt shaft diameter as 16.2 cm.

**Example 7.6.** *A belt driven cost iron pulley 120 cm diameter overhangs the nearest bearing by 30 cm. The pulley is driven from below and belt ends are vertical and parallel. The tension on tight side of pulley is 360 kg and the ratio of tight side tension to stock side tension is 3. If the weight of pulley is 100 kg and permissible shear stress in shaft is 500 kg/cm$^2$, determine the diameter of the shaft. Shock and fatigue factor for bending is 1.5 and for torque is 1.3.*

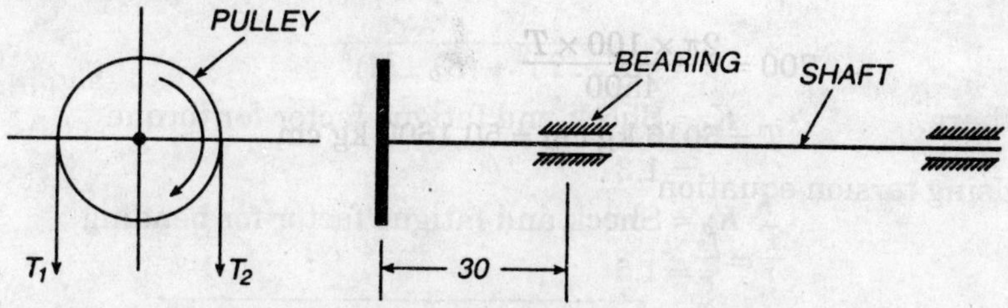


Fig. 7.10

**Solution.** The arrangement is shown in Fig. 7.10.

Let $T_1$ = Tension on tight side of belt

= 360 kg

$T_2$ = Tension on slack side of belt

$W$ = Weight of pulley

= 100 kg

$D$ = Diameter of pulley

= 120 cm

$R$ = Radius of pulley

= 60 cm

$f_s$ = Shear stress in shaft

= 500 kg/cm$^2$

$$\frac{T_1}{T_2} = 3$$

$$T_2 = \frac{T_1}{3} = \frac{360}{3}$$

= 120 kg.

Torque $(T) = (T_1 - T_2) \times R$

= (360 − 120) × 60

= 14,400 kg cm.

$W_1$ = Total downward load on shaft.

$= T_1 + T_2 + W$

= 360 + 120 + 100

= 580 kg

$M$ = Bending moment

= 580 × 30 = 17,400 kg cm.

(*i*) To find shaft diameter on the basis of torque

$T_e$ = Equivalent torque

$$= \sqrt{(K_s \cdot T)^2 + (K_b \cdot M)^2}$$

where $K_s$ = Shock and fatigue factor for torque

$= 1.3$

$K_b$ = Shock and fatigue factor for bending

$= 1.5$

$$T_e = \sqrt{(1.3 \times 14400)^2 + (1.5 \times 17400)^2}$$

$= 24100$ kg cm.

Use torsion equation

$$\frac{T_e}{I} = \frac{f_s}{r}$$

where $I$ = Moment of inertia of shaft

$$= \frac{\pi}{32} d^4$$

$f_s$ = shear stress in shaft

$r$ = radius of shaft $= d/2$

$$\frac{24{,}100}{\frac{\pi}{32} d^4} = \frac{500}{\frac{d}{2}}$$

$\therefore \quad d = 6.3$ cm.

(*ii*) To find shaft diameter on the basis of bending

$M_e$ = Equivalent bending moment

$$= \frac{1}{2}[K_b M + \sqrt{(K_b M)^2 + (K_s \cdot T)^2}]$$

$$= \frac{1}{2}[1.5 \times 17400 + \sqrt{(1.5 \times 17400)^2 + (1.3 \times 14400)^2}]$$

$= 36300$ kg cm

Use bending equation

$$\frac{M_e}{I_1} = \frac{f}{y}$$

where $I_1$ = Moment of inertia

$$= \frac{\pi}{64} d^4$$

$f$ = Bending stress

$= 800$ kg/cm$^2$

$$y = d/2$$

$$\frac{36{,}300}{\frac{\pi}{64}d^4} = \frac{\frac{800}{d}}{2}$$

$$d = 7.7 \text{ cm.}$$

Hence shaft diameter = 7.7 cm.

**Example 7.7.** *A shaft is supported by self aligning bearings at the ends and carries a V-belt sheave which contributes a radial load of 200 kg to the shaft and a gear which contributes a radial load of 60 kg. (Fig. 7.11). Calculate the diameter of shaft if the permissible stress is limited to 700 kg/cm².*

**Solution.**

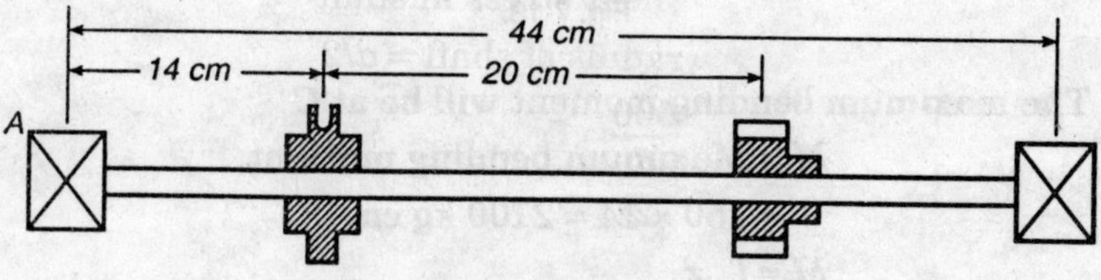


Fig. 7.11

Let $\qquad d$ = Shaft diameter

As the bearings are self aligning, the shaft is assumed to be simply supported with concentrated reactions at the bearings.

As shown in Fig. 7.12.

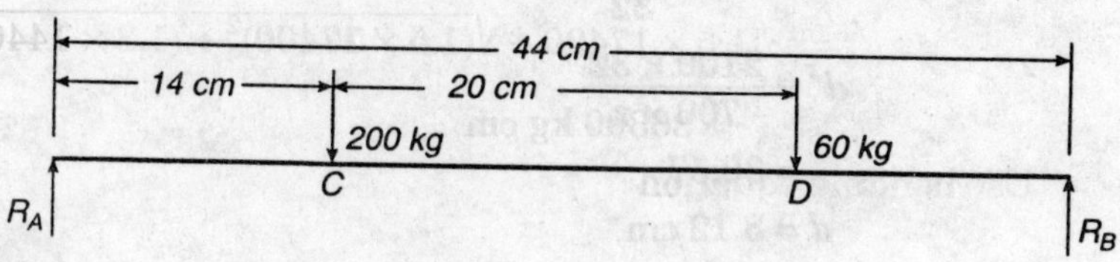


Fig. 7.12.

Let $\qquad R_A$ = Reaction at $A$

$R_B$ = Reaction at $B$

To calculate $R_A$, take moments about $B$.

$$R_A \times 44 = 60 \times 10 + 200 \times 30$$

$$R_A = \frac{600 + 6000}{44} = 150 \text{ kg.}$$

To find $R_B$ take moments about $A$

$$R_B \times 44 = 200 \times 14 + 60 \times 34$$

$$R_B = \frac{2800 + 2040}{44}$$

$$= 110 \text{ kg.}$$

Fig. 7.13 shows shear force diagram

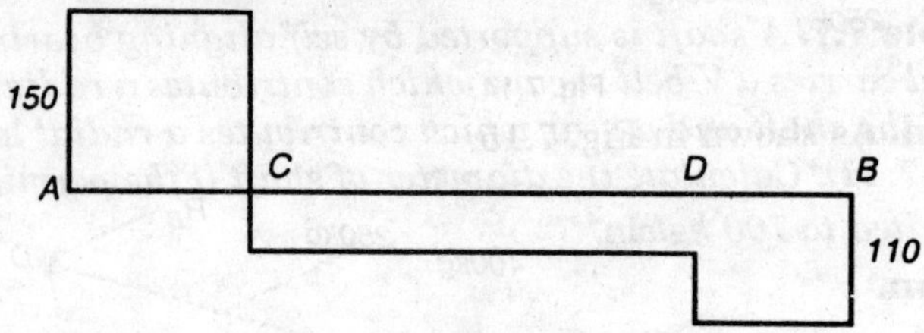


Fig. 7.13.

The maximum bending moment will be at $C$

$$M = \text{Maximum bending moment.}$$

$$= 150 \times 14 = 2100 \text{ kg cm}$$

$$M = f \cdot z$$

where $f$ = Allowable stress = 700 kg/cm$^2$

$z$ = Section modulus for shaft

$$= \frac{\pi}{32} d^3$$

$$2100 = 700 \times \frac{\pi}{32} d^3$$

$$d^3 = \frac{2100 \times 32}{700 \times \pi}$$

$$= 30.57$$

$$d = 3.12 \text{ cm.}$$

**Example 7.8.** *A rotating shaft 3 cm. diameter supports pulleys M and N. The pulley M is of 15 cm. diameter and pulley N is 10 cm. diameter. The tensions in belt of pulley M are vertical and tensions in belt of pulley N are horizontal. Determine principal stresses in shaft neglecting the weight of shaft land pulleys. Take AB = CD = 12 cm. and BC = 24 cm. (Fig. 7.14).*

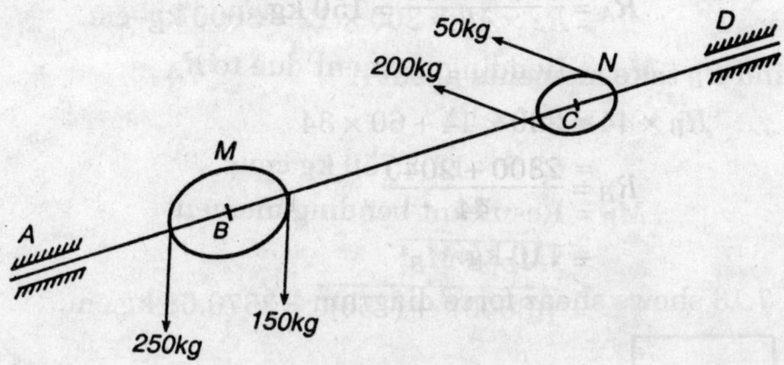


Fig. 7.14.

**Solution.** As shown in Fig. 7.15.

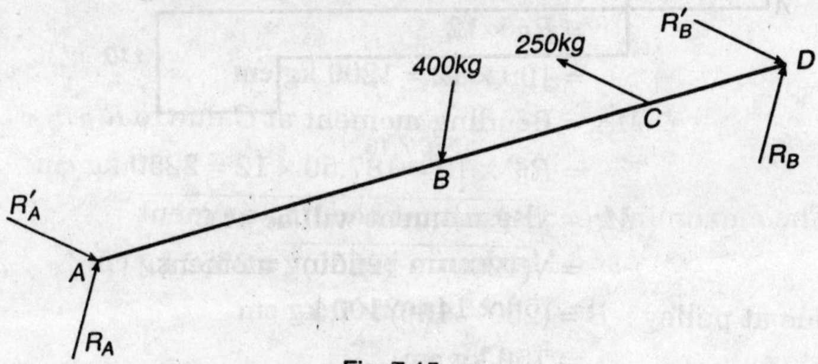


Fig. 7.15.

Let $R_A$ = Vertical reaction at $A$

$R_B$ = Vertical reaction at $B$

$R_A'$ = Horizontal reaction at $A$

$R_B'$ = Horizontal reaction at $B$.

To find $R_A$ take moments about $D$

$$R_A \times 48 = 400 \times 36$$

$$R_A = 300 \text{ kg.}$$

$$R_B = 400 - 300 = 100 \text{ kg.}$$

To find $R_A'$ take moments about $D$.

$$R_A' \times 48 = 250 \times 12$$

$$R_A' = \frac{250 \times 12}{48}$$

$$= 62.5 \text{ kg}$$

$$R_B' = 250 - 62.5 = 187.5 \text{ kg.}$$

Bending moment at $B$.

$$M_{B_1} = \text{Bending moment due to } R_A$$

$= R_A \times 12 = 300 \times 12 = 3600$ kg–cm.

$M_{B_2}$ = Bending moment due to $R_A'$

$= R_A' \times 12$

$= 62.5 \times 12 = 750$ kg cm.

$M_B$ = Resultant bending moment

$= \sqrt{M_{B_1}^2 + M_{B_2}^2}$

$= \sqrt{(3600)^2 + (750)^2} = 3676.68$ kg.cm

Bending moment at $C$

$M_{C_1}$ = Bending moment at $C$ due to $R_B$

$= R_B \times 12$

$= 100 \times 12 = 1200$ kg cm.

$M_{C_2}$ = Bending moment at $C$ due to $R'_B$

$= R_B' \times 12 = 187.50 \times 12 = 2250$ kg cm

$M_C = \sqrt{\text{Resultant bending moment}}$

$= \sqrt{(1200)^2 + (2250)^2} = 2552$ kg cm

Torque at pulley $B = (250 - 150) \times 7.5$

$= 750$ kg cm.

Torque at pulley $C = (200 - 50) \times 5$

$= 750$ kg cm

Hence maximum torque ($T$)

$= 750$ kg cm

Maximum bending moment ($M$)

$= 3676.68$ kg cm

Let $f_b$ = Bending stress

$d$ = Shaft diameter = 3 cm

$r$ = Radius of shaft = 1.5 cm

$$\frac{M}{I} = \frac{f_b}{y}$$

$$f_b = \frac{M \times y}{I}$$

$$= \frac{M \times \frac{d}{2}}{\frac{\pi}{64} d^4} = \frac{3676.68 \times \frac{3}{2}}{\frac{\pi}{64} \times 3^4}$$

$$= \frac{3676.68 \times 3 \times 64}{2 \times \pi \times 3^4} = 1387 \text{ kg/cm}^2.$$

Let $f_s$ = Shear stress

$$\frac{T}{I} = \frac{f_s}{r}$$

$$f_s = \frac{T}{I} \times r = \frac{750 \times \frac{3}{2}}{\frac{\pi}{32} d^4} = \frac{750 \times 3 \times 32}{2 \times \pi \times 3^4}$$

$$= 141.47 \text{ kg/cm}^2$$

$f_1$ = Principal stress (maximum)

$$= \frac{1}{2} \times f_b + \frac{1}{2}\sqrt{f_b^2 + 4f_s^2}$$

$$= \frac{1}{2} \times 1387 + \frac{1}{2}\sqrt{(1387)^2 + 4 \times (141.47)^2}$$

$$= 693.5 + \frac{1}{2} \times 1415.6 = 693.5 + 707.8$$

$$= 1401.3 \text{ kg/cm}^2$$

$f_2$ = Principal stress (minimum)

$$= \frac{1}{2} f_b - \frac{1}{2}\sqrt{f_b^2 + 4f_s^2}$$

$$= \frac{1}{2}\, 1387 - \frac{1}{2}\sqrt{(1387)^2 + 4 \times (141.47)^2}.$$

$$= 14.3 \text{ kg/cm}^2.$$

**Example 7.9.** *A steel shaft is supported between two bearings A and B and carries a pulley and a gear. The tensions in the belt of pulley are horizontal and the gear mounted on the shaft is driven by another gear directly behind it. The pulley is of 40 cm. diameter and gear is of 20 cm. diameter. If the ratio of tensions in the belt is 2 : 1 and gears transmit 36 H.P. and shaft rotates at 300 R.P.M., calculate the shaft diameter assuming stresses not to exceed 600 kg/cm² in shear and 1000 kg/cm.² in tension. Given AB = 30 cm.; CD = 40 cm. and DB = 20 cm.*

**Solution.**

$T$ = Torque at $D$

$$= \frac{\text{H.P.} \times 4500}{2\pi \text{ N}}$$

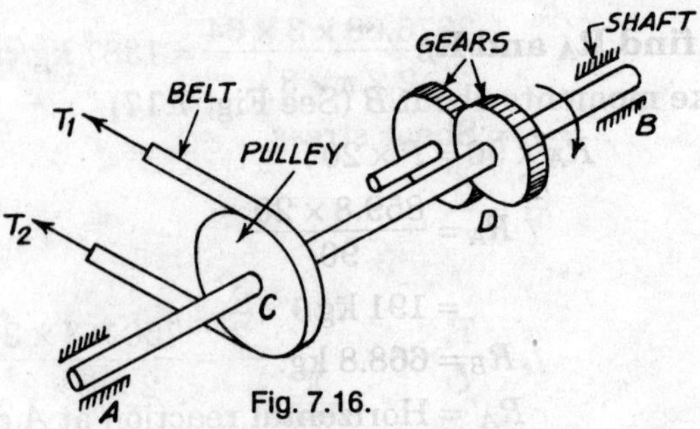


Fig. 7.16.

where $N$ = R.P.M. of shaft

H.P. = Horse power transmitted

$$T = \frac{36 \times 4500}{2\pi \times 300}$$

$$= 85.98 \text{ kg m} = 8598 \text{ kg cm.}$$

Let $T_1$ = Tension on tight side of belt

$T_2$ = Tension on loose side of belt.

$$\frac{T_1}{T_2} = 2 \qquad \text{...( 1)}$$

$$T = (T_1 - T_2) \times R$$

where $R$ = Radius of pulley = 20 cm

$$8598 = (T_1 - T_2) \times 20$$

$$8598 = (2T_2 - T_2) \times 20$$

as $T_1 = 2T_2$

$$T_2 = 430 \text{ kg.}$$

$$T_1 = 860 \text{ kg}$$

$F$ = Total horizontal force at $C$

$= T_1 + T_2 = 1290$ kg

$P$ = Vertical force at $D$

$$= \frac{T}{R_1}$$

where $R_1$ = Pitch circle radius of gear mounted on shaft = 10 cm.

$$P = \frac{8598}{10} = 859.8 \text{ kg.}$$

Let $R_A$ = Vertical reaction at $A$ due to $F$

$R_B$ = Vertical reaction at $B$ due to $F$

**To find $R_A$ and $R_B$**

Take moments about $B$ (See Fig. 7.17)

$$R_A \times 90 = P \times 20$$

$$R_A = \frac{859.8 \times 20}{90}$$

$$= 191 \text{ kg}$$

$$R_B = 668.8 \text{ kg.}$$

Let $R_A'$ = Horizontal reaction at $A$ due to $F$

$R_B'$ = Horizontal reaction at $B$ due to $F$

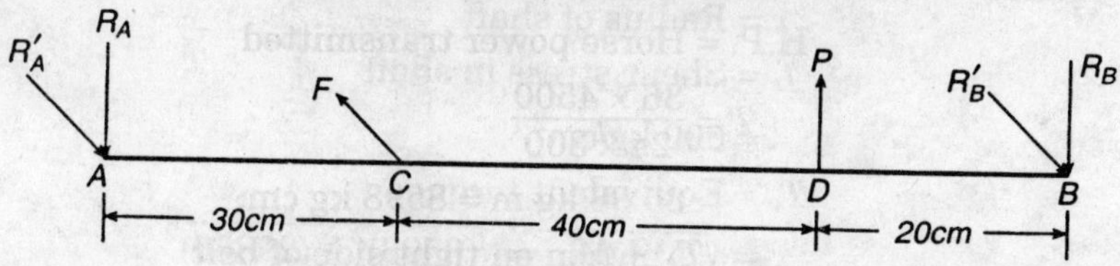


Fig. 7.17.

To find $R_A'$ take moments about $B$.

$$R_A' \times 90 = F \times 60$$

$$R_A' = \frac{1290 \times 60}{90} = 860 \text{ kg.}$$

$$R_B' = 1290 - 860 = 430 \text{ kg.}$$

Bending moment at $C$

$M_{C_1}$ = Bending moment due to $R_A$

$$= R_A \times 30 = 191 \times 30$$

$$= 5730 \text{ kg cm.}$$

$M_{C_2}$ = Bending moment due to $R_A'$

$$= R_A' \times 30 = 860 \times 30$$

$$= 28{,}800 \text{ kg cm.}$$

$M_C$ = Resultant bending moment at $C$.

$$= \sqrt{M_{C_1}^2 + M_{C_2}^2}$$

$$= \sqrt{(5730)^2 + (28800)^2}$$

$$= 29{,}360 \text{ kg cm.}$$

$M_{D_1}$ = Bending moment at $D$ due to $R_B$

$$= R_B \times 20 = 668.8 \times 20 = 13{,}376 \text{ kg cm.}$$

$M_{D_2}$ = Bending moment at $D$ due to $R_B'$

$$= R_B' \times 20$$

$$= 430 \times 20 = 8600 \text{ kg cm..}$$

$$M_D = \text{Resultant bending moment at } D$$

$$= \sqrt{M_{D_1}^2 + M_{D_2}^2}$$

$$= \sqrt{(13{,}376)^2 + (8600)^2}$$

$$= 15{,}900 \text{ kg cm.}$$

This shows that bending moment at the point $C$ is more.

**To find shaft diameter**

Let $d$ = Shaft diameter

$r$ = Radius of shaft

$f_s$ = Shear stress in shaft

$= 600 \text{ kg/cm}^2$.

$T_e$ = Equivalent torque

$$= \sqrt{T_e^2 + M_C^2} = \sqrt{(8598)^2 + (29360)^2}$$

$$= 30{,}510 \text{ kg cm.}$$

Using torsion equation

$$\frac{T_e}{I} = \frac{f_s}{r}$$

$$T_e = I \times \frac{f_s}{r} = \frac{\pi}{32} d^4 \times f_s \times \frac{2}{d}$$

$$= \frac{\pi}{16} f_s \cdot d^3$$

$$30{,}510 = \frac{\pi}{16} \times 600 \times d^3$$

$$d = 6.37 \text{ cm.}$$

Let $f_b$ = Bending stress

$= 1000 \text{ kg/cm}^2$

$M_e$ = Equivalent bending moment

$$= \frac{1}{2}[M_C + \sqrt{M_C^2 + T_e^2}]$$

$$= \frac{1}{2}[29360 + \sqrt{(29360)^2 + (8598)^2}]$$

$$= 29{,}935 \text{ kg cm.}$$

$$\frac{M_e}{I} = \frac{f_b}{y}$$

$$M_e = I \times \frac{f_b}{y}$$

where $I$ = Moment of inertia of shaft $= \frac{\pi}{64} d^4$

$$y = \frac{d}{2}$$

$$29{,}935 = \frac{\pi}{64} d^4 \times \frac{1000}{d} \times 2$$

$$= \frac{\pi}{32} \times 1000 \times d^3$$

$$d = 6.73 \text{ cm., say } 6.8 \text{ cm.}$$

Hence, shaft diameter = 6.8 cm.

**Example 7.10.** *Fig. 7.18 shows a mild steel shaft supported on self aligning bearing A and B. This shaft carries two pulleys C and D. The pulley C is of 24 cm diameter and pulley D is of 48 cm diameter. The tension in tight side of pulley C is 380 kg and tension on tight side of pulley D is 100 kg. Pulley C weighs 20 kg and pulley D weighs 40 kg. The shaft transmits 6 H.P. at 300 R.P.M. Calculate suitable shaft diameter if the allowable shear stress in shaft is 400 kg/cm².*

**Solution.**

$$\text{H.P.} = 6$$

$$N = \text{R.P.M.} = 300$$

$$\text{H.P.} = \frac{2\pi NT}{4500}$$

$$= \frac{2\pi \times 300 \times T}{4500}$$

$$T = 1433 \text{ kg cm.}$$

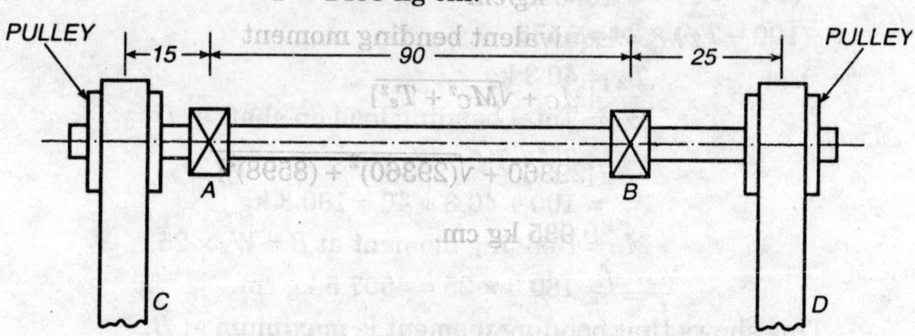


Fig. 7.18.

Let $T_1$ = Tension on tight side of pulley $C$ = 180 kg.

$T_2$ = Tension on loose side of pulley $C$

$D_1$ = Diameter of pulley $C$ = 24 cm

$R_1$ = Radius of pulley $C$ = 12 cm

$W_C$ = Weight of pulley $C$ = 20 kg.

$$(T_1 - T_2) \times R_1 = T$$

$$(180 - T_2 \times 12) = 1433$$

$$180 - T_2 = 119.4$$

$$T_2 = 60.6 \text{ kg.}$$

$W_1$ = Total bending load on shaft at $C$

$$= T_1 + T_2 + W_C$$

$$= 180 + 60.6 + 20 = 260.6 \text{ kg.}$$

$M_A$ = Bending moment at $A$

$$= W_1 \times 15$$

$$= 260.6 \times 15$$

$$= 3909 \text{ kg cm.}$$

Let $T_1'$ = Tension on tight side of belt at pulley $D$ = 100 kg.

$T_2'$ = Tension on loose side of belt at pulley $D$

$D_2$ = Diameter of pulley $D$ = 48 cm.

$R_2$ = Radius of pulley $D$ = 24 cm.

$W_d$ = Weight of pulley $D$ = 40 kg.

$$(T_1' - T_2') \times R_2 = T$$

$$(100 - T_2') \times 24 = 1433$$

$$T_2' = 40.3 \text{ kg}$$

$W_2$ = Total bending load on shaft at $D$

$$= T_1' + T_2' + W_d$$

$$= 100 + 40.3 + 40 = 180.3 \text{ kg}$$

$M_B$ = Bending moment at $B = W_2 \times 25$

$$= 180.3 \times 25 = 4507.5 \text{ kg cm.}$$

This shows that bending moment is maximum at $B$.

$$T_e = \text{Equivalent torque}$$
$$= \sqrt{T^2 + M_B^2} = \sqrt{(1433)^2 + (4507.5)^2}$$
$$= 4729 \text{ kg cm.}$$

Using tension equation

$$\frac{T_e}{I} = \frac{f_s}{r} \;;\; T_e = \frac{\pi}{32} d^4 \times f_s \times \frac{2}{d} = \frac{\pi}{16} f_s\, d^3$$

$$4729 = \frac{\pi}{16} \times 400 \times d^3$$

$$d = 3.92$$

We adopt, $d = 4$ cm.

**Example 7.11.** *A mild steel shaft carries two gears, C and D located at distances 24 cm. and 38 cm respectively from the centre lines of the left and right bearings as shown in Fig. 7.19. The diameter of gear C is 58 cm. and diameter of gear D is 18 cm. The power is delivered to gear C and taken out at gear D in such a manner that tooth pressures $P_c$ and $P_e$ at gear C and D respectively act vertically downward. If the shaft transmits 14 H.P. at 100 R.P.M. Calculate the diameter of shaft. Safe tensile stress is 800 kg/cm$^2$. Gear C weighs 100 kg and gear D weighs 40 kg.*

**Solution.**

Let $R_A$ = Reaction at $A$

$R_B$ = Reaction at $B$

$W_C$ = Weight of gear $C$ = 100 kg.

$W_d$ = Weight of gear $D$ = 40 kg.

H.P. = 14

$N$ = 100 R.P.M.

$f$ = Safe stress = 800 kg/cm$^2$.

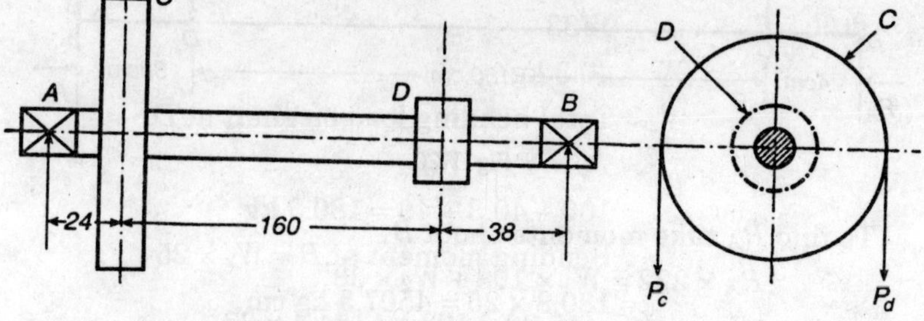


Fig. 7.19.

**(*i*) To find torque (T)**

$$\text{H.P.} = \frac{2\pi NT}{4500}$$

$$14 = \frac{2\pi \times 100 \times T}{4500}$$

$$T = \frac{14 \times 4500}{2\pi \times 100}$$

$$= 100.3 \text{ kg m} = 10030 \text{ kg cm.}$$

**(*ii*) To find maximum bending moment (M)**

$P_C$ = Vertical force at $C$

$$= \frac{T}{R_C}$$

where $R_C$ = Radius of gear $C$

$$= \frac{10030}{29} = 345.86 \text{ kg}$$

$P_D$ = Vertical force at $D = \dfrac{T}{R_D}$

where $R_D$ = Radius of gear $D$ = 9 cm.

$$= \frac{10030}{9} = 1114.4 \text{ kg.}$$

$W_1$ = Total vertical load at $C$

$$= 345.86 + 100 = 445.86 \text{ kg}$$

$W_2$ = Total vertical load at $D$

$$= P_D + W_D = 1114.4 + 40 = 1154.4 \text{ kg.}$$

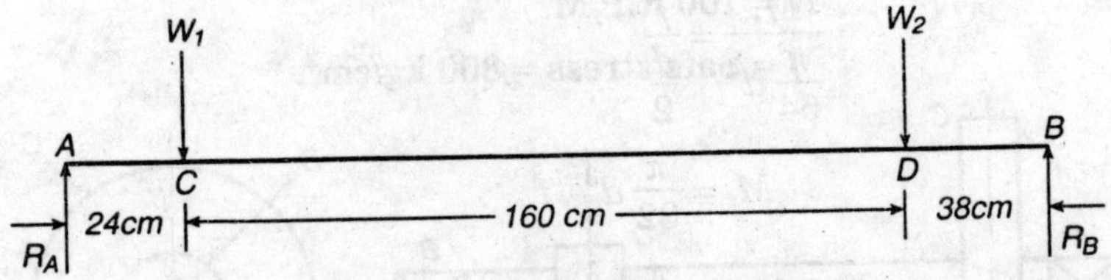


Fig. 7.20.

To find $R_A$ take moments about $B$

$$R_A \times 222 = W_1 \times 198 + W_2 \times 38$$

$$R_A = \frac{445.86 \times 198 + 1154.4 \times 38}{222} = 595.3 \text{ kg.}$$

Similarly $R_B = \dfrac{W_1 \times 24 + W_2 \times 184}{222}$

$= \dfrac{445.86 \times 24 + 1154.4 \times 184}{222}$

$= 1004.96$ kg.

Maximum bending moment will be either at $C$ or at $D$

$M_C = R_A \times 24$

$= 595.3 \times 24 = 14287.2$ kg cm.

$M_D =$ Bending moment at $D$

$= R_B \times 38$

$= 1004.96 \times 38 = 38188.48$ kg cm.

$M =$ Maximum bending moment is at $D$

$= 38188.48$ kg cm.

$M_e =$ Equivalent bending moment

$= \frac{1}{2}[M + \sqrt{M^2 + T^2}$

$= \frac{1}{2}[38188.8 + \sqrt{(38188.48)^2 + (10030)^2}$

$= 38,835$ kg cm.

*(iii)* **To find shaft diameter, *d***

Using bending equation

$$\frac{M_e}{I} = \frac{f}{y}$$

$$\frac{M_e}{\frac{\pi}{64} d^4} = \frac{f}{\frac{d}{2}}$$

$$M_e = \frac{\pi}{32} d^3 . f$$

$$38,835 = \frac{\pi}{32} d^3 \times 800$$

$$d^3 = \frac{38,835 \times 32}{\pi \times 800} = 494.71$$

$$d = 7.9 \text{ cm.}$$

**Example 7.11.** *A propeller shaft is to transmit 90 H.P. at 150 R.P.M. without a significant bending. The efficiency of propeller is 75% at 10 knots (1 knot = 1085 km ph). If* $\frac{L}{K} < 40$*, determine the diameter of shaft.*

**Solution.** $\text{H.P.} = \frac{2\pi NT}{4500}$

$$90 = \frac{2\pi \times 150 \times T}{4500}$$

$$\therefore \quad T = 42.994 \text{ kgm}$$

$P$ = Axial load on shaft

$V$ = Speed

$$= \frac{10 \times 1.85 \times 1000}{60 \times 60} = 51.3 \text{ m/sec.}$$

$\eta$ = Efficiency = 0.75

$$\text{H.P.} = \frac{P \times V}{75 \times \eta}$$

$$90 = \frac{P \times 5.13}{75 \times 0.75}$$

$$P = 987 \text{ kg.}$$

Take $k_s$ = 1.5 for suddenly applied load with minor shocks

Now, $\frac{L}{k} = 40$

$$\alpha = \frac{1}{1 - 0.0044\left(\frac{L}{k}\right)}$$

$$= \frac{1}{1 - 0.0044 \times 40} = 1.21$$

$D$ = shaft diameter cm

$f_s$ = shear stress in shaft

$$= \frac{16 \,.\, k_s \,.\, T}{\pi D^3}$$

$$= \frac{16 \times 1.5 \times 42994}{\pi D^3}$$

$$= \frac{328 \times 10^3}{D^3} \text{ kg/cm}^2$$

$M$ = Bending moment = 0

$f$ = Direct stress

$$= \alpha \,.\, \frac{P}{A} = \alpha \,.\, \frac{987}{\pi \times D^2} \times 4$$

$$= \alpha \,.\, \frac{1257}{D^2} \text{ kg/cm}^2$$

$$= \frac{1.21 \times 1257}{D^2} = \frac{1521}{D^2} \text{ kg/cm}^2$$

$(f_s)_{max}$ = 570 kg/cm$^2$ for commercial shafts

$$570 = \sqrt{(f_s)^2 + \frac{1}{2} \times (f)^2}$$

$$= \sqrt{\left(\frac{328 \times 10^3}{D^3}\right)^2 + \frac{1}{4}\left(\frac{1521}{D^2}\right)^2}$$

This gives $D$ = 8.4 cm. by trial.

**Example 7.11.** *A machine shaft is to transmit 80 H.P. at 900 RPM with mild shock. The shaft is subjected to an axial thrust of 6000 kg and to a maximum bending moment of 9200 kg/cm. The shaft is supported at intervals of 2.4 cm. Determine shaft diameter when designed according to code.*

**Solution.** $N$ = R.P.M. of shaft = 900

$T$ = Torque

$$\text{H.P.} = \frac{2\pi NT}{4500}$$

$$80 = \frac{2\pi \times 900 \times T}{4500}$$

$T$ = 63.7 kg m = 6370 kg cm

$M$ = Bending moment = 9200 kg cm

$P$ = Axial thrust = 6000 kg.

According to code, the shaft is made of a ductile material whose ultimate tensile strength is twice the ultimate shear strength.

$k_s$ = shock and fatigue factor for shear

= 1.5

$k_b$ = shock and fatigue factor for bending

= 1.8

The shaft diameter is controlled by maximum shear stress theory

$$f_{s\,(max)} = 560 \text{ kg/cm}^2.$$

$$D = \text{shaft diameter.}$$

Now maximum shear stress is given by

$$f_{s\,(max)} = \sqrt{\left(\frac{16.k_s.T}{\pi D^3}\right)^2 + \frac{1}{4}\left(\frac{k_b.32M}{\pi D^3} + \frac{\alpha.4.P}{\pi D^2}\right)^2} \quad ...(1)$$

It is difficult to solve this equation because constant $\alpha$ is not known.

Therefore the problem should be solved by trial and error method neglecting $P$.

$$T_e = \text{Equivalent torque} = \sqrt{(k_b M)^2 + (k_s T)^2}$$

$$= \sqrt{(1.8 \times 9200)^2 + (1.5 \times 6370)^2}$$

$$= 17.7 \times 10^3 \text{ kg cm}$$

$$T_e = \frac{\pi}{16} f_s D^3$$

$$17.7 \times 10^3 = \frac{\pi}{16} \times 560 \times D^3$$

$$D = 5.44 \text{ cm.} = 5.5 \text{ cm (say)}$$

$$k = \text{Radius of gyration}$$

$$= \frac{D}{4} = \frac{5.5}{4} = 1.37 \text{ cm}$$

$$L = \text{Length of shaft between bearings}$$

$$= 240 \text{ cm}$$

$$\frac{L}{K} = \frac{240}{1.37} = 175$$

This is more than 115.

Therefore, $$\alpha = \frac{f_{yc}\left(\frac{L}{k}\right)^2}{n.\pi^2.E}$$

where $n = 1$ for hinged ends

$$E = 2.1 \times 10^6 \text{ kg/cm}^2$$

$$f_{yc} = 3000 \text{ kg/cm}^2 \text{ for C 45 steel annealed}$$

$$\alpha = \frac{3000 \times 175^2}{1 \times \pi^2 \times 2.1 \times 10^6} = 0.44$$

$f_s$ = shear stress as per equation (1) is

$$= \sqrt{\left(\frac{16 \times 1.5 \times 6370}{\pi \times 5.5^3}\right)^2 + \frac{1}{4}\left(\frac{1.8 \times 32 \times 9200}{\pi \times 5.5^3} + \frac{0.44 \times 4 \times 6000}{\pi \times 5.5^2}\right)^2}$$

$$= 540 \text{ kg/cm}^2$$

This is less than 560 kg/cm$^2$. Therefore it is safe.

## 7.7 Couplings

Couplings are used to connect two shafts together so that they act as a single unit and power can be transmitted directly from one shaft to another. Couplings provide a permanent connection of shafts. Couplings are of two types :

(*i*) Rigid couplings. (*ii*) Flexible couplings.

Rigid couplings are used where shafts are properly aligned. They are of the following types :

(*a*) Muff coupling. (*b*) Clamp coupling. (*c*) Flange coupling.

Flexible couplings take care of small misalignment in the shaft axes, lateral or angular. They are of the following types :

(*a*) Bushed pin type coupling.

(*b*) Universal coupling.

(*c*) Oldham coupling.

## 7.8 Sleeve or Muff Coupling

In this type of coupling a sleeve or muff of steel or cast iron is fitted on the shaft and keyed to both the shafts. The key used generally is a taper rectangular sunk key. It is also called a box coupling. Fig. 7.21 shows a sleeve coupling. In this coupling the various dimensions may be assumed as follows :

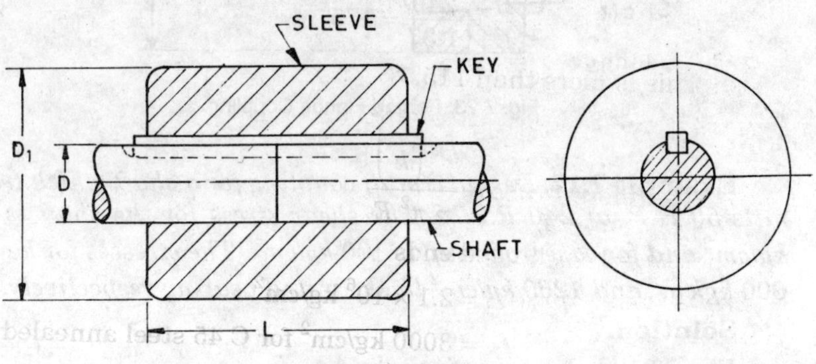


Fig. 7.21. Sleeve coupling.

$D$ = Shaft diameter

$D_1$ = Diameter of sleeve = $2D + 1.3$ cm

$L$ = Length of sleeve = $3.5\ D$

Fig. 7.22 shows a half lap muff coupling.

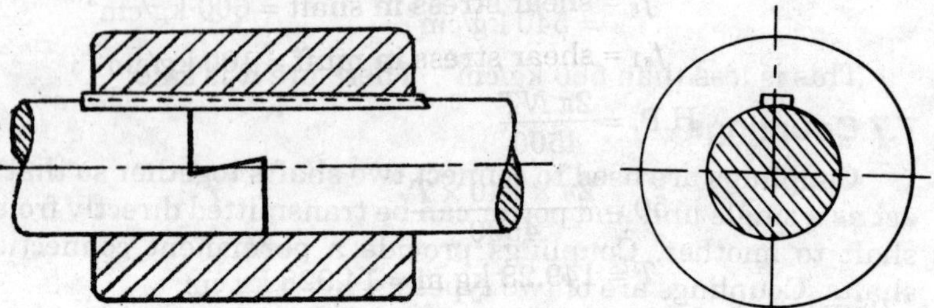

Fig. 7.22. Half lap muff coupling.

## 7.9 Solid Coupling or Forge Coupling or Marine Type Coupling

In this coupling the ends of shafts are forged to form flanges. To ensure alignment of shafts, a spigot is formed in one of the flanges and corresponding recess is provided in other flange. This coupling is used for marine propellor shafts. Fig. 7.23 shows a solid coupling.

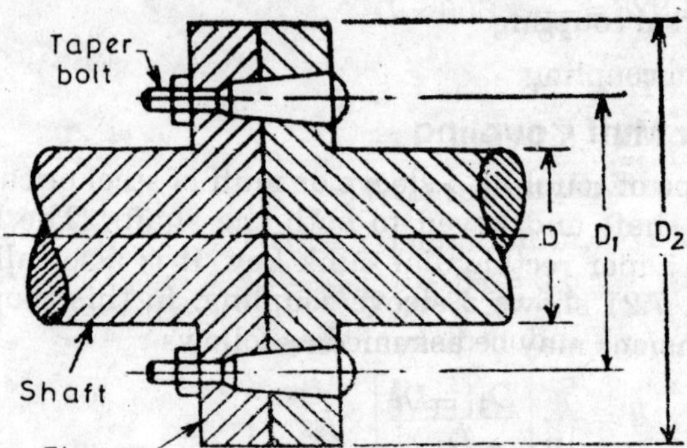


Fig. 7.23. Forged Flange Coupling.

**Example 7.12.** *Design a muff coupling for a shaft which transmits 50 H.P. at 240 R.P.M. The shear stress for the shaft is 600 kg/cm² and for cast iron muff is 100 kg/cm². The stresses for key are 600 kg/cm² and 1260 kg/cm² in shear and bearing respectively.*

**Solution.**

Fig. 7.21 shows a muff coupling

$$H.P. = 50$$

$$N = 240 \text{ R.P.M.}$$

$$f_s = \text{shear stress in shaft} = 600 \text{ kg/cm}^2$$

$$f_{s1} = \text{shear stress in muff} = 100 \text{ kg/cm}^2$$

$$H.P. = \frac{2\pi NT}{4500}$$

$$50 = \frac{2\pi \times 240 \times T}{4500}$$

$$T = 149.28 \text{ kg m} = 14{,}928 \text{ kg cm.}$$

**(*i*) To find shaft diameter (D)**

$$\frac{T}{I} = \frac{f_s}{R}$$

where $R = \text{shaft radius} = \dfrac{D}{2}$

$$T = I \cdot \frac{f_s}{R} = \frac{\pi}{32} D^4 \times \frac{f_s}{(D/2)} = \frac{\pi}{16} f_s D^3$$

$$14{,}928 = \frac{\pi}{16} \times 600 \times D^3$$

$$D^3 = 126.77$$

$$D = 5.1 \text{ cm.}$$

**(*ii*) To find muff diameter ($D_1$)**

$$D_1 = \text{muff diameter} = 2D + 1.3 \text{ cm}$$

$$= 2 \times 5.1 + 1.3 = 11.5 \text{ cm.}$$

Let $f_{s2}$ = Induced shear stress in muff

$$T = \frac{\pi}{16}\left[\frac{D_1^4 - D^4}{D_1}\right] \times f_{s2}$$

$$14{,}928 = \frac{\pi}{16}\left[\frac{(11.5)^4 - (5.1)^4}{11.5}\right] \times f_{s2}$$

$$f_{s2} = 52.1 \text{ kg/cm}^2$$

This is less than the allowable shear stress 100 kg/cm$^2$ in muff. Hence safe.

**(*iii*) To find length of muff**

$$L = \text{Length of muff} = 3.5\ D$$

$$= 3.5 \times 5.1 = 17.85 \text{ cm}$$

*(iv)* **To design key**

Use a rectangular sunk key

$b$ = Width of key

$t$ = Thickness of key

$l$ = Length of key in each shaft

$$= \frac{1}{2} \times \text{Length of muff}$$

$$= \frac{1}{2} \times 17.85 = 8.925 \text{ cm.}$$

$P$ = Tangential load at shaft radius

$$= \frac{T}{R} = \frac{14{,}928 \times 2}{5.1} = 5854 \text{ kg.}$$

Consider shearing failure of key

$A$ = Area under shear $= l \times b$

$$P = A \times f_{s_3} = 8.925 \times b \times 600$$

$$5854 = 8.225 \times b \times 600$$

$$b = 1.1 \text{ cm}$$

$f_e$ = Crushing stress in key = 1260 kg/cm$^2$.

Consider crushing failure of key

$A$ = Area under crushing

$$= l \times \frac{t}{2}$$

$$P = A \times f_c$$

$$= l \times \frac{t}{2} \times f_c$$

$$5854 = 8.925 \times \frac{t}{2} \times 1260$$

$$t = 1 \text{ cm.}$$

Taper in key = 1 : 100.

**Example 7.13.** *Design a forged flange coupling for a marine engine shaft which is required to transmit 3000 H.P. at 100 R.P.M. The allowable shear stress in shaft and bolt is 600 kg/cm$^2$.*

**Solution.**

Fig. 7.23 shows a forged flange coupling

$$\text{H.P.} = \frac{2\pi NT}{4500}$$

$$3000 = \frac{2\pi \times 100 \times T}{4500}$$

$$T = 21{,}496 \text{ kg m} = 21{,}49{,}600 \text{ kg cm.}$$

(*i*) **To calculate shaft diameter**

$D$ = Shaft diameter

$f_s$ = Shear stress in shaft = 600 kg/cm.$^2$

$$T = \frac{\pi}{16} f_s D^3$$

$$21{,}49{,}600 = \frac{\pi}{16} \times 600 \times D^3$$

$$D = 26.3 \text{ cm.}$$

We adopt $D = 27$ cm.

(*ii*) **To design bolts**

$D_1$ = Pitch circle diameter of bolts

$= 1.6\, D = 1.6 \times 27 = 43.2$ cm.

$R_1$ = Pitch circle radius

$$= \frac{D_1}{2} = \frac{43.2}{2} = 21.6 \text{ cm.}$$

$d$ = Mean diameter of bolt.

$n$ = Number of bolt

$n$ = 8 (Assume)

$F$ = Shear force on each bolt

$$= \frac{T}{R_1 \times n}$$

$$= \frac{21{,}49{,}600}{21.6 \times 8} = 12{,}440 \text{ kg.}$$

The bolt is in single shear

$A$ = Area under shear

$$= \frac{\pi}{4} d^2$$

$f_s$ = Shear stress in bolt = 600 kg/cm$^2$.

$$F = A \times f_s$$

$$12{,}440 = \frac{\pi}{4} d^2 \times 600$$

$$d = 5.14 \text{ cm.}$$

Taper in bolt $= 1 : 24.$

***(iii)* To design flange**

$$D_2 = \text{Outside diameter of flange}$$
$$= 2\,D = 2 \times 27 = 54 \text{ cm}$$
$$t = \text{Thickness of flange}$$
$$= \frac{D}{3} = \frac{27}{3} = 9$$
$$P = \text{Shear force at shaft radius}$$
$$= \frac{T}{\text{Shaft radius}}$$

The flange may get sheared off at the circumference of shaft

$$P = \frac{T}{13.5} = \frac{2149600}{13.5} = 159230 \text{ kg}$$
$$P = \text{Shear Area} \times \text{Shear stress}$$
$$159230 = \pi\,Dt \,.\, f_{s_1} = \pi \times 27 \times 9 \times f_{s_1}$$
$$f_{s_1} = 209 \text{ kg/cm}^2 \text{ which is safe.}$$

## 7.10 Protected Type Flange Coupling

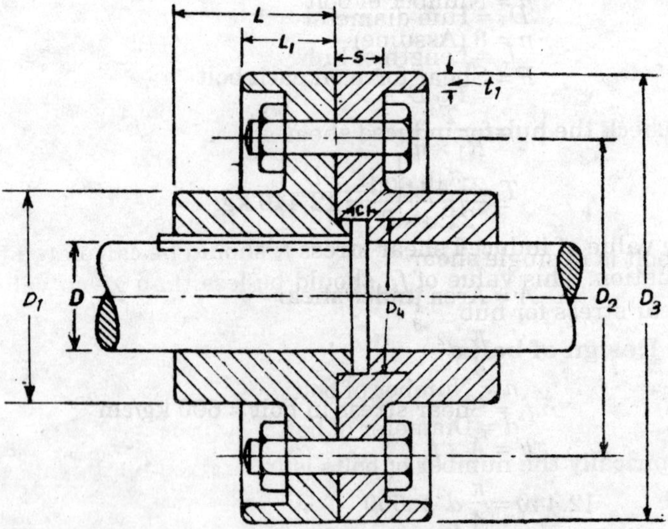


Fig. 7.24. Protected Type Flange Coupling.

It consists of two hubs keyed on the ends of two shafts. The hubs extend into flanges whose faces are brought together and connected by means of bolts. Bolts are guarded by giving projections at the flanges. Fig. 7.24 shows a protected type of flange coupling. This is the most commonly used coupling. Hubs are made of cast iron whereas shafts, keys and bolts are made up of mild steel.

$D$ = Diameter of shaft

$D_2$ = Pitch circle diameter of bolt = 3 $D$

$D_1$ = Hub diameter = 2 $D$

$D_3$ = Diameter of flange = 4 $D$

H.P. = Horse power transmitted by shaft

$N$ = R.P.M. of shaft

$f_s$ = Safe shear stress in shaft keys.

(*i*) **To find shaft diameter (D)**

$$\text{H.P.} = \frac{2\pi NT}{4500}$$

where $T$ = Torque (kg m)

$$T = \frac{\pi}{16} f_s D^3$$

The shaft diameter $D$ is calculated from this relation.

(*ii*) **Design of hub**

$D_1$ = Hub diameter = 2 $D$

$L$ = Length of hub

= 1.5 $D$

To check the hub for induced shear stress

$$T = \frac{\pi}{16} f_{s_1} \left[ \frac{D_1^4 - D^4}{D_1} \right]$$

The value of induced shear stress $f_s$ should be calculated from this equation. This value of $f_{s_1}$ should be less than given value of safe shear stress for hub.

(*iii*) **Design of bolts**

$n$ = Number of bolts

$d$ = Diameter of bolt

Empirically the number of bolts is to be fixed by the following relation

$$n = \frac{4}{15} D + 3$$

where $D$ is shaft diameter in cm.

The number of bolts for some of shaft diameters is as follows :

$n = 3$ for shaft diameter upto 4 cm

$= 4$ for shaft diameter upto 10 cm

$= 6$ for shaft diameter up to 18 cm.

$F$ = Force on each bolt

$$= \frac{T}{n \times R_2}$$

where $R_2$ = Pitch circle radius of bolt

$$= \frac{D_2}{2}$$

$f_{s2}$ = Safe shear stress in bolts

The bolt is in single shear

$A$ = Area under shear

$$= \frac{\pi}{4} d^2$$

$$F = \frac{\pi}{4} d^2 \times f_{s2}$$

The diameter $d$ can be found from this equation.

(*iv*) **To design key**

$l$ = Length of key

= Length of hub + 6 mm

$b$ = width of key $= \frac{D}{4}$

$t$ = Thickness of key $= \frac{D}{6}$

To find induced shear stress ($f_{s3}$) in key consider shearing of key

$A$ = Area under shear

$= l \times b$

$P$ = Tangential force at shaft radius

$$= \frac{T}{\text{Shaft radius}}$$

$$P = A \times f_{s3} = l \times b \times f_{s3}.$$

The value of $f_{s3}$ calculated from this equation should be less than allowable shear stress in key.

To find induced crushing stress ($f_{c1}$) in key.

$$P = l \times \frac{t}{2} \times f_{c_1}$$

T... $f_{c_1}$ calculated from this equation should be less than safe ... crushing stress in key.

**...gn of flange**

$$D_3 = \text{Diameter of flange} = 4\,D$$

$$S = \frac{D}{4} + 1 \text{ cm}$$

$$L_1 = \frac{D}{2} + 1.25 \text{ cm}$$

$$t_1 = 0.1\,D + 0.5 \text{ cm}$$

$$C = 0.1\,D + 0.25 \text{ cm.}$$

**Example 7.14.** *Design a flange coupling of protected type for a mild steel which is to transmit 80 H.P. at 240 R.P.M. The maximum torque is 30% greater than the mean torque. The allowable shear stress in cast iron hub is 60 kg/cm$^2$ and allowable shear stress in shaft and key is 400 kg/cm$^2$. The allowable shear stress in bolt is 300 kg/cm$^2$. Crushing stress in key is 1250 kg/cm$^2$.*

**Solution.**

Fig. 7.24 shows a protected type flange coupling.

$$\text{H.P.} = \frac{2\pi NT}{4500}$$

$$80 = \frac{2\pi \times 240 \times T}{4500}$$

Mean torque, $T = 238.85 \text{ kg m} = 24{,}885 \text{ kg cm.}$

$$T_m = \text{Maximum torque} = 1.3 \times T$$

$$= 1.3 \times 23{,}885 = 31{,}050 \text{ kg cm.}$$

**(*i*) To calculate shaft diameter (D)**

$$f_s = \text{Shear stress in shaft}$$

$$= 400 \text{ kg/cm}^2$$

$$\frac{T_m}{T} = \frac{f_s}{R}$$

$$T_m = \frac{\pi}{32} D^4 \times \frac{f_s}{D/2}$$

$$T_m = \frac{\pi}{16} f_s D^3$$

$$3150 = \frac{\pi}{16} \times 400 \times D^3$$

$$D = 7.3 \text{ cm.}$$

(*ii*) **To design hub**

$$D_1 = \text{Hub diameter} = 2\,D$$

$$= 2 \times 7.3 = 14.6 \text{ cm.}$$

$$L = \text{Length of hub} = 1.5\,D$$

$$= 1.5 \times 7.3 = 10.95 \text{ cm.}$$

Let $f_{s_1}$ = Induced shear stress in hub

$$T_m = \frac{\pi}{16} f_{s_1} \left[\frac{D_1^4 - D^4}{D_1}\right]$$

$$31050 = \frac{\pi}{16} f_{s_2} \left[\frac{(14.6)^6 - (7.3)^4}{14.6}\right]$$

$$f_{s_1} = 54.2 \text{ kg/cm}^2.$$

This is less than allowable shear stress 60 kg/cm$^2$ in hub. Hence safe.

(*iii*) **To design bolts**

$$d = \text{Diameter of bolt}$$

$$n = \text{Number of bolts}$$

$$= \frac{4}{15} D + 3$$

$$= \frac{4}{15} \times 7.3 + 3 = 4.95$$

We adopt 6 bolts.

$$\therefore \quad n = 6$$

$$D_2 = \text{Pitch circle diameter of bolt}$$

$$= 3\,D = 3 \times 7.3$$

$$= 21.9 \text{ cm.}$$

$$R_2 = \text{Radius of pitch circle}$$

$$= \frac{D_2}{2} = \frac{21.9}{2}$$

$$= 10.95 \text{ cm.}$$

$$f_{s_2} = \text{Shear stress in bolt} = 300 \text{ kg/cm}^2.$$

$$F = \text{Force on each bolt}$$

$$= \frac{T_m}{n \,.\, R_2}$$

$$= \frac{31{,}050}{6 \times 10.95} = 472.6 \text{ kg.}$$

The bolt is in single shear

$$A = \text{Area under shear} = \frac{\pi}{4} d^2$$

$$F = A \times f_{s_2}$$

$$472.6 = \frac{\pi}{4} d^2 \times 300$$

$$d = 1.41 \text{ cm.}$$

(*iv*) **To design key**

Use a rectangular key

$$l = \text{Length of key}$$

$$= \text{Length of hub} + 6 \text{ mm}$$

$$= 10.95 + 0.6 = 11.55 \text{ cm}$$

$$b = \text{Width of key}$$

$$= \frac{D}{4} = \frac{7.3}{4}$$

$$= 1.82 \text{ cm} = 1.9 \text{ cm (say)}$$

$$t = \text{Thickness of key} = \frac{D}{6}$$

$$= \frac{7.3}{6} = 1.2 \text{ cm.}$$

$$f_{s_3} = \text{Shear stress induced in key}$$

$$f_{c_1} = \text{Crushing stress induced in key}$$

$$P = \text{Tangential load at shaft radius}$$

$$= \frac{T_m}{R}$$

where $R$ = Shaft radius

$$= \frac{7.3}{2} = 3.65 \text{ cm.}$$

$$P = \frac{31{,}050}{3.65} = 8507 \text{ kg.}$$

Consider shearing failure of key.

$$A = \text{Area under shear} = l \times b$$

$$P = l \times b \times f_{s_2}$$

$$8507 = 11.55 \times 1.9 \times f_{s_3}$$

$$f_{s_3} = 387.6 \text{ kg/cm}^2.$$

This is less than allowable shear stress 400 kg/cm² in key. Hence safe.

Consider crushing of key

$$A = \text{Area under crushing}$$

$$= l \times \frac{t}{2}$$

$$P = A \times f_{c_1}$$

$$8507 = l \times \frac{t}{2} \times f_{c_1} = 11.55 \times \frac{1.2}{2} \times f_{c_1}$$

$$f_{c_1} = 1227 \text{ kg/cm}^2.$$

This is less than the allowable crushing stress 1250 kg/cm² in key. Hence safe.

Taper in key = 1 : 100.

**(*iv*) Design of flange**

$$D_3 = \text{Diameter of flange} = 4\,D$$

$$= 4 \times 7.3 = 29.2 \text{ cm}$$

$$D_4 = 1.5\,D$$

$$= 1.5 \times 7.3 = 11 \text{ cm}$$

$$S = \frac{D}{4} + 1 \text{ cm}$$

$$= \frac{7.3}{4} + 1 = 2.8 \text{ cm}$$

$$L_1 = \frac{D}{2} + 1.25 \text{ cm} = \frac{7.3}{2} + 1.25 = 4.9 \text{ cm}.$$

$$t_1 = 0.1\,D + 0.5 \text{ cm}$$

$$= 0.1 \times 7.3 + 0.5 = 1.23 \text{ cm}$$

$$C = 0.1\,D + 0.25 \text{ cm}$$

$$= 0.1 \times 7.3 + 0.25 = 0.98 \text{ cm}$$

## 7.11 Pin Type Flexible Coupling

This coupling has the ability to absorb shocks. Flexible coupling can be used to connect shafts permitting some non-alignment to exist between them. It is used to connect a machine to a prime mover for direct drive. Fig. 7.25 shows a pin type flexible coupling.

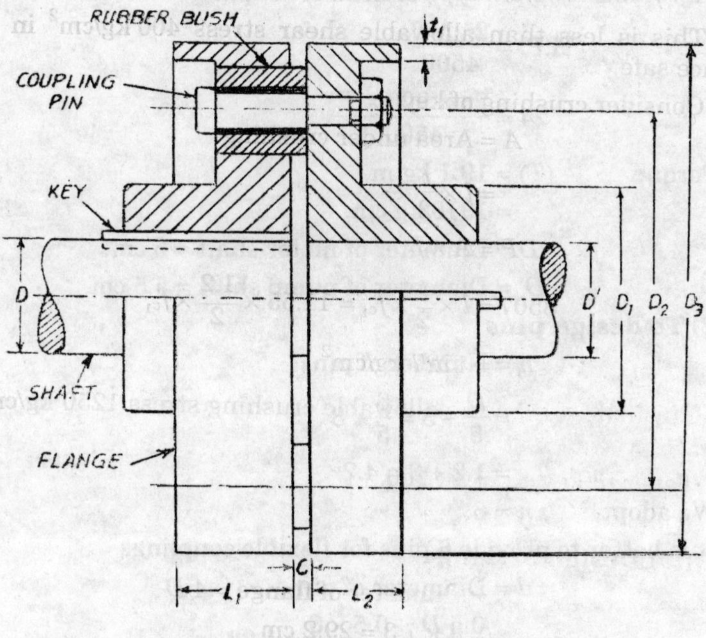


Fig. 7.25. Pin type flexible coupling.

In this coupling bolts are known as pins having special shape as shown in the figure. Coupling pin is shown in Fig. 7.26.

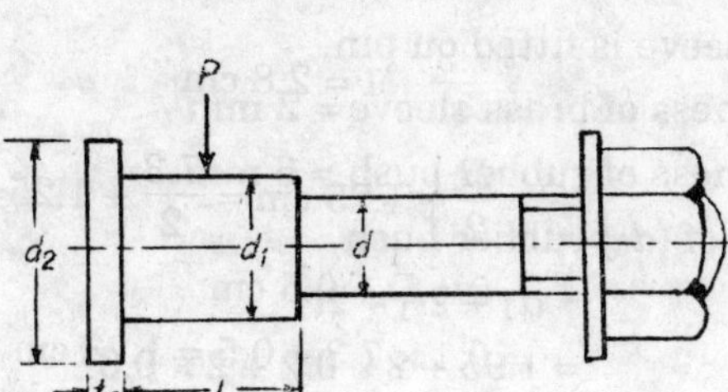


Fig. 7.26. Coupling pin.

**Example 7.15.** *Design a bushed pin type of flexible coupling for connecting motor and centrifugal pump shafts, the diameters of motor and pump shafts being 6 cm and 5.5 cm respectively. The power to be transmitted is 24 at a speed of 900 R.P.M. The allowable* *shear stress in pins is 190 kg/cm² and the bearing pressure on rubber bush is 3 kg/cm². Allowable shear stress in key is 400 kg/cm².*

**Solution.**

Fig. 7.25 shows pin type of flexible coupling.

$$\text{H.P.} = \frac{2\pi NT}{4500}$$

$$24 = \frac{2\pi \times 900 \times T}{4500}$$

Torque $(T) = 19.1$ kg m.

$= 1910$ kg cm.

$D$ = Diameter of motor shaft = 6 cm.

$D'$ = Diameter of pump shaft = 5.5 cm.

(*i*) **To design pins**

$n$ = Number of pins

$$= \frac{D}{5} + 3 = \frac{6}{5} + 3$$

$$= 1.2 + 3 = 4.2$$

We adopt, $n = 6$.

It is better to provide 6 pins for flexible couplings

$d$ = Diameter of pin

$$= \frac{0.5\,D}{\sqrt{n}} = \frac{0.5 \times 6}{\sqrt{6}} = 1.22 \text{ cm.}$$

$\approx 1.3$ cm (say)

$d_1 = 1.5\,d = 1.5 \times 1.3$

$= 1.95$ cm.

A brass sleeve is fitted on pin.

$(t_1)$ Thickness of brass sleeve = 2 mm

$(t_2)$ Thickness of rubber bush = 6 mm.

Diameter of $(d_3)$ rubber bush

$= d_1 + 2t_1 + 2t_2$

$= 1.95 + 2 \times 0.2 + 2 \times 0.6$

$= 3.55$ cm.

$D_2$ = Diameter of pitch circle of pins

$= 3\,D = 3 \times 6 = 18$ cm.

$L$ = Length of bush

$A$ = Bearing area of bush = $L \times d_3$

$P$ = Driving force on each pin

$$= \frac{T}{n \times R_2}$$

where $R_2$ = Pitch circle radius

$$= \frac{D_2}{2} = \frac{18}{2} = 9 \text{ cm}$$

$$P = \frac{1910}{6 \times 9} = 35.37 \text{ kg.}$$

$f_b$ = Bearing pressure on rubber bush

$= 3 \text{ kg/cm}^2$

$$P = A \times f_b = L \times d_3 \times f_b$$

$$35.37 = L \times 3.55 \times 3$$

$$L = 3.32 \text{ cm}$$

$t_2$ = Thickness of pin head = 3 mm (assume)

$d_2$ = diameter of pin

$= d_3 - t_2 = 3.55 - 0.3 = 3.23$ cm

$C$ = Clearance between flanges

$= 0.1\,D = 0.1 \times 6 = 0.6$ cm

**Stresses in Pin**

$$f_s = \text{Direct shear stress} = \frac{P}{\frac{\pi}{4} d^2}$$

$$= \frac{35.4}{\frac{\pi}{4} (1.3)^2} = 26.66 \text{ kg/cm}^2.$$

Since the pin is not rigidly held in left hand face and the rubber is compressible the force $P = 35.37$ kg at the enlarged portion will exert a bending action on the pin. Assuming a uniform distribution of load $P$ along the bush as shown in Fig. 7.25, the arm of bending moment will be,

$$\frac{L}{2} + C = \frac{1}{2} \times 3.32 + 0.6$$

$$= 1.66 + 0.6 = 2.26 \text{ cm}$$

$M$ = Bending moment

$= P \times 2.26 = 35.37 \times 2.26 = 76.4$ kg cm

$f_t$ = Bending stress

$$= \frac{M}{\frac{\pi}{32} d^3} = \frac{76.4}{\frac{\pi}{32}(1.3)^3} = 354 \text{ kg/cm}^2$$

$$f_1 = \text{Maximum principal stress}$$

$$= \frac{1}{2}\left[f_t + \sqrt{f_t^2 + 4f_s^2}\right]$$

$$f_1 = \frac{1}{2}[354 + \sqrt{(354)^2 + 4 \times (26.66)^2}]$$

$$= 356 \text{ kg/cm}^2 \text{ which is safe.}$$

$$f_{s(max)} = \text{Maximum shear stress}$$

$$= \frac{1}{2}\sqrt{f_t^2 + 4f_s^2} = \frac{1}{2}\sqrt{(354)^2 + 4 \times (26.66)^2}$$

$$= 179 \text{ kg/cm}^2$$

which is within safe limit of 190 kg/cm$^2$.

(*ii*) **To design key**

Use a square key

$$b = \text{Width of key}$$

$$= \frac{D}{4} = \frac{6}{4} = 1.5 \text{ cm}$$

$$t = \text{Thickness of key} = 1.5 \text{ cm}$$

$$l = \text{Length of key}$$

$$f_{s_1} = \text{Shear stress in key}$$

$$= 400 \text{ kg/cm}^2$$

$$F = \text{Tangential load at shaft radius}$$

$$= \frac{T}{\text{Shaft radius}}$$

$$= \frac{1910}{3} = 636.6 \text{ kg.}$$

Consider shear failure of key

$$F = l \times b \times f_{s_1}$$

$$636.6 = l \times 1.5 \times 400$$

$$l = 1 \text{ cm.}$$

Generally $l$ is not kept less than 1.2 $D$

$$\therefore \quad l = 1.2\, D = 1.2 \times 9 = 7.2 \text{ cm.}$$

(*iii*) **To design Flange**

$L_1$ = Width of flange on left hand side

$$= \frac{D}{2} + 1.25$$

$$= \frac{6}{2} + 1.25 = 4.25 \text{ cm}$$

$L_2$ = Width of flange on right hand side

$$L_2 = \frac{D'}{2} + 1.25$$

$$= \frac{5.5}{2} + 1.25 = 4 \text{ cm}$$

$D_3$ = Diameter of flange

$$= 4 \times D = 4 \times 6 = 24 \text{ cm}$$

$t_1$ = Thickness of flange

$$= 0.1\,D = 0.1 \times 6 = 0.6 \text{ cm.}$$

(*iv*) **To design hub**

Length of left hand hub

$$= 1.5\,D = 1.5 \times 6 = 9 \text{ cm.}$$

Length of right hand hub

$$= 1.5\,D' = 1.5 \times 5.5 = 8.25 \text{ cm.}$$

$D_1$ = Diameter of hub

$$= 2\,D = 2 \times 6 = 12 \text{ cm.}$$

## 7.12 Clamp or Compression Coupling or Split Muff Coupling

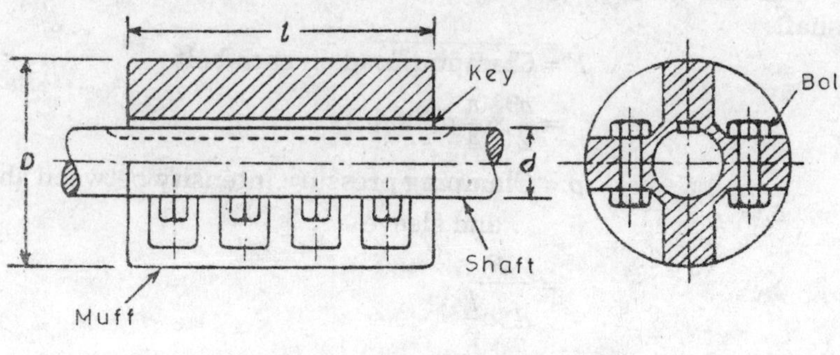


Fig. 7.27. Clamp or Compression Coupling.

It is also called a split muff coupling. In this coupling muff is split into two semi-cylindrical halves which are joined together by means of nuts and bolts used in recesses formed in muff. (Fig. 7.27). This two shafts are joined with muff by means of a key. This coupling can be readily assembled and disassembled very easily. It is conveniently used for the line shaft service and can easily transmit heavy torque.

(*i*) **To design shaft**

Let $T$ = Torque to be transmitted

$N$ = R.P.M. of shaft

$d$ = Diameter of shaft

$f_s$ = Shear stress in shaft

$$T = \frac{\pi}{16} f_s \cdot d^3$$

Shaft diameter ($d$) is found from this relation.

(*ii*) **To design bolts.**

$d$ = Core diameter of bolt

$f_t$ = Allowable tensile stress in bolt.

$n$ = Number of bolts.

$A$ = Area of cross–section of bolt

$$= \frac{\pi}{4} d^2$$

$P$ = Tensile load per bolt

$$= A \times f_t$$

$$= \frac{\pi}{4} d_c^2 \times f_t.$$

As half the member of bolts will give clamping pressure on each shaft.

$F$ = Clamping load on each bolt

$$= \frac{n}{2} \times \frac{\pi}{4} d_c^2 \times f_t.$$

$p$ = Clamping pressure intensity between shaft and sleeve.

$$= \frac{F}{d \times \frac{l}{2}}$$

where $l$ = Length of sleeve (muff)

$$p = \frac{\frac{n}{2} \cdot \frac{\pi}{4} d_e^2 \cdot f_t}{d \cdot \frac{l}{2}} = \frac{n \cdot \pi \, d_c^2 \cdot f_t}{4 \times d \cdot l}$$

Let $\mu$ = Coefficient of friction between shaft and sleeve.

$p_1$ = Tangential frictional force per unit area of shaft perisphery

$$= \mu \cdot p = \frac{\mu \cdot n \cdot \pi d_c^2 \cdot f_t}{4 \times d \cdot l}$$

$T$ = Torque that can be transmitted by the coupling

$= p_1 \times$ peripheral area of shaft $\times$ Radius of shaft.

$$= \frac{\mu \cdot n \cdot \pi \cdot d_s^2 \cdot f_t}{4 \cdot d \cdot l} \times \frac{\pi d \cdot l}{2} \times \frac{d}{2}$$

$$T = \frac{\mu \cdot n \cdot \pi^2 \, d_c^2 \cdot d \, f_t}{16} \quad \text{...(i)}$$

$P$ = Load which can be taken by each bolt.

$$= \frac{\pi}{4} d_c^2 \cdot f_t \quad \text{...(ii)}$$

Substituting this value of $P$ in equation (*i*) we get

$$P = \frac{4T}{\mu \cdot \pi \cdot n \cdot d} \quad \text{...(iii)}$$

The diameter of coupling bolt is found using equation (*ii*) and equation (*iii*).

**(*iii*) To design muff**

$D$ = Muff diameter = $2d$

$l$ = Length of muff = $3.5\,d$.

**(*iv*) To design key**

Use a rectangular shunk key

$L$ = Length of key on each shaft

$= \frac{1}{2} \times$ muff length

$= \frac{1}{2} \cdot l.$

$f_s$ = Shear stress in key

$f_c$ = Crushing stress in key

Considering shearing failure of key

$$A = \text{Area under shear} = L \times b$$

$$P_1 = \text{Shear force}$$

$$= \frac{T}{\text{shaft radius}}$$

$$P_1 = A \times f_s = L \times b \times f_s.$$

The width ($b$) of key can be found from this relation.

Let $t$ = Thickness of key

Considering crushing of key

$$P_1 = L \cdot \frac{t}{2} \cdot f_c$$

The thickness of key is found from this relation.

**Example 7.16.** *Design a clamp coupling for a shaft of diameter 6 cm. The H.P. to be transmitted by the shaft is 40 at 200 R.P.M. The allowable shear stress in shaft and key is 400 kg/cm² and the permissible tensile stress in bolt is 500 kg/cm² The coefficient of friction between shaft and muff is 0.3. The two halves of the coupling are to be connected by 8 bolts. Crushing stress in key is 1000 kg/cm²*

**Solution.**

Fig. 7.27 shows a clamp coupling.

(*i*) **To design shaft**

$d$ = Diameter of shaft

$N$ = R.P.M. of shaft = 200 R.P.M.

H.P. = 40

$f_s$ = Shear stress in shaft

= 400 kg/cm²

$$\text{H.P.} = \frac{2\pi NT}{4500}$$

$$40 = \frac{2\pi \times 200 \times T}{4500}$$

$$T = \frac{40 \times 4500}{2\pi \times 200}$$

= 143.31 kg cm. = 14331 kg cm.

$$T = \frac{\pi}{16} f_s\, d^3$$

$$14331 = \frac{\pi}{16} \times 400 \times d^3$$

$$d = 5.67 \text{ cm.}$$

We adopt, $d = 5.7$ cm.

(*ii*) **To design bolts**

Let $d_c$ = Core diameter of bolt.

$n$ = Number of bolts = 8

$A$ = Area of cross–section of bolt

$$= \frac{\pi}{4} d_c^2$$

$f_t$ = Allowable tensile stress in bolt.

$P$ = Tensile load per bolt = $A \times f_t$.

$$= \frac{\pi}{4} d_c^2 \times f_t.$$

But
$$P = \frac{4T}{\mu \,.\, \pi n \,.\, d}$$

$$= \frac{4 \times 14331}{0.3 \times \pi \times 8 \times 5.7} = 1334 \text{ kg.}$$

$$P = \frac{\pi}{4} d_c^2 \times f_t$$

$$1334 = \frac{\pi}{4} d_c^2 \times 650$$

$$d_c = 1.62 \text{ cm}$$

Out side diameter of bolt

$$= \frac{d_c}{0.84} = \frac{1.62}{0.84} = 1.93 \text{ cm.}$$

(*iii*) **To design muff**

$D$ = Diameter of muff

$= 2\,d = 2 \times 5.7 = 11.4$ cm.

$l$ = Length of muff

$= 3.5\,d = 3.5 \times 5.7 = 19.95$ cm.

(*iv*) **To design key**

Use a rectangular key of width ($b$) and thickness ($t$)

$L$ = Length of key

$$= \frac{1}{2} \times \text{muff length} = \frac{1}{2} \times 19.95 = 9.975 \text{ cm.}$$

$f_s$ = Shear stress in key

= 400 kg/cm$^2$.

$f_c$ = Crushing stress in key

= 1000 kg/cm$^2$.

$P_1$ = Tangential force at shaft radius

$$= \frac{\text{T}}{\text{Shaft radius}} = \frac{14331}{5.7} \times 2 = 5028 \text{ kg.}$$

Considering shearing of key

$$P_1 = L \times b \times f_c$$

$$5028 = 9.975 \times b \times 400$$

$$b = 1.26 \text{ cm.}$$

Again considering crushing of key

$$P_1 = L \cdot \frac{t}{2} \cdot f_c$$

$$5028 = 9.975 \times \frac{t}{2} \cdot 1000$$

$$t = 1 \text{ cm.}$$

Taper in key = 1 : 100.

## 7.13 Universal Coupling

It is used to connect together shafts whose axis will intersect if produced. This coupling consists of two forks which are keyed to the shafts. The two forks are pin joined to a centre block having two arms at right angles to each other. In this coupling the angle between the shafts should not be more than 45° Fig. 7.28 shows a universal coupling.

**Example 7.17.** *Design a universal coupling to transmit a torque of 45,000 kg cm. The safe shear stress in shaft is 600 kg/cm$^2$ and the safe shear stress in pin is 310 kg/cm$^2$.*

**Solution.**

(*a*) **To find shaft diameter**

$T$ = Torque = 45000 kg cm.

$D$ = Shaft diameter.

$f_s$ = Safe shear stress in shaft = 600 kg/cm$^2$.

$$T = \frac{\pi}{16} f_s \times D^3$$

$$45000 = \frac{\pi}{16} \times 600 \times D^3$$

$$D = 7.25 \text{ cm.}$$

(*b*) **To find pin diameter**

$d$ = Diameter of pin.

$f_{s_1}$ = Shear stress in pin = 310 kg/cm$^2$.

The pin in double shear

$$T = 2 \times \frac{\pi}{4} \times d^2 \,.\, f_{s_1} \,.\, D$$

$$45000 = 2 \times \frac{\pi}{4} \times d^2 \times 310 \times 7.25$$

$$d = 3.57 \text{ cm} = 3.6 \text{ cm (say).}$$

(*c*) **Dimensions of rectangular key**

Length $= 1.5D = 1.5 \times 7.25 = 10.87$ cm.

Width $= \frac{D}{4} = \frac{7.25}{4} = 1.81$ cm.

Thickness $= \frac{D}{6} = \frac{7.25}{6} = 1.21$ cm.

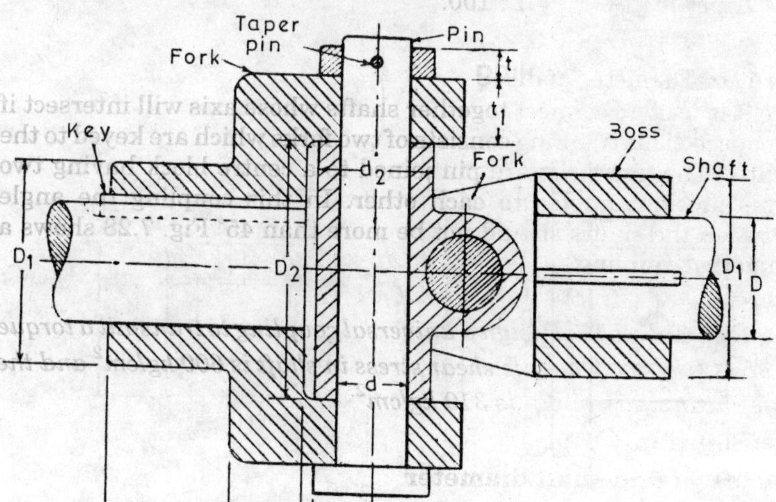


Fig. 7.28. Universal coupling.

Other dimensions are as follows

$$d_1 = 1.5d = 1.5 \times 3.6 = 5.4 \text{ cm.}$$
$$D_1 = 1.75\,D = 1.75 \times 7.25$$
$$= 10.875 \text{ cm.}$$
$$d_2 = L_1 = D = 7.25 \text{ cm.}$$
$$L_2 = 0.5D = 3.625 \text{ cm.}$$
$$t = 0.5d = 3.625 \text{ cm.}$$
$$D_2 = 2D = 14.50 \text{ cm.}$$

## 7.14 Oldham Coupling

It can be used for shafts which are not in alignment but whose axes are parallel. It falls in the category of rigid slip couplings. It consists of two flanges keyed or screwed to the two respective shafts. A slot is cut in each flange so that when attached to the shafts the slots are perpendicular to each other. A disc having perpendicular tongues on both sides is inserted between the two flanges.

Fig. 7.29 shows various parts of Oldham coupling whereas Fig. 7.30 shows assembled oldham coupling. Fig. 7.31 shows pressure distribution in an Oldham coupling

$S$ = Distance from centre line to the pressure area centroid

$$= \frac{D}{3}$$

where $D$ = Diameter of disc

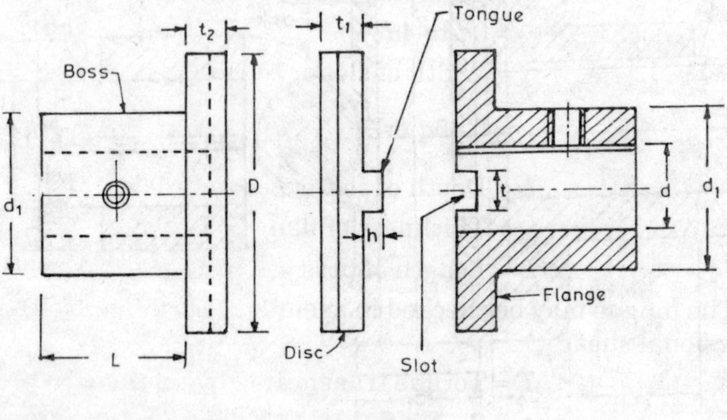


Fig. 7.29

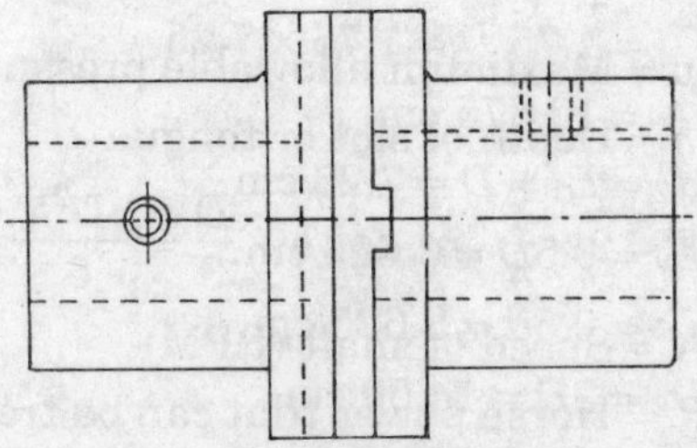

Fig. 7.30

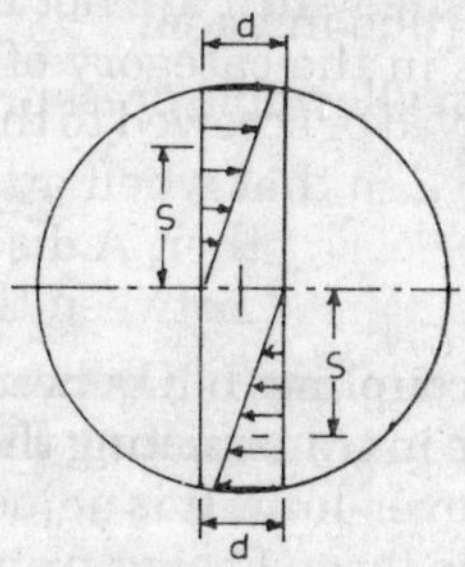


Fig. 7.31

The various dimensions of the Oldham coupling are as follows:

$d$ = Shaft diameter

$d_1$ = Diameter of boss = $2d$

$D$ = Diameter of disc or flange

$= 3d$ to $4d$

$t$ = Width of slot or tongue

$= 0.45d$ or $\dfrac{D}{6}$

$h$ = Depth of slot or tongue = $0.5t$

$t_1$ = Thickness of flange = $0.75d$

$L$ = Length of boss = $1.75d$

The tongue may be checked in shear and crushing and the boss in torsional shear

$T$ = Torque transmitted by coupling

$= 2 \,.\, F \times S$

where $F$ = Total force on each side

$$= \frac{1}{4} . p . D . h$$

where $p$ = Maximum allowable pressure

$h$ = Depth of slot or tongue

$$T = 2 \times \frac{1}{4} . p . D . h \times \frac{D}{3} = \frac{pD^2h}{6}$$

Let $N$ = Speed of shaft (RPM)

H.P. = Horse power that can be transmitted

$$= \frac{2\pi NT}{4500}$$

where $T$ = Torque in kg–m.

The value of maximum allowable pressure ($p$) should not exceed 7 to 8.5 N/mm$^2$.

## 7.15 Slip Coupling

Fig. 7.32 shows a slip coupling. It has two flanges having friction material lining which help in transmitting the torque. This coupling is a safety device against over-load. It is adjusted in such a way that it starts slipping when the torque being transmitted exceeds by 10 to 20 of the maximum rated torque.

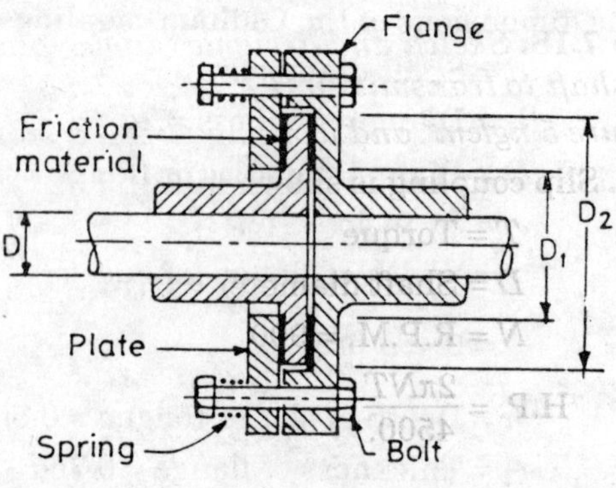


Fig. 7.32

$P_a$ = Axial force exerted by the spring

$$= \frac{\pi}{4} (D_2^2 - D_1^2) \times p$$

$P_t$ = Tangential force for two pairs of friction surfaces = $2 \mu . P_a$

where $p$ = Bearing pressure

$\mu$ = Coefficient of friction

$T_f$ = Frictional torque transmitted by the coupling $P_t \times R_m$

where $R_m$ = Mean radius

$$= \frac{1}{2}\left(\frac{D_1 + D_2}{2}\right) = \frac{D_1 + D_2}{4}$$

$$\therefore \quad T_f = P_t \times R_m = 2 \,.\, \mu \,.\, P_a \,.\, R_m$$

$$= 2 \,.\, \mu \,.\, \frac{\pi}{4}(D_2^2 - D_1^2)p \times \frac{D_1 + D_2}{4}$$

$$= \frac{\pi}{8}\mu\,(D_2^2 - D_1^2)(D_1 + D_2)\,p$$

The following values may be assumed

$$\frac{D_2}{D_1} = 1.5 \text{ to } 1.75$$

$p$ = Permissible bearing pressure

= 4 to 5 kg/cm$^2$

$\mu$ = 0.15 for cast iron on cast iron

$n$ = Number of springs = $0.04D + 4$

where $D$ = Shaft diameter.

**Example 7.18.** *Sketch and design a slip coupling to connect 6 cm diameter shaft to transmit 30 H.P. at 900 RPM. Given $\mu = 0.16$, bearing pressure 5 kg/cm$^2$ and working stress in bolts 400 kg/cm$^2$.*

**Solution.** Slip coupling is shown in Fig. 7.32.

$T$ = Torque

$D$ = Shaft diameter = 6 cm.

$N$ = R.P.M. = 900

$$\text{H.P.} = \frac{2\pi NT}{4500.}$$

(*i*) **To find torque**

$$30 = \frac{2\pi \times 900 \times T}{4500}$$

$T$ = 23.8 kg–m = 2380 kg–cm.

**(ii) To find $D_1$ and $D_2$**

$$\frac{D_2}{D_1} = 1.5$$

$$D_2 = 1.5\,D_1$$

$$\mu = 0.16$$

$$p = \text{Safe bearing pressure} = 5 \text{ kg/cm.}^2$$

We know that $T = \frac{\pi}{8} \cdot (D_2^2 - D_1^2)(D_1 + D_2)p$

$$2380 = \frac{\pi}{8} \times 0.15[(1.5D_1)^2 - D_1^2](D_1 + 1.5D_2) \times 5$$

$$D_1 = 14.2 \text{ cm.}$$

$$D_2 = 1.5D_1 = 1.5 \times 14.2 = 21.3 \text{ cm.}$$

$$D_m = \text{Mean diameter} = \frac{D_1 + D_2}{2}$$

$$= \frac{14.2 + 21.3}{2} = 17.8 \text{ cm.}$$

**(iii) To find diameter of bolt**

$$n = \text{Number of bolts} = 6$$

Axial force $P_a = \frac{\pi}{4}(D_2^2 - D_1^2)\,p = \frac{\pi}{4}(21.3^2 - 14.2^2) \times 5 = 989$ kg

Let $d_c$ = Core diameter of bolt

$$n \times \frac{\pi}{4} d_c^2 \times f_t = P_a$$

$$6 \times \frac{\pi}{4} d_c^2 \times 400 = 989$$

$$d_c = 0.73 \text{ cm}$$

$$d = \text{Outside diameter of bolt}$$

$$= \frac{d_c}{0.84} = \frac{0.73}{0.84} = 0.87 \text{ cm.}$$

$$D = \text{Shaft diameter} = 6 \text{ cm.}$$

Diameter of boss $= 2D = 2 \times 6 = 12$ cm

$$D_0 = \text{Outside diameter of coupling}$$

$$= D_2 + 2 \times d + 2 \times c$$

where $c$ = Clearance = 1 cm (say)

$$D_0 = 21.3 + 2 \times 0.87 \times 2 + 2 \times 1 = 26.8 \text{ cm.}$$

## PROBLEMS

**7.1.** State the function of key. Sketch any four types of keys.

**7.2.** Sketch and discuss the design of a muff coupling.

**7.3.** Sketch and discuss the design of a solid coupling.

**7.4.** Design and draw a protected type of C.I. flange coupling for a steel shaft transmitting 20 h.p. at 200 r.p.m. and having an allowable shear stress of 400 kgf/cm$^2$. The working stress in bolts should not exceed 3000 kgf/cm$^2$. Assume that the same material is used for shaft and key and that the crushing stress is twice the value of its shear stress and the maximum torque is 25% greater than the full load torque. Take shear stress for C.I. as 40 kgf/cm$^2$.

**7.5.** Design a shaft to transmit power from an electric motor to a lathe headstock through a pulley by means of a horizontal belt drive. The pulley weighs 20 kg and is located at 100 mm from the centre of the nearest bearing. Diameter of the pulley is 200 mm. Maximum power transmitted is 1.5 h.p. at 120 r.p.m. Angle of lap of belt is 180$^o$ and the coefficient of friction between pulley is 0.3. Shock factors in bending and torsion are 1.5 and 2 respectively. Allowable shear stress in the shaft is 3.5 kg/sq mm. The pulley is mounted overhung on the shaft. *(A.M.I.E., 1980)*

**7.6.** Design and draw a clamp coupling for a shaft of diameter 7.0 cm. The torque to be transmitted is 24000 kg cm. The number of bolt used is 6 and the allowable stress in the material of the bolt is limited to 700 kg/cm$^2$. The coefficient of friction between the shaft and muff material is 0.3. The allowable stress in shaft and key is 580 kg/cm$^2$.

**7.7.** Determine suitable diameter as a mild steel shaft to transmit 50 H.P. at 300 R.P.M. if the anlge of twist is not to exceed 0.1$^o$ per meter length of shaft. Modulus of rigidity for shaft material is $0.84 \times 10^6$ kg/cm$^2$ and shear stress is 400 kg/cm$^2$.

**7.8.** A shaft 120 cm long is supported at the ends in bearings. Two pulleys each of weight 5 kg and each of diameter 100 cm is mounted on the shaft is 15 cm from each end of shaft. The pulleys are belt driven from below and angle of lap for each pulley is 160$^o$. If the shaft transmits 12 H.P. at R.P.M. Calculate suitable diameter of shaft. Take $\mu = 0.3$ and $f_s =$ 400 kg/cm$^2$.

**Hint.** $$\frac{T_1}{T_2} = e^{\mu\theta}$$

$$(T_1 - T_2) R = T$$

The vlaue of $T_1$ and $T_2$ can be found from these two equations,

where $T_1$ = Tension on tight side of belt

$T_2$ = Tension on slake side

$T$ = Torque

$\mu$ = Coefficient of friction between belt and pulley.

$\theta$ = Angle of lap

$R$ = Radius of pulley

**7.9.** A solid steel shaft is subject to a bending moment of 2000 kg cm and a twisting moment of 12500 kg cm. If the safe tensile stress is 800 kg/cm$^2$. Calculate the diameter of shaft.

**7.10.** What are flexible couplings and what are their applications ? Illustrate your answer with suitable examples and sketches.

Design a bushed-pin type flexible coupling for connecting a motor shaft to a pump-shaft for the following service conditions :

h.p. to be transmitted - 50
r.p.m. of motor shaft - 1000
Diameter of the motor shaft - 50 mm
Diameter of the pump shaft - 45 mm

Draw a neat dimensionsed sketch of the coupling.

Bearing pressure in the rubber bush and the allowable stress in the pins are to be limited to 4.5 and 250 kg/cm$^2$ respectively.

**7.11.** Write short notes on the following :

(*i*) Oldham coupling ; and

(*ii*) Slip coupling.

# 8

# Bolts, Nuts and Screws

## 8.1 Introduction

Screw threads are helical in form and helical ridges are formed by cutting or rolling a groove into the surface of a cylindrical bar thus producing what is known as screw. The form of a screw mainly depends upon the purpose for which it is to be used and the system to which it belongs.

The threads cut on the surface of a screw are called external threads whereas those cut in a hole are called internal threads. Screws, nuts and bolts are used to connect parts together in such a manner that they can be disconnected easily. Screws are also used for transmission of power such as lead screw on machine tools and screws in presses. Threaded joints are highly reliable in operation and can be obtained in a wide range suitable for different conditions. They are relatively cheap to produce due to standardisation and efficient methods of manufacturing. Ordinarily screwed fastenings remain tight under static loads, however, many of these fasteners become loose under the action of cyclic loads or machine vibrations.

## 8.2 Parts of a Screw Thread

A screw thread (Fig. 8.1) has the following parts :

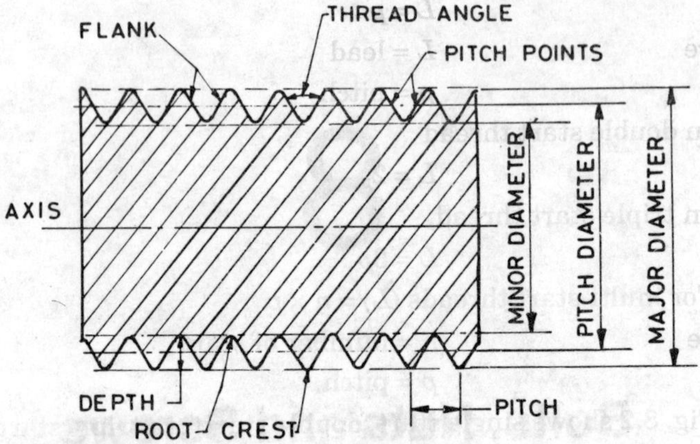


Fig. 8.1

(*i*) **Pitch.** It is the distance between the corresponding points on the consecutive thread measured parallel to the axis of screw.

(*ii*) **Lead**. It is distance that a nut will advance along the axis of thread in one turn or revolution. In single start thread (Fig. 8.2) lead in equal to pitch.

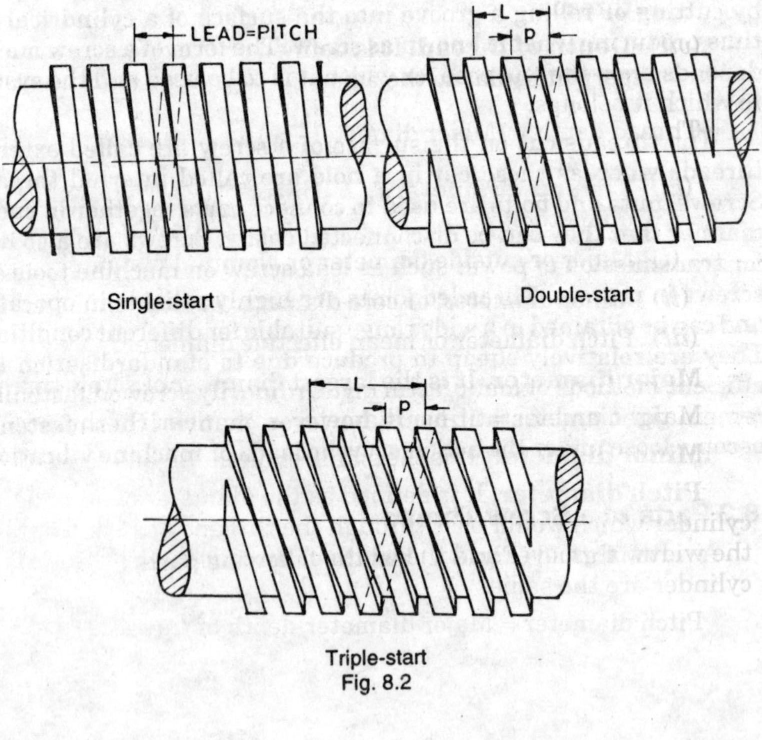


Fig. 8.2

$$L = p$$

where $L$ = lead

$p$ = pitch

In double start thread

$$L = 2_p$$

and in triple start thread,

$$L = 3p$$

For multi-start threads $(L) = n \times p$

where $n$ = number of start

$p$ = pitch.

Fig. 8.2 shows single start, double start and triple start thread.

(*iii*) **Angle of thread.** The angle included between the sides of the thread is known as angle of thread.

(*iv*) **Crest.** Creast is the top surface joining the two sides of a thread.

(*v*) **Root.** It is the bottom surface joining the sides of two adjacent threads.

(*vi*) **Flank.** It is the surface between the crest and the root of thread.

(*vii*) **Depth of thread.** It is defined as the distance measured perpendicular to the axis.

$$\text{Thread depth} = (\text{Major diameter} - \text{MinorDiameter}) \times \frac{1}{2}$$

(*ix*) **Thread diameters.** A thread has following three diameters:

(*i*) Major or outside diameter or Nominal diameter.

(*ii*) Minor diameter, or core diameter or Root diameter.

(*iii*) Pitch diameter or mean effective diameter.

**Major diameter.** It is the largest diameter of screw thread.

Major diameter = Minor diameter + 2 × depth of thread.

**Minor diameter.** It is the smallest diameter of a screw thread.

**Pitch diameter.** It is defined as the diameter of an imaginary cylinder which would pass through the threads at such points that the width of grooves and the width of threads cut by the surface of cylinder are the same.

Pitch diameter = Major diameter-depth of thread.

## 8.3 Left Hand and Right Hand Threads

A left hand thread advances into a thread hole when turned anti-clockwise.

In this thread, $h$ = height of thread

$= 0.64\,p$

where $p$ = pitch of thread.

Slope of thread $= \frac{p}{2}$

Fig. 8.3 shows conventional representation of left hand thread.

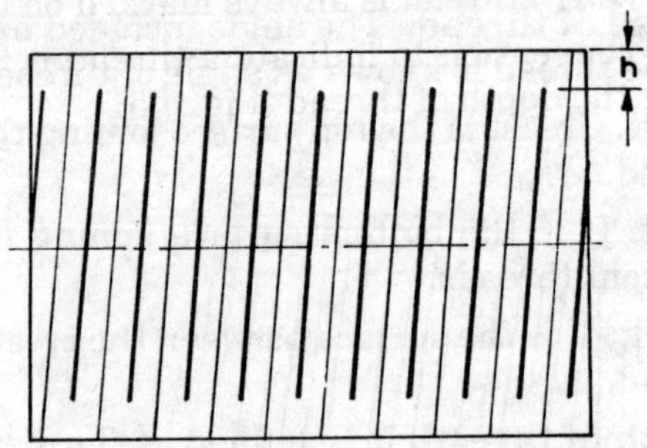


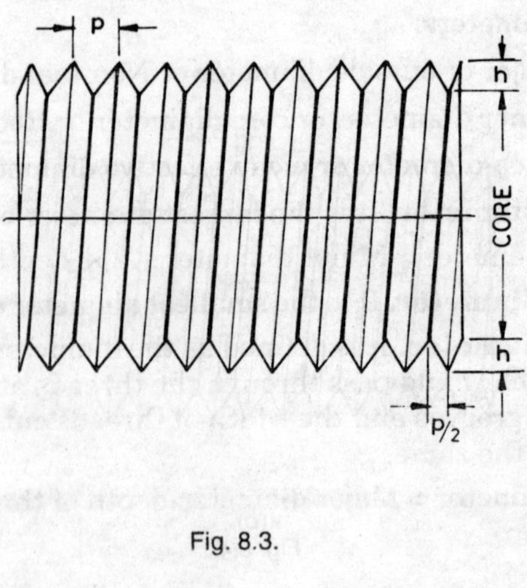


Fig. 8.3.

## 8.4 Right Hand Threads

A thread is said to be right hand thread if it advances into a threaded hole when turned clockwise. In right hand thread

$$h = 0.64\,p$$

where $p$ = pitch of thread.

Fig. 8.4 shows conventional representation of right hand thread.

If not specified a thread is always considered to be right hand thread.

A thread is always considered to be right hand thread if it not otherwise specified.

A left hand (L.H.) thread is always marked on drawing.

The simple convention to indicate a thread is by drawing two lines indicating the depth of thread (Fig. 8.5).

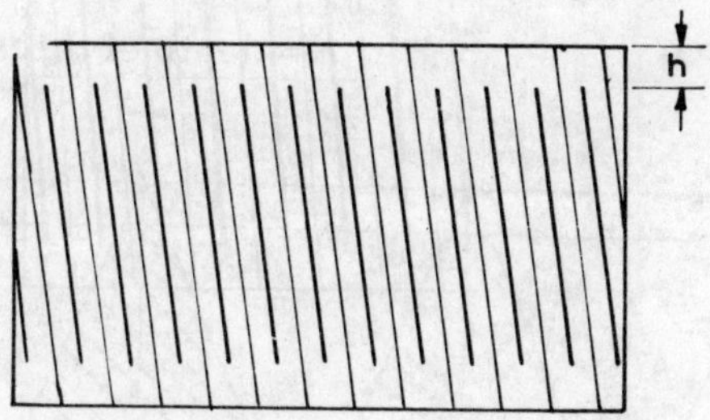


(a)

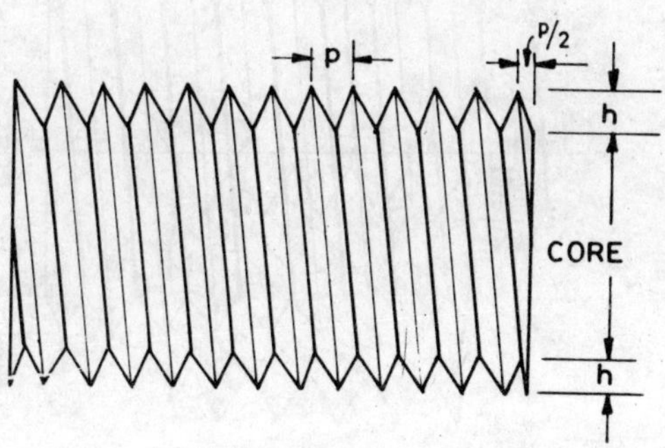


(b)

Fig. 8.4.

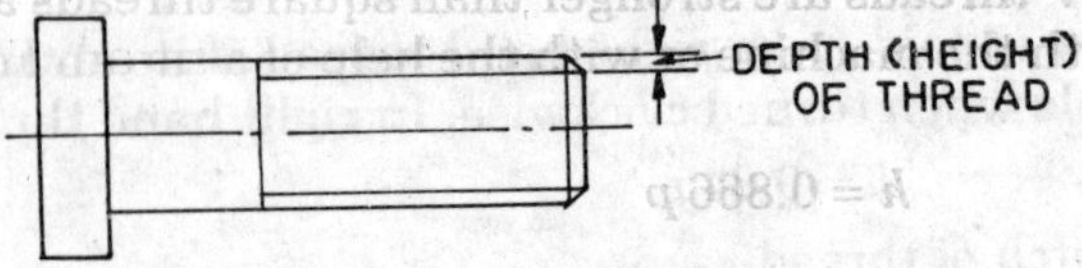


Fig. 8.5.

## 8.5 Types of Threads

The various types of threads in common use are as follows :

(*i*) **British association (B.A.) thread.** They are rounded *V* threads. They have fine pitches. They are used on screws for precision work such as instruments. In this thread (Fig. 8.6)

$$h = 0.6\,p$$

$$H = 1.136\,p$$

$$H_1 = 0.236\,H$$

where $p$ = pitch $h$ = depth of threads

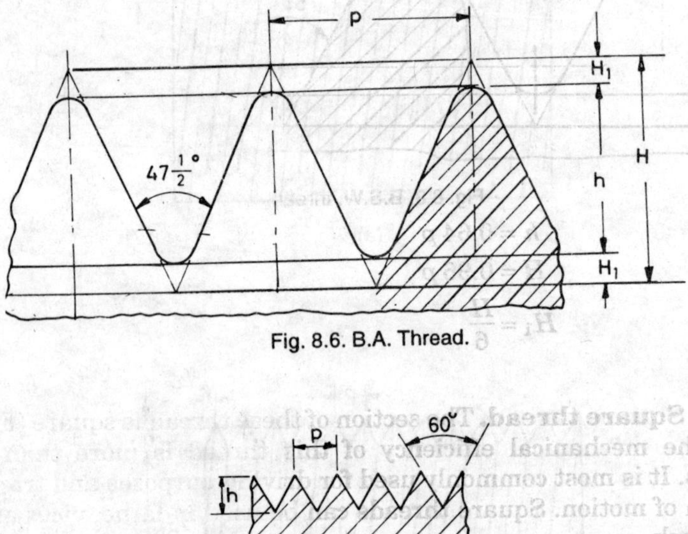


Fig. 8.6. B.A. Thread.

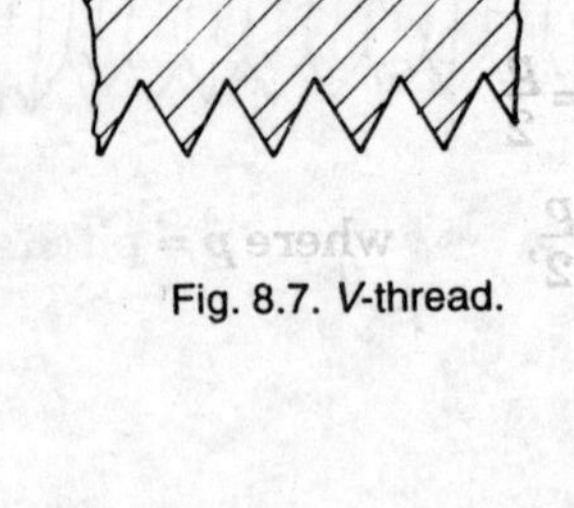


Fig. 8.7. *V*-thread.

*(ii)* **V-threads.** Fig. 8.7 shows a single *V* thread. The thread angle is 60°. *V* threads are stronger than square threads and can be easily cut with the machine or with the help of a tap and die. In the thread,

$$h = 0.866\,p$$

*(iii)* **British standard Whitworth (B.S.W.) thread.** They are rounded *V* threads and have an angle of 55°. Its rounded top or crest is not so easily abraled as in *V* thread and the rounded groove bottom reduces the stress concentration that occurs at sharp corners. They are used on bolts, screwed fastenings and British standard pipe threads. In this thread (Fig. 8.8)

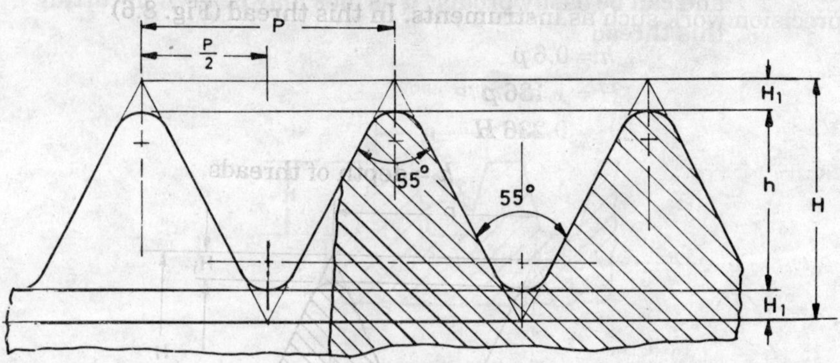


Fig. 8.8. B.S.W. thread.

$$h = 0.64\,p$$

$$H = 0.96\,p$$

$$H_1 = \frac{H}{6}$$

*(iv)* **Square thread.** The section of these thread is square (Fig. 8.9). The mechanical efficiency of this thread is more than *V* threads. It is most commonly used for driving purposes and transmission of motion. Square threads can be used in lathe, vices and screw jack.

In this thread.

Depth of thread, $h = \frac{p}{2}$

Width of thread $= \frac{p}{2}$, where $p$ = pitch.

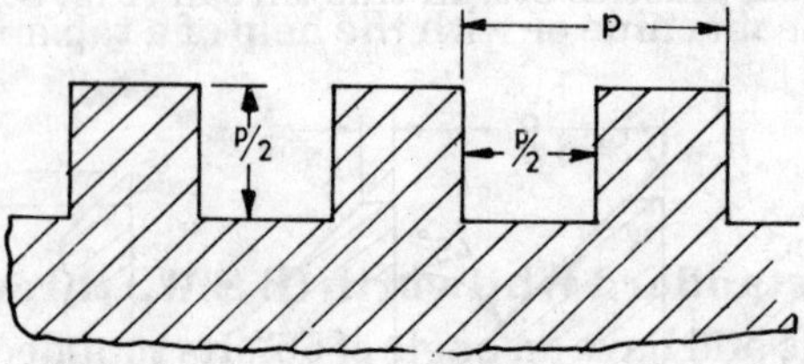


Fig. 8.9. Square thread.

(*v*) **Acme thread.** This thread is stronger than square thread and can be easily produced as dies may be used in cutting this thread.

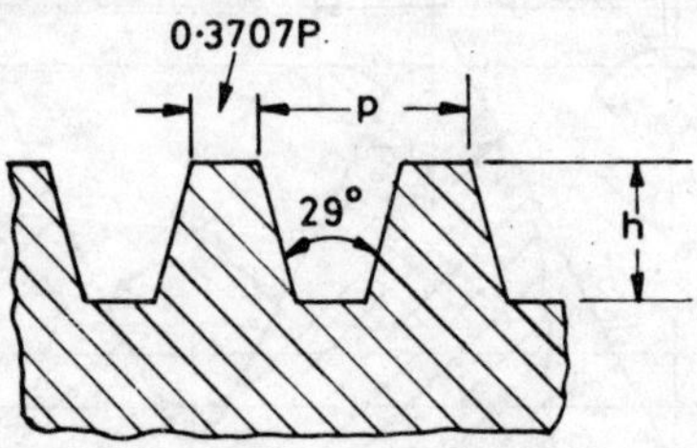


Fig. 8.10. Acme thread.

In this thread $h = \frac{p}{2} + 0.25$ mm

Thread angle $= 29°$.

This thread is used on lead screws of lathes as it is easier to engage a splitnut with this thread (Fig. 8.10).

(*vi*) **Buttress thread.** These threads (Fig. 8.18) are used to resist axial loads in one direction only. The spindles of bench vices have buttress threads. Buttress thread has the efficiency of square thread.

In this thread, $h$ = height (depth) of thread),

$$= \frac{3}{4} p.$$

(*vii*) **Knuckle thread.** It can easily resist greater strain and rough use. It can be easily cast or rolled but cannot be easily made on machine. It is used in railway carriage coupling screws and in electric bulbs and sockets, and on objects made up of glass, plastics etc. In this thread (Fig. 8.12)

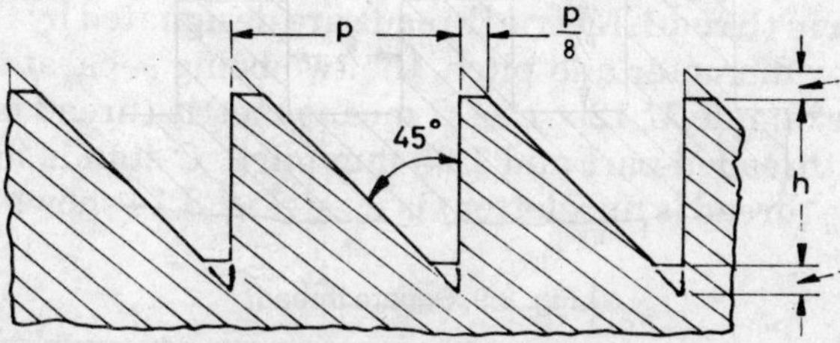


Fig. 8.11. Buttress thread.

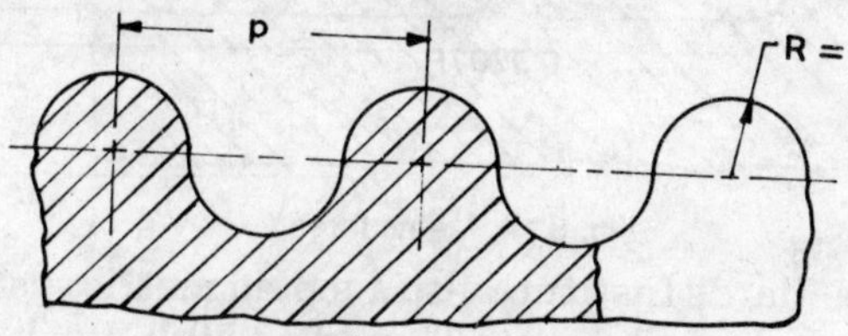


Fig. 8.12. Knuckle thread.

Radius at top and bottom $= \dfrac{p}{2}$

Depth $\qquad h = \dfrac{p}{2}$

(*viii*) **American (National) standard thread.** This thread (Fig. 8.13) is similar to V-thread in which 60° angle has been retained but the tap and root have been flattened. This thread is used for nuts, bolts, screws and stapped holes. In this thread

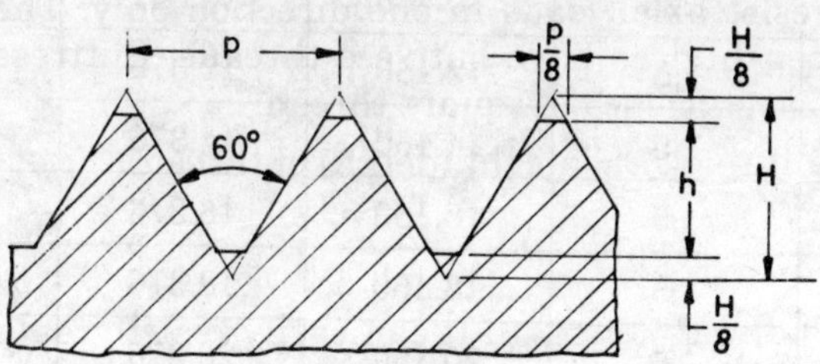


Fig. 8.13. American (National) Standard Thread.

$$H = 0.896\,p$$

$$h = \frac{3}{4}H$$

(*ix*) **Metric thread.** Metric threads are designated by the letter *M* followed by diameter and pitch, the two being separated by the sign *X*. For example *M* 12 × 1.24 *C* means metric thread of 12 mm diameter of threaded part and 1.25 mm pitch. *C* stands for coarse thread. If the thread is fine, letter *f* is used. Fig. 8.14 shows a metric thread.

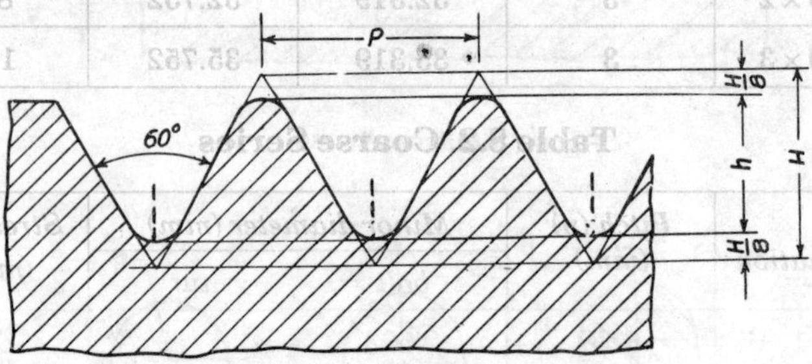


Fig. 8.14. Metric thread.

Indian Standards Institute also adopted metric system of screw threads as the Indian Standard Thread on 29th April, 1958.

As recommended by IS : 4218 (Part VI) 1967 the screw threads for screws, bolts and nuts for fine series and coarse series as shown in Tables 8.1 and 8.2.

**Table 8.1. Fine Series**

| *Designation* | *Pitch p (mm)* | *Minor diameter* | | *Stress area ($mm^2$)* |
|---|---|---|---|---|
| | | *bolt (mm)* | *Nut (mm)* | |
| M 8 × 1 | 1 | 6.773 | 6.918 | 39.2 |
| M 10 × 1.25 | 1.25 | 8.466 | 8.647 | 61.6 |
| M 12 × 1.25 | 1.25 | 10.466 | 10.647 | 92.1 |
| M 14 × 1.5 | 1.5 | 12.160 | 12.376 | 125 |
| M 16 × 1.5 | 1.5 | 14.160 | 14.376 | 167 |
| M 18 × 1.5 | 1.5 | 16.160 | 16.376 | 216 |
| M 20 × 1.5 | 1.5 | 18.160 | 18.376 | 272 |
| M 22 × 1.5 | 1.5 | 20.160 | 20.376 | 333 |
| M 24 × 2 | 2 | 21.546 | 21.835 | 384 |

*Contd...*

| Designation | Pitch p (mm) | Minor diameter | | Stress area ($mm^2$) |
|---|---|---|---|---|
| | | bolt (mm) | Nut (mm) | |
| M 27 × 2 | 2 | 24.546 | 24.835 | 496 |
| M 30 × 2 | 2 | 27.546 | 27.835 | 621 |
| M 33 × 2 | 2 | 30.546 | 30.835 | 761 |
| M 36 × 2 | 3 | 32.319 | 32.752 | 865 |
| M 39 × 3 | 3 | 35.319 | 35.752 | 1028 |

**Table 8.2. Coarse Series**

| Designation | Pitch (p) (mm) | Minor diameter (mm) | | Stress area ($mm^2$) |
|---|---|---|---|---|
| | | bolt | nut | |
| M 1 | 0.25 | 0.693 | 0.729 | 0.460 |
| M 1.1 | 0.25 | 0.793 | 0.829 | 0.58 |
| M 1.2 | 0.25 | 0.893 | 0.929 | 0.732 |
| M 1.4 | 0.30 | 1.032 | 1.075 | 0.83 |
| M 1.6 | 0.35 | 1.171 | 1.221 | 1.27 |
| M 1.8 | 0.35 | 1.371 | 1.421 | 1.70 |
| M 2 | 0.40 | 1.509 | 1.567 | 2.07 |
| M 2.2 | 0.45 | 1.648 | .713 | 2.48 |
| M 2.5 | 0.45 | 1.948 | 2.013 | 3.39 |
| M 3 | 0.5 | 2.387 | 2.459 | 5.03 |
| M 3.5 | 0.6 | 2.764 | 2.850 | 6.78 |
| M 4 | 0.7 | 3.141 | 3.242 | 8.78 |
| M 4.5 | 0.75 | 3.580 | 3.688 | 11.3 |
| M 5 | 0.8 | 4.019 | 4.134 | 14.2 |
| M 6 | 1 | 4.773 | 4.918 | 20.1 |
| M 7 | 1 | 5.773 | 5.918 | 28.9 |
| M 8 | 1.25 | 6.466 | 6.647 | 36.6 |
| M 10 | 1.5 | 8.160 | 8.376 | 58.0 |

*Contd...*

| *Designation* | *Pitch (p) (mm)* | *Minor diameter (mm)* | | *Stress area* $(mm^2)$ |
|---|---|---|---|---|
| | | *bolt* | *nut* | |
| M 12 | 1.75 | 9.853 | 10.106 | 84.3 |
| M 14 | 2 | 11.546 | 11.835 | 115 |
| M 16 | 2 | 13.546 | 13.835 | 157 |
| M 18 | 2.5 | 14.933 | 15.294 | 192 |
| M 20 | 2.5 | 16.933 | 17.294 | 245 |
| M 22 | 2.5 | 18.933 | 19.294 | 303 |
| M 24 | 3 | 20.320 | 20.752 | 353 |
| M 27 | 3 | 23.320 | 23.752 | 459 |
| M 30 | 3.5 | 27.706 | 27.211 | 561 |
| M 33 | 3.5 | 28.706 | 29.211 | 694 |
| M 36 | 4 | 31.093 | 31.670 | 817 |
| M 39 | 4 | 34.093 | 34.670 | 976 |

Table 8.3 indicates proportions of square threads.

**Table 8.3.**

| *FINE SERIES* | | | *COARSE SERIES* | | |
|---|---|---|---|---|---|
| *Nominal Diameter mm* | *Common difference mm* | *Pitch mm* | *Nominal Diameter mm* | *Common difference mm* | *Pitch mm* |
| 10 - 22 | 2 | 2 | 20 - 28 | 2 | 8 |
| 22 - 62 | 2 | 3 | 30 - 38 | 2 | 10 |
| 65 - 110 | 5 | 4 | 40 - 52 | 2 | 12 |
| 115 - 175 | 5 | 6 | 55 - 58 | 3 | 14 |
| 180 - 200 | 5 | 8 | 58 - 62 | 2 | 14 |
| 200 - 240 | 10 | 8 | 65 - 80 | 5 | 16 |
| 250 - 300 | 10 | 12 | 80 - 82 | 2 | 16 |
| 300 - 400 | 20 | 12 | 85 - 95 | 5 | 18 |
| 420 - 500 | 20 | 18 | 95 - 98 | 3 | 18 |
| 520-640 | 20 | 24 | 100-110 | 5 | 20 |

*Contd...*

| *FINE SERIES* | | | *COARSE SERIES* | | |
|---|---|---|---|---|---|
| *Nominal Diameter mm* | *Common difference mm* | *Pitch mm* | *Nominal Diameter mm* | *Common difference mm* | *Pitch mm* |
| | | | 115 - 130 | 5 | 22 |
| | | | 135 - 155 | 5 | 24 |
| | | | 160 - 180 | 5 | 28 |
| | | | 185 - 200 | 5 | 32 |
| | | | 210 - 240 | 10 | 36 |
| | | | 250 - 280 | 10 | 40 |
| | | | 290 - 300 | 10 | 44 |
| | | | 300 - 340 | 20 | 44 |
| | | | 360 - 400 | 20 | 48 |

There are three series of ISO metric threads :

1. Coarse series
2. Fine series
3. Extra fine series.

Coarse series is used for general purpose where jerks and vibrations are not very important, detachment is frequent and tapped holes are in a metal other than steel.

Fine threads series is used for automotive and air-craft parts where jerks and vibrations are predominant, fine adjustment is important and tappled holes are in steel.

Extra fine series is used for aeronautic equipment for threading in thin walled components and where fine adjustments are required and vibrations are excessive.

## 8.6 Screw Fastenings

These are temporary fasteners which hold the parts together through the medium of a screw thread. These are used in pairs for their action. A nut and a boltor stud comprise a screwed pair various types of screw fasteners are as follows.

(*a*) Through bolts
(*b*) Studs
(*c*) Cap screws
(*d*) Machine screws
(*e*) Set screws.

## 8.7 Through Bolt

Bolt is a bar with threads at one end and a head at the other end. Bolts are extensively used for connecting the two machine parts. The main parts of a bolt are head, shank and threaded portion.

The threading is either partly done on the shank or on the complete length of the shank depending upon the thickness of two parts to be joined. The shank may be of cylindrical shape or a part of it may be square just adjoining the head. The square portion gets fitted into cavity in the parts to be connected and thus avoids the rotation of bolt when the nut is tightened on bolt. The shape of head varies.

Fig. 8.15 shows a hexagonal head bolt. It passes through the holes in the two parts to be joined and is held in place by a nut and is called a through bolt.

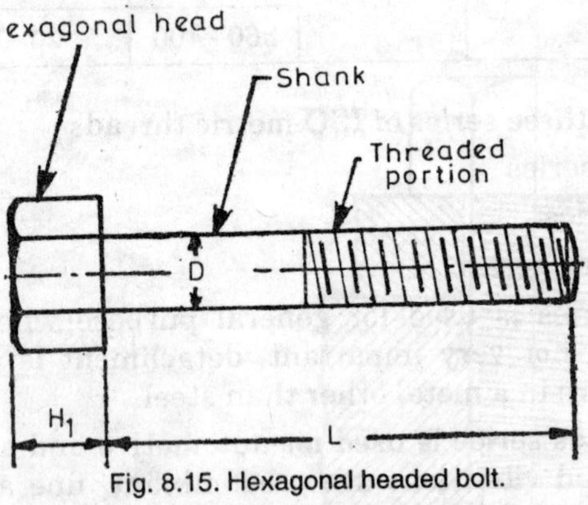


Fig. 8.15. Hexagonal headed bolt.

Fig. 8.16 shows two parts joined by through bolt.

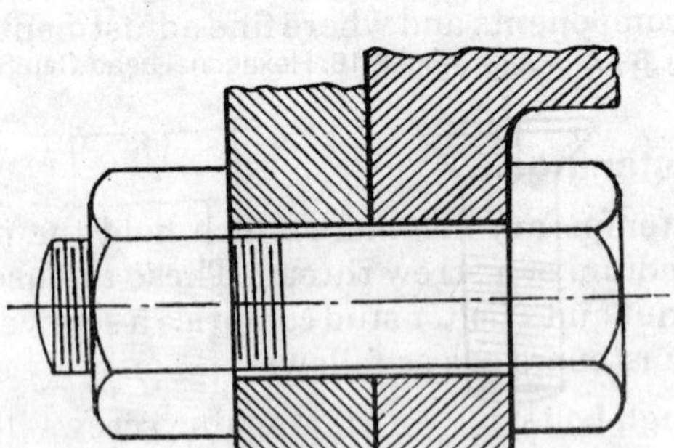

Fig. 8.16. Through bolt.

## 8.8 Studs

Stud is a round rod threaded on both ends. It is used where through bolts are undesirable. The threads are either of coarse or fine series depending on the material into which the stud is screwed. The middle portion is made square, or left plain or is provided with a collar. The threads cut on both ends are of same hand. The stud is first screwed into the machine part and then other part to be connected is placed on first part and a nut is tightened on the other end of stud.

Fig. 8.17 shows two parts joined by a stud.

## 8.9 Cap Screw

Cap screws make an excellent fastening for machine parts that do not require frequent removal. The holding is due to the pressure exerted by the head of screw (Fig. 8.18).

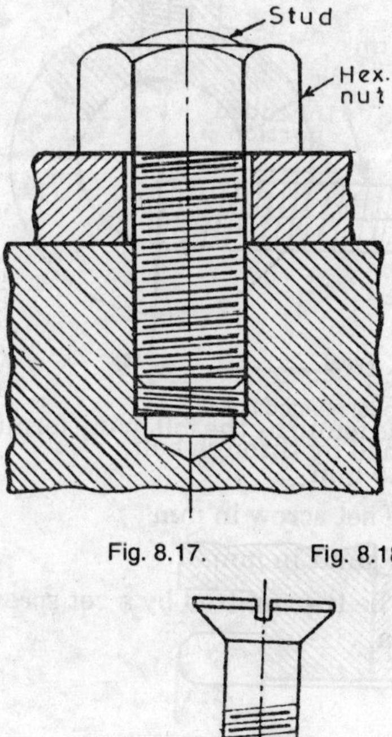


Fig. 8.17.

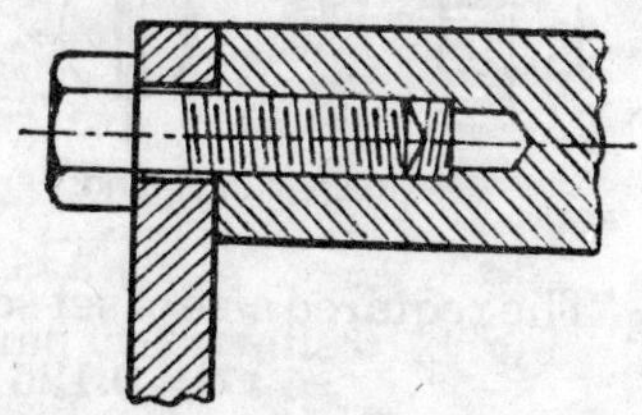

Fig. 8.18. Hexagonal head Cap Screw.

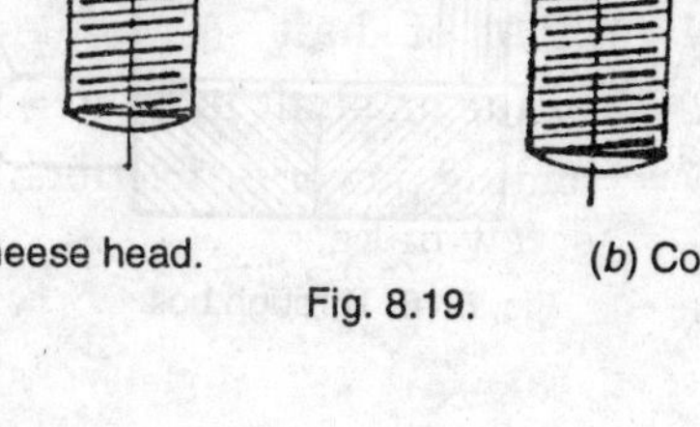

(*a*) Cheese head. (*b*) Countersunk.

Fig. 8.19.

### 8.9.1 Machine Screws.

Machine screws are used in machine tools, discs for fastening together various parts. Fig. 8.19 shows two types of machine screws.

## 8.10 Set Screws

They are used to prevent rotation or sliding of one part on another. For example gudgeon pin and piston of internal combustion engine or a collar on a shaft. A set screw is screwed into one part until the end of the screws presses firmly against the other part.

Fig. 8.20 (*a*) and (*b*) shows two types of set screws. Fig. 8.20 (*c*) shows the use of a set screw.

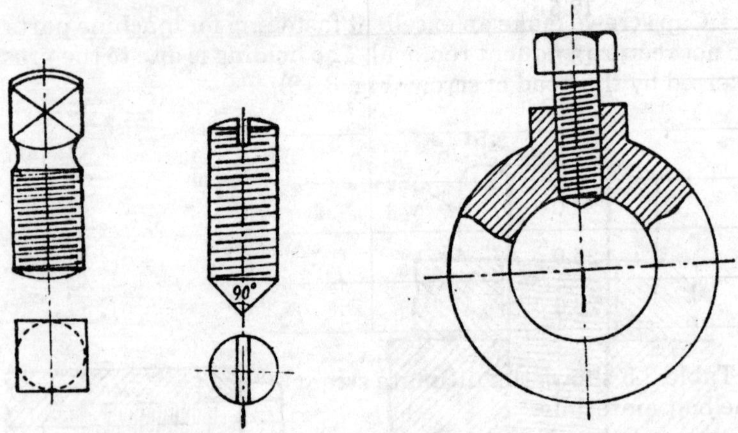


(*a*) Oval or Round (*b*) Conical. (*c*)

Fig. 8.20.

The required size of set screws is found by the following formula.

$$d = 0.125\,D + 7.5 \text{ mm.}$$

where $d$ = Diameter of set screw in mm

$D$ = Diameter of shaft in mm.

Horse power (H.P.) which can be transmitted by a set screw is calculated by the following formula.

$$\text{H.P.} = \frac{2\pi NT}{4500}$$

where $N$ = R.P.M. of shaft

$T$ = Torque on shaft in kg m = $F \times R$

where $F$ = Holding power or frictional resistance of set screw in kg.

$R$ = Radius of shaft in metre.

Table 8.4 shows holding power of set screws.

**Table 8.4.**

| *Diameter of set screw (mm)* | *Holding power (kg)* |
|---|---|
| 7.5 | 75 |
| 9.0 | 116 |
| 10.5 | 165 |
| 12.5 | 225 |
| 13.5 | 300 |
| 15.0 | 390 |
| 18.5 | 585 |
| 21.0 | 835 |
| 25.0 | 1140 |
| 28.0 | 1500 |

Table 8.5 shows the ultimate strength and endurance limit for some bolt materials.

**Table 8.5**

| *Material* | *Ultimate Strength ($kg/cm^2$)* | *Endurance Limit ($kg/cm^2$)* |
|---|---|---|
| Low Carbon Steel (Hot rolled)<br>C — 0.10 to 0.20 | 4,250 | 1,700 |
| Low Carbon Steel (Hot rolled)<br>C — 0.20 to 0.30 | 4,690 | 2,600 |
| Medium Carbon Steel (Annealed)<br>C0 — 0.30 to 0.40 | 4,900 | 2,450 |
| Ni-steel (Heat treated drawn at 1000° F)<br>Ni — 3.25 to 3.75<br>C — 0.35 to 0.45 | 8,820 | 3,500 |
| Ni — Cr. Steel (Heat treated drawn at 1000° F)<br>Ni — 1.00 to 1.5<br>C — 0.35 to 0.45 Cr - 0.45 to 0.75 | 10,500 | 5,600 |

## 8.11 Stresses in Screws Fastenings

The following stresses due to static load should be considered in screw fastenings.

(*a*) Initial stresses due to screwing up.

(*b*) Stresses due to external forces.

(*c*) Stress due to the combination of screwing up and external forces.

## 8.12 Initial Stresses due to Screwing up

The various stresses produced in a bolt, screw or stud due to screwing up tightly are as follows.

(*i*) Tensile stress due to stretching of bolt.

(*ii*) Compressive stresses on the thread.

(*iii*) Shearing stresses across threads.

(*iv*) Torsional shear stresses due to frictional resistance of the threads.

(*v*) Bending stresses if the surface under the head or nut are not perfectly to the bolt axis.

Above mentioned stresses can not be determined accurately and therefore bolts are designed on the basis of direct tensile stress, and using a high factor of safety to allow for tightening stresses.

For bolts used to make fluid tight joints the initial tension is calculated as follows.

$$P = 284\ d \text{ kg (MKS units)}$$

where $P$ = Initial tension

$d$ = Nominal diameter of bolt in mm

It is desirable that for fluid tight joint bolts less than $M$ 16 should not be used as they are likely to rupture during tightening.

Compressive stresses or bearing stresses and shearing stresses are calculated by using formulas for simple stresses when tightening load is estimated.

When a bolt is acted upon by a force perpendicular to its axis and tending to cut it across its right section, the bolt is under shear. In such a case the involved area should be the body area and not the root area.

The torsional stress is calculated as follows :

$$f_s = \frac{16\,T}{\pi\, d_c^3}$$

where $f_s$ = Torsional shear stress

$T$ = Torque applied

$d_c$ = Core diameter of thread

Fig. 8.21 (*a*) shows bending of a stud. It is observed that greater the shank length less is the bending stress in the bolt or stud. It is further observed that effect of bending stress due to misalignment at angles of misalignment $\theta \le 2$ degrees the static strength of bolts made from steels of low strength changes but little.

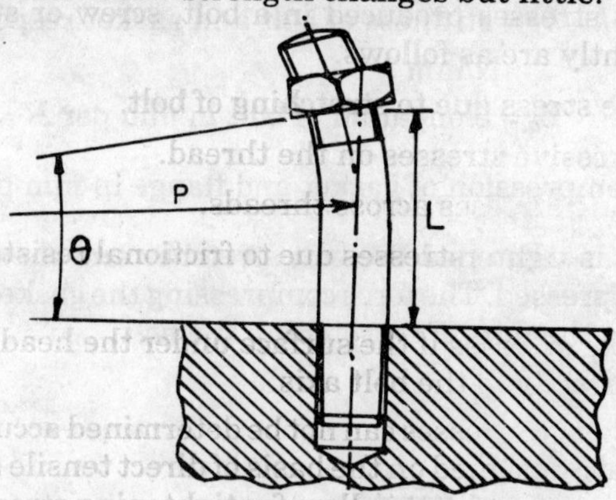


Fig. 8.21 (*a*)

Bending stresses induced in the shank of bolts is calculated as follows :

$$f = \frac{x\,.\,E}{2L}$$

where $f$ = Bending stress

$x$ = Difference in height between the extreme corners of the nut or head

$E$ = Modulus of elasticity of bolt materials.

$L$ = Length of the shank of the bolt.

### 8.12.1 Pre loading of Bolts

In case of pressure vessels and cylinder covers it is required to apply the initial tightening torque to make a joint leak proof. The initial tightening elongates the bolt and compresses the connected members.

Pre loading of bolts has the following advantages :

1. It stops the leakage in the pressure vessels.

2. It reduces the amplitude of fluctuation in load thereby improving the fatigue strength of the parts.

Fig. 8.21 (*b*) shows a bolted joint with flexible gasket.

Let $F$ = External load

$L_g$ = Length of gasket

$L_b$ = Length of bolt

$F_i$ = initial load due to tightening of the bolt

$F_g$ = compression load on the gasket

$F_b$ = combined load on the bolt

$k_b, k_g$ = stiffness of bolt and gasket respectively in N/mm

$\delta_b$ = elongation of bolt in mm per $N = 1/k_b$

$\delta_g$ = compression of gasket and flange in mm per $N = \frac{1}{k_g}$.

When bolt is tightened the bolt stretches and the flanges and gasket are compressed. The force compressing the gasket and flange will be equal to the force $F_i$, stretching the bolt.

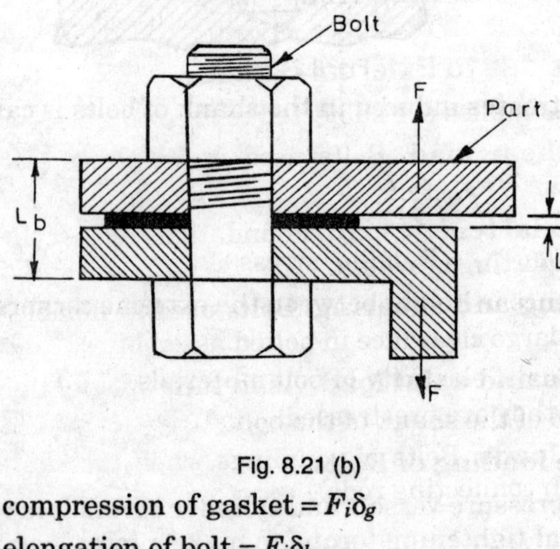


Fig. 8.21 (b)

Initial compression of gasket = $F_i\delta_g$

Initial elongation of bolt = $F_i\delta_b$.

When the load $F$ is applied, increase in length of bolt or gasket will be $(F_b - F_i)\,\delta_b$.

Final deformation of gasket

$$F_g\delta_g = F_i\delta_g - (F_b - F_i)\,\delta_b$$

Final compressive load on the gasket

$$F_g = F_i - (F_b - F_i)\,\frac{\delta_b}{\delta_g}$$

Combined load on the bolt

$$F_b = F_g + F = F_i - (F_b - F_i)\,\frac{\delta_b}{\delta_g} + F$$

$$= F_i + \left(\frac{\delta_g}{\delta_g + \delta_b}\right) F = F_i + CF.$$

where $$C = \frac{\delta_g}{\delta_g + \delta_b} = \frac{k_b}{k_b + k_g}$$

Hence $$F_g = F_i - \left(\frac{k_g}{k_g + k_b}\right) F$$

Now $$\delta_b = \frac{l_b}{A_b\, E_b} = \frac{1}{k_b}$$

where $l_b$ and $A_b$ are the length and diameter of the bolt, and $k_b$ and $k_g$ are the stiffnesses for the bolt, gasket and flange respectively. For the gasket with an area $A_g$ and a thickness $t$, and the flange having an area $A_f$ and a thickness $l_f$.

$$\delta_g = \frac{t}{A_g E_f} + \frac{l_f}{A_f E_f} = \frac{1}{k_g}$$

## 8.13 Stresses due to External Forces

Bolts in assemblies are subjected to following types of loads.

(*i*) **Pure shear load.** Bolts used in couplings, eccentrically loaded brackets.

(*ii*) **Pure axial tensile load.** Foundations bolts, cylinder cover bolts, bolts supporting brackets.

(*iii*) **Bending and shearing.** Bolts used in flexible couplings where there is large clearance in bolted assemblies.

(*iv*) **Torque and axial load.** As in turn buckle, tightening of the bolts when they are prestressed.

(*v*) **Cyclic loads.** Bolts in couplings when the shafts are not co-axial, bolts in connecting rods.

Indian standard for mechanical fasteners are as follows :

IS : 4218 - 1967 I.S.O. Metric threads.

IS : 4694 - 1968 Basic dimensions for square threads.

IS : 1362 - 1967 Black hexagonal bolts, nuts and lock nuts.

IS : 2585 - 1968 Black square bolts and nuts.

IS : 1821 - 1967 Dimensions for clearance hole for bolted joints.

IS : 2186 - 1967 Dimensions for external interference fit threads.

A bolt subjected to externally applied tensile force will cause tensile stress in the bolt.

Let $P$ = Tensile force

$$P = \frac{\pi}{4} d_c^2 \times f_t \quad ...(i)$$

where $d_c$ = Diameter at the root of the thread

$f_t$ = Allowable tensile stress in the bolt material.

The equation (*i*) can be solved to find $d_c$ and then nominal diameter to found as follows :

$d$ = Nominal diameter of bolt

$d_c = 0.84\, d$ for coarse threads

$= 0.88\, d$ for fine threads.

The equation (*i*) may also be solved to find area at the root of the threads and from tables supplied for coarse series and fine series of metric threads the suitable diameter of threads can be selected.

## 8.14 Stresses due to Combined Load

When the bolt are subjected to combined load due to initial tightening and external forces the resultant load on the bolt is calculated as follows :

$$P = P_1 + kP_2$$

where $P$ = Resultant load on the bolt

$P_1$ = Initial tightening load on the bolt

$P_2$ = External load on the bolt

$$K = \frac{K_b}{K_b + K_c}$$

where $K_b$ = Stiffness constant for the bolt

$K_c$ = Stiffness constant for the compressed member.

Table 8.6 shows the values of $K$ for different types of joints.

Table 8.6

| *Type of joint* | *K* |
|---|---|
| Metal to metal joint | 0.00 to 0.10 |
| Hard copper gasket | 0.25 to 0.50 |
| Soft copper gasket | 0.50 to 0.75 |
| Soft thick gasket | 0.75 to 1.00 |

The number of bolts used are multiples of 2 or 3 and the pitch of bolts is generally not more than 5 times the diameter of bolt to make the joints steam tight.

## 8.15 Bolts of Uniform Strength

Bolts subjected to shock or impact loads should be designed to absorb impact energy as well as to resist torque. The stresses are higher in threaded part of bolt and therefore major part of the energy is absorbed in threaded portion of the bolt. In order to make the bolt of uniform strength the shank of the bolt should be reduced in diameter. The shank diameter is reduced in the following manners.

(*i*) Turning down the shank (Fig. 8.21).

(*ii*) Drilling a hole in the shank (Fig. 8.22).

Let $d_1$ = Diameter of hole to be drilled

$d$ = Nominal diameter of bolt

$d_c$ = Core diameter of bolt

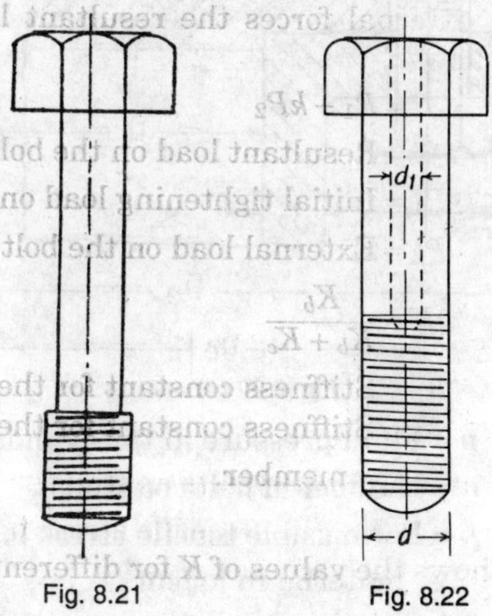


Fig. 8.21 Fig. 8.22

$$A = \text{Nominal area of bolt} = \frac{\pi}{4}\, d^2$$

$$A_c = \text{Root area of bolt} = \frac{\pi}{4}\, d_c^{\,2}$$

$$A_1 = \text{Area of hole} = \frac{\pi}{4}\, d_1^{\,2}$$

$$A - A_c = A_1$$

$$\frac{\pi}{4} d^2 - \frac{\pi}{4} d_c^{\,2} = \frac{\pi}{4} d_1^{\,2}$$

$$d_1 = \sqrt{d^2 - d_c^{\,2}}.$$

### 8.15.1 To design bolts or studs for cylinder covers.

Bolts or studs are used to tighten the cylinder covers. Fig. 8.22 (*a*) shows the cylinder covered secured by bolts whereas Fig. 8.22 (*b*) shows the use of studs to hole the cylinder cover in its position.

Following procedure should be adopted to determine the size and number of bolts or studs. The bolts or studs are screwed up tightly along with metal gasket or asbestos packing to provide a leak proof joint.

Let $D$ = Diameter of cylinder in cm

$d$ = Nominal diameter of bolt or stud

$d_c$ = Core diameter of bolt or stud

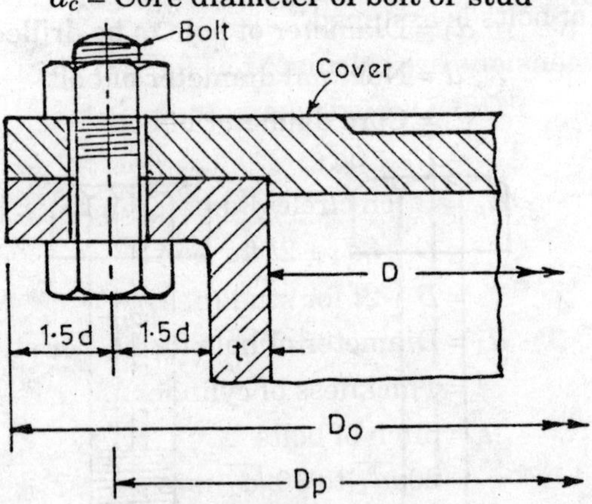


Fig. 8.22 (*a*)

$p$ = Fluid pressure in the cylinder in kg/cm$^3$

$n$ = Number of bolts or studs

$f_t$ = Permissible tensile stress for bolt or stud material in kg/cm$^2$

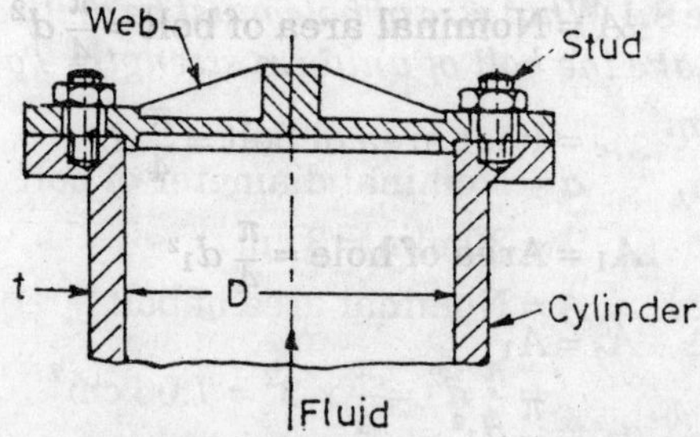


Fig. 8.22 (*b*)

$P$ = Force acting on the cylinder cover

$$= \frac{\pi}{4} D^2 \times p$$

$F$ = Resistance force offered by bolts or studs

$$= P/n$$

$$F = \frac{\pi}{4} d_c^2 \cdot f_t \cdot n$$

$$P = F = \frac{\pi}{4} d_c^2 \cdot f_t \cdot n$$

From above equation the number of bolts or studs may be obtained if the size of the bolt or stud is known and *vice versa*. Usually size of bolts is assumed.

Other dimensions are calculated as follows.

$D_o$ = Out side diameter of cover

$= D_p + 3d_1$

$D_p$ = Pitch circle diameter of bolts

$= D + 3d_1 + 2t$ for bolt

$= D + 2t$ for stud (nearly)

where $d_1$ = Diameter of hole for bolt or stud

$t$ = Thickness of cylinder

$s$ = pitch of bolts

$= 20\sqrt{d_1}$ to $30\sqrt{d_1}$ mm

where $d_1$ is in mm.

Usually a bolt of less than 1.6 cm diameter is not used because tightening produces sufficient tensile stress and bolts of smaller size (less than 1.6 cm diameter) get broken.

**Example 8.1** *What size of hole must be drilled in a standard 30 mm bolt to make the bolt of uniform strength. Take root area of the bolt as 5.61 cm².*

**Solution.** $d$ = Nominal diameter of bolt

$= 30 \text{ mm} = 3 \text{ cm}$

$A$ = Nominal area of bolt

$$= \frac{\pi}{4} d^2 = \frac{\pi}{4} \times 3^2 = 7.06 \text{ cm}^2$$

$A_c$ = Root area of bolt = 5.61 cm²

$A_1$ = Area of hole be drilled

$$= A - A_c = 7.06 - 5.61 = 1.45 \text{ cm}^2$$

$d_1$ = Diameter of hole

$$A_1 = \frac{\pi}{4} d_1^2$$

$$1.45 = \frac{\pi}{4} . d_1^2$$

$$d_1 = 1.36 \text{ cm.}$$

**Example 8.2.** *Calculate the safe load which can be carried by M 30 bolt assuming the safe tensile stress 600 kg/cm².*

**Solution.** $f_t$ = Safe tensile stress = 600 kg/cm²

$P$ = Safe load = $A_c \times f_t$

where $A_c$ = Stress area of bolt

= 5.61 cm² (From Table 8.2)

$$P = A_c \times f_t = 5.61 \times 600 = 3366 \text{ kg.}$$

**Example 8.3.** *A standard M 36 bolt is subjected to a tensile load that sets up with in an induced tensile stress of 600 kg/cm².*

(*a*) *What tensile load is carried by the bolt ?*

(*b*) *To what shearing load is the bolt head subjected ?*

(*c*) *If a standard semifinished hexagonal bolt head is used what is the unit shearing stress induced therein ?*

**Solution.** From table

(*a*) $d_c$ = Root diameter of bolt

$= 31.093 \text{ mm} = 3.1093 \text{ cm}$

$$A_c = \text{Root area} = \frac{\pi}{4}(3.1093)^2 = 7.59 \text{ cm}^2$$

$$f_t = \text{Tensile stress} = 600 \text{ kg/cm}^2$$

$$P = \text{Tensile load} = A_c \times f_t$$

$$= 600 \times 7.59 = 4554 \text{ kg.}$$

(*b*) $F_s$ = Shear load on bolt head

$$= P = 4554 \text{ kg}$$

(*c*) $d$ = Nominal diameter of bolt = 36 mm = 3.6 cm

Let $H$ = Height of bolt head

= Nominal diameter of bolt

= 36 mm = 3.6 cm.

$$A = \text{Area in shear} = \pi d H$$

$$= \pi \times 3.6 \times 3.6 = 40 \text{ cm}^2$$

$f_s$ = Shear stress

$$F_s = A \times f_s$$

$$f_s = \frac{F_s}{A} = \frac{4554}{40.7} = 111.9 \text{ kg/cm}^2.$$

**Example 8.4.** *In a steam engine the diameter of cylinder is 24 cm and steam pressure acting on the cylinder head is kg/cm². The cylinder head is held in position by 12 bolts of size M16 × 2C and a soft copper gasket is used to make the joint leak proof. Calculate the stress produced in the bolts. Sketch the joint and dimension it.*

**Solution.** $D$ = Cylinder diameter = 4 cm

$d$ = Diameter of bolt = 16 mm

$P_1$ = Initial tension due to tightening of bolt

$$= 284\, d = 284 \times 16 = 4544 \text{ kg}$$

$p$ = Steam pressure

$P_2$ = External load on each bolt

$$= \frac{\frac{\pi}{4} D^2 p}{n}$$

where $n$ = Number of bolts = 12

$$= \frac{\frac{\pi}{4} \times 24^2 \times 8}{12} = 302 \text{ kg}$$

$P$ = Resultant load on each bolt

$= P_1 + kP_2$

where $k$ = Constant = 0.5 (say)

$P = 4544 + 0.5 \times 302 = 4695$ kg

$A$ = Stress area of bolt

$= 157\ \text{mm}^2$ (From table 8.2)

$f$ = Stress in bolt

$$= \frac{P}{A} = \frac{4695}{1.57} = 2990\ \text{kg/cm}^2.$$

Fig. 8.22 (*a*) shows a typical joint used to hold the cylinder head in position.

Let $d_1$ = hole diameter for bolt

$= d + 1$ mm = 16 + 1

= 17 mm = 1.7 cm

$D_p$ = pitch circle diameter

$= D + 3d_1 + 2t$

Assume, $t = 1.0$ cm

$D_p = 24 + 3 \times 1.7 + 2 \times 1$

= 31.7 cm

$p_1$ = pitch of bolts

$$= \frac{\pi D_p}{n}$$

$$= \frac{\pi \times 31.7}{12} = 8.3\ \text{cm} = 83\ \text{mm}$$

$p_1$ is also given by

$p_1 = 20\sqrt{d_1}$ to $30\sqrt{d_1}$ mm

$= 20\sqrt{17}$ to $30\sqrt{17}$

= 82.4 to 123.7 mm.

Since the pitch found lies between these two limits hence satisfactory

$D_o$ = out side diameter of cover

$= D_p + 3d_1 = 31.7 + 3 \times 1.7$

= 36.8 cm

**8.15.1 Eye bolt.**

It is used to lift heavy parts. Eye bolts are usually forged from mild ductile steel. It consists of a ring of circular section material having a screwed shank forged integral with it. The average proportions of an eye bolt are shown in Fig. 8.23.

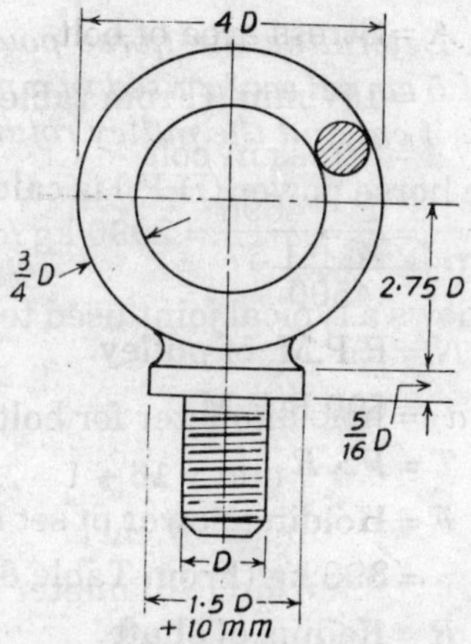


Fig. 8.23. Eye Bolt.

**Example 8.5.** *A machine part weighing 3000 kg is to be lifted by a mild steel eye bolt. Design the eye bolt if the safe tensile stress in bolt material is 800 kg/cm$^2$.*

**Solution.**

Fig. 8.23 shows an eye bolt

$D$ = Nominal diameter of bolt

$f_t$ = Tensile stress = 800 kg/cm$^2$

$P$ = Tensile load = 3000 kg

$d_c$ = Core diameter of bolt

$$P = A \times f_t$$

where $A$ = Core area required at the bottom of thread

$$3000 = A \times 800$$

$$A = 3.75 \text{ cm}^2$$

$$= \frac{\pi}{4} d_c^2$$

$$d_c = 2.18 \text{ cm} = 21.8 \text{ mm}$$

Using coarse threads,

We adopt M27 bolt which has core diameter of 23.320 mm.

(From Table 8.2)

$\therefore \qquad D = 27$ mm.

The other dimensions in terms of $D$ are indicated in Fig. 8.23.

**Example 8.5.** *Determine the horse power that can be transmitted safely by a 1.5 cm set screw used in a pulley installation. The diameter of shaft is 4 cm and the pulley rotates at 600 R.P.M.*

**Solution.** The horse power (H.P.) is calculated as follows :

$$\text{H.P.} = \frac{2\pi NT}{4500}$$

$$N = \text{R.P.M. of pulley}$$
$$= 600 \text{ R.P.M.}$$

Torque, $\qquad T = F \times R$

where $\qquad F$ = Holding power of set screw

= 390 kg (From Table 8.2)

$R$ = Radius of shaft

= 2 cm

$$= \frac{2}{100} \text{ m.}$$

$$T = 390 \times \frac{2}{100} \text{ kg m.}$$

$$\text{H.P.} = 2\pi \times 600 \times 390 \times \frac{2}{100} \times \frac{1}{4500}$$
$$= 6.53$$

**Example 8.6.** *In a steam engine the maximum steam pressure is 12 kg/cm$^2$ absolute and the back pressure is 0.15 kg/cm$^2$ absolute. Determine the diameter of screwed end of the piston rod if the cylinder diameter is 32 cm and the allowable tensile stress in the piston rod material is 500 kg/cm$^2$.*

**Solution.**

$p_1$ = Maximum steam pressure

= 12 kg/cm$^2$

$p_2$ = Back pressure of steam

= 0.15 kg/cm$^2$

$d$ = Diameter of cylinder

= 32 cms

$$f_t = \text{Safe tensile stress}$$
$$= 500 \text{ kg/cm}^2$$
$$P = \text{Maximum tensile force on piston}$$
$$= \frac{\pi}{4} D^2 (p_1 - p_2) = \frac{\pi}{4} \times 32^2 \times (12 - 0.15)$$
$$= \frac{\pi}{4} \times 32^2 \times 11.85 = 9525 \text{ kg.}$$

Let $d_c$ = Core diameter of screwed end of piston

$$P = \frac{\pi}{4} d_c^2 \times f_t$$
$$9525 = \frac{\pi}{4} d_c^2 \times 500$$
$$d_c = 4.93$$
$$d = \text{Nominal diameter of screwed end}$$
$$= \frac{d_c}{0.84} = \frac{4.93}{0.84} = 5.87 \text{ cm.}$$

## 8.16 Boiler Stays

Stay bolts are used to join together parallel plates of boilers. They may be screwed through the bolts and nuts may be used. In order to reduce local stresses the body of the stay is generally turned to a diameter smaller than the root diameter of threads. The various types of stays are as follows :

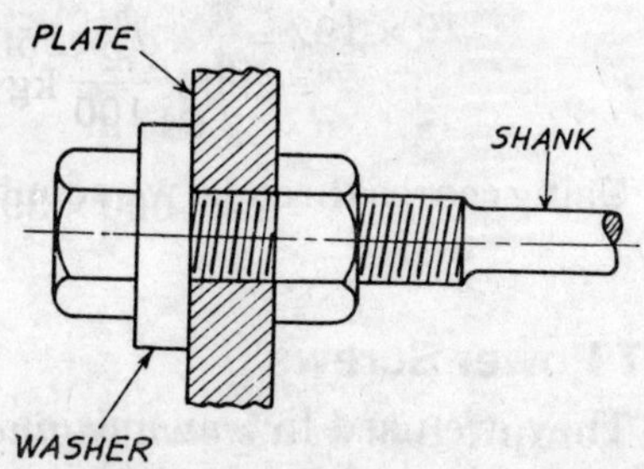

Fig. 8.24.

(*a*) Gusset stays
(*b*) Diagonal stays
(*c*) Longitudinal stays
(*d*) Stay bolts.

Fig. 8.24 shows a through stay with a bolt and nut.

The diameter of stay bolt is calculated as follows :

Let $p$ = Steam pressure acting on plate

$A$ = Area of plate supported by the stay

$f_t$ = Design stress in tension in stay bolt

$$d_c = \text{Core diameter of stay bolt}$$

$$p \times A = \frac{\pi}{4} d_c^2 \times f_t$$

The value of $d_c$ can be found from this equation. Nominal diameter corresponding to $d_c$ can be found from table 8.2.

**Example 8.7** *Calculate the diameter of a stay bolt for a boiler to support an area of 16 cm × 12 cm when the steam pressure is 10 kg/cm² gauge and the design stress in tension in stay bolt is 350 kg/cm².*

**Solution.** $p$ = Steam pressure = 10 kg/cm²

$A$ = Area to be supported by stay bolt

= 16 × 12 = 192 cm²

$f_t$ = Design stress in tension in stay bolt

$d_c$ = Core diameter of screwed end of stay bolt

$$p \times A = \frac{\pi}{4} d_c^2 \times f_t$$

$$10 \times 192 = \frac{\pi}{4} \times d_c^2 \times 350$$

$$d_c = 2.64 \text{ cm}$$

Using coarse threads, we adopt $M$ 30 diameter stay. (From table 8.2).

## 8.17 Power Screws

They are used to transmit power in screw operated machines such as screw jack, press, lathe etc. A power screw converts rotary motion into rectilinear motion. A power screw should possess high resistance to wear and retain its precision for a long time. The design of a power screw requires consideration of strength of screw in tension or compression, shearing of screw itself or of threads, wearing of threads and power requirement. The following thread forms are used for power screws

(*i*) Square threads

(*ii*) Acme threads

(*iii*) Buttress threads.

Square threads have maximum efficiency but it is quite difficult to cut these threads. Acme threads are slightly less efficient than square threads but it is easier to cut acme threads. Acme thread is quite commonly used in machine tools such as in lead screws of lathes. Buttress threads can transmit power only in one direction and are commonly used in screw jacks, vices etc. Buttress threads can be easily cut and have high efficiency.

For larger lead and high efficiency multiple threads are used.

## 8.18 Force Analysis on Power Screws

While designing a power screw the following two considerations should be taken into account.

(*i*) Torque required to turn the screw or nut

(*ii*) Mechanical efficiency of power screw drive.

(*a*) **Square thread.** Fig. 8.25 shows a square thread. The helix angle of the thread is calculated as follows (Fig. 8.26)

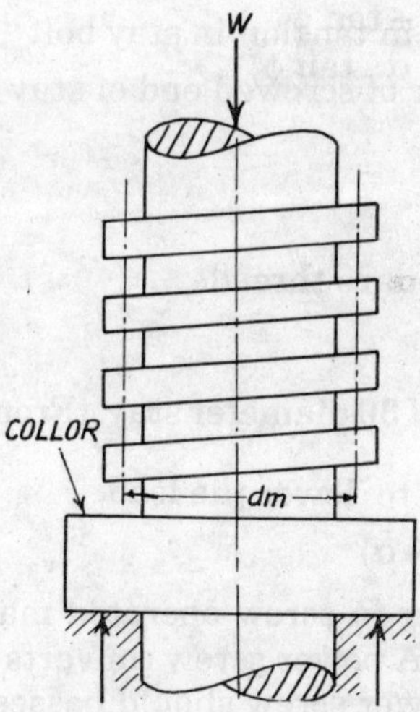


Fig. 8.25.

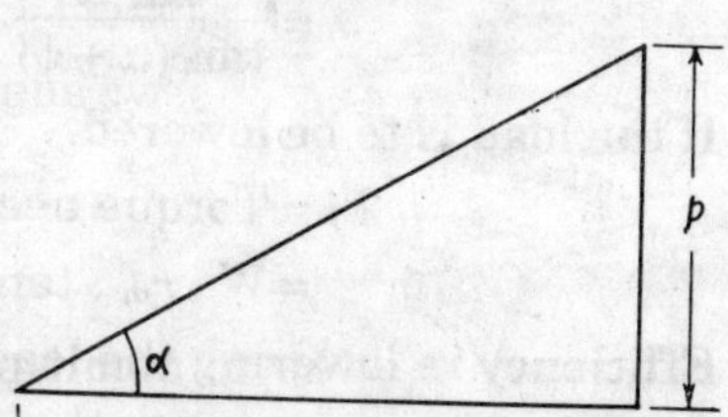


Fig. 8.26.

$$\tan \alpha = \frac{L}{\pi d_m}$$

where $\alpha$ = Helix angle

$L$ = Lead = $\eta p$

$\eta$ = Number of starts

$p$ = Pitch of threads

$d_m$ = Mean diameter of screw

When the nut of screw is moved against axial load $W$, the load on the nut is transferred to the screw as a distributed load on the surface of the threads in contact.

$W$ = Weight of load.

$P$ = Tangential source required to raise the load

$= W \cdot \tan(\alpha + \phi)$

where $\mu$ = Coefficient of friction

$\phi$ = Angle of friction

$\mu = \tan \phi$

$T$ = Torque needed to raise the load

$= P \times r_m$

where $r_m$ = Mean radius of screw

$$T = W \cdot r_m \tan(\alpha + \phi)$$

$$T = W \cdot r_m \cdot \frac{\tan \alpha + \tan \phi}{1 - \tan \alpha \cdot \tan \phi}$$

where $\tan \alpha = \dfrac{L}{\pi d_m}$

$\tan \phi = \mu$

$\eta$ = Efficiency of square threads

$$= \frac{\tan \alpha}{\tan(\alpha + \phi)}$$

If the load is to be lowered.

$T_1$ = Torque needed to lower the load

$= W \cdot r_m \cdot \tan(\phi - \alpha)$

Efficiency in lowering the load

$$= \frac{\tan \alpha}{\tan(\phi - \phi)}.$$

(*b*) **Acme threads and trapezoidal threads.** In these threads torque is found as follows :

$T$ = Torque required to raise the load

$$= W \cdot r_m \cdot \left[\frac{\tan \alpha \cdot \cos\beta + \tan \phi}{\cos \beta - \tan \alpha \cdot \tan \phi}\right]$$

where $\beta$ = Half the included angle of thread

$2\beta$ = Thread angle.

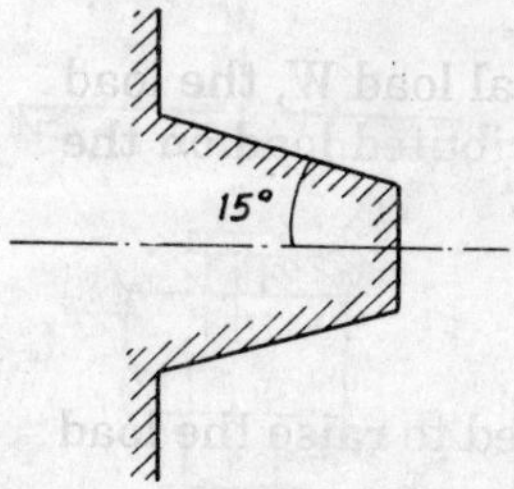


Fig. 8.27.

$= 29^\circ$ for acme thread.

$= 30^\circ$ for trapezoidal thread.

Fig. 8.27 shows section of trapezoidal thread.

$\eta$ = Efficiency

$$= \frac{\tan \alpha (1 - \tan \phi \cdot \sec \beta \cdot \tan \alpha)}{\tan \alpha + \tan \phi \cdot \sec \beta}$$

Table 8.7 indicates the coefficient of friction ($\mu$) for power screws.

**Table 8.7**

| *Lubricant* | $\mu$ |
|---|---|
| Machine oil and graphite | 0.17 |
| Lard oil | 0.11 |
| Heavy machine oil | 0.14 |

Table 8.8 indicates the safe bearing pressure in power screws.

**Table 8.8**

| *Service* | *Material* | | *Safe Bearing pressure kg/cm²* | *Remarks* |
|---|---|---|---|---|
| | *Screw* | *Nut* | | |
| Hand Press | Steel | Bronze | 175 to 245 | Low speed well lubricated |
| Jack Screw | Steel | C.I. | 126 to 175 | Low speed not over 2.4m/min |
| Jack Screw | Steel | Bronze | 112 to 175 | Low speed not over 3m/min. |
| Hosting Screw | Steel | C.I. | 41 to 70 | Medium speed 6 to 12 m/min. |
| Hoisting Screw | Steel | Bronze | 56 to 98 | Medium speed (6 to 12 m/min). |
| Lead Screw | Steel | Bronze | 10.5 to 16.8 | High Speed 15m/min and over. |

In a thrust collar (Fig. 8.28) having $R_1$ and $R_2$ as outer and inner radii and $\mu_1$ the coefficient of collar friction, the torque is calculated as follows

$$T = \frac{2}{3} \mu_1 W \left[ \frac{R_1^3 - R_2^3}{R_1^2 - R_2^2} \right]$$

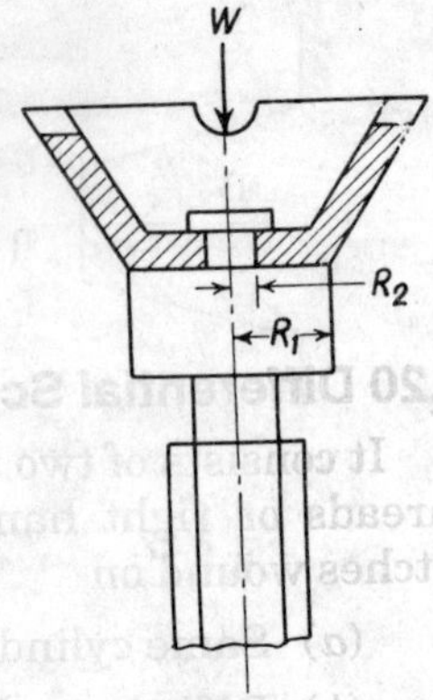


Fig. 8.28. Collar friction

## 8.19 Compound Screw

It consists of a right hand and a left hand thread wound on.

(*i*) Some cylinder (Fig. 8.29)

(*ii*) Different cylinders. (Fig. 8.30).

If the thread is wound on the same cylinder two nuts are used whereas when threads are wound on different cylinders one nut is used. During one revolution of screw two nuts move towards one another a distance equal to sum of two pitches.

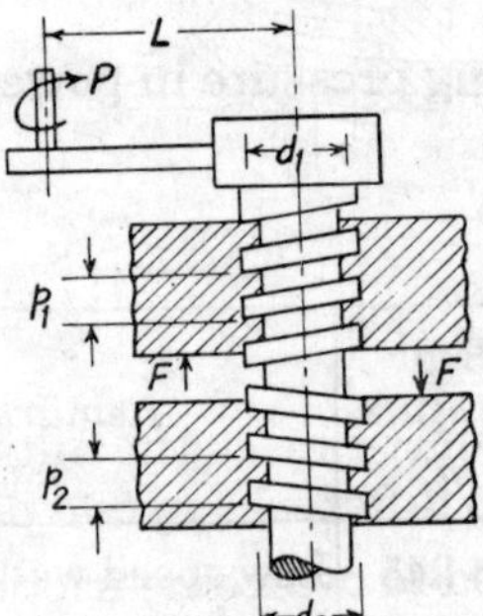


Fig. 8.29.

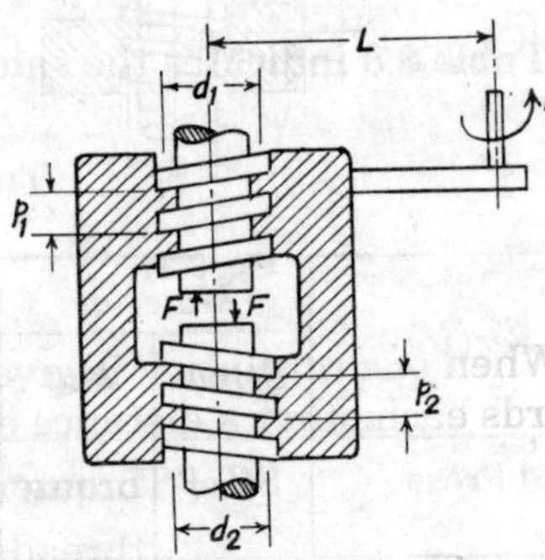


Fig. 8.30

Let $\quad p_1, p_2$ = Pitch of threads

$\mu_1, \mu_2$ = Coefficient of friction of the threads

$d_1, d_2$ = Means diameter of screw threads

$T$ = Torque required to overcome friction at the thread surfaces

$$= PL = F \left[ \frac{p_1 + \mu_1 \cdot \pi d_1}{\pi d_1 - \mu_1 p_1} \times \frac{d_1}{2} + \frac{p_2 + \mu_2 \cdot \pi d_2}{\pi d_2 + \mu_2 p_2} \times \frac{d_2}{2} \right]$$

$T_1$ = Ideal torque when coefficient of friction is zero

$$= \frac{F(p_1 + p_2)}{2\pi}$$

$$\eta = \text{Efficiency} = \frac{T_1}{T}$$

## 8.20 Differential Screw

It consists of two threads of the same hand *i.e.* either left hand threads or right hand threads but the threads are of different pitches wound on

(*a*) Same cylinder (Fig. 8.31).

(*b*) Different cylinders (Fig. 8.32).

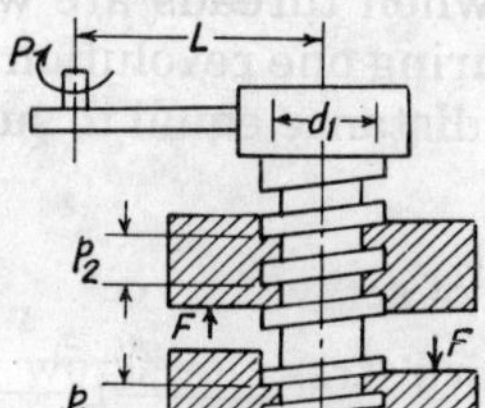


Fig. 8.31.

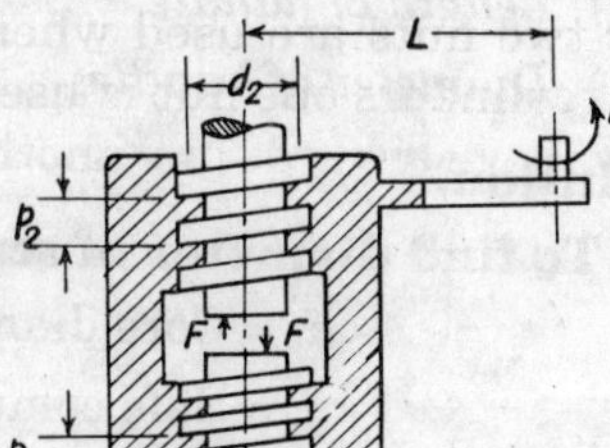


Fig. 8.32.

When one revolution is given to nut it causes the nuts to move towards each other a distance equal to difference of two pitches.

$T$ = Torque required to overcome friction at the thread surfaces

$$= PL = F\left[\frac{p_1 + \mu_1 \pi d_1}{\pi d_1 - \mu_1 p_1} \times \frac{d_1}{2} + \frac{\mu_2 \pi d_2 - p_2}{\pi d_2 + \mu_2 p_2} \times \frac{d_2}{2}\right]$$

$T_1$ = Ideal torque when coefficient of friction is zero

$$= \frac{F \cdot (p_2 - p_1)}{2\pi}$$

$$\eta = \text{Efficiency} = \frac{T_1}{T}$$

**Example 8.8** *Fig. 8.33 shows a nut and screw clamp. The compressive load is 2400 kg and a force of 35 kg is required to be* *applied at the end of handle to operate the screw. The safe compressive stress for screw is 1100 kg/c m² and coefficient screw threaded friction is 0.13. A friction torque 280 kg cm acts at pad M. If bearing pressure for screw and nut is 200 kg/cm², and bending stress in handle is 800 kg/cm², calculate the following :*

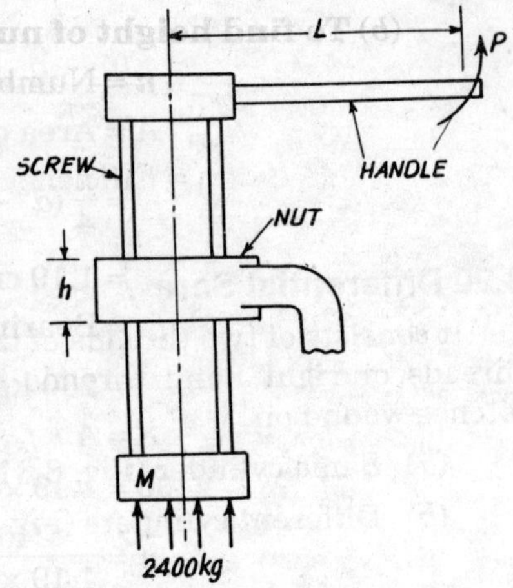

Fig. 8.33.

(*a*) *Diameter of screw.*

(*b*) *Height of nut.*

(*c*) *Length of handle.*

(*d*) *Diameter of handle.*

**Solution.**

(*a*) **To find diameter of screw**

$d_c$ = Core diameter of screw

$f_c$ = Safe compressive stress for screw

= 1100 kg/cm²

$F$ = Compressive force = 2400 kg

$A$ = Area of screw under compression

$$= \frac{\pi}{4} d_c^2$$

$$F = A \times f_c$$

$$2400 = \frac{\pi}{4} = d_c^2 \times 1100$$

$d_c$ = 1.67 cm.= 1.7 cm (say)

We adopt single start square threads having 4 mm pitch.

$d_m$ = Mean diameter of screw

$$= d_c + \frac{p}{2}$$

= 1.7 + 0.2 + 1.9 cm

where $p$ = pitch = 4 mm

$d$ = out side diameter of screw

$= d_c + p = 1.7 + 0.4 = 2.1$ cm.

**(b) To find height of nut *h***

$n$ = Number of threads in nut

$A$ = Area of each thread under bearing

$$= \frac{\pi}{4}(d^2 - d_c^2) = \frac{\pi}{4}(2.1^2) - (1.7^2)$$

$$= 1.19 \text{ cm}^2.$$

$f_{c_1}$ = Bearing stress in screw and nut

$$= 200 \text{ kg/cm}^2$$

$$F = A \times f_{c_1} \times n$$

$$2400 = 1.19 \times 200 \times n$$

$$n = \frac{2400}{1.19 \times 180} = 10$$

$$h = \text{Height of nut} = n \times p$$

$$= 10 \times 4 = 40 \text{ mm}$$

$D$ = Out side diameter of nut

$$= 2\,d = 2 \times 2.1 = 4.2 \text{ cm.}$$

**(c) To find length of handle**

$\mu$ = Coefficient of friction = 0.13

$\alpha$ = Helix angle of thread

$\phi$ = Friction of angle

$$\tan \alpha = \frac{p}{\pi\, d_m} = \frac{0.4}{\pi \times 1.9} = 0.067$$

$$\tan \phi = \mu = 0.13$$

$r_m$ = Mean radius

$$= \frac{d_m}{2} = \frac{1.9}{2} = 0.95 \text{ cm}$$

$T$ = Torque required to overcome friction at the nut

$$= F \times r_m \times \tan(\alpha + \phi)$$

$$= F \,.\, r_m \,.\, \frac{\tan\alpha + \tan\phi}{1 - \tan\alpha \,.\, \tan\phi}$$

$$= 2400 \times 0.95 \times \frac{0.067 + 0.13}{1 - 0.067 \times 0.13}$$

$$= 2400 \times 0.95 \times 0.198 = 451 \text{ kg cm.}$$

Let $P$ = Force applied at the end of handle

$$= 35 \text{ kg}$$

$L$ = Length of handle

$T_1$ = Torque required to overcome friction at pad

= 280 kg cm

$T_2$ = Total torque = $T + T_1$

= 450 + 280 = 730 kg cm

$$T_2 = P \times L$$

$$730 = 35 \times L$$

$$L = \frac{730}{35} = 20.85 \text{ cm.}$$

(*d*) **To find diameter of handle**

$d_1$ = Diameter of handle

$f_b$ = Bending stress in handle

= 800 kg/cm$^2$

$$T_2 = \frac{\pi}{32} d_1^3 \times f_b$$

$$730 = \frac{\pi}{32} d_1 \times 800$$

$$d_1^3 = 9.3$$

$$d_1 = 2.1 \text{ cm.}$$

**Example 8.9.** *It is required to lift a load of 300 kg by a double start acme thread of 6 mm pitch and 40 mm diameter at the rate of 0.6 m / min. The end of the screw is carried on a thrust collar 50 mm outside diameter and 28 mm inside diameter. If coefficient of friction is 0.13. Calculate the H.P. of the motor to drive the slide.*

**Solution.**

$d$ = Nominal diameter of thread = 40 mm

$p$ = Pitch = 6 mm

For double start thread

$L$ = Lead = $2p$

= 2 × 6 = 12 mm = 1.2 cm

Distance through which slide is elevated in one revolution is equal to lead.

$N$ = Speed of rotation of screw

$$= \frac{0.6 \times 100}{L}$$

$$= \frac{0.6 \times 100}{1.2} = 50 \text{ R.P.M.}$$

$W$ = Load to be lifted = 300 kg

Now $T_1$ = Torque required to overcome friction at the thread surfaces

$$= W \,.\, r_m \,.\, \tan(\alpha + \phi)$$

$d_m$ = Mean diameter of thread

$$= d - \frac{p}{2} = 40 - \frac{6}{2} = 37 \text{ mm}$$

$r_m$ = Mean radius of thread

$$= \frac{d_m}{2} = \frac{37}{2} = 18.5 \text{ mm} = 1.85 \text{ cm.}$$

$\alpha$ = Helix angle

$$\tan \alpha = \frac{L}{\pi d_m}$$

$$= \frac{12}{\pi \times 37} = 0.103$$

$\phi$ = Friction angle

$$\tan \phi = \mu = 0.13$$

$$T_1 = W \,.\, r_m \, f_{an} \, (\alpha + \phi)$$

$$= W \,.\, r_m \frac{\tan \alpha + \tan \phi}{1 - \tan \alpha \,.\, \tan \phi}$$

$$= 300 \times 1.85 \times \frac{0.103 + 0.13}{1 - 0.103 \times 13}$$

$$= 300 \times 1.85 \times 0.236 = 131 \text{ kg cm}$$

$T_2$ = Torque required to overcome friction at the collar surface

$$= \frac{2}{3} \mu W \left[ \frac{R_1^3 - R_2^3}{R_1^2 - R_2^2} \right]$$

where $R_1$ = outside radius of collar

$$= \frac{50}{2} = 25 \text{ mm} = 2.5 \text{ cm}$$

$R_2$ = Inside radius of collar

$$= \frac{28}{2} = 14 \text{ mm} = 1.4 \text{ cm}$$

$$T_2 = \frac{2}{3} \times 0.13 \times 300 \left[ \frac{2.5^2 - 1.4^3}{2.5^2 - 1.4^3} \right] = 78 \text{ kg cm.}$$

$T$ = Total torque required to overcome friction at threads and collor surface

$= T_1 + T_2 = 131 + 78 = 209$ kg cm

$= 2.09$ kgm

$$\text{H.P.} = \frac{2\pi NT}{4500}$$

$$= \frac{2\pi \times 50 \times 2.09}{4500} = 0.14.$$

**Example 8.10.** *A square threaded transmission screw used in a screw jack has a root diameter of 60 mm and a lead of 12 mm. It is double thread and is designed to lift a load of 12,000 kg. The coefficient of friction is 0.15. Determine the following :*

(*a*) *Pitch of screw*

(*b*) *Mean radius of thread*

(*c*) *Efficiency of the screw*

(*d*) *Unit compressive stress in the screw*

(*e*) *Bearing pressure on the projected area of the threads in contact.*

(*f*) *Is the screw self locking ?*

**Solution.**

(*a*) $d_c$ = Root diameter of screw

$= 60$ mm $= 6$ cm

$p$ = Pitch

$L$ = Lead

$12 = 2p$

$p = 6$ mm.

(*b*) $d_m$ = Mean diameter of screw

$$= d_c + \frac{p}{2} = 60 + \frac{6}{2} = 63 \text{ mm}$$

$r_m$ = Mean radius

$$= \frac{d_m}{2} = \frac{63}{2} = 31.5 \text{ mm.}$$

(*c*) $\eta$ = Efficiency of screw

$$= \frac{\tan \alpha}{\tan (\alpha + \phi)}$$

where $\alpha$ = Helix angle.

$$\tan \alpha = \frac{L}{\pi\, d_m} = \frac{12}{\pi \times 63} = 0.06$$

$$\phi = \text{Friction angle}$$

$$\tan \phi = \mu = 0.15$$

$$\eta = \frac{\tan \alpha}{\tan (\alpha + \phi)} = \frac{\tan \alpha\, [1 - \tan \alpha \times \tan \phi]}{\tan \alpha + \tan \phi}$$

$$= \frac{0.06[1 - 0.16 \times 0.15]}{0.06 + 0.15}$$

$$= \frac{0.06 \times 0.991}{0.21} = 0.283 = 28.3\%$$

(*d*) $W$ = Load to be lifted

$= 12000$ kg

$f_c$ = Compressive stress in the screw

$A$ = Area of screw under compression

$$= \frac{\pi}{4} d_e^2$$

$$W = A \times f_e$$

$$W = \frac{\pi}{4} d_e^2 \times f_e$$

$$12000 = \frac{\pi}{4} \times 6^2 \times f_e$$

$$f_b = 424.62 \text{ kg/cm}^2.$$

(*e*) $f_b$ = Bearing pressure on the thread

$\eta$ = Number of threads

$= 12$ Bearing

$W$ = Load on the threads

$= 12{,}000$ kg

$d$ = Nominal diameter of screw

$= d_e + p = 60 + 6 = 66$ mm

$= 6.6$ cm

$A$ = Bearing area

$$= \frac{\pi}{4}(d^2 - d_e^2) \times n$$

$$W = A \times f_b$$

$$12{,}000 = \frac{\pi}{4}[d^2 - d_c^2] \times f_b \times n$$

$$= \frac{\pi}{4}[6.6^2 - 6^2] \times f_b \times 12$$

$$12{,}000 = \frac{\pi}{4} \times 7.56 \times f_b \times 12$$

$$f_b = 168.5 \text{ kg/cm}^2.$$

(*f*) $\tan \alpha = 0.06$

$$\alpha = 3^\circ - 27'$$

$$\tan \phi = \mu = 0.15$$

$$\phi = 8^\circ - 32'.$$

As friction angle is greater than helix angle, the screw is self locking.

**Example 8.11.** *Design a screw jack to lift a load of 4000 kg through a height of 30 cm. The allowable shear stress in gun metal nut is 260 kg/cm² and allowable bearing pressure for screw threads is 120 kg/cm². The coefficient of friction of the threads and collor is 0.13. The screw is made up of mild steel for which Rankine's constants are 3300 kg/cm² and* $\frac{1}{7500}$. *For column pin jointed at both ends. The safe compressive stress in screw is 500 kg/cm².*

**Solution.** Fig. 8.34 shows a screw jack.

(*i*) **To design screw**

$f_c$ = Safe compressive stress in screw

= 500 kg/cm²

$W$ = Load to be lifted

= 4000 kg

$d_c$ = Core diameter of screw

The screw is under direct compression

$A$ = Area under compression

$$= \frac{\pi}{4} d_c^2$$

$$W = A \times f_c = \frac{\pi}{4} d_c^2 \times f_c$$

$$4000 = \frac{\pi}{4} d_c^2 \times 500$$

$$d_c = 3.2 \text{ cm.}$$

We adopt square threads having a pitch of 6 mm.

$p$ = Pitch of threads = 6 mm

= 0.6 cm

$d$ = Out side diameter of screw

$= d + p \qquad = 3.2 + 0.6 = 3.8$ cm.

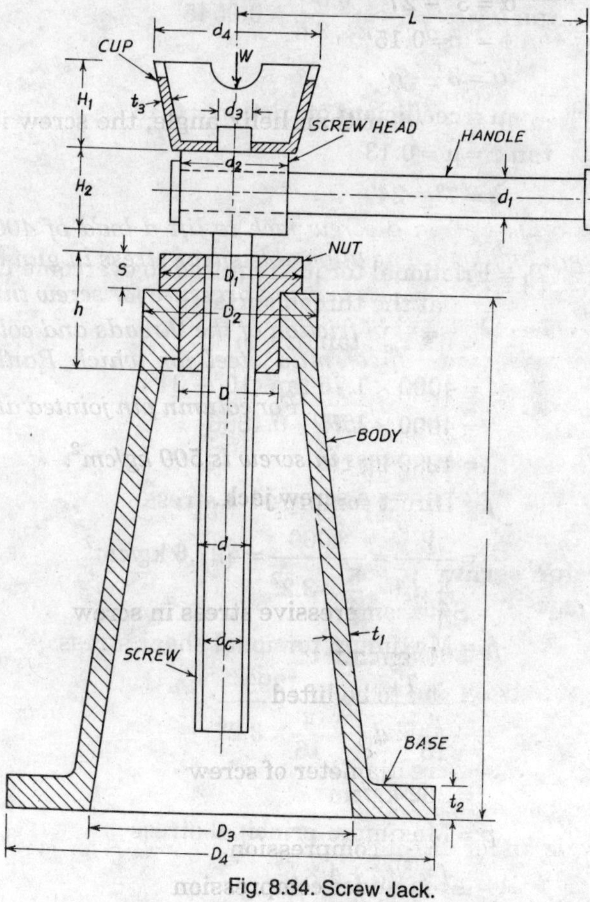


Fig. 8.34. Screw Jack.

$d_m$ = Mean diameter of screw

$$= d_c + \frac{p}{2} = 3.2 + \frac{0.6}{2}$$

$$= 3.5 \text{ cm}$$

$$d_m = \frac{d + d_c}{2} = \frac{3.8 + 3.2}{2} = 3.5 \text{ cm}$$

$r_m$ = Mean radius of screw

$$= \frac{3.5}{2} = 1.75 \text{ cm.}$$

To check the screw for principal stress, proceed as follows :

$\phi$ = Friction angle

$\alpha$ = Helix angle

$$\tan \alpha = \frac{p}{\pi\, d_m} = \frac{0.6}{\pi \times 3.5} = 0.0545$$

$$\alpha = 3^\circ - 7'$$

$\mu$ = coefficient of friction = 0.13

$$\tan \phi = \mu = 0.13$$

$$\phi = 7^\circ - 24'$$

$T_1$ = Frictional torque required to overcome friction at the thread surfaces

$$= W \,.\, r_m \,.\, \tan(\alpha + \phi)$$

$$= 4000 \times 1.75 \tan(10^\circ - 31')$$

$$= 4000 \times 1.75 \times 0.1856$$

$$= 1299 \text{ kg cm}$$

$f$ = Direct compressive stress

$$= \frac{W}{\frac{\pi}{4} d_c^2} = \frac{4000}{\frac{\pi}{4} \times 3.2^2} = 497.6 \text{ kg/cm}^2$$

$f_s$ = Maximum torsional shear stress

$$= \frac{T_1}{\frac{\pi}{16} \times d_c^3} = \frac{1299}{\frac{\pi}{16} \times 3.2^3}$$

$$= 202 \text{ kg/cm}^2$$

$p$ = Maximum principal stress

$$= \frac{f + \sqrt{f^2 + 4 \times f_s^2}}{2}$$

$$= \frac{497.6 + \sqrt{497.6^2 + 4 \times 202^2}}{2}$$

$$= 569 \text{ kg/cm}^2$$

The screw is made up of mild steel for which ultimate strength is about 4000 kg/cm$^2$.

$$\text{Factor of safety} = \frac{4000}{569}$$

$$= 7, \text{ which is adequate}$$

(*ii*) **To design cup**

$d_2$ = Diameter of head of screw

$= 1.75 \times d = 1.75 \times 3.8$

$= 6.65$ cm.

Diameter of seat of cup

$= d_2 = 6.65$ cm.

$r_2$ = Radius of seat of cup = 3.325 cm.

The cup is fitted with a pin which remains loose fit in the cup.

$d_3$ = Diameter of pin

$$= \frac{d_2}{3} \text{ (say)} = \frac{6.65}{3}$$

$= 2.22$ cm.

$$r_3 = \text{Radius of pin} = \frac{2.22}{2} = 1.11 \text{ cm}$$

$T_2$ = Frictional torque at the cup

$$= \frac{2}{3} \mu W \left[ \frac{r_2^3 - r_3^3}{r_2^2 - r_3^2} \right]$$

$$= \frac{2}{3} \times 0.13 \times 4000 \left[ \frac{3.325^3 - 1.11^3}{3.325^2 - 1.11^2} \right]$$

$$= \frac{2}{3} \times 0.13 \times 4000 \times 3.62 = 1255 \text{ kg cm.}$$

$T$ = Total torque to be applied by the handle

$= T_1 + T_2$

$= 1299 + 1255 = 2554$ kg cm.

(*iii*) **To design handle**

Let $d_1$ = Diameter of handle

$f_b$ = Allowable bending stress in handle

$= 1100 \text{ kg/cm}^2$ (say)

Considering bending of handle

$$T = \frac{\pi}{32} d_1^3 \times f_b$$

$$2544 = \frac{\pi}{32} d_1^3 \times 1100$$

$$d_1^3 = 23.56$$

$$d_1 = 2.86 \text{ cm}$$

$H_2$ = Height of screw head

$$= 2 \times d_1 = 2 \times 2.86 = 5.72 \text{ cm.}$$

To find length of handle, assume that one person can apply a load of 60 kg at the end of the lever

$$F = 60 \text{ kg}$$

$L$ = Length of handle

$$F \times L = T$$

$$60 \times L = 2554$$

$$L = 42.56 \text{ cm.}$$

Allowing some length for grapping

$$L = 45 \text{ cm (say)}$$

(*iv*) **To design nut.**

The nut is made of gun metal

$n$ = Number of threads in the nut

$A$ = Bearing area for thread

$$= \frac{\pi}{4}(d^2 - d_c^2) = \frac{\pi}{4}(3.8^2 - 3.2^2)$$

$$= 3.3 \text{ cm}^2$$

$f_{b_1}$ = Bearing stress in threads = 120 kg/cm²

$$W = n \times A \times f_{b_1}$$

$$n = \frac{W}{A \times f_{b_1}} = \frac{4000}{3.3 \times 120} = 10.1$$

We adopt 12 threads

$\therefore$ $n = 12$

$h$ = Height of nut

$$= n \times p$$

$$= 12 \times 0.6 = 7.2 \text{ cm.}$$

$D$ = Outer diameter of nut = $2d$
$= 2 \times 3.8 = 7.6$ cm
$S$ = Thickness of collar
$= \frac{D}{4}$ (say) $= \frac{7.6}{4} = 1.9$ cm
$D_1$ = Outer diameter of collar
$= 1.25\, D$ (say) $= 1.25 \times 7.6 = 9.5$ cm.

The collor of the nut rests on the castings of the main body and it may be crushed under load being lifted.

$A$ = Crushing area between collar of nut and the body

$$= \frac{\pi}{4}[D_1^2 - D^2] = \frac{\pi}{4}[9.5^2 - 7.6^2]$$

$= 25.5$ cm$^2$

$f_{c_1}$ = Crushing stress

$W = f_c \times A$

$$f_{c_1} = \frac{4000}{25.5} = 156.86 \text{ kg/cm}^2$$

which is reasonably low.

To calculate the shear stress ($f_{s_1}$) induced in the collar, consider shearing of collar

$A$ = Area that resist shearing of collar
$= \pi \,.\, D \,.\, S = \pi \times 7.6 \times 1.9$
$= 45.34$ cm$^2$

$W = A \times f_{s_1}$

$$f_{s_1} = \frac{W}{A} = \frac{4000}{45.34} = 88.22 \text{ kg/cm}^2$$

This stress is less than allowable shear stress of 260 kg/cm$^2$ in the nut, hence safe.

(*v*) **To design body**

$L_1$ = Length of threaded portion of screw
= Lift + Height of nut
$= 30 + 7.2 = 37.2$ cm
$t_1$ = Thickness of body
$= 0.25 \times d = 0.25 \times 3.8 = 0.95$ cm
$t_2$ = Thickness of base $= 2t_1$

$= 2 \times 0.95 = 1.9$ cm

$D_2$ = Diameter of body at top = $1.5\ D_1$

$= 1.5 \times 9.5 = 14.25$ cm

$H$ = Height of body

$= L_1 + 5$ cm (say)

$= 37.2 + 5 = 42.2$ cm

$D_3$ = Inside diameter of body at base

$= 2.25 \times D_1 = 2.25 \times 9.5 = 21.37$ cm

$D_4 = 1.5\ D_3 = 1.5 \times 21.37 = 32$ cm.

To check the body against toppling, proceed as follows

$H_1$ = Distance from base of body at which effort will be acting

$=$ Lift $+ H + d_1$

$= 30 + 42.2 + 2.86 = 75.06$ cm

$y$ = Distance from the centre of base at which resultant meets

$$y \times W = H_1 \times F$$

$$y \times 4000 = 75.06 \times 60$$

$$y = 0.89 \text{ cm.}$$

Therefore, the body is stable against toppling.

(*vi*) **To check the screw against bucking.** The screw can be checked for stability against buckling by the use Rankine-Gordon formula

$P$ = Critical load causing failure

$$P = \frac{f_c \, . \, A}{1 + \frac{1}{a}\left(\frac{l}{k}\right)^2}$$

where $f_c = 3300$ kg/cm$^2$

$$A = \frac{\pi}{4} d_c^2 = \frac{\pi}{4} \times (3.2)^2 = 8 \text{ cm}^2.$$

When the maximum lift is attained the screw can be looked upon as a strut fixed at the lower end and free at the top. The end fixity coefficient for this column will be 0.25

$$\therefore \quad \frac{1}{a} = \frac{1}{7500 \times 0.25} = \frac{1}{1875}$$

$l$ = length of screw which is unsupported

$$= \text{Lift} + \text{Height of head of screw}$$
$$= 30 + H_2 = 30 + 5.72 = 35.72 \text{ cm}$$
$$P = \frac{3300 \times 8}{1 + \frac{1}{1875}\left(\frac{35.72 \times 4}{3.2}\right)^2}$$
$$= 12{,}815 \text{ kg}$$

Using $k = \frac{d_c}{4}$

Factor of safety $= 3$

Permissible buckling load

$$= \frac{12{,}815}{3} = 427.16 \text{ kg.}$$

As the permissible buckling load is more than load to be lifted, therefore the screw is safe against buckling.

Other dimensions are as follows.

$$t_s = \text{Thickness of cup} = \frac{t_1}{2}$$
$$= \frac{0.95}{2} = 0.475 \text{ cm}$$
$$d_5 = 1.5\, d_1 = 1.5 \times 2.86 = 4.29 \text{ cm.}$$

## 8.21 Eccentric Loading of Bolted Joints

Bolted joints may be subjected to eccentric load such as a bracket attached to a wall, a pillar crane etc. There are two cases of eccentric loading on bolts.

(*i*) Loading parallel to the axis of bolt

(*ii*) Loading perpendicular to the axis of bolt.

In first case only tensile stress is induced in the bolts whereas in second case both tensile and shear stress is induced in the bolts.

(*i*) **Loading parallel to the axis of bolt.** Fig. 8.35 shows fastening of a bracket with 4 bolts. The load tends to rotate the bracket about the edge line. In general the most heavily loaded bolt are those which are at the greatest distance from edge of turning.

Let $F$ = Eccentric load

$S$ = Distance of load $F$ from the tilting edge

$S_1$ = Distance of nearest bolts from tilting edge

$S_2$ = Distance of farthest bolt from tilting edge

$w$ = Load in a bolt at unit distance from tilting edges $M\text{–}M$.

Then the load in a bolt at a distance $S_1$ from edge $M\text{-}M$ will be $w \times S_1$ and the moment of this load about the edge $M\text{-}M$ will be $w \times S_1 \times S_1 = w \times S_1^2$.

Now there are two bolts at bolt line 1 and therefore the resisting moment of these two bolts at bolt line 2 will be $2\, w\, S_1^2$.

Similarly the resisting moment of two bolts at the bolt line 2 will be $2\, wS_2^2$.

Turning moment due to load

$$F = F \times S$$

$$F \times S = 2w \times S_1^2 + 2w \times S_2^2 \qquad \text{...}(i)$$

From this equation, the load $w$ can be found.

Thus load in a bolt at bolt line 2 will be $w \times S_2$ and load in a bolt at line 1 will be $w \times S_1$.

The bolts at line 2 will be heavily loaded

$F_1$ = Direct tensile load on each bolt $= \dfrac{F}{n}$

where $n$ = Number of bolts

$F_2$ = Load in a bolt at line 2

$F_2 = w \times S_2$

$P$ = Total tensile load in the most heavily loaded bolt

$= F_1 + F_2$

The bolt is designed for load $P$.

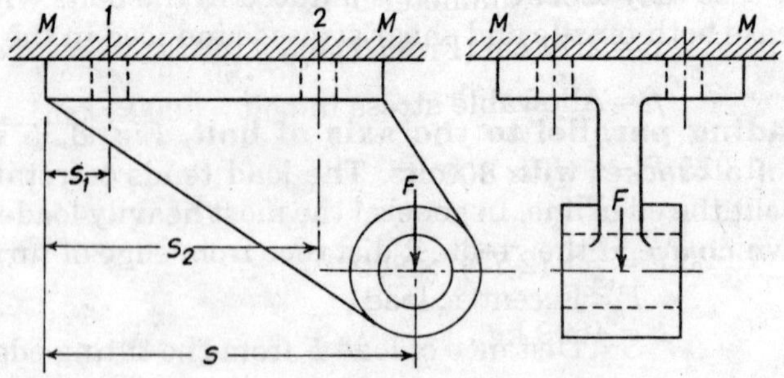


Fig. 8.35.

**Example 8.12.** *A bracket shown in Fig. 8.35 is used to support a load F kg. Calculate the load F if allowable stress in the bolt is M* 30 × 35.

*Take* $S_1 = 5$ *cm*, $S_2 = 25$ *cm*, $S = 40$ *cm.*

**Solution.** $n$ = Number of bolts = 4

$F$ = Eccentric load

$S_1 = 5$ cm

$S_2 = 25$ cm

$S$ = Distance of load from the tilting edge = 40 cm

$F_1$ = Direct tensile load in each bolt

$$= \frac{F}{n} = \frac{F}{4} = 0.25\, F \text{ kg}$$

$w$ = Load in a bolt at unit distance from tilting edge $M$–$M$

$$F \times S = 2\omega\, S_1^2 + 2w\, S_2^2$$

$$F \times 40 = 2w \times 5^2 + 2\omega \times 25^2$$

$$w = 0.031\, F$$

The bolt at line 2 is heavily loaded

$F_2$ = Load in a bolt at line 2

$$= w \times S_2 = w \times 25$$

$$= 0.031\, F \times 25 = 0.775\, F$$

$P$ = Total tensile load in the most heavily loaded bolt

$$= F_1 + F_2 = 0.25\, F + 0.775\, F = 1.025\, F$$

$d_c$ = Core diameter of bolt $M$ 30

= 2.77 cm (From Table 8.2)

$f_t$ = Allowable stress in bolt = 800 kg/cm$^2$

$$1.025\, F = \frac{\pi}{4}\, d_c^2 \times 800$$

$$1.025\, F = \frac{\pi}{4} \times (2.77)^2 \times 800$$

$$F = 4699 \text{ kg.}$$

(*ii*) **Loading perpendicular to the axis of the bolt.** Fig. 8.36 shows a bracket fastened to a flange by mean of 4 bolts.

Let $F$ = Eccentric load

$S$ = Distance of load $F$ from tilting edge

$S_1$ and $S_2$ are the distances from the turning edge $M$-$M$ to the centre of bolt line 1 and 2 respectively.

$n$ = Number of bolts°

$F_s$ = Average shear load on each bolt

$$= \frac{F}{n}$$

Turning moment about edge $M$-$M$ due to load

$$F = F \times S$$

$w$ = Load in a bolt at unit distance from tilting edge $M$–$M$.

$$F \times S = 2w \times S_1^2 + 2w \times S_2^2$$

From this equation the load $w$ can be found.

Now the bolts in line 2-2 are heavily loaded.

$F_t$ = Tensile load in each bolt at line 2 – 2

$$= w \times S_2$$

$F_1$ = Equivalent tensile load

$$= \frac{1}{2}\left[F_t + \sqrt{F_t^2 + 4\,F_s^2}\right]$$

$F_2$ = Equivalent shear load

$$= \frac{1}{2}\left[\sqrt{(F_t^2 + 4\,F_s^2}\right]$$

The bolts are now designed for tensile load $F_1$ and shear load $F_2$.

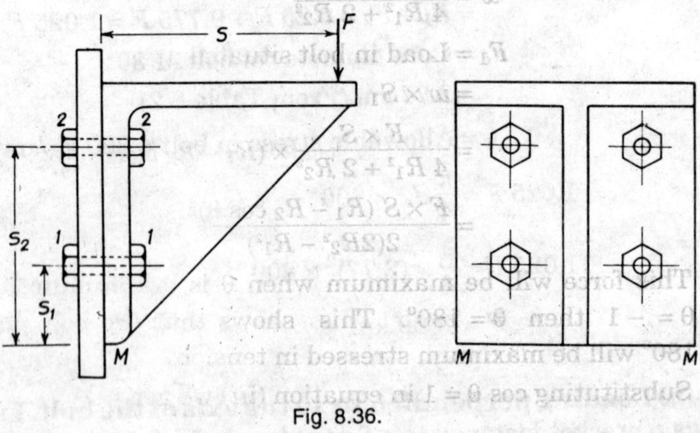


Fig. 8.36.

**Eccentric load perpendicular to bolt axis for a circular base.** Fig. 8.37 shows a circular base bracket and a flanged bearing fastened together by means of bolts.

$F$ = Eccentric load

$S$ = Distance of load $F$ from turning point $M$

$n$ = Number of bolts

$w$ = Load in each bolt per unit surface from turning point.

$S_1$, $S_2$, $S_3$ and $S_4$ are the distances of the bolt centres from turning point $M$ of bolt 1, 2, 3 and 4 respectively.

Moment due to applied load $= F \times S$

Resisting moment due to load on all bolts

$$= w\, S_1^2 + w\, S_2^2 + w\, S_3^2 + w\, S_4^2$$

$$F \times S = w(S_1^2 + S_2^2 + S_3^2 + S_4^2)$$

The load $w$ is calculated from the equation.

$$w = \frac{F \times S}{S_1^2 + S_2^2 + S_3^2 + S_4^2} \qquad ...(i)$$

Let $R_1$ = Radius of the column flange

$R_2$ = Radius of bolt pitch circle from the figure

$$S_1 = R_1 - R_2 \cos\theta$$

$$S_2 = R_1 + R_2 \sin\theta$$

$$S_3 = R_1 + R_2 \cos\theta$$

$$S_4 = R_1 - R_2 \sin\theta$$

Substituting these values in equation (*i*) we get

$$w = \frac{F \times S}{4\,R_1^2 + 2\,R_2^2} \qquad ...(ii)$$

$F_1$ = Load in bolt situated at 1

$$= w \times S_1$$

$$= \frac{F \times S}{4\,R_1^2 + 2\,R_2^2} \times (R_1 - R_2 \cos\theta)$$

$$= \frac{F \times S\,(R_1 - R_2 \cos\theta)}{2(2R_2^2 - R_1^2)} \qquad ...(iii)$$

This force will be maximum when θ is a minimum or when $\cos\theta = -1$ then $\theta = 180^\circ$. This shows that the bolt placed at $\theta = 180^\circ$ will be maximum stressed in tension.

Substituting $\cos\theta = 1$ in equation (*iii*) we get

$$\text{Maximum force} = \frac{F \times S(R_1 + R_2)}{2\,(2R_1^2 + R_2^2)}$$

Let $n$ = Number of bolts

In such case the general expression for the load in a bolt is as follows :

$$\text{Load in a bolt} = \frac{2FS\,(R_1 - R_2 \cos\theta)}{n(2R_1^2 + R_2^2)}$$

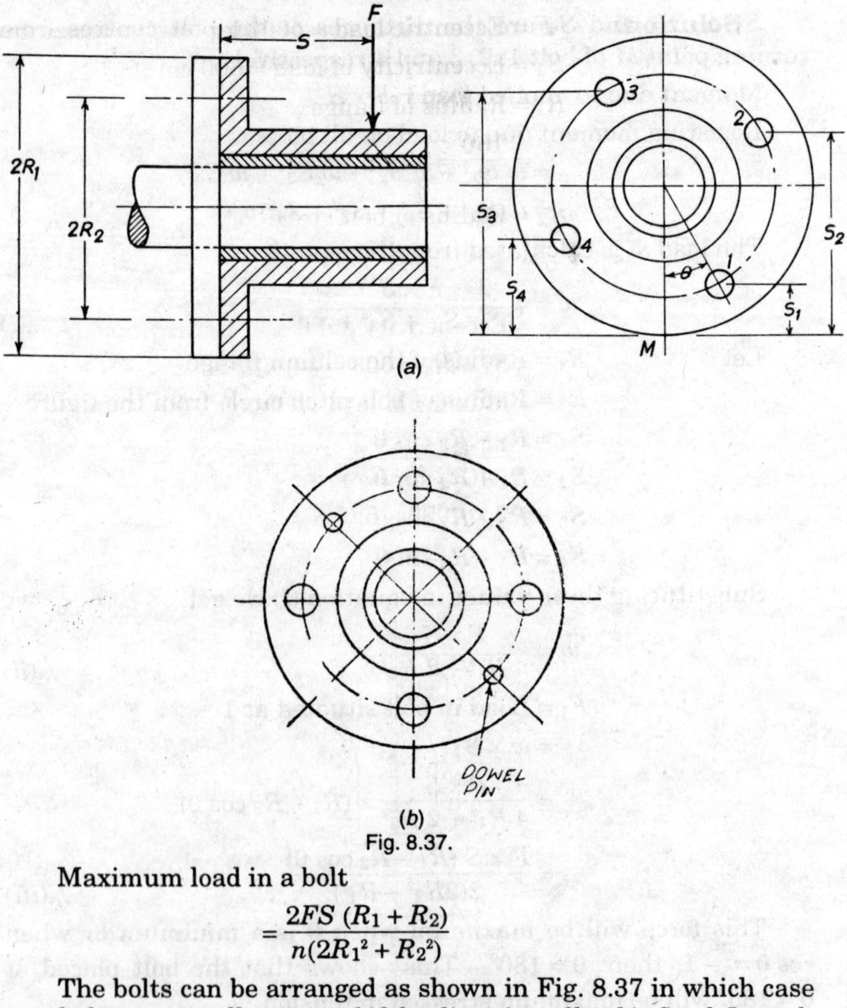


(a)

(b)

Fig. 8.37.

Maximum load in a bolt

$$= \frac{2FS\,(R_1 + R_2)}{n(2R_1^2 + R_2^2)}$$

The bolts can be arranged as shown in Fig. 8.37 in which case two bolts are equally stressed if the direction of load is fixed. In such case the maximum load is calculated as follows :

$$\text{Maximum load} = \frac{2FS\left[R_1 + R_2 \cos\left(\frac{180}{n}\right)\right]}{n(2R_1^2 + R_2^2)}$$

**Example 8.13.** *A pillar crane is fastened to foundation by 6 bolts spaced equally on a bolt circle diameter is 140 cm and diameter of flange is 160 cm determine the size of bolt (Fig. 8.38). Take allowable stress intensity in bolt material as 920 kg/cm$^2$.*

**Solution.** $F$ = Eccentric load = 4000 kg

$S_1$ = Eccentricity of load = 600 cm

$R_1$ = Radius of flange

$$= \frac{160}{2} = 80 \text{ cm}$$

$R_2$ = Radius of bolt circle

$$= \frac{140}{2} = 70 \text{ cm.}$$

$S$ = Eccentricity of load from turning edge $M$

$$= S_1 - R_1 = 600 - 80 = 520 \text{ cm}$$

$P$ = Maximum load on a bolt

$$= \frac{2FS \times (R_1 + R_2)}{n(2R_1^2 + R_2^2)}$$

$$= \frac{2 \times 4000 \times 520(80 + 70)}{6(2 \times 80^2 + 70^2)} = 5875 \text{ kg}$$

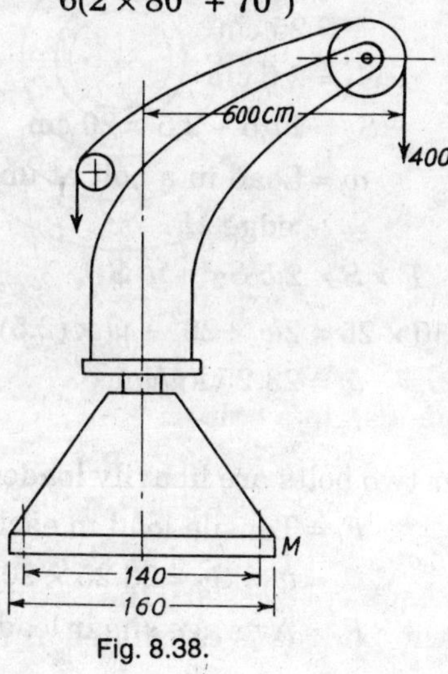


Fig. 8.38.

Let $d_c$ = Core diameter of bolt

$f_t$ = Allowable stress in bolt

$= 920 \text{ kg/cm}^2$

$$P = \frac{\pi}{4} d_c^2 \times f_t$$

$$5875 = \frac{\pi}{4} d_c^2 \times 920$$

$$d_c = 2.85 \text{ cm} = 28.5 \text{ mm}$$

From Table 8.2 the standard size of bolt is M 33 × 3.5 *C* where *C* indicates coarse series.

**Example 8.14.** *Calculate the size of the bolts for the three hole bracket as shown in Fig. 8.39. Use coarse threads and the allowable tensile stress 270 kg/cm² and allowable shear as stress as 120 kg/cm².*

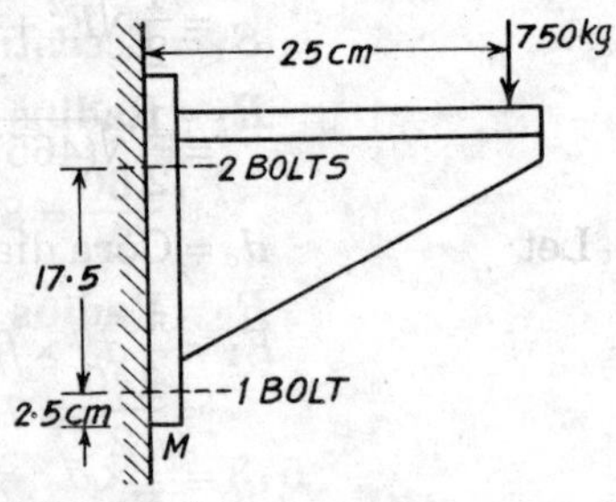


Fig. 8.39

**Solution.**

$n$ = Number of bolts

$F$ = Eccentric load

= 750 kg

$S$ = Distance of load $F$ from tilting edge

= 25 cm

$S_1$ = 2.5 cm

$S_2$ = 17.5 + 2.5 = 20 cm

$w$ = Load in a bolt at unit distance from tilting edge $M$

$$F \times S = 2w\, S_2^2 + w\, S_1^2$$

$$750 \times 25 = 2w \times 20^2 + w \times (2.5)^2$$

$$w = 23.25 \text{ kg/cm.}$$

The upper two bolts are heavily loaded.

$F_t$ = Tensile load in each of upper bolt

$= w \times S_2 = 23.25 \times 20 = 465$ kg

$F_s$ = Average shear load on each bolt

$$= \frac{750}{3} = 250 \text{ kg}$$

$$F_1 = \text{Equivalent tensile load}$$

$$= \frac{1}{2} [ F_t + \sqrt{F_t^2 + 4 F_s^2} ]$$

$$= \frac{1}{2} [ 465 + \sqrt{(465)^2 + 4 \times (250)^2} ] = 573 \text{ kg}$$

$$F_2 = \text{Equivalent shear load}$$

$$= \frac{1}{2} \sqrt{F_t^2 + 4 F_s^2}$$

$$= \frac{1}{2} \sqrt{(465)^2 + 4 \times (250)^2} = 340 \text{ kg}$$

Let $d_c$ = Core diameter of bolt

$$F_1 = \frac{\pi}{4} d_c^2 \times f_t$$

$$573 = \frac{\pi}{4} \times d_c^2 \times 270$$

$$d_c = 1.644 \text{ cm} = 16.44 \text{ mm}.$$

From Table 8.2 we select $M\ 20 \times 2.5$ bolt.

$$f_{s_1} = \text{Shear stress induced in bolt}$$

$$F_2 = \frac{\pi}{4} d^2 \times f_{s_1}$$

where, $d$ = Nominal diameter of bolt = 2 cm

$$f_{s_1} = \frac{F_2 \times 4}{\pi \times 2^2} = \frac{340 \times 4}{\pi \times 2^2} = 108.3 \text{ kg/cm}^2.$$

which is less than allowable shear stress of 120 kg/cm$^2$, hence safe.

**Example 8.15.** *A bracket is attached to a column by means of 4 bolts as shown in Fig. 8.40. Calculate the size of bolts used if the permissible tensile stress and shear stress is 800 kg/cm$^2$ and 600 kg/cm$^2$ respectively.*

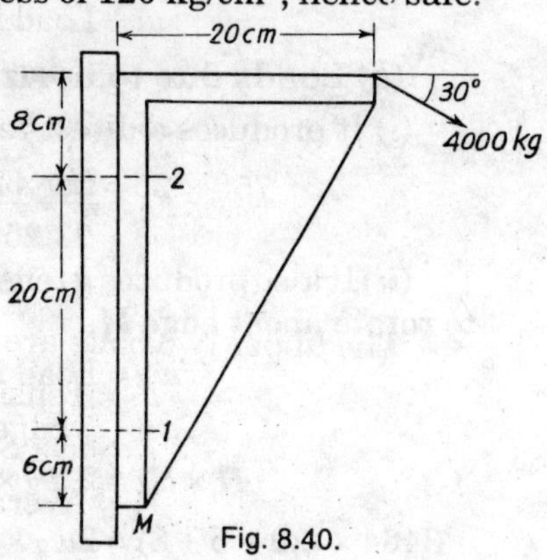

Fig. 8.40.

**Solution.** There are two bolts at line 1 and two bolts at line 2.

$n$ = Number of bolts = 4

$P$ = Load 4000 kg.

$F$ = Vertical component of $P$

$$= P \sin 30 = 4000 \times \frac{1}{2} = 2000 \text{ kg}$$

$H$ = Horizontal component of $P = P \cos 30$

$$= 4000 \times \frac{\sqrt{3}}{2} = 3464 \text{ kg.}$$

**(a) Loads due to vertical load of 2000 kg.**

(i) $F_s$ = Shear load on each bolt

$$= \frac{2000}{n} = \frac{2000}{4} = 500 \text{ kg.}$$

(ii) Vertical load also produces a tensile load on each bolt due to its tendency to its rotate about edge $M$. It is calculated as follows.

$w_1$ = Load in a bolt at unit distance from tilting edge $M$.

$$F \times S = 2\, w_1 S_1^2 + 2\, w_1 S_2^2$$

where $S$ = 20 cm.

$S_1$ = 6 cm.

$S_2$ = 26 cm.

$$2000 \times 20 = 2\, w_2 \times 6^2 + 2w_1 \times 26^2$$

$$w_1 = 28 \text{ kg.}$$

The bolts at line 2 are heavily loaded.

$F_1$ = Tensile load in each bolt at line 2

$$= w_1 \times S_2 = 28 \times 26 = 728 \text{ kg.}$$

**(b) Loads due to horizontal load 3464 kg.**

(i) It produces a direct tensile load ($F_2$) on each bolt.

$$F_2 = \frac{H}{n} = \frac{3464}{4} = 866 \text{ kg.}$$

(ii) It also produces a tensile load on each bolt due to its tendency to rotate about edge $M$.

$w_2$ = Load in a bolt at unit distance from tilting edge $M$

$$H \times S_3 = 2\, w_2 \times S_1^2 + 2\, w_2 \times S_2^2$$

$$3464 \times (20 + 6 + 8) = 2w_2 \times 6^2 + 2w_2 \times 26^2$$

$$3464 \times 34 = 2\, w_2 \times 36 + 2\, w_2 \times 676$$

$$w_2 = 82.7 \text{ kg.}$$

The bolt at line 2 is heavily loaded.

$F_3$ = Tensile load on each bolt at line 2

$= w_2 \times S_2 = 82.7 \times 26 = 2150$ kg.

$F_4$ = Maximum tensile load on a bolt at line 2

$= F_1 + F_2 + F_3$

$= 728 + 866 + 2150 = 3744$ kg.

$F_t$ = Equivalent tensile load

$$= \frac{1}{2}[F_4 + \sqrt{F_4^2 + 4F_s^2}]$$

$$= \frac{1}{2}[3744 + \sqrt{(3744)^2 + 4 \times (500)^2}]$$

$$= \frac{1}{2}[3744 + 3876] = 3810 \text{ kg.}$$

$F_{S_1}$ = Equivalent shear force

$$= \frac{1}{2}\sqrt{F_4^2 + 4F_s^2}$$

$$= \frac{1}{2} \times 3876 = 1938 \text{ kg.}$$

$f_t$ = Allowable tensile stress in bolt

$= 800$ kg/cm$^2$

$d_c$ = Core diameter of each bolt

$$F_t = \frac{\pi}{4} d_c^2 \times f_t$$

$$3810 = \frac{\pi}{4} d_c^2 \times 800$$

$$d_c = 2.46 \text{ cm.}$$

From Table 8.2, for coarse series the standard size of bolt will by $M\ 30 \times 3.5$.

$\therefore$ $d = 30$ mm

Let $f_{s1}$ = shear stress induced in the bolt

$$F_{s1} = \frac{\pi}{4} d^2 \times f_{s1}$$

$$1938 = \frac{\pi}{4} d^2 \times f_{s1} = \frac{\pi}{4} \times 3^2 \times f_{s1}$$

$$f_{s1} = 274.3 \text{ kg/cm}^2.$$

This is less than the allowable shear stress 600 kg/cm$^2$ hence the bolt is safe against shearing.

**Example 8.16.** *The screw of a shaft straightener is subjected to a maximum load of 2000 kg. Determine the size of the two bolts required to fasten the straightener to the base, assuming allowable stress to be 600 kg/cm$^2$ Neglect tightening up stresses (Fig. 8.41).*

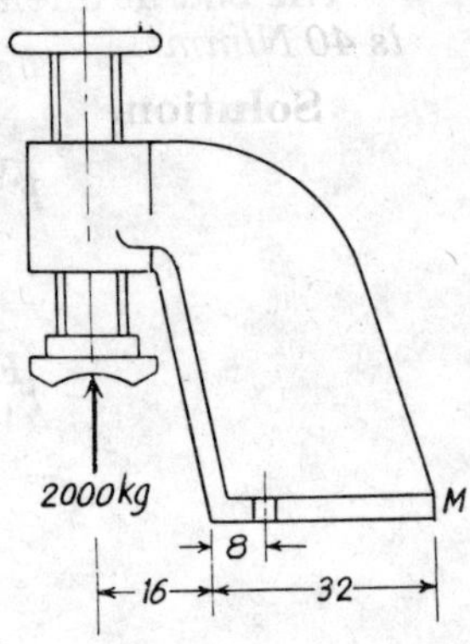


Fig. 8.41.

**Solution.**

$P$ = Load = 2000 kg

$n$ = Number of bolts = 2

$F$ = Direct tensile force on each bolt

$$= \frac{P}{n} = \frac{2000}{2} = 1000 \text{ kg}$$

$F_1$ = Force on each bolt due to tendency of $P$ to produce moment about pivot $M$.

Taking moment about $M$

$$P \times (16 + 32) = 2 \times F_1(32 - 8)$$

$$2000 \times 48 = 2F_1 \times 24$$

$$F_1 = 2000 \text{ kg}$$

Total load on each bolt

$$= F + F_1 = 1000 + 2000$$

$$= 3000 \text{ kg}$$

Let $d_c$ = Core diameter to bolt

$$\frac{\pi}{4} d_c^2 \times 600 = 3000$$

$$d_c = 2.52 \text{ cm}$$

$d$ = Nominal diameter of bolt

Using coarse threads, we adopt

$d$ = 30 mm (From Table 8.2)

**Example 8.16.** *(a) A pulley bracket is supported by 4 bolts as shown in Fig. 8.42. The load applied is 20 kN and weight of pulley and bracket is 1 kN. Determine the size of bolts. Safe stress in bolts is 40 N/mm$^2$.*

**Solution.** $P$ = Load applied = 20 kN

$W$ = Weight of pulley and bracket

$F$ = Total load = $P + W = 20 \times 2 + 1 = 41$ kN

$n$ = Number of bolts = 4

$F_S$ = Direct shear load on each bolt

$$= \frac{F}{n} = \frac{41}{4} = 10.25 \text{ kN.}$$

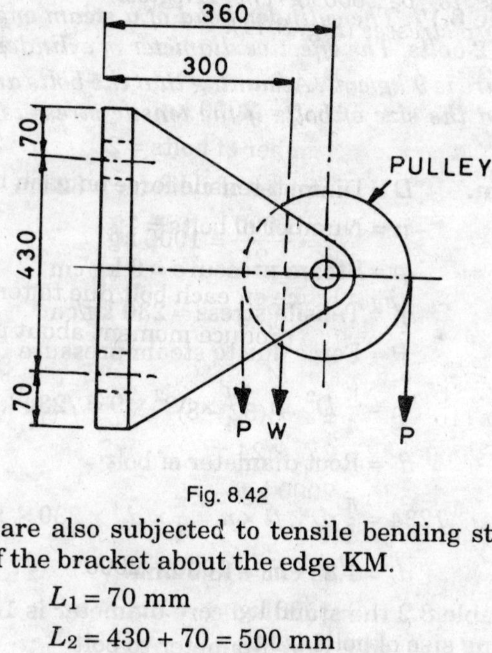


Fig. 8.42

The bolts are also subjected to tensile bending stress due to tilting effect of the bracket about the edge KM.

$L_1$ = 70 mm

$L_2$ = 430 + 70 = 500 mm

$F_1$ = Load on each of bolt at the top

$$= \frac{(W \times 300 + 2 \times P \times 360) \times 500}{2(L_1^2 + L_2^2)}$$

$$= \frac{(1 \times 300 + 2 \times 20 \times 360) \times 500}{2\,(70^2 + 500^2)} = 14.4 \text{ kN}$$

$F_e$ = Equivalent shear load

$$= \frac{1}{2}\sqrt{F_1^2 + 4F_s^2}$$

$$= \frac{1}{2}\sqrt{14.4^2 + 4 \times 10.25^2} = 12.5 \text{ kN}$$

$\sigma$ = Safe stress in bolt = 40 N/mm$^2$

$d$ = Diameter of bolt

$$F_e = \frac{\pi}{4} d^2 \cdot \sigma$$

$$12.5 \times 10^3 = \frac{\pi}{4} d^2 \times 40$$

$d$ = 20 mm.

**Example 8.17.** *The cylinder head of a steam engine is held in position by 12 bolts. The effective diameter of cylinder is 32 cm and steam pressure is 9 kg/cm$^2$. Assuming that the bolts are not initially stressed, find the size of bolts if the tensile stress is not to exceed 230 kg/cm$^2$.*

**Solution.** $D$ = Diameter of cylinder = 32 cm

$n$ = Number of bolts = 12

$p$ = Steam pressure = 9 kg/cm$^2$

$f_t$ = Tensile stress = 230 kg/cm$^2$

$P$ = Force due to steam pressure

$$= \frac{\pi}{4} D^2 \cdot p = \frac{\pi}{4} \times 32^2 \times 9 = 7234 \text{ kg}$$

Let $d_c$ = Root diameter of bolt

$$7234 = \frac{\pi}{4} d_c^2 \cdot ft \times n = \frac{\pi}{4} \times d_c^2 \times 230 \times 12$$

$d_c$ = 1.83 cm = 18.3 mm.

From Table 8.2 the standard core diameter is 18.933 mm and corresponding size of bolts is $M_{22}$.

**Example 8.18.** *The cylinder head of a steam engine is subjected to a steam pressure of 0.8 N/mm$^2$ and is held in position by means of 10 bolts. A soft copper gasket is used to make the joint leak proof.*

*The effective diameter of cylinder is 320 mm. If the stress in bolts is not to exceed N/cm$^2$ find the size of bolts.*

**Solution.** Let, $D$ = Diameter of cylinder = 320 mm

$p$ = Steam pressure = 0.8 N/mm$^2$

$R$ = Steam force

$= \frac{\pi}{4} D^2 . p = \frac{\pi}{4} \times 320^2 \times 0.8$

= 64307 N

$P$ = External load on each bolt

$= \frac{R}{n}$ where $n$ = Number of bolts

$= \frac{64307}{10} = 6430.7$ N

$P_1$ = Initial tension due to tightening of bolt

= 2840 $d$, where $d$ = Nominal diameter of bolt

$P$ = Resultant axial load on the bolt

$= P_1 + KP_2$

where $k$ = Constant = 0.5 (say)

$P = (2840\, d + 0.5 \times 6430.7)$ N

Let $d_c$ = Core diameter of bolt

$f_t$ = Tensile stress = 120 N/mm$^2$

$P = \frac{\pi}{4} d_c^2 . f_t$

$$2840\, d + 0.5 \times 6430.7 = \frac{\pi}{4} d_c^2 \times 120 \quad ...(1)$$

Let $d_c = 0.84\, d$

Substituting this in equation (1) we get

$$2840\, d + 0.5 \times 6430.7 = \frac{\pi}{4} (d \times 0.84)^2 \times 120.$$

$$2840\, d + 3215.35 = 66.46\, d^2$$

Solving this quadratic equation we get

$d = 49.8$

Therefore size of bolt is M 50.

**Example 8.19.** *Calculate the bending stress induced in a M 20 bolt that should hold two plates together having a combined thickness of 8.5 cm and are so placed that the gap x as in Fig. 8.42 is 0.03 cm. Given* **E** $= 2 \times 10^6$ *kg/cm*$^2$.

**Solution.** $\sigma_b$ = Bending stress $= \dfrac{x \,.\, E}{2L}$

where $x$ = Gap = 0.03 cm

$L$ = Effective length of shank of bolt

= 5.8 cm

$$\sigma_b = \frac{0.03 \times 2 \times 10^6}{2 \times 5.8} = 5172 \text{ kg/cm}^2.$$

This shows that bending stress produced is very high. Therefore it is very important to have outside surface true to reduce the bending stress.

**Example 8.20.** *Determine the diameter of the fastening bolt for a pulley block shown in Fig. 8.43. The maximum load to be lifted by the pulley is 2000 kg. The bolt is made of C15 mild steel having a yield stress of 24 kg/mm².*

**Solution.** The bolt is subjected to tensile load.

Let, factor of safety = 2

$\sigma_y$ = Yield stress

$\sigma_t$ = Safe tensile stress $= \dfrac{\sigma_y}{2} = \dfrac{24}{2}$

= 12 kg/mm².

Let $d_c$ = Root diameter of bolt

$d$ = Nominal diameter of bolt

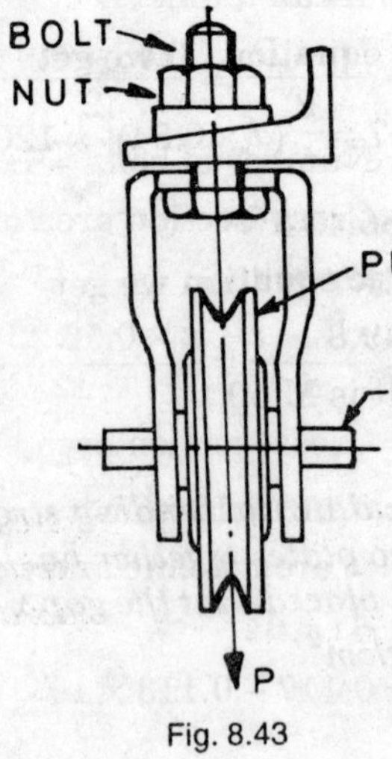


Fig. 8.43

$$P = \text{Tensile load} = 2000 \text{ kg}$$

$$P = \frac{\pi}{4} d_c^2 \cdot \sigma_t$$

$$2000 = \frac{\pi}{4} \cdot d_c^2 \times 12$$

$$d_c = 14.57$$

From Table 8.2 we select $d = 18$

Bolt size $= M18 \times 2.5$.

**Example 8.21.** *The lid of a cast iron pressure vessel is kept in position by twelve M 12 steel bolts having an initial tightening load of 24 kN when the vessel is at 23°C and the initial pressure is atmospheric. Find the load in each bolt :*

*(a) When pressure is increased to 1.5 MPa.*

*(b) When the vessel is heated to 124°C with atmospheric internal pressure.*

*(c) When the vessel is heated to 124°C with an internal pressure of 1.5 MPa.*

*Take E for steel = 208 GPa*

*E for Cast iron = 84 GPa*

*E for zinc = 84 GPa*

*Linear co-efficient* ($\alpha$) *for steel* $= 12 \times 10^{-6}/°K$, *for cast iron* $= 10 \times 10^{-6}/°K$ *and for zinc* $= 30 \times 10^{-6}/°K$.

**Solution.** *(a)* $D_m$ = Mean diameter of flange

$$= \frac{D_1 + D_2}{2} = \frac{0.48 + 0.64}{2} = 0.56 \text{ m}$$

$n$ = Number of bolts = 12

$A_1$ = Cross–section area of flange and zinc gasket per bolt

$$= \frac{\pi D_m \cdot t}{n} = \frac{\pi \times 0.56 \times 0.08}{12} = 0.0117 \text{ m}^2$$

$A_2$ = Cross–section area of M12 bolt

$$= 0.113 \times 10^{-3} \text{ m}^2$$

$A$ = Net area of zinc and cast iron flange per bolt

$$= A_1 - A_2$$

$$= 0.117 - 0.113 \times 10^{-3} = 0.0115 \text{ m}^2$$

Now $\frac{\text{Stress}}{\text{Strain}} = E$

$$\text{Stress} = \text{Strain} \times E$$

$$\frac{P}{A} = \frac{\Delta L}{L} \times E$$

$$\frac{\Delta L}{P} = \frac{L}{AE} = \text{Deflection per } N \text{ of load}$$

$$t = 28,\ t_1 = 7 \text{ mm}$$

For zinc, $\frac{L}{AE} = \frac{t_1}{A \times E}$

$$= \frac{7 \times 10^{-3}}{0.115 \times 84 \times 10^{9}} = 7.42 \times 10^{-12} \text{ m/N}$$

$(1 \text{ GPa} = 10^{8} \text{ N/m}^2)$

For cast iron, $\frac{L}{AE} = \frac{t}{A \,.\, E}$

$$= \frac{56 \times 10^{-3}}{0.0115 \times 84 \times 10^{-9}} = 58 \times 10^{-12} \text{ m/N}$$

For bolt, $\frac{L}{AE} = \frac{63 \times 10^{-3}}{0.113 \times 10^{-3} \times 208 \times 10^{9}}$

$$= 2.68 \times 10^{-9} \text{ m/N}$$

$m$ = Sum of deflection of bolted members

$$= 7.42 \times 10^{-12} + 58 \times 10^{-12}$$

$$= 65.42 \times 10^{-12} \text{ m/N}$$

$b$ = Deflection of bolt

$$= 2.61 \times 10^{-9} \text{ m/N}$$

$$\frac{m}{m+b} = \frac{65.42 \times 10^{-12}}{65.42 \times 10^{-12} + 2.68 \times 10^{-9}}$$

$$= 2.36 \times 10^{-2}$$

$p$ = Fluid pressure

$$= 1.5 \text{ MPa} = 1.5 \times 10^{6} \text{ N/m}^2$$

$P_2$ = Load per bolt due to fluid pressure

$$= \frac{\frac{\pi}{4} D_1^2 + p}{n} = \frac{\frac{\pi}{4} (0.48)^2 \times (1.5) \times 10^{6}}{12}$$

$$= 2.26 \times 10^{4} \text{ N}$$

$$P_1 = \text{Initial tightening load}$$
$$= 24 \text{ kN} = 24000 \text{ N}$$
$$P = \text{Total load}$$
$$= P_1 + \frac{m}{m+b} \cdot P_2$$
$$= 24000 + 2.36 \times 10^{-2} \times 2.26 \times 10^4$$
$$= 24228 \text{ N} = 24.228 \text{ kN}$$

(*b*) The increase in length due to temperature change is found as follows,

For zinc, $\Delta L = \alpha \cdot L \cdot \Delta T$

$$= 30 \times 10^{-6} \times 7 \times 10^{-3} \times 101$$
$$= 2.12 \times 10^{-5} \text{ m}$$

For C.I., $\Delta L = \alpha \cdot L \cdot \Delta T$

$$= 10 \times 10^{-6} \times 2 \times 0.028 \times 101$$
$$= 5.65 \times 10^{-5} \text{ m}$$

For bolt, $\Delta L = \alpha \cdot L \cdot \Delta T$

$$= 12 \times 10^{-6} \times 63 \times 10^{-3} \times 101$$
$$= 7.63 \times 10^{-5} \text{ m}$$
$$\Delta L_1 = (\Delta L)_{zinc} + (\Delta L)_{CI.}$$
$$= 2.12 \times 10^{-5} + 5.65 \times 10^{-5}$$
$$= 7.67 \times 10^{-5} \text{ m}$$

$\Delta L_2$ = Total increase in length of bolt

= Increase in length due to load + Increase in length due to temperature change

$$= \frac{(P_3 - P_1) \cdot L}{AE} + 7.36 \times 10^{-5}$$

where $P_3$ = New initial load on bolt

$$\Delta L_2 = \frac{(P_3 - 24000) \times 63 \times 10^{-3}}{0.113 \times 10^{-9} \times 208 \times 10^9} + 7.36 \times 10^{-5}$$
$$= (2.68 \times 10^{-3})(P_3 - 24000) + 7.36 \times 10^{-5}$$

$\Delta L_3$ = Total increase in length of zinc and C.I. flanges due to load $P_3$

$$= \frac{(P_3 - 24000) \times 63 \times 10^{-3}}{0.0115 \times 84 \times 10^9} + \Delta L_1$$

$$\Delta L_3 = (P_3 - 24000) \times 65.2 \times 10^{-12} + 7.67 \times 10^{-5}$$

Now $\Delta L_2 = \Delta L_3$

$$2.68 \times 10^{-9}(P_3 - 24000) = 65.2 \times 10^{-12}(P_3 - 24000) + 7.67 \times 10^{-5} + 7.36 \times 10^{-5}$$

Solving we get $P_3 = 24900\ N$

This is the new initial load on bolt.

(c) Resultant load $= P_3 \dfrac{m}{m+b} \times P_2$

$$= 24900 + 2.36 \times 10^{-2} \times 2.26 \times 10^4 = 25433 \text{ N.}$$

**Example 8.22.** *The cylinder head of a steam engine is subjected to a steam pressure of 16 kg/cm² and is held in position by 10 bolts. The diameter of cylinder is 32 cm. The bolts have a yield stress of 3200 kg/cm² and an endurance limit of 2200 kg/cm². The bolts are tightened with an initial preload of 1.4 times that of steam load. A soft copper gasket is used to make the joint leak proof. Assuming a stress concentration factor of 2.6 and a factor of safety 2 find the size of bolts.*

**Solution.** $D$ = Diameter of cylinder = 32 cm

$n$ = Number of bolts = 10

$P_2$ = Steam force per bolt

$$= \frac{\frac{\pi}{4} D^2 \,.\, P}{n}$$

where $p$ = Steam pressure $= \dfrac{\frac{\pi}{4} 32^2 \times 16}{10} = 1286$ kg

$P_1$ = Initial tightening load

$$= \frac{\frac{\pi}{4} D^2 \,.\, p \times 1.4}{n}$$

$$P_1 = \frac{\frac{\pi}{4} \times 32^2 \times 16 \times 1.5}{10}$$

= 1929 kg = Minimum load on each bolt

$P$ = Maximum load on bolt

$= P_1 + KP_2$

where $K = 0.5$ (say)

$$= 1929 + 0.5 \times 1286 = 2572 \text{ kg}$$

$P_{av}$ = Average load on bolt

$$= \frac{P + P_1}{2} = \frac{2572 + 1929}{2} = 2250.5 \text{ kg}$$

$P_v$ = Variable load on bolt

$$= \frac{P - P_1}{1} = \frac{2572 - 1929}{2} = 321.5 \text{ kg}$$

Let $d$ = Nominal diameter of bolt

$d_c$ = Core diameter of bolt

$A$ = Stress area of bolt $= \frac{\pi}{4} d_c^2$

$\sigma_{av}$ = Average stress on bolt

$$= \frac{P_{av}}{A} = \frac{2250.5}{A}$$

$\sigma_v$ = Variable stress on bolt

$$= \frac{P_v}{A} = \frac{321.5}{A}$$

$\sigma_e$ = Endurance limit = 2200 kg/cm$^2$

we know according to Soderberg criterion

$$\sigma_v = \sigma_c \times \left[\frac{1}{\text{F.S.}} - \frac{\sigma_{av}}{\sigma_y}\right]$$

where F.S. = Factor of safety

$\sigma_y$ = Yield stress

$$\frac{321.5}{A} = 2200\left[\frac{1}{2} - \frac{2250.5}{A \times 3200}\right]$$

Solving this equation, we get

$$A = 1.76 \text{ cm}^2$$

Now $A = \frac{\pi}{4} d_c^2$

$$1.76 = \frac{\pi}{4} d_c^2$$

$$d_c = 1.49 \text{ cm} = 14.9 \text{ mm.}$$

From Table 8.2 the bolt with this core diameter is M18.

**Example 8.23.** *An M12 steel bolt 240 mm long is subjected to an impact load and required to absorb a kinetic energy of 5 J.*

*Determine (a) Stress in the shank of bolt if there is no threaded portion between the nut and the bolt head.*

*(b) Stress in the shank of the area of the shank is reduced to that of root area of the threads. Take E = 210* GPa.

**Solution.** (*a*) $U$ = Energy of impact = 5 J

$A$ = Cross section area of M12 bolt

$$= \frac{\pi}{4} \times 12^2 = 113 \text{ mm}^2 = 0.113 \times 10^{-3} \text{ m}^2$$

$P$ = Impact load

$\delta$ = Extension

$$U = \frac{1}{2} . P . \delta = \frac{1}{2} . P . \left(\frac{PL}{AE}\right) = \frac{P^2L}{2AE}$$

$$P = \sqrt{\frac{2\,AEU}{L}}$$

$$= \sqrt{\frac{2 \times 0.113 \times 10^{-3} \times 210 \times 10^9 \times 5}{0.24}}$$

$$= 31.4 \times 10^3 \text{ N} = 31.4 \text{ kN}$$

$d_c$ = Root diameter

$$A_c = \text{Root area} = \frac{\pi}{4} \times 9.853^2 = 76.2 \text{ mm}^2$$

$$A_c = 76.2 \times 10^{-6} \text{ m}^2$$

$\sigma$ = Stress = $P/A$

$$= \frac{31.4 \times 10^3}{76.2 \times 10^{-6}} = 412 \times 10^6 \text{ N/m}^2 = 412 \text{ MPa}$$

This value has neglected stress concentration.

(*b*) When diameter of shank of bolt is reduced to root diameter.

$$A_c = \text{root area} = 76.2 \times 10^{-6} \text{ m}^2$$

Using this value of area we have

$$P = \sqrt{\frac{2\,A_C\,.\,E\,.\,U}{L}}$$

$$= \sqrt{\frac{2 \times 76.2 \times 10^{-6} \times 210 \times 10^6 \times 5}{0.24}}$$

$$= 25.8 \times 10^3 \text{ N} = 25.8 \text{ kN}$$

$$\sigma = \frac{25.8 \times 10^3}{AC} = \frac{25.8 \times 10^3}{76.2 \times 10^{-6}}$$

$$= 338.5 \times 10^6 \text{ N/m}^2 = 338.5 \text{ MPa}.$$

**Example 8.24.** *A 26 mm single start square threaded screw with pitch 5 mm is 380 mm long between the nut and collar. It is subjected to an axial load of 30 kN. The coefficient of friction between the screw and nut is 0.14. The yield stress is 360 MPa. Determine factor of safety.*

**Solution.** $D$ = Out side dia of threads

$D_c$ = Core (Root) diameter of threads

$p$ = Pitch

$$D = D_c + p$$

$$26 = D_c + 5$$

$$D_c = 21 \text{ mm}$$

$D_m$ = Mean diameter

$$= \frac{D + D_c}{2} = \frac{26 + 21}{2} = 23.5 \text{ mm}$$

$$R_m = \text{Mean radius} = \frac{D_m}{2}$$

$\alpha$ = Thread angle

$$\tan \alpha = \frac{p}{\pi D_m} = \frac{5}{\pi \times 23.5}$$

$$\alpha = 4.04^\circ$$

$\mu$ = Coefficient of friction between screw and nut

$= 0.14$

$\phi$ = Friction angle

$$\tan \phi = \mu = 0.14$$

$$\phi = 7.97$$

$p$ = Force = 30 kN

$T$ = Torque

$$= P.R_m \tan(\alpha + \phi)$$

$$= 30000 \times \frac{23.5}{2} \tan(4.04 + 7.97)$$

$$= 70875 \text{ N mm}$$

$f_s$ = Shear stress

$$= \frac{16 \, . \, T}{\pi \, . \, D_c^3} = \frac{16 \times 70875}{\pi \times 21^3}$$

$$= 39 \text{ MPa}$$

$L$ = Length of screw

$= 380$

$K$ = Radius of gyration

$$= \frac{D_c}{4} = \frac{21}{4}$$

$\frac{L}{K}$ = Slenderness ratio

$$= \frac{380 \times 4}{21} = 72.4$$

This is actual value of $\frac{L}{K}$.

$f_y$ = Yield stress

Find $\frac{L}{K}$ using the following relation.

$$\frac{L}{K} = \sqrt{\frac{2\,C\,\pi^2\,E}{f_y}}$$

$$= \sqrt{\frac{2 \times 1 \times \pi^2 \times 2 \times 10^5}{360}} = 109$$

This calculated value is more than actual value 72.4. So following J.B. Johnson relation is used to find the compressive stress.

$\delta_c$ = Compressive stress

$$= \frac{P}{A} \times \frac{1}{\left[\dfrac{1 - f_y \, . \left(\dfrac{L}{K}\right)^2}{4C\,\pi^2\,E}\right]}$$

where $C$ = Constant

It depends on end conditions.

$C = 1$ (assume)

$$A = \text{Area} = \frac{\pi}{4} D_c^2$$

$$\sigma_C = \frac{30000 \times 4}{\pi \times (21)^2} \times \left[ \frac{1}{\dfrac{1 - 360\ (72.4)^2}{(4 \times 1 \times \pi^2 \times 2 \times 10^5}} \right]$$

$$= 112.4 \text{ MPa}$$

$$f_{max} = \text{maximum shear stress}$$

$$= \frac{1}{2} \sqrt{\sigma_c{}^2 + 4.f_s{}^2}$$

$$= \frac{1}{2} \sqrt{(112.4)^2 + 4 \times 39^2}$$

$$= 66 \text{ MPa}$$

$$f_{ys} = \text{Yield shear stress}$$

$$= \frac{f_y}{2} = \frac{360}{2} = 180$$

$$n = \text{Factor of safety}$$

$$= \frac{f_{ys}}{f_{max}} = \frac{180}{66}$$

$$= 2.72.$$

**Example 8.25.** *A triple start square theraded screw is used to raise a load of 48kN. The nominal diameter of the screw is 52 mm and the pitch is 6 mm. Height of nut is 42 mm and coefficient of friction between the screw and the nut is 0.14 and there is no collar friction. Determine*

(*a*) *Maximum shear stress induced in the screw*

(*b*) *Transverse shear stress induced in the screw and nut threads*

(*c*) *Bearing pressure between the screw and the nut*

**Solution.**

Let $D$ = Nominal diameter of screw

$= 52$ mm

$p$ = Pitch

$= 6$ mm

$D_c$ = Core or root diameter screw threads

$$D = D_c + p$$

$$52 = D_c + 6$$

$$D_c = 46 \text{ mm}$$

$D_m$ = Mean diameter of screw threads

$$= \frac{D + D_c}{2} = \frac{52 + 46}{2} = 49 \text{ mm}$$

$\alpha$ = Thread angle

$$\tan \alpha = \frac{3p}{\pi D_m} \text{ as it is triple start} = \frac{3 \times 6}{\pi \times 49}$$

$$\alpha = 6.67^\circ$$

$\mu$ = Coefficient of friction = 0.14

$\phi$ = Friction angle

$$\tan \phi = \mu = 0.14$$

$$\phi = 7.96^\circ$$

$P$ = Load = 48 kN

$T$ = Torque to overcome friction

$$= P . \frac{D_m}{2} \tan (\alpha + \phi)$$

$$= 48000 \times \frac{49}{2} \tan (6.67 + 7.96) = 305760 \text{ N mm}$$

$f_s$ = Shear stress

$$= \frac{16\, T}{\pi D_c^3} = \frac{16 \times 305760}{\pi \times 46^3} = 16 \text{ MPa}$$

$\sigma_c$ = Compressive stress

$$= \frac{P}{\frac{\pi}{4} D_c^2} = \frac{\frac{48000}{\pi}}{4} \times 46^2$$

$$= 28.9 \text{ MPa}$$

$f_{sm}$ = Maximum shear stress

$$= \frac{1}{2} \sqrt{\sigma_c^2 + 4 f_s^2} = \frac{1}{2} \sqrt{28.9^2 + 4 \times 16^2}$$

$$= 21.5 \text{ MPa}$$

$$= \frac{\text{Height of nut}}{\text{Pitch}} = \frac{42}{6} = 7$$

$p_b$ = Bearing pressure = $\frac{P}{A}$

$$= \frac{P}{\frac{\pi}{4} (D^2 - D_c^2) \times \eta} = \frac{48000}{\frac{\pi}{4} (52^2 - 46^2) \times 7}$$

$$= 14.85 \text{ MPa}$$

$$t = \text{Thickness of thread} = \frac{p}{2} = \frac{6}{2} = 3 \text{ mm}$$

$$f_{st} = \text{Transverse shear stress in screw}$$

$$= \frac{P}{\pi D_c \, . \, t \, . \, \eta} = \frac{48000}{\pi \times 46 \times 3 \times 7} = 15.82 \text{ MPa.}$$

**Example 8.26.** *A cast iron cylinder is fastened to a cylinder of bore 480 mm with 6 stud bolts. The maximum pressure inside the cylinder is 2.3 MPa. The stiffness of part is three times the stiffness of bolt. Determine the initial tightening load so that the joint is leak-proof.*

**Solution.**

$$n = \text{Number of bolts} = 6$$

$$\delta = \text{Maximum pressure}$$

$$= 2.3 \text{ MPa}$$

$$D = \text{Bore size}$$

$$= 480 \text{ mm}$$

$$P = \text{Force}$$

$$= \frac{\pi}{4} D^2 \times \sigma = \frac{\pi}{4} \times 480^2 \times 2.3 = 416 \times 10^3 \text{ N}$$

$$F_o = \text{Load per bolt} = \frac{P}{\eta} = \frac{416 \times 10^3}{4}$$

$$= 69.3 \times 10^3 \text{ N}$$

$$K_p = \text{Stiffness of the part}$$

$$K_b = \text{Stiffness of the bolt}$$

$$K_p = 2\, K_b$$

$$F_i = \text{Initial tightening load}$$

$$= F_o \left( \frac{K_p}{K_p + K_b} \right) = F_o \left( \frac{3\, K_b}{3\, K_b + K_b} \right)$$

$$= F_o \left( \frac{3}{3+1} \right) = 69.3 \times 10^3 \times \frac{3}{4} = 52 \times 10^3 \text{ N}$$

**Example 8.27.** *Fig. 8.43.1 shows a part attached to the support by means of a bolt and subjected to load P. The bolt is M 10 × 1.5 having stress area 58 mm². The bolt material has a yield stress of 320 N/mm² and endurance limit of 200 N/mm². The stress concentration factor for the threads is 3.6. The load continuously fluc-*

*tuates between zero and 8 kN. The steel part has a net area of 280 mm$^2$. Determine.*

*(a) Factor of safety for the bolt when no initial force is present.*

*(b) The minimum required value of initial tightening force to prevent loss of compression in the part.*

*(c) The factor of safety for the bolt when initial tightening force exists.*

*(d) Minimum force in the part for the given loading and initial tightening force.*

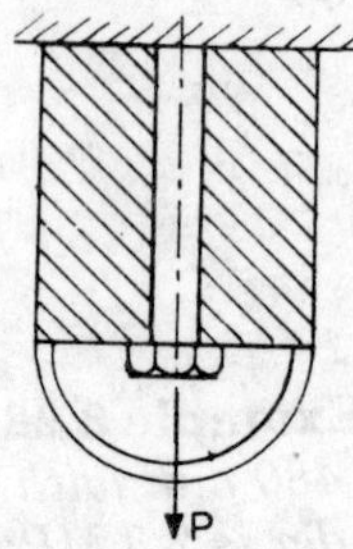


Fig. 8.43.1

**Solution.**

(a)
$$P_m = \text{Mean load} = \frac{0+8}{2} = 4 \text{ kN}$$

$$P_a = \text{Alternating load} = 4 \text{ kN}$$

$$A = \text{Bolt stress area} = 58 \text{ mm}^2$$

$$\sigma_m = \text{Mean stress} = \frac{P_m}{A} = \frac{4 \times 10^3}{58} = 69 \text{ N/mm}^2$$

$$\sigma_a = \text{Alternating stress}$$

$$= \frac{P_a}{A} = \frac{4 \times 10^3}{58} = 69 \text{ N/mm}^2$$

$$K_t = \text{Stress concentration factor} = 3.6$$

$$K_t \times \sigma_a = 69 \times 3.6 = 248.4 \text{ N/mm}^2$$

Plotting $\sigma_m$ and $K_t \times \sigma_a$ in Fig. 8.43 (*a*), it is observed that bolt loading is unsafe.

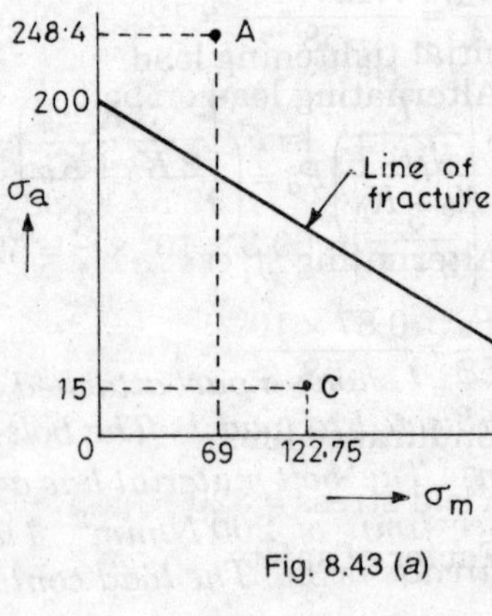


Fig. 8.43 (*a*)

(b)

$K_p$ = Stiffness of part

$K_b$ = Stiffness of bolt

$A_1$ = Gross area of bolt

$$= \frac{\pi}{4}(10)^2 = 78.54 \text{ mm}^2$$

$A_s$ = Net area of steel part = 280 mm$^2$

$F_i$ = Initial tightening force

$$= \left(\frac{K_p}{K_p + K_b}\right) P_{max}$$

where $P_{max}$ = Maximum force

= 8 kN

$L$ = Length of bolt

= Length of part.

For bodies of equal length and modulic the spring constants (stiffness) are proportional to the cross-sectional area

$$F_1 = \left(\frac{A_s}{A_1 + A_s}\right) \times P_{max} = \left(\frac{280}{78.54 + 280}\right) \times 8$$

$$= 6.25 \text{ kN}$$

(c)

$P_1$ = Average bolt load

$$= P_{m.}\left(\frac{K_b}{K_b + K_p}\right) + F_i = 4\left[\frac{78.54}{78.54 + 280}\right] + 6.25$$

$$= 7.12 \text{ kN}$$

$\sigma_1$ = Average stress in bolt

$$= \frac{P_1}{A} = \frac{7.12 \times 10^3}{58} = 122.75 \text{ N/mm}^2$$

$P_2$ = Alternating load on bolt

$$= \left(\frac{K_b}{K_b + K_p}\right) P_a = \left(\frac{78.54}{78.54 + 280}\right) \times 4 = 0.87 \text{ kN}$$

$\sigma_2$ = Alternating stress in bolt

$$= \frac{P_2}{58} = \frac{0.87 \times 10^3}{58} = 15 \text{ N/mm}^2$$

$\sigma_e$ = Endurance limit = 200 N/mm$^2$

$\delta_y$ = Yield stress = 320 N/mm$^2$

$N$ = Factor of safety

$$\frac{\sigma_y}{N} = \delta_1 + \left[\frac{K_t \cdot \sigma_y}{\sigma_e}\right] \times \sigma_2$$

$$\frac{320}{N} = 122.75 + \left[\frac{3.6 \times 320}{200}\right] \times 15$$

$$N = 1.3$$

(*d*) $P_{min}$ = Minimum force on the part

$$= \left[\frac{K_p}{K_p + K_b}\right] P_{\max} - F_i$$

$$= \left[\frac{280}{280 + 78.54}\right] \times 8 - 6.25$$

$$= -0.01 \text{ kN.}$$

## PROBLEMS

**8.1.** Sketch and discuss the following types of threads.

(*a*) Square thread, (*b*) Buttress thread
(*c*) Acme thread (*d*) Knuckle thread
(*e*) Metric thread.

**8.2.** Write short notes on the following :

(*a*) Through bolts (*b*) Studs
(*c*) Cap screws (*d*) Machine screws
(*e*) Set screws.

**8.3.** Sketch and discuss the following :

(*a*) Eye bolt (*b*) Boiler stays
(*c*) Power screws.

**8.4.** Define the efficiency of the following :

(*a*) Compound screw (*b*) Differential screw.

**8.5.** A square threaded transmission screw used in a jack has a root diameter of 50 mm and a load of 18 mm. It is triple threaded and is designed to lift a load of 8000 kg. The coefficient of friction is assumed to be 0.14. Determine the following :

(*a*) Pitch of screw
(*b*) Mean radius of screw
(*c*) Efficiency
(*d*) Unit compressive stress in screw
(*e*) Unit shear stress at the thread if there are 12 threads in the nut.
(*f*) Bearing pressure on the projected area of the threads in contact.
(*g*) Is the screw self locking.

**8.6.** What horse power can be transmitted by two 15 mm set screws employed in a pulley installation if the rotative speed of the pulley is 250 R.P.M. and diameter of shaft is 62 mm.

**8.7.** Two bolts are used to fasten a crane runway bracket as shown in Fig. 8.44. Determine the size of bolts if the design stress in bolt material is 500 kg/cm$^2$.

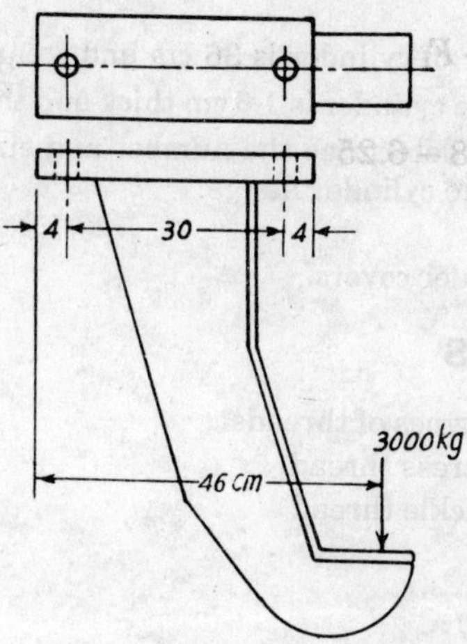


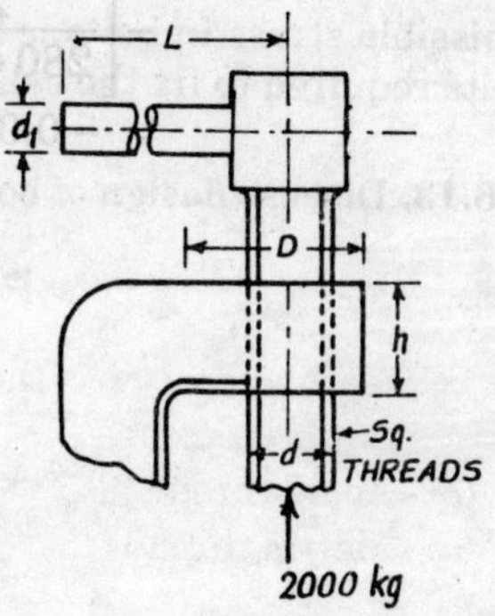


Fig. 8.44 Fig. 8.45

**8.8.** A pillar crane is used to lift a load of 5700 kg by arm of crane which is 80 cm long. The pillar crane has a circular base 58 cm in diameter and is secured to a concrete base by four bolts equally spaced on a bolt circle of 48 cm diameter. Calculate the size of bolts if the stress is not to exceed 600 kg/cm$^2$.

**8.9.** Fig. 8.45 shows the screw of a small hand punch. If the maximum force required for punching is 2000 kg determine the size $D$, $d$, $d_1$, $h$ and $L$ if the punch is operated by one man. The following data are supplied :

Coefficient of thread friction = 0.13.

Coefficient of collar friction = 0.11.

Bearing pressure for the threads = 160 kg/cm$^2$.

Safe stress in tension and compression in screw and handle = 700 kg/cm$^4$

Safe stress in shear in screw and handle = 400 kg/cm$^2$.

Collar diameter = 3.7 cm.

**8.10.** A square threaded screw 30 mm. Core diameter has on efficiency of 72% when raising a weight of 2000 kg. The coefficient of friction for the threads is 0.11 with collar friction negligible. Find the torque that the brake mounted on the screw should exert when the load is being lowered at a uniform rate.

**8.11.** Name the usual materials used for screw and nut of screw and nut of screw jack.

**8.12.** In a steam engine the diameter of cylinder is 36 cm and steam pressure in the cylinder is 16 kg/cm$^2$. If the cylinder is 1.6 cm thick and the permissible stress in bolts is 280 kg/cm$^2$, determine the number and size of bolts required to fix the cylinder cover to cylinder flange.

**8.13.** Discuss design of bolts for cylinder covers.

# 9

# Springs

## 9.0 Introduction

A spring is an elastic body whose primary function is to deflect or distort under load. When the load is removed, the spring recovers its original shape. Springs are quite commonly used in watches, valves, railway carriages, motor-cars etc. The important functions of springs according to their uses are as follows :

(*i*) To absorb the energy of suddenly applied loads.

(*ii*) To store and redistribute energy as in clock mechanisms.

(*iii*) To measure forces as in spring balances.

(*iv*) To exert forces or torques in mechanisms.

Springs frequently operate with high values for working stresses and with loads which are continuously varying.

## 9.1 Types of Springs

The various types of springs are as follows :

(*i*) **Helical Springs.** These springs are made of circular or non-circular wire coiled into a helical form, the load being applied along the axis of the helix. In a tension helical spring (Fig. 9.1)

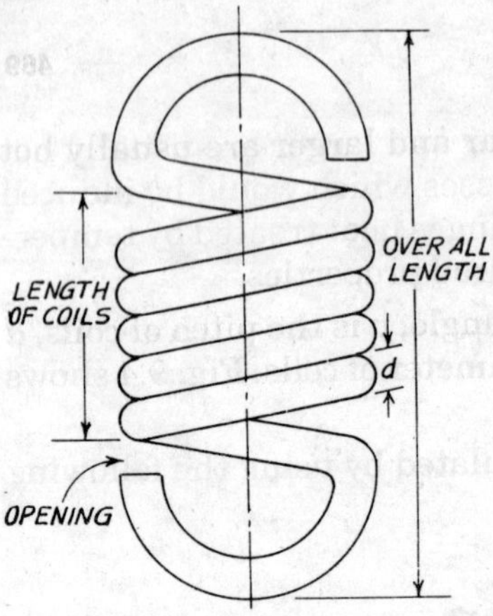


Fig. 9.1

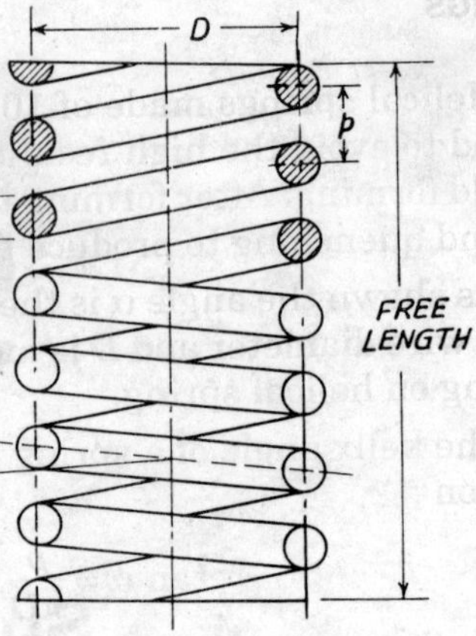


Fig. 9.2

the coils are close to each other where as in a compression helical spring the coils are separate from each other. In these springs the major stress is shear stress due to twisting. Fig. 9.2 shows helical compression spring of circular wire and Fig. 9.3 shows helical spring of rectangular wire.

The helical springs may be

(*i*) close-coiled ; and

(*ii*) open coiled.

If the helix angle is more than 5 degrees then the springs are usually called open coiled helical springs.

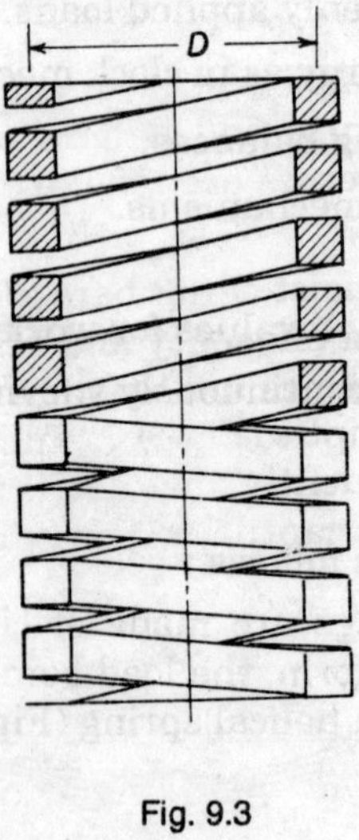


Fig. 9.3

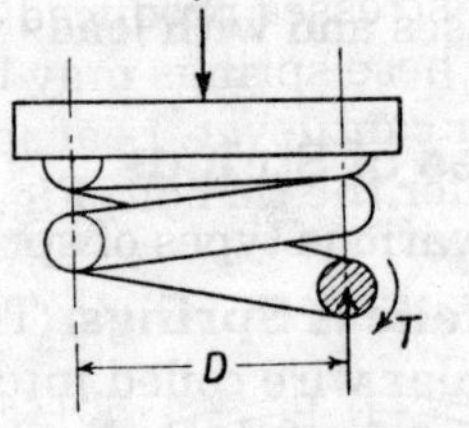


Fig. 9.4

Helical springs made of 10 mm bar and larger are usually hot wound to avoid the high residual stresses which would be induced by cold forming. After forming the spring is heat treated by tempering and quenching to produce the desired properties.

As shown the angle $\alpha$ is the helix angle, $p$ is the pitch of coils, $d$ is the wire diameter and $D$ is mean diameter of coils. Fig. 9.4 shows loading on helical spring.

The helix angle of a spring is calculated by using the following relation :

$$\tan \alpha = \frac{p}{\pi D}.$$

(*ii*) **Spiral springs.** These springs are made of flat strip wound in the form of spiral and loaded in torsion. In these springs the major stresses are tensile and compressive due to bending. Fig. 9.5 shows spiral spring.

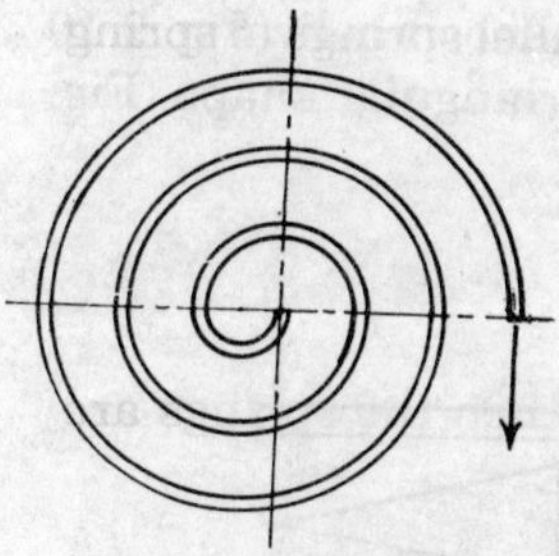

Fig. 9.5. Spiral spring.

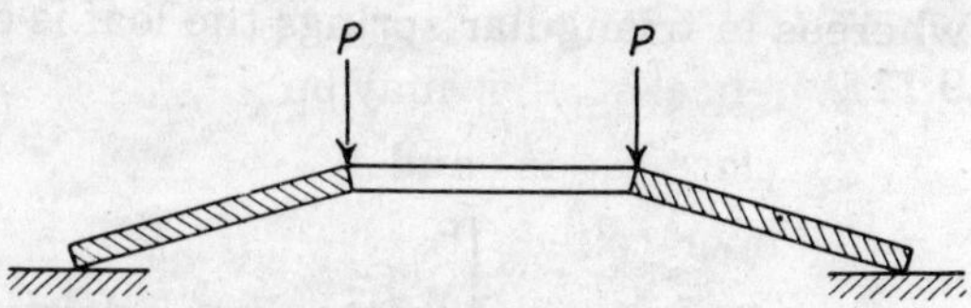


Fig. 9.6. Belliville spring.

(*iii*) **Belliville springs.** These springs consist of coned discs which may be stacked up to give a variety of load deflection characteristics. In these springs the major stresses are tensile and compressive. Fig. 9.6 shows belliville spring.

(*iv*) **Leaf springs.** These springs consist of flat bars of varying lengths clamped together so as to obtain efficiency and resilience. The major stresses produced in such springs are tensile and compressive. These springs may be semi-elliptic (Fig. 9.7), full elliptic (Fig. 9.8) or cantilever. Leaf springs frequently have a hole through the leaves for the tie bolt. Fig. 9.9 shows cantilever leaf spring.

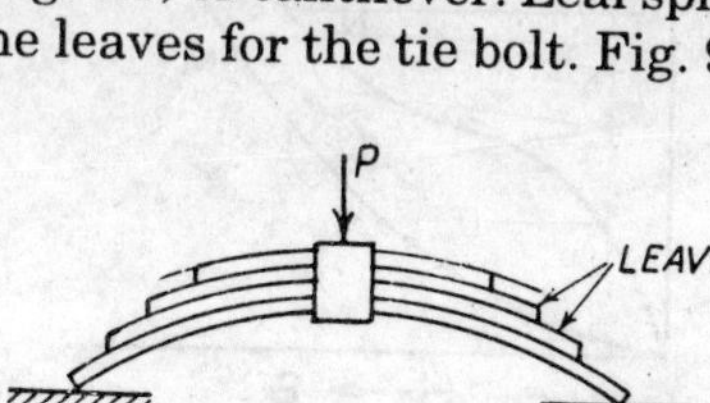


Fig. 9.7. Semielliptic spring.

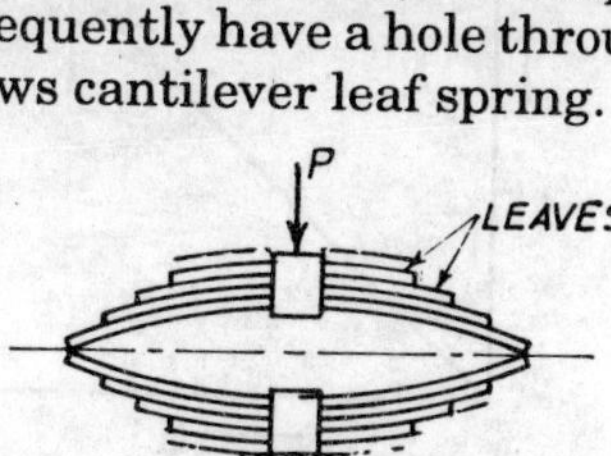


Fig. 9.8. Elliptic spring.

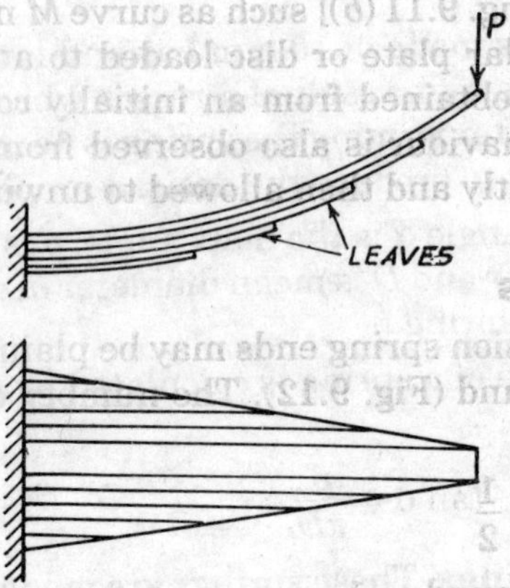


Fig. 9.9. Cantilever leaf spring.

(*v*) **Flat springs.** These springs may be parallel the triangular types. The leaf is of uniform width in flat parallel springs (Fig. 9.10 whereas in triangular springs the leaf is of triangular shape (Fig. 9.11).

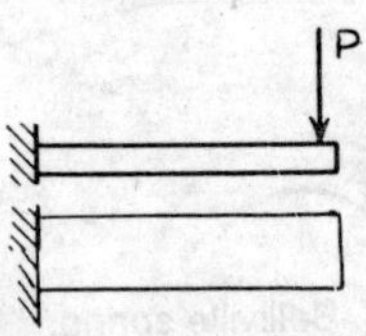


Fig. 9.10. Flat parallel spring.

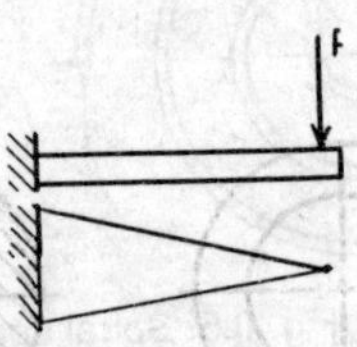

Fig. 9.11. Triangular spring.

### 9.1.1. Load Deflection (P -δ) Diagram.

The load deflection diagram is usually straight line if the material of the spring is not stressed beyond the elastic limit [see Fig. 9.11 (*a*)]. However in some cases load deflection diagram may

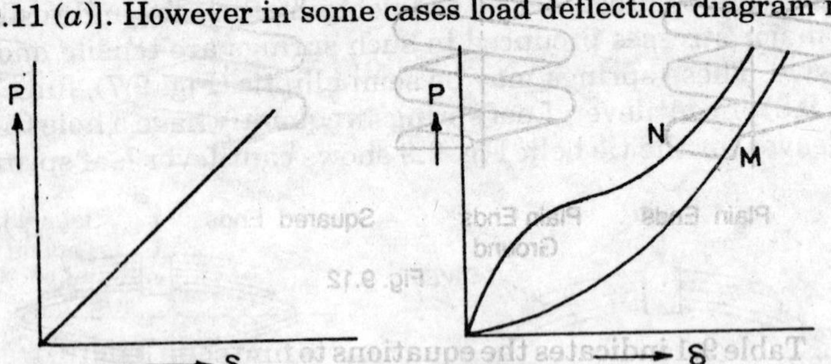


(a) (b)

Fig. 9.11

be as shown in [Fig. 9.11 (*b*)] such as curve *M* may be obtained with a thin, flat circular plate or disc loaded to a large deflection and curve *N* may be obtained from an initially coned disc (Belleville) springs. This behaviour is also observed from clock power spring when wóund tightly and then allowed to unwind.

## 9.2 Spring Ends

The compression spring ends may be plain, ground, squared or squared and ground (Fig. 9.12). The number of inactive turns are as follows :

Plain ends — $\frac{1}{2}$

Plain ends ground — 1

Square ends — 2

Square and ground ends — 2

Let $d$ = Wire diameter

$n$ = Number of active coils

$p$ = Pitch of coils

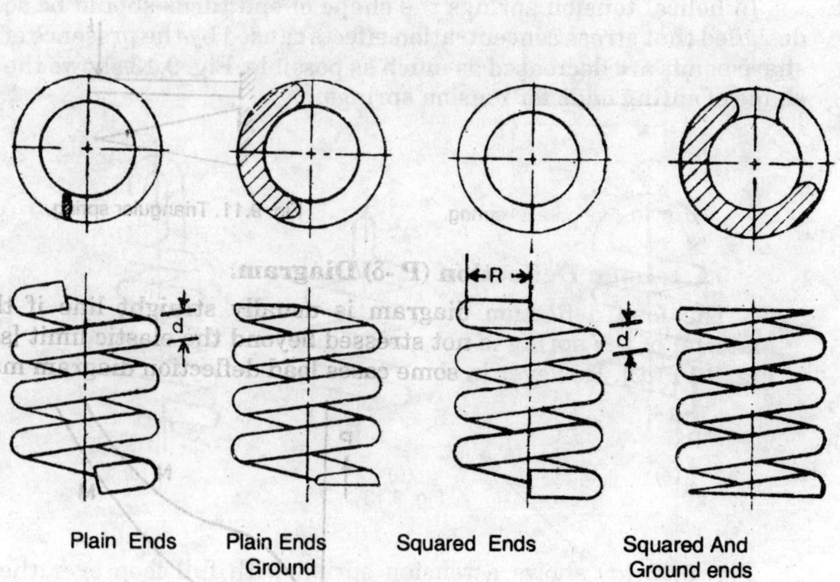


Fig. 9.12

Table 9.1 indicates the equations to find solid length, free length etc.

**Table 9.1**

| *Type of end* | *Actual number of turns* ($n_1$) | *Solid Length* | *Free Length* |
|---|---|---|---|
| Plain Ends | $n$ | $(n + 1) d$ | $np + d$ |
| Ground Ends | $n$ | $nd$ | $np$ |
| Square Ends | $n + 2$ | $(n + 3)d$ | $np + 3d$ |
| Square and ground | $n + 2$ | $(n + 2)d$ | $np + 2d$ |

The plain ends are most economical to produce. But in this case the spring gets bowed sideways and the loading deviates considerably from the axial loading and the stress produced on one side of the spring may be considerably higher than calculated.

Squared and ground ends provide axial loading where as maximum deviation from the axial loading is given by the squared end but left unground.

In helical tension springs the shape of end turns should be so designed that stress concentration effects caused by the presence of sharp bends are decreased as much as possible. Fig. 9.13 shows the shape of spring ends for tension springs.

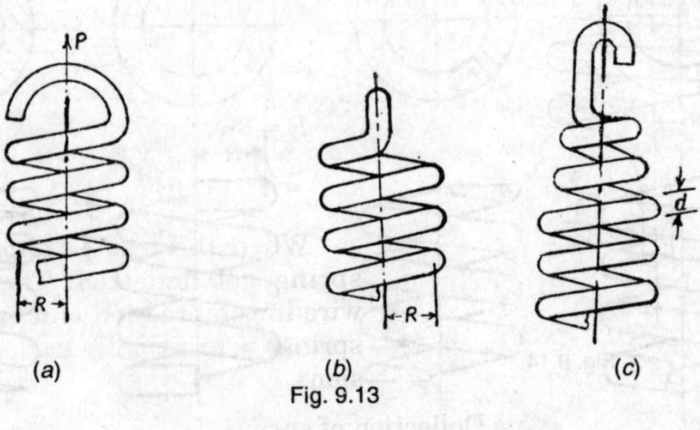


Fig. 9.13

Fig. 9.13 ($d$) shows a tension spring with full loop over the centre. The commonly used dimensions are as follows.

$$H = C$$
$$= \text{Inside coil diameter}$$

$$A = \frac{H}{3}, L = \frac{d}{n+1}$$

where $n$ = Number of turns in dimension $L$ between the points where loop begins and ends.

Number of active turns = $n + 1$

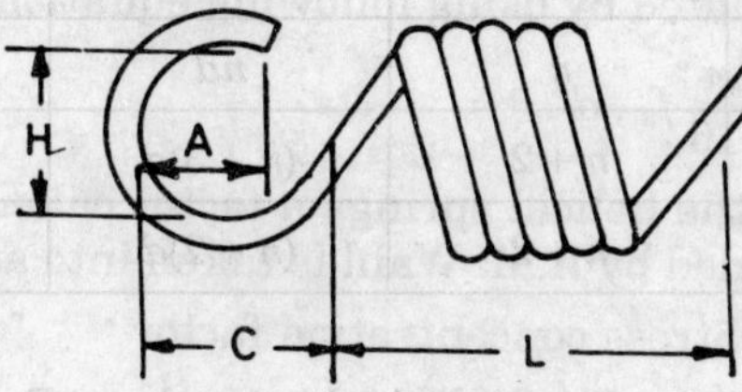


Fig. 9.13.(*d*)

## 9.3 Close Coiled Helical Spring Subjected to Axial Loading

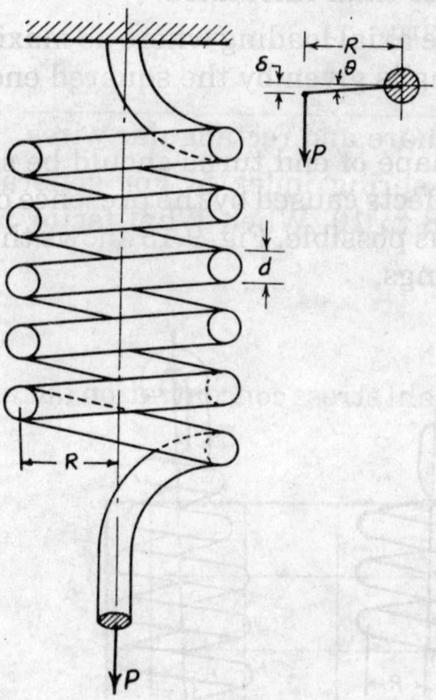


Fig. 9.14

Fig. 9.14 shows a close coiled helical spring made of circular wire and subjected to axial loading.

Let $P$ = Axial load

$d$ = Diameter of spring wire

$D$ = Mean diameter of coils

$n$ = Number of active coils

$r$ = Radius of wire

$= \frac{d}{2}$

$R$ = Mean radius of coils

$= \frac{D}{2}$.

When the load is applied the spring get deflected. The spring wire in compression and extension springs is principally loaded in torsion.

Let $\delta$ = Deflection of spring

$\theta$ = Angle of twist

$G$ = Modulus of rigidity

$f_s$ = Torsional shear stress induced in the wire

$$L = \text{Length of spring wire} = 2\pi R \,.\, n$$

**(i) Twisting Moment**

$T$ = Twisting moment on any section of spring $= P \times R$

The maximum value of shear stress (*f*) induced in the spring material can be calculated by using following equation

$$T = \frac{\pi}{16} f_s \,.\, d^3$$

While designing the helical springs a factor called stress concentration factor defined by A.M. Wahl is taken into account

$K$ = Stress concentration factor

$$= \frac{4C-1}{4C-4} + \frac{0.615}{C}$$

where $C$ = Spring index

$$= \frac{D}{d} \text{ for circular wire}$$

$$= \frac{D}{\text{Radial thickness of wire for square and rectangular wires}}$$

Clutch and valve springs have spring index 5. For general industrial uses the spring index is 8 to 10. When Whal factor is taken into account.

$$T = \frac{1}{K} \times \frac{\pi}{16} f_s \, d^3.$$

Fig. 9.15 shows the variation of Wahl stress concentration factor ($k$) with spring index ($C$).

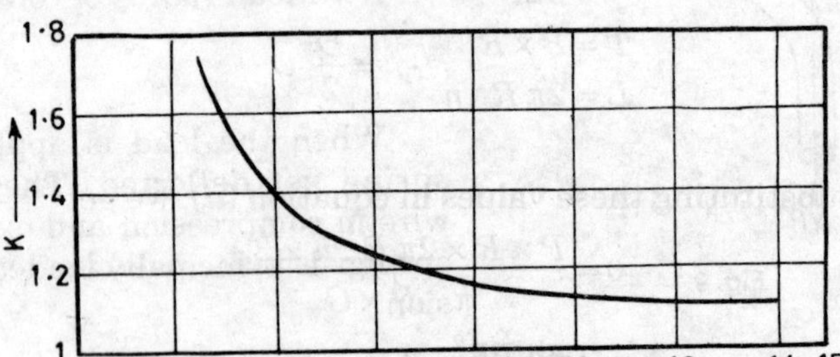


Fig. 9.15

For square and rectangular section wire springs, the spring index is defined as the ratio of mean diameter of coil ($D$) and radial thickness of wire.

Wahl stress concentration factor is a correction factor due to the combined effect of stress concentration at the inner spring coil curvature and the effect of transverse shear.

The values of Wahl stress concentration factor ($K$) for different values of spring index ($C$) are indicated in Table 9.1 ($a$).

**Table 9.1** ($a$)

| $C$ | $K$ |
|---|---|
| 4 | 1.4 |
| 5 | 1.31 |
| 6 | 1.25 |
| 7 | 1.21 |
| 8 | 1.18 |

(*ii*) **Deflection of spring.** The value of deflection (1) is calculated as follows :

$$\frac{T}{I_p} = \frac{f_s}{r} = G\frac{\theta}{L} \qquad ...(i)$$

$$\theta = \frac{T \cdot L}{I_p \times G} \qquad ...(ii)$$

where $I_p$ = Polar moment of inertia for spring wire

$$= \frac{\pi}{32} d^4$$

$$T = P \times R$$

$$L = 2\pi R \cdot n$$

Substituting these values in equation (*ii*), we get

$$\theta = \frac{P \times R \times 2\pi R \cdot n \times 32}{\pi \cdot d^4 \times G}$$

$$= \frac{64\, PR^2 \cdot n}{Gd^4}$$

From (Fig. 9.14), $\delta = R\theta$

$$\delta = \frac{R \times 64\, PR^2\, n}{Gd^4}$$

$$= \frac{64\,P\,R^3\,n}{Gd^4}$$

$$= \frac{8\,PD^3\,n}{Gd^4}$$

If the spring material is not stressed beyond the elastic limit the usual type of spring will have a straight line load deflection diagram as shown in Fig. 9.16.

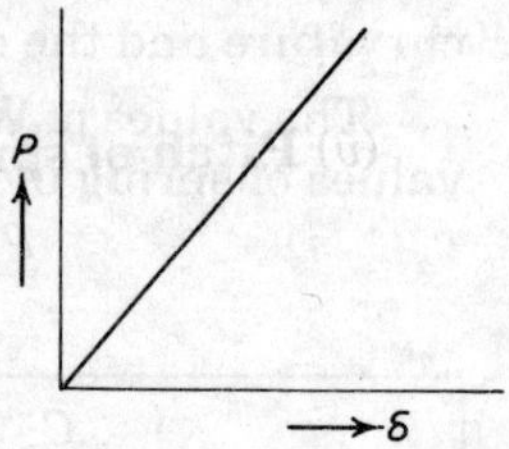


Fig. 9.16

(*iii*) **Stiffness (S) of spring**

$$S = \text{Stiffness of spring} = \frac{P}{\delta}$$

$$= \frac{P}{64\,P\,R^3\,n} \times Gd^4 = \frac{Gd^4}{64\,R^3\,n}$$

(*iv*) **Energy stored in spring**

$$E = \text{Energy stored in spring}$$

$$= \frac{1}{2}\,.\,P\,.\,\delta = \frac{1}{2}\,.\,P \times R\theta = \frac{1}{2}\,.\,T\,\theta.$$

Now $$T = \frac{\pi}{16} f_s\, d^3$$

$$\theta = \frac{L\,.\,f_s}{r\,.\,G} \text{ from torsion equation } (i)$$

$$= \frac{2L\,.\,f_s}{Gd}$$

$$\therefore \quad E = \frac{1}{2}\,.\,T\,.\,\theta$$

$$= \frac{1}{2}\,.\,\frac{\pi}{16} f_s d^3 \times \frac{2f_s\,.\,L}{G\,.\,d}$$

$$= \frac{f_s^{\,2}\,.\,\pi d^2\,.\,L}{16 \times G}$$

$$= \frac{f_s^{\,2}}{4G} \times \frac{\pi}{4} d^2 \times L = \frac{f_s^{\,2}}{4G} \times V$$

where $V$ = Volume of spring wire

$$= \frac{\pi}{4} d^2\,.\,L$$

Energy ($E_1$) stored per unit volume is given by

$$E_1 = \frac{E}{V} = \frac{f_s^2 \cdot V}{4G \times V} = \frac{f_s^2}{4G}.$$

(*v*) **Pitch of spring**

$p$ = Pitch of spring

$= \frac{L_1 - L_2}{n_1} + d$

$n_1$ = Actual number of turns

where $L_1$ = Free length

= Length of spring compressed under load

$P$ + Deflection under load + Clash allowance which is 15 percent of deflection

$L_2$ = Solid length

$= n_1 \times d.$

While choosing the pitch of the coils the following points should be taken care of :

(*a*) The spring must not close up before the maximum service load is reached.

Compression springs are seldom designed to close up under the maximum working load. An allowance called clash allowance of 15% of the maximum working deflection is usually adequate to avoid clashing of the coils during service.

(*b*) The pitch of the coils should be such that the stress does not exceed the yield point stress in torsion when the spring gets compressed accidentally.

(*vi*) **Solid length.** Solid length of a spring is defined as the length of the spring measured parallel to the axis when the spring is so compressed that all the coils touch each other.

(*vii*) **Free length.** It is the length of a spring measured parallel to the axis when the load is removed from the spring.

## 9.4 Helical Springs of Non-circular Wire

Square wires or rectangular wires are also used for making helical springs.

Let $b$ = Width of rectangular wire

$t$ = Thickness of wire

$f_s$ = Maximum torsional shear stress in the spring

$$f_S = \frac{K \cdot P \cdot D\,(3b + 1.8t)}{2b^2t^2}$$

$$\delta = \frac{2.45PD^3n}{Gt^2(b - 0.56t)}$$

For square wire spring,

$$b = t = a$$

$$f_s = \frac{2.4K \cdot P \cdot .D}{a^3}$$

$$\delta = \frac{5.58\,PD^3n}{G_a^4} = \frac{5.58PC^3n}{G_a}$$

where $C$ = Spring index = $\frac{D}{a}$.

## 9.5 Close Coiled Helical Spring with Axial Couple

Fig. 9.17 shows a close coiled helical spring under an axial couple $M$.

$M$ = Bending moment on wire at all sections

$f$ = Maximum bending stress

$Z$ = Section modulus

$$= \frac{\pi}{16} d^3$$

$$f = \frac{M}{Z} = \frac{32\,M}{d^3}$$

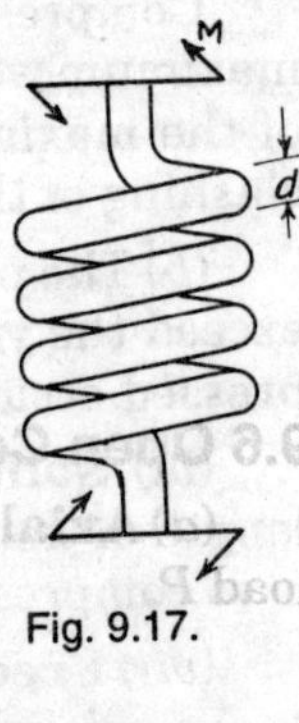


Fig. 9.17.

Let the number of coils change from $n$ to $n_1$ and radius of curvature change from $R$ to $R_1$ due to the bending moment $M$.

$$M = EI\left(\frac{1}{R_1} - \frac{1}{R}\right) \text{ approximately}$$

$L$ = Length of wire

$$= 2\pi R \cdot n = 2\pi R_1 n_1$$

$$\therefore \quad \frac{1}{R} = \frac{2\pi n}{L}$$

$$\frac{1}{R_1} = \frac{2\pi n_1}{L}$$

$$\therefore \qquad M = EI\left[\frac{2\pi n_1}{L} - \frac{2\pi n}{L}\right] = EI \,.\, \frac{2\pi}{L}\,[n_1 - n]$$

$$\phi = \text{Angle of twist of spring} = 2\pi(n_1 - n)$$

$$\therefore \qquad M = \frac{EI}{L} \times \phi$$

$$\phi = \frac{ML}{EI}$$

where $I$ = Moment of inertia of spring

$$= \frac{\pi}{64}\, d^4$$

$$\phi = \frac{64\, ML}{\pi d^4 E} = \frac{64M \times \pi D\,.\,n}{\pi d^4 E}$$

$$= \frac{64M\,.\,D\,.\,n}{Ed^4}$$

The strain energy ($U$) of spring due to bending is given by

$$U = \frac{M^2\, L}{2EI}$$

$$= \frac{64M^2\, \pi\,.\,D\,.\,n}{2E\,.\,\pi d^4} = \frac{32M^2\, D^n}{Ed^4}$$

$$= \left(\frac{32\, M}{\pi d^3}\right)^2 \times \frac{\pi^2 Dnd^2}{32E}$$

$$= f^2 \times \frac{1}{8E} \times \frac{\pi}{4} d^2 \times \pi D_n = \frac{f_2}{8E} \times \text{Volume.}$$

## 9.6 Open Coiled Helical Springs

(*a*) **Axial load.** Fig. 9.18 shows part of springs subjected to axial load $P$.

$L$ = Length of wire = $2\pi Rn \sec \alpha$

$\alpha$ = Helix angle of wire

$P$ = Axial load

$T$ = Moment applied to wire = $P \times R$

The moment can be resolved into components perpendicular and parallel to the wire

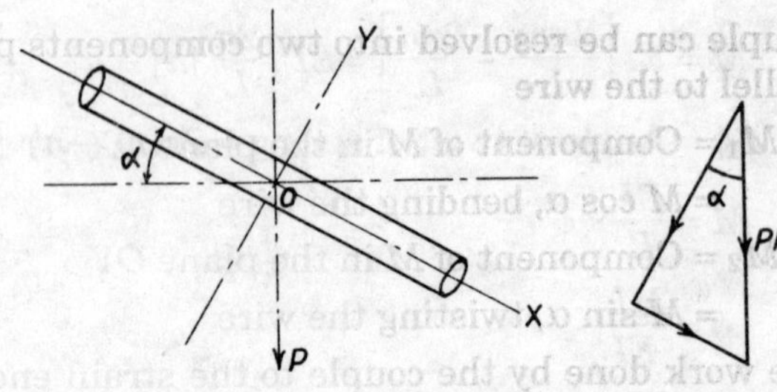

(a) (b)

Fig. 9.18

$T_1$ = Component in plane $OX$

$= T \sin \alpha = PR \sin \alpha$, bending the wire

$T_2$ = Component in plane $OY$

$= T \cos \alpha' = PR \cos \alpha$. twisting *the wire}*.

Equating the work done by the load to the strain energy in the wire

$$\frac{1}{2} . P . \delta = \frac{T_1^2 L}{2EI} + \frac{T_2^2 L}{2GI_p}$$

where $G$ = Modulus of rigidity

$I_p$ = Polar moment of inertia

$$\frac{1}{2} P\delta = \frac{(PR \sin \alpha)^2 L}{2EI} + \frac{(PR \cos \alpha)^2 . L}{2GI_p}$$

$$\delta = PR^2 L \left[ \frac{\sin^2 \alpha}{EI} + \frac{\cos^2 \alpha}{GI_p} \right].$$

(*b*) **Axial couple.** Fig. 9.19 shows part of the spring subjected to an axial couple $M$

$\alpha$ = Helix angle of wire

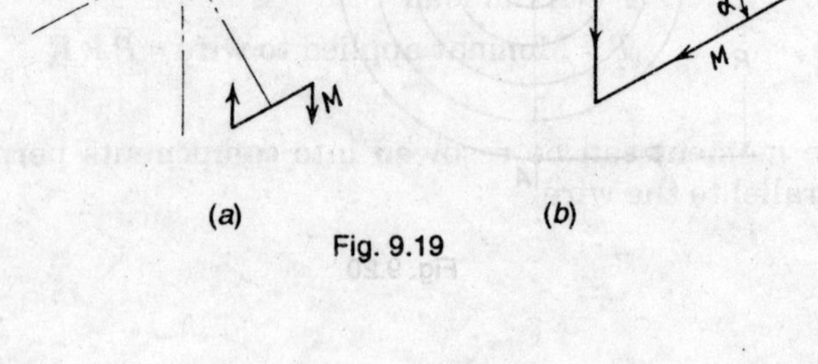

(a) (b)

Fig. 9.19

The axial couple can be resolved into two components perpendicular and parallel to the wire

$$M_1 = \text{Component of } M \text{ in the plane } OX$$
$$= M \cos\alpha, \text{ bending the wire}$$
$$M_2 = \text{Component of } M \text{ in the plane } OY$$
$$= M \sin\alpha, \text{ twisting the wire}$$

Equating the work done by the couple to the strain energy in the wire

$$\frac{1}{2} M\phi = \frac{M_1^2 \,.\, L}{2EI} + \frac{M_2^2 \, L}{2GI_p}$$

$$\phi = ML\left[\frac{\cos^2\alpha}{EI} + \frac{\sin^2\alpha}{GI_p}\right]$$

$$= M 2\pi Rn \sec\alpha \left[\frac{\cos^2\alpha \times 64}{E \,.\, \pi d^4} + \frac{\sin^2 \times 32}{G \,.\, \pi \,.\, d^4}\right]$$

$$= \frac{64MRn \sec\alpha}{d^4}\left[\frac{2\cos^2\alpha}{E} + \frac{\sin^2\alpha}{G}\right]$$

$$\delta = \text{Axial extension}$$

$$= MR \sin\alpha \,.\, \cos\alpha \,.\, L\left[\frac{1}{GI_p} - \frac{1}{EI}\right].$$

## 9.7 Flat Spiral Springs

Fig. 9.20 shows a flat spiral spring made of rectangular section strip of breadth $b$ and thickness, $t$. The winding torque $T$ is applied at the centre arbor $O$ and the other end of the spring is pinned at $A$.

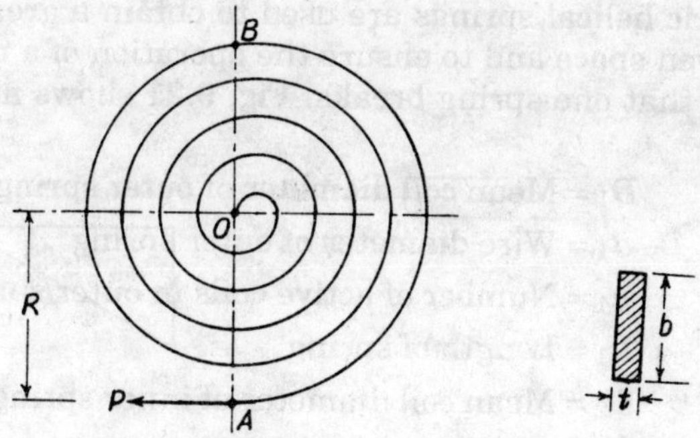


Fig. 9.20

$P$ = Force acting at distance $R$

$T$ = Torque = $P \times R$

$L$ = Length of wire forming spring

$\theta$ = Angular deflection in radians

$E$ = Modulus or elasticity of the material of the spring

Maximum bending moment occurs at point $B$ which is diametrically opposite to pinned end $A$.

Maximum bending moment at $B$

$$= P \times 2R = 2PR$$

$f$ = Maximum flexural stress

$$= \frac{2PR \times 6}{bt^2} = \frac{12PR}{bt^2} = \frac{12T}{bt^2}$$

The values of $\theta$ and $\delta$ are calculated using the following relations.

$$\theta = \frac{PRL}{EI} = \frac{TL}{EI} = \frac{12TL}{Ebt^3}$$

$$\delta = R\theta = \frac{PR^2 L}{EI}$$

$U$ = Strain energy of the spring

$$= \frac{f^2}{24E} \times V$$

where $V$ = Volume of the spring.

## 9.8 Concentric Helical Springs

Concentric helical springs are used to obtain a greater spring force in a given space and to ensure the operation of a mechanism in the event that one spring breaks. Fig. 9.21 shows a concentric spring.

Let $D_1$ = Mean coil diameter of outer spring

$d_1$ = Wire diameter of outer spring

$n_1$ = Number of active coils in outer spring

$L_1$ = Length of spring

$D_2$ = Mean coil diameter of inner spring

$d_2$ = Wire diameter of inner spring

$n_2$ = Number of active coils in inner spring

$$L_2 = \text{Length of spring}$$

Assuming same material for both springs

$$f_s = \text{Permissible shear stress}$$

$$= \frac{8P_1D_1}{\pi d_1^3} = \frac{8P_2D_2}{\pi d_2^3} \qquad ...(1)$$

$\therefore$ Both the springs when compressed until the adjacent coils meet, have the same solid height

$$n_1d_1 = n_2d_2 \qquad ...(2)$$

If both springs are of same initial height, they will have same deflection

$$\delta_1 = \delta_2$$

$$\frac{8P_1D_1^3n_2}{Gd_1^4} = \frac{8P_2D_2^3n_2}{Gd_2^4}$$

$$\frac{8\,P_1\,D_1^3\,n_1}{d_1^4} = \frac{8\,P_2\,D_2^3\,n_2}{d_2^4} \qquad ...(3)$$

From equation (1) and (3) we get

$$\frac{D_1^2n_1}{d_1} = \frac{D_2^2n^2}{d_2} \qquad ...(4)$$

From equations (2) and (4) we get

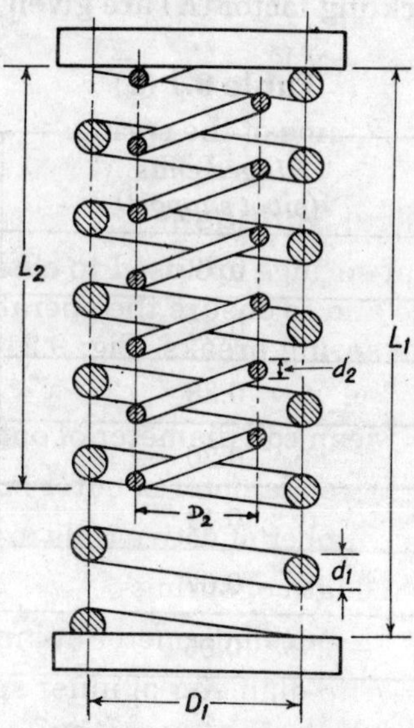


Fig. 9.21 Concentric springs.

$$\frac{D_1^2}{d_1} = \frac{n_2}{n_1} \cdot \frac{D_2^2}{d_2} = \frac{d_1}{d_2} \cdot \frac{D_2^2}{d_2}.$$

$$\frac{D_1^2}{d_1^2} = \frac{D_2^2}{d_2^2}$$

and $$\frac{D_1}{d_1} = \frac{D_2}{d_2} = C$$

This shows that in concentric springs the load should be so distributed that their spring indexes are same.

**9.8.1 Buckling of Compression Springs.** Buckling of compression helical springs takes place usually when free length of spring is more than four times the pitch diameter. In such case the buckling load is calculated as follows

$$P_c = S \times L_1 \times K$$

where $P_c$ = Critical (buckling) load

$S$ = Spring scale (kg/cm)

$L_1$ = Free length of spring (cm)

$K$ = Buckling factor. It depends on the ratio of $L_1/D$

where $D$ = Pitch diameter

The values of buckling factor ($K$) are given in Table 9.1 ($a$).

**Table 9.1 ($a$)**

| $L_1/D$ | *Hinged ends (pivot support)* | *Built in ends (square and ground)* |
|---|---|---|
| 1 | 0.72 | 0.72 |
| 2 | 0.63 | 0.70 |
| 3 | 0.38 | 0.68 |
| 4 | 0.20 | 0.63 |
| 5 | 0.11 | 0.53 |
| 6 | 0.07 | 0.38 |
| 7 | 0.05 | 0.25 |

Fig. 9.21 ($a$) shows buckling of a helical spring with fixed ends.

### 9.8.2 Vibrations of Surging of Helical Springs.

When a compressive load is applied suddenly to a helical spring, the coil at the contact end gets deflected and sends a compression wave that travels along the spring up to the supported end where it gets reflected and travels back to the deflected end. This wave travels along the spring in definitely. The material is subjected to higher stresses which may cause early fatigue failure.

Fig. 9.21 (*a*)

The natural frequency (*f*) of vibrations of the spring is given by the formula

$$f = \frac{d}{2\pi D^2 n_1}\sqrt{\frac{6G \cdot g}{\rho}}$$

where $D$ = Mean diameter of coil

$d$ = Diameter of spring wire

$n_1$ = Number of active coils

$G$ = Modulus of rigidity

$\rho$ = Density of spring material

$g$ = Acceleration due to gravity.

## 9.9 Materials for Springs

The springs are commonly made from high carbon steels with carbon 0.7 to 1% medium carbon alloy steels, phosphor bronze, brass or 18/8 stainless steel. Helical springs are either cold formed or hot formed depending on the size of wire. Small sizes are wound cold, but larger diameter wires are wound hot. After winding the spring is given a stress relieving heat treatment.

Table 9.2 indicates the safe stress and modulus of rigidity for some of the material for springs.

According to IS standards and spring wires are indicated in Table 9.2 (A) with modulas of rigidity ($G$).

Higher values of stress can be used with smaller sizes wires because of the relatively deeper penetration of the hardening due to drawing. If the spring carries a steady load or is subjected to but few stress cycle during its normal life. The service would be considered light. Severe service covers fatigue conditions of continuously varying load where maximum stress is at least twice the minimum.

## Table 9.2

| *Material* | *Safe shear stress* *($kg/cm^2$)* | *Modulus of rigidity* *(G) ($kg/cm^2$)* |
|---|---|---|
| High carbon wire<br>C = 0.85 to 0.95<br>Mn = 0.25—0.6 | 4800 | $0.8 \times 10^6$ |
| Oil tempered wire<br>C = 0.60—0.70<br>Mn = 0.60—0.90 | 4000 | $0.8 \times 10^6$ |
| Music wire<br>C = 0.7—1.00<br>Mn = 0.30—0.60 | 4600 | $0.8 \times 10^6$ |
| Chrome vanadium alloy steel<br>C = 0.45—0.55<br>Mn = 0.50—0.80<br>Cr = 0.24—1.10<br>C = 0.15—0.18 | 4050 | $0.8 \times 10^6$ |
| Stainless steel (18 - 8)<br>Cr = 17—20<br>Ni = 7—10<br>C = 0.08—0.15<br>Mn = 2 (max.) | 3250 | $0.7 \times 10^6$ |
| Nickel silver<br>Cu = 56<br>Zn = 25<br>Ni = 18 | 2500 | $0.39 \times 10^6$ |
| Phosphor bronze<br>Cu = 91—93<br>Sn = 7—9 | 2250 | $0.44 \times 10^6$ |
| Monel<br>Ni = 64<br>Cu = 26<br>Mn = 2.5<br>Fe = 2.25 | 2500 | $0.67 \times 10^6$ |
| Beryllium copper<br>Cu = 98<br>Be = 2 | 2250 | $0.45 \times 10^6$ |

Table 9.2 (A)

| *Material* | *G N/mm*$^2$ |
|---|---|
| Patented and cold drawn steel wires-unalloyed, Grades 1, 2, 3 and 4 as per IS : 4454 (Part I)—1981 | 81,370 |
| Oil harened and tempered spring steel wire and valve spring wire-unalloyed, Grades SW and VW as per IS : 4454 (Part II)-1975. | 81,370 |
| Alloyed, oil hardened and tempered valve spring wire and spring steel wire for use under moderately, elevated temperatures, Grades IS, 2S, 1D and 2D as per IS : 4454 (part III)—1975 | 81,370 |
| Hot rolled steel for hot formed springs, Grades 1, 2 as per IS : 3431—1965 | 80,000 |
| Hot rolled steel for hot formed springs, Grades 98C6, 113 C6, 55 Si 7, 60 Si 7, 50 Cr 4V2 and 60 Cr 4V2 as per IS : 3195—1975 | 80,000 |
| Stainless spring steel wire, as per IS : 4454 (Part IV)—1975. | |
| Grade 1 : Tempered | 73,530 |
| Untempered | 69,610 |
| Grad 2 : Tempered | 78,430 |
| Untempered | 73,530 |
| Hard drawn brass wires as per IS : 4076-1967 | 35,000 |
| Phosphor bronze wires as per IS : 1385-1968 | 42,000 |

## 9.10 Design Procedure

Helical springs are designed on the basis of following :

(*i*) Strength

(*ii*) Bucking

(*iii*) Surging due to resonance when cyclic disturbances are present.

Following data usually should be known to design helical spring:

(*i*) Load on spring

(*ii*) Deflection

(*iii*) Commercial tolerances such as :

(*a*) free length tolerance

(*b*) coil diameter tolerance

(c) spring rate tolerance

(d) load tolerance.

Tolerances should be specified as widely as the proper functioning of the spring permits especially for these dimensions that are not critical.

(iv) When the loading on the spring is continuously fluctuating due allowance must be made in the design fair fatigue and stress concentration.

(v) Space limitations.

(vi) The spring index should be greater than 3 to avoid stress concentration, when no space limitations are imposed value of spring index 8 may be used.

(viii) Material of spring.

### 9.10.1 Surging and Natural Frequency

With compression springs used in machines, engines and devices running at high speed, resonance may occur. This phenomenon is known as surging of a springs. In order to avoid resonance, the designer must know the natural frequency of a spring. The "fundamental frequency" of a compression spring guided at both ends and periodically compressed by the same stroke is given by :

$$f_m = \frac{d}{2\pi\, i_f\, D_m^2}\sqrt{\frac{Gg}{2_\gamma}}\ Hz$$

where $\gamma$ = specific weight of spring material , N/m$^3$

$g$ = acceleration due to gravity, m/s$^2$

For the spring having one end fixed and the other free, the fundamental frequency is :

$$f_n = \frac{d}{4\pi\, i_f\, D_m^2}\sqrt{\frac{G}{2_\rho}}\ \text{Hz}$$

where $\rho = \frac{\gamma}{g}$ is the density of spring material, kg/cm$^3$

$D_m$ = Mean coil diameter in mm

$G$ = Modulus of rigidity

$d$ = Diameter of spring wire, mm

$i_f$ = Number of working (active) coils

$f_n$ = Fundamental frequency, Hz

**Example 9.1.** *A closed coil helical spring is subjected to a load of 35 kg. The spring stiffness is 2.5 kg / cm and spring index is 7. If the maximum shear stress in the spring is 5500 kg / cm determine the following :*

(*a*) *Diameter of wire.*

(*b*) *Mean diameter of coil.*

(*c*) *Number of active coils.*

(*d*) *Solid length of the spring.*

*Take* $G = 0.84 \times 10^6$ *kg/cm*$^2$.

**Solution.** (*a*) **To calculate wire diameter**

$P$ = Load = 35 kg.

$D$ = Mean diameter of coil.

Mean radius, $R = \dfrac{D}{2}$

$d$ = Wire diameter.

$f_s$ = Allowable stress in spring material

$= 5500 \text{ kg/cm}^2$

$n$ = Number of active coils.

$G$ = Modulus of rigidity

$= 0.84 \times 10^6 \text{ kg/cm}^2$.

$T$ = Twisting moment

$$= P \times R$$

$$= P \times \frac{D}{2}$$

$$= 35 \times \frac{D}{2}$$

$$= 17.5\, D$$

$$= \frac{\pi}{16} f_s d^3$$

$$17.5\, D = \frac{\pi}{6} f_s d^3$$

$$17.5 \frac{D}{d} = \frac{\pi}{16} f_s \,.\, d^2$$

$C$ = Spring index

$$= \frac{D}{d} = 7$$

$$17.5.\ C = \frac{\pi}{16} f_s \cdot d^2$$

$$17.5 \times 7 = \frac{\pi}{16} \times 5500 \times d^2$$

$$d = 0.336 \text{ cm.}$$

(*ii*) **To calculate the coil diameter**

$$\frac{D}{d} = 7$$

$$D = 7 \times 0.336 = 2.352 \text{ cm.}$$

$$R = \text{Radius} = \frac{D}{2} = 1.176 \text{ cm.}$$

(*c*) **To calculate number of coils**

$$S = \text{Spring stiffness} = 2.5 \text{ kg/cm}$$

$$\delta = \frac{P}{S} = \frac{35}{2.5} = 14 \text{ cm}$$

$$\delta = \frac{64\, P\, R^3\, n}{Gd^4}$$

$$14 = \frac{64 \times 35 \times 1.176^3 \times n}{0.84 \times 10^6 \times (0.336)^4}$$

$$n = 42.$$

(*d*) **To calculate solid length.** Assuming squared and ground ends.

Solid length $= (n + 2)\, d = (42 + 2) \times 0.336 = 14.78$ cm.

**Example 9.2.** *A closed coil helical spring is required for a safety valve of 7 cm diameter which is to below off at a pressure of 11kg/cm$^2$. The mean diameter of coil is 15 cm and maximum lift of valve is 1.2 cm. The initial compression of the spring is 2.5 cm. If the allowable shear stress in the spring material is 4300 kg/cm$^2$ and modulus of rigidity is 0.84 × 10$^3$kg/cm$^2$, determine the following :*

*(a) Stiffness of spring.*

*(b) Diameter of wire.*

*(c) Number of active coils.*

*(d) Solid length.*

**Solution.** (*a*) **To find stiffness of spring**

$$d_1 = \text{Valve diameter}$$

$P$ = Load on valve

$p$ = Steam pressure

$$P = \frac{\pi}{4} d_1^2 \times p = \frac{\pi}{4} \times 7^2 \times 11 = 423 \text{ kg.}$$

Initial compression = 2.5 cm.

$$S = \text{Stiffness of spring} = \frac{P}{2.5}$$

$$= \frac{423}{2.5} = 169.2 \text{ kg/cm}$$

**(b) To find wire diameter**

Maximum compression of spring

= Initial compression + Maximum lift of valve.

Maximum compression ($\delta$)

$= 2.5 + 1.2 = 3.7$ cm

Maximum load ($F$) on the spring $= S \times \delta$

$= S \times 3.7 = 169.2 \times 3.7 = 626$ kg

Let $d$ = Wire diameter

$$C = \text{Spring index} = 7 = \frac{D}{d}$$

$k$ = Wahl concentration factor

$$= \frac{4C-1}{4C-4} + \frac{0.615}{C} = \frac{4 \times 7 - 1}{4 \times 7 - 4} + \frac{0.615}{7} - 1.213$$

$D$ = Mean coil diameter = $7d$

$f_s$ = Allowable shear stress

$T$ = Twisting moment.

$$T = \frac{1}{k} \cdot \frac{\pi}{16} f_s \cdot d^3$$

$$P \times R = \frac{1}{k} \cdot \frac{\pi}{16} f_s \cdot d^3$$

$$626 \times (3.5\, d) = \frac{1}{1.213} \times \frac{\pi}{16} \times 4300 \times d^3$$

$d = 1.77$ cm.

**(c) To calculate active number of turns**

$n$ = Number of active turns in the spring.

$$D = 7\,d = 7 \times 1.77 = 12.39 \text{ cm.}$$

$$R = \frac{D}{2} - \frac{12.39}{2} = 6.195 \text{ cm.}$$

$$S = \frac{G\,d^4}{64\,R^3 n}$$

$$169.2 = \frac{0.84 \times 10^6 \times (1.77)^4}{64 \times (6.195)^3 \times n}$$

$$n = \frac{0.84 \times 10^6 \times 9.81}{64 \times 237.75 \times 169.2}$$

$$= 3.2$$

Assuming squared and ground ends

$n_1$ = Actual member of turns

$= 3.2 + 2 - 5.2$

(*d*) **To calculate free length**

$L_1$ = Free length

$= L_2 + \delta_2 + C_1$

$L_2$ = Solid length

$= n_1 \,.\, d = 5.2 \times 1.77 = 9.2$ cm

$\delta$ = Maximum compression = 3.7 cm

Assuming a clearance of 1 mm between adjacent coils.

$C_1$ = Clearance between adjacent coils

$= 4 \times 0.1 = 0.4$ cm

$L_1 = 9.2 + 3.7 + 0.4 = 13.3$ cm.

**Example 9.3.** *Design a closed coil helical compression spring for a service load ranging from 225 kg to 227 kg. The axial deflection of the spring for the load is 6 mm. Assume a spring index of 6, permissible shear stress intensity of 4200 kg/c $m^2$ and $G = 0.84 \times 10^6$ kg/cm$^2$. Neglect the effect of stress concentration.*

**Solution.** (*a*) **To calculate wire diameter**

$D$ = Mean diameter of coil

$P$ = Maximum load = 275 kg

$d$ = Wire diameter

$C$ = Spring index

$$= 6 = \frac{D}{l}$$

$f_s$ = Permissible shear stress

$= 4200 \text{ kg/cm}^2$

$T$ = Twisting moment $= P \times \frac{D}{2}$

$$P \times \frac{D}{2} = \frac{\pi}{16} f_s d^3$$

$$\frac{275}{2} \times \left(\frac{D}{d}\right) = \frac{\pi}{16} \times 4200 \times d^2$$

$$\frac{275}{2} \times 6 = \frac{\pi}{16} \times 4200 \times d^2$$

$d = 1$ cm

Because $D = 6\,d = 6$ cm

Outside diameter of spring $= D + d$

Inside diameter of spring $= D - d$

**(*b*) To calculate number of turns**

$F$ = Loading producing deflection

$= 275 - 225 = 50$ kg

$R = 3$ cm

$\delta$ = Deflection $= \frac{64\,P\,R^3 n}{G\,.\,d^4}$

$$0.6 = \frac{64 \times 50(3)^3 \times n}{0.84 \times 10^6}$$

$n = 5.8 = 6$ (say)

**(*c*) To calculate maximum deflection**

$\delta_m$ = Maximum deflection

$$= \frac{275}{275 - 225} \times 0.6 = 3.3 \text{ cm}$$

**(*d*) To calculate free length**

Assuming square and ground ends.

$n_1$ = Actual number of turns $= n + 2 = 8$

Assume a clearance between adjacent coils

$= 0.1$ mm

$L_1$ = Free length

= Solid length + Maximum compression

+ Clearance between adjacent coils

$= n_1 \times d + \delta_m + (n_1 - 1) \times 0.1 = 12$ cm.

**Example 9.4.** *It is required to design a spring to absorb 2000 kg cm of energy. The spring index is 6 and the initial compression of the spring is 3 cm and the spring gets compressed by additional 5 cm while absorbing energy. The safe stress in the spring material is 3600 kg/cm$^2$ and $G = 0.84 \times 10^6$ kg/cm$^2$.*

**Solution.** (*a*) **To calculate wire diameter**

$E$ = energy = 2000 kg cm

$C$ = Spring index = 6

$D$ = Mean coil diameter

$d$ = Wire diameter

$$6 = \frac{D}{d}$$

$S$ = Stiffness of spring

$\delta^1$ = Initial compression = 3 cm

$P_1$ = Initial load on the spring

$$S = \frac{P_1}{\delta_1}$$

$P_1 = S \times \delta_1 = S \times 3 = 3S$ kg

$\delta_2$ = Compression of.spring while absorbing energy = 5 cm.

Maximum compression

$= \delta_1 + \delta_2 = 5 + 3 = 8$ cm

$P_2$ = Maximum load on the spring

$= 5 \times (\delta_2 + \delta_1) = 8\ S$ kg.

$P$ = Mean force during compression

$$= \frac{P_1 + P_2}{2} = \frac{3S + 8S}{2} = 5.5\ S$$

$E_1$ = Energy absorbed during shock

$= P \times \delta_2 = 5.5 \times S \times 5$

$E = E_1$

$$2000 = 5.5 \times S \times 5$$

$$S = 72.7 \text{ kg/cm.}$$

$$P_2 = \text{Maximum load on the spring}$$

$$= 8 \times 72.7 = 581.6 \text{ kg.}$$

$$f_t = \text{Safe shear stress in spring}$$

$$= 3600 \text{ kg/cm}^2$$

$$C = \frac{D}{d}$$

$$D = 6 \times d$$

$$R = \text{Mean radius of coil}$$

$$= \frac{D}{2} = \frac{6\,d}{2} = 3\,d$$

$$T = \text{Twisting moment}$$

$$= P_2 \times R = 581.6 \times R = 581.9 \times 3\,d.$$

Now $$T = \frac{\pi}{16} f_s\, d^3$$

$$581.6 \times 3d = \frac{\pi}{16} f_s\, d^3$$

$$581.6 \times 3d = \frac{\pi}{16} \times 3600 \times d^3$$

$$d = 1.57 \text{ cm.}$$

(*b*) **To calculate mean diameter of coil**

$$D = 6d = 6 \times 157 = 9.42 \text{ cm.}$$

(*c*) **To find number of turns.**

$$S = \frac{G\,d^4}{64\,R^3\,n}$$

$$72.7 = \frac{0.84 \times 10^6 \times 1.57^4}{64(4.71)^3 \times n}$$

$$n = 10.5.$$

**Example 9.5.** *A composite spring has two close coiled springs in series. Each spring has a mean coil diameter 10 times its wire diameter. The diameter of wire of one spring is 0.28 cm and this spring has 18 coils. The second spring has 14 coils. The stiffness of composite spring material is 3600 kg/cm$^2$ and G = $0.8 \times 10^6$ kg/cm. Determine the following :*

(a) *The diameter of wire of second spring.*

(b) *Limiting axial load far composite spring*

(c) *Extension of composite spring under limiting load.*

**Solution.**

(a) **To calculate wire diameter.** Fig. 9.21 shows the composite spring

$D_1$ = Mean diameter of coil of spring 1

$d_1$ = Wire diameter of spring 1 = 0.28 cm

$D_2$ = Mean diameter of coil of spring 2

$d_2$ = Mean diameter of spring 2

$$10 = \frac{D_1}{d_1} = \frac{D_2}{d_2}$$

Let $\delta$ = Deflection of composite spring

$\delta_1$ = Deflection of spring 1

$\delta_2$ = Deflection of spring 2

$S, S_1, S_2$ are of stiffness of composite spring, spring 1 and spring 2 respectively.

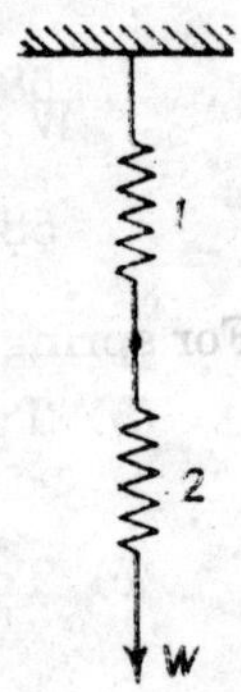

Fig. 9.21

$W$ = Load applied to spring

$$\delta = \delta_1 + \delta_2$$

$$\frac{W}{S} = \frac{W}{S_1} + \frac{W}{S_2}$$

$$\frac{1}{S} = \frac{1}{S_1} + \frac{1}{S_2} \qquad ...(i)$$

$$S = 1.2 \text{ kg/cm}$$

$$\frac{1}{S_1} = \frac{64\, R_1^3\, n_1}{G\, d^4}$$

where $R_1 = \frac{D_1}{2} = \frac{10\, d_1}{2} = 5\, d_1 = 5 \times 0.28$ cm

$$\frac{1}{S_2} = \frac{64\, R_2{}^3 n^2}{G} d_2 d^4$$

where $R_2 = \frac{D_2}{2} = \frac{10\, d_2}{2} = 5d_2$

$n_1$ = Number of active turns in spring 1 = 18

$n_2$ = Number of active turns in second spring = 14

$$\frac{1}{S}=\frac{1}{S_1}+\frac{1}{S_2}$$

$$\frac{1}{1.2}=\frac{64(5\times0.28)^3\times18}{0.8\times10^6\times(0.28)^4}+\frac{64(5\,d_2)^3\times14}{0.8\times10^6\times(d_2)^4}$$

$$\frac{0.8\times10^6}{1.2\times64\times5^3}=\frac{18}{0.28}+\frac{14}{d_2}$$

$$d_2 = 0.73 \text{ cm}$$

$$D_2 = 10\times d_2 = 7.3 \text{ cm}$$

$$R_2 = 3.65 \text{ cm.}$$

(*b*) **To calculate limiting load.** For spring 1,

$$T = \text{Twisting moment}$$

$$= W\times R_1 = W\times5\times0.28 \text{ kg cm}$$

$$f_s = \text{Safe stress} = 3600 \text{ kg/cm}^2$$

$$T=\frac{\pi}{16}f_s\,d_1^3$$

$$W\times5\times0.28=\frac{\pi}{16}\times3600\times(0.28)^3$$

$$W = 11.1 \text{ kg.}$$

For spring 2 $\quad T=\frac{\pi}{16}f_s\,d_2^3$

$$W\times R_2=\frac{\pi}{16}f_2\,d_2^3$$

$$W\times3.65=\frac{\pi}{16}\times3600(0.73)^3$$

$$W = 75.3 \text{ kg.}$$

$\therefore$ $\quad W$ = Limiting axial load for the spring

$$= 11.1 \text{ kg}$$

$$\delta=\frac{W}{S}=\frac{11.2}{1.2}=9.25 \text{ kg/cm.}$$

**Example 9.6.** *A closed coil helical spring B is placed inside the coils of a second helical spring A having same number of coils, axial free length and same materials. The mean diameters of coils of the spring A and B are 12 cm and 10 cm respectively and spring A is made of 1.4 cm diameter wire and spring B is made of 0.9 cm* *diameter wire. Determine the load taken and maximum stress in each spring if the two springs are compressed by an axial load of 300 kg.*

**Solution. Spring A :**

$D_1$ = Mean diameter of.coil = 12 cm

$R_1$ = 6 cm

$d_1$ = Wire diameter = 1.4 cm

$P_1$ = Load shared by spring.

**Spring B :**

$D_2$ = Mean diameter of coil = 12 cm

$R_2$ = Mean radius = 5 cm

$d_2$ = Wire diameter = 0.9 cm

$P_2$ = Load shared by spring

$P$ = Total load = 300 = $P_1 + P_2$ ...(*i*)

**(*a*) To calculate $P_1$ and $P_2$**

$$\delta_1 = \delta_2$$

$$\frac{64\, P_{1R_1}{}^3 n_1}{G\, d_1^4} = \frac{64\, P_2 R_2^3 n_2}{G d_2^4}$$

As both springs have same member of coils

$$n_1 = n_2$$

$$\frac{P_1}{P_2} = \left(\frac{R_2}{R_1}\right)^3 \left(\frac{d_1}{d_2}\right)^4$$

$$= \left(\frac{5}{6}\right)^3 \times \left(\frac{1.4}{0.9}\right)^4$$

$$= 3.4 \qquad \text{...(ii)}$$

From (*i*) and (*ii*) equations

$P_1$ = 231.82 kg

$P_2$ = 68.18 kg

**(*b*) To calculate shear stress**

$f_{s_1}$ = Shear stress in spring *A*

$T_1$ = Twisting moment

$$= P_1 R_1 = \frac{\pi}{16} f_{s_1} d_1^3$$

$$231.82 \times 6 = \frac{\pi}{16} f_{s_1} \times (1.4^3)$$

$$f_{s_1} = 2583 \text{ kg/cm}^2$$

$f_{s_2}$ = Shear stress in spring $B$

$T_2$ = Twisting moment = $P_2R_2$

$$= \frac{\pi}{16} f_{s_2} d_2^3$$

$$68.18 \times 5 = \frac{\pi}{16} f_{s_2} \times 0.9^3$$

$$f_{s_2} = 2382.8 \text{ kg/cm}^2.$$

**Example 9.7.** *A truck weighing 2000 kg and moving at 0.69 m/sec² has to be brought to rest by a buffer. Find how many spring each of 15 coils will be required to store the energy of motion during compression of 15 cm. The diameter of wire of spring is 2 cm and the mean radius of coil is 10 cm and G = 0.8 × 10⁵kg/cm². Also determine stiffness of spring.*

**Solution.**

$R$ = Mean radius of coil = 10 cm

$P$ = Maximum force on each spring

$\delta$ = Deflection in each spring = 15 cm

$N$ = Number of springs

$n$ = Number of coils = 15

$d$ = Wire diameter = 2 cm

$$\delta = \frac{64 P R^3 n}{G d^4}$$

$$15 = \frac{64 P \times 10^3 \times 15}{0.8 \times 10^6 \times 2^4}$$

$P$ = 200 kg

$E$ = Kinetic energy of moving truck

$W$ = Weight of truck = 2000 kg

$V$ = Velocity of truck = 0.69 m/sec

$$E = \frac{1}{2} \frac{W}{g} V^2$$

$$= \frac{1}{2} \times \frac{2000}{9.81} \times (0.69)^2$$

$$= 48.52 \text{ kg m}$$

$$= 4852 \text{ kg cm}$$

$E_1$ = Energy stored in $N$ springs

$$= N \times P \frac{\delta}{2}$$

$$= N \times 200 \times \frac{15}{2} = 1500\, N \text{ kg cm.}$$

$$E = E_1$$

$$4852 = 1500\, N$$

$$N = \frac{4852}{1500} = 3.23$$

Hence $N$ = Number of springs in buffer = 4 (say)

$$\text{Stiffness of spring } = \frac{P}{\delta} = \frac{200}{15} = 13.33 \text{ kg/cm.}$$

**Example. 9.8.** *A close coiled helical spring made of square section wire is subjected to an axial load of 38 kg. The allowable shear stress in spring material is 3000 kg/cm² and spring index is 5. The modulus of rigidity is $0.8 \times 10^6$ kg/cm². determine the following :*

(*a*) *Size of square section.*

(*b*) *Mean diameter of coil.*

(*c*) *Number of active turns if the deflection of spring is 1 cm.*

**Solution.**

(*a*) **To determine size of wire**

$P$ = Axial load = 38 kg

$f_s$ = Shear stress = 3000 kg/cm²

$G = 0.8 \times 10^6$ kg/cm²

Let $a$ = Side of square section of the spring

$D$ = Mean diameter of coil

$$\text{Spring index } C = \frac{D}{a} = 5$$

$$D = 5\, a$$

$k$ = Stress concentration factor

$$= \frac{4C-1}{4C-4} + \frac{0.615}{C}$$

$$= \frac{4 \times 5 - 1}{4 \times 5 - 4} + \frac{0.615}{5} = 1.31$$

$$f_s = \frac{2.4\,k\,PD}{a^3}$$

$$3000 = \frac{2.4 \times 1.31 \times 38 \times 5a}{a^3} = \frac{597.36}{a^2}$$

$$a = \frac{597.36}{3000} = 0.2 \text{ cm}$$

$$D = 5 \times a = 5 \times 0.2 = 1 \text{ cm.}$$

(*ii*) **To calculate active number of turns**

$n$ = Number of active turns

$S$ = Stiffness of spring

$$= \frac{P}{\delta} = \frac{38}{1} = 38 \text{ kg/cm}$$

$$\delta = \frac{5.58\,PD^3 n}{G\,.\,d^4}$$

$$1 = \frac{5.58 \times 38 \times 1^3 \times n}{0.8 \times 10^6 \times 0.2^4}$$

$$n = 6.$$

**Example 9.9.** *To particulars of concentric helical spring are as follows :*

| | *Wire diameter* | *Mean diameter of coil* | *n* | *Free length* |
|---|---|---|---|---|
| *Inner spring* | *0.4 cm* | *3.2 cm* | *7* | *8.5 cm* |
| *Outer spring* | *0.5 cm* | *4 cm* | *9* | *10 cm* |

*If the spring is subjected to a load of 45 kg determine for each spring.*

*(a) Load carried.*

*(b) Change in length.*

*(c) Shear stress induced in spring wire.*

*Assume* $G = 0.84 \times 10^6$ *kg/cm²*.

**Solution.**

(*a*) **To find load carried.** As the free length of outer spring is more than free length of inner spring therefore outer takes the whole load until its compression is, 10 – 8.5 = 1.5 cm after which both the springs are compressed together.

For outer spring

$$P_1 = \text{Load}$$
$$D_1 = 4 \text{ cm}$$
$$d_1 = 0.5 \text{ cm}$$
$$n_1 = 9$$
$$\delta_1 = 1.5 \text{ cm}$$
$$\delta_1 = \frac{8 P_1 D_1^3 n_1}{G d_1^4}$$
$$1.5 = \frac{8 \times P_1 \times 4^3 \times 9}{(0.84) \times 10^6 \times (0.5)^4}$$
$$P_1 = 17.1 \text{ kg}$$
$$P = 45 - 17.1 = 27.9 \text{ kg.}$$

This load $P$ will be now proportionately shared by the two springs.

$$\delta = \text{Further compression of outer springs}$$
$$= \text{Deflection of inner spring}$$
$$P_2 = \text{Additional load taken be the outer spring}$$
$$= \frac{17.1 \times \delta}{1.5} = 11.4\ \delta$$
$$P_3 = \text{Load taken by inner spring}$$
$$= \delta \times \text{Stiffness of inner spring}$$
$$= \frac{\delta \times G d_2^4}{8 D_2^3 n_2}$$
$$= \frac{\delta \times 0.84 \times 10^6 \times (0.4)^4}{8 \times (3.2)^3 \times 7} = 11.7\ \delta$$
$$P = P_2 + P_3 = 11.4\ \delta + 11.7\ \delta$$
$$27.9 = 23.1\ \delta$$
$$\delta = 1.2 \text{ cm}$$

Load shared by outer spring

$$= P_2 + P_1 = 11.4 \times \delta + P_1$$
$$= 11.4 \times 1.2 + 17.1 = 30.78 \text{ kg.}$$

**(b) To find change in length**

Change in length of inner spring

$= \delta = 1.2$ cm

Change in length of outer spring

$= \delta_1 + \delta = 1.5 + 1.2 = 2.7$ cm

**(c) To find shear stress induced**

$f_{s_1}$ = Shear stress induced in outer spring

$T_1$ = Twisting moment

$= 30.78 \times R_1 = 30.78 \times 2$

$= 61.56$ kg cm

$$61.55 = \frac{\pi}{16} f_{s_1} d_1^3 = \frac{\pi}{16} f_{s_1} \times (0.5)^3$$

$f_{s_1} = 2509.45$ kg/cm$^2$

$f_{s_2}$ = Shear stress induced in inner spring

$T_2 = 14.22 \times R_2 = 14.22 \times 1.6$

$= 22.75$ kg cm

$$22.75 = \frac{\pi}{16} f_{s_2} d_2^3$$

$$22.75 = \frac{\pi}{16} f_{s_2} \times (0.4)^3$$

$f_{s_2} = 1811.3$ kg/cm$^2$.

**Example 9.10.** *A close coiled helical spring made of 3 cm diameter wire is to absorb the energy of a truck weighing 6000 kg moving at 1m/sec. If the safe shear stress in spring material is 3000 kg/cm$^2$ and $G = 0.84 \times 10^6$ kg/cm$^2$ determine the following :*

(a) *Volume of spring.*

(b) *Weight of spring if density of spring material is 7.3 gm/cm$^2$.*

(c) *Number of active turns if spring index is 8.*

**Solution.**

**(a) To calculate volume of spring**

$W$ = Weight of truck = 6000 kg

$V$ = Velocity of truck = 1 m/sec

= 100 cm/sec.

$f_s$ = Safe shear stress = 3000 kg/cm$^2$

$V_1$ = Volume of spring

$E$ = Strain energy of spring

$$= \frac{f_s^2 \cdot V_1}{4G}$$

$E_1$ = Kinetic energy of moving truck

$$= \frac{1}{2} \cdot \frac{W}{g} \cdot V^2$$

$$E = E_1$$

$$\frac{f_s^2 \cdot V_1}{4G} = \frac{1}{2} \frac{W}{g} V^2$$

$$\frac{(3000)^2 \times V_1}{4 \times 0.84 \times 10^6} = \frac{1}{2} \times \frac{6000}{981} \times (100)^2$$

$$V_1 = 11400 \text{ cm}^3$$

(*b*) **To find weight of spring**

$W_1$ = Weight of spring = $V_1$ × density

$$= 11400 \times \frac{7.3}{1000} = 83.22 \text{ kg.}$$

(*c*) **To calculate number of turns**

$n$ = Number of active coils

$$C = 8 = \frac{D}{d}$$

$d$ = Wire diameter = 3 cm

$$V_1 = n \cdot \frac{\pi}{4} d^2 \times \pi D$$

$$1140 = n \times \frac{\pi}{4}(3)^3 \times \pi(8 \times 3)$$

$$n = 21.4.$$

**Example 9.10.** (*a*) *It is required to design a spring for the value of a petrol engine using following data :*

*Maximum inside diameter of string = 2.3 cm*

*Spring load when valve is open = 34 kg*

*Spring load when valve is closed = 20 kg*

*Length of spring when valve is open = 4 cm*

*Length of spring when valve is closed = 4.8 cm*

*Maximum permissible shear stress in spring material 3800 kg/cm$^2$ and modulus of rigidity is $0.8 \times 10^6$ kg/cm$^2$. Also calculate the dangerous engine speed. Density of spring material is 0.007 kg/cm$^3$.*

**Solution.**

(*a*) **To find wire diameter (*d*)**

Let $d$ = Wire diameter

$D$ = Mean coil diameter

= Inside diameter of coil + $d$ = $(2.3 + d)$ cm.

$f_s$ = Shear stress = 3800 kg/cm$^2$

$$R = \text{Mean radius} = \frac{D}{2} = \frac{1}{2}(2.3 + d)$$

$P_1$ = Maximum load = 34 kg

$T$ = Torque = $p_1 \times R$

$$P_1 \times R = \frac{\pi}{16} f_s d^3$$

$$34 \times \frac{1}{2}(2.3 + d) = \frac{\pi}{16} \times 3800 \times d^3$$

$d$ = 0.38 cm

$\therefore$ $D = 2.3 + 0.38 = 2.68$ cm

$R$ = 1.34 cm.

(*b*) **To find maximum deflection**

$\delta$ = Compression of spring

= 4.8 − 4 = 0.8 cm

$P_1$ = Maximum load = 34 kg

$P_2$ = Maximum load = 20 kg

$\delta_1$ = Maximum deflection under 34 kg load

$$= \frac{\delta \times P_1}{P_1 - P_2} = \frac{0.8 \times 34}{34 - 20} = 1.94 \text{ cm}$$

(*c*) **To find number of turns**

$$\delta_1 = \frac{64 P_1 R^3 n}{G d^4}$$

$$1.94 = \frac{64 \times 34 \times (1.34)^3 n}{0.8 \times 10^6 \times (0.38)^4}$$

$$n = 6.18 = 7 \text{ (say)}$$

Assuming square and ground ends.

$$n_1 = \text{Total number of turns}$$
$$= n + 2 = 7 + 2 = 9.$$

(*d*) **To find length**

Solid length $= n_1 \times d = 9 \times 0.38 = 3.42$ cm

Free length of spring = Solid length + Deflection under the load + crash allowance

$$= 3.42 + \delta_1 + 0.15 \times \delta_1$$
$$= 3.42 + 1.94 + 0.15 \times 1.94 = 5.65 \text{ cm.}$$

(*e*) **To find pitch**

$$p = \text{Pitch of coils}$$
$$= \frac{\text{Free length} - \text{solid length}}{n_1} + d$$
$$= \frac{5.65 - 3.42}{9 + 0.38} = 0.62 \text{ cm.}$$

(*f*) **To find critical speed**

The frequency of natural vibrations is given by

$$f = \frac{d}{2\pi D^2 n_1}\sqrt{\frac{6\,G\,.\,g}{\rho}}$$

where $\rho = 0.007$ kg/cm³.

$$f = \frac{0.38}{2\pi(2.68)^2 \times 9}\sqrt{\frac{6 \times 0.8 \times 10^6 \times 981}{0.007}}$$
$$= 243 \text{ vibration per second (VPS)}$$
$$= 14580 \text{ VPM.}$$

**Example 9.11.** *The spring load against which a value is opened is provided by an inner helical spring arranged within and concentric with an outer helical spring. Both springs are of steel, closely coiled and the free length of the inner spring is 7 mm longer than that of the outer spring. The outer springs has 12 coils of 25 mm mean diameter, wire diameter being 3 mm and the initial compression of spring is 5 mm when the valve is closed. Find the stiffness of the inner spring if the greatest force required to open the valve 10 mm is 14 kg.*

(*a*) *Also calculate the mean diameter of coils of the inner spring if* $G = 0.8 \times 10^6$ *and radial clearance between the springs is 1.6 mm and wire diameter is 2 mm.*

**Solution.**

(*a*) **To calculate stiffness**

$\delta_2$ = Initial compression of outer spring = 0.5 cm.

$\delta_1$ = Initial compression of inner spring

= 0.7 cm + 0.5 = 1.2 cm

$x$ = Distance through which valve is to be opened = 1 cm

When the valve is open 1 cm

$\delta_3$ = Compression of outer spring

$= \delta_2 + x = 0.5 + 1 = 1.5$ cm

$\delta_4$ = Compression of inner spring

$= \delta_1 + x = 1.2 + 1 = 2.2$ cm

$d_2$ = Wire diameter of outer spring = 0.3 cm

$D_2$ = Mean diameter of outer spring = 2.5 cm

$n_2$ = Number of coils = 12

$P_2$ = Force exerted

$$= \frac{\delta_3 \times G d_2^4}{8 D_2^3 n_2}$$

$$= \frac{1.5 \times 0.8 \times 10^6 \times (0.3)^4}{8 \times (2.5)^3 \times 12}$$

= 6.48 kg

$P$ = Total load = 14 kg

$P_1$ (Force exerted by inner spring)

$= P - P_2 = 14 - 6.48 = 7.52$ kg.

Stiffness of inner spring

$$S_1 = \frac{P_1}{\delta_4} = \frac{7.52}{2.2} = 3.4 \text{ kg/cm.}$$

(*b*) **To calculate mean diameter**

$d_1$ = Wire diameter of inner spring = 0.2 cm

$y$ = Radial clearance between springs = 1.6 mm

$$D_1 = D_2 - (d_1 + d_2 + 2 + y)$$
$$= 2.5 - (0.2 + 0.3 + 2 \times 0.16) = 1.6 \text{ cm.}$$

**Example 9.12.** *Fig.9.22 shows a compression spring to carry maximum axial tensile load 3000 kg. Calculate d, $d_1$, $d_2$ and L when spring is free and total number of coils of spring. The spring index is 7, allowable stress in spring material is 5000 kg/cm$^2$ and spring deflection is 1.2 cm when load changes from 2800 kg to 3000 kg. Allowable stress in the rod is 800 kg/cm$^2$. Take $G = 0.8 \times 10^6$ kg/cm$^2$.*

**Solution.** (*a*) **To calculate, $d_1$**

$P$ = Maximum tensile load = 3000 kg

$f_t$ = Safe tensile stress in rod = 800 kg/cm$^2$

Consider tensile failure of threaded rod.

$d_c$ = Core diameter of threaded part

$d_1$ = Nominal diameter

$$A = \text{Area under tension} = \frac{\pi}{4} d_c^2$$

$$P = A \times f_t$$

$$3000 = \frac{\pi}{4} d_c^2 \times 800$$

$$d_e = 2.18 \text{ cm}$$

$$d_1 = \frac{d_c}{0.8} = \frac{2.18}{0.8} = 2.73 \text{ cm.}$$

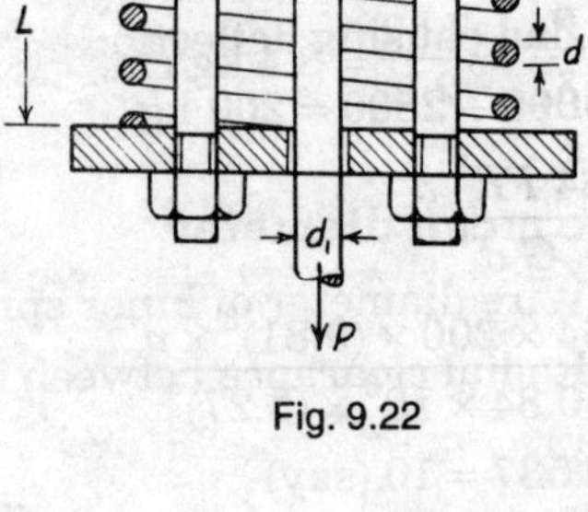


Fig. 9.22

(*b*) **To calculate $d_2$.** The rod of diameter $d_2$ is bent in U-shape and is threaded at the ends.

$d_{c_1}$ = Core diameter at threaded portion of rod

The rod is under tension

$$2 \times \frac{\pi}{4} d_{c_1}^2 \times f_t = P$$

$$2 \times \frac{\pi}{4} d_{c_1}^2 \times 800 = 3000$$

$$d_{c_1} = 1.09 \text{ cm}$$

$$d_2 = \frac{1.09}{0.8} = 1.36 \text{ cm.}$$

(*c*) **To calculate diameter of spring wire**

$d$ = Diameter of spring wire

$D$ = Mean diameter of coil

$R$ = Mean radius of coil = $D/2$

$$\frac{D}{d} = \text{Spring index} = 7$$

$$D = 7\,d$$

$$R = 3.5\,d$$

$T$ = Twisting moment = $P \times R$

$$P \times R = \frac{\pi}{16} \cdot f_s \cdot d^3$$

$$3000 \times 3.5\,d = \frac{\pi}{16} \times 5000 \times d^3$$

$$d = 3.27 \text{ cm}$$

$$R = 3\,d = 3.27 \times 3 = 9.81 \text{ cm.}$$

(*d*) **To calculate number of turns**

$n$ = Number of turns

$\delta$ = Deflection = 1.2 cm

$F$ = Load causing deflection

= 3000 − 2800 = 200 kg

$$\delta = \frac{64\,FR^3\,n}{G\,d^4}$$

$$1.2 = \frac{64 \times 200 \times (9.81)^3 \times n}{0.84 \times 10^6 \times (3.27)^4}$$

$$n = 9.537 = 10 \text{ (say)}$$

(*e*) **To calculate free length of spring**

Assuming square and ground ends

$n_1$ = Total number of turns

$= n + 2 = 10 + 2 = 12$

$C_1$ = Clearance between adjacent coils

= 0.1 cm (say)

$\delta_m$ = Maximum deflection

$$= \frac{3000}{3000 - 2800} \times \delta$$

$$= \frac{3000}{200} \times \delta = 15\,\delta$$

$= 15 \times 1.2 = 18$ cm.

Free length $= (n_1 - 1) \times c_1 + n_1\, d + \delta_m$

$= (12 - 1) \times 0.1 + 12 \times 3.27 + 18$

$= 58.34$ cm.

**Example 9.13.** *A flat strip 1.5 cm wide, 0.13 cm thick and 200 cm long is used for making a flat spring. If the maximum stress at the point of maximum bending moment is 8000 kg/cm² and* $E = 2 \times 10^6$ *kg/cm², calculate :*

(*i*) *Bending moment*

(*ii*) *Number of turns to wind up the spring*

(*iii*) *Strain energy stored in the spring.*

**Solution.**

$b$ = Width = 1.5 cm

$t$ = Thickness = 0.13 cm

$f$ = Stress = 800 kg/cm²

$E = 2 \times 10^6$ kg/cm²

$T$ = Torque

(*a*) **To find torque**

$$f = \frac{12\,T}{bt^2}$$

$$8000 = \frac{12\,T}{1.5 \times (0.13)^2}$$

$T = 16.9$ kg cm.

(*b*) **To find number of turns**

$n$ = Number of turns

$\theta$ = Angular deflection in radians

$$= \frac{12\,TL}{E\,bt^3} = \frac{12 \times 16.9 \times 200}{2 \times 10^6 \times 1.5 \times (0.13)^3}$$

$$= 8 \text{ radians}$$

$$n = \frac{\theta}{2\pi}.$$

(*c*) **To calculate strain energy**

$U$ = Strain energy

$$= \frac{f^2}{24\,E} \times \text{Volume of spring}$$

$$= \frac{f^2}{24} E\,.\,b\,.\,t\,.\,L = \frac{(8000)^2 \times 1.5 \times 0.13 \times 200}{24 \times 2 \times 10^6}$$

$$= 6.5 \text{ kg cm.}$$

## 9.10.2. Torsion Helical Springs

These springs are used for the transmission of small torques and are commonly used in door hunges, levers, automobile starters etc. The primary stress developed in such springs is flexural as compared to torsional shear stress developed in helical tension or compression springs. Fig. 9.23 shows a helical torsion spring. The spring may be made of circular wire, rectangular wire or square cross-section wire.

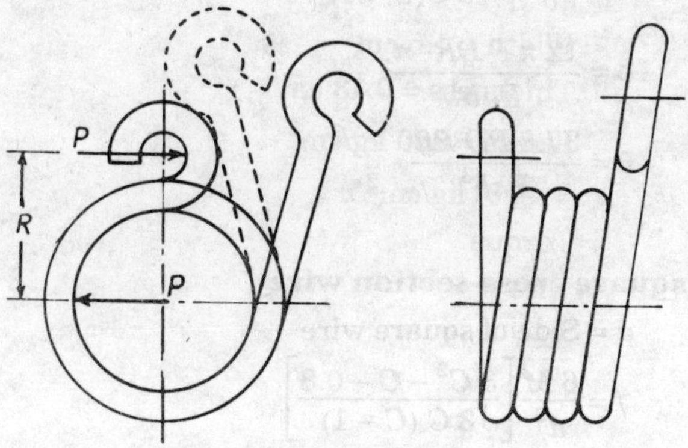


Fig. 9.23.

Let $P$ = Load acting

$R$ = Moment arm of load

= Distance from load line to spring axis

$M$ = Bending moment

$= P \times R$

$\theta$ = Angle of twist (radians)

$\delta$ = Deflection

$C$ = Spring index

$n$ = Number of effective coils

$f$ = Flexural stress

$E$ = Young's modulus of elasticity

$D$ = Mean diameter of coil

**(*a*) For circular cross-section wire**

$d$ = Diameter of wire

$$f = \frac{32\,M}{\pi\,d^3}\left[\frac{4\,C^2 - C - 1}{4\,C(C-1)}\right]$$

$$\delta = \frac{64\,P\,D\,R^2\,n}{Ed^4}$$

$$\theta = \frac{64\,PD\,Rn}{Ed^4}$$

**(*b*) For rectangular cross-section wire ($h \times b$)**

$h$ = Wire dimension parallel to axis

$b$ = Wire dimension perpendicular to axis

$$f = \frac{6\,M}{hb^2}\left[\frac{3\,C^2 - C - 0.8}{3\,C(C-1)}\right]$$

$$\delta = \frac{12\,\pi\,P\,DR^2\,n}{Ehb^3}$$

$$\theta = \frac{37.8\,PD\,Rn}{Ehb^3}$$

**(*c*) For square cross-section wire**

$a$ = Side of square wire

$$f = \frac{6\,M}{d^3}\left[\frac{3\,C^2 - C - 0.8}{3\,C\,(C-1)}\right]$$

$$\delta = \frac{12\,\pi\,PD\,R^2 n}{Ed^4}$$

$$\theta = \frac{37.8\, PD\, Rn}{Ed^4}$$

Torsion springs should be installed such that the application of load winds up the wire as a result of the diameter will be reduced and clearance should be provided when the spring operates around a material.

**Example 9.14.** *In a torsion spring made of circular wire the mean diameter of coil is 5 cm. The spring index is 7 and number of active coils is 6. If the torque applied is 800 kg cm and permissible stress in the spring is 5500 kg/cm² determine diameter of wire and angle of twist of spring.*

*Take* $E = 2 \times 10^6$ kg/cm²

**Solution.**

$M$ = 800 kg cm

$f$ = Permissible stress = 5500 kg/cm²

$d$ = Wire diameter

$D$ = Mean diameter of coil = 5 cm

$C$ = Spring index = 7

$n$ = Number of active coils = 6

$E = 2 \times 10^6$ kg/cm²

(*a*) **To determine, d**

$$f = \frac{32\, M}{\pi\, d^3}\left[\frac{4\, C^2 - C - 1}{4\, C(C-1)}\right]$$

$$5500 = \frac{32 \times 800}{\pi\, d^3}\left[\frac{4 \times 7^2 - 7 - 1}{4 \times 7(7-1)}\right]$$

$d$ = 1.18 cm.

(*b*) **To determine angle of twist**

$\theta$ = Angle of twist

$$= \frac{64\, P\, D\, R\, n}{E\, d^4} = \frac{64\, (P \times R)\, D \times n}{E\, d^4}$$

$$= \frac{64\, M\, D \times n}{E\, d^4} = \frac{64 \times 800 \times 5 \times 6}{2.1 \times 10^6 \times (1.18)^4}$$

= 0.377 radian.

## 9.11 Leaf Springs

They are made up of number of leaves. Fig. 9.24 shows cantilever type leaf spring made from number of strips placed one above the other. Fig. 9.25 shows a cantilever leaf spring using triangular plate.

Let $f$ = Maximum stress in the spring

$P$ = Load applied

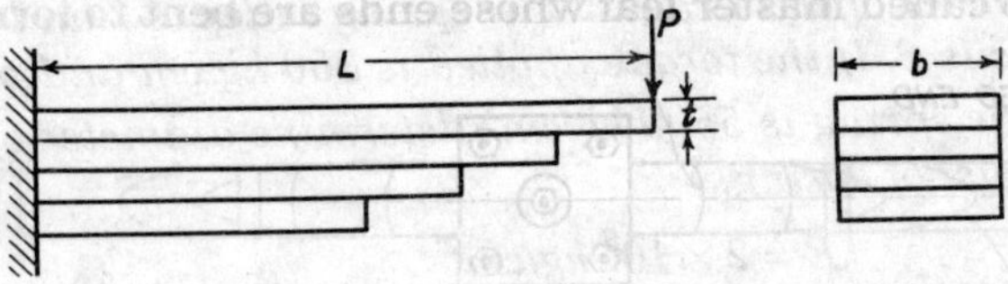


Fig. 9.24

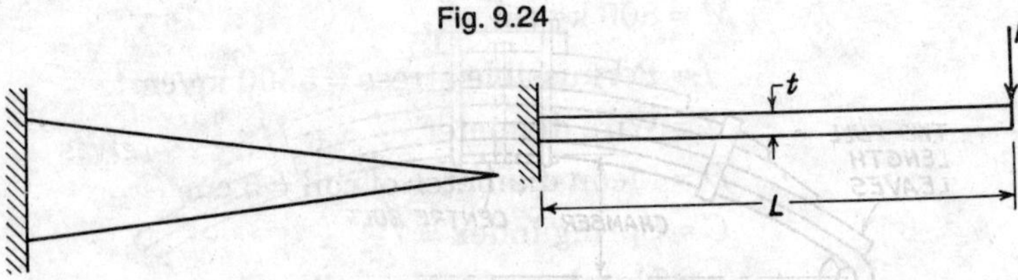


Fig. 9.25

$t$ = Thickness of each leaf

$b$ = Width of each leaf

$n$ = Number of leaves

$L$ = Length of cantilever spring

$\delta$ = Deflection of spring

$$= \frac{6\,PL^3}{E_n\,bt^3}$$

The value of stress is found by using the following formula ;

$$f = \frac{6\,PL}{n\,.\,bt^3}$$

$U$ = Strain energy of spring $= \dfrac{f^2}{6\,E} \times V_1$

where $V_1$ = Volume of spring $= \dfrac{n\,.\,L\,bt}{2}$

$E$ = Modulus of elasticity.

**Semi elliptical leaf springs.** This spring consists of number of leaves which are held together by U-clips and a bolt passing through the centre. The diameter of bolt should be subtracted from the width of plate when making calculations for strength of the spring. These springs are quite commonly used in railway wagons and road vehicles. Fig. 9.26 shows semi-elliptical leaf spring which may be considered as two cantilevers. These springs are made up of highly hardened plain carbon steels, silico manganese steels and vanadium steel. In these springs the long leaf fastened to the supports is called master leaf whose ends are bent to form an eye.

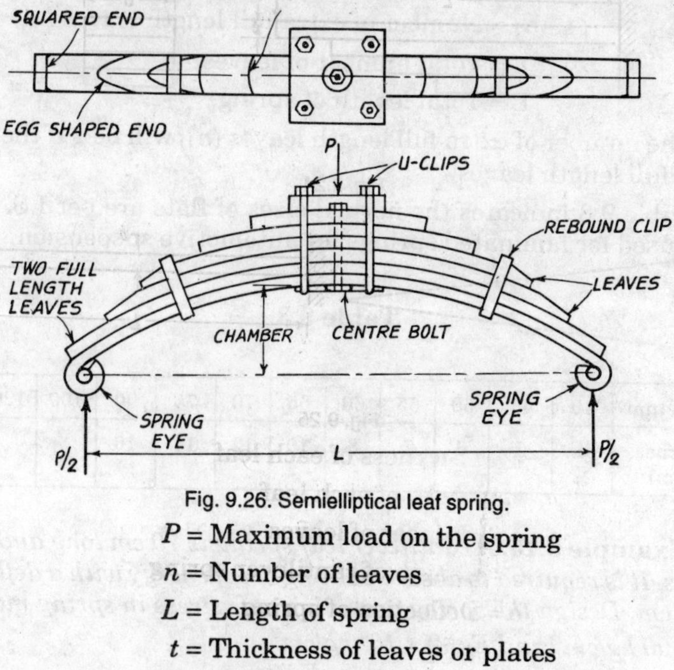

Fig. 9.26. Semielliptical leaf spring.

Let $P$ = Maximum load on the spring

$n$ = Number of leaves

$L$ = Length of spring

$t$ = Thickness of leaves or plates

$b$ = Width of leaves

$f$ = Maximum stress

$\delta$ = Camber or deflection of the spring.

The various values are calculated as follows :

$$\delta = \frac{f L^2}{4 E t} \quad ...(i)$$

$$f = \frac{3 PL}{2 bt^2 n} \quad ...(ii)$$

Substituting value of $f$ from equation (*ii*) in equation (*i*), we get

$$\delta = \frac{3\,PL^3}{8\,En\,bt^3}$$

These formulae are true when the spring is without extra full length leaves. When extra full length leaves are provided then the deflection is calculated as follows :

$$\delta = \frac{3\,PL^3}{4\,(2+k)\,En\,bt^3} = \frac{L^2 f}{2(2+k)\,Et}$$

where $k = \frac{n_1}{n}$

where $n_1$ = Number of extra full length leaves

$n$ = Total number of leaves

$L$ = Total length of spring.

The number of extra full length leaves ($n_1$) will be 2 if there are three full length leaves.

Table 9.3 indicates the normal sizes of flats are per I.S. 3431-1965 used for laminated springs for automotive suspension.

**Table 9.3**

| Width (nm) | 40 | 45 | 50 | 55 | 60 | 65 | 70 | 75 | 90 | 100 | 120 | 150 |
|---|---|---|---|---|---|---|---|---|---|---|---|---|
| Thickness (mm) | 4 | 5 | 6 | 7 | 8 | 10 | 12 | 14 | 16 | | | |

**Example 9.15.** *A cantilever leaf spring is 70 cm long and has 8 leaves. It is required to absorb 8100 kg cm of energy with a deflection of 18 cm. Design the spring assuming safe stress in spring material as 8000 kg/cm² and E = 2 × 10⁶ kg/cm².*

**Solution.** (*a*) **To calculate load**

$P$ = Load on spring

$L$ = Length of spring = 70 cm

$\delta$ = Deflection = 18 cm.

$f = 8000$ kg/cm$^2$

$E = 2 \times 10^6$ kg/cm$^2$

$E_1 = \text{Energy} = \frac{1}{2} . P . \delta$

$$8100 = \frac{1}{2} \times P \times 18$$

$$P = 900 \text{ kg.}$$

(*b*) **To calculate thickness and width of leaf**

Let

$b$ = Width of each leaf

$t$ = Thickness of each leaf

$n$ = Number of leaves = 8

$$f = \frac{6 \cdot P \cdot L}{n \cdot bt^2}$$

$$8000 = \frac{6 \times 900 \times 70}{8 \times bt^2}$$

$$bt^2 = \frac{189}{32} \quad ...(i)$$

$$E_1 = \text{Energy of spring} = \frac{f^2 \times V_1}{6} E$$

where $V_1$ = Volume of spring $= \dfrac{n \cdot b \cdot t \cdot L}{2}$

$$E_1 = \frac{f^2 \times n \cdot b \cdot t \cdot L}{2 \times 6 \times E}$$

$$8100 = \frac{(8000)^2 \times 8 \times b \times t \times 70}{2 \times 6 \times 2 \times 10^6}$$

$$b \times t = \frac{2430}{448} \quad ...(ii)$$

By dividing equation (*i*) by (*ii*), we get

$$t = \frac{189}{32} \times \frac{448}{2430} = 1.1 \text{ cm.}$$

Now

$$b \times t = \frac{2430}{448}$$

$$b \times 1.1 = \frac{2430}{448}$$

$$b = 4.95 \text{ cm} = 5 \text{ cm (say)}$$

**Example 9.16.** *A semi-elliptical laminated vehicle spring to carry a load of 295 kg is to consist of 7 leaves 7.35 cm wide, two of the leaves extending the full length of spring. The spring is to be 10.9 cm in length and attached to the axle by U-bolts 7.26 cm apart. These bolts hold the central portion of the spring so rigidly that they may* *be considered equivalent to a band having a width equal to the distance between the bolts. The leaves are to be silico-manganese steel. Assuming an allowable stress at 3500 kg/cm$^2$ and $E = 2.1 \times 10^6$, determine the following :*

(*a*) *Thickness of leaves*

(*b*) *Eye diameter*

(*c*) *Deflection*

(*d*) *Length of the other five leaves.*

**Solution.** (*a*) **To calculate thickness**

$P = 295$ kg

$b$ = Width of each leaf = 7.35 cm.

Length of spring = 109 cm

$x$ = Width of band

= Distance between centre of U–bolts 7.62 cm

$L$ = Effective length of spring

= 109 – 7.92 = 101.38 cm

$n$ = Number of leaves = 7

$n_1$ = Extra full length leaf = 2 – 1 = 1

$$f = \text{Maximum stress} = \frac{3\,Lp}{2n \times bt^2}$$

$$3500 = \frac{3 \times 101.38 \times 295}{2 \times 7 \times 7.35 \times t^2}$$

$t = 0.5$ cm.

(*b*) **To calculate eye diameter**

Let $d$ = Eye diameter = Diameter of pin

$l$ = Length of pin = Width of leaf = 7.35 cm

Considering bearing of pin for eye

Area under bearing = $l \times d$

Taking bearing stress ($f_b$) as 100 kg/cm$^2$ and load on pin as $\dfrac{P}{\cos 45}$.

$$\frac{P}{\cos 45} = l \times d \times f_b$$

$$\frac{295}{1} \times \sqrt{2} = 7.35 \times d \times 100$$

$$d = 0.5 \text{ cm}$$

The pin can be checked in shear

$$\text{Area under shear} = 2 \times \frac{\pi}{4} d^2$$

$$f_{s_1} = \text{Induced shear stress}$$

$$\frac{P}{\cos 45} = 2 \times \frac{\pi}{4} d^2 \times f_{s_1}$$

$$f_{s_1} = \frac{295 \times \sqrt{2} \times 2}{\pi \times 0.5^2} = 1082 \text{ kg/cm}^2$$

This is quite within limits, hence safe.

(*c*) **To calculate deflection**

$$k = \frac{n}{n_1} = \frac{1}{7}$$

$$\delta = \text{Deflection} = \frac{3\, PL^3}{4(2+k)\, En\, bt^3}$$

$$= \frac{3 \times 295 \times (101.38)^3}{4\left(2 + \frac{1}{7}\right) \times 2.1 \times 10^6 \times 7 \times 7.35 \times 0.5^3}$$

$$= 7.97 \text{ cm.}$$

(*d*) $N_f$ = Full length leaves = 2

$n_g$ = Number of graduated leaves = 5

$n$ = Total leaves = 7

If $n_f = 1$, then the number of leaves to be cut is $n$ and if $n_f = 2$ the number of leaves to be cut is $(n - 1)$ and two of full length leaves will be of small length (this includes the master leaf).

For $n_f = 2$

$$L_1 = \text{Smallest leaf length} = \frac{\text{Effective length}}{\text{n} - 1} + x$$

$$= \frac{L}{n-1} + x = \frac{101.38}{6} + 7.62 = 24.52 \text{ cm}$$

$$L_2 = \text{Length of second graduated leaf}$$

$$= \frac{L}{n-1} \times 2 + x = \frac{101.38}{6} \times 2 + 7.62 = 41.42 \text{ cm}$$

$$L_3 = \text{Length of third graduated leaf}$$

$$= \frac{L}{n-1} \times 3 + x$$

$$= \frac{101.38}{6} \times 4 + 7.62 = 58.32 \text{ cm}$$

$L_4$ = Length of fourth graduated leaf

$$= \frac{L}{n-1} \times 4 + x = \frac{101.38}{6} \times 4 + 7.62 = 75.22 \text{ cm}$$

$L_5$ = Length of fifth graduated leaf

$$= \frac{L}{n-1} \times 5 + x = \frac{101.38}{6} \times 5 + 7.62 = 92.12 \text{ cm.}$$

Sixth and seventh leaves will be of full length and seventh leaf will act as master leaf.

$$\text{Length of sixth leaf} = \frac{L}{n-1} \times 6 + x = \frac{L}{6} \times 6 + x = L + x$$

$$= 101.38 + 7.62 = 109 \text{ cm.}$$

Length of seventh leaf *i.e.* master leaf

= Span length of spring + Allowances for eye

$= 109 + 2\pi(d + t) = 109 + 2\pi(0.5 + 0.5)$

$= 115.28$ cm

where $d$ = Inside diameter of the eye at each end

$t$ = Thickness of master leaf

**Example 9.17.** *A helical compression spring is to carry a fluctuating load varying from 400 N to 600 N. The spring index is 7 and factor of safety is 2.3, yield stress in shear is 640 MPa and endurance limit is 350 MPa. If deflection due to variation in load is 3.5 mm, determine*

*(a) Spring wire diameter*

*(b) Number of effective turns in the spring.*

**Solution.**

$C$ = Spring Index = 7

$P_{max}$ = Maximum force = 600 N

$P_{min}$ = Minimum force = 400 N

$P_m$ = Mean force $= \frac{1}{2}(P_{max} + P_{min})$

$$P_m = \frac{1}{2}(600 + 400) = 500 \text{ N}$$

$P_v$ = Variable force

$$= \frac{1}{2}[P_{max} - P_{min}] = \frac{1}{2}[600 - 400] = 100 \text{ N}$$

$K_v$ = Variable Wahl correction factor

$$= \frac{4C - 1}{4C - 4} = \frac{4 \times 7 - 1}{4 \times 7 - 4} = 1.12$$

$K_m$ = Mean Wahl correction factor

$$= 1 + \frac{0.615}{C} = 1 + \frac{0.615}{7} = 1.08$$

$d$ = Wire diameter

$f_m$ = Mean stress

$$= \frac{8\, k_m \,.\, p_m \,.\, C}{\pi d^2} = 8 \times 1.08 \times 500 \times \frac{7}{\pi d^2} = \frac{9630}{d^2}$$

$f_v$ = Variable stress

$$= \frac{8\, K_v \,.\, P_v \,.\, C}{\pi d^2}$$

$$= \frac{8 \times 1.12 \times 100 \times 7}{\pi d^2} = \frac{1997}{d^2}$$

$f_{ys}$ = Yield stress in shear = 640 MPa

$f_{es}$ = endurance limit = 350 MPa

$n$ = Factor of safety = 2.3

According to Soderberg formula

$$\frac{\frac{f_v}{f_{es}}}{2} = \frac{\frac{f_{ys}}{n} - f_m}{f_{ys} - \frac{f_{es}}{2}}$$

$$\frac{\frac{1997}{d^2}}{\frac{350}{2}} = \frac{\frac{640}{2} - \frac{9630}{d^2}}{640 - \frac{350}{2}}$$

$d$ = 5.3 mm

$\delta$ = Deflection = 3.5 mm

$F$ = Load which causes deflection

= 600 – 400 = 200 N

$G$ = Modulus of rigidity = $0.8 \times 10^5$ N/mm

$n$ = Number of turns

$$= \frac{G \cdot d \cdot \delta}{8 F C^3} = \frac{0.8 \times 10^5 \times 5.3 \times 3.5}{8 \times 200 \times 7^3} = 2.8 = 3 \text{ (say)}.$$

**Example 9.18.** *A load of 4 KN is dropped from a height of 60 mm axially on a helical spring made of steel wire of diameter 18 mm. If the spring index is 7 and number of active coils are 8, calculate the stress induced in the spring.*

**Solution.**

$n$ = Number of coils = 8

$C$ = Spring index = 7

$d$ = Wire diameter = 18 mm

$G$ = Modulus of rigidity = $0.8 \times 10^5$ N/mm$^2$

$\delta$ = Deflection of spring

$P$ = Effective load on the spring

$$\delta = \frac{8 Pc^3 \cdot n}{G d} = \frac{8 \times P \times 7^3 \times 8}{0.8 \times 10^5 \times 10} = 0.027 \text{ P}$$

$W$ = Falling weight = 5 kN = 4000 N

$h$ = Height through which weight falls = 60 mm

$$W(h + \delta) = \frac{1}{2} \cdot P \cdot \delta$$

$$4000(60 + 0.027P) = \frac{1}{2} \times P \times 0.027P$$

$P$ = 10560 N

$k$ = Wahl stress concentration factor

$$= \frac{4C - 1}{4C - 4} + \frac{0.615}{C} = \frac{4 \times 7 - 1}{4 \times 7 - 4} + \frac{0.615}{7} = 1.21$$

$\tau$ = Shear stress

$$= \frac{8 k PC}{\pi d^2} = \frac{8 \times 1.21 \times 10560 \times 7}{\pi \times 18^2} = 703 \text{ MPa}.$$

## PROBLEMS

**9.1.** (*a*) State the functions of a spring. (*b*) Describe with sketches the various types of springs.

**9.2.** (*a*) State the factors governing choice of materials for springs. (*b*) What are the commonly used materials for springs ?

**9.3.** Discuss the following terms in connection with spring :

(*a*) Free length (*b*) Solid length

(*c*) Wahl's stress concentration factor

(*d*) Load-deflection diagram

(*e*) Buckling of compression springs

(*f*) Surging of springs.

**9.4.** A closed coil spring is subjected to a load of 80 kg. The deflection at this load is 7 cm. The mean diameter of load is 6 cm. The allowable stress in the material of spring is 3000 kg/cm$^2$ and $G = 0.84 \times 10^6$ kg/cm$^2$.

(*a*) Wire diameter

(*b*) Number of coils

(*c*) Length of spring if minimum clearance between the adjacent coils is 1.7 cm.

**9.5.** A weight of 60 kg is to drop on the centre of a platen from a height of 34 cm. The platen is supported on four helical springs. If the deflection allowed for each spring is 5 cm and spring index is 6, determine the following.

(*a*) Wire diameter (*b*) Mean diameter of coil

(*c*) Number of coils.

Take safe stress in spring 3200 kg/cm$^2$.

**9.6.** The larger of two concentric helical springs is made of 35 mm diameter round bar stock and has 245 mm mean coil diameter and 6 active coils. The inner spring is of 25 mm bar, has 9 active coils and mean diameter of coils and 150 mm. The free height of outer spring is 18 mm more than the inner spring. Find the deflection of each spring for a load of 9000 kg. Find the load carried by each spring.

**9.7.** A helical spring is made from rectangular wire 12 mm by 6 mm. With the narrow side parallel to the helix axis. Mean diameter of coil is 75 mm. The static load is 80 kg.

(*a*) Find the value of maximum stress and the deflection if the number of active coils is 8.

(*b*) Repeat (*a*) with the spring wound with long side of the section parallel to the axis.

**9.8.** A close coiled helical spring consists of 12 coils. The mean diameter of coils is 10 cm and spring is made of 1.2 cm diameter wire. It is subjected to an axial load of 120 kg. If $G = 0.84 \times 10^6$ kg/cm$^2$, determine the following:

(*a*) Shear stress in the spring, (*b*) Deflection of spring.

**9.9.** A weight of 15 kg falls from a height of 60 cm on a closely wound spring which is compressed by a maximum amount of 8 cm under the impact. The spring is made of steel rod of 2.7 cm diameter and mean diameter of coils is 1.8 cm. Take $G = 0.84 \times 10^6$ kg/cm$^2$. Determine the following :

(*a*) Instantaneous stress produced by the impact

(*b*) Number of coils in the spring.

**9.10.** A locomotive semi-elliptical laminated spring has an overall length of 100 cm and is acted on by a load of 7000 kg at its centre. The spring has 3 full length leaves and 15 graduated leaves with a central band of 10 cm width. All the leaves are to be stressed to 400 kg/cm$^2$ when fully loaded. The ratio of the total spring depth to that of the width is two. Assume $E = 2 \times 10^2$ kg/cm$^2$. Determine the width and thickness of the leaves.

*(A.M.I.E.1978)*

**9.11.** Design a close coiled helical spring of silicon manganese steel for the value of an I.C. engine capable of exerting a net force of 6.5 kg. When the value is open and 5.4 kg when it is closed. The internal and external diameters are governed by space limitations as it has to fit over a bushing 19 mm outside diameter and go inside a space of 38 mm diameter. The valve lift is 6 mm. Using the following data :

$G = 0.8 \times 10^6$ kg /cm$^2$

Elastic limit in shear (12 mm diameter) = 6650 kg/cm$^2$.

Factor of safety of ordinary work =2

Factor of safety for continuous service and rapid stress change =3

Size factor to allow for the change in elastic limit with change in wire diameter (cm) $= \dfrac{0.86 + 0.7 \times 2.5}{d}$

$$k = \text{Wahl stress concentration factor}$$

$$= \frac{4\,C - 1}{4\,C - 4} + \frac{0.615}{C}$$

where $C$ = Spring index **(A.M.I.E. 1980)**

**9.12.** A cantilever spring has an effective length of 60 cm and has two full length leaves and six graduated leaves each 54 mm wide. The spring is to sustain a load of 430 kg. The allowable stress in spring material is 3400 kg/cm$^2$. Determine.

(*a*) Thickness of spring leaves.

(*b*) Deflection of spring.

**9.13.** A flat spiral spring is to give a maximum torque of 16 kg cm for a maximum stress of 6500 kg/cm$^2$. If the space considerations limit the width of wire to 17 mm determine thickness and length of spring to give threes complete turns of motion when stress decreases from 6500 to zero.

**9.14.** The following particulars refer to the valve spring of a petrol engine.

Length of the spring when the valve is open = 41 mm

Length of the spring when the valve is closed = 49 mm

Spring load when valve is open = 36 kg

Spring load when valve is closed = 22 kg.

Maximum inside diameter of spring = 25 mm

Evaluate

(*i*) Size of wire for the maximum operating stress of 4000 kg/cm$^2$ and

$$G = 8.3 \times 10^5 \text{ kg/cm}^2$$

(*ii*) Number of active coils

(*iii*) Pitch of the spring. **(A.M.I.E. 1971)**

**9.15.** A close coil helical spring compresses 12 cm in bringing to rest a body of weight 660 kg moving at 65 m/min. The spring index is 7 and $G = 0.84 \times 10^6$ kg/cm$^2$. Determine.

(*a*) Wire diameter if $f_s$ = 3000 kg/cm$^2$

(*b*) Number of active turns.

**9.16.** Two steel springs each of 10 active coils of 2.8 mm wire have mean radius of helix 8 mm and support a bar as shown in Fig. P-9.16. The right hand spring has a free length 10 mm more than left spring. When load is acting the bar is level. Find distance *S*.

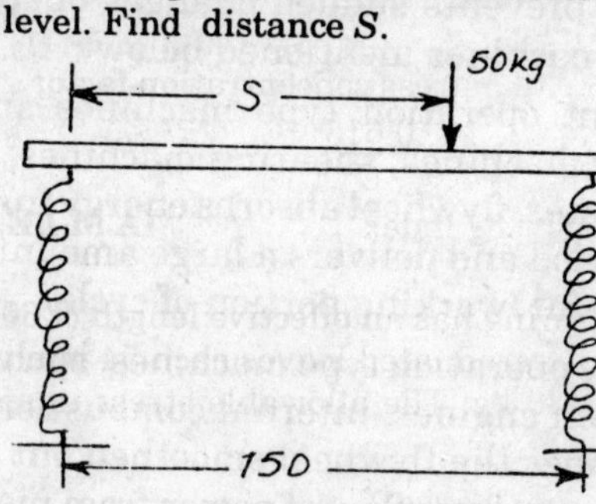


Fig. P-9.16

# 10

# Flywheels and Pulleys

## 10.0 Flywheel

A flywheel is attached at the end of the shaft. It acts as a energy reservoir. Flywheel stores energy at some time and gives up when desired. Flywheel prevents sudden changes of speed. Flywheel is needed for two of machines mentioned below :

(*i*) Intermittent operation type machines such as punching machines riveting machines, shearing machines, presses, crushes etc. In these machines, flywheel absorbs energy from a power source during the idle period and delivers a large amount of stored energy in a very short useful (working portion of cycle).

(*ii*) Continuous operation type machines, such a steam engines, internal combustion engines, internal combustion engines, pumps etc. In such machines the flywheel smoothen out the sped fluctuation caused by non-uniform flow of power from piston during working stroke.

Flywheels may be either made solid in one piece or the flywheel may be made rim coupled to shaft by arms (Fig. 10.2). Flywheels may be cast solid in one piece or different parts joined by both depending upon the size of flywheel. Fig. 10.2 shows a flywheel with a solid web. Stud both may be used to make the rim connection (Fig. 10.3).

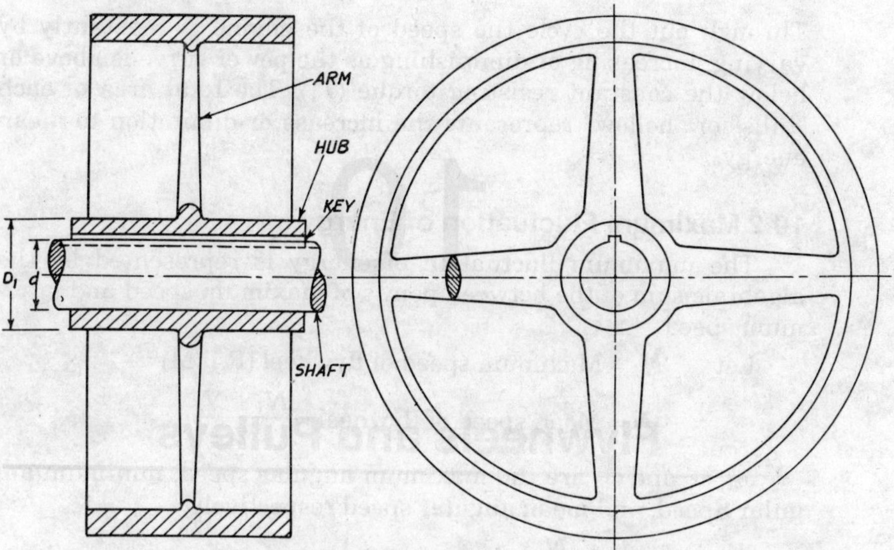


Fig. 10.1. Fly wheel.

An armed type flywheel is able to store more energy than solid disc type flywheel for the same mass, speed and material of flywheel.

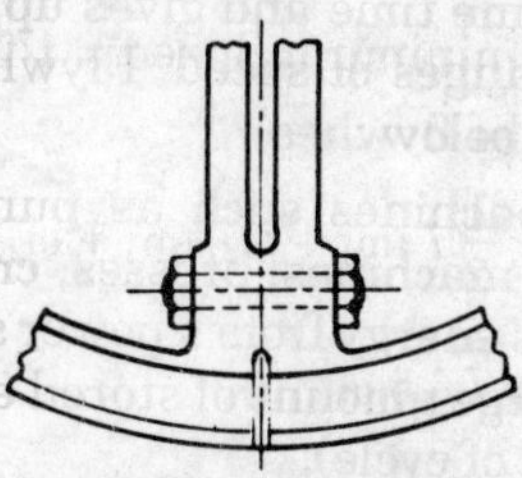

Fig. 10.2

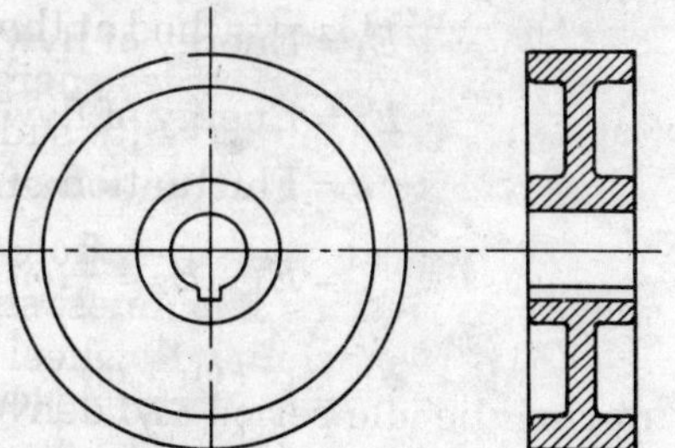

Fig. 10.3

## 10.1. Turning Moment Diagram

This diagram shows the variation of torque ($T$) corresponding to the angle of rotation (0) of crank from the inner dead centre positon. The area under the turning moment diagram represent the work done. Consider a case where turning moment diagram is as show in Fig. 10.4.

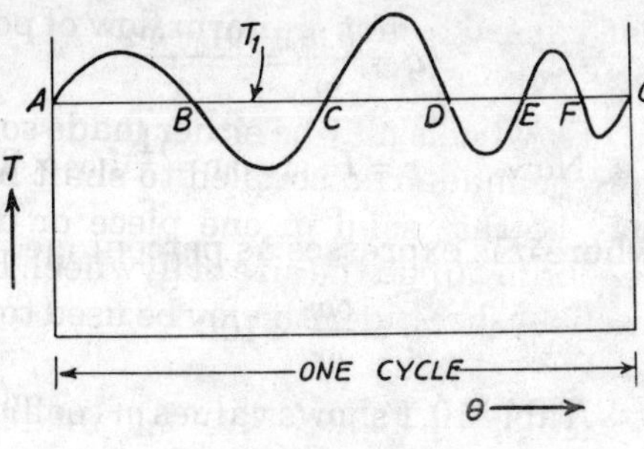


Fig. 10.4.

Through out the cycle the speed of the engine is constantly by varying, increasing or diminishing as the power curve is above or below the constant resisting torque ($T_1$). The total area of each "hills" or "hollow" represents the increase or diminition to mean energy.

## 10.2 Maximum Fluctuation of Energy

The maximum fluctuation of energy is represented by the algebraic sum of the between points of maximum speed and minimum speed.

Let $N_1$ = Maximum speed of flywheel (R.P.M)

$N$ = Mean speed of flywheel $= \dfrac{N_1 + N_2}{2}$

$\omega_1$, $\omega_2$ and $\omega_3$ are the maximum angular speed, minimum angular Speed, and mean angular speed respectively.

$$\omega = 2\pi \frac{N}{60}$$

$I$ = Moment of inertia of flywheels

$E$ = Energy of flywheel at mean speed ($N$) = $1/2\,.I\,.\omega^2$

$E_1$ = Energy of flywheel at maximum speed = $1/2\, I\, \omega_1^2$

$E_2$ = Energy of flywheel at minimum Speed = $1/2\, I\, \omega_2^2$

$e$ = Fluctuation of energy of flywheel

$$= E_1 - E_2 = \frac{1}{2} I \omega_1^2 - \frac{1}{2} \omega_2^2 = \frac{1}{2} I\, (\omega_1 + \omega_2)\, (\omega_1 + \omega_2)$$

$$= I\,.\left(\frac{\omega_1 + \omega_2}{2}\right)(\omega_1 - \omega_2) = I\omega\, \delta\, \omega$$

where $\delta\, \omega$ = Maximum permissible fluctuation of speed

$= \omega_1 - \omega_2$

### 10.2.1 Coefficient of fluctuation of speed (q)

$$q = \frac{\delta\, \omega}{\omega} = \frac{\omega_1 - \omega_2}{\omega}$$

Now $\quad e = I\,.\,\omega\,.\,\delta\omega = \dfrac{1}{2} I \omega_2 \times 2 \times \delta \dfrac{\omega}{\omega} = \dfrac{2Eq}{100}$

where $q$ is expresses as percentage.

$$q = \frac{\delta\omega}{\omega} \times 100$$

Table 10.1 shows values of coefficient of fluctuation of speed ($q$).

**Table 10.1**

| *Engines operating* | $q = \delta\frac{\omega}{\omega}$ |
|---|---|
| Hammers | 0.2 |
| Punches and shears | 0.1 to 0.15 |
| Gear wheel transmission | 0.02 |
| Machine shop drive | 0.025 to 0.028 |
| Engines with belt transmission | 0.03 |
| D.C. generators | 0.0065 |

## 10.3 Stresses in the Rim of Flywheel

The various stresses in the flywheel rim is induced due to the following reasons :

(*a*) Centrifugal stresses.

(*b*) Stresses due to change of speed and load.

(*c*) Shrinkage, stresses caused by the unequal cooling rates of the metal in the hub, arms and rim.

Centrifugal stress in the flywheel rim is given by

$$f = \rho\frac{v^2}{g} \text{ kg/cm}^2$$

where $f$ = Centrifugal stress

$\rho$ = Density of material inkg/sm$^3$

= 7.26 gm/cm$^3$ for cast iron = 7.8 gm per /cm$^3$ for cast steel.

$v$ = Mean velocity in cm/sec.

$g$ = Acceleration due to gravity in cm per sec$^2$

The practical design formula to determine centrifugal stress ($f$) is follows :

$$f = 0.0737\ v^2 \text{kg/cm}^2$$

where $v$ = Rim velocity in m /sec.

$f < 70$ kg /cm$^2$ for C. I. flywheel

$< 280$ kg /cm$^2$ for C. S. flywheel.

The bending stress$f_b$ is calculated as follows :

$$f_b = \frac{\pi^2 D\rho\, v^2}{2g \times n^2 h}$$

where $D$ = Mean diameter of rim; $h$ = Rim thickness

$n$ = Number of arms

The resultant stress $f_r$ in the rim at the junctions with the arms may be taken as

$$f_r = \frac{3}{4} f + \frac{1}{4} f_b$$

## 10.4. Design o Flywheel

(*a*) **Shaft.** The diameter of flywheel shaft ($d$) is calculated based upon the maximum torque it is to transmit.

(*b*) **Hub.**

Diameter of hub = $2 \times d$

Length of hub = $2d$ to$2.5d$.

(*c*) **Key.** A rectangular or square sunk key may be used.

For a square sunk key

$$\text{Width of key} = \text{Thickness of key} = \frac{d}{4}$$

Length of key can be found out on the basis of maximum torque.

(*d*) **Arms.** The arms of elliptical cross-section whose major axis ($a$) is twice the minor axis ($b$) (Fig. 10.5) are usually used in the flywheel. The major axis of the ellipse is in the plane of rotation to give arams greater resistance to bending.

The arms are never attached directly on the hub and the rim but a circumferential rib is provided at the hub and rim. (Fig. 10.6).

$$b_1 = \text{Width of rib} = 0.67\,a$$
$$h_1 = \text{Height of rib} = 0.67\,b_1$$

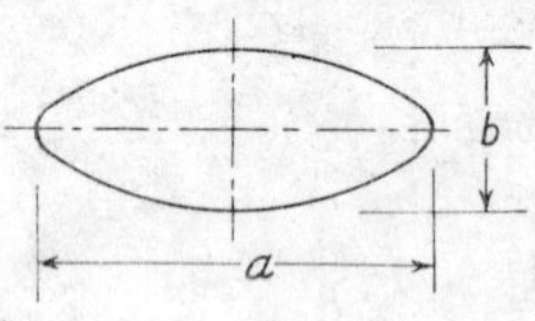


Fig. 10.5.

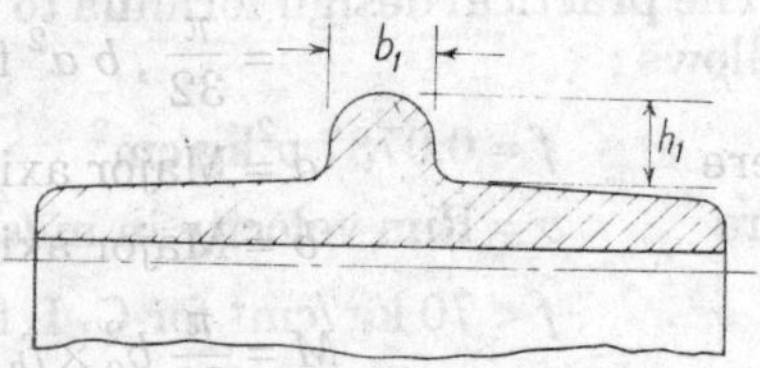


Fig. 10.6.

$D$ = Mean diameter of rim

$n$ = Number of arms

= 4 if $D < 400$ mm

= 6 if $400 < D < 3000$ mm

$$= 8 \text{ if } D > 3000 \text{ mm}$$

Sometimes even upto 12 arms may be used.

The arms are designed based on maximum bending moment.

$M$ = Maximum bending moment on the arm at hub

$$= \frac{T_m}{n} \times \frac{D - D_1}{D}$$

where $T$ = Maximum torque acting on the rim

$n$ = Number of arms

$D_1$ = Outside diameter of hub

Use bending equation

$$\frac{M}{I_1} = f\frac{b}{y}$$

where $I$ = Moment of inertia of elliptical section

$$= \frac{\pi}{64} b\, d^3$$

$$y = \frac{d}{2}$$

$Z$ = Section modulus

$$= \frac{I}{y} = \frac{\frac{\pi}{64} ba^3}{a/2} = \frac{\pi}{32} b\, a^2$$

$$M = f_b \times Z$$

where $f_b$ = Maximum bending stress

$Z$ = Section modulus of the arm cross section at the hub

$$= \frac{\pi}{32},\ b\, a^2 \text{ for elliptical section}$$

where $a$ = Major axis of elliptical section

$b$ = Major axis of elliptical section

$$M = \frac{\pi}{32} b_a^2 \times f_b$$

The values of $a$ and $b$ are calculated from this relation using

$$a = 2\, b$$

For pulleys upto 200 mm diameter, use webs.

For pulleys above 200 mm diameter and upto 450 mm diameter, use 4 arms.

Small pulleys are provided with webs with holes for handling convenience instead of arms or spokes. Since the arms are subjected to complete reversal of stress, a factor of safety of at least 8 (eight) should be provided. The allowable stress for cast 21 Mpa as the ultimate tensile strength of cast iron is 120 to 200 Mpa.

(*e*) **Rim.** Rim dimensions are calculated as follows :

$$W = \text{Weight of flywheel}$$

$$I = \text{Moment of inertia of flywheel}$$

$$= \frac{W}{g} \cdot k^2$$

where $k$ = reduce of gyration of flywheel. It is usual practice to consider the weight of flywheel to be concentrated at the mean radius of the rim and finally to make adjustment for the flywheel to effect of the hub and ram of the flywheel.

For the solid disc flywheel radius of gyration is found by the relation.

$$k^2 = \frac{D^2}{8}$$

$$k = \frac{D}{2\sqrt{2}}$$

where $D$ = Diameter of flywheel

If the thickness of rim is small as compared to radius of rimn the radius of gyration of rim may be taken equal to the mean radius of rim ($R$) without much error $k = R$.

Let $h$ = Thickness of rim in cm

$s$ = Width of rim in cm

$D$ = Mean diameter of wheel in cm

$W$ = Volume of rim × Density of material

$= \pi D \times h \times s \times P$

where $\rho$ = Density.

The section of rim is usually rectangular.

The ratio of width to height of rim section is as follows

$$\frac{s}{h} = 0.6 \text{ to } 2$$

**Rim speed.** The stress in the rim depends upon the rim speed ($v$). The safe rim speeds are indicated in Table 10.2.

**Table 10.2.**

| *Type of engine* | $v$*(m/min)* |
|---|---|
| For C.I. flywheel of engines under 1000 H.P. | 1500 |
| For larger machines C.I. flywheel | 1800 |
| For cast iron steel flywheel | 3600 |
| For steel flywheels of automotive engines | 6000 |

## 10.5. Flywheel for Punches

In case of presses punches, shears etc. the energy is consumed at a very high variable rate although energy is supplied at a comparatively constant rate by the motor. Nearly 80% of the energy supplied during a working cycle is consumed in about 1/5th of cycle. The excess energy needed is supplied by the flywheel and this causes reduction in flywheel speed.

$\rho$ = Force required to punch a hole in a plate

$= \pi . d .t\, fsu$

where $d_1$ = Diameter of hole

$t$ = Thickness of plate

$fsu$ = ultimate shear strength of plate material

Work done punching a hole average force $\times t = \frac{1}{2} P. t.$

The capacity of the flywheel can be increased by increasing weight, diameter or the velocity. To help the weight and diameter of flywheel with in reasonable limits the flywheel should be mounted on a high speed auxiliary shaft.

**Example 10.1.** *Design a cast iron flywheel for a single cylinder double acting steam engine that delivers 200 H P. at 120 R.P.M. The fluctuation of speed ±1.5% of the mean speed and the maximum fluctuation of energy per revaluation is 12%. The mean diameter of the rim is 2 m. The density of the cast iron is 7.25 gm/cm*$^2$*. Working stress in shaft 400 kg/cm*$^2$*.*

**Solution.** ($a$) **To calculate weight of rim**

$$H.P. = 200$$

$$N = \text{Mean speed} 120 \text{R. P .M}$$

$$E = \text{Energy delivered per revolution}$$

$$E = \text{H.P} \times \frac{4500}{N}$$

$$= 200 \times \frac{4500}{120} = 7500 \text{ kgm}$$

$$e = \text{Fluctuation of energy of flywheel}$$

$$= \frac{12}{100} \times E$$

$$= \frac{12}{100} \times 7500 = 900 \text{ kg}cm$$

$$\omega = \frac{2\pi N}{60} = \frac{2\pi \times 120}{60}$$

$$= 4\ \pi \text{ radian per sec}$$

$$\delta\ \omega = \frac{3}{100} \times \omega = \frac{3}{100} \times 4\pi$$

$$= 12\frac{\pi}{100} \text{ radian/sec.}$$

$$e = I\ .\ \omega\ .\ \delta\omega$$

$$900 = I \times 4\pi \times \frac{12\pi}{100}$$

$$I = 190.17 \text{ kg m sec}^2$$

$$k = \text{Radius of gyration} = 1m$$

$$W = \text{Weight of rim}$$

$$I = \frac{W}{g}\ k^2$$

$$190.17 = \frac{W}{9.81} \times 1^2$$

$$W = 1864 \text{ kg.}$$

(*b*) **To find rim diameters**

$$h = \text{Thickness of rim}$$

$$s = \text{Width of rim}$$

$$D = \text{Mean diameter of rim} = 2\text{m} = 200 \text{ cm}$$

$$rhp = \text{Density} = 7.25 \text{ gm/cm}^3 = 0.00725 \text{ kg/cm}^2$$

$$W = \pi D\ hs \times \rho$$

Using $s = 2h$, we get

$$1864 = \pi \times 200 \times h \times 2h \times 0.00725$$

$$h = 14.3 \text{ cm}$$

$$s = 2h = 2 \times 14.3 = 28.6 \text{ cm}$$

(c) **To calculate shaft diameter**

$$d = \text{Shaft diameter}$$

$$\text{H.P.} = 2\pi \frac{NT}{4500}$$

$$200 = \frac{2\pi \times 120 \times T}{4500}$$

$$T = 1194.26 \text{ kg}m = 119{,}426 \text{ kgcm.}$$

Let us take maximum torque ($T_m$) 50% more that mean torque ($T$)

$$T_m = 119{,}426 \times 1.5 = 179{,}139 \text{ kgcm}$$

$$T_m = \text{Safe shear stress in shaft} = 400 \text{ kg/cm}^2$$

$$T_m = \frac{\pi}{16} f_s d^3$$

$$179{,}139 = \frac{\pi}{16} \times 400 \times d^3$$

$$d = 13.16 \text{ cm} = 13.5 \text{ cm } (say)$$

(d) **Hub**

Diameter $(D_1) = 2d = 2 \times 13.5 = 27$ cm

Length $= 2.5d = 2.5 \times 13.5 = 33.75$ cm.

(e) **Key.** Using a rectangular sunk key

Width of key ($B$) $= \frac{d}{4} = \frac{13.5}{6} = 3.375$ cm

Thickness of Key $= \frac{d}{6} = \frac{13.5}{6} = 2.25$ cm

$$L = \text{Length of key}$$

$$P = \text{Force acting on key}$$

$$= \frac{T_m}{\text{Radius of key}} = \frac{179139}{6.75}$$

$$= 26{,}539 \text{ kg}$$

Considering shearing action of the key

$$P = L \times B \times f_s$$

$$26{,}539 = D \times 3.375 \times 400$$

$$L = 19.66 \text{ cm.}$$

(*f*) **To design arms.** We adopt 6 arms of elliptical cross section whose axis (*a*) is twise the minor axis (*b*)

$$n = \text{Number of arms} = 6$$

$$M = \text{Maximum bending moment on the arm will be near the hub}$$

$$= \frac{T_m}{n} \times \frac{D - D_1}{D}$$

where $D_1$ = Diameter of hub

$$M = \frac{179{,}139}{6} \times 200 - \frac{27}{200} = 25.826 \text{ kg cm}$$

$$M = f_b \times Z$$

$$f_b = \text{Safe flexural stress}$$

$$= 150 \text{ kg/cm}^2 \text{(say)}$$

$$Z = \text{Section modulus}$$

$$= \frac{\pi}{32} b\, a^2 \text{ for elliptical section}$$

$$= \frac{\pi}{32}\left(\frac{a}{2}\right) a^2 = \frac{\pi}{64} a^3$$

$$25{,}826 = 150 \times \frac{\pi}{64} a^3$$

$$a = 15.2 \text{ cm}$$

$$b = \frac{15.2}{2} = 7.6 \text{ cm.}$$

**Example 10.2.** *A cast iron flywheel is to store 40,000 kg m of energy at 150 R.P.M. Determine the following :*

(*a*) *Diameter of a mild steel shaft if energy is being transmitted at the rate of 240 H.P. The safe shear stress in shaft and key is 400kg/cm². Maximum torque is 40% more than mean torque.*

(*b*) *Diameter of hub.*

(*c*) *Diameter of a rectangular sunk key.*

(*d*) *Weight, widht and thickness of rim assuming that 90% of energy is stored in the rim. Width of rim is twise the thickness of rim.*

(*e*) *Dimensions of six elliptical section arms. The safe stress is 160kg/cm².*

*The radius of gyration is 80 cm and sensity of cast iron is 0.00072kg/cm*$^2$.

**Solution.**

$$\text{H.P.} = 2pi\frac{NT}{4500}$$

$$240 = 2\pi \times 150 \times \frac{T}{4500}$$

$$T = 1146.5 \text{ kgm} = 114{,}650 \text{ kgcm}$$

$$T_m = \text{Maximum torque}$$

$$= 1.4 \times 114{,}650 = 160{,}510 \text{ kgcm}$$

(*a*) **To calculate shaft diameter**

$d$ = Shaft diameter

$f_s$ = Safe shear stress in shaft = 400 kg/cm$^2$

$$T_m = \frac{\pi}{16} f_s\, d^3$$

$$160{,}510 = \frac{\pi}{16} \times 400 \times d^3$$

$$d = 12.7 \text{ cm} = 13 \text{ cm(say)}$$

(*b*) **Diameter of hub**

$D_1$ = Diameter

$= 2d = 2 \times 13 = 26$ cm

Length $= 2.5d = 2.5 \times 13 = 32.5$ cm

(*c*) **To find dimensions of rectangular sunk key**

$B$ = Width of key

$$= \frac{d}{4} = \frac{13}{4} = 3.25 \text{ cm}$$

Thickness $= \frac{d}{6} = \frac{13}{6} = 2.16$ cm

Length $= L$

$P$ = Force acting on key

$$= \frac{T_m}{r}$$

where $r$ = Radius of shaft

$$= \frac{13}{2} = 6.5 \text{ cm}$$

$$P = \frac{160{,}510}{6.5} = 24{,}694 \text{ kg}$$

Consider shearing action of key

$$P = L \times B \times f_s$$

$$24{,}694 = L \times 3.25 \times 400$$

$$L = 19 \text{ cm}$$

(*d*) **To find rim dimensions**

$W$ = Weight of rim

$E$ = Energy stored

$= 40{,}000 \times 0.9 = 36{,}000$ kg–m

$N$ = 150 R.P.M.

$\omega$ = Angular speed

$$\omega = 2\pi \times \frac{150}{60} = 15.7 \text{ radius/sec.}$$

$k$ = Radius of gyration = 0.8 m

$I$ = Moment of inertia

$$= \frac{1}{2}\frac{W}{g}k^2$$

$$E = \frac{1}{2} I . \omega^2$$

$$36{,}000 = \frac{1}{2} \times \frac{W}{9.81} \times (0.8)^2 \times (15.7)^3$$

$W$ = 4477 kg

$S$ = Width of rim

$h$ = Thickness on rim

$rhp$ = Density of rim = .0072 kg/cm$^2$

$D$ = Diameter of rim

$= 80 \times 2 = 160$ cm.

$$W = \pi D \times s \times h \times \rho$$

$$4477 = \pi \times 160 \times s \times \frac{s}{2} \times .0072$$

$$s = 49.75 \text{ cm}$$

$$h = \frac{s}{2} = \frac{49.45}{2} = 24.875 \text{ cm.}$$

(*e*) **To calculate dimensions of arms.**

$n$ = Number of arms = 6

$a$ = Major axis of elliptical section

$b$ = Minor axis of elliptical section

$a = 2\,b$

$M$ = Maximum bending moment on arms

$$= \frac{T_m}{n} \times \left(\frac{D - D_1}{D}\right)$$

$$= \frac{160{,}510}{6} \times \left(160 - \frac{26}{160}\right)$$

$$= 22{,}404 \text{ kg cm}$$

$$M = f_b \times Z$$

$$= 160 \times \frac{\pi}{32}\, ba^2$$

$$22{,}404 = 160 \times \frac{\pi}{32}\left(\frac{a}{2}\right) \times a^2$$

$$22{,}404 = 160 \times \frac{\pi}{64}\, a^3$$

$$a = 14.2 \text{ cm.}$$

$$b = \frac{a}{2} = \frac{14.2}{2} = 7.1 \text{ cm.}$$

**Example 10.3.** *For a reciprocating rngine the areas above and below the mean turning moment line taken in under are 5.3, 3.3, 3.8, 4.7,1.8, 3.6, 3.5 and 2.8 sq.cm.*

*The diagram has been drawn to the following scales.*

*Turning moment 1 cm = 1000kgm*

*Crank angle 1cm = 60°*

*Design a suitable cast iron flywheel for the engine. The mean R.P.M is 150 and total fluctuation of speed is 3.5% of the mean speed. The density of cast iron is 7.25gm/cm$^2$.*

*The safe shear stress in shaft and key is 400kg/cm$^2$ and also calculate the centrifugal or stress produces in the rim of the flywheel if the peripheral velocity of flywheel is to 15 metre per second.*

**Solution.**

(*a*) **To calculate diameter of flywheel.**

Let $E$ the energy of the flywheel in $cm^2$ of crank affort diagram (Fig.10.7 at the beginning of cycle. We calculate the energy at the other points.

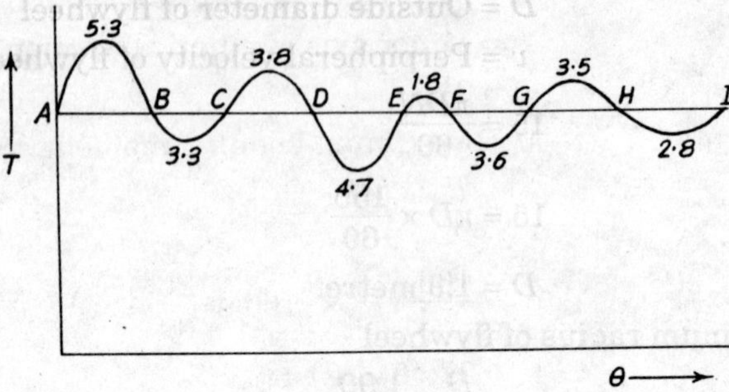


Fig. 10.7

Energy at $A$, $E_A = E$

$B$, $E_B = E + 5.3$

$C$, $E_c = E + 5.3 - 3.3 = E + 2$

$D$, $E_D = E + 2 + 3.8 = E + 5.8$

$E$, $E_E = E + 5.8 - 4.7 = E + 1.1$

$F$, $E_F = E + 1.1 = 1.8 = E + 2.9$

$G$, $E_G = E + 2.9 - 3.6 = E - 0.7$

$H$, $E_H = E - 7 + 3.5 = E + 2.8$

$I$, $E_I = E + 2.8 - 2.8 = E$

Maximum energy at $D$ at minimum energy is at $G$.

The energy scale of the the diagram is and follows :

$$1 \text{ cm}^2 = 1000 \times \frac{\pi}{3} = 1046.66 \text{ kg m.}$$

$e$ = Maximum fluctuation of energy

$= (E + 5.8) - (E - 0.7)$

$= 6.5$ sup2 $= 6.5 \times 1046.66$

$= 6803.3$ kgm

$\omega$ = Mear speed of flywheel

$$= 2\pi\frac{N}{60} = 2\pi \times \frac{150}{60} = 15.7 \text{ radian/sec}$$

$\delta_\omega$ = Maximum fluctuation of speed

$$= \frac{3.5}{100} \times 15.7 = 0.55 \text{ radian/sec}$$

$$e = I \,.\, \omega \,.\, \delta_\omega$$

$$6803 = I \times 15.7 \times 0.55$$

$$I = 787.87 \text{ kg m sec}^2$$

$D$ = Outside diameter of flywheel

$v$ = Perpipheral velocity of flywheel

$$15 = \frac{\pi DN}{60}$$

$$15 = \pi D \times \frac{150}{60}$$

$$D = 1.9 \text{ metre.}$$

Maximum radius of flywheel

$$= \frac{D}{2} = \frac{1.90}{2} = 0.95 \text{ m} = 95 \text{ cm}$$

We adopt 90 cm of meman radius of flywheel.

**(b) To find calculate weight of flywheel**

$W$ = Weight of flywheel

$K$ = Radius of gyration of flywheel

= 90 cm = 0.9 m

$$I = \frac{W}{g} k^2$$

$$787.87 = \frac{W}{9.81} \times (0.9)^2$$

$$W = 9542 \text{ kg.}$$

**(c) To find rim dimensions**

Let $P$ = Density of C.I

$s$ = Width of rim

$h$ = Height of rim

$= \frac{s}{2}$ (say)

Mean diameter $D_1$ = 180 cm

$$W = \pi D_1 \times h \times s \times \rho$$

$$9542 = \pi \times 180 \times \frac{s}{2} \times s \times 0.00725$$

$$s = 68 \text{ cm}$$

$$h = 34 \text{ cm}$$

**(d) To calculate hoop stress (f)**

$$f = 0.0737\, v^2$$

$$= 0.0737 \times 15^2 = 16.58 \text{ kg/cm}^2.$$

**Example 10.4.** *Design a flywheel for a punching machine to punch 24 holes of 18 mm diameter per minute in steel plate 12 mm thick mild steel plate. The ultimate shear stress of plate material is 340 kg/cm². The actual punching operation is to last for 1/2 of angular rotation of the crank shaft. The crankshaft is powered by a flywheel shaft through a reduction gearing having ratio of italic 1: 10.*

*The flywheel is made of cast iron weighing 7.25 gm/cm². Hub and spokes provide for italic 5% of rotational inertia of the wheel. The diameter of flywheel must not exceed 120 cm due to space dimensions.*

*Estime the horse poiver needed for the driving motor assuming a mechanical efficiency of 70%.*

**Solution.**

(*a*) **To calculate H.P. of driving motor**

$d^1$ = Diameter of hole = 18 mm = 1.8 cm

$n_1$ = Number of holes = 24

$t$ = Plate thickness = 1.2 cm

$f_{s_1}$ = Ultimate shear stress

= 3400 kg/cm²

$P$ = Maximum punching force

$= \pi\, d_1 t_1 \times f_s$

$= \pi \times 1.8 \times 1.2 \times 3400 = 23{,}060$ kg

$W_1$ = Work done in punching a hole

= Average force × Plate thickness

$= \dfrac{1}{2} \times P \times t = \dfrac{1}{2} \times 23{,}060 \times 1.2$

= 13,836 kg cm = 138.36 kg cm.

As 24 holes are produced per minute and one hole is produced in every crank shaft rotation

$N_1$ = Crank shaft speed = 24 R.P.M.

Since reduction gear has a ratio 1 : 10

∴ $N$ = Speed of flywheel shaft

$= 24 \times 10 = 240$ R.P.M.

$\eta$ = Mechanical efficiency = 0.7

H.P. of driving motor

$$= W_1 \times \frac{N_1}{\eta} \times 4500 = 138.36 \times \frac{24}{0.7} \times 4500$$

$$= 1.1$$

(*b*) **To calculate weight of flywheel rim.** Let us adopt mean diameter of flywheel as 110 cm

$$D = 110 \text{ cm}$$

As punching is done only during $\frac{1}{5}$ rotation of crank shaft

$$e = \text{Maximum fluctuation of flywheel energy}$$

$$= \left(1 - \frac{1}{5}\right) \times W_1 = \frac{4}{5} \times 13{,}836$$

$$= 1{,}069 \text{ kg cm} = 110.69 \text{ kg m}$$

$$\omega = \text{Mean speed of flywheel}$$

$$= \frac{2\pi N}{60} = \frac{2\pi \times 240}{60} = 25.16 \text{ radius/sec.}$$

Let permissible coefficient of fluctuation of speed

$$= 0.1$$

$$\delta_\omega = \text{Fluctuation of speed}$$

$$= 0.1 \times \omega = 0.1 \times 25.12$$

$$= 2.512 \text{ radians/sec}$$

$$W = \text{Weight of flywheel rim}$$

Since hub and spoked provide for 5% of rotation inertia of flywheel

$$0.95 \times e = I \, . \, \omega \, . \, \delta_\omega = \frac{W}{g} k^2 \times \omega \times \delta_\omega$$

$$0.95 \times 110.69 = \frac{W}{9.81} \times (0.5)^2 \times 25.12 \times 2.512$$

$$W = 54 \text{ kg}$$

(*c*) **To calculate rim dimensions**

$$s = \text{Width of rim}$$

$$h = \text{Thickness of rim}$$

Let $s = 1.5\, h$

$$W = \pi D s h \rho$$

$$54 = \pi \times 110 \times 1.5 \times h \times s \times 0.00725$$

$$h = 3.8 \text{ cm}$$

$$s = 1.5\,h = 1.5 \times 3.8 = 5.70 \text{ cm}$$

(*d*) **To check for total stress**

$v$ = Mean speed of flywheel

$$= \pi \frac{DN}{60} = \pi \times 120 \times \frac{240}{60}$$

1507.2~roman cm roman / roman sec

$$f = \text{Hoop stress} = \frac{\rho\, v^2}{g}$$

$$= \frac{0.000725 \times (1507.2)^2}{981} = 16.78 \text{ kg/cm}^2$$

Let $n$ = Number of arms = 6

$f_b$ = Bending stress

The flywheel is mounted on shaft supported in bearing (Fig. 10.8).

Overhang of flywheel ($I$)

$$= \frac{s}{2} + x + y$$

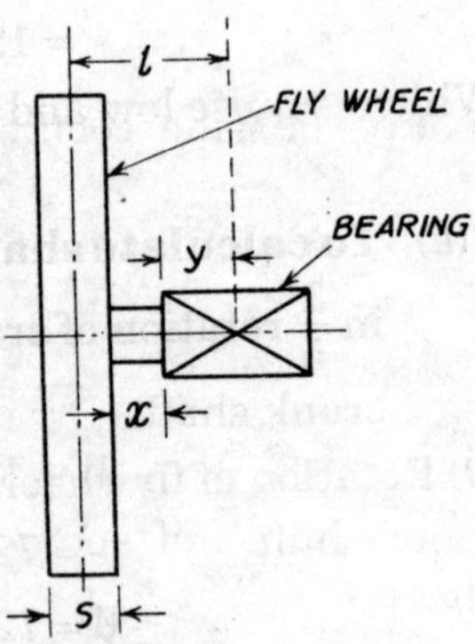

Fig. 10.8.

$s$ = Rim width

$x$ = Clearance

= 1.5 cm (say)

$y$ = Half of bearing length

= 6 cm (say)

$$I = \frac{5.7}{2} + 1.5 + 6$$

= 10.35 cm

$M$ = Bending moment = $W \times l$

= 54 × 10.35 = 559 kg cm

$T_e$ = Equivalent torque

$$= \sqrt{T^2 + M^2} = \sqrt{(1101.6)^2 + (559)^2}$$

= 1235 kg cm

Let $d_1$ = Shaft diameter

$f_{s_1}$ = Allowable shear stress in shaft

= 300 kg/cm$^2$ (say)

$$T_e = \frac{\pi}{16} f_s\, d^3$$

$$1235 = \frac{\pi}{6} \times 300 \times d^3$$

$$d = 2.76 \text{ cm} = 3 \text{ cm (say)}$$

The value of $T$ is calculated at part (*e*)

$$f_b = \frac{\pi^2 D\rho\, v^2}{2g\, n^2\, h}$$

$$= \frac{\pi^2 \times 120 \times 0.00725 \times (1507.2)^2}{2 \times 981 \times 6^2 \times 3.8}$$

$$= 72.6 \text{ kg/cm}^2$$

$f_r$ = Resultant stress in the rim

$$= \frac{3}{4} f + \frac{1}{4} f_b$$

$$= \frac{3}{4} \times 16.78 + \frac{1}{4} \times 72.6$$

$$= 12.58 + 18.15 = 30.73 \text{ kg/cm}^2$$

Which is quite low and hence safe.

(*e*) **To calculate shaft diameter.** As the punching operation in $\frac{1}{5}$ rotation of crank shaft i.e. in 72 degree of rotation of crank shaft.

(*0*) Rotation of flywheel shaft

$$= 72 \times 10$$

$$\theta = 720^\circ = 4\pi$$

$T_m$ = Maximum torque on shaft

$W_1$ = Work done = $T_m \times \theta$

$$13{,}836 = T_m \times 4\pi$$

$$T_m = \frac{13{,}836}{4}\pi = 1101.6 \text{ kg cm}$$

(*f*) **To find key dimensions.**

$B$ = Width of key

$$= \frac{d}{4} = \frac{3}{4} = 0.75 \text{ cm}$$

Thickness of key $= \frac{d}{6} = \frac{3}{6} = 0.5$ cm

$r$ = Radius of shaft = 1.5 cm

$F$ = Force on key

$$= \frac{T_m}{r} = \frac{1101.6}{1.5} = 735.6 \text{ kg}$$

$L$ = Length of key

Considering shearing action of key

$$L \times B \times f_s = 734.4$$

$$L = 3.26 \text{ cm}$$

But Length of key should be minimum equal to 1.5 $d$.

$\therefore$ Length of key $= 1.5 \times 3 = 4.5$ cm.

**Example 10.5.** *A machine shaft running at a speed of 240 R.P.M requires a torque which increases uniformly from 14,000 kg cm to 40,000 kg cm during the first ¼ revolution, remains constant during next ½ revolution, decreases uniformly to 14,000 kg cm during the next ¼ revolution and then remains constant for the following ½ revolution, the cycle being then repeated. It is directly coupled to a motor which exerts a constant torque and has a rotor weighing 600 kg and radius of gyration 36 cm. It is desired to limit the total fluctuation of speed to 4% by providing additional flywheel whose mean speed is limited to 1200 metre per minute. Calculate the weight of flywheel rim.*

**Solution.** The variation of torque ($T$) in kg cm and crank angle ($0$) is shown in Fig. 10.9.

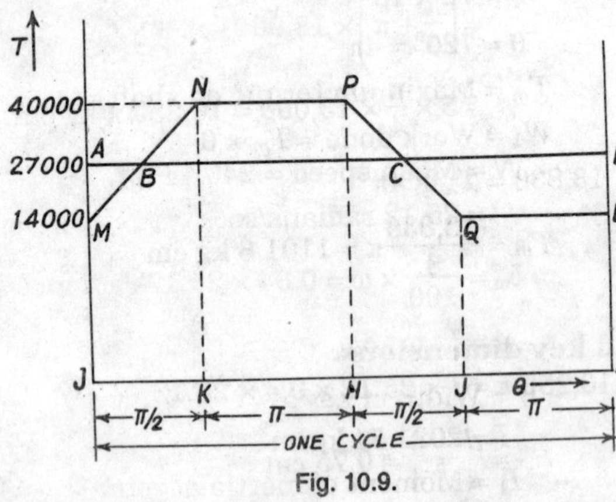


Fig. 10.9.

Area of diagram M N P Q E.

= Area of trapezium $MNKJ$ + Area of rectangle $NPHK$ + Area of trapezium $PQJH$ + Area of rectangle $QEFJ$.

$$= \left(\frac{14,000 + 40,000}{2}\right) \times \frac{\pi}{4} + 40,000 \times \pi + \left(\frac{14,000 + 40,000}{2}\right) \times \frac{\pi}{2} + 14,000 \times \pi$$

$$= 81,000 \times \pi \text{ kg cm.}$$

$T$ = Mean torque

$\theta_m$ = Crank angle per cycle = $3\pi$

$$T \times 3\pi = 81,000 \times \pi$$

$$T = 27,000 \text{ kg cm.}$$

Maximum fluctuation of energy ($e$) is given by the area of turning moment and crank angle $T - \theta$ diagram above the mean torque line $AD$.

$e$ = Fluctuation of energy

= Area of trapezium $BNPC$

$$e = \frac{1}{2} \times \frac{\pi}{4} \times (40,000 - 27000) + (40,000 - 27,000) \times \pi + \frac{1}{2} \times \frac{\pi}{4} (40,000 - 27,000)$$

$$= \frac{\pi}{8}(13,000) + 13,000\,\pi + 13,000 \times \frac{\pi}{8}$$

$$= \left(\frac{\pi}{4} + \pi\right) \times 13,000$$

$$= 5 \times \frac{\pi}{4} \times 13,000 = 16,250\,\pi \text{ kg cm.}$$

$N$ = Mean speed = 240R.P.M.

= 25.12 radians/sec.

$$\delta_\omega = \frac{4}{100} \times \omega = 0.04 \times 25.12 \text{ radians/sec.}$$

$$e = I \, . \, \omega \, . \, \delta_\omega$$

$$16,250\,\pi = I \times 25.12 \times 0.4 \times 25.12$$

$$I = 2021.54 \text{ kgcm}^2$$

$I_1$ = Moment of inertia of rotor

$$= \frac{500}{981} \times 30^2 = 458.7 \text{ kg cm}^2$$

$I_2$ = Moment of inertia of flywheel

$= I - I_1 = 2021.54 - 458.7$

$= 1562.84$ kg cm$^2$

$V$ = Peripheral velocity of flywheel

= 1200 metre min

$D$ = Diameter of flywheel

$1200 = \pi DN = \pi D \times 240$

$D = 1.59$ m = 159 cm.

Assume, $k$ = Radius of gyration of flywheel

$$= \frac{D}{2} = \frac{159}{2} \text{ cm} = 79.5 \text{ cm.}$$

$W$ = Weight of flywheel rim

$$I_2 = \frac{W}{g} k^2$$

$$1562.84 = \frac{W}{981} \times (79.5)^2$$

$W = 242.57$ kg.

**Example 10.5** *(a) A cast iron flywheel is to be designed to store 6800 kg-m of energy at 180 RPM. Determine*

*(a) Weight and thickness of rim if width of rim is 36 cm and radius of gyration is 1.3 m. (Assume whole energy in the rim). Density is 0.007 kg/cm$^2$.*

*(b) Diameter of shaft and size of key if 300 H.P. is to be transmitted and safe stress in shaft and key is 380 kg/cm$^2$.*

*(c) Dimensions of arms. Minor axis is 0.6 major axis. Safe stress arms is 160 kg/cm$^2$. Use 6 arms.*

*(d) Dimensions of hub (boss).*

**Solution.** *(a)* To find size of rim

$W$ = Weight

$s$ = Width of rim = 36 cm

$h$ = Thickness of rim

$K$ = Radius of gyration = 1.3 m

$E$ = Energy to be stored.

$$E = \frac{1}{2} I\omega^2$$

where $\omega$ = Angular speed

$$= 2\pi \times \frac{180}{60} = 18.8 \text{ rad/sec}$$

$$I = \text{Moment of inertia} = \frac{W}{g}K^2$$

$$E = \frac{1}{2} \cdot \frac{W}{g} K^2 \cdot \omega^2$$

$$68000 = \frac{1}{2} \times \frac{W}{9.81} \times (1.3)^2 \times (18.8)^2$$

$$W = 2234 \text{ kg}$$

Weight of rim = Weight of flywheel = 2234 kg

$\rho$ = Density of flywheel material

$D$ = Flywheel diameter

$$= 2\,k = 2 \times 1.3$$

$$= 2.6 \text{ m} = 260 \text{ cm.}$$

$$W = \pi D \,.\, s \,.\, h \times \rho$$

$$2234 = \pi \times 260 \times 36 \times h \times 0.007$$

$$h = 11 \text{ cm}$$

(*b*) To find shaft and key size

$d$ = Shaft diameter

$f_s$ = Shear stress in shaft = 380 kg/cm$^2$

$$\text{H.P.} = \frac{2\pi NT}{4500}$$

$$300 = 2\pi \times 180 \times \frac{T}{4500}$$

$T$ (Torque) = 1194 kg–m = 119400 kg cm

Use torsion equation

$$\frac{T}{J} = \frac{f_s}{r}$$

where $r$ = shaft radius

$$\frac{119400}{\frac{\pi}{32} d^4} = \frac{380}{\frac{d}{2}}$$

$$d = 11.7 \text{ cm}$$

Let us use a square key

$$\text{Width} = \text{Thickness}$$

$$= \frac{d}{4} = \frac{11.7}{4} = 2.9 \text{ cm}$$

$$L = \text{Length of key}$$

$$F = \text{Force on key}$$

$$= \frac{T}{\quad} = \frac{119400}{5.86} = 20410 \text{ kg}$$

$$F = L \times \text{Width} \times f_s$$

$$20410 = L \times 2.9 \times 380$$

$$L = 18.5 \text{ cm}$$

(*c*) To find dimensions of arms, use elliptical arms

$$a = \text{Major arms}$$

$$b = \text{Minor axis} = 0.6\,a$$

$$f = \text{Safe stress in arms} = 160 \text{ kg/cm}^2$$

$$n = \text{Number of arms} = 6$$

$$M = \text{Bending moment on arms}$$

$$= \text{Torque on shaft} = 119400 \text{ kg cm}$$

$$M_A = \text{Bending moment per arm}$$

$$= \frac{119400}{6} = 19900 \text{ kg cm}$$

$$\frac{MA}{I} = \frac{f}{y}$$

where $I = \text{Moment of inertia} = \frac{\pi}{64} b a^3$

$$y = \frac{a}{2}$$

$$\frac{19900}{\frac{\pi}{64}(0.6\,a)\,a^3} = \frac{160}{\frac{a}{2}}$$

$$a = 12.8 \text{ cm}$$

$$b = 0.6 \times 12.8 = 7.68 \text{ cm}$$

Taper for major axis = 2 cm per metre length of arm

$$= 2 \times K = 2 \times 1.3 = 2.6 \text{ cm}$$

Taper for minor axis = 1 cm per metre length

$$= 1 \times K = 1 \times 1.3 = 1.3 \text{ cm}$$

$\therefore$ Major axis at rim $= a - 2.6 = 12.8 - 2.6 = 10.2$ cm

$\therefore$ Minor axis at rim

$$= b - 1.3 = 7.68 - 1.3 = 6.38 \text{ cm}$$

(*d*) To find dimensions of hub.

Diameter of hub $= 2\,d = 2 \times 11.7 = 23.4$ cm

Length of hub $= 2.5\,d = 2.5 \times 11.7 = 29.25$ cm

## 10.6 Pulleys

Belt and pulleys arrangement is used to transmit power form driving shaft to driven (follower) shaft (Fig.10.10). The pulleys are keyed to the shafts and one or more continuous belts and passed over each pair of pulleys. The pulleys are made up of cast iron, pressed steel, welded steel and wood in standard sizes. Cast iron pulleys are generally used to transmit power. The pulleys are of the following types.

(*a*) Flat belt pulleys (*b*) V-belt pulleys

(*c*) Rope pulleys.

A pulley may be of solid or split construction. The various parts of a pulleys are as follows :

(*i*) Hub or boss (*ii*) Arms

(*iii*) Rim.

The hub or the boss is the inner portion of the pulley which enclosed the shaft which it is keyed. The outside surface of the hub is slightly tapered. The rim is the outer portion on which the belt comes. In flat pulleys rims are often given camber on the surface.

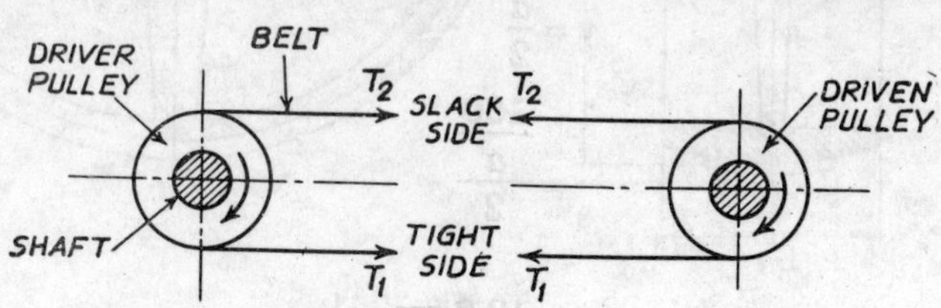


Fig. 10.10

The camber is called crowning or draw. The crowning or draw. The crowning does not allow the belt to slip off the pulley when it rotated crowning for cast iron and steel pulleys is indicated in table 10.3 as per IS 1691-1963 hub or arms connect the rim and hub. The arms of the pulley may be straight or curved and may be of circular cross section, rectangular cross section or elliptical cross section. The arms with elliptical cross section are quite commonly used. All types of arms taper from hub to rim.

**Table 10.3**

| *Nominal diameter (mm)* | *Crowning (mm)* |
|---|---|
| 40-112 | 0.3 |
| 125 and 140 | 0.4 |
| 160 and 180 | 0.5 |
| 250 and 280 | 0.8 |
| 315 and 355 | 1.0 |

Fig. 10.11 shows a cast iron pulley with straight arms.

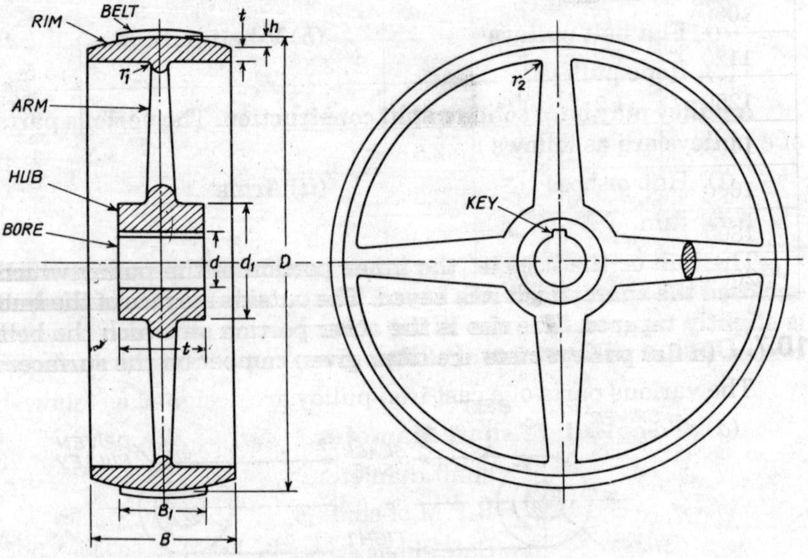


Fig. 10.11

**Table 10.3.1** Indicates crown of cast and mildsteel pulleys as per Is 1691-1980

**Table 10.3.1**

| *Nominal diameter (mm)* | *Crown of pulleys of width(mm)* | | | | | | |
|---|---|---|---|---|---|---|---|
| | *125 and smaller* | *140 and 160* | *180 and 200* | *224 and 250* | 280 and 315 | *355* | *400 and larger* |
| 400 | 1 | 1.2 | 1.2 | 1.2 | 1.2 | 1.2 | 1.2 |
| 450 | 1 | 1,2 | 1.2 | 1.2 | 1.2 | 1.2 | 1.2 |
| 500 | 1 | 1.5 | 1.5 | 1.5 | 1.5 | 1.5 | 1.5 |
| 560 | 1 | 1.5 | 1.5 | 1.5 | 1.5 | 1.5 | 1.5 |
| 630 | 1 | 1.5 | 2 | 2 | 2 | 2 | 2 |
| 710 | 1 | 1.5 | 2 | 2 | 2 | 2 | 2 |
| 800 | 1 | 1.5 | 2 | 2.5 | 2.5 | 2.5 | 2.5 |
| 900 | 1 | 1.5 | 2 | 2.5 | 2.5 | 2.5 | 2.5 |
| 1000 | 1 | 1.5 | 2 | 2.5 | 3 | 3 | 3 |
| 1120 | 1.2 | 1.5 | 2 | 2.5 | 3 | 3 | 3.5 |
| 1250 | 1.2 | 1.5 | 2 | 2.5 | 3 | 3.5 | 4 |
| 1400 | 1.5 | 2 | 2.5 | 3 | 3.5 | 4 | 4 |
| 1600 | 1.5 | 2 | 2.5 | 3 | 3.5 | 4 | 5 |
| 1800 | 2 | 2.5 | 3 | 3.5 | 4 | 4.5 | 5 |
| 2000 | 2 | 2.5 | 3 | 3.5 | 4 | 4.5 | 6 |

## 10.7. Design of Cast Iron Pulley

The various parts of a cast iron pulley are designed as follows :

(*a*) **To calculate shaft diameter**

$d$ = shaft diameter

$N$ = R.P.M of shaft

$f_s$ = Safe shear stress in shaft material

$r$ = Shaft radius = $\frac{d}{2}$

$$\text{H.P} = 2\pi \frac{NT}{4500} \text{ where } T = \text{Torque (kgm)}$$

$$\frac{T}{\frac{\pi}{32}d^4} = \frac{f_s}{r}$$

$$\therefore \qquad T = \text{Torque} = \frac{\pi}{16} f_s d^3$$

(*b*) **Hub.**

$d_1$ = Outer diameter of hub = $2d$

Length of hub $(L) = 1.5d$ to $2d$

or $L = \frac{2}{3} B$ to $B$

where $B$ = Width of pulley rim

(*c*) **Key.** A rectangular parallel sunk key may be used.

Thickness of key = $d/4$

Width of key = $d/6$

Length = Length of hub + 6 mm

(*d*) **Arms.** The number of arms in a pulley depend up the pulley diameter

$D$ = Diameter of pulley

$n$ = Number of arms

= 4 when $D$ = 20 to 60 mm

= 6 when $D$ = 61 to 150 cm

= 8 when $D$ is more than 150 cm

The number of arms can also be calculated using the following formula

$$n = 1.7\sqrt{\frac{D}{100}}$$

where $D$ is in millimeters.

For elliptical section of arms

Let $a$ = Major axis of elliptical section

$b$ = Minor axis of elliptical section

Assuming that only half the number of arms effective as the belt wraps itself around the pulley through 180*supo*. Assuming that the arms act as cantilevers and that arms extend upto centre of pulley

$$M = \text{Bending moment on each arm} = \frac{T}{n_1}$$

where $n_1 = \frac{n}{2}$

$f$ = Permissible stress in arms material

$M = f \times Z$

where $Z$ = Section modulus of an ellipse $= \frac{\pi}{64} a^3$

where $a = 2b$

$$M = f \times \frac{\pi}{64} a^3.$$

From this equation the value of major axis ($a$) is found

$$b = \frac{a}{2}$$

Major axis is placed in the plane of rotation.

These dimensions are at the hub.

The taper in terms is usually $\frac{1}{48}$ to $\frac{1}{32}$.

Arms taper from hub to rim small pulleys are provided with web or web with holes.

For $D$ = 20 cm use web

Since the arms are subjected to complete reversal of stress a factor of safety of about 8 should be used

$f$ = Safe stress for C.I. arms

= 140 to 210 kg/cm$^2$.

For pulleys above 450 mm diameter, use 6 arms. The cross-section of arms is generally elliptical with minor axis half of the major axis.

Major axis of arm near boss is given by :

$$b = 2.94 \sqrt[3]{\frac{a_1 D}{4n}} \text{ for single belt}$$

$$= 2.94 \sqrt[3]{\frac{a_1 D}{2n}} \text{ for double belt}$$

The cross-section of arm near the rim may be taken as 2/3rd of that near the boss or a taper of 4 mm per 100 mm may be provided.

Radius of the cross-section of arms,

$$= \frac{3}{4} b$$

Radius, $r_1 = r_2$ near rim $= b/2$

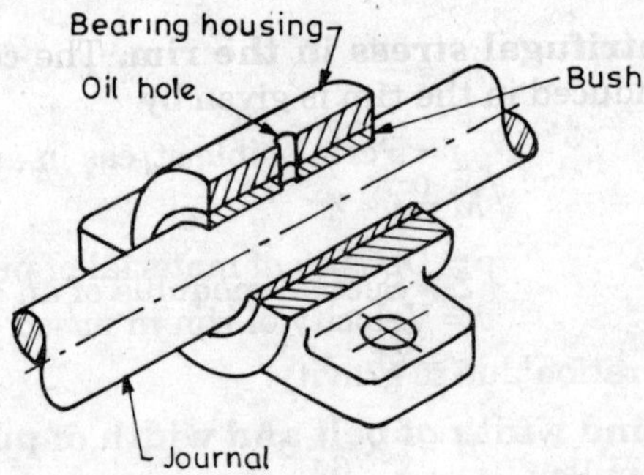


Fig. 10.1(d)

Fig. 12.1(d) shows pictorial view of journal bearing.

(*e*) **Rim.** $t$ = Thickness of pulley rim

$$= \frac{D}{300} + 2 \text{ mm to } \frac{D}{300} + 3 \text{ mm}$$

where $D$ = Diameter of pulley in'mm

Width of rim ($B$) is about 25% more than width ($B_1$) of belt

$h$ = Crowning in rim

The permissible rim speed is indicated in Table 10.

**Table 10.4.**

| *Type of pulley* | *Rim speed m/min* |
|---|---|
| (*i*) Mild steel pulleys sold or split with flat or crown face and mild steel spokes. | 1500 |
| (*ii*) Cast iron pulleys | |
| (*a*) Solid with flat or crown face | 1500 |
| (*b*) Split with flat or crown face | 1000 |

## 10.8. Preferred Nominal Diameter (mm) of Pulleys

40, 45, 56, 63, 71, 80, 90, 100, 112, 122, 140, 160, 180, 200, 224, 250, 280, 315, 355, 400, 450, 500, 560, 630, 710, 800, 900, 1000, 1120, 1250, 1400, 1600, 1800, 2000.

(*e*) **Centrifugal stress in the rim.** The centrifugal stress ($f_s$) induced in the rim is given by

$$f_s = \rho \frac{v^2}{g}$$

where $\rho$ = Density of material of pulley

$v$ = Velocity of rim in m/sec

$g$ = Acceleration due to gravity.

(*f*) **To find width of belt and width of pulley.** Fig. 10.12 shows belt on pulley.

Let $T_1$ = Tension on tight side of belt (kg)

$T_2$ = Tension on loose side (kg)

$\mu$ = Coefficient of friction between belt and pulley

$\theta$ = Angle of lab

$R$ = Pulley radius

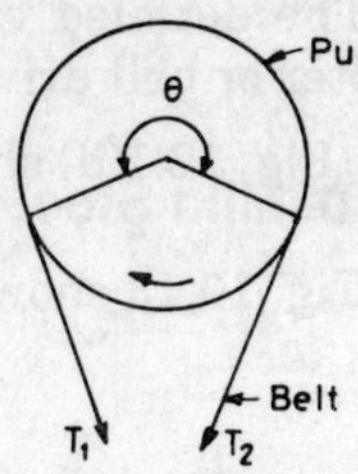


Fig. 10.12.

$$\frac{T_1}{T_2} = e^{\mu\theta} \quad \text{....(1)}$$

$$(T_1 - T_2) \times R = \text{Torque}$$

From (1) and (2) value of $T_1$ and $T_2$ can be found.

Let $F$ = Permissible tension in belt (kg/cm)

$$B_1 = \text{Width of belt} = \frac{T_1}{F} \text{ cm}$$

$$= \text{Width of pulley} = 1.2\, B_1 \text{ (say)}$$

Table 10.5 indicates the pulley width [I.S.2122 (Part I)-1973].

**Table 10.5.**

| *Width of belt (mm)* | *Width of pulley in excess of width of belt (mm)* |
|---|---|
| Up to 125 | 13 |
| 125 to 250 | 25 |
| 250 to 375 | 38 |
| 375 to 500 | 50 |

The face of the pulleys rim is crowned to keep the belt on the pulley. The crowning forces the belt to return to the centre of pulley.

## 10.9. Coefficient of Friction

The coefficient of friction between belt and pulley depends on the following factors :

(*i*) Material of belt (*ii*) Material of pulley

(*iii*) Belt speed (*iv*) Belt slip.

The coefficient of friction for I.C. and steel pulleys foe leather oak tanned belt is

$$\mu = 0.25 - \text{Dry} = 0.2 - \text{Wet} = 0.15 - \text{Greasy}$$

The detailed values of coefficient of friction are given in the chapter or belt drive.

## 10.10. Mild Steel Pulley

Fig. 10.13 shows a mild steel pulley. In this pulley

$$L = \text{Length of boss} = \frac{a}{2}$$

where $a$ = Width of pulley

$t$ = Thickness of rim = 5 mm (average value)

The spokes provided on mild steel pulley depend on diameter of pulley. Table 10.7 indicates the spokes provided on pulleys of different diameters.

**Table 10.7**

| *Diameter of pulley* | *Number of spokes (mm)* | *Diameter of spoke (mm)* |
|---|---|---|
| 280-500 | 6 | 19 |
| 560-710 | 8 | 19 |
| 860-1000 | 10 | 22 |
| 1120 | 12 | 22 |
| 1250 | 14 | 22 |
| 1400 | 16 | 22 |
| 1600 | 18 | 22 |
| 1800 | 20 | 22 |
| 2000 | 22 | 22 |

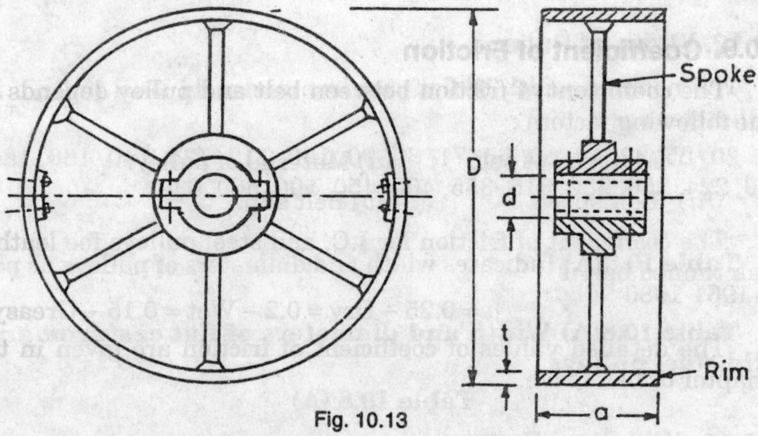


Fig. 10.13

Steel pulleys have the following advantages :

(*i*) They are strong and durable.

(*ii*) They are lighter in weight than C.I. pulleys.

## 10.11. Pulley Diameters

The nominal diameters of C.I. and mild steel pulleys for given belt speeds and plied are indicated in Table 10.8.

**Table 10.8.**

| *Numbers of Plies* | *Maximum belt speed m/sec* | | | | |
|---|---|---|---|---|---|
| | 10 | 15 | 20 | 25 | 30 |
| 2 | 50 | 63 | 80 | 90 | 112 |
| 3 | 90 | 100 | 112 | 140 | 180 |
| 4 | 140 | 160 | 180 | 200 | 250 |
| 5 | 200 | 224 | 250 | 315 | 355 |
| 6 | 250 | 315 | 355 | 400 | 450 |
| 7 | 355 | 400 | 450 | 500 | 560 |
| 8 | 450 | 500 | 560 | 630 | 710 |
| 9 | 560 | 630 | 710 | 800 | 900 |
| 10 | 630 | 710 | 800 | 900 | 1000 |

## 10.12. Width of Pulleys

The nominal width of flat cast iron and mild steel pulleys in millimeter are :

20, 25, 32, 40, 50, 63, 71, 80, 90, 100, 112, 125, 140, 160, 180, 200, 224, 250, 280, 315, 355, 400, 450, 500, 560, 630.

**Table 10.8(A)** Indicates width and diameters of pulleys as per IS-1961-1980

**Table 10.8(A) Width and diameters of flat cast iron and mild steel pulleys**

**Table 10.8 (A)**

| *Width, mm* | Tolerance, mm | Nominal dia, mm | Tolerance, mm |
|---|---|---|---|
| 20 25 32 | ± 1 | 40 | ± 0.5 |
| 40 50 63 71 | | 45, 50 | ± 0.6 |
| 80 90 100 | ± 1.5 | 56, 63 | ± 0.8 |
| 112 121 140 | | 71, 80 | ± 1.0 |
| 160 180 200 | ± 2 | 90, 100, 112 | ± 1.2 |
| 224 250 280 315 | | 125 140 | ± 1.9 |
| 355 490 450 | ± 3 | 160, 180, 200 | ± 2.0 |
| 500 560 630 | | 224, 250 | ± 2.5 |
| Material of C.I. Pulley | | 280, 315, 355 | ± 3.0 |
| Grade FG 200 of IS : 210--1978 | | 400, 450, 500 | ± 4.0 |
| | | 560, 630, 710 | ± 5.0 |
| | | 800, 900, 1000 | ± 6.3 |
| Material for M.S. pulley : | | 1120 1250 1400 | ± 8.0 |
| IS :226--1975 | | 1600 1800 2000 | ± 10.0 |

## 10.13. Belt Speed

For efficient power transmission recommended belt speeds vary from 18 m/*sec* to 23 metre per second.

## 10.14. Material of Pulleys

The material commonly used for making pulleys are as follows:

(*i*) **C.I. pulley.** Grade 20 fo I.S. 210--1970.

(*ii*) **M.S. pulleys.** I.S. 226--1969.

**Example 10.6.** *Design a cast iron pulley 70 cm in diameter to transmit 40 H.P at 300 R.P.M. The safe shear stress in shaft material is 400kg/cm² and pulley has four elliptical arms. The safe working stress in the arms is 160kg/cm². The coefficient of friction between belt and pulleys is 0.3 and angle of lap is 120°. The permissible tension per cm width of belt is 28 kg per cm.*

**Solution.** (*a*) **To calculate shaft diameter**

$$N = 300 \text{ R.P.M}$$

$$\text{H.P.} = 40$$

$$\text{H.P.} = 2\pi\frac{NT}{4500}$$

$$T = 40 \times \frac{4500}{2}\pi \times 300 = 95.54 \text{ kg m}$$

$$= 9554 \text{ kg cm}$$

$$d = \text{Shaft diameter}$$

$$f_s = \text{Safe shear stress in shaft material}$$

$$= 400 \text{ kg/cm}^2$$

$$T = \frac{\pi}{16} f_s d^3$$

$$9554 = \frac{\pi}{16} \times 400 \times d^3$$

$$d = 4.95 \text{ cm} = 5 \text{ cm (say)}$$

(*b*) **Hub.** Hub diameter

$$= 2d = 2 \times 5 = 10 \text{ cm}$$

Hub length $= \frac{oi}{2} \times d = \frac{\pi}{2} \times 5 = 7.85$ cm

To check the hub, use torsion equation

$$\frac{T}{J} = \frac{f_{s1}}{r_1}$$

where $r_1 = \text{Hub radius} = \dfrac{d_1}{2}$

$J = \text{Polar moment of inertia} = \dfrac{\pi}{32}(d_1^4 - d^4)$

$d_1 = \text{Hub diameter}$

$f_{s1} = \text{Induced shear stress}$

$$\frac{T}{\frac{\pi}{32}(d_{s1} - d^4)} = \frac{f_{s1}}{\frac{d_1}{2}}$$

$$\frac{9554}{\frac{\pi}{32}(10^4 - 5^4)} = \frac{f_{s1}}{\frac{10}{2}}$$

$$f_{s1} = 45 \text{ kg/cm}^2$$

Which is less than permissible shear stress (about 50–60 kg/cm$^2$) in C.I. hub.

Hence hub is safe.

(*c*) **To find width of pulley**

Let $T_1 = \text{Tension on tight side of belt}$

$T_2 = \text{Tension on loose side of belt}$

$D = \text{Diameter of pulley} = 70 \text{ cm}$

$R = \text{Radius of pulley} = \dfrac{70}{2} = 35 \text{ cm}$

$$T = (T_1 - T_2) \times R$$

$$9554 = (T_1 - T_2) \times 35$$

$$T_1 - T_2 = 273 \text{ kg} \qquad \text{...}(i)$$

$\mu = \text{Coefficient of friction} = 0.3$

$\Theta = \text{Angle of lap} = 120^o$

$= \pi \times \dfrac{120}{180} \times \dfrac{2}{3}\pi \text{ radians}$

$= \dfrac{T_1}{T_2} = e^{\mu}\,\Theta = e^{0.3 \times 2/3\pi} = e^{(0.628)}$

$$\frac{T_1}{T_2} = 1.88 \qquad \text{...}(ii)$$

From eqns. (*i*) and (*ii*)

$$T_1 = 583 \text{ kg}$$

$$T_2 = 310 \text{ kg}$$

$F$ = Permissible tension in belt

= 28 kg per cm

Width ($B_1$) of belt $= \dfrac{T_1}{f} = \dfrac{583}{28}$

= 20.82 cm

$B$ = Width of pulley face

$= 1.2 \times 20.82 = 25$ cm

As the width of pulley face is 25 cm but the length of hub calculated is 7.85 cm which is too small therefore we adopt length of hub $= \dfrac{2}{3}B = \dfrac{2}{3} \times 25 = 16.66 = 17$ cm (say)

(*d*) **To find arms dimensions**

$n$ = Number of arms

= 4

$a$ = Major axis of elliptical section

$b$ = Minor axis of elliptical section

$a = 2\,b$ (say)

$M$ = Bending moment on each arm

$$= \frac{T}{n_1}$$

where $n_1 = \dfrac{n}{2} = \dfrac{4}{2} = 2$

$$M = \frac{954}{2} = 4777 \text{ kg cm}$$

$f$ = Permissible stress in arms

= 160 kg/cm$^2$

$Z$ = Modulus of section of ellipse

$$= \frac{\pi}{64} a^3$$

$$M = f \times Z$$

$$4777 = 160 \times \frac{\pi}{64} a^3$$

$$a = 8.47 \text{ cm.}$$

$$b = \frac{a}{2} = \frac{8.47}{2} = 4.235 \text{ cm}$$

(*e*) **Key.** The dimensions for a rectangular sunk key are as follows :

$$\text{Width of key} = \frac{d}{4} = \frac{5}{4} = 1.25 \text{ cm}$$

$$\text{Thickness of key} = \frac{a}{6} = \frac{5}{6} = 0.833 \text{ cm}$$

$$\text{Length of key}(L_1) = \text{Length of hub} = 17 \text{ cm}$$

$$P = \text{Force on key}$$

$$= \frac{T}{\text{Shaft radius}} = \frac{9554}{2.5} = 3821.6 \text{ kg}$$

$$f_{s_1} = \text{Induced shear stress in key}$$

Considering shearing of key

$$P = L_1 \times \text{width of key} \times f_{s_1}$$

$$3821.6 = 17 \times 1.25 \times f_{s_1}$$

$$f_{s_1} = 179.84 \text{ kg/cm}^2$$

This is within limits, hence safe

$$t = \text{Rim thickness}$$

$$= \frac{D}{300} + 2 \text{ mm} = \frac{700}{300} + 2 = 4.33 \text{ mm.}$$

**Example 10.7.** *A cast iron pulley is to transmit 30 H.P. at 240 R.P.M. The diameter of pulley is 80 cm. Determine the following :*

*(a) The diameter of the shaft if the safe shear stress in shaft is limited to 450kg/cm$^2$.*

*(b) The width of the pulley assuming that tension on tightside of belt is twise the tension on slack side of belt and the permissible tension per cm width of belt is 24 kg.*

*(c) Dimensions of 6 elliptical arms at the hub if the safe stress in arms is 150kg/cm$^2$.*

*(d) Dimensions of hub and a rectangular key.*

*(e) Thickness of rim.*

**Solution.** (*a*)**To calculate shaft diameter**

$$d = \text{Shaft diameter}$$

$$\text{H . P.} = 2\pi \frac{NT}{4500}$$

$$30 = 2\pi \times 240 \times \frac{T}{4500}$$

$$T = 89.57 \text{ kg m} = 8957 \text{ kg cm}$$

$$T = \frac{\pi}{16} f_s \, d^3$$

$$8957 = \frac{\pi}{16} \times 450 \times d^3$$

$$d = 4.66 \text{ cm} = 4.75 \text{ cm (say)}$$

(*b*) **To calculate width of pulley**

$D$ = Diameter of pulley = 80 cm.

$R$ = Radius of pulley = 40 cm.

$T_1$ = Tension on tight side of belt

$T_2$ = Tension on loose side of belt

$$\frac{T_1}{T_2} = 2 \qquad \text{...}(i)$$

$$(T_1 - T_2) \times R = T$$

$$(T_1 - T_2) \times 40 = 8957$$

$$T_1 + T_2 = 224 \text{ kg.} \qquad \text{...}(ii)$$

From equation (*i*) and (*ii*)

$T_1$ = 448 kg.

$T_2$ = 224 kg.

$F$ = Tension per cm width of belt = 24

$B_1$ = Width of belt

$$= \frac{T_1}{F} = \frac{448}{24} = 18.67 \text{ cm.}$$

Assuming width of pulley face 20% more than the width of belt

$B$ = Width of pulley

$$= 1.2 \times B_1 = 1.2 \times 18.67 = 22.4 \text{ cm.}$$

(*c*) **To find arm dimensions**

$n$ = Number of arms = 6

The arms are of elliptical section with major axis (*a*) and minor axis (*b*) with $a = 2b$.

$M$ = Bending moment on each arm

$$= \frac{I}{n_1} \text{ where } n_1 = \frac{n}{2} = \frac{6}{2} = 3$$

$$= \frac{8957}{3} = 2986 \text{ kg cm}$$

$$f = \text{Permissible stress in arms} = 150 \text{ kg/cm}^2$$

$$Z = \text{Section modulus} = \frac{\pi}{64} d^3$$

$$M = f \times Z$$

$$2986 = 150 \frac{\pi}{64} d^3$$

$$a = 7.4 \text{ cm}$$

$$b = \frac{a}{2} = \frac{7.4}{2} = 3.7 \text{ cm.}$$

(*d*) **Hub**

Diameter of hub

$$= 2d = 2 \times 4.75 = 9.50 \text{ cm.}$$

Length of hub $= \frac{2}{3} \times B$

$$= \frac{2}{3} \times 22.4 = 14.93 \text{ cm} = 15 \text{ cm (say).}$$

(*e*) **Key**

The dimensions of a rectangular key are as follows :

$$\text{Width} = \frac{d}{4} = \frac{4.75}{6} = 1.18 \text{ cm.}$$

$$\text{Thickness} = \frac{d}{6} = \frac{4.75}{4} = 0.79 \text{ cm.}$$

Length of key = Length of hub = 15 cm

Let $f_{s_1}$ = Induced shear stress in key

$P$ = Force on key

$$= \frac{T}{2.375} = \frac{8957}{2.375} = 3771 \text{ kg.}$$

Considering shearing of key

$$P = \text{Length} \times \text{Width} \times f_{s_1}$$

$$3771 = 15 \times 1.18 \times f_{s_1}$$

$$f_{s_1} = 139.6 \text{ kg/cm}^2$$

which is within limits, hence safe

(*f*) **Rim size**

$$t = \text{Rim thickness}$$

$$= \frac{D}{300} + 2 \text{ mm} = \frac{800}{300} + 2 = 4.67 \text{ mm.}$$

## PROBLEMS

**10.1.** The areas of turning moment diagram for one revaluation of a multi-cylinder engine with reference to the mean turning moment below and above the line are -0.32, +4.8, -2.62, +3.33, -3.1, +2.26, -3.74, +2.6 and -2.44 cm$^2$. The scales for abscissa and ordinate are 1 cm = 24°, and 1 cm = 650 kg m respectively. The mean speed is 300 R.P.M. with a percentage speed fluctuation of ± 1.5%. If the hoop stress in the material of the rim is not to exceed 56 kg/cm$^2$ determine suitable diameter and cross-section of flywheel assuming that width is 4 times the thickness. The density of the material may be taken as 0.0072 kg/cm$^3$. Neglect the effect of loss and arms. *(A.M.I.E.,1980)*

**10.2.** A machine is driven by an electric motor and has a cyclic load which approximately represented by the torque angle graph as shown in Fig.10.14. The speed of the machine must not vary during the cycle by more that ± 15% of the mean speed of 450 R.P.M. A cast iron flywheel is mounted on machine shaft. If space considerations limit the diameter of flywheel to 70 cm determine the following :

(*a*) Diameter of machine shaft if safe shear stress in shaft material is 400 kg/cm$^2$.

(*b*) House power of motor allowing 20% over load.

(*c*) Size of flywheel rim if width is twise th thickness. Density of cast iron is 7025 gm/cm$^3$. Neglect the enertia of hub and arms.

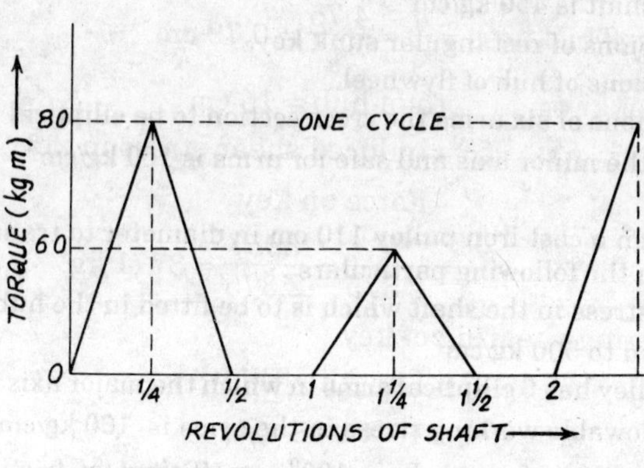


Fig. 10.14

**10.3.** Design a cast iron flywheel for a multi-cylinder I.C engine working on four stroke cycle that develops 40 H.P. at 450 R.P.M. Mean velocity of flywheel rim is 1200 m/min. The maximum energy variation is 25% of mean energy per cycle and total speed variation is 2%.

**10.4.** Design a flywheel for a 4 cylinder 50 H.P. engine running at 1000 R.P.M. The variation of speed is to be within ± 1.5% of the mean speed and fluctuation of energy may be assumed to be $\frac{1}{3}$ of that of one revolution. The diameter of flywheel should not exceed 70 cm. The allowable shear stress in steel is 400 kg/cm$^2$ and density of cast iron is 7.25 gm/cm$^3$. Assume a square cross-section of rim.

**10.5.** A machine has to carry out punching operation at the rate of 12 holes per minute. It does 60 kg m of work per sq.cm of the sheared area in cutting 3 cm diameter holes in 1.5 cm thick plates. A flywheel is fitted to the machine shaft which is driven by a constant torque. The fluctuation of speed is between 150 and 200 R.P.M. Actual punching takes 2 seconds. Fractional losses are equivalent to 1/6 of work done during punching calculate the following :

(*a*) H.P. required to drive the machine.

(*b*) Weight of flywheel if radius of gyration is 50 cm.

**10.6.** A cast iron flywheel is to store 20,000 kg m of energy at 240 R.P.M. If the tensile stress is 60 kg/cm$^2$ and total fluctuation of speed is 2% determine the following :

(*a*) Weight of flywheel if density is 0.0072 kg/cm$^2$.

(*b*) Thickness of rim if width is twise the thickness.

(*c*) Diameter of shaft if 300 H.P is transmitted.

The $f_s$ for shaft is 450 kg/cm$^2$

(*d*) Dimensions of rectangular sunk key.

(*e*) Dimensions of hub of flywheel.

(*f*) Dimensions of six arms the cross section to be elliptical with major axis 0.5 times the minor axis and safe for arms is 160 kg/cm$^2$.

**10.7.** Design a cast iron pulley 110 cm in diameter to trans 60 h.p. at 350 r.p.m. with the following particulars :

(*a*) Shear stress in the shaft which is to be fitted in the hubbore of the pulley is limited to 500 kg/cm$^2$.

(*b*) The pulley has 6 elliptical arms in which the major axis is twise the minor axis. Allowable working stress in the arms is 160 kg/cm$^2$.

(*c*) Angle of lap of the belt is 100$^\circ$ , coefficient of friction 0.3 and permissible tension per cm width of the belt is 27 kg.

**10.8.** Design a cast iron pulley to transmit 15 H.P. at 200R.P.M. The pulley has four section with major axis twise the minor axis. The centrifugal stress in the rim is limited to 50 kg/cm$^2$ and density of cast iron is 7.25 gm/cm$^2$. The safe stress in arms is 160 kg/cm$^2$and safe shear stress in shaft is limited to 420 kg/cm$^2$.

**10.9.** A pulley of 90 cm diameter revolving at 150 r.p.m. is to transmit 16 horse power. Find the width of a leather belt if the maximum tension is not to exceed 14.0 kg/cm width. The tension on the tight side is twice that on the slack side. Determine the dimensions of the various parts of the pulley assuming it to have 6 arms. Maximum shear stress not to exceed 500 kg/cm$^2$.

**10.10.** (*a*) What is a pulley ? Name the various materials commonly used for the making pulleys. (*b*) What is crowning of pulleys ?

**10.11.** (*a*) What is the function of flywheel (*b*)Discuss the general design of a flywheel.

**10.12.** Write short notes on the following :

(*a*) Centrifugal stress in the rim of a pulley

(*b*) Turning moment diagram for a flywheel.

(*c*) Coefficient of friction between belt and pulley.

(*d*) Mild steel pulley

(*e*) Belt speed

(*f*) Materials for pulleys.

# 11

# Gears

## 11.1. Introduction

Gears are used to transmit power. They transmit power positively without slip and at a constant velocity ratio. They are useful for high torque transmission. They have high efficiency, reliable service and simple operation.

## 11.2. Types of Gears

They are classified as follows :

(*i*) Gears which connect parallel shafts such as spur gears, helical gears, double helical gears, and herring bone gears.

(*ii*) Gears which connect inclined shafts such as bevel gears.

(*iii*) Gears which connect non parallel and non inter-secting shafts such as spiral gears, worm and worm wheels.

(*iv*) Based on peripheral velocity ($V$) gears are classified as follows :

(*a*) Low velocity, $V < 3$ m/s

(*b*) Medium velocity, $V = 3$ to15 m/s.

(*c*) High velocity, $V > 15$ m/s.

(*v*) Based on accuracy of manufacture, there are 12 degrees of accuracy of manufacture of gears, one being the highest.

(*vi*) Based on number of steps the gears are classified as follows:

(*a*) One-step gear

(*b*) Two-step gear

(*c*) Three-step gears and so on.

The gears drives have the following advantages :

1. Gear drives provide positive drives.
2. They have high efficiency and high reliability.
3. They can take up heavier loads.
4. They are capable of driving loads subjected to shock at speeds up to 1200 mpm.
5. Their operation is simple.

However gear drives are not suitable for larger distances.

The comparison of single mesh gears is indicated in Table 1.1

$r$ = Gear ratio range

$n$ = Efficiency

$V$ = Maximum pitch line velocity.

**Table 11.1**

| *Type of gearing* | *r* | *n(%)* | *V (mpm)* |
|---|---|---|---|
| Spur | 1 to 10 | 98 | 600 |
| Helical and double helical | 1 to 15 | 98 | 9000 |
| Straight Bevel | 1 to 6 | 98 | 300 |
| Spiral Bevel | 1 to 9 | 98 | 2400 |
| Worm | 3½ to 90 | 50 to 90 | 1800 |

## 11.3. Spur Gears

They are used to connect shafts whose axes are parallel to each other. In these gears teeth are straight and parallel to the shaft axis. Spur gears are most commonly used, they are simple in design and easy to manufacture. Fig. 11.1 shows two spur gears in contact.

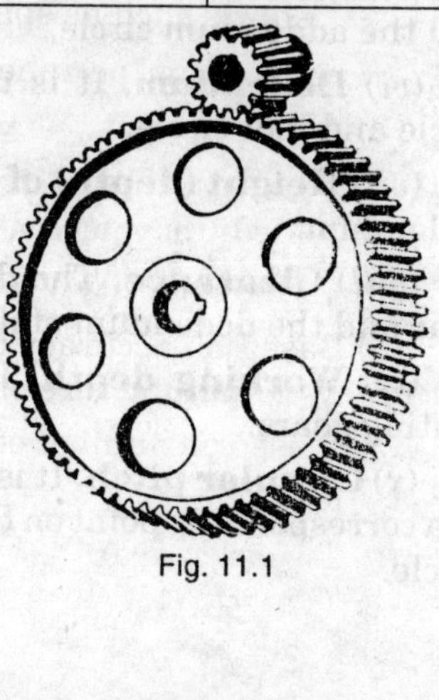

Fig. 11.1

## 11.4 Spur Gear Nomenclature

Fig. 11.2 shows a few teeth of a spur gears. The various terms in connection with spur gear are as follows.

(*i*) **Pinion and gear.** When two gears come in contact the smaller gear wheel is called pinion and the bigger one is called gear.

(*ii*) **Pitch circle.** The pitch cylinders of a pair of gears in mesh are the imaginary friction cylinders which will roll together without slip when one gear drives the other. Pitch circle is a section of a pitch cylinder by a plane at right angles to the axis.

(*iii*) **Addendum circle.** It is the circle which bounds the outer ends of the teeth.

(*iv*) **Dedendum circle.** (Root circle). It is the circle which bounds the bottom ends of teeth.

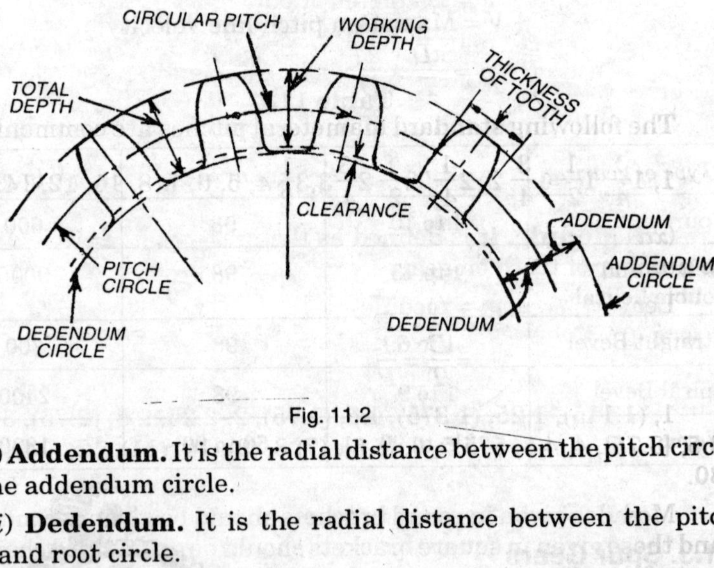


Fig. 11.2

(*v*) **Addendum.** It is the radial distance between the pitch circle and the addendum circle.

(*vi*) **Dedendum.** It is the radial distance between the pitch circle and root circle.

(*vii*) **Height (depth) of teeth.** It is the sum of addendum and dedendum.

(*viii*) **Clearance.** The difference between the addendum of a gear and the dedendum of its mating gear is called clearance.

(*ix*) **Working depth.** It is the depth of engagement of two mating gears.

(*x*) **Circular pitch.** It is the distance from a point on one tooth to a corresponding point on the adjacent tooth measured along pitch circle.

Let, $\quad p =$ Circular pitch

$$= \frac{\pi D}{T}$$

where $\quad D =$ Pitch circle diameter (P.C.D.)

$T =$ Number of teeth on gear

The following standard circular pitches are commonly used.

$$\frac{1}{16}, \frac{1}{8}, \frac{3}{16}, \frac{1}{4}, \frac{5}{16}, \frac{3}{8}, \frac{7}{16}, \frac{1}{2}, \frac{9}{16}, \frac{5}{8}, \frac{11}{16}, \frac{3}{4}, \frac{13}{16}, \frac{7}{8}, \frac{15}{16}, 1, 1\frac{1}{2}, 1\frac{3}{8},$$

$$1\frac{1}{2}, 1\frac{5}{8}, 1\frac{3}{4}, 1\frac{7}{8}, 2, 2\frac{1}{4}, 2\frac{1}{2}, 2\frac{3}{4}, 3.$$

*(xi)* **Diameteral pitch.** It is defined as the ratio of number of teeth to pitch circle diameter.

$$P = \text{Diameter pitch} = \frac{T}{D}$$

$$P \times p = \frac{\pi D}{T} \times \frac{T}{D} \times \pi$$

The following standard diameteral pitches are commonly used.

$$1, 1\frac{1}{4}, 1\frac{1}{2}, 1\frac{3}{4}, 2, 2\frac{1}{4}, 2\frac{1}{2}, 2\frac{3}{4}, 3, 3\frac{1}{2}, 4, 5, 6, 7, 8, 10, 12, 14, 16.$$

*(xii)* **Module.** It is defined as the ratio of pitch circle diameter to number of teeth on gear.

Let $\quad m =$ module

$$= \frac{D}{T} = \frac{1}{P}$$

1, (1.115), 1.25, (1.375), 1.5, (1.75), 2, 2.25, 2.5, (2.75), 3, [3.25], 3.5, [3.75], 4, 4.5, 5, 5.5, 6, [6.5], (7) 8, (9), 10, (11), 12, (14), 16, (18), 30.

Modules given in round brackets should be given second choice, and those given in square brackets should be given third choice. The rest of the values are preferred modules, which are generally used.

Let addendum $= m$

$D_a =$ Addendum circle diameter

$= D + 2 \times$ Addendum

$= D + 2\,m = mT + 2m = m(T + 2)$

where $\quad T =$ Number of teeth on gear

*(xiii)* **Pressure angle.** (Angle of obiquity). It is defined as the angle made by a normal drawn at the point of contact of the mating

gears with the tangent to two pitch circles at the pitch point. The standard pressure angles are $14\frac{1}{2}°$ and $20°$.

(*xiv*) **Face.** It is the part of tooth surface which is above pitch surface. (Fig. 11.3).

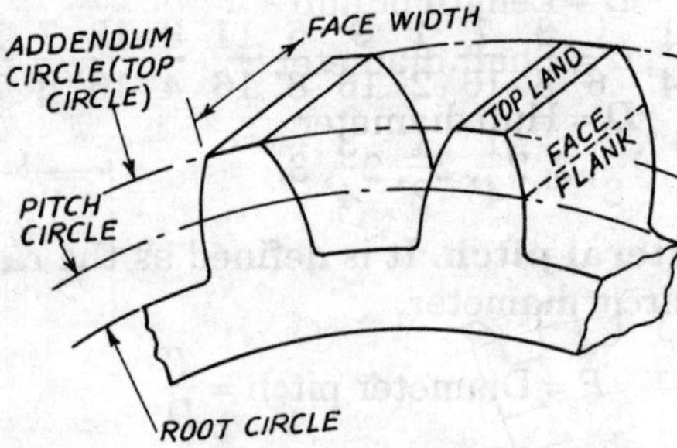


Fig. 11.3.

(*xv*) **Flank.** It is the part of tooth surface lying below the pitch surface.

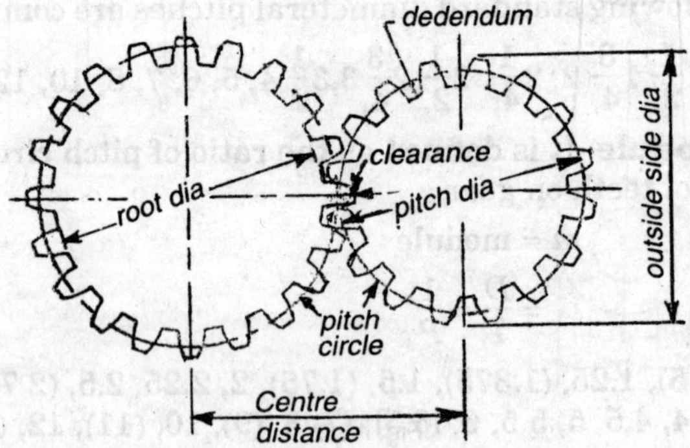


Fig. 11.4.

(*xvi*) **Profile.** It is the curve forming face and flank.

(*xvii*) **Centre distance.** It is the distance between the centres of two mating gears. (Fig.11.4).

$$C = \text{Centre distance}$$

$$= \frac{D_1}{2} + \frac{D_2}{2}$$

where $D_1$ = P. C. D. of gear 1

$D_2$ = P. C. D. of gear 2

$$C = \frac{D_1}{2} + \frac{D_2}{2} = \frac{mT_1}{2} + \frac{mT_2}{2}$$

$$= \frac{m}{2}(T_1 + T_2)$$

where $T_1$ and $T_2$ are teeth on gear 1 and gear 2 respectively.

Fig. 11.5 shows a gear. In the spur gear shown

$b$ = Face width

$L$ = Length of hub

$d$ = Shaft diameter

$D$ = Hub diameter

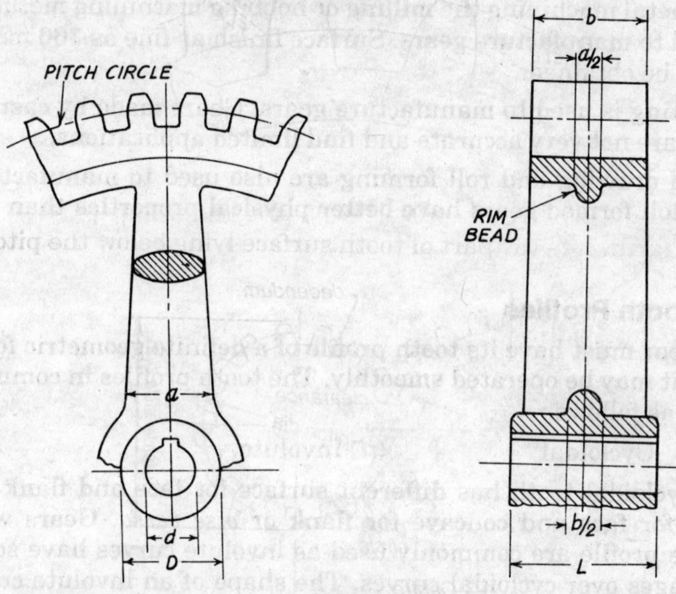


Fig. 11.5

(*xviii*) **Thickness of tooth.** It is the thickness of tooth measured along the pitch circle.

(*xix*) **Tooth space.** It is the width of empty space in between the two consecutive teeth measured on the pitch circle.

(*xx*) **Backlash.** It is the difference between the tooth space and thickness of tooth as measured on the pitch circle.

In a spur gear $m$ = Module

$a$ = Addendum = $m$

$d$ = Dedendum = 1.25 m

Clearance = 0.25 m

Working depth = Total depth – Clearance = $a + d$ – Clearance

$$= m + 1.25\ \text{m} - 0.25\ \text{m} = 2\ \text{m}$$

### 11.4.1. Manufacturing Methods

The commonly methods employed for manufacturing gears are as follows :

(*i*) Metal machining,

(*ii*) Casting,

(*iii*) Forming.

In metal machining the milling or hobbing machining methods are used to manufacture gears. Surface finish as fine as 160 micro cms can be obtained.

Casting is used to manufacture gears. Gears made by casting process are not very accurate and find limited applications.

Cold drawing and roll forming are also used to manufacture gears. Roll formed gears have better physical properties than cut teeth.

## 11.5. Tooth Profiles

A gear must have its tooth profile of a definite geometric form so that it may be operated smoothly. The tooth profiles in common use are as follows :

(*i*) Cycloidal (*ii*) Involute.

A cycloidal tooth has different surface for face and flank *i.e.* convex for face and concave for flank or *vise versa.* Gears with involute profile are commonly used as involute curves have some advantages over cycloidal curves. The shape of an involute curve depends upon the diameter of base circle. It is easier to manufacture involute gears, they work correctly even if the centre distance is not exact and angle of pressure remains constant from beginning to engagement to its end. Whereas in cycloidal gears angle of pressure is maximum when engagement starts, reduces to zero at the pitch point and then increases to maximum at the end of engagement. Further it is difficult to manufacture cycloidal gears.

All members of an interchangeable set of involute spur gears must have

(*i*) The same diameter pitch and hence the same circular pitch.

(*ii*) The same angle of obliquity.

Whereas in case of an interchangeable set of cycloidal spur gears all members should have,

(*i*) The same diameteral pitch and hence the same circular pitch.

(*ii*) The faces and flanks of their teeth generated by the same rolling or generating circle the diameter of which is equal to the radius of the pitch circle of the smallest gear of the set.

## 11.6. Spur Gear Tooth Forms

American Standard Association and American Gear Manufacturers' Association (AGMA) have recommended the following forms of gear teeth.

(*i*) The 14½° composite system

(*ii*) The 14½° full depth involute system

(*iii*) The 20° full depth involute system

(*iv*) The 20° stub involute system.

The 14½°composite system is a combination of cycloidal curves at the top and bottom and involute at the middle. This form is quite different to manufacture. The 14½° full depth involute system is quite satisfactory under cutting begins when the number of teeth on pinion is less than 32. Th 20° full depth involute system has the same proportions as the 14½° involute except that pressure angle has been increased to 20° to avoid interference and undercutting. The undercutting will begin if number of teeth on pinion is less than 18. In 20° stub involute system the tooth is made shorter than full depth and tooth is more strong so that heavy loads can be taken up by gears. This system is quite commonly used in automotive industry because of its raggedness.

Table 11.2 shows standard tooth proportions of spur gears.

**Table 11.2**

**Standard Tooth Proportions of Involute Spur Gears**

| *Tooth characteristics* | *Cast teeth* | *14½° system* | *Full depth 20° system* | *Stub teeth system* |
|---|---|---|---|---|
| Pressure angle (deg) | 15 | 14½ | 20 | 20 |
| Addendum (cm) | 0.943 m | *m* | *m* | 0.8 m |

| | | | | |
|---|---|---|---|---|
| Minimum dedendum (cm) | 1.257 m | 1.157 m | 1.157 m | m |
| Minimum total depth (cm) | 2.2 m | 2.157 m | 2.157 m | 1.8 m |
| Minimum clearance (cm) | 0.314 m | 0.157 m | 0.157 m | 0.2 m |
| Thickness of the tooth (cm) | 1.493 m | 1.571 m | 1.571 m | 1.571 m |
| Approximate fillet radius (cm) | 0.209 m | 0.209 m | 0.209 m | 0.209 m |
| Outside diameter | $(T + 2)$ m | $(T + 2)$ m | $(T + 2)$ m | $(T + 1.6)$m |
| Backlash | 0.157 m | 0 | 0 | 0 |

## 11.7. Base Circle

The radius of base circle is found as follows :

Draw the pitch circle with centre $O$ (Fig. 11.6). Draw a tangent $T_1T_2$ at $P$ which is perpendicular to $OP$. Now draw $N_1N_2$ passing through $P$ and inclined at pressure angle ($\psi$) to $T_1T_2$. From $O$ draw a perpendicular $OS$ to $N_1N_2$. Then $OS$ is the radius of base circle. With $O$ as centre and $OS$ as radius draw the base circle

$OS = R_1$ = Base circle radius

$OP = R$ = pitch circle radius

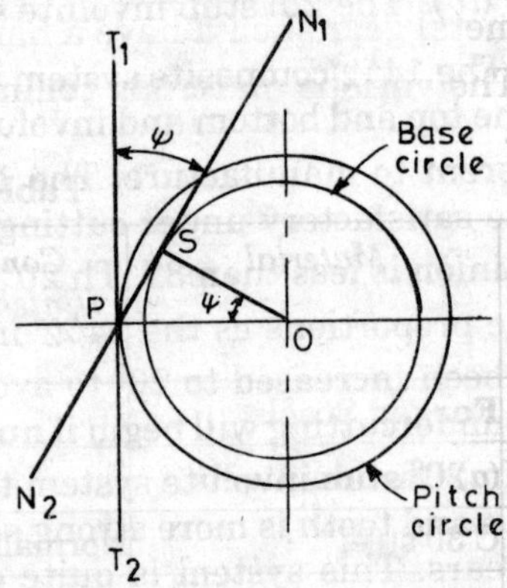

Fig. 11.6.

From right angle triangle $OSP$

$$OS/OP = \cos \psi$$

$$OS = OP \cos \psi$$

$$R_1 = R \cos \psi$$

where $\psi$ = Pressure angle.

## 11.8. Materials

The selection of materials used for gears depends upon the following factors :

(*a*) Degree of accuracy desired, (*b*) Type of service, (*c*) Allowable stress, (*d*) Shock resistance, (*e*) Wear resistance, (*f*) Peripheral speed, and (*g*) Weight of the drive.

Gears are commonly made of steel, cast iron, Bronze or phenolic resins. The great variety of materials available provides the designer with the opportunity of obtaining the optimum materials for any particular requirement whether it be high strength, a long wear life, quietness of operation or high reliability.

Steel gears have high strength and low cost. When gear is to be quenched and tempered C 40 to C 60 plain carbon steels can be used whereas C 20 plain carbon steels can be used for gears to be case hardened. Cast iron gears have good wear resistance whereas bronze gears have more corrosion resistance and are quite useful for reducing friction and wear when the sliding velocity is high. Nonmetallic gears are mated with steel or cast iron gears to obtain the greatest load carrying capacity. To secure good wear resistance the metal gear should have a hardness of at least 300 BHN.

The various materials commonly used are indicated in Table 11.3.

**Table 11.3**

| *S. No.* | *Material* | *Condition (finished gear)* | *Min tensile strength kg/mm²* | *BHN* |
|---|---|---|---|---|
| (*i*) | **Forged Steels** | | | |
| | (*a*) **Carbon Steels** | | | |
| | C 30 steel | Normalised | 50 | 143 |
| | C 30 steel | Hardened and Tempered | 60 | 152 |
| | C 40 steel | Normalised | 58 | 152 |
| | C 40 steel | Hardened and Tempered | 60 | 179 |
| | C 55 Mn 75 steel | Normalised | 22 | 201 |
| | C 55 Mn 75 steel | Hardened and Tempered | 70 | 223 |
| | C 55 Mn 75 steel | — | 80 | 248 |
| | (*b*) **Carbon Chromium Steels** | | | |
| | 55 Cr 70 steel | Hardened and Tempered | 90 | 125 min. |

*Contd...*

| S. No. | *Material* | *Condition (finished gear)* | *Min tensile strength kg/mm²* | *BHN* |
|---|---|---|---|---|
| | 55 Cr 70 steel | ,, | 100 | 285 ” |
| | 40 Cr 1 steel | ,, | 80 | 229 ” |
| | **(c) Carbon Manganese Steels** | | | |
| | 27 Mn 2 steel | Normalised | 55 | — |
| | 27 Mn 2 steel | Hardened and Tempered | 60 | 170 ” |
| | 37 Mn 2 steel | ,, | 70 | 201 ” |
| | 37 Mn 2 steel | ,, | 70 | 201 ” |
| | 37 Mn 2 steel | ,, | 80 | 229 ” |
| | **(d) Manganese Molybdenum Steel** | | | |
| | 35 Mn 2 Mo 28 steel | Hardened and Tempered | 70 | 201 min. |
| | 35 Mn 2 Mo 28 steel | ” | 80 | 229 ” |
| | 35 Mn 2 Mo 45 steel | ” | 80 | 229 ” |
| | **(e) Chromium Molybdenum Steels** | | | |
| | 40 Cr 1 Mo 28 steel | Hardened and Tempered | 70 | 201 min. |
| | 40 Cr 1 Mo 28 steel | ” | 80 | 229 ” |
| | 40 Cr 1 Mo 28 steel | ” | 100 | 285 ” |
| | 40 Cr 1 Mo 60 steel | ” | 90 | 248 ” |
| | 15 Cr 3 Mo 55 steel | ” | 90 | 265 ” |
| | **(f) Nickel Steels** | | | |
| | 40 Ni 3 steel | ” | 80 | 229 ” |
| | 40 Ni 3 steel | ,, | 90 | 255 min |
| | **(g) Nickel Chromium Steel** | | | |
| | 30 Ni 4 Cr 1 steel | ” | 154 | 444 min. |
| | **(h) Nickel Chromium molybdenum Steel** | | | |

*Contd...*

| S. No | Material | Condition (finished gear) | Min tensile strength $kg/mm^2$ | BHN |
|---|---|---|---|---|
| | 40 Ni 2 Cr 1 Mo 28 steel | „ | 90 | 255 ” |
| | 31 Ni 3 Cr 65 Mo 55 steel | „ | 90 | 255 ” |
| | 31 Ni 3 Cr 65 Mo 55 steel | „ | 155 | 244 ” |
| | 31 Ni 3 Cr 65 Mo 55 steel | „ | 110 | 311 ” |
| | 31 Ni 3 Cr 65 Mo 55 steel | „ | 100 | 285 ” |
| | 31 Ni 3 Cr 65 Mo 55 steel | „ | 155 | 444 ” |
| (ii) | **Surface Hardened Steel** | | | |
| | (a) **Carbon Steel** | | | |
| | C 40 steel | — | 55.12 | 145 Core |
| | | | | 460 Case |
| | C 55 steel | — | 70.86 | 200 Core |
| | | | | 520 Case |
| | (b) **C-Cr Steel** | | | |
| | C 55 Cr steel | — | 86.61 | 250 Core |
| | | | | 500 Case |
| | 1% Cr steel | — | 70.86 | 500 Case |
| | (c) **Ni-Steel** | | | |
| | $3\frac{1}{2}$% Ni steel | — | 70.86 | 200 Core<br>300 Case |
| | (d) Ni-Cr steel | | | |
| | $3\frac{1}{2}$ % Ni-Cr steel | — | 86.61 | 250 Core |

*Contd...*

| S No | Material | Condition (finished gear) | Min tensile strength $kg/mm^2$ | BHN |
|---|---|---|---|---|
| | | — | | 500 Case |
| | $1\frac{1}{2}$% Ni 1% Cr steel | — | 86.61 | 250 Core |
| (iii) | **Case Hardened steel** | | | |
| | (a) **C-Steels** | | | |
| | 0.12 to 0.22% C steel | — | 50.39 | 650 Case |
| | 0.15 % C steel | — | 50.39 | 140 Core |
| | 0.20% C steel | — | 50.39 | 140 Core |
| | | | | 640 Case |
| | (b) Ni Steel | | | |
| | 3% Ni steel | — | 70.86 | 200 Case |
| (iv) | **Malleable C.I** | | | |
| | (a) White heat casting (grade B) | — | 28 | 217 |
| | (b) Black heat casting (grade B) | — | 32 | 149 |
| (v) | **Cast iron** | | | |
| | Grade 20 | As Cast | 20 | 179 Min |
| | Grade 25 | „ | 25 | 197 ” |
| | Grade 35 | „ | 35 | 207 ” |
| (vi) | **Cast Steel** | | | |
| | Grade 1 | — | 55 | 145 |
| (vii) | **Phosphor Bronze** | Sand Cast | 16 | 60 |
| | | Chilly Cast | 24 | 70 |

Table 11.4 indicates the allowable static stress for some of the gear material.

Table 11.4

| *Material* | *f (kg/cm$^2$)* | *BHN* |
|---|---|---|
| Cast iron grade 20 | 480 | 200 |
| Cast iron grade 35 | 575 | 225 |
| Cast steel 0.2% C (heat treated) | 1970 | 250 |
| Bronze | 700 | 80 |
| Manganese Bronze | 1410 | 100 |
| Forged steel C = 0.3% (Heat treated) | 2200 | 200 |
| Alloy steel, case hardened | 3500 | 640 |
| Cr-Ni steel *C* = 0.45% (Heat treated) | 5250 | 450 |
| Plastic | 600 | — |

The safe stress in MPa is indicated in Table 11.4 (A)

Table 11.4 (A)

| *Material* | *f (MPa)* | *Hardness (BHN)* |
|---|---|---|
| Cast iron, ordinary | 56 | 180 |
| Cast iron, good grade | 70 | 180 |
| Cast iron, High grade | 105 | 180 |
| Cast steel, untreated | 140 | 180 |
| Cast steel, heat treated | 196 | 250 |
| Forged steel, C—30 | 175 | 150 |
| Steel C—30, heat treated | 224 | 300 |
| Steel C—40 untreated | 210 | 150 |
| Alloy steel, case hardened | 350 | 650 |
| Cr-Ni steel, heat treated | 455 | 475 |
| Cr-Va steel heat treated | 525 | 450 |

| Manganese Bronze | 140 | 100 |
|---|---|---|
| Aluminium Bronze | 154 | 180 |
| Phosphor Bronze | 84 | 100 |

## 11.9. Accuracy of Gears

Accuracy in cutting of gears is estimated for the normal operation of drive. The degree of accuracy depends upon kind of service of the gear. The gears are rated according to the accuracy which they are cut. According to international standards which has been adopted by India also there are twelve degree of accuracy1 to 12,1 being the highest. The degrees of accuracy 6 to 10 are commonly used.

Table 11.5 gives the relationship between peripheral speeds of gears and degree of accuracy.

**Table 11.5**

| *Degree of accuracy* | *Peripheral speed of gears (m/s)* |
|---|---|
| 1—6 | >15 |
| 6—7 | 7.5—15 |
| 7—8 | 5—7.5 |
| 8—9 | 2.5—5 |
| 10—12 | Below 2.5 |

Degree of accuracy commonly used for various types of machines is indicated in Table 11.6.

**Table 11.6**

| *Type of machine* | *Degree of accuracy* |
|---|---|
| Metal cutting machine tools | 3—8 |
| Automobiles | 5—8 |
| Trucks | 7—9 |
| General purpose reduction gears | 6--9 |
| Crane mechanisms | 7--10 |

## 11.9. (a) Surface Durability

Failure of the surfaces of the gear teeth generally called wear may take place in following ways.

(i) **Pitting.** This type of failure takes place due to many repetitions of high contact stresses.

(ii) **Scoring.** It takes place due to lubrication failure.

(iii) **Abrasion.** This type of wear due to presence of foreign materials.

To assure a satisfactory life, the gears design should be such that the dynamic surface stresses are within the surface endurance limit of the material.

## 11.10. Velocity Ratio

The velocity ratio is defined as the number of revolutions of the driver gear to the number of revolution of driven gear. For a single mesh gear drive velocity ratio is given by the following relation.

$$\text{V.R.} = \text{Velocity ratio} = \frac{N_1}{N_2} = \frac{D_2}{D_1} = \frac{T_2}{T_1}$$

where $N_1$ = R.P.M. of driving gear

$D_1$ = P.C.D. of driving gear

$T_1$ = Number of teeth on driven gear

$N_2$ = R.P.M. of driven gear

$D_2$ = Pitch circle diameter (P.C.D) of driven gear

$T_2$ = Number of teeth on driven gear

The angular velocity, peripheral velocity and other dimensions of gear always refer to the pitch diameter of the gear.

## 11.11. Design Considerations of Spur Gears

The following data are usually given for the design of a gear drive.

(i) Horse power to be transmitted

(ii) Velocity ratio

(iii) Centre distance between shafts.

While designing a gear drive the following requirements should be fulfilled.

(i) The gear teeth should be strong enough to withstand the static as well as dynamic loading on the drive.

(ii) The material used for gears should be economical

(*iii*) The teeth should have good wear resistance.

(*iv*) Gears should be provided with proper lubrication arrangements.

## 11.12. Strength of Gear Teeth

When a gear is rotating the gear tooth is considered to be subjected to a load $Q$ acting along the line as shown in Fig. 11.7. The load $Q$ has two components namely a tangential load $F$ tending to break the tooth by bending and a radial force $N$ trying to produce a compressive stress in the tooth. The compressive stress being produced by $N$ is comparatively small as compared to tensile stresses produced due to $F$ therefore the stress due to $F$ need be considered.

$$F = Q \cos \psi$$

$$N = Q \sin \psi$$

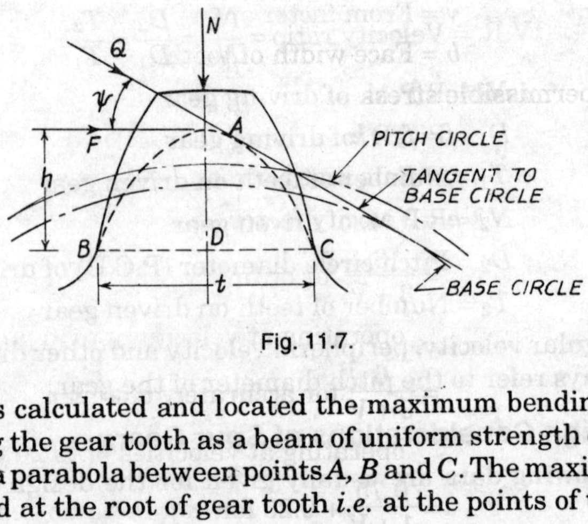


Fig. 11.7.

Lewis calculated and located the maximum bending stress by assuming the gear tooth as a beam of uniform strength obtained by drawing a parabola between points $A$, $B$ and $C$. The maximum stress is induced at the root of gear tooth *i.e.* at the points of tangency at $B$ or $C$.

$$M = \text{Bending moment} = F \times h$$

Now $$\frac{M}{I} = \frac{f}{y_1}$$

$$M = I \times \frac{f}{y_1}$$

$$= \frac{\frac{b\,t^2}{12} \times f}{t/2}$$

$$= f \times \frac{bt^2}{6}$$

$$\therefore \quad F \times h = f \,.\, \frac{bt^2}{6}$$

$$F = f \,.\, b \,.\, \frac{t^2}{6h}$$

The quality $\frac{t^2}{6h}$ is replaced by $p \times y$

$$F = f\,b\,py.$$

This equation is called as Lewis equation.

where $f$ = Permissible working stress

$p$ = Circular pitch

$y$ = From factor or tooth factor

$b$ = Face width of tooth

The permissible stress

$$f = f_s \times k$$

where $f_s$ = Safe static stress

$k$ = Velocity factor

$= \frac{3}{3 + V}$ for ordinary industrial gears operating at velocity upto10 m/sec.

$= \frac{6}{6 + V}$ for accurately cut gear operating at velocities upto 20 m/sec

$= \frac{0.75}{1 + V} + 0.25$ for non-metallic gears

where $V$ = Pitch line velocity in m/*sec*

$y$ = Tooth factor

$= 0.124 - \frac{0.684}{T}$ for14½ involute full depth

$= 0.154 - \frac{0.912}{T}$ for 20° involute full depth

$$= 0.175 - \frac{0.841}{T} \text{ for } 20^\circ \text{ stub involute tooth}$$

where $T$ = Number of teeth on gear

The strength of the tooth determined from Lewis equation is called beam strength of the tooth.

Table 11.7 indicates the value of form factor ($y$)

**Table 11.7.**

| *No. of teeth* | *Form Factor* | | |
|---|---|---|---|
| | *14½°* | *20° full depth* | *20° stub* |
| 12 | 0.067 | 0.078 | 0.099 |
| 13 | 0.071 | 0.083 | 0.103 |
| 14 | 0.075 | 0.088 | 0.108 |
| 15 | 0.078 | 3.092 | 0.111 |
| 16 | 0.081 | 0.094 | 0.115 |
| 17 | 0.084 | 0.096 | 0.117 |
| 18 | 0.086 | 0.098 | 0.120 |
| 19 | 0.088 | 0.100 | 0.123 |
| 20 | 0.090 | 0.102 | 0.125 |
| 21 | 0.092 | 0.104 | 0.127 |
| 22 | 0.093 | 0.105 | 0.129 |
| 24 | 0.095 | 0.107 | 0.132 |
| 26 | 0.098 | 0.110 | 0.135 |
| 28 | 0.100 | 0.112 | 0.137 |
| 30 | 0.101 | 0.114 | 0.139 |
| 34 | 0.104 | 0.118 | 0.142 |
| 38 | 0.106 | 0.122 | 0.145 |
| 43 | 0.108 | 0.126 | 0.147 |
| 50 | 0.110 | 0.130 | 0.151 |
| 60 | 0.113 | 0.134 | 0.154 |

| No. of teeth | Form Factor | | |
|---|---|---|---|
| | 141/2° | 20° full depth | 20° stub |
| 75 | 0.115 | 0.138 | 0.158 |
| 100 | 0.117 | 3.142 | 0.161 |
| 150 | 0.119 | 0.146 | 0.165 |
| 300 | 0.122 | 0.150 | 0.170 |
| rack | 0.124 | 0.154 | 0.175 |

## 11.13. Service Factor

The Lewis equation is applicable for gears operating under-steady load conditions. For gears subjected to shock and in continuous operation for more than 10 hours per day the tangential load ($F$) is calculated as follows.

$$F = \frac{\text{H. P.} \times 4500}{V \times C_1}$$

where $V$ = Pitch line velocity in m/min

$C_1$ = Service factor

The value of service factor is indicated in Table 11.8.

**Table 11.8.**

| Type of Load | Type of service | | |
|---|---|---|---|
| | 24 hrs per day | 8-10 hrs per day | Intermittent 3 hrs per day |
| Light shock | 0.65 | 0.80 | 1.00 |
| Medium shock | 0.55 | 0.65 | 0.80 |
| Heavy shock | 0.50 | 0.55 | 0.65 |
| Steady | 0.8 | 1.00 | 1.25 |

The value of $V$ is 10 to 12 m/sec for super gears. The pitch line velocity is limited to 3 m/sec for cast teeth.

## 11.14. Face Width of Tooth

The width of face ($b$) is related to circular pitch as follows.

$$b = 2p \text{ for cast gears}$$
$$= 3.5p \text{ for cut gears}$$
$$= 5p \text{ for precisions cut gears}$$

The face width generally varies from 8 m to 12.5 m for well proportional gears.

## 11.15. Dynamic Load on Gear Teeth

When a pair of gear wheels rotate, some times a jerky motion is observed which causes hammering effect on gears teeth. This causes the increase in load on the teeth more than the normal steady theoretical load under ideal conditions of drive. The load gets increased due to the dynamic action. The total dynamic load at the pitch line is given by the following reaction.

$$F_d = F + F_v$$
$$= F + \frac{0.112\,V\,(b \times C_1 + F)}{0.112V + \sqrt{b\,C_1 + F}}$$

where $F_d$ = Dynamic load

$F_v$ = Variable load

$V$ = Pitch line velocity in m/min

$b$ = Face width in cm

$C_1$ = Factor depending upon machinery errors

$$= \frac{k.e}{\frac{1}{E_p} + \frac{1}{E_g}}$$

where $k$ = a constant depending upon tooth form

$= 0.107$ for $14\frac{1^\circ}{2}$ Tooth

$= 0.111$ for $20^\circ$ full depth tooth

$= 0.115$ for $20^\circ$ stub tooth

$E_p$ = Young's modulus for pinion

$E_g$ = Young's modulus for gear (kg/cm$^2$)

$e$ = Tooth action error in cm

Table 11.9 indicates the values of $e$ in cm.

**Table 11.9**

| *Module (m) mm* | *Class I Industrial* | *Class II Accurate* | *Class III Precision* |
|---|---|---|---|
| 4 | 0.00508 | 0.00254 | 0.00127 |
| 5 | 0.00555 | 0.00277 | 0.0015 |
| 6 | 0.00652 | 0.00316 | 0.00172 |
| 7 | 0.00712 | 0.00353 | 0.00195 |
| 8 | 0.00778 | 0.00389 | 0.00198 |

Class-I gears are ordinary commercial quantity gears made with a form cutter whereas class-II gears are accurately hobbed or generated gears and class-III gears are precision gears precision gears as resulting from shaving, grinding or lapping operations.

## 11.16. Limit Load for Wear

Gears may wear due to improper lubrication or foreign particles in the lubricant. According to Buckingham the load limit for wear is expression by the equation.

$$F_d = k \cdot D_p \cdot b \cdot Q$$

where $F_\omega$ = Limiting load for wear in kg

$k$ = Material combination factor

$$= \frac{f_{se}^2 \times \sin\psi}{1.4}\left[\frac{1}{E_p} + \frac{1}{E_g}\right]$$

$f_{se}$ = Surface endurance limit of a gear pair in kg/cm$^2$

$\psi$ = Pressure angle

$E_p$ = Modulus of elasticity for pinion in kg/cm$^2$

$E_g$ = Modulus of elasticity for gear in kg/cm$^2$

$D_p$ = Pitch circle diameter of pinion in cm

$b$ = Face width of gear in cm

$Q$ = Ratio factor

$$= \frac{2T_g}{T_g + T_p} \text{ for external gears}$$

$$= \frac{2T_g}{T_g - T_p} \text{ for internal gears}$$

$T_g$ = Number of teeth on gear

$T_p$ = Number of teeth on pinion

The value of $f_{se}$ is calculated as follows

$$f_{se} = 28 \times \text{B.H.N.} - 700 \text{ kg/cm}^2 \text{ for steel}$$

where B.H.N. is hardness of gear material

$$f_{se} = 6300 \text{ kg/cm}^2 \text{ for C.I}$$

It should be ensured that the wear load ($F_\omega$) should be more than dynamic load ($F_d$).

Only the weaker gear should be checked. A weaker gear is one with smaller value of strength factor ($f \times y$) of gear.

## 11.16. (*a*). Gear Blank Design

Gear blanks can be produced by different manufacturing methods such as casting, forging and machining from a solid blank. Some of the factors to be considered while designing a gear blank are as follows :

(*i*) Rigidity is almost always a prime consideration.

The arms or webs should have rigidity to maintain uniform load across the face. Therefore arms or webs must be thick enough for adequate support. The rim bead gives additional rigidity and strength to the rim.

(*ii*) The hub should have sufficient thickness to maintain a proper fit with the shaft to provide sufficient metal for key slot and to transmit torque through the hub to the web or spokes without serious stress concentration. The length of hub should be at least equal to face width of gear. The hub bead is used to brace the arms and reduce stress concentration caused by the torque transmitted from the hub to the arms.

(*iii*) The arms are usually made of elliptical section but they may also be designed with an *H* or *I* section or any other suitable shape depending on stiffness and strength desired.

## 11.17. Design of Gears

The various parts of a gear are designed as follows :

(*i*) **Shaft** $d$ = Diameter of shaft

$f_s$ = Safe shear stress in shaft

$$T_e = \frac{\pi}{16} f_s \cdot d^3$$

where $T_e$ = Equivalent torque = $\sqrt{T^2 + M^2}$

$M$ = Bending moment acting on shaft

$$H.P = \frac{2\pi NT}{4500}$$

$N$ = Shaft R.P.M.

$T$ = Torque.

*(ii)* **Hub.** The gear hubs are either made solid or split. The dimensions of hub in terms of shafts diameter are indicated in Table 11.10.

**Table 11.10.**

| *Type of service* | *Diameter of hub* | | *Length of hub* |
|---|---|---|---|
| | *Cast iron* | *Cast steel* | |
| Light load without shock | $1\frac{5}{8}d + 3$ mm | $1\frac{1}{2}d + 5$ mm | 1.75 $d$ to 2.5 $d$ |
| Medium load and medium shock | $1\frac{3}{4}d + 6$ mm | $1\frac{5}{8}d + 6$ mm | " |
| Heavy load and heavy shock | 2 $d$ | $1\frac{3}{4}d + 3$ mm | " |

*(iii)* **Arms.** Small gears up to 25 cm diameter are built with a solid web joining hub and rim. The thickness of the web is generally equal to half the circular pitch.

The number of arms in a gear depend upon the pitch circle diameter. The arms used are indicated in Table 11.11.

**Table 11.11.**

| *Pitch circle diameter* | *Number of arms* |
|---|---|
| up to 50 cm | 4 |
| 50 to 150 cm | 6 |
| 150 to 200 cm | 8 |
| Above 200 cm | 10 |

Fig. 11.8 shows different sections of the arms of the gears.

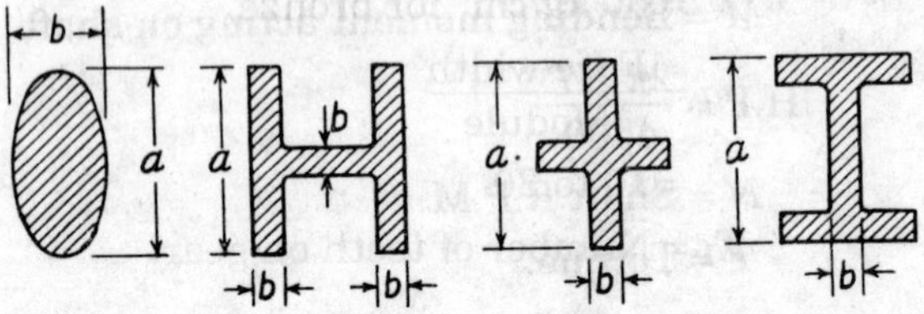


Fig. 11.8.

Arms of elliptical cross section are used in gears for light loads whereas H-sections arms are generally used for heavy gears. In elliptical arms the major axis ($a$) is twice the minor axis ($b$) and the major axis lies in the plane to rotation.

(*iv*) **Rim.** The rim thickness ($t$) is calculated as follows.

$$t = m\sqrt{\frac{T}{2 \times n}}$$

where $m$ = Module in mm

$T$ = Number of teeth on gear

$n$ = Number of arms

(*v*) **Weight of gear.**

$W$ = Weight of gear = $kTbp^2$

where $k$ = 0.012 for spur gears

= 0.10 for bevel gears

$T$ = Number of gears

$b$ = Face width in cm

$p$ = Circular pitch in cm

When both pinion and gear are made of same material the pinion is the determining factor.

(*vi*) **Boch's formula to calculate module.** According to Boch the module ($m$) is given by

$$m = 0.88\sqrt[3]{\frac{T}{C^2 \,.\, q \times T_1}}$$

where $T$ = Torque on the gear

$C_2$ = Strength coefficient

= 40 kg/cm$^4$ for C.I.

$= 60$ to $80$ kg/cm$^2$ for steel

$= 50$ kg/cm$^2$ for bronze

$$q = \frac{\text{Face width}}{\text{Module}}$$

$= 10$ to $30$

$T_1$ = Number of teeth on gear.

(*vii*) **Design load for gears.** Design load ($F_0$) for gears is found from the following relation :

$$F_o = \frac{C_o \times C_R}{C_v \times C_L} \times F$$

where $F_o$ = Design load

$C_o$ = Over load factor

$= 1$ to1.75 uniform power source

$= 1.25$ to $2.0$ for light shock

$= 1.5$ to $2.25$ for medium shock

$C_R$ = Reliability factor

$= 0.7 - 0.8$ for low reliability

$= 1.0 - 1.25$ for medium reliability

$= 1.5 - 3.0$ for high reliability

$C_V$ = velocity factor

$= \frac{366}{366 + V}$ for very accurately cut and ground metallic gears.

$= \frac{43}{43 + \sqrt{V}}$ for hardened steel, ground and lapped gears.

$$C_V = \frac{45}{60 + V_m} + 0.25 \text{ for non metallic gears}$$

where $V$ is speed in mpm.

$C_L$ = Life factor

It depends on number of cycles

$C_L = 3 - 4.0$ for $10^3$ cycles

$C_L = 1.1 + 1.4$ for $10^6$ cycles

$= 0.9 - 1$ for $10^8$ cycles

For helical gears velocity factor $C_v$ is given by

$$C_v = \frac{925}{915 + V} \text{ for } V = 600 \text{ to} 1200 \text{ mpm}$$

$$= \frac{43}{43 + \sqrt{V}} \text{ for } V > 1200 \text{ mpm}$$

$$= \frac{65}{60 + V} + 0.25 \text{ for non.metallic gears.}$$

If above factors are taken into account then gears should be designed for $F_o$.

**Example 11.1.** *A shaft running at 240 R.P.M. is driven by a 16 H.P., 960% R.P.M. motor through a pair of 14½° involute spur gears. The centre distance is approximately 40 cm. The gear is to be made of cast steel and pinion of forged steel. Design the gears assuming the following data :*

*Safe static stress for gear= 1400 kg/cm².*

*Safe static stress for pinion = 2000 kg /cm².*

*Service factor = 0.65.*

*Check the gear for wear assuming B.H.N. of cast steel 165.*

**Solution.**

(*a*) **To calculate P.C.D.**

H.P = 16

$C_1$ = Service factor = 0.65

$D_p$ = P.C.D. of pinion

$D_G$ = P.C.D. of gear

$C$ = Centre distance = 40 cm

$N_p$ = R.P.M. of pinion = 960

$N_G$ = R.P.M. of gear = 240

$$\frac{D_p}{2} + \frac{D_g}{2} = 40$$

$$D_p + D_g = 80 \qquad \text{...}(i)$$

$$\frac{D_g}{D_p} = \frac{N_p}{N_g} = \frac{960}{240} = 4$$

$$D_G = 4D_p$$

From (*i*) and (*ii*) equations

$$D_g = 64 \text{ cm}$$
$$D_p = 16 \text{ cm}$$

**(b) To calculate tangential load**

As the gear is weaker than pinion so gear should be designed.

$$V = \text{Pitch line velocity}$$
$$= \frac{\pi D_g \,.\, N_g}{60} = \frac{\pi \times 64 \times 240}{60 \times 100}$$
$$= 8 \text{ m/sec} = 480 \text{ m/min}$$
$$F = \text{Tangential load}$$
$$= \frac{\text{H.P.} \times 4500}{\text{V} \times \text{C}_1} = \frac{16 \times 4500}{480 \times 0.65} = 231 \text{ kg.}$$

**(c) To find teeth proportions**

According to Lewis equation

$$F = f \,.\, p \,.\, y \,.\, b$$
$$f = \text{Permissible safe stress}$$
$$= 1400 \times \text{velocity factor}$$
$$= 1400 \times \frac{3}{3 + V}$$

where $V$ is in metre per sec.

$$= 1400 \times \frac{3}{3 + 8}$$
$$= 382 \text{ kg/cm}^2$$
$$p = \text{Circular pitch} = \pi\, m$$
$$m = \text{Module}$$
$$y = 0.124 - \frac{0.684}{T_g} \quad \text{for } \psi = 14½°.$$
$$= 0.124 - \frac{0.684}{D_g} \times m$$
$$= 0.124 = \frac{0.684}{64} \times m$$

where $T_g$ = Number of teeth on gear

$$m = \frac{D_g}{T_g}$$
$$T_g = \frac{D_g}{m} = \frac{64}{m}$$

$b$ = Face width of tooth

$= 3.5 \times p \ (say) = 3.5 \times \pi m$

Now $F = f \, . \, p \, . \, y \, . \, b$

$$321 = 382 \times \pi \times m \times (0.124 - \frac{0.64}{64} \times m) \times 3.5 \, \pi \, m$$

The value of module ($m$) should be so chosen that R.H.S.is at least equal to L.H.S.or greater but not less than L.H.S.

when $m = 3$ mm ; R.H.S. = 142.37

$m = 4$ mm ; R.H.S. = 252.46

$m = 4.5$ mm ; R.H.S. = 318.2

Although $m = 4.5$ gives a sufficient higher value but the module ($m$) should be taken equal to 4 mm.

$m = 4$ mm

$T_p$ = Number of teeth on pinion

$$= \frac{D_p}{m} = \frac{160}{4} = 40$$

$$\frac{T_g}{T_p} = \frac{D_g}{D_p} = \frac{N_p}{N_g} = \frac{960}{240} = 4$$

$T_g = 4 \times T_p = 4 \times 40 = 160.$

Gear teeth proportions :

Addendum $= m = 4$ mm

Dedendum $= 1.157 \times \text{m} = 1.157 \times 4$

$= 4.628$ mm

Total depth = Addendum + Dedendum

$=.4 + 4.628 = 8.628$ mm

Clearance $= 0.157 \times 4 = 0.628$ mm

Face width $= 3.5 \times \pi \times m \times 0.4 = 4.4$ cm

Diameter of gear blank $= D_g + 2\text{m}$

$= 640 + 2 \times 4 = 648$ mm

Diameter of pinion blank $= D_p + 2 \times 4$

$= 160 + 8 = 168$ mm.

(*d*) **Check for wear**

$F_\omega$ = Limiting load due to wear

$= K \, . \, D_p \, b \, . \, Q$

where $D_p$ = P.C.D. of pinion in cm

$$= 16 \text{ cm}$$

$$b = \text{Face width}$$

$$= 3.5 \times \pi \times m$$

$$= 3.5 \times \pi \times 0.40 = 4.4 \text{ cm}$$

Ratio factor, $Q = 2\dfrac{T_g}{T_g + T_p}$

$$= \frac{2 \times 160}{160 + 40} = \frac{320}{200}$$

$$= 1.6$$

$$K = \text{Load stress factor}$$

$$K = \frac{f_{se}^2 \times \sin\psi}{1.4}\left[\frac{1}{E_p} + \frac{1}{E_g}\right]$$

$$f_{se} = \text{Surface endurance limit}$$

$$= 28 \times \text{B.H.N.} - 700$$

$$= 28 \times 165 - 700$$

$$= 3920 \text{ kg/cm}^2$$

$$\sin\psi = \sin 14\tfrac{1}{2}^\circ = 0.25$$

$$E_p = E_g = 2 \times 10^6 \text{ kg/cm}^2 \text{ (Assume)}$$

$$K = \frac{(3920)^2 \times 0.25}{1.4}\left[\frac{1}{2 \times 10^6} + \frac{1}{2 \times 10^6}\right]$$

$$= 2.74$$

$$F_\omega = 2.74 \times 16 \times 4.4 \times 1.6$$

$$= 308.6 \text{ kg}$$

This is more than the tangential load of 231 kg. hence gears are safe from the view point of wear load.

**Example 11.2.** *A motor shaft transmits 20 H.P. at 1200 R.P.M. to a low speed shaft with a speed reduction of 3.1. The teeth are 14½° involute with 24 teeth on the pinion. Both gear and pinion are made of steel heat treated and the maximum allowable static stress in gear and pinion is 2200kg/cm$^2$. The starting torque is 30% more than running torque and the safe shear stress in shaft and key is 450 kg/cm$^2$. Design a suitable spur gear drive.*

**Solution.** (*a*) **To find pitch circle diameters**

$$N_p = \text{R.P.M. of pinion} = 1200$$

$N_g$ = R.P.M. of gear

$T_g$ = Number of teeth on gear

$T_p$ = Number of teeth on pinion = 24

$$\frac{N_g}{N_p} = \frac{1}{3}$$

$$N_g = N_p \times \frac{1}{3} = 1200 \times \frac{1}{3} = 400 \text{ R.P.M.}$$

$$\frac{T_g}{T_p} = \frac{N_p}{N_g} = 3$$

$$T_g = 3 \times T_p = 3 \times 24 = 72$$

Let, module ($m$)= 5 mm

$D_g$ = Pitch circle diameter of pinion

$D_g$ = Pitch circle diameter of gear

$$m = \frac{D_g}{T_g}$$

$$D_p = m \ . \ T_g$$

$$= 5 . \times 72 = 360 \text{ mm}$$

$$D_p = m \ . \ T_p$$

$$= 5 \times 24 = 120 \text{ mm.}$$

**(*b*) To calculate tooth dimensions**

As the starting torque is 30% more than running torque, the spur gears should be designed for

$$1.3 \times 20 = 26 \text{ H.P}$$

$V$ = Pitch line velocity

$$= \frac{\pi \, D_p \ . \ N_p}{60} = \frac{\pi \times 12 \times 1200}{60 \times 100}$$

$$= 7.54 \text{ m/sec.}$$

$F$ = Tangential load

$$= \frac{\text{H.P} \times 75}{\text{V}} = \frac{26 \times 75}{7.54} = 259 \text{ kg.}$$

According to Lewis equation

$$F = f \ . \ p \ . \ y \ . \ b$$

$f$ = Static stress × velocity factor

$$= 2200 \times \frac{3}{3 + V}$$

$$= 2200 \times \frac{3}{3 + 7.54}$$

$$= 626.2 \text{ kg/cm}^2$$

$p$ = Circular pitch = $\pi$ m

$= \pi \times 0.5 = 1.57$ cm

$b$ = Face width of tooth

$$b = \text{form factor} = 0.124 - \frac{0.684}{T_p}$$

$$= 0.124 - \frac{0.684}{24} = 0.095$$

$F = f \,.\, p \,.\, y \,.\, b$

$259 = 626.1 \times 1.57 \times 0.095 \times b$

$b = 2.77$ cm

$= 3$ cm (say)

Addendum = Module = 5 mm

Dedendum = 1.257 m = 5.785 mm

The particulars of the drive will be as follows :

| *Item* | *Number of teeth* | *P.C.D (mm)* | *Module (m)(mm)* | *Teeth width (mm)* | *Addendum (mm)* | *Dedumdum (mm)* | *Clearance (mm)* | *Blank Diameter (mm)* |
|---|---|---|---|---|---|---|---|---|
| Gear | 72 | 360 | 5 | 30 | 5 | 1.157 m=5.785 mm | 0.175 m=0.785 | 370 |
| Pinion | 24 | 120 | 5 | 30 | 5 | 5.785 (mm) | 0.785 | 130 |

**(c) To calculate shaft diameter and hub diameter**

$d$ = Shaft diameter

$f_s$ = Safe shear stress in shaft

$= 450 \text{ kg/cm}^2$

$\psi$ = Pressure angle = $14\frac{1}{2}^\circ$

$Q$ = Maximum thrust

$$= \frac{F}{\cos\psi}$$

$$= \frac{259}{\cos 14\frac{1}{2}^\circ} = \frac{259}{0.9681} = 267.5 \text{ kg}$$

$W$ = Weight of gear

$= k \,.\, T_g \,.\, b \,.\, p^2 = 0.012 \times 72 \times 3 \times (1.57)^2$

$= 6.4$ kg

Figs. 11.9 and 11.9 (*a*) show various forces acting on a pair of gears.

The resultant of $Q$ and $W$ is given by

$$R = \sqrt{Q^2 + W^2 + 2QW \cos \psi}$$

$$= \sqrt{(267.5)^2 + (6.4)^2 + 2 \times 267.5 \times 6.4 \times \cos 14\frac{1}{2}^\circ}$$

$= 274$ kg

We assume that the gear is overhang on the shaft by 15 cm.

$M$ = Bending moment

$= R \times 15 = 274 \times 15 = 4110$ kg cm

$T$ = Twisting moment

$= F \times$ Pitch circle radius of gear

$= 259 \times 18 = 4662$ kg cm

Equivalent torque, $T_e = \sqrt{T^2 + M^2} = \sqrt{(4662)^2 + (4110)^2}$

$= 6215$ kg cm

$$T_e = \frac{\pi}{16} f_s \, d^3$$

$$6210 = \frac{\pi}{16} \times 450 \times d^3$$

$d = 4.13$ cm. $= 4.25$ cm (say).

Similarly diameter of pinion shaft can be calculated. It can be taken equal to 3 cm.

Gear hub diameter $= 1\frac{1}{2}d + 6$ mm

$= 1\frac{1}{2} \times 4.25 + 0.6 = 6.975$ cm

Hub length $= 2d = 2 \times 4.25 = 8.5$ cm.

**(*d*) To design arms**

$n$ = Number of arms

$= 4$ (say).

Let the arms be of elliptical cross section with $a$ as major axis and $b$ as minor axis and $a = 2b$.

$$M_1 = \text{Maximum bending moment on each arm}$$
$$= \frac{T}{n}$$
$$= \frac{4662}{4}$$
$$= 1165.5 \text{ kg cm}$$
$$f = \text{Permissible bending stress in arms}$$
$$= 400 \text{ kg/cm}^2 \text{ (assume)}$$
$$Z = \text{Modulus of section of elliptical arm}$$
$$= \frac{\pi}{64} a^3$$
$$M_1 = f \,.\, Z$$
$$1165.5 = 400 \times \frac{\pi}{64} a^3$$
$$a = 3.9 \text{ cm}$$
$$b = \frac{a}{2}$$
$$= \frac{3.9}{2}$$
$$= 1.95 \text{ cm.}$$

Thus the elliptical section of the arm at the hub is 3.9 × 1.95 cm. Fig. 11.10 shows the details of gears.

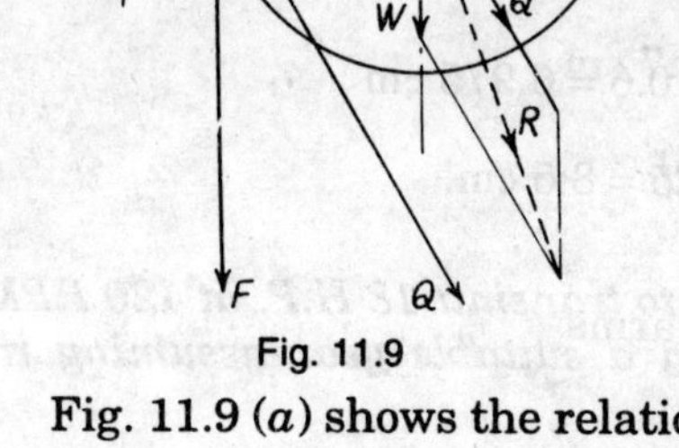

Fig. 11.9

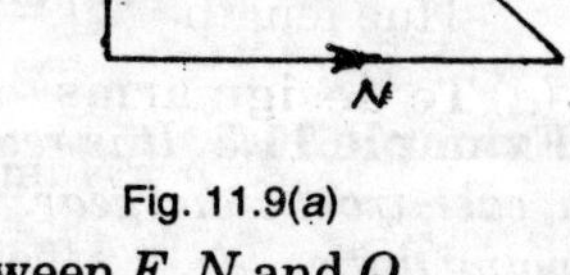

Fig. 11.9(a)

Fig. 11.9 ($a$) shows the relation between $F$, $N$ and $Q$.

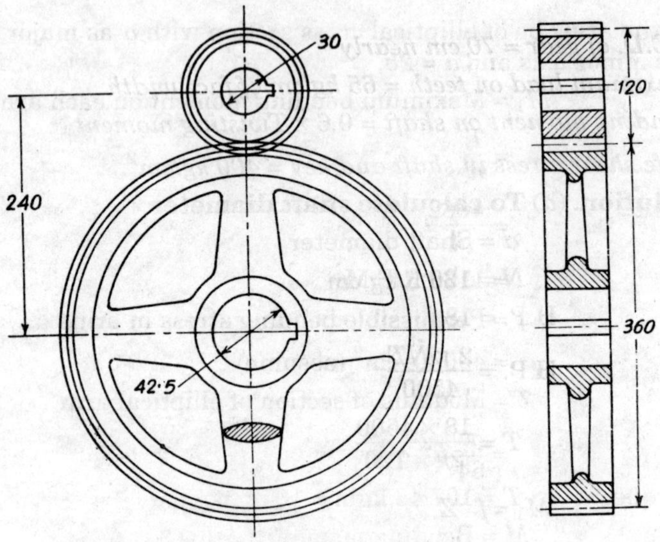


Fig. 11.10.

$$\frac{F}{Q} = \cos \psi$$

$$\frac{N}{F} = \tan \psi$$

where $F$ = Tangential load

$Q$ = Maximum thrust

$N$ = End thrust.

(*e*) **Key size.** Use rectangular key

Length = Length of hub + 6 mm

= 8.5 + 0.6 = 9.01 cm

$$\text{Width} = \frac{d}{4} = \frac{4.25}{4} = 1.06 \text{ cm}$$

$$\text{Thickness} = \frac{d}{6} = \frac{4.25}{6} = 0.7 \text{ cm}$$

Taper 1 : 100.

**Example 11.3.** *It is required to transmit 18 H.P. at 120 RPM. by a cast iron spur gear. Design a suitable gear assuming the following data :*

*P.C.D. of gear = 70 cm nearly*

*Maximum load on teeth = 65 kg/cm of face width*

*Bending moment on shaft = 0.6 × Twisting moment*

*Safe shear stress in shaft and key = 400 kg/cm².*

**Solution.** (*a*) **To calculate shaft diameter**

$d$ = Shaft diameter

$N$ = 120 R.P.M.

H.P. = 18

$$\text{H.P.} = \frac{2\,\pi\, NT}{4500}$$

$$T = \frac{18 \times 4500}{2\pi \times 120}$$

Torque, $T$ = 107.48 kgm = 10748 kg cm

$M$ = Bending moment = $0.6 \times T$

$= 0.6 \times 10748 = 6445$ kg cm.

$T_e$ = Equivalent torque = $\sqrt{T^2 + M^2}$

$= \sqrt{10748^2 + 6445^2} = 12532$ kg cm.

$f_s$ = Safe shear stress in shaft and key

= 400 kg/cm² (Assume)

$$T_e = \frac{\pi}{16} f_s \,.\, d^3$$

$$12532 = \frac{\pi}{16} \times 400 \times d^3$$

$d = 5.42 = 5.5$ cm (say).

(*b*) **Hub**

Diameter of hub = 1½ $d$ + 6 mm = 1.5 × 5.5 + 0.6

= 8.85 cm = 9 cm (say)

Length of hub = $2d$ = 2 × 5.5 = 11 cm.

(*c*) **Key.** For a rectangular parallel sunk key

Length of key = Length of hub + 6 mm

= 11.6 cm.

$$\text{Width} = \frac{d}{4} = \frac{5.5}{4} = 1.375 \text{ cm}$$

$$\text{Thickness} = \frac{d}{6} = \frac{5.5}{4} = 0.91 \text{ cm}$$

To check the key in shear, consider shearing failure of key

$f_{s_1}$ = Induced shear stress in key

$P$ = Force acting on key

$$= \frac{T_e}{\text{Shaft radius}} = \frac{12532}{5.5} \times 2 = 4557 \text{ kg.}$$

$P$ = Length of key × Width × $f_{s_1}$

$$4557 = 11 \times 1.375 \times f_{s_1}$$

$$f_{s_1} = 301 \text{ kg/cm}^2$$

which is safe, hence O.K.

(*d*) **Teeth dimensions**

$T$ = Torque = 10748 kg cm

$D$ = P.C.D = 70 cm

$$T_g = \text{Number of teeth} = \frac{D}{m} = \frac{70}{m}$$

$N_g$ = R.P.M. of gear

According to Boch the module ($m$) is given by

$$m = 0.88 \sqrt[3]{\frac{T}{C_2 \cdot q \cdot T_g}}$$

where $C_2$ = Strength coefficient

= 40 for C.I.

$$q = \frac{\text{Face width}}{\text{Module}} = 10 \text{ (say)}$$

$$m = (0.88)\ ^{uo}303\sqrt{\frac{10748 \times m}{40 \times 10 \times 70}}$$

$$m^3 = (0.88)^3 \times \frac{10748 \times m}{40 \times 10 \times 70}$$

$$m^2 = \frac{(0.88)^3 \times 10748}{400 \times 70}$$

$$m = 0.51 \text{ cm} = 5.1 \text{ mm.}$$

We adopt standard value of module as 5.5 mm

$$m = 5.5 \text{ mm.}$$

$$m = \frac{D_g}{T_g}$$

$$5.5 = \frac{700}{T_g}$$

$$T_g = \frac{700}{5.5} = 127.27 = 128 \text{ (say)}.$$

**Gear tooth proportions**

Addendum = $m$ = 5.5 mm

Dedendum = 1.157 m = 1.157 × 5.5

= 6.36 mm

Clearance = 0.157 m

= 0.157 × 5.5 = 0.86 m

Total depth = Addendum + Dedendum

= 5.5 + 6.36 = 11.86 mm

Outside diameter = $(T_g + 2) \times m$

= (128 + 2).× 5.5 = 715 mm

Tooth thickness = 1:571 m

= 1.151 × 5.5 = 8.64 mm

Face width = 10 m = 10 × 5.5 = 55 mm.

(*e*) **Arms.** For 70 cm P.C.D. the number of arms will be 6

$n$ = Number of arms = 6

Let the arms be of elliptical cross section whose major axis ($a$) is twice the minor axis.

$M$ = Bending moment of each arm

$$= \frac{T}{n} = \frac{10748}{6} = 1791.3 \text{ kg cm}$$

$f$ = Allowable bending stress in Arms

= 180 kg/cm$^2$ (assume)

= Modulus of section

$$= \frac{\pi}{64} a^3$$

$$M = f \times Z$$

$$1791.3 = 180 \times \frac{\pi}{64} a^3$$

$a$ = 5:88 cm

$$b = \frac{a}{2} = \frac{5.88}{2} = 2.94 \text{ cm}.$$

The taper in the arms from hub to rim be taken as 1 in 32.

Check for maximum load on tooth is carried out as follows :

$R$ = Pitch circle radius

$= \frac{70}{2} = 35$ cm.

$F$ = Tangential load

$= \frac{T}{R} = \frac{10748}{35} = 307$ kg.

Face width = 5.5 cm

Load on tooth $= \frac{F}{\text{Face width}} = \frac{307}{5.5}$

= 55.8 kg per cm of face width

This is less than the given on tooth *i.e.*, 65 kg/cm of face width. Hence safe

(*f*) **Rim** $t$ = Rim thickness

$= m\sqrt{\frac{T_g}{2 \times n}} = 5.5\sqrt{\frac{128}{2 \times 6}}$

= 17.96 mm = 18 mm (say).

## 11.18. Helical Gears

In helical gears teeth are cut in the from of a helix about the axis of rotation. One of the gear has a right hand helix and the mating gear has a left hand helix. The mating gear have same helix angle. The twisted teeth allow more teeth in contact at one time distributing the load more widely. These gears have the following characteristics.

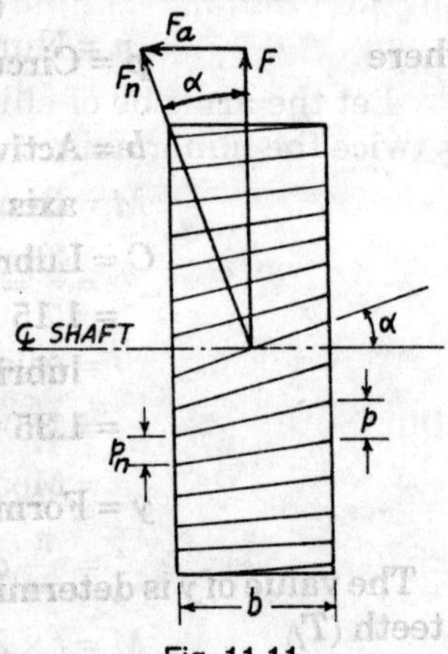


Fig. 11.11.

(*i*) They are used for heavy loads.

(*ii*) They are used for high pitch line velocities of the order of 1200 to 3000 m/min.

(*iii*) They are less noisy.

They are commonly used in automobile gear boxes, and in steam and gas turbines for speed reduction.

Fig. 11.11 shows a helical gear having helical angle (α).

The normal tooth force $F_n$ has two components.

$F$ = Tangential driving force

$F_\alpha$ = End thrust or axial load = $F \cdot \tan \alpha$.

The end thrust produced should be supported by thrust bearing (roller or ball type). The usual range of helix angle used is 15° and 30°, although for very high speed higher value of helix angle may be used.

$p$ = Circular pitch in the plane of rotation. (Plane perpendicular to gear axis)

$p_n$ = Normal circular pitch (circular pitch in the plane normal to the teeth)

$p_n = p \cos \alpha$.

In order that contact may be maintained across the entire active face of the gear minimum value of face width ($b$) is given by

$$b = \frac{p}{\tan \alpha}.$$

## 11.19. Strength of Helical Gears

$$F = \frac{f \cdot p \cdot y \cdot b}{C}$$

where $p$ = Circular pitch

$b$ = Active face width parallel or along the axis of rotation

$C$ = Lubrication factor

= 1.15 for enclosed gears, continuously lubricated

= 1.35 for scantly lubrication

$$y = \text{Form factor} = 0.154 - \frac{0.912}{T_f}$$

The value of $y$ is determined for the virtual or formative number of teeth ($T_f$)

$$T_f = \frac{T}{\cos^3 \alpha}$$

where $T$ = Actual number of teeth

$f$ = Allowable stress

= Static stress × Velocity factor

$$\text{Velocity factor} = \frac{4.5}{4.5 + V} \text{ when } V \text{ is up to 5 m/sec}$$

$$= \frac{6}{6+V} \text{ when } V \text{ is up to 10 m/sec}$$

$$= \frac{15}{15+V} \text{ when } V \text{ is up to 20 m/sec}$$

$$= \frac{5.5}{5.5+\sqrt{V}} \text{ when } V \text{ is more than 20 m/sec}$$

where $V$ = Pitch line velocity in m/sec.

## 11.20. Dynamic Load

Dynamic load on helical gears is given by the following relation

$$F_d = \frac{F + 0.112\, V\,(bC_1 \cos^2 \alpha + F) \cos \alpha}{0.112\, V + \sqrt{bC_1 + F}}$$

The various symbols used have the same meaning as in case of spur gear

## 11.21. Limit Load for Wear

The wear load ($F_w$) is given by the following relation

$$F_w = k \,.\, D_p \,.\, b \,.\, Q$$

where

$$k = \frac{f_{se}^2 \,.\, \sin\psi}{1.4 \cos^2 \alpha}\left[\frac{1}{E_p} + \frac{1}{E_g}\right]$$

$$Q = \frac{2\, T_g}{T_g + T_p}$$

$D_p$ = P.C.D. of pinion in cm

$b$ = Face width of gear in cm

$f_{se}$ = Surface endurance limit of gear pair in kg/cm$^2$.

## 11.22. Horse Power Rating and Load Rating

(*i*) **H.P. on strength basis.** The horse power rating of a spur gear with 20° pressure angle and helical gears for strength is given by

$$\text{H.P. (strength)} = \frac{k_1 \,.\, k_2 \,.\, k_3\, bm^2\, TN}{25.4} \times \frac{1774}{108}$$

where $k_1$ = Speed factor

It depends upon the following :

(*a*) R.P.M. of gear

(b) Running time in hour per day

$k_2$ = Strength factor for gears

$k_3$ = Bending stress factor

$b$ = Face width of gear in mm

$m$ = Module in mm

$T$ = Number of teeth on gear

$N$ = R.P.M. of gear

The allowable tangential load in kg per mm of face width for strength is given by

$$F = \frac{k_1 \, . \, K_2 \, . \, k_3 \, m}{25.4}$$

(ii) **H.P. on wear basis.** The horse power rating of a spur gear with 20° pressure angle and helical gears for wear is given by

$$\text{H.P. (wear)} = \frac{k_1' \, . \, k_2' \, . \, k_3' \, bm \, NT}{k} \times \frac{1774}{108}$$

where $k_1'$ = Speed factor for wear

$k_2'$ = Zone factor

$k_3'$ = Surface stress factor

$k$ = Pitch factor

The allowable tangential load ($F_w$) in kg/mm of face width for wear is calculated as follows :

$$F_w = \frac{k_1' \, . \, k_2' \, . \, k_3'}{k}.$$

## 11.23. Double Helical or Herringbone Gears

A double helical gear (Herringbone gear) is equivalent to two helical gears of opposite hand mounted side by side on the same shaft. They develop opposite end thrust and this cancel out thrust load. This is the major advantage of using double helical gears. The main disadvantage of single helical gears is the side thrust on shaft bearings. Fig. 11.12 shows a herringbone gear. The usual helix angles are 20° to 30° for industrial gears and up to 45° for turbine drives.

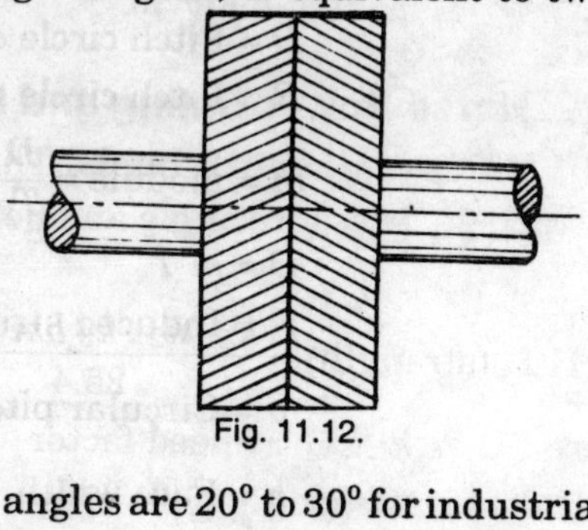

Fig. 11.12.

**Example 11.4.** *A cast iron helical gear with 30° helix angle has to transmit 30 H.P. at 1200 R.P.M. The safe static stress for cast iron is 550 kg/cm². The width of face is 3.5 times circular pitch. If the gear has 24 teeth determine the following for 20° full depth teeth.*

*(a) Module*

*(b) Pitch diameter*

*(c) Width of face*

*(d) End thrust.*

*Assume lubrication factor =1.15.*

**Solution.** (*a*) **To calculate module (m)**

$$\text{H.P.} = 30$$

$$N = 1200 \text{ R.P.M.}$$

$$\text{H.P.} = \frac{2\pi NT}{4500}$$

$$30 = \frac{2\pi \times 1200 \times T}{4500}$$

$$T = 17.91 \text{ kg cm.} = 1791 \text{ kg cm}$$

$T_g$ = Number of teeth on gear

$\alpha$ = Helix angle = 30°

$T_f$ = Formative number of teeth

$$= \frac{T_g}{\cos^3 \alpha} = \frac{24}{\cos^3 30}$$

$$= \frac{24}{(0.866)^3} = 37$$

$$y = 0.154 - \frac{0.912}{T_f} = 0.154 - \frac{0.912}{37} = 0.127$$

$D$ = Pitch circle diameter in cm

$R$ = Pitch circle radius

$$m = \text{module} = \frac{D}{T_g}$$

$$D = m\, T_g$$

$f_1$ = Induced stress in gear

$$p = \text{Circular pitch} = \pi \frac{D}{T_g} = \pi m$$

$b$ = Face width

$$= 3.5\, p = 3.5 \times \pi m$$

$$F = \frac{T}{R} = \frac{T \times 2}{m\ T_g} = \frac{2T}{m\ T_g}$$

$C$ = Lubrication factor = 1.15

$$F = \frac{f_1 \cdot p \cdot y \cdot b}{C}$$

$$f_1 = \frac{C \cdot F}{p \cdot y \cdot b} = \frac{2\,TC}{m\ T_g \cdot p \cdot y \cdot b}$$

$$= \frac{2\,TC}{m\ T_g \times \pi\ m \times y \times 3.5\ \pi\ m}$$

$$f_1 = \frac{2\,TC}{m^3\ \pi^2 \times 3.5 \times T_g \times y}$$

$$= \frac{2 \times 1791 \times 1.15}{m^3 \times \pi^2 \times 3.5 \times 24 \times 0.127} = \frac{39.16}{m^3}$$

$f$ = Allowable stress

= Static stress × Velocity factor

$$= 550 \times \left(\frac{6}{6+V}\right)$$

$V$ = Pitch line velocity

$$= \pi\frac{Dn}{60} = \frac{\pi\ m\ T_g\ N}{60 \times 100}\ \text{m/sec}$$

$$= \frac{\pi \times 24 \times m \times 1200}{60 \times 100}$$

= 15 $m$ metre per second.

$$f = 550\left(\frac{6}{6+15\ m}\right)$$

In order that design should be safe the allowable stress should be more than induced stress

$$f \geq f_1$$

$$550\left(\frac{6}{6+15\ m}\right) \geq \frac{39.16}{m^3}$$

when $m$ = 6 mm *i.e.* 0.6 cm and, $f$ = 220

$f_1$ = 181.3

when $m$ = 5 mm *i.e.* 0.5 cm and $f$ = 244.44

$f_1$ = 313.28

Hence $m$ = 6 mm

$D = m\ .\ T_g = 6 \times 24 = 144$ mm = 14.4 cm.

$$b = \text{Face width} = 3.5 \times \pi\, m$$
$$= 3.5 \times \pi \times 0.6 = 6.6 \text{ cm}$$

End thrust $= F_\alpha = F \tan \alpha.$

Now $$F = \frac{\text{H.P} \times 4500}{V}$$

$$V = \frac{\pi DN}{100} = \frac{\pi \times 14.4 \times 1200}{100}$$
$$= 542.6 \text{ metre/min.}$$
$$F = \frac{4500 \times \text{H.P.}}{V} = \frac{4500 \times 30}{542.6}$$
$$= 248.8 \text{ kg.}$$
$$F_a = \text{End thrust}$$
$$= F \,.\, \tan \alpha = 248.8 \tan 30$$
$$= 248.8 \times 0.577 = 143.56 \text{ kg.}$$

**Example 11.5.** *A pair of helical gears has teeth of 20° involute full depth, 30° helix angle, 5 mm module and 100 mm face width. The pinion has 24 teeth and transmission ratio is 8 : 1. The speed of the gear is 500 R.P.M. and pinion and gear are made up of same material and the pair is to run for 24 hours continuously. Determine H.P. rating of pair of gears considering strength only.*

*Bending stress factor = 14.05*

*Speed factor = 0.165 for pinion*

*= 0.28 for gear*

*Strength factor = 0.8 for pinion*

*= 0.7 for gear.*

*Also check the gears against wear.*

**Solution.**

$$m = \text{Module} = 5 \text{ mm}$$
$$b = \text{Face width} = 100 \text{ mm}$$
$$N_g = \text{R.P.M. of gear} = 500$$
$$N_p = \text{R.P.M. of pinion} = 500 \times 8 = 4000$$
$$T_p = \text{Number of teeth on pinion} = 24$$
$$T_g = \text{Number of teeth on gear}$$
$$= 24 \times 8 = 192$$
$$k_1 = \text{Speed factor}$$

$= 0.165$ for pinion

$= 0.28$ for gear

$k_2 =$ Strength factor

$= 0.8$ for pinion $= 0.7$ for gear

$k_3 =$ Bending stress factor $= 14.05$

For gear, the horse power on strength basis is given by

$$\text{H.P.} = \frac{k_1 \,.\, k_2 \,.\, k_3\, bm^2\, T_g\, N_g}{25.4} \times \frac{1774}{108}$$

$$= \frac{0.28 \times 0.7 \times 14.05 \times 100 \times 5^2 \times 192 \times 500}{25.4} \times \frac{1774}{108} = 461.6$$

For pinion

$$\text{H.P.} = \frac{k_1 \,.\, k_2 \,.\, k_3\, bm^2\, T_p\, N_p}{25.4} \times \frac{1774}{108}$$

$$= \frac{0.65 \times 0.8 \times 14.05 \times 100 \times 5^2 \times 24 \times 4000}{25.4} \times \frac{1774}{108} = 311$$

As the gear and pinion are made up of same material, the pinion is weaker in strength. Hence H.P. rating of the pair is 311,

**To check the pinion for wear**

$T_p = 24$

$N_p = 4000$ R.P.M.

$m =$ Module $= 5$ mm

$$m = \frac{D_p}{T_p}$$

$$5 = \frac{D_p}{24}$$

$D_p = 120$ mm $= 12$ cm

$$V = \text{Velocity} = \frac{\pi\, D_p\, N_p}{1000}$$

$$= \frac{\pi \times 120 \times 4000}{1000} = 1507 \text{ mpm}$$

$$\text{H.P.} = \frac{F \times V}{4500}$$

$$311 = \frac{F \times 1507}{4500}$$

$F = 928$ kg

$$\psi = 20^{\circ}$$

$$F_{\omega} = \text{Wear load} = \frac{D_p \,.\, b \,.\, K \,.\, Q}{\cos^2 \psi}$$

where $b$ = Face width

$= 100 \text{ mm} = 10 \text{ cm}$

$$K = \frac{f_{se}^2 \,.\, \sin \psi}{1.4}\left[\frac{1}{E_p} + \frac{1}{E_g}\right]$$

$f_{se} = 28 \times \text{B.H.N.} - 700$

$= 28 \times 152 - 700 = 3556 \text{ kg/cm}^2$

$E_p$ = Modulus of elasticity for pinion

$= 2 \times 10^6 \text{ kg/cm}^2 \text{ (say)} = E_g$

B.H.N. = 152 (Assume)

$$k = \frac{3556^2 \times \sin 20}{1.4} \times \left[\frac{1}{2 \times 10^6} + \frac{1}{2 \times 10^6}\right] = 3.1.$$

$$Q = \frac{2 \,.\, T_g}{T_p + T_g} = \frac{2 \times 192}{24 + 192} = 1.8$$

$$F_{\omega} = \frac{12 \times 10 \times 3.1 \times 1.8}{\cos^2 20} = 1012 \text{ kg.}$$

Since $F_{\omega}$ is more than $F$ therefore gears are safe against wear.

**Example 11.5.** *(a) A pair helical gears has a transmission ratio of 10 : 1. The teeth are 20° full depth involute 5 mm module. The pinion has 24 teeth and rotates at 4500 R.P.M. The active face width is 7.2 cm. The material of gear is C 40 steel untreated and wear and lubrication factor 1.25. Determine H.P. capacity of the gear drive. Reliability factor is 1.75.*

**Solution.** According to Lewis equation

$$F = \frac{f \,.\, p \,.\, y \,.\, b}{C_w}$$

$b$ = Face width = 7.2 cm

$T$ = Number of teeth on pinion = 24

$p$ = Circular pitch

$= \pi \times m = \pi \times 5 = 1.57 \text{ cm}$

$C_w$ = Wear and lubrication factor = 1.25

$$Y = 0.154 - \frac{0.912}{T}$$

$$= 0.154 - \frac{0.912}{24} = 1.116$$

$$f = \text{Safe stress}$$

$$= \frac{\text{Ultimate stress}}{\text{K}} \times \text{Velocity factor}$$

Ultimate stress for C 40 steel = 5800 kg/cm$^2$ (From Table 11.3)

$$D_P = \text{Pinion pitch circle diameter}$$

$$= m \times T = 5 \times 24 = 120 \text{ mm}$$

$$C_V = \text{Velocity factor}$$

$$= \frac{43}{43 + \sqrt{V}}$$

where $V = \pi D_P N_P$ mpm

$$= \pi \times \frac{120}{1000} \times 4500$$

$$= 1696 \text{ mpm}$$

where $N_P$ = P.R.M of pinion = 4500

$$C_V = \frac{43}{43 + \sqrt{1696}} = 0.51$$

$$f = \frac{5800 \times 0.51}{K}$$

where $K$ = Reliability factor = 1.75

$$= \frac{5800 \times 0.51}{1.75} = 1696 \text{ kg/cm}^2$$

$$F = \frac{f \,.\, p \,.\, y \,.\, b}{C_w}$$

$$= \frac{1690 \times 1.57 \times 0.116 \times 7.2}{1.25} = 1772 \text{ kg}$$

$$\text{H.P.} = \frac{F \times V}{4500} = \frac{1772 \times 1696}{4500} = 667.8.$$

## 11.24. Bevel Gears

They are used to transmit power between two shafts whose axes intersect at a certain angle. The pitch surfaces are conical in bevel gears (Fig. 11.13). A pair of bevel gears is called Miter gears when their shafts make an angle of 90 degrees with each other and have the same rotative speed. The pair of mitre gears must be of same size and have same number of teeth. Bevel gears are known as angular gears if the axes of shafts of bevel gears intersect at any angle other than 90 degrees. Figs. 11.14 and Fig. 11.15 show two bevel gears in contact. Bevel gears are not interchangeable and are designed in pair.

## 11.25. Bevel Gear Nomenclature

(*i*) **Pitch cone.** In a bevel gear pitch surfaces are conical. Pitch cone is the cone containing the pitch elements of the teeth.

Bevel gear
Fig. 11.13

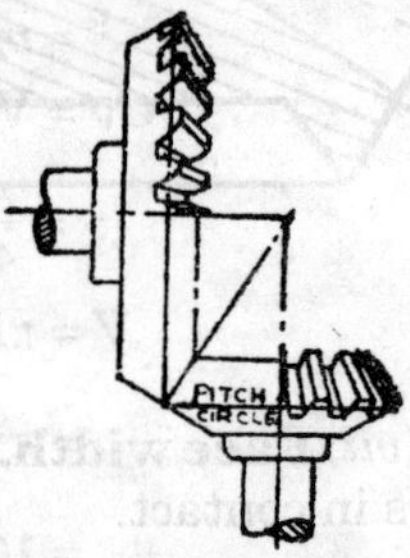


Fig. 11.14.

(*ii*) **Cone centre.** It is the point where the axes of two mating gears intersect each other or it is the apex of the pitch cone. As shown in Fig.10.15, the point *C* is cone centre.

(*iii*) **Cone radius (R).** It is the length of pitch cone element.

(*iv*) **Pitch angle.** It is the angle made by the pitch line with the gear axis.

$$\gamma = \text{Pitch angle}$$

(*v*) **Root angle or cutting angle.** It is the difference between pitch angle dedendum angle. It is also called cutting angle.

$$\delta = \text{Root angle} = \gamma - \text{Dedendum angle}$$

(*vi*) **Face angle.** It is the angle between the addendum element of a tooth and the axis of gears. It is equal to sum of pitch angle and addendum angle.

$$\text{Face angle} = \gamma + \text{Addendum angle}$$

As shown in Fig. 11.16.

$R_1$ is the back cone radius.

The height $H_1$ is called Backing height.

The height $H_2$ is called Crown height.

$H$ is called Mounting height = $H_1 + H_2$.

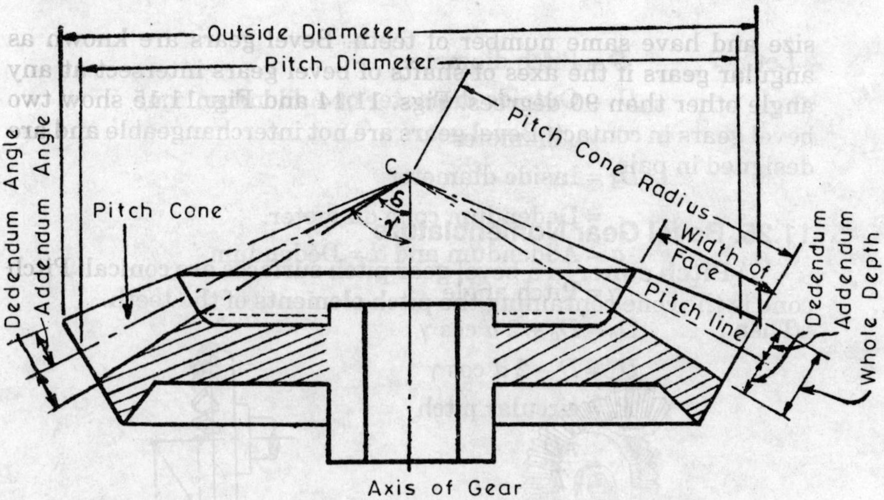


Fig. 11.15.

(*vii*) **Face width.** It is indicated by $b$. Fig. 11.16 shows two bevel gears in contact.

The angle between the axes of two shafts is indicated by angle $\theta$.

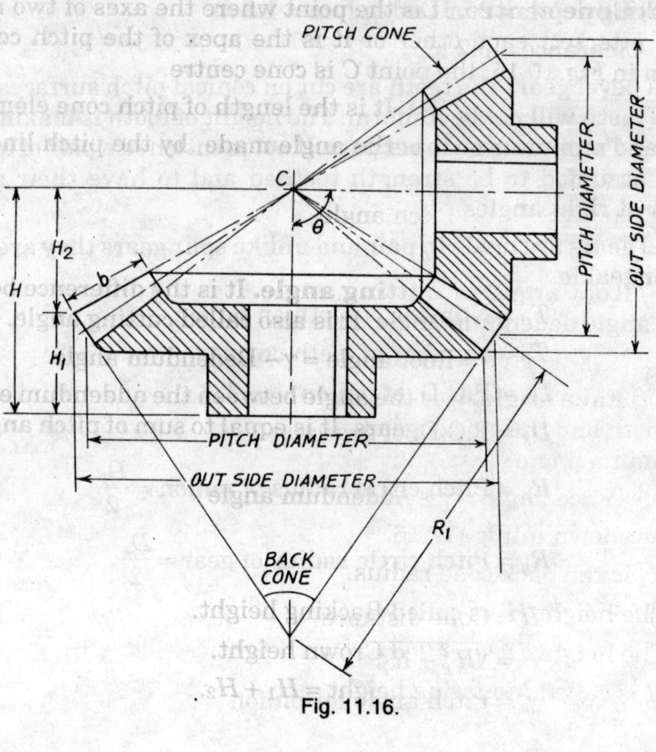


Fig. 11.16.

Let $D$ = Pitch diameter

$D_o$ = Outside diameter or Addendum cone diameter

$D_1$ = Inside diameter

= Dedendum cone diameter

$a$ = Addendum and $d$ = Dedendum.

$\gamma$ = Pitch angle

Then $D_o = D_o + 2\, a \cos \gamma$

$D_1 = D - 2\, d \cos \gamma$

$P_c$ = circular pitch

$= \dfrac{\pi D}{T}$

where $T$ = number of teeth

$m = \text{Module} = \dfrac{D}{T}$

Addendum = $m$ Thickness of tooth = 1.57 m

Working depth = 2 m Dedendum = 1.2 m

Clearance = 0.2 m.

As in bevel gears the teeth are cut on conical pitch surfaces the height of teeth will not be uniform. The height of tooth is maximum at outer and minimum on inner part. If not mentioned a pair of bevel gears is assumed to be strength toothed and to have their axes intersect at right angles.

Bevel gears are made in pair and unlike spur gears they are not interchangeable.

$T_p$ = Number of teeth on pinion

$T_g$ = Number of teeth on gear

$D_p$ = P.C.D. of pinion = $m\, T_p$

$D_g$ = P.C.D. of gear = $m\, T_g$

$R_p$ = Pitch circle radius of pinion = $\dfrac{D_p}{2}$

$R_g$ = Pitch circle radius of gear = $\dfrac{D_g}{2}$

(*viii*) $R$ = Cone distance

$= \sqrt{R_g^2 + R_p^2}$

(*ix*) $\gamma_p$ = Pitch angle for pinion

$$= \tan^{-1} \frac{\sin \theta}{\frac{T_g}{T_p} + \cos \theta}$$

$$\tan \gamma_p = \frac{T_p}{T_g}$$

if $\theta = 90^o$

(*x*) $\gamma_p$ = Pitch angle of gear

$$= \tan^{-1} \frac{\sin \theta}{\frac{T_p}{T_g} + \cos \theta}$$

$$\tan \gamma_g = \frac{T_g}{T_p}$$

if $\theta = 90^o$

(*xi*) $\theta$ = Shaft angle = $\gamma_p + \gamma_g$.

(*xii*) Face angle of gear

$$= \gamma_g + \tan^{-1} \frac{2 \sin \gamma_g}{T_g}$$

$$= \gamma_g + \tan^{-1} \frac{\text{addendum}}{\text{cone distance}}$$

(*xiii*) $\delta_g$ = Root angle of pinion

$$= \gamma_p - \tan^{-1} \frac{\text{dedendum}}{\text{cone distance}}$$

$N_p$ = R.P.M. of pinion

$N_g$ = R.P.M. of gear

(*xiv*) Velocity ratio

$$= \frac{N_p}{N_g} = \frac{D_g}{D_p}.$$

## 11.26. Strength of Bevel Gear Teeth

The Lewis equation for bevel gear is as follows :

$$F = f \,.\, p \,.\, b \,.\, y \left( 1 - \frac{b}{R} \right)$$

where $F$ = Equivalent tangential force at large end

$R$ = Length of cone distance

$y$ = Form factor for virtual member of teeth or formative number of teeth ($T_f$)

$$y = 0.154 - \frac{0.912}{T_f}$$

$b$ = Face width = 6 m to 10 m

It should lie between $R/4$ and $R/3$.

$T_f$ = Formative number of teeth

$$= \frac{\text{Actual number of teeth}}{\cos \gamma}$$

where $\gamma$ = Pitch cone angle

$$\cos \gamma_g = \frac{R_g}{R}$$

and $$\cos \gamma_p = \frac{R_g}{R}$$

where $R_p$ = Pitch circle radius of pinion

$R_g$ = Pitch circle radius of gear

$f$ = Allowable stress = Static stress × Velocity factor

Velocity factor $= \frac{183}{183 + V}$ for full depth teeth finished with form cutters

$= \frac{366}{366 + V}$ for generated system teeth

where $V$ is pitch line velocity in metre per minute. It is usually taken as 360—390 metre per minute for ordinary cut teeth and about 600 mpm for generated teeth.

**Bevel factor.** $\left(1 - \frac{b}{R}\right)$ is called bevel factor.

**11.26.1. Wear load on bevel gear teeth.** The limiting load for wear is given by the following relation

$F_w$ = Limiting load for wear

$$= \frac{D_p \,.\, b \,.\, k \,.\, Q}{\cos\gamma_p}$$

where ratio factor,

$$Q = \frac{2\, T_g \cos \gamma_p}{T_p \cos \gamma_g + T_g \cos \gamma_p}$$

The other terms have the same nomenclature as in spur gears.

## 11.27. Bearing Loads on Bevel Gears

Fig. 11.17 shows various forces on a bevel gear. The tangential effort ($F$) is the component of total normal ($Q$) on the teeth.

$$Q = \frac{F}{\cos\psi}$$

Force ($Q$) has another component $R = Q \sin\psi$ and $Q$ can be again resolved into components as follows :

(i) $F_x$ = End thrust on gear

= Radial force on pinion = $F \tan\psi \sin\gamma_g$

(ii) $F_y$ = End thrust on pinion

= Radial force on pinion = $F \tan\psi \cos \gamma_p$

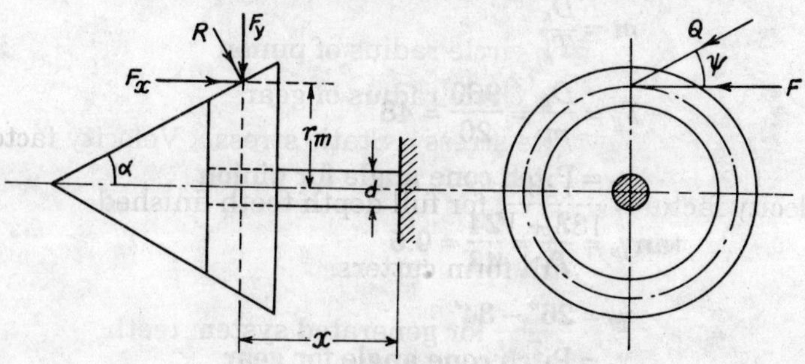


Fig. 11.17.

(iii) $F$ = Turning force as determined by Lewis equation

$\psi$ = Pressure angle

**Example 11.6.** *Design a bevel gear drive between two shafts whose axis are at right angles. The horse power at gear shaft is 80 and the gear is made of forged steel with an allowable static stress of 1600 kg/cm$^2$. The speed of pinion shaft is 300 R.P.M. and that of gear shaft is 150 R.P.M. Pinion has 24 full depth teeth of 20 mm module and pressure angle 20°. Neglect overhang of gears.*

**Solution.**

(a) **To find face width**

$N_p$ = R.P.M. of pinion = 300

$N_g$ = R.P.M. of gear = 150

$m$ = Module = 20 mm

$$D_g = \text{P.C.D. of gear}$$

$$D_p = \text{P.C.D. of pinion}$$

$$T_g = \text{Number of teeth on pinion} = 24$$

$$D_p = m\ .\ T_p = 20 \times 24$$

$$= 480 \text{ mm} = 48 \text{ cm}$$

$$\frac{D_p}{D_g} = \frac{N_g}{N_p}$$

$$D_g = D_p \times \frac{N_p}{N_g} = 48 \times \frac{300}{150}$$

$$= 96 \text{ cm}$$

$$T_g = \text{Number of teeth on gear}$$

$$m = \frac{D_g}{T_g}$$

$$T_g = \frac{D_g}{.m} = \frac{960}{20} = 48$$

$$\gamma_p = \text{Pitch cone angle for pinion}$$

$$\tan\gamma_p = \frac{T_p}{T_g} = \frac{24}{48} = 0.5$$

$$\gamma_p = 26^\circ - 34'$$

$$\gamma_g = \text{Pitch cone angle for gear}$$

$$= 90 - \gamma_p = 90 - (26^\circ - 34') = 63^\circ - 26'$$

$$R = \text{Cone distance}$$

$$= \sqrt{R_g^2 + R_p^2} = \sqrt{48^2 + 24^2}$$

$$= 53.66 \text{ cm}$$

$$V = \text{Pitch line velocity}$$

$$= \frac{\pi\, D_g\ .\ N_g}{100}$$

$$= \frac{\pi \times 96 \times 150}{100} = 452 \text{ m/m}$$

$$\text{Velocity factor} = \frac{183}{183 + V}$$

$$= \frac{183}{183 + 452} = 0.29$$

$$F = f\ .\ p\ .\ y\ .\ b \left(1 - \frac{b}{R}\right)$$

$$f = \text{allowable stress}$$

$$= 1600 \times \text{velocity factor}$$

$$= 1600 \times 0.29 = 464 \text{ kg/cm}^2$$

$$p = \pi m = \pi \times 2 = 6.28 \text{ cm}$$

$$T_f = \text{Formative number of teeth on gear}$$

$$= \frac{\text{Actual number of teeth on gear}}{\cos\gamma_g}$$

$$= \frac{48}{\cos 63^\circ - 26'} = \frac{48}{0.447} = 104$$

$$y = 0.154 - \frac{0.912}{T_f}$$

$$= 0.154 - \frac{0.912}{104} = 0.146$$

$$F = \frac{\text{H.P.} \times 4500}{\text{V}}$$

$$= \frac{80 \times 4500}{452} = 796.4 \text{ kg}$$

$$F = f \, . \, p \, . \, y \, . \, b\left(1 - \frac{b}{R}\right)$$

$$= 464 \times 6.28 \times 0.146 \times b\left(1 - \frac{b}{53.66}\right)$$

$$796.4 = 425.4 \, b\left(1 - \frac{b}{53.66}\right)$$

$$b^2 - 53.66b + 100.4 = 0$$

$$b = \frac{53.66 \pm \sqrt{(53.66)^2 - 4 \times 100.4}}{2}$$

$$= \frac{53.66 - 49.76}{2}$$

$$= \frac{53.66 - 49.76}{2} = 1.95 \text{ cm.}$$

Now $b$ should lie between $\frac{R}{4}$ and $\frac{R}{3}$. *i.e.* between $\frac{53.66}{2}$ and $\frac{53.66}{3}$. Thus the calculated value is very low. Hence we adopt

$$b = 13 \text{ cm.}$$

**(*b*) Check for wear**

$$F_w = \text{Limiting load due to wear}$$

$$= \frac{D_p \cdot b \cdot k \cdot Q}{\cos \gamma_p}$$

$$D_p = 58 \text{ cm}$$

$$b = 13 \text{ cm}$$

$$Q = \frac{2 \times T_{gf}}{T_{gf} + T_{pf}}$$

where $T_{gf}$ = Formative number of the teeth on gear

$$= \frac{T_g}{\cos \gamma_g} = \frac{48}{\cos 63^\circ - 26'}$$

$$= 104$$

$T_{pf}$ = Formative number of teeth on pinion

$$= \frac{24}{\cos \gamma_p} = \frac{24}{\cos 26^\circ - 34'}$$

$$= \frac{24}{0.894} = 26.84 = 27 \text{ (say)}$$

$$Q = \frac{2 \times 104}{27 + 104} = 1.58$$

$$k = \frac{f_{se}^2 \times \sin\psi}{1.4}\left[\frac{1}{E_p} + \frac{1}{E_g}\right]$$

$$f_{se} = 28 \times \text{B.H.N} - 700$$

$$= 28 \times 200 - 700 = 4900 \text{ kg/cm}^2$$

Assuming B.H.N. = 200

$$\sin\psi = \sin 20 = 0.342$$

$$\psi = \text{Pressure angle} = 20^\circ$$

$$E_p = 2 \times 10^6 \text{ kg/cm}^2$$

$$E_g = 2 \times 10^6 \text{ kg/cm}^2 \text{ (assume)}$$

$$k = \frac{4900^2 \times 0.342}{1.4} = \left[\frac{1}{2 \times 10^6} + \frac{1}{2 \times 10^6}\right]$$

$$= 5.86$$

$$F_w = \frac{D_p \times b \times k \cdot Q}{\cos \gamma_p}$$

$$= \frac{48 \times 13 \times 5.86 \times 1.58}{0.894} = 6462 \text{ kg.}$$

This is more than $F$, hence safe.

**Tooth proportions**

Addendum$(a) = m = 2$ cm

Dedendum$(d) = 1.2$ m $= 1.2 \times 2 = 2.4$ cm

Total depth $= a + d = 2 + 2.4 = 4.4$ cm

Circular pitch

$$\pi m = 3.14 \times 2 = 6.28 \text{ cm.}$$

Blank diameter of gear

$$= D_g + 2\,a \cos \gamma_g$$
$$= 96 + 2 \times 2 \times \cos 63° 26'$$
$$= 96 + 4 \times 0.447 = 97.788 \text{ cm}$$

Blank diameter of pinion

$$= D_p + 2a \cos \gamma_p = 48 + 2 \times 2 \times \cos 26° 34'$$
$$= 48 + 4 \times 0.894 = 51.576 \text{ cm}$$

**Gear shaft**

Let $d$ = Gear shaft diameter

$$\text{H.P.} = 2\pi N_g \cdot \frac{T}{4500}$$

$$80 = \frac{2\pi \times 150 \times T}{4500}$$

$$T = 382.16 \text{ kg m} = 38216 \text{ kg cm}$$

$f_s$ = Shear stress in shaft

$= 400$ kg/cm$^2$ (assume)

$$T = \frac{\pi}{16} f_s \cdot d^3$$

$$38216 = \frac{\pi}{16} \times 400 \times d^3$$

$$d = 7.86 \text{ cm}$$

$T_1$ = Torque transmitted by pinion

$$\text{H.P.} = \frac{2\pi N_g T_1}{4500}$$

$$80 = \frac{2\pi \times 300 \times T_1}{4500}$$

$$T_1 = 191 \text{ kgm} = 19100 \text{ kg cm}$$

$d_1$ = Diameter of pinion shaft

$$T_1 = \frac{\pi}{16} \times 400 \times d_1^3$$

$$19100 = \frac{\pi}{16} \times 400 \times d_1^3$$

$$d_1 = 6.24 \text{ cm.}$$

The gears should be provided with 4 arms. The standard keys should be provided in gear and pinion hubs.

**Example 11.7.** *A machine shaft is driven at 1200 R.P.M. by a 22 H.p. motor running at 800 R.P.M. through a pair of bevel gears. The gear on the motor shaft is made of cast steel having a pitch diameter meter 24 cm with a face width of 5 cm. The pinion is made of forged steel. The safe static stress for cast steel is 1300 kg/cm² and for forged steel the safe static stress is 1900 kg /cm². The teeth are 14½° full height form. Take*

$$y = 0.124 - \frac{0.684}{\text{Number of teeth}}$$

$$\text{Velocity factor} = \frac{6}{6 + V}$$

*Determine the following :*

*(a) Module,*

*(b) Radial pressure on pinion.*

*(c) End thrust on the gear.*

**Solution.** (*a*) **To find module (m).**

$$D_g = \text{P.C.D. of gear} = 24 \text{ cm}$$

$$N_g = \text{R.P.M of gear} = 800$$

$$V = \text{Pitch line velocity}$$

$$= \frac{\pi D_g \cdot N_g}{100} = \frac{\pi \times 24 \times 800}{100}$$

$$= 603 \text{ mpm} = 10.04 \text{ m/sec.}$$

$$\text{H.P.} = 22$$

Gear is weaker than pinion

$$F_1 = \text{Induced force in gear}$$

$$= \frac{\text{H.P.} \times 4500}{V}$$

$$= \frac{22 \times 4500}{V} = \frac{22 \times 4500}{603}$$

$$= 164.18 \text{ kg}$$

$$F_2 = \text{Allowable force}$$

$$= f \,.\, p \,.\, y \,.\, b \left(1 - \frac{b}{R}\right)$$

$$\text{Velocity factor} = \frac{6}{6 + V}$$

$$f = \text{Safe stress} = 1300 \times \frac{6}{6 + V}$$

$$= 1300 \times \frac{6}{6 + 10.5} = 486 \text{ kg/cm}^2$$

$$D_p = \text{P.C.D. of pinion}$$

$$\frac{D_p}{D_g} = \frac{N_g}{N_p}$$

$$D_p = D_g \times \frac{N_g}{N_p}$$

$$= 24 \times \frac{800}{1200} = 16 \text{ cm}$$

$$R_p = \text{Pitch circle radius of pinion} = 8 \text{ cm}$$

$$R_g = \text{Pitch circle radius of gear} = 12 \text{ cm}$$

$$R = \text{Cone distance} = \sqrt{R_p^2 + R_g^2}$$

$$= \sqrt{8^2 + 12^2} = 14.42 \text{ cm}$$

$$T_g = \text{Number of teeth on gear}$$

$$T_f = \text{Formative number of teeth on gear}$$

$$= \frac{T_g}{\cos \gamma_g}$$

$$\cos \gamma_g = \frac{R_p}{R}$$

$$= \frac{8}{14.42} = 0.554$$

$$m = \text{module} = \frac{D_g}{T_g}$$

$$T_g = \frac{D_g}{m} = \frac{24}{m}$$

$$T_f = \frac{T_g}{\cos \gamma_g}$$

$$= \frac{24}{m \times 0.554} = \frac{43.3}{m}$$

$$y = 0.124 - \frac{0.684}{T_f} = 0.124 - \frac{0.684 \times m}{43.3}$$

$b$ = Face width = 5 cm

$p$ = Circular pitch = $\pi m$

$$F_2 = 486 \times \pi m \times 5 \times \left(0.124 - \frac{0.684 \times m}{43.3}\right)\left(1 - \frac{5}{14.42}\right)$$

$$F_2 = 618 \text{ m} - 78.73 \text{ m}^2$$

In order that design is safe

$$F_2 \geq F_1$$

$$618 \text{ m} - 78.73 \text{ m}^2 = 164.18$$

Choose suitable value of $m$.

when $m = 3$ mm

$F_2 = 178.4$

$F_1 = 164.18$

when $m = 2.5$ mm (0.25 *cm*)

$F_2 = 149.6$

$F_1 = 164.18$

Hence we adopt,

$m = 3$ mm

(*b*) **To find radial pressure on pinion ($F_x$)**

$$F_x = F_1 \tan \psi \sin \gamma_g$$

$$= 164.18 \tan 14\frac{1}{2} \times \frac{R_g}{R}$$

$$= 164.18 \times 0.258 \times \frac{R_g}{R}$$

$$= 164.18 \times 0.3153 \frac{12}{14.42}$$

$= 43$ kg = End thrust on gear. **Ans.**

**Example 11.8.** *A bevel gear is required to transmit a maximum torque of 5000 kg cm and is provided with 4 arms of T-section. Suggest suitable dimensions of arms if the safe stress in arm material is 560 kg/cm*$^2$.

**Solution.** Let the $T$-section (Fig. 11.18) have

$t$ = Thickness of flange

$h$ = Width of flange = 6 $t$ (say)

$n$ = Number of arms = 4

Assuming that only half of arms carry the tangential load.

$M$ = Bending moment be resisted by T–section

$$= \frac{5000}{2} = 2500 \text{ kg cm}$$

$f$ = Safe stress = 560 kg/cm$^2$

$Z$ = Modulus of section

$$= \frac{1}{6} . t . h^2$$

$$= \frac{1}{6} \times t \times (6\,t)^2$$

$$= 6\,t^3$$

$$M = f . Z$$

$$2500 = 560 \times 6\,t^3$$

$$t = 0.9 \text{ cm}$$

$$h = 6t = 6 \times 0.9 = 5.4 \text{ cm.}$$

The vertical leg may be made 0.9 cm thick.

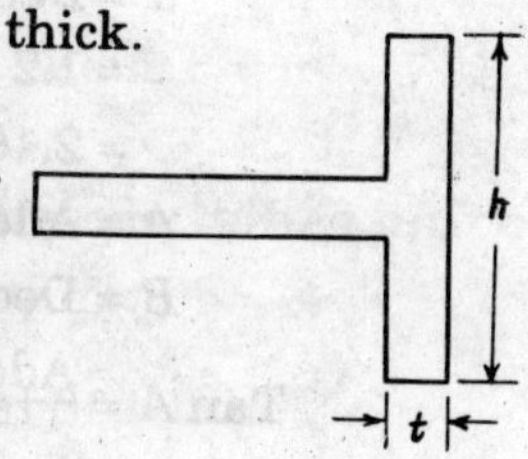


Fig. 11.18.

**Example 11.8** *(a) Design a pair of bevel gears whose axes are at 90° .The pinion has 36 teeth and gear has 72 teeth with a module of 1.8 mm. Sketch gear and indicate various angles.*

**Solution.**

$D_g$ = P.C.D. of gear

$T_g$ = Number of teeth on gear = 72

$m$ = Module = 1.8 mm

$T_p$ = Number of teeth on pinion = 36

$$m = \frac{D_g}{T_g}$$

$$1.8 = \frac{D_g}{72}$$

$$D_g = 129.6 \text{ mm}$$

Similarly $D_p$ = P.C.D. of pinion

$$= m \times T_p = 1.8 \times 36$$

$$= 64.8 \text{ mm}$$

$\gamma_g$ = Pitch cone angle of gear

$$\text{Tan } \gamma_g = \frac{T_g}{T_p} = \frac{72}{36} = 2$$

$$\gamma_g = 63^\circ - 26'$$

$\theta$ = Shaft angle = $90^\circ$

$\gamma_g$ = Pitch cone angle of pinion

$$= 90 - \gamma_g = 90 - 63^\circ - 26'$$

$$= 26^\circ - 34'$$

$R$ = Pitch cone radius = $\sqrt{R_g^2 + R_g^2}$

$$= \sqrt{\left(\frac{129.6}{2}\right)^2 + \left(\frac{64.8}{2}\right)^2}$$

$$= 72.5 \text{ mm}$$

$a$ = Addendum for both pinion and gear

$$= m = 1.8 \text{ mm}$$

$d$ = Dedendum for both pinion and gear

$$= 1.2 \text{ m} = 1.2 \times 1.8$$

$$= 2.16 \text{ mm}$$

$A$ = Addendum angle

$B$ = Dedendum angle

$$\text{Tan } A = \frac{\text{Addendum}}{R} = \frac{1.8}{72.5}$$

$$A = 1^\circ - 25'$$

$$\text{Tan } B = \frac{\text{Dedendum}}{R} = \frac{2.16}{72.5}$$

$$B = 1^\circ - 42'$$

Tooth thickness at pitch line = $1.57 \times m$

$$= 1.57 \times 1.8$$

$= 2.83$ mm

Whole depth at large end of tooth

$= \text{Addendum} + \text{Dedendum} = 1.8 + 2.16$

$= 3.96$ mm

Root angle or cutting angle of gear

$= \gamma_g - B = 63^\circ\ 26' - 1^\circ\ 42' = 60^\circ\ 44'$

Cutting angle of pinion $= \gamma_p - B$

$= 26^\circ\ 34' - 1^\circ\ 42' = 24^\circ\ 52'$

$D_1$ = Outside diameter of gear

$= D_g + 2a \cos \gamma_g = 129.6 + 2 \times 1.8 \cos 63^\circ\ 26'$

$= 131.2$ mm

$D_2$ = Outside diameter of pinion

$= D_p + 2a \cos \gamma_p = 64.8 + 2 \times 1.8 \times \cos 26^\circ\ 34'$

$= 68$ mm

Angular addendum of gear = Addendum $\times \cos \gamma_g$

$= 1.8 \times \cos 63^\circ\ 26' = 1.8 \times 0.4472 = 0.8$ mm

Angular addendum of pinion

$= \text{Addendum} \times \cos \gamma_p$

$= 1.8 \times \cos 26^\circ\ 34' = 1.8 \times 0.8948 = 1.6$ mm

Fig. 11.18 (*a*) shows a bevel gear and various angle are indicated in it.

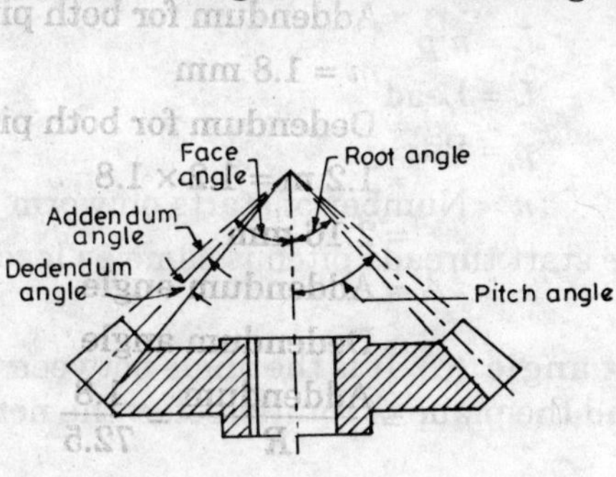


Fig.11.18 (*a*)

## 11.28. Worm and Worm Wheel

Worm and worm wheel arrangement is used to transmit power between shafts with perpendicular non-intersecting axes. The worm is usually of cylindrical form and resembles a screw and the worm wheel is similar to a spur gear except that teeth have been twisted and curved to conform to the shape of worm. When the worm rotates its thread presses against the teeth in the rim of worm wheel causing it to rotate. Velocity ratio from 10 : 1 upto 100 : 1 are generally employed and ratios as high as 500 : 1 have been used in single reduction. The most commonly used material for worm wheels is hard phosphor bronze working with a hardened steel worm.

## 11.29. Worm and Worm Gear Nomenclature

The tooth shape, addendum, dedendum etc. for a worm and worm wheel will be same as for spur gears.

**Worm.** Fig.11.19 shows worm.

(*i*) **Pitch.** It is the distance between corresponding points on adjacent threads measured parallel to the axis. The pitch of the worm must exactly equal to the circular pitch of worm wheel.

(*ii*) **Lead.** It is the distance a thread advances for complete revolution of worm.

$$L = n\,p$$

where $L$ = Lead

$p$ = Pitch

$n$ = Number of starts on worm

For single start threads pitch is same as lead.

(*iii*) **Helix angle** ($\alpha$). It is the angle between the tangent to the pitch helix and the plane of rotation of or the normal to the axis of the worm.

$$\tan\alpha = \frac{L}{\pi D_w}$$

where $D_w$ = Pitch diameter of worm

(*iv*) **Face length** ($S$). It is the length of the threaded portion of worm.

The various dimensions of worm are indicated in Table 11.11.

**Table 11.11**

| | *Symbol* | *Single and double threads* | *Tripple and quadruple threads* |
|---|---|---|---|
| Normal pressure angle | $\psi$ | 14½° | 20° |
| Pitch diameter (Bored with shaft) | $D_w$ | $2.4p + 2.8$ | $2.4\ p + 2.8$ |
| Pitch diameter integral with shaft (cm) | $D_w$ | $2.35\ p + 1$ | $2.35\ p + 1$ |
| Depth of tooth (m) | $h$ | $0.686\ p$ | $0.686p$ |
| Face length (cm) | $S$ | $(4.5 + 02\ T_w)\ p$ | $(4.5 + 0.02\ T_w)\ p$ |
| Hub diameter (cm) | $D_1$ | $1.66\ p + 2.5$ | $1.726\ p + 2.5$ |
| Addendum (cm) | $a$ | $0.318\ p$ | $0.286\ p$ |

Maximum bore for shaft $(d_w) = p + 1.35$

(*v*) **Tooth pressure angle** ($\psi$). It is measured in a plane containing the axis of worm and is equal to one half of thread profile angle. Its standard values are $14\frac{1}{2}^o$, $20^o$, $25^o$ and $30^o$.

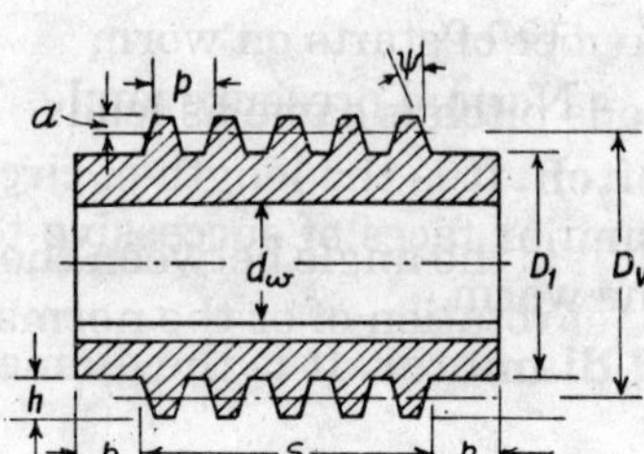


Fig. 11.19. Worm

**Worm wheel.** Fig. 11.20 shows worm and worm wheel.

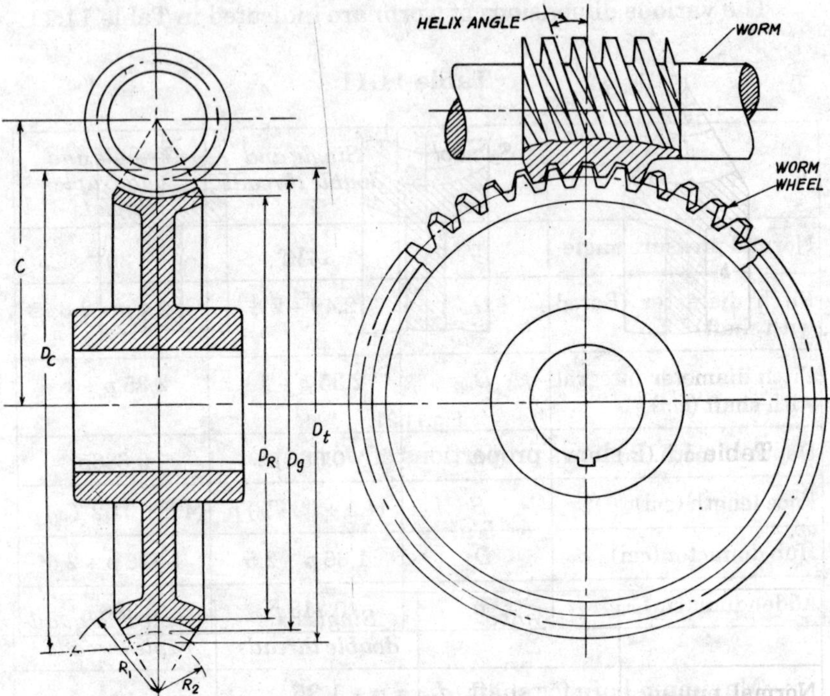


Fig. 11.20.

(*i*) **Face angle** (θ). The face angle ranges from 60° to 75°, the 60° degrees being the usual angle.

$$\tan\frac{\theta}{2} = \frac{\tan \psi_n}{\tan \alpha}.$$

where $\psi_n$ = Normal pressure angle.

(*ii*) **Circular pitch.** It is the length of circular arc of the pitch cylinder between similar faces of successive teeth and is equal to the axial pitch of the worm.

(*iii*) **Pitch and diameter.** It is the diameter of pitch cylinder of worm wheel.

The various rim constructions of worm wheel are shown in Fig. 11.21. The concave faced (Fig. 11.21 *a*) worm gear is the most commonly used form and is used for all heavy service and general industrial purposes. The hobbed strength face (Fig. 11.21 *b*) is used for light loads and strength faced worm gear (Fig. 11.21 *c*) is used for very light loads.

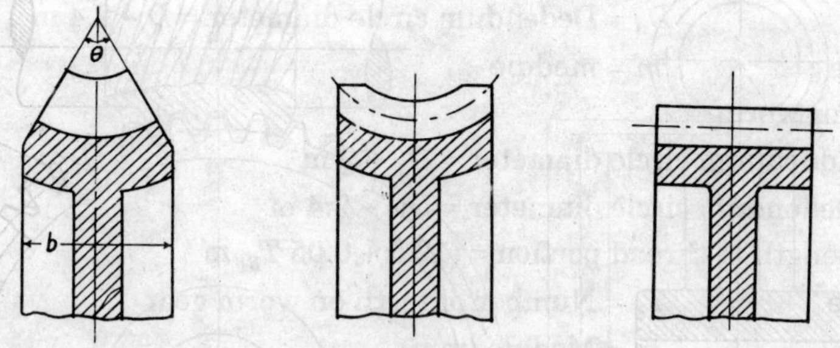


Fig.11.21.

Table 11.12 shows proportions of worm gear.

**Table 11.12**

| | *Symbol* | *Single and double threads* | *Triple and quadruple threads* |
|---|---|---|---|
| Normal pressure angle | $\psi$ | $14\frac{1}{2}^{o}$ | $20^{o}$ |
| Out side diameter (cm) | $D_\theta$ | $D_g + 1.0135\,p$ | $D_g + 0.8903\,p$ |
| Throat diameter (cm) | $D_t$ | $D_g + 0.036\,p$ | $D_g + 0.572\,p$ |
| Face width (cm) | $b$ | $2.38\,p + 0.65$ | $2.15\,p + 0.5$ |
| Radius of gear rim (cm) | $R_1$ | $2.2\,p + 1.4$ | $2.1\,p + 1.4$ |
| Face radius (cm) | $R_2$ | $0.882\,p + 1.4$ | $0.914\,p + 1.4$ |

$p$ = Circular pitch

$D_g$ = Gear pitch diameter

$D_R$ = Root diameter

(*iv*) **Worm and Worm gear proportions.** For worm gear

$$D_g = m \times T_g$$

$D_a$ = Addendum circle diameter = $D + 2$ m

$D_d$ = Dedendum circle diameter = $D - 2.4$ m

where $m$ = module

For worm

Addendum circle diameter = $D_\omega + 2$ m

Dedendum circle diameter = $D\omega - 2.4$ m

Length of thread portion = $(12.5 + 0.05\ T_g)$ m

where $T_g$ = Number of teeth on worm gear

$m$ = Module (mm)

## 11.30. Velocity Ratio ($r$)

It is given by the following relation

$$r = \frac{N_w}{N_g} = \frac{T_g}{T_m} = \frac{D_g}{D_w \tan\alpha}$$

where $N_w$ = R.P.M. of worm

$N_g$ = R.P.M. of gear

$T_g$ = Number of teeth on gear

$T_w$ = Number of threads in parallel on worm

$D_g$ = Pitch diameter of gear

$D_w$ = Pitch diameter of worm, $\alpha$ = Helix angle

Let $V_\omega$ = Linear velocity of worm = $\dfrac{L\,.\,N_\omega}{60}$

$V_g$ = Linear velocity of worm gear = $\dfrac{\pi\,.\,D_g N_g}{60}$

Now, $V_\omega = V_g$

$$\frac{LN_w}{60} = \frac{\pi\, D_g\,.\,N_g}{60}$$

$$LN_w = \pi\, D_g\,.\,N_g$$

$$\frac{N_w}{N_g} = \frac{\pi\, D_g}{L} = r$$

$$p = \text{Circular pitch} = \frac{\pi D_g}{T_g}.$$

**11.31.1. Helix Angle.** For a compact design the helix angle is given by

$$\cot\alpha = \sqrt[3]{r}$$

The helix able ($\alpha$) less than 90° results in a rapid wear and safe value is $12\frac{1}{2}^{\circ}$. The value of $\alpha$ varies from 9° to 45°.

## 11.31. Centre Distance (C)

The centre distance is given by the following relation :

$$C = \frac{D_w + D_g}{2} = \frac{L}{2\pi}(\cot \alpha + r)$$

Now normal load $(L_n)$

$$= L \cos \alpha$$

where $L$ = Axial lead

$$\therefore \quad \frac{C}{L_n} = \frac{1}{2\pi}\left[\frac{1}{\sin \alpha} + \frac{r}{\cos \alpha}\right]$$

where $r$ = Velocity ratio.

## 11.32. Number of Threads on Worm

The number of threads on worm ($n$) according to velocity ratio are indicated in Table 11.12 ($a$).

**Table 11.12 ($a$)**

| $r$ | $n$ |
|---|---|
| 4-10 | 6 |
| 6-12 | 4 |
| 8-12 | 3 |
| 12-36 | 2 |
| 20 and over | 1 |

## 11.33. Beam Strength of Worm Gear Teeth

The strength of teeth is determined by the Lewis equation

$$F = f \cdot p \cdot y \cdot b$$

where $f = \text{Safe static stress} \times \left(\frac{3}{3 + V_g}\right)$

$V_g$ = Velocity of worm gear in m /sec

$p$ = Circular pitch

$b$ = Face width

When the sum of teeth in worm and wheel exceeds 40 the following values of $y$ as indicated in Table 11.13 may be used.

**Table 11.13**

| $\psi$ *(Degrees)* | y |
|---|---|
| 14½ | 0.1 |
| 20 | 0.125 |
| 25 | 0.15 |
| 30 | 0.175 |

The static stress of 370 kg/cm$^2$ for cast iron and 550 kg/cm$^2$ for bronze are the usual values.

## 11.34. Limiting Load for Wear

The tooth pressures in worm gearing are frequently very high. Worms of steel should be hardened to atleast 250 B.H.N. The limit load for wear is given by the equation.

$F_w$ = Limit load for wear

$= D_g \cdot b \cdot k$

where $D_g$ = Pitch diameter of worm gear

$b$ = Face width

$k$ = Constant

The value of constant $k$ depends upon the kind of material used for wheel. The values of $k$ are indicated in Table 11.14.

**Table 11.14**

| *Material of wheel* | $k$ |
|---|---|
| Cast iron | 3.5 |
| Manganese bronze | 5.6 |
| Phosphor bronze | 7 |
| Non-metallic | 8.75 |

## 11.35. Dynamic Tooth Load

It is calculated by using the following relation.

$$F_d = \text{Dynamic tooth load}$$

$$= F\left(\frac{6+V_g}{6}\right) \text{ for metallic gears}$$

$$= \frac{F \times (3+V_g)}{3+0.25\,V_g} \text{ for non metallic gears}$$

where $V_g = \dfrac{L \times N_w}{100}$

$L$ = Lead of worm in cm

$N_w$ = R.P.M. of worm.

## 11.36. Analysis of Forces in Worm Gearing

The various forces acting in worm wheel arrangement are shown in Fig.11.22. The normal force is $Q$ on the gear tooth and the normal pressure angle is $\psi_n$.

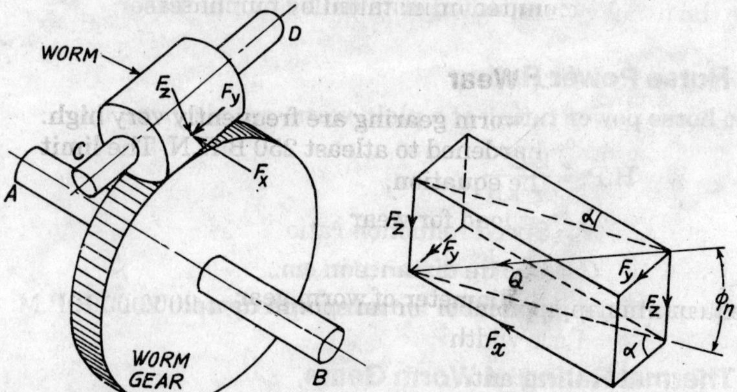


Fig.11.22

$$\tan \psi_n = \tan \psi \cos \alpha$$

$$F_x = \text{Tangential force on the worm}$$

$$= \text{End thrust on gear}$$

$$= Q \cos \psi_n \sin \alpha + \mu Q \cos \alpha$$

$$F_y = \text{Tangential force on gear}$$

$$= \text{End thrust on worm}$$

$$= Q \cos \psi_n \cos \alpha - \mu Q \sin \alpha$$

$F_z$ = Force tending to separate the worm and gear apart

$F_z = Q \sin \psi_n$

where $\mu$ = Coefficient of friction

$F = Q \sin \psi_n \cos \alpha$.

## 11.37. Efficiency

The efficiency ($\eta$) of worm and gear is calculated by using the following relation.

$$\eta = \frac{\tan \alpha (\cos \psi_n - \mu \tan \alpha)}{\cos \psi_n \tan \alpha - \mu}$$

The efficiency will be maximum

when $\tan \alpha = \sqrt{1 + \mu^2} - \mu$

$\eta = 100 - \frac{r}{2}$ for commercial worm gear reducers

$= 100 - r$ for worm gear sets without cases. mounted or installed by purchaser.

## 11.38. Horse Power Rating

The horse power rating of a plain worm gear is given by

$$\text{H.P.} = \frac{2\,C^{1.7}}{r + 5}$$

$r$ = Speed reduction ratio

where $C$ = Centre distance in cm

This equation is applicable for worm speeds upto 2000 R.P.M.

## 11.39. Thermal Rating of Worm Gears

The heat produced ($H$) by friction is dissipated by means of artificial cooling in the form of cooling coils in the gear box housing or by means of external oil coolers.

$$H = k \,.\, A \,.\, (T_1 - T_2)$$

where $k$ = Co–efficient of heat dissipation in kcal per min .per sq. metre per °C.

$A$ = Housing area in $m^2$

$T_1$ = Temperature of lubricant (°C)

$T_2$ = Ambient temperature (°C).

**Example 11.9**. *Determine the helix angle for a double threaded worm having an axial pitch of 2 cm and a pitch diameter of 8 cm.*

**Solution.**

$$p = \text{Pitch} = 2 \text{ cm}$$

$$L = \text{Lead} = 2p = 2 \times 2 = 4 \text{ cm.}$$

$$D_w = \text{Pitch diameter of worm} = 8 \text{ cm}$$

$$\alpha = \text{Helix angle}$$

$$\tan \alpha = \frac{L}{\pi D_w} = \frac{4}{\pi \times 8} = 0.1592$$

$$\alpha = 9^\circ 3'$$

**Example 11.10.** *A triple threaded steel worm drives a bronze worm wheel. The wheel rotates at 120 R.P.M. and width of face of wheel is 2.25 times the circular pitch which is 3.5 cm. If the pressure angle is 20° and velocity ratio is 10 : 1 and safe static stress for bronze is 400 kg/cm², determine H.P. transmitted.*

*Assume,* $$y = 0.154 - \frac{0.912}{\text{Number of teeth}}$$

**Solution.**

$$F = \text{Tangential turning force}$$

$$= f \cdot p \cdot y \cdot b$$

where $$f = \text{allowable stress}$$

$$f = \text{Static stress} \times \left(\frac{3}{3+V}\right)$$

$$V = \text{Pitch line velocity in m/sec.}$$

$$N_g = \text{R.P.M. of worm wheel} = 120$$

$$T_g = \text{Number of teeth on gear}$$

$$D_g = \text{Pitch diameter of worm wheel}$$

$$n = \text{Number of worm starts} = 3$$

$$r = \text{Velocity ratio} = 10 = \frac{T_g}{n}$$

$$T_g = n \times 10 = 3 \times 10 = 30$$

$$p = \text{Circular pitch} = \frac{\pi D_g}{T_g}$$

$$D_g = \frac{p \times T_g}{\pi} = \frac{3.5 \times 30}{\pi}$$

$$V = \frac{\pi . D_g N_g}{100} \text{ metre/min}$$

$$= \frac{\pi D_g . N_g}{100 \times 60} \text{ m/sec.}$$

$$= \frac{\pi \times 3.5 \times 30}{\pi} \times \frac{120}{100 \times 60}$$

$$= \left[\frac{3.5 \times 30 \times 120}{100 \times 60}\right] = 2.1 \text{ m/sec.}$$

$$f = \text{Allowable stress}$$

$$= \text{Static stress} \times \left(\frac{3}{3 + V}\right)$$

$$= 400 \times \left(\frac{3}{3 + 2.1}\right) = 235.3 \text{ kg/cm}^2$$

$$b = \text{Face width} = 2.25 \times p$$

$$= 2.25 \times 3.5 = 7.87 \text{ cm}$$

$$y = 0.154 - \frac{0.912}{T_g} = 0.154 - \frac{0.912}{30}$$

$$= 0.124$$

$$F = f . p . y . b$$

$$= 235.3 \times 3.5 \times 0.124 \times 7.87$$

$$= 803.68 \text{ kg.}$$

$$\text{H.P.} = \frac{F \times V}{75}$$

$$= \frac{803.68 \times 2.1}{75}$$

$$= 22.5.$$

**Example 11.11.** *A 20° involute worm and gear have a speed reduction ratio of 15 : 1. The distance between shafts is about 30 cm. Axial pitch of threads may be about 3 cm. Determine the following :*

*(a) Helix angle*

*(b) Module*

*(c) Number of teeth on gear*

*(d) Pitch diameter, addenum circle diameter, and length of threaded portion of worm.*

*(e) Pitch diameter, addendum circle diameter, and face width of worm wheel.*

**Solution.**

**(a) To calculate helix angle**

$C$ = Centre distance = 30 cm

$\alpha$ = Helix angle

$r$ = Velocity ratio = 15 : 1

$$\cot \alpha = \sqrt[3]{15} = 2.46$$

$$\alpha = 22^\circ\ 7'.$$

**(b) To calculate module**

$L_n$ = Normal load

$$\frac{C}{L_n} = \frac{1}{2\pi}\left[\frac{1}{\sin \alpha} + \frac{r}{\cos \alpha}\right]$$

$$\frac{30}{L_n} = \frac{1}{2\pi}\left[\frac{1}{0.3768} \times \frac{15}{0.9264}\right]$$

$$= 3$$

$$L_n = \frac{30}{3} = 10 \text{ cm}$$

$L$ = Axial load

$$= \frac{L_n}{\cos \alpha} = \frac{10}{0.9264} = 10.8 \text{ cm}$$

$p$ = Axial pitch of worm is about 4 cm

$n$ = Number of worm starts

$$= \frac{L}{p} = \frac{10.8}{4} = 2.7$$

Hence we adopt, triple start threads

$n$ = 3 (say)

$p$ = axial pitch

$$= \frac{L}{n} = \frac{10.8}{3} = 3.6 \text{ cm}$$

$m$ = Module

$$p = \pi m$$

$$m = \frac{p}{\pi} = \frac{3.6}{\pi}$$

$$= 1.146 \text{ cm} = 11.46 \text{ mm}$$

Taking standard module of 12 mm

$$m = 12 \text{ mm}.$$

**(c) To calculate number of teeth on gear**

$p$ = Axial pitch = $\pi \times 12$

= 37.68 mm = 3.768 cm

$L = n \times p = 3 \times 3.768 = 11.3$ cm

$L_n$ = Normal load

$= L \times \cos \alpha = 11.3 \times 0.9264 = 10.47$ cm

$$\frac{C}{L_n} = \frac{2}{2\pi}\left[\frac{1}{\tan \alpha} + \frac{r}{\cos \alpha}\right]$$

$$= \frac{1}{2\pi}\left[\frac{1}{0.3764} + \frac{15}{0.9264}\right] = 3$$

$C = L_n \times 3$

$= 10.47 \times 3 = 31.41$ cm

$T_g$ = Number of teeth on gear

$$r = \frac{T_g}{n}$$

$T_g = r \times n = 15 \times 3 = 45.$

**(d) To calculate worm dimensions**

$D_w$ = Pitch diameter of worm

$$\tan \alpha = \frac{L}{\pi D_\omega}$$

$$D_w = \frac{L}{\pi \times \tan \alpha} = \frac{11.3}{\pi \times 0.4064} = 8.85 \text{ cm}$$

Addendum = $m$ = 1.2 cm

Addendum circle diameter

$= D_w + 2m = 8.85 + 2 \times 1.2 = 11.25$ cm

Dedendum circle diameter

$= D_w - 2.4$ m $= 8.85 - 2.4 \times 1.2 = 5.97$ cm

$r$ = Speed reduction ratio = 27

$h$ = Depth of tooth

$= 0.623 \times p = 0.623 \times 3.768$

= 2.35 cm

$S$ = Length of threaded portion of worm

$\geq (11 + 0.06\, T_g)\, m$ for single and double threads

$\geq (12.5 + 0.09\, T_g)\, m$ for triple and quadruple threads where $m$ = Module in mm

$$S \geq (12.5 + 0.09\ T_g) \times m$$
$$\geq (12.5 + 0.09 \times 45) \times 12$$
$$\geq 198.6 \text{ mm}$$

Allowing about 20 mm for the feed marks produced by grinding wheel as it leaves the thread root

$$S = 198.6 + 20 = 218.6 \text{ mm}$$
$$= 220 \text{ mm (say).}$$

(*e*) **To find worm gear dimensions**

$m$ = Module = 12 mm

$D_g$ = Pitch diameter

$$m = \frac{D_g}{T_g}$$

$$D_g = 12 \times 45 = 540 \text{ mm}$$

Addendum = Module = $m$ = 12 mm

Addendum circle diameter

$$= D_g + 2\ m = 540 + (2 \times 12) = 564 \text{ mm}$$

$$b = \text{Face width} = 2.15\ p + 0.5$$
$$= 2.15 \times 3.798 + 0.5 = 8.6 \text{ cm.}$$

**Example 11.12.** *Design a suitable worm gearing with the following data :*

*H.P. to be transmitted = 5*

*Speed reduction = 27*

*Pressure angle = 14½°*

*Centre distance = 18 cm*

*Speed of worm = 1200 R.P.M.*

*The worm is made up of hardened steel and wheel of phosphor bronze for which the material combination factor for phosphor bronze is 7 kg/cm² and static stress for wheel is 530 kg/cm².*

**Solution.**

(*a*) **To calculate pitch diameters**

$C$ = Centre distance

$D_w$ = Pitch diameter of worm

$$D_w = \frac{C^{0.875}}{1.89} \text{ cm} = \frac{18^{0.875}}{1.89} = 6.64$$

$p$ = Circular pitch

$$D_w \approx 3\,p$$

$$6.64 = 3 \times p$$

$$p = 2.21 \text{ cm}$$

$r$ = Speed relation ratio = 27

$T_g$ = Number of teeth on gear

$$= r \times n = 27 \times 2 = 54$$

Assuming double starts threads for which $n = 2$

$D_g$ = Pitch diameter of gear

$$C = \frac{D_w + D_g}{2}$$

$$18 = \frac{6.64 + D_g}{2}$$

$$D_g = 29.36 \text{ cm}$$

$p$ = Nearest circular pitch

$$= \frac{\pi D_g}{T_g} = \frac{\pi \times 29.36}{54} = 1.7 \text{ cm}$$

$m$ = Module

Now $p = \pi m$

$$m = \frac{1.70}{\pi} = \frac{1.7}{3.14} = 0.54 \text{ cm} = 5.4 \text{ mm}$$

We adopt standard module of 6 mm

$$m = 6 \text{ mm}$$

$$p = \pi m = \pi \times 6 = 18.84 = 1.884 \text{ cm}$$

$D_g$ = Pitch circle diameter of worm wheel

$$p = \frac{\pi D_g}{T_g}$$

$$D_g = \frac{p \times T_g}{\pi} = \frac{1.884 \times 54}{\pi} = 32.4 \text{ cm}$$

$D_w$ = Pitch diameter of worm

$$C = \frac{D_g + D_w}{2}$$

$$D_w = 2C - D_g$$

$$= 36 - 32.4 = 3.6 \text{ cm.}$$

**(*b*) To calculate H.P. transmitted**

$$F = f \cdot p \cdot y \cdot b$$

$$N_g = \text{R.P.M. of gear}$$

$$N_w = \text{R.P.M. of worm} = 1200$$

$$N_g = \frac{1200}{r} = \frac{1200}{27}$$

$$V = \text{Pitch line velocity}$$

$$= \frac{\pi D_g N_g}{100 \times 60}$$

$$= \pi \times 32.4 \times \frac{1200}{27} \times \frac{1}{100} \times \frac{1}{60}$$

$$= 0.75 \text{ m/sec}$$

$$f = \text{Safe stress}$$

$$= 530 \times \left(\frac{3}{3+V}\right) = 530 \times \left(\frac{3}{3+0.75}\right)$$

$$= 424 \text{ kg/cm}^2$$

$$p = 1.884 \text{ cm}$$

$$y = \text{Form factor for } 14\tfrac{1}{2}^\circ \text{ involute profile}$$

$$= 0.124 - \frac{0.684}{T_g} = 0.124 - \frac{0.684}{54}$$

$$= 0.112$$

$$b = \text{Face width} = 2.38\,p + 0.65$$

$$= 2.38 \times 1.884 + 0.65 = 5.13 \text{ cm}$$

$$F = f \cdot p \cdot y \cdot b$$

$$= 424 \times 1.884 \times 0.112 \times 5.13 = 459 \text{ kg}$$

Horse power rating from strength point of view is given by

$$\text{H.P.} = \frac{F \times V}{75} = \frac{459 \times 0.75}{75} = 4.59$$

**(*c*) To check for wear**

$$F_w = \text{Wear load} = D_g \times b \times k$$

where $k$ = Material combination factor

$$= 7 \text{ kg/cm}^2$$

$$F_w = 32.4 \times 5.13 \times 7 = 1163.5 \text{ kg}$$

This is more than $F$, hence safe.

(*d*) **To check for heat dissipation.** The permissible input power from heat dissipation view point is as follows :

$$\text{H.P.} = \frac{2\,C^{1.7}}{r+5} = \frac{2 \times 18^{1.7}}{27+5} = 8.5$$

This is more than H.P. transmitted hence the design is safe as against heat dissipation.

(*e*) **To find efficiency** ($\eta$)

$$\eta = (0.95 - 0.96)\frac{\tan \alpha}{\tan(\alpha + \phi_1)}$$

where $\phi_1$ = Reduced friction angle

$$\tan \phi_1 = \mu_1$$

where $\mu_1$ = Reduced co–efficient of friction

$$= 0.025 + \frac{V_\omega}{18000}$$

where $V_w$ = Sliding velocity or rubbing velocity

$$= \frac{\pi\, D_w\, N_w}{100 \cos \alpha}$$

For economical design $\cot^3\alpha = r = 27$

$$\cot \alpha = \sqrt[3]{27}$$

$$\alpha = 18^\circ - 24'$$

$$V_\omega = \frac{\pi \times 3.6 \times 1200}{100 \cos 18^\circ - 4'} = 143 \text{ mpm}$$

$$\mu_1 = 0.025 + \frac{143}{18000} = 0.033$$

$$\tan \phi_1 = \mu_1$$

$$\phi_1 = 1^\circ - 54'$$

$$\eta = \frac{0.95 \tan 18^\circ - 24'}{\tan(20^\circ - 18')} = 0.84.$$

(*f*) **To find worm shaft diameter**

$T_1$ = Torque acting on worm wheel shaft

$$= \frac{\text{H.P.} \times 4500}{2\pi \times \text{N}_g} = \frac{5 \times 4500 \times 27}{2\pi \times 1200}$$

$$= 80.6 \text{ kg m} = 8060 \text{ kg cm}$$

$T_2$ = Moment on worm shaft

$$= \frac{T_1}{r \times n} = \frac{80.6}{27 \times 0.84}$$

= 3.56 kg m = 356 kg cm

Turning force on worm

= Axial force on worm wheel

$$F_2 = \frac{T_2}{R_\omega}$$

where $R_w = \frac{D_w}{2} = 1.8$ cm

$$= \frac{3.56}{1.8} \times 100 = 198 \text{ kg}$$

Axial force on worm = Turning force on wheel

$$F_1 = \frac{T_1}{R_g}$$

where $R_g = \frac{D_g}{2} = 16.2 \text{ cm} = \frac{80.6 \times 100}{16.2} = 497$ kg

$N$ = Radial force on worm

$$= F_1 \tan \psi = 497 \times \tan 14\frac{1}{2} = 129 \text{ kg}$$

$S$ = Distance between bearing of worm shaft

= $D_g$ (say) = 32.4 cm

$M_1$ = Bending moment due to $N$ in vertical plane

$$= \frac{N \times S}{4} = \frac{129 \times 32.4}{4} = 1045 \text{ kg cm.}$$

$M_3$ = Bending moment due to $F_1$ in vertical plane

$$= F_1 \times \frac{D_w}{4} = \frac{497 \times 3.6}{4}$$

= 447 kg cm

$M_3$ = Total bending moment in vertical plane

$= M_1 + M_2 = 1045 + 447 = 1492$ kg cm

$M_4$ = Bending moment due to $F_2$ in horizontal plane

$$= F_2 \times \frac{S}{4} = 198 \times \frac{32.4}{4} = 1604 \text{ kg cm}$$

$M$ = Resultant bending moment on worm shaft

$$= \sqrt{M_3^2 + M_4^2} = \sqrt{1492^2 + 1604^2} = 2200 \text{ kg cm}$$

Let $d_1$ = Diameter of worm shaft

$f_s$ = Shear stress for shaft = 450 kg/cm$^2$.
(assume)

$T_e$ = Equivalent torque

$$= \sqrt{T_2^2 + M^2} = \sqrt{356^2 + 2200^2} = 2200 \text{ kg cm}$$

$$T_e = \frac{\pi}{16} f_s d_1^3$$

$$2229 = \frac{\pi}{16} \times 450 \times d_1^3$$

$$d_1 = 1{:}47 \text{ cm.}$$

(*g*) **To find worm wheel shaft diameter**

$F_2$ = Axial force on worm wheel
= 198 kg

$F_1$ = Turning force on worm wheel = 497 kg

$N$ = Radial force on worm wheel = 129 kg

$M_1$ = Bending moment due to $F_2$ in vertical plane

$$= F_2 \times \frac{D_g}{4} = 198 \times \frac{32.4}{4} = 1604 \text{ kg cm}$$

Let, $S_1$ = Distance between bearing centres of worm wheel shaft = 25 cm

$M_2$ = Bending moment due radial force in vertical plane

$$= \frac{N \times S_1}{4} = \frac{129 \times 25}{4} = 806 \text{ kg cm}$$

$M_3$ = Total bending moment in vertical plane

$$= M_1 + M_2 = 1604 + 806 = 2410 \text{ kg cm}$$

$M_4$ = Bending moment due to turning force in horizontal plane

$$M_4 = F_1 \times \frac{S_1}{4} = 497 \times \frac{25}{4} = 3106 \text{ kg cm}$$

$M$ = Resultant bending moment on wheel shaft

$$= \sqrt{M_4^2 + M_3^2}$$

$$= \sqrt{3106^2 + 1492^2} = 3376 \text{ kg cm}$$

$T_e$ = Equivalent torque

$$= \sqrt{M^2 + T_1^2} = \sqrt{3376^2 + 8060^2} = 8684 \text{ kg cm}$$

$$T_e = \frac{\pi}{16} f_s d_2^3$$

where $d_2$ = Diameter of worm wheel shaft

$$8684 = \frac{\pi}{16} \times 450 \times d_2^3$$

$$d_2 = 4.6 \text{ cm.}$$

**Example 11.13.** *A pair of spur gears is used to transmit 18 kW at 1400 R.P.M. of pinion. The gear ratio is 4 and tooth profile is 20° stub. Gear is made of C.I and pinion is made of C.S.*

*Determine (a) Module, (b) Face width.*

**Solution.** $m$ = Module

$G$ = Gear ratio = 4

Addendum $= m$

$T_p$ = Minimum number of teeth on pinion

$$= \frac{2 \, . \, a \, \omega \, . \, G}{\sqrt{1 + \frac{1}{G}\left(\frac{1}{G} + 1\right)\sin^2\phi} - 1}$$

$$= \frac{2 \times 1 \times \frac{1}{4}}{\sqrt{1 + \frac{1}{4}\left(\frac{1}{4} + 2\right)\sin^2 20} - 1} = 15.4 = 16 \text{ (say)}$$

$T_g$ = Number of teeth on gear

$= G \times T_p$

$= 4 \times 16 = 64$

Let $\sigma_p$ = Stress in pinion

$= 90$ MPa

$\sigma_g$ = Stress in gear

$= 75$ MPa

$y_g$ = Form factor for gear

$$= 0.175 - \frac{0.841}{T_g}$$

$$= 0.175 - \frac{0.841}{64} = 0.16$$

$$\psi = \text{Pressure angle} = 20^\circ$$

$$y_p = \text{Form factor for pinion}$$

$$= 0.175 - \frac{0.841}{16} = 0.12$$

$$\sigma_p \,.\, y_p = 90 \times 0.12 = 10.8 \text{ and } \sigma_g\, y_g = 75 \times 0.16 = 12$$

Thus pinion may be designed.

$$V = \text{Speed} = \pi\, D_p \,.\, N_p$$

where $D_p$ = Pitch circle diameter

$$m = \frac{D_p}{T_p}$$

$$D_p = m \times T_p = m \times 16$$

$$N_p = \text{R.P.M. of pinion} = 1400$$

$$V = \frac{\pi \times m \times 16 \times 1400}{60 \times 1000}$$

$$= 1.17\, m \text{ metre/sec.}$$

$$k = \text{Velocity factor}$$

$$= \frac{3}{3 + V} = \frac{3}{3 + 1.17\, m}$$

$$P = \text{Power transmitted} = 18 \text{ kW}$$

$$p = F \times V$$

$$18000 = F \times V$$

$$F = \frac{18000}{1.17\, m}$$

$$G = \text{Face width} = 10 \text{ m (say)}$$

According to Lewis equation

$$F = \text{Tangential load}$$

$$= k \,.\, \sigma_p \,.\, y_p \,.\, b \,.\, p$$

$$\frac{18000}{1.17\, m} = \left(\frac{3}{3 + 1.17\, m}\right) 90 \times 0.12 \times 10\, m \times \pi\, m$$

$$m = 4.8 \text{ mm}$$

$$b = \text{Face width} = 10 \text{ m}$$

$$= 10 \times 4.8 = 48 \text{ mm.}$$

**Example 11.14.** *In a worm gear speed reducer the centre distance should not exceed 240 mm. The gear ratio is 10, the worm speed is 2400 RPM. Determine the dimensions and the capacity of the reducer. Assume 14½° involute teeth.*

*Also determine the capacity of the gear drive based on wear and heat dissipation.*

**Solution.**

Let $D_w$ = Pitch diameter of worm

$$= \frac{C^{(0.875)}}{2.48} \text{ where } C = \text{Centre distance}$$

$$= \frac{(0.24)^{(0.875)}}{2.48} = 0.11 \text{ m} = 110 \text{ mm}$$

$p$ = circular pitch

$$D_w = 3p$$

$$p = \frac{D_w}{3} = \frac{0.11 \times 1000}{3} = 36.7 \text{ mm}$$

$m$ = Module

$$p = \pi \times m$$

$$36.7 = \pi \times m$$

$$m = 11.7 \text{ mm} = 12 \text{ mm (say)}$$

$T_g$ = Worm gear teeth

= 25 for double start worm gear

$D_g$ = P.C.D. of worm gear

$$m = \frac{D_g}{T_g}$$

$$12 = \frac{D_g}{25}; D_g = 300 \text{ mm}$$

$$N_g = \text{R.P.M. of gear} = \frac{2400}{10} = 240$$

$F_t$ = Tangential force

$$= K_v \,.\, \sigma \,.\, y \,.\, b \,.\, p$$

$V_g$ = Pitch velocity

$$= \frac{\pi\, D_g \,.\, N_g}{60 \times 1000}$$

$$= \frac{\pi \times 300 \times 240}{60 \times 1000} = 3.77 \text{ m/s}$$

$$K_v = \text{Velocity factor}$$

$$= \frac{6}{6 + V_g} = \frac{6}{6 + 3.77} = 0.64$$

$\sigma$ = 50 MPa for phosphor bronze gear (assume)

$\text{Y} = \text{Pressure angle} = 14\frac{1}{2}^{\circ}$

$y$ = Form factor

$= 0.1$ for $\psi = 14\frac{1}{2}^{\circ}$ from Table 11.13

$b = \text{Face width} = 0.73 \times D_w = 0.73 \times 110$

$= 80.3$ mm

$$F_t = 0.64 \times 50 \times 0.1 \times 36.7 \times 80.3$$

$$= 9430 \text{ N}$$

Power based on beam strength

$$= \frac{F_t \times V_g}{1000} = \frac{9430 \times 3.77}{1000} = 35.5 \text{ kW}$$

$P_1$ = Power capacity based on heat dissiption

$$= \frac{3650 \times C^{(1.7)}}{R + 5}$$

where $R$ = Transmission ratio

$= 10$

$C$ = Centre distance = 0.24 m

$$P_1 = \frac{3650 \times 0.24^{(1.7)}}{10 + 5} = 21.5 \text{ kW}$$

$P_2$ = Power rating based on wear

$$= \frac{N_w}{R} \cdot k \cdot Q \cdot V.$$

where $N_w$ = Speed of worm = 2400

$K$ = Pressure constant = 0.8 (Assume)

$V_w$ = Velocity of worm

$$= \frac{\pi \, d_w \cdot N_w}{60 \times 1000} = \frac{\pi \times 110 \times 2400}{60 \times 1000} = 13.8 \text{ m/s}$$

$$V = \frac{2.3}{2.3 + V_w + \dfrac{3 \, V_w}{R}}$$

$$= \frac{2.3}{2.3 + 13.8 + \dfrac{3 \times 13.8}{10}} = 0.12$$

$$Q = \frac{R}{R + 2.5} = \frac{10}{10 + 2.5} = 0.81$$

$$P_2 = \frac{N_w \,.\, k \,.\, Q \,.\, V}{R}$$

$$= \frac{2400 \times 0.8 \times 0.81 \times 0.12}{10} = 18.7 \text{ kW}$$

Thus power input is limited by wear criteria and should be 18.7 kW.

**Example 11.15.** *In a spur gear drive a 20° full depth steel pinion meshes with a C.I. gear with 230 BHN. Centre distance is 240 mm and speed ratio is 3 : 1. The speed of the pinion is 600 RPM. The module is 5 mm and face width of teeth 54 mm. The wear load factor is 0.9 N/mm² and the dynamic tooth factor is 7.5 N/mm/micron. The tooth error is $7 + 0.6\,(m + 0.25\sqrt{d})$ where m is module in mm and d is the pitch circle diameter (p.c.d.) of the gear in mm. The permissible static stress for pinion is 110 MPa and for gear 50 MPa. Determine the maximum safe power that can be transmitted by the spur gear pair.*

**Solution.**

Let $d_p$ = Pitch circle diameter of pinion

$d_g$ = Pitch circle diameter of the gear

$C$ = Centre distance

$m$ = Module = 5 mm

$$C = \frac{d_g + d_p}{2} \quad \text{and} \quad \frac{d_g}{d_p} = 3$$

$$240 = \frac{d_g + d_p}{2} = \frac{3\,d_p + d_p}{2} = \frac{4\,d_p}{2}$$

$$d_p = 120 \text{ mm}$$

$$d_g = 360 \text{ mm}$$

$T_p$ = Number of teeth on pinion

$$m = \text{module} = \frac{d_p}{T_p}$$

$$5 = \frac{120}{T_p}$$

$$T_p = \frac{120}{5} = 24$$

$T_g$ = Number of teeth on gear

$$\frac{T_g}{T_p} = 3$$

$$T_g = 3 \times 24 = 72$$

$$y_p = 0.154 - \frac{0.912}{T_p}$$

$$= 0.154 - \frac{0.912}{24} = 0.116$$

$y_g$ = From factor for gear

$$= 0.154 - \frac{0.912}{T_g}$$

$$= 0.154 - \frac{0.912}{72} = 0.142$$

Now $\sigma_p$ = Safe static stress for pinion

= 110 MPa

$\sigma_p$ = Safe static stress for gear = 50 MPa

$$\sigma_p \times y_p = 110 \times 0.116 = 12.76$$

$$\sigma_g \times y_g = 50 \times 0142 = 7.1$$

Thus gear is weaker

$V$ = Pitch line velocity

$$= \frac{\pi \, d_p \, . \, N_p}{60} = \frac{\pi \times 120 \times 600}{1000 \times 60}$$

= 3.77 m/sec

$b$ = Face width = 54 mm

$p$ = Circular pitch = $\pi \times m = \pi \times 5$

$F$ = Tangential load

$$= \sigma_g \, . \, y_g \, . \, b \, . \, p$$

$$= 50 \times 0.142 \times 54 \times \pi \times 5$$

= 6019.38 N

$F_w$ = Wear load

$$= k.. \, d_p \, . \, b \, . \, Q$$

where $K$ = Load stress factor for wear

= 0.90 N/mm$^2$

$Q$ = Ratio factor

$$= \frac{2\,T_g}{T_g + T_p}$$

$$= \frac{2 \times 72}{72 + 24}$$

$$= 1.5$$

$$F_\omega = 0.90 \times 120 \times 54 \times 1.5$$

$$= 8748 \text{ N}$$

**Since $F_w$ is more than $F$, so the gears are safe.**

**Now** $F_o$ = **Design load**

$= F = 6019.38$

$C$ = **Dynamic tooth factor**

$= 7.5$ **N/mm/micron.**

**According to Buckingam formula**

$$F_o = \frac{21\,V\,(b\,C + F_t)}{21\,V + \sqrt{b\,C + F_t}} + F_t$$

$e$ = **Tooth pitch error for gear and pinion**

$$= 8 + .63(m + 0.25\sqrt{d_g}) + 8 + .63(m + 0.25\sqrt{d_p})$$

$$= 16 + 0.63(5 + 0.25\sqrt{360}) + 0.63(5 + 0.25\sqrt{120})$$

$$= 29.8$$

$$C = 7.5 \times e = 7.5 \times 29.8 = 223.5$$

$$F_o = 6019.38$$

$$= \frac{21 \times 3.77 \times (54 \times 223.5 + F_t)}{21 \times 3.77 + \sqrt{54 \times 223.5 + F_t}} + F_t$$

$$F_t = 1471 \text{ N}$$

$$p = \text{Power transmitted} = \frac{F_t \times V}{1000} = \frac{1471 \times 3.77}{1000}$$

$$= 5.54 \text{ kW.}$$

## PROBLEMS

**1.** Name the different types of gears in use. State their individual applications.

**2.** Sketch the tooth profile of spur gear and explain the various terms associated with it.

**3.** What are helical gears. In what way they are preferable to spur gears?

**4.** What kinds of curves are used for the profiles of gear teeth ?

**5.** What is so called number of teeth of a bevel gear.

**6.** State the difference between a miter bevel gears and angular gears.

**7.** What is an interchangeable set of spur gears ?

**8.** A cut semi-steel spur gear has 14½° involute teeth, a diameter material pitch of 3, a pitch diameter of 24 cm and a length of tooth of 7 cm. It runs at 250 R.P.M. The static stress for semi-steel is 500 kg/cm². Determine:

(*a*) Circular pitch (*b*) Pitch line velocity
(*c*) Number of teeth on gear (*d*) Form factor
(*e*) Tooth pressure (*f*) Torque in gear shaft
(*g*) Horse power that can be transmitted safety.

**9.** Draw sketches to illustrate a pair of helical gears and bevel gears and indicate the nature and directions of forces acting on the bearing of the gear and pinion shafts in each case.

**10.** A pair of straight spur gears is to transmit 30 H.P. when the pinion rotates at 303 R.P.M. The velocity ratio is 1:3. The allowable static stress for the pinion and gear materials are 1200 kgcm² respectively. The pinion has 15 teeth and its face width is 14 times the module.

The tooth form factor $y$ can be taken as

$$y = 0.154 - \frac{0.912}{\text{Number of teeth}}$$

$$C_v = \text{Velocity factor}$$

$$= \frac{3}{3 + V}$$

where $V$ = Peripheral velocity of gear in m/sec.

Determine (*a*) Module

(*b*) Pitch width.

(*c*) Pitch circle diameter of both pinion and gear form the stand point of strength only taking into consideration the effect of dynamic loading.

**11.** A pair cast steel annealed spur gears with cast teeth have velocity ratio of 3 and transmit 30 H.P. at 120 R.P.M. of pinion. The pitch diameter of pinion is approximately 20 cm. Calculate module, face width of gears and correct pitch diameters and number of teeth on gear and pinion.

**12.** Design a pair of spur gears for the following duty.

H.P. transmitted = 50

R.P.M. of input shaft = 900

R.P.M of output shaft

$= 150$

Static stress for steel pinion $= 2100$ Pinion

Static stress for cast iron gear $= 800$ kg/cm$^2$

$$\text{Velocity factor}(C_v) = \frac{3}{3 + V}$$

$$\text{Lewis form factor } (y) = 0.124 - \frac{0.684}{N}$$

where $N$ = Number of teeth

Stress fatigue factor = 144

Both pinion and gear are provided with $14\frac{1}{2}^o$ full depth involute teeth.

Give a neat dimensioned sketch of gear and pinion.

**13.** Design a spur gear drive to transmit 30 H.P. at 900 R.P.M. Speed reduction is 2.5. The centre distance between the drive is 35 cm. Materials for pinion and wheel are steel and cast iron respectively. The pressure angle of 20°. Design stress for pinion material is 840 kg/cm$^2$ and surface endurance limit for pinion material is 6000 kg/cm$^2$. Modulus of elasticity of pinion material is $2 \times 10^6$ kg/cm$^2$ and that of gear is $1 \times 10^6$ kg/cm$^2$, check the gears for wear.

**14**. Design a pair of helical gears to transmit 30 H.P. at 1800 R.P.M. of the pinion. The velocity ratio is 3. The helix angle is 30°. The gear teeth are 20° full depth involute system. The pinion has 24 teeth. Both gears are made of cast steel with working stress of 500 kg/cm$^2$. Design the gears from the stand point of strength. Find the end thrust on gear.

**15**. A pair of helical gears connecting parallel shafts is to transmit 4500 kg cm torque at 1800 R.P.M. of pinion. The teeth on to be 20° stub of heats treated alloy steel. The width of face is limited to 42 mm. The driven gear rotates at 900 R.P.M. If the helix angle is 30°. Calculate the following :

(*a*) Module

(*b*) Axial thrust

Check the gears for wear.

**16.** (*a*) In a pair of helical gears the pinion has 27 teeth and rotates at 2800 R.P.M. The velocity ratio is 7 and the teeth are to be 20° full depth involute. The diameteral pitch is 2 and active face width is 8 cm. The allowable stress for the materials of the gears is 800 kg/cm$^2$. The helix angle is 15°. Determine the power that can be transmitted by the gear.

**17**. Design a pair of helical gears with the following data.

Centre distance = 40 cm

Power to be transmitted = 110
R.P.M. of pinion = 720
Speed reduction ratio = 4 : 1.

**18.** Design a pair of bevel gears to transmit 60 H.P. at 600 R.P.M. The output shaft speed is 300 R.P.M. and is at $75^{\circ}$ to the input shaft. The pinion has 27 teeth of $14\frac{1}{2}^{\circ}$ involute. The permissible shear stress in shaft material is 450 kg/cm$^2$. The safe static stress in gear and pinion is 900 kg/cm$^2$. The bending moment for gear is 40 % of twisting moment and that for pinion is to be neglected.

**19.** Two shafts at right angles to each other are connected by a pair of $20^{\circ}$ full depth straight involute tooth bevel gears. The velocity ratio is 3 : 1. The pinion is made of steel having an allowable static stress of 1000 kg/cm$^2$ and gear is of cast steel with safe stress of 700 kg/cm$^2$. The pinion transmits 50 H.p. at 750 R.P.M. If the pinion has 20 teeth determine module, face width and pitch diameters of gear wheels from the stand point of strength taking velocity factor into consideration. Assume face width to be ⅓ of the length of the pitch cone element. The form factor ($y$) is given by

$$y = 0.154 - \frac{0.912}{N}$$

where $N$ is formative number of teeth and velocity factor ($C_\theta$) is given by

$$C_\theta = \frac{3}{3 + V}$$

where $V$ is pitch line velocity in metre/sec.

If the pinion shaft over hangs be 15 cm determine is diameter for a safe shear stress of 450 kg/cm$^2$.

**20.** A spindle of a drilling machine is to be driven by means of a pair of strength bevel gears. The pinion is to be mounted on the horizontal drive shaft. The reduction ratio 5 : 1. If the drill requires 2000 kg cm at 300 R.P.M.determine proportions of gears with $20^{\circ}$ stub teeth. Both gear and pinion are made of steel having safe static stress of 1400 kg/cm$^2$.

Lewis from factor is

$$y = 0.175 - \frac{0.841}{T_f}$$

where $T_f$ = Formative number of teeth

**21.**A pair of straight bevel gears are required to transmit 15 H.P. at 1200 R.P.M. of 24 tooth pinion. speed reduction is 4 : 1. The teeth are to be 14½° full depth. Determine.

(*a*) Module (*b*) Gear face width

(*c*) Pitch diameters

(*d*) Pitch cone angles for both gears.

Select the materials to obtain compact design.

**22.** Determine the helix angle for a double threaded worm having a pitch diameter of 15 cm and an axial pitch of 3 cm.

**23.** A hardened steel worm transmits power to a phosphor bronze gear with a transmission ratio of 12 : 1. Supporting bearings of worm and worm gear are placed 20 cm centres and the worm rotates at 1200 R.P.M. Design the worm gear drive and estimate the horse power ratings from the stand point of strength, wear and heat disspation. The teeth are $14\frac{1}{2}^\circ$ involute full depth system.

**24.** A triple threaded cast iron worm runs at 300 R.P.M. and is having 8 H.P. at its supply end. The distance between worm and worm wheel shafts is 24 cm. The speed reduction ratio is 12 : 1 and the worm has $14\frac{1}{2}^\circ$ pressure angle and helix angle should be greater than $15^\circ$. If the total efficiency of worm and its bearings is 80%, determine the following :

(*a*) Worm shaft diameter if the safe stress in shaft is 450 kg/cm$^2$.

(*b*) Axial thrust and tangential pressure on worm wheel and worm.

**25.** Explain the various terms used for the worm and worm wheel. What are their special field of application ?

**26.** A worm gear reducer unit is to have 40 cm centre distance. Determine horse power input rating in order to prevent over heating if the transmission ratio is 24.

**27.** Two steel bevel gears having a B.H.N. 250 connect shafts at $90^\circ$. The number of teeth on pinion and gears are 27 and 45. The teeth are $14\frac{1}{2}^\circ$ full depth and module is 5 mm. Face width is 36 mm. Find wear load.

**28.** A pair of bevel gears having $14\frac{1}{2}^\circ$ composite teeth is to transmit 10 kW. Find module and diameters of gears. Given :

| | *Pinion* | *Gear* |
|---|---|---|
| No. of teeth | 24 | 48 |
| Speed (R.P.M.) | 1200 | 400 |
| Material | Steel | Cast Iron |

# 12

# Bearings

## 12.1. Introduction

Bearing is a machine part which supports a rotating shaft and confines its motion. Bearings are mainly classified as follows :

(*a*) Journal bearings (*b*) Pivot bearings

(*c*) Thrust bearings (*d*) Ball and roller bearings.

Depending on nature of contact between working surfaces, the bearings may be classified as follows :

(*i*) Sliding contact bearings.

(*ii*) Rolling contact bearings.

Fig. 12.1 shows various types of bearings.

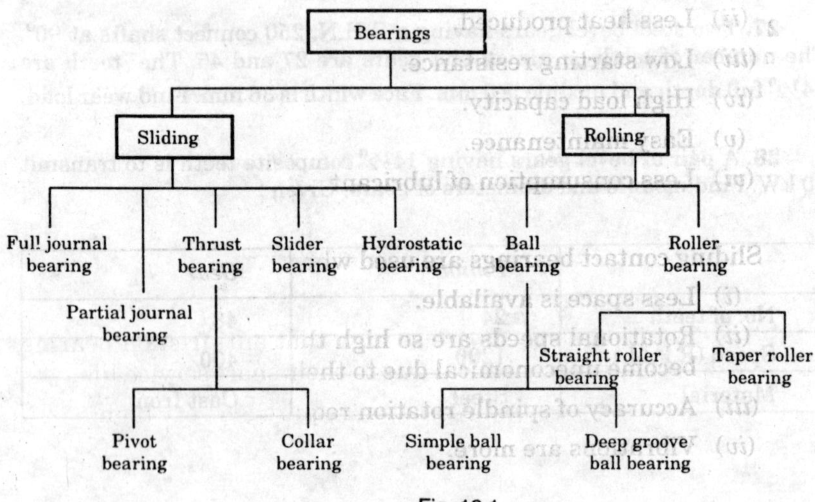


Fig. 12.1

In sliding contact bearings also called plain bearings the lubricant is introduced between the surfaces moving relative to one another whereas in rolling contact rolling motion is utilised to minimise friction.

Sliding contact bearings may be further classified as :

(*a*) Full journal bearings.

(*b*) Partial journal bearings.

(*c*) Thrust bearing.

(*i*) Pivot or step bearings.

(*ii*) Collar or conical bearing.

(*d*) Slider bearings.

(*e*) Hydro static bearings.

Rolling bearings may be:

(*a*) Ball bearings :

(*i*) Simple ball bearings.

(*ii*) Deep groove ball bearing

(*b*) Roller bearing :

(*i*) Straight roller bearing.

(*ii*) Taper roller bearing.

Rolling contact bearings also called anti-friction bearings are most commonly used bearings. The distinguishing features of these bearings are as follows :

(*i*) Low frictional torque.

(*ii*) Less heat produced.

(*iii*) Low starting resistance.

(*iv*) High load capacity.

(*v*) Easy maintenance.

(*vi*) Less consumption of lubricant.

Sliding contact bearings are used when :

(*i*) Less space is available.

(*ii*) Rotational speeds are so high that anti-friction bearings become uneconomical due to their short service life.

(*iii*) Accuracy of spindle rotation required is very high.

(*iv*) Vibrations are more.

The in-herent damping of vibrations of sliding bearings is considerably greater than that of anti-friction bearings.

## 12.2 Journal Bearings

In journal bearings, journal is the shaft that runs in the bushing or sleeve which is usually stationary and supports the bearing. In these bearings the *bearing pressure* is at right angles to the shaft axis. Examples of journal bearing are shown in Fig. 12.2.

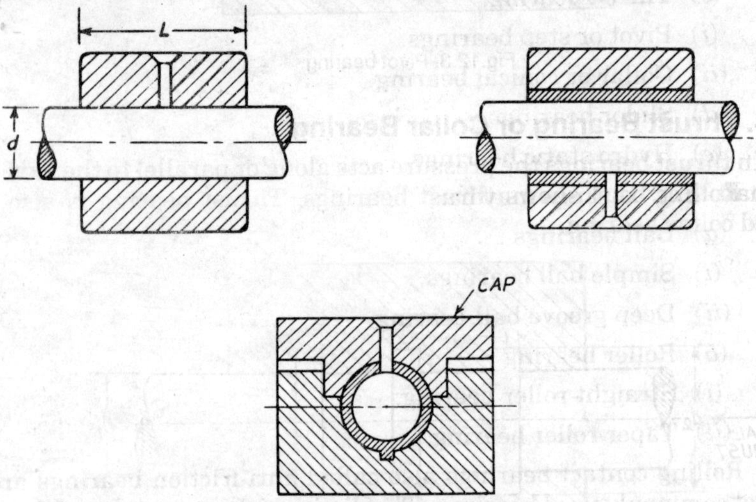


Fig. 12.2 Journal bearings.

For light loads and low speeds the bearing which is generally of cast iron may be unlined but otherwise a separate insert or bushing is usually provided to form the bearing surface for supporting the shaft. It is made up of material such as habitt or bronze which is known to have desirable qualities of high load capacity and low friction. The journal is usually made of steel and may be hardened. Its surface is accurately finished and highly polished.

Each of the journal bearings is tapped on the upper side so that an oil or grease cup can be screwed into the tapped hole. The lubricant thus gains access to the upper part of the bearing and is carried by the rotating journal to the lower bearing surface.

## 12.3. Pivot Bearings

In pivot bearings, bearing pressure acts parallel to the axis of shaft. Fig. 12.3 shows a pivot bearing.

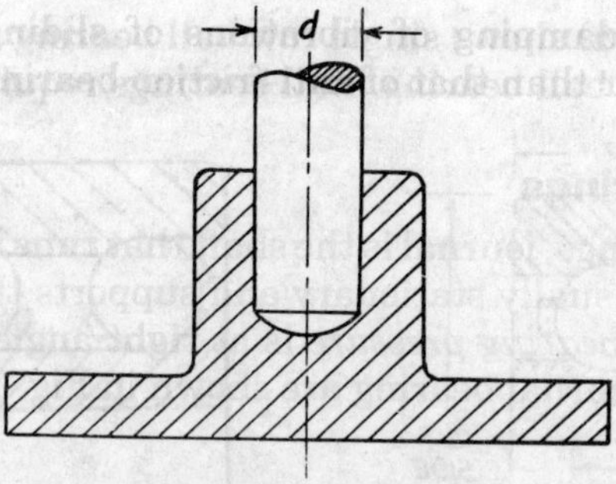


Fig.12.3. Pivot bearing.

## 12.4. Thrust Bearing or Collar Bearing

In thrust bearings the pressure acts along or parallel to the axis of shaft. Fig. 12.4 shows thrust bearings. Thrust bearing is also called collar bearing.

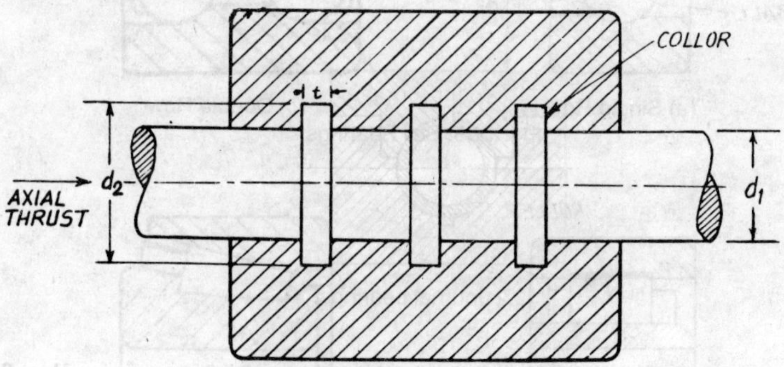


Fig.12.4. (*a*) Thrust bearing.

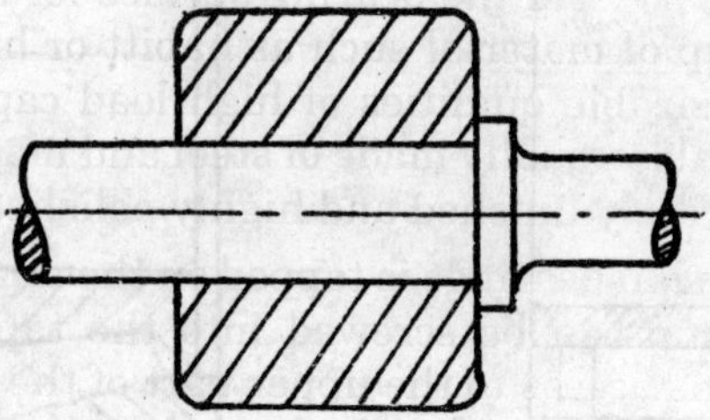

Fig.12.4 (*b*) Thrust bearings.

## 12.5. Ball and Roller Bearings (Anti-friction Bearings)

Ball and roller bearings provide better lubrication. They can resist heavy loads and higher speeds for sufficient time without failure. Fig. 12.5 (*a*) shows single row ball bearing and Fig.12.5 (*b*) shows double row ball bearing. Ball bearings require less space.

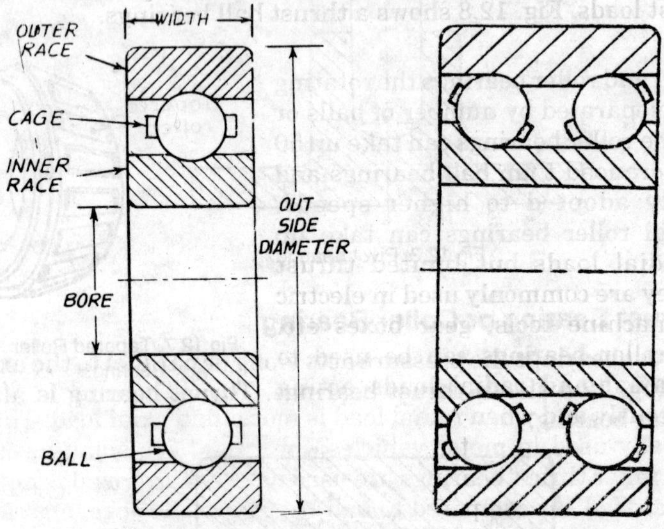


Fig. 12.5. Ball Bearings.

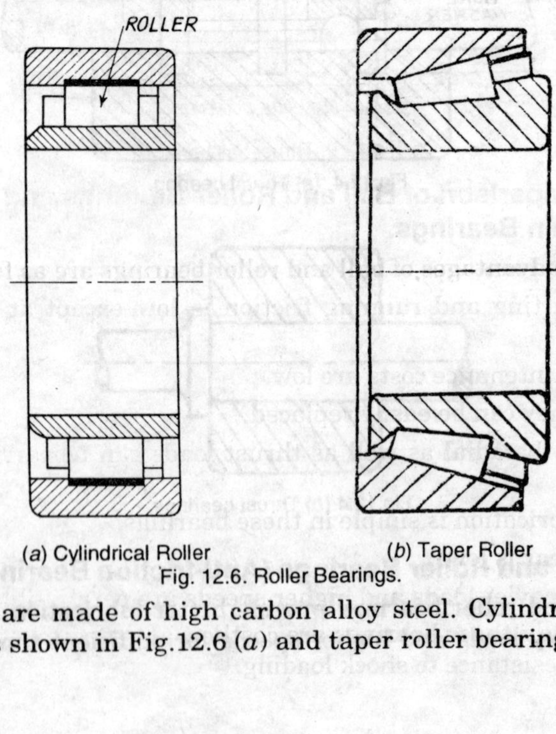


Fig. 12.6. Roller Bearings.

Balls are made of high carbon alloy steel. Cylindrical roller bearing is shown in Fig.12.6 (*a*) and taper roller bearing is shown in Fig. 12.6 (*b*) and Fig. 12.7. Roller bearings can take up both radial and thrust loads. Fig. 12.8 shows a thrust ball bearings.

In ball and roller bearings the rotating pairs are separated by number of balls or rollers. The roller bearings can take up 50 to 70% more load than ball bearings and are easily adopted to higher speeds. Cylindrical roller bearings can take up heavy radial loads but limited thrust loads. They are commonly used in electric motors, machine tools, gear boxes etc. Tapered roller bearings can be used to support axial and radial loads acting simultaneously and when radial load is more than axial load. They are generally used in motor vehicles, machine tools spindles etc. Spherical roller thrust bearings are used where thrust load is more than radial load. As compared to ball bearings roller bearings are costlier, more sensitive to misalignment and dirt.

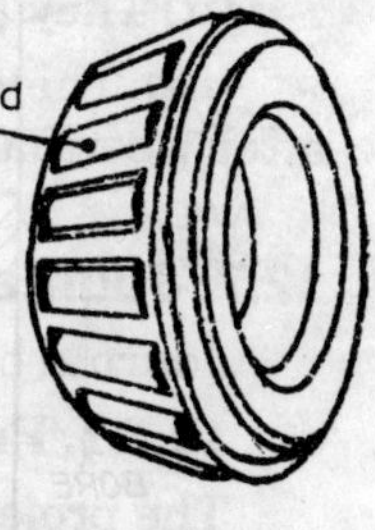


Fig 12.7. Tapered Roller Bearing.

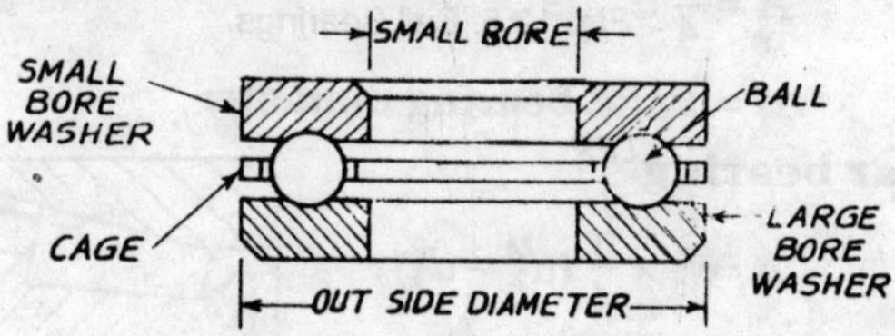


Fig.12.8. Thrust ball bearing.

## 12.6. Comparison of Ball and Roller Bearings and Plain Bearings.

Some advantages of ball and roller bearings are as follows :

(*i*) Starting and running friction is low except at very high speeds.

(*ii*) Maintenance costs are low.

(*iii*) They can be easily replaced.

(*iv*) Both radial as well as thrust loads can be carried by the bearings.

(*v*) Lubrication is simple in these bearings.

(*vi*) Wear is low.

(*vii*) Heavier loads and higher speeds are permissible.

However, these bearings are costlier, are sensitive to dirt and have low resistance to shock loading.

Advantages of pain bearings are as follows :

(*i*) Their first cast is low.

(*ii*) They are better suited to over load and shock conditions.

(*iii*) Their operation is quieter than ball bearings especially after wear has taken place.

## 12.7. Journal Bearing Design

Journal bearing or sleeve bearings are designed as follows :

### 12.7.1. Projected area

The projected area is calculated as follows :

(*a*) **Journal bearings**

$$A = \text{Projected area} = L \times d$$

where $L$ = Length of bearing

$d$ = Diameter of journal bearing

(*b*) **Pivot bearing**

$$A = \frac{\pi}{4} d^2$$

where $d$ = Pivot bearing diameter.

(*c*) **Collar bearing**

$$A = n \times \frac{\pi}{4} (d_2^2 - d_1^2)$$

where $n$ = Number of collars

$d_1$ = Inside diameter of collar

$d_2$ = Outside diameter of collar

**12.7.2. Total load on journal bearing.** It is calculated as follows :

$$P = \text{Total load} = A \times p$$

where $p$ = Intensity of pressure

**12.7.3. Lubrication of bearings.** The friction loss of energy in a bearing is turned into heat and because of this the bearing gets heated up which will reduce the power transmission. It is therefore essential to lubricate the bearings so that heat produced is removed. Under steady operating conditions the heat is removed from a bearing at the same rate at which it is produced. The heat however must be dissipated at a sufficiently rapid rate to maintain an operating temperature low enough so that no harm will come to the lubricant. The various lubricants commonly used are as follows :

(*i*) Liquid (lard oil, mineral oil, spurn oil etc.)

(*ii*) Semisolid (grease)

(*iii*) Solid (graphite)

The principal factors that influence the choice of a lubricant are as follows :

(*i*) Temperature, (*ii*) Intensity of pressure and (*iii*) Speed.

Sometimes cooling coils are provided for large and important bearings. Majority of the bearings in use depend upon the surrounding air as the cooling medium. Many bearings are constructed in the form of a self contained unit with an oil reservoir in the base or pedestal. The clearance between journal and bearing should completely be filled with oil at all times.

### 12.7.3 (*a*) Properties of a good lubricant

The lubricant should possess the following properties :

(*i*) The lubricant should have sufficient viscosity.

(*ii*) The lubricant must possess sufficient oiliness.

(*iii*) During working the lubricant must not produce any gases etc.

(*iv*) When the lubricant comes in contact with air, gases or water etc. it must not produce deposits or sludge which shall hamper the lubrication.

### 12.7.3. (*b*) Methods of lubrication

The various methods used for lubrication are as follows :

(*i*) Bottle oiling system

(*ii*) Ring oiling

(*iii*) Splash oiling.

Bottle oiler is used where small but continuous flow of lubrication is required Fig. 12.8 (*a*) shows bottle lubricator. The arrangement is used for light and medium size shaft bearings. The up and down motion is given to the needle only when the shaft is in motion and thus bearing is lubricated only when the shaft is revolving and actual bearing action is taking place.

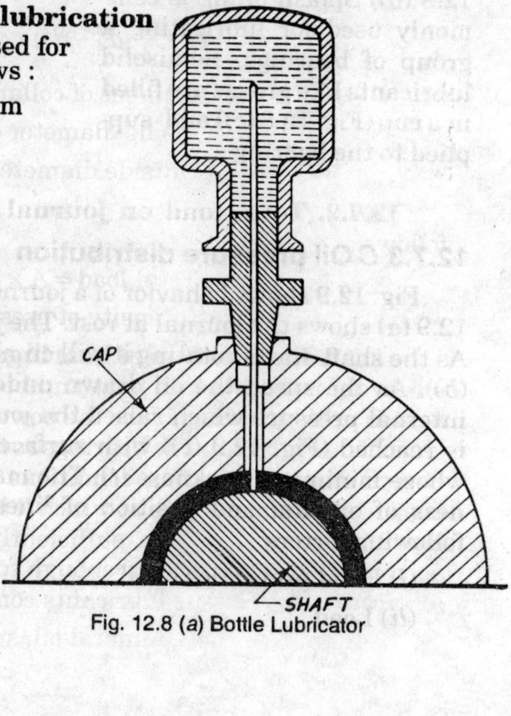

Fig. 12.8 (*a*) Bottle Lubricator

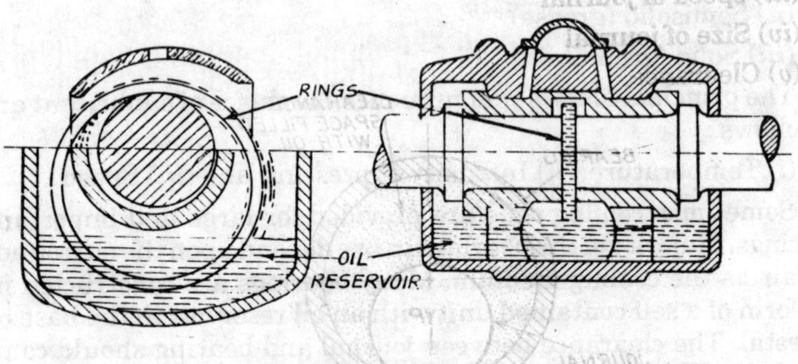


Fig. 12.8 (*b*) Ring Oil Lubricator.

Lubrication by means of rings used as lubricant carrier is commonly used in electric motors generators and steam turbines, Oil is stored in an oil reservoir forming the lower part of the bearing. The rings dip into oil in the reservoir and revolve along with the shaft and carry oil to the shaft. (Fig. 12.8 (*b*)) Splash oiling is commonly used for lubricating a group of bearings. Semisolid lubricants like grease are filled in a cup (Fig. 12.8 (*c*)) and supplied to the bearing.

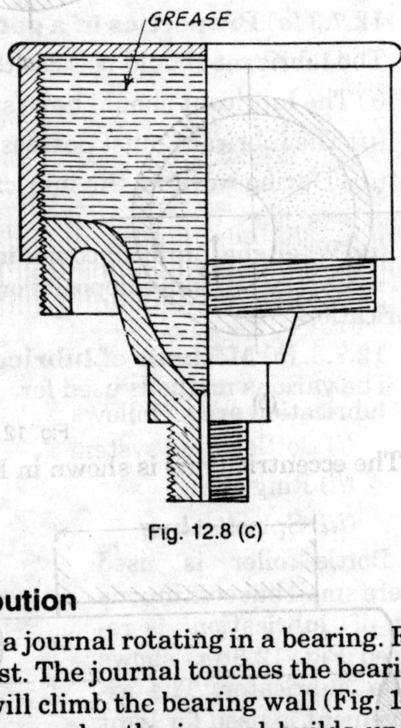


Fig. 12.8 (c)

### 12.7.3 *C* Oil pressure distribution

Fig. 12.9 shows behavior of a journal rotating in a bearing. Fig. 12.9 (*a*) shows the journal at rest. The journal touches the bearing. As the shaft starts rotating it will climb the bearing wall (Fig. 12.9 (*b*)). As the speed the oil drawn under the journal builds up an internal pressure which raised the journal up till the equilibrium is reached (Fig. 12.9 (*c*)) with surfaces separated by a film of oil whose minimum thickness (*t*). The magnitude of minimum thickness of oil film and position of lines of centres depend on the following factors.

(*i*) Fluid properties of oil

(*ii*) Load

(*iii*) speed of journal

(*iv*) Size of journal

(*v*) Clearance.

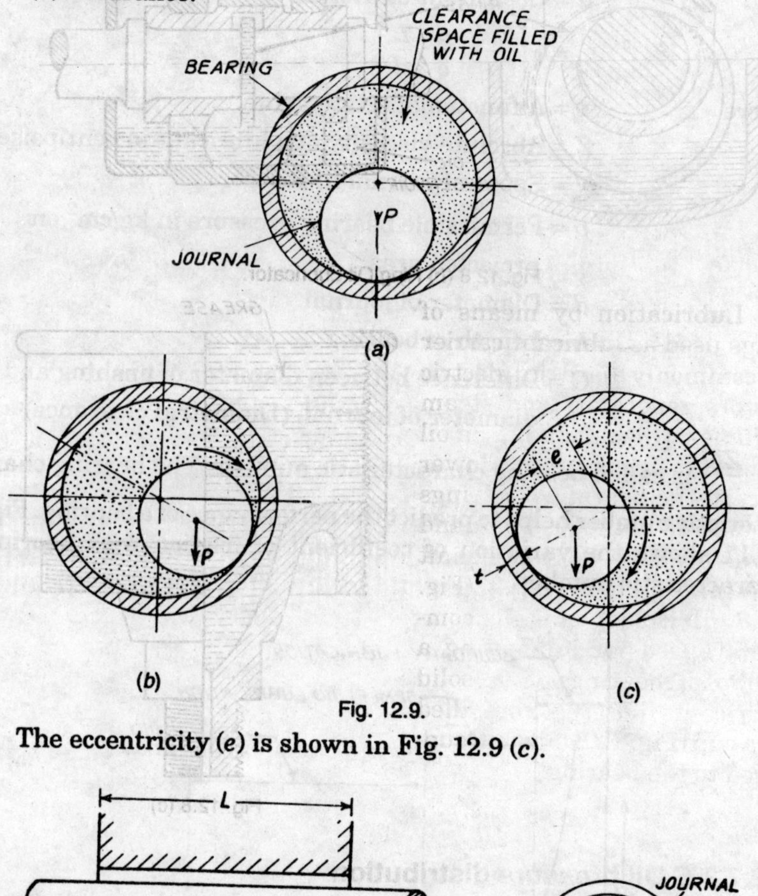


Fig. 12.9.

The eccentricity (*e*) is shown in Fig. 12.9 (*c*).

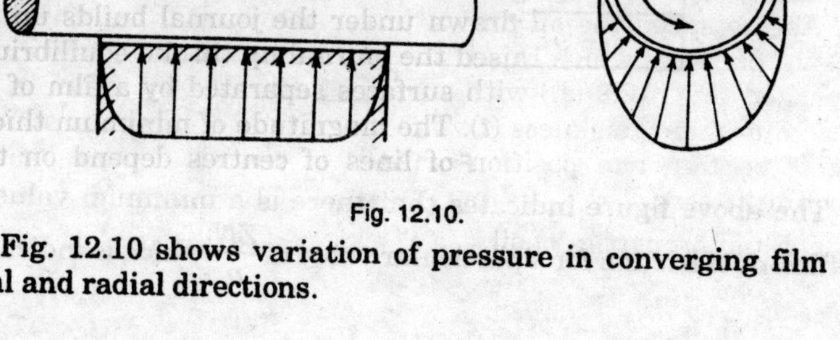


Fig. 12.10.

Fig. 12.10 shows variation of pressure in converging film in axial and radial directions.

**12.7.4. Bearing constants.** The coefficient of friction for a complete film lubrication is expressed as follows :

$\mu$ = Coefficient of friction

$$= \phi\left(\frac{ZN}{p}, \frac{d}{c} \cdot \frac{L}{d}\right)$$

where $\phi$ = A functional relationship

$Z$ = Absolute viscosity of a lubricant in centipoise

$N$ = Speed of journal in R.P.M.

$p$ = Permissible bearing pressure in kg/cm$^2$ on projected area

$d$ = Diameter of journal

$L$ = Length of bearing

$C$ = Difference between diameter of bushing and diameter of journal. (Diametral clearance)

$\frac{ZN}{p}$ is called bearing characteristic number. The bearing characteristic number helps to predict the performance of a bearing. Fig. 12.11 shows the variation of coefficient of friction with bearing characteristic number.

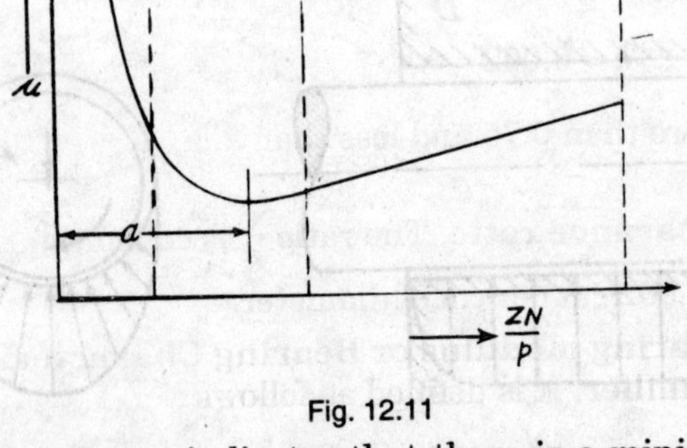


Fig. 12.11

The above figure indicates that there is a minimum value of coefficient of friction for a particular value of $\frac{ZN}{p}$ which is indicated by α. When $\frac{ZN}{p}$ is more than α the bearing may operate with complete film lubrication, when $\frac{ZN}{p}$ is less than α. The oil film gets ruptured and there is metal to metal contact. The value of $\frac{ZN}{p}$ is called modules when the oil film ruptures. To prevent such conditions the bearing should operate at value of $\frac{ZN}{p}$ at least three times the minimum value of α and for large fluctuations and heavy impact the values of $\frac{Zn}{p}$ may be as high as 15 α.

**Viscosity.** It determines the load carrying capacity of an oil. Viscosity decreases with an increase in oil, temperature. The standard unit of viscosity is 'Centipoise'.

$$1 \text{ centipoise} = \frac{1}{100} \text{ of a poise}$$

$Z$ = Absolute viscosity = ρ(0.225 – 180/s)

ρ = Specific gravity of oil

$S$ = Saybolt reading in seconds.

**12.7.5. Coefficient of friction.** For self contained bearings for hydrodynamic lubrication the coefficient of friction is given empirically as below

$$\mu = \frac{33}{10^{10}}\left(\frac{ZN}{p}\right)\left(\frac{d}{c}\right) + k$$

where $k$ = Correction factor

Its value depends upon $\frac{L}{D}$ ratio

$$k = 0.002$$

when $\frac{L}{D}$ is more than 0.75 and less than 2.8

**12.7.6. Clearance ratio**. The ratio $\frac{c}{d}$ is called clearance ratio. It is 0.001 to 0.002 cm per cm of diameter.

**12.7.7. Bearing modulus or Bearing Characteristics number.** It is defined as follows :

$$\text{Bearing modulus} = \frac{ZN}{p}$$

where $Z$ = Viscosity of lubricating oil in centipoise

$N$ = R.P.M. of journal

$p$ = Bearing pressure in kg/cm$^2$

For any given bearing there is a value for bearing modulus indicated by $\alpha$ for which coefficient of friction is minimum. It is desirable that the bearing should not be operated at this value of bearing modulus to avoid wear and heating. The average value of bearing modulus should be $\frac{ZN}{p} \geq 3\alpha$. For large fluctuations and heavy impact $\frac{ZN}{p} = 15\ \alpha$.

**12.7.8. Sommerfeld number.** This number ($S$) is quite useful in the design of sleeve bearings. It is defined as follows :

$$S = \frac{ZN}{p}\left(\frac{d}{c}\right)^2 \quad \text{where} \quad c = \text{Diametral clearance.}$$

**12.7.9. Critical pressure.** The minimum operating pressure (critical pressure) is the pressure at which the oil film breaks and metal to metal contact takes place.

It is given by the following relation.

$p_c$ = Critical pressure

$$= \frac{ZN}{475 \times 10^6}\left(\frac{d}{c}\right)^2\left(\frac{L}{d+L}\right)$$

**12.7.10. Oil Flow and temperature rise.** Flow of oil through a bearing depends on the way in which oil is introduced into its journal speed, load which it carries and oil viscosity. This temperature at a given journal speed is function of rate of flow and oil film thickness which are dependent on viscosity. Fig. 12.12 shows variation of temperature rise, oil flow and viscosity with radial clearance.

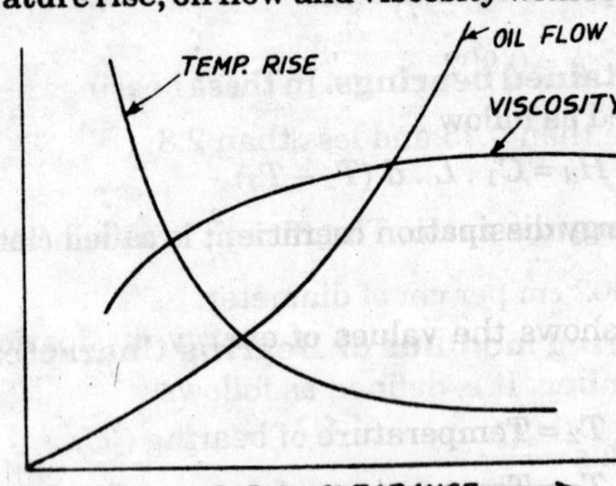


Fig. 12.12.

**12.7.11. Clearance.** There is always some clearance between shaft and bearing. The clearance depends on desired quality. Small clearances can be maintained with high grade workmanship but when costs must be reduced, the clearance are usually made larger. The clearance must be adequate to allow for expansion due to temperature and must allow sufficient space for entrance of the lubricant.

**12.7.12. Length to diameter ratio.** The ratio of length of journal to its diameter depends upon the application of bearing. For general industrial machinery the ratio $\frac{L}{d}$ varies from 1 to 2.

**12.7.13. Heating of bearings.** The frictional work is converted into heat. The heat energy thus produced at the bearings must be continuously dissipated otherwise the heat produced will result in rise in temperature will break down the lubricant and result in destruction of bearing. The usual operating temperature for bearings varies from 50 to 80°C. Heat generated ($H$) at the bearings is calculated as follows :

$$H = \frac{\mu . P . V}{427} \text{ kcal/min}$$

where $\mu$ = Coefficient of friction

$P$ = Load on bearing in kg

$V$ = Rubbing velocity in metre/min.

The rate of heat dissipation depends upon the method of lubrication. It is calculated as follows :

(*i*) **Self contained bearings.** In these bearings heat dissipated ($H_d$) is calculated as follow :

$$H_d = C_1 . L . d\ (T_2 - T_1)$$

where $C_1$ = Energy dissipation coefficient kcal/min/cm²/°C.

Table 12.1 shows the values of energy dissipation coefficient ($C_1$).

$T_2$ = Temperature of bearing (°C)

$T_1$ = Temperature of surrounding (°C)

**Table 12.1**

| *Bearing condition* | $C_1$ |
|---|---|
| Heavy duty (oil lubricated) | |
| Quiet air | 0.00042 to 0.00056 |
| Simple pillow block bearing | |
| Quiet air | 0.00021 to 0.00035 |
| Air at 150 mpm | 0.0007 to 0.0011 |

In these bearings heat generated in oil is transmitted to the bearing body from where it is dissipated to surrounding area.

$T_2$ = Temperature of bearing may be taken as

$$T_2 = T_1 + \frac{1}{2}(T_0 - T_1)$$

$$T_2 - T_1 = T_1 + \frac{1}{2}(T_0 - T_1) - T_1 = \frac{1}{2}(T_0 - T_1)$$

where $T_0$ = oil temperature.

For usual industrial applications, the upper limit of permissible oil temperature ranges from 70°C to 82°C. If the temperature is higher, bearing is cooled by water circulating through coils built in the bearing or using pressure feeding of the lubricant.

*(ii)* **Pressure Fed bearings.** In these bearings the heat removed by circulating oil is given by

$$H_d = \rho \,.\, \phi \,.\, Q(T_2 - T_1)$$

where $\rho$ = Specific gravity of oil in kg/litre

$\phi$ = Specific heat of oil in kcal/kg/°C

$Q$ = Quantity of oil in litre/min

$T_1$ = Inlet temperature of oil in °C

$T_2$ = Outlet temperature of oil in °C.

In these bearings the oil is supplied at pressure ranging from 0.7 to 7 kg/cm$^2$.

The heat dissipated should be at least equal to heat generated.

## 12.8. Bearing Materials

Bearing material should possess the following requirements.

(*i*) It should be of high compressive strength.

(*ii*) It should have low coefficient of friction.

(*iii*) It should have thermal conductivity so as to allow the rapid removal of heat produced due to friction.

(*iv*) It should have high resistance to corrosion.

(*v*) It should have sufficient fatigue strength.

(*vi*) It should have the ability to embed solid particles in oil thereby avoiding wear of shaft.

(*vii*) The material should be soft with a low modulus of elasticity.

(*viii*) Bearing material should not get weld easily to the journal material.

The bearing metal should be able to resist the temperature, it is designed for without lossing strength.

The following materials are commonly used as bearing material:

(*i*) **Lead base babbit.** It contains lead 74%, tin 10%, antimony 15%, arsenic 0.5% and Cu 0.25%.

It has excellent resistance to seizure and has good corrosion resistance. It is used for split bushings made from strip or gravity cast bearings. It should not be used above 115°C.

(*ii*) **Tin base babbit.** Its composition is as follows :

Tin = 80%

Antimony = 7.5%

Copper = 3.25%

It is slightly harder than lead babbit. It is also used for split bushings.

(*iii*) **Lead bronze.** A typical composition of lead bronze used as bearing material is as follows :

Copper = 72%

Lead = 25%

Tin = 3%

(*iv*) **Copper lead alloy.** A typical composition of copper lead alloy used as bearing material is as follows :

Cu = 55%

Lead = 45%

Table 12.1 (A) indicates some of bearing materials and their applications.

**Table 12.1 (A)**

| *Composition* | | | | *Applications* |
|---|---|---|---|---|
| *Tin* | *Antimony* | *Copper* | *Lead* | |
| 93 | 3.5 | 3.5 | — | Motor and aero engines. |
| 86 | 10.5 | 3.5 | — | Main bearings, motor and aero engines. |
| 80 | 11 | 3 | 6 | Bearing for heavy loads and high speeds. |
| 60 | 10 | 1.5 | 28.5 | Bearings for engines and electric machines, railways and tramways. |
| 40 | 10 | 1.5 | 48.5 | Heavy pressure and bearing speed. |
| 20 | 15 | 1.5 | 63.5 | Medium pressure and speed. |
| 5 | 15 | — | 80 | Long bearings with medium load. |

**12.8.1. Bearing properties.** The essential bearing properties of bearing materials are as follows :

(*i*) Wettability

(*ii*) Anti-seizure or antifrictional properties

(*iii*) Embeddability

(*iv*) Deformability.

The property of bearing metal to form an oil film to avoid metal to metal contact is called wettability.

Large amount of heat may be generated when there is metal to metal contact in a bearing and this may lead to welding or seizure of the contacting surfaces. This can result in a piece of bearing being torn out subsequently causing galling or scoring. The property of the metal that prevents such happenings is called antifrictional or antiseizure property. Bearing metals having high thermal conductivity have high antiseizure property.

Embeddability is the property by which the bearing metal can embed in itself dirt, grit or filing often present in lubricating oil. It is because of this property that these foreign materials do not spoil the shaft or gain it in the bearing. This property comes from low yield strength and softness of the metal. Some time due to some manufacturing defects the shaft is not aligned inside the bearing and produces a famming effect. The bearing metal should be able to deform itself to some extent for accommodating deflection. Bearing metals with low yield strength and low modulus of elasticity possess high deformability.

## 12.9. Bearing Caps and Bolts

Bearing caps are provided when bearings are used in two halves. The bearing cap (Fig.12.13) is designed as a simple beam loaded at the centre and supported at bolt centres.

Let $P$ = Load

$a$ = Distance between bolt centres

$L$ = Bearing length.

$t$ = cap thickness

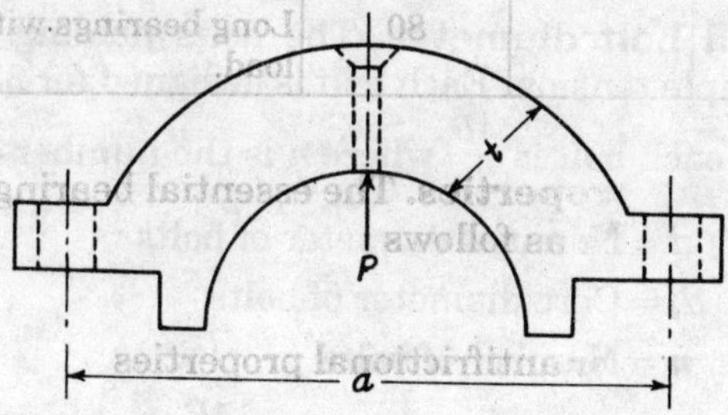


Fig. 12.13.

**(i) To find cap thickness**

$M$ = Maximum bending moment at the centre

$$= \frac{Pa}{4}$$

$$Z = \text{Section modulus} = \frac{1}{6} L t^2$$

$f$ = Bending stress

$$M = f \times Z = \frac{Lt^2}{6} \times f$$

$$\frac{Lt^2}{6} \cdot f = \frac{Pa}{4}$$

$$t = \sqrt{\frac{3\,Pa}{2\,Lf}}$$

When oil hole is provided in the cap, the length will be the bearing cap length less the diameter of oil hole.

The deflection ($y$) of the cap is given by the relation

$$y = \frac{Pa^3}{48\,EI}$$

where $I$ = Moment of inertia

$E$ = Modulus of elasticity

$$y = \frac{Pa^3}{48\,E} \times \frac{12}{Lt^3} = \frac{Pa^3}{4ELt^3}$$

$$t = \sqrt[3]{\frac{Pa^3}{4ELy}} = 0.63\,a\,\sqrt[3]{\frac{P}{ELy}}$$

(*ii*) **To find bolt diameter.** The bolts holding the cap are designed in simple tension. Each bolt is designed for 33% over load *i.e.* the load on each bolt is $\frac{4P}{3n}$ where $n$ is the number of bolts.

Let $d$ = Nominal diameter of bolts

$d_e$ = Core diameter of bolts

$n$ = Number of bolts

$F$ = Force on each bolt = $\frac{4P}{3n}$

$f_t$ = Safe tensile stress in bolts

Bolts are in tension

$$F = \frac{\pi}{4} d_c^2 \cdot f_t$$

$$d = \frac{d_c}{0.8}$$

## 12.10. Designed Parameters

Some of the design parameters for various types of bearings are given in Table 12.2.

**Table 12.2.**

| *Application* | *Bearing* | *P (kg/cm²)* | $\frac{L}{a}$ | *Z (centipoise)* | $\frac{ZN}{p}$ |
|---|---|---|---|---|---|
| Machine tools | Wrist pin | 3.5-21 | 1-3 | 10-20 | 1430-2850 |
| Punching machine | Crank pin | 350-560 | 1-2 | 100 | 115-215 |
| | Crank shaft main bearings | 140-270 | 1-2 | 100 | 115-215 |
| Automobile | Crank shaft main bearing | 20-120 | 0.8-1.5 | 25-30 | 280-430 |
| | Crank pin | 105-240 | 0.5-1.5 | 8 | 143 |
| Gas turbine | Crank shaft main bearings | 35-70 | 0.5-2 | 20-60 | 285-430 |
| | Crank pin | 85-125 | 0.8-1.5 | 20-60 | 145-285 |
| Line shafts of centrifugal pumps | Wrist pin | 7-14 | 1-2 | 25 | 430-1430 |
| Railway car | Axle | 21-35 | 1.8-2 | 500 | 700-1430 |

## 12.11. Selection of Bearings

The selection of bearings depends upon the following factors.

1. Mechanical requirements
   - (*i*) Load
   - (*ii*) Speed
   - (*iii*) Starting friction
   - (*iv*) Space requirements
   - (*v*) Type of lubrication
   - (*vi*) Power consumption
2. Environment conditions
3. Economics

(*i*) Life (*ii*) Maintenance

(*iii*) Cost

Table 12.2 (*a*) may be used as a guide for the selection of bearings.

**Table 12.2 (*a*)**

| *Service factor* | *Characteristics* | *Sliding* | *Rolling* |
|---|---|---|---|
| 1. Mechanical requirements | Load | | |
| | Unidirectional | Good | Excellent |
| | Cyclic | Good | Excellent |
| | Shock | Fair | Excellent |
| | Emergency | Fair | Fair |
| | Speed : | | |
| | Limited by | Turbulence and temperature rises | Centrifugal loading and dynamic effects |
| | Starting Friction | Poor | Good |
| | Space Requirements | | |
| | (Radial Bearings) | | |
| | Radial Dimension | Small | Large |
| | Axial Dimension | $\frac{1}{4}$ to 2 times the shaft diameter | 1/5 to $\frac{1}{2}$ times the shaft diameter |
| | Types of failure | Often permits limited emergency operation after failure | Limited operation may continue after fatigue failure but not after lubricant failure |
| | Damping of Vibrations | Good | Poor |
| | Type of Lubricant | Oil or other fluid grease dry lubricants an or gas | Oil or grease |
| | Quantity of Lubricant | Large | Small |

(*Contd...*)

| *Service factor* | *Characteristics* | *Sliding* | *Rolling* |
|---|---|---|---|
| | Noise | Quiet | May be noisy, depending upon quality of bearing and resonance of mounting |
| | Power Consumption | Depends on bearing geometry and speed | Usually lower than slider bearings |
| 2. Economics | Life | Unlimited except for cycle loading | Limited by fatigue properties of bearing metal. |
| | Maintenance | CLean lubricant is required with continuous attention | Clean Lubricant required only occasional attention grease. |
| | Cost | Very small in mass production | Intermediate |
| | Ease of replacement | Function of design and installation | Function of type of installation |
| 3. Environment conditions | Low temp. Starting High Temp. operation | Poor Limited by lubricant | Good Limited by lubricant |

**Example 12.1.** *It is required to design a journal bearing for a centrifugal pump running at 1200 R.P.M. The journal is 8 cm and load on each journal is 1800 kg. The factor* $\frac{ZN}{p}$ *for bearing is 2600. The length and diameter ratio is 1.2. Take correction factor as 0.002. The bearings and atmospheric temperatures are 80°C and 30°C respectively.*

**Solution.** (*a*) **To calculate bearing pressure**

$d$ = Diameter of journal = 8 cm

$L$ = Length of journal

$$\frac{L}{d} = 1.2$$

$L = 1.2\,d = 1.2 \times 8 = 9.6$ cm

$P$ = Load on bearing = 1800 kg

$A$ = Projected area = $L \times d$

$= 9.6 \times 8 = 76.8\ \text{cm}^2$

$p$ = Bearing pressure

$P = p \times A$

$$p = \frac{P}{A} = \frac{1800}{76.8} = 23.4 \text{ kg/cm}^2$$

**(b) To find viscosity**

$N$ = R.P.M. of journal = 1200

Now $\frac{NZ}{p} = 2600$

$$Z = \text{Viscosity} = p \times \frac{2600}{N}$$

$$= \frac{23.4 \times 2600}{1200} = 50.7 \text{ Centipoise}$$

**(c) To calculate coefficient of friction**

$\mu$ = Coefficient of friction

$$= \frac{33}{10^{10}}\left(\frac{ZN}{p}\right)\left(\frac{d}{c}\right) + k$$

where $\frac{c}{d}$ = Clearance ratio = 0.001 (say)

$k$ = Correction factor = 0.002

$$\mu = \frac{33}{10^{10}} \times 2600 \times \frac{1}{0.001} + 0.002 = 0.01058$$

**(d) To calculate heat generated and heat dissipated.**

$H$ = Heat generated

$$= \frac{\mu \,.\, P \,.\, V}{427} \text{ kcal/min}$$

$\mu = 0.01058$

$P$ = Load on bearing = 1800 kg

$$V = \frac{\pi dN}{100} = \pi \times \frac{8}{100} \times 1200 = 301.44 \text{ m/min}$$

$$H = \frac{0.01058 \times 1800 \times 301.44}{427}$$

$= 13.44$ kcal/min

$H_d$ = Heat dissipated

$= C_1 \, . \, L \, . \, d \, . \, (T_2 - T_1)$

$C_1$ = Energy dissipation coefficient

= 0.0012 (assume)

$T_2$ = Bearing temperature = 80°C

$T_1$ = Atmospheric temperature = 30°C

$H_d = 0.0012 \times 9.6 \times 8 \, (80 - 30)$

= 4.6 kcal/min.

As the rate of heat dissipation is less than rate of heat generation therefore the bearing should be cooled artificially.

**Example 12.2.** *A full journal bearing of 5 cm diameter and 10 cm length is to carry a load of 700 kg. The journal speed is 900 R.P.M. The Diametral clearance is 0.005 cm. The bearing is lubricated with oil whose absolute viscosity at the operating temperature of 75°C may be taken as 11 centipoise. The room temperature is 35°C. Calculate the power loss due to friction and the mass of oil required to dissipate the heat generated during operation. Take specific heat of oil as 0.45 kcal/kg/°C.* *(A.M.I.E. 1982)*

**Solution.** **(*a*) To calculate power loss due to friction**

$d$ = Diameter of shaft = 5 cm

$L$ = Length of shaft = 10 cm

$P$ = Load = 700 kg

$N$ = Journal speed = 900 R.P.M.

$p$ = Bearing pressure

$$= \frac{P}{L \, . \, d} = \frac{700}{10 \times 5} = 14 \text{ kg/cm}^2$$

$Z$ = Viscosity of oil

= 11 centipoise

$V$ = Rubbing velocity at the bearing

$$= \frac{\pi \, dN}{100} = \frac{\pi \times 5 \times 900}{100}$$

= 141.3 m/min

$c$ = Diametral clearance

= 0.005 cm

$k$ = Correction factor

= 0.002 (say)

$$\mu = \frac{33}{10^{10}}\left(\frac{ZN}{p}\right)\left(\frac{d}{c}\right) + k$$

$$= \frac{33}{10^{10}} \times \frac{11 \times 900}{14} \times \frac{5}{0.005} + 0.002$$

$$= 0.0043$$

$H$ = Heat generated due to friction in horse power units

$$= \frac{\mu\, PV}{4500} = \frac{0.0043 \times 700 \times 141.3}{4500}$$

$$= 0.0945 \text{ H.P.}$$

**(*b*) To calculate mass of oil**

$H$ = Heat generated

$$= \frac{\mu\, PV}{427} = \frac{0.0043 \times 700 \times 141.3}{427}$$

$$= 0.996 \text{ kcal /min.}$$

Heat generated at the bearing is taken away the lubricating oil.

Let $m$ = Mass of lubricating oil flow through the bearing per minute

$T_1$ = Inlet temperature of oil

= Room temperature = 35°C

$T_2$ = Outlet temperature of oil

= Operating temperature of bearing = 75°C

$\phi$ = Specific heat of oil

= 0.45 kcal/kg/°C

$$H = m \,.\, \phi \,.\, (T_2 - T_1)$$

$$0.996 = m \times 0.45 \times (75 - 35)$$

$$m = 0.06 \text{ kg/min.}$$

**Example 12.3.** *A journal bearing 8 cm diameter and 12 cm long supports a load of 600 kg at 900 R.P.M. If the radial clearance is 0.004 cm and frictional horse power is 1.2 calculate the viscosity of the lubricating oil.*

**Solution.**

$d$ = Diameter of journal = 8 cm

$L$ = Length of journal = 12 cm

$P$ = Load on bearing = 600 kg

$N$ = 900 R.P.M.

$p$ = Bearing pressure

$$= \frac{P}{L \times d} = \frac{600}{12 \times 8}$$

$$= 6.25 \text{ kg/cm}^2$$

$V$ = Rubbing velocity

$$= \frac{\pi dN}{100} = \frac{\pi \times 8 \times 900}{100}$$

= 226 m/min.

$c$ = Diametral clearance

= 0.004 × 2 = 0.008 cm

$K$ = 0.002

$\mu$ = Coefficient of friction.

$$= \frac{33}{10^{10}}\left(\frac{ZN}{p}\right)\left(\frac{d}{c}\right) + K$$

$$= \frac{33}{10^{10}} \times Z \times \frac{900}{6.25} \times \frac{8}{0.008} + 0.002$$

$$= 0.00047\,Z + 0.002$$

$$\text{H.P.} = \frac{\mu \,.\, P \,.\, V}{4500}$$

$$1.2 \times 4500 = (0.00047\,Z + 0.002) \times 600 \times 226$$

$$Z = 80.4 \text{ centipoise.}$$

**Example 12.4.** *Design the bearing cap for a journal bearing with journal diameter of 10 cm. The length of bearing is 15 cm. The distance between bolts centres is 14 cm. The load on the cap is 1200 kg. The cap is made up of cast iron with an allowable tensile strength of 270 kg/cm². The dafe tensile stress in bolts is 360 kg/cm².*

**Solution.** (*a*) **To calculate cap thickness**

$a$ = Distance between bolts centres = 14 cm.

$L$ = Length of bearing = 15 cm

$P$ = Load = 1200 kg

$f$ = Safe tensile stress in cap

= 270 kg/cm²

$t$ = Cap thickness

$$= \sqrt{\frac{3\,Pa}{2\,L_f}} = \sqrt{\frac{3 \times 1200 \times 14}{2 \times 15 \times 270}}$$

$$= 2.5 \text{ cm.}$$

**(b) To calculate bolt diameter**

Let $d$ = Nominal diameter of bolt

$d_1$ = Core Diameter of bolt

$n$ = Number of bolts = 2

$F$ = Load on each bolt

$$= \frac{P}{2} \times \frac{4}{3}$$

Assuming that each bolt will take up a load of 4/3 times the usual load

$$F = \frac{1200}{2} \times \frac{4}{3} = 800 \text{ kg.}$$

$f_t$ = Safe tensile stress in each bolt = 360 kg/cm$^2$

The bolts are in tension

$$F = \frac{\pi}{4} d_1^2 \times f_t$$

where $d_1$ = Core diameter of bolt.

$$800 = \frac{\pi}{4} d_1^2 \times 360\,,\; d_1 = 1.68 \text{ cm.}$$

and $$d = \frac{d_1}{0.8} = \frac{1.68}{0.8} = 2.1 \text{ cm.}$$

**Example 12.5.** *A full journal bearing has journal of diameter 5 cm. The bearing length is 7 cm and radial load of the bearing is 2200 kg. The journal rotates at 1400 R.P.M. If the radial clearance is 0.005 cm and minimum oil film thickness is 0.0012 cm determine the mean viscosity of lubricating oil.*

**Solution.**

$d$ = Diameter of journal = 5 cm

$L$ = Bearing length = 7 cm

$P$ = Load = 2200 kg

$N$ = R.P.M. of journal = 1400 R.P.M..

$t$ = Oil film thickness = 0.0012 cm

$C_r$ = Radial clearance

$$= 0.005 \text{ cm}$$

$V$ = Rubbing velocity

$$= \pi \frac{dN}{60} = \pi \times 5 \times \frac{1400}{60} = 366 \text{ cm/sec.}$$

$r$ = Radius of journal = 2.5 cm

$Z$ = Viscosity of lubricating oil in kg sec/cm$^2$

$e$ = Eccentricity ratio

$$= 1 - \frac{t}{C_r} = 1 - \frac{0.0012}{0.005}$$

$$= 0.76.$$

The load carrying capacity of a bearing is given by

$$P = \frac{12 \pi ZVL r^2 e}{C_r^2 (\sqrt{(1-e^2)} (2+e^2)}$$

$$2200 = \frac{12 \pi Z \times 366 \times 7 \times (2.5)^2 \times 0.76}{(0.005)^2 \sqrt{1-(0.76)^2} \times (2+0.76)^2}$$

On simplification this will give

$$Z = 0.2 \times 10^{-6} \frac{\text{kg sec}}{\text{cm}^2}$$

$$= 0.2 \times 10^{-2} \frac{\text{kg sec}}{\text{m}^2}$$

Now $\frac{1 \text{ kg sec}}{\text{m}^2} = 98.1 \times 10^2$ centipoise

$$Z = 0.2 \times 10^{-2} \times 98.1 \times 10^2$$

$$= 19.62 \text{ centipoise.}$$

**Example 12.6.** *Design a collar bearing to take a thrust of 18,000 kg. The bearing pressure is 10 kg/cm$^2$ when the shaft rotates at 150 R.P.M. The bearing collars are of 32 cm internal and 42 cm external diameter. The effective friction area of bearing pad is 85%, of collar area and coefficient of friction is 0.03. The safe shear stress in collars is 300 kg/cm$^2$.*

**Solution.** (*a*) **To calculate the number of collars**

$d_1$ = Inside diameter of collar = 32 cm

$d_2$ = Outside diameter of collar = 42 cm

$n$ = Number of collars

$t$ = Thickness of collar

$p$ = Bearing pressure = 10 kg/cm$^2$

$\mu = 0.03$

$N$ = 150 R.P.M.

$P$ = 18,000 kg.

$A$ = Effective friction area

$$= n \times \frac{\pi}{4}(d_2^2 - d_1^2) \times 0.85$$

$$= n \times \frac{\pi}{4}(42^2 - 32^2) \times 0.85 = n \times 494 \text{ cm}^2$$

$$P = A \times p$$

$$18{,}000 = n \times 494 \times 10$$

$$n = 3.64$$

We adopt 4 collars

$$\therefore \quad n = 4$$

Collar Bearing is shown in Fig. 12.4 (*a*)

**(*b*) To calculate thickness of collar**

Consider shearing failure of collars

$f_s$ = Safe shear stress in each collar = 300 kg/cm$^2$

$A$ = Shearing area = $n \times \pi\, d_1 \times t = 4 \times \pi \times 32 \times t = 402\, t$ cm$^2$

$$P = A \times f_s$$

$$18{,}000 = 402 \times t \times 300$$

$$t = 0.15 \text{ cm}$$

As it is too small, we adopt

$$t = 0.5 \text{ cm.}$$

**(*c*) To calculate H.P. lost in friction**

$T$ = Torque required to overcome friction at the collar bearing.

$$= \frac{2}{3}\mu \,.\, P \,.\left[\frac{r_2^3 - r_1^3}{s_2^2 - r_1^2}\right]$$

$$= \frac{2}{3} \times 0.03 \times 18000\left[\frac{21^3 - 16^3}{21^2 - 16^2}\right]$$

$$= 10{,}051 \text{ kg cm} = 100.51 \text{ kg m.}$$

$$\text{H.P.} = 2\pi \frac{NT}{4500} = \frac{2\pi \times 150 \times 100.51}{4500} = 21.$$

**Example 12.7.** *Make a dimensioned sketch of a foot step bearing of a simple design proportioning the bearing surface so that the vertical shaft carry a load so 800 kg while running at a speed of 120 R.P.M. Allow a maximum bearing presume of 16 kg/cm². If the coefficient of friction is 0.04, calculate the power lost in friction at the bearing.*

**Solution.** (*a*) **To calculate shaft diameter**

$d$ = Shaft diameter

$p$ = Bearing pressure = 16 kg/cm²

$P$ = Load = 800 kg

$$P = \frac{\pi}{4} d^2 \times p$$

$$800 = \frac{\pi}{4} d^3 \times 16$$

$$d = 8 \text{ cm}$$

(*b*) **To calculate horse power lost in friction**

$T$ = Friction torque $= \frac{2}{3} \mu \,.\, P \,.\, r$

$r$ = Radius of shaft = 4 cm

$\mu$ = Coefficient of friction = 0.04

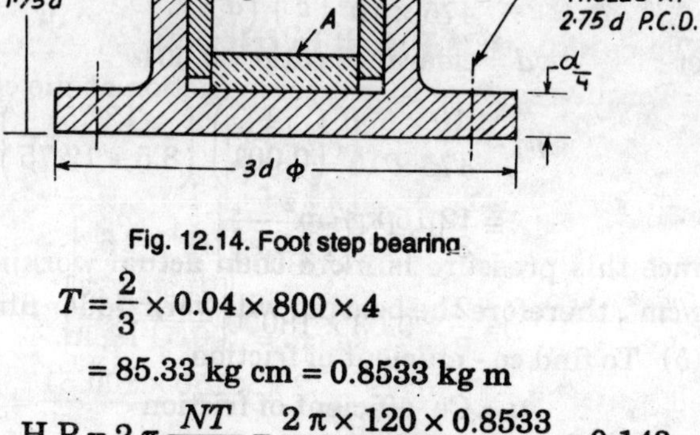


Fig. 12.14. Foot step bearing.

$$T = \frac{2}{3} \times 0.04 \times 800 \times 4$$

$$= 85.33 \text{ kg cm} = 0.8533 \text{ kg m}$$

$$\text{H.P} = 2\,\pi \frac{NT}{4500} = \frac{2\,\pi \times 120 \times 0.8533}{4500} = 0.143$$

Fig. 12.14. shows a foot step bearings. It has a steel disc A of thickness $\frac{d}{4}$ and a brass bush *B* to reduce friction.

**Example 12.7.** *(a) A journal bearing is to support a load of 460 kg at 600 RPM using a hardened steel journal and a bronze backet babbit bearing. If room temperature is 20°C and oil temperature 78°C. Design the bearing for a machine tool.*

**Solution.** (*a*) **To find bearing pressure.** From Table 12.2

Let $\frac{ZN}{p} = 1430$

$Z = 10$ (centipoise)

$N = 600$ RPM

$$\frac{ZN}{p} = 1430.$$

$$\frac{10 \times 600}{p} = 1430.$$

$$p = 4.2 \text{ kg/cm}^2$$

Let $L$ = Length of journal

$d$ = Diameter of journal

$L = 1.5\, d$ (say)

$P$ = Load = 460 kg

$$460 = L \,.\, d \,.\, p = 1.5\, d \times d \times p = 1.5 \times d^2 \times 4.2$$

$$d = 8.5 \text{ cm}$$

$$L = 1.5 \times 8.5 = 12.75 \text{ cm}$$

$p_1$ = permissible bearing pressure

$$= \frac{ZN}{475 \times 10^6}\left(\frac{d}{c}\right)^2\left(\frac{L}{d+L}\right)$$

Let $c/d$ = clearance ratio = 0.001

$$p_1 = \frac{10 \times 600}{475 \times 10^6}\left(\frac{1}{0.001}\right)^2\left(\frac{12.75}{8.5 + 12.75}\right)$$

$$= 12.15 \text{ kg/cm}^2$$

Since this pressure is more than actual working pressure of 4.2 kg/cm², therefore the bearing will work under film lubrication.

(*b*) To find co - efficient of friction

$\mu$ = Co–efficient of friction

$$= \frac{33}{10^{10}} \times \frac{ZN}{p} \times \frac{d}{c} + K$$

$$\mu = \frac{33}{10^{10}} \times \frac{10 \times 600}{4.2} \times 1000 + 0.002 = 0.006$$

(*c*) **To find heat generated and heat dissipated.**

$$H = \text{Heat generated}$$

$$= \frac{\mu PV}{427} \text{ K cal/min} \qquad \text{where } V = \pi dN$$

$$= \frac{0.006 \times 460 \times \pi}{427} \times \frac{8.5}{100} \times 600$$

$$= 1.04 \text{ K cal/min}$$

$$H_4 = \text{Heat dissipated} = C_1 \,.\, L.\, d.\, (T_2 - T_1)$$

where $C_1 = 0.00056$

$L = 12.75$ cm

$d = 8.5$ cm

$T_1$ = Temperature of surroundings = 20°C

$T_2$ = Temperature of bearing = $T_1 + ½\,(T_0 - T_1)$

where $T_0$ = oil temperature

$$T_2 - T_1 = T_1 + \frac{1}{2}(T_0 - T_1) - T_1 = \frac{1}{2}(T_0 - T_1)$$

$$= \frac{1}{2}(78 - 20) = 29°\text{C}$$

$$H_d = 0.00056 \times 8.5 \times 12.75 \times 29 = 1.76 \text{ K cal/min}$$

Since $H_d$ is more than $H$, hence design is safe.

## 12.12. Ball and Roller Bearings

They provide rolling friction in place of sliding friction and hence lower the friction resistance. The case and simplicity of lubrication in these so called antifriction bearings is quite noteworthy. In these bearings a supply of oil or grease placed in the housing of the bearing need not be replenised for about six months if bearings is protected properly from dirt and moisture. They can easily take up both radial and thrust loads simultaneously. These bearings can accommodate themselves to rather heavy overloads for sufficient time. In ball bearings the balls are made up of high carbon alloy steels and inner and outer races are made up of high carbon chrome alloy steel.

## 12.13. Standard Dimensions and Designation of Ball Bearings

The ball bearings are available in standard dimensions. Bearings are made in five standard series as follows :

(*i*) **Extra light (100 series) bearings.** They are able to take up less load.

(*ii*) **Light (200 series) bearings.** They are used for medium loads.

(*iii*) **Medium (300 series) bearings.**

(*iv*) **Heavy (400 series) bearings.** Medium (300 series) are used for relatively heavy load whereas heavy (400 series) bearings are used for still heavier loads.

(*v*) **Extra heavy (500 series) bearings.** They are used to carry very heavy loads.

The dimensions of some standard ball bearings are given in Table 12.3.

**Table 12.3**

| *Bearing Number* | *d (mm)* | *D (mm)* | | | b (*mm*) | | |
|---|---|---|---|---|---|---|---|
| | | *200 Series* | *300 Series* | *400 Series* | *200 Series* | *800 Series* | *400 Series* |
| 00 | 10 | 30 | 35 | | 9 | 11 | |
| 01 | 12 | 32 | 37 | | 10 | 12 | |
| 02 | 15 | 35 | 42 | | 11 | 13 | |
| 03 | 17 | 40 | 47 | 62 | 12 | 14 | |
| 04 | 20 | 47 | 52 | 72 | 14 | 15 | |
| 05 | 25 | 52 | 62 | 80 | 15 | 17 | 21 |
| 06 | 30 | 62 | 72 | 90 | 16 | 19 | 23 |
| 07 | 35 | 72 | 80 | 100 | 17 | 21 | 25 |
| 08 | 40 | 80 | 90 | 110 | 18 | 23 | 27 |
| 09 | 45 | 85 | 100 | 120 | 19 | 25 | 29 |
| 10 | 50 | 90 | 110 | 130 | 20 | 27 | 31 |
| 11 | 55 | 100 | 120 | 140 | 21 | 29 | 33 |

(*Contd...*)

| 12 | 60 | 110 | 130 | 150 | 22 | 31 | 35 |
|---|---|---|---|---|---|---|---|
| 13 | 65 | 120 | 140 | 160 | 23 | 33 | 37 |
| 14 | 70 | 125 | 150 | 180 | 24 | 35 | 42 |
| 15 | 75 | 130 | 160 | 190 | 25 | 37 | 45 |
| 16 | 80 | 140 | 170 | 200 | 26 | 39 | 48 |
| 17 | 85 | 150 | 180 | 210 | 28 | 41 | 52 |
| 18 | 90 | 160 | 190 | 225 | 30 | 43 | 54 |
| 19 | 95 | 170 | 200 | 240 | 32 | 45 | |
| 20 | 100 | 180 | 215 | 250 | 34 | 47 | |

$d$ = Bore

$D$ = Outside diameter

$b$ = Width of races.

## 12.14. Bearing Life

Ball or roller bearing life is defined as the number of revolutions (or hours at some given constant speed) that 90% of a group of apparently identical bearings will complete or exceed before the signs of fatigue appear in the material of one of the races or any of the rolling element. Life of a bearing is a function of load. It is observed that life of a bearing ($L$) is inversely proportional to the $n$ power of the equivalent bearing load ($P$).

$$L \propto \frac{1}{P^n}$$

$$\frac{L_1}{L_2} = \left(\frac{P_2}{P_1}\right)^n$$

where $n = 3$ for ball bearings

and $n = \frac{10}{3}$ for roller bearings.

## 12.15. Dynamic Load Ratings

It is also called basic dynamic capacity and is defined as the radiant load that a ball bearing can withstand for one million revolutions of the inner ring with 10% failure.

$C$ = Dynamic load rating

$$P = \text{Load}$$

Rating life, $L = \left(\frac{C}{P}\right)^3$ millions of revolutions

$$P = C \times \left(\frac{1}{L}\right)^{\frac{1}{3}}$$

If, $N = R.P.M.$

$L$ = Life in hours

Then the value of equivalent load is found from the following relation :

$$P = C\left(\frac{10^6}{60NL}\right)^{1/3}$$

$$\frac{C}{P} = \text{Loading ratio}$$

Bearing life is generally referred to as $L_{10}$ life on a 10% of failure or 90% survival rate. A bearing with $5L_{10}$ life means life is $5 \times 10^6$ revolutions

$$C = \left(\frac{L}{L_{10}}\right)^{1/n} \times P$$

where $L_{10}$ = Life of bearing for 90% survival at one million revolution

$n = 3$ for ball bearings

$= \frac{10}{3}$ for roller bearings

The bearing life for various types of machines is given in Table 12.4.

**Table 12.4**

| *Type of machine* | *Life (hours)* |
|---|---|
| Machines working continuously for 24 hours | 40,000—60,000 |
| Machines working for 24 hours continuously with high degree of reliability | 1,00,000—2,00,000 |
| Machines for use 8 hours a day and fully utilised | 20,000—30,000 |
| Machines is used for 8 hours but not fully utilised | 12,000—20,000 |
| Air craft engines | 1,000—2,000 |

The fatigue life of the bearings is considerably reduced by temperature rise. This should be taken into account if bearings are to be operated at high temperature.

Table 12.4 (*a*) indicates the decrease in capacity of bearings operated at high temperature.

**Table 12.4** (*a*)

| *Bearing temperature* °C | *Decrease in capacity (%)* |
|---|---|
| 125 | 5 |
| 150 | 10 |
| 175 | 15 |
| 200 | 25 |
| 225 | 35 |

## 12.16. Static Load Rating

It is defined as a load acting on a non-rotating bearing under which permanent deformation should appear in balls and race ways. The static equivalent load is defined as that static load which if applied would cause the same total permanent deformation as that which occurs under the actual conditions of loading.

The basic static load rating ($C_0$) for ball bearing is given by the following formula :

$$C_0 = f_1 \cdot I \cdot z \cdot d_1^2 \cdot \cos\alpha$$

where $f_1$ = 0.34 for self aligning ball bearings

= 1.25 for radial contact and angular contact ball bearings.

$I$ = Number of rows of balls in any one bearing.

$z$ = Number of balls per row

$d_1$ = Ball diameter in mm.

$\alpha$ = Nominal angle of contact–the angle between line of action of ball load and a plane perpendicular to bearing axis.

## 12.17. Load Calculation for Radial Ball Bearings

The limiting load ($P$) for various types of bearing is calculated as follows :

(*i*) **Stastically loaded bearings.** These bearings rotate at very slow speed,

$$P = \frac{4.37\,F}{z}$$

where $F$ = Radial load on bearing

$z$ = Number of balls in bearing

When the bearing is subjected to both radial and thrust loads the equivalent bearing load ($P$) is calculated as follows :

$$P = XF + YQ$$

where $F$ = Actual constant radial load

$X$ = Radial factor of bearing

$Y$ = Thrust factor of bearing

$Q$ = Actual constant thrust load

The values of $X$ and $Y$ are given in Table 12.5.

**Table 12.5**

| *Bearing type* | | *Single row bearing* | | *Double row bearing* | |
|---|---|---|---|---|---|
| | | $X$ | $Y$ | $X$ | $Y$ |
| Angular | $\alpha = 20^\circ$ | 0.5 | 0.42 | 1 | 0.84 |
| Contact | $\alpha = 25^\circ$ | 0.5 | 0.38 | 1 | 0.76 |
| Groove ball | $\alpha = 38^\circ$ | 0.5 | 0.33 | 1 | 0.66 |
| Bearings | $\alpha = 40^\circ$ | 0.5 | 0.26 | 1 | 0.52 |
| Radial contact groove ball bearing | | 0.6 | 0.5 | 0.6 | 0.5 |
| Self aligning ball bearings | | 0.5 | $0.22 \cot \alpha$ | 1 | $0.14 \cot \alpha$ |

(*ii*) **Dynamically loaded bearings.** For dynamically loaded bearings under the combined action of radial and thrust loads the equivalent load ($P$) is given by

$$P = X_1 V F + Y_1 Q$$

where, $X_1$ = Radial factor, $Y_1$ = Thrust factor

$X_1 = 1, Y_1 = 1.5$ for radial ball bearings

$X_1 = 0.5, Y_1 = 1$ for angular contact bearings

$X_1 = 0.5, Y_1 = 2.5$ for self aligning bearings.

$V$ = Rotation factor

= 1 for self–aligning bearings

= 1.2 for all types of bearings except self aligning bearings if inner race is stationary.

A simplified formula to find equivalent load is

$$P = \frac{F + 3Q}{2} \quad \text{if } Q => \frac{1}{3} F$$

$$= \frac{F + 4Q}{3} \quad \text{if } Q > \frac{1}{2} F$$

(*iii*) **Thrust ball bearings.** The basic static load ($C_{0\,\alpha}$) rating in kg for thrust ball bearing is given by

$$C_{0\,\alpha} = f \,.\, z \,.\, d_1^2 \sin \alpha$$

where $f$ = Constant = 5

$z$ = Number of balls carrying thrust in one direction

$d_1$ = Ball diameter in mm

$\alpha$ = Normal angle of contact.

## 12.18. Roller Bearings

The rating life ($L$) in millions of revolution is related to equivalent bearing load ($P$) as follows :

$$L = \left(\frac{C}{P}\right)^{10/3} \text{ million revolutions}$$

The basic static load ($C_0$) rating for radial roller bearings is given by the following relation :

$C$ = Basic static load rating

$= f_1 \,.\, z \,.\, L_e \,.\, d_1 \,.\, \cos \alpha \,.\, I$

where $L_e$ = Effective length of contact between one roller. and that ring where the contact is shortest.

$I$ = Number of rows of balls in any one bearing.

$f_1$ = Constant = 2.2

$z$ = Number of ball per row.

The static equivalent load ($P$) for radial roller bearings subjected to combined radial and thrust loads is given by the formula

$$P = XF + YQ$$

where, for self aligning and tapered roller bearings ($\alpha \neq 0^o$).

$X = 0.5$ Single row bearings

$Y = 0.22 \cot \alpha$

$X = 1$ Double row bearings

$Y = 0.44 \cot \alpha$

For self-aligning and tapered roller bearings subjected to constant radial and constant thrust loads, the equivalent load is calculated as follows :

$$P = XVF + YQ$$

The values of factors $X$, $Y$ and $V$ are indicated in Table 12.6.

## 12.19. Design Load for Ball Bearings

The design load for ball bearings is calculated as follows :

$$W = \text{Design load in kg}$$
$$= P \cdot K_L \cdot K_A \cdot K_T$$

where $P$ = Equivalent load in kg

$K_L$ = Speed factor

$K_A$ = Application factor or service factor

$K_T$ = Thrust factor

The values of $K_A$ are indicated in Table 12.7.

**Table 12.6.**

| Bearing Type | V | | X | | | | Y | | | | e |
|---|---|---|---|---|---|---|---|---|---|---|---|
| | If in Relation to the load the inner Ring is Rotating | Stationary | Single-Row Roller Bearings | | Double-Row Roller Bearings | | For Single-Row Roller Bearings | | For Double-Row Roller Bearingss | | For Single and Double row Roller Bearings |
| | | | when $\frac{Q}{VF} \le e$ | when $\frac{Q}{VF} > e$ | when $\frac{Q}{VF} \le e$ | when $\frac{Q}{VF} > e$ | when $\frac{Q}{VF} \le e$ | when $\frac{Q}{VF} > e$ | when $\frac{Q}{VF} \le e$ | when $\frac{Q}{VF} > e$ | |
| Self-aligning roller bearings and tapered roller bearing $a \neq 0$ | 1 | 1.2 | 1 | 0.4 | 1 | 0.67 | 0 | 0.4 cot $a$ | 0.45 cot $a$ | 0.67 cot $a$ | 1.5 tan $a$ |

**Table 12.7.**

| Type of service | | $K_A$ |
|---|---|---|
| | *Ball bearing* | *Roller bearing* |
| Heavy shock load | 2.5 | 1.7 |
| Moderate shock load | 2 | 1.3 |
| Light shock load | 1.5 | 1 |
| Steady load | 1 | 1 |

$K_S$ = Speed factor

$$= \sqrt[3]{\frac{N_A}{N_C}}$$

where $N_A$ = Rotation speed of bearing in R.P.M.

$N_C$ = Catalogue speed of bearing, RPM

$K_L$ = Life factor

$$= \sqrt[3]{\frac{L}{L_C} \times K_R}$$

where $L$ = Desired life of bearing (hours)

$L_C$ = Catalogue life of bearings (hours)

$K_R$ = Reliability factor.

The values of $K_R$ depend upon the per cent bearings which will not fail during catalogue rated life and are indicated in Table 12.8.
$A$ = Per cent bearings which will not fail during catalogue rated life

**Table 12.8.**

| $A$ | |
|---|---|
| 0 | ∞ |
| 10 | 14.5 |
| 20 | 10 |
| 30 | 8 |
| 40 | 6.4 |

*(Contd...)*

| A | |
|---|---|
| 50 | 5 |
| 60 | 4 |
| 70 | 3 |
| 80 | 2 |
| 90 | 1 |
| 100 | 0 |

Values of thrust factor ($K_T$) are indicated in Table 12.9.

**Table 12.9. Thrust Factor ($K_T$)**

| *Ratio thrust load / Radial load* | *Single row bearings* | *Double row bearings* |
|---|---|---|
| 0.1 | 1 | 1.1 |
| 0.2 | 1 | 1.2 |
| 0.4 | 1.1 | 1.4 |
| 0.6 | 1.4 | 1.6 |
| 0.8 | 1.7 | 1.8 |
| 1 | 2.0 | 2 |
| 2 | 3.5 | 3 |
| 3 | 5.0 | 4 |
| 4 | 6.50 | 5 |
| 5 | 8.0 | 6 |

## 12.20. Loading Ratio

The loading ratio $\frac{C}{P}$ for different lives expressed in million of revolutions is indicated in Table 12.10 for ball bearings and in Table 12.11 for roller bearings.

**Table 12.10.**

| *Life in millions of revolutions (L)* | $\frac{C}{P}$ |
|---|---|
| 0.5 | 0.793 |
| 1 | 1 |
| 2 | 1.26 |
| 4 | 1.59 |
| 8 | 2 |
| 16 | 2.52 |
| 20 | 2.71 |
| 50 | 3.68 |
| 100 | 4.64 |
| 200 | 5.85 |
| 400 | 7.37 |
| 1000 | 10 |
| 2000 | 12.6 |
| 8000 | 15.9 |
|  | 20 |

**Table 12.11.**

| *Life in millions of revolutions (L)* | $\frac{C}{P}$ |
|---|---|
| 0.5 | 0.812 |
| 1 | 1 |
| 2 | 1.24 |
| 4 | 1.52 |
| 8 | 1.87 |
| 20 | 2.46 |
| 50 | 3.23 |
| 100 | 3.98 |
| 200 | 4.9 |
| 400 | 6.03 |
| 1000 | 7.94 |
| 2000 | 9.78 |
| 4000 | 12 |
| 8000 | 14.8 |

## 12.21. Radial Load Capacity

Table 12.12 shows typical radial capacity of ball bearings based on an average life of 10,000 hours and Table 12.13 indicates radial capacity of roller bearings.

## Table 12.12.

| Bearing No. | Bore mm | Radial-load capacity lb. at 500 R.P.M. | | | | | | | | | | | | | | | | |
|---|---|---|---|---|---|---|---|---|---|---|---|---|---|---|---|---|---|---|
| | | *Deep-groove type* | | | | *Filling slot type* | | | *Angular type* | | | *Two-row spherical type* | | | *Two-row angular type* | | |
| | | *Series* | | | | *Series* | | | *Series* | | | *Series* | | | *Series* | | |
| | | 100 | 220 | 300 | 400 | 200 | 300 | 400 | 200 | 300 | 400 | 200 | 300 | 400 | 200 | 300 | 400 |
| 00 | 10 | 167 | 190 | 330 | — | — | — | — | 265 | 330 | — | 205 | 310 | — | — | — | — |
| 01 | 12 | 185 | 220 | 380 | — | — | — | — | 330 | 410 | — | 250 | 360 | — | 335 | — | — |
| 02 | 15 | 200 | 260 | 470 | — | — | — | — | 415 | 515 | — | 290 | 430 | — | 470 | — | — |
| 03 | 17 | 214 | 330 | 560 | 910 | — | — | — | 455 | 610 | 1025 | 360 | 505 | 770 | 515 | 930 | 1690 |
| 04 | 20 | 366 | 400 | 650 | 1380 | — | 970 | — | 615 | 735 | 1550 | 495 | 640 | 1050 | 770 | 1020 | 2080 |
| 05 | 25 | 395 | 500 | 910 | 1610 | — | 1200 | — | 660 | 1025 | 1900 | 610 | 770 | 1140 | 840 | 1530 | 2610 |
| 06 | 30 | 544 | 610 | 1190 | 1945 | 940 | 1460 | — | 1020 | 1335 | 2290 | 760 | 1050 | 1370 | 1160 | 2020 | 3090 |
| 07 | 35 | 677 | 850 | 1500 | 2290 | 1270 | 1820 | — | 1270 | 1685 | 2690 | 880 | 1240 | 1740 | 1550 | 2540 | 4010 |
| 08 | 40 | 717 | 1000 | 1840 | 2630 | 1560 | 2200 | — | 1675 | 2070 | 3285 | 1000 | 1460 | 1960 | 1660 | 3120 | 4980 |
| 09 | 45 | 920 | 1110 | 2220 | 3070 | 1660 | 2880 | — | 1775 | 2245 | 3615 | 1210 | 1870 | 2360 | 1820 | 3740 | 5640 |
| 10 | 50 | 972 | 1220 | 2490 | 3510 | 1840 | 3850 | — | 1950 | 2905 | 4270 | 1300 | 2120 | 2870 | 2120 | 4450 | 6780 |

| Bearing No. | Bore mm | Radial-load capacity lb. at 500 R.P.M. | | | | | | | | | | | | | | | | |
|---|---|---|---|---|---|---|---|---|---|---|---|---|---|---|---|---|---|---|
| | | *Deep-groove type* | | | | *Filling slot type* | | | *Angular type* | | | Two-row spherical type | | | *Two-row angular type* | | |
| | | *Series* | | | | Series | | | *Series* | | | *Series* | | | *Series* | | |
| | | *100* | *200* | *300* | *400* | *200* | *300* | *400* | *200* | *300* | *400* | *200* | *300* | *400* | *200* | *300* | *400* |
| 11 | 55 | 1320 | 1540 | 2940 | 4000 | 2300 | 3850 | — | 2250 | 3430 | 4870 | 1590 | 2530 | 3100 | 2540 | 5950 | 7490 |
| 12 | 60 | 1390 | 1640 | 3050 | 4510 | — | — | — | 2520 | 4000 | 5595 | 1850 | 2900 | 3390 | 3110 | 6320 | 8770 |
| 13 | 65 | 1457 | 1890 | 3990 | 5050 | — | — | — | 2935 | 4595 | 6145 | 1970 | 3110 | 3920 | 3220 | 7650 | 9650 |
| 14 | 70 | 1840 | 2070 | 4500 | 6210 | — | — | — | 3330 | 5240 | 7550 | 2250 | 3650 | 4800 | 3640 | 8240 | 11000 |
| 15 | 75 | 1925 | 2280 | 4800 | 6820 | — | — | — | 3740 | 5610 | 8305 | 2360 | 3920 | 5080 | 3980 | 8700 | 12400 |
| 16 | 80 | 2280 | 2490 | 5070 | 7470 | — | — | — | 4050 | 6180 | 9080 | 2570 | 4330 | 5350 | 4430 | 10300 | 14900 |
| 17 | 85 | 2485 | 2940 | 5680 | 8130 | — | — | — | 4550 | 7090 | 9895 | 2880 | 4780 | 6700 | 5150 | 10500 | 16000 |
| 18 | 90 | 2750 | 3140 | 6200 | 8825 | — | — | — | 5140 | 7560 | 10740 | 3340 | 5480 | 7980 | 5900 | 12400 | 16600 |
| 19 | 95 | 2880 | 3620 | 6980 | 10280 | — | — | — | 5905 | 8750 | 12510 | 3740 | 6100 | 8500 | 6700 | 12900 | 20300 |
| 20 | 100 | 3000 | 3920 | 7680 | 11825 | — | — | — | 6740 | 9290 | 14390 | 4100 | 7100 | 10600 | 7160 | 16100 | 22700 |
| 21 | 105 | 3380 | 4120 | 8400 | — | — | — | — | 7115 | 10480 | — | 4460 | 7450 | — | 8500 | 17500 | — |

**Note :-** The values should be multiplied by 0.45 to have load in kg.

**Table 12.13.**
**(Capacity in lb)**

| | | *Load capacity at 500 R.P.M.* | | |
|---|---|---|---|---|
| *Bearing No.* | *Bore (mm)* | *Series 200* | *Series 300* | *Series 400* |
| 00 | 10 | 370 | 616 | — |
| 01 | 12 | 415 | 795 | — |
| 02 | 15 | 460 | 895 | — |
| 03 | 17 | 595 | 1090 | 2040 |
| 04 | 20 | 745 | 1290 | 2680 |
| 05 | 25 | 895 | 1760 | 3370 |
| 06 | 30 | 1320 | 2450 | 4150 |
| 07 | 35 | 1540 | 2660 | 5000 |
| 08 | 40 | 1840 | 3220 | 6000 |
| 09 | 45 | 2150 | 4050 | 7070 |
| 10 | 50 | 2450 | 4980 | 8240 |

The above values should be multiplied by 0.45 to have load in kg.

## 12.22. Lubrication of Rolling Bearings

Proper lubrication is needed to protect the bearings against corrosion, to remove heat generated for meeting load, speed and temperature requirements.

Greases are quite suitable

$$L_f = K\left[\frac{14 \times 10^6}{N\sqrt{d}} - 4d\right]$$

where $L_f$ = Service life of grease or lubrication interval (hours)

$K$ = Factor dependent on type of bearing

$N$ = R.P.M.

$d$ = Bearing bore diameter (mm)

The values of factor $K$ are indicated in Table 12.14.

**Table 12.14.**

| *Bearing type* | *K* |
|---|---|
| Spherical roller and taper roller bearings | 1 |
| Cylindrical roller and needle roller bearings | 6 |
| Radial ball bearings | 10 |

**Example 12.8.** *Select a suitable single row radial ball bearing to carry a radial load of 150 kg and a thrust load of 120 kg at 900 R.P.M. The bearing is to be used 7 hours per day and average service life of 8 years is desired.*

**Solution.** $F$ = Radial load = 150 kg

$Q$ = Thrust load = 120 kg

$P$ = Equivalent load

As $Q > \frac{1}{2} \times F$

$$\therefore \quad P = \frac{F + 4Q}{3} = \frac{150 + 4 \times 120}{3} = 210 \text{ kg}$$

Desired life = 8 × 300 × 7

$L$ = 16,800 hours

Assuming 300 working days per year

$$K_S = \text{Speed factor} = \sqrt[3]{\frac{N_A}{N_C}}$$

where $N_A$ = Rotational speed of bearing = 900 R.P.M.

$N_C$ = Catalogue speed of bearing

= 500 R.P.M. (see Table 12.12)

$$K_S = \sqrt[3]{\frac{900}{500}} = 1.2$$

$K_L$ = Life factor

$$= \sqrt[3]{\frac{L}{L_C \times K_R}}$$

where $L$ = Desired life = 16,800 hours

$L_C$ = Catalogue life of bearing

= 10,000 hours (see Table 12.12)

$K_R$ = Reliability factor

$= 1$ (see Table 12.8)

$$K_L = \sqrt[3]{\frac{16{,}800}{10{,}000} \times 1} = 1.18$$

$K_T$ = Thrust factor = 1.7

Thrust factor depends upon ratio of $= \dfrac{\text{Thrust load}}{\text{Radial load}}$

(see Table 12.9)

$K_A$ = Application factor

$= 1.5$ (see Table 12.7)

$W$ = Design load for bearing

$= P \, . \, K_L \, . \, K_S \, . \, K_A \, . \, K_T$

$= 210 \times 1.18 \times 1.2 \times 1.5 \times 1.7$

$= 758.3$ kg.

For this load bearing No.308 deep groove type with a capacity of 1840 kg may be selected (see Table 12.12).

**Example 12.9.** *A ball bearing has a desired life of 8000 hours (for 90% of the bearing) for a speed of 400 R.P.M. and a radial load of 420 kg. Determine the specific dynamic capacity.*

**Solution.**

$L$ = Desired life = 8000 hours

$= 8000 \times 400 \times 60$

$= 192 \times 10^6$ Revolutions

$$= 192 \times \frac{10^6}{10^6}$$

$= 192$ millions of revolutions

$P$ = Equivalent bearing load = 420 kg

$C$ = Dynamic load rating

$$L = \left(\frac{C}{P}\right)^3$$

$C = L^{1/3} \times P$

$= (192)^{1/3} \times 420 = 5.67 \times 420$

$= 2381.4$ kg.

**Example 12.10.** *Design a suitable ball bearing for an axial flow compressor to carry radial load of 260 kg and thrust load of 150 kg. The service imposes light shock and bearing will be in use for 35 hours per week for 4 years. The speed of shaft is 900 R.P.M. and diameter of shaft in 54 mm.*

**Solution.** As both radial and axial loads are to be resisted by the bearing, therefore a single row angular contact bearing can be used.

$L$ = Life of bearing in revolution

$= 60 \times N \times h \times w \times n$

where $N$ = R.P.M. = 900

$h$ = Hours in use per week = 35

$w$ = Week per year = 52

$n$ = Number of years = 4

$L = 60 \times 900 \times 35 \times 52 \times 4 = 393 \times 10^6$

$P$ = Equivalent load $= (XF + YQ) \times K_S$

where $K_S$ = Service factor

= 1.1 to 1.5 for rotary machines

= 1.3 to 1.9 for reciprocating machines

= 1.6 to 4.0 for impact loads

Let us take $K_S = 1.4$

From Table 12.5

$X$ = Radial factor = 0.5

$Y$ = Thrust factor = 0.42

$F$ = Radial load = 260 kg

$Q$ = Thrust load = 150 kg

$P = (0.5 \times 260 + 0.42 \times 150) \times 1.4 = 270$ kg

$C$ = Dynamic load capacity

$$P = \left(\frac{L}{L_{10}}\right)^{1/K}$$

where $K$ = 3 for ball bearings

$L_{10}$ = Life of bearing for 90% survival at one million ($10^6$) revolutions.

$$C = 270\left(\frac{393 \times 10^6}{10^6}\right)^{1/3} = 1978 \text{ kg.}$$

## PROBLEMS

**1.** Define a bearing. How will you:

(*a*) Classify various types of bearings,

(*b*) What is the difference between a radial bearing and thrust bearings?

**2.** Name and sketch various journal bearings.

**3.** (*a*) What are so called antifriction bearings ?

(*b*) What is the difference between ball bearings and roller bearings ?

**4.** State the advantages of ball bearings over journal bearings.

**5.** (*a*) Define a lubricant.

(*b*) State the purpose of lubrication of bearings.

**6.** Write short notes on the following :

(*a*) Bearing modulus.

(*b*) Design load of a ball bearing.

(*c*) Sommer field number of a bearing.

(*d*) Bearings materials.

(*e*) Lubrication of rolling bearings.

(*f*) Selection of bearings.

**7.** Design a journal bearing for the following data :

Journal diameter = 7 cm

Journal speed = 450 R.P.M.

Clearance = 0.0025 cm/cm

Oil used has a viscosity = 10 centipoise at 75°C

Ambient temperature = 27°C

Specific gravity of oil = 0.9.

**8.** Design a multiple collar bearing for a rotary pump shaft 5 cm diameter rotating at 900 R.P.M. and to take up a load of 350 kg. Coefficient of friction is 0.035. The ratio of outside diameter to inside diameter of each thrust area is 1.6 and maximum bearing pressure is 20 kg/cm$^2$.

**9.** Write short notes on the following :

(*a*) Critical pressure for journal bearings.

(*b*) Static load rating.

(*c*) Dynamic load rating.

**10.** Design a bearing cap to with stand a load of 1200 kg. The journal is 12 cm diameter and 18 cm long. A hole 1 cm in diameter is provided at the bearing cap centre and there are two flying bolts on each side of the shaft axis. The allowable tensile stress in cap and bolt material is 390 kg/cm$^2$.

**11.** Select a roller contact bearing having a life of 10,000 hours for spindle of a drilling machine with journal of 5 cm diameter and carrying an axial load of 800 kg at an angular speed of 28 radians/sec.

**12.** A shaft is supported by two bearings 400 mm apart and carries a level gear of 200 mm P.C.D. at one end. Overhanging beyond the nearer bearing by 150 mm. The gear produces a radial load of 1000 kg and a thrust load or 300 kg when the speed is 600 R.P.M. Determine :

(*a*) The shaft diameter if the shaft is made if steel for which design shear stress is 300 kg/cm$^2$.

(*b*) The dynamic capacity of ball bearings to be used. The desired life is 2 years at 50 hours per week.

**13.** (*a*) What are rolling contact bearings ? Discuss their advantages over journal bearings.

(*b*) Discuss the effect of clearance on heat dissipation in a journal bearing. How is the clearance decided for optimal performance with reference to film thickness, friction and heat dissipation ?

**14.** A 8 cm shaft running at 300 r.m.p. is supported by a collar bearing having 6 collars, each of 12 cm outside diameter. Calculate the average bearing pressure and H.P. lost in friction if the axial lead is 300 kg and coefficient of friction is 0.04

**15.** State the properties of a lubricant. Describe any three methods of lubrication used for bearings.

# 13

# Belt, Rope and Chain Drives

## 13.1. Introduction

Belts, ropes and chains are used for power transmission from one shaft to another shaft. Rope drive is best suited for application where large amount of power is to be transmitted over longer distances. Chain drive operates without slipping and can be used for transmission of power over considerable distance.

## 13.2. Belt Drive

Belt drives are quite commonly used in industry for transmission of power. A belt drive is usefully empolyed when an exact velocity ratio is not an important.

Belt drive consists of an endless belt fitted over two pulleys. The motion from driving pulley is transmitted to the driven pulley by frictional resistance between the belt and the surface of the pulleys.

Four types of belts are commonly used :

(*i*) Flat belt

(*ii*) V-belt

(*iii*) Ribbed belt

(*iv*) Toothed belt.

Selection of belt depends on the following factors :

(*i*) Power to be transmitted

(*ii*) Centre distance

(*iii*) Space available
(*iv*) Spread of driver and driven shafts
(*v*) Reduction ratio
(*vi*) Positive drive requirements
(*vii*) Service conditions.

**13.2.1. Flate Belt drives.** They are classified as follows :

(*i*) **Open belt drive.** In this drive a belt passes over two pulleys, as shown in Fig. 13.1 (*a*). The pulleys rotate in the same direction. When the centre distance between the shafts is quite large the tight side of the belt should be the lower one.

(*ii*) **Cross belt drive.** Fig. 13.1 (*b*) shows a cross belt drive. In this drive the pulleys rotate in the opposite direction. In this drive wear is more. To reduce wear the speed should be kept 15 m/sec and the centre distance should be more than 20 times width of belt.

(*iii*) **Jockey pulley drive.** A flat belt with idler pulley also called Jockey pulley drive is shown in Fig. 13.1 (*c*). This type of drive is used when high velocity ratio is desired in short distance.

(*iv*) **Belt drive with guide pulley.** It is shown in Fig. 13.1 (*d*). It is used to transmit power from one shaft to several shafts arranged in parallel.

(*v*) **Quarter twist belt drive.** Fig. 13.1 (*e*) shows this drive. It is used for shafts at right angles.

(*vi*) **Right angle drive.** In this, drive shown in Fig. 13.1 (*f*) a guide pulley is used to transmit power between shafts at right angles.

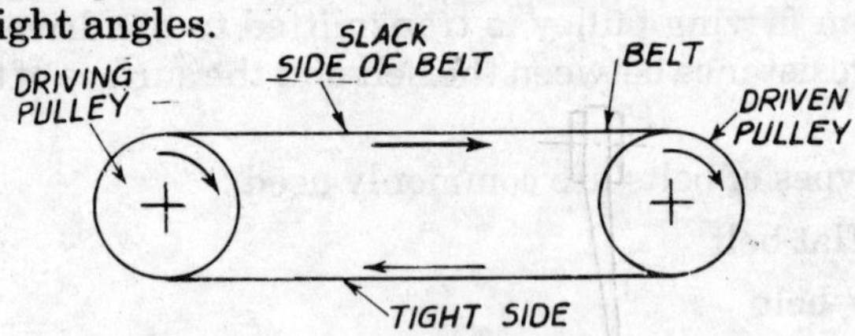

(*a*) Open belt drive.

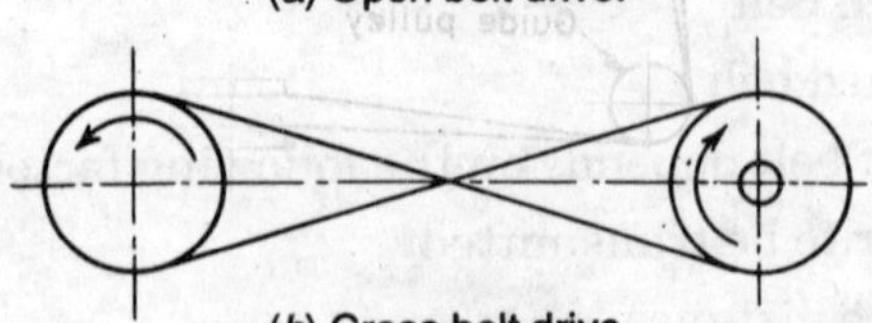
(*b*) Cross belt drive.

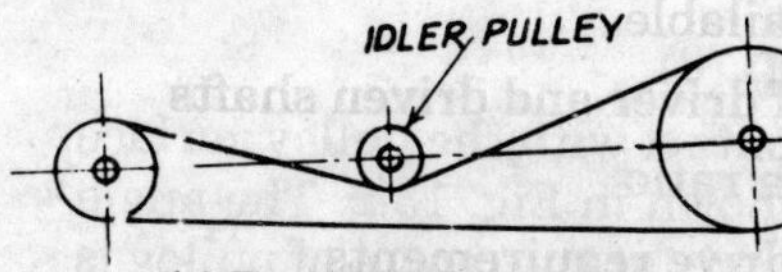


(*c*) Flat belt with idler pulley.

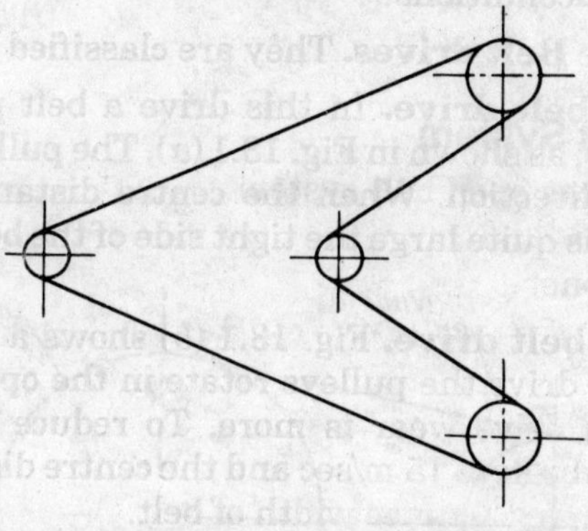

(*d*) Belt drive with guide pulley and many other pulleys

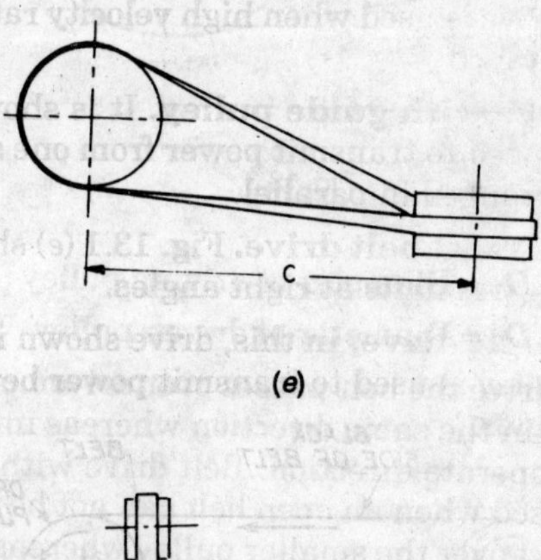


(*e*)

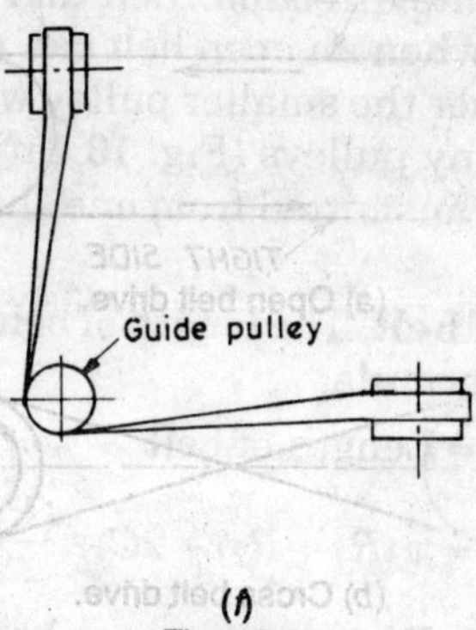


(*f*)

Fig. 13.1

## 13.3. Angle of Lap (θ)

A belt makes contact with the pulley surface over an arc *xy* as shown in Fig. 13.2. The angle which the arc subtends at the centre of pulley is called angle of lap or angle of contact (θ)

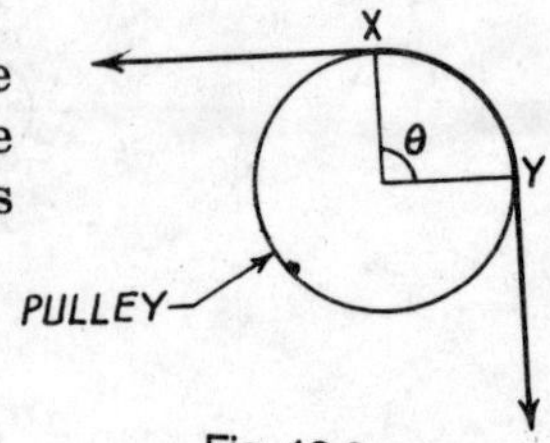


Fig. 13.2

## 13.4. Open Belt System

Fig. 13.3 shows open belt system.

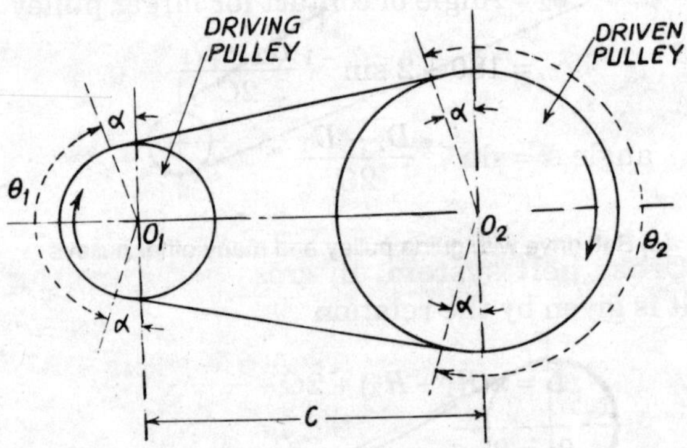


Fig. 13.3.

$D_1$ = Diameter of driving pulley

$D_2$ = Diameter of driven pulley

In open belt, drive the belt passes over driven pulleys and both the pulleys rotate in the same direction whereas in cross belt drive pulleys rotate in operate direction. Belt drive with an idler pulley [Fig. 13.1 (*c*)] is used when an open belt can not be used because of small arc of contact over the smaller pulley whereas belt drive with guide pulleys and many pulleys (Fig. 13.1 *d*) arrangement is used when power is to be transmitted from one shaft to several shafts in parallel.

**13.4.1. Length of belt.** The length of belt required for open belt system given by the formula,

$$L = \text{Length of belt}$$

$$= \pi (R_1 + R_2) + 2C + \frac{(R_1 - R_2)^2}{C}$$

where $C$ = Distance between centres of pulleys.

$R_1$ = Radius of driving pulley

$$= \frac{D_1}{2}$$

$R_2$ = Radius of driven pulley

$$= \frac{D_2}{2}$$

$\theta_1$ = Angle of contact on smaller pulley

$$= 180 - 2 \sin^{-1} \frac{D_2 - D_1}{2C} \text{ degrees}$$

$\theta_2$ = Angle of contact for larger pulley

$$= 180 + 2 \sin^{-1} \frac{D_2 - D_1}{2C}$$

where angle $\alpha = \sin^{-1} \frac{D_2 - D_1}{2C}$

**13.4.2. Cross belt system.** In cross belt drive (Fig. 13.3 *a*) length of belt is given by the relation

$$L = \pi(R_1 + R_2) + 2C + \frac{(R_1 + R_2)^2}{C}$$

$$\theta_1 = \theta_2$$

$$= 180 + 2 \sin^{-1} \frac{D_2 + D_1}{2C} \text{ degrees.}$$

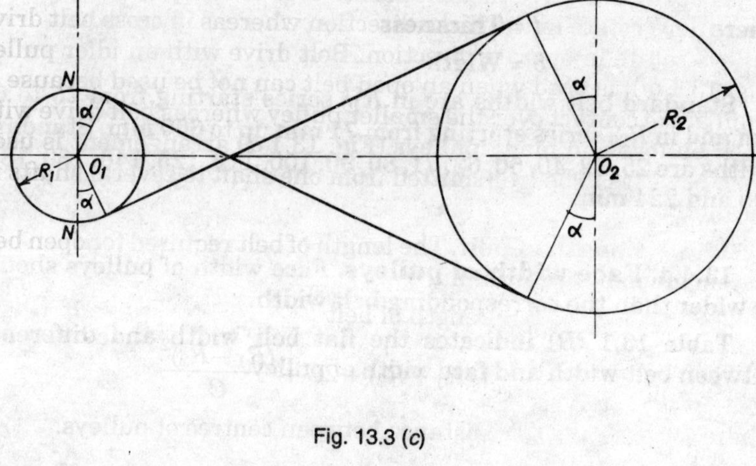


Fig. 13.3 (*c*)

The centre distance in flat belt drives may be as high as 15 m but generally centre distance ($C$) between pulleys is kept between 6 to 8 m. The centre distance can also be calculated from the following relations :

$$C \geq 3.5\, D_2$$

$$\geq (1.5 - 2)\,(D_1 + D_2)$$

where $D_1$ = Diameter of smaller pulley

$D_2$ = Diameter of bigger pulley.

**13.4.3. Thickness and width of flat belt.** Standard flat belt thicknesses are :

5, 6.5, 8, 10 and 12 mm

Table 13.1 ($A$) indicates the thickness and corresponding belt widths commonly used.

**Table 13.1 (*A*)**

| *t (mm)* | *b (mm)* |
|---|---|
| 5 | 25 to 63 |
| 6.5 | 50 — 140 |
| 8.0 | 90 — 224 |
| 10.0 | 125 — 400 |
| 12.0 | 250 — 600 |

where $t$ = Thickness

$b$ = Width

Standard belt widths are in $R_{10}$ series starting from 25 to 63 mm and in $R_{20}$ series starting from 71 mm up to 600 mm. Standard widths are 25, 32, 40, 50, 63, 71, 80, 90, 100, 112, 125, 140, 160, 180, 200 and 224 mm.

**13.4.4. Face width of pulleys.** Face width of pulleys should be wider than the corresponding belt width.

Table 13.1 ($B$) indicates the flat belt width and difference between belt width and face width of pulley.

**Table 13.1 (*B*)**

| *Belt Width (mm)* | *Difference (mm)* |
|---|---|
| up to 125 | 15 |
| 125-250 | 25 |
| 250-375 | 40 |
| 375-500 | 50 |

The aim of designed should be to choose a thin wide belt.

## 13.5. Flat Belt Materials

The material commonly used for making flat belts are as follows:

(*i*) Leather belts

(*ii*) Cotton and canves belts

(*iii*) Rubber belts

(*iv*) Balata belts

(*v*) Nylon core belts.

Leather belts made from Oak tanned leather or chrome leather. Oak tanned leather does not have as good friction as chrome leather. The modulus of elasticity of leather varies from 1400 to 3150 kg/cm$^2$. The ultimate strength of leather of high quality is 280 kg/cm$^2$. The thickness of single leather strip varies from 3 to 5.5 mm. Double ply belts are obtained by cementing together two strips of leather. Similarly three ply belts are obtained by cementing together three strips to leather.

Cotton and canvas belts are cheap and are made by stitching together three or more plies or layers of canvas or cotton layers. Modulus of elasticity of cotton belts varies from 4900 to 14,000 kg/cm$^2$ and have a strength of 350 to 500 kg/cm$^2$.

Rubber belts are resistant to moisture, acids, alkalis etc. They are made up of plies consisting of fabric or cord strength members impregnated with vulcanised rubber. They have ultimate strength of about 60 to 100 kg/cm$^2$ and modulus of elasticity varies from 9000 to 14,500 kg/cm$^2$.

Balata belts are about 25% more stronger than rubber belts and are made in the same manner as the rubber belts except that balata is substituted for rubber. These belts are acid proof and water proof.

Nylon core belts have tensile strength about 8 times that of leather and are made with leather on both outside plies.

**13.5.1. Density of belt materials.** The density of some of belt materials is shown in Table 13.1(*C*)

**Table 13.1 (*C*)**

| *Material* | *Density* |
|---|---|
| Leather | 1000 kg/m$^3$ |
| Rubber | 1400 kg/m$^3$ |
| Balata | 1110 kg/m$^3$ |
| Canvas | 1220 kg/m$^3$ |

## 13.6. Coefficient of Friction

The coefficient of friction (μ) between belt and pulley depends upon the material of belt pulley. Table 13.2 shows coefficient of friction for some of belt and pulley materials.

**Table 13.2**

| *Belt Material* | *Pulley material* | | | | |
|---|---|---|---|---|---|
| | *Cast Iron, Steel* | | | Wood | *Paper* |
| | *Dry* | *Wet* | *Greasy* | | |
| Oak tanned leather | 0.25 | 0.20 | 0.15 | 0.30 | 0.33 |
| Chrome tanned leather | 0.40 | 0.35 | 0.25 | 0.45 | 0.55 |
| Canves stitched | 0.2 | 0.15 | 0.12 | 0.23 | 0.25 |
| Balata | 0.32 | 0.20 | - | 0.35 | 0.38 |
| Cotton woven | 0.22 | 0.15 | 0.12 | 0.25 | 0.28 |
| Rubber | 0.30 | 0.18 | - | 0.32 | 0.35 |

## 13.7. Belt Speeds

For efficiency and longer life belt speeds of 15-20 metres per second should be used.

On the basis of belt speeds the belt drives are classified as follows :

(*i*) **Right drives.** They are used to transmit small powers at belt speeds up to 12 m/s. These drives are used in small machine tools and agricultural machines.

(*ii*) **Medium drives.** The belt speed in such drives varies from 12 to 24 m/s. They are also used in machine tools.

(*iii*) **Heavy drives.** These drives are used to transmit large powers. The belt speeds are above 24 m/s. These are quite suitable for compressors, generators and main drives.

## 13.8. Strength of Belts

It is usual to use factor of safety of 6 to 8. The working stress can be obtained by dividing the ultimate strength by factor of safety. Table 13.3 shows strength of belt materials.

## 13.9. Belt Joints

The ends of belt are joined together by different types of fasteners. Table 13.4 indicates the various types of joints and their efficiency.

**Table 13.3**

| *Belt Material* | *Ultimate tensile strength* (kg/cm$^2$) |
|---|---|
| Chrome leather (Single ply) | 525—800 |
| Oak leather-Single ply | 280—380 |
| -Double ply | 175—350 |
| Convas with rubber impregnation | 310 |

**Table 13.4**

| *Type of joints* | *Efficiency (%)* |
|---|---|
| Cemented by belt maker | 100 |
| Wire laced by machine | 90 |
| Wire laced by hand | 82 |
| Metal hooks | 35 |

Fig. 13.4 (*a*) shows cemented joint and Fig. 13.4 (*b*) shows joints made by metal hooks.

Fig. 13.4 (*a*)

13.4 (*b*)

Safe allowable stress for belt joints

$$= \text{Working stress} \times \eta$$

where $\eta$ = Efficiency of joint

$$\text{Working stress} = \frac{\text{Ultimate stress}}{\text{Factor of safety}}.$$

## 13.10. Velocity Ratio

It is defined as the ratio of speed of driven shaft to that of driving shaft.

Let $N_1$ = R.P.M of driving shaft

$N_2$ = R.P.M of driven shaft

$D_1$ = Diameter of driving pulley

$D_2$ = Diameter of driven pulley

If the belt has negligible thickness and if the belt does not slip over the surface of pulley then

$V_1$ = Peripheral velocity of driving pulley in m/sec

$$= \frac{\pi D_1 N_1}{60}$$

$V_2$ = Peripheral velocity of driven pulley

$$= \frac{\pi D_2 N_2}{60}$$

Now $$V_1 = V_2$$

$$\frac{\pi D_1 N_1}{60} = \frac{\pi D_2 N_2}{60}$$

$$\frac{N_2}{N_1} = \frac{D_1}{D_2}$$

If we take percentage of total slip of belt drive ($S$) into account then,

$$\text{Velocity ratio} = \frac{N_2}{N_1} = \frac{D_1}{D_2}\left(\frac{100 - S}{100}\right)$$

If thickness of belt is also taken into account then

$$\text{Velocity ratio} = \frac{N_2}{N_1} = \frac{D_1 + t}{D_2 + t}\left(\frac{100 - S}{100}\right)$$

where $t$ = Thickness of belt

$S$ = Total percentage slip between driver and driven shaft.

Let $S_1$ = Percentage of slip between belt and driving pulleys

$S_2$ = Percentage of slip between belt and driven pulley

$$\left(\frac{100 - S}{100}\right) = \left(\frac{100 - S_1}{100}\right)\left(\frac{100 - S_2}{100}\right)$$

The slip in belt drive depends of material of belt and pulley and on effective tension in the belt.

The usual values of velocity ratios are as follows :

Velocity ratio ≤ 5 for open flat belt drive

≤ 10 for flat belt drive with an idler pulley

≤ 8 to 15 for V–belt drive.

Amount of slip increases if the belt is over-loaded. It has been found that a slip of upto about 3 per cent increases the coefficient of friction. Under normal conditions, a slip of about $1\frac{1}{2}$ to 2 per cent is present. Due to slip, the belt speed is less than the peripheral speed to the driving pulley and slightly more than the peripheral speed of the driven pulley.

Creep is the phenomenon caused by the elasticity of the material. The belt is stretched more on the tight side than on the slack side.

In practice the combined effect of slip and creep is called simply slip and the combined effect should not exceed 3 per cent.

## 13.11. Ratio of Driving Tension and Power Transmitted

The horse power transmitted by belt drive depends upon tensions in the belt coefficient of friction between belt and pulleys and linear speed of belt.

Let $T_1$ = Tension in tight side of belt in kg

$T_2$ = Tension in slack side of belt in kg

$\mu$ = Coefficient of friction between belt and pulley

$\theta$ = Angle of lap on smaller pulley in radians.

H.P. = Horse power transmitted

$$= \frac{(T_1 - T_2)\,V}{4500} = \frac{T_1\left(1 - \dfrac{T_2}{T_1}\right)V}{4500}$$

$$= \frac{T_1\left(1 - \dfrac{1}{e^{\mu\theta}}\right)V}{4500}$$

where $V$ = Speed of belt in metre/min

$$\frac{T_1}{T_2} = e^{\mu\theta}$$

The centrifugal tension in the belt becomes of consequence at high speeds and should be taken into account while calculating width of belt

$T_c$ = Centrifugal tension in kg

$$= \frac{w\,.\,v^2}{g}$$

where $w$ = Weight per metre length of belt in kg

$v$ = Linear speed of belt in metre per second

Tension on tight side of belt = $T_1 + T_c$

Tension on slack side of belt = $T_2 + T_c$.

When the effect of centrifugal tension is considered the horse power transmitted is given by the relation,

$$\text{H.P.} = \frac{(T - T_c)\left(1 - \dfrac{1}{e^{\mu\theta}}\right) \times V}{4500}$$

$T$ = Maximum permissible tension in belt

$= T_1 + T_c$

where $V$ = Linear speed of belt in metre per minute

Design H.P. = H.P. to be transmitted × Service factor

Service factor = 1.2 for jerky loads

= 1.4 for shock and reversed loads.

## 13.12. Maximum Permissible Velocity of Belt

The maximum permissible velocity of belt at which maximum horse power can be transmitted is calculated as follows :

$$V_m = \text{Maximum velocity} = \sqrt{\frac{T \times g}{3w}}$$

where $T$ = Maximum permissible tension in belt

At maximum speed of belt $T = 3\,T_C$.

## 13.13. Initial Tension in the Belt

It is calculated as follows :

$$T_0 = \frac{T_1 + T_2}{2}$$

where $T_0$ = Initial tension

## 13.14. Design of Belt Dimensions

Let $t$ = Thickness of belt in cm

$b$ = Width of belt in cm

$f_t$ = Safe stress in tension in kg/cm$^2$

If centrifugal tension is neglected

$$T_1 = f_t \,.\, t \,.\, b.$$

If centrifugal tension is taken into account

Maximum tension = $T = T_1 + T_c = f_t \,.\, t \,.\, b$

It is sometimes customary to express the safe stress ($f$) in belt terms of kg per cm width of belt.

$b = \dfrac{T_1}{f}$ if centrifugal tension is neglected

$= \dfrac{T_1 + T_c}{f}$ when centrifugal tension is taken into account.

## 13.15. Rockwood Drive

In this drive (Fig. 13.4) the weight of motor is used to maintain belt tension. The motor is bolted to an intermediate base which is pivoted on the pin $A$. The moment equation can be written by multiplying forces $T_1$, $T_2$ and $W$ by their respective arms measured from the pivot at $A$.

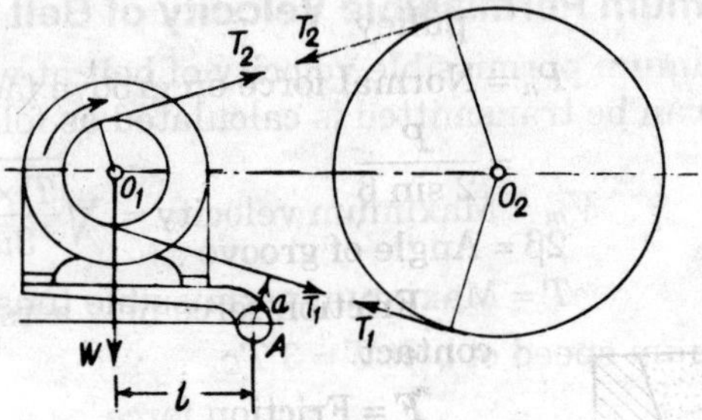


Fig. 13.4.

$$T_1 a + T_2 e = W \cdot l$$

where $W$ = Weight of motor

In this drive the lever arm ($l$) of weight of motor is kept very large so that most of belt tension is due to product of weight and lever arm.

## 13.16. V-belt Drives

They are used for short centre industrial drives for medium and heavy power transmission V-belts have trapezoidal cross section and are used with grooved pulleys. When power to be transmitted in large a number of V-belts can be arranged in different grooves side by side. The number of belts should not exceed 8 to 12.

They are made of fabrics and cords moulded in rubber and covered with fabrics (Fig. 13.5). The included angle of groove of pulley is about 30–40°. They are made endless so that difficulty with splicing devices is avoided. The belt speed should range from 5 to 10 metre per second.

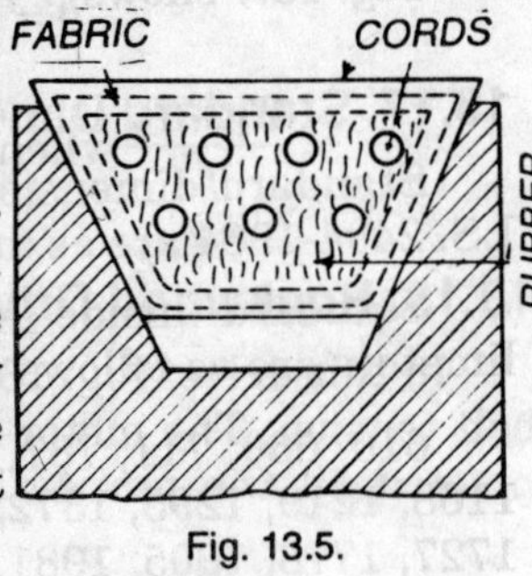


Fig. 13.5.

All belts in the drive should stretch at the same rate in order to keep the load equally divided between them. When one of the belts breaks the entire group may usually be replaced. V-belts transmit more power without slip as compared to flat belts.

**13.16.1. V-belt Forces.** Fig. 13.6 shown the cross section of a V-belt drive.

Let $\mu$ = Coefficient of friction between belt and pulley

$P_n$ = Normal force on groove face

$$= \frac{P}{2 \sin \beta}$$

$2\beta$ = Angle of groove

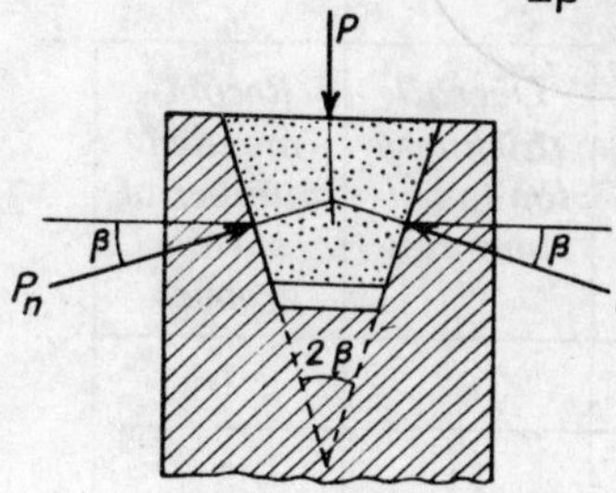

Fig. 13.6.

Friction force now acts on both sides of contact.

$$F = \text{Friction force}$$

$$= \mu \,.\, 2 \,.\, P_n$$

$$= \mu \,.\, 2 \,.\, \frac{P}{2 \sin \beta}$$

$$= \frac{\mu P}{\sin \beta}$$

$$= \mu' \,.\, P$$

where $\mu'$ = Equivalent coefficient of friction

$$= \frac{\mu}{\sin \beta}$$

$T_1$ = Tension on tight side of belt

$T_2$ = Tension on slack side of belt

$$\frac{T_1}{T_2} = e^{\mu \theta}$$

$$= e^{\frac{\mu \theta}{\sin \beta}}$$

where $\theta$ = Angle of lap.

Fig. 13.7 shows a V-belt pulley.

Fig. 13.7

## 13.17. Standard Dimensions of V-belts

Standard dimensions of V-belts according to I.S. 2494-1964 are as follows :

Standard inside lengths of V-belts in millimeters are as follows :

610, 660, 711, 787, 813, 889, 914, 965, 991, 1016, 1067, 1092, 1168, 1219, 1295, 1372, 1397, 1422, 1473, 1524, 1600, 1626, 1651, 1727, 1778, 1905, 1981, 2032, 2057, 2159, 2286, 2438, 2464, 2540,

2667, 2845, 3048, 3150, 3251, 3404, 3658, 4013, 4115, 4394, 4572, 4953, 5334, 6045, 6807, 7569, 8331, 9093, 9885, 10617, 12141, 13665, 15189, 16713 mm.

The V-belts are classified as *A, B, C, D* and *E*. The pitch length of V-belts is found by adding to inside length 36 mm for A-belts, 43 mm for *B* belt, 56 mm for *C* type of belt, 79 mm for *D* belt and 92 mm for *E* belt.

**Table 13.5**

| *Belt Section* | *H.P* | *Min. dia of pulley mm* | *Width of belt at top (mm)* | *Overall thickness top to bottom mm* | *Recommended number of sheave grooves* |
|---|---|---|---|---|---|
| *A* | 1-5 | 71 | 13 | 8 | 6 |
| *B* | 3-20 | 125 | 17 | 11 | 9 |
| *C* | 10-100 | 200 | 22 | 14 | 14 |
| *D* | 30-200 | 315 | 32 | 19 | 14 |
| *E* | 40-350 | 500 | 38 | 23 | 20 |

**Table 13.6**

| *Groove Cross section* | *Pitch width (a) mm* | *x Min. mm* | *y mm* | *s mm* | *b mm* | *Pulley pitch diameter (D) mm* | *Angle (2β) Degrees* |
|---|---|---|---|---|---|---|---|
| *A* | 11 | 3.3 | 8.7 | 15 | 10 | Under 75 | 32 |
| | | | | | | 75 to 125 | 34 |
| | | | | | | Above 125 | 38 |
| *B* | 14 | 4.2 | 10.8 | 19 | 12.5 | Under 125 | 32 |
| | | | | | | 125 to 200 | 34 |
| | | | | | | Above 200 | 38 |
| *C* | 19 | 5.7 | 14.3 | 25.5 | 17 | Under 200 | 34 |
| | | | | | | 200 to 300 | 36 |
| | | | | | | Above 300 | 38 |

| | | | | | | | |
|---|---|---|---|---|---|---|---|
| *D* | 27 | 8.1 | 19.9 | 37 | 24 | Under 300 | 34 |
| | | | | | | 300 to 500 | 36 |
| | | | | | | Above 500 | 38 |
| *E* | 32 | 9.6 | 23.4 | 44.5 | 29 | — | — |

Table 13.5 shows the various dimensions of different types of V-belts. A belt is completely designated by cross section and nominal inside length. For example a V-bolt designated by C 2032 IS 2494 means belt is of *C* type and has an inside length of 2032 mm and has a width of 22 mm and overall thickness 14 mm. The belt pitch length will be

$$2032+56 = 2088 \text{ mm}$$

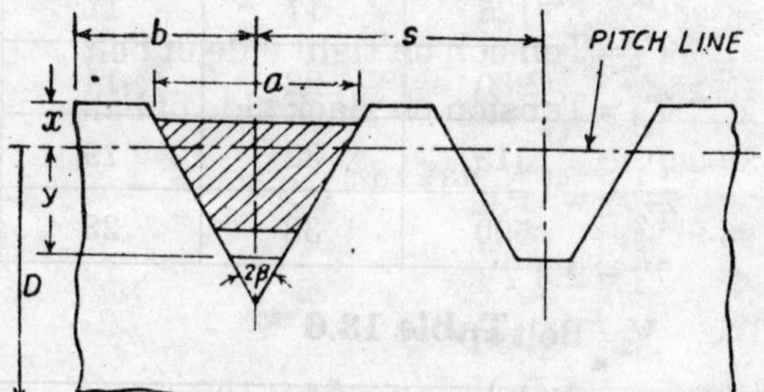


Fig. 13.8.

Fig. 13.8 shows various dimensions of a V-belt pulley. The values are indicated in Table 13.6.

**Example 13.1** *In an open belt drive the diameter of a pulley on the driving shaft is 54 cm and the pulley rotates at 150 R.P.M. A counter shaft is to be driven at 300 R.P.M. If the centre distance between shaft is 250 cm and* $\mu = 0.3$, *determine width of belt so that 5 H.P. is transmitted. The safe permissible stress is 16 kg/cm width of belt.*

**Solution.**

$D_1$ = Diameter of driving pulley = 54 cm

$N_1$ = Speed of driving pulley = 150 R.P.M.

$D_2$ = Diameter of driven pulley

$N_2$ = R.P.M. of driven pulley = 300 R.P.M.

$$\frac{N_2}{N_1} = \frac{D_1}{D_2}$$

$$\frac{300}{150} = \frac{54}{D_2}$$

$$D_2 = 27 \text{ cm}$$

$\theta$ = Angle of lap of smaller pulley = $180 - 2\,\alpha$

where $$\sin \alpha = \frac{D_2 - D_1}{2\,C} = \frac{54 - 27}{250}$$

$$= 0.108$$

$$\alpha = 6^\circ\ 12'$$

$$\theta = 180 - 2\alpha = 180 - 12^\circ\ 24'$$

$$= 167^\circ - 36' = 2.923 \text{ radians}$$

$$\mu = 0.3$$

$T_1$ = Tension on tight side of belt

$T_2$ = Tension on slack side of belt

$$\frac{T_1}{T_2} = e^{\mu\theta} = e^{0.3 \times 2.923} = 2.4$$

$$T_1 = 2.4\ T_2$$

$V$ = Belt speed

$$= \frac{\pi\ D_1 N_1}{100} = \frac{\pi \times 54 \times 150}{100}$$

$$= 254 \text{ m/min}$$

$$\text{H.P.} = \frac{(T_1 - T_2) \times V}{4500}$$

$$5 = \frac{(2.4\ T_2 - T_2) \times 254}{4500}$$

$$T_2 = 63.3 \text{ kg}$$

$$T_1 = 2.4\ T_2 = 2.4 \times 63.3 = 152 \text{ kg}$$

$b$ = Width of belt

$f$ = Safe stress in belt = 16 kg/cm

$$b = \frac{T_1}{f} = \frac{152}{16} = 9.5 \text{ cm.}$$

**Example 13.2.** *A leather belt transmits 16 H.P. from a pulley 90 cm diameter running at 450 R.P.M. The density of belt material* *is 0.004 kg/cm² and maximum stress in belt is 50 kg/cm². The angle of lap is 165° and μ = 0.27. The belt is 0.4 cm thick. Calculate width of belt.*

**Solution.**

$D$ = Diameter of pulley = 90 cm.

$N$ = R.P.M. of pulley = 450

$V$ = Belt speed

$$= \frac{\pi DN}{60}$$

$$= \frac{\pi \times 0.9 \times 450}{60} = 21.2 \text{ m/sec.}$$

$b$ = Width of belt in cms

$t$ = Thickness of belt

= 0.4 cm.

$T_c$ = Centrifugal tension

$$= \frac{w}{g} . V^2$$

where $w$ = Weight of belt per metre length

$= 0.004 \times b \times t \times 100$

$= 0.004 \times b \times 0.4 \times 100$

$$T_c = \frac{0.004 \times b \times 0.4 \times 100 \times (21.2)^2}{9.81}$$

$= 7.3\, b$ kg.

$\mu = 0.27$

$\theta$ = Angle of lap = 165°

$$e^{\mu\theta} = e^{0.27 \times \frac{165 \times \pi}{180}} = 2.17$$

$T_1$ = Maximum tension = $50 \times b \times t$

$= 50 \times b \times 0.4 = 20\, b$ kg.

$$\text{H.P.} = \frac{(T_1 - T_c)\left(1 - \frac{1}{e^{\mu\theta}}\right) \times V}{75}$$

$$16 = \frac{(20\, b - 7.3\, b)\left(1 - \frac{1}{2.17}\right) \times 2.12}{75}$$

$b = 8.25$ cm.

**Example 13.3.** (*a*) *An electric motor drives a pump. The motor pulley is 28 cm in diameter and runs at 750 R.P.M. The pump pulley is 140 cm in diameter. The shaft centre distance is 160 cm. The flat belt used is 1 cm thick and of 20 cm width. Calculate horse power capacity neglecting the centrifugal tension.*

$\mu = 0.24$ *for larger pulley and belt*

$= 0.28$ *for smaller pulley and belt*

*Safe stress in belt* $= 24\ kg/cm^2$

*An idler pulley is used to make angle of lap* $210°$ *on smaller pulley and* $260°$ *on larger pulley.*

(*b*) *Determine the horse power capacity if motor pulley is a V-pulley with the following data :*

*Groove angle* $= 40°$

$\mu = 0.24$

*Assume maximum tension is same as in flat belt and also the pitch diameter of V-belt pulley and pitch diameter of larger pulley remain same as for flat belt.*

**Solution.** (*a*) **To determine H.P. capacity of flat belt.**

**Smaller pulley**

$\theta_1$ = Angle of lap = 210°

$\mu_1$ = Coefficient of friction between belt and pulley = 0.28

$T_1$ = Tension on tight side of belt

$T_2$ = Tension on slack side of belt

$$\frac{T_1}{T_2} = e^{\mu_1 \theta_1}$$

$$= e^{\frac{0.28 \times 210 \times \pi}{180}} = 2.787$$

**Larger pulley**

$\mu_1 = 0.24$

$\theta_2 = 260°$

$$\frac{T_1}{T_2} = e^{\mu_2 \theta_2}$$

$$= e^{\frac{0.24 \times 260 \times \pi}{180}} = 2.96$$

Therefore, horse power capacity of the drive depends upon smaller pulley.

$b$ = Width of belt = 20 cm

$t$ = Thickness of belt = 1 cm.

$f_t$ = Safe stress in belt = 24 kg/cm$^2$

$T_1$ = Maximum tension

$= 24 \times b \times t = 24 \times 20 \times 1 = 480$ kg

$$\frac{T_1}{T_2} = 2.787$$

$$T_2 = \frac{T_1}{2.787} = \frac{480}{2.787}$$

$= 172.23$ kg

$D_1$ = Diameter of motor pulley

= 28 cm.

$N_1$ = R.P.M. of motor pulley

= 750.

$V$ = Speed of belt

$$= \frac{\pi D_1 N_1}{100} = \frac{\pi \times 28 \times 750}{100}$$

= 659.4 m/min.

$$\text{H.P.} = \frac{(T_1 - T_2) \times V}{4500} = \frac{(480 - 172.23) \times 659.4}{4500}$$

= 45 cm.

**(b) To determine H.P. capacity of V-flat drive**

$\theta_1$ = Angle of lap on smaller pulley without idler pulley.

$C$ = Centre distance = 160 cm

$$\theta_1 = 180 - 2 \sin^{-1} \frac{D_2 - D_1}{2C}$$

$$= 180 - 2 \sin^{-1} \frac{140 - 28}{2 \times 160} = 139^\circ$$

$\theta_2$ = Angle of lap for larger pulley

$$= 180 + 2 \sin^{-1} \frac{D_2 - D_1}{2C}$$

$$= 180 + 2 \sin^{-1} \frac{140 - 28}{2 \times 160} = 221^\circ$$

In this case idler pulley has not been used and therefore sum of $\theta_1$ and $\theta_2$ should be 360°

$$\theta_1 + \theta_2 = 139 + 221 = 360^\circ$$

$$2\,\beta = \text{Groove angle for pulley} = 40^\circ$$

$$\beta = 20^\circ$$

$$\mu = 0.24$$

For smaller pulley $= e^{\frac{\mu\theta_1}{\sin\beta}}$

$$= e^{0.24 \times \frac{139 \times \pi}{180} \times \frac{1}{\sin 20}} = e^{1.7} = 5.48.$$

For larger pulley,

$$\frac{T_1}{T_2} = e^{\mu\theta_2} = e^{0.24 \times \frac{221 \times \pi}{180}} = 2.52$$

This shows that horse power capacity of drive is governed by larger pulley

$$T_1 = 480$$

$$\frac{T_1}{T_2} = 2.52$$

$$T_2 = \frac{T_1}{2.52} = \frac{480}{2.52} = 190.47 \text{ kg}$$

$$V = \text{Speed of belt} = 659.4 \text{ m/min}$$

$$\text{H.P. capacity} = \frac{(T_1 - T_2) \times V}{4500} = \frac{(480 - 190.47) \times 659.4}{4500} = 42.4.$$

**Example 13.4.** *A flat belt is required to transmit 40 H.P. at 600 R.P.M. to a machine pulley 120 cm diameter. The distance between the pulley centres is 300 cm and speed reduction is 3.1. Service factor is 1.5. The belt is 1 cm thick and the safe stress in belt material is 25 kg/cm². Assume μ = 0.3. Determine width and length of belt.*

**Solution.** (*a*) **Find width of belt**

Let $C$ = Centre distance = 300 cm

$$D_1 = \text{Diameter of smaller pulley}$$

$$D_2 = \text{Diameter of bigger pulley reduction ratio} = 3$$

$$D_1 = \frac{D_2}{3}$$

$$= \frac{120}{3} = 40 \text{ cm}$$

$$\frac{T_1}{T_2} = e^{\mu\theta}$$

where $\theta$ = Angle of lap for smaller pulley

$$= 180 - 2 \sin \frac{D_2 - D_1}{2C}$$

$$= 180 - 2 \sin^{-1} \frac{120 \times 40}{2 \times 300}$$

$$= 164.7^{\circ}$$

$\mu$ = Coefficient of friction = 0.3

$$\frac{T_1}{T_2} = e^{\mu\theta}$$

$$= e^{0.3 \times \frac{\pi \times 164.7^{\circ}}{180}} = 2.36$$

$N_1$ = R.P.M. of smaller pulley = 600 R.P.M.

Design H.P. = Rated H.P. × Service factor

$$= 40 \times 1.5 = 60$$

$V$ = Speed of belt

$$= \frac{\pi D_1 N_1}{100} = \frac{\pi \times 40 \times 600}{100} = 753.6 \text{ m/min}$$

$$\text{H.P.} = \frac{(T_1 - T_2)}{4500}$$

$$60 = \frac{(T_1 - T_2) \times 753.6}{4500}$$

$$T_1 - T_2 = 358.3$$

Now $T_1 = 2.36\, T_2$

$$\therefore \quad (2.36\, T_2 - T_2) = 358.3$$

$$T_2 = 263.7 \text{ kg}$$

$$T_1 = 2.36 \times T_2 = 2.36 \times 263.7 = 622 \text{ kg}$$

$f_t$ = Safe stress in belt material = 25 kg/cm²

$b$ = Width of belt, $t$ = Thickness of belt

$$T_1 = b \times t \times f_t$$

$$622 = b \times 1 \times 25$$

$$b = 24.88 \text{ cm.}$$

**(b) To find length of belt**

$L$ = Length of belt

$$= \pi (R_1 + R_2) + 2C + \frac{(R_2 - R_1)^2}{C}$$

$$= \pi (20 + 60) + 2 \times 300 + \frac{(60 - 20)^2}{300}$$

$$= \pi \times 80 + 600 + .\frac{40^2}{300} = 605.33 \text{ cm}$$

The length should be reduced by 1% of allow initial tension in the belt.

$$\therefore \quad \text{Length} = 605.33 - \frac{1}{100} \times 605.33 = 599.28 \text{ cm.}$$

**Example 13.5.** *A flat belt 12 cm wide and 1 cm thick has a belt speed of 660 m / min. The ratio of tight side tension and slack side tension is 2. If the safe permissible stress in the belt material is 24 kg/cm² and density of belt material is 1 gm/cm³ determine the following :*

(a) *H.P. transmitted*

(b) *Speed of belt at which maximum horse power is transmitted.*

(c) *Maximum horse power transmitted.*

**Solution.** (*a*) **To determine horse power**

$b$ = Width of belt = 12 cm

$t$ = Thickness of belt = 1 cm

$T_1$ = Tight side tension

$T_2$ = Slack side tension

$$\frac{T_1}{T_2} = 2 = k$$

$f_t$ = Safe permissible stress in belt

$= 24 \text{ kg/cm}^2$

Maximum tension in belt

$$T = b \times t \times f_t = 12 \times 1 \times 24 = 288 \text{ kg}$$

$T_c$ = Centrifugal tension = $wv^2/g$

where $w$ = Weight of belt material per metre length

$$= \frac{1 \times b \times t \times 100}{1000}$$

$$= \frac{1 \times 12 \times 1 \times 100}{1000}$$

$= 1.2$ kg/metre

$$v = \text{Belt speed} = 660/\text{min}$$

$$= \frac{660}{60} \text{ m/sec} = 11 \text{ m/sec}$$

$$T_c = \frac{wv^2}{g} = \frac{1.2 \times 11^2}{9.81} = 14.8 \text{ kg}$$

$$\text{H.P. transmitted} = \frac{(T - T_c)\left(1 - \frac{1}{k}\right)V}{4500}$$

$$= \frac{(288 - 14.8)\left(1 - \frac{1}{2}\right) \times 660}{4500} = 20$$

(*b*) **To find maximum permissible speed**

$$V_m = \text{Maximum permissible speed of belt}$$

At maximum speed of belt

$$T_c = \frac{T}{3} = \frac{288}{3} = 96 \text{ kg}$$

$$T_c = \frac{w\,V_m^2}{g}$$

$$V_m = \sqrt{\frac{T_c \times g}{w}} = \sqrt{\frac{96 \times 9.81}{1.2}}$$

$$= 28 \text{ m/sec} = 1680 \text{ m/min.}$$

(*c*) **To find maximum horse power**

Maximum H.P. transmitted

$$= \frac{(T - T_c)\,(1 - \frac{1}{k}) \times V_m}{4500}$$

$$= \frac{(288 - 96)(1 - \frac{1}{2}) \times 1680}{4500}$$

$$= 35.84.$$

**Example 13.6.** *In a flat belt drive the driving pulley is of 60 cm diameter and runs at 300 R.P.M. and the driven pulley runs at 200 R.P.M. The belt is 8 mm thick and the slip between belt and each pulley is 2%. Determine the following :*

(*a*) *Diameter of driven pulley*

(*b*) *Percentage of total effective slip.*

**Solution.** (*a*) **To find diameter**

$D_1$ = Diameter of driving pulley = 60 cm

$N_1$ = 300 R.P.M.

$N_2$ = R.P.M. of driven pulley = 200

$t$ = Thickness of belt = 0.8 cm

$S_1$ = Percentage of slip = 2%

$V_1$ = Speed of driving pulley

$$= \frac{\pi (D_1 + t) N_1}{60} (100 - S_1)$$

$$V_1 = \frac{\pi(60 + 0.5)300}{60}\left(\frac{100-2}{100}\right)$$

$= 931$ cm/sec

$V_2$ = Speed of second pulley

$$= V_1 \times \left(\frac{100 - S_2}{100}\right)$$

where $S_2$ = Percentage slip of driven pulley

$= 2\%$

$$V_2 = 931\left(\frac{100-2}{100}\right) = 912 \text{ cm/sec.}$$

$D'_2$ = Effective diameter of driven pulley

$$\frac{\pi D_2' N_2}{60} = 912$$

$$D'_2 = \frac{60 \times 912}{200 \times \pi} = 87 \text{ cm}$$

$D_2$ = Actual diameter of pulley

$= D_2' - t = 87 - 0.8 = 86.2$ cm

(*b*) **To calculate total percentage of effective slip**

$S$ = Total percentage of effective slip

$$\left(\frac{100 - S}{100}\right) = \left(\frac{100 - S_1}{100}\right)\left(\frac{100 - S_2}{100}\right)$$

$$1 - 0.1\, S = (1 - 0.01\, S_1)\,(1 - 0.01\, S_2)$$

$$= .1 - .01\, S_1 - 0.01\, S_2 + 0.0001\, S_1 S_2$$

$$S = S_1 + S_2 - 0.01\, S_1 S_2$$

$$S = 2 + 2 - 0.01 \times 2 \times 2$$

$$= 4 - 0.04 = 3.96\%.$$

**Example 13.6 (A).** *In an open belt drive the diameters of driving and driven pulleys are 100 cm and 130 cm respectively. The output of driven shaft is 160 H.P. and centre distance is 3 metres. Assuming coefficient of friction as 0.32, belt speed 20 m/s, slip as 1.6 percent at each pulley, and friction loss at each shaft as 4%, calculate the following.*

(*a*) *R.P.M. of each shaft*

(*b*) *Tensions in belt*

(*c*) *Size of wire laced leather belt*

(*d*) *Shaft size assuming an allowable stress of 500 kg/cm*$^2$.

(*e*) *Net efficiency of drive.*

**Solution.**

Let $D_1$ = Diameter of driving pulley

$N_1$ = R.P.M. of driving pulley

$D_2$ = Diameter of driven pulley

$N_2$ = Diameter of driven pulley

$C$ = Centre distance

$S$ = Slip = 0.016

$V$ = Belt speed = 20 m/s

(*a*)
$$V = \frac{\pi D_1 N_1}{60}(1 - S)$$

$$20 = \frac{\pi \times 1 \times N_1}{60}(1 - 0.016)$$

$$N_1 = 388 \text{ R.P.M.}$$

Again
$$V = \frac{\pi D_2 N_2}{60}(1 - S)$$

$$20 = \frac{\pi \times 1.3 \times N_2}{60}(1 - 0.016)$$

$$N_2 = 310 \text{ R.P.M.}$$

(*b*) For driven shaft

$$\text{H.P.} = \frac{2\pi N_2 T}{4500}$$

$$160 = \frac{2\pi \times 310 \times T}{4500}$$

$$T = 369.8 \text{ kg m} = 36980 \text{ kg cm.}$$

Friction loss = 4%

$T_m$ = Torque transmitted by belt

$= 1.04 \times T = 1.04 \times 36980 = 38459$ kg cm.

$R_2$ = Radius of driven shaft = 65 cm.

$T_1$ = Tight side tension

$T_2$ = Loose side tension

$(T_1 - T_2) \times R_2 = T_m$

$$T_1 - T_2 = \frac{T_m}{R_2} = \frac{38459}{65} = 592 \text{ kg.}$$

(c) $\theta$ = Angle of contact

$$= 180 - 2\sin^{-1}\frac{D_2 - D_1}{2C}$$

$$= 180 - 2\sin^{-1}\left(\frac{130 - 100}{2 \times 300}\right)$$

$\theta = 170$ degrees

$$= \frac{170 \times \pi}{180} = 2.97 \text{ radians}$$

Now $$\frac{T_1}{T_2} = e^{\mu\theta}$$

where $\mu = 0.32$

$$= e^{0.32 \times 2.97} = 2.47$$

$T_1 = 2.47\, T_2$

and $T_1 - T_2 = 592$

$\therefore$ $T_1 = 994$ kg.

As the belt speed more than 10 m/s therefore centrifugal stress should be taken into account.

$f_c$ = Centrifugal stress

$$= \frac{\omega V^2}{g}$$

For leather, $\omega = 1 \text{ gm/cm}^2 = 0.001 \text{ kg/cm}^2$

$V = 20$ m/s

$$f_c = \frac{0.001 \times (20 \times 100)^2}{981} = 4 \text{ kg/cm}^2$$

Let $\eta$ = Efficiency of joint = 0.9 (say)

$f_t$ = Tensile stress for leather

$= 28 \text{ kg/cm}^2$ (assume)

$f$ = Net safe stress

$= f_t \times \eta = 28 \times 0.9 = 25.2\ \text{kg/cm}^2$

$b$ = Width of belt

$t$ = Thickness of belt

$$b.t = \frac{T_1}{f - f_c} = \frac{994}{25.2 - 4} = 46.8\ \text{cm}^2$$

Now $\quad t = \frac{D_1}{50} = \frac{100}{50} = 2\ \text{cm}$

$$b \times 2 = 46.8$$

$$b = \frac{46.8}{2} = 23.4\ \text{cm.}$$

(*d*) Let $\quad d_1$ = Diameter of driving shaft

$d_2$ = Diameter of driven shaft

For driven shaft

$$T_m = \frac{\pi}{16} f_s\, d_2^3$$

$$38459 = \frac{\pi}{16} \times 500 \times d_2^3$$

$$d_2 = 7.3\ \text{cm.}$$

$R_1$ = Radius of driving pulley

$= 50$ cm

$T_d$ = Torque on driving pulley

$= (T_1 - T_{2)} \times R_1 \times 1.04$

$= 592 \times 50 \times 1.04 = 30.784$ kg cm.

$$30784 = \frac{\pi}{16} f_s\, d_1^3 = \frac{\pi}{16} \times 500 \times d_1^2$$

$$d_1 = 6.8\ \text{cm.}$$

(*e*) Total loss in efficiency

$= 2$ (slip + friction) $= 2(1.6 + 4)$

$= 11.2$ per cent

Net efficiency of drive

$= 100 - 11.2 = 88.8$ per cent.

**Example 13.6. (B)** *Two shaft one metre apart are connected by a V-belt drive to transmit 80 kw at 1000 RPM of a driver pulley of 280 mm effective diameter. The driven pulley rotates at 250 R.P.M.*

*The angle of groove is 45° and coefficient of friction between belt and pulley rim is 0.24. Area of belt section is 380 mm² and permissible stress is 2 MPa. Density of belt material is 1100 kg/m³.*

*Determine (a) Number of belts required.*

*(b) Length of belt.*

**Solution.**

$A$ = Area of belt section = 380 mm²

$D_1$ = Driver pulley diameter

= 280 mm

$N_1$ = R.P.M. of driver pulley

= 1000

$V$ = Driver pulley speed

$$= \frac{\pi D_1 N_1}{1000 \times 60}$$

$$= \frac{\pi \times 280 \times 1000}{1000 \times 60} = 14.65 \text{ m/s}$$

$\omega$ = Mass/unit length = $1100 \times A$

$$= \frac{1100 \times 380}{1000 \times 1000} = 0.42 \text{ kg/m}$$

$T_c$ = centrifugal tension

$= \omega v^2$

$= 0.42 \times 14.65^2 = 90.14\ N$

$\sigma$ = Permissible stress

= 2.0 MPa

$T$ = Maximum tension

$= 2 \times 380$

$= 760\ N$

$T_1$ = Tight side tension = $T - T_c$

$= 760 - 90.14 = 669.86\ N$

$D_2$ = Diameter of driver pulley

$N_2$ = R.P.M. of driver pulley = 250

$$\pi D_1 N_1 = \pi D_1 N_2$$

$$\pi \times 280 \times 1000 = \pi D_2 \times 250$$

$$D_2 = 1120 \text{ mm}$$

$c$ = Centre distance between pulleys = 1 m

$\theta$ = Angle of lap for smaller pulley

$$= 180 - 2\sin^{-1}\frac{D_2 - D_1}{2C}$$

$$= 180 - 2\sin^{-1}\frac{1120 - 280}{2 \times 1000}$$

= 130.4 degrees

$\mu$ = Coeff. of friction = 0.24

$T_2$ = Loose side tension

$\alpha$ = Angle of groove = 40°

$$\frac{T_1}{T_2} = e^{\frac{\mu\theta}{\sin\frac{\alpha}{2}}}$$

$$= e^{0.24 \times \frac{\pi \times 130.4}{180} \times \text{cosec } 20} = 4.95$$

$$T_2 = \frac{T_1}{4.95}$$

$$= \frac{669.86}{4.95} = 135.3\ N$$

$P_1$ = Power = $(T_1 - T_2)\ V$

= (669.86 – 135.3) × 14.65

= 7831 $W$ = 7.831 kW

$P$ = Total power to be transmitted = 80 kW

Number of belts required $= \frac{P}{P_1} = \frac{80}{7.831}$

= 10.2 = 11 (say)

$L$ = Length of belt

$$= \pi(R_1 + R_2) + 2C + \frac{(R_1 - R_2)^2}{C}$$

where $R_1$ = Radiues $= \frac{D_1}{2}$

$$= \frac{280}{2} = 140 \text{ mm}$$

$$R_2 = \frac{D_2}{2} = \frac{1120}{2} = 560 \text{ mm}$$

$$L = \pi(140 + 560) + 2 \times 1000 + \frac{(560 - 140)^2}{1000}$$

= 4374.4 mm.

## 13.18. Chain Drives

They are used to transmit power between parallel shafts comparatively at a longer distances. A chain drives (Fig. 13.9) consists of an endless chain running over two sprockets. Sprockets are wheels provided with teeth of special profile. Chain drive has the following advantages.

(*i*) Chain drive can transmit more power than belt drive.

(*ii*) Chain drive provides positive non-slip drive.

(*iii*) Maintenance cost of chain drive is low.

(*iv*) Efficiency of chain drive is high (upto 98%).

(*v*) Chain drive can be operated under adverse temperature and atmospheric conditions.

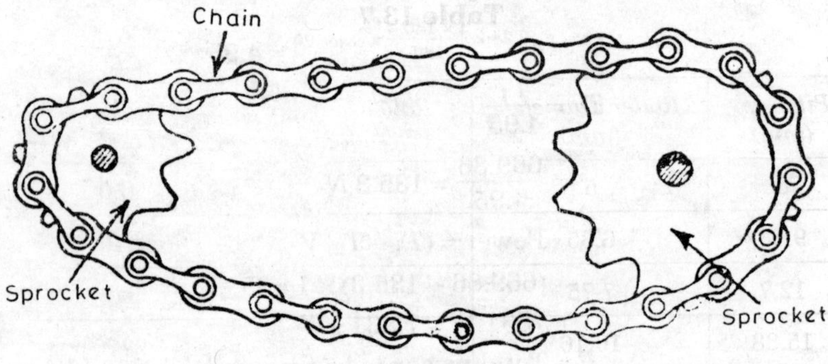


Fig. 13.9

**13.18.1. Types of chain.** A chain is made of links, pit bushings. The following two types of chains are most commonly used.

(*i*) Roller chain.

(*ii*) Toothed (silent) chain.

(*iii*) Bush chains.

Roller chain is shown in Fig. 13.10. In this chain rollers are housed between connecting links and rotate freely on bushes. Distance between two consecutive pins must be equal to pitch ($p$) of sprocket wheel. Table 13.7 indicates the various sizes of B.S. simplex roller chain.

Silent chain provide a comparatively noiseless and uniform drive. In this chain a row of toothed links is connected through bushes.

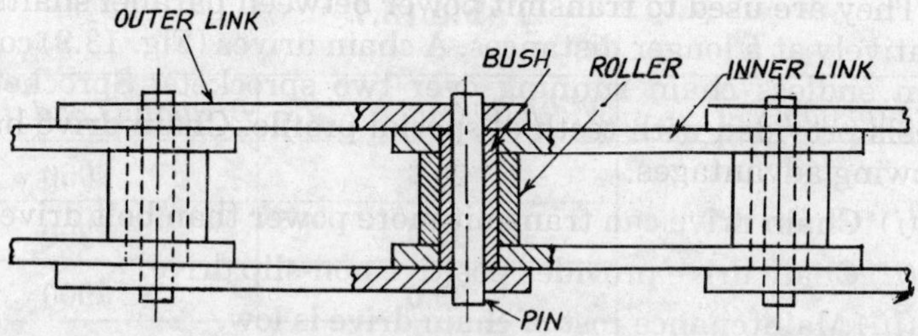


Fig. 13.10. Roller chain.

**Table 13.7**

| *Pitch (p) (mm)* | *Roller diameter (mm)* | *Roller length (mm)* | *Bearing load (kg)* |
|---|---|---|---|
| 8 | 5 | 3 | 450 |
| 9.53 | 6.35 | 5.7 | 910 |
| 12.7 | 7.75 | 3.3 | 910 |
| 15.88 | 10.16 | 9.7 | 2270 |
| 19.05 | 12.07 | 11.7 | 2950 |
| 25.40 | 15.88 | 17.0 | 4540 |
| 31.75 | 19.05 | 19.6 | 6580 |
| 38.10 | 25.40 | 25.4 | 10890 |
| 44.45 | 27.94 | 31.0 | 13150 |
| 50.8 | 29.21 | 31.0 | 16780 |

Fig. 13.11 shows silent chain system.

Table 13.8 indicates breaking load for toothed chain for typical values of width and pitch.

## Table 13.7

| Pitch (p) (mm) | Width (b) (mm) | Breaking Load (kg) |
|---|---|---|
| 12.7 | 20.5 | 2050 |
| | 33.0 | 3300 |
| | 39.0 | 3900 |
| | 51.5 | 5150 |
| | 63.0 | 6300 |
| | 91.0 | 9100 |
| 15.87 | 26.5 | 3180 |
| | 33.0 | 3960 |
| | 39.0 | 4680 |
| | 51.5 | 6180 |
| | 63.0 | 7560 |
| | 91.0 | 10920 |
| | 123.0 | 14760 |
| 19.5 | 33.0 | 4900 |
| | 39.0 | 5800 |
| | 51.5 | 7700 |
| | 63.0 | 9445 |
| | 91.0 | 13600 |
| | 123.0 | 18400 |
| | 148.0 | 22200 |
| | 198.0 | 29700 |
| 25.4 | 51.5 | 8700 |
| | 93.0 | 15800 |
| | 101.0 | 17100 |
| | 121.0 | 20500 |
| | 154.0 | 26200 |
| | 204.5 | 34700 |

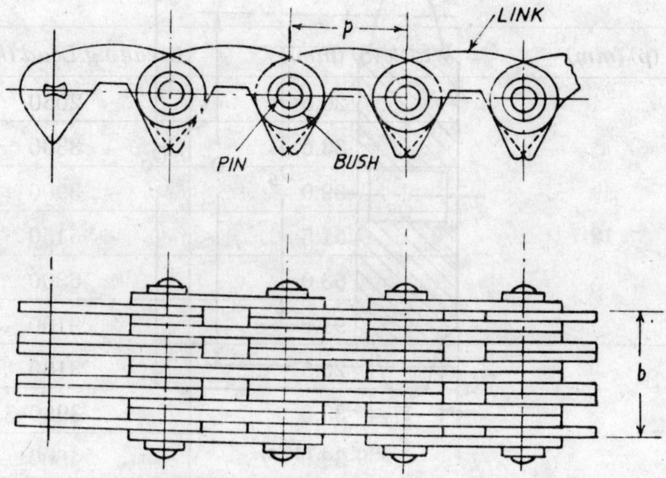


Fig. 13.11.

Roller chains and bush chains are recommended for low and medium speed service whereas silent chain is employed for high speed ratios due to its more smooth and quiet operation.

$$d = \text{Roller diameter} = \frac{5}{8} \times \text{pitch}$$

$$d_p = \text{Pin diameter} = \frac{5}{16} \times \text{pitch}$$

$b$ = Chain width (Distance between roller link plates)

$$= \frac{5}{8} \text{ pitch}$$

$t$ = Thickness of link plates = $p/8$

$h_o$ = Maximum height of pin link plates (outer plates) = 0.82 p

$h_1$ = Maximum height of roller link plates (Inner plates) = 0.95 p

$l$ = Length of roller = 0.9 $b$ – 0.15

According to Indian Standards (IS 2403 - 1964) roller chains are designated by roller diameter and number of strands.

Fig. 13.11 ($a$) shows types of silent chain joints.

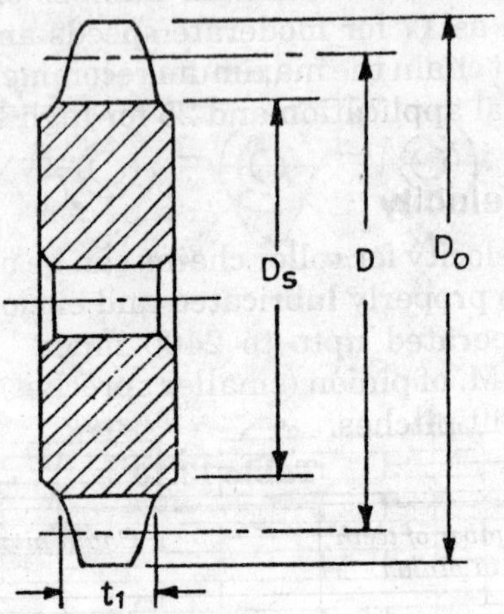


Fig. 13.11 (*a*)

## 13.19. Velocity Ratio

The velocity ratio ($r$) of a chain drive is given by

$$r = \frac{N_p}{N_G} = \frac{T_g}{T_p}$$

where

$N_P$ = Speed of rotation of sprocket pinion (smaller) in R.P.M.

$N_G$ = Speed of rotation of sprocket wheel (larger wheel)

$T_P$ = Number of teeth on pinion

$T_g$ = Number of teeth of sprocket wheel

## 13.20. Teeth of Pinion

Table 13.9 shows number of teeth in a pinion (smaller sprocket) for different values of velocity ratio. For example, the number of teeth on pinion for roller chain at velocity ratio 6 to 17.

**Table 13.9**

| *Type of chain* | *Velocity ratio* | | | | | |
|---|---|---|---|---|---|---|
| | *1* | *2* | *3* | *4* | *5* | *6* |
| Roller chain | 31 | 27 | 25 | 23 | 21 | 17 |
| Silent chain | 40 | 35 | 31 | 27 | 23 | 19 |

In roller chains the maximum number of teeth for pinion is recommmended as 17 for moderate speeds and 21 for high speed drives. For silent chain the maximum recommended teeth on pinion are 21 for general application and 25 for high speed applications.

## 13.21. Chain Velocity

The chain velocity for roller chains can be as high as 1200 mpm if the chains are properly lubricated and enclosed. Whereas silent chain can be operated upto to 2400 mpm. Table 13.10 shows permissible R.P.M. of pinion (smaller sprocket) for roller and silent chains as different pitches.

**Table 13.10**

| *Type of chain* | *Number of teeth in pinion* | *Chain pitch (p) (mm)* | | | | |
|---|---|---|---|---|---|---|
| | | *12* | *15* | *20* | *25* | *30* |
| | 15 | 2300 | 1900 | 1350 | 1150 | 1100 |
| | 19 | 2400 | 2000 | 1450 | 1200 | 1050 |
| Roller chain | 23 | 2500 | 2100 | 1500 | 1250 | 1100 |
| | 27 | 2550 | 2150 | 1550 | 1300 | 1100 |
| | 30 | 2600 | 2200 | 1550 | 1300 | 1100 |
| Silent chain | 17-35 | 3000 | 2650 | 2200 | 1650 | 1300 |

For roller chains the maximum number of revolutions and the maximum chain speed is indicated in Table 13.10 (*A*).

**Table 13.10 (*A*)**

| *Pitch mm* | *Max. RPM* | *Chain speed m/s* |
|---|---|---|
| 9.525 | 3500 | 13.7 |
| 12.7 | 2500 | 13.4 |
| 15.875 | 2300 | 12.0 |
| 19.05 | 1800 | 10.9 |
| 25.4 | 1500 | 9.7 |
| 31.75 | 1000 | 8.1 |
| 38.1 | 800 | 7.3 |
| 44.45 | 600 | 6.5 |
| 50.8 | 400 | 6.0 |
| 63.5 | 300 | 4.7 |

## 13.22. Pitch

The pitch for roller chains varies from 6 mm to 75 mm and for silent chains it varies 3 mm to 75 mm.

The selection of pitch depends on the following :

(*i*) Power to be transmitted

(*ii*) Chain speed

(*iii*) Number of revolutions of the smallest chain wheel.

(*a*) For bushed and roller chains $p = R_1 \sqrt[3]{\dfrac{\text{H.P.} \times k}{T_p \times w_1 \times pb.x}}$ mm

(*b*) For silent chains $p = R_2 \sqrt[3]{\dfrac{\text{H.P} \times k}{T_p\, w_1 \,.\, pb.b}}$ mm

where $p$ = Pitch

$R_1 = 30 \;;\; R_2 = 280$

H.P. = Power in $kW$

$K$ = Load factor

$\omega_1$ = Angular speed of driving sprocket

$x$ = Number of chain strands

$b$ = Width of chain (mm)

$pb$ = Allowable bearing pressure chains

$= 3.5$ to $1.37$ kg/mm$^2$ for roller chains

When $N$ = 50 to 2800 R.P.M.

$pb = 2$ to $0.75$ kg/mm$^2$ for silent chains

Another formula to find pitch is given by

$$p = \frac{C}{30 \text{ to } 60}$$

The standard pitch used are 6.25, 8, 9.525, 12.7, 15.875, 19.05, 25.4, 31.75, 38.1, 44.75, 50.8, 63.5, 76.2 mm

Fig. 13.11 (*b*) shows sectional view of a sprocket

$TS$ = Shroud diameter

$$= p \cot \frac{180^\circ}{T} - 1.3 \times h_1$$

where $h_1$ = Maximum height of inner plates

$= 0.95 \times p$

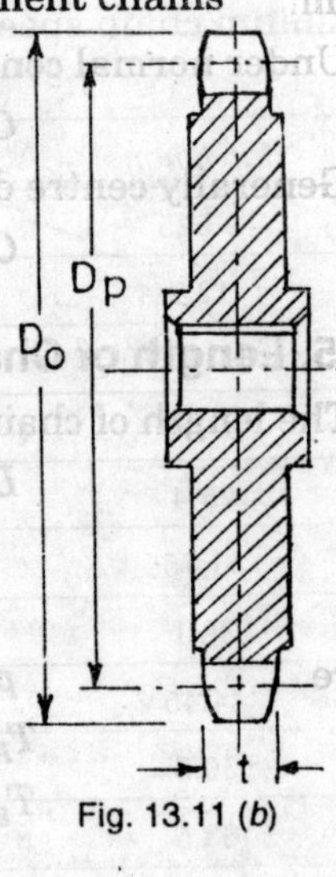

Fig. 13.11 (*b*)

$t_1$ = Tooth Width
$= 0.91\, b$

where $b$ = chain width.

## 13.23. Pitch Diameter of Sprocket

The pitch diameter ($D$) of sprocket is given by

$$D = \frac{p}{\sin \dfrac{\pi}{T}}$$

where $T$ = Number of teeth on sprocket
$p$ = Pitch
$D_o$ = Outside diameter of sprocket
$= D + 0.8\, d$

where $d$ = Roller diameter.

## 13.24. Centre Distance

The centre distance ($C$) between sprockets centres is calculated as follows :

$C_{min}$ = Minimum centre distance

$$= \frac{D_1 + D_2}{2} + 30 \text{ to } 50 \text{ mm}$$

where $D_1$ and $D_2$ are the diameter of addendum circle of the sprocket in mm.

Under normal conditions

$$C = 30\,p \text{ to } 50\,p$$

Generally centre distance is kept less than 80 $p$.

$$C < 80\,p$$

## 13.25. Length of Chain

The length of chain required is calculated as follows :

$L$ = Length of chain

$$= \frac{T_P + T_g}{2} + \left(\frac{T_g - T_p}{2\pi}\right)^2 \frac{p}{C} + \frac{2C}{p}$$

where $p$ = Pitch
$T_p$ = Number of teeth on pinion
$T_g$ = Number of teeth on sprocket wheel

$C$ = Centre distance between sprockets

Length of chain is also given by

$$L = n \cdot p$$

where $n$ = Number of chain links

Accurate centre distance is given by

$$C = \left[\frac{p}{4} n - \frac{T_g + T_p}{2} + \sqrt{\left(n - \frac{T_g + T_p}{2}\right)^2 - 8\left(\frac{T_g - T_p}{2\pi}\right)^2}\right]$$

**13.25.1. Number of chain links.** The number of chain links is given by the following relation.

$$n = \frac{2C}{p} + \frac{T_g + T_p}{2} + p\,\frac{(T_g - T_p)^2}{4\pi^2 c}.$$

## 13.26. Driving Force

The driving force *i.e.* tension on tight side treating tension on slacks side as zero is calculated as follows :

$P$ = Driving force

$$= \text{H.P.} \times \frac{4500}{V}$$

$V$ = Chain velocity in mpm

H.P. = Horse power transmitted

$F$ = Total load on driving side of chain is given by

$$= P + P_c + P_f$$

where $P_c$ = Chain tension due to centrifugal action

$$= \frac{\omega V^2}{g}$$

where $\omega$ = Weight per meter of chain length

$V$ = Chain velocity (mpm)

$P_f$ = Tension due slagging

$$= k_f \cdot \omega \cdot C.$$

where $k_f$ = Coefficient that takes into account the arrangement of chain drive.

= 1.0 for vertical position

= 2.0 for centre line inclined at an angle up to 45°

$k_f = 4.0$ for horizontal drives

$$\text{Factor of safety} = \frac{Fb}{F}$$

where $Fb$ = Breaking strength of chains.

$= 1060\, p^2$ kg where p is in cm for roller chains.

$= 1060\, p$ kg per cm width of chain for silent.

chains

**13.26.1. Lubrication.** Lubrication plays an import role in increasing life of chain drive. A chain is usually lubricated by an oil. However, for low running chain drives grease lubrication can also be used.

Table 13.10 (*B*) indicates the type of lubrication for different chain speeds.

**Table 13.10 (*B*)**

| *Chain speed (m/s)* | *Lubrication* | |
|---|---|---|
| | *Favourable,* | Admissible |
| up to 4 | Right dropwise | Grease |
| 4-7 | Submersion in oil bath. | Dropwise |
| 7-12 | Forced | Oil bath |
| more than 12 | Spray type | Forced feed |

SAE 20 and SAE 30 oils are used for shorter pitches and SAE 40 for heavier types of chains.

Method of lubrication depends on the following factors :

(*i*) Speed of chain

(*ii*) Magnitude of power to be transmitted.

## 13.27. Check for Wear and Bearing Pressure

Due to tension and dynamic loads during operation, wear of chain takes place and pitch increases. The chain elongation should be restricted to 3%. The chain should be checked for wear.The bearing pressure on rollers is calculated as follows :

$$f_c = \frac{P \, . \, K}{A}$$

where $f_b$ = Bearing pressure in kg/cm$^2$

$P$ = Driving force

$A$ = Projection of joint bearing surface

For roller chains, $A$ = Roller diameter × Chain width within the inner plates

For silent chains,

$A = 0.76 \times$ Diameter of joint pivot × Chain width

$k$ = Load factor

$= k_1 . k_2 . k_3$

where $k_1$ = 1 to 1.4 that takes into account nature of load

$k_2$ = 1 to 1.5 that takes into account method of lubrication

$k_3$ = 1 to 1.45 that takes into account service conditions.

The usual value of $f_b$ (bearing pressure) is 3.5 kg/mm$^2$ when sprocket speed is less than 50 R.P.M. and its value is 1.4 kg/mm$^2$ when sprocket speed is 2800 R.P.M. for roller chains and for silent chains the value of bearing pressure is about 2 to 0.75 kg/mm$^2$.

## 13.28. Bearing Strength of Chains

The beraing strength ($F_b$) of chain is calculated as follows :

For roller chain $F_b = 1060\, p^2$ kg

where $p$ = Pitch in cm

For silent chains

$F_b = 1060\, p$ kg per cm width of chain.

## 13.29. Total Load on Chain

The total load on driving side of chain is calculated as follows :

$$F = P + P_c + P_f$$

where $F$ = Total load driving side of chain

$P$ = Net driving force

$$= \frac{\text{H.P.} \times 4500}{\text{V}}$$

$P_e$ = Chain tension due to centrifugal force

$$= \frac{w}{g} \cdot v^2$$

where $w$ = weight per metre length of chain

$v$ = Chain speed in metre/sec

$P_f$ = Tension due to sagging = $k \cdot w \cdot C$

where

$k$ = Constant which takes into account the arrangement of chain drive

= 2 to 6 when chain drive is inclined with respect to horizontal at tan than 40°

= 1 to 1.5 when angle of inclination is more than 40°.

## 13.30. Factor of Safety

It is defined as the ratio of bracking strength ($F_b$) to total load on driving side of chain ($F$).

$$\text{Factor of safety} = \frac{F_b}{F}$$

Table 13.11 indicates factor of safety for chain drives.

**Table 13.11**

| *Type of chain* | *R.P.M. of Pinion* | | | | | | | |
|---|---|---|---|---|---|---|---|---|
| Roller Chain : | 50 | 200 | 400 | 600 | 800 | 1000 | 1200 | 1600 |
| $p$ = 12 – 15 mm | 7 | 7.8 | 8.55 | 9.35 | 10.2 | 11.0 | 11.7 | 13.2 |
| = 20 – 25 mm | 7 | 8.2 | 9.35 | 10.3 | 11.7 | 12.9 | 14.0 | 16.3 |
| = 30 – 35 mm | 7 | 8.55 | 10.2 | 13.2 | 14.8 | 16.3 | 19.5 | — |
| Silent Chains : | | | | | | | | |
| $p$ = 12.7 – 15.87 mm | 20 | 22.2 | 24.4 | 28.7 | 29.0 | 31.0 | 33.4 | 37.8 |
| = 19.05 – 25.04 mm | 20 | 23.4 | 26.7 | 30.0 | 33.4 | 36.8 | 40.0 | 46.5 |

**13.30.1 Design prodcedure of chain drive.** The design of chain drive is carried out as follows :

(*i*) Select type of chain

(*ii*) Find teeth on sprocket pinion

(*iii*) Fix chain speed

(*iv*) Find pitch

(*v*) Determine total force acting on driving side of chain and find factor of safety

(*vi*) Find sprocket size

(*vii*) Check the chain for wear

(*viii*) Desireable speed ratio 6 : 1 and should not exceed 9 : 1. Smallest sprocket should have at least 23 teeth and there should not be more than 100 teeth on large sprocket.

**Example 13.7.** *A roller chain derive is required to actuate a compressor from 16 H.P. electric motor running at 1000 R.P.M., the compressor speed being 250 R.P.M. The minimum centre distance is 60 cm. The weight per metre length of chain is 2.5 kg and the compressor operates in two shafts. Determine.*

(*a*) *Number of teeth on sprockets*

(*b*) *Pitch diameters of sprockets*

(*c*) *Factor of safety*

(*d*) *Length of chain*

(*e*) *Sprocket pinion outside diameter.*

**Solution.** (*a*) **To find number of teeth**

$$\text{Velocity ratio} = \frac{\text{R.P.M. of motor}}{\text{R.P.M. of compressor}} = \frac{1000}{250} = 4$$

From Table 13.8, we select the teeth for sprocket pinion as 23 corresponding to velocity ratio 4.

$$T_P = \text{Number of teeth on pinion} = 23$$

$$T_g = \text{Number of teeth on sprocket gear}$$

$$\doteq 23 \times \frac{1000}{250} = 92.$$

(*b*) **To find pitch diameter of sprockets**

Assume, $P = \text{Pitch} = 15 \text{ mm} = 1.5 \text{ cm}$

$$D_p = \text{Pitch diameter of pinion}$$

$$= \frac{p}{\sin\frac{\pi}{T_p}} = \frac{15}{\sin\frac{180}{23}}$$

$$= \frac{15}{\sin 7.8^o} = \frac{15}{0.1357} = 110 \text{ mm}$$

$D_g$ = Pitch diameter of sprocket gear

$$= \frac{p}{\sin\frac{\pi}{T_g}} = \frac{15}{\sin\frac{180}{92}} = \frac{15}{\sin 1.95^o} = 441 \text{ mm}$$

(c) $N_P$ = R.P.M. of pinion = 1000

$V$ = Pitch line velocity

$$= \frac{\pi D_P T_P}{60} = \frac{\pi \times 110 \times 1000}{60 \times 1000}$$

= 5.75 m/*sec* = 345 m/min

$$p = \text{Driving force} = \frac{\text{H.P.} \times 4500}{\text{V}}$$

$$P = \frac{16 \times 450}{345} = 209 \text{ kg}$$

$F$ = Total load on driving side of chain

$= P + P_c + P_f$

$P_c$ = Chain tension due to centrifugal force

$$= \frac{w}{g} v^2$$

$w$ = Weight for metre length of chain

= 2.5 kg

$$P_e = \frac{2.5 \times (5.75)^2}{9.81} = 8.42 \text{ kg.}$$

$C$ = Centre distance = 60 cm

$P_f = k \cdot w \cdot C$

$k$ = Constant = 4 (say)

$$P_f = 4 \times 2.5 \times \frac{60}{100} = 6 \text{ kg}$$

$$F = P + P_c + P_f = 209 + 8.42 + 6 = 223.42 \text{ kg}$$

$F_b$ = Breaking strength of chain = $1060\, p^2$

where $p$ = Pitch in cm

$$F_b = 1060 \times (1.5)^2 = 2385 \text{ kg}$$

$$\text{Factor of safety} = \frac{f_b}{F} = \frac{2385}{223.42}$$

= 10.67 = 11 (say)

**(*d*) To find length of chain**

$$L = \text{Length of chain}$$

$$= \frac{T_P + T_g}{2} + \left(\frac{T_g - T_P}{2\pi}\right)^2 \frac{p}{C} + \frac{2C}{p}$$

$$= \frac{23 + 92}{2} + \left(\frac{92 - 23}{2\pi}\right)^2 \times \frac{1.5}{60} + \frac{2 \times 60}{1.5}$$

$$= 140.5 \text{ cm.}$$

**(*e*) To find sprocket pinion outside diameter**

$$D_0 = \text{Outside diameter of sprocket pinion}$$

$$= D_P + 0.8\, d$$

where $d$ = Roller diameter

$$= \frac{5}{8} \times p \text{ (Assume)} = \frac{5}{8} \times 15$$

$$= 9.375 \text{ mm} = 10 \text{ mm (say)}$$

$\therefore$ $D_0 = D_p + 0.8\, d = 110 + 0.8 \times 10 = 118$ mm

$$b = \text{Chain width} = \frac{5}{8} \times p = \frac{5}{8} \times 15 = 9.37 \text{ mm.}$$

$$t_1 = \text{Tooth width}$$

$$= 0.91\, b = 0.91 \times 9.37 = 8.52 \text{ mm}$$

$$D_r = \text{Shroud diameter of proket pinion}$$

$$= p \cot \frac{180}{T_p} - 1.3\, h_1$$

where $h_1 = 0.95\, p = 0.95 \times 15 = 14.25$ mm

$$D_r = 15 \cot \frac{180}{23} - 1.3 \times 14.25 = 101 \text{ mm.}$$

## 13.31. Rope Drive

Rope drive is successfully used where large amount of power is to be transmitted over longer distances. The ropes are made up of the following materials :

(*a*) Fibre ropes (*b*) Wire ropes.

**Fibre ropes.** Fibrous material commonly used are hemp and manila and cotton. Manila ropes are more durable and stronger than cotton ropes. Hemp ropes have less strength as compared to manila rope. Hemp ropes are commonly used for hand operated hoisting machinery. The fibre ropes operate successfully for a centre distance of about 60 m. The diameter of manila and cotton ropes used for power transmission usually varies from 38 mm to 50 mm. The size of ropes is usually designated by its circumference. The ultimate tensile strength of cotton ropes is about 350 $d^2$ kg whereas the ultimate tensile strength of manila ropes is 500 $d^2$ kg where $d$ is rope diameter in cm. Both manila and cotton ropes are suitable where small powers to be transmitted. The velocity of fibrous ropes varies from 900 to 1800 metre per minute.

Fibre ropes have the following properties :

(*i*) Rapid abrasion

(*ii*) In adequate strength

(*iii*) Rapid damage from sharp objects and atmospheric effects.

These poor properties make them suitable only for hand operated hoisting machinery, rope pulleys.

## 13.32. Wire Ropes

Wire ropes are made of various grades of steels such as cast steel, plow steel, alloy steel and wrought iron. Wire ropes are manufactered from steel wires with an ultimate strength ranging from 110 to 225 kg/cm$^2$. A number of wires such as 7, 19 or 37 are first twisted into a strand. A number of strands usually 6 or 8 are then twisted about a core or centre to form the rope. Cores may be of hemp or of wire. The ropes are designated as 6 × 7, 6 × 37 and so on A 6 × 7 rope means a rope made from six strands with seven wires in each strand. Fig. 13.12. shows a 6 × 7 rope and 6 × 19 steel wire rope.

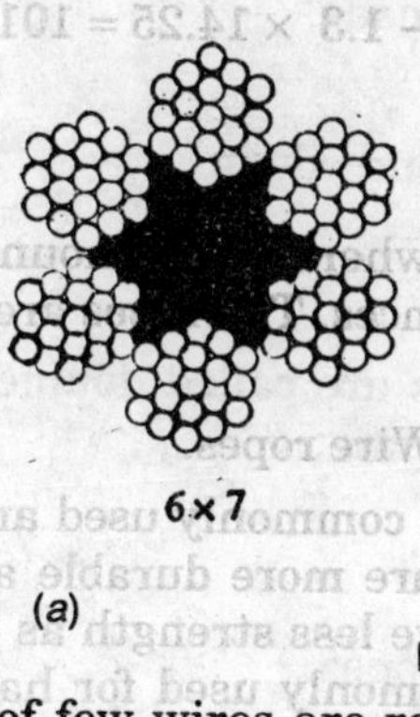

6 × 7

(*a*)

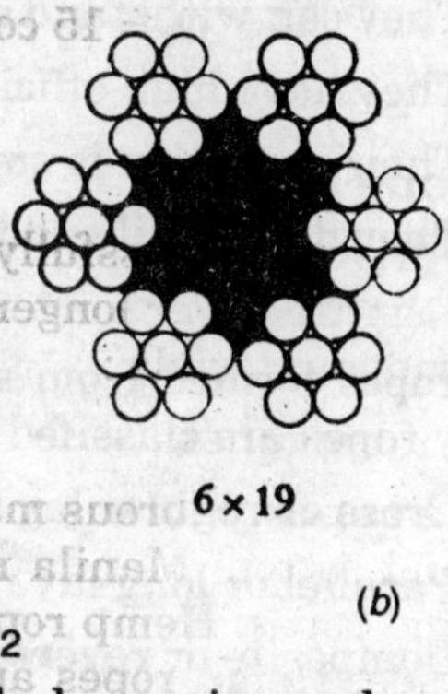

6 × 19

(*b*)

Fig. 13.12

Ropes of few wires are relatively large size such as 6 × 7 are used for guy wires but are too stiff for hoisting service unless the sheaves have very large diameters. The 6 × 19 and 6 × 37 types are the most widely used ropes for hoisting services. The diameter of rope and diameter of wire are related as follows :

$$d = 1.5\, d_1 \sqrt{n}$$

where $d$ = Diameter of rope

$d_1$ = Diameter of wire

$n$ = Number of wires in the rope

Table 13.12 indicates the effective cross-sectional area ($A$), average sheave diameter ($D$) and weight ($w$) kg/m (approximately) for different types of ropes where $d$ is rope diameter in cm.

**Table 13.12**

| *Rope* | $w$ | $d_1$ | $A$ | $D$ |
|---|---|---|---|---|
| 6 × 7 | $0.347\, d^2$ | $0.106\, d$ | $0.38\, d^2$ | $75\, d$ |
| 6 × 19 | $0.363\, d^2$ | $0.063d$ | $0.38\, d^2$ | $45\, d$ |
| 6 × 37 | $0.35\, d^2$ | $0.05\, d$ | $0.38\, d^2$ | $27\, d$ |
| 8 × 19 | $0.346\, d^2$ | $0.050\, d$ | $0.35\, d^2$ | $31\, d$ |

## 13.33. Wire Ropes have the Following Advantages

(*i*) Wire ropes are more reliable.

(*ii*) They can withstand shock loads.

(*iii*) They have high efficiency.

(*iv*) Their operation is smooth and silent.

(*v*) They do not fail suddenly.

Wire ropes formed from strands are called double lay ropes. Double lay ropes are classifed as follows :

(*i*) Cross or regular lay ropes.

(*ii*) Parallel or long lay ropes.

(*iii*) Composite or reverse laid ropes.

Fig. 13.12 (*a*) shows double lay ropes.

Fig. 13.12 (*a*)

## 13.34. Factor of Safety

In rope drive a high factor of safety (F.O.S.) is recommended. It is defined as follows :

$$\text{F.O.S.} = \frac{P_1}{P_2}$$

where $P_1$ = Ultimate tensile strength

$P_2$ = Normal working load on rope

Table 13.13 indicates the tensile strength of steel wire ropes used for haulage purpose in mines.

**Table 13.13**

| *Type of Rope* | *Nominal wire diameter (mm)* | *Tensile strenght (kg)* | |
|---|---|---|---|
| | | *Tensile strength of wire 160 kg/mm²* | *Tensile strength of wire 180 kg/mm²* |
| 6 × 7 | 8, 9, 10, 11, 12, 13, 14, 16, 18, 19, 20, 21, 22, 24, 25, 26, 27, 28, 29, 31, 35 | 5300 $d^2$ | 5975 $d^2$ |
| 6 × 19 | 13, 14, 16, 18, 19, 20, 21, 22, 24, 25, 26, 28, 29, 32, 35, 36, 38 | 5300 $d^2$ | 5950 $d^2$ |

$d$ = Rope diameter in cm.

## 13.35. Rope Speed

*(i)* **Wire ropes.** The wire ropes have the following speeds for the various application as indicated below.

Rope speed = 80 – 400 mpm for elevators
= 60 mpm for track cables, guys and cranes
= 350 – 500 mpm for mining ropes

*(ii)* **Fibrous ropes.** The velocity of ropes varies between 900-1800 mpm. Commonly used velocity being 1200-1500 mpm.

Table 13.14 indicates the factor of safety for different types of ropes.

**Table 13.14**

| *Type of ropes* | *F.O.S.* |
|---|---|
| Cotton rope | 30 |
| Manila rope | 36 |
| Wire rope : | |
| *(i)* Elevators | 8-12 |
| *(ii)* Cranes | 4-6 |
| *(iii)* Track cables, guys | 4 |
| *(iv)* Electric hoists | 7 |

## 13.36. Rope Fasteners

Various types of fasteners are in used Fig. 13.13 shows thimble and clamps used as fastener and Fig. 13.14 shows eye shoe with rivets as rope fastener.

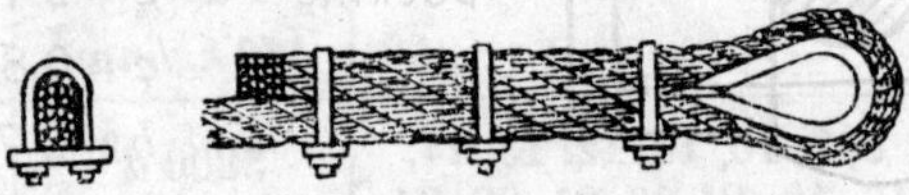

Fig. 13.13.

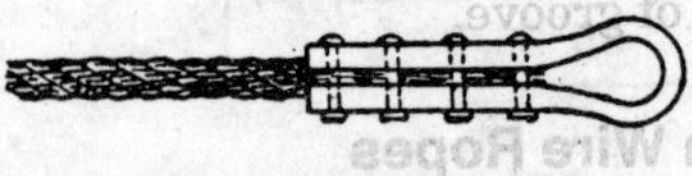

Fig. 13.14.

## 13.37. Rope Pulleys

(*i*) **For fibrous rope.** Rope pulleys are grooved to carry one or more ropes. For fibrous ropes the diameter of pulley is 40 $d$ and the minimum value is 30 $d$ where $d$ is the diameter of rope. Fig. 13.15 shows typical fibrous rope sheave rim. The various dimensions are as follows :

$$d = \text{Rope diameter}$$

$$a = \frac{d}{4}$$

$$d = d + \frac{d}{12}$$

$$a = 0.8\ d$$

$$e = 0.5\ d$$

Groove angle $(\alpha) = 45^\circ$ (commonly used).

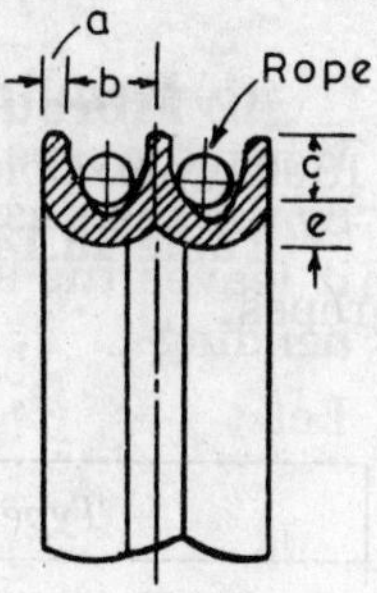


Fig. 13.15.

(*ii*) **For steel rope.** The rim of a wire rope sheave is shown in Fig. 13.16. The bottom of groove is packed with soft materials like leather or gutta purcha to minimise slipping. The various dimensions in terms of rope diameter are as follows:

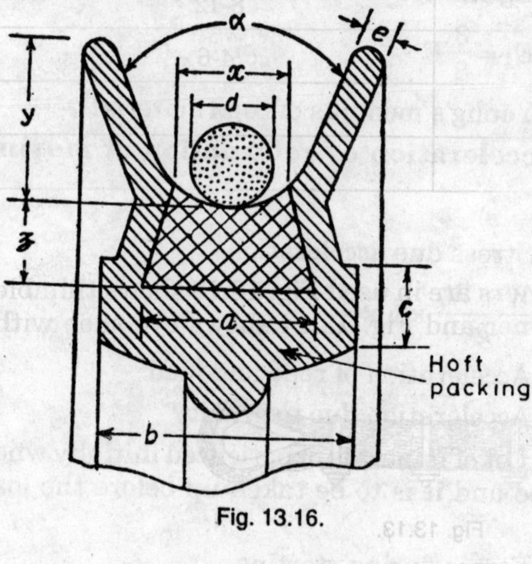


Fig. 13.16.

$d$ = Rope diameter

Groove angle $(\alpha) = 60^\circ$

$x = 1.5\ d$

$y = 1.5\ d + 17.5$

$z = 0.7\ d + 7$

$c = 0.8\ d + 10$

$b = 2.7\ d + 10$

$a = 2.4\ d + 5$

$e = 0.2\ d + 6$

A cotton rope rests on the sides of groove while a steel wire rope rests on the bottom of groove.

## 13.38. Stresses in Wire Ropes

The various types of stresses in a wire rope are as follows :

(*a*) Direct stress due to weight to be lifted and weight of rope.

Let $A$ = Area of rope

$W$ = Weight to be lifted

$W_r$ = Weight of rope

$$f = \text{Direct stress} = \frac{W + W_r}{A}$$

(*b*) **Bending stress due to bending of ropes over sheaves.** When the rope passes over the sheave, the bending stress is relieved by the readjustment of wires but when the rope is straightened as it leaves the sheave, the inner wires are subjected to tension in bending

Let $d_1$ = Wire diameter in cm

$D$ = diameter of sheave in cm

$F_b$ = Bending stress

$$= E_1 \times \frac{d}{D}$$

where $E_1$ = Modulus of elasticity of rope in kg/cm$^2$

$E_1 = 8.4 \times 10^5$ kg/cm$^2$ for ropes of ordinary construction

It is observed that $E_1 = \frac{3}{8} E$

where $E$ = Young's modulus of rope material

(*c*) **Stress due to acceleration or retardation of moving masses.**

$f_a$ = Stress due acceleration

$$= \frac{W + W_r}{g} \times a \times \frac{1}{A}$$

where $a$ = Acceleration of rope and load

$g$ = Acceleration due to gravity

(*d*) **Starting stress.** Lot of impact is experienced initially when there is slack in the rope and it is to be taken up before the load begins to move.

$f_s$ = Stress during starting

$$= \frac{W + W_r}{A_r}\left[1 + \sqrt{1 + \frac{2\,ah\,E_1}{f \,.\, l \,.\, g}}\right]$$

where $L$ = Length of rope

$h$ = Slack during starting

$a$ = Acceleration of rope

Effective stress in rope

$= f_s + f_b$ during starting

$= f + f_t$ during normal working

$= f + f_b + f_a$ during acceleration of load

The sum of these stresses should be less than ultimate strength divided by factor of safety.

## 13.39. Selection of Wire-Ropes

Selection of wire ropes depends on the following factor :

(i) Strength

(ii) Abrasion resistance

(iii) Corrosion resistance

(iv) Flexibility

(v) Fatigue strength

(vi) Resistance to crushing.

## 13.40. Systems of Rope Driving

The two systems commonly used in rope driving are as follows.

(i) Multiple system

(ii) Continuous system.

In multiple system one or more independend ropes run side by side in the groove of the sheaves. Each ropes is supposed to transmit the same amount of power.

In continuous system only one rope is wound round the driving and driven pulleys several times.

## 13.41. Length of Rope

The length of rope is given by the following formula :

$$L = \frac{\pi}{2}(D_1 + D_2) + (D_2 - D_1)\sin^{-1}\frac{D_2 - D_1}{2C} + 2C\cos\frac{\alpha}{2}$$

where $D_1$ = Diameter of smaller pulley

$D_2$ = Diameter of larger pulley

$\alpha$ = Groove angle.

## 13.42. Ultimate Tensile Breaking Load

The ultimate tensile breaking load of the manila ropes may be taken as 500 $d^2$ kg where $d$ is the diameter of rope in cm. For cotton ropes it may be taken as 310 $d^2$ kg.

## 13.43. Strength of Wire used for Ropes

The grade of wire is the minimum tensile strength of the wire used. Table 13.15 indicates the grade of wires and their tensile strength.

**Table 13.15**

| *Grade of wire* | *Tensile strength range (kg/mm$^2$)* |
|---|---|
| 120 | 120-150 |
| 140 | 140-170 |
| 160 | 160-190 |
| 180 | 180-210 |
| 200 | 200-240 |

Table 13.16 indicates the strength of wire ropes for lifts and hoists.

**Table 13.16**

| *Construction* | *Dia mm* | *Approx. wt. kg/m* | *Nominal breaking strength (tonnes)* | |
|---|---|---|---|---|
| | | | *Tensile strength of wire (kg/sq mm)* | |
| | | | *110 to 125* | *125 to 140* |
| 6 × 19 group | | | | |
| 6 × 12/6/1 | 6 | 0.15 | 1.5 | 1.7 |
| 6 × 19(12/6/1) | 8 | 0.25 | 2.3 | 2.7 |
| 6 × 19(6 + 6 F/1) | 10 | 0.40 | 4.0 | 4.5 |
| 6 × 19(9/9/1) | 12 | 0.55 | 5.5 | 6.0 |
| | 14 | 0.75 | 7.7 | 8.8 |
| | 16 | 0.95 | 9.6 | 11.0 |
| | 18 | 1.25 | 12.7 | 14.2 |
| | 20 | 1.45 | 15.0 | 17.0 |

*Contd...*

| Construction | Dia mm | Approx. wt. kg/m | Nominal breaking strength (tonnes) Tensile strength of wire (kg/sq mm) | |
|---|---|---|---|---|
| | | | 110 to 125 | 125 to 140 |
| | 22 | 1.85 | 18.8 | 21.2 |
| | 25 | 2.25 | 23.0 | 26.0 |
| 8 × 19 group | | | | |
| 8 × 10 filler | 8 | 0.20 | 2.2 | 2.5 |
| wire | 10 | 0.35 | 3.8 | 4.3 |
| *i.e.* 8 × 12.6 | 12 | 0.50 | 5.0 | 5.5 |
| + 6 F/1) | 14 | 0.70 | 7.0 | 8.1 |
| 8 × 10(9/9/1) | 16 | 0.85 | 9.0 | 10.0 |
| scale | 18 | 1.10 | 11.5 | 13.5 |
| | 20 | 1.35 | 14.0 | 15.5 |
| | 22 | 1.70 | 18.5 | 21.0 |

**Example 13.8.** *Design a 6 × 19 steel wire rope for a vertical mine hoist to lift 1400 tonnes of coal from a depth of 600 metres in each 8 hours shaft. The rope velocity is 600 mpm and acceleration and deceleration periods are 10 seconds and a rest period of 12 seconds for discharging and loading. The safety factor should be at least 6. Assume a two compartment shaft with the hoisting skips in balance.*

**Solution.** (*a*) **To find diameter of rope**

$S$ = Distance travelled by hoist during acceleration

$v$ = Rope velocity = 600 mpm

$t$ = Acceleration time = 10 seconds

$$S = \frac{V \cdot t}{2} = \frac{600}{60} \times \frac{10}{2} = 50 \text{ metres}$$

= Distance travelled during deceleration period

$$a = \text{Acceleration} \frac{V}{t} = \frac{600}{60} \times \frac{1}{10}$$

$= 1 \text{ m/sec}^2$

$$S_1 = \text{Total distance travelled at full speed}$$
$$= 600 - 2 \times 50 = 500 \text{ metres}$$
$$T_1 = \text{Time required for } S_1$$
$$= \frac{S_1 \times 60}{600} = \frac{500 \times 60}{600} = 50 \text{ seconds}$$
$$T = \text{Time required for one trip.}$$
$$T_1 = 10 \text{ sec. (Acceleration period)}$$
$$T_2 = 10 \text{ seconds (Deceleration period)}$$
$$T_3 = 50 \text{ seconds (Full speed time)}$$
$$T_4 = 15 \text{ seconds (Discharging and loading time)}$$
$$= T_1 + T_2 + T_3 + T_4 = 85 \text{ seconds}$$

Number of hours in a shift = 8

Number of trips in a shift

$$= \frac{8 \times 3600}{85} = 339 \text{ trips}$$
$$W = \text{Total load to be lifted} = 1400 \text{ tonnes}$$
$$W_1 = \text{Load to be liffed in each trip}$$
$$= \frac{W}{N_1} = \frac{1400}{339} = 4.13 \text{ tonnes}$$
$$W_2 = \text{Weight of hoisting skip}$$
$$= 0.6 \times W_1 \text{ (Assume)}$$
$$W_2 = 0.6 \times 4.13 = 2.478 = 2.5 \text{ tonnes (say)}$$
$$W_3 = \text{Total load to be hoisted}$$
$$= W_1 + W_2 = 4.1 + 2.5 = 6.6 \text{ tonnes}$$

Assume a factor of safety of 15. The real safety factor will be checked.

$$W_4 = \text{Ultimate load}$$
$$= 15 \times W_3 = 15 \times 6.6 = 99 \text{ tonnes}$$

The ultimate strength of 6 × 19 rope is 5950 $d^2$ where $d$ is rope diameter in cm.

$$\therefore \quad 5950\, d^2 = 99 \times 1000$$
$$d^2 = 16.53$$
$$d = 4.1 \text{ cm.}$$

(*b*) **To calculate wire diameter**

$$d_1 = \text{Wire diameter}$$

$= 0.063\ d = 0.063 \times 4.1 = 0.26$ cm

(c) **To find factor of safety**

$w$ = Weight per metre $= 0.363\ d^2$ kg/m

$= 0.363 \times 4.4 = 6.1$ kg/m

$A$ = Area $= 0.38\ d^2 = 0.38 \times (4.1)^2 = 6.39\ \text{cm}^2$

$W_r$ = Weight of rope $= w \times H$

where $H$ = Depth = 600 metre

$$W_r = \frac{6.1 \times 600}{1000} = 3.66 \text{ tonnes}$$

$F_a$ = Stress due to acceleration

$$= \frac{W_3 + W_r}{g} \times a \times \frac{1}{A}$$

$P_1$ = Equivalent load due to acceleration of load and rope

$= f_a \times A$

$$P_1 = \frac{W_3 + W_r}{g} \times a = \frac{6.6 + 3.66}{9.81} \times 1$$

$= 1.04$ tonnes

$P_2$ = Equivalent bending load

$$= E_1 \times \frac{d}{D} \times A$$

where $E_1$ = Modulus of elasticity of rope

$$= \frac{3}{8} E = \frac{3}{8} \times 8.4 \times 10^5$$

$= 3.15 \times 10^5\ \text{kg/cm}^2$

Assuming $E = 8.4\ 10^5\ \text{kg/cm}^2$

$D$ = Sheave diameter

$= 45\ d$ (From table 13.11)

$= 45 \times 4.1 = 184.5$ cm

$$P_2 = 10^5 \times 3.15 \times \frac{4.1}{184.5} \times 6.39 \times \frac{1}{1000}$$

$= 4.47$ tonnes

$P$ = Total load $= W_3 + P_1 + P_2 + W_r$

$= 6.6 \times 1.04 + 4.47 + 3.66 = 15.77$ tonnes

$$\text{Factor of safety} = \frac{F}{P}$$

where $F$ = Ultimate strength of rope

$= 5950\, d^2 = 5950 \times (4.1)^2$ kg

$$\text{Factor of safety} = \frac{5950 \times (4.1)^2}{15.77 \times 1000} = 6.34$$

**Example 13.9** *Determine the number of ropes required for a rope drive to transmit 240 H.P. at 900 mpm.*

**Solution.**

$P$ = Total effective pull

$V$ = Velocity = 900 mpm

$$\text{H.P.} = \frac{P \times V}{4500}$$

$$240 = \frac{P \times 900}{4500}$$

$$P = 1200 \text{ kg}$$

Let $T_1$ = Tension on tight side

$T_2$ = Tension on loose side

$$\frac{T_1}{T_2} = e^{\mu e \theta}$$

where $\theta = 180^\circ$ (say) $= \pi$

$\mu_e$ = Equivalent coefficient of friction

$\alpha$ = Angle of groove = 45° (say)

$\mu$ = Coefficient of friction = 0.18 (say)

$$\mu_e = \frac{\mu}{\sin\frac{\alpha}{2}} = \frac{0.18}{\sin 22.5} = 0.47$$

$$\frac{T_1}{T_2} = e^{0.47 + \pi} = 4.3$$

$$P = T_1 - T_2$$

$$1200 = 4.3\, T_2 - T_2$$

$$T_2 = 363 \text{ kg}$$

$$T_1 = 1563 \text{ kg.}$$

Let factor of safety = 30 (F.O.S.)

$F$ = Ultimate tensile breaking load per rope

$= 500\, d^2$

where $d$ = Rope diameter in cm

$= 3.2$ cm (say)

$F_S$ = Allowable tensile load per rope

$$\frac{F}{\text{F.O.S.}} = \frac{500\, d^2}{30}$$

$$= \frac{500 \times 3.2^2}{30} = 170 \text{ kg}$$

$F_C$ = Centrifugal effect $= \dfrac{\omega V_1^2}{g}$

where, $\omega$ = Weight of rope per metre length

$= 0.07\, d^2$ kg/m

$\omega = 0.07\ 3.2^2 = 0.71$ kg/m

$V_1$ = Speed (m/s) $= \dfrac{V}{60} = \dfrac{900}{60} = 15$ m/s

$$F_C = \frac{0.71 \times 15^2}{9.81} = 16 \text{ kg}$$

$W$ = Net effective tensile load per rope

$= F_S - F_C = 170 - 16 = 154$ kg

$n$ = Number of ropes $= \dfrac{T_1}{W}$

$$= \frac{1563}{154} = 10.14 = 11 \text{ (say)}.$$

**Example 13.10.** *A leather belt 120 mm wide and 6 mm thick is required to transmit power from a pulley of diameter 700 mm at 450 RPM. Angle of lap for smaller pulley is 140°, coefficient of friction is 0.28, mass of belt is 1000 kg/m³ and maximum permissible stress is 3.0 MPa. Find the maximum power that can be transmitted.*

**Solution.**

$P$ = Power to be transmitted

$D$ = Pulley diameter

$= 700$ mm

$N$ = RPM

$= 450$

$\mu = 0.28$

$\sigma$ = Permissible stress

$= 3.0$ MPa

$V$ = Belt speed

$$= \frac{\pi \times 700 \times 450}{60 \times 1000} = 16.5 \text{ m/s}$$

$T_C$ = Centrifugal tension = $mV^2$

where $m$ = Mass of belt per unit length

$= \rho \,.\, b \,.\, t \,.$

where $\rho$ = Density of leather belt = 1000 kg/m$^2$

$b$ = width of belt = 120 mm

$t$ = Thickness of belt = 6 mm

$$T_C = \rho \,.\, b \,.\, t \,.\, V^2$$

$$= 1000 \times \frac{120}{1000} \times \frac{6}{1000} \times 16.5^2 = 196 \text{ N}$$

$T$ = Total tension

$= \sigma \,.\, b \,.\, t$

$$= 3 \times 10^6 \times \frac{120}{1000} \times \frac{6}{1000} = 2160 \text{ N}$$

$T_1$ = Tight side tension

$= T - T_C = 2160 - 196$

$= 1964$ N

$T_2$ = Loose side tension

$$\frac{T_1}{T_2} = e^{\mu\,\theta}$$

$$\frac{1964}{T_2} = e^{0.28 \times \frac{\pi \times 140}{180}}$$

$T_2 = 997$ N

$P$ = Power transmitted

$$= \frac{(T_1 - T_2) \times V}{1000}$$

$$= \frac{(1964 - 997) \times 16.5}{1000} = 16 \text{ kW.}$$

**Example 13.11.** *Design a leather belt to drive a winch from an electric motor of 10 kW power. Speed of motor shaft is 700 RPM, speed ratio is 4,slip is 2%. Belt position is horizontal and there is considerable variation of load. Coefficient of friction is 0.3.*

**Solution.**

Let $D_1$ = Diameter of motor shaft pulley

$D_2$ = Diameter of driven pulley

$N$ = R.P.M. of motor shaft = 700

$P$ = Power = 10 kW

$$D_1 = 1.2\sqrt[3]{\frac{P}{N}} = 1.2\sqrt[3]{\frac{10}{700}} = 0.29 \text{ m}$$

$S$ = slip = 2% = 0.02

V.R. = Velocity ratio = 4

$$\text{V.R.} = \frac{D_2}{D_1(1-S)}$$

$$4 = \frac{D_2}{0.29(1-.02)}$$

$$D_2 = 4 \times 0.29 \times 0.98$$

$$= 1.14 \text{ m}$$

$C$ = Centre distance

$$= 2(D_1 + D_2) = 2(1.14 + 0.29)$$

$$= 2.86 \text{ m}$$

$L$ = Length of belt

$$= 2C + \frac{(D_2 - D_1)^2}{4C} + 1.57(D_2 + D_1)$$

$$= 2 \times 2.86 + \frac{(1.14 - 0.29)^2}{4 \times 2.86} + 1.57(1.14 + 0.29)$$

$$= 8.04 \text{ m}$$

$$V = \text{Belt speed} = \frac{\pi D_1 N_1}{60} = \frac{\pi \times 0.29 \times 700}{60}$$

$$= 10.6 \text{ m/}S$$

$\theta$ = Angle of contact of smaller pulley

$$= 180 - 2\sin^{-1}\frac{D_2 - D_1}{2C}$$

$$= 180 - 2\sin^{-1}\frac{1.14 - 0.29}{2 \times 8.04} = 174^\circ$$

$\mu = 0.3$

Let $T_1$ = Tight side tension

$T_2$ = Loose side tension

$$\frac{T_1}{T_2} = e^{\mu\,\theta}$$

$$= e^{0.3 \times \frac{\pi \times 174}{180}}$$

$$= 2.48 \qquad \text{...(1)}$$

$$\frac{(T_1 - T_2) \times V}{1000} = P$$

$$\frac{(T_1 - T_2) \times 10.6}{1000} = 10 \qquad \text{...(2)}$$

Solving equation (1) and (2)

$T_1 = 1850$ N

$T_2 = 746$ N

$f_t$ = working stress in leather belt

= 3 MPa (Assume)

$f_C$ = Centrifugal stress

$= \rho V^2$

where $\rho$ = Density of belt material

$= 1000 \text{ kg/m}^3$

$f_C = 1000 \times (10.6)^2 = 0.112$ MPa

Let $b$ = Belt width

$t$ = Belt thickness

$= 0.02 \times 0.29 = 0.0058$ m $= 5.8$ mm

= 6 mm (say)

$$b \times t = \frac{T_1}{(f_t - f_C) \times C_1}$$

where $C_1$ = Correction factor

= 1 for horizontal drive

$$b = \frac{1850}{6(3 - 0.112)}$$

= 106 mm.

## PROBLEMS

**1.** (*a*) What are the various types of belts ? (*b*) Classify belt drives and state their fields of application.

**2.** Write short notes on the following :

(*a*) Belt materials.

(*b*) Belt slip.

(*c*) Maximum permissible velocity of belt.

**3.** A flat belt drive is required to be designed for an A.C. motor which is to drive an air compressor. The following data are supplied :

Motor H.P. = 15

Motor R.P.M. = 600

Compressor R.P.M. = 150

Diameter of motor pulley = 36 cm

Centre distance = 120 cm.

Slip = 3%.

**4.** State the advantages of V-belts over flat belts.

**5.** A V-belt drive is required to actuate a centrifugal pump from an electric motor. The drive consists of three *B* type V-belts. The motor pulley has a 15 cm pitch diameter and pump pulley has a pitch diameter of 45 cm. The motor runs at 900 R.P.M. the centre distance is 100 cm. Calculate what horse power can be transmitted ?

**6.** State the advantages and disadvantages of chain drive.

**7.** What are various types of

(*a*) Chains used in chain drive ?

(*b*) State the normal and maximum chain velocities for roller and silent chain drives.

**8.** Write short notes on the followings :

(*a*) Number of teeth on sprockets

(*b*) Chain materials.

(*c*) Lubrication of chain drive.

**9.** A roller chain drive is required to transmit 50 H.P. from an electric motor to a compressor. The motor speed is 600 R.P.M. and compressor shaft speed is 150 R.P.M. Determine size of sprockets, the pitch and number of strands required.

**10.** (*a*) What is rope drive ?

(*b*) Describe fibre ropes and wire ropes.

**11.** Write short notes on the following :

(*a*) Rope pulleys

(*b*) Stresses in wire ropes

(*c*) Rope fasteners.

**12.** Determine the equivalent bending load for a 60 mm. $6 \times 19$ steel rope to lift a cage from a mine 200 metre deep. The cage acceleration is 2 m/sec$^2$ and rope sheave diameter is 2.5 metre.

**13.** A compressor requiring 120 H.P. is to be run at about 250. R.P.M. The drive is by V-belts from an electric motor running at 75 R.P.M. The diameter of pulley on the compressor shaft must not be greater than 1 metre while the centre distance between pulleys is limited to 1.75 m. The belt speed should not exceed 1600 m/min.

Determine number of V-belts required to transmit the power if each belt has a cross sectional area of 3.75 cm$^2$ and weighs 0.001 kg per cm$^2$ and has an allowable tensile stress of 25 kg/cm$^2$. The groove angle of pulley is 35°. The coefficient of friction between belt and pulley is 0.25. Calculate also the length required of each belt.

**14.** Distinguish clearly giving examples between, belt drive, chain drive and rope drive.

**15.** Design a V-belt for a 12 H.P., 1200 R.P.M. induction motor to drive a pump at about 400 R.P.M. The minimum centre distance between sheaves is 1200.

**16.** Write short notes on the following :

(*i*) Systems of rope drives

(*ii*) Selection of wire ropes

(*iii*) Double lay ropes.

# 14

# Brakes and Clutches

## 14.1. Brakes

Brake is a device which is used to bring to rest or slow down a moving body. In process of performing this function the brake is required to absorb the kinetic energy of moving parts or the potential energy of the objects being lowered by hoists, elevators, and then dissipate the energy in the form of heat. The brake capacity depends upon the following factors :

(*i*) Intensity of pressure between braking surfaces.

(*ii*) Coefficient of friction.

(*iii*) Ability of brake to dissipate heat equivalent to energy absorbed.

## 14.2. Types of Brakes

The various types of brakes are as follows :

(*i*) Hydraulic brakes

(*ii*) Electric brakes.

(*iii*) Mechanical brakes.

(*a*) Block brake

(*b*) Band brake

(*c*) Block and band brake

(*d*) External and internal shoe brake.

## 14.3. Energy to be Absorbed by the Brake

When a brake is applied to moving body it will absorb energy of moving body.

The motion of the body can be of the following types :

(*i*) Pure translation

(*ii*) Pure rotation

(*iii*) A combination of translation and rotation.

When the motion of the body is pure translator the kinetic energy ($E_1$) is to be absorbed by the brake is as follows :

$$E_1 = \frac{1}{2} . \frac{W}{g} . (V_1^2 - V_2^2) \text{ kg m}$$

where $W$ = Weight of body in kg

The body moving with velocity $V_1$ m/sec is retained to velocity $V_2$ m/sec by braking action.

When the body is rotating about it centre of rotation the kinetic energy of body ($E_2$) to be absorbed by the brake is calculated as follows :

$$E_2 = \frac{1}{2} . I . (\omega_1^2 - \omega_2^2) \text{ kg m}$$

where $I$ = Moment of inertia of mass of body about its axis of rotation

$\omega_1$ and $\omega_2$ are angular velocities in radians/sec. before and after braking. For a rolling body, the kinetic energy ($E$) is given by

$$E = E_1 + E_2$$

$$= \frac{1}{2} \frac{W}{g} (V_1^2 - V_2^2) + \frac{1}{2} I (\omega_1^2 - \omega_2^2) \text{ kg m.}$$

The capacity of a brake is stated in terms of the amount of frictional work it can absorb in a particular time.

When the brake is applied if $F$ is the frictional force and the body is brought to rest in a distance $S$ then the frictional work is calculated as follows :

$$\text{Frictional work} = F \times S = F \times \pi DN$$

where $D$ = Diameter of brake drum

$N$ = Number of turns of the drum during which the body is brought to rest.

Now $F \times \pi DN$ = Total kinetic energy absorbed

$T$ = Frictional torque in kg m.

$$= F \times R_1$$

where $R_1$ = Radius of brake drum = $D/2$

## 14.4. Block or Shoe Brake

It consists of a block which is passed against the revolting drum by means of a lever. The normal reaction ($R_n$) between block and drum is concentrated at the centre of block. (Fig. 14.1). The lever is pivoted about the pin $A$.

$P$ = Brake actuating force

$F$ = Frictional force or braking force

$= \mu R_n$

$R_n$ = Normal reaction between block and drum.

$R$ = Pin reaction

$r$ = Radius of drum

Fig. 14.1 ($b$) shows force triangle.

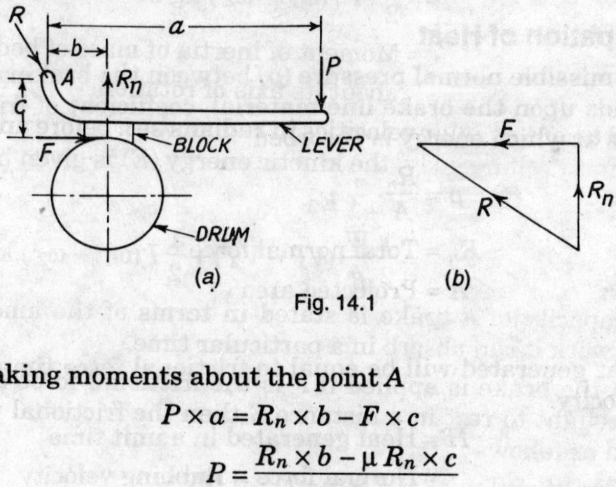


Fig. 14.1

Taking moments about the point $A$

$$P \times a = R_n \times b - F \times c$$

$$P = \frac{R_n \times b - \mu R_n \times c}{a}$$

$$= \frac{R_n \times (b - \mu \cdot c)}{a} = \frac{F}{\mu \times a} [b - \mu \cdot c]$$

When the friction acts so as to assist in applying the brake, the brake is said to be self energising. The brake shall be self locking when

$$\mu \cdot c \geq b$$

$$T = \text{Braking torque} = F \times r$$

When angle of contact between block and drum is less than 60°, the normal pressure is assumed to be uniform between them. But when angle of contact is more than 60° it is assumed that the unit pressure is less at the ends than at the centre and wear in the direction of applied force is uniform. In such case we use equivalent coefficient of friction.

$$\mu_c = \text{Equivalent co–efficient of friction}$$

$$= \frac{4\,\mu\,.\,\sin\theta/2}{\theta + \sin\theta}$$

where $\theta$ = Angle of contact in radian

$\mu$ = Actual coefficient of friction.

In block brake the blocks (shoes) are made of cast iron provided with special brake linings which may be secured with rivets or with counter sunk screws. Brake levers are made of die forged or cast steel. Depending on the size of brake the safe bending stress in evers is taken from 400 to 800 kg/cm$^2$. Brake wheels are made of cast iron. The width of wheel should be more than width of shoe by about 5 mm to 10. Brake wheels should be finned for better heat dissipation.

## 14.5. Dissipation of Heat

The permissible normal pressure ($p$) between the braking surfaces depends upon the brake line material, coefficient of friction and the rate at which energy is absorbed.

$$p = \frac{R_n}{A}$$

where $R_n$ = Total normal force

$A$ = Projected area

The heat generated will be equal to frictional force times the rubbing velocity.

$H$ = Heat generated in a unit time

= Normal force × Rubbing velocity

$= \mu\,.\,R_n \times V$

$$= \frac{\mu\,.\,p \times A \times V}{427}\ \text{kcal/min}$$

where $A$ = Contact area in cm$^2$

$p$ = Bearing pressure in kg/cm$^2$

$V$ = Peripheral velocity of drum in m/min.

This shows that heat generated depends upon $p \times V$. For shoe brakes the design value of $p \times V$ is often specified. (See Table 14.1).

**Table 14.1**

| *Application* | $pV$ |
|---|---|
| For continuous service with short rest periods and poor heat dissipation | 570 |
| For intermittent service with long rest periods and poor heat dissipation | 1100 |
| For continuous service and good heat dissipation | 1660 |

Table 14.1 indicates the value of $pV$ in kg m per cm$^2$ of projected area per minute.

H.P. absorbed per sq. cm of projected area

$$= \frac{\mu \cdot p \times V}{4500}$$

where $p$ = Bearing pressure in kg/cm$^2$

$V$ = Rubbing velocity in metre per minute

The product $p \times V$ is called design coefficient.

## 14.6. Brake Linings Materials

Brake lining material should have a high coefficient of friction and should effectively resist wear and should be able to retain braking capacity at temperature up to 300°C. Its cost should be low. The material should have high heat conductivity.

Table 14.2 indicates the value of coefficient of friction ($\mu$) and allowable pressure ($p$) for various unlubricated lining materials. The friction materials may be used either dry or in oil.

**Table 14.2**

| *Materials in contact* | $\mu$ | $p$ (*kg/cm*$^2$) |
|---|---|---|
| Cast iron on cast iron | 0.15 — 0.2 | 10 — 17 |
| Steel on cast iron | 0.25 — 35 | 8.0 — 13.5 |
| Wood on cast iron or steel | 0.2 — 0.35 | 4.0 — 6.0 |
| Cork on metal | 0.35 | 0.55 — 1 |
| Leather on cast iron | 0.2 | 0.7 — 2.8 |

*Contd...*

| *Materials in contact* | μ | *p* ($kg/cm^2$) |
|---|---|---|
| Bronze on cast iron | 0.17 | 5.6 — 8.4 |
| Fiber on steel | 0.17 | 0.7 — 2.8 |
| Asbestos on cast iron or steel | 0.30 — 0.4 | 5.3 — 7 |
| Carbon graphite on steel | 0.25 | 20 |

**Example 14.1.** *In the block brake (Fig. 14.2) the block is made of cast iron with a coefficient of friction 0.2, If the braking torque is 4000 kg cm, calculate the force P and the position of pivot so as to make the brake self energising. The diameter of drum is 40 cm.*

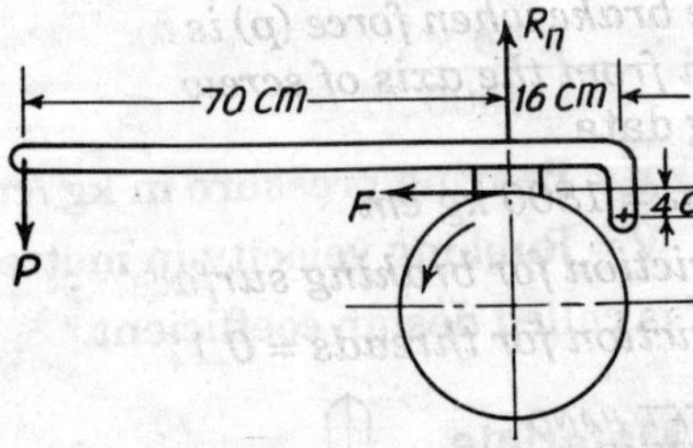


Fig. 14.2.

**Solution.** (*a*) **To find *P***

$$T = \text{Braking torque} = 4{,}000 \text{ kg–cm}$$

$$P = \text{Brake actuating force}$$

$$F = \text{Braking force}$$

$$R_1 = \text{Radius of drum} = 20 \text{ cm}$$

$$R_n = \text{Normal reaction}$$

$$F = \frac{T}{R_1} = \frac{4{,}000}{20} = 200 \text{ kg}$$

Taking moments about the pivot

$$P \times 86 + F \times 4 = R_n \times 16$$

$$P \times 86 + F \times 4 = \frac{F}{\mu} \times 16$$

$$P \times 86 + 200 \times 4 = \frac{200}{0.2} \times 16$$

$$P = 176.74 \text{ kg}$$

(*b*) **To find position of pivot**

Let the distance of line of action of $F$ from pivot be $S$.

Taking moments about the pivot.

$P \times 86 + F \times S - R_n \times 16 = 0$

In order that the brake is self energising $F \times S$ should be at least equal to $R_n \times 16$ so that $P$ is zero.

$$\therefore \quad F \times S = R_n \times 16$$

$$\mu R_n \times S = R_n \times 16$$

$$0.2 \times S = 16$$

$$S = \frac{16}{0.2} = 80 \text{ cm.}$$

**Example 14.2.** *In a double block brake shown in Fig. 14.3, the blocks are pivoted at $O_1$ and $O_2$ and the blocks move closer to each other and apply the brake when force (p) is applied at the hand lever at a distance 30 cm from the axis of screw. Determine this force (p) using the following data.*

*Torque on drum = 1800 kg cm*

*Coefficient of friction for braking surface = 0.25*

*Coefficient of friction for threads = 0.17*

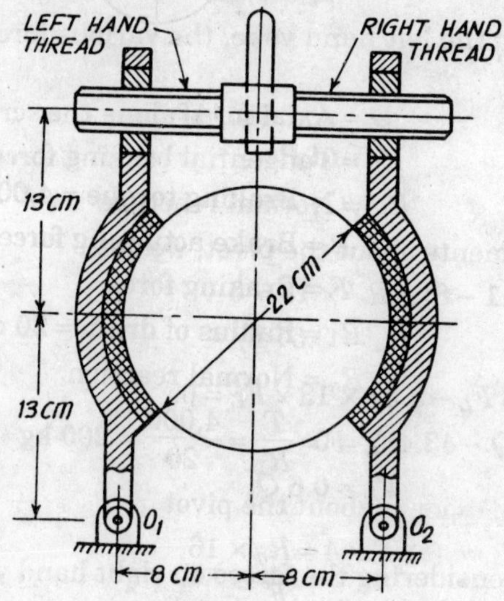


Fig. 14.3

*Angle subtended by each block = 90*

*Diameter of block drum = 22 cm*

*The screw has six square threads with a mean diameter of 2.5 cm. and a lead of 6 cm.*

**Solution.**

$\theta$ = Angle subtended by block = $\pi/2$

$\mu$ = Coefficient of friction for braking surface = 0.25

$\mu_e$ = Equivalent coefficient of friction

$$= \frac{4\,\mu\,.\,\sin\frac{\theta}{2}}{\theta + \sin\theta}$$

$$= \frac{4 \times 0.25 \times \sin 45}{\frac{\pi}{2} + \sin\frac{\pi}{2}} = 0.28$$

$R_n$ = Normal reaction between block and brake drum

$F$ = Tangential braking force

$$F = \mu_e R_n$$

$$R_n = \frac{F}{\mu_e} = \frac{F}{0.28} = 3.57\,F$$

**Considering the left hand yoke, the various force acting are as follows :**

$Q$ = Axial force along the screw

$K_L$ = Tangential braking force

$R_n'$ = Normal reaction.

**Taking moments about the pivot, we get**

$$26\,Q + F_L(11 - 8) - R_n' \times 13 = 0$$

Now $R_n' = 3.57\,F_L$

$$\therefore\ 26\,Q + 3\,F_L - 3.57 \times 13 \times F_L = 0.$$

$$26Q - 43.4F_L = 0$$

$$F_L = 0.6\,Q.$$

**Similarly considering the forces on right hand yoke and taking moments about right hand pivot.**

$$26\,Q - (11 - 8)F_R - R_n'' \times 13 = 0.$$

$$26\,Q - 3F_R - Rn'' \times 13 = 0\ .$$

But $Rn'' = 3.57\,F_R$

$$26\,Q - 3\,F_R - 3.57 \times 13 \times F_R = 0,$$

$$F_R = 0.53\,Q$$

$$R_1 = \text{Radius of drum} = 11 \text{ cm}$$

$$T = \text{Braking torque}$$

$$= (F_L + F_R) \times R_1$$

$$1800 = (0.6\,Q + 0.53\,Q) \times 11$$

$$Q = 144.8 \text{ kg}$$

$T_1$ = Torque required to over-come friction surfaces

$$= 2 \times Q \times \frac{d}{2} \tan(\alpha + \phi)$$

where $d$ = Mean diameter of screw = 2.5 cm.

$\alpha$ = Thread angle

$$\tan \alpha = \frac{L}{\pi\, d}$$

where $L$ = Load = 6 cm

$$\tan \alpha = \frac{6}{\pi \times 2.5} = 0.7643$$

$$\alpha = 37^\circ\, 23'$$

$\phi$ = Friction angle

$\tan \phi = \mu_1$ = Coefficient of friction for threads

$$= 0.17$$

$$\phi = 9^\circ\, 39'$$

$$T_1 = 2 \times Q \times \frac{d}{2} \tan(\alpha + \phi)$$

$$= 2 \times 144.8 \times \frac{2.5}{2} \tan(47^\circ\, 2')$$

$$= 387.34 \text{ kg cm}$$

Let, $P$ = Force applied at hand lever at a distance of 30 cm.

$$\therefore \quad P \times 30 = T_1$$

$$P \times 30 = 387.34$$

$$P = 12.9 \text{ kg.}$$

**Example 14.3.** *Calculate the horse power absorbed per sq. cm of projected area by a brake of* $\mu = 0.2$ *and* $pV = 1100$*.*

**Solution.** $$\text{H.P.} = \frac{\mu \cdot P \cdot V}{4500} = \frac{0.2 \times 1100}{4500} = 0.049$$

**Example 14.4.** *Calculate the average bearing pressure and horse power for the brake shown in Fig. 14.4. The diameter of drum is 40 cm and it rotates at 200 R.P.M. Coefficient of the friction is 0.2 and wheel width is 7.5 cm.*

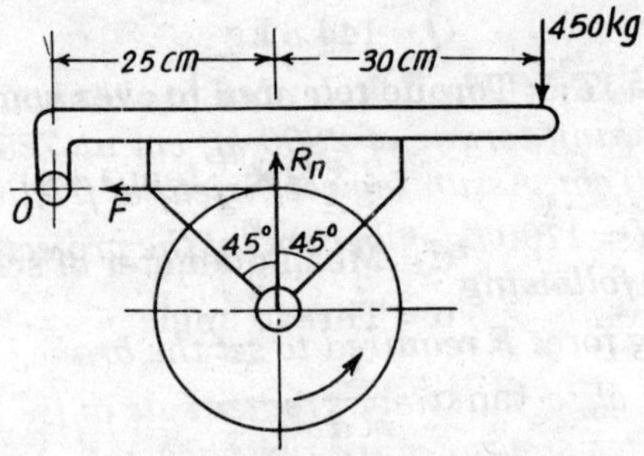


Fig. 14.4.

**Solution.** (*a*) **To find average bearing pressure**

$P$ = Brake actuating force = 450 kg

$R_n$ = Normal reaction

$\mu$ = Coefficient of friction = 0.2

$r$ = Wheel radius = 20 cm

$F$ = Friction force

$b$ = Wheel width = 7.5 cm

Taking moments at the pivot $O$

$$P \times 55 = R_n \times 25$$

$$R_n = \frac{450 \times 55}{25} = 990 \text{ kg}$$

$A$ = Projected area of block

$= b(r \sin 45 + r \sin 50)$

$= 7.5 \times 20(\sin 45 + \sin 50)$

$= 221 \text{ cm}^2$

$P$ = Average bearing pressure

$$= \frac{R_n}{A} = \frac{990}{221} = 4.48 \text{ kg/cm}^2$$

(*b*) **To find horse power**

$T$ = Braking torque

$$= F \times r = \mu R_n \, . \, r$$

$$= 0.2 \times 990 \times \frac{20}{100} = 39.6 \text{ kg m}$$

$$N = 200 \text{ R.P.M.}$$

$$\text{H.P.} = \frac{2\pi NT}{4500} = \frac{2\pi \times 200 \times 39.6}{4500} = 11.05.$$

**Example 14.5.** *The double shoe brake shown in Fig. 14.4 must provide a braking torque of 2800 kg cm at 720 R.P.M. The drum diameter is 30 cm. Assuming coefficient of friction 0.3 for the brake lining and pV = 1100 kg m per cm² of the projected area per minute. Calculate the following :*

*(a) Spring force P required to set the brake.*

*(b) Which shoe will have greater rate of wear and what will be the ratio of rates of wear of the two shoes.*

*(c) Width of shoes.*

**Solution.**

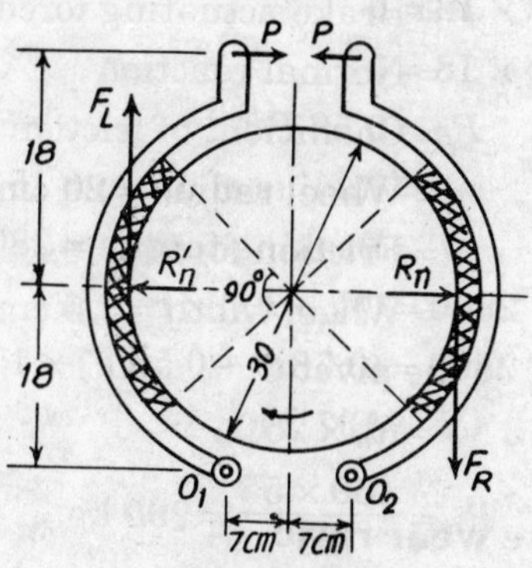


Fig. 14.5

$\mu$ = Coefficient of friction

$\theta$ = Angle of contact of each shoe = 90°

$\mu_e$ = Equivalent coefficient of friction

$$= \frac{4\mu \, . \, \sin \frac{\theta}{2}}{\theta + \sin \theta}$$

$$= \frac{4 \times 0.3 \times \sin 45}{\frac{\pi}{2} + \sin 90}$$

$= 0.33$

$Rn$ = Normal reaction between shoe and drum

$F$ = Braking force = $\mu_e R_n$

$$R_n = \frac{F}{\mu_e} = \frac{F}{0.33} = 3F$$

(*a*) **To calculate spring force**

$P$ = Spring force

$F_L$ = Braking force due to left shoe

$R_n'$ = Normal reaction on left shoe

Taking moments about left pivot $O_1$

$$P \times 36 + (15 - 7) \times F_L - R_n' \times 18 = 0$$

$$36\,P + 8\,F_L - 3F_L \times 18 = 0$$

$$F_L = 0.78\,P$$

Let $F_R$ = Brake force due to right shoe

$R_n''$ = Normal reaction on right shoe

Taking moments about right pivot $O_2$

$$P \times 36 - 8\,F_R - R_n'' \times 18 = 0$$

$$36\,P - 8\,F_R - 3F_R \times 18 = 0$$

$$F_R = 0.58\,P$$

$r$ = Radius of drum = 15 cm

$T$ = Braking torque = 2800 kg cm

$$2800 = (F_L + F_R) \times r$$

$$2800 = (0.78\,P + 0.58\,P) \times 15$$

$$P = 137.3 \text{ kg.}$$

(*b*) **To calculate wear ratio**

$$F_L = 0.78\,P = 0.78 \times 137.3 = 107 \text{ kg}$$

$$F_R = 0.58\,P$$

$$= 0.58 \times 137.3 = 79.7 \text{ kg}$$

Therefore left side shoe will have greater wear

$$\text{Ratio of wear} = \frac{F_L}{F_R} = \frac{107}{79.7} = 1.34.$$

(*c*) **To determine width of shoe**

$b$ = Width of shoe in cm

$$R_n' = 3\,F_L = 3 \times 107 = 321 \text{ kg}$$

$$R_n'' = 3\,F_R = 3 \times 79.7 = 239.1 \text{ kg}$$

Maximum normal force

$$= R_{n'} = 321 \text{ kg}$$

$$V = \text{Rubbing velocity}$$

$$= \frac{\pi DN}{100} = \frac{\pi \times 30 \times 720}{100}$$

$$= 678 \text{ m pm}$$

$$A = \text{Projected area of one shoe}$$

$$= 2\,.\,r\,.\,\sin\frac{\theta}{2} \times b$$

$$= 2 \times 15 \times \sin 45 \times b = 21.2\,b \text{ cm}^2$$

$$p = \text{Unit pressure on shoe}$$

$$= \frac{R_n'}{A} = \frac{321}{21.2\,b} = \frac{15.14}{b} \text{ kg/cm}^2$$

Now $pV = 1100$

$$\frac{15.14}{b} \times 678 = 1100$$

$$b = 9.33 \text{ cm.}$$

**Example 14.6.** *In a pivot shoe brake (Fig. 14.6) the braking torque is 400 kg cm. The coefficient of friction is 0.3 and the drum rotates at 120 R.P.M. If the brake angle is 90° and the brake is to be self energising, calculate the following :*

(*a*) *Brake lever pivot point $O_1$ or $O_2$.*

(*b*) *The brake actuating force (P).*

(*c*) *H.P. absorbed.*

**Solution.** (*a*) **To determine pivot point**

In the pivoted shoe, brake the distance $h$ is calculated as follows:

$$h = \frac{4\,.\,r\,.\,\sin\frac{\theta}{2}}{\theta + \sin\theta}$$

where $\theta$ = Brake shoe angle = 90°

$r$ = Radius of brake drum = 15 cm

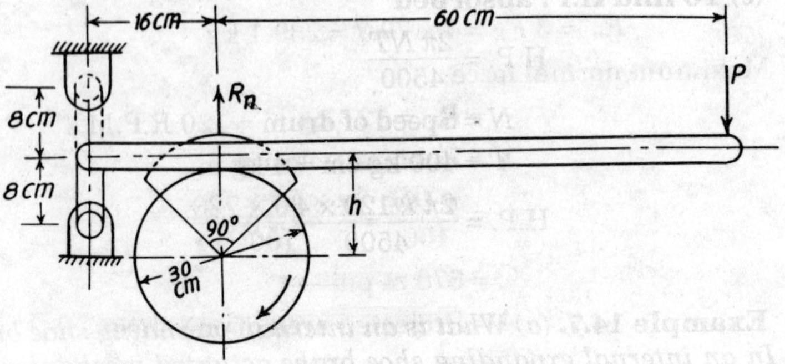


Fig. 14.6.

$$h = \frac{4 \times 15 \times \sin 45^\circ}{\frac{\pi}{2} + \sin 90^\circ} = 18.62 \text{ cm}$$

$P$ = Brake actuating forces

$\mu$ = Coefficient of friction = 0.3

$R_n$ = Normal reaction

$P$ = Braking force or frictional force = $\mu R_n$

$T$ = Braking torque = $F \times h = \mu R_n \cdot h$

$400 = 0.3 \times R_n \times 18.62$

$R_n = 71.6$ kg

Taking moments about pivot $O_1$

$$P(60 + 16) - R_n \times 16 - F \times 8 = 0 \qquad ...(1)$$

Taking moments about pivot $O_2$

$$P(60 + 16) - R_n \times 16 + F \times 8 = 0 \qquad ...(2)$$

From equations (1) and (2) we find that when the lever is pivoted at $O_2$ the moments due to frictional force ($F$) helps the applied force. Hence the brake is self energising. Therefore pivot point is $O_2$.

(*b*) **To find the force (P).** From equation (2), we have

$P(76) - R_n \times 16 + F \times 8 = 0$

$P \times 76 - 71.6 \times 16 + \mu R_n \times 8 = 0$

$P \times 76 - 71.6 \times 16 + 0.3 \times 71.6 \times 8 = 0$

$P = 12.8$ kg.

**(c) To find H.P. absorbed**

$$\text{H.P.} = \frac{2\pi NT}{4500}$$

$N$ = Speed of drum = 120 R.P.M.

$T$ = 400 kg cm = 4 kg m

$$\text{H.P.} = \frac{2\pi \times 120 \times 4}{4500} = 0.67.$$

**Example 14.7.** *(a) What is an internal expanding shoe brake ? (b) In an internal expanding shoe brake actuated mechanically by cam and lever arrangement, each shoe subtents an angle of* $90^\circ$ *at the drum centre. The drum diameter is 32 cm and coefficient of friction 0.28. Calculate the braking force if a braking torque of 6000 kg-cm is required assuming that forces exerted by cam ends on two shoes are equal. The various distances are as follows :*

*Distance between points where the cam acts on two brake shoes = 4 cm*

*Distance between fulcrum centres=10 cm*

*Distance of line of action force from the cam axis = 12 cm.*

*Distance of fulcrum centres* and *that of cam axis, both from the drum centre* = *14* cm.

**Solution.** Internal expanding shoe brakes are commonly used in automobiles. In these brakes each of the two brake shoes is pivoted at one end about a fixed fulcrum.

The outer surfaces of shoes are lined with some friction material like asbestos. When a braking force is applied at the end of an arm keyed to the cam spindle, the shoes come in contact with the inside cylindrical surfaces of brake drum and brake gets applied.

$R$ = Radial of drum = 16 cm

$\mu$ = Coefficient of friction = 0.28

In this brake the reaction $R_1$ and $R_2$ act tangential on a circle called friction circle as shown in Fig. 14.7.

$r$ = Radius of friction circle

$= \mu \,.\, R = 0.28 \times 16$

$= 4.48$ cm

$S_1 = S_2 = S$

= Force applied by cam on each shoe

$a$ = Distance between cam axis and $S_1$ and $S_2$

$$= \frac{4}{2} = 2 \text{ cm}$$

$h$ = Distance of line of action of braking force cam axis = 12 cm

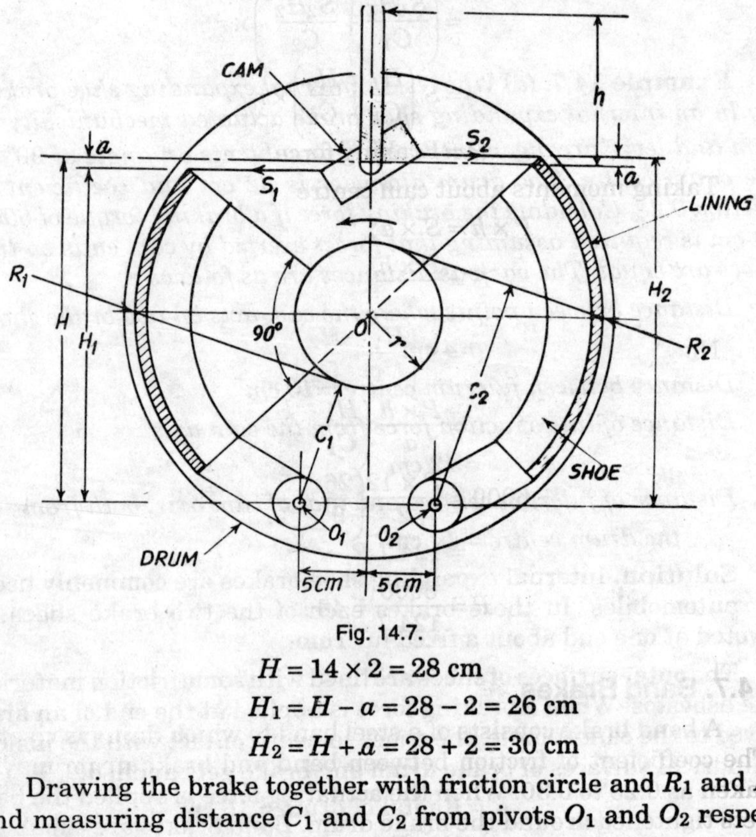


Fig. 14.7.

$$H = 14 \times 2 = 28 \text{ cm}$$

$$H_1 = H - a = 28 - 2 = 26 \text{ cm}$$

$$H_2 = H + a = 28 + 2 = 30 \text{ cm}$$

Drawing the brake together with friction circle and $R_1$ and $R_2$ and measuring distance $C_1$ and $C_2$ from pivots $O_1$ and $O_2$ respectively, we get

$$C_1 = 9 \text{ cm}$$

$$C_2 = 17 \text{ cm}$$

Taking moments about $O_1$

$$S \times H_1 = R_1 \times C_1$$

$$R_1 = \frac{S_1 H_1}{C_1}$$

Taking moments about fulcrum $O_2$.

$$S_2H_2 = R_2 \times C_2$$

$$R_2 = \frac{S_2 \, . \, H_2}{C_2}$$

$$T = \text{Braking torque}$$

$$= (R_1 + R_{2)} \times r$$

$$= \left(\frac{S_1H_1}{C_1} + \frac{S_2H_2}{C_2}\right) \times r$$

$$= S\left(\frac{H_1}{C_1} + \frac{H_2}{C_2}\right) \times r$$

$$P = \text{Braking force}$$

Taking moments about cam centre

$$P \times h = S \times a$$

$$S = \frac{P \times h}{a}$$

Now

$$T = S\left(\frac{H_1}{C_1} + \frac{H_2}{C_2}\right) \times r$$

$$= \frac{P \times h}{a}\left(\frac{H_1}{C_1} + \frac{H_2}{C_2}\right) \times r$$

$$6000 = \frac{P \times 12}{2}\left(\frac{26}{9} + \frac{30}{17}\right) \times 4.48$$

$$= 124.7 \, P$$

$$P = \frac{6000}{124.7} = 48 \text{ kg.}$$

## 14.7. Band Brakes

A band brake consists of a steel band to which lining is riveted. The coefficient of friction between band and brake drum may be taken as 0.25 to 0.30. When the actuating force is applied the band gets tightened around the brake drum. Band brakes are capable of exerting large torques. Careful attention must be paid to details so that the band seats properly on the drum when absorbing energy and remains free and clear when not in use. The tight side of band is rigidly fixed and slack side is made adjustable. The bearings pressure between band and brake may be taken between 4 to 15 kg/cm$^2$. Other details for a band brake are as follows :

$$f_t = \text{Permissible tensile stress in steel band}$$

$$= 500 \text{ to } 800 \text{ kg/cm}^2$$

$t$ = Thickness of band = 0.005 $D$

The thickness of band varies from 3 to 10 mm.

$W$ = Width of band

= 10 cm for $D < 100$ cm

= 15 cm for $D > 100$ cm

where $D$ = Diameter of drum

Fig. 14.8 shows a simple band brake. The action of band while in contact with the drum is identical to that of belt wrapped around its pulley.

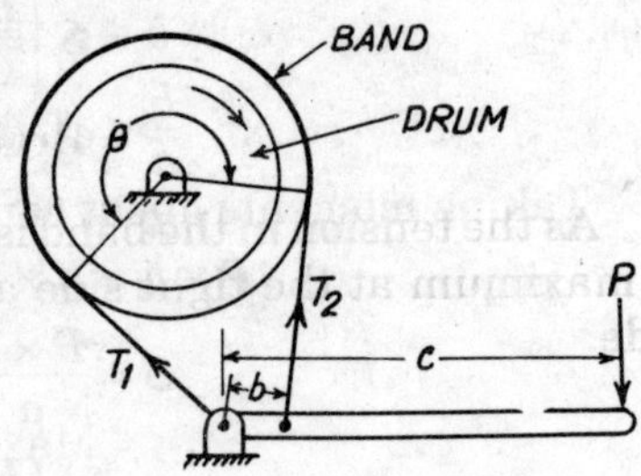

Fig. 14.8. Simple band brake.

$T_1$ = Tension on tight side of band

$T_2$ = Tension on slack side of band

$\theta$ = Angle of contact between band and brake drum

$\mu$ = Coefficient of friction between band and drum

$T_1 - T_2$ = Total friction force on band

$$\frac{T_1}{T_2} = e^{\mu^{\theta}}$$

$T$ = Braking torque

$= (T_1 - T_2) \times r$

where $r$ = Radius of drum

The sum of moments about to fulcrum should be zero

$$P \times C - T_2 b = 0$$

$$P = T_2 \cdot \frac{b}{C}$$

## 14.8. Differential Band Brake

In this brake the lever is pivoted and the band is attached to two points of the lever at a distance $a$ and $b$ from the pivoted point (Fig. 14.9).

$P$ = Brake actuating force

$$\frac{T_1}{T_2} = e^{\mu^{\theta}}$$

$$T = (T_1 - T_2) \times r$$

Consider the equilibrium of lever

$$P \times C + T_1 \times a - T_2 \times b = 0$$

$$P = \frac{T_2 b - T_1 a}{C} = \frac{T_2 b - T_2 . e^{\mu^\theta} . a}{C}$$

$$= T_2 \left[ \frac{b - e^{\mu^\theta} . a}{C} \right]$$

In order that brake should be self locking $P = 0$ or negative. This gives

$$\therefore \quad b \le a . e^{\mu^\theta}$$

$$\frac{b}{a} \le e^{\mu^\theta} \text{ (condition for self lock)}$$

As the tension in the band is not constant therefore the pressure is maximum at the tight side and minimum pressure at the slack side.

$$p_1 = \text{Maximum pressure} = \frac{T_1}{w . r}$$

$$p_2 = \text{Minimum pressure}$$

$$= \frac{T_2}{w . r}$$

$$f_t = \text{Safe stress in tension in band material}$$

$$= \frac{T_1}{w . t}$$

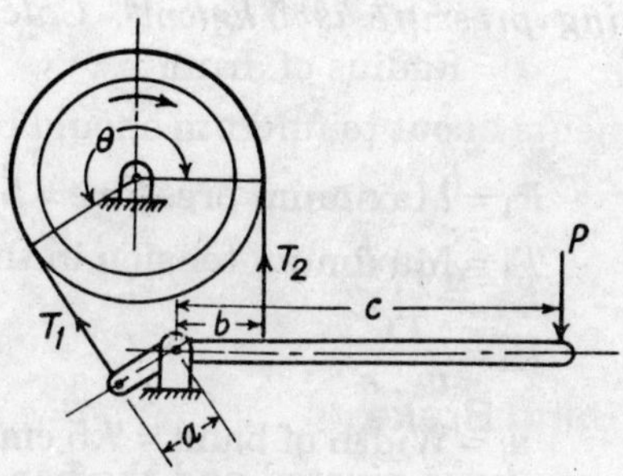


Fig. 14.9. Differential band brake.

where $w$ = Width of band

$t$ = Thickness of band

$r$ = Radius of drum.

## 14.9. Band and Block Brake

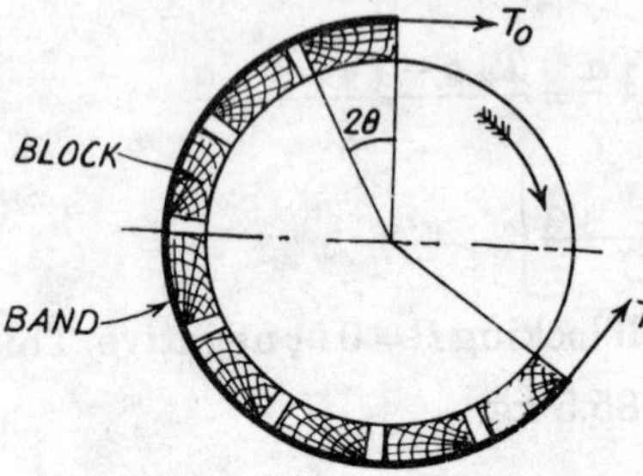


Fig. 14.10. Band and block brake.

In this brake a steel band is lined with a number of wooden blocks. The friction between blocks and drum produces the brake torque.

$T_o$ = Tension on slack side of belt

$T_n$ = Tension after nth block, on tight side of the brake

$n$ = Number of blocks

$2\theta$ = Angle subtended by one block at the centre

$\mu$ = Coefficient of friction

$$\frac{T_n}{T_o} = \left[\frac{1 + \mu \tan \theta}{1 - \mu \tan \theta}\right]$$

Fig. 14.10 Shows a band and block brake.

**Example 14.8.** *In a simple band brake shown in Fig. 15.8 has a drum of 40 cm diameter and a width of lining equal to 7.5 cm. The angle of contact is 270° and $\mu = 0.4$. The distance c = 24 cm and b = 7 cm. The drum rotates at 200 R.P.M. in the clockwise direction. The maximum lining pressure is 5 kg/cm². Calculate the force, torque horse power.*

**Solution.**

$P_1$ = Maximum pressure = 5 kg cm²

$T_1$ = Maximum tension in the band

$$P_1 = \frac{T_1}{w \cdot r}$$

$w$ = Width of band = 7.5 cm

$r$ = Radius of drum = 20 cm

$$T_1 = p_1 \cdot w \cdot r = 5 \times 7.5 \times 20 = 750 \text{ kg}$$

$\mu$ = Coefficient of friction

$\theta$ = Angle of contact = 270°

$$e^{\mu\theta} = e^{\frac{0.2 \times 270 \times \pi}{180}} = 2.56$$

$$\frac{T_1}{T_2} = e^{\mu^\theta}$$

$$\frac{750}{T_2} = 2.56$$

$$T_2 = 293 \text{ kg}$$

$$P = T_2 \cdot \frac{b}{c}$$

$$= \frac{293 \times 7}{24} = 85.5 \text{ kg.}$$

(*b*) **To calculate torque**

$$T = \text{Torque} = (T_1 - T_2) \times r$$

$$= (750 - 293)\ 20$$

$$= 9140 \text{ kg cm} = 91.40 \text{ kg m}$$

(*c*) **To find H.P.**

$$\text{H.P.} = \frac{2\pi NT}{4500}$$

$$= \frac{2\pi \times 200 \times 91.40}{4500} = 25.5.$$

**Example 14.9.** *A differential hand brake shown in Fig. 14.9 has an angle of contact between its cast iron drum and leather lined steel band of 270°. The drum is of 40 cm diameter and μ = 0.3. The moments arms c, a and b are 60 cm, 3 cm, and 15 cm respectively. The brake is to sustain a torque of 5000 kg cm. Determine the operation force P.*

**Solution.**

$$\mu = 0.3$$

$$\theta = 270^\circ = \frac{270 \times \pi}{180} \text{ radians}$$

$$e^{\mu\,\theta} = e^{0.3 \times 270 \times \frac{\pi}{180}}$$

$$= e^{1.41} = 4.1$$

$$\frac{T_1}{T_2} = e^{\mu^\theta} = 4.1$$

$$r = \text{Radius of drum} = 20 \text{ cm}$$

$$T = \text{Braking torque} = 500 \text{ kg cm}$$

$$5000 = (T_1 - T_2) \times r$$

$$5000 = (4.1\, T_2 - T_2) \times 20$$

$$T_2 = 80.6 \text{ kg}$$

$$T_1 = 80.6 \times 4.1 = 331 \text{ kg};$$

$P$ = Brake operating force

$a = 3$ cm ; $b = 12$ cm

Consider the equilibrium of lever

$$P \times C + T_1 \times a - T_2 \times b = 0$$

$$P = \frac{T_2\, b - T_1\, a}{c}$$

$$= \frac{80.6 \times 15 - 331 \times 3}{60} = 3.6 \text{ kg}$$

Friction clutches generate heat as a result of relative motion of the parts but the amount of sliding is not ordinarily as great as in brake.

**Example 14.9.1.** *In the band brake shown in Fig 14.10 (a) the maximum lining pressure at any point in the brake is limited to 0.58 MPa. Find the torque capacity and the force F of the coefficient of friction is 0.16. Drum diameter is 240 mm and band width is 50 mm*

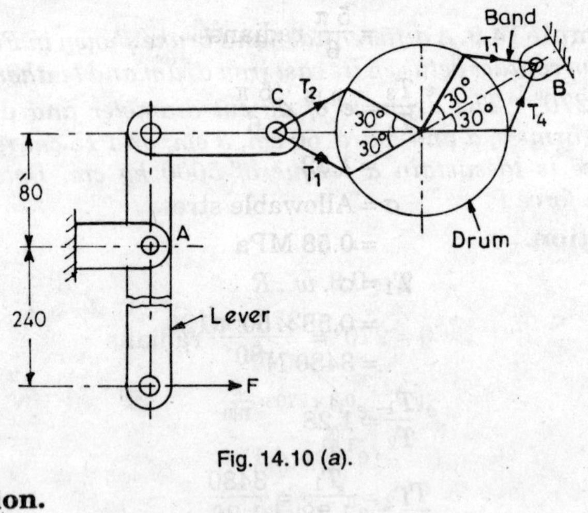


Fig. 14.10 (*a*).

**Solution.**

$F$ = Force

$\mu$ = Coefficient of friction

$= 0.16$

Let $T_1$ , $T_2$ , $T_3$ and $T_4$ be the tensions.

$$D = \text{Drum diameter}$$
$$= 240 \text{ mm}$$
$$R = \text{drum radius}$$
$$= \frac{D}{2} = \frac{240}{2}$$
$$= 120 \text{ mm}$$
$$W = \text{Width of band}$$
$$= 50 \text{ mm}$$
$$T_2 = T_3$$
$$\frac{T_1}{T_2} = e^{\mu\theta}$$

where $\theta = 90^\circ = \frac{\pi}{2}$

$$\frac{T_1}{T_2} = e^{0.16 \times \frac{\pi}{2}} = 1.28$$
$$\frac{T_3}{T_4} = e^{\mu\,\theta_1}$$

where $\theta_1 = 150^\circ = \frac{150 \times \pi}{180}$

$$= \frac{5\,\pi}{6} \text{ radians}$$
$$\frac{T_3}{T_4} = e^{0.16} \times \frac{5\,\pi}{6}$$
$$= 1.52$$
$$\sigma = \text{Allowable stress}$$
$$= 0.58 \text{ MPa}$$
$$T_1 = \sigma \,.\, w \,.\, R$$
$$= 0.58 \times 50 \times 120$$
$$= 3480 \text{ N}$$
$$\frac{T_1}{T_2} = 1.28$$
$$T_2 = \frac{T_1}{1.28} = \frac{3480}{1.28}$$
$$= 2718 \text{ N}$$
$$T_3 = T_2 = 2718$$

$$\frac{T_3}{T_4} = 1.52$$

$$T_4 = \frac{T_3}{1.52}$$

$$= \frac{2718}{1.52} = 1788 \text{ N}$$

$$T = \text{Torque} = (T_1 - T_4) \, . \, R$$

$$= \frac{3480 - 1788 \times 120}{1000} = 203 \text{ Nm}$$

To determine the force ($F$) take moments about the hings $A$

$$F \times 240 = [T_2 \cos 30 + T_3 \cos 30] \times 80$$

$$= [2718 \cos 30 + 2718 \cos 30] \times 80$$

$$= 1571 \text{ N}$$

**Example 14.9.2.** *Sketch and describe a pivoted type shoe brake.*

**Solution.** Fig. 14.10 (*b*) shows a pivoted type shoe brake. This brake is not commonly used because of the following draw backs.

1. It is difficult to locate the pivot close to the drum

2. It is difficult to maintain shoe and pivot position as the lining wears.

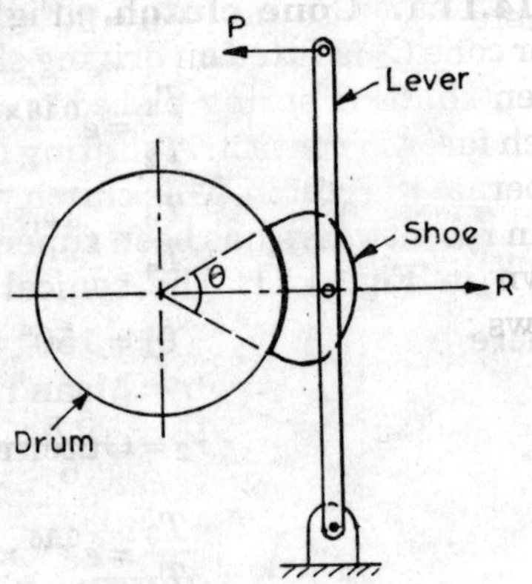


Fig. 14.10 (*b*)

In this brake

$$T = \text{Frictional torque}$$

$$= \mu \, . \, R \, . \, r \, . \left[ \frac{4 \sin \frac{\theta}{2}}{\theta + \sin \theta} \right]$$

where $\mu$ = Coefficient of friction

$R$ = Normal reaction between shoe and drum

$r$ = Radius of drum

$\theta$ = Shoe angle.

## 14.10. Clutches

A clutch is a device which is used to connect shafts in such a way that the shafts can be ready engaged and disengaged clutches are classified as follows.

(*a*) Friction clutches

(*b*) Positive contact clutches.

## 14.11. Friction Clutches

They transmit torque by virtue of a friction force. The various types of friction clutches are as follows :

(*i*) Cone clutch

(*ii*) Disk or plate clutch.

**14.11.1. Cone clutch.** Fig.14.11 shows a cone clutch. The outer cone $C_1$ is fitted on driving shaft and inner cone $C_2$ is fitted on driven shaft. A spring placed on driven shaft is used to hold the clutch faces in contact. A shifting lever provided in groove $C$ is used to operate the clutch. This clutch was formerly used in automobiles but in recent years has been superseded in that field disk clutch, as shown in Fig.14.11. The conical surface has various radius as follows :

$$r = \text{Mean radius} \; ; \; r_1 = \text{Inner radius}$$
$$r_2 = \text{Outer radius}$$

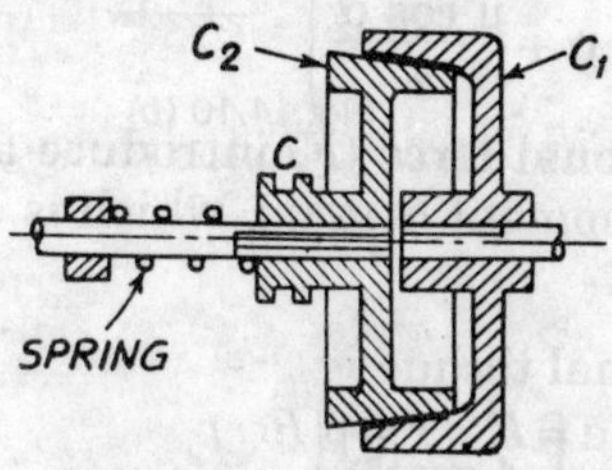


(*a*) Cone clutch

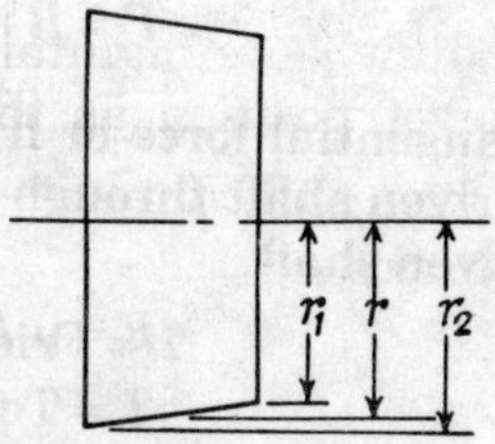


(*b*)

Fig. 14.11.

The design of cone clutch rests primarily obtaining mean radius ($r$) and width ($b$) of contact surfaces. Fig. 14.12 shows forces acting on a cone clutch.

Let $\qquad \alpha$ = Cone Angle of clutch

$\mu$ = Coefficient of friction

$A$ = Area of contact surface of clutch

$P$ = Axial force

$R$ = Total normal force between contact surfaces

$F$ = Frictional resistance, a tangential force

$b$ = Width of clutch

The axial force ($P$) forces the inner cone against the outer cone. The normal force ($R$) is assumed to be concentrated at the two points $A$ and $C$. So that half of $R$ *i.e.* $\frac{R}{2}$ acts at each point. In the parallelogram $A\,B\,C\,D$ of forces $B\,D$ represents $P$.

In right angle triangle $BOA$

$$\sin\alpha = \frac{OB}{AB} = \frac{P/2}{R/2}$$

$$= P/R$$

$$\therefore \quad P = R\sin\alpha.$$

This is true for steady operation after the clutch is engaged. If the engagement takes place when one shaft is rotating and other is stationary there appears an additional force resisting engagement of magnitude $\mu\cos\alpha$. But is observed that the force $\mu\cos\alpha$ is only 25% effective.

$$P = R\left(\sin\alpha + \frac{\mu\cos\alpha}{4}\right)$$

The tangential force or frictional force ($F$) introduce a torque into the driven shaft through a moment arm ($r$) which is equal to that in driven shaft.

$$F = \mu R.$$

and $$T = \text{Torque} = F \times r = \mu R \,.\, r$$

$$= \mu \,.\, \frac{P}{\sin\alpha} \,.\, \frac{r_1 + r_2}{2}$$

$$= \frac{\mu P \times (r_1 + r_2)}{2\sin\alpha} = \frac{\mu \,.\, P}{\sin\alpha} \times r$$

where $r$ = Mean radius = $\frac{r_1 + r_2}{2}$

$r_1$ = In side radius

$r_2$ = out side radius of friction surface.

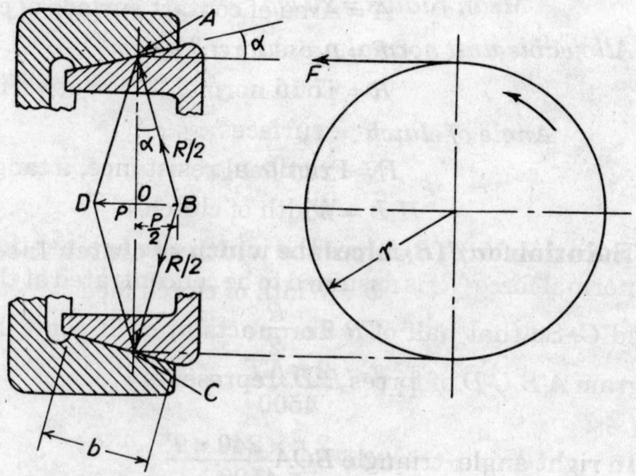


Fig. 14.12

The area of conical friction is equal to the product of its mean circumference and its slant height

$$A = 2\pi\, r.b.$$

$p$ = Allowable unit normal pressure between contact surface

$$= \frac{R}{A},\ p = \frac{R}{2\pi\, r\, b},\ b = \frac{R}{2\pi\, r\, p}.$$

The ratio $r/b$ varies from 2.25 to 4. In cone clutch the angle of clutch ($\alpha$) varies from $8^{\circ}$ to $30^{\circ}$ depending upon the clutch facing material and type of service required. The most common angle is $12^{\circ}$. The contact surfaces of the clutch may present metal to metal contact but more often the male member is lined with some such material as wood, leather, cork or an asbestos composition.

In a cone clutch the important zerometric design parameters are as follows :

(*i*) Cone angle ($\alpha$)

(*ii*) Face width of cone.

If the cone angle is too small say less than about $8^{\circ}$ then the force required to disengage the clutch may be quite large. And the wedging effect lessens rapidly when large cone angles are used.

**Example 14.10.** *In a cast iron cone clutch, calculate the width of clutch face and axial force using the following data.*

*Mean radius = 20 cm*

*Allowable unit normal pressure = 3 kg/cm*$^2$

$\mu$ -: *1.15*

*Angle of clutch = 12°*

*N = 240 R.P.M.*

*H.P. = 30*

**Solution.** (*a*) **To calculate width of clutch face**

$b$ = Width of clutch face

$T$ = Torque

$$\text{H.P.} = \frac{2\,\pi\,NT}{4500}$$

$$30 = \frac{2\,\pi \times 240 \times T}{4500}$$

$T$ = 89.6 kg m = 8960 kg cm.

$r$ = Mean radius = 20 cm.

$F$ = Tangential force

$$= \frac{T}{r} = \frac{8960}{20} = 448 \text{ kg.}$$

$R$ = Normal force

Now $F = \mu\,R$

$448 = 0.15\,R$

$$R = \frac{448}{0.15} = 2986 \text{ kg.}$$

$A$ = Area of contact surface of clutch

$= 2\,\pi\,.\,r\,.\,b$

$= 2\pi \times 20 \times b$

$= 125.6\;b$ cm$^2$.

$p$ = Allowable unit normal pressure = $R/A$

$$3 = \frac{2986}{125.6}\,b$$

$b$ = 7.92 cm.

(*b*) **To calculate axial force**

$P$ = Axial force

$$P = R\left[\sin\alpha + \frac{\mu\cos}{4}\right]$$

$$= 2986\left[\sin 12 + \frac{0.15 \cos 12}{4}\right]$$

$$= 2986\left[0.2079 + \frac{0.15 \times 0.981}{4}\right] = 730 \text{ kg}$$

**Example 14.11.** *A leather faced cone clutch is to transmit 30 H.P. at 600 R.P.M. from an electric motor to an air compressor. If the intensity of pressure is 1.1 kg/cm² and $\mu = 0.2$ calculate the following :*

*(a) Shaft diameter*

*(b) Face width*

*(c) Minimum axial force*

*(d) Spring dimensions.*

**Solution.** *(a)* **To find shaft diameter**

$d$ = Shaft diameter

$f_s$ = safe stress in shaft material

$= 400 \text{ kg/cm}^2$ (say)

$$\text{H.P.} = 2\frac{\pi NT}{4500}$$

$$30 = \frac{2\pi \times 600 \times T}{4500}$$

$$T = 35.8 \text{ kg m} = 3580 \text{ kg cm.}$$

Assuming maximum torque 50% more than average torque

$T_{max}$ = Maximum torque

$= 1.5 \times 3580 = 5370$ kg cm

$$T_{max} = \frac{\pi}{16} f_s d^3$$

$$5370 = \frac{\pi}{16} \times 400 \times d^3$$

$$d^3 = 68.4$$

$$d = 4.1 \text{ cm.}$$

*(b)* **To find face width**

$R$ = Normal force $= p \times 2\pi r \times b$

$r$ = Mean radius

$b$ = Face width

$\mu = 0.2$

$$p = 1.1 \text{ kg/cm}^2$$

$$F = \text{Tangential force}$$

Now $T = F \times r = \mu R \,.\, r = \mu \,.\, p \times 2\pi r \,.\, b \,.\, r$

$$5370 = 0.2 \times 1.1 \times 2\pi \times r^2 \,.\, b$$

Let $\dfrac{r}{b} = 3$

$\therefore$ $5370 = 0.2 \times 1.1 \times 2\pi \times (3b)^2 \,.\, b$

$$5370 = 0.2 \times 1.1 \times 2\pi \times 9b^3$$

$$b = 7.56 \text{ cm}$$

$$r = 3b = 3 \times 7.56 = 22.68 \text{ cm.}$$

In commercial clutches $r$ varies from 2.5 to 5 $d$

$$\frac{r}{d} = \frac{22.68}{4.1} = 5.53 \text{ which is safe}$$

$$\text{Mean diameter} = 2r = 2 \times 22.68 = 45.36 \text{ cm}$$

$$\alpha = \text{Angle of } (D) \text{ clutch} = 12^\circ \text{ (say)}$$

$$D_1 = \text{Small cone diameter}$$

$$= D - b \sin\alpha = 45.36 - 7.56 \sin 12$$

$$= 45.36 - 7.56 \times 0.2079$$

$$D_1 = 43.79 \text{ cm}$$

$$D_2 = \text{Outside cone diameter}$$

$$= D + b \sin\alpha$$

$$= 45.36 + 7.56 \times 0.2079 = 46.93 \text{ cm}$$

Corresponding face width ($b$)

$$= \frac{D_2 - D_1}{2\sin\alpha} = \frac{46.93 - 43.79}{2 \times 0.2079}$$

$$= 7.55 \text{ cm approx.}$$

(*c*) **To find minimum axial force**

$$P = \text{Minimum axial force}$$

$$= R \sin\alpha = p \,.\, 2\pi r \,.\, b \,.\, \sin\alpha$$

$$= 1.1 \times 2\pi \times 22.68 \times 7.56 \times 0.2079$$

$$= 246.24 \text{ kg.}$$

(*d*) **Spring design.** Helical spring is necessary to keep the clutch engaged and to do so must exert a force $P$ which is 246.14 kg. The spring will be made of heat treated steel wire circular in section.

The helical coil spring can now be designed as discussed in Chapter 9.

**14.11.2. Disc or plate clutches.** They are quite commonly used in automobiles, machine tools, tractors etc. Disc clutches are of two types.

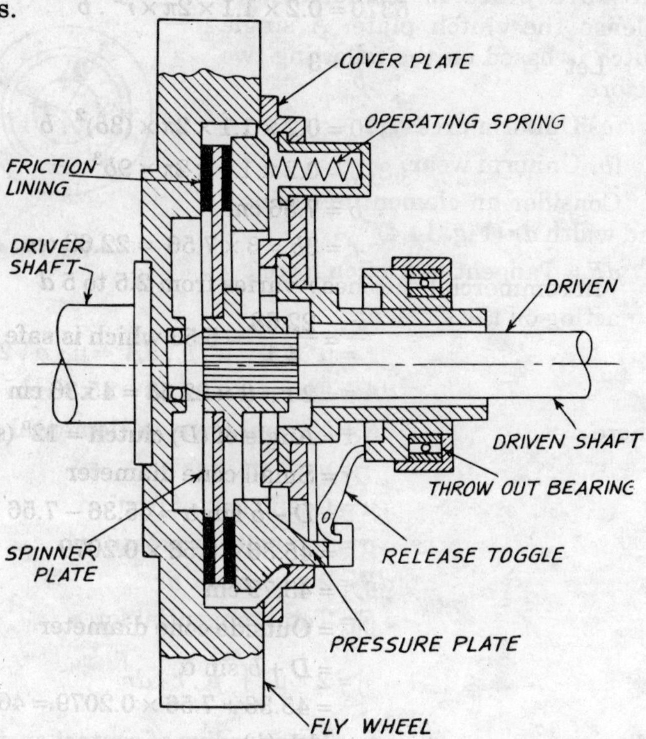


Fig. 14.13.

(*i*) Single disc clutch

(*ii*) Multi disc clutch.

Disc clutches have the following advantages :

(*i*) Large load carrying capacity with small over all dimensions.

(*ii*) Smooth engagement

(*iii*) Capacity can be easily varied by increasing or decreasing the number of discs. Generally the number of discs does not exceed 10—12.

A typical single disc clutch is shown in Fig. 14.13. The driven shaft is splined at the end to take the spinner plate which is situated between driving and pressure plates. A friction lining material like asbestos. Ferodo is fastened to both sides of spinner plate. Engagement of clutch is effected by the use of springs. To disengage the clutch the pressure plate is withdrawn to release the clutch plate. A single clutch is based on the following two factors.

(*a*) Uniform pressure

(*b*) Uniform wear.

Consider an element of radius $r$ and width $dr$ (Fig. 14.4)

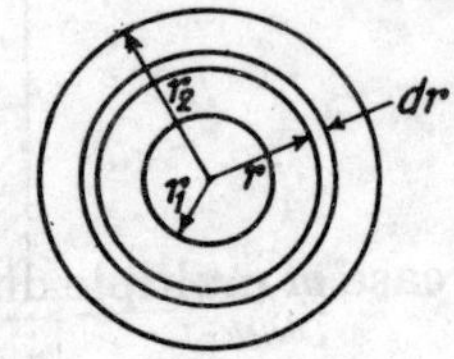


Fig. 14.14.

$dF$ = Tangential friction force acting on the element

$$= \mu \,.\, dR = \mu \,.\, p \,.\, dA = \mu \,.\, p \,.\, 2\pi r \,.\, dr$$

$dA$ = Elemental area = $2\pi r \,.\, dr$

where $dR$ = Normal force on elemental area

$$= p \,.\, 2\pi r \,.\, dr$$

$\mu$ = Coefficient of friction

$p$ = Intensity of pressure

$$dF = 2\pi\mu \,.\, p \,.\, r \,.\, dr$$

$F$ = Total tangential force

$$= 2\pi\mu \,.\, \int_{r_1}^{r_2} p \,.\, r \,.\, dr$$

where $r_1$ = Inner radius of contact surfaces

$r_2$ = Outer radius of contact surfaces

$dT$ = Friction torque on the elemental area

$$= dF \,.\, r$$

$$= 2\pi\mu \,.\, p \,.\, r^2 \,.\, dr$$

$T$ = Total friction torque

$$= 2\pi\mu \int_{r_1}^{r_2} pr^2 \,.\, dr$$

**Uniform pressure.** In this case the normal force $R$ will be uniformly distributed over the entire area

$$p = \frac{R}{A}$$

$$= \frac{R}{\pi(r_2^2 - r_1^2)}$$

Now $$T = 2\pi\mu p \int_{r_1}^{r_2} r^2\, dr = \frac{2}{3}\pi\mu p \,.\, (r_2^3 - r_1^3)$$

$$= \frac{2}{3}\pi\mu \,.\, \frac{R}{\pi(r_2^3 - r_1^3)} \times (r_2^3 - r_1^2)$$

$$= \frac{2}{3} \,.\, \mu R \,.\, \frac{(r_2^3 - r_1^2)}{(r_2^2 - r_1^2)}$$

In case of multiple disc clutches,

If $n$ = Number of friction surfaces

$$T = \frac{2}{3} \,.\, \mu R \,.\, n \,.\, \frac{(r_2^3 - r_1^3)}{(r_2^2 - r_1^2)}$$

If $r_m$ = Mean radius for each pair of active surfaces

$$T = n \,.\, F \,.\, r_m$$

$$= n \,.\, \mu \,.\, R \,.\, r_m$$

where $R$ = Normal force on clutch disc i.e. the axial force

$$\therefore \quad n \,.\, \mu R \,.\, r_m = \frac{2}{3} \,.\, \mu \,.\, R \,.\, n \,.\, \frac{r_2^3 - r_1^3}{r_2^2 - r_1^2}$$

$$\therefore \quad r_m = \frac{2(r_2^3 - r_1^3)}{3\; r_2^2 - r_1^2}$$

**Unifrom wear.** The rate of wear depends on intensity of pressure and rubbing velocity between contact surfaces. Since clutch is essentially a power transmission unit unifrom wear will be assumed unless it is specified otherwise.

$$R = \text{Total normal force}$$

$$= \int p \,.\, dA$$

$$= \int_{r_1}^{r_2} p \,.\, 2\pi r \,.\, dr$$

$$= 2\pi \int_{r_1}^{r^2} .\, 2p \,.\, r \,.\, dr$$

As the rate of wear depends upon intensity of pressure and the rubbing velocity and as the rubbing velocity is directly proportional to radius ($r$) therefore the rate of wear varies as $p \times r$. And after the components have run for some time the conditions are reached when $pr$ = constant.

$\therefore$ For unifrom wear $p \times r = C$

where $C$ = Constant

$$R = 2\pi \int_{r_1}^{r_2} p \, . \, r \, . \, dr = 2\pi \, . \, C \, . \int_{r_1}^{r_2} dr$$

$$\therefore \quad R = 2\pi \, . \, C \, . \, (r_2 - r_1)$$

$$C = \frac{R}{2\pi (r_2 - r_1)}$$

Now

$$T = 2\pi\mu \, . \int_{r_1}^{r_2} p \, . \, r^2 \, . \, dr = 2\pi \, . \, \mu \, . \, C \, . \int_{r_1}^{r_2} r \, dr$$

$$T = 2\pi\mu \, . \, C \, . \, \frac{r_2^2 - r_1^2}{2}$$

$$= \pi \, . \, \mu \, . \, C \, . \, (r_2^2 - r_1^2)$$

$$= \pi \, . \, \mu \, . \, \frac{R}{2\pi(r_2 - r_1)} \times (r_2^2 - r_1^2)$$

$$= \mu \, . \, R \, . \, \frac{r_2 + r_1}{2}$$

If there are $(n)$ friction surfaces

$$T = n \, . \, \mu R \, . \left(\frac{r_2 + r_1}{2}\right)$$

Again

$$T = n \, . \, F \, . \, r_m = n \, . \, \mu \, . \, R \, . \, r_m$$

$$\therefore \quad n \, . \, \mu R \, . \, r_m = n \, . \, \mu \, . \, R \, . \, \frac{r_2 + r_1}{2}$$

$$\therefore \quad r_m = \frac{r_2 + r_1}{2.}$$

A multiple disc clutch is of the same principle as single disc clutch but it uses several pairs of flat contact surfaces instead of one pair. In general by increasing the number of pairs in contact surfaces the unit normal pressure required to transmit a given torque is reduced. This increases the life of clutch plates. But however multiple disc clutch with a large number of discs presents an undersirable characteristic in having a heavy rotating mass.

**14.11.3. Thickness of clutch plates.** The thickness of clutch plates or discs depends on the following :

(*i*) Thickness of steel core.

(*ii*) Thickness of friction material face.

Thickness of steel core depends on diameter of the disc. Table 14.3 indicates the typical values of core thickness for some of the values of clutch diameter.

**Table 14.3.**

| *Clutch diameter (mm)* | *Core Thickness ,(mm)* |
|---|---|
| 0.150 | 0.75 |
| 150 - 300 | 1.5 |
| 300 - 450 | 2.25 |
| 450 - 600 | 3.2 |

The usual thickness of friction faces is about 0.735 to 1 mm for wet friction sintered metal friction face and it may be as large as 6 mm for simple disc clutch.

Fig. 14.14 (*a*) shows a clutch plate.

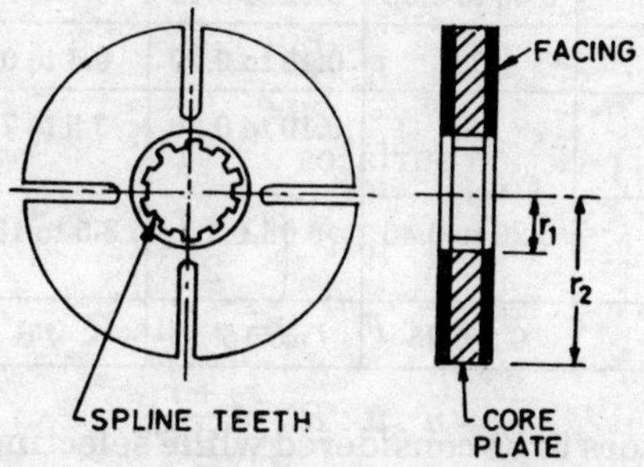


Fig. 14.14. (*a*)

## 14.12. Friction Materials

The friction material used in brakes or clutches should possess the following characteristics.

(*i*) They should have high and uniform coefficient of friction.

(*ii*) They should have high resistance to wear.

(*iii*) They should have high heat conductivity

(*iv*) They should be able to resist high temperature.

The friction materials may be used either dry or in oil. Some of the friction materials are cork, felt, asbestos, sintered metal linings (*e.g.* copper on iron base with lead, tin, graphite and or silica in the mixture). Now-a-days brake linings are made of mixture of asbestos and a binder moulded or woven with or without wire or metal chips of brass or copper.

Table 14.4 indicates the maximum unit pressure ($p$) and coefficient of friction ($\mu$) for some material combinations for clutches.

**Table 14.4**

| *Contact Wearing* | *Surface Mating* | *Friction coefficient* | | *Max. Unit pressure (kg / sq. cm)* | *Max. Operating Temperature* °C |
|---|---|---|---|---|---|
| | | *Dry* | *Wet* | | |
| Cast iron | Cast iron | 0.15 to 0.20 | 0.05 | 10.5 to 17.5 | 315 |
| Cast iron | Steel | | 0.06 | 8.4 to 14.0 | 260 |
| Powder metal | Cast iron or steel | 0.10 to 0.40 | 0.05 to 0.10 | 10.5 | 535 |
| Leather | -Do- | 0.30 to 0.50 | 0.12 to 0.15 | 0.7 to 2.8 | 93 |
| Cork | -Do- | Do- | 0.15 to 0.20 | 0.5 to 0.9 | 93 |
| Woven asbestos | -Do- | Do- | 0.10 to 0.20 | 3.5 to 7.0 | 180 |
| Moulded asbestos | -Do- | 0.20 to 0.40 | 0.08-0.12 | 3.5 to 10.5 | 260 |
| Wood | -Do- | 0.2-0.35 | 0.16 | 4-6 | 150 |

The three factors to be considered while selecting a material for facing of friction clutches are as follows :

(*i*) Coefficient of friction

(*ii*) Unit pressure

(*iii*) Maximum operating temperature.

**Example 14.12.** *In a multiple disc clutch four pairs of contact surfaces whose outer diameter is 30 cm and inner diameter is 20 cm are used. If* $\mu = 0.2$ *and unit normal pressure is 1.3 kg/cm*$^2$. *Calculate the following :*

(*a*) *Axial force*

(*b*) *H.P. transmitted at 450 R.P.M.*

**Solution.** *(a)* **To find axial force**

$r_1$ = Inner radius = 10 cm

$r_2$ = Outer radius = 15 cm

$\mu = 0.2$

$p$ = Unit normal pressure

$= 1.3 \text{ kg/cm}^2$

$n$ = Number of friction surfaces = 4

$R$ = Total normal force

$= n \, . \, p \, . \, \pi \, (r_2^2 - r_1^2)$

$= 4 \times 1.3 \times \pi \, (15^2 - 10^2)$

$= 2041$ kg.

$P$ = Axial force for one friction surface

$$= \frac{R}{n} = \frac{2041}{4}$$

$= 510.25$ kg.

*(b)* **To find H.P.**

For uniform wear, $T$ = Torque = $\mu \, . \, R \, . \, rm.$

$$T = \mu \, . \, R \, . \, \frac{r_1 + r_2}{2}$$

where $r^m$ = mean radius $= \dfrac{r_1 + r_2}{2}$

$$= 0.2 \times 2041 \times \frac{15 + 10}{2}$$

$= 5102$ kg cm $= 51.02$ kg m

$N = 450$ R.P.M.

$$\text{H.P.} = \frac{2\pi \, NT}{4500}$$

$$= \frac{2\pi \times 450 \times 51.02}{4500} = 32.$$

**Example 14.13.** *In a single disc clutch the outside diameter of contact surface is 28 cm and inside diameter is 18 cm. If $\mu = 0.2$ and the allowable normal pressure is 1.2 kg/cm$^2$, calculate*

*(a) Axial force*

*(b) H.P. transmitted at 900 R.P.M.*

**Solution.** *(a)* **To find axial force**

$r_1$ = Inner radius = 9 cm

$r_2$ = Outside radius = 14 cm.

$\mu = 0.2$

$p$ = Allowable normal pressure = 1.2 kg/cm$^2$

$R$ = Normal force

$= p \cdot \pi (r_2^2 - r_1^2)$

$= 1.2 \times \pi (14^2 - 9^2) = 433$ kg

$P$ = Axial force = $R$ = 433 kg

(*b*) **To find H.P.**

For uniform wear $T$ = Torque

$n$ = No. of surfaces = 2

$$T = \mu \cdot R \cdot \frac{r_1 + r_2}{2} \times n$$

$$= 0.2 \times 433 \times \frac{14 + 9}{2} \times 2$$

$= 19.92$ kg cm = 19.92 kg m

$N$ = 900 R.P.M.

$$\text{H.P.} = \frac{2\pi NT}{4500}$$

$$= \frac{2\pi \times 900 \times 19.92}{4500} = 25.$$

(*ii*) **For uniform pressure**

$T$ = Torque = $\mu \cdot R\, rm\, n$

where $rm$ = Mean radius

$$= \frac{2}{3}\left[\frac{r_2^3 - r_1^3}{r_2^3 - r_1^2}\right]$$

$$T = \mu \cdot R \cdot n \times \frac{2}{3}\left[\frac{r_2^3 - r_1^3}{r_2^2 - r_1^2}\right]$$

$$= 0.2 \times 433 \times 2 \times \frac{2}{3}\left[\frac{14^3 - 9^3}{14^2 - 9^2}\right]$$

$= 2026$ kg cm = 20.16 kg m

$$\text{H.P.} = \frac{2\pi NT}{4500} = \frac{2\pi \times 900 \times 20.26}{4500}$$

$= 25.4.$

**Example 14.14.** *A multi-disc clutch uses 4 steel and 3 bronze discs of 26 cm outer diameter and 16 cm inner diameter. If the unit normal pressure is 12 kg/cm$^2$ and $\mu = 0.2$. Calculate*

*(a) Axial force*

*(b) H.P. transmitted at 600 R.P.M.*

**Solution.** (*a*) **To find axial force**

$R$ = Normal force on clutch discs *i.e.* the axial forces

$= n \cdot p \cdot \pi(r_2^2 - r_1^2)$

where $n$ = Number of contact surfaces

$= n_1 + n_2 - 1$

$n_1$ = Number of steel disc = 4

$n_2$ = Bronze discs = 3

$n = 4 + 3 - 1 = 6$

$p$ = Unit normal pressure = 1.2 kg/cm$^2$

$r_1$ = Inner radius = 8 cm

$r_2$ = Outer radius of discs

$= \frac{26}{2} = 13$ cm

$R = n \cdot p \cdot \pi(r_2^2 - r_1^2)$

$= 6 \times 1.2 \times \pi \times (13^2 - 8^2) = 2373$ kg.

(*b*) **To find H.P.**

For uniform wear, $T$ = Torque transmitted

$= \mu \cdot R \cdot \frac{r_1 + r_2}{2}$

$= 0.2 \times 2373 \times \frac{13 + 8}{2}$

$= 4983$ kg cm $= 49.83$ kg m

$N = 600$ R.P.M.

$$\text{H.P.} = \frac{2\pi NT}{4500} = \frac{2\pi \times 600 \times 49.83}{4500}$$

$= 41.72.$

**Example 14.15.** *A dry single plate clutch is to transmit 25 H.P. at 100 R.P.M. The number of springs to be used is 4 and ratio of* *mean radius of friction faces and radial width of friction faces is 1.5. Calculate.*

(*a*) *Mean radius*

(*b*) *Radial width of friction faces*

(*c*) *Dimensions of spring assuming mean coil diameter 6 times diameter of wire.*

**Solution.** (*a*) **To find mean radius**

$n$ = Number of friction surfaces = 2

$b$ = Radial width of friction faces

$= r_2 - r_1$

$A$ = Area of friction faces $= 2\pi\, r_m \,.\, b$

$R$ = Axial force

$= p \,.\, 2\pi\, r_m \times b$

where $r_m$ = Mean radius

$$= \frac{r_1 + r_2}{2}$$

$p$ = Unit normal pressure

$= 0.8$ kg/cm$^2$ (say)

$$\therefore \frac{r_m}{b} = 5 \quad \because \quad \frac{r_m}{5} = b$$

$$R = p \times 2\pi r_m \,.\, b$$

$$= p \,.\, 2\pi \,.\, r_m \times \frac{r_m}{5}$$

$$= p \,.\, 2\pi \,.\, \frac{rm^2}{5}$$

Assuming uniform wear

$T$ = Torque $= n \,.\, \mu\, R \,.\, r_m$

$$\text{H.P} = \frac{2\pi NT}{4500}$$

$$25 = \frac{2\pi \times 1000 \times T}{4500}$$

$T = 17.91$ kg m $= 1791$ kg cm

$\mu$ = Coefficient of friction = 0.2 (say)

$$T = n \,.\, \mu \,.\, R\, r_m$$

$$= 2 \times 0.2 \times p \times 2\pi \times \frac{r_m^{\,3}}{5} \times r_m$$

$$1791 = 2 \times 0.2 \times 0.8 \times 2\pi \times \frac{r_m^3}{5}$$

$$r_m = 16.45 \text{ cm.}$$

(*b*) **To find radial width**

$$b = \text{Radial width of friction faces}$$

$$\frac{r_m}{b} = 5$$

$$b = \frac{r_m}{5} = \frac{16.45}{5} = 3.29 \text{ cm}$$

(*c*) **To design spring**

$$T = \mu \,.\, R \,.\, r_m \,.\, n$$

$$1791 = 0.2 \times R \times 16.45 \times 2$$

$$R = 272 \text{ kg}$$

$$n_1 = \text{Number of springs} = 4$$

$$W = \text{Load per spring}$$

$$= \frac{R}{n_1} = \frac{272}{4} = 68 \text{ kg.}$$

The spring used will be helical spring of circular wire and can be designed as discussed in Chapter 9.

**Example 14.16.** *A multiple disc clutch, steel on bronze is to transmit 6 HP at 640 RPM. The average allowable pressure is 3.6 kg/cm² and the inner and outer radius of contact are 3.6 cm and 6.8 cm respectively. If the clutch operates in oil with an effective coefficient of friction 0.12. Calculate the following :*

(*a*) *Number of discs required*

(*b*) *Axial force.*

**Solution.** (*a*) **To find number of discs**

$$r_1 = \text{Inner radius of contact}$$

$$= 3.6 \text{ cm}$$

$$r_2 = \text{Outer radius} = 6.8 \text{ cm}$$

$$\mu = 0.12$$

$$p = 3.6 \text{ kg/cm}^2$$

$$P = \text{Force} = p \,.\, \pi(r_2^2 - r_1^2)$$

$$= 3.6 \times \pi \times (6.8^2 - 3.6^2) = 379 \text{ kg}$$

$$T = \text{Torque}$$

$$H.P = \frac{2\pi NT}{4500}$$

$$6 = \frac{2\pi \times 640 \times T}{4500}$$

$$T = 6.72 \text{ kgm} = 672 \text{ kg cm}$$

$n$ = Number of pair of contact surfaces

$$T = n \times \mu \,.\, P \,.\, r_m$$

where $r_m$ = mean radius

$$= \frac{r_1 + r_2}{2}$$

$$672 = n \times 0.12 \times 379 \times \frac{3.6 + 6.8}{2}$$

$$n = 2.73$$

Number of contact surface must be even

$n = 4$ (say)

$n_1$ = Number of steel discs

$= 3$

$n_2$ = Number of bronze discs = 2

**(*b*) To find axial force (P)**

$$T = n \times \mu \,.\, P \,.\, \frac{r_1 + r_2}{2}$$

$$672 = 4 \times 0.12 \times P \times \frac{3.6 + 6.8}{2}$$

$$P = 259 \text{ kg.}$$

**Example 14.17.** *A plate clutch is to transmit 130 kW at 400 RPM. The plate clutch has maximum diameter of 540 mm with maximum lining pressure 0.3 MPa. The coefficient of friction is 0.28. Determine inside diameter and spring force to engage the clutch. If safe shear stress for the spring material is 560 MPa, the spring index is 7 and six springs are used, determine spring wire diameter.*

**Solution.** $P$ = Power

$= 130 \text{ kW} = 130 \times 1000 \text{ W}$

$N$ = RPM = 400

$$P = \frac{2\pi NT}{60}$$

where $T$ = Frictional torque

$$130 \times 1000 = \frac{2\pi \times 400 \times T}{60}$$

$$T = 3105 \text{ Nm}$$

Now $T = \mu \cdot \pi p \cdot r_1 \cdot (r_2^2 - r_1^2)$

where $r_1$ = Inner radius

$r_2$ = Outer radius = 270 mm

$P$ = Maximum lining pressure

= 0.3 MPa

$$3105 \times 10^3 = 0.28\,\pi \times 0.3 \times (270^2 - r_1^2) \times r_1$$

$r_1$ = 142,196 mm

Using $r_1$ = 196 mm

$p$ = Axial force required to apply the clutch

$= 2\pi\, p \cdot r_1 \cdot (r_2 - r_1)$

$= 2\pi \times 0.3 \times 196\,(270 - 196)$

= 27325 N

$n$ = Number of springs = 6

$F$ = Load on each spring

$$= \frac{P}{n}$$

$$= \frac{27325}{6} = 4554 \text{ N}$$

$C$ = Spring index = 7

$K$ = Wall stress concentration factor

$$= \frac{4C - 1}{4C - 4} + \frac{0.625}{C}$$

$$= \frac{4 \times 7 - 1}{4 \times 7 - 4} + \frac{0.625}{7}$$

= 1.215

$d$ = Spring wire diameter

$f_s$ = Shear stress

$$= \frac{8\,KFC}{\pi\, d^2}$$

$$= \frac{8 \times 1.215 \times 4554 \times 7}{\pi \cdot d^2}$$

$d$ = 13.27 mm.

**Example 14.18.** *A plate clutch is required to transmit 70 kW at 200 RPM. The maximum pressure intensity is 0.8 MPa and coeff. of friction is 0.26. The ratio of O.D to ID is 1.3. Calculate the dimensions of the friction surface with single pair of mating friction surfaces.*

**Solution.**

$$P = \text{Power} = 70 \text{ kW}$$

$$T = \text{Torque}$$

$$N = \text{RPM} = 1200$$

$$P = \frac{2\pi NT}{60}$$

$$70 \times 10^3 = \frac{2\pi \times 1200 \times T}{60}$$

$$T = 557.3 \text{ Nm}$$

$$\mu = 0.26$$

$$r_1 = \text{Inside radius}$$

$$p = \text{Pressure intensity} = 0.8 \text{ MPa}$$

$$r_2 = \text{Outside radius} = 1.3\, r_1$$

$$T = \pi \,.\, \mu \,.\, p \,.\, r_1\, [r_2^2 - r_1^2]$$

$$557.3 = \frac{\pi \times 0.26 \times 0.8 \times r_1\, [(1.3\, r_1)^2 - r_1^2]}{1000}$$

$$r_1 = 107.34 \text{ mm}$$

$$r_2 = 1.3\, r_1 = 1.3 \times 107.34$$

$$= 139.5 \text{ mm.}$$

## 14.13. Positive Contact Clutches

They operate by meshing jaws or teeth of driving member with the corresponding elements of the driven member. They have the following advantages.

(*i*) They do not slip.

(*ii*) They are smaller in size and less costly as compared to friction clutches for a given capacity.

(*iii*) No heat is produced during their operation.

Various types of positive contact clutches are as follows :

(*a*) Jaw clutch

(*b*) Tooth clutch.

**14.3.1 Jaw clutches.** They are frequently used in sprocket wheels, gears and pulleys. Jaw clutches are of two types :

(*i*) Square jaw clutch

(*ii*) Spiral jaw clutch.

A jaw clutch is device that through the direct contact of inter locking lugs or jaws permits one shaft to drive another. A square jaw clutch is shown in Fig. 14.15. It consists of two halves, one half having projects jaws or claues and other half having corresponding recesses. The fixed half is fastened to shaft by a sunk key while sliding half is fastened to the shaft by a feather key and is provided with a recess in which forked end of operating lever fits. It can transmit power in either direction of rotation. It is used where engagement and disengagement in motion and under load is not necessary.

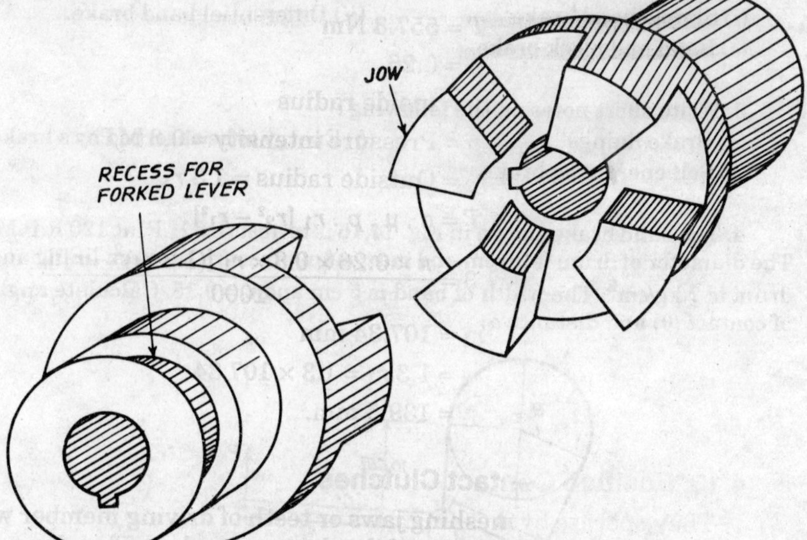

Fig. 14.15 Square Jaw clutch

These clutches have the following characteristics :

(*i*) There is no slip

(*ii*) They are positive contact clutches

(*iii*) No heat is produced

(*iv*) Engagement is accompanied by shock

(*v*) They can not be engaged at high speeds.

The spiral jaw clutch is made with either left hand or right hand spiral jaws since power can be transmitted by them in one direction only. Running engagement is possible in this clutch.

**14.3.2 Tooth clutch.** It has multiple teeth modified in various ways to provide strength. Running engagement is possible in this clutch.

## PROBLEMS

**1.** What is a brake. What are the various types of brakes ?

**2.** Sketch and describe the following types of brakes.

(*a*) Shoe brake

(*i*) External shoe brake (*ii*) Internal shoe brake.

(*b*) Band brake.

(*i*) Simple band brake (*ii*) Differential band brake.

(*c*) Band and block brake.

**3.** Write short notes on the following :

(*a*) Brake linings (*b*) Energy to be absorbed by a brake

(*c*) Self energising brake.

**4.** The band brake shown in Fig. 14.16 is to absorb 8 H.P. at 120 R.P.M. The diameter of drum is 30 cm and maximum pressure between lining and drum is 7 kg/cm$^2$. The width of band is 5 cm and $\mu = 0.15$. Calculate angle of contact ($\theta$) and distance *a*.

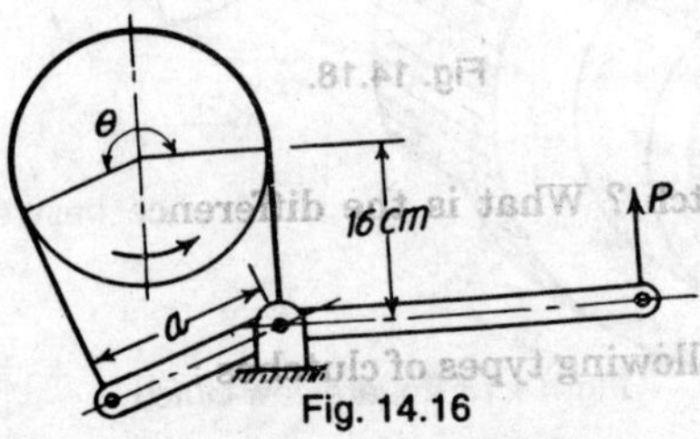


Fig. 14.16

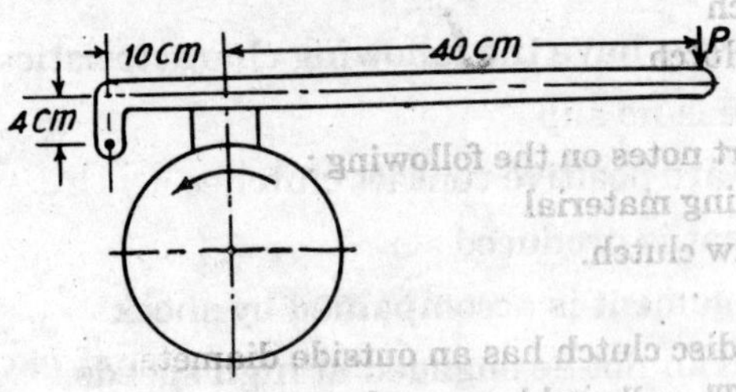


Fig. 14.17

**5.** The block brake shown in Fig. 14.17 is to resist a torque of 12,000 kg cm. If the coefficient of friction is 0.25, calculate the operating force $P$. The drum is of 60 cm diameter. Can this brake be made self acting. If so, state the change in dimensions.

**6.** In the double shoe brake for an electric crane shown in Fig. 14.18. the diameter of drum is 40 cm and each brake shoe is 14 cm long. The permissible average bearing pressure is 4 kg/cm$^2$ and $\mu = 0.28$. If the operating force is 50 kg, determine the following :

(*a*) Braking torque

(*b*) Width of brake shoes.

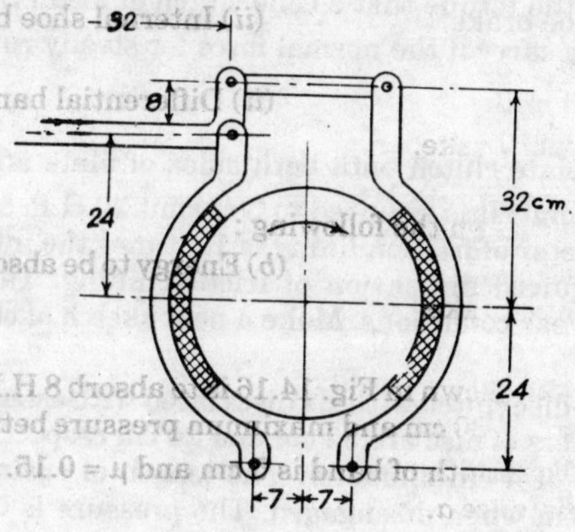


Fig. 14.18.

**7.** What is a clutch ? What is the difference between a clutch and coupling ?

**8.** Describe the following types of clutches :

(*a*) Cone clutch

(*b*) Disc clutch

(*c*) Positive clutch.

**9.** Write short notes on the following :

(*a*) Brake lining material

(*b*) Square jaw clutch.

**10.** A single disc clutch has an outside diameter of 24 cm and in side diameter 18 cm. The allowable normal pressure is 1.6 kg/cm$^2$ and $\mu = 0.2$. Find :

(*a*) Axial force
(*b*) H.P. transmitted at 900 R.P.M.

**11.** A cone clutch is used to connect two 25 mm diameter shafts whose safe shearing stress is 400 kg/cm$^2$. The angle of clutch is 12° and width of clutch is 6 cm. The unit normal pressure is 0.8 kg/cm$^2$ and $\mu = 0.25$. Determine,

(*a*) Torque transmitted by the clutch
(*b*) H.P. transmitted at 900 R.P.M.
(*c*) Radius of clutch
(*d*) Axial force required.

**12.** Calculate the torque that a cone clutch of mean radius 15 cm and clutch angle 8° can carry if the normal force for steady running is 200 kg. Take $\mu = 0.2$.

**13.** A single plate clutch with both sides of plate effective the axial pressure is 0.3 kg/cm$^2$. It is required to transmit 20 H.P. at 1800 R.P.M. If the external diameter of friction lining is 1.4 times the internal diameter. Calculate the required dimension of friction lining. Take $\mu = 0.25$ and assume uniform wear conditions. Make a neat sketch of clutch.

**14.** In a multi-disc clutch with six discs faced with asbestos. The outside and inside diameters of disc are 32 cm and 20 cm respectively. The clutch uses four springs of 4 cm diameter. The length of spring is 8 cm when engaged and 7.2 cm when disengaged. The pressure is 50% higher than when engaged. The maximum stress in spring is limited to 4300 kg/cm$^2$. Determine H.P. transmitted at 900 R.P.M. assuming 0.8 kg/cm$^2$ pressure on discs.

**15.** A cone clutch has a width of face of 5 cm and a mean diameter of 36 cm. The cup of clutch is made of cast iron and the cone is faced with a fibrous material. If the normal pressure is 2.2 kg/cm$^2$ angle of clutch is 10° and $\mu = 0.24$, calculate the following :

(*a*) Area of contact surfaces
(*b*) Frictional force or tangential force.

**16.** A 60 cm outer diameter plate clutch has a lining pressure of 3 kg/cm$^2$. If 140 H.P. is to be transmitted at 450 R.P.M. and $\mu = 0.28$, find inside diameter and spring force required to keep the clutch engaged.

# 15

# Levers

## 15.1. Introduction

A lever is a rigid rod hinged or pivoted at a point and capable of turning about the pivot. A lever is used to lift heavy load by applying a small force. The lever is loaded at one place and the force (effort) is applied at the other place to lift the load. A lever may be a straight or curved link. A lever works on the principle of moments. Fig. 15.1 shows a simple lever having one fulcrum ($C$)

Let $W$ = Load to be lifted

$P$ = Effort applied to lift the load

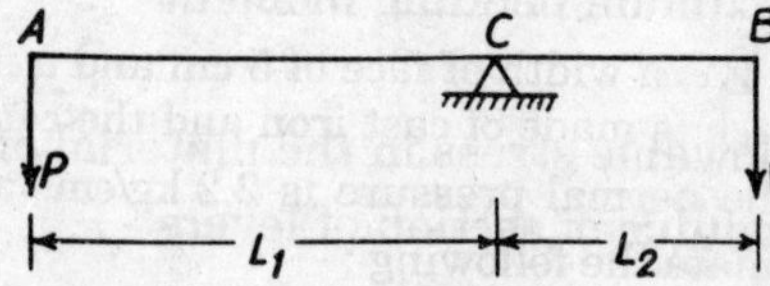


Fig. 15.1.

$L_1$ = Distance between $P$ and fulcrum

$L_2$ = Distance between $W$ and fulcrum

Taking moments about fulcrum ($C$)

$$P \times L_1 = W \times L_2$$

$$\frac{W}{L_1} = \frac{P}{L_2}$$

$$\frac{W}{P} = \frac{L_1}{L_2}$$

$\frac{W}{P}$ is called mechanical advantage and the ratio $\frac{L_1}{L_2}$ is called leverage. The perpendicular distance $L_1$ and $L_2$ of forces from the fulcrum are called arms of lever. Levers are of two types :

(*a*) Simple levers (*b*) Compound levers.

A simple lever has only one fulcrum whereas compound lever has more than one fulcrum. The compound levers are used in cases where the effort arm should be very big to obtain high mechanical advantage but the space is limited. The compound levers may be made up of straight pieces which may be attached with one another by means of pin joints.

## 15.2. Design of Levers

The section of the lever arm may be rectangular, elliptical circular or I-section. Fig. 15.2 shows a lever having rectangular section with fulcrum at $C$. The section of lever at which maximum bending moment occurs is calculated as follows :

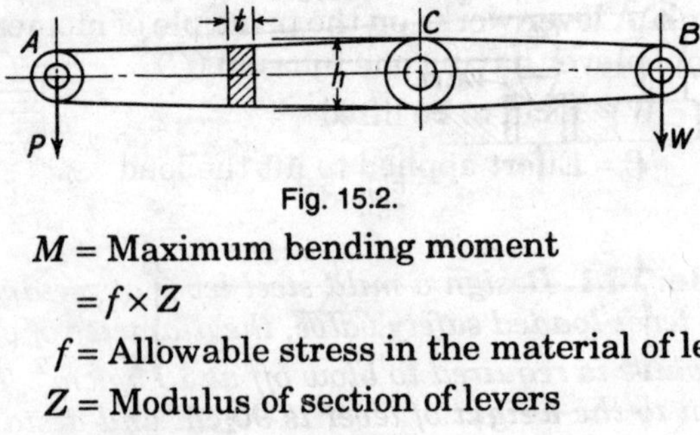


Fig. 15.2.

$M$ = Maximum bending moment

$= f \times Z$

where $f$ = Allowable stress in the material of lever

$Z$ = Modulus of section of levers

$= \frac{1}{6} th^2$ for rectangular section

where $t$ = Thickness of lever

$h$ = Height of lever

$Z = \frac{\pi}{32} b\, a^2$ for elliptical section

where $a$ = Length of major axis of ellipse

$b$ = Length of minor axis of ellipse

Usually $\frac{a}{b} = 2$ to 2.5

$$Z = \frac{\pi}{32} d^3 \text{ for circular section}$$

where $d$ = Diameter of lever

The pin at fulcrum is designed for bearing and bending considerations with a proper check for shear and some times deflection also. The section of lever arm is tapered from the fulcrum to the end. The taper depends upon type of free end and taper is provided in height and not in thickness. As shown in the figure the maximum bendings moment occurs at fulcrum and goes on reducing towards ends. That is why the lever is suitably tapered from fulcrum towards ends.

## 15.2. Lever of Lever Loaded Safety Valve

Fig. 15.3 shows a lever loaded safety valve used in steam boilers. The valve gets opened by steam pressure when the pressure reaches a certain maximum valve up to which it is safe to operate the valve. The controlling force for the valve is provided by weights put at free end of lever which is provided at fulcrum by a pin to the toggle. In spring balance type of safety valve the controlling force is provided by the spring attached at the end of lever.

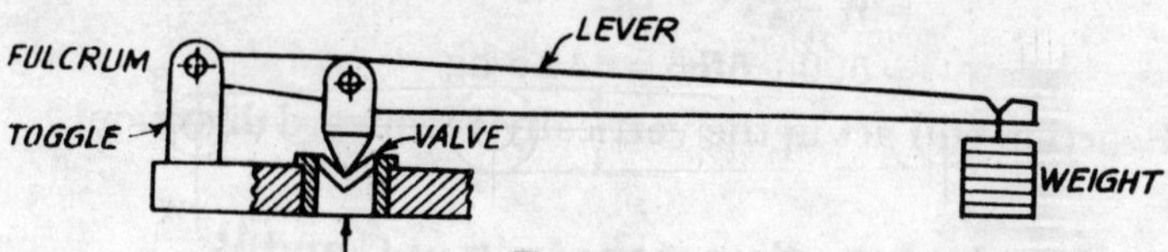


Fig. 15.3.

**Example. 15.1.** *Design a mild steel lever of rectangular cross-section for a lever loaded safety valve, the diameter of valve being 7 cm and the valve is required to blow off at 13 kg/cm². The distance from fulcrum to the weight of lever is 90 cm and distance between fulcrum and pin connecting valve spindle links to the lever is 10 cm. The safe stresses are 400 kg/cm, 260 kg/cm² and 600 kg/cm² in tension, shear and crushing respectively. The permissible bearing pressure for the pin may be taken as 210 kg/cm².*

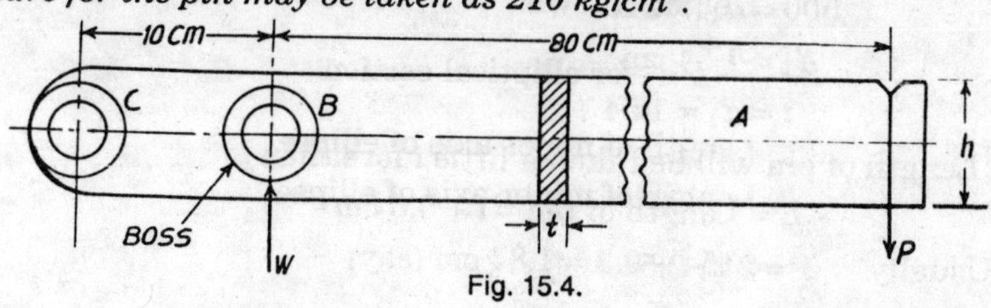


Fig. 15.4.

**Solution. (*a*) To find force at C and B**

Fig. 15.4 shows lever of a safety valve

$$W = \text{Steam load acting upward at } B$$

$$= \frac{\pi}{4} D^2 \times p$$

where $D$ = Diameter of valve = 7 cm

$p$ = Steam pressure = 13 kg/cm$^2$

$$W = \frac{\pi}{4} \times 7^2 \times 13 = 500 \text{ kg}$$

$P$ = Force applied at $A$

To find $P$, take moments about fulcrum $C$

$$P \times 90 = W \times 10$$

$$P = \frac{W \times 10}{90} = \frac{W}{9}$$

$$= \frac{500}{9} = 55.5 \text{ kg}$$

$R$ = Reaction at $C$

$$= W - P$$

$$= 500 - 55.5 = 444.5 \text{ kg}$$

Reaction will act in the vertically downward direction.

**(*b*) To calculate diameter of pin at C and B**

Let $d_1$ = Diameter of pin at $B$

$f_b$ = Bearing pressure on pin = 210 kg/cm$^2$

$W$ = Load at $B$ = 500 kg

$t$ = Thickness of lever

Considering bearing of the pin

$$W = d_1 \cdot t \cdot f_b$$

$$500 = d_1 \times d_1 \times f_b \text{ assuming } t = d_1$$

$$500 = d_1^2 \times 210$$

$$d_1 = 1.54 \text{ cm}$$

$$t = d_1 = 1.54$$

Length of pin will be taken a little more than $t$.

$L$ = Length of pin = $t$ + 0.3 cm

= 154 + 0.3 = 1.84 cm (say)

$d_2$ = Diameter of pin at $C$

As the difference between load at $B$ and $C$ is not large therefore we take diameter of pin at $C$ same as that of diameter of pin at $B$.

$\therefore \quad d_2 = d_1 = 1.54$ cm

We provide a gun metal bush of 1.5 mm thickness at each pin.

$d_3$ = Diameter of gun metal bush for pins at $C$ and $B$

$$= d_1 + \frac{1.5 \times 2}{10}$$

$$= 1.54 + \frac{3}{10} = 1.84 \text{ cm}$$

$d_4$ = Diameter of boss = $2 \times d_3$

$= 2 \times 1.84$

$= 3.68$ cm

Fig. 15.5 shows section at fulcrum

(c) **To determine section of lever**

$t$ = Thickness of lever

$h$ = Height of lever

Maximum bending moment on lever will occur near boss at $B$.

$M$ = Maximum bending moment

$$= P\left(82 - \frac{d_4}{2}\right)$$

$$= 55.5\left(82 - \frac{3.68}{2}\right)$$

$= 4449$ kg cm

$f$ = Safe bending stress in lever

$= 400$ kg/cm$^2$

$Z$ = Modulus of section = $\frac{1}{6} th^2$

$M = f \times Z$

$$4449 = 400 \times \frac{1}{6} \times th^2 = 400 \times \frac{1}{6} \times 1.54 \times h^2$$

$h = 6.6$ cm

Check the lever aganist induced shear stress. The maximum load occurring on lever is between $C$ and $B$ where cross-section will be $h \times t$.

$f_{s_1}$ = Induced shear stress

$$= \frac{W}{h \times t} = \frac{500}{6.6 \times 1.54} = 49.2 \text{ kg/cm}^2$$

This is less than given shear stress of 260 kg/cm². Hence safe.

Fig. 15.5 shows section of lever at *B*.

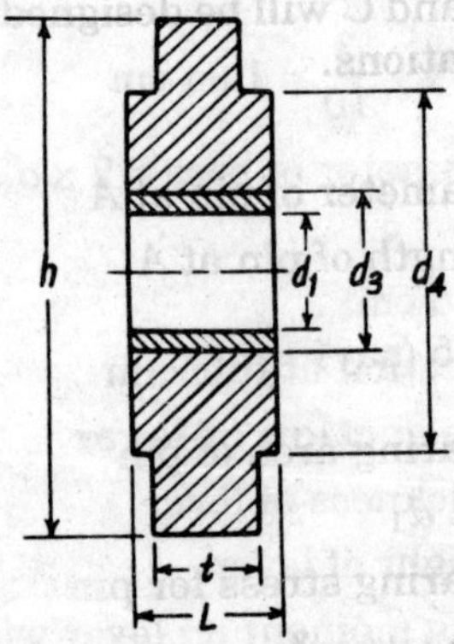


Fig.15.5.

**Example 15.2.** *Design a right angled bell crank lever to raise a load of 200 kg acting on a pin at the end of 12 cm long arm and the effort is applied at the end of an arm 16 cm long through a pin and fork. The following stresses apply both to pin and lever :*

Allowable stress in tension = *700 kg/cm²*

Allowable stress in shear = *500 kg/cm²*

Allowable stress in compression = *1100 kg/cm²*

Allowable bearing pressure for pin = *160 kg/cm²*

**Solution.**

**(a) To find pin diameters**

Fig.15.6 shows bell crank lever.

$W$ = Load = 200 kg

Let $P$ = Force to be applied at $A$

Taking moments about $C$

$$P \times 16 = W \times 12$$

$$P = \frac{200 \times 12}{16} = 150 \text{ kg}$$

$R$ = Reaction at $C$

$$= \sqrt{P^2 + W^2}$$

$$= \sqrt{150^2 + 200^2}$$

$$= 250 \text{ kg}$$

The pins at $A$, $B$ and $C$ will be designed in bearing and checked by shearing considerations.

**Pin at A.**

Let $d_1$ = Diameter of pin at $A$

$L_1$ = Length of pin at $A$

$$\frac{L_1}{d_1} = 1.25 \text{ (say)}$$

$A$ = Bearing area of pin

$= L_1 \,.\, d_1$

$f_b$ = Bearing stress for pin

$= 160 \text{ kg/cm}^2$

Fig. 15.6. Bell crank liver.

$$L_1 \times d_1 \times f_b = P$$

$$1.25\, d_1 \times d_1 \times 160 = 150$$

$$1.25\, d_1^2 \times 160 = 150$$

$$d_1 = 0.86 \text{ cm}$$

$$= 0.9 \text{ cm (say)}$$

$L_1$ = Length of pin

$$= 1.25 \times 0.9$$

$$= 1.125 \text{ cm}$$

The pin can be checked in shear.

$A$ = Area of pin in double shear

$$= 2 \times \frac{\pi}{4} d_1^2$$

$$P = 2 \times \frac{\pi}{4} \times d_1^2 \times f_{s_1}$$

$$150 = 2 \times \frac{\pi}{4} \times (0.9)^2 \times f_{s_1}$$

$$f_{s_1} = 118 \text{ kg/cm}^2$$

Therefore the induced shear stress ($f_{s_1}$) is less than allowable shear stress of 500 kg/cm$^2$. Hence safe

$$d = \text{Boss diameter}$$
$$= 2 \times d_1 = 2 \times .0.9 = 1.8 \text{ cm}$$

A brass bush should be pressed into boss. The bush should be 1.5 mm to 3 mm thick.

Fig.15.7 shows pin, bush and boss size.

$$d_b = \text{Bush diameter}$$
$$d_1 + 0.3 \text{ cm}$$
$$= 1.2 \text{ cm}$$

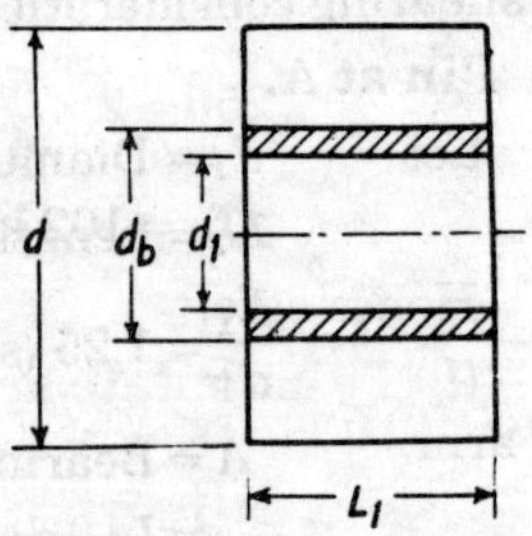

Fig. 15.7.

**Pin at B.**

Let $d_2$ = Diameter of pin at $B$

$L_2$ = Length of pin

$$\frac{L_2}{D_2} = 1.25$$

$$L_2 \,.\, d_2 \,.\, f_b = W$$

$$1.25\, d_2 \times d_2 \times 160 = 200$$
$$d_2 = 1 \text{ cm}$$
$$L_2 = 1.25\, d$$
$$= 1.25 \times 1 = 1.25, \text{cm}$$

Boss diameter $= 2d_2 = 2 \times 1 = 2$ cm

Let $f_{s_2}$ = Induced shear stress in pin

$$2 \times \frac{\pi}{4} d_2^2 \times f_{s_2} = W$$

$$2 \times \frac{\pi}{4} \times 1^2 \times f_{s_2} = 200$$

$$f_{s_2} = 127 \text{ kg/cm}^2$$

This is less than allowable shear stress, hence safe.

A bush 1.5 mm thick should be provided.

**Pin at C.**

Let $d_3$ = Diameter of pin at $C$

$L_3$ = Length of pin

$$L_3 \times d_3 \times f_b = R$$

$$1.25\, d_3 \times d_3 \times 160 = 250$$

$d_3 = 1.25$ cm

A bush 1.5 mm thick can be provided.

$L_3 = 1.25 \times d_3$

$= 1.25 \times 1.25 = 1.56$ cm

Boss diameter $= 2\, d_3$

$= 2 \times 1.25 = 2.5$ cm

Let $f_{s3}$ = Induced shear stress in pin

$$R = 2 \times \frac{\pi}{4} d_3^2 \times f_{s3}$$

$$250 = 2 \times \frac{\pi}{4} \times (1.25)^2 \times f_{s3}$$

$$f_{s3} = 102 \text{ kg/cm}^2.$$

Hence safe.

(*b*) **To calculate arm section.** Let us take rectangular section of arm.

$t$ = Thickness of arm

$b$ = Width of arm

$= 3t$ (assume)

$M$ = Maximum bending moment

$= P \times 16 = 150 \times 16$

$= 2400$ kg cm

$M = f \,.\, Z$

where $f$ = Allowable bending stress

= Allowable tensile stress

$= 700$ kg/cm$^2$

$Z$ = Modulus of section

$$= \frac{t \,.\, b^2}{6}$$

$$M = f \times Z$$

$$2400 = 700 \times \frac{1}{6} \,.\, t \,.\, b^2$$

$$= 700 \times \frac{1}{6} \,.\, t \,.\, (3t)^2$$

$t = 1.3$ cm

$b = 3t = 3 \times 1.3 = 3.9$ cm.

At each pin a brass bush is pressed into boss so that pin can take up wear and renewal is simple when wear occurs.

**Example 15.3.** *(a) What is hand lever ? (b) In a hand lever load of 30 kg is applied at 80 cm from centre of shaft. The allowable shear stress in shaft is 300 kg/cm$^2$ and the permissible stress in lever is limited to 700 kg/cm$^2$. The shaft overhang is 3 cm. Calculate*

*(i) Shaft diameter*

*(ii) Section of lever*

*(iii) Boss size*

*(iv) Twist of shaft per metre length.*

**Solution.** (*a*) A hand lever commonly used in various machines is shown in Fig. 15.8. The force $F$ is applied at a distance $L$ called effective length of lever. Generally height of lever ($H$) near boss is taken five times the thickness ($t$) of lever.

$$H = 5\,t$$

The height of lever is tapered from the boss to the handle. The thickness is kept constant.

The force exerted by a man may be normally taken as 30 kg.

(*b*) **To calculate shaft diameter**

$d$ = Shaft diameter

The shaft is subjected to combined bending and twisting

$T_e$ = Equivelent torque

$= \sqrt{M^2 + T^2}$

where $M$ = Bending moment

$= F \times S = 30 \times 7$

$= 210$ kg cm

$F$ = Force applied = 30 kg

$S$ = Overhang of shaft = 7 cm

$T$ = Twisting moment

$= F \times L = 30 \times 80$

$= 2400$ kg cm

$L$ = Effective length of lever = 80 cm

$T_e = \sqrt{(210)^2 + (2400)^2}$

$= 2410$ kg cm

$f_s$ = Shear stress in shaft

$$= 300 \text{ kg/cm}^2$$

$$T_e = \frac{\pi}{16} f_s \,.\, d^3$$

$$2410 = \frac{\pi}{16} \times 300 \times d^3$$

$$d = 3.45 \text{ cm}$$

$$= 3.5 \text{ cm (say)}$$

$D$ = Boss diameter

$$= 1.6\, d = 1.6 \times 3.5$$

$$= 5.6 \text{ cm}$$

$L_1$ = Length of boss

$$= 1.25\, d = 1.25 \times 3.5$$

$$= 4.37 \text{ cm.}$$

(*c*) **To find section of lever. Assuming that lever will extend to the centre of shaft.**

Let $H$ = Height of lever

$t$ = Thickness of lever near the boss

$M$ = Maximum bending moment = $F \times L$

$$= 30 \times 80 = 2400 \text{ kg cm}$$

$$M = f \times Z$$

where $f$ = Permissible bending stress in lever

$$= 700 \text{ kg/cm}^2$$

$Z$ = Modulus of section

$$= \frac{1}{6} \,.\, t \,.\, H^2$$

$$H = 5t \text{ (say)}$$

$$2400 = 700 \times \frac{1}{6} \,.\, t\, H^2$$

$$2400 = 700 \times \frac{1}{6} \times t \,.\, (5\,t)^2$$

$$t = 0.93 \text{ cm}$$

$$= 1 \text{ cm (say)}$$

$$H = 5t = 5 \times 1$$

$$= 5 \text{ cm.}$$

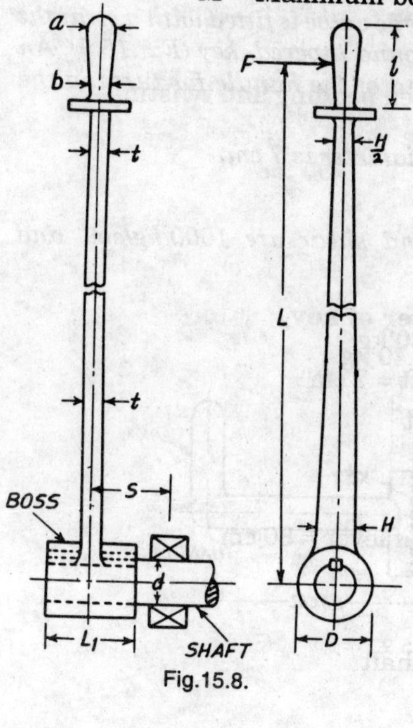


Fig.15.8.

(*d*) **Dimensions of handle are as follows**

$$l = 125 \text{ mm}$$
$$a = 32 \text{ mm}$$
$$b = 25 \text{ mm}$$

(*e*) **To calculate twist of shaft**

$\theta$ = Angle of twist

$L_2$ = Length of shaft = 100 cm

$f_s$ = Shear stress in shaft

= 300 kg/cm$^2$

$C$ = Modulus of rigidity

= $0.8 \times 10^6$ kg/cm$^2$ (say)

$r$ = Radius of shaft = 1.75 cm

$$\frac{C^{\theta}}{L_2} = \frac{f_s}{r}$$

$$\frac{0.8 \times 10^6 \times \theta}{100} = \frac{300}{1.75}$$

$$\theta = 0.0214 \text{ radians.}$$

**Example 15.4.** *A spindle of a large valve is fitted with a straight double ended handle by means of round tapered key (Fig.15.9). An effort of 40 kg is applied at each end of the handle for turning the spindle. Calculate*

*(a) Diameter of key if spindle diameter is 7 cm.*

*(b) Diameter of handle.*

*Allowable stress in tension and shear are 1000 kg/cm$^2$ and 470 kg/cm$^2$ respectively.*

**Solution.** (*a*) **To find diameter of key**

$P$ = Force applied = 40 kg

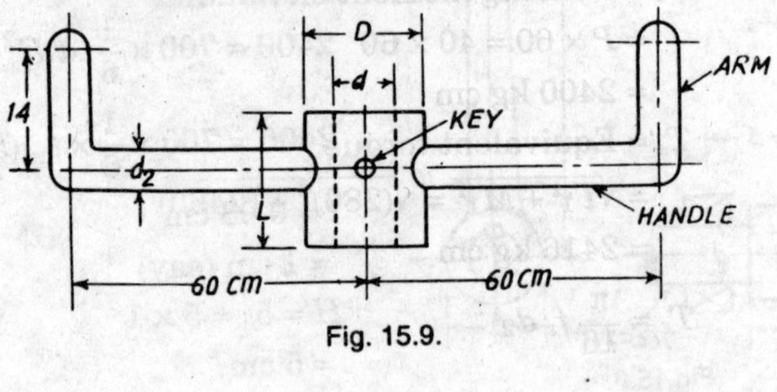


Fig. 15.9.

$d_1$ = Diameter of tapered key

$d$ = Diameter of spindle = 7 cm

$T$ = Torque to be resisted by spindle

$= 2 \times P \times 60$

$= 2 \times 40 \times 60 = 4800$ kg cm

$f_s$ = Safe shear stress in key

= 470 kg/cm$^2$

$r$ = Radius of spindle = 3.5 cm

The key is in double shear

$F$ = Shear force on key

$$= 2 \times \frac{\pi}{4} d_1^2 \times f_s$$

Torque to be resisted by tapered key $= F \times r$

$$= 2 \times \frac{\pi}{4} \times d_1^2 \times f_s \times r$$

$$\therefore \quad 4800 = 2 \times \frac{\pi}{4} \times d_1 \times f_s \times r$$

$$4800 = 2 \times \frac{\pi}{4} \times d_1^2 \times 470 \times 3.5$$

$d_1$ = 1.36 cm = 1.4 cm (say).

(*b*) **To determine diameter of handle.** Assuming that force ($P$) acts at centre of arm.

Let $d_2$ = Diameter of handle

$T_1$ = Torque on handle

$$= P \times \frac{14}{2} = P \times 7$$

$= 40 \times 7 = 280$ kg cm

$M_1$ = Bending moment on handle

$= P \times 60 = 40 \times 60$

= 2400 kg cm

$T_e$ = Equivalent torque

$$= \sqrt{T_1^2 + M_1^2} = \sqrt{(280)^2 + (2400)^2}$$

= 2416 kg cm

$$T_e = \frac{\pi}{16} f_s d_2^3$$

$$2416 = \frac{\pi}{16} \times 470 \times d_2^3$$

$$d_2 = 2.97 \text{ cm} = 3 \text{ cm (say)}$$

$$L = \text{Length of boss}$$

$$= = 2\,d_2 = 2 \times 3 = 6 \text{ cm}$$

$$D = \text{Diameter of boss}$$

$$= 2\,d = 2 \times 7 = 14 \text{ cm}$$

**Example 15.5.** *A rocker arm of forged steel for exhaust valve for a gas engine is shown in Fig.15.10. Maximum force of 240 kg acts on roller B. Angle between arms 135° and bearing pressure for the pin is 60 kg/cm². The allowable stress for rocker arm is 780 kg/cm². Determine.*

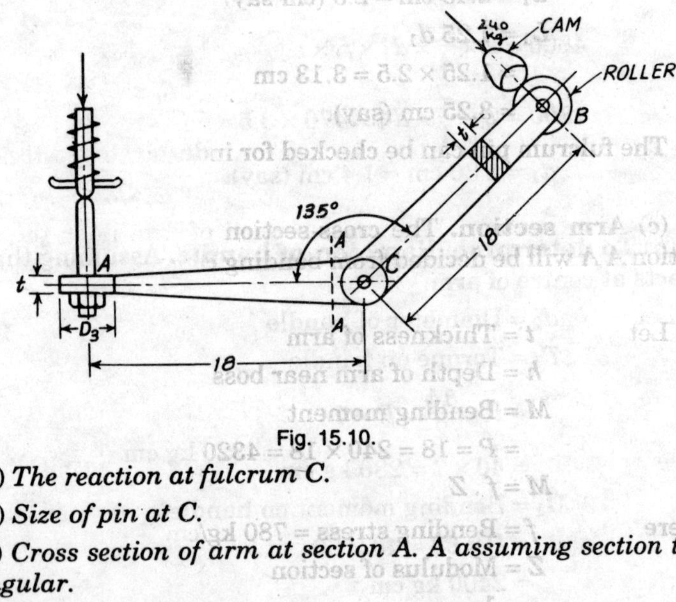


Fig. 15.10.

*(a) The reaction at fulcrum C.*

*(b) Size of pin at C.*

*(c) Cross section of arm at section A. A assuming section to be rectangular.*

*(d) Size of pin at roller*

*(e) Size to tappet screw.*

**Solution.** **(*a*) To find reaction at fulcrum.**

$P$ = Load at $B$ = 240 kg.

Let $R$ = Reaction of fulcrum

Since the arms of lever are of equal length the force at the two ends of rocker arm will be equal

$$= \sqrt{P^2 + P^2 - 2P \times P \times \cos 135}$$

$$= \sqrt{240^2 + 240^2 - 2 \times 240 \times 240 \cos 135}$$

$$= 443 \text{ kg.}$$

(*b*) **To find diameter of pin at fulcrum.**

Let $d_1$ = Diameter of pin at $C$

$L_1$ = Length of pin

$\frac{L_1}{d_1} = 1.25$ (say).

$f_b$ = Bearing stress = 60 kg/cm$^2$

Considering bearing of fulcrum pin.

$$L_1 . d_1 . f_b = R$$

$$1.25\, d_1 \times d_1 \times 60 = 443$$

$$d_1 = 2.43 \text{ cm} = 2.5 \text{ (cm say)}$$

$$L_1 = 1.25\, d_1$$

$$= 1.25 \times 2.5 = 3.13 \text{ cm}$$

$$= 3.25 \text{ cm (say).}$$

The fulcrum pin can be checked for induced shear stress ($f_{s_1}$).

(*c*) **Arm section.** The cross-section of arm near the boss at section *A A* will be decided from bending consideration.

Let $t$ = Thickness of arm

$h$ = Depth of arm near boss

$M$ = Bending moment

$= P = 18 = 240 \times 18 = 4320$ kg cm

$$M = f . Z$$

where $f$ = Bending stress = 780 kg/cm$^2$

$Z$ = Modulus of section

$$= \frac{1}{6} . t\, h^2$$

Assume $\frac{h}{t} = 5$

$$M = f . Z$$

$$4320 = 780 \times \frac{1}{6} . t . (5\,t)^2$$

$$t = 1.88 \text{ cm} = 2 \text{ cm (say)}$$

$$h = 5t = 5 \times 2 = 10 \text{ cm.}$$

(*d*) **To determine diameter of roller pin.**

Let $d_2$ = Diameter of pin

$L_2$ = Length of pin

$$\frac{L_2}{d_2} = 1.25 \text{ (say)}$$

The pin is in double shear

$$R = 2 \times \frac{\pi}{4} d_1{}^2 \times f_{s_1}$$

$$443 = 2 \times \frac{\pi}{4} \times (2.5)^2 \times f_{s_1}$$

$$f_{s_1} = 45 \text{ kg/cm}^2$$

which is quite safe.

$D_1$ = External diameter of boss

$= 2d_1 = 2 \times 2.5 = 5$ cm

A brass bush 3 mm thick will be inserted in the boss.

$d$ = Dia of bush

$= d_1 + 0.3 \times 2$

$= 2.5 + 0.6$

$= 3.1$ cm.

Fig. 15.11 shows size of pin, bush, boss etc.

$P$ = Load at roller

$= 240$ kg

$f_b$ = Bearing stress

$= 60 \text{ kg/cm}^2$.

Considering bearing of pin

$$P = L_2 . d_2 . f_b$$

$$240 = 1.25\, d_1 \times d_2 \times 60$$

$$d_2 = 1.78 \text{ cm}$$

$$= 1.8 \text{ cm (say)}$$

$$L_2 = 1.8 \times 1.25 = 2.3 \text{ cm}$$

$D_2$ = Overall diameter of eye

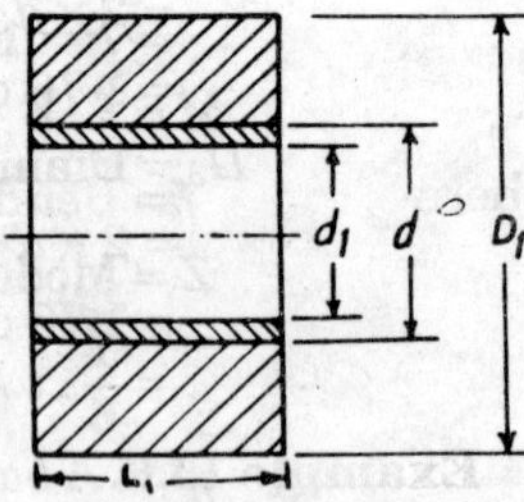

Fig.15.11.

$$= 2 \,.\, d_2 = 2 \times 1.8 = 3.6 \text{ cm}$$

The pin can be checked for induced shear stress. The pin is in double shear.

Let $f_{s_2}$ = Induced shear stress

$$240 = 2 \times \frac{\pi}{4} d_2^3 \times f_{s_2}$$

$$240 = 2 \times \frac{\pi}{4} \times (1.8)^2 \times f_s^2$$

$$f_{s_2} = 47 \text{ kg/cm}^2$$

which is quite safe.

(*e*) **Adjustable tappet screw size.** The screw has to carry a load of 240 kg in compression.

Let $d_c$ = Core diameter of screw

$d_3$ = Outside diameter of screw

$f_s$ = Compressive stress in screw

$= 550 \text{ kg/cm}^2$ for M.S. screw (say)

$$240 = \frac{\pi}{4} d_c^2 \,.\, f_c$$

$$240 = \frac{\pi}{4} d_c^2 \times 550$$

$$d_c = 0.74 \text{ cm}$$

$$d_3 = \frac{d_c}{0.84} = \frac{0.74}{0.84}$$

$$= 0.88 \text{ cm}$$

$t_1$ = Depth at screw end

$= 2 \times d_3 = 2 \times 0.88$

$= 1.76$ cm.

$D_3$ = Diameter of screw end

$= 2 \times d_3 + 2 \times 0.88$

$= 1.76$ cm.

**Example 15.6.** *A band brake shown in Fig. 15.11 (a) is required to balance a torque of 2800 kg/cm on the drum shaft. The drum diameter is 34 cm. The band is lined with asbestos having coefficient of friction 0.28. The arc of contact is 270°. The allowable stresses in* *tension, compression and shear may be taken as 800 kg/cm*$^2$ *1000 kg* cm$^2$ *and 480 kg/cm*$^2$ *respectively. Determine (a) size of pins and (b) size of lever.*

**Solution.** (*a*) **To find tensions.**

$T$ = Torque = 2800 kg cm

$\theta$ = Angle of contact

$= 270^\circ = 270 \times \dfrac{\pi}{180}$

= 4.7 radians

$\mu$ = Coefficient of friction

= 0.28

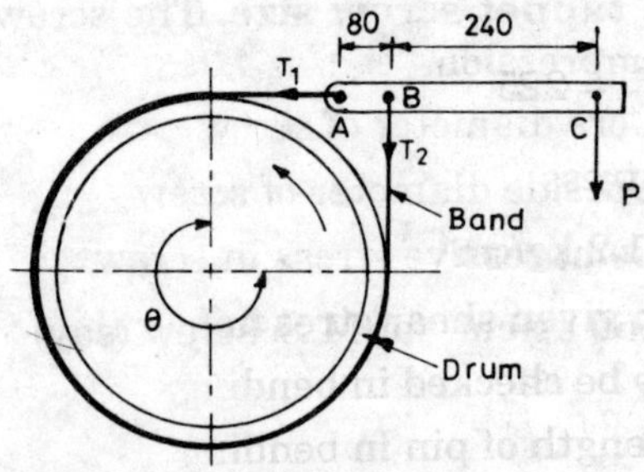


Fig. 15.11 (*a*)

$T_1$ = Tight side tension (kg)

$T_2$ = Loose side tension (kg)

$$\frac{T_1}{T_2} = e^{\mu}\,\theta = e^{0.28 \times 4.7} = 3.72 \qquad ...(1)$$

$R$ = Radius of drum

= 17 cm

$$(T_1 - T_2) \times 17 = T = 2800 \qquad ...(2)$$

Solving Eqs. (1) and (2)

$T_1$ = 225 kg

$T_2$ = 60.5 kg.

(*b*) **To find size of pins.**

Both pins at $A$ and $B$ are designed for tension $T_1$

Let $d$ = diameter of pin

$l$ = Length of pin

$= 1.25\ d$ (say)

Consider bearing of pin

$l \times d \times p = T_1$

where $p$ = Bearing pressure between pin and lever

$= 90$ kg/cm$^2$ (say)

$1.25\ d \times d \times 90 = 225$

$d = 1.42$ cm

$l = 1.25 \times 1.42 = 1.78$ cm.

The pin can be checked in double shear

$$2 \times \frac{\pi}{4} d^2 \times f_{s_1} = 225$$

$$2 \times \frac{\pi}{4} \times 1.42^2 \times f_{s_1} = 225$$

Induced shear stress

$f_{s_1} = 71.2$ kg/cm$^2$

This is less than given shear stres hence safe.

The pin can also be checked in bending

$L$ = Length of pin in bending

$= l + t_1 \times 2$

where $t_1$ = Thickness of each eye end

$= \frac{1}{2}$ (say)

$$L = l + 2t^3$$

$$= l + 2 \times \frac{l}{2} = 2l$$

$= 2 \times 1.78 = 3.56$ cm

$$M = \text{Bending moment} = \frac{T_1 \times L}{4}$$

$$= \frac{225 \times 3.56}{4}$$

$= 200$ kg cm

$f$ = Bending stress

$Z$ = Section modulus

$$= \frac{\pi}{32} d^3 = \frac{\pi}{32} \times 1.42^3$$

$$f = \frac{M}{Z} = 714 \text{ kg/cm}^2$$

This is less than allowable value, hence safe.

**(c) To find size of boss**

Boss will be made at pin joints.

Diameter of boss = $2d = 2 \times 1.42 = 2.84$ cm

Length of boss = $l = 1.78$ cm

**(d) To find section of lever.**

The lever can be considered as cantilever supported at $A$

$P$ = Effort applied at $C$

Taking moments about the fulcrum $A$

$$P \times (24 + 8) = T_2 \times 8 = 60.5 \times 8$$

$$P = 15 \text{ kg}$$

$M_1$ = Bending moment of $P$ about $A$

$$= P \times 32 = 15 \times 32$$

$$= 480 \text{ kg cm.}$$

Taking lever rectangular in section

Let, $h$ = height of lever

$t$ = Thickness of lever

$= \frac{h}{2}$ (say)

$f_b$ = Bending stress

= Tensile stress (say)

= 800 kg/cm²

$$M_1 = f_b \times Z_1$$

where $Z_1$ = section modulus

$$M_1 = f_b \times \frac{tr^2}{6}$$

$$480 = \frac{800 \times t \times (2t)^2}{6}$$

$$t = 0.96 \text{ cm}$$

$$h = 2t = 1.92 \text{ cm.}$$

## PROBLEMS

**1.** (*a*) What is a lever ? (*b*) What do you understand by mechanical advantage and leverage of a lever ? (*c*) Why are levers usually tapered ? (*d*) Why are bushes of softer material inserted in the eyes of lever ?

**2.** Sketch a right angled bell crank lever and discuss its design.

**3.** Design a right angled bell crank lever which has its both the arms at an equal angle with the horizontal plane. The longer arm is 30 cm long and carries a vertically downward effort while the shorter arm is 10 cm long and carries a vertically downward load of 1700 kg. The fulcrum and the ends work in forked ends. The safe stresses in tension, shear and crushing are 800 kg/cm$^2$, 500 kg/cm$^2$ and 1100 kg/cm$^3$ respectively. The bearing stress for the pin is 80 kg/cm$^2$.

Make a neat sketch of lever.

**4.** Design and sketch a lever for a lever loaded safety valve to satisfy the following particulars :

Blow off pressure = 14 kg/cm$^2$
Diameter of valve = 9 cm.
Leverage ratio = 8
Distance of axis of fulcrum from valve axis = 10 cm
Safe tensile stress = 600 kg/cm$^2$.
Allowable bearing pressure for pin
= 80 kg/cm$^2$.

**5.** Fig. 15.12 shows a mild steel crank lever. A force of 45 kg is applied on pin at 17 cm away from the centre line of crank web. A square hole is made in boss to connect the lever with the square end of crank shaft. Design the lever.

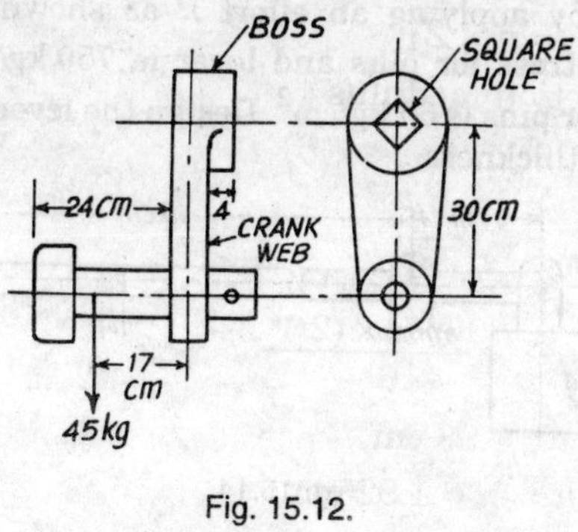


Fig. 15.12.

**6.** Sketch a hand lever and discuss its design.

**7.** Fig. 15.13 shows rocker arm for operating an inlet value of an internal combustion engine. The pivoted point $C$ is mounted on bracket. A spring is provided to overcome the forces at end $A$. The allowable stresses for forged steel rocker arm are 700 kg/cm$^2$, 500 kg/cm$^2$ and 900 kg/cm$^2$ respectively in tension, shear and crushing. The pin at $C$ is of mild steel having allowable bearing stress 50 kg/cm$^2$. Maximum load ($P$) on valve is 400 kg. Design.

(*a*) Pin at $C$.

(*b*) Rocker arm assuming it to be of rectangular section.

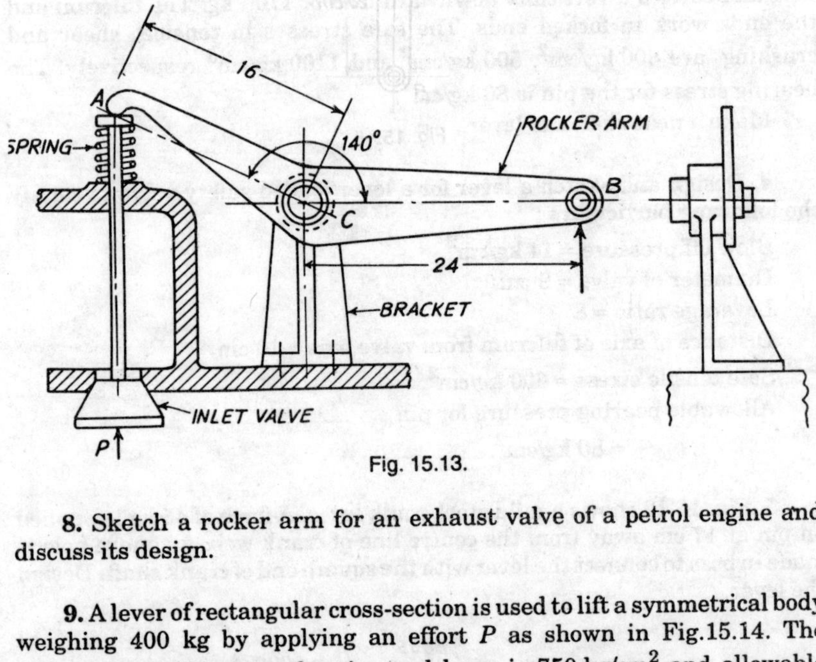


Fig. 15.13.

**8.** Sketch a rocker arm for an exhaust valve of a petrol engine and discuss its design.

**9.** A lever of rectangular cross-section is used to lift a symmetrical body weighing 400 kg by applying an effort $P$ as shown in Fig.15.14. The allowable tensile stress for pins and lever is 750 kg/cm$^2$ and allowable bearing pressure for pins is 60 kg/cm$^2$. Design the lever assuming depth of lever two times its thickness.

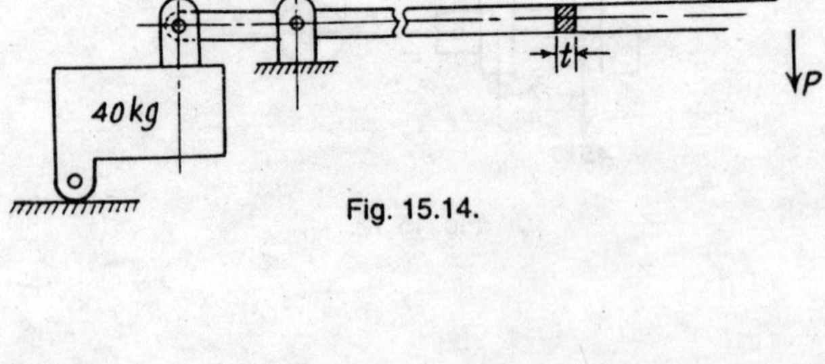


Fig. 15.14.

**15.10.** A mild steel angular lever shows in Fig.15.15 is used in a printing press. A force of 150 kg is applied at *A*. Design the lever and pins at *A*, *B* and *C*.

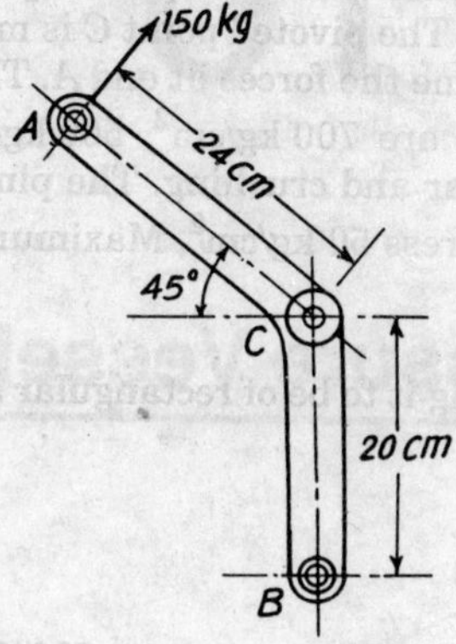


Fig. 15.15.

# 16

# Pressure Vessels

## 16.1. Pressure Vessels

Pipes and cylindrical vessels in general are used to transmit and store liquids, vapours and gases which are under a considerable pressure. The thickness of pressure vessel such as tanks, cylinders pipes etc. must be such that the stresses induced in them are within safe limits. Pressure vessels should be designed very carefully because rupture of a pressure vessel means an explosion with the accompanying possibility of loss of the life and property.

## 16.2. Thin Cylinders

A cylinder is said to be a thin cylinder if the ratio $t/d = 0.05$ or less where $t$ is the thickness of shell and $d$ is the internal diameter of shell.

Thin cylinders such as liquid storage tanks, steam boilers, air vessles, gas or water pipes are subjected to internal fluid pressures uniformly distributed over their internal surface area. Thin cylinders are frequently subjected to pressures up to 300 kg/cm$^2$.

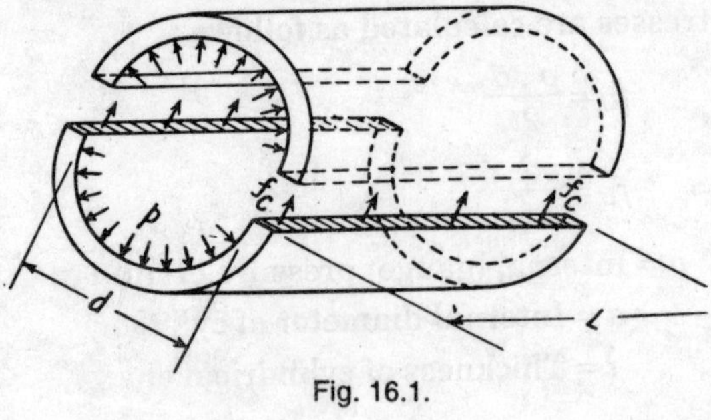


Fig. 16.1.

As the fluid pressure ($p$) acts equally in all direction of the radials vectors. Fig. 16.1 shows that there is a tendency to rupture the cylinder along the longitudinal section or the cylinder may fail across a transverse section as shown in Fig. 16.2. Due to internal fluid pressure the stresses set up in cylindrical vessels are of two types.

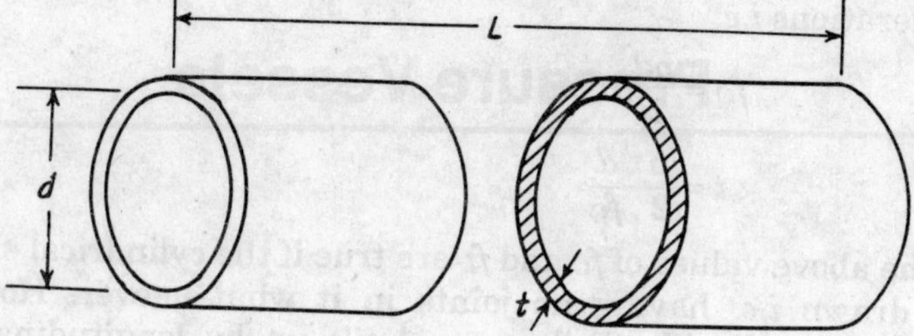


Fig. 16.2.

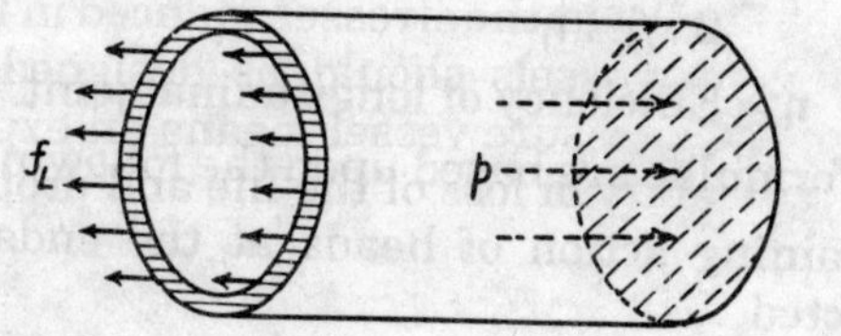


Fig. 16.3.

(*a*) Hoop stress or circumferential stress ($f_C$) acting across longitudinal section (Fig. 16.1).

(*b*) Longitudinal stress $f_L$ acting parallel to axis of cylinder. (Fig. 16.3).

These stresses are calculated as follows :

$$f_C = \frac{p \cdot d}{2t}$$

$$f_L = \frac{pd}{4t}$$

where $p$ = Internal (gauge) pressure of fluid in the cylinder

$d$ = Internal diameter of cylinder

$t$ = Thickness of cylindrical shell

$f_L$ = Longitudinal stress

$f_C$ = Hoop stress

This shows that stress ($f_L$) in cylinder wall parallel to its axis is half of hoop stress ($f_C$). For this reason longitudinal joint in the boiler shell is made stronger.

The thickness of cylinder wall is calculated using hoop stress considerations *i.e.*

$$f_C = \frac{pd}{2t}$$

$$t = \frac{p \cdot d}{2 \cdot f_C}$$

The above values of $f_C$ and $f_L$ are true if the cylindrical shell is solid drawn *i.e.* having no joints in it what-so-ever. However cylindrical shells like boilers are built up by longitudinal and circumferential riveted or welded joints. Therefore while designing the thickness of pressure vessels the efficiency of the joints should be considered. In that case

$$t = \frac{p \cdot d}{2 \cdot f_C \cdot \eta}$$

where $\eta$ = Efficiency of longitudinal joint

The above formulae are based upon the following assumptions.

(*i*) Restraining action of heads at the ends of cylinder is neglected.

(*ii*) The stress induced in cylinder wall is uniform throughout its thickness

(*iii*) Effect of curvature of cylinder wall is neglected.

**Boiler code.** According to this code the minimum plate thickness ($t$) for boilers is as follows :

$$t = 6 \text{ mm} \quad \text{if } d \leq 900 \text{ mm}$$

$$= 7.5 \text{ mm} \quad \text{if } d = 925 \text{ to } 1350 \text{ mm}$$

$$= 10 \text{ mm} \quad \text{if } d = 1275 \text{ to } 1800 \text{ mm}$$

$$= 12.5 \text{ mm if } d > 1800 \text{ mm.}$$

where $d$ = Boiler diameter

The minimum ultimate stresses for steel plates are as follows :

$$f_t = 3850 \text{ kg/cm}^2$$

$$f_s = 3080 \text{ kg/cm}^2$$

$$f_c = 6650 \text{ kg/cm}^2$$

A factor of safety of 5 is recommended.

## 16.3. Thin Spherical Shells

The diameter of thin spherical shells is calculated from the storage capacity of the shell

$V$ = Storage capacity of shell

$d$ = Internal diameter of shell

$$V = \frac{\pi}{6} \cdot d^2$$

Consider a spherical shell of diameter ($d$) and thickness ($t$) as shown in Fig. 16.4 subjected to internal gauge pressure $p$.

$F_1$ = Force tending rupture the shell along diametral plane

$$= \frac{\pi}{4} d^2 \cdot p$$

$F_2$ = Force that resists of rupture of shell

$$= \pi d \cdot t \cdot f_t$$

$$F_1 = F_2$$

$$\frac{\pi}{4} d^2 \cdot p = \pi \cdot d\, t \cdot f_t$$

$$t = \frac{pd}{4 \cdot f_t}$$

where $f_t$ = Permissible tensile stress in shell material

For boilers with dished ends (Fig. 16.5) the thickness is calculated as follows :

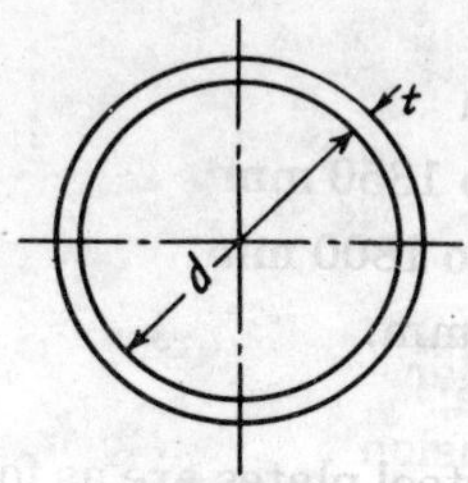


Fig. 16.4.
Spherical shell.

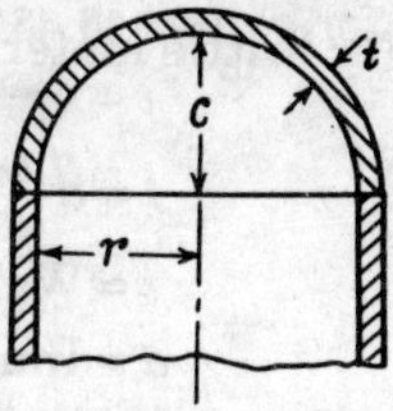


Fig. 16.5.
Dished end cylinder.

$f_t$ = Permissible tensile stress in material of dished ends

$$= p \cdot \frac{(r^2 + c^2)}{4 \cdot t \cdot c}$$

where $c$ = Camber

$r$ = Radius of cylindrical base

$t$ = Thickness of plate

$p$ = Pressure of steam.

The thickness is calculated from this relation the spherical shells are used to store fluids. Spherical shells are stronger than cylindrical shells.

The various considerations in the design of a pressure vessel are as follows :

(*i*) To select suitable material capable of withstanding effects of pressure and thermal loads.

(*ii*) To decide the stress induced in the vessel material due to pressure and temperature.

(*iii*) To take into account the effect of concentration of stresses due to geometric discontinuities.

(*iv*) To identify the most likely modes of failure.

(*v*) Spherical shells are stronger than cylindrical shells therefore semi-spherical head (dished head).

## 16.4. Thick Cylinders

A thick cylinder is subjected to a very high internal fluid pressure. The walls of cylinder are extremely thick. In thick cylinders the stress across the wall thickness can not be assumed to be uniform as in case of thin cylinders. Wall thickness of cylinder is calculated as follows :

(*i*) For brittle materials

$$t = a\left[\sqrt{\frac{f+p}{f-p}} - 1\right]$$

where $t$ = Wall thickness

$a$ = Inner radius of cylinder

$f$ = Working stress in tension

$p$ = Internal pressure in cylinder

This equation called Lame's formula is applicable to both open and closed ended cylinders.

$$f = \frac{1}{8} f_{ut.} \text{ (nearly)}$$

where $f_{ut.}$ = ultimate tensile stress

(*ii*) **For ductile materials**

(*a*) Cylinders with closed ends.

According to Clavarino's equation the thickness for closed end thick walled cylinders is given by

$$t = a\left[\sqrt{\frac{f + (1-2\sigma)\,p}{f - (1+\sigma)\,p}} - 1\right]$$

where $\sigma$ = Poisson's ratio

Thick cylinders include hydraulic press, cylinder, steel tank for shipping gas etc.

(*b*) **Cylinders with open ends.** In such cylinders the thickness is calculated using Birnie equation

$$t = a\left[\sqrt{\frac{f + (1-\sigma)\,p}{f + (1+\sigma)\,p}} - 1\right]$$

where $a = \frac{d}{2}$

where $d$ = Inner diameter of cylinder $f$ may be taken as

$$f = 0.8\, f_{yt}$$

where $f_{yt}$ = Tensile stress at yield point.

## 16.5. Pipes

The pipes are generally made of wrought iron, cast iron, steel and brass. Cast iron pipes are mainly used for water and sewage systems whereas steel and wrought iron pipes are used for conveying steam, air and oil. Stainless steel, copper, brass pipes are used for media causing considerable corrosion. Majority of pipes used for pressure purposes are lap welded. A pipe is designated by its diameter, wall thickness and material.

The diameter of pipe is calculated as follows :

$$Q = \frac{\pi}{4} d^2 \,.\, v$$

where $Q$ = Quantity of fluid to be carried by pipe by volume per unit time

$v$ = Velocity of fluid in pipe

$d$ = Internal diameter of pipe.

The thickness of pipe is calculated as follows :

$$t = \frac{p \cdot d}{2 \cdot f_t}$$

where $p$ = Pressure of fluid

$f_t$ = Permissible stress

If corrosion of pipe is taken into account

$$t = \frac{pd}{2 \cdot f_t} + c$$

where $c$ = Allowance for corrosion

= 1 mm when $t < 6$ mm

= 0.18 $t$ when $t > 6$ mm.

Weisbach has recommended the following values of C indicated in Table 16.1

**Table 16.1**

| *Pipe material* | *C* |
|---|---|
| Steel | 0.3 cm |
| C.I. | 0.9 cm |
| Zinc | 0.4 cm |
| Copper | 0.4 cm |

**Example 16.1.** *A boiler shell is subjected to a steam pressure of 16 kg/cm² and is made of 12 mm thick plate having a limiting tensile stress of 1000 kg/cm². Determine the maximum diameter of shell if the circumferential and longitudinal efficiencies are 40% and 85% respectively.*

**Solution.**

$p$ = Steam pressure

= 16 kg/cm²

$t$ = Thickness of shell plate

= 1.2 cm.

$\eta_c$ = Circumferential efficiency = 0.4

$$\eta_t = \text{Longitudinal efficiency} = 0.85$$

The diameter of shell should be so selected that neither $f_c$ nor $f_t$ exceed 1000 kg/cm$^2$.

$$f_c = \frac{pd}{2t \cdot \eta_\tau}$$

$$1000 = \frac{16 \times d}{2 \times 1.2 \times 0.85}$$

$$\therefore \quad d = 127.5 \text{ cm}$$

Again $$1000 = \frac{16 \times d}{4 \times 1.2 \times 0.4}$$

$$\therefore \quad d = 120 \text{ cm.}$$

Hence $$d = 120 \text{ cm.}$$

**Example 16.2.** *A steam boiler 120 cm in diameter generates steam at a gauge pressure of 7 kg/cm$^2$. Calculate the thickness of shell if the ultimate stress in tension is 4000 kg/cm$^2$ and factor of safety is 5. The efficiency of riveted joint used is 70%.*

**Solution.**

$d$ = Internal diameter of shell

= 120 cm

$p$ = Steam pressure

= 7 kg/cm$^2$ (gauge)

$\eta$ = Efficiency = 0.7

$f_t$ = Safe stress in tension

$$= \frac{4000}{5} = 800 \text{ kg/cm}^2$$

$t$ = Thickness of shell

The thickness of shell is calculated as follows :

$f_c$ = Circumferential stress

$$= \frac{pd}{2 \cdot t \cdot \eta}$$

$$t = p \cdot \frac{d}{2 \cdot f_c \cdot \eta}$$

$$= \frac{7 \times 120}{2 \times 800 \times 0.7}$$

$$= 0.75 \text{ cm}$$

**Example 16.3.** *An air vessel is 60 cm in diameter and is designed for a maximum working pressure of 14 kg/cm$^2$. The thickness of vessel plate is 12 mm. Determine the maximum and minimum stresses in the material of vessel when*

*(a) It is seamless.*

*(b) It is built up with circumferential and longitudinal joints of efficiency 70% and 80% respectively.*

**Solution.**

$$p = 14 \text{ kg/cm}^2$$
$$d = 60 \text{ cm}$$
$$t = 1.2 \text{ cm}$$

(*a*)
$$f_C = \text{Maximum stress}$$
$$= \frac{pd}{2t} = \frac{14 \times 60}{2 \times 1.2}$$
$$= 350 \text{ kg/cm}^2$$
$$f_L = \text{Minimum stress}$$
$$= \frac{pd}{4t} = \frac{14 \times 60}{4 \times 1.2}$$
$$= 175 \text{ kg/cm}^2$$

(*b*)
$$\eta_C = 0.7$$
$$\eta_L = 0.8$$
$$f_C = \text{Maximum stress}$$
$$= \frac{pd}{2 \,.\, t\, \eta_L}$$
$$= \frac{14 \times 60}{2 \times 1.2 \times 0.8}$$
$$= 437 \text{ kg/cm}^2$$
$$f_L = \text{Minimum stress}$$
$$= \frac{pd}{4 \,.\, t \,.\, \eta_c} = \frac{14 \times 60}{4 \times 1.2 \times 0.7}$$
$$= 250 \text{ kg/cm}^2.$$

**Example 16.4.** *A hydraulic accumulator is to store 200 litres of water at a pressure of 180 kg/cm$^2$. If length of stroke of ram is 2.8 metre, calculate the following :*

*(a) Diameter of ram*

*(b) Internal diameter of cylinder*

*(c) Thickness of cylinder wall.*

*The safe stress for the cylinder should not exceed 550 kg/cm$^2$.*

**Solution.**

$p$ = Water pressure = 180 kg/cm$^2$

$V$ = volume = 200 litres

= 200 × 0.001 cubic metre

= 0.2 cubic metre

(*a*) **To find diameter of ram**

$D$ = Diameter of ram

$L$ = Length of stroke = 2.8 m

$$V = \frac{\pi}{4} D^2 . L$$

$$0.2 = \frac{\pi}{4} \times D^2 \times 2.8$$

$D$ = 0.3 metre = 30 cm.

(*b*) $D_1$ = Internal diameter of cylinder

$= D + 2 \times c$

where $c$ = Clearance = 3 cm (say)

$D_1 = D + 2c$

$= 30 + 2 \times 3$

= 36 cm.

(*c*) **To find thickness of cylinder**

$f$ = Safe stress in cylinder

= 550 kg/cm$^2$

$a$ = Radius of cylinder

$$= \frac{D_1}{2} = \frac{36}{2} = 18 \text{ cm}$$

$t$ = Thickness of cylinder by Lame's formula is given by

$$t = a\left[\sqrt{\frac{f+p}{f-p}} - 1\right]$$

$$= 18\left[\sqrt{\frac{550+180}{550-180}} - 1\right]$$

= 7.2 cm.

**Example 16.5.** *A cast iron pipe 25 cm in diameter is to carry compressed air at 8 kg/cm$^2$ and at a velocity of air 6 metre per second. If the permissible tensile stress in pipe material is 170 kg/cm$^2$, determine*

*(a) Amount of air flowing per second*

*(b) Thickness of pipe.*

**Solution.**

(*a*) $d$ = Inside diameter of pipe

$= 25$ cm $= 0.25$ metre

$p$ = Air pressure

$= 8$ kg/cm$^2$

$v$ = Velocity of air

$= 6$ m/sec.

$Q$ = Amount of air flowing per second

$$Q = \frac{\pi}{4} . d^2 \times v$$

$$= \frac{\pi}{4} \times (0.25)^2 \times 6$$

$= 0.29$ cu. metre/sec

(*b*) $f_t$ = Permissible stress

$= 170$ kg/cm$^2$

$$f_t = \frac{p . d}{2 . t}$$

$$170 = \frac{8 \times 25}{2 \times t}$$

$t = 0.588$ cm.

**Example 16.6.** *A spherical shell of 200 cm diameter is subjected to an internal pressure of 12 kg/cm$^2$. The permissible stress in the shell material is 600 kg/cm$^2$. If the joint efficiency is 75%, calculate thickness of shell plate.*

**Solution.**

$p = 12$ kg/cm$^2$

$f_t$ = Permissible tensile stress

$= 600$ kg/cm$^2$

$d = 200$ cm

$$\eta = 0.75$$

$$f_t = \frac{p \,.\, d}{4 \,.\, t \,.\, \eta}$$

$$600 = \frac{12 \times 200}{4 \times t \times 0.75}$$

$$t = 0.75 \text{ cm.}$$

**Example 16.7.** *A thin cylindrical pressure vessel of 100 cm diameter generates steam at a pressure of 15 kg/cm². Find minimum wall thickness if*

*(a) Longitudinal stress does not exceed 250 kg/cm²*

*(b) Circumferential stress does not exceed 390 kg/cm².*

**Solution.**

(*a*) $d$ = Diameter of vessel = 100 cm

$p$ = Steam pressure

= 15 kg/cm²

$f_L$ = Longitudinal stress

$$= \frac{pd}{4 \,.\, t}$$

$$250 = \frac{15 \times 100}{4 \,.\, t}$$

$$t = 1.5 \text{ cm}$$

$f_C$ = Circumferential stress

$$= \frac{pd}{2t}$$

$$390 = \frac{15 \times 100}{2t}$$

$$t = 1.92 \text{ cm.}$$

Hence thickness of pressure vessel is 1.92 cm. This will keep both stresses within limits.

**Example 16.8.** *The maximum force exerted by a small hydraulic press is 50,000 kg. The working pressure of the fluid is 200 kg/cm². Determine the diameter of the plunger operating the table. Also suggest the suitable thickness for the cast steel cylinder in which plunger operates if the permissible stress for cast steel is 1000 kg/cm².*

**Solution.** (*a*) **To find diameter of plunger**

$P$ = Force

= 50,000 kg

$p$ = Fluid pressure = 200 kg/cm$^2$

$d$ = Diameter of plunger

$$P = \frac{\pi}{4} d^2 . p$$

$$50{,}000 = \frac{\pi}{4} \times d^2 \times 200$$

$$d = 17.84 \text{ cm}$$

(*b*) **To find thickness of cylinder**

$D_1$ = Diameter of cylinder

where $c$ = Clearance = 3 cm (say)

$$D_1 = 17.84 + 2 \times 3$$

$$= 23.84 \text{ cm}$$

$$a = \text{Radius of cylinder} = \frac{D_1}{2}$$

$$= \frac{23.84}{2} = 11.92 \text{ cm}$$

$f$ = Allowable tensile stress

= 1000 kg/cm$^2$

$t$ = Thickness of cylinder

$$= a\left[\sqrt{\frac{f+p}{f-p}} - 1\right]$$

$$= 11.92\left[\sqrt{\frac{1000+200}{1000-200}} - 1\right]$$

$$= 2.62 \text{ cm.}$$

**Example 16.8** (*a*) *A cast iron pipe is to deliver water at the rate of 2500 litres per second and at a low rate of 0.5 m/s. Determine diameter of pipe and wall thickness is the maximum pressure in the pipe is not to exceed 90 k Pa. The permissible stress in cast iron is 16.5 MN/m$^2$.*

**Solution.**

$Q$ = Discharge

$= 2500$ litres/s

$= \frac{2500}{1000}$ m$^3$/s

$= 2.5$ m$^3$/s

$d$ = Diameter of pipe

$v$ = Velocity of flow = 0.5 m/s

$A$ = Area of pipe

$Q = A \times V$

$$2.5 = \frac{\pi}{4} d^2 \times 0.5$$

$d = 2.53$ m

$f$ = Safe stress

$= 16.5$ MN/m$^2$

$= 16.5 \times 10^2$ N/m$^2$

$p$ = Pressure

$= 100$ k Pa $= 100 \times 10^3$ Pa

$= 100 \times 10^3$ N/m$^2$

$t$ = Thickness

$$t = \frac{pd}{2 . ft}$$

$$= \frac{100 + 10^3 \times 2.53}{2 \times 16.5 \times 10^6}$$

$= 0.076$ m $= 7.6$ cm.

**Example 16.9.** *A pressure vessel shown in Fig. 16.6 is used as a digester in a chemical process. It is to be designed to withstand a fluid pressure of 2 kg/cm$^2$. The vessel and its cover are made of cast iron. All other links are of steel. The cover is held tightly against the vessel by means of a screw B which is turned down through the tapped hole in the beam A so that the end of the screw presses firmly against the cover. The beam has rectangular cross section in which $h = 2b$. The rectangular section is opened up at the centre to take up the tapped hole. The beam is attached by pins C and D to links G and H which are secured by pins E and F to the extension cast on to the vessel. If vessel stress ($f_t$) for cast iron is 175 kg/cm$^2$ and $f_t$, $f_c$ and $f_s$ for steel are 500 kg/cm$^2$, 500 kg/cm$^2$ and 400 kg/cm$^2$ respectively, design vessel, cover, screw, beam, pin, link and C.I. extension.*

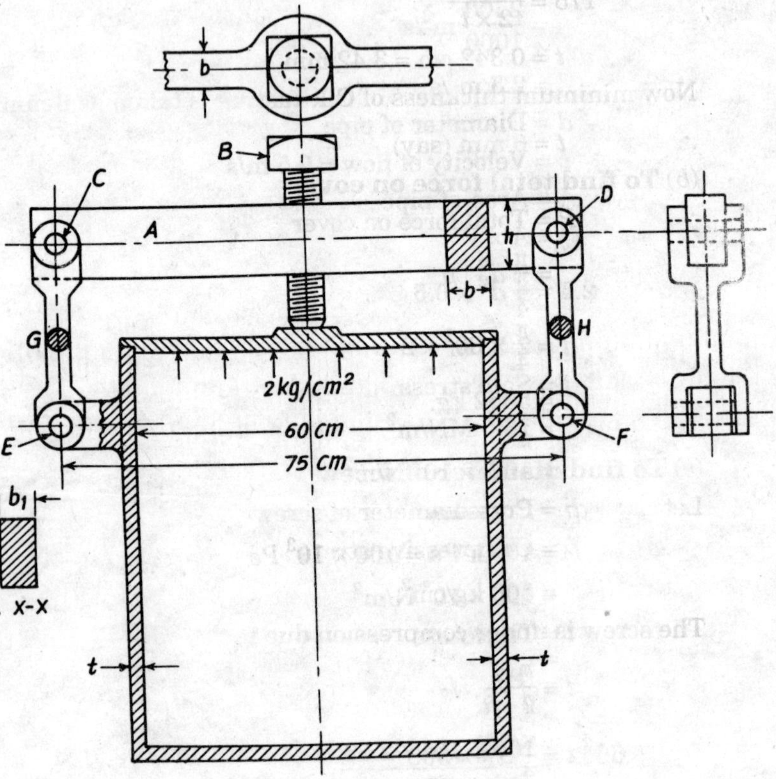


Fig. 16.6.

**Solution.**

$d$ = Diameter of pressure vessel = 60 cm

$p$ = Fluid pressure

= 2 kg/cm$^2$

**(a) To find thickness of cylinder wall**

$t$ = Thickness of cylinder wall

$f_t$ = Tensile stress for cast iron

= 175 kg/cm$^2$

$$f_t = \frac{pd}{2 \, . \, t}$$

$$175 = \frac{2 \times 60}{2 \times t}$$

$$t = 0.342 \text{ cm} = 3.42 \text{ mm}$$

Now minimum thickness of C.I. casting is taken as 6 mm

$$\therefore \quad t = 6 \text{ mm (say)}$$

**(b) To find total force on cover**

$$P = \text{Total force on cover}$$

$$= \frac{\pi}{4} d^2 . p$$

$$= \frac{\pi}{4} \times 60^2 \times 2$$

$$= 5652 \text{ kg.}$$

**(c) To find diameter of screw**

Let $d_c$ = Core diameter of screw

$f_c$ = Compressive stress

$= 500 \text{ kg/cm}^2$

The screw is under compression due to force $P$.

$$P = \frac{\pi}{4} d_c^2 . f_c$$

$$5652 = \frac{\pi}{4} d_c^2 \times 500$$

$$d_c = 3.8 \text{ cm}$$

$$d = \text{Outside diameter}$$

$$= \frac{d_c}{0.84}$$

$$= \frac{3.8}{0.84}$$

$$= 4.50 \text{ cm} = 45 \text{ mm.}$$

Hence a standard screw $M$ 45 with pitch of 4.5 mm can be used.

**(d) To determine section of beam**

The beam has rectangular section

$h$ = height

$b$ = Width

$h = 2b$.

The beam is a simple beam with a single concentrated load ($P$) at its centre.

$$M = \text{Maximum bending moment}$$

$$= \frac{PL}{4} \text{ where } L = 75 \text{ cm}$$

$$= \frac{5652 \times 75}{4}$$

$$= 105{,}975 \text{ kg cm}$$

$$M = f \,.\, Z$$

where $f$ = Bending stress

$$= f_t = 500 \text{ kg/cm}^2$$

$Z$ = Section moduleus

$$= \frac{bh^2}{6}$$

$$105{,}975 = 500 \times \frac{bh^2}{6}$$

$$= \frac{500 \times b \times (2b)^2}{6}$$

$$b = 6.82 \text{ cm} = 7 \text{ cm (say)}$$

$$h = 2b = 2 \times 7 = 14 \text{ cm.}$$

The diameter of tapped hole is 4.5 cm.

Width of section at tapped hole

$$= b + 4.5$$

$$= 7 + 4.5$$

$$= 11.5 \text{ cm.}$$

As the axis of screw is parallel to dimensions $h$ it will remain same.

(*e*) **To find diameter of pins at C and D**

Let $d_1$ = Diameter of pins

$$F = \text{Force on each pin} = \frac{P}{2}$$

$$= \frac{5652}{2} = 2826 \text{ kg}$$

$f_s$ = Shear stress

$$= 400 \text{ kg/cm}^2$$

The pin is in double shear

$$F = 2 \times \frac{\pi}{4} d_1^2 \times f_s$$

$$2826 = 2 \times \frac{\pi}{4} d_1^2 \times 400$$

$$d_1 = 2.12 \text{ cm}$$

$$= 2.2 \text{ (cm } (say))$$

Now the links $G$ and $H$ are subjected to tension. This causing shearing of pins $E$ and $F$. The pins $E$ and $F$ are subjected to same shear force as pins $C$ and $D$

$\therefore$ Diameter of pin $E$ or $F$ = Diameter of pin $C$

$= 2.2$ cm

**(f) To find diameter of link**

Links $G$ and $H$ are of circular cross-section.

Let $d_2$ = Diameter of links $G$ or $H$

$f_t$ = Tensile stress = 500 kg/cm$^2$

The links are under tension due to force $F$.

$$F = \frac{\pi}{4} d_2^2 f_t$$

$$2826 = \frac{\pi}{4} d_2^2 \times 500$$

$$d_2 = 2.6 \text{ cm.}$$

**(g) To find section of extensions**

The extensions on vessel act as cantilever and are of equal length and sustain equal end load ($F$)

$L_1$ = Length of extension

$$= \frac{75}{2} \left( \frac{60}{2} + t \right)$$

$$= 37.5 - (30 + 0.6)$$

$$= 6.9 \text{ cm.}$$

$M_1$ = Bending moment

$$M_1 = F \times L_1$$

$$= 2826 \times 6.9$$

$$= 19{,}500 \text{ kg cm}$$

$$M_1 = f \times Z_1.$$

where $f$ = Safe tensile stress for cast iron

$= 175$ kg/cm$^2$

$$Z_1 = \frac{b_1 \cdot h_1^2}{6} = \frac{(b_1\, 2b_1)^2}{6}$$

$$= \frac{4}{6} b_1^3 = \frac{2}{3} b_1^3$$

$$M_1 = f \cdot Z_1$$

$$19{,}500 = 175 \times \frac{2}{3} b_1^2$$

$$b_1 = 5.5 \text{ cm}$$

$$h_1 = 2\, b_1 = 11 \text{ cm.}$$

## 16.6. Heads or Ends for Pressure Vessels

The end closures for pressure vessels may be formed into any of the following shapes :

(*i*) Dished and flanged

(*ii*) Semi-spherical

(*iii*) Semi-ellipsoidal

(*iv*) Flat.

**16.6.1. Flat heads.** Such heads are commonly used for pistons, cylinders, boilers etc. Flat plates forming the heads may be cast integral with supporting a members or fixed to them by means of bolts, welds or rivets.

The flat plates forming heads of pressure vessels can be divided into two types :

(*i*) Simply supported at the edges or centre

(*ii*) Rigidly fixed to the supporting members.

Flat plates generally used are of two types

(*a*) Rectangular flat plate

(*b*) Circular flat plate.

### Rectangular flat plate

(*a*) **Uniform load.** With uniform load the thickness of plate is calculated as follows :

$t$ = Thickness of plate

$$= s_1 \cdot s_2 \cdot c_1 \sqrt{\frac{P}{f_t\,(s_1^2 + s_2^2)}}$$

where $s_1$ = Larger side of rectangle

$s_2$ = Smaller side of rectangle

$c_1$ = Constant

For C.I., $c_1 = 0.75$, for freely supported plate

$= 0.62$, for fixed plate

For M.S., $c_1 = 0.60$, for freely supported plate

$f_t$ = Allowable design stress

(*b*) **Rectangular flat plate with concentrated load.** The thickness of plate under such conditions is calculated as follows :

$$t = c_2 \, . \sqrt{\frac{s_1 \, . \, s_2 \, . \, p}{f_t \, . \, (s_1^2 + s_1^2)}}$$

where, for C.I., $c_2 = 4.3$ (for freely supported plate)

$= 4.0$ (for fixed plate)

For M.S. $c_2 = 3.45$ (for freely supported plate and 3 for fixed plate)

**Circular flat plates. In these plates also two types of loads may act.**

(*i*) **Plates with uniformly distributed load.** The thickness of plate is found as follows :

$$t = k_1 \, . \, d \, . \sqrt{\frac{P}{f_t}}$$

where $k_1$ = Constant

For C.I., $k_1 = 0.54$, for freely supported plate

$= 0.44$, for fixed plate

For M.S. $k_1 = 0.42$, for freely supported plate

$= 0.35$, for fixed plate

(*ii*) **Plate loaded centrally only.** In such case thickness is found as follows :

$$t = 3 \times \sqrt{\left(\frac{1 - 0.67 \, d_1}{d}\right)\frac{P}{f_t}}$$

[For freely supported plate]

$$= 1.65 \times \sqrt{\frac{P}{f_t} \log_e \left(\frac{d}{d_1}\right)}$$

[For fixes plate]

where the load $P$ is distributed uniformly on plate over an area of $\frac{\pi}{4} d_1^2$

The thickness of circular plates can be found by using following formula also.

$$t = \sqrt{\frac{3P(3+\sigma)}{8\pi . f}}$$

for plates with edges freely supported

$$= \sqrt{\frac{3P}{4\pi f}}$$

for plates with edges rigidly fixed.

where $P$ = Total load on plate

$$= P + \pi r^2$$

where $r = \frac{d}{2}$

$\sigma$ = Poisson's ratio.

**16.6.2 Dished heads.** A dished head Fig. (16.7) is quite strong and is most commonly used. The thickness is found as follows :

$t$ = thickness

$$= \frac{8.33\, p, R_1}{2f}$$

where $f$ = Ultimate stress of material

$R$ = Radius of curvature of head

$= 0.8d$ if $R < 0.8\, d$

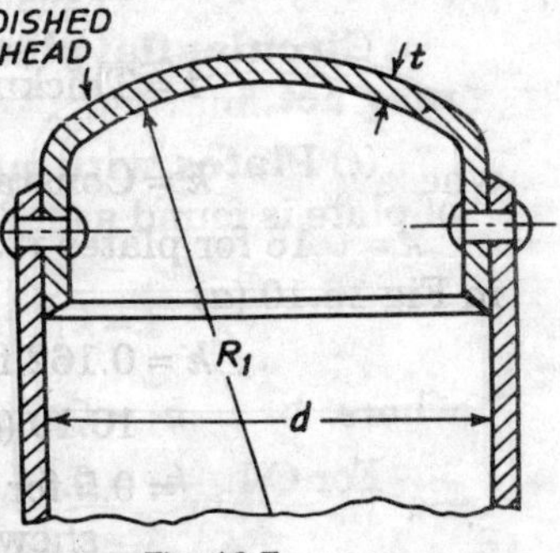


Fig. 16.7.

**16.6.3 Semi-Ellipsoidal cover**. It may be integral or welded. Fig. 16.8 shows ellipsoidal cover.

$d$ = Inside diameter

$t$ = Thickness of plate

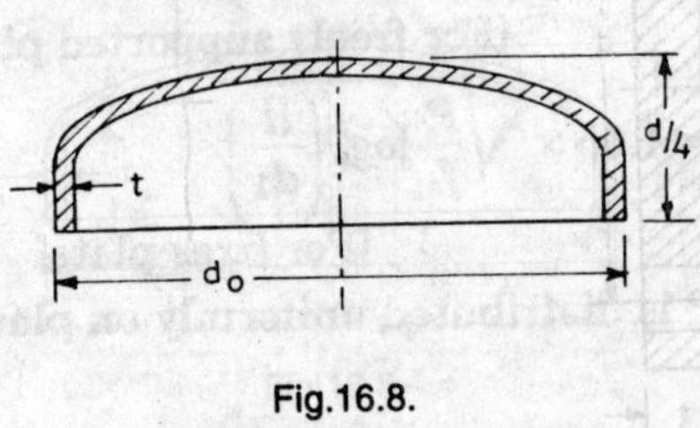


Fig.16.8.

**16.6.4 Hemi-spherical cover.** It may also be integral or welded. Fig. 16.9 shows a hemi-spherical cover.

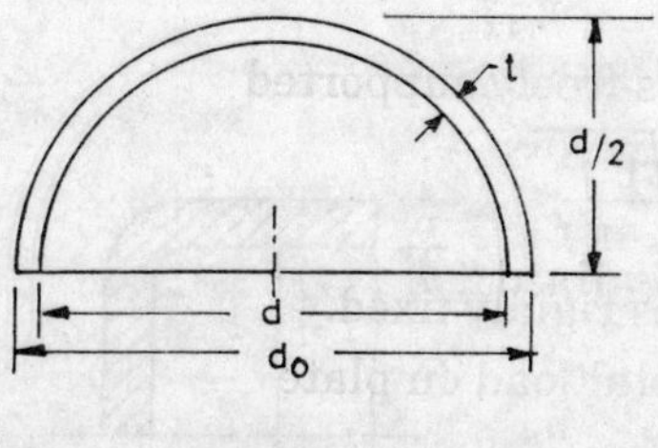


Fig. 16.9.

**16.6.5 Bolted and welded heads.** Fig. 16.10 shows some types of bolted and welded heads and covers for pressure vessels.

$$t = \text{Thickness of coverplates} = d.\sqrt{\frac{k\,.\,p}{f}}$$

where $k$ = Constant that depends on type of joint.

$k = 0.16$ for plates riveted or bolted rigidly to flanges as shown in Fig 16.10 (*a*)

$k = 0.162$ for integral flat heads as shown in Fig. 16.10 (*d*)

$= 0.5$ for plate fusion welded with fillet weld as shown in Fig. 16.10 (*c*)

$= 0.3$ for flanged heads attached to the shell by a lap joint as shown in Fig. 16.10 (*e*)

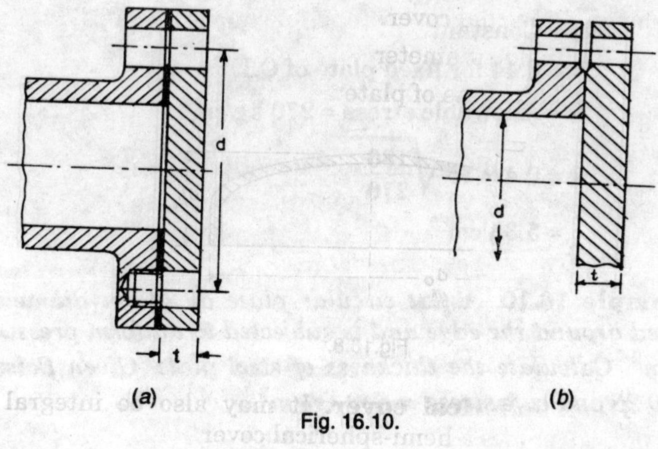


Fig. 16.10.

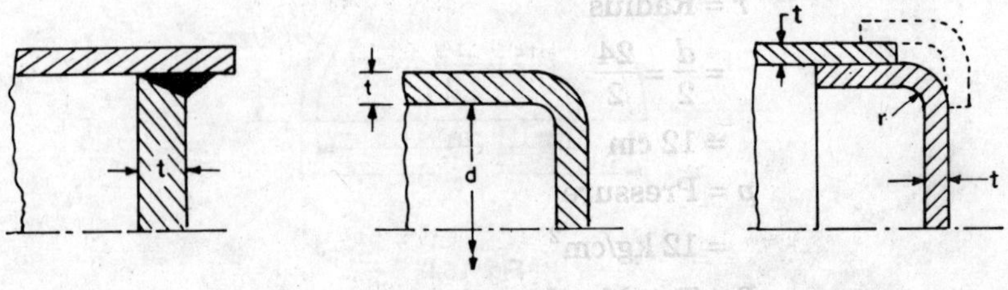

(c) (d) (e)

Fig. 16.10.

**Example 16.9**. *A cast iron cylinder is subjected to an internal fluid pressure of 180 kg/cm² and is to have a flat head cast integral with the cylinder walls. The inside diameter is 12 cm. Calculate thickness of head. The permissible working stress is 270 kg/cm².*

**Solution.**

$d$ = Inside diameter

$d$ = 12 cm

$p$ = 180 kg/cm².

A circular flat plate with uniformly distributed load will be used as head of cylinder

$t$ = Thickness of circular plate

$= k_1 . d . \sqrt{\frac{p.}{f_t.}}$

where $k_1$ = Constant

= 0.44 for fixed plate of C.I.

$f_t$ = Allowable stress = 270 kg/cm²

$t = 0.4 \times 15\sqrt{\frac{180}{270}}$

= 5.35 cm.

**Example 16.10**. *A flat circular plate of 24 cm diameter is supported around the edge and is subjected to uniform pressure of 12 kg/cm². Calculate the thickness of steel plate. Given Poisson's ratio = 0.28 and safe stress = 640 kg/cm².*

**Solution.**

$d$ = Diameter of plate

= 24 cm

$r$ = Radius

$$= \frac{d}{2} = \frac{24}{2}$$

= 12 cm

$p$ = Pressure

= 12 kg/cm$^2$

$P$ = Total load on plate $= p \times \pi r^2$

$$= 12 \times \pi \times 12^2 = 5426 \text{ kg}$$

$\sigma$ = Poisson's ratio

= 0.28

$f$ = Safe stress

= 640 kg/cm$^2$

$t$ = Thickness of plate

$$= \sqrt{\frac{3P(3+\sigma)}{8\pi f}}$$

$$= \sqrt{\frac{3 \times 5426(3+0.28)}{8\pi \times 640}} = 1.8 \text{ cm.}$$

## PROBLEMS

**1.** What do you understand by a thin shell ? How does it differ from thick shell ?

**2.** Discuss the salient features in the design of pressure vessel.

**3.** Derive a formula for the thickness of a thin spherical shell subjected to an internal fluid pressure.

**4.** A steam boiler 120 cm in diameter generates steam at a gauge pressure of 18 kg/cm$^2$. If the safe tensile stress is 800 kg/cm$^2$, calculate the thickness of shell. Efficiency of the joint is 85%.

**5.** A standard 25 cm wrought iron pipe has an outside diameter of 28 cm. What unit tensile stress is created by internal pressure of 10 kg/cm$^2$.

How many cubic metre of steam per minute can be carried by the pipe if the velocity of flow of steam is 2000 metre per minute.

**6.** Calculate the thickness of cylinder of hydraulic accumulator of the internal pressure is 60 kg/cm$^2$ and the tensile stress is limited to 300 kg/cm$^2$. The internal diameter of cylinder is 50 cm.

**7.** A hydraulic press is to exert a maximum force of 60 tonnes. The working pressure of fluid 180 kg/cm$^2$. Determine the diameter of plunger operating the table. Also determine thickness of cast steel cylinder in which plunger operates if the permissible stress for the cast steel is 900 kg/cm$^2$.

**8.** A spherical vessel is made of 1.2 cm thick plate. If it is subjected to internal pressure of 12 kg/cm$^2$ and permissible stress in the material is 500 kg/cm$^2$, determine diameter of shell. Take joint efficiency as 70%.

**9.** A pressure vessel of 60 cm internal diameter is subjected to an internal fluid pressure of 120 kg/cm$^2$. If the safe tensile stress 450 kg/cm$^2$, calculate

(*a*) Thickness of shell of vessel

(*b*) Thickness of hemispherical cover for the vessel.

**10.** Design a hydraulic press of 50 tonnes capacity water pressure is 160 kg/cm$^2$. Other particulars are as follows :

Distance between centre lines of pillars=90 cm. Distance between top plate and top of supporting platform when ram is in its downward position=100 cm.

For C.I. $f_t = 300$ kg cm$^2$

For M.S., $F_t = 600$ kg/cm$^2$.

**11.** A tank is subjected to an internal fluid pressure of 100 kg/cm$^2$ and is provided with a dished head. Calculate thickness of head of the radius of curvature is 24 cm and the ultimate stress is 2300 kg/cm$^2$.

**12.** Sketch and describe any two type of heads for a pressure vessel.

# 17

# Engine Parts

## 17.1. Pistons for Steam Engines

The various types of pistons generally used in steam engine are shown in Fig. 17.1. Box piston (Fig. 17.1 (*a*) is used for small engine whereas lightness is required such as in locomotive engine and marine engine, the plate piston and conical plate pistons are preferred. Steam engine pistons are made of cast iron. Materials like wrought iron, cast steel and bronze may also be used. The various dimensions of steam engine pistons are taken empirically as follows :

$$t = \text{Thickness of walls} = \frac{D}{40} + 1 \text{ cm}$$

$$b = \text{Width of face} = 0.5\,D\ ;\ D_1 = 1.6\,d$$

$$b_1 = \text{Width of piston ring} = 0.3\,D \text{ to } 0.06\,D$$

$$t_1 = \text{Thickness of piston rings} = 0.03\,D$$

$$\alpha = 30^\circ \text{ for conical piston}$$

where $D$ = Diameter of cylinder

$d$ = Diameter of piston rod

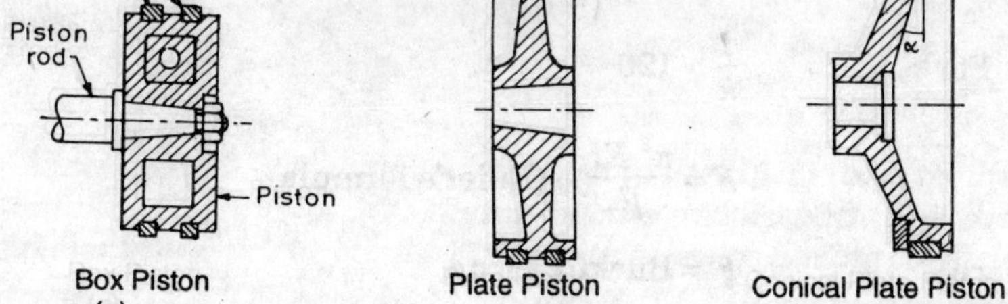


Box Piston (*a*) Plate Piston (*b*) Conical Plate Piston (*c*)

Fig. 17.1.

The piston generally has a tapered hole in which the tapered portion of piston rod accurately fits and a nut is screwed on the threaded end. In order to prevent leakage two or more rings of square or rectangular section are sprung over the piston in grooves provided for the purpose.

## 17.2. Piston Rod of Steam Engine

Piston rods are made of mild steel. Piston rod is subjected to alternate tensile and compressive forces. The diameter of piston rod is calculated as follows :

$$P = \text{Force due to steam pressure}$$

$$= \frac{\pi}{4} . D^2 . p$$

where $p$ = Steam pressure

$D$ = Diameter of cylinder of steam engine

$l$ = Length of piston rod

$d$ = Diameter of piston rod.

**Case I :** $P = \frac{\pi}{4} d^2 \times f_t$

where $f_t$ = Allowable tensile stress in piston rod material

The above formula is applied when piston rod is of short length *i.e.*, $\frac{l}{d}$ is less than 20 or slenderness ratio is upto 40.

**Case II :** The diameter of piston rod is calculated as follows if slenderness ratio is more than 40. The piston is designed as a column with both ends fixed.

For $\frac{l}{k} = 40 \text{ to } 120$

$$F = \frac{f_c . A}{l + a\left(\frac{l}{k}\right)^2} \quad \text{(Rankine–Gorden formula)}$$

For $\frac{l}{k} > 120$

$$F = \frac{\pi^2 EI}{l^2} \quad \text{(Euler's formula)}$$

where $F$ = Buckling load

$k$ = Least radius of gyration of rod section

$E$ = Young's modulus of elasticity

$f_c$ = Yield compressive stress

$= 3300 \text{ kg/cm}^2$ for M.S.

$A$ = Area of cross–section of rod

$c$ = Constant

$= \frac{1}{7500}$ for M.S.

$I$ = Moment of inertia

$= \frac{\pi}{64} d^4$ for cylindrical pistons.

**Example 17.1.** *Design the piston rod and cross-head pin of a double acting steam engine from the following date.*

*Diameter of the cylinder = 28 cm*

*Stroke = 45 cm*

*Steam pressure at the beginning of the stroke*

*= 10 kgf/sq.cm*

*Back pressure of steam = 1.25 kgf/sq. cm*

*Crank–shaft speed = 150 r.p.m.*

*Connecting rod length = 4.5 × the crank radius.*

*Materials used for piston rod, cross-head pin and bearings are forged steel, and gun metal respectively. Maximum permissible working stresses for forged steel are 890 kgf/sq. cm in tension and compression and 600 kgfsq. cm in shear. For high carbon steel it is 1100 kgf/sq. cm in tension. The constant a of the Rankine formula for steel column having pin ends is*

$$a = \frac{1}{7500}$$

**Solution.** (*a*) **To find piston rod diameter**

$p$ = Difference of pressure on the two sides of piston

$= 10 - 1.25 = 8.75 \text{ kg/cm}^2$

$D$ = Diameter of cylinder = 28 cm

$P$ = Actual load on piston

$$= \frac{\pi}{4} D^2 . p$$

$$= \frac{\pi}{4} \times 28^2 \times 8.75$$

$$= 5385 \text{ kg.}$$

Stroke length = 45 cm

Piston rod length = 45 + 20 = 65 cm

Allowing 20 cm for length of stuffing box and gland.

Using Rankine formula

$$P = \frac{f_c \, . \, A}{1 + a\left(\frac{l}{k}\right)^2}$$

where $f_c$ = Compressive stress

$= 800 \text{ kg/cm}^2$

$d$ = Diameter of piston rod

$$A = \frac{\pi}{4} d^2$$

$$a = \frac{1}{7500} \text{ for M.S.}$$

$l$ = Equivalent length of piston rod

$$= \frac{65}{2} = 3.25 \text{ cm}$$

Assuming both ends of rods as fixed.

$k$ = Radius of gyration

$$I = A\, k^2$$

$$\frac{\pi}{64} d^4 = \frac{\pi}{4} d^2 \, . \, k^2$$

$$k = \frac{d}{4}$$

$$5385 = \frac{800 \times \frac{\pi}{4} d^2}{1 + \frac{1}{7500}\left(\frac{32.4}{d} \times 4\right)^2}$$

This gives

$$d^4 - 8.6\, d^2 - 19.3 = 0$$

$$d^2 = 10.45$$

$$d = 3.25 \text{ cm}$$

(*b*) **To design cross head pin**

Let $d_1$ = Diameter of cross head pin

$l_1$ = Length of bearing

$$\frac{l_1}{d_1} = 1.25 \text{ to } 2.25$$

$p_b$ = Bearing pressure in pin

$= 70$ to $100\ \text{kg/cm}^2$.

The force on the slide and thrust in connecting rod are maximum when angle between crank connecting rod is 90°

As shown in Fig 17.2.

$$AB = \text{Crank radius}$$

$$= r = \frac{1}{2} \times \text{Stroke}$$

$$= \frac{1}{2} \times 45 = 22.5 \text{ cm}$$

$$B.C. = \text{Length of connecting rod}$$

$$= L = 4.5 \times r$$

$$= 4.5 \times 22.5 = 101.25 \text{ cm}$$

$$\cos \phi = \frac{BC}{AC} = \frac{L}{\sqrt{L^2 + r^2}}$$

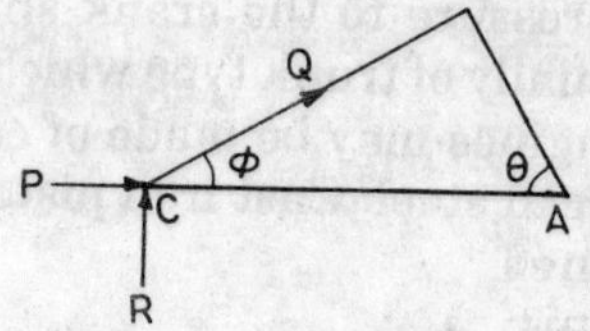

Fig. 17.2.

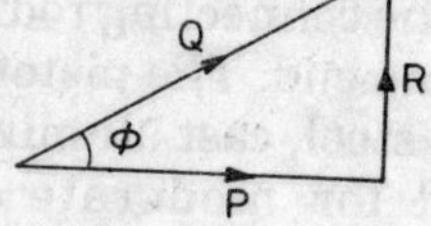

Fig. 17.3.

$$= \frac{101.25}{\sqrt{(101.25)^2 + (22.5)^2}}$$

$$= 0.976$$

$$\phi = 12^\circ\ 36'$$

As shown in Fig. 17.3,

$$Q = \text{Thrust in connecting rod}$$
$$= \frac{P}{\cos \phi} = \frac{5385}{0.976}$$
$$= 5517 \text{ kg}$$
$$R = \text{Reaction of slide}$$
$$= Q \sin \phi = 5517 \times 0.2181 = 1203 \text{ kg}$$

Considering bearing on pin

$$Q = l_1 \,.\, d_1 \,.\, p_b$$
$$= 1.5\, d_1 \times d_1 \times 80$$
$$5517 = 120\, d_1^2$$
$$d_1 = 6.78 \text{ cm}$$
$$l_1 = 1.5\, d_1 = 1.5 \times 6.78 = 10.2 \text{ cm}$$

The total length of pin is double the length of bearing.

The pin is in double shear.

Let $f_{s_1}$ = Induced shear stress in the pin

$$Q = 2 \times \frac{\pi}{4} d_1^2 \times f_{s_1}$$
$$5517 = 2 \times \frac{\pi}{4} \times (6.78)^2 \times f_{s_1}$$
$$f_{s_1} = 6.5 \text{ kg/cm}^2.$$

This is less than given shear stress hence safe.

## 17.3 Piston for I.C. Engine

A piston is used to transmit gas pressure to the crank shaft through the connecting rod. Piston is usually of trunk type which is open at one end. The pistons for I.C. engines may be made of cast iron, cast steel, cast aluminium and forged steel. Cast iron pistons are used for moderate rated engines whereas aluminium alloys give light pistons and for better heat dissipation.

Aluminium alloys pistons are used for highly rated engines. Piston should have sufficient bearing area in order to prevent undue wear and it should form an effective seal to avoid gases form leaking to oil side or oil to gas side. A piston should have minimum weight and should have good qualities of heat dissipation. Piston should

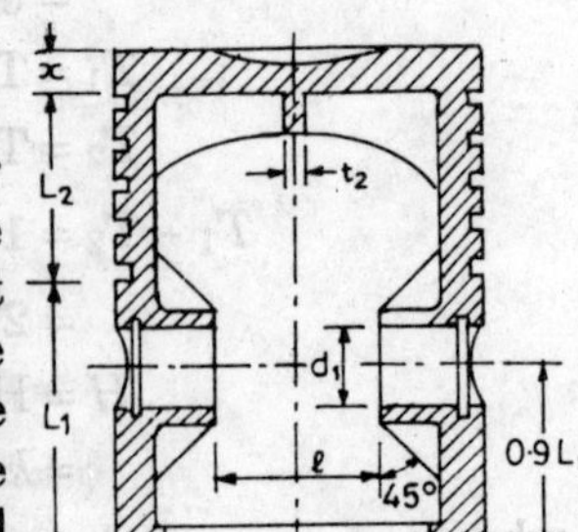


Fig. 17.4.

have rigid construction to withstand thermal and mechanical distortion.

Fig. 17.4 shows a piston for I.C. engines. The various parts are designed as follows.

*(i)* **Piston Head.** Piston head is subjected to uniformly distributed load due to maximum intensity of gas pressure. Thickness of head is calculated as follows.

*(a)* Based on strength thickness is given by

$$t = \sqrt{\frac{3 . p . D^2}{16 . f_t}}$$

where $t$ = Thickness of head in cm

$p$ = Maximum gas pressure in kg/cm$^2$

$D$ = Cylinder bore in cm

$f_t$ = Allowable stress in bending

= 350 to 370 kg/cm$^2$ for C.I.

= 600 kg/cm$^2$ for nickel, cast iron and aluminium alloy

= 850 kg/cm$^2$ for forged steel.

*(b)* Based on heat dissipation thickness is found as follows.

$$t = \frac{H}{16 . C . (T_1 - T_2) \times \frac{\pi}{4}}$$

where $C$ = Constant

= 1.5 for aluminium alloys

= 0.45 for steel

= 0.4 for grey cast iron

$T_1$ = Temperature at the centre of piston

$T_2$ = Temperature near the edge of piston

$T_1 - T_2$ = 111°C for aluminium

= 222°C for C.I.

$H$ = Heat flowing through the load

= $k . W \times C_v \times$ B.H.P. kcal/hour

where $k$ = constant based on portion of heat supplied to

the engine which is absorbed by piston = 0.05

$C_v$ = High calorific value of fuel

$W$ = Weight of fuel used in kg per B.H.P. per hour

B.H.P. = Brake horse power of engine per cylinder

Table 17.1 indicates the thickness of head in terms of cylinder bore ($D$).

**Table 17.1.**

| *Type of engine* | *Piston material* | *Thickness* | |
|---|---|---|---|
| | | *Four Stroke* | *Two Stroke* |
| Compression ignition | C.I. | 0.11 $D$ to 0.13 $D$ | 0.16 $D$ to 0.18 $D$ |
| Compression ignition | Al | 0.13 $D$ to 0.16 $D$ | 0.17 $D$ to 0.20 $D$ |
| Spark ignition gas engines | C.I. | 0.12 $D$ to 0.14 $D$ | 0.20 $D$ to 0.23 $D$ |

(*ii*) **Piston rings.** Piston rings are generally made of cast iron and alloy cast iron due to their good wearing qualities. Piston rings inserted at top function as compression rings and may be 3, 4, 5, 6, or 7 in number. These rings transfer heat from piston to cylinder linear and absorb part of piston fluctuations due to side thrust. The rings inserted below the compression rings are called oil scraper or oil control rings and are used to provide proper lubrication. The compression rings are usually made of rectangular cross section. A part of the ring is cut off in order to permit it to go into cylinder against the liner wall. Square cut rings are quite commonly used. Fig. 17.5 shows pistons ring with angle cut ring. Fig. 17.6 shows square cut ring.

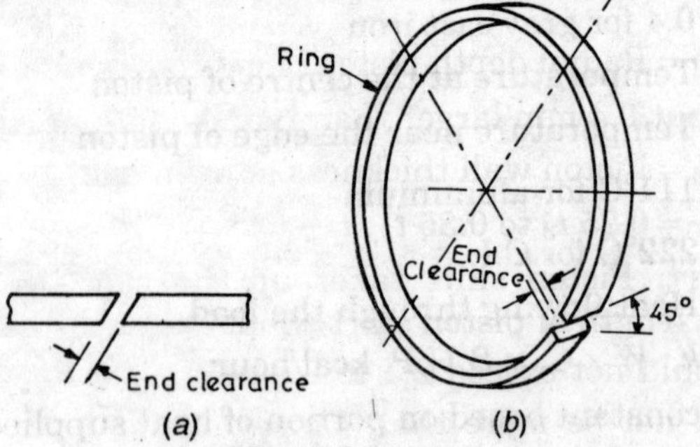


Fig. 17.5.

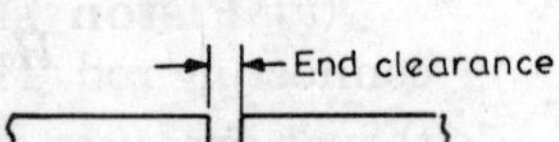


Fig. 17.6.

The clearance between th ends should be sufficient so that even at highest temperature they will not touch each other.

The radial width ($b$) of ring is selected as follows.

$$b = \sqrt{\frac{3 \cdot p_1}{f_t}} \times D$$

where

$b$ = Radial width of ring in cm

$p_1$ = Wall pressure in kg/cm$^2$

$f_t$ = Allowable stress in bending

= 850 to 1100 kg/cm$^2$ for C.I.

$t_1$ = Axial thickness of ring

= 0.7 $b$ to $b$

It is also calculated as follows.

$$t_1 \text{ (Minimum)} = \frac{D}{10\, n}$$

where $n$ = Number of rings

The land between ring grooves are made equal to or slightly less than ring axial thickness ($t_1$).

$x$ = Distance of first ring groove from top

= $t$ to 1.2 $t$

(*iii*) **Ribs.** Ribs are provided to transmit side thrust from connecting rod to the skirt through the piston pin boss. Radial may be 4 in number.

$t_2$ = Thickness of rib

$$= \frac{t}{3} \text{ to } \frac{t}{2}$$

(*iv*) **Piston barrel.** The maximum thickness of barrel ($t_3$) is calculated as follows :

$$t_3 = 0.45 + 0.03\, D + b_1 \text{ cm}$$

where $b_1$ = Radial depth piston ring grooves and is about 0.4 mm larger than radial width of ring ($b$)

$t_4$ = Piston wall thickness at open end

= 0.25 $t_3$ to 0.35 $t_3$,

(*v*) **Piston shirt.** Piston skirt takes up the side thrust of connecting rod. The length of piston skirt should be such that side thrust pressure should not exceed 2.1 to 2.8 kg/cm$^2$ for low speed engines and should not be more than 4.9 kg/cm$^2$ for high speed engines skirt is the name given to portion of piston barrel below the ring section upto open end.

$$P = \text{Maximum force due to gas}$$

$$= \frac{\pi}{4} D^2 \times p$$

where $p$ = Maximum gas pressure

$F$ = Side thrust

$= \mu \, . \, p$

where $\mu$ = Coefficient of friction between liner and skirt

Let $L_1$ = Length of skirt in cm

$p_s$ = Side pressure in kg/cm$^2$

$$F = L_1 \, . \, D \, . \, p_s$$

$L$ = Length of piston

$= L_1 + L_2 + L_3$

where $L_2$ = Length of ring section

$L_3$ = Length of top land

A longer piston runs more smoothly. Empirically length is calculated as follows

$$L = D \text{ to } 1.45\, D.$$

(*vi*) **Gudgeon pin or piston pin.** Piston pin is made of case hardened alloy steel containing nickel, chromium, molybdenum or vanadium with a safe tensile strength of about 900 to 1200 kg/cm$^2$.

$l_1$ = Length of pin

$d_1$ = Diameter of pin

$$\frac{l_1}{d_1} = 1.5 \text{ to } 2$$

$p_b$ = Bearing stress in pin

= 150 to 300 kg/cm$^2$

Considering bearing of pin

$$l_1 \times d_1 \times p_b = P$$

The pin is subjected to bending moment. The maximum bending stress is calculated as follows considering the pin to be a beam uniformly loaded for a distance of $l_1$.

$M$ = Maximum bending moment

$$= \frac{P \cdot D}{8}$$

$$M = f \cdot Z$$

where $f$ = Bearing stress

$Z$ = Section modulus

$$= \frac{\pi}{32} d_1^3$$

The pin is placed at a distance of about $\frac{L_1}{2}$ from the edge of open end of piston.

(*vii*) **Piston clearances.** The clearance to be provided between piston and liner depends upon types of engine and piston diameter. The clearance is about 0.15 mm at the bottom open end and clearance near the head is about 0.875 mm whereas clearance near bottom most oil ring groove is 0.2 mm. Clearance is the essential because of thermal expansion or distortion under load.

Fig. 17.7 shows piston and connecting rod connection.

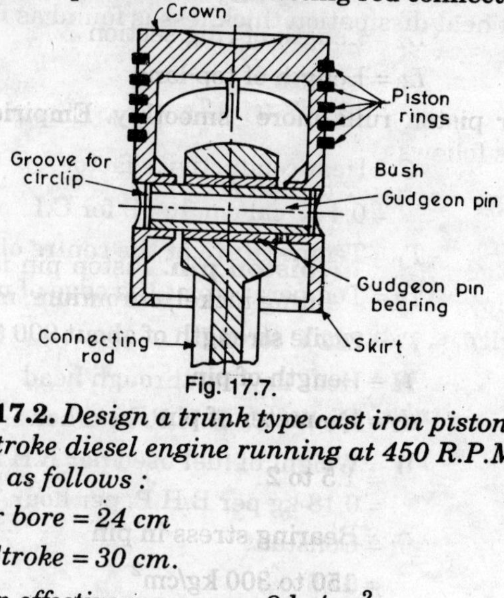

Fig. 17.7.

**Example 17.2.** *Design a trunk type cast iron piston for a single cylinder four stroke diesel engine running at 450 R.P.M. The other particulars are as follows :*

*Cylinder bore = 24 cm*

*Stroke = 30 cm.*

*Brake mean effective pressure = 8 kg/cm²*

*Maximum gas pressure = 50 kg/cm²*

*Fuel consumption = 0.18 kg per B.H.P. per hour*

*H.C.V. of fuel = 1100 kcal/kg.*

**Solution.** $D$ = Cylinder bore = 24 cm

$L$ = Stroke.length = 30 cm

$p$ = Maximum gas pressure = 50 kg/cm$^2$

$p_m$ = Brake mean effective pressure = 8 kg/cm$^2$.

$C_c$ = High calorific value (H.C.V.) of fuel

= 11000 kcal/kg

(*i*) **Position head.** Based on strength

Let $t$ = Thickness of head

$$= \sqrt{\frac{3 \cdot p \cdot D^2}{16\, f_t}}$$

$$= \sqrt{\frac{3 \times 50 \times 24^2}{16 \times 350}} = 3.93 \text{ cm} = 4 \text{ cm (say)}$$

where $f_t$ = Allowable stress in bearing

= 350 kg/cm$^2$ (say)

Based on heat dissipation thickness is found as follows :

$$t = \frac{H}{16 \cdot C \cdot (t_1 - T_2) \times \frac{\pi}{4}}$$

where $C$ = Heat conductivity factor

= 0.4 K. cal/cm. hr °C for C.I.

$T_1$ = Temperature at the centre of piston

$T_2$ = Temperature at the edge of piston

$T_1 - T_2$ = 222°C for C.I.

$H$ = Heat flowing through head

= $K \cdot W \cdot C_v$. B.H.P. kcal/hour

where, $W$ = Weight of fuel used per B.H.P. per hour

= 0.18 kg per B.H.P. per hour

$k$ = Constant

= 0.05

B.H.P. = Braking horse power of engine per cylinder

$$= \frac{p_m \cdot L \cdot A \cdot N}{4500}$$

$L$ = Stroke length.

= 0.3 metre

$$A = \frac{\pi}{4} D^2 = \frac{\pi}{4} \times 24^2 \text{ cm}^2$$

$$= 452 \text{ cm}^2$$

$$N = \frac{450}{2} \text{ for four stroke engine}$$

$$= 225 \text{ R.P.M.}$$

$$\text{B.H.P.} = \frac{8 \times 0.3 \times 452 \times 225}{4500}$$

$$= 54$$

$$H = 0.05 \times 0.18 \times 11,000 \times 54$$

$$= 5346 \text{ kcal/hour}$$

$$t = \frac{H}{16c \,.\, (T_1 - T_2) \times \frac{\pi}{4}}$$

$$= \frac{5346}{16 \times 0.4 \times 222 \times \frac{\pi}{4}}$$

$$= 4.8 \text{ cm} = 5 \text{ cm (say)}$$

Hence $t$ = Thickness = 5 cm.

*(ii)* **Piston rings.** Let the pistons have 3 sealing rings and 2 oil rings.

$b$ = Radial width of ring

$$= \sqrt{\frac{3 \,.\, p_1}{f_t}} \times D$$

where $p_1$ = Wall pressure

= 0.24 to 0.42

= 0.3 kg/cm$^2$ (say)

$f_t$ = Allowable stress in bending

= 850 kg/cm$^2$ for C.I. (say)

$$b = 24\sqrt{\frac{3 \times 0.3}{850}}$$

$$= 0.77 \text{ cm} = 0.8 \text{ cm (say)}$$

$t_1$ = Axial thickness of ring

$$= 0.7\, b = 0.7 \times 0.8$$

$$= 0.56 \text{ cm} = 0.6 \text{ cm (say)}$$

$\therefore$ Section of ring is 8 mm × 6 mm.

Empirically the maximum axial width is given by

$$t = \frac{D}{10n}$$

where $n$ = Number of rings = 5

$$= \frac{24}{10 \times 5} = 0.48 \text{ cm}$$

Hence O.K.

$x$ = Distance of first ring groove from top

$= t$ to $1.2\,t = t$ (say)

$= 5$ cm

Width of other ring lands

$= 0.75\,t_1$ to $t_1 = t_1 = 0.6$ cm

(*iii*) **Ribs.** Four radial ribs may be provided.

$t_2$ = Thickness of rib

$$= \frac{t}{2} = \frac{5}{2} = 2.5 \text{ cm.}$$

(*iv*) **Piston barrel.** The thickness of barrel is found as follows:

$t_3$ = Thickness

$= 0.45 + 0.03\,D + b_1$

where $b_1$ = Radial depth of piston wrong grooves

$= b + 0.4$ mm

$= 0.8 + 0.04$ cm $= 0.84$ cm

$t_3 = 0.45 + 0.03 \times 24 + 0.84 = 2$ cm

$t_4$ = Piston wall thickness at open end

$= 0.25\,t_3 = 0.25 \times 2$

$= 0.5$ cm.

(*v*) **Piston skirt.** The length of piston skirt is found as follows:

$F$ = Side thrust

$$= \mu \,.\, P = \mu \times \frac{\pi}{4} D^2 \times p$$

$$= 0.1 \times \frac{\pi}{4} \times 24^2 \times 50$$

$= 2260$ kg

Assuming,

$\mu$ = Coefficient of friction = 0.1

$L_1$ = Length of skirt

Projected area = $L_1 \times D$

$p_s$ = Side pressure = 2.5 kg/cm$^2$ (say)

$F = L_1 . D . p_s$

$2260 = L_1 \times 24 \times 2.5$

$L_1$ = 37.66 = 38 cm (say)

$L$ = Piston length = $L_1 + L_2 + L_3$

where $L_2$ = Length of ring section

$= 2 \times 5 . t_1 = 10 \times 0.6 = 6$ cm

$L_3$ = Length of top land

$= x = 5$ cm

$L = 38 + 6 + 5 = 49$ cm.

(*vi*) **Gudgeon pin**

Let $d_1$ = Diameter of pin

$l_1$ = Length of pin

$$\frac{l_1}{d_1} = 1.5 \text{ (say)}$$

$p_b$ = Bearing pressure on pin

= 200 kg/cm$^2$ (say)

$P$ = Maximum force due to gas pressure

$$P = \frac{\pi}{4} D^2 . p$$

$$= \frac{\pi}{4} \times (24)^2 \times 50 = 22{,}600 \text{ kg}$$

Considering bearing of pin

$226 = l_1 . d_1 . p_b$

$22{,}600 = 1.5\, d_1 \times d_1 \times 200 = 300\, d_1^2$

$d_1 = 0.868 = 8.7$ cm

$l_1 = 1.5 \times 8.7 = 13$ cm

The pin is also subjected to bending

$M$ = Maximum bending moment

$$= \frac{\text{P . D}}{8} = \frac{22{,}600 \times 24}{8} = 67{,}800 \text{ kg cm.}$$

$$f = \text{Bending stress in pin}$$
$$= 1050 \text{ kg/cm}^2 \text{ (Say)}$$
$$M = f \times Z$$
$$Z = \frac{M}{f}$$
$$= \frac{67{,}800}{1050} = 64.5$$

Now $$64.5 = \frac{\pi}{32} d_1^3$$

$\therefore$ $$d_1 = 8.67 \text{ cm}$$

which is less than 8.7 cm.

Hence $$d_1 = 8.7 \text{ cm is O.K.}$$

The pin is placed at a distance of about $\frac{L_1}{2}$ from the edge of open end of piston.

(*vii*) **Piston clearances.** Proper clearance should be provided between piston and liner. Too little a clearance will cause seizing of the piston. Clearance near head is about 0.85 mm, near bottom most oil ring groove is about 0.2 mm whereas the clearance at the bottom open end is about 0.15 mm.

## 17.4. Connecting Rod

It transmits force of gases from the piston to the crank shaft. Fig. 17.8 shows a connecting rod commonly used in internal combustion engine. The connecting rod has an eye at small end for the piston pin bearing and a big end opening which is usually split to take the crank pin bearing. Arrangements are provided for lubrication of both big and small ends. Bolts or studs are used at big end to fasten the cap. The bushes are made of phosphor bronze. The materials commonly used for making connecting rod range from mild steel to alloy steels. Connecting rods are made of mild steel for low speed engines, of chrome nickel alloy steel for high speed powerful engines and of aluminium alloys for high speed light weight engines. Connecting rods are mostly manufactured by drop forging. The connecting rod may be of circular section, rectangular section or I-section. Fig. 17.9 shows typical connecting rod sections. Connecting rods of circular and rectangular sections are generally used in low speed engines whereas in high speed engines connecting rod I-section is preferred because of lightness required.

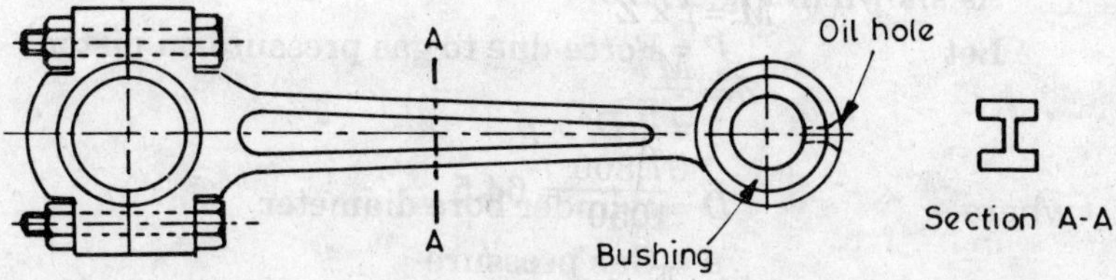


Connecting Rod
Fig. 17.8.

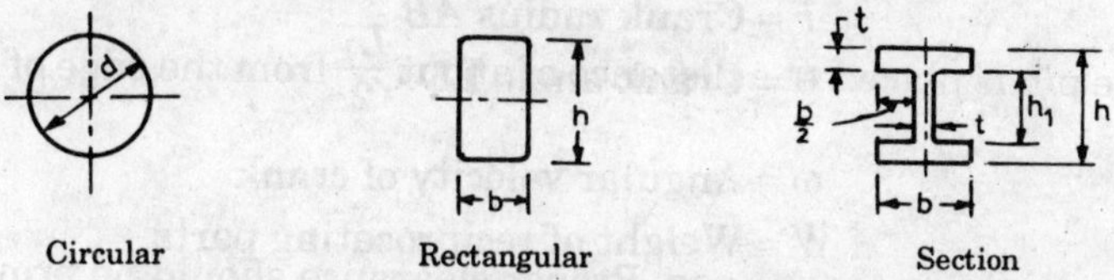


Fig. 17.9.

### 17.4.1 Stresses in the Connecting Rod

The connecting rod is usually of I-section for high speed engines as I-section fulfills the most desirable conditions such as adequate strength and stiffness with minimum weight. A connecting rod is subjected to alternating tension and compression, the compressive stress being much greater than tensile stress and is therefore designed mainly as a strut. Connecting rod has a lateral oscillation in addition to its longitudinal motion. The various forces acting on a connecting rod are as follows :

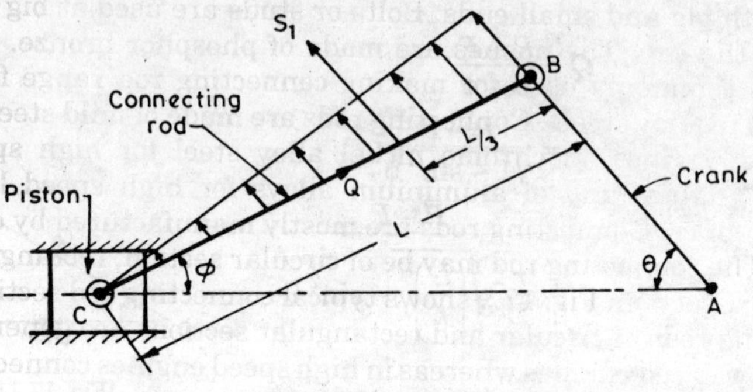


Fig. 17.10.

(*i*) Direct load on piston due to gas pressure and inertia of reciprocating parts.

As shown in Fig. 17.10.

Let $P$ = Force due to gas pressure on piston

$$= \frac{\pi}{4} D^2 \times p$$

where $D$ = cylinder bore diameter

$p$ = Gas pressure

$F$ = Force due to inertia of reciprocating parts

$$= \frac{W}{g} r\omega^2 \left(\cos\theta + \frac{r}{L}\cos 2\theta\right)$$

where $L$ = Connecting rod length

$r$ = Crank radius $AB$

$\theta$ = Crank angle I.D.C.

$\omega$ = Angular velocity of crank

$W$ = Weight of reciprocating parts

$= W_1 + W_2 + W_3$

where $W_1$ = weight of piston and rings

$W_2$ = Weight of piston pin

$W_3$ = Weight of one third portion of connecting rod (small end portion which can be assumed to reciprocate).

The thrust ($Q$) along the connecting rod at any instant will be gas load minus the inertia force. The actual thrust $Q$ in the connecting rod will be more than the net load ($P - F$) due to angularity of the rod.

As shown in Fig. 17.11 the load $Q$ will be maximum when $\theta = 90^\circ$.

$$Q = \frac{P-F}{\cos\phi}$$

$$= \frac{P-F}{\sqrt{1-\sin^2\phi}}$$

$$= \frac{P-F}{\frac{r}{L}\sqrt{\left(\frac{L}{r}\right)^2 - \sin^2\theta}}$$

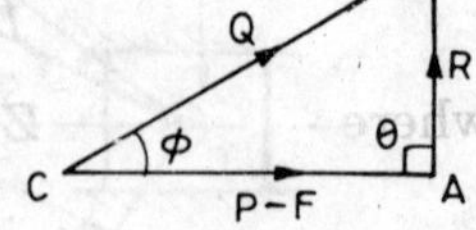


Fig. 17.11.

as $\sin\theta = \frac{L}{r} \sin\phi$

$R$ = Vertical reaction.

(*ii*) **Force due to inertia of connecting rod.** The inertia of connecting rod produces two types of forces namely longitudinal force along the rod and a force normal to connecting rod called normal force. The longitudinal force has already been considered by taking into account one third portion of connecting rod on small end side as reciprocating. The remaining two third can be assumed as rotating with crank which produces a normal force and due to normal load a centrifugal force will act on connecting rod which tries to bend the connecting rod.

$S$ = Maximum centrifugal force

$$= \frac{\sigma \cdot A \cdot \omega^2 r}{g}$$

where $\sigma$ = Density of connecting rod material

$A$ = Area of cross section of connecting rod

$r$ = Crank radius

$\omega$ = Angular speed

$S_1$ = The resultant normal force on connecting rod

$$= \frac{1}{2} \cdot S \cdot L$$

$$= \frac{\sigma A \omega^2 r}{g} \times \frac{L}{2}$$

This force will act at a distance ⅔ $L$ from the piston pin.

It is observed that maximum bending moment occurs at a distance $\frac{L}{\sqrt{3}}$ from the piston pin and is calculated as follows :

$M$ = Maximum bending moment

$= 0.128\, S_1 \times L$

$f$ = Maximum bending stress $= \frac{M}{Z}$

where $Z$ = Section modulus of connecting rod.

The bending force is zero at piston pin and minimum at crank pin as shown in Fig.17.11. The bending stress is maximum when crank and connecting rod are at right angle to each other.

(*iii*) **Force due to friction of piston and piston rings.** This force is quite small and can be neglected. It is calculated by using the following formula :

$$S_2 = \text{Force of friction}$$
$$= n \,.\, \mu \,.\, b\, \pi D \,.\, p_1$$

where $n$ = Number of rings

$\mu$ = Coefficient of friction = 0.1 (about)

$b$ = Axial width of rings

$D$ = Cylinder bore

$p_1$ = Pressure of rings

= 0.24 to 0.4 kg/cm$^2$.

(*iv*) **Friction at piston pin bearing and crank pin bearing.** The friction at the two end bearing tries to bend the connecting rod and tries to increase the compressive stress on the connecting rod due to direct load.

**Design procedure.** The various steps used in design of connecting rod are as follows :

(*i*) To find section of connecting rod, use Rankine-Gorden formula as indicated below :

$$\text{Buckling load} = \frac{f_c \,.\, A}{1 + a\left(\dfrac{L}{k}\right)^2}$$

where $f_c$ = Ultimate crushing stress (kg/cm$^2$)

$a$ = Constant

$A$ = Section area in cm$^2$

$L$ = Equivalent length of connecting rod in cm

$k$ = Radius of gyration about the axis of buckling in cm.

$a$ = constant

$$= \frac{1}{1600} \text{ for C.I.} = \frac{1}{7500} \text{ for M.S.}$$

Buckling load = Factor of safety × Maximum gas load

Factor of safety = 6 to 15 for heavy shock

= 4 to 7 for light shock

= 3 to 5 for steady load.

The allowable stresses for the material used for connecting rods are as follows :

$$\text{Alloy steel} = 1200 \text{ to } 1800 \text{ kg/cm}^2$$

$$\text{Carbon steel} = 800 \text{ to } 1200 \text{ kg/cm}^3$$

(*ii*) Use $\frac{L}{r} = 4$ to 5.

(*iii*) Crank pin and small end pin are designed in bearing.

$$e = 1.25 \text{ to } 1.5 \text{ for big end pin}$$

$$= 1.5 \text{ to } 2 \text{ for small end pin}$$

where $$e = \frac{\text{Length of pin}}{\text{Diameter of pin}}$$

Allowable bearing pressure

$$= 50 \text{ to } 105 \text{ kg/cm}^2 \text{ for crank pin}$$

$$= 105 \text{ to } 150 \text{ kg/cm}^2 \text{ for gudgeon pin end}$$

Higher value of stress may be used depending upon the quality of the bearing material.

(*iv*) Bolts for big end cap are made of M.S. with a safe stress of about 1000 kg/cm$^2$.

(*v*) Design cap for big end based upon the maximum bending moment due to inertia force.

**Example.17.3.** *Design a connecting rod for a petrol engine from the following data :*

*Diameter of piston = 110 mm*

*Weight of reciprocating parts = 2 kg*

*Length of connecting rod from centre to centre*

*= 325 mm*

*Stroke = 150 mm*

*R.P.M. = 1500 with possible over speed of 2500*

*Compression ratio = 4 : 1*

*Maximum explosion pressure*

*= 25 kg/cm$^2$.*

**Solution.** (*a*) **To determine section of rod**

The connecting rod used in I.C. engines is mostly of I-section with the proportions shown in Fig. 17.12.

$$D = \text{Piston diameter} = 11 \text{ cm}$$

$p$ = Gas pressure = 25 kg/cm$^2$

$P$ = Gas pressure on piston

$$= \frac{\pi}{4} D^2 . p$$

$$= \frac{\pi}{4} \times 1^2 \times 25$$

$$= 2375 \text{ kg}$$

$H$ = Depth = $5t$

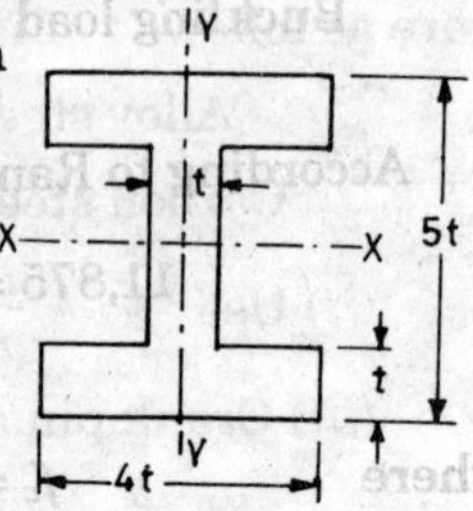


Fig. 17.12.

$B$ = Width = $4t$ ($t$ = thickness)

$A$ = Cross–sectional area of rod

$$= 2(4t \times t) + 3t \times t = 11t^2$$

$I_{xx}$ = Moment of inertia about $X$–$X$ axis

$$= \frac{BH^3}{12} - \frac{bh^3}{13}$$

where $b = B - t = 3t$

$h = H - 2t = 5t - 2t = 3t$

$$= \frac{4t \times (5t)^3}{12} - \frac{3t \times (3t)^3}{12} = \frac{419}{12} t^4$$

$I_{yy}$ = Moment of inertia of $Y$–$Y$ axis

$$= \frac{tB^3}{12} \times 2 + \frac{ht^3}{12}$$

$$= \frac{t \times (4t)^3}{12} \times 2 + \frac{3t \times t^2}{12} = \frac{131}{12} t^4$$

$k$ = Radius of gyration

$$4k_x^2 = I_{xx}$$

$$k_x^2 = \frac{I_{xx}}{A} = \frac{419}{12} t^4 \times \frac{1}{11t^2} = 3.18\, t^2$$

$$k_y^2 = \frac{I_{yy}}{A} = \frac{131\, t^4}{12} \times \frac{1}{11\, t^2} = 0.995\, t$$

$$\frac{k_x^2}{k_y^2} = \frac{3.18}{0.995} = 3.2.$$

This shows that $k_x^2$ is nearly four times $k_y^2$. Therefore, proportions shown in Fig. 17.12 are satisfactory.

Buckling load = $P$ × Factor of safety

Factor of safety = 5 (say)

Buckling load $= P \times 5$

$= 2375 \times 5 = 11875$ kg.

According to Rankine-Gordon formula

$$11{,}875 = \frac{f_c \cdot A}{1 + 1\left(\frac{L}{K}\right)^2}$$

where $f_c$ = Ultimate crushing stress

$= 3300$ kg/cm² for M.S.

$A = 11\, t^2$

$a = \text{Constant} = \frac{1}{7500}$ for M.S.

$L$ = Length of connecting rod

$= 32.5$ cm for hinged ends

$k^2 = 3.18\, t^2$

$$11{,}875 = \frac{33{,}000 \times 11\, t^2}{1 + \frac{1}{7500}\left[\frac{(32.5)^2}{3.18\, t^2}\right]}$$

$69\, t^4 - 22.57\, t^2 - 1 = 0$

$t^2 = 0.366$

$t = 0.6$ cm

$\therefore$ $H = 5t = 5 \times 0.6 = 3$ cm

$B = 4t = 4 \times 0.6 = 2.4$ cm.

**(*b*) To design pin for small end**

Let $d_1$ = Diameter of small end pin *i.e.*, piston pin or guedon pin

$L_1$ = Length of pin

$\frac{L_1}{d_1} = 1.5$ to $2$

$= 1.5$ (say)

$p_b$ = Bearing pressure = 150 kg/cm² (say)

Considering bearing of pin

$L_1 \cdot d_1 \cdot p_b = P$

$1.5\, d_1 \times d_1 \times 150 = 2375$

$$d_1 = 3.25 \text{ cm}$$
$$L_1 = 1.5\, d_1 = 1.5 \times 3.25$$
$$= 4.87 \text{ cm.}$$

A bronze bush about 3 mm thick is provided as piston pin bearing.

**(c) To design pin for big end**

Let $L_2$ = Length of pin

$d_2$ = Diameter of pin at big end

$$\frac{L_2}{d_2} = 1.3 \text{ (say)}$$

$p_b$ = Bearing pressure

$= 90 \text{ kg/cm}^2$ (say)

Considering bearing of pin

$$L_2 \,.\, d_2\, p_b = 2375$$
$$1.3\, d_2 \times d_2 \times 90 = 2375$$
$$d_2 = 4.5 \text{ cm}$$
$$L_2 = 1.3 \times 4.5 = 5.85 \text{ cm.}$$

**(d) To find diameter of bolts for big end cap**

Let $d_c$ = Core diameter of bolts

$n$ = Number of bolts = 2

$W$ = Weight of reciprocating parts = 2 kg

$F$ = Inertia force

$$= \frac{W}{g} r\omega^2 \left(\cos\theta + \frac{r}{L}\cos^2\theta\right)$$

$$= \frac{W}{g} r\omega^2 \left(1 + \frac{r}{L}\right)$$

Now, $\theta$ = Crank angle = $0^\circ$

As inertia force is maximum when crank angle ($\theta$) is zero degree.

$N$ = Maximum R.P.M. = 2500

$\omega$ = Angular speed

$$= \frac{2\pi N}{60} = \frac{2\pi \times 2500}{60}$$

$= 261.66$ radians/sec.

$$r = \text{Crank radians} = \frac{\text{Stroke}}{2} = \frac{15}{2} = 7.5 \text{ cm}$$

$$F = \frac{W}{g} r\omega^2 \left(1 + \frac{r}{L}\right)$$

$$= \frac{2}{9.81} \times \frac{7.5}{100} \times (261.66)^2 \left(1 + \frac{7.5}{32.5}\right)$$

$$= 1288 \text{ kg.}$$

The bolts are under tension

$$f = \text{Safe shear in bolts}$$

$$= 1000 \text{ kg/cm}^2 \text{ (say)}$$

$$F = 2 \times \frac{\pi}{4} d_c^2 \times f$$

$$1288 = 2 \times \frac{\pi}{4} \times d_c^2 \times 1000$$

$$d_c = 0.9 \text{ cm}$$

$$d = \text{Outer diameter}$$

$$= \frac{0.9}{0.84} = 1.1 \text{ cm.}$$

(*e*) **To find thickness of big end cap**

The cap is treated as beam freely supported at bolt centres and loaded in between uniformly distributed load and centrally concentrated load. In such case the maximum bending moment is calculated as follows :

$$M = \text{Maximum bending moment}$$

$$= \frac{F \times c}{6}$$

where $c$ = Distance between bolt centres

$$= d_2 + 2_{c_1} + d + c_2$$

where $d_2$ = Diameter of bolt at big end

$$= 4.5 \text{ cm}$$

$c_1$ = Thickness of bearing liner

= Thickness of shell + Thickness of bearing metal

$\doteq 0.4 \times$ Cylinder bore + 1 mm

$= 0.04 \times 110 + 1$

$= 5.4$ mm $= 0.54$ cm.

$$d = \text{Diameter of bolt}$$
$$= 1.1 \text{ cm}$$
$$c_2 = \text{Clearance} = 1.5 \text{ mm (say)}$$
$$c = d_2 + 2_{c_1} + d + c_2$$
$$= 4.5 + 2 \times 0.54 + 1.1 + 0.15$$
$$= 6.83 \text{ cm.}$$
$$M = \frac{F \cdot c}{6} = \frac{1288 \times 6.83}{6}$$
$$= 1466 \text{ kg cm.}$$
$$M = f_b \times Z$$

where $f_b$ = Bending stress

$$= 1100 \text{ kg/cm}^2 \text{ (say)}$$
$$Z = \text{Section modulus}$$
$$= \frac{b \cdot t^2}{6}$$

where $b$ = Width of cap

$$= \text{Length of bearing}$$
$$\doteq L_2 = 5.85 \text{ cm}$$
$$t = \text{Thickness of cap}$$
$$M = f_b \cdot Z$$
$$1466 = 1100 \times \frac{5.85 \times t^2}{6}$$
$$t = 1.17 \text{ cm.}$$

**Example 17.4.** *(a) Design an overhung crank for a gas engine having the following particulars :*

*Cylinder diameter = 24 cm*

*Stroke = 40 cm*

*Connecting rod length = 5 × Crank length*

*Engine speed = 180 R.P.M.*

*Explosion pressure = 12 kg/cm²*

*Bearing pressure on crank pin = 80 kg/cm².*

(*b*) *Also find maximum stress in the crank when the crank is at $30^\circ$ and gas pressure is 8 kg/cm$^2$.*

*Assume suitable values for the missing data.*

*Make a near sketch of crank.*

**Solution.**

Fig. 17.13 shows over hung crank.

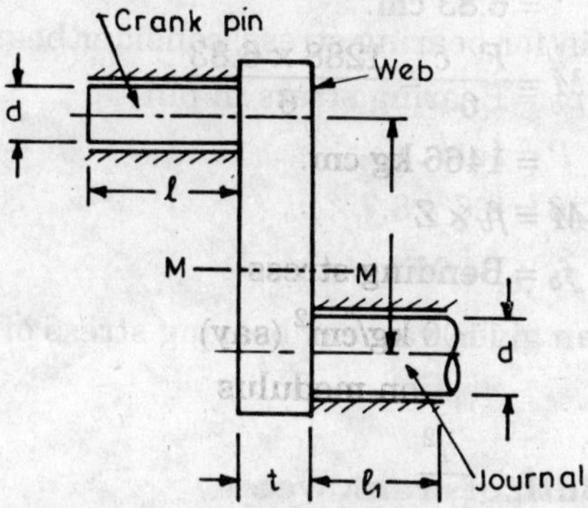


Fig. 17.13.

(*a*) **To calculate diameter of crank pin**

Let $d$ = Diameter of crank pin

$l$ = Length of crank pin

$$\frac{l}{d} = 0.7 \text{ to } 1.1$$

$$\frac{l}{d} = 1.1\, d \text{ (assume)}$$

$D$ = Cylinder diameter

$p$ = Explosion pressure

$P$ = Load on piston

$$= \frac{\pi}{4} D^2 \times p$$

$$= \frac{\pi}{4} \times 24^2 \times 12 = 5426 \text{ kg.}$$

The load on piston ($P$) may not be evenly distributed over the crank pin length.

$M$ = Bending moment on pin

$$= 0.75 \,.\, P \,.\, l$$

$$= 0.75 \times 5426 \times 1.1\, d = 4476\, d \text{ kg cm}$$

$$f_b = \text{Safe stress in bending} = 600 \text{ kg/cm}^2 \text{ (say)}$$

$$M = \frac{\pi}{32} d^3 . f_b$$

$$4476\, d = \frac{\pi}{32} d^3 \times 600$$

$$d = 8.7 \text{ cm}$$

$$l = 1.1\, d = 1.1 \times 8.7 = 9.6 \text{ cm}$$

To check the pin for bearing stress, consider bearing of pin.

$$p_b = \text{Bearing stress in pin}$$

$$P = l \,.\, d \,.\, p_b$$

$$5426 = 9.6 \times 8.7 \times p_b$$

$$p_b = 64.96 \text{ kg/cm}^2.$$

This is less than given value of bearing stress of 80 kg/cm$^2$.

Hence safe.

**([illegible]) To find width of crank web**

$$t = \text{Thickness of crank web}$$

$$= 0.6\, d = 0.6 \times 8.7$$

$$= 5.22 \text{ cm.}$$

$$b = \text{Width of crank web}$$

$$M = \text{Bending moment on crank web}$$

$$= P\left(0.75\, l + \frac{t}{2}\right)$$

$$= 5426\left(0.75 \times 9.6 + \frac{5.22}{2}\right) = 53{,}175 \text{ kg cm}$$

$$Z = \text{Section modulus} = \frac{bt^2}{6}$$

$$f = \text{Bending stress} = \frac{M}{Z}$$

$$= \frac{53{,}175}{bt^2} \times 6 = \frac{53{,}176 \times 6}{b \times (5.22)^2} = \frac{11{,}709}{b}$$

$$A = \text{Cross sectional area} = b \times t$$

$$f_1 = \text{Direct compressive stress}$$

$$= \frac{P}{A} = \frac{5426}{b \,.\, t} = \frac{5426}{b \times 5.22} = \frac{1039}{b}$$

$$\text{Total stress} = f + f_1 = \frac{11,709}{b} + \frac{1039}{b}$$

Assume, total stress on web

$$= 800 \text{ kg/cm}^2$$

$$800 = \frac{11,709}{b} + \frac{1039}{b}$$

$$b = 16 \text{ cm.}$$

(*c*) **To calculate journal diameter**

$d_1$ = Diameter of crank shaft journal

$l_1$ = Length of journal = 1.5 $d$ to 2$d$

Let $l_1 = 1.5\,d = 1.5 \times 8.7$

$= 13$ cm.

$M$ = Bending moment on journal

$$= P\left(0.75\,l + t + \frac{l_1}{2}\right)$$

$$= 5426\left(0.75 \times 9.6 + 5.22 + \frac{13}{2}\right)$$

$$= 102,660 \text{ kg cm.}$$

$f_t$ = safe stress in journal = 800 kg/cm$^2$

$$M = \frac{\pi}{32} d_1^3 \times f_t$$

$$102,660 = \frac{\pi}{32} d_1^3 \times 800$$

$$d_1 = 11 \text{ cm.}$$

(*d*) **To calculate maximum stress**

$$n = \frac{L}{r} = 5$$

where $L$ = Length of connecting rod

$r$ = Crank radius

As shown in Fig. 17.14.

$$\sin \phi = \frac{\sin \theta}{n}$$

$$= \frac{\sin 30}{5} = 0.1$$

$$\phi = 5^\circ\, 45'$$

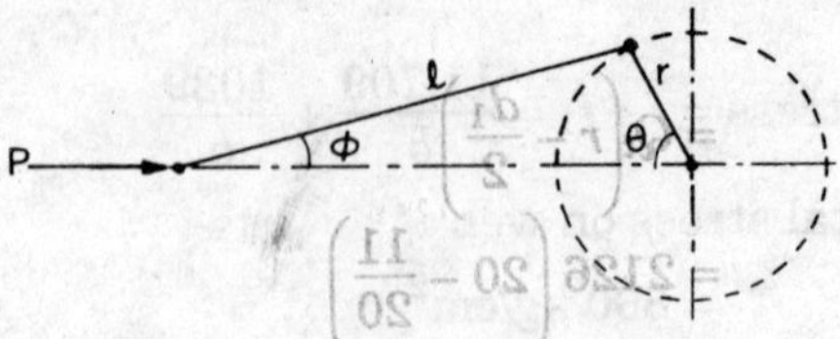


Fig. 17.14.

$$\cos \phi = 0.9949$$

$$p_1 = \text{Pressure}$$

$$= 8 \text{ kg/cm}^2$$

$$P_1 = \frac{\pi}{4} D^2 \times p_1$$

$$= \frac{\pi}{4} \times 24^2 \times 8$$

$$= 3617 \text{ kg.}$$

$$Q = \text{Thrust in connecting rod}$$

$$= \frac{P_1}{\cos \phi} = \frac{3617}{0.9949}$$

$$= 3635 \text{ kg.}$$

This thrust has two components namely $Q_t$ (tangential) and $Q_r$ (radial) to the crank respectively.

$$Q_t = Q \sin (\theta + \phi)$$

$$= 3635 \sin (30 + 5^\circ 45')$$

$$= 2126 \text{ kg}$$

$$Q_r = Q \cos (\theta + \phi)$$

$$= 3635 \cos (30^\circ + 5^\circ 45')$$

$$= 2950 \text{ kg.}$$

The weakest section of the crank web is *M-M* where the crank web joins the crank shaft. At this section web is subjected to bending and torsion due to force $Q_t$ and bending and direct compressive stress due to $Q_r$.

$$r = \text{Crank radius} = \frac{1}{2} \times \text{Stroke}$$

$$= \frac{1}{2} \times 40 = 20 \text{ cm}$$

$$f_1 = \text{Bending stress due to } Q_t$$

$$M_1 = \text{Bending moment due to } Q_t$$

$$= Q_t\left(r - \frac{d_1}{2}\right)$$

$$= 2126\left(20 - \frac{11}{20}\right)$$

$$= 30{,}827 \text{ kg cm.}$$

$$f_1 = \frac{\frac{M_1}{b^2 t}}{6} = \frac{6\,M_1}{b^2\,t} = \frac{6 \times 30{,}827}{16^2 \times 5.22}$$

$$= 138 \text{ kg/cm}^2$$

$f_2$ = Bending stress due to $Q_r$

$M_2$ = Bending moment due to $Q_r$

$$= Q_r\,(0.75\,l + 0.5\,t)$$

$$= 2950\,(0.75 \times 9.6 + 0.5 \times 5.22)$$

$$= 28{,}910 \text{ kg cm.}$$

$$f_2 = \frac{M_2}{bt^2} = \frac{6\,M_2}{bt^2} = \frac{6 \times 28{,}910}{16 \times (5.22)^2}$$

$$= 398 \text{ kg/cm}^2$$

$f_3$ = Direct compressive stress due to $Q_r$

$$= \frac{Q_r}{b\,.\,t} = \frac{2950}{16 \times 5.22} = 35 \text{ kg/cm}^2$$

= Total stress at the upper left corner of crank

$$f = f_1 + f_2 + f_3$$

$$= 138 + 398 + 35$$

$$= 571 \text{ kg/cm}^2$$

The force $F_t$ causes torsion

$T$ = Twisting moment due to $F_t$

$$= F_t\,(0.75\,l + 0.5\,t)$$

$$= 2126\,(0.75 \times 9.6 + 0.5 \times 5.22)$$

$$= 20{,}834 \text{ kg cm}$$

$Z$ = Polar section modulus

$$= \frac{bt^2}{4.5}$$

$f_s$ = Torsional shear Stress due to $T$

$$= \frac{T}{Z} = \frac{20.834}{bt^2} \times 4.5$$

$$= \frac{20,834 \times 4.5}{16 \times (5.22)^2}$$

$$= 215 \text{ kg/cm}^2.$$

$f_m$ = Maximum principal stress

$$= \frac{1}{2}[f + \sqrt{f^2 + 4 f_s^2}]$$

$$= \frac{1}{2}[571 + \sqrt{(571)^2 + 4 \times (215)^2}]$$

$$= 643 \text{ kg/cm}^2.$$

**Example 17.5.** *Determine the main dimensions of an overhung crank shaft with two main bearings for an I.C. engine. The cylinder diameter is 24 cm and stroke is 40 cm. The connecting rod length is five times the crank radius. A flywheel weighing 800 kg is placed between the main bearings. The maximum gas pressure is 12 kg/cm². For maximum torque the crank angle is 30° from I.D.C. when the pressure is 8 kg/cm². Bearing pressure on crank pin is 80 kg/cm².*

*Make a neat sketch of crank shaft.*

**Solution.**

Fig. 17.15 shows an overhung crank shaft with two main bearings and a flywheel placed between the bearings.

(*a*) **To find crank pin diameter**

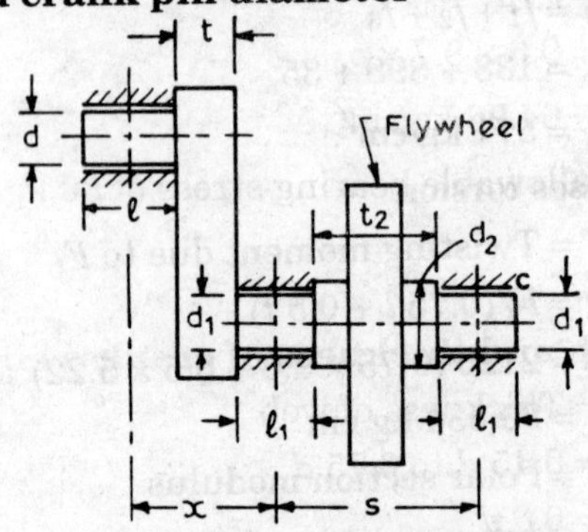


Fig. 17.15.

Let $d$ = Diameter of crank pin

$l$ = Length of crank pin

$$\frac{l}{d} = 1.1 \text{ (say)}$$

$l = 1.1\ d$

$D$ = Cylinder diameter = 24 cm

$p$ = Maximum gas pressure

$= 12\ \text{kg/cm}^2.$

$P$ = Load on piston

$$= \frac{a}{4} D^2 \times p = \frac{\pi}{4} \times (24)^2 \times 12$$

$= 5426$ kg

$M$ = Bending moment on pin

$= 0.75\ P\ .\ l$

$= 0.75 \times 5426 \times 1.1\ d$

$= 4476\ d$ kg cm.

$f_b$ = Safe Stress in bending in pin material

$= 600\ \text{kg/cm}^2$ (say)

$$M = f_b \times \frac{\pi}{32} d^3$$

$$4476\ d = 600 \times \frac{\pi}{32} d^3$$

$d = 8.7$ cm, $l = 1.1\ d = 1.1 \times 8.7 = 9.6$ cm

To check the pin for bearing stress. Consider bearing of pin

$p_b$ = Bearing stress in pin

$P = l\ .\ d\ .\ p_b$

$5426 = 9{,}6 \times 8.7 \times p_b$

$p_b = 64.96\ \text{kg/cm}^2.$

This is less than allowable bearing stress of 80 kg/cm$^2$. Hence safe.

(*b*) **To find width and thickness of crank web**

$t$ = Thickness of web

$= 0.45\ d$ to $0.75\ d$

Let $t = 0.6\ d$

$= 0.6 \times 8.7$

$= 5.22$ cm

$b$ = Width of crank web

= 16 cm as discussed in example 17.4.

**(c) To find reactions on bearings**

Let width of flywheel = 20 cm

Allowing for certain clearances

$$l_2 = 24 \text{ cm (say)}$$

$$l_1 = 1.5\,d = 1.5 \times 8.7 = 13 \text{ cm}$$

The gas load $P$ gives two horizontal reactions

$H_1$ = Horizontal reaction at bearing $B$

$H_2$ = Horizontal reaction at bearing $C$

$s$ = Centre distance between bearings

$$= l_2 + \frac{l_2}{2} + \frac{l_1}{2}$$

$$= 24 + 6.5 + 6.5 = 37 \text{ cm}$$

$x$ = Distance between centre of crank pin bearing and centre of bearing $B$.

$$= \frac{l_1}{2} + \frac{l}{2} + t$$

$$= 6.5 + 4.8 + 5.22$$

$$= 16.52 \text{ cm}$$

$$= 17 \text{ cm (say)}$$

$W$ = Weight of flywheel

$= 800$ kg

$$H_1 = \frac{P\,.\,(x+s)}{s}$$

$$= \frac{5426(17+37)}{37} = 7919 \text{ kg}$$

$$H_2 = \frac{5426(17)}{37} = 2493 \text{ kg}$$

There are two vertical reactions due to weight of flywheel.

$$V_1 = V_2 = \frac{W}{2}$$

$$= \frac{800}{2} = 400 \text{ kg.}$$

**(d) To find diameter of journals**

$d_1$ = Diameter of both the journals

$= 11$ cm as calculated in example 17.4.

To calculate the induced bearing pressure in journal, proceed as under.

$H_1$ = Horizontal reaction
= 7919 kg.
$V_1$ = Vertical reaction
= 400 kg.
$R$ = Resultant reaction

$$= \sqrt{H_1^2 + V_1^2}$$
$$= \sqrt{(7919)^2 + (400)^2}$$
$$= 7929 \text{ kg.}$$

Consider bearing of journal

$$F = l_1 \,.\, d_1 \,.\, p_b$$

$p_b$ = Bearing pressure

$$= \frac{F}{l_1 \,.\, d_1} = \frac{7929}{11 \times 13}$$
$$= 55.45 \text{ kg/cm}^2.$$

Now the allowable bearing pressure in journals usually varies from 32 to 87 kg/cm$^2$.

Hence the induced bearing pressure ($p_b$) in journals is safe.

(*e*) **To calculate diameter $d_2$**

$d_2$ = Diameter of portion of crankshaft under the flywheel
$l_2$ = Length of portion of crankshaft under flywheel
= 24 cm
$M$ = Bending moment due to weight of flywheel

$$= \frac{W \,.\, l_2}{4}$$
$$= \frac{800 \times 24}{4} = 4800 \text{ kg cm.}$$

$T$ = Twisting moment due to $F_t$

$$= F_t \times r$$
$$= 2126 \times 20$$
$$= 42{,}520 \text{ kg cm}$$

where $r$ = Crank radius = 20 cm
$F_t$ = 2126 kg as calculated in example 17.4
$T_e$ = Equivalent torque

$$= \sqrt{T^2 + M^2} = \sqrt{(42520)^2 + (4800)^2}$$

$$= 42{,}790 \text{ kg cm}$$

$f_3$ = Safe shear stress in crankshaft = 300 kg/cm$^2$

$$T_e = \frac{\pi}{16} \cdot d_2{}^3 \times f_s$$

$$42790 = \frac{\pi}{16} d_2{}^3 \times 300$$

$$d_2 = 11.32 = 11.5 \text{ cm (say)}$$

(*f*) **To find maximum stress when $\theta = 30^\circ$**

$f_m$ = Maximum stress

= 643 kg/cm$^2$ as calculated in example 17.4.

**Example 17.6.** *(a) What is an eccentric ? (b) Design a single throw eccentric for a steam engine using the following data :*

*Steampressure = 12 kg/cm$^2$*

*Effective area of face of value = 28 cm × 20 cm*

*Travel of value = 14 cm*

*Diameter of crankshaft = 16 cm*

*Coefficient of friction between value* and *port face = 0.15*

*The safe stores in strap bolts is 210 kg/cm$^2$ and maximum tensile stress in straps is 550 kg/cm$^2$ whereas the bearing pressure between strap and sheave is 7 kg/cm$^2$. Safe stress in rod is 320 kg/cm$^2$.*

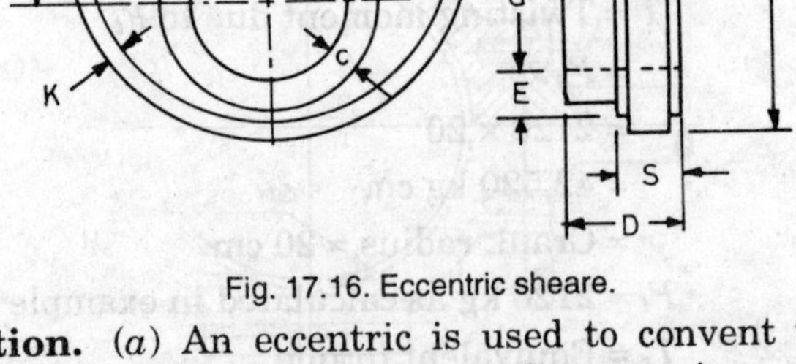


Fig. 17.16. Eccentric sheare.

**Solution.** (*a*) An eccentric is used to convent the circular motion of the crankshaft into the rectilinear reciprocating motion of the slide valve of a steam engine. An eccentric consists of a sheave and a step in two halves. Sheaves are made of cast iron and straps of worught iron. A split sheave is made in two parts which as held together by studs. Fig. 17.16 shows eccentric sheave and Fig. 17.17 the eccentric straps.

**(*b*) To find sheave dimensions**

Let $D$ = Diameter of sheave

$s$ = width of sheave

$r$ = Radius of eccentric

$= \frac{1}{2} \times \text{Travel of valve} = \frac{1}{2} \times 14 = 7 \text{ cm}$

$d$ = Crankshaft diameter = 16 cm

$$E = \frac{d}{5} + 0.5 \text{ cm} = \frac{16}{5} + 0.5 = 3.7 \text{ cm}$$

$$D = 2\left[E + \frac{d}{2} + r\right] = 2\left(3.7 + \frac{16}{2} + 7\right) = 37.4 \text{ cm}$$

$P$ = Force required move the valve = $\mu \cdot p \cdot A$

where $A$ = Area of valve

$\mu$ = Coefficient of friction

$p$ = Steam pressure

$P = 0.15 \times 12 \times 28 \times 20 = 1008$ kg

$P = s \cdot D \cdot p_1$

where $p_1$ = Bearing pressure between strap and sheave

$= 7 \text{ kg/cm}^2$

$1008 = s \times 37.4 \times 7$

$s = 3.85$ cm = 4 cm (say)

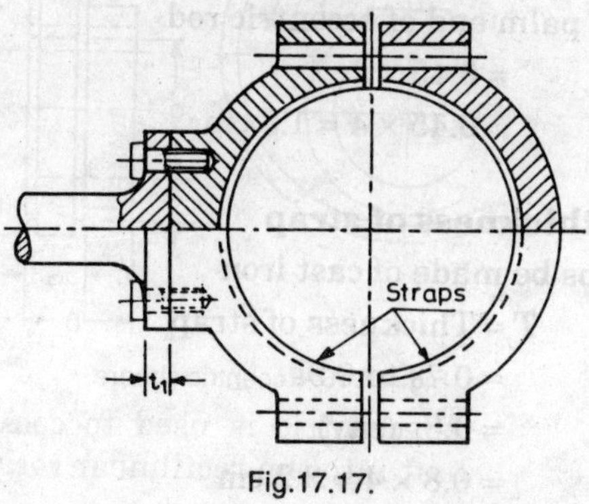


Fig.17.17.

The other dimensions are calculated as follows :

$$B = s \text{ to } 1.6\,s$$
$$= 1.6\,s \text{ (say)}$$
$$= 1.6 \times 4 = 6.4 \text{ cm}$$
$$A \doteq 0.65s = 0.65 \times 4 = 2.6 \text{ cm}$$
$$C = 0.4s = 0.4 \times 4 = 1.6 \text{ cm}$$
$$k = 0.13s \doteq 0.13 \times 4 = 0.52 \text{ cm}$$
$$F = 0.55s = 0.55 \times 4 = 2.2 \text{ cm}$$
$$H = 0.32s = 0.32 \times 4 = 1.28 \text{ cm}$$
$$Z = 0.55s = 0.55 \times 4 = 2.2 \text{ cm.}$$

Diameter of set screws $= 0.32 \times s$

$$= 0.32 \times 4$$
$$= 1.28 \text{ cm.}$$

**(c) To find valve rod diameter**

Let $d_1$ = Core diameter of threaded portion

$$P = \frac{\pi}{4} \cdot d_1^2 \times f$$

where $f$ = Safe stress in valve rod

$$= 320 \text{ kg/cm}^2$$
$$1008 = \frac{\pi}{4} d_1^2 \times 320$$
$$d_1 = 2 \text{ cm}$$

$d$ = Nominal diameter

$$= \frac{2}{0.8} = 2.5 \text{ cm}$$

Thickness of palm end of eccentric rod

$$= 0.45 \times s$$
$$= 0.45 \times 4 = 1.8 \text{ cm.}$$

**(d) To find thickness of strap**

Let the straps be made of cast iron

$T$ = Thickness of strap

$$= 0.7s \text{ to } 0.9s$$
$$= 0.8s \text{ (say)}$$
$$= 0.8 \times 4 = 3.2 \text{ cm}$$

$$M = \text{Maximum bending moment on strap}$$

$$= \frac{PL}{4}$$

where $L$ = Distance between strap bolt axis

$$= D + 2T = 37.4 + 2 \times 3.2 = 43.8 \text{ cm}$$

$$= 44 \text{ cm (say)}$$

$$M = \frac{1008 \times 44}{4} = 11{,}088 \text{ kg cm}$$

$$M = \frac{1}{6} \cdot s \cdot T^2 \times f_t$$

where $f_t$ = Maximum tensile stress in strap = 550 kg/cm$^2$

$$11{,}088 = \frac{1}{6} \times 4 \times T^2 \times 550$$

$$T = 5.5 \text{ cm}$$

$$t_1 = 0.45\ T$$

$$= 0.45 \times 5.5$$

$$= 2.48 \text{ cm.}$$

Empirical formula for $T$ is as follows :

$$T = 0.7s \text{ to } 0.9s \text{ for C.I.}$$

$$= 0.5s \text{ to } 0.6s \text{ for steel}$$

$$= 0.6s \text{ to } 0.8s \text{ for brass.}$$

**(e) To find strap bolts**

$d_2$ = Diameter of bolts

Number of bolts = 2

$d_c$ = Core diameter of bolts

$$P = 2 \times \frac{\pi}{4} d_c^2 \times f_t$$

where $f_t$ = Safe stress in bolts

$$= 210 \text{ kg/cm}^2$$

$$1008 = 2 \times \frac{\pi}{3} \times d_c^2 \times 210$$

$$d_c = 1.75 \text{ cm.}$$

$$d_2 = \frac{1.75}{0.8}$$

$$= 2.18 \text{ cm.}$$

## PROBLEMS

**1.** Discuss the design of piston for an I.C. engine.

**2.** Design a trunk type cast iron piston for I.C. engine from the following data :

Diameter of the cylinder = 10 cm
Stroke = 15 cm
Maximum explosion pressure = 35 kg/sq. cm
Maximum permissible tension for cast iron for the design of head thickness is 300 kg/sq. cm and the flexural stress for the pin may be taken from 900 to 1,200 kg/sq. cm. The gudgeon pin should be hardened and ground and should turn in phosphor bronze bushing. Bearing pressure should be limited to 200 kg/sq. cm.

Sketch the piston (cross-section) inserting important dimensions of the piston pin, piston rings and scraper ring in position.

Check the design from heat transfer view point.

**3.** State the functions of the following in an I.C. engine piston
(*a*) Ribs
(*b*) Piston rings
(*c*) Piston pin.

**4.** Determine the size of a piston rod subjected to total load having cyclic fluctuation from 15,000 kg in compression to 25,000 kg in tension. The endurance limit is 3600 kg/cm$^2$ and yield strength is 4000 kg/cm$^2$. Take impact factor=1.25, factor of safety 1.5, surface finish factor 0.88 and stress concentration factor 2.25.

**5.** Sketch and discuss the design of an overhung crank.

**6.** (*a*) It is required to design an overhung crank for an I.C. engine. Using the following data :

Cylinder diameter = 30 cm
Stroke = 50 cm
Connecting rod length = 4.5 × Crank radius
Explosion pressure = 20 kg/cm$^2$

(*b*) Find the maximum stress when crank is at 40$^\circ$ from I.D.C. while gas pressure is 13 kg/cm$^2$.

**7.** A D-slide valve of a steam engine has an effective area of 26 cm by 20 cm. The maximum steam pressure is 10.0 kg/cm$^2$ gauge and the co-efficient of friction between the valve and its seat is 0.2. If the length of the rod driving the valve is 160 cm and its section is circular, determine the section of the rod. The rod may be assumed to have both ends hinged. The modulus of elasticity of the rod material is $2.0 \times 10^6$ kg/cm$^2$. If the eccentric rod is held to the strap by means of two M.S. studs, determine the size of the studs. Also calculate eccentric sheave and strap dimensions. Sketch the sheave and straps.

Assume factor of safety 8.

**8.** Design completely a connecting rod for a four cylinder internal combustion engine given the following data :

Piston diameter = 100 mm
Length of connecting rod = 30 cm
Stroke of piston = 12 cm
Probable explosion pressure = 28 kg/cm$^2$
R.P.M. of engine = 2000
Weight of reciprocating parts = 2 kg
Assume :
The yield stress in compression for connecting rod material

= 3300 kg/cm$^2$

Allowable stress in bolts = 800 kg/cm$^2$
Allowable bearing pressure :

For big end 110 kg/cm$^2$

For small end = 200 kg/cm$^2$
Draw a dimensioned sketch of connecting rod.

# 18

# Miscellaneous Parts

## 18.1. Machine Frames

The machine frames should be strong enough to resist the induced stress and be rigid enough to maintain accurate alignment. Machine frames are generally made from cast iron as it can be easily machined and has good wear resistance. Cast steel frames are preferred for heavy machines. Machine frames of box section are quite commonly used. Frames of presses, reveters, crane hooks etc. are designed on the principles of curved beams. In curved beams the neutral axis is shafted towards the centre of curvature of the section and is nearer to the centre of curvature than centroidal axis. Table 18.1 indicates the values of radius of curvature ($R_n$) of natural axis for different shapes of sections commonly used in machine frames.

$R_n$ = Radius of curvature of neutral axis

$R$ = Radius of curvature of centroidal axis

Line $y_1 y_2$ indicates the centre line of curvature. (See Table 18.1.)

**Example 18.1.** *The frame of a punching press is shown in Fig. 18.1. It is of T section and is required to resist a force of 8000 kg. Determine the maximum stress in frame.*

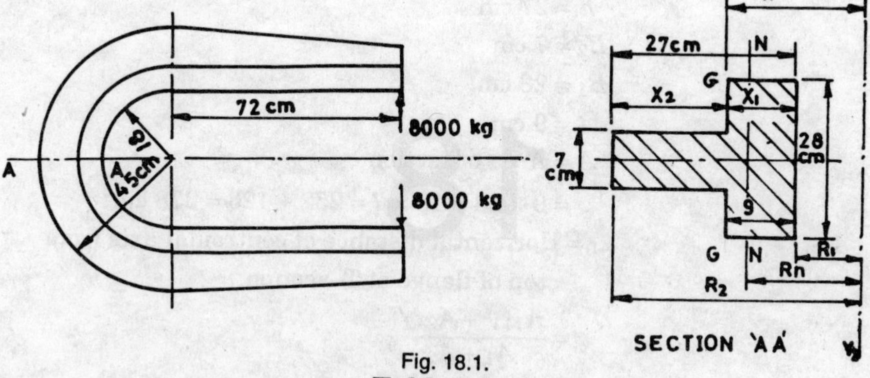


Fig. 18.1.

**Table 18.1.**

| *Shapes of section* | $R_n$ |
|---|---|
| 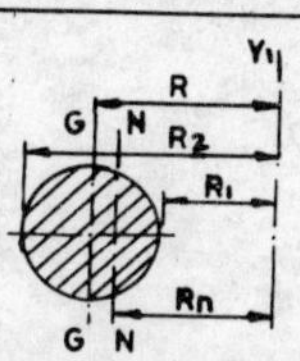 | $\dfrac{(\sqrt{R_2}+\sqrt{R_1})^2}{4}$ |
| 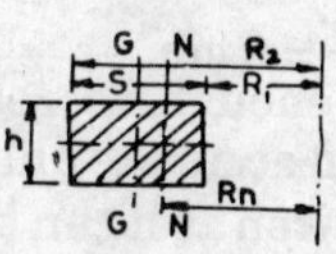 | $\dfrac{S}{\log_e \dfrac{R_2}{R_1}}$ |
| 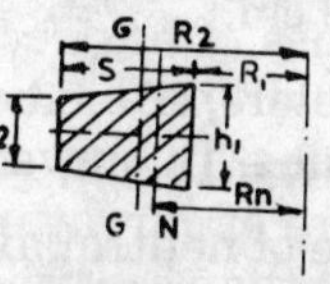 | $\dfrac{\left(\dfrac{h_1+h_2}{2}\right) h\,(R_2-R_2)}{\left(\dfrac{h_1 R_2 - h_2 R_1}{R_2-R_1}\right)\log_e \dfrac{R_2}{R_1} - (h_1-h_2)}$ |
| 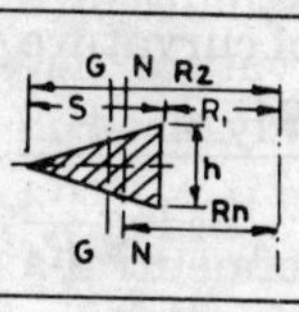 | $\dfrac{\dfrac{h(R_2-R_1)}{2}}{\dfrac{h\,R_2}{R_2-R_1}\log \dfrac{R_2}{R_{1-h}}}$ |
| 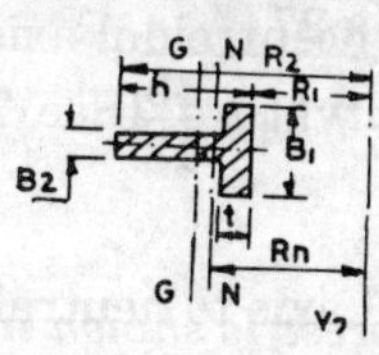 | $\dfrac{(B_1-B_2)\,t + B_2\,.\,h}{\dfrac{(B_1-B_2)\log R_1 + t}{R_1} + B_2 \log \dfrac{R_2}{R_1}}$ |

**Solution.** The dimensions of section at $AA$ are :

$h = 27$ cm

$B_2 = 7$ cm

$B_1 = 28$ cm

$t = 9$ cm.

$A$ = Area of section

$= 9 \times 28 + 18 \times 7 = 252 + 126 = 378 \text{ cm}^2$

Let $x_1$ = Horizontal distance of centroidal axis from top of flange of T–section.

$$= \frac{A_1 x_1' + A_2 x_2'}{A_1 + A_2}$$

where $A_1 = 28 \times 9 = 252 \text{ cm}^2$

$$x'_1 = \frac{t}{2} = \frac{9}{2} = 4.5 \text{ cm.}$$

$$A_2 = (27 - 9) \times 7 = 126 \text{ cm}^2$$

$$x_2' = t + \frac{18}{2}$$

$$= 9 + 9 = 18 \text{ cm.}$$

$$x_1 = \frac{252 \times 4.5 + 126 \times 18}{252 + 26} = 9 \text{ cm.}$$

$$x_1 + x_2 = h$$

$$x_1 + x_2 = 27 \text{ cm}$$

$$x_2 = 27 - x_1 = 27 - 9 = 18 \text{ cm.}$$

$R_1$ = Inner radius = 18 cm (given)

$R_2$ = Outer radius = $R_1 + h = 18 + 27 = 45$ cm

$R_n$ = Radius of curvature of neutral axis] NN from the centre line of curvature $y_1\, y_1$

$$= \frac{(B_1 - B_2)\, t + B_2 \,.\, h}{(B_1 - B_2) \log_e \dfrac{R_1 + t}{R_1} + B_2 \log \dfrac{R_2}{R_1}}$$

$$= \frac{(28 - 7) \times 9 + 7 \times 27}{(28 - 7) \log_e \dfrac{18 + 9}{18} + 7 \log_e \dfrac{45}{18}}$$

$$= 25.5 \text{ cm.}$$

$e$ = Distance from centroidal axis to neutral axis.

$$= R - R_n$$
$$= (R_1 + x_{1)} - R_n$$
$$= (18 + 9) - 25.5 = 1.5 \text{ cm}$$
$$h_1 = x_1 - e = 9 - 2.5 = 6.5 \text{ cm}$$
$$h_2 = x_2 + e = 18 + 2.5 = 20.5 \text{ cm.}$$
$$P = \text{Load} = 8000 \text{ kg}$$
$$L = 32 \text{ cm}$$
$$M = \text{Bending moment of section}$$
$$= P(L + R_{n)}$$
$$= 8000(72 + 25.5)$$
$$= 78 \times 10^4 \text{ kg cm.}$$
$$f = \text{Direct stress} = \frac{P}{A}$$
$$= \frac{8000}{378} = 21.2 \text{ kg/cm}^2$$
$$f_1 = \text{Stress at inner surface}$$
$$= \text{Direct stress} + \text{Bending stress}$$
$$= f + \frac{Mh_1}{Ae\,(R_n - h_1)}$$
$$= 21.2 + \frac{78 \times 10^4 \times 6.5}{378 \times 2.5\,(25.5 - 6.5)}$$
$$= 303.6 \text{ kg/cm}^2$$
$$f_2 = \text{Stress at outer fibre}$$
$$= f - \frac{Mh_2}{Ae\,(R_n + h_2)}$$
$$= 21.2 - \frac{78 \times 10^6 \times 20.5}{378 \times 2.5(25.5 + 20.5)}$$
$$= -825 \text{ kg/cm}^2 \text{ (compressive).}$$

**Example 18.2.** *An offset link shown in Fig. 18.2 is subjected to a force of 600 kg. The link cross-section has 6 cm height and 1.7 cm width. The eccentricity of force is 1.5 cm. Determine the maximum stress in the link.*

**Solution.**

$$P = \text{Force}$$
$$= 600 \text{ kg}$$

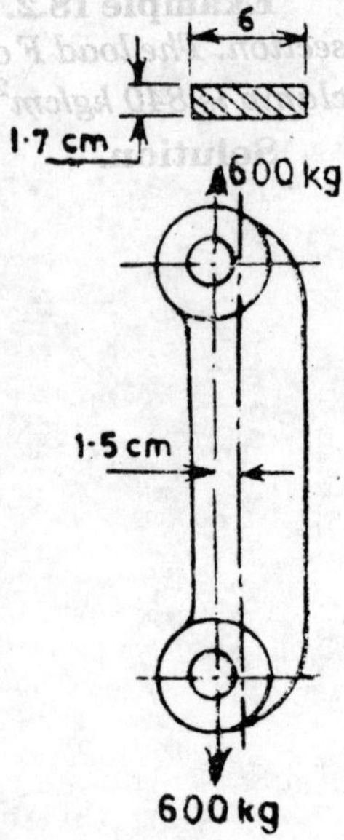

Fig 18.2.

$e$ = Eccentricity
$= 1.5 \text{ cm}$
$b$ = Weight = 1.7 cm
$s$ = Height = 6 cm.
$A$ = Area of link section
$= b \times s$
$= 1.7 \times 6$
$= 10.2 \text{ cm}^2$
$f$ = Direct stress

$$= \frac{P}{A} = \frac{600}{10.2}$$

$= 58.8 \text{ kg/cm}^2$
$M$ = Bending moment
$= P \times e$
$= 600 \times 1.5 = 900 \text{ kg cm}$
$f_b$ = Bending stress.

The bending stress will be tensile at inner edge and compressive at outer edge.

$$f_b = \frac{M}{Z}$$

where $Z$ = Section modulus

$$= \frac{bs^2}{6} = 1.7 \times \frac{6^2}{6}$$

$= 10.2 \text{ cm}^2$

$$f_b = \frac{900}{10.2}$$

$= 88.3 \text{ kg/cm}^2$
$f_1$ = Maximum stress (tensile at inner edge
$= f + f_b = 58.8 + 88.3$
$= 147.1 \text{ kg/cm}^2$
$f_2$ = Stress (compressive) at outer edge
$= f + f_b = 58.8 + 88.3$
$= 29.5 \text{ kg/cm}^2$

**Example 18.2.** (*a*) *Fig. 18.2 (a) shows a C-clamp of rectangular section. The load F on the clamp is 2000 kg and the safe stress in the clamp is 840 kg/cm². Design a suitable section for the clamp.*

**Solution.**

$$F = \text{Load} = 2000 \text{ kg}$$

$$h = 2\,b \text{ (say)}$$

$$e = \text{Eccentricity of load} = 16 \text{ cm}$$

$$A = \text{Area} = h \times b = 2b \times b = 2b^2 \text{ cm}^2$$

$$f_d = \text{Direct stress} = \frac{F}{A} = \frac{2000}{2b^2} = \frac{1000}{b^2} \text{ kg/cm}^2$$

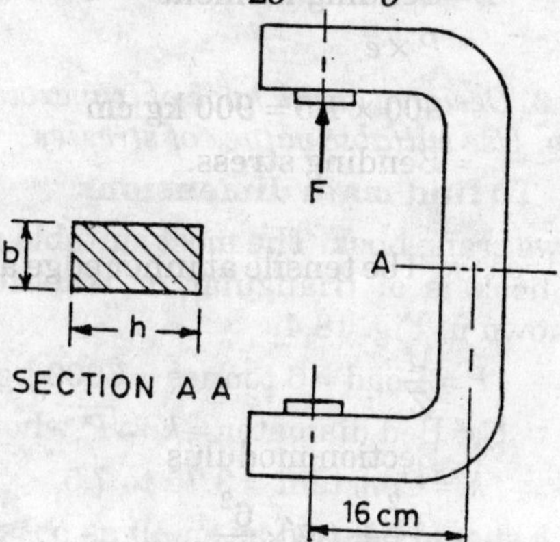


Fig. 18.2.(*a*)

$$M = \text{Bending moment} = F \times e = 2000 \times 16 = 32000 \text{ kg cm}$$

use bending equation

$$\frac{M}{I} = \frac{f_b}{y}$$

where

$$f_b = \text{Bending stress}$$

$$I = \text{Moment of inertia} = \frac{bh^3}{12} = b \times \frac{(2b)^3}{12} = \frac{2}{3}b^4$$

$$y = \frac{h}{2} = \frac{2b}{2} = b$$

$$z = \frac{I}{y} = \frac{2}{3}\frac{b^4}{b} = \frac{2}{3}b^3$$

$$M = Z.f_b = \frac{2}{3}b^3 \times f_b$$

$$f_b = \frac{3 \times 32000}{2b^3} = \frac{48000}{b^3} \text{ kg/cm}^2$$

$$f = \text{Safe stress} = 480 \text{ kg/cm}^2$$

Now $$f = f_a + f_b$$

$$840 = \frac{1000}{b^2} + \frac{48000}{b^3}, \text{ by trial we get}$$

$$b = 3.5 \text{ cm and } h = 2b = 2 \times 3.5 = 7 \text{ cm.}$$

**Example 18.3.** *Design a crank hook of trapezoidal cross-section for 6 tonnes crane. Use suitable values of stresses.*

**Solution.** (*a*) **To find main dimensions**

Fig. 18.3 shows crane hook. The most suitable practical section for the body of hook is of triangular or trapezoidal from with proportions as shown in Fig. 18.4.

$$P = \text{Load} = 6 \text{ tonnes} = 6000 \text{ kg}$$

$$C = \text{Bed diameter} = k \,.\, \sqrt{P} \text{ where } P \text{ is in tonnes}$$

where $$k = \text{Constant} = 3.75 \text{ to } 7.5$$

The value of $k$ should be used as small as possible for economy of material

$$c = 3.75\sqrt{6} = 9.185 = 9.2 \text{ cm (say)}$$

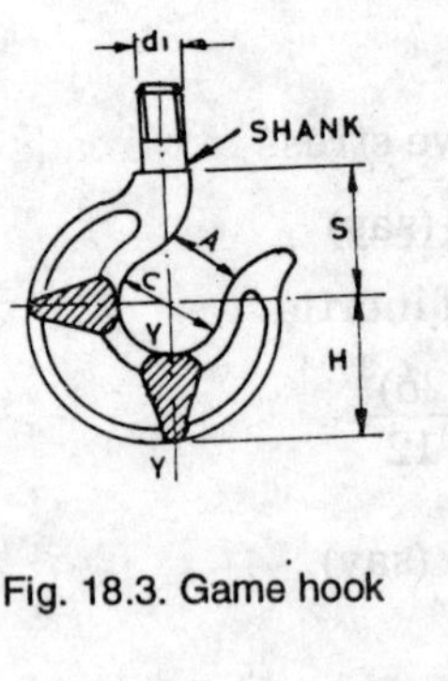


Fig. 18.3. Game hook

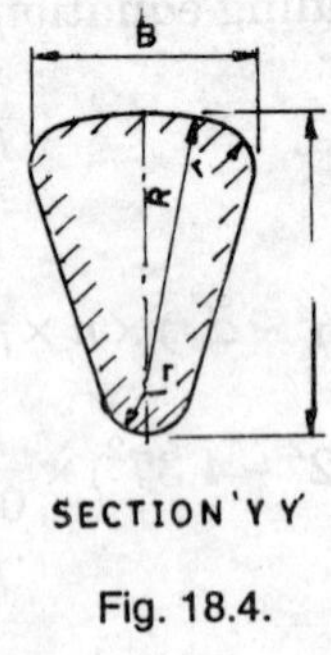


Fig. 18.4.

Let $d$ = Depth of section from intrados to extrados.

$$= (3.125\sqrt{P} + 0.1\,c) \text{ cm}$$
$$= 125\sqrt{6} + 0.1 \times 9.2$$
$$= 8.57 \text{ cm} = 8.6 \text{ cm (say)}$$

This value of $d$ is at horizontal and vertical centre lines of hook. The dimension is increased by about 8% at a plane midway between the horizontal and vertical centre lines. Thus at a plane at 45° the value of $d$ will be 8.6 + 0.7 = 9.3 cm.

Now shank has threads.

Let $d_c$ = Core diameter of shank

$d_1$ = Full diameter of shank

$f_t$ = Safe stress in shank

= 400 kg/cm² (say)

$$\frac{\pi}{4} d_c^2 \times f_t = P$$

$$\frac{\pi}{4} d_c^2 \times 400 = 6000$$

$$d_c = 4.37 \text{ cm}$$

$$d_1 = \frac{d_c}{0.84} = \frac{4.37}{0.84} = 5.2 \text{ cm.}$$

To find height of hook nut.

The nut is fastened on threads provided on shank.

Let $h$ = Height of threads

$p$ = Pitch of threads

= 5 mm (say)

$n$ = Number of threads in height $h$

$$n \times p = h$$

$$n = \frac{h}{p}$$

$f_c$ = Compressive stress in threads

= 500 kg/cm² (say)

$$\frac{\pi}{4}(d_1^2 - d_c^2) \times n \times f_c = p$$

$$\frac{\pi}{4}(5.2^2 - 4.37^2) \times \frac{h}{0.5} \times 500 = p$$

$$h = 0.96 = 1 \text{ cm (say)}$$

$$R_1 = \text{Radius of intrados curve}$$
$$= 0.75\,d = 0.75 \times 8.6 = 6.45 \text{ cm}$$
$$r = \text{Corner radius} = \frac{d}{8}$$
$$= \frac{8.6}{8} = 1.1 \text{ cm (say)}$$
$$B = \text{Width at intrados}$$
$$= 0.65\,d = 0.65 \times 8.6 = 5.6 \text{ cm}$$
$$A = \text{Throat} = 0.75 \times c$$
$$= 0.75 \times 9.2 = 7 \text{ cm.}$$

**(*b*) To find maximum stress at intrados**

The trapezoidal section will have dimensions as shown in Fig. 18.5.

$$B = 5.6 \text{ cm}$$
$$d = 8.6 \text{ cm}$$
$$E = 2.2 \text{ cm}$$

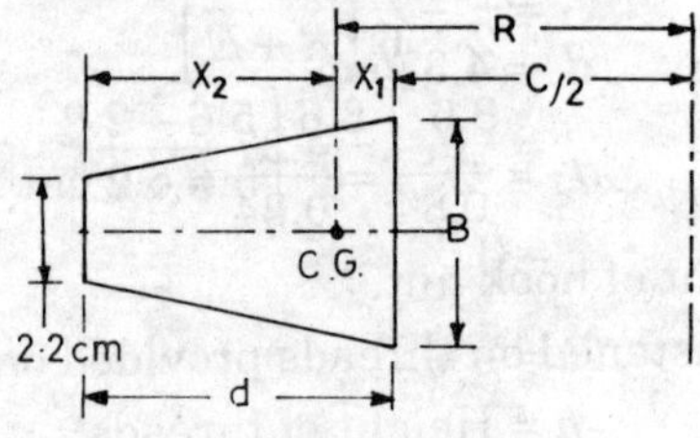


Fig. 18.5.

where $E = \text{Width of section at extrados}$

$$= \frac{d}{4} = \frac{8.6}{4} = 2.2 \text{ cm (say)}$$
$$A = \text{Area of trapezoidal section}$$
$$= \frac{1}{2}(5.6 + 2.2) \times 8.6$$
$$= 33.54 \text{ cm}^2$$
$$R_n = \text{Radius of curvature of neutral axis}$$

$$= \frac{\dfrac{(x_1 + x_2)\,(B + E)}{2}}{\left[\left\{\dfrac{B(R + x_2) - E(R - x_1)}{x_1 + x_2}\right\} \log_e \dfrac{R + x_2}{R - x_1}\right] - (B - E)}$$

where $\quad R$ = Radius of curvature of centroidal axis

Now

$$R - x_1 = \frac{c}{2}$$

$$= \frac{9.2}{2} = 4.6 \text{ cm}$$

$$R + x_2 = \frac{c}{2} + d$$

$$= \frac{9.2}{2} + 8.6 = 1.32 \text{ cm.}$$

$$x_1 + x_2 = d = 8.6 \text{ cm}$$

$$R_n = \frac{\dfrac{8.6 \times 5.6 + 2.2}{2}}{\left[\left\{\dfrac{5.6(13.2) - 2.2(4.6)}{8.6}\right\} \log \dfrac{13.2}{4.6}\right] - (5.6 - 2.2)}$$

$$= 7.53 \text{ cm.}$$

Now

$$x_1 = \frac{d}{2} - \frac{d}{6}\left[\frac{B - E}{B + E}\right]$$

$$= \frac{8.6}{2} - \frac{8.6}{6}\left[\frac{5.6 - 2.2}{5.6 + 2.2}\right]$$

$$= 3.68 \text{ cm}$$

$$R = \frac{c}{2} + x_1$$

$$= \frac{9.2}{2} + 3.68$$

$$= 8.28 \text{ cm}$$

$$e = \text{Eccentricity} = R - R_n$$

$$= 8.28 - 7.53 = 0.75 \text{ cm}$$

$$h_1 = x_1 - e = 3.68 - 0.75 = 2.93 \text{ cm}$$

$$f = \text{Direct stress} = \frac{P}{A}$$

$$= \frac{6000}{33.54} = 179 \text{ kg/cm}^2$$

$$f_1 = \text{Maximum stress at intrados}$$

$$= \text{Direct stress} + \text{Bending stress}$$

$$= f + \frac{Mh_1}{A \,.\, e \times (R_n - h_1)}$$

where $\quad M$ = Maximum bending moment = $P \times R_n$

$$= P \times \text{Eccentricity of load}$$
$$= 6000 \times 7.53$$
$$= 49{,}680 \text{ kg cm}$$
$$f_1 = 179 + \frac{49680 \times 2.93}{33.54 \times 0.75 \times (7.53 - 2.93)}$$
$$= 1437 \text{ kg/cm}^2.$$

## 18.2. Valve Gear of an I.C. Engine

Valve gear mechanism of an I.C. engine consists of those parts which atuate the inlet valves, exhaust valves at the required time with respect to position of piston and crank pin. Fig. 18.6 shows the valve gear arrangement for horizontal engines. Fuel is admitted to the engine by the inlet valve and burnt gases escape through the exhaust valve. The moment of valve is actuated by a can moving on a rotating can shaft through a rocker arm. The rocker arm moving on a fulcrum pin moves the tappet which further operates the valve stem. Valves is modern I.C. engines are usually of mushroom shaped poppet valves (Fig. 18.7). A spring holds the valve tightly against the seat and allows no leakage of gas from the cylinder.

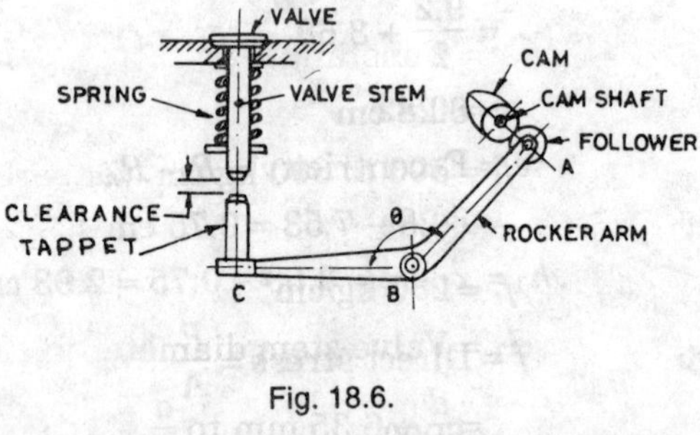


Fig. 18.6.

Both inlet and exhaust valves are subjected to high temperature of burning gases. The temperature at inlet valve is less as compared to exhaust valve. Special heat resisting alloys are therefore used in the construction of exhaust valves.

Inlet valves are made of carbon steel, nickel steel, or chrome nickel steel whereas exhaust valves are made of austenitic type of chrome nickel steels which possess high heat resisting properties.

Valve springs are made of manganese steels and cams are made of case hardened carbon steel.

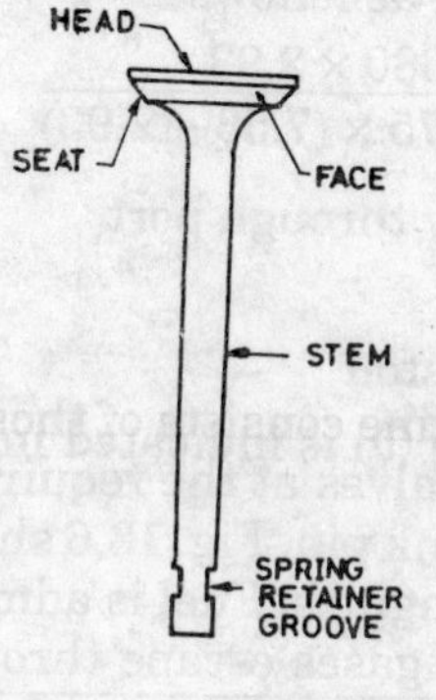


Fig. 18.7 Poppet value.

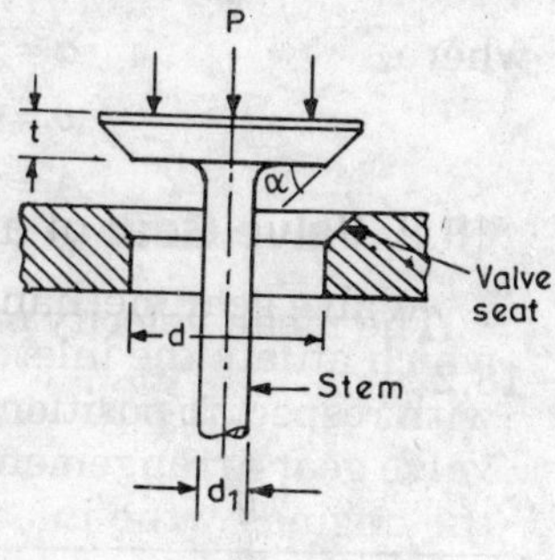


Fig. 18.8.

As shown in Fig. 18.8.

Let $p$ = Maximum gas pressure in kg/cm$^2$

$d$ = Port diameter in cm

$f_t$ = Allowable stress in bending in valve material in kg/cm$^2$

$t$ = Thickness of valve disc or head

$$= c \,.\, d \,.\, \sqrt{\frac{p}{f_t}}$$

$c$ = Constant

For steel, $c = 0.42$

and $f_t$ = 500 to 600 kg/cm$^2$ for carbon steel

For C.I, $c = 0.54$

and $f_t$ = 280 kg/cm$^2$

$d_1$ = Valve stem diameter in cm

$$= \frac{d}{8} + 6.35 \text{ mm to } \frac{d}{8} + 11 \text{ mm}$$

The maximum lift of valve is found as follows

$h$ = lift of valve

$$\pi d \,.\, h \cos \alpha = \frac{\pi}{4} d^2$$

$$h = \frac{d}{4} \cos \alpha$$

where $\alpha$ is the angle at which valve disc seat is tapered

$$\alpha = 30 \text{ to } 45^\circ$$

The size of valve opening is calculated as follows

$$a \times v = A \times V$$

where $a$ = Port area

$v$ = Mean gas velocity through port

$A$ = Area of piston

$V$ = Mean speed of piston

The mean velocity of gas flow velocity ($v$) is indicated in Table 18.2

**Table 18.2**

| *Type of engine* | *v(m/sec)* | |
|---|---|---|
| | *Inlet valve* | *Exhaust valve* |
| Low speed | 33—40 | 40—50 |
| High speed | 80—90 | 90—100 |

The total load for which spring is designed is calculated as follows.

$F$ = Total load on spring

$= F_1 + F_2$

where $F_1$ = Initial load

= Force on the valve tending to draw it into the cylinder on suction stroke

$F_2$ = Load at full lift

= Full lift × Stiffness of spring

**Example 18.5.** *Design rocker arm, spring, roller and tappet for valve gear mechanism of an I.C. engine using the following data.*

*Maximum back pressure when exhaust valve opens*

$= 5 \ kg/cm^2$

*Maximum suction pressure*

$= 0.3 \ kg/cm^3$ *below atmospheric*

*Diameter of valve* = 10 *cm*

*Lift of valve = 3 cm*

*R.P.M. of crank shaft = 1200*

*Angle of action of cam shaft*

*= 100°*

*Weight of parts associated with valve = 0.5 kg*

*Effective length of each arm of rocker arm = 20 cm*

*Angle between two arms of rocker arm = 130°*

*The rocker arm is I-section.*

*Motion of valve is simple harmonic motion without dwell in fully opened position.*

**Solution.** (*a*) **To design rocker arm**

$d$ = Valve diameter = 10 cm

$h$ = Lift of valve = 3 cm

$p$ = Maximum back pressure

= 5 kg/cm$^2$

$p_1$ = Maximum gas load

$$= \frac{\pi}{4} d^2 \times p = \frac{\pi}{4} \times 10^2 \times 5$$

= 393 kg.

$N$ = Speed of cam shaft

$$= \frac{1200}{2} = 600 \text{ R.P.M.}$$

$\beta$ = Half angle of action of cam

$$= \frac{100}{2} = 50^\circ$$

$W$ = Weight of parts associated with valve

= 0.5 kg

Lift of valve = 3 cm

$$r = \frac{3}{2} = 1.5 \text{ cm}$$

$P_2$ = Force required to accelerate the valve at the beginning of stroke

$$= \frac{0.5}{981} \times 1.5 \times \left(2\pi \times \frac{600}{60} \times \frac{180}{50}\right)^2$$

= 39 kg

$p_1$ = Maximum suction pressure
= 0.3 kg/cm$^2$

$P_3$ = Force on valve tending draw it into cylinder on suction stroke

$$= \frac{\pi}{4} \cdot d^2 \cdot p_1$$

$$= \frac{\pi}{4} \times 10^2 \times 0.3$$

= 23.6 kg

$P$ = Total maximum force on rocker arm
$= P_1 + P_2 + P_3$
= 393 + 39 + 23.6
= 455.6 kg.

Fig. 18.6. shows valve gear arrangement.

$L = AB = BC$
= Effective length of each arm
= 20 cm.

As the arms are of equal length therefore force at the cam end will also be 455.6 kg.

The rocker arm is of I-section. Let the dimensions of I-section be as shown in Fig. 18.9.

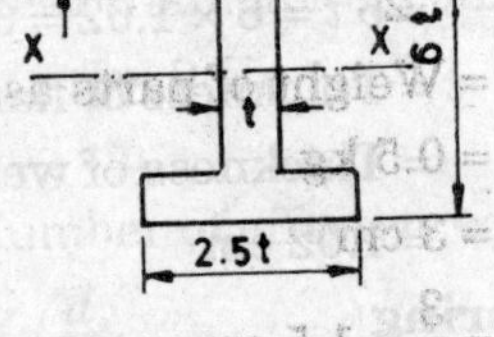


Fig. 18.9.

$I_{xx}$ = Moment of inertia about $xx$ axis

$$= \frac{1}{12}(B_1 H_1^3 - B_2 H_2^3)$$

where $B_1 = 2.5\,t$

$$H_1 = 6\,t$$

$$B_2 = 1.5\,t$$

$$H_2 = 4\,t$$

$$I_{xx} = \frac{1}{12}[2.5\,t \times (6t)^3 - 1.5\,t \times (4t)^3]$$

$$= \frac{444\,t^4}{12}$$

$Z_{xx}$ = Section modulus

$$= \frac{I_{xx}}{y} = \frac{444\,t^4}{12 \times 3t}$$

$$\doteq 12.33\,t^3$$

$M$ = Maximum bending moment

$$= P \times L = 455.6 \times 20$$

$$= 9112 \text{ kg cm}$$

$f_t$ = Safe stress in rocker arm

$$= 700 \text{ kg/cm}^2 \text{ (say)}$$

$$M = f_t \times Z_{xx}$$

$$9112 = 700 \times 12.33\,t^3$$

$$t = 1.02 \text{ cm}$$

$B_1$ = Width of I–section

$$= 2.5\,t = 2.5 \times 1.02$$

$$= 2.55 \text{ cm.}$$

$H_1$ = Depth of I–section

$$= 6\,t = 6 \times 1.02 = 6.12 \text{ cm}$$

$t$ = Thickness of flange

= Thickness of web

= 1.02 cm

(*b*) **To design spring**

$F$ = Total load on spring

$$= F_1 + F_2$$

where $F_1 = P_3 = 23.6$ kg

$F_2$ = Load on full lift

= Lift of valve × Stiffness of spring

$$F_2 = h \times s$$

where $s$ = Stiffness of spring

$= 8$ kg/cm (say)

$F_2 = 3 \times 8 = 24$ kg

$F = 23.6 + 24 = 47.6$ kg

$D$ = Mean Diameter of coil

$C$ = Spring index

$= \dfrac{D}{d} = 7$ (say)

$k$ = Stress concentration factor

$$= \frac{4C - 1}{4C - 4} + \frac{0.615}{C}$$

$$= \frac{4 \times 7 - 1}{4 \times 7 - 4} + \frac{0.615}{7}$$

$= 1.213$

Let $d$ = Diameter of wire

$f_s$ = Torsional shear stress

$= 3800$ kg/cm$^2$ (say)

$R$ = Mean radius of coil

$T$ = Torque $= F \times R$

$= 47.6 \times 4\, d$

$$T = \frac{\pi}{16} \frac{f_s}{k} d^3$$

$$47.6 \times 4d = \frac{\pi}{16} \times \frac{3800}{1.213} \times d^3$$

$d = 0.55$ cm.

$D$ = Mean diameter of coil

$= 7d = 7 \times 0.55$

$= 4.05$ cm.

Let $n$ = Number of effective coils

$$= \frac{G \,.\, d}{8\, C^3\, I}$$

where $G$ = Modulus of rigidity

$= 0.8 \times 10^6$ kg/cms (say)

$C$ = Spring index = 7

$s$ = Spring stiffness

$= 8$ kg/cm

$$n = \frac{0.8 \times 10^6 \times 0.55}{8 \times 7^3 \times 8} = 20$$

Since the spring is to be used as compression spring two more coils should be provided to allow for bearings at the ends.

Total number of coils

$$= n + 2 = 20 + 2 = 22.$$

(*c*) **To design roller.** Roller provided at rocker arm end is carried by a pin.

Let $d_1$ = Diameter of pin

$l_1$ = Length of pin

$$\frac{l_1}{d_1} = 1.2 \text{ (say)}$$

$p_b$ = Bearing stress in pin

= 80 kg/cm$^2$ (say)

Considering bearing of pin

$$P = l_1 \,.\, d_1 \,.\, p_b$$

$$455.6 = 1.2\, d_1 \times d_1 \times 80$$

$$d_1 = 2.17 \text{ cm}$$

$$l_1 = 1.2\, d_1$$

$$= 1.2 \times 2.17 = 2.6 \text{ cm}$$

$d_2$ = Outer diameter of roller

$$= 2\, d_1 = 2 \times 2.17$$

$$= 4.37 \text{ cm.}$$

(*d*) **To design tappet.** Tappet is a threaded rod and is provided with a lock nut. It is under compression.

Let $d_c$ = Core diameter of thread part of tappet

$f_c$ = Safe compressive stress

= 600 kg/cm$^2$ (say)

$$P = \frac{\pi}{4}\, d_c^2 \,.\, f_c$$

$$455.6 = \frac{\pi}{4} \,.\, d_c^2 \times 600$$

$$d_c = 0.98 \text{ cm}$$

$d$ = Nominal diameter

$$= \frac{d_c}{0.8} = \frac{0.98}{0.8}$$

$$= 1.2 \text{ cm.}$$

The rocker arm end which carries tappet is made circular and its dimensions are taken as follows.

Diameter $= 2d = 2 \times 1.2 = 2.4$ cm

Height $= 2d = 2 \times 1.2 = 2.4$ cm.

**Example 18.6.** *The valve of an I.C. engine is 6 cm in diameter and is subjected to a maximum gas pressure of 40 kg/cm². The safe stress in bending in valve material is 460 kg/cm². Determine*

(*a*) *Thickness of valve head*

(*b*) *Stem diameter*

(*c*) *Maximum lift of valve.*

**Solution. (*a*) To find thickness of valve head**

$p$ = Maximum gas pressure

$= 40$ kg/cm$^2$

$d$ = Diameter of valve

$= 6$ cm

$f_t$ = Safe stress

$= 460$ kg/cm$^2$

$t$ = thickness of valve head

$$= c \, . \, d \, . \sqrt{\frac{P}{f_t}}$$

where $c$ = Constant = 0.42 for steel valve

$$t = 0.42 \times 6 \times \sqrt{\frac{40}{460}} = 0.75 \text{ cm.}$$

**(*b*) To find valve stem diameter**

$d_1$ = Valve stem diameter in cm

$$= \frac{d}{8} + 6.35 \text{ cm}$$

$$= \frac{6}{8} + 0.635$$

$$= 1.39 \text{ cm.}$$

(*c*) **To find lift of valve**

$$h = \text{Lift of valve}$$

$$= \frac{d}{4 \cos \alpha}$$

where $\alpha$ = Angle at which valve disc is tapered

$$= 30^{\circ} \text{ (say)}$$

$$h = \frac{d}{4 \cos \alpha}$$

$$= \frac{6}{4 \times 0.867}$$

$$= 1.73 \text{ cm.}$$

## 18.3. Pipe Joints

Pipes are used to carry fluids. Various types of pipes are used depending on nature of fluid, quantity of fluid, pressure of fluid, and service conditions. Pipes are made of cast iron, wrought iron, steel, copper and brass. The sizes of pipes are standardised.

Pipes are joined together by different types of joints some commonly used pipe joints are as follows:

(*i*) **Socket joint.** The two pipes to be jointed together have external threads on the ends. A socket having internal threads connects the two pipes together (Fig. 18.10).

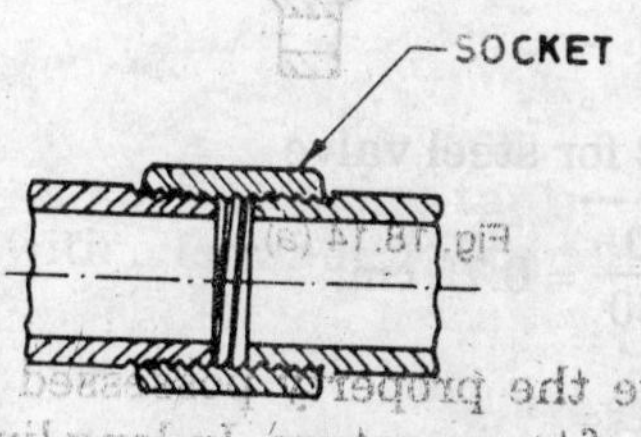


Fig. 18.10. Socket joint.

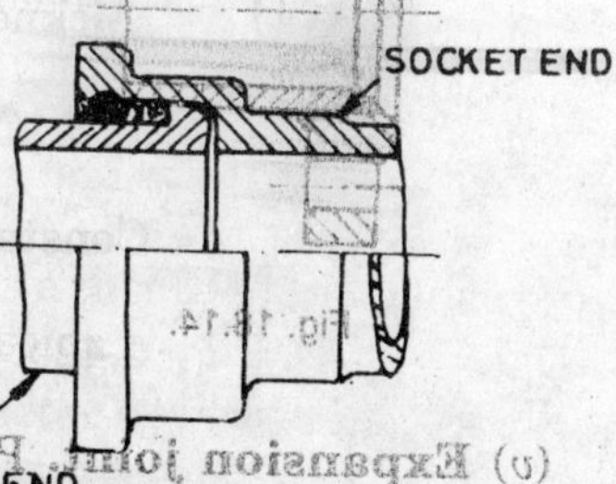


Fig. 18.11.

(*ii*) **Socket and spigot joint.** This joint is mainly used to connect underground cast iron pipes. The joint (Fig. 18.11) is made by partly filling the space between spigot end and socket end with jute yarn and the remaining space is then filled with molten lead which is firmly caulked after cooling.

(*iii*) **Welded joint.** Pipes can be joined by welded joint (Fig. 18.12).The pipes cannot be disassembled. Welded pipe joints are more reliable where pressure tightness and strength are concerned.

Fig. 18.12.

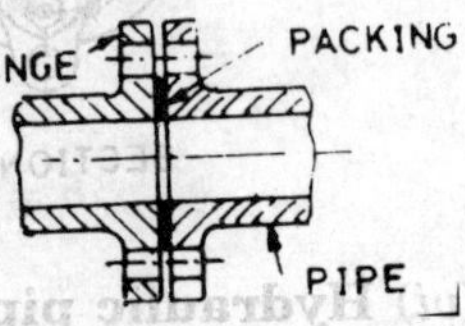


Fig. 18.13.

(*iv*) **Cast iron flanged joint.** In this joint separate flanges at ends are cast integral with the pipes (Fig. 18.13). Bolts and nuts are used to connect the flanges together. In order to make the joint free from any leakage packing of some soft material such as Indian rubber or convas is introduced between the flanges. Flat welded flanges (Fig. 18.14) and butt welded flanges as shown in Fig. 18.14 (*a*) are also used.

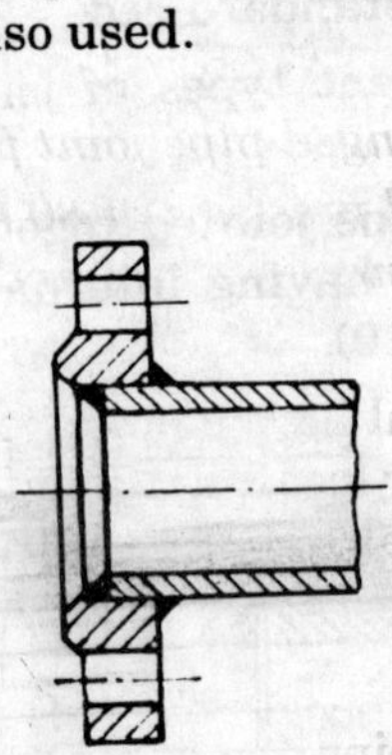

Fig. 18.14.

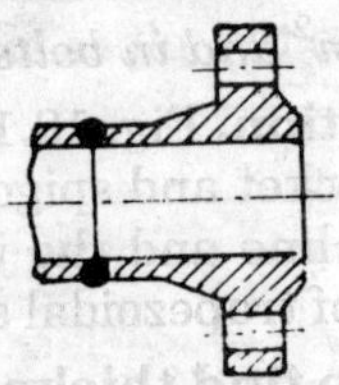

Fig. 18.14 (*a*).

(*v*) **Expansion joint.** Pipes have the property possessed by materials of expanding with increase of temperature. In long lines the expansion is permitted by the use of suitable joints or bends. The expansion of straight run of a pipe can be treated as pure linear expansion resulting from temperature change. Expansion joints take up expansion at one point be allowing relative motion of the two sections of pipe connected by the joint. Fig. 18.15 shows an expansion joint. When expansion is to be taken by the flexibility of pipe itself various types of pipes bends are used.

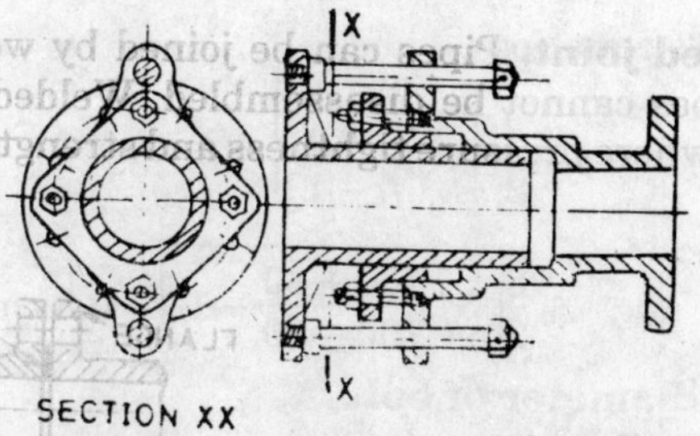


Fig. 18.15.

(*vi*) **Hydraulic pipe joints.** These joints are used for pipes carrying fluids at high pressure. For hydraulic pressures upto 85 kg/cm$^2$ and pipe bore from 5 to 17.5 cm flanges and pipes are cast integrally, the flanges are of oval shapes and are connected by two bolts.

Fig. 18.16 shows a hydraulic pipe joint with oval shaped flanges. For pipes having fluid pressure above 85 kg/cm$^2$ and with bores of 5 cm or below the flanges may be screwed or welded on pipes and are made square and screwed by four bolts.

**Example 18.7.** *Design an oval flanged pipe joint for a pipe of 50 mm bore subjected an internal fluid pressure of 80 kg/cm$^2$. The maximum tensile stress in pipe material is not to exceed 700 kg/cm$^2$ and in bolts 600 kg/cm$^2$.*

**Solution.** Fig. 18.16 shows the oval flanged pipe joint. In this joint a socket and spigot is provided for locating the pipe bore in a strength line and the joint is made leak proof with the help of a packing of trapezoidal section.

(*a*) **To find thickness of pipe**

$t$ = Thickness of pipe

$d$ = Bore = 5 cm

$f_t$ = Safe stress in pipe material = 700 kg/cm$^2$

$p$ = Fluid pressure = 80 kg/cm$^2$.

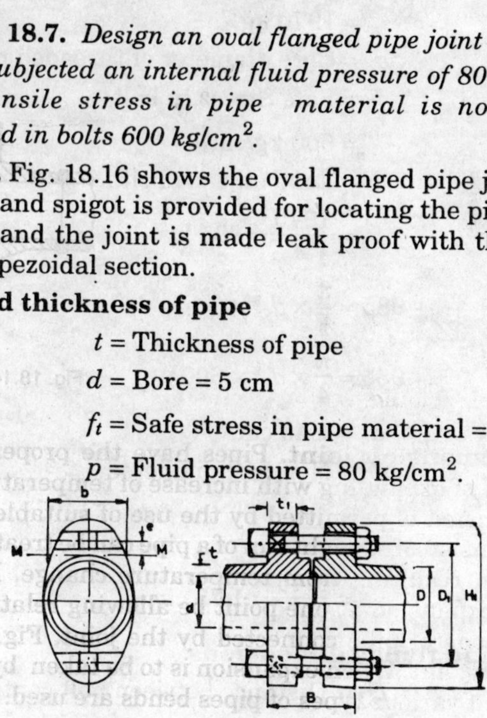


Fig. 18.16.

Using Lame's equation

$$t = \frac{d}{2}\left[\sqrt{\frac{f_t + p}{f_t - 1}}\right]$$

$$= \frac{5}{2}\left[\sqrt{\frac{700 + 80}{700 - 80}} - 1\right] = 0.3 \text{ cm.}$$

(*b*) **To find diameter of bolt**

$n$ = Number of bolt = 2

The flanges are of oval shape

$D$ = Outside diameter of packing

$= d + 2 \times t$

$= 5 + 2 \times 0.3 = 5.6$ cm.

$P$ = Load on joint

$$= \frac{\pi}{4} \cdot D^2 \cdot p$$

$$= \frac{\pi}{4} \times (5.6)^2 \times 80$$

= 1970 kg.

Let $d_c$ = Core diameter of threaded part of bolt

$f_1$ = Safe Stress in bolt

= 600 kg/cm$^2$

$F$ = Load on each bolt

$$= \frac{1970}{2} = 985 \text{ kg}$$

$$985 = \frac{\pi}{4} \times d_c^2 \times f_1$$

$$985 = \frac{\pi}{4} \times d_c^2 \times 600$$

$d_c = 1.45$ cm.

$d_1$ = Nominal diameter

$$= \frac{d_c}{0.84}$$

$$= \frac{1.45}{0.84} = 1.73 \text{ cm.}$$

(*c*) **To find flange dimensions**

Let $D_1$ = Distance between bolt centres

$= d + 2t + S + h$

where $S$ = Distance across corners of bolts

$\doteq 2 \times d_1$ (say)

$= 2 \times 1.73 = 3.46$ cm.

$h$ = Extra allowance for inaccuracies

$= 0.6$ cm (say)

$D_1 = 5 + 2 \times 0.3 + 3.46 + 0.6 = 9.66$ cm

$H_1$ = Overall major axis of flange

$= D_1 + 2 \times d_1$

$= 9.66 + 2 \times 1.73$

$= 13.12$ cm

$H_2$ = Minor axis of flange

$= d + 2 \times t$ + Extra allowance

$= 5 + 2 \times 0.3 + 1.2$

$= 6.8$ cm

$t_1$ = Thickness of flange.

The thickness of flange is found by considering the bending action of bolt on the flange at various sections where fracture is most likely to occur. The line of fracture is at $MM$

$e$ = Eccentricity

= Distance between bolt line and line of fracture $MM$

$b$ = Width of flange at section $MM$

The flange is drawn to scale as shown in Fig. 18.17. The valves of $e$ and $b$ are measured from the figure of flange and are found to be as follows :

$e = 2$ cm approximately

$b = 4.8$ cm approximately

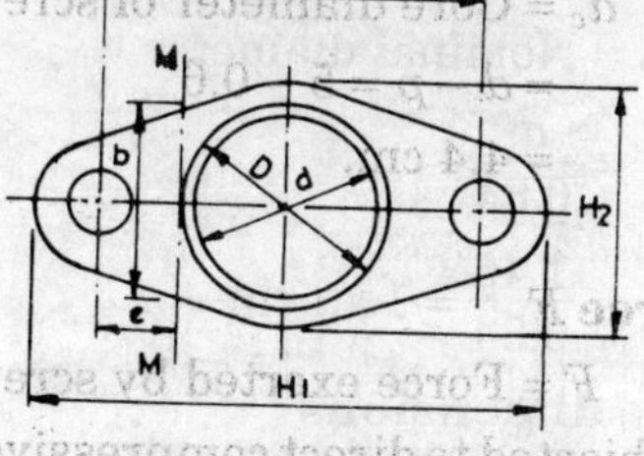


Fig. 18.17.

$M$ = Bending moment

$= F \times e = 985 \times 2$

$= 1970$ kg cm.

$M = f_t \times Z$

where $Z$ = Section modulus of flange

$= \dfrac{b \cdot t_1^2}{6}$

$f_t$ = Safe stress = 700 kg/cm$^2$

$$1970 = 700 \times \frac{b\, t_1^2}{6}$$

$$1970 = 700 \times 4.8 \times \frac{t_1^2}{6}$$

$t_1 = 1.9$ cm

$B = 4\,t + 1.75$ cm

$= 4 \times 0.3 + 1.75 = 2.95$ cm.

**Example 18.8.** *A bracket clamp is shown in Fig. 18.18 (a). The screw has square threads of 6 mm pitch. The outside diameter of screw is 5 cm. If the coefficient of friction is 0.6 and the compressive stress in screw is limited to 1000 kg/cm$^2$ determine the following :*

(*a*) *Core diameter of screw.*

(*b*) *Force F that the screw can exert.*

(*c*) *Bearing stress coming on threads.*

(*d*) *Efficiency of screw.*

**Solution.** (*a*) **To find core diameter**

$d$ = Outside diameter of screw

$= 5$ cm

$p$ = Pitch = 0.6 cm

$d_c$ = Core diameter of screw

$= d - p = 5 - 0.6$

$= 4.4$ cm.

(*b*) **To find force** $F$

$F$ = Force exerted by screw

The screw is subjected to direct compressive stress and torsional shear stress. Therefore the principle stress should be considered to find $F$. But the torsional shear stress is not given therefore we design the screw for lower value of stress say 700 kg/cm$^2$

$f_c$ = Compressive stress in screw

$= 700$ kg/cm$^2$ (say)

$$F = \frac{\pi}{4} \cdot d_c^2 \cdot f_c$$

$$= \frac{\pi}{4} \times (4.4)^2 \times 700$$

$= 10{,}638$ kg.

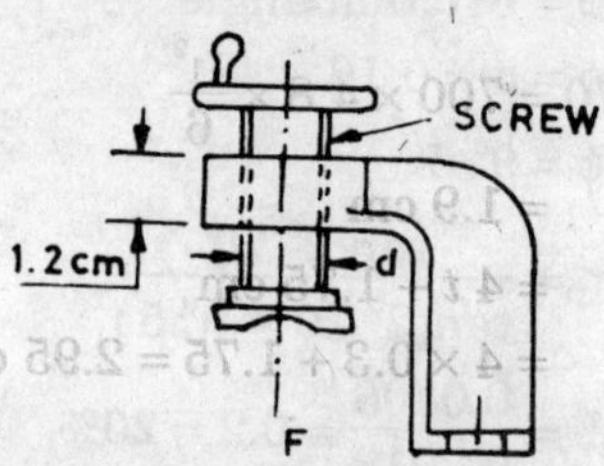


Fig. 18.18 (*a*).

(*c*) **To find bearing stress**

$p$ = Bearing stress coming on threads

$h$ = Height of nut

$= 12$ cm

$A$ = Bearing area

$$= n \times \frac{\pi}{4}(d^2 - d_c^2)$$

where $n$ = Number of threads

$$= \frac{h}{p} = \frac{12}{0.6} = 20$$

$$F = n \times \frac{\pi}{4}[5^2 - (4.4)^2] \times p$$

$$10{,}638 = 20 \times \frac{\pi}{4}[5^2 - (4.4)^2] \times p$$

$p = 120$ kg/cm$^2$.

(*d*) **To find efficiency of screw**

$\eta$ = Efficiency of screw

$$= \frac{\tan \alpha}{\tan (\alpha + \phi)}$$

where $\alpha$ = Helix angle

$$d_m = \text{Mean diameter of screw} = \frac{5 + 4.4}{2} = 4.7 \text{ cm}$$

$$\tan \alpha = \frac{p}{\pi d_m} = \frac{0.6}{\pi \times 4.7} = 0.0406$$

$$\alpha = 2^\circ 20'$$

$$\mu = \text{Coefficient of friction} = 0.16$$

$$\phi = \text{Friction angle}$$

$$\tan \phi = \mu = 0.16$$

$$\phi = 9^\circ 5'$$

$$\eta = \frac{\tan 2^\circ 20'}{\tan(2^\circ 20' + 9^\circ 5')}$$

$$= \frac{0.0406}{0.2019} = 0.2 = 20\%.$$

## 18.4. Cross Head for Stem Engine

It is used to connect piston rod to the connecting rod. It is supported by guide bars in which it slides to and fro. Cross heads main body is made of cast steel forged steel, or cast iron. The brasses are housed in the body and are kept in position by strip made of cast iron or cast steel. The strip and main body are held together by means of two mild steel bolts. Fig. 18.18 (*b*) shows cross head for vertical steam engine.

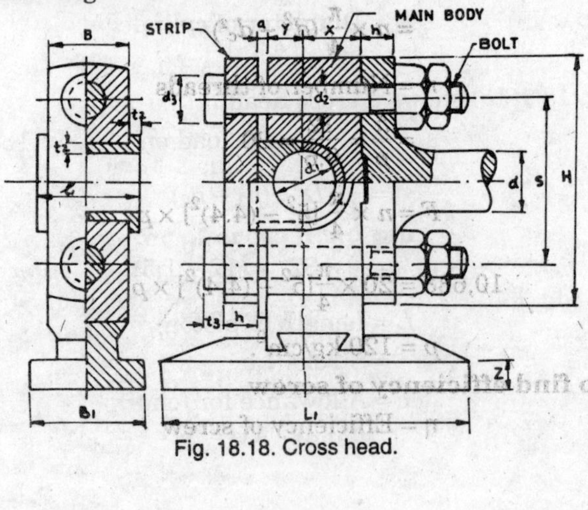


Fig. 18.18. Cross head.

**Example 18.9.** *Sketch and design a cross head having one slide for a double acting steam engine. The cross head pin is made of bronze, bolts are made of carbon steel and other parts are made of forged steel. The other particulars are as follows :*

*Steam pressure at inlet*

$= 12 \ kg/cm^2$

*Back pressure* $= 1.5 \ kg/cm^2$

*Diameter of cylinder* $= 32$ *cm*

*Stroke* $= 64$ *cm*

*R.P.M. of engine* $= 150$

*Allowable stress for carbon steel*

$= 1000 \ kg/cm^2$

*Allowable stress for forged steel*

$= 800 \ kg/cm^2$ *in tension* and *compression*

$= 600 \ kg/cm^2$ *in shear*

*Allowable bearing pressure for slide*

$= 4 \ kg/cm^2$

*The connecting rod length is five times the length of crank.*

**Solution.** (*a*) **To find piston rod diameter**

$p_1$ = Steam pressure at inlet

$= 12$ kg/cm$^2$

$p_2$ = Back pressure

$= 1.5$ kg/cm$^2$

$D$ = Diameter of cylinder

$= 32$ cm

Fig. 18.18(*b*) shows a cross head.

$P$ = Maximum load on piston rod

$$= \frac{\pi}{4} \cdot D^2 \cdot (p_1 - p_2)$$

$$= \frac{\pi}{4} \times 32^2 \times (12 - 1.5) = 8440 \text{ kg.}$$

$L$ = Length of piston rod

= Stroke + $c$

where $c$ = Allowance for length of stuffing box and glands

$= 18$ cm (say)

$L = 64 + 18 = 82$ cm

$d$ = Diameter of piston rod.

The piston rod diameter is calculated by treating it as a column with both ends fixed. According to Rankine's formula

$$P = \frac{f_c \cdot A}{1 + a\left(\frac{l}{k}\right)^2}$$

where $f_c$ = Allowable compressive stress = 800 kg/cm$^2$

$A$ = Area of piston rod

$= \frac{\pi}{4} d^2$

$a$ = Rankine constant

$= \frac{1}{7500}$

$l$ = Equivalent length

$= \frac{L}{2}$ for both ends fixed

$= \frac{82}{2} = 41$ cm

$k$ = Radius of gyration

$= \frac{d}{4}$ for circular section.

$$8440 = \frac{800 \times \frac{\pi}{4} d^2}{1 + \frac{1}{7500}\left(\frac{41}{d} \times 4\right)^2}$$

$$d^4 - 13.44\, d^2 - 48.2 = 0$$

$d = 4.2$ cm.

**(b) To find diameter of cross head pin**

Let $d_1$ = Diameter of cross head pin

$l_1$ = Length of pin

$\frac{l_1}{d_1} = 1.25$ to $2.25$

$= 1.5$ (say).

The thrust in the connecting rod and reaction on slide are maximum when the connecting rod and crank are at right angle. (Fig. 18.19).

$r$ = Crank length

$L_2$ = Connecting rod length

$$\sin \phi = \frac{r}{L_2}$$

$$= \frac{1}{5} \text{ (Given)}$$

$$\sin \phi = 0.2$$

$$\phi = 11^\circ 32'$$

$$\cos \phi = 0.98$$

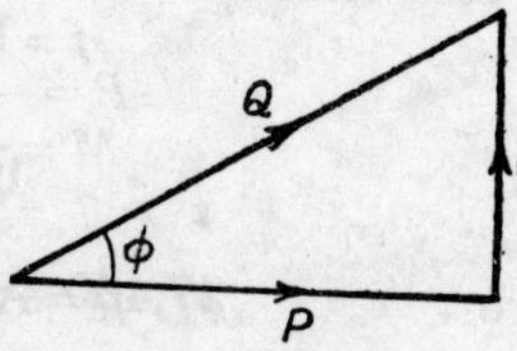


Fig. 18.19.

$Q$ = Thrust in connecting rod

$$\frac{P}{Q} = \cos \phi$$

$$\frac{P}{\cos} \phi = Q$$

$$\frac{8440}{0.98} = Q$$

$$Q = 8612 \text{ kg}$$

$R$ = Reaction on slide

$= Q \sin \phi$

$= 8612 \times 0.2 = 1722$ kg

$p_b$ = Bearing stress on pin

$= 80$ kg/cm$^2$ (say)

Considering bearing of pin

$$Q = p_b \times l_1 \times d_1$$

$$8612 = 80 \times 1.5\, d_1 \times d_1$$

$$d_1 = 8.47 \text{ cm}$$

$$= 8.5 \text{ cm (say)}$$

$$l_1 = 1.5\, d_1$$

$$= 1.5 \times 8.5 = 12.75 \text{ cm.}$$

The pin should be checked against bending and shearing.

Considering pin to be simply supported at the centres of fork sides of connecting rod small end.

$M$ = Maximum bending moment

$$= Q\frac{l_1}{4} = \frac{8612 \times 12.75}{4}$$

$= 27{,}450$ kg cm

$f$ = Induced bending stress in pin

$$M = \frac{\pi}{32} d_1^3 \times f$$

$$27{,}450 = \frac{\pi}{32} \times (8.5)^3 \times f$$

$$f \doteq 456 \text{ kg/cm}^2.$$

This is less than given safe stress of 800 kg/cm² hence safe.

The pin is in double shear.

$$2 \times \frac{\pi}{4} d_1^2 \times f_s = Q$$

$$2 \times \frac{\pi}{4} \times (8.5)^2 \times f_s = 8612$$

$$f_s = 76 \text{ kg/cm}^2$$

This is less than given safe shear stress of 600 kg/cm², hence safe.

**(c) To design brasses**

$t_1$ = Thickness of brasses in the direction of load

$= 0.1\, d_1 + 0.3$ cm

$= 0.1 \times 8.5 + 0.3$

$= 1.15$ cm.

$t_2$ = Thickness of brasses at right angle to the load direction

$= 0.75\, t_1 = 0.75 \times 1.15$

$= 0.87$ cm.

**(d) To find diameter of bolt**

Let $d_c$ = Core diameter of bolt

$n$ = Number of bolts = 2

The bolts are in tension

$f_t$ = Allowable stress in bolts

$= 1000$ kg/cm²

$$P = 2 \times \frac{\pi}{4} d_c^2 \times f_t$$

$$8440 = 2 \times \frac{\pi}{4} \times d_c^2 \times 1000$$

$$d_c = 2.32 \text{ cm}$$

$$= 2.4 \text{ cm (say)}$$

$d_2$ = National diameter of bolt

$$= \frac{d_c}{0.84} = \frac{2.4}{0.84}$$

$$= 2.86 \text{ cm}$$

$s$ = Distance between centre lines of bolts

$$= d_1 + 2\,t_2 + d_2 + c_1$$

where $c_1$ = Metal thickness of 1 cm on each side

$$= 2 \times 1 = 2 \text{ cm (say)}$$

$$s = 8.5 + 2 \times 0.87 + 2.86 + 2$$

$$= 15.10 \text{ cm}$$

$d_3$ = Diameter of bolt head

$$= 1.5\,d_2 = 1.5 \times 2.86$$

$$= 4.3 \text{ cm.}$$

$t_3$ = Thickness of bolt head

$$= 0.75\,d_2 = 0.75 \times 2.86$$

$$= 2.15 \text{ cm.}$$

**(*e*) To design keep plate (strip)**

$B$ = Width of keep plate

= Length of brasses – $2 \times t_2$

$$= l_1 - 2\,t_2$$

$$= 12.75 - 2 \times 0.87$$

$$= 11.01 \text{ cm.}$$

$H$ = Length of keep plate

= $S + 2\,d_2$ + Metal thickness of 1 cm on each side

$$= 15.10 + 2 \times 2.86 + 2 \times 1$$

$$= 22.82 \text{ cm.}$$

$h$ = Thickness of keep plate

The thickness of keep plate is found by considering the plate freely supported at bolt centres and loaded in the manner intermediate between concentrated loading and uniformly distributed loading.

$M$ = Maximum bending moment

$= \frac{Q \times S}{6}$

$= \frac{8612 \times 15.10}{6}$

$= 21.674$ kg cm.

$M = f_b \, . \, Z$

where $Z$ = Section modulus of keep plate

$= B \frac{h^2}{6}$

$f_t$ = Safe stress in keep plate

$= 800$ kg/cm$^2$

$$21674 = \frac{11.01 \times h^2}{6} \times 800$$

$h = 3.84$ cm $= 3.9$ cm (say)

$t_4$ = Thickness of $T$ head of piston rod

$= h = 3.9$ cm.

**(*f*) To design slide**

$R$ = Reaction on slide = 1722 kg

$f_b$ = Bearing stress in slide

$= 4$ kg/cm$^2$

$A$ = Bearing area of slide

$= \frac{R}{f_b} = \frac{1722}{4} = 430$ cm$^2$

$L_1$ = Length of slide

$B_1$ = Width of slide

$= 0.4\, L_1$ (say)

$A = L_1 \times B_1$

$430 = L_1 \times 0.4 \times L_1$

$L_1 = 32.8$ cm.

$B_1 = 0.4 \times 32.8$

$\doteq 13.12$ cm.

The slide should be made detachable so that it can be easily replaced on being worn out with minimum cost.

The outer dimensions are kept as follows :

$$a = 5 \text{ to } 7 \text{ mm}$$

$$x = \frac{d_1}{2} + 1.25 \text{ cm.} \qquad y = \frac{d_1}{2}$$

$$Z = 1 \text{ cm to } 1.5 \text{ cm.}$$

**Example 18.10.** *Sketch and design a hydraulic press using the following data.*

*Press capacity = 30 tonnes*

*Water pressure = 180 kg/cm²*

*Friction factor* for *gland = 1.2*

*Allowable tensile stress* for *C.I. = 300 kg/cm²*

*Allowable tensile stress* for *M.S. = 600 kg/cm²*

*Allowable tensile stress* for *C.S. = 1000 kg/cm².*

*Distance between centres of pillars = 60 cm.*

**Solution.** Fig 18.20 shows a hydraulic press.

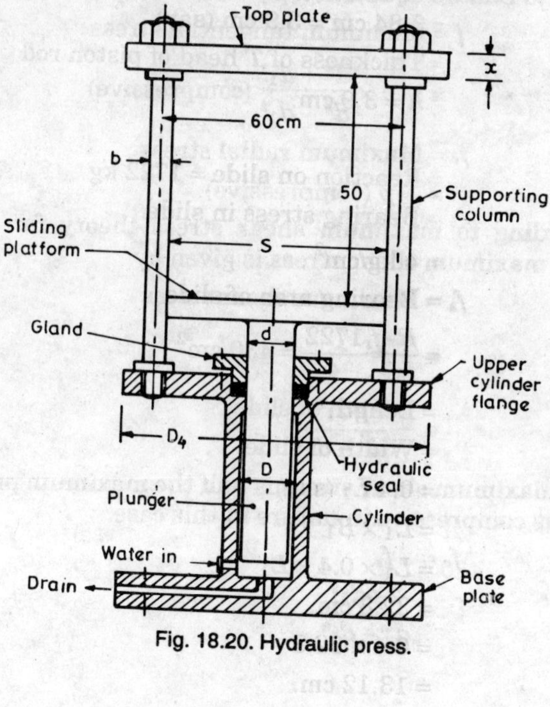


Fig. 18.20. Hydraulic press.

$P$ = Press capacity
= 30 tonnes
= 30,000 kg.

(*a*) **To find diameter of plunger**

$d$ = Diameter of solid plunger
$p$ = Water pressure
= 180 kg/cm$^2$

$$\frac{\pi}{4} d^2 \times p = P$$

$$\frac{\pi}{4} \times d^2 \times 180 = 30{,}000$$

$$d = 14.57 \text{ cm}$$
$$= 14.6 \text{ cm (say)}$$

In order to reduce the weight the plunger it can be made hollow Fig. (18.21).

Let $d_1$ = Inside diameter of plunger

The plunger can be treated as a thick cylinder subjected to external pressure.

According to Lame's equation if $p_1$ = Internal pressure = 0

then, $f$ = Maximum tangential stress

$$= -p \times \frac{d^2 + d_1^2}{d^2 - d_1^2} \text{ (compressive)}$$

$f_r$ = Maximum radial stress
= $-p$ (compressive)

But according to maximum shear stress theory for ductile materials the maximum shear stress is given by

$f_s$ = Maximum shear stress

$$= \frac{f - f_r}{2}$$

$$= -\frac{p d_1^2}{d^2 - d_1^2}$$

Now the maximum shear stress is half the maximum principal stress which is compressive in nature in this case.

$$f_c = 2 f_s$$

$$= \frac{2 p d_1^2}{d^2 - d_1^2}$$

Let $$\frac{d}{d_1} = n$$

$$f_c = \frac{2p}{n^2 - 1}$$

$$n^2 - 1 = \frac{2p}{f_e}$$

$$n^2 = 1 + \frac{2p}{f_c}$$

$$= 1 + \frac{2 \times 180}{600} = 1.6$$

$$n = 1.265$$

$$\therefore \quad \frac{d}{d_1} = 1.265$$

$$d_1 = \frac{d}{1.265}$$

$$= \frac{14.6}{1.265} = 11.54 \text{ cm.}$$

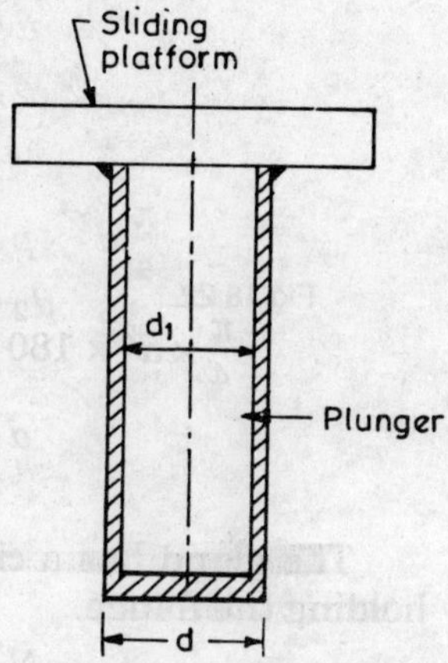

Fig. 18.21.

(*b*) **To find diameters of cylinder**

The cylinder is made of cast iron (C.I.)

$D_1$ = Inside diameter of cylinder

$= d + 2$ cm (say) $= 14.6 + 2 = 16.6$ cm.

$f_t$ = Safe stress for cast iron

$= 300$ kg/cm$^2$

The cylinder is designed as a thick cylinder

$t$ = Thickness of cylinder

$$= \frac{D_1}{2}\left[\sqrt{\frac{f_t + p}{f_t - p}} - 1\right]$$

$$= \frac{16.6}{2}\left[\sqrt{\frac{300 + 180}{300 - 180}} - 1\right]$$

$$= 8.3 \text{ cm}$$

$D_2$ = Outside diameter of cylinder

$$= D_1 + 2t$$

$$= 16.6 + 2 \times 8.3$$

$$= 33.2 \text{ cm.}$$

(*c*) **To find size of gland.** Fig. 18.22 shows gland.

$t_1$ = Thickness of gland

$$= \sqrt{\frac{d}{2.5}} \text{ to } 1.25\sqrt{\frac{d}{2.5}}$$

$$= \sqrt{\frac{d}{2.5}} \text{ (say)} = \sqrt{\frac{14.6}{2.5}}$$

= 2.41 cm

= 2.5 cm (say)

Fig 18.22. $d_2$ = Outside diameter of gland

$= d + 2t_1$

$= 14.6 + 2 \times 2.5$

= 19.6 cm.

The gland has a circular flange. Eight studs may be used for holding the flange.

$N$ = Number of studs = 8

$F$ = Total load on gland

$$= \frac{\pi}{4} (d_2^2 - d^{2)} \times p \times \text{friction factor}$$

$$= \frac{\pi}{4} (19.6)^2 - (14.6)^2 \times 1.2 \times 180$$

= 28,995 kg.

$R$ = Load on each stud

$$= \frac{F}{N} = \frac{28,995}{8}$$

= 3624 kg.

Studs are made of M.S.

Let $d_c$ = Core diameter of stud

$f_t$ = Safe stress for M.S.

= 600 kg/cm$^2$

$$\frac{\pi}{4} d_c^2 \times f_t = R$$

$$\frac{\pi}{4} d_c^2 \times 600 = 3364$$

$d_c$ = 2.77 cm

= 27.7 mm

Outside diameter ($d_o$)

$$= \frac{27.7}{0.84} = 32.97 \text{ mm.}$$

Thus studs will be M 33 with a pitch of 3.5 mm

$d_0$ = Outside diameter of stud

= 3.3 cm.

$D_3$ = Pitch circle diameter of studs

$= d_2 + 3d_o$

$= 19.6 + 3 \times 3.3 = 29.5$ cm.

$D_4$ = Outside diameter of flange

$= D_3 + 3d_0 = 29.5 + 3 \times 3.3 = 39.4$ cm

$t_2$ = Thickness of gland flange

$= 1.3\ d_0 = 1.3 \times 3.3 = 4.29$ cm.

$h = 3\ d_0 = 3 \times 3.3$

= 9.9 cm.

(*b*) **To calculate diameter of supporting column.** The supporting column are made of M.S. Let there be four supporting columns.

Load per supporting column

$$= \frac{30{,}000}{4} = 7500 \text{ kg.}$$

The columns are subjected to tensile force.

$a$ = Core diameter of column

$f_t$ = Safe tensile stress for column

= 600 kg/cm$^2$

$$\frac{\pi}{4} \cdot a^2 \cdot f_t = 7500$$

$$\frac{\pi}{4} \cdot a^2 \cdot 600 = 7500$$

$a$ = 4 cm.

$b$ = Outside diameter of column

$$= \frac{a}{0.84} = \frac{a}{0.84} = 4.76 \text{ cm} = 4.8 \text{ cm (say).}$$

(*e*) **To find thickness of upper cylinder flange**

Let, $t_3$ = Thickness of upper cylinder flange

$C$ = Centre to centre distance of supporting columns

= 60 cm.

Let us consider the flange as a cantilever connected to the cylinder at the outer diameter.

$L$ = Arm of cantilever

$$= \frac{C - D_2}{2} = \frac{60 - 33.2}{2}$$

= 13.4 cm.

$M$ = Maximum bending moment on the flange where it joins the cylinder

$= P \,.\, L = 30{,}000 \times 13.4$

$= 40.2 \times 10^4$ kg cm

$$M = f \times Z$$

where $f$ = Allowable tensile stress in flange

= 300 kg/cm$^2$

$$Z = \frac{\pi D_2 \,.\, t_3^2}{6}$$

$$40.2 \times 10^4 = \frac{\pi \times 33.3 \times t_2^3}{6} \times 300$$

$t_2$ = 4.26 cm

= 5 cm (say)

$D_4$ = Outer diameter of cylinder flange

= $C$ + 3 × Outer diameter of column

= 60 + 3 × $b$ = 60 + 3 × 4.8

= 74.4 cm.

**(f) To find thickness of sliding platform**

$T$ = Thickness of sliding platform

The sliding platform is a square plate supporting at centre and loaded uniformly. Its thickness is calculated by considering it a circular plate for which Grashof formula is as follows :

$$T^2 = \frac{p_1 \,.\, s^2}{4 \,.\, f_t}\left[2 \log \frac{s}{d} + \frac{1}{4}\right]$$

where $s$ = Diameter of plate

$= C - b$

$$= 60 - 4.8 = 55.2 \text{ cm}$$

$$f_t = \text{Safe stress for M.S.} = 600 \text{ kg/cm}^2$$

$$p_1 = \text{Intensity of pressure}$$

$$= \frac{P}{\frac{\pi}{4 \times s^2}} = \frac{30{,}000}{\frac{\pi}{4} \times (55.2)^2}$$

$$= 12.54 \text{ kg/cm}^2$$

$$d = \text{Diameter of plunger}$$

$$= 14.6 \text{ cm}$$

$$T^2 = \frac{12.54 \times (55.2)^2}{4 \times 600}\left[2 \log \frac{55.2}{14.6} + \frac{1}{4}\right]$$

$$T_2 = 15.9[2.8 + 0.25]$$

$$T = 6.96 \text{ cm}$$

$$= 7 \text{ cm (say).}$$

(*g*) **To find thickness of top plate.** Top plate is designed as a rectangular flat plate uniformly loaded and supported at four corners.

$$\text{Size of top plate} = C$$

$$= 60 \text{ cm}$$

$$x = \text{Thickness of top plate}$$

$$= L_1 \,.\, L_2 \,.\, \sqrt{\frac{P_2}{2 \,.\, f_t \,.\, (L_1^2 + L_2^2)}}$$

where $L_1 = L_2 = C = 60$ cm

$$p_2 = \text{Intensity of pressure}$$

$$= \frac{P}{L_1 \times L_2} = \frac{30{,}000}{60 \times 60}$$

$$= 8.34 \text{ kg/cm}^2$$

The plate is assumed to be made of cast steel (C.S.)

$$f_t = \text{Safe tensile stress for C.S.}$$

$$= 1000 \text{ kg/cm}^2$$

$$x = 60 \times 60 \sqrt{\frac{8.34}{2 \times 1000 \times (60^2 + 60^2)}}$$

$$= 2.75 \text{ cm.}$$

**Example 18.11.** *Fig. 18.23 shows a bracket supporting a vertical load of 2700 kg and riveted to a vertical plate. Determine the load on each rivet. Also determine the maximum load and the rivet on which it acts.*

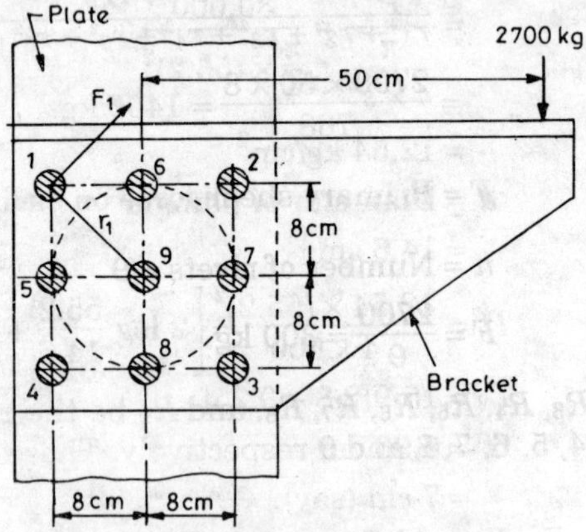


Fig. 18.23.

**Solution.** $P$ = Vertical load = 2700 kg

$e$ = Eccentricity = 50 cm.

The centre of gravity of the rivet system is at the centre of rivet 9.

$r_1$ = Distance of centre of rivet 1 from centre of gravity

$= \sqrt{8^2 + 8^2} = \sqrt{128} = 11.3$ cm.

Now $r_1 = r_2 = r_3' = r_4 = 11.3$ cm.

$r_5 = r_6 = r_7 = r_8 = 8$ cm.

Let $F_1, F_2, F_3, F_4, F_5, F_6, F_7, F_8,$ and $F_9$ be the forces due to couple on rivet 1, 2, 3, 4, 5, 6, 7, 8 and 9 respectively.

Turning moment = $P \cdot e$ .

$$\therefore \quad P \times e = \frac{F_1}{r_1}\left[r_1^2 + r_2^2 + r_3^2 + r_4^2 + r_5^2 + r_6^2 + r_7^2 + r_8^2 + r_9^2\right]$$

$$2700 \times 50 = \frac{F_1}{11.3}[(11.3)^2 + (11.3)^2 + (11.3)^2 + (11.3)^2 + 8^2 + 8^2 + 8^2 + 8^2]$$

$$= \frac{F_1 \times 768}{11.3}$$

$$\therefore \quad F_1 = \frac{2700 \times 50 \times 11.3}{768} = 1986 \text{ kg.}$$

Now $F_1 = F_2 = F_3 = F_4 = 1986$ kg

$$F_5 = F_6 = F_7 = F_8$$

$$= \frac{P \cdot e \cdot r_5}{r_1^2 + r_2^2 + r_3^2 + r_4^2 + r_5^2 + r_6^2 + r_7^2 + r_8^2}$$

$$= \frac{2700 \times 50 \times 8}{768} = 1406 \text{ kg.}$$

$$F = \text{Primary shear force on each rivet} = \frac{P}{n}$$

where $n$ = Number of rivets = 9

$$F = \frac{2700}{9} = 300 \text{ kg.}$$

Let $R_1$, $R_2$, $R_3$, $R_4$, $R_5$, $R_6$, $R_7$, $R_8$, and $R_9$ be the resultant load on rivet 1, 2, 3, 4, 5, 6, 7, 8 and 9 respectively. These are indicated in Fig. 18.24.

As forces $F_1$, $F_2$, $F_3$, and $F_4$ are equal and are inclined at 45° to the horizontal their vertical ($v$) and horizontal components ($H$) are equal disregarding the signs

$$H = F_1 \cos 45 = 1986 \times \frac{1}{\sqrt{2}} = 1404 \text{ kg}$$

$$V = F_1 \sin 45$$

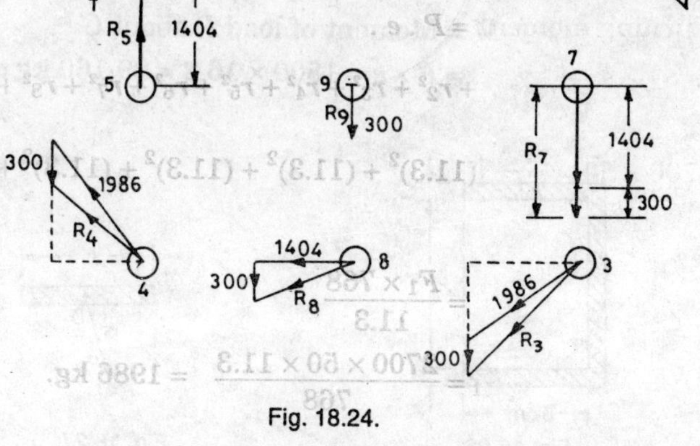


Fig. 18.24.

$$= 1986 \times \frac{1}{\sqrt{2}} = 1404 \text{ kg.}$$

$$R_1 = R_4 = \sqrt{H^2 + (V - 300)^2}$$

$$= \sqrt{(1404)^2 + (1104)^2} = 1786 \text{ kg}$$

$$R_2 = R_3 = \sqrt{(1404)^2 + (1404 + 300)^2} = 2208 \text{ kg}$$

$$R_5 = 1406 - 300 = 1106 \text{ kg}$$

$$R_6 = R_8 = \sqrt{(1406)^2 + (300)^2} = 1438 \text{ kg}$$

$$R_7 = 1406 + 300 = 1706 \text{ kg}$$

$$R_9 = 300 \text{ kg.}$$

The maximum load is 2208 kg and acts on rivet 2 and 3.

**Example 18.12**. *Fig. 18.25 shows a bracket carrying a load of 1800 kg and welded on to a stanchion by three fillets. Calculate necessary throat thickness if working stress is not to exceed 800 kg/cm².*

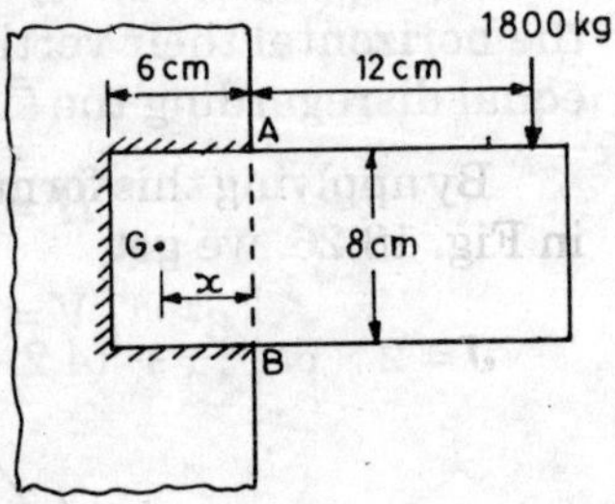

Fig. 18.25

**Solution.**

$P$ = Applied load = 1800 kg

$t$ = Throat thickness

Let $G$ be the centroid

$\bar{x}$ = Distance of $G$ from $AB$

Take moments about $AB$

$$(2 \times 6t + 8t)\,\overline{xx} = 2 \times 6t \times 3 + 8t \times 6$$

$$\bar{x} = 4.2 \text{ cm}$$

$e$ = Eccentricity of load

$= \bar{x} + 12 = 4.2 + 12 = 16.2$ cm.

$M$ = Moment of load $P$ about $G$

$= P \times e = 1800 \times 16.2 = 29{,}160$ kg cm.

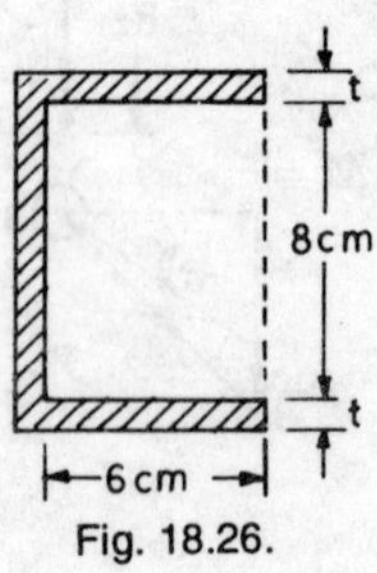

Fig. 18.26.

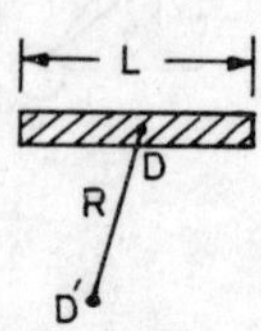

Fig. 18.27.

As shown in Fig. 18.27 the polar moment of inertia for a rectangle of length $L$ and width $t$, where $t$ is very small and having an area '$a$' is given by the following relation.

$J_1$ = Polar moment of inertia about an axis passing through the centroid $D$ and perpendicular to plane of paper

$$= \frac{aL^2}{12}$$

$J$ = Polar moment of interia about a parallel axis passing through $D'$

$$= J_1 + aR^2$$

where $R$ is perpendicular distance between the axis

$$J = a\frac{L^2}{12} + a\,R^2$$

$$= a\left[\frac{L^2}{12} + R^2\right]$$

By applying this formula to the three rectangular area as shown in Fig. 18.26. we get

$$J = 2 \times 6t\left[\frac{6^2}{12} + \{(4.2-3)^2 + 4^2\}\right] + 8t\left[\frac{8^2}{12} + (6-4.2)^2\right]$$

$$= 12t\,[3 + (1.2)^2 + 4^2] + 8t\left[\frac{16}{3} + (1.8)^2\right]$$

$$= 12\,t[20.44] + 8t[8.57]$$

$$= 313.84\,t \text{ cm}^4$$

$f_1$ = Direct stress due to applied load

$$= \frac{P}{\text{Area}}$$

$$\text{Area} = 2 \times 6t + 8t = 20\,t$$

$$f_1 = \frac{1800}{20}\,t = \frac{90}{t}$$

$$f = \text{Stress due to } M = \frac{M}{J}\cdot y$$

$$= \frac{29{,}160}{313.84\,t} \times y$$

$$= \frac{93}{t}\cdot y$$

The resultant is maximum at $A$ and $B$ where $y$ has its maximum value. The vertical ($V$) and horizontal ($H$) components of this stress are as follows :

$$V = f + f_1 = \frac{93\,y}{t} + \frac{90}{t} = \frac{93 \times 4.2}{t} + \frac{90}{t}$$

$$= \frac{390.6}{t} + \frac{90}{t} = \frac{480.6}{t}$$

As $$y = \bar{x} = \frac{480.6}{t}$$

$$H = \frac{93}{t}\,y$$

where $$y = \frac{8}{2} = 4 \text{ cm } H = \frac{93 \times 4}{t} = \frac{372}{t}$$

$$s = \text{resultant stress} = \sqrt{V^2 + H^2}$$

$$s = \sqrt{\left(\frac{480.6}{t}\right)^2 + \left(\frac{372}{t}\right)^2} = \frac{607}{t}$$

But $$s = 800 \text{ kg/cm}^2 \text{ (given)}$$

$$800 = \frac{607}{t}$$

$$t = 0.76 \text{ cm.}$$

**Example 18.13.** *Calculate the maximum stress on the section RN of the clamp shown in Fig. 18.28 when a force (P) of 240 kg is exerted by the screw. The section is rectangular 24 mm × 10 mm.*

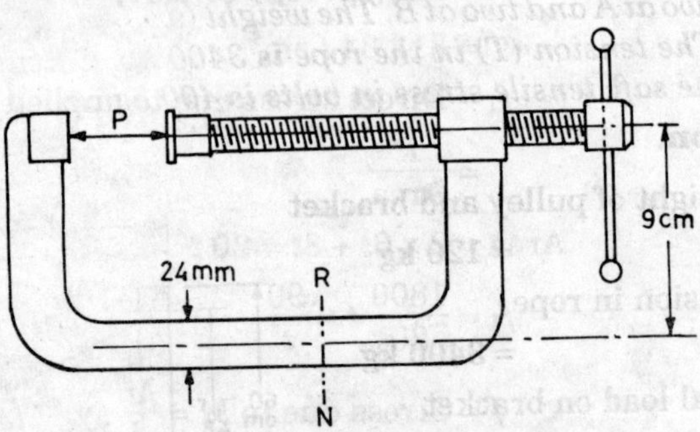


Fig. 18.28.

**Solution.** $P$ = Force = 240 kg

$A$ = Area of cross–section

$= 2.4 \times 1 = 2.4 \text{ cm}^2$

The section $RN$ is subjected to a force of 240 kg and a bending moment

$(M)$ of $240 \times 9 = 2160$ kg cm.

$$f = \text{Direct tensile stress}$$

$$= \frac{P}{A} = \frac{240}{2.4} = 100 \text{ kg/cm}^2$$

$$I = \text{Second moment of area}$$

$$= \frac{1 \times (2.4)^3}{12} = 1.5 \text{ cm}^4$$

$$\sigma = \text{Bending stress}$$

$$\frac{M}{I} = \frac{\sigma}{y}$$

where $y = \frac{2.4}{2} = 1.2$ cm

$$\frac{2160}{1.15} = \frac{\sigma}{1.2}$$

$$\sigma = 2353 \text{ kg/cm}^2$$

$p_1$ = Maximum tensile stress on the section.

$$= \sigma + f = 2253 + 100 = 2353 \text{ kg/cm}^2$$

$p_2$ = Maximum compressive stress

$$= \sigma - f = 2253 - 100 = 2153 \text{ kg/cm}^2.$$

**Example 18.14.** *Fig. 18.29 shows a pulley bracket supported by four bolts, two at A and two at B. The weight (w) of pulley and bracket is 120 kg. The tension (T) in the rope is 3400 kg. Calculate the size of bolts if the safe tensile stress in bolts is 400 kg/cm.*

**Solution.**

$W$ = Weight of pulley and bracket

= 120 kg

$T$ = Tension in rope

= 3400 kg

$F$ = Total load on bracket

$= 2T + W$

$= 2 \times 3400 + 120$

= 6920 kg

$n$ = Number of bolts = 4

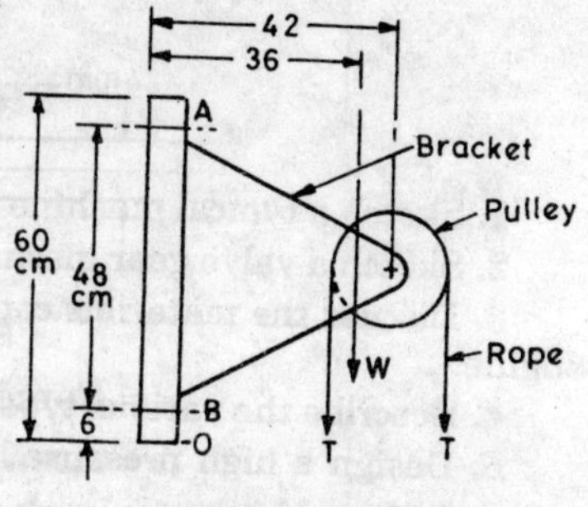


Fig. 18.29.

$$R = \text{Direct shear force on each bolt}$$

$$= \frac{F}{n} = \frac{6920}{4} = 1730 \text{ kg}$$

$P$ = Force per bolt due to turning moment per unit distance from the edge $O$

$$P_1 = \text{Load shared by bolts at } A$$

$$= P \times \text{Distance of } A \text{ from } O = P \times 54 = 54P$$

$$P_2 = \text{Load shared by bolts at } B$$

$$= P \times \text{Distance of } B \text{ from } O = P \times 6 = 6P$$

$$\therefore \quad \frac{P_1}{P_2} = \frac{54P}{6P} = 9$$

To find $P_1$ and $P_2$ take moments about $O$

$$W \times 36 + 2T \times 42 = 2[P_1 \times 54 + P_2 \times 6]$$

$$120 \times 36 + 2 \times 3400 \times 42 = 2[9\,P_2 \times 54 + P_2 \times 6]$$

$$P_2 = 295 \text{ kg}$$

$$P_1 = 9P_2 = 9 \times 295 = 2655 \text{ kg}$$

$$S = \text{Force on each bolt at } A$$

$$= R + P_1 = 1730 + 2655 = 4385 \text{ kg}$$

$$f = \text{Safe stress in bolts}$$

$$d_c = \text{Core diameter of bolt}$$

$$s = \frac{\pi}{4} d_c^2 \times f$$

$$4385 = \frac{\pi}{4} d_c^2 \times 400$$

$$d_c = 3.74 \text{ cm}$$

$$d = \text{Normal diameter} = \frac{d_c}{0.8} = 4.67 \text{ cm.}$$

## PROBLEMS

**1. Sketch a typical machine frame and discuss its design.**

**2. Sketch a valve gear mechanism of an I.C. engine.**

**3. Discuss the materials commonly used for making valves of an I.C. engine.**

**4. Describe the various types of pipe joints.**

**5. Design a high pressure hydraulic pipe joints to connect two steel pipes of 60 mm bore at a working pressure of 150 kg/cm$^2$. The allowable**

stress in pipe material is 800 kg/cm$^2$ and allowable stress in bolts is 600 kg/cm$^2$. Allowable stress in flanges is 850 kg/cm$^2$.

**6.** Design a crane hook of trapezoidal cross-section for 8 tonnes crane. Assume suitable values of stresses. The weight of hook and weight of other accessories on the hook is 0.6 tonnes.

**7.** Sketch and design an oval flanged pipe joint to connect two pipes of 40 mm bore subjected to a fluid pressure of 70 kg/cm$^2$. The stresses are as follows :

Allowable stress in pipes = 700 kg/cm$^2$

Allowable stress in bolts = 600 kg/cm$^2$

Allowable stress in flanges = 750 kg/cm$^2$.

**8.** Name the materials commonly used for the following parts :

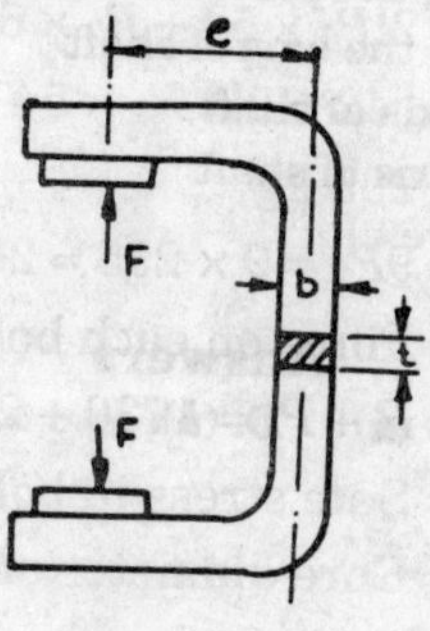


Fig. 18.30.

(*a*) Pipes (*b*) Rocker arm (*c*) Crane hook.

**9.** Fig. 18.30 shows C-clamp. The load ($F$) on the clamp is 4000 kg. If $e$ = 18 cm and $b = 3t$, calculate the dimension $b$ and $t$ assuming safe stress in the clamp as 900 kg/cm$^2$.

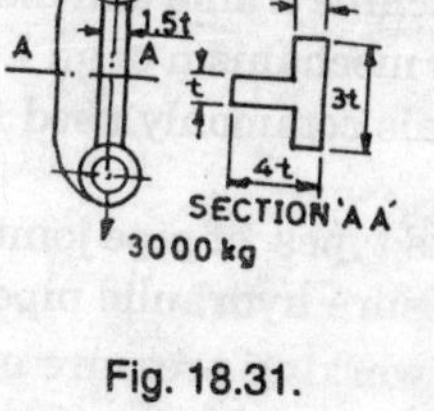


Fig. 18.31.

**10.** Fig. 18.31 shows a cast iron link. Determine the dimension *t* if safe stress in link is 800 kg/cm$^2$.

**11.** Tick mark the correct answer.

(*A*) The eccentric straps are made somewhat thicker at the point where they are bolted in order to avoid.

(*a*) Torsion (*b*) Shear
(*c*) Bending (*d*) None of the above.

(*B*) The flywheel hub diameter usually various between

(*a*) 2*d* to 2.5*d* (*b*) 2.5*d* to 3.5*d*
(*c*) 3.5*d* to 4*d* (*d*) none of the above.

(*C*) The pulley hub length usually various between

(*a*) *B*/3 to *B* (*b*) *B* to 1.5*B*
(*c*) 1.5*B* to 2*B*

where *B* is width of pulley rim.

(*D*) In foot step bearing the pressure acts

(*a*) Perpendicular to the axis of shaft
(*b*) Parallel to the axis of shaft
(*c*) Inclined to the axis of shaft
(*d*) None of the above.

## Answers

**A.** (*c*) **B.** (*a*) **C.** (*a*) **D.** (*b*).

# 19

# Manufacturing Considerations in Design

## 19.1. Introduction

While designing a component it should be ensured that it will be easier to manufacture the component. Manufacturing of components should be economical to reduce the cost of the component.

Following measures help in reducing the manufacturing cost of a component.

(*i*) Improved materials, tools and processes.

(*ii*) Automation wherever it contributes to greater efficiency.

(*iii*) **Standardisation.** Use of as many standard parts as possible should be made. Standardised products have better quality and are more reliable giving higher service in life.

(*iv*) Provide as large a tolerance on the components as possible consistent with functional requirements.

(*v*) Such features which are difficult to machine and require the use of special tools or fixtures should be avoided.

(*vi*) The cost of the component should be low, cost of production is costly associated with the following ;

(*a*) Material

(*b*) Manufacturing process.

(*c*) Quality.

(*vii*) Design the component so that workpiece when gripped in the work holding device is sufficiently by rigid to withstand the machining forces.

(*viii*) Assembly of components should be easier. For this :

(*a*) Ensure that each operating machined surface on a component has a corresponding machined surfaces on the mating component.

(*b*) Ensure that internal corners do not interfere with a corresponding external corner on the mating component.

(*ix*) Initial design should be based on kinematic principles and then modified to suit load and wear requirements.

## 19.2. Design Principles of or Manufacture

Some of the design principles which should be considered while deciding the manufacturing of components by different manufacturing methods are as follows. They help in reducing manufacturing cost.

(*i*) **Drilling.** It is not desirable to design a component in which drilling is to be carried out as shown in Fig. 19.1. It is easier to drill a component with flat surfaces as shown in Fig. 19.2.

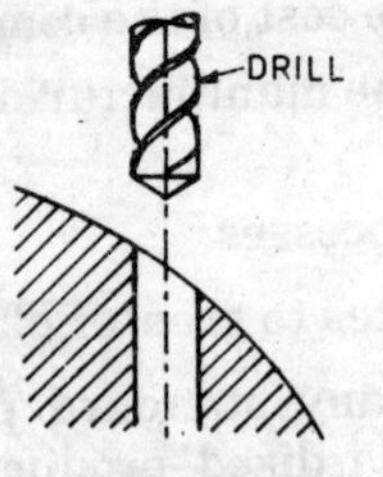


Fig. 19.1.

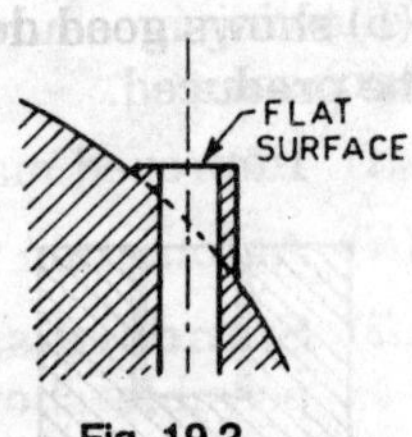


Fig. 19.2.

Similarly drill may snag as shown in (Fig. 19.3 (*a*)] as compared to part shown in [Fig. 19.3 (*b*)] which is a better design for drilling.

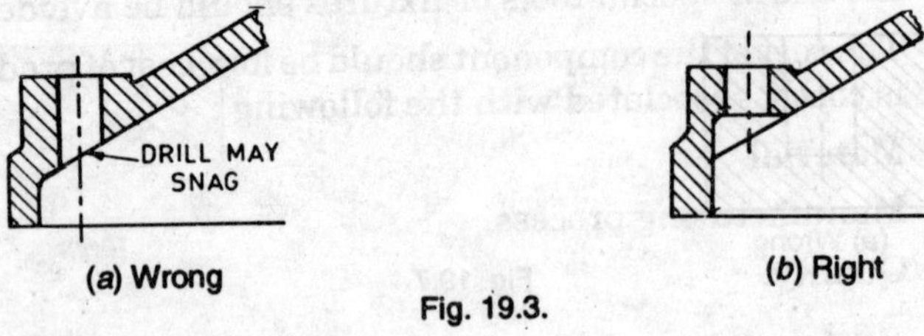


(*a*) Wrong (*b*) Right

Fig. 19.3.

Fig 19.4.(*a*) shows poor design of a flange in which hole is to be drilled. Fig. 19.4 (*b*) shows better design.

(*a*) Poor (*b*) Good

Fig. 19.4.

(*ii*) **Under cut.** It is desirable to design an under cut for tool run out when threading up to shoulders (See Fig. 19.5).

(*a*) Poor (*b*) Good

Fig. 19.5

Fig. 19.6 (*a*) shows a poorly designed component whereas Fig. 19.6 (*b*) shows good design of the same component in which a hole is to be produced.

(*a*) (*b*)

Fig. 19.6

It is easier to produce internal threads as shown in Fig. 19.7 (*b*) as compared to producing internal threads shown in Fig. 19.7 (*a*).

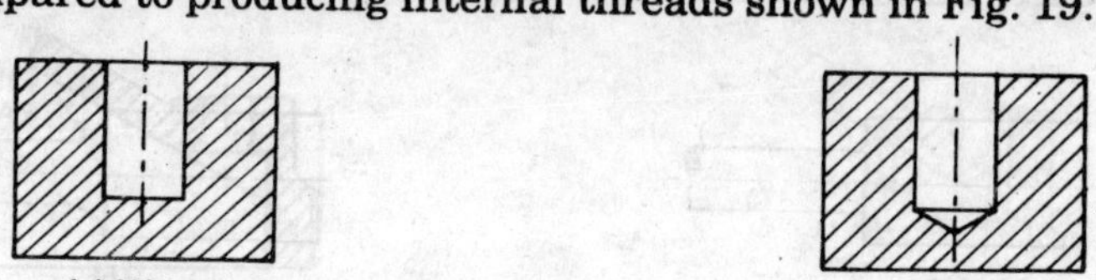

(*a*) Wrong (*b*) Right

Fig. 19.7

Fig. 19.8.

It is different to grind surface $AB$ of work piece as shown in Fig. 19.9 ($a$) whereas by providing an undercut to allow tool travel it becomes easier to grind surface $AB$ as shown in Fig. 19.9 ($b$).

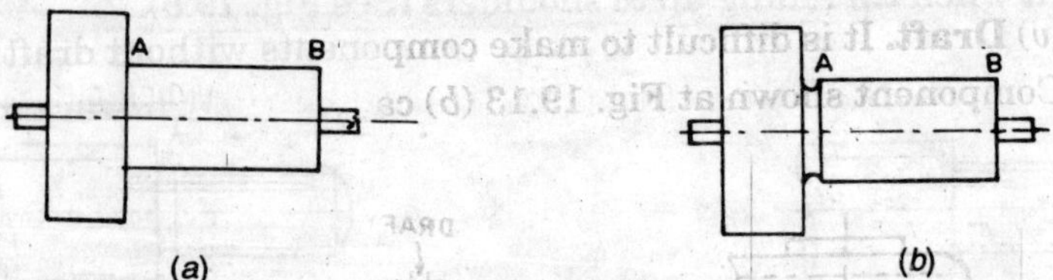


Fig. 19.9.

It is easier to hold the component shown in Fig. 19.10 ($b$) as compared to component shown in Fig. 19.10 ($a$) because the component shown in Fig. 19.10 ($b$) can be easily held at $AB$ and $CD$ during machining.

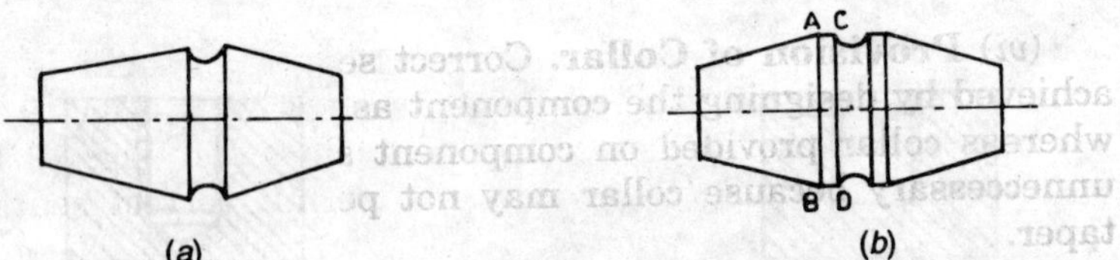


Fig. 19.10.

(*iii*) **Fillet.** A shaft with fillet is preferred Fig. 19.11 ($b$) as component to a shaft without a fillet Fig. 19.11 ($a$) because there will be less stress concentration in shaft with fillet.

Fig. 19.11.

(*iv*) **Boss.** It is better to omit outside boss as shown in Fig. 19.12 (*b*).

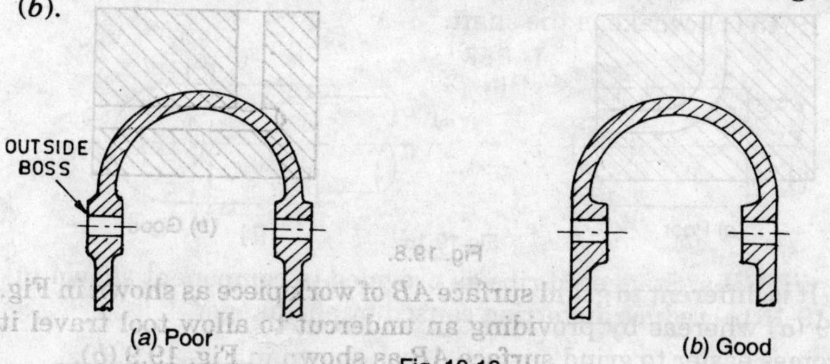


Fig. 19.12

(*v*) **Draft.** It is difficult to make components without draft. Component shown at Fig. 19.13 (*b*) can be easily produced.

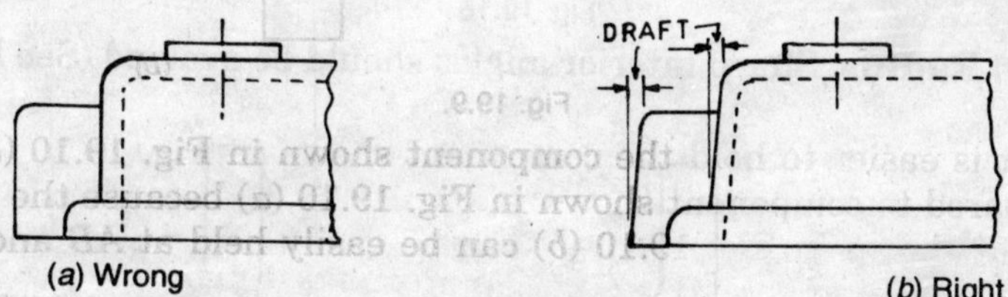


Fig. 19.13.

(*vi*) **Provision of Collar.** Correct seating of taper is better achieved by designing the component as shown in Fig. 19.14 (*a*) whereas collar provided on component shown in Fig. 19.14 (*b*) unneccessary because collar may not permit correct seating of taper.

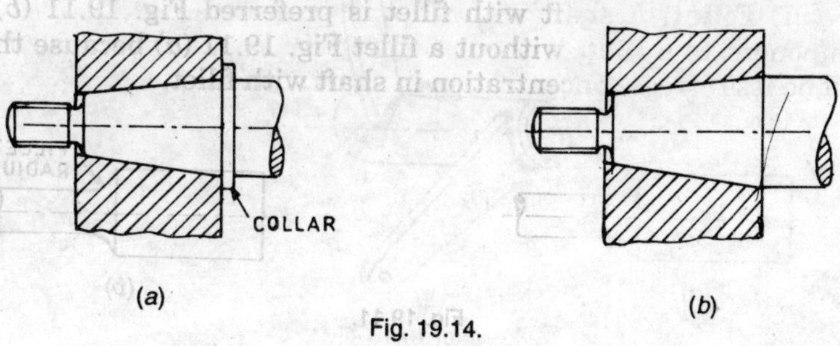


Fig. 19.14.

(*vii*) **Use of taper pin.** Use of taper pin through centre of shaft [Fig. 19.15 (*a*)] weakens the shaft.

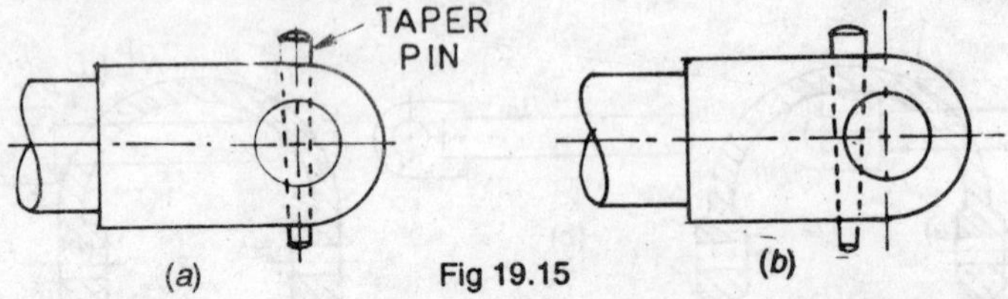


Fig 19.15

(*viii*) **Ribs.** Staggered ribs as provided in component shown in Fig. 19.16 (*b*) reduce distortion caused by shrinkage.

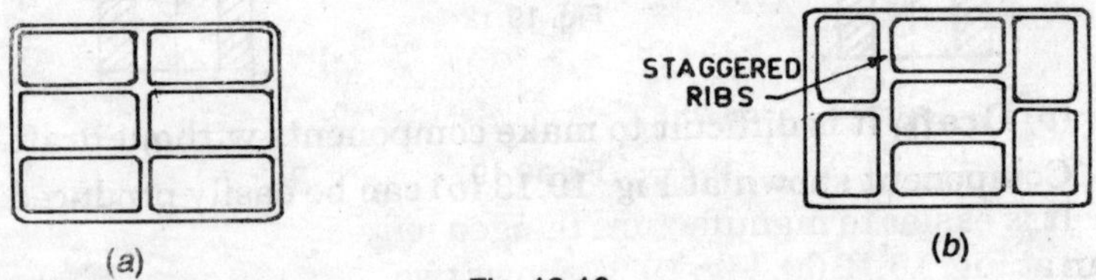


Fig. 19.16

(*ix*) **Radius.** Sharp interior angles should be avoided (See Fig. 19.17).

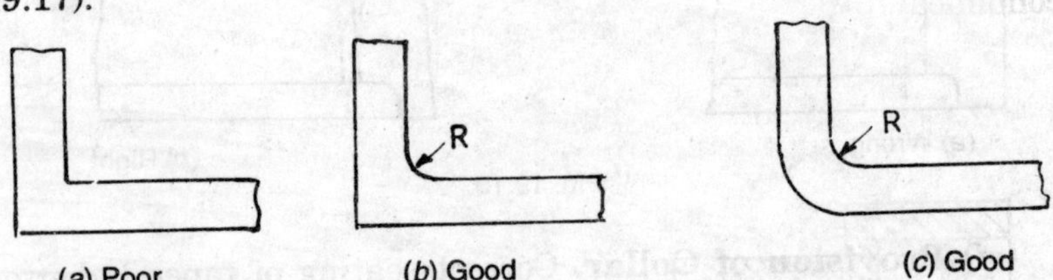


Fig. 19.17

(*x*) **Use of economical manufacturing method.** As far as possible manufacturing method cost should be low. The lever shown at Fig. 19.18 should be fabricated by welding as compared to making the lever by casting process to keep the initial cost low.

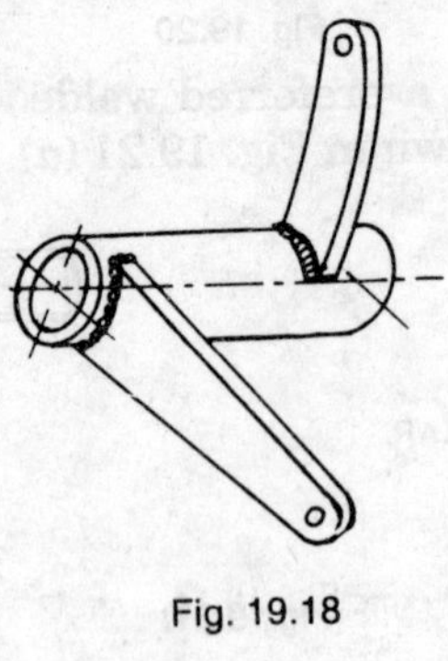

Fig. 19.18

Fig 19.19 shows a component that can be made in three ways. However cost of making component by welding will be low.

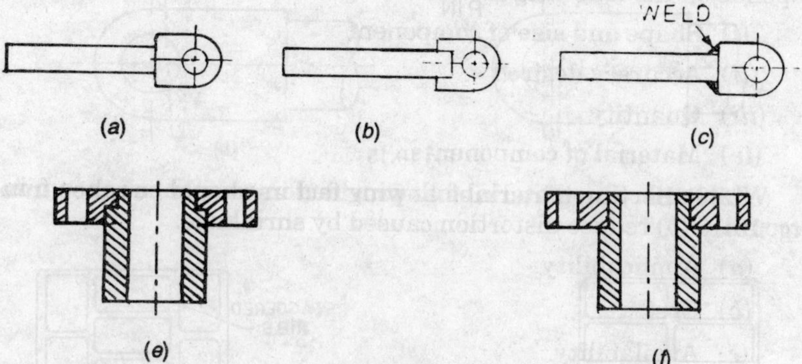


Fig 19.19

It is easier to manufacture flanged joint shown in Fig. 19.19 (*d*) than at Fig. 19.19 (*c*). Fig. 19.20 shows two methods namely machining and fabrication by welding of manufacturing a component. Fabrication by welding making use of tubular stock may be economical.

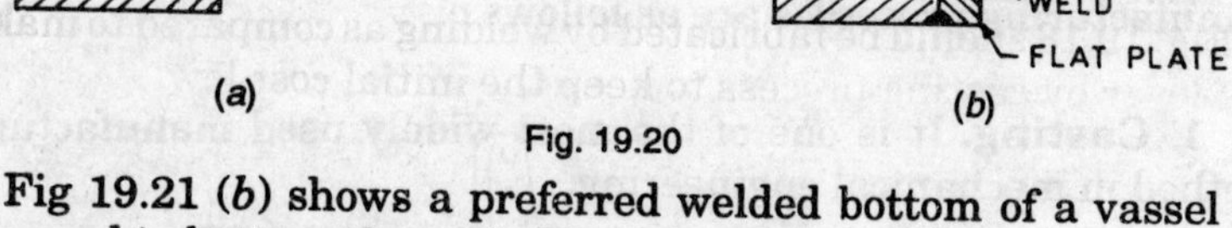


Fig. 19.20

Fig 19.21 (*b*) shows a preferred welded bottom of a vassel as compared to bottom shown in Fig. 19.21 (*a*).

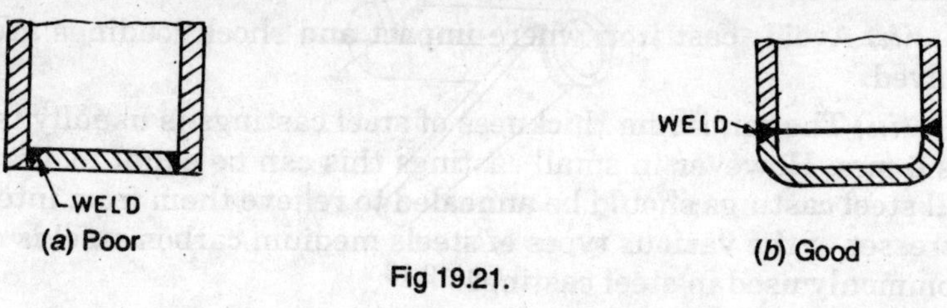


Fig 19.21.

## 19.3. Manufacturing Processes

The manufacturing processes used to manufacture component depends on the following factors :

(*i*) Shape and size of component

(*ii*) Accuracy desired

(*iii*) Quantity

(*iv*) Material of components.

While selecting material following factors should be taken into account :

(*a*) Applicability

(*b*) Cost

(*c*) Availability

(*d*) Machinability.

(*e*) Amount of machining required.

(*f*) Utilise raw material in the standard form supplied out of machining, welding, casting, forging etc. that method should be used for manufacturing a component which had least cost keeping into view quality.

For example frames and housings of machine tools can be economically manufactured by casting as compared to welding and machining methods.

Sections of castings below 3 mm in thickness is different to cast and in such cases a minimum of 3 mm can be provided even through lesser values may withstand the loads.

Some of the points to be considered during design for different manufacturing processes are as follows :

1. **Casting.** It is one of the most widely used manufacturing method in mechanical engineering.

(*i*) Cast iron is much stronger in compression. Therefore cast iron castings should be loaded in compression as far as possible.

(*ii*) Avoid cast iron where impact and shock loadings are involved.

(*iii*) The minimum thickness of steel castings is usually taken as 6 mm. However in small castings this can be equal to 4.5 mm. All steel castings should be annealed to relieve them from internal stresses of the various types of steels medium carbon steel is most commonly used in steel castings.

(*iv*) Only certain non-ferrous alloys can be economically cast such as zinc, aluminium.

(*v*) Due to high cost of dies and machines, die casting is economical only for mass production.

Die castings are made by forcing molten metal under high pressure into a metal could called a die.

(*vi*) Patterns should be provided with ample draft for their early withdrawal from the mould.

2. **Forging.** Forged parts can be manufactured with fairly close dimensional tolerances. This method results in substantial saving in material.

(*i*) Adequate draft should be provided to permit easy removal of the forgings from the dies. Inside draft angle is about 7 – 10° and out side draft angle is 56 – 70°.

(*ii*) The parting line, if possible, should divide the forging about in half.

(*iii*) Sections should not be thin as to restrict the flow of metal.

(*iv*) Ample fillet and curvatures should be given to the forgings.

3. **Welding.** Welding is especially suitable for low quantity production to reduce time and cost to and to avoid a foundry pattern or a forging die. Low carbon steels can be easily welded. It results in saving in material and manufacturing cost while designing welded structures following factors should be considered.

(*i*) Welds should not be subjected to bending.

(*ii*) A weld should not be located at the point of maximum deformation.

(*iii*) Parts to be welded should be arranged so that there is sufficient clearance for the welding operation.

(*iv*) For general machine elements most welds are fillet welds though but welds are used a great deal in designing pressure vessels.

(*v*) Limit the number of welds used.

4. **Machining.** Machined parts can have better surface finish. The machining operations giving high class of accuracy and surfaces finish will be more expensive whenever two machine parts are assembled. The type of joint and class of accuracy will depend on

the surface roughness of the mating surfaces. Machining methods like turning, shaping, milling, drilling etc. produce components having sufficient accuracy.

## 19.4. Tolerances

Tolerances in design influence the producibility of the end product in many ways. Tolerances cover dimensional variations and surfaces roughness range and also the variation in mechanical properties resulting from heat treatment and other processing operations. Large tolerances help in easy manufacturing and also lasser parts will be rejected during inspection process.

## 19.5. Surface Roughness

Selection of class of accuracy and surface finish is a vital stage in design. Higher the accuracy required in the part manufactured high will be the class of surface finish which means smaller irregularities of the surface.

There are two methods of assessing the surface roughness.

(*i*) Root mean square (R.M.S.) method

(*ii*) Centre Line Average (C.L.A.) method.

In both these methods the surface roughness is measured as the average deviation from a nominal surface.

Tolerance provided should be as large as possible to keep manufacturing cost low.

Table 19.1 indicates the surface roughness values for some of the manufacturing methods.

**Table 19.1**

| *S. No.* | *Manufacturing Process* | *Surface roughness (microns)* |
|---|---|---|
| 1. | Lapping | 0.012 to 0.016 |
| 2. | Honoring | 0.025 to 0.40 |
| 3. | Cylinder grinding surface grinding, diamond turning, Diamond boring | 0.063 to 5 |
| 4. | Reaming broaching | 0.4 to 3.2 |
| 5. | Turning | 0.32 to 25 |

*(Contd...)*

| *S. No.* | *Manufacturing Process* | *Surface roughness (microns)* |
|---|---|---|
| 6. | Boring | 0,4 to 6.3 |
| 7. | Milling | 0.32 to 25 |
| 8. | Planning, shaping, drilling | 1.6 to 25 |
| 9. | Press work | 2.5 to 50 |
| 10. | Forging | 1.6 to 2.5 |
| 11. | Sand casting | 5 to 50 |
| 12. | Die casting | 0.8 to 3.2 |

## 19.6. Standardisation

Standardisation is defined as the establishing of desirable criteria with respect to the size, shape, quality etc. of a product. A standard is a set of specifications for parts, materials or processes intended to achieve, unformity, efficiency and a specified quality shapes and dimensions of the following parts are standardised in order to make their use in standard form.

(*i*) Fasteners such as nuts, bolts, keys, screws, revets, cotters.

(*ii*) Power transmission devices like belts, ropes, couplings, electric motors.

(*iii*) Pumps.

(*iv*) Bearings.

Various advantages of standardisation are as follows:

(*i*) Standardisation of manufacturing method helps to reduce manufacturing cost.

(*ii*) Standardisation of testing methods helps in improving quality of product.

(*iii*) Use of standard parts, materials etc. helps in reducing labour cost.

(*iv*) Replacement of worn out or damaged parts by standard ones reduces maintenance cost.

(*v*) Standardisation products have better quality and are more reliable giving higher service life.

## PROBLEMS

**1.** Discuss the relative merits and demerits of following manufacturing methods.

(*a*) Machining (*b*) Welding

(*c*) Casting (*d*) Forging.

**2.** State the factors which help in reducing manufacturing cost of a component.

**3.** Discuss some of design principles for the manufacturing of a component.

**4.** Write short notes on :

(*i*) Standardisation

(*ii*) Surface roughness.

# 20

# Seals and Gaskets

## 20.1: Seals

They are used to prevent leakage of liquids, and gases. They are also used to seal dirt and contaminants. The selection of seal depends on the following factors.

(*i*) Pressure of fluid.

(*ii*) Temperature of fluid.

(*iii*) Corrosive atmosphere.

(*iv*) Shaft speed.

## 20.2. Types of Seals

The various types of seals are as follows :

(*i*) Face seals.

(*ii*) Dynamic shaft seals.

(*iii*) Split ring seals.

(*iv*) Diaphragm seal.

(*v*) Labyrinth seal.

1. **Face Seals.** They provide a pressure tight seal between shaft and housing. They can operate successfully both statically and dynamically and under wide diversity of medium, temperature, pressure and speeds. The shaft material, finish, roughness and hardness are not highly critical.

Two basic elements of a complete seal are as follows :

(*i*) **Seal head unit.** Tins incorporates the housing, end face member and the spring assembly.

(*ii*) **Seal seat.** This is the mating member.

Seal head may be stationary or rotating. These seals can be used up to the 210 kg/cm$^2$ for speeds as high as 15000 mpm and for temperature between – 200°C to 50°C.

Face seals may be made of :

(*i*) Resin (*ii*) Carbon

(*iii*) Ceramic (*iv*) Metal.

Resin seals can resist temperature. – 15°C to 100°C. Ceramic and carbon seals can be used up to 260°C. Metal seals can also be used up to 260°C. The metals used may be bronze, satellite, steel. They can be used with oils, fuels, and fuels compatible with corrosion resistance of the metal.

2. **Dynamic shaft seals.** These seals are quite commonly used in more dynamic applications because of the following reasons.

(*i*) They have the versatility of meeting requirements of shaft speed, pressure and temperature.

(*ii*) They have relatively high insensitivity to dimensional variations.

(*iii*) They have positive sealing ability.

(*iv*) The can work successfully in varying lubricating conditions.

(*v*) Low cost.

They are often referred to as oil seals or shaft seals.

The common materials used for shaft seals are as follows :

(*i*) Nitrile

(*ii*) Poly acrylic

(*iii*) Leather

(*iv*) Silicon.

Nitrile can be used from – 1°C to 77°C and it has excellent abrasion resistance.

Polyacrylic seals can be used from – 1°C to 180°C and have fair resistance to abrasion.

Leather can be used from – 10°C to 96°C. It has excellent resistance to abrasion.

The temperature range for silicon seals is – 27°C to 260°C.

Radial lip seals for rotating shafts are of following types :

(*i*) Single lip

(*ii*) Single lip spring loaded

(*iii*) Double lip spring loaded.

Fig. 20.1 shows an oil seal for rotating shaft.

*A* indicates rubber seal. *B* indicates metal reinforcement whereas spring is indicated by *C*.

Table 20.1 indicates the various dimensions of an oil seal.

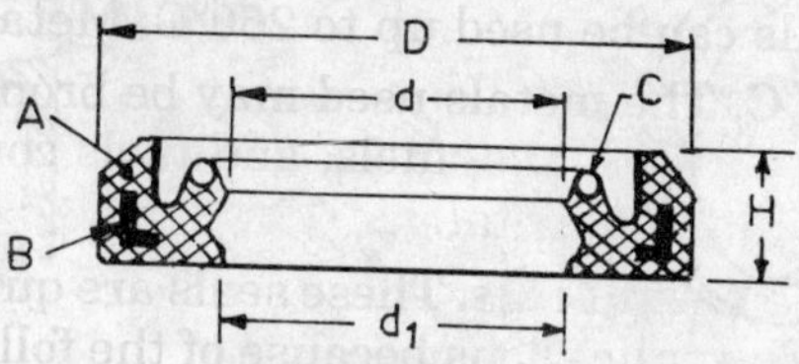


Fig. 20.1.

**Table 20.1**

| *Shaft Diameter* | | | | |
|---|---|---|---|---|
| *(mm)* | *d (mm)* | $d_1$*(mm)* | *D (mm)* | *H (mm)* |
| 6 | 5.8 | | 22 | 7 |
| 10 | 9.8 | — | 25 | 7 |
| 15 | 14.8 | — | 30 | 7 |
| 20 | 19.8 | 19 | 40 | 10 |
| 25 | 24.8 | 24 | 42 | 10 |
| 30 | 29.7 | 29 | 52 | 10 |
| 35 | 34.7 | 34 | 58 | 10 |
| 40 | 39.7 | 39 | 60 | 10 |
| 50 | 49.7 | 49 | 70 | 10 |
| 70 | 69.7 | 69 | 95 | 10 |
| 90 | 89.7 | 89 | 120 | 12 |
| 100 | 99.6 | 99 | 125 | 12 |
| 150 | 149.5 | 148.5 | 180 | 15 |
| 200 | 199.5 | 198.5 | 240 | 15 |

3. **Split ring seals.** These seals are used commonly in internal combustion engines, steam engines, compressor etc. They are usually of rectangular cross-section and are split to make them resilient as shown in Fig. 20.2. They are slipped over the piston whose surface has grooves of same profile as the ring seals.

Fig. 20.3 shows split ring seals in position on a piston of steam engine.

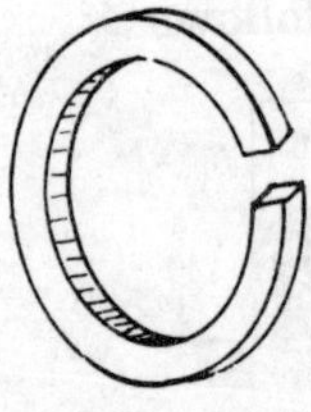

Fig. 20.2.

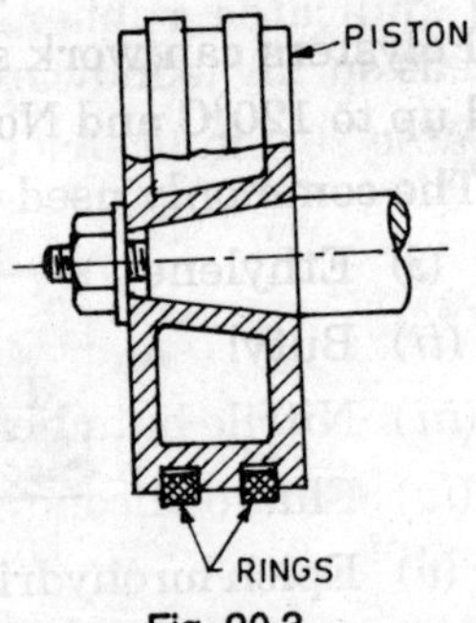


Fig. 20.3.

4. **Felt Seals.** They are the sealing devices which are applied in large quantities to prevent leakage of oil or grease from relatively simple systems. They serve two purposes.

(*i*)To prevent dust and dirt from penetrating into closed system.

(*ii*)To prevent lubricants from leakage to atmosphere.

Fig. 20.4 (*a*) shows a conventical belt seal and Fig. 20.4 (*b*) shows cupped ring type felt seal.

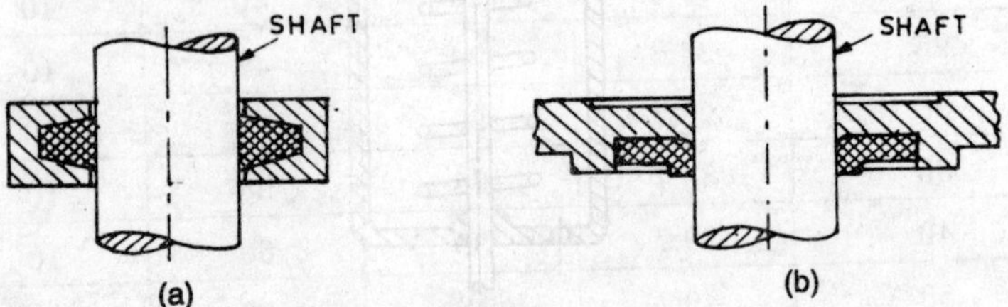


Fig. 20.4.

5. **Diaphragm seals.** They are used in two types.

(*i*) Flat diaphragm seals.

(*ii*) Rolling diaphragm seals.

Flat diaphram has got no convolutions or convolutions less than 180°. A rolling diaphragm has full 180° convolutions. A rolling diaphragm is used as a long travel bellow or redially sealed hydraulic piston with zero leakage.

A diaphragm is made of fabric which is impregnated with an elastomer for impermeability.

The commonly used fabrics are as follows :

(*i*) Polysters
(*ii*) Nylon
(*iii*) Nomex.

Polysters can work successfully up to 180°C whereas nylon is used up to 120°C and Nomex fabric can resist temp. up to 260°C.

The commonly used elastomers are as follows :

(*i*) Ethylene
(*ii*) Butyl
(*iii*) Nitrile butadiene
(*iv*) Fluorosilicone
(*v*) Epich lorohydrin.

Fig. 20.5 shows a rolling diaphragm seal.

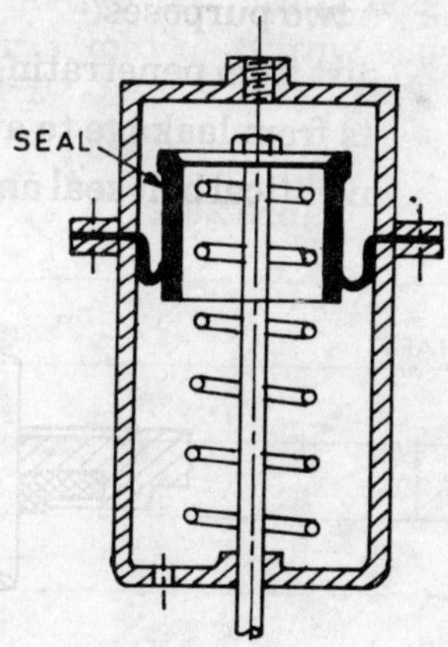


Fig. 20.5.

6. **Labyrinth seals.** These are dynamic types of seals. They are mostly used in heavy industrial power and air craft applications where relatively high leakage rates can be tolerated and design simplicity is a necessity. They are also called clearance seals because these limit the leakage by closely controlling the annular

clearance between a rotating or reciprocating shafts and its relatively stationary housing.

Fig. 20.5 shows various types of Labyrinth seals.

Fig. 20.6 (*a*) shows seal with axial clearance whereas Fig. 20.6 (*b*) shows seal with radial clearance. Fig. 20.6 (*c*) shows interlocking seal.

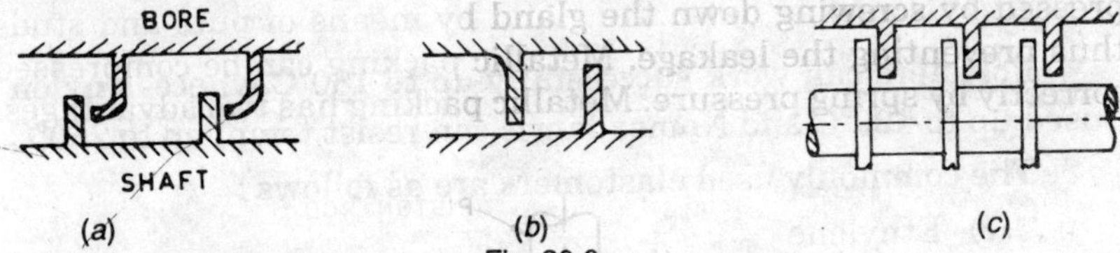


Fig. 20.6.

These seals have the following advantages:

(*i*) Reliability

(*ii*) Simplicity

(*iii*) Flexibility.

## 20.3. Packings

They are used to seal static and dynamic components. The various packing materials with their temperature limitations are shown in Table 20.2.

**Table 20.2.**

| *Material* | *Temperature* (°C) |
|---|---|
| Cotton | 100 |
| Asbestos and TFE Filament | 260 |
| Synthetic rubber | – 180 to 260 |
| Lead | 230 |
| Aluminium | 540 |
| Leather | 82 |
| Fabric reinforced rubber | 120 |

## 20.4. Compression Packings

They are used in pumps, valves, piston to seal hot water, steam and other hot fluids.

Packings are made of hempen rope, asbestos, rubber rope, or soft metals. The compression packings are placed between shaft and housing. Fig. 20.7 shows a tuffing box for steam engine. It uses a compression packing which is placed in the annular space surrounding the piston rod between bush and gland. The packing is compressed by screwing down the gland by means of nuts and studs thus preventing the leakage. Metallic packing can be compressed correctly by spring pressure. Metallic packing has two advantages.

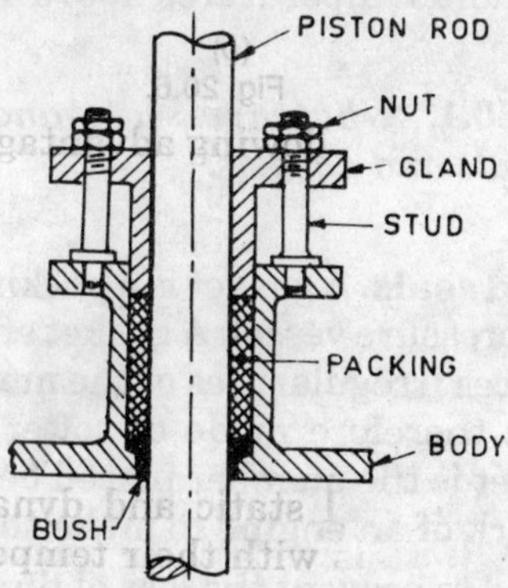


Fig. 20.7.

(*i*) It can be successfully used for high pressure steam.

(*ii*) It is not burnt by intense heat.

## 20.5. Moulded Packings

The packings usually do not need gland adjustment. Fig.20.8 shows a commonly used cup packing.

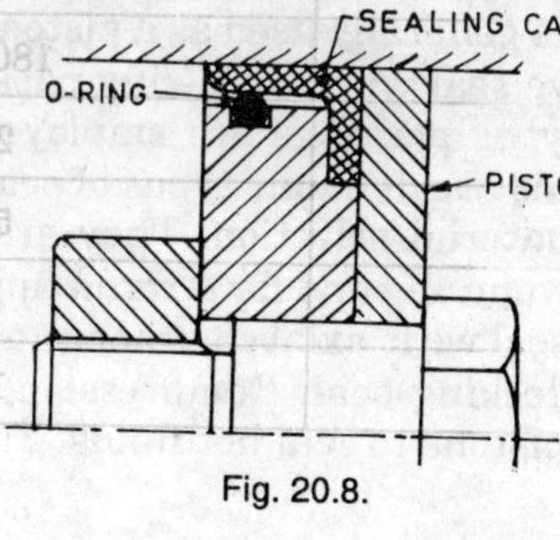


Fig. 20.8.

## 20.6. Gaskets

They provide sealing by deforming and filling surface irregularities of the members between which they are placed. Gaskets may be made of the following materials.

(*i*) **Metals.** The metals commonly used for making gaskets are copper, aluminium, soft iron, monel metal, lead, brass.

(*ii*) **Non-metals.** Non-metals used for making gaskets are cork, rubber, paper, leather, and asbestos products cork and rubber gaskets can resist temperature up to 70°C whereas asbestos products gaskets can resist temperature upto 260°C. Generally a non-metallic gasket should not be used for pressures in excess of about 85 kg/cm$^2$ and temperatures above 450°C and below – 18°C.

**Example. 20.1.** *What are seals and Gaskets. Sketch and describe some seals and gaskets.*

**Solution.**

**Gaskets and seals.** A gasket is a packing and is used to prevent loss of fluid in a pressure vessel. A gasket effects a seal by deforming and filling surfaces irregularities of the members between which it is placed and is therefore made of softer material. The common example of gasket is the member placed between the cylinder head and cylinder block of an engine to make the joint tight.

A seal is used to prevent the loss of fluid in a sliding or rotating joint. Seals are also used to seal out dirt and fluids and to allow a controlled atmosphere within a sealed volume. The selection of a seal depends upon the following factors :

(*i*) Type and properties of medium to be sealed.

(*ii*) Temperature and pressure of sealed medium.

(*iii*) Speed and direction of movement of sealed parts.

Fig. 20.9 shows various types of gaskets and seals.

The O-ring seal is generally used as a piston seal in a hydraulic cylinder or as a valve seal whereas V-ring packing are assembled in multiples. Cup types packings are employed for reciprocating parts. Labyrinth seals are dynamic types of seals and are reliable, simple flexible in material selection. They are generally used in heavy industrial power units and for aircraft applications. Fig. 20.9 (*e*) shows labyrinth seal with axial clearance and Fig. 20.9 (*f*) shows labyrinth non-interlocking seal. Compression packing is used in pumps, valves and pistons to seal hot fluids. Fig. 20.10 shows ring type flange joint for pressure service. To maintain a fluid tight joint it is necessary that the parts be tightly bolted together.

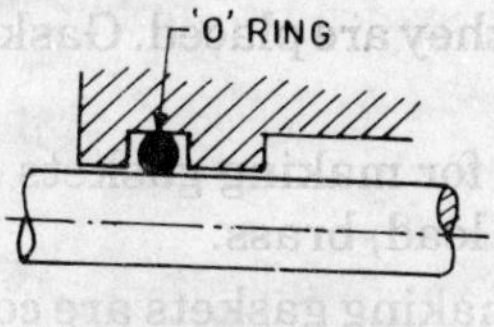


(*a*) O-ring packing

(*b*) V-Ring packing

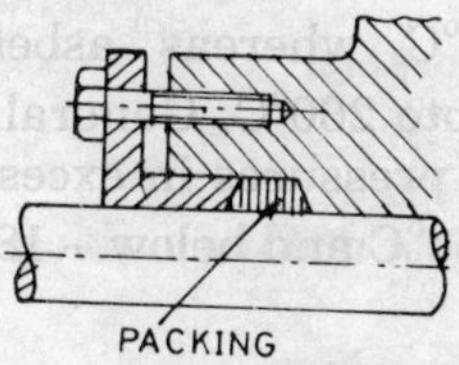


(*a*) Compression packing

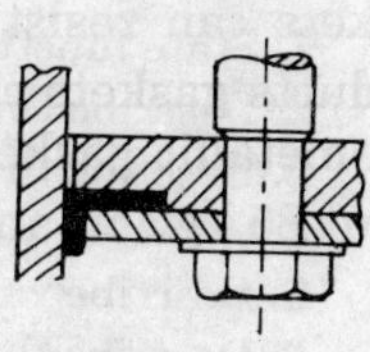

(*b*) Cup packing

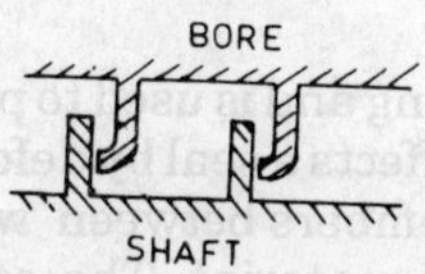


(*e*) Labyrinth seals

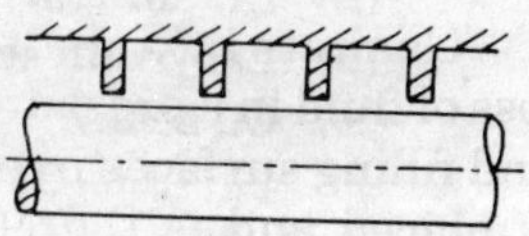

(*f*)

Fig. 20.9.

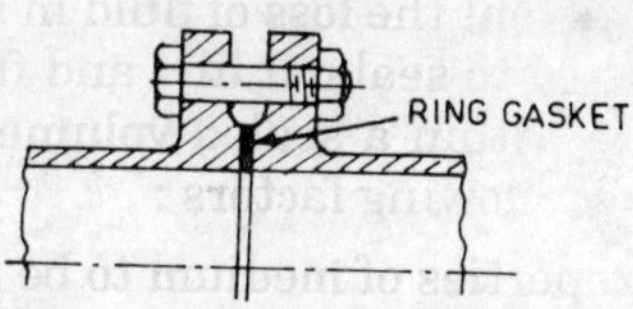


Fig. 20.10.

**Materials.** Materials used for gaskets should possess the following requirements :

(*i*) They should have high permeability.

(*ii*) They should be resistance to environmental deterioration.

(*iii*) They should have the ability to flow into joint irregularities on being compressed.

Gaskets may be made of non-metallic materials or metallic materials. The non-metallic materials commonly used are cork, rubber, asbestos. Such gaskets are quite commonly used up to 80 kg/cm$^2$ and 450 kg/cm$^2$. The metallic gaskets are generally made of copper, brass, aluminium, stainless steel, lead, and low carbon steels.

Seals may be made of resin, carbon, synthetic rubber, brass, stainless steel etc.

## PROBLEMS

**1.** State functions of seals, packings and gaskets.
**2.** Describe the various types of seals.
**3.** Describe the various materials used for seals.
**4.** What are the materials commonly used for making packing.
**5.** Describe various types of packings.
**6.** Describe the materials used for making gaskets.
**7.** Write short notes on the following :
(*i*) Compression packing
(*ii*) Diaphragm seal
(*iii*) Labyrinth seal
(*iv*) Oil seal.

# 21

## Objective Type Problems

1. The taper provided on a cotter is

(*a*) 1 : 25 (*b*) 1 : 30

(*c*) 1 : 40 (*d*) None of the above.

2. A cotter is generally made of

(*a*) Cast iron (*b*) High speed steel

(*c*) Gun metal (*d*) Mild steel.

3. In snap head of a rivet the height of head is

(*a*) 0.7 *d* (*b*) 0.9 *d*

(*c*) 0.5 *d*

where *d* is rivet diameter.

4. The polar moment of inertia of a circular shaft of diameter (*d*) is given by

(*a*) $\frac{\pi}{64} d^4$ (*b*) $\frac{\pi}{32} d^4$

(*c*) $\frac{\pi}{16} d^3$ (*d*) None of the above.

5. Modulus of resilience is given by

(*a*) $\frac{f^2}{4E}$ (*b*) $\frac{f^2}{2E}$

(c) $\frac{f^2}{6E}$ (d) None of the above

where $f$ is the stress and $E$ modulus of elasticity.

6. The standard taper on a taper pin is
   (a) 1 : 30 (b) 1 : 25
   (c) 1 : 48 (d) None of the above.

7. State whether the following statements are true or false
   (a) Most brittle materials have considerably higher value for ultimate strength in compression than for tension
   (b) Cotters are always inserted at right angle to the axis of the parts to be joined together
   (c) A brittle material has less resistance to separation than resistance to sliding
   (d) A ductile material is one whose resistance to sliding is smaller than its resistance to separation
   (e) A limit of about 5% elongation is usually taken as dividing line between ductile materials and brittle materials
   (f) In self locking screws the angle of friction is greater than the helix angle.

8. In worm gearing the axial pitch of worm ($p_a$) is related to circular pitch ($p$) of the gear as follows :
   (a) $p_a > p$ (b) $p_a < p$
   (c) $p_a = p$ (d) None of the above.

9. In worm gearing worm wheel is generally made of
   (a) Cast iron (b) Hard phosphor bronze
   (c) Brass (d) Wrought iron.

10. **Statements**
   (a) Bevel gears are not inter-changeable and are designed in pairs
   (b) The simplest type of a bearing to take a radial load is a plain journal bearing

(c) Ball and roller berings are known as antifriction bearings.

11. The maxin.um static load ($P_1$) which can be carried out by a roller bearing is given by

(a) $P_1 = 4.6\,F$ (b) $P_1 = \dfrac{5.6\,F}{z}$

(c) $P_1 = \dfrac{6\,6\,F}{z}$

where $F$ is the radial load and $z$ is number of balls per row.

12. State the advantages and disadvantages of worm gear drives.

13. **Statements**

(a) Ball bearings as compared to roller bearings are usually preferred for heavy loads

(b) Unlike roller bearings ball bearings present no problem of end thrust

(c) Horizontal belt drives should be arranged to run with tight side on the bottom

(d) Cast iron pipe is best suited for underground water lines and sewage

(e) Silent chains are used for high speed ratios whereas roller chains are used for low and medium service

(f) The addendum of a spur gear is greater than dedendum.

14. State the in hours for the ball bearings and roller bearings used for the following duties

(i) Domestic electrical appliances

(ii) Small fans

(iii) Light motor cycles

(iv) Heavy motor cycles and light cars

(v) Heavy cars and light trucks

(vi) Axle bearing for passenger train

(vii) Machine tool gears

(viii) Rope pulleys for conveyors.

15. **Fill in the blanks**

(*a*) The economical centre distance for flat belt drive is ....

(*b*) Fibre ropes can be used to transmit power up to a centre distance of about.....

(*c*) Wire ropes can be used to transmit power up to a centre distance of......

(*d*) The economical speed of fibrous ropes is....

(*e*) The commonly used angle of groove in pulley rim for cotton rope is.....

(*f*) V-belts should not be used at speeds above.....

16. State three limitations of V-belt drive as compared to flat belt drive.

17. Brake levers are manufactured from

(*a*) Cast steel (*b*) Cast iron

(*c*) Wrought iron.

18. The radius of friction circle ($r$) in an internal expanding shoe brake is given by

(*a*) $r = \mu R$ (*b*) $r = \frac{\mu}{R}$

(*c*) $r = \frac{R}{\mu}$

where $R$ is brake drum radius and $\mu$ is coefficient of friction.

19. The coefficient of friction for asbestos on cast iron as materials in contact in brakes is

(*a*) 0.2 to 0.25 (*b*) 0.15 to 0.2

(*c*) 0.3 to 0.4.

20. The most common value of cone face angle of cone clutch is

(*a*) 6.5° (*b*) 12.5°

(*c*) 18.5°.

21. **Statements**

(*a*) The square jaw clutch can be driven in both the directions of rotation

(*b*) Spiral jaw clutch can be driven in one direction only

(*c*) A brake is said to be self energising when the moment of frictional force is in the same direction as by that the brake actuating force

(*d*) A brake is said to be self locking when the brake gets applied only by frictional force without the application of actuating force.

(*e*) Now-a-days all automotive brakes are pivoted internal shoe brakes.

(*f*) More the angle of twist more will be the stiffness of shaft.

22. In bell crank lever the height of lever ($h$) is related to its thickness $t$ as

(*a*) $h = 5t$ (*b*) $h = 10t$

(*c*) $h = 15t$ (*d*) None of the above.

23. The bearing pressure for pin at fulcrum in rocker arm for exhaust valve of a gas engine varies from

(*a*) 10 to 20 kg/cm$^2$ (*b*) 30 to 60 kg/cm$^2$

(*c*) 100 to 150 kg/cm$^2$ (*d*) None of the above.

24. The ratio length ($L$) and diameter ($D$) of pin at fulcrum of bell crank lever is usually taken as

(*a*) $\frac{L}{D} = 1.25$ (*b*) $\frac{L}{D} = 2.25$

(*c*) $\frac{L}{D} = 3.25$.

25. The ratio of internal diameter ($d$) and thickness ($t$) usually considered a line of demarcation between thin and thick cylinders is

(*a*) 40 (*b*) 60

(*c*) 20 (*d*) None of the above.

26. Name three non-metallic materials used for gaskets.

27. Fill in the blanks.
   (*a*) Generally a non-metallic gasket should not be used for pressures in excess of about..... and temperatures above.....
   (*b*) Cork and rubber gaskets are best suited at temperature below....
   (*c*) In a pressure vessel the longitudinal stress is.... the circumferential or hoop or tangential stress.

28. Name the materials commonly used for the following components :
   (*a*) Cylinder of a hydraulic press
   (*b*) Connecting rod of high speed power fuel engine
   (*c*) Piston of an I.C. engine
   (*d*) Piston rod of steam engine
   (*e*) Piston of steam engine
   (*f*) Eccentric sheaves, straps and eccentric rod.

29. For cast iron yield strength is quite often assumed to be
   (*a*) 0.6 × ultimate strength
   (*b*) 0.3 × ultimate strength
   (*c*) 0.9 × ultimate strength.

30. Compare horse power transmitted, peripheral speed and speed ratio of the following power transmission drives
   (*a*) Flat belt (*b*) V-belt
   (*c*) Spur gears (*d*) Chain drive.

31. The rocker arm of valve gear mechanism of an I.C. engine is made of
   (*a*) Gun metal (*b*) Cast steel
   (*c*) Wrought iron.

32. The module ($m$) of a spur gear is given by

(a) $\frac{T}{D}$ (b) $\frac{D}{T}$

(c) $D \times T$ (d) None of the these

where $D$ is P.C.D. of gear and $T$ is the number of teeth.

33. The bolts of a flange coupling are designed in

(a) Shear (b) Tension

(c) Compression.

34. In the formula H.P. = $\frac{2\pi NT}{4500}$ the torque ($T$) obtained as

(a) Minimum (b) Maximum

(c) Average.

35. The thickness of a cylindrical shell is designed on the basis of

(a) Hoop stress (b) Longitudinal stress

(c) None of the above.

36. It is preferred to use cast iron for machine parts subjected to

(a) Compressive load (b) Tensile load

(c) Impact load.

37. Spring index ($c$) is defined as

(a) $\frac{d}{D}$ (b) $\frac{D}{d}$

(c) $D \times d$ (d) None of the above

where $D$ is mean diameter of coil and $d$ is the diameter of spring wire.

38. State three application of riveted joints.

39. The thickness ($t_1$) of cover plates in double cover plates butt joints is given by

(a) $t_1 = \frac{5}{8} t$ (b) $t_1 = \frac{9}{7} t$

(c) $t_1 = \frac{3}{8} t$

where $t$ is the thickness of plates to be joined together.

40. The efficiency of single riveted lap joint is about

(a) 75 to 85% (b) 65 to 75%

(c) 45 to 65%.

41. The hydraulic pipe joint having oval flanges is used to connect pipes subjected to a maximum fluid pressure of

(a) 145 kg/cm² (b) 85 kg/cm²

(c) 45 kg/cm² (d) None of the above.

42. State the difference between key and cotter.

43. The frames of heavy duty machines are made of

(a) Cast iron (b) Cast steel

(c) High speed steel (d) None of the above.

44. Define the following :

(a) Journal (b) Key

(c) Rack.

45. The usual value of drive ratio for salient chains is

(a) The usual value ratio for salient chains is

(b) 6 : 1 (b) 12 : 1

(c) 18 : 1 (d) None of the above.

46. The Poisson's ratio $\left(\frac{1}{m}\right)$ is related to lateral strain ($e_1$) and liner strain ($e_2$) as

(a) $\frac{1}{m} = \frac{e_1}{e_2}$ (b) $\frac{1}{m} = \frac{e_2}{e_1}$

(c) $\frac{1}{m} = e_1 \times e_2$ (d) None of the above.

47. The effective length ($l$) of a column hinged at both ends as compared to its actual length ($L$) is

(*a*) $l = 2L$ (*b*) $l = L$

(*c*) $l = \frac{L}{\sqrt{2}}$ (*d*) $l = \frac{L}{2}$.

48. Foot step bearing is used to support

(*a*) Vertical shaft (*b*) Horizontal shaft

(*c*) Both (*a*) and (*b*).

49. Which of the following cast iron is more machinable

(*a*) White cast iron (*b*) Grey cast iron

(*c*) Malleable cast iron.

50. The threads provided on the screw of screw jack are generally of form

(*a*) Vee (*b*) Square

(*c*) Acme (*d*) Any other type.

51. In the formula $\frac{T_1}{T_2} = e^{\mu\theta}$, the angle (θ) should be taken in open belt drive

(*a*) For smaller pulley

(*b*) For larger pulley

(*c*) Either of larger or smaller pulley.

52. Name the physical properties of material which should be studied while selecting a material for making a component.

53. Enumerate the factors and properties of materials a designer is required to consider while designing a machine part.

54. A saddle key is used for the transmission of

(*a*) Small steady torque (*b*) Medium torque

(*c*) Heavy torque.

55. State the function of the following

(*a*) Rivet (*b*) Flywheel.

56. Name a few stress raisers.

57. State whether the following statements are true or false

(*a*) Ductile materials fail by yielding

(*b*) Brittle materials fail by fracture

(*c*) A reduction of stress concentration can be had by using fillets of elliptical shape

(*d*) The compressive strength of brittle materials is many times greater than their tensile strength.

58. Maximum normal stress theory is used to predict failure of

(*a*) Brittle materials (*b*) Ductile materials.

59. Statements

(*a*) Machine parts subjected to continuously varying load fail at stresses which are considerably below the yield point

(*b*) Fatigue failure usually takes place across the crystals

(*c*) Helical gears subject the shaft bearings to both radial and axial thrust loads.

60. Pure aluminium has a tensile strength of

(*a*) 30 MPa (*b*) 60 MPa

(*c*) 90 MPa

where $P_a$ = Pascal = 1 N/m$^2$.

61. Density of steel is

(*a*) 9750 kg/m$^3$ (*b*) 7750 kg/m$^3$

(*c*) 5750 kg/m$^3$.

62. Density of aluminium is

(*a*) 2770 kg/m$^3$ (*b*) 3770 kg/m$^3$

(*c*) 5770 kg/m$^3$.

63. Define the following
  (*a*) Power screw  (*b*) Life of ball bearing
  (*c*) Basic load rating for ball bearing
  (*d*) Rating life of a group of identical ball bearings.

64. State the factors which affect coefficient of friction between screw and nut

65. Name the anti-friction bearings used for the following types of loads
  (*a*) Heavy axial loads
  (*b*) Combined radial and axial loads
  (*c*) Heavy radial loads at high speeds.

66. A pan head rivet of 8 mm diameter and length 40 mm is designed as
  (*a*) Pan head rivet 40 × 8 IS : 2155
  (*b*) Pan head rivet 8 × 40 IS : 2155
  (*c*) None of the above.

67. State the endurance limit ($\sigma_e$) in terms of ultimate tensile stress for the following materials
  (*a*) Aluminium and magnesium (materials having no defined endurance limit)
  (*b*) Cast iron and cast steel
  (*c*) Steels with hardness less than 400 BHN ($\sigma_4$ < 140 kg/mm$^2$).

68. State the type of load that can be taken up by the following types of bearings
  (*a*) Cylindrical roller bearing
  (*b*) Taper roller bearing
  (*c*) Simple radial ball bearings
  (*d*) Angular contact ball bearings
  (*e*) Ball thrust bearings.

69. State the distinguishing features of anti-friction bearings as compared to sliding bearings.

70. Tick mark the correct answers

(*A*) The stiffness of a spring is a measure of

(*a*) The amount of a spring gets compressed by the application of load

(*b*) Load which produces unit deflection in the spring.

(*c*) Capacity of the spring that can be stored in it

(*d*) Strength of spring

(*B*) A bearing in which the oil film is maintained by supplying oil under pressure is called

(*a*) Journal bearing

(*b*) Roller bearing

(*c*) Hydrodynamic bearing

(*d*) Hydrostatic bearing.

(*C*) Key way cut in a shaft affects the strength of shaft due to

(*a*) Length of key way

(*b*) Stress concentration at and near the corners of key way

(*c*) Shearing of key way

(*d*) None of the above.

(*D*) A fastener used to hold the pulleys wheels etc. On the rotating shaft to prevent relative rotary motion between the pair is called

(*a*) Stud

(*b*) Set screw

(*c*) Cotter

(*d*) Key.

(*E*) The convexity provided on the rim of pulley to prevent slipping the belt off the pulley is called

(*a*) Crowing

(*b*) Webbing

(*c*) Wringing

(*d*) Caulking.

(*F*) A bearing in which the oil film pressure is generated only by rotation of journal is called

(*a*) Bushed bearing

(*b*) Hydrodynamic bearing

(*c*) Journal bearing

(*d*) None of the above.

71. Statements

(*a*) A key resists shear over a longitudinal section

(*b*) A cotter resists shear over a transverse section

(*c*) Flanges of flange coupling are made of cast iron

(*d*) The pin of knuckle joint is made of cast iron

(*e*) Flywheel rim is made heavier as compared to a pulley.

72. The shafts are usually made from carbon steel of grade

(*a*) C10 (*b*) C15

(*c*) C25 (*d*) None of the above.

73. The bearing pressure in roller chains is

(*a*) 1 – 1.5 kg/cm$^2$ (*b*) 8 – 9 kg/cm$^2$

(*c*) 3.5 – 1.7 kg/cm$^2$ (*d*) None of the above.

74. Chain length (*L*) in chain drive is given by

(*a*) $L = m \times p$ (*b*) $L = m \times 2p$

(*c*) $L = m \times \frac{p}{2}$ (*d*) None of the above.

where $p$ = pitch and $m$ = number of chain links.

75. State the value of the following in terms of pitch ($p$) for chain drive

(*a*) Thickness of link plates

(*b*) Chain width

(*c*) Maximum height of roller link plates (inner plates).

76. The ulitmate tensile strength of steel wires used for making ropes varies from

(*a*) 40 – 80 kg/mm² (*b*) 120 – 240 kg/mm²

(*c*) 320 – 500 kg/mm² (*d*) None of the above.

77. **Statements**

(*a*) A steel wire rope designed by 6 × 19 has six strands and nineteen wires

(*b*) Cotton ropes are available in two constructions

(*i*) Hawser laid or plain laid

(*ii*) Cable laid.

(*c*) Manila ropes are available in three constructions

(*i*) Hawser laid or pailn laid

(*ii*) Shroud laid

(*iii*) Cable laid.

78. Diameter ($D$) of wire rope is given by

(*a*) $D = 1.5\, dw \sqrt{n}$ (*b*) $D = 1.5 \,.\, dw \,.\, n$

(*c*) $1.5 \,.\, dw\, n^2$ (*d*) None of the above

where $dw$ = Diameter of wire

$n$ = Number of wires in rope

79. The most commonly used pulley groove angle for rope drive is

(*a*) 30° (*b*) 45°

(*c*) 60° (*d*) None of the above.

80. Name two main types of couplings.

81. State three factors which affect the coefficient of friction between belt and pulley.

82. The endurance limit ($\sigma_e$) and ultimate tensile stress ($\sigma_{ut}$) for steels are related as follows

(*a*) $\sigma_e = 0.5\, \sigma_{ut}$ (*b*) $\sigma_e = 0.75\, \sigma_{ut}$

(*c*) $\sigma_e = 0.9\ \sigma_{ut}$ (*d*) $\sigma_e = 1.2\ \sigma_{ut}$.

83. State three reasons for failure of bearings.

84. How does surface failure takes place in gears.

85. Define full journal bearing and partial journal bearing.

## ANSWERS

1. (*a*) 2. (*d*) 3. (*a*) 4. (*a*)

5. (*b*) 6. (*e*)

7. (*a*) True (*b*) True (*c*) True (*d*) True (*e*) True (*f*) True

8. (*c*) 9. (*b*) 10. (*a*) True (*b*) True (*c*) True

11. (*a*)

12. Advantages (*a*) Small size (*b*) Noiseless operation (*c*) High speed ratios. Disadvantages : (*a*) Low efficiency (*b*) Low power capacity

13. (*a*) True (*b*) True (*c*) True (*d*) True (*e*) True (*f*) False.

Table 21.1 gives the internationally accepted life of ball and roller bearing for the different applications.

**Table 21.1**

| *Application* | *Life (hours)* |
|---|---|
| Domestic electrical appliances | 1000 — 2000 |
| Small Fans | 2000 — 4000 |
| Light Motor Cycles | 600 — 1200 |
| Heavy Motor Cycles or Light Cars | 1000 — 2000 |
| Heavy Cars or Light Trucks | 1500 - 2500 |
| Axle bearing for Passenger Train | 25000 |
| Machine tool gears | 20000 |
| Rope pulleys for Conveyors | 40000 — 60000 |

15. (*a*) 8 m (*b*) 60 m (*c*) 150 m (*d*) 1500 mpm (*e*) 45° (*f*) 50 metre/sec.

16. (*a*) V-belt cannot be used with large centre distances.

(*b*) V-belt are not as durable as flat belts.

(*c*) The design of V-belt is more complicated as compared to flat belts.

17. (*a*) 18. (*a*)

19. (*c*) 20. (*b*)

21. (*a*) True (*b*) True (*c*) True (*d*) True (*e*) True (*f*) True

22. (*a*) 23. (*b*)

24. (*a*) 25. (*c*)

26. (*a*) Cork (*b*) Rubber (*c*) Asbestos.

27. (*a*) 80 kg/cm$^2$, 450°C (*b*) 70°C (*c*) Half

28. (*a*) Cast iron

(*b*) Chrome nickel alloy with ultimate tensile strength of about 9400–13500 kg/cm$^2$.

(*c*) The various materials generally used for I.C. engine piston are as follows :

(*i*) Cast iron

(*ii*) Cast aluminium

(*iii*) Cast steel

(*d*) M.S.

(*e*) Cast iron

(*f*) Eccentric sheaves--C.I.

Eccentric straps--W.I.

Eccentric rod--F.S.

29. (*a*)

30. The horse power (H.P.), peripheral speed ($V$) and speed ratio ($r$) are compared as shown in Table 21.2 in maximum values are indicated in bracket.

## Table 21.2

| *Type of drive* | *H.P.* | *V (m/s)* | *r* |
|---|---|---|---|
| Flat belt | Upto 130 (2500) | 5--30 | Upto 4 (10) |
| V-belt | Upto 70 (1500) | 5--30 | Upto 7 (15) |
| Spur gears | 13000 | 25 | 6--10 |
| Chain drive | 275 (5000) | Upto 25 | Upto 15 |

31. (*b*) 32. (*b*)
33. (*a*) 34. (*c*)
35. (*a*) 36. (*a*)
37. (*b*)
38. Riveted joints are widely used in
(*i*) Roof trusses (*ii*) Boilers (*iii*) Bridges
39. (*a*) 40. (*c*)
41. (*b*)
42. A key is driven parallel to the axis of shaft subjected to torsional stress whereas cotter is driven at right angles to the axes of the connect parts subjected to axial load only.
43. (*b*)
44. (*a*) **Journal.** The portion of a shaft or axle within the bearing is called journal. N.P. (*b*) **Key.** A key is a machine member used at the interface of pair of matching male and female circular cross-sectioned members to prevent relative angular motion between these mating members. (*c*) **Rack.** It is a spur gear of infinite diameter. Its pitch line is a strength line and pitch surface is a plane surface.
45. (*b*) 46. (*a*)
47. (*b*) 48. (*a*)
49. (*b*) 50. (*b*) and (*c*)
51. (*a*)
52. (*i*) Specific heat (*ii*) Melting point (*iii*) Thermal conductivity (*iv*) Electrical conductivity (*v*) Coefficient of thermal expansion.

53. The various properties to the considered strength, stiffness, ductility, fatigue resistance, corrosion resistance, casting and forging properties, hardness, machinability, thermal conductivity etc.
The machine part designed should possess the following characteristics : (*i*) It should be sufficiently rugged to function properly for a reasonable life.

(*ii*) It should incorporates safety measures.

(*iii*) It should be pleasing external appearance.

(*iv*) Cost of servicing and installation should be low.

(*v*) The overall cost should be minimum.

54. (*a*)

55. (*i*) **Rivet.** A rivet is used to connect metal plates together permanently. It is cylindrical in form and is forged with a head at one end, the other end being made by a machine or by hand when the rivet which is red hot is placed in position through the plates.

(*ii*) **Flywheel.** It can be considered as an energy reservoir which stores energy at some time and gives up energy when desired.

56. Sharp corners, threads, rough surface.

57. (*a*) True (*b*) True (*c*) True (*d*) True

58. (*a*) 59. (*a*) False (*b*) False (*c*) True

60. (*a*) 61. (*b*)

62. (*a*)

63. (*a*) **Power Screw.** Power transmitting device to convert rotary motion to linear.

(*b*) **Life of ball bearing.** Life of ball bearing is the number of resolutions that the bearing runs before the first evidence of fatigue in either ring or ball.

(*c*) **Basic load rating for ball bearing.** The basic load rating is that radial load which corresponds to a total permanent deformation of rolling element and race at the most heavily stressed contact of 0.0001 of the ball diameter.

(*d*) **Rating life of a group of identical ball bearings.** It is inversely proportional to the cube of equivalent dynamic load.

64. Material of screw and nut and their surface condition.

65. (*a*) Axial thrust bearing

(*b*) Taper roller bearing

(*c*) Roller bearing

66. (*a*)

67. (*a*) 0.35 (*b*) 0.4 to 0.5 (*c*) 0.5

68. (*a*) High loads

(*b*) High radial and axial loads at moderate to high speeds

(*c*) To support radial loads

(*d*) Higher radial load and a high unidirectional thrust load

(*e*) For axial load.

69. Starting friction torque is low, ease of lubrication, less axial space for comparable shaft diameter, early warning of impending failure, readily replaceable stock items etc.

70. (*A*) (*b*) (*B*) (*a*)

(*C*) (*b*) (*D*) (*d*)

(*E*) (*a*) (*F*) (*b*)

71. (*a*) True (*b*) True (*c*) True (*d*) False (*e*) True

72. (*d*)

73. (*d*)

74. (*a*)

75. (*a*) *p*/8 (*b*) *p*/2 (*c*) 3*p*/8

76. (*b*)

77. (*a*) True (*b*) True (*c*) True

78. (*a*)

79. (*b*)

81. (*i*) material (*ii*) surface finish

(*iii*) working conditions

82. (*a*)

83. (*i*) fatigue (*ii*) spelling (*iii*) lubrication failure

84. Due to rolling and sliding action of the gear teeth the following types of surface destruction may occur.

1. **Abrasive wear.** A failure due to the pressure of foreign material in the lubricant that can scratch the tooth surface.

2. **Corrosive wear.** A failure due to chemical reaction on the tooth surface.

3. **Pitting.** A fatigue failure due to repeated application of stress cycles.

4. **Scoring.** A failure due to metal-to-metal contact on account of lubricant failure.

Abrasion, wear and scoring are clearly failures that are the results of improper lubrication and gear enclosure. Pitting is a form of wear that occurs chiefly near the pitch line and is probably caused by fatigue failure of the material just under the surface where the pressure between two curved surfaces produces the maximum shear stress. When the material below the surfaces develops a fatigue crack, the sliding action of the tooth surfaces will pull the surface material out, forming a pit. In soft materials, wear may occur by the sliding action of the teeth pushing the metal toward the pitch line where the sliding action becomes pure rolling and then reverses in direction. This action produces a hump near the pitch line and causes excessive noise.

85. When the shaft is totally encased by the bearing sleeve, the bearing is said to be a full journal bearing, and when it is partly encased, the bearing is said to be a partial journal bearing.

**Table 1**
**Permissible Bearing Pressures for Power Screws**

| *Application* | *Material Combination* | | *Bearing Pressure* | *Working Condition* |
|---|---|---|---|---|
| | *Screw* | *Nut* | *kg/cm²* | Low speed 3 m/min |
| Screw Jack | Steel | C.I. | 120-160 | |
| | Steel | Bronze | 105-170 | Medium speed |
| Hoisting Screw | Steel | C.I. | 40-70 | |
| | Steel | Bronze | 50-95 | 6—13 m/min |
| Lead Screw | Steel | Bronze | 10-16 | High speed > 15 m/min |

**Table 2. Permissible Rim Speeds of Pulleys**

| *Type of Pulley* | *Maximum Rim speed (metre per min)* |
|---|---|
| (*a*) Cast iron pulley<br>(*i*) Solid with flat or crown face<br>(*ii*) Split with flat or crown face | 1450 |
| (*b*) Mild steel pulleys | 1000 |
| (*i*) Solid or split with flat or crown face and mild steel spokes | 1500 |

## Table 3
## Preferred width of pulleys in millimeter

20, 25, 32, 40, 50, 63, 71, 80, 90, 100, 112, 125, 140, 160, 180, 200, 224, 250, 280, 315, 355, 400, 450, 500, 560, 630.

## Table 4
## Preferred nominal diameter (mm) of pulleys

40, 45, 56, 63, 71, 80, 90, 100, 112, 122, 140, 160, 180, 200, 224, 250, 280, 315, 355, 400, 450, 500, 560, 630, 710, 800, 900, 1000, 1120, 1250, 1400, 1600, 1800, 2000.

## Table 5
## Width of Flat Pulleys

| *Width of Belt (B) (mm)* | *Width of pulley in Excess of B* |
|---|---|
| upto 125 mm | 12 min minimum |
| 125 to 250 mm | 25 mm minimum |
| 250 to 375 mm | 38 mm minimum |
| 375 to 500 mm | 50 mm minimum |

## Table 6
## Mechanical Properties and Applications of Cast Iron and Cast Steels

| *IS Designation* | *Tensile Strength kg/mm²* | *Stress kg/mm²* | *Elongation Per-cent (Gauge length 5.65√A)* | *BHN* | *Typical Applications* |
|---|---|---|---|---|---|
| **Grey C.I. Castings** | | Transverse Rupture Stress | | | Machine tools beds and frames, flywheels, pulleys, low speed gears etc. |
| Grade--15 | 13 to 19 | 28.5 to 41.7 | -- | 146 to 197 | |
| 20 | 17 to 24 | 33.5 to 46.4 | -- | 179 to 223 | |
| 25 | 22 to 28 | 38.6 to 51.0 | -- | 197 to 241 | |
| 30 | 27 to 31 | 43.6 to 52.5 | -- | 207 to 241 | |
| 35 | 32 to 35 | 55.3 to 57.3 | -- | 207 to 241 | |
| 40 | 37 to 40 | 62.7 to 63.7 | -- | 241 to 320 | |

(*Contd...*)

| **Speroidal or Nodular Graphite Cast Iron** | | Minimum Proof Stress (0.2 percent) | | | Intricate casting, frames for machines, dies for press formings, shafts etc. |
|---|---|---|---|---|---|
| IS Grade-- SG 80/2 | 80 | 48 | 2 | 260 to 330 | |
| SG 60/2 | 60 | 40 | 2 | 210 to 280 | |
| SG 42/12 | 42 | 28 | 12 | ·187 max. | |
| **Cast Steels** | | Yield strength | | | Complicated castings, cast part, can be welded. |
| — | | (0.5 percent proof stress) | | | |
| IS-CS 65 | 65 | 40 | 17 | 190 | |
| CS 85 | 85 | 71 | 12 | 248 | |
| CS 125 | 125 | 102 | 5 | 363 | |
| **Alloy Cast Iron** | | Yield Strength | | | Castings, where toughness, strengh, wear-resistance is required as in crank shafts of automobile engines |
| Nickel C.I. | 25 | 12 | — | 180 min. | |
| Ni-Mo C.I. | 30 | 18 | — | 220 min., | |